TRIOEDD YNYS PRYDEIN

Peniarth 16, fo. 50*r*.

Reproduced by kind permission of The National Library of Wales.

TRIOEDD YNYS PRYDEIN

THE TRIADS OF THE ISLAND OF BRITAIN

Edited with
Introduction, Translation and Commentary
by

RACHEL BROMWICH

Published on behalf of the Language and Literature Committee of the University of Wales Board of Celtic Studies

CARDIFF
UNIVERSITY OF WALES PRESS
2006

First Edition, 1961
Second Edition, 1978
Third Edition, 2006

British Library Cataloguing-in-Publication Data
A catalogue record for this book is available from the British Library.

ISBN 0-7083-1386-8

Printed in Great Britain by Cromwell Press, Trowbridge, Wiltshire

Cyflwynir y gwaith hwn
i'm hen athro annwyl
SYR IFOR WILLIAMS

CONTENTS

ILLUSTRATIONS

PREFACE

This third edition of *Trioedd Ynys Prydein* contains a complete revision of the work of the earlier editions. Whereas in the second edition of 1978 revisions and new references were added at the end of the volume, in this edition revisions and additions have been incorporated into the text. A new triad (triad 97) has been added to the corpus and the orthography of the texts of the triads has been emended in the light of the critique published by Kenneth Hurlstone Jackson in *Welsh History Review*, Special Number (1963), 82–7. The Introduction, Textual Notes and Notes on Personal Names have been revised and augmented. The fifth Appendix of the earlier editions, 'North Welsh Genealogical Triads', has been omitted. References to relevant works published before 2000, and to the volumes of the two series, *Beirdd y Tywysogion* and *Beirdd yr Uchelwyr*, published by the Centre for Advanced Welsh and Celtic Studies to date, have been incorporated in the Notes.

Dr Bromwich, who was ninety in July 2005, has worked on this edition for many years but has unfortunately been too unwell to supervise the preparation of the volume in its final stages. Close friends who were in contact with Dr Bromwich, however, have been at hand to undertake the tasks necessary to complete the work. Care has been taken to comply with what were considered the intentions of Dr Bromwich, so that this volume in its entirety must be considered to be essentially her work. Dr Bromwich's son Brian and his family have supported the whole enterprise.

Finally it has been my privilege to be on hand when need arose to write this Preface: *Disgybl wyf, hi a'm dysgawdd.*

Morfydd E. Owen

Bryneithin, Llanfarian, 2006

INTRODUCTION

I. MANUSCRIPTS AND VERSIONS

This edition of *Trioedd Ynys Prydein* is based upon a full collation of the manuscripts. The text reproduced is in the first instance that of Peniarth MS. 16, which represents the oldest version of TYP that has come down to us, with the exception of a fragment of four *Trioedd y Meirch* preserved in the *Black Book of Carmarthen*. I have called this the 'Early Version'. The text of Pen. 16 ends with triad 46, so that this manuscript includes less than half of the total of ninety-seven triads contained in this volume. The remaining triads are those not found in Pen. 16, but which appear in the later collections, as follows:

Triads 47–69 are from the White Book, *Llyfr Gwyn Rhydderch*; and where the fragmentary text of TYP contained in this manuscript is defective, from the complete version of the same series preserved in the Red Book, *Llyfr Coch Hergest*. This version is designated WR.

Triads 70–80 are from Pen. 47, and triads 81–6 from Pen. 50, while triads 87–97 consist of miscellaneous additions to *Trioedd Ynys Prydein* which appear for the first time in one or other of the late manuscript collections.

I have given precedence to preserving the order of the triads as these appear in Pen. 16, although to do so has involved subordinating to this order, the order in which the triads are given in the much more extensive collection of WR. The reason for this choice is that I believe Pen. 16 to preserve an older arrangement and grouping of *Trioedd Ynys Prydein*; see below, pp. lxxxviii–lxxxix. The table given on pp. xiii–xv may be consulted as a guide to the grouping of the triads in the chief manuscripts, and as an indication of the sources of individual triads. (A list of manuscript sources is also given beneath the text of each triad.) The construction of a satisfactory *stemma* of TYP is not possible because of the nature of the material: all manuscripts omit triads which are represented in other manuscripts, and numerous intermediary texts have undoubtedly been lost. But the distinction between the two main versions, the Early Version (Pen. 16 and 45) and that of WR (*White Book of Rhydderch* and *Red Book of Hergest*), remains a valid one for the texts of TYP as a whole: in following the grouping of one or other version the later manuscripts also present a text whose affinities are with this version. But I hope to show in the following pages that each of the manuscripts employed for the basic texts of triads 1–87 draws on written sources other than those that have come down to us, some of which are of at least equal antiquity with those which have survived. There is evidence that some at least of the triads which are represented in both of the main versions go back ultimately to a common *written* source (see below, pp. lxxxix–xc).

Triads 1–90 include all the triads contained in the first and second series of *Trioedd Ynys Prydain* in the *Myvyrian Archaiology of Wales* (MA^2 388–99). The first series represents the collection of *Trioedd Ynys Prydain* made by Robert Vaughan of Hengwrt (1592–1666) from older manuscript sources. An account of the formation of the Myvyrian text will be found below, pp. xxxix–xliv. The Myvyrian second series reproduces the triads from the *Red Book of Hergest*. The third series (MA^2 400–11) is the work of Iolo Morganwg, who in the late eighteenth century rewrote many of the older triads in an expanded form, with the introduction of some fresh material. The investigation of these triads belongs properly to the study of Iolo's sources and methods; and as such, it falls outside the scope of this book.[1] In the notes I have referred to the triads from the third series only occasionally, and incidentally.

In the appendices, I–IV, I have brought together certain documents which have either remained hitherto unpublished, or of which the published texts are not easily accessible: the subject-matter is in each case relevant to *Trioedd Ynys Prydein*, although the documents vary considerably in date. To print the texts in full has saved the necessity for constant quotation, both in the notes to the triads and in the Notes to Personal Names. In including these documents in an edition of *Trioedd Ynys Prydein* I may claim to be following the distinguished precedent of Robert Vaughan and Moses Williams, each of whom included a part of this material in their manuscript collections of TYP. The content of the appendices is discussed below, pp. c ff.

A fuller discussion of the manuscript sources of TYP follows.

[1] Translations from the Myvyrian text of Iolo Morganwg's 'Third Series' of *Trioedd Ynys Prydain* were published i) by William Probert (1790–1837) as an appendix to his *Ancient Laws and Institutes of Wales* in 1823, (reprinted as *The Triads of Britain* by Malcolm Smith, London, 1977); and ii) by J. H. Parry in *The Cambro-Briton* for 1820–22. The English translation which Iolo himself made of his 'Third Series' has come down in *Iolo Aneirin Williams MS. 71*, preserved in the National Library of Wales. For an annotated edition of Iolo's own translations of his triads, see R. Bromwich, 'Trioedd Ynys Prydain: the Myvyrian Third Series', THSC 1968, pp. 299–388; ibid., 1969, pp. 127–56. See further R. Bromwich, *Trioedd Ynys Prydain in Welsh Literature and Scholarship* (Darlith Goffa G. J. Williams, Cardiff, 1969).

PLAN SHOWING THE RELATION BETWEEN THE MAIN TEXTS OF *TRIOEDD YNYS PRYDEIN*

On the left the triads are numbered serially as in this volume. The numbers on the right show the order in which they appear in the manuscripts. Vertical lines denote 'floating sections', see pp. xxv, lxxxviii.
Triads in the WR series which are absent from the text of W are italicized.

	Pen. 16	Pen. 45	Pen. 47	Pen. 50	WR	Pen. 51	Pen. 77	Car. 18	NLW 6434 and DC
1. lleithiclwyth	1	1	—	40	—	—	1	—	—
2. hael	2	2	—	21	34	22	—	—	1
3. gwyndeyrn	3	3	2	22	*8*	25	—	—	2
4. deifnyawc	4	4	3	23	23	11	—	—	3
5. post cat	5	5	4	24	33	—	—	—	4
6. tarw catuc	6	6	5	25	—	—	—	—	5
7. tarw vnben	7	7	17	{ 26	29	17	—	—	6
8. lledyf vnben	8	8	18	{ 26	37	31	—	—	7
9. vnben llys A.	9	9	19	—	28	16	—	—	8
10. vnben deivyr a brennych	10	10	20	—	30	18	—	—	9, 38
11. gva(y)vrud beird	11	11	21	27	50	43	—	—	10, 36
12. overveird	12	—	—	28	*9*	26	—	—	—
13. cynweissyat	13	12	22	—	22	10	—	—	—
14. llyghessavc	14	13	23	—	27	15	—	—	45
15. llyghes kynniweir	15	—	24	—	*13*	2	—	—	39
16. gwrduaglavc	16	14	25	—	—	—	—	—	—
17. hualawc	17	15	1	18	45	38	—	3	31
18. catvarchavc	18	16	26	—	60	—	2	4	11
19. galovyd	19	17	10	—	38	32	3	5	27
20. rudvoawc	20	18	—	29	26	14	—	7	44
21. taleithyavc cat	21	19	7	30	25	13	4	8	12

	Pen. 16	Pen. 45	Pen. 47	Pen. 50	WR	Pen. 51	Pen. 77	Car. 18	NLW 6434 and DC
22. glew	22	20	—	48	35	29	5	9	26
23. trahauc	23	21	27	31	36	30	6	10	—
24. ysgymyd aereu	24	22	28	49	39	33	7	11	—
25. aeruedawc	25	—	29	—	32	21	—	6	48
26. gwrdueichyat	26	23	30	—	58	50	8	23	—
27. lletvrithavc	27	24	31	—	—	—	—	22	13
28. prif hut	28	25	32	32	21	9	—	21	14
29. diweir deulu	29	26	33	19	43	36	—	20	15
30. anyweir deulu	30	27	34	20	44	37	—	19	16
31. gosgord adwy(n)	31	28	35	—	*20*	8	—	18	—
32. mat gyflavan	32	29	—	34	*30*	—	—	17	46
33. anvat gyflavan	33	30	36	33	*31*	19	—	15	47
34. anvat vwyallawt	34	31	37	—	*34*	20	—	14	—
35. cyfor er enys hon	35	32	—	10	*5*	1	—	13	38
36. gormes a doeth yr enys hon	36	33	—	9	—	—	—	1	—
37. cud a datcud	37	34	14	11	10, 11	27	—	2	51
38. rodedicvarch	38	rest of page illegible	51, 52	—	52	44	—	16	17
39. pryf edystir	39		54	—	53	45	—	—	18
40. anreithvarch	40		48	53	54	46	—	—	19
41. gorderchvarch	41		50	54	56	48	—	—	20
42. gohoew edystyr	42		46	—	55	47	—	—	21, 37
43. tom edystyr	43		47	—	—	—	—	—	22
44. marchlwyth	44		53	50	*12*	28	—	—	23
45. pryf ychen	45		55	51	—	—	—	—	24
46. pryf vuch	46		56	52	—	—	—	—	25
47. kedernit adaf.	—	—	—	—	*1*	—	12	—	—
48. pryt adaf.	—	—	—	—	*2*	—	13	—	—
49. doethineb adaf	—	—	—	—	*3*	—	14	—	—
50. pryt eva	—	—	39	—	*4*	—	15	—	—
51. trywyr gwarth	—	—	—	—	*46*	23	—	—	52
52. goruchel garcharawr	—	—	—	17	7, 51	24	—	—	—
53. gwith balfawt	—	—	—	35	14	3	—	—	40

54. drud heirfa	—	—	—	12	15	4	11	—	—
55. neges o bowys	—	—	—	—	16	—	—	—	—
56. prif riein A.	—	—	43	43	17	5	—	—	41
57. karedic wreic	—	—	44	44	18	6	—	—	42
58. gwrvorwyn	—	—	45	—	19	7	—	—	43
59. anvat gyghor	—	—	—	14	24	12	—	—	53
60. gweith perllan vangor	—	—	—	—	40	33a	—	—	28
61. eur gelein	—	—	—	—	41	34	—	—	29
62. hualhogeon deulu	—	—	—	15	42	35	—	—	30
63. tarw ellyll	—	—	—	—	46	39	—	—	32
64. gwyd ellyll	—	—	—	—	47	40	—	—	33
65. trwydedawc	—	—	—	—	48	41	9	—	34
66. diweir	—	—	41	38	49	42	—	—	35
67. eurgryd	—	—	—	—	61	—	—	—	—
68. brenhin o veibon eillon	—	—	—	—	62	—	—	—	—
69. budyr hafren	—	—	—	—	63	—	—	—	—
70. gwyndorllwyth	—	—	6	36	—	—	—	—	—
71. serchawc	—	—	8	37	—	—	—	—	—
72. cyndynyawc	—	—	9	—	—	—	—	—	—
73. gogyfurd llys A.	—	—	11	—	—	—	—	—	—
74. anheol	—	—	12	47	—	—	—	—	—
75. dyn goreu wrth osp a phellenigynon	—	—	13	46	—	—	—	—	—
76. engiryawl	—	—	15	—	—	—	—	—	—
77. anhynodawc llys A.	—	—	16	—	—	—	—	—	—
78. gwenriein	—	—	38	—	—	—	—	—	—
79. gohoywriein	—	—	40	—	—	—	—	—	—
80. aniweir wreic	—	—	42	39	—	—	—	—	—
81. santeidd linys	—	—	—	1	—	—	—	—	—
82. gwestei gwynvydedic	—	—	—	2	—	—	—	—	—
83. corff a wnaeth duw er Theilaw	—	—	—	3	—	—	—	—	—
84. overgat	—	—	—	13	—	—	10	—	—
85. prif lys A.	—	—	—	41	—	—	—	—	—
86. marchawc a enillawd y greal	—	—	—	45	—	—	—	—	50

PENIARTH 16 (formerly Hengwrt 54). This is a composite vellum manuscript, made up of several fragments varying in date between the thirteenth and fifteenth centuries (*Rep.* I, p. 337). The section which contains *Trioedd Ynys Prydein*[2] and *Bonedd y Saint* (folios 50–54b) is a detached portion of the same manuscript as that which contains the Dingestow Court *Brut y Brenhinedd*, NLW 5266B (ed. H. Lewis, Cardiff, 1942; referred to hereafter as BD); and the triads are written in the same hand as the *Brut*. A page which contained the opening words of TYP is however missing, so that the text begins in the middle of triad 1. A certain difference of opinion has been expressed as to the date of this manuscript. Gwenogvryn Evans states (*Rep.* I, p. 337; see also RBB xiii) that this section (iv) of Pen. 16 was written during the early years of the thirteenth century. But the editor of BD gave it as the opinion of the British Library authorities, Robin Flower and Idris Bell, that the manuscript belongs to the end of the thirteenth century rather than to its beginning (BD xxiii), though he does not state the grounds on which this opinion was formed. E. D. Jones, when Librarian of the National Library of Wales, after re-examining the two manuscripts, agreed that the hand of this portion of Pen. 16 is identical with that of the Dingestow *Brut*, and kindly gave me permission to quote his opinion that the work is to be dated to the third quarter[3] of the thirteenth century. In his words 'One notices the predominantly medial punctuation in Dingestow, the dotting of the *y*, and the turn to the left of the first stroke of the *y*.' Nevertheless, as Henry Lewis has shown, the language of the Dingestow *Brut* is of the early thirteenth century (BD xxix, xxxv), so that it is apparent that the manuscript is a copy of an earlier text. The same conclusion is to be drawn from a study of the linguistic features of the Pen. 16 text of *Trioedd Ynys Prydein*, as will be seen from the evidence cited below.

Orthography of Peniarth 16. The normal spelling employed is that which is common to the *Llyfr Gwyn*, the *Llyfr Coch*, and other manuscripts of the thirteenth and fourteenth centuries (see PKM xiii). The following outline will indicate the main differences from Modern Welsh:

Final *-t* represents *-d*: *kynwyt* (triad 6), *cat* (triad 21), *coet* (triad 26), *hut* (triad 28), *oet* (triad 30).

Final *-d* represents *-dd*: *teyrned* (triad 1), *Nud* (triad 2), *bard* (triad 11), *galouyd* (triad 19), *teirg6aed* (triad 27).

[2] I edited the text of *Trioedd Ynys Prydein* from Pen. 16 in B XII, pp. 1–15, with variants from Pen. 45. *Bonedd y Saint* from Pen. 16 is printed in LBS IV, pp. 369–71. For a more recent *variorum* edition of *Bonedd y Saint*, see EWGT 51–67.

[3] Similarly Daniel Huws 'ail hanner y 13g.' *Nat. Lib. of Wales Journal* XXVIII, p. 19. See also AW 9. On the close relationship between the two manuscripts, see further B. F. Roberts, 'Fersiwn Dingestow o *Brut y Brenhinedd*', B XXVII, p. 332.

Medially the value of *-t-*, *-d-*, is ambiguous: *-t-* = *-d-* in *Tutclyt* (triad 2), *Catwalla6n* (triad 11), *lleturitha6c* (triad 27), etc.

Medial *-d-* = *d* in *Mordaf* (triad 2), *Carada6c* (triad 18), but = *dd* in *Ryderch* (triad 2), *Guendoleu* (triad 29), *Ywerdon* (triad 29), *Gledyfrud* (triads 24, 40), *edystyr* (triad 42), etc. Hence the uncertainty in triad 31 as to whether *adwy* 'gap' or *adwy(n)* = *addwyn* 'splendid' is intended (see note to triad 31).

Final *-c* = *-g*: *wledic* (triad 3), *trahauc* (triad 23), *caduc* (triad 6), etc.

Medial *-y-* = *-i-* (vocalic): *Anyweir* (triad 30), *Aneiryn* (triad 34), *pryf* (triads 35, 37, 45, 46), and *i̯* (consonantal): *deifnya6c* (triad 4), *cynweissyat* (triad 13), *Meirchya6n* (triads 14, 26), etc.

Besides representing *u* (see below) *6* is employed for *w*: *h6ch* (triad 26), *Duna6t*, *Einya6n*, *Keida6*, *Gwalla6c*, etc., and for *f*: *Kyn6arch* (triad 6), *o6er6eird* (triad 12), *6renhin* (triad 32). etc.

Besides representing *w* (see below), *u* is employed for *f*: *ruduoa6c* (triad 20), *aeruaeu* (triad 24), *Cynuelyn* (triad 5), etc., as well as for *u*: *Run* (triad 3), *Nud* (triad 31); and has both these values in turn in *Ruua6n* (= *Rhufawn*) (triad 3), and in reverse order in *a uuant* (= *a fuant*, triad 29).

In addition, Pen. 16 preserves traces of a different and perhaps older system of orthography, similar to that of the *Black Book of Carmarthen* (middle and later 13th cent.); see D. Huws, *Nat. Lib. of Wales Journal* XXVIII, p. 19.

e for *y* (obscure). This appears in the contraction *e. p.* (= *enys prydein*) used throughout; in the definite article *Er, E* (= *Yr, Y*, triad 44), *henyf* (triad 1b), *eman* (triad 36), *emyl* (triad 35a), *Kenyr* (triad 21), *Brennych* (triad 16), *Brennach* (triad 26), *Ewein* (triads 3, 13, 40), *Lledanwyn* (triad 8), *Kenan* (triad 25).

e for *y* (clear) in *ell deu* (triad 30), *ell tri* (triads 7, 10, 21).

6 for *u* in *6ryen* (triads 6, 33), *6thyr* (triad 28), *6nben* (triad 7).

u for *w* in *Caurdaf* (triad 13), *Gueir* (triad 19), *Guendoleu* (triad 29), *Rahaut* (triad 12), *guelwgan* (triad 41), *ymchuelassant* (triad 30).

Even older are *-i-* for *-u-* in *Dina6t* (triad 16; cf. Bede's abbot *Dinoot*), and *t* for *th* in *eu hewytyr* (triad 35c), which recalls the orthography of the *Black Book of Chirk*. Other instances of the retention of an older system of spelling are obscured by uncertainty as to the correct form of certain proper names. Thus *e* may represent *ei* in *Enygan* (triad 33), where the other manuscripts read *Einygan*. It is likely that *o* represents *w* in *Naomon* (triad 44) and in *godwf* (triad 42b, see note), while in *Govrowy* (= *Gobrwy*, triad 9) the scribe apparently altered the medial *-b-* in his prototype to *-v-*, but had already copied the second *-o-* before concluding that this should be a *-w-* in his own system of spelling. In *Gwythelin* (triad 28) it is possible that medial *-th-* has been wrongly restored from *-t-* which in the archetype could denote both *d* and *th*, and that the name should be *Gwyddelin*; cf.

Pen. 45's *Gwydelyn*. But the correct derivation of this name remains uncertain (see under Notes to Personal Names). Another archaic feature is the absence of lenition in the epithets following certain proper names, *Pabo Post Prydein* (triad 5), *Kyn6a6r Catgaduc* (triad 6), *Goronwy Peuyr* (triad 30), *Eliffer Gosgordua6r* (triad 8), beside the more normal lenited forms, *Echel 6ordwytwll* (triad 9), *G6ga6n Gledyfrud* (triad 24), *Cynuelyn Drwsgyl* (triad 5), *Riwallawn Wallt Banhadlen* (triad 4). Non-lenition of such epithets is found in the *Gododdin* and in the *Historia Brittonum*, see CA lxxix–lxxx. The fact that such non-lenited forms tend (with few exceptions) to remain static throughout the different texts of TYP favours the belief that a number of triads which occur in both the two main versions of TYP are derived ultimately from a common manuscript tradition (see below, pp. lxxxix–xc).

There are no instances in Pen. 16's text of TYP of the use of *w* for *v* (*f*), or of final *-t* for *-dd* and *-d* for *-d*, all of which are characteristic of the orthography of the *Black Book of Carmarthen*, and of which the editor of *Brut Dingestow* cites a number of instances. But in view of the fact that the text of TYP is so much shorter, the proportion of early forms in it is as great as in BD, and points similarly to an exemplar of the early thirteenth century. Whether this exemplar was the same manuscript as that which contained the prototype of *Brut y Brenhinedd* is of course a different question.

PENIARTH 45 (formerly Hengwrt 536). The text of *Trioedd Ynys Prydein* contained in this manuscript (pages 293–301) bears the title *Trioed Arthur ai Wyr*. This text is closely related to that of Pen. 16. It was printed with an English translation by W. F. Skene in 1868 as an appendix to volume II of his *Four Ancient Books of Wales*, pp. 456–64. Skene's text is on the whole reliable, though it contains certain minor errors; while his translation is in accordance with the standard of knowledge of Early Welsh of his time. Like Pen. 16, this manuscript combines TYP with a text of *Brut y Brenhinedd* and one of *Bonedd y Saint*. It contains also the earliest version of the *Trioedd Arbennig* (see p. xxv, n. 14 below) and the unique text of the early version of *Bonedd Gwŷr y Gogledd* (see App. II below). J. G. Evans dated Pen. 45 as 'late thirteenth-century' (*Rep.* I, p. 379), though E. D. Jones told me that he would confidently place it as earlier than the *Book of Taliesin*—(*circa* 1275). The style of writing appears to be of slightly later date than that of Pen. 16.[4] The contraction *y. p.* (*ynys prydein*) is employed

[4] Punctuation is almost though not entirely on the line; *y* is not dotted, and the back-stroke of the *y* is a prolongation of the second element, as in the *Book of Taliesin*; the vertical stroke of the *t* begins slightly above the cross-bar, but is less pronounced than in

throughout, and we have the spellings *Ywein* (triad 3) and *Owein* (triad 13) for earlier *Ewein*. Certain triads are omitted which are present in Pen. 16 (nos. 12, 15, 25), evidently as a result of carelessness in copying. There is an instance of *homoeoteleuton* or *achub y blaen* at the end of triad 11, where *Ryhawt eil Morgant* is added as an extra name: this is in fact the last name in Pen. 16's version of triad 12. From the middle of triad 37 to the end of the series (triad 46) this text is illegible, because the last page is much worn, shrivelled and dirty, having served as an outer cover; infra-red light has failed to render legible any more of the remainder of the text than the red initial letter which marks the beginning of *Trioedd y Meirch*. Evidently it was already in this condition in Robert Vaughan's day, since he ends his transcript of Pen. 45 at triad 36. But, in compensation for its mutilated ending, Pen. 45 provides the complete text of triad 1, of which the beginning is lacking in Pen. 16, since it was written at the end of a page which is lost. I have thus been able to supply the opening words of the text from this manuscript.

It is clear that this version of TYP is not a direct copy of Pen. 16, but rather that it has some other manuscript as its source. In triad 26c the sentence *Ac yna yd aeth yny mor* occurs in this text, but is absent from Pen. 16. Since the words are necessary to complete the sense of the passage, it is likely that the scribe of Pen. 16 may have failed to copy them. Similarly in triad 30c, the explanatory sentence includes minor additions which are lacking in Pen. 16. Nevertheless the two manuscripts are very close, and it is likely that they have a common source. Pen. 45's misreading *Manawydyan* in triad 8b, where Pen. 16 has *Manawdyan* suggests that the *y* in this name was already misplaced in the common archetype. It is to be noted that this manuscript preserves a number of early readings which are absent from Pen. 16, and which may be attributed to the common archetype. These consist of:

o for *w*: *deorath* wledic, triad 3 (= Pen. 16, *dewrarth W.*); *gordodo*, triad 26c (= Pen. 16, *gordody*, probably due to a misreading of the *-o* in the original as *e*).

u for *w*: *porthuawr gadu*, triad 9 (Pen. 16, *portha6r gadw*).

t for *th*: *Maton6y*, triad 28 (Pen. 16, *Mathonwy*).

e for *y*: *gwenenen*, triad 26c (Pen. 16, *g6enynen*).

Confusion of final *-c* and *-t*: *Betwyr m. Bedravt*, triad 21 (Pen. 16, *m. Bedra6c*). In this last case it is not certain which is the correct form.

BT. More recently, D. Huws, *Nat. Lib. of Wales Journal* XXVIII, p. 20 dates Pen. 45 to the first half of the fourteenth century.

Absence of lenition:

after prepositions: *ar keneu, ar kyw*, triad 26c (Pen. 16, *ar geneu, ar gyw*);

medially: *Henpen*, triad 22 (Pen. 16, *Henben*); *catcaduc*, triad 6 (Pen. 16, *catgaduc*);

initially: *diweir teulu*, triad 29 (Pen. 16, *d. deulu*);

of a possessive genitive after a feminine noun: *Cath Paluc*, triad 26c (Pen. 16, *cath baluc*);

of epithets: *Rua6n Peuyr*, triad 3 (Pen. 16, *R. Beuyr*); *Gwgawn Cledyfurud*, triad 24 (Pen. 16, *G. Gledyfrud*).

Another feature of this text is the consistent omission of medial consonantal *y* (= *i̯*), where this is present in Pen. 16. Examples: *deifna6c* (triad 4), *cynweissat* (triad 13), *Meircha6n* (triads 14, 26), *g6rdveichat* (triad 26), *Aranrot* (triad 35c), *Einavn* (triad 23), *taleithavc* (triad 21).

The Version of the Llyfr Gwyn and the Llyfr Coch (= WR). The *Llyfr Gwyn Rhydderch* (W) is dated *circa* 1350, the *Llyfr Coch Hergest* (R) *circa* 1400.[5] These two manuscripts contain a version of *Trioedd Ynys Prydein* which differs in marked respects from the Early Version as given in Pen. 16 and Pen. 45. The text of W is found in the detached fragment of the *Llyfr Gwyn* (formerly Pen. 12, now rebound correctly with the main volume; *Rep.* I, p. 324; see further D. Huws, 'Llyfr Gwyn Rhydderch', CMCS 21, p. 29). It begins (p. 117) in the middle of *Trioedd Ynys Prydein*, and this fragmentary text of TYP is followed by *Bonedd y Saint*, proverbs, gnomic and general triads, etc. The whole was published by Phillimore, *Cy.* VII, pp. 123–54. Thirteen triads are missing at the beginning of W's text, but since the order and grouping of the triads in the remainder corresponds exactly with the arrangement of these in the full version of the same series contained in the *Llyfr Coch*, and is entirely different from the arrangement of the Early Version, it will be easier to discuss the characteristics of this version after listing the contents of R. In the *Llyfr Coch Hergest*, cols. 588–600, the text of *Trioedd Ynys Prydein* is subdivided into the following groups, each introduced under a separate heading:

(1) Col. 588. *Tri dynyon a gavssant gampeu adaf.* A list of the men and women who possessed the qualities of Adam and Eve, comprising triads 47–50 in this book.

(2) Cols. 588–90. *Pan aeth llu y Lychlyn* introduces two triads, nos. 35

[5] For a description of the two manuscripts see the note contributed by Daniel Huws, AW 10–12; and for a detailed palaeographical and historical discussion of the *Llyfr Gwyn Rhydderch* see the same writer's article CMCS 21, pp. 1–37.

and 51 below; to the first of which alone R's subheading is applicable. (For the relation of this pair of triads to each other, see note to triad 51.)

(3) Cols. 590–2. *Dechreu y Trioed y6 y rei hynn.* This section comprises triads 52, 3, 12, 37, 44, 15, 53, 54, followed by triad 55 which is introduced by a red initial letter, as though it were the beginning of a new group.

(4) Cols. 592–6. *Trioed y6 y rei hynn.* Triads 56, 57, 58, 31, 28, 13, 4, 59, 21, 20, 14, 9, 7, 10, 33, 25, 5, 2, 22, 23, 8, 19, 24, 60, 61, 62, 29, 30, 17, 63, 64, 65, 66, 11, 52 (second version).

(5) Cols. 596–8. *Trioed y Meirch y6 y rei hynn.* Triads 38, 39, 40, 42, 41, *Tri Penn uarch* (see triad 44; and note that triad 44 is itself misplaced and occurs in the middle of section 3); 26, 18, 67, 68, 69.

(6) Col. 600.[6] *Enweu Ynys Prydein ae rac ynyssed.* See App. I below.

The Red Book text of *Trioedd Ynys Prydein* was printed by J. Rhŷs and J. G. Evans on pp. 297–309 of the *Red Book Mabinogion* (Oxford, 1887); also by Rhŷs in *Cy.* III, pp. 52–61. See now G. Charles-Edwards, 'The Scribes of the Red Book of Hergest', *Nat. Lib. of Wales Journal* XXI, pp. 246–56.

The text of the White Book begins in the middle of section 3 above,[7] and in the middle of triad 53. It continues with the triads contained in sections 4, 5, and 6, under similar headings, and in an order which corresponds with that of R in everything except in the fact that section 6 (*Enweu Ynys Prydein*) is introduced at the end of section 3, and is followed by the poem *Anrec Uryen* (RBP col. 1049), before the scribe returns to section 4 of TYP. As Phillimore pointed out (*Cy.* VII, p. 98), the textual resemblance between W and R is so close that one must conclude either that R is a copy of W or that both texts stem almost immediately from a common source. This closeness is apparent in the fact that in the following examples the grossest textual errors are repeated in both W and R:

Triad 4, *gwall ap gvyar* (Pen. 16, *Gwalchmei m. G.*); triad 30, *ar lan fergan* (Pen. 16, *alan fyrgan*); triad 11, *selen ap kynan* (elsewhere *Selyf m. K.*); ibid., *auan vedic* (Pen. 16, *Auan 6erdic*, the 'little bard'); triad 33, *Aneirin G6a6t Ryd merch teyrnbeird* (Pen. 16, *A. Gwa6tryd Mechdeyrn Beird*, see note). In

[6] Between sections 5 and 6 there is given a brief group of general triads (pp. 598–9) under the heading *Trioed heuyt y6 y rei hynn.* These also occur in W (*Cy.* VII, pp. 136–8), but they are not relevant to the present discussion except in so far as their occurrence in the manuscript emphasizes the clear differentiation into separate groups of triads which is a feature of this version of *Trioedd Ynys Prydein.*

[7] The text of TYP in Pen. 51 derives ultimately from that of W (see p. xxix below); and from it we may conclude that section 2 and the first part of section 3 above were present in the *Llyfr Gwyn*, but that R's section 1—the *Tri dyn(yon) a gawsant gampeu Adaf*—was not represented in this manuscript. The triad of the 'Women who received Eve's beauty' (triad 50) was unknown to the *Gogynfeirdd*, and is certainly an addition to the original triple group of triads, being based on *Dares Phrygius* (Welsh version *circa* 1300). It is quoted earliest by Dafydd ap Gwilym (GDG no. 50).

triad 55 W's *o vein Gvyned* is altered by R to *owein Gwyned*—a careless slip made by a scribe who was not considering the sense of what he was writing. But it caused at least one early scholar to believe that this triad must date from the time of Owain Gwynedd (see *Cy*. VII, p. 98). Both manuscripts leave a space for the third item of triad 54, *Teir Drut Heirua*, to be filled in later: in W this item has been supplied from another version in a sixteenth-century hand. In 54a there is an instance in which R supplies a better reading than W, where R gives *treulei* for the meaningless *trewyllyei*. This reading is supported by the other manuscripts and must be correct (see note to triad 54). Similarly in triad 9 R corrects W's *a Chaedyrleith* to the intelligible form *a Chaedyrieith*. But an intelligent scribe could have supplied these emendations on his own initiative: they are not sufficient in themselves to prove that W and R derive independently from a common source. However, in an important introduction to the re-issue (1973) of the *Llyfr Gwyn Rhydderch*, first published by Gwenogvryn Evans in 1907; R. M. Jones lays stress (pp. vi–xii) on the amount of evidence offered by the variant spellings in W and R, which indicate that they derive from different copies of the tales. The same is likely to be true of the texts of TYP in the two manuscripts. Cf. also CO(2) x–xi.

In spite of late features and additions to the text (see below) the WR version preserves certain traces of copying from an exemplar which must have been at least as old, and probably older, than that of Pen. 16 and Pen. 45. Certain early orthographical features are common to both W and R; although, as one would expect, they are more numerous in W, and the scribe of R shows a tendency to modernize his exemplar.[8] Below are listed instances in which W preserves traces of an orthography similar to that of the *Black Book of Carmarthen*. Later forms given in R are added in brackets; where there are no such additions, the readings of W and R are identical:

i for *y*: *na cheissint*, triad 8 (R, *-ynt*);

e for *y*: *esgemyd*, triad 24 (Pen. 16, *ysgymyd*); *Dreon*, triad 31 (Pen. 16, *Dryon*); *Heiden*, triad 33 (Pen. 16, *Eidyn*); *Selef*, *aeruedogeon*, triad 25 (R, *Selyf*, *eruedogyon*); *Degynelw*, triad 11 (Pen. 16, *dygynnelw*); *hualhogeon*, *Belen*, triad 62; *melen*, triad 64; *Echemeint*, triad 52 (R, *Echymeint*).

w for *v* (= *f*): *catwarchawc*, triad 18 (R, *catuarchavc*).

[8] Nevertheless the *Gogynfeirdd* seem to have been more familiar with the names and word-forms in the WR version of TYP than with those of the Early Version, in those instances where it is possible to make a distinction. On this point see my chapter 'Cyfeiriadau Traddodiadol a Chwedlonol y Gogynfeirdd', ch. 11 in M. E. Owen and B. F. Roberts (eds), *Beirdd a Thywysogion* (Caerdydd, 1996), pp. 211–12.

In addition this version preserves a number of forms which are paralleled in the language of the ninth-century glosses, and in the *Black Book of Chirk*:

e for *ae*: *y tatmeth*, triad 26a (R, *y datmaeth*, and altered to *y datmaeth* in the following line in W);

e for *ei*: *a thelu*,[9] triad 30b (R, *a theulu*); *yd hanuyde*, triad 26c (R, *hanuydei*);

s for *d* (= *dd*): *Arderys*, triad 31;

c for *ch*: *bryneic*, triad 10; cf. also (*B*)*reat*, triad 26c, where -*t* = -*c* for -*ch* (see note);

absence of prosthetic *y*-: *Sgafnell*, triad 10;

confusion of *th* and *ch*: *meirthion*, triad 14 (R, *meirchyon*); *Tri tharw ellyll*, triad 63 (R *tri charv e.*), where either form is possible.

The medial vowel is preserved in *Tutawal*, triad 2 (R, *Tutwal*, cf. O.W. *Tutagual*, Harl. Gen. VI), and medial -*g*(*u*) in the form *y Vergaed*, triad 26c (Pen. 16, *y Venwaed*), see n.

The following instances of non-lenition of epithets following proper names occur (see p. xx above): *G6ga6n kledyfrud*, triad 40 (R, *gledyfrud*); *G6rtheyrn G6rtheneu*, triad 37d, 51 (in R only; both triads are lacking from W). Non-lenition after the possessive pronoun is preserved in W's *y tatmeth*, triad 26a (R, *y datmaeth*). In triad 30c both texts preserve the old construction by which a lenited accusative directly follows a verb of motion, without intervening preposition, in *yn mynet Gamlan* (see note to triad 30c).

The WR version regularly preserves the Ml.W. lenition of proper names following *verch*, see triads 53, 56–8. This has led to much confusion as to the correct forms of the names by later copyists of the group of triads 56–8 (see note to triad 56).

A striking feature of the WR version in contrast to the Early Version is the addition of comments to a number of triads, which purport to explain the meaning of the key epithets. Such additions are made to triads 8, 17, 25; and some additional explanatory matter about the characters and stories referred to is appended also in this version to triads 20, 22, 26, 28, 33. I have discussed these additions in detail in the notes to the triads concerned. Nothing of the kind is found in the Early Version,[10] and (with the exception of triad 52 where something similar occurs) it is to be noted that the explanations which are added in the WR version are confined to such triads as are attested as existing in a simpler form in the Early Version. In the case of triads 8, 17, 25, these explanatory comments are

[9] *Telu* is found for *teilu* in the Juvencus *englynion* (B VI, pp. 102, 106). The word later became *teulu* under the influence of the *u* in the final syllable.

[10] Unless it may be in the explanation offered for *Tri Aryanllu*, triad 35; see note.

plainly inept,[11] and reveal ignorance on the part of their original redactor as to the real meaning of the key epithet. Nor do the additions made to triads 20, 22, 28, seem likely to contain any genuine additional knowledge as to the stories referred to. But the strange addition made to triad 33 concerning the death of the poet Aneirin may conceivably reflect an early tradition about the *Cynfardd*—if so, it is the more tantalizing that it has come down in so corrupt a form.[12]

The instances of older orthography preserved in the additions to triads 8 and 25 (see above) suggest that these comments are not the work of the scribe of W, but that they have a manuscript history which may take them back at least a century before the date of the *Llyfr Gwyn*. Further, there is a suggestion that the additions made in this version to triads 8, 26, and 28 are inspired by a desire to bring certain references in these triads into conformity with events narrated in the *Mabinogi* in its extant form (see notes to these triads). In contrast to this, I have suggested in my note to triad 67 that the prior existence of this triad (which is preserved only in the version of WR) in an oral form has itself been instrumental in moulding the precise shape given to two incidents in the extant *Mabinogi* (see pp. lxxiii–lxxiv below). But it seems certain that this attempt to bring the two into conformity goes back to a considerably earlier date than that of the *Llyfr Gwyn* itself. If my arguments in this matter are accepted, they lead us to the conclusion that the manuscript transmission of the WR version of TYP has continued in close company with the text of the *Pedeir Keinc* over

[11] In his essay 'On the Justification of Ordering in TYP', SC XVI/XVII, pp. 104–9, E. P. Hamp has queried my support of the original serial arrangement of the triads in Pen. 16 and 45 (the Early Version) as against the arrangement found in WR. Two problems are involved here: one is that of the original listing of TYP when the triads were first committed to writing, and the other is that of the antiquity of individual triads. Evidence for the high antiquity of a part of TYP is to be found in the citation of ten triads in the *Four Branches of the Mabinogi* (PKM xxv), as well as of a few others in the *Hengerdd* (see nn. to triads 13, 18 and 76). Investigation arising from the publication of *Cyfres Beirdd y Tywysogion* has convinced me that the *Gogynfeirdd* drew their allusions to TYP from the original of the WR series, rather than from that of the Early Version (see my chapter 'Cyfeiriadau Traddodiadol a Chwedlonol y Gogynfeirdd' in M. E. Owen and B. F. Roberts (eds), *Beirdd a Thywysogion*. But I adhere to my former conclusion that the serial arrangement of TYP in the Early Version represents the primary written arrangement of the triads. Here nos. 1–25 of the series all present the names and patronymics of three traditional heroes, grouped together under a complimentary, but designedly ambiguous epithet. When first drawn up, the whole series was inaugurated by the *Tri Hael*, as in the sixteenth-century printed version *Y Diarebion Camberäec* (below p. xxxiv), and this was undoubtedly the most popular and the most frequently quoted of all the triads. Before expanding the series, the redactor of the WR version added some explanatory comments of his own to some of the earlier triads, and these comments tend to be either ignorant or merely inept.

[12] On the triad and other early references to the poet Aneirin see M. E. Owen, 'Hwn yw e Gododin. Aneirin ae cant', *Ast. H.* 134ff.

a number of years previous to the appearance of both in the *Llyfr Gwyn*—and that each has had a significant influence upon the other.[13]

PENIARTH 47, PART III. Fifteenth century (*Rep.* I, p. 381); pages 17–25. This text contains most of the triads found in the Early Version, with certain important additions (triads 70–80). Although the triads are not given in the same order as in the Early Version, yet it will be seen from the table, pp. xiii–xv above, that certain 'floating sections' are preserved intact in Pen. 47, as they are also in Pen. 50. These are sufficient in themselves to prove that the affinities of both manuscripts are with the Early Version rather than with that of WR. A further comparison of the manuscript readings shows that the text of Pen. 47 is related more closely to that of Pen. 45 than to that of Pen. 16. Cf. the following examples in which the two correspond as against Pen. 16: *Bedravt*, triad 21 (Pen. 16, *Bedra6c*); *a phlewdvr fflam*, triad 9 (Pen. 16, *fleudur flam*); *gwenenen*, triad 26C (Pen. 16, *gwenynen*); *Llocheu*, triad 4 (Pen. 45, *llecheu*, with confusion of *o* and *e*; Pen. 16, *Llacheu*). It is however unlikely that Pen. 45 was the immediate source of this manuscript. It is to be noted that Pen. 47 gives the WR version of triad 18 *Tri Chatvarchawc* in preference to that of the Early Version, and contains in addition a few triads which are represented in WR but not in the Early Version: nos. 50, 56, 57, 58. These belong to a group of eight triads which are designated in the manuscript of Pen. 47 as *Trioedd y Gwragedd*; cf. the note appended in the manuscript to the end of triad 58: *hyt hyn y dywetpwyt y trioed arbennic*[14] *a thrioed y milwyr a thrioed y gvraged. traethvn bellach trioed y meirch*. The version of *Trioedd y Meirch* which follows is one of especial interest. It is certainly not dependent on the text of the Early Version, but shares certain features in common with the fragment of *Trioedd y Meirch* which is preserved in the *Black Book of Carmarthen* (see below, p. lxxxv, n. 136). These consist in the inclusion of the name of Gwalchmai's horse (Pen. 47, *Meingalet*; LlDC, *Kein Caled*; see triad 46A and variants of triad 42), and the name *Bacheslwm serch* [*sic*], triad 40—this is the only manuscript to give any

[13] In this connection it is perhaps not an insignificant detail that it is only in the *Pedeir Keinc* and in TYP that the epithet *bendigeit* 'blessed' is found attached to the name of *Brân vab Llŷr* (see note). I have suggested (note to triad 37) that the original significance of this epithet is directly related to the episode of Brân's burial which is described both in triad 37 and in *Mabinogi Branwen*. See also note to *Katwalad(y)r Vendigeit*.

[14] This group of triads does not in fact accompany TYP in this manuscript, but the note makes it clear that the *Trioed Arbennic* must have been present in the exemplar from which the scribe was copying. From the content of this list it is clear that *arbennic* in the title has the meaning of 'sacred', since a combination of religious, pseudo-learned, and proverbial matter follows. The *Trioed Arbennic* precede TYP in the versions of Pen. 45, Pen. 50, and Pen. 77, thus claiming for these triads a superior status. See edn. and discussion of 'Y Trioedd Arbennig' by M. E. Owen, B XXIV, pp. 434–50.

equivalent epithet for BBC's *Bucheslom seri*. Pen. 47's *Ruhyr reon tuthvleid* (variant of 41a) looks like a corruption of BBC's *Ruthir ehon tuth bleid* (variant of 42a) and is closer to this form than any of the variants of the name which appear in the other manuscripts. This adds interest to the additional *Trioedd y Meirch* (triads 46A and B) which appear in the text of Pen. 47 alone. Triad 46A is evidently a version of the BBC triad *Tri gohoev etystir* (variant of triad 42), but substitutes the name *Myngrwn march Gwedw*—this is the *Guyn Mygtwn march Gwedw* of CO ll. 689, 1006, 1177, who is not elsewhere included in *Trioedd y Meirch*. There is no reason to suppose that triads 46A and B are not as old as the rest of the group to which they belong; and it is not improbable that both offer names which were included in the lost part of the BBC text.

Finally, this text preserves certain echoes of the older poetry which are not found in the other manuscripts of TYP. Pen. 47's reading in triad 45 *ych brychbras y beuren* recalls *ych brychbras y penrvy*, BT 55.21–3. *Ysgwydvrith march llemenic* (variant of triad 43c) is paralleled only in the *Canu y Meirch* (BT 48), which has *Yscvydurith yscodic gorwyd llemenic* (see below, p. lxxxii). The key epithet *Tri engiriaul* of triad 76 would seem to be related to the reference in the *Gododdin* to *tridid engiriaul* (CA l. 1252), although the names in the triad as we have it have plainly been altered (see note). But the explanation of these things may simply lie in the fact that the original redactor of the Pen. 47 series had worked over the *hengerdd*. (For some further light on the provenance of this manuscript see below, pp. xliii–xliv.)

Among the additions to TYP found in this manuscript is *Tri Gwyndorllwyth* (triad 70). This triad can be shown on linguistic and textual evidence to be as old, in its original form, as any of the triads in the earlier manuscripts (see note), although a certain amount of alteration in the names in the triad as we have it in Pen. 47 has partially obscured its original nucleus, and it happens that Pen. 50 preserves a better version. There are a few other instances in which Pen. 47 preserves traces of an older orthography, which are not paralleled in the texts of the corresponding triads in Pen. 16 or Pen. 45, and which indicate an exemplar at least as old as the prototype of this text:

e for *y*: *(m)enydawc*, triad 31 (Pen. 16, *Mynyda6c*); *Manawedan*, triad 8; *Keheret*, triad 39 (showing also confusion of *o*, *e*; Pen. 16, W: *Ky(h)oret*);

w for *v* (= *f*): *bethewnos*, triad 29c;

o for *w*: *porthavr gado*, triad 9 (Pen. 16, *-gadw*).

Non-lenition of an epithet which is lenited in the other versions appears in triad 9: *Echel mordvytwll* (see below p. xc).

Triads 71, 72, 73, are combined in this manuscript in a group with triads 19, 21, all of which include the name of *Drystan* (*m. Tallwch*). They bear witness to the increase in the popularity of *Drystan* (= *Tristan*) as a result of the romances, at the time when the Pen. 47 collection was formed.

PENIARTH 50, pages 149–60 (the end of TYP is wanting). This is the famous manuscript known as *Y Cwta Cyfarwydd* (the 'Short Guide') which contains a large collection of prose and poetry, written in the first half of the fifteenth century, somewhere in west Morgannwg or Gower—perhaps by a certain *Dauyd* (whose name occurs on p. 114), and who may have been a monk at Neath abbey (see *Rep.* I, p. 389; G. J. Williams, *Traddodiad Llenyddol Morgannwg*, pp. 11, 192). Dates ranging between the years 1425–56 are found on different pages of the manuscript. Professor Williams points out that the scribe of this manuscript had a first-hand knowledge of the *Book of Llan Dâv*: he quotes the *Llyfr Teilo* and gives a Welsh translation of one of its charters as evidence for the ancient boundaries of the kingdom of Morgannwg (for the passage see *Cy.* IX, pp. 325–6; LL 247–9). Of the additional triads (nos. 81–6) which (with the exception of 84) are found only in this manuscript, it is to be noted that triads 82 and 83 betray a strong interest in St Teilo and in Llan Dâv: triad 83 is indeed a direct quotation from the passage in the *Vita* of the saint contained in LL, which describes the miracle of St Teilo's triple body. We may probably conclude that these two triads, which he prefixed to the beginning of his collection, are the personal contribution of the scribe of this manuscript.

This text of TYP shows affinities in its grouping of the triads with Pen. 47, and the two manuscripts contain in common some additions to the Early Version which (with a single exception) do not appear in any other text (nos. 70,[15] 71, 74, 75). There is a case of *achub y blaen* between triads 7 and 8, where the title *Tri tharw unben y. p.* of triad 7 is followed by the names which belong to triad 8: this offers confirmation for the fact that the scribe was here following an exemplar with grouping similar to that of the Early Version. But Pen. 50 is not a copy of Pen. 47, and it has already been pointed out that this manuscript contains a better and older version of triad 70 than does Pen. 47. It contains a version of *Enweu Ynys Prydein* (App. I) as well as certain other triads which are found in the WR version (nos. 52, 53, 54, 59), but which do not appear in manuscripts of the Early Version. A few instances of the preservation of an archaic orthography in the text of Pen. 50 may be noted:

[15] Triad 70 is found in C 6, but this manuscript may be derived in part from Pen. 50; see pp. xxxi–xxxii below.

w for *v* (= *f*) *Morwyd*, triads 70, 71;
e for *y* in *Brecheina6c*, triad 81; *Kenvawr*, triad 6; *Mynedawc*, triad 33;
e for *ei* in *Geryoet*, triad 52c.

The interest in ecclesiastical legend already observed, combined with an interest in literary romance material, is conspicuous elsewhere in this text of TYP. The version of triad 70 (*Tri Gwyndorllwyth*) given in this manuscript brings out clearly the nucleus around which this triad was evolved, in a reference to the miraculous fertility of *Nevyn* daughter of *Brychan Brecheniauc*, as this is expounded in the early document *De Situ Brecheniauc* (see EWGT 15 (14)). The same interest in the family of Brychan is evinced in triad 81, *Tri Santeidd Linys*. The substitution here of *llinys Joseph o Arimathia* for that of *Caw o Brydyn* in older versions of this triad may probably also be regarded as the work of the scribe of the manuscript, and the interest thus betrayed in the subject matter of *Y Seint Greal* is repeated in another of Pen. 50's additions, triad 86, *Tri Marchawc a enillawd y Greal.* No other text of TYP (except Vaughan's transcript of Pen. 50) has this latter triad in quite the same form, and I think it probable that this triad also is the work of the scribe himself. It is interesting to find that the triad implies a wider knowledge of the French Vulgate Arthurian romances than the writer could have obtained merely from a knowledge of *Y Seint Greal*, the Welsh translation of one 'branch' only of these romances (see note to triad 86). We know that two copies of *Y Seint Greal* were in existence in this part of South Wales during the fifteenth century (*Traddodiad Llenyddol Morgannwg*, pp. 12–13, 148)—one in the possession of the Glamorgan *bonheddig* Hopcyn ap Tomas, and the other in that of Trahaern ap Ieuan ap Meurig, who lived near Caerleon, and to whom Guto'r Glyn addressed his *cywydd* begging for the loan of the book on behalf of the abbot of Glyn y Groes (Valle Crucis) (GGl, pp. 303–4). It is evident that a copy of *Y Seint Greal*, the romance so highly esteemed in Glamorgan at the time, was at the disposal of the scribe of *Y Cwta Cyfarwydd.* Interest in the romances and in Geoffrey of Monmouth's *Historia Regum* appears in the substitution of *Caerllion* in triad 85 as the site of one of Arthur's *teir prif lys*, in place of *Aberffraw* in the older version of this triad (App. I, 4); and again in the addition made in this manuscript to triad 35, which alludes to Geoffrey's tale of St Ursula and thc virgins of Cologne (see *var. lccta* to triad 35). It seems however that the scribe had some additional knowledge of the legend of St Ursula which he could not have derived from Geoffrey (see note to *Dunawt tywyssawc Kernyw*).

Perhaps the enterprise of this scribe in bringing new ecclesiastical and secular material into the time-honoured framework of *Trioedd Ynys Prydein* is to be explained in relation to the fact noted by Professor G. J.

Williams (*Traddodiad Llenyddol Morgannwg*, p. 147), that it became the custom in the fourteenth and fifteenth centuries for *boneddigion* to pay copyists—probably in many cases ecclesiastics—to compile for them manuscript codices of prose and poetry.

PENIARTH 51, pages 170–85 (*Rep.* I, p. 399). This manuscript is in the autograph of the *pencerdd* Gwilym Tew of Morgannwg, who was at the height of his career *circa* 1470[16] (*Bywgraffiadur*). It contains a mixed collection of prose and verse, including a copy of the *dwned* or bardic grammar, genealogies, a list of words from the *Gododdin*, and the oldest copy of the *Tri Thlws ar Ddeg* (App. III). It is interesting as being the earliest manuscript extant which is known to be the work of a bard and not of an ecclesiastic (see G. J. Williams, *Traddodiad Llenyddol Morgannwg*, p. 48). Ifor Williams has pointed out the ineptitude of the 'explanations' given in the word-list from the *Gododdin* (B I, pp. 216 ff.): evidently by the latter part of the fifteenth century much of the old bardic vocabulary had passed into oblivion, even among the *penceirddiaid*. This fact is relevant in relation to the very confused and corrupt text of TYP given in this manuscript. It is apparent that Gwilym Tew was content to copy mechanically the text which lay before him, even when what he wrote conveyed little or no meaning. The version of TYP here given is that of WR, with certain omissions and some slight alterations in the order of the triads. Section I of the *Llyfr Coch* (= triads 47–50, see p. xx above) is not included, and the text begins with section 2: *Porth a aeth gan yrp luyddiawc* [*sic*]. The text is so inaccurate that it seems impossible that it could have been taken down directly from either W or R. But since it contains certain names which have dropped out of R (triad 56b, *Vthr ap Greidiol*; triad 33, *Iago ap peli*) and on occasion preserves W's readings where these differ from those of R (cf. triad 63), it would appear that Gwilym Tew's exemplar stood closer to the text of W than to that of R. It is therefore of interest to find that, except for section 1 of the WR series (see p. xx above), this text includes all those triads which, though represented in R, are lacking from the lost beginning of W (nos. 3, 12, 15, 35, 37, 44, 51, in the numbering of this book, see table; pp. xiii–xv). Pen. 51 therefore indicates that these triads were originally contained in W as well as in R; but it suggests that section 1 (*Tri Dyn a gauas Kedernit Adaf*, etc.) was absent from the *Llyfr Gwyn*. It is possible, therefore, that in spite of the corrupt state of the text, Pen. 51's version of the triads listed above may preserve some of the lost readings contained in W. This suggestion gives particular significance to

[16] R. S. Loomis quotes the opinion of Sir W. Ll. Davies, former Librarian of the National Library of Wales, that Pen. 51 dates from '*circa* 1460' (WAL 46, n. 23).

Pen. 51's version of triad 51 which, instead of *Trywyr Gwarth*, is entitled *Tair Gormes Ynys Prydain*—the title of triad 36. In my note to triad 51 I have shown that *Trywyr Gwarth*, which is based entirely on the narrative of the *Brut*, has been substituted in the WR version for the *Teir Gormes* of the Early Version, and that both triads deal essentially with the same theme, that of the successive invasions which entered Britain. Pen. 51 adds at the end of this triad a reference to *Iddaw*(*c*) *Cor*(*dd*) *Prydein* as plotting the battle of Camlan. But if this allusion to a character distinctive of *Breudwyt Ronabwy* was derived from an earlier version of the triad, it is difficult to see why it did not make its way into the *Llyfr Coch* collection—more probably it is an addition by the scribe.

Throughout the text of TYP a number of corrections have been subsequently added above the line, in a darker ink and in a later hand. These corrections are from a much better text, which is either that of R itself or a copy, since where any distinction exists, the readings correspond with those of R as against W (triad 60c, *Gwiwawn* = *Gviavn* in W; triad 54a, *nis treulei* = *nis trewyllei* in W).

Gwilym Tew's copy offers one interesting variant. This is in triad 34, where one of the *Teir Anvat 6wyalla6t* is the blow which *talhaearn a trewis e veirin yni ffen* [*sic*]. The other texts state that a certain (*H*)*eidyn* slew Aneirin. The manuscript readings of this version are too corrupt for us to put much faith in them, yet the suggestion here given that W's confused rendering of the *Tair Bwyellawd* really conceals a tradition that Aneirin was slain by another of the famous *Cynfeirdd* offers an intriguing possibility. Gwilym Tew certainly did not recognize Aneirin's name in the allusion, or surely he would not have written it in this manner.

Peniarth 27, Part II. This manuscript belongs to the latter half of the fifteenth century (*Rep.* I, p. 355; see also B XV, p. 99, n.). Pages 87–8 contain a finely-written, complete, and fairly accurate copy of *Trioedd y Meirch* alone, not accompanied by the rest of TYP. The order of the triads does not correspond with that of any of the other versions: triads 38–44 in this book appear in the order 2, 7, 4, 5, 6, 3, 1, in Pen. 27.

Peniarth 77, pp. 304–6. The part of the manuscript containing TYP was written in 1576 by Sir Thomas Wiliems of Trefriw (*Rep.* I, p. 509). The text is only fragmentary, and gives TYP after the list entitled *Trioed Arbennic*[17] (p. 303). There are however several points of interest about this text of TYP. It combines a grouping which, with omissions, represents that of the

[17] See p. xxv, n. 14 above. Morfydd Owen tells me that the version of this text given here corresponds closely with that found in Pen. 45 and 50.

Early Version (cf. nos. 1, 18–26, on the table, pp. xiii–xv). In addition it includes triads 47–50, which constitute section 1 of the version of TYP contained in the *Llyfr Coch* (p. xx above), and which do not appear in the Early Version. Moreover this text of the group *Tri dynyon a gawssant gampeu adaf*, etc. (triads 47–50) is remarkable in that it preserves a variant of triad 49 with names paralleled only in Prydydd y Moch's quotation of the triad (see n. to triad 47). Evidently, therefore, this variant is independent of, and earlier than, the text of R. Pen. 77 includes also a complete text of *Teir Drut Heirua* (triad 54), which is defective in WR, and is absent from the Early Version. It is apparent therefore that this manuscript owes nothing to the text of the *Llyfr Gwyn* or the *Llyfr Coch*, but that from an independent source it presents certain of the triads which are characteristic of the WR version. Pen. 77 also contains (p. 213) a text of the *Tri Thlws ar Ddeg* (App. III) and (p. 209) of the *Pedwar Marchog ar Hugain* (App. IV).

British Library Additional 31,055, p. 26 (= BL[1]), and Peniarth 240, p. 93. The former manuscript was written by Sir Thomas Wiliems in 1594–6 (*Rep.* II, p. 1053), and is the source of the fragment of TYP contained in Pen. 240, which was written by the Revd W. Wynn about 1755. The writer of this manuscript states that the triads he gives are 'allan o Lyfr Mr Tho. Wiliams Physygwr llythyren am lythyren'. This version is based on that of WR, as is apparent from the grouping of the triads. It includes *Enweu Ynys Prydein* (App. I), in the form in which this appears in W, and follows the reading of W against that of R in triad 56b. It is evident therefore that it is derived ultimately from the text of the *Llyfr Gwyn*. The triads presented are nos. 8, 18, 23, 24, 26, 54–8, 67, 68, 69.

Peniarth 252. Seventeenth century. On pp. 169–70 is a fragment of TYP. The triads included are nos. 11, 15, 35, 37, 51, 59, 63–6, with two additions, triad 46c (an addition to the *Trioedd y Meirch*, not represented elsewhere) and triad 87 (see note). The version followed is that of WR, but the text is very corrupt, and the manuscript much stained, and in places difficult to decipher. The beginning is torn. A point of interest is the title given to triad 35, *Tri Arianllu Ynys Brydain*, which serves to link the text with NLW 6434 (see below, p. xxxviii), and so with the lost *Book of Sir Richard Wynn of Gwydir*.

Hafod 3. Early seventeenth century (*Rep.* II, p. 302). On p. 178 is given as an isolated unit triads 47–50, *Tri dyn a gafas kadernyd adda* = section 1 in the *Llyfr Coch* (see p. xx above).

Cardiff 6. *circa* 1550. Pages 1–6 contain a fragment of TYP presenting the following triads: nos. 2, 5, 6, 10, 11, 17, 29, 30, 52, 53, 62, 70. Later in the same manuscript (p. 105) the short version (see pp. xxxvii–xxxviii below) of *Trywyr Gwarth* (triad 51) occurs by itself. Apart from the fact that here—as in all versions of TYP—triads 29, 30, are kept together as a pair, nothing can be deduced from the order of the triads in this manuscript as to its affiliations. C 6 combines triads which are characteristic of each of the two main series, and it does not seem possible to show that it is related exclusively to the one rather than to the other. The text of those triads which are represented in the Early Version is closer to that of Pen. 50 than to any other extant manuscript (cf. *var. lecta* of triads 5, 6, 62, 70). On the other hand this manuscript has the WR version of triad 29 and includes triad 51, which is absent from the Early Version. Interesting variants found in this version are those which appear in the text of triad 30 concerning the *teulu* of *Alan Fyrgan* (see note to triad 30), and the variant in the title of triad 70, *Tri aur dorllwyth*. The compound *aurdorllwyth* occurs in a poem by Iolo Goch (GIG no. V.38n.), where its use may well be reminiscent of the triad (see note to triad 70). This version also adds a triad which is found in no other manuscript. This is triad 91, *Tri Diofnog*, which is based on part II of *Y Seint Greal* (= *Perlesvaus*, see note to triad 91). This triad should be compared with triad 86 which is based on *Y Seint Greal*, part I, and which, as suggested above (p. xxviii), was probably contributed to TYP by the scribe of Pen. 50. Since C 6 betrays a relation with Pen. 50 in its readings in a number of other triads, it is tempting to believe that this triad also was made by the scribe of Pen. 50, and that it was included among the triads in that manuscript which were represented in the concluding pages of TYP which have been lost.

CARDIFF 18. Late sixteenth and early seventeenth century (*Rep.* II, p. 172). On p. 59 the triad *Tair Gwragedd a fu i Vrychan Vrycheiniog* (triad 96) is prefixed to genealogical material. On pp. 72–5 is a selection of TYP (see p. xv above). The affinities are with the Early Version, and the text is closer to Pen. 16 than to Pen. 45; but there are differences in the order of the triads. The variant *adfwyn* in triad 31 presents the reading of WR as against the *adwy* of the Early Version.

Y DIAREBION CAMBERÄEC and the BOOK OF SIR RICHARD WYNN OF GWYDIR. One of the earliest printed books to be published in Welsh contains a version of *Trioedd Ynys Prydain*. This is *Y Diarebion Camberäec*, the second edition of William Salesbury's *Oll Synnwyr Pen*[18] (1547), of which

[18] See D. J. Bowen, *Gruffudd Hiraethog a'i Oes* (Caerdydd, 1958), p. 55, and references cited below. Triads whose demonstrable source is the printed text in *Y Diarebion Camberäec* are cited by Wm. Camden in his *Britannia* (1586); see R. Bromwich, B XXIII, pp. 14–17.

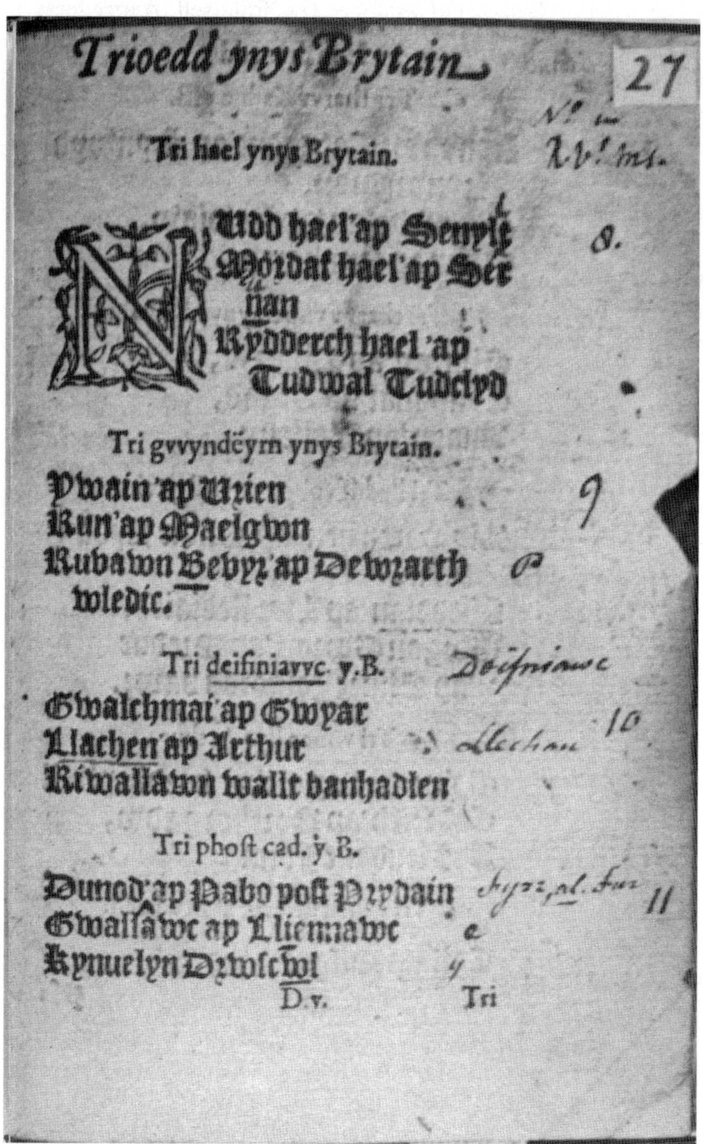

Trioedd ynys Brytain.

Tri hael ynys Brytain.

Nudd hael ap Senyllt
Mordaf hael ap Servan
Rydderch hael ap Tudwal Tudclyd

Tri gvvyndeyrn ynys Brytain.

Owain ap Urien
Run ap Maelgwn
Rubawn Bebyr ap Dewrarth wledic.

Tri deifiniavvc y.B.

Gwalchmai ap Gwyar
Llachen ap Arthur
Riwallawn wallt banhadlen

Tri phost cad. y B.

Dunod ap Pabo post Prydain
Gwallawc ap Lliennawc
Kynuelyn Drwscbol

D.v. Tri

First page of *Trioedd Ynys Prydein* in *Y Diarebion Camberäec* (1567?). Reproduced by kind permission of The National Library of Wales.

a single mutilated copy has so far come to light, which is preserved in the British Library. This work contains a corrected and slightly expanded version of the proverbs in *Oll Synnwyr Pen*, followed by a version of TYP, which includes in addition a few general and proverbial triads. The book lacks not only the title-page[19] but also a section of the proverbs, and a number of pages at the end, which comprised the conclusion of TYP. Alun Mathias has shown[20] that the original contents of the volume can be reconstructed from a manuscript copy of the full printed text which has come down in NLW 6434 'Llyfr Thomas Wynn o'r Dyffryn', which was written in 1577, partly by a professional copyist named Ieuan Llwyd.[21] The contents of this manuscript bear the title 'Crynodab or Diarebion Sathredig: Trioedd Ynys Prydain a Thalm or Philosophi neu'r hen athronddysg Camberaig'.[22] A date of publication for *Y Diarebion Camberäec* between the years 1565 and 1568, and probably in the year 1567, is to be deduced from the *Llythyr Annerch* to Richard Langford which Salesbury prefixed to the work, and which is preserved in NLW 6434.[23]

A comparison of the text of TYP in DC with that in NLW 6434 places beyond doubt the fact that the two are very closely related; and Mr Mathias has demonstrated conclusively that NLW 6434 represents a copy of the printed text, by showing that the presence of eight triads in DC, which are absent from the manuscript version, is to be explained as due to the fact that the copyist inadvertently turned over two pages at once, thus passing from the middle of the triad *Tri Eurgelein* (no. 61 in this book) to one of the *Trioedd y Meirch* (no. 42), so that his text reads:

> Tri aur gelain y. B. madoc ap Brwyn. kyngain ap pelliawc. ellwyd march alser ap maelgwyn.[24]

[19] Since the title-page is missing the work has come to be known by the title which appears on the top of the first page, *Y Diarebion Camberäec*. For this text of TYP I employ the abbreviation DC.

[20] Alun Mathias, 'Astudiaeth o Weithgarwch Llenyddol William Salesbury', (University of Wales M.A. thesis, 1949), pp. 191 ff.; *Journal of the Welsh Bibliographical Society* VII, pp. 125–33.

[21] *Handlist of Manuscripts in the National Library of Wales*, vols I/II (1940–51), p. 180.

[22] In addition to the proverbs and TYP the manuscript contains the following texts: (i) *Geirie Gwir Taliesin*, (ii) *llyma XXIIII Gwell*, (iii) *llyma Gas Bethau Owain Kyveiliog*, (iv) *Traethawt o Athronddysg Gamberaig*, (v) *Traethawt o Gymmendawt Camberaig*, (vi) *Y Diarebion Cambereg*.

[23] Alun Mathias, op. cit., pp. 192–4. For the text of the *Llythyr Annerch* see Garfield H. Hughes (ed.), *Rhagymadroddion 1547–1659* (Caerdydd, 1951), pp. xi–xii; T. H. Parry-Williams (ed.), *Rhyddiaith Gymraeg: Y Gyfrol Gyntaf 1488–1609* (Caerdydd, 1954), pp. 69–71.

[24] Cf. triad 42 below, and A. Mathias, 'William Salesbury—Ei Fywyd a'i Weithiau', in G. Bowen (ed.), *Y Traddodiad Rhyddiaith yn yr Oesau Canol* (Llandysul, 1970), pp. 49–51.

The eight triads in DC which do not appear in NLW 6434 correspond in serial order with the triads numbered in this volume as follows: 62, 17, 63, 64, 65, 66, 11, 42. The other triads in this volume of which the printed text has come down in DC are numbers 2–11, 18, 19, 21, 22, 27–30, 38–46, 60, 61. The remaining triads found in NLW 6434 (amounting to 15 of TYP together with some of the proverbial triads) were presumably found also in DC, though they were on the pages which have since been lost. (For these see table, pp. xiii–xv above.) In the textual notes I have recorded the few instances in which the text of NLW differs from that of DC.

Robert Vaughan knew of the existence of DC, though he was unable to obtain a copy of the work. He refers to it in a letter to Archbishop Ussher dated November 1653: 'I am tould (and think it true) that it (the Triades) hath beene printed long since together with some Welshe proverbs, but I cannot learne where any printed copy is to be found.'[25] At a much later date the book was known and used by the *Myvyrian* editors, who quote variants from 'Ll. Argraff' in the footnotes to the first series of triads.[26] Evan Evans refers to 'the old printed copy of the Triades' for the variant reading *gwawdrwy* (triad 11) in his copy of Lewis Morris's translation of TYP in Panton 29 (p. 71, see p. li below).

Some further light on the source of the version of TYP printed by Salesbury in DC may be derived from certain later copies of this version. Three eighteenth-century manuscripts present the same text, either in complete form, or in the form of a list of textual variants which correspond

[25] Quoted in *Journal of the Welsh Bibliographical Society* VII, p. 133. For Vaughan's letter to Ussher see C. R. Elrington, *The Whole Works of the Most Reverend James Ussher* (Dublin, 1847–64), xvi, 597; and T. Emrys Parry, '*Llythyrau Robert Vaughan, Hengwrt*, gyda rhagymadrodd a nodiadau' (University of Wales M.A. thesis, Bangor, 1961). On the encouragement given by Archbishop Ussher to Vaughan to collect and afterwards to translate TYP, see my *Trioedd Ynys Prydain in Welsh Literature and Scholarship*, pp. 6–8, and refs there given.

[26] MA^2 388–94. In a few instances the editors have erroneously labelled as 'Ll. Argraff' variants which do not correspond with the readings of the printed text. These are p. 389, col. 2, where 'Ll. Argraff' is cited for *Ffleidur* (DC: *Ffleuddvr*), *Dyssyfndod* (DC: *Dysgyfedawc*), *Avan Ferddig* (DC: *Auan Uerdeic*), *Hyd au* (DC: *byd a ei*), p. 391, col. 2: *Echemeint* (absent from DC and NLW), p. 394, col. 1: *Lles* (DC: *lleu*), *trwyddawc* (DC: *Arwyddawc*). That the *Myvyrian* editors used the identical copy of DC now preserved in BL, which was defective then as now, is demonstrated by the fact that no variants are cited from the latter part of the text which has come down only in NLW 6434. Conclusive proof of this is to be found in a note which Owen Jones prefixed to his copy of the triads from DC in BL Addl. 15,023 (see p. lii below), which accurately describes the imperfect condition of the volume, and states that its owner at the time was Richard Morris. Traces of the work of William Owen Pughe(?) are found in the margins, where the number of the triad in 'RV's MS.' [*sic*] is added to each triad, and a number of the variant readings in the text have been underlined, while the corresponding forms from Vaughan's manuscript have been written in the margin (see plate, p. xxxiii). See further G. J. Williams, *Journal of the Welsh Bibliographical Society* X, p. 9.

with the readings of DC and NLW, and each of these manuscripts refers to the source of this version as the 'Book of Sir Richard Wynn of Gwydir'. Harley MS. 4181 was written by the herald Hugh Thomas about the year 1700. On pp. 1–6 is found a copy of TYP from the *Llyfr Coch*, which is followed on p. 6 by another version, corresponding both textually and in the order of the triads with DC, which is introduced as follows:

> There is another History under the same title with this, now or late in the custody of Sir Richard Win of Gwider, collected by a learned Priest called Thomas ap Ieuan ap David ap Kynrig ap Iorwerth, who was a greate traviler, and had some time studied at Rome as himselfe saith, and wrote with all integrity imaginable about the year 1500.

Variant readings from the same text are quoted by Moses Williams in C 36[27] and in his collection of TYP in Ll. 65 (see below, p. xlvii). In C 36 there is found the same superscription as is quoted above. A note in Ll. 65 states that the *Book of Sir Richard Wynn* was in the possession of Sir John Wynn, the fifth baronet, in the year 1717. The original owner of the work may have been either the second baronet (1588–1649) or the fourth baronet, to whom Robert Vaughan dedicated his *British Antiquities Revived* in 1662 (see *Bywgraffiadur* 1032).

The superscription which is prefixed to this version of TYP in both Harl. 4181 and C 36 can hardly be taken as implying that the *Book of Sir Richard Wynn* was a printed copy of *Y Diarebion Camberäec*. On the contrary, it suggests that the original of Salesbury's text was a collection of *Trioedd* made *circa* 1500 by the 'Learned Priest' referred to as *Thomas ap Ieuan*, etc., and it is possible that the lost pages of the printed version originally contained a note to this effect. But if this is so, it is surprising that no note of the kind has been reproduced in NLW 6434. And there are other difficulties as well. The version of TYP contained in Harl. 4181 reproduces the same error in the text of *Tri Eurgelein* as has already been noted (p. xxxiv) as occurring in NLW 6434, and contains in consequence the same lacuna of eight triads; and we can only conclude from this that Harl. 4181 is itself ultimately dependent on the copy of the printed text represented by NLW 6434. Since the two other eighteenth-century manuscripts referred to above merely quote variants from the *Book of Sir Richard Wynn*, it is impossible to tell whether the text on which they are based contained the same omission.

[27] This is a manuscript of the early eighteenth century (*Rep.* II, p. 231). The date '26 Nov. 1717' is appended to the triads. On pp. 1–28 are triads from the *Llyfr Coch* with variants in another hand, which I judge to be that of Moses Williams. It seems probable that C 36 is a rough draft for the collated text of TYP which Moses Williams wrote later in Ll. 65 (see below, pp. xlvii ff.).

But it must remain in doubt whether the attribution of this version to *Thomas ap Ieuan*, etc., appeared in Salesbury's text, or in its original, or whether it became appended to this version at some subsequent period.

The three eighteenth-century copies of this version share in common certain other additions to the text of TYP, some of which do not appear either in DC or in NLW. Two additional triads (which I have not included in this volume) are introduced among the general triads in NLW, but head the collection of TYP in Harl. 4181, as follows:

Tri Thywysogion y syth: Michael a Gabriel a Raphael.
Tri Thywysog Saint: Adha, Moeses, a Pheter.[28]

The three eighteenth-century manuscripts also present some North Welsh genealogical triads, and both Harl. 4181 and C 36 claim that the source of these was the *Book of Sir Richard Wynn*. These manuscripts also contain a text of the *Pedwar Marchog ar Hugain* (App. IV) which was apparently derived from the same source. App. IV and the two triads which head Harl. 4181 may be late additions to this version of TYP; while the rest of the series, in common with Salesbury's printed version, may go back to a manuscript collection of TYP which originated in the manner described, and which came into the possession of the second or fourth baronet whose name it later bore, at a date subsequent to the publication of DC.

The version of TYP represented by DC, NLW, and Harl. 4181, is a 'contaminated' version. The text of the triads contained in it adheres in the main to the readings of the Early Version, though there are a few exceptions (e.g. the extraordinary error *Aneirin merch teyrnbeird* in triad 33 which persists only in the WR version and the transcripts based upon it). Certain groups recur in the order of their presentation in the Early Version (nos. 2–11, 17–25 in this book, see table on pp. xiii–xv above), while nos. 56–61, 62–6 (the latter found in DC only, see above) present a sequence which occurs only in the WR version. In addition there are certain triads (nos. 14, 15, 20, 22, 33, 35) which occur in both versions, but in which the text here presented is closer to WR than to the Early Version. The composite nature of the DC text is further illustrated by the fact that it contains two separate versions of triads 10, 11, 42. An interesting feature of this version is that both DC and NLW head the series of TYP with the *Tri Hael* (triad 2), and I have suggested (see n. to triad 2) that this triad originally headed the series in the Early Version.

[28] In this text there appears the following ill-conceived attempt to create a new triad. After triad 21 are the following words: *Tri Abedrawg oedh Nonn. . . .* Attempts to elucidate the epithet *abedrawg* failed until I noted that at the corresponding place in NLW were the words *A bedrawc oedd hvnv* (cf. triad 21: *Bedwyr m. bedra6c oed h6nn6*). The copyist took these words to be the beginning of a new triad.

Other features of the *Book of Sir Richard Wynn* as represented by NLW and the three later manuscripts are the following: (i) in this version triad 35 was given its variant title *Tri Arianllu Ynys Prydain* (see note); (ii) this manuscript contained a shortened version of triad 51, *Trywyr Gwarth*, which agreed with the version of this triad found in C 6 (a variant of triad 51 below, after that of the *Llyfr Coch*); (iii) it contained a shortened and distinctive version of triad 86 (see *var. lecta*); (iv) it contained the triad *Tri Hynaif Byd* (triad 92). Nos. (iii) and (iv) appear only in this group of manuscripts. P. C. Bartrum, *Nat. Lib. of Wales Journal* XIII, p. 144, would identify *The Book of Sir Richard Wynn* with Pen. 127.

Note. An additional text of this version of TYP is to be found in BL Addl. 15,047, folios 54 v.–74 r. (See *Catalogue of Additions to the Manuscripts in the British Museum* for the year 1844, p. 78.) This manuscript was written by the Radnorshire bard Hywel ap Syr Mathew in the years 1575–6. The interest of the version of TYP which it contains consists in the fact that while this version corresponds closely with DC and NLW both in its textual readings and in the order of the triads, it is plainly derived from an independent source. Under the heading *Trioedd Ynys Brydain weithan a gair* there follows the *Tri Hael* and all subsequent triads (omitting only triad 4) in the order in which they appear in NLW, plus the eight triads referred to above as missing from NLW, which are preserved in DC. As in DC and NLW, a group of proverbial triads is interpolated into the middle of the text of TYP. The series concludes with a number of triads which are found in the older collections, but which do not appear either in NLW or in DC. Included in it also are the two triads *Tri Thywysogion* and *Tri Thywysog Saint*, which I have referred to (p. xxxvii) above as appearing in the manuscripts of this version. Appendix IV is not included, however, nor does this text contain the superscription found in the eighteenth-century manuscripts, associating this version with the *Book of Sir Richard Wynn*. I am indebted to P. C. Bartrum for directing me to this manuscript, which unfortunately came to my knowledge too late for me to include reference to it in the table showing the relation between the main manuscripts (pp. xiii–xv above), which its importance undoubtedly merits. I have referred to this manuscript as BL^2 in my list of sources for individual triads, but I have been unable to include full references to it among the *variæ lectiones*. Since its readings correspond very closely with DC and NLW, I have confined myself to citing BL^2 only in those instances in which it offers a reading which differs markedly from these texts. In all other instances it may be concluded that the readings of BL^2 correspond with those of DC and NLW.

The Collections

Three extensive collections of *Trioedd Ynys Prydein* were made by antiquarian scholars of the seventeenth and early eighteenth centuries. They were based almost entirely upon the earlier manuscripts already discussed. Two of these collections still remain in manuscript, while the third, that of Robert Vaughan of Hengwrt, became the basis for the first series of triads in the *Myvyrian Archaiology of Wales* (second edition, pp. 388–94). In the order of their date of composition these collections are the work of:

John Jones Gelli Lyfdy, in Peniarth 267[29]
Robert Vaughan of Hengwrt, in Peniarth 185; and
Moses Williams, in Llanstephan 65.

Peniarth 267. This manuscript was written during John Jones's detention in the Fleet prison in the years 1635–41 (*Rep.* I, p. 1077). The following note occurs on p. 251 of the manuscript, at the close of the section of TYP naming the men who inherited Adam's qualities (triads 47–50 below), and which John Jones took from the copy of Simwnt Vychan which is bound up with Pen. 16: *Ag fal hynn a esgrifennais if ddiwaethaf o law Simwnt fychan y terfyna y 2. dydd o fis chwefror* 1640. Although Jones gives no other specific indications as to his sources, yet there is no difficulty in identifying these, since the original manuscripts have all survived; moreover he was a faithful copyist and preserved the order of the triads in his originals. The manuscripts used by him were as follows: pp. 123–42, TYP from Pen. 50;[30] pp. 228–30, *Trioedd y Meirch* from Pen. 27; pp. 231–45, TYP from Pen. 16. On p. 245 there occurs the following note: *Y Trioedd uchod a gefeis if yn ysgrifenedig ar femrwn, mewn llaw ewingrwn, a esgrifennessid uwchlaw chwechan mlynedd kynn no hynn,*

[29] See Lhuyd, *Arch. Brit.* 262, col. 1, where a manuscript of 'Mr Jones o'r Gelhy Lyvdy' is entitled the *Hanesyn Vlodeuog* 'gan deked yr ysgrifen'. The description is well deserved, and the list of contents given by Lhuyd makes it clear that the manuscript intended can be no other than Pen. 267 or Wynnstay 10 (see note below).

[30] J. Jones examined Pen. 50 in the year 1612 (G. J. Williams, *Traddodiad Llenyddol Morgannwg*, pp. 153–4). Since writing the first edition I have found that a collection of TYP by an amanuensis of J. Jones, corresponding in all particulars with that in Pen. 267, is found in Wynnstay 10. Folios 98–106 reproduce the version of Pen. 50; folios 107–8 that of Pen. 27; folios 108–13, Pen. 16; folios 114–15 *Pedwar Marchog ar hugain*. Even the note and date and colophon correspond with those in Pen. 267. In this manuscript the source of the Pen. 50 version of TYP is acknowledged as being *Ex Cwtta Cyfarwydd*. See E. D. Jones, *Nat. Lib. of Wales Journal* II, p. 30. (I am indebted to Nesta Lloyd who has contributed this information.) See further the note 'C' on Pen. 50 in SC XXX, p. 200.

ag a gollassei eu dechreuad hwynt, ond kymaint ag a gefais mi ai hesgrifennais yn y mod y kefais. This is a description of Pen. 16, which has lost the opening words of the first triad; and a comparison of the readings proves that this was the manuscript which Jones had before him. On pp. 245–50 there follows *Pedwar Marchog ar Hugain Llys Arthur* (App. IV), from the text of Simwnt Vychan, now bound up with Pen. 16.

In addition to his main collection of TYP in Pen. 267, reference may be made to an earlier manuscript of John Jones, Pen. 216. This manuscript is not written in the distinctive orthography used later by Jones, and it bears the date 1611 on p. 156 (see triad 90 below). A few separate triads are found scattered through the text in different places, as follows: p. 33 a version of *Pedwar Marchog ar Hugain* (App. IV); p. 136, *Tri Phorthor Perllan Vangor fawr ymaelawr* (triad 60); p. 156, *Tri Dyfal Gyfangan* (triad 90), said to be taken *allan o hen lyfr Kymraec medd Sr. Tom ap Wil.* (the reference is to Thomas Wiliems of Trefriw, *Dict. Latino-Cambricum* (Pen. 228) I, p. xxii); p. 158, *Tri Chudd a Thri Datcudd* (triad 37). I have noted the variant readings from the triads in this manuscript, which are of a certain interest, since with the exception of triad 90 the source from which John Jones derived them is not clear. The readings of triads 37, 60, correspond with those of the *Book of Sir Richard Wynn* of Gwydir (pp. xxxvi–xxxvii above).

Peniarth 185 (= V). This is a small octavo volume containing the collection of *Trioedd Ynys Prydein* made by Robert Vaughan of Hengwrt (1592–1666). The manuscript bears no date.[31] The *Trioedd* are bound up

[31] I am indebted to Emrys Parry for referring me to a letter of Robert Vaughan's to Archbishop Ussher, preserved in *Trin. Coll. Dublin* C. 2. 22, and printed in C. R. Elrington (ed.), *The Whole Works of the Most Reverend James Ussher* (Dublin, 1847–64), XVI, pp. 591–2. This is dated 22 June 1653, and contains the following passage: 'As concerning the translating and explicating of the British Triades, to speak the truth, it was the thing I aimed at the last year for you, but after that I had gathered together, out of sundry fragments, some number of them, about Allhallentide last, I applied myself wholly to reading them and other ancient British antiquities, for my better understanding of them, until after Christmas; at what time I perceived that I could do no good in it, and therefore, lest I should shame myself and discredit the book, I laid it aside, and took an easier matter in hand . . . Truly I am very diffident of my own sufficiency to meddle with the Triades; nevertheless if you think that I can perform anything to the purpose, I will willingly make a second trial, hoping to prevail more by prayers than by skill and knowledge.' (In November of the same year Vaughan was once more occupied with the subject of the triads, cf. his letter to Ussher referred to p. xxxv, n. 25 above). It seems a natural conclusion to draw from this letter that Pen. 185 represents the 'sundry fragments' which Vaughan gathered together with the purpose of elucidating TYP for the benefit of the archbishop; and in this case the manuscript is to be dated November 1652. Vaughan's notes on *Trioedd Ynys Prydein* in NLW 7857 (see below) are no doubt the fruit of the 'second trial' which he made at the archbishop's instigation. Edward Jones, Bardd y Brenin, states in a note (NLW Addl. 111B, p. 47) that Vaughan 'did not live to finish his notes and explanations of *Trioedd Ynys Prydein*'.

with two other fragments: the *Testamentum Wulfrici* (an extract from Domesday Book in Anglo-Saxon script and probably also in Vaughan's own hand), and a fragment of an English journal of a voyage made in the Atlantic and Indian oceans in the year 1627. *Trioedd Ynys Prydein* cover pp. 1–60[32] and comprise 107 triads, including *Enweu Ynys Prydein* (App. I) and *Pedwar Marchog ar Hugain* (App. IV). The title-page reads as follows: '*Trioedd Ynys Prydein* or the *British Triades*, collected by Robt. Va^{n} Esqr out of several Manuscripts on Parchment'. ('A copy of this MS. was taken by me Lewis Morris, July 1738. Bendith dduw gida thi. Vale bene vale.' 'And by me Aneurin Owen, July 1829.') This collection is the source of the first series of *Trioedd Ynys Prydein* in the *Myvyrian Archaiology of Wales* (second edition, pp. 388–94) which was taken from William Morris's copy[33] of his brother Lewis Morris's transcript of Pen. 185. Pages 1–29 contain an alphabetical list of the proper names in TYP, followed by an alphabetical list of the triads according to their key epithet; p. 26 is left blank; p. 30 lists Vaughan's sources, and the number of triads contained in each (see MA^2 388). These are given as follows:

Llyfr John Balmer, 70 trioedd;
Llyfr Robert Vaughan, 34 trioedd;
Y Llyfr Cwta, 56 trioedd;
Llyfr Maredudd Llwyd,[34] 56 trioedd (y 4 hyn ar femrwn);
a Llyfr o Law John Jones o'r Gelli Lyfdy, 53 trioedd;
Achwaneg o'r 24 Marchog Llys Arthur, 8 trioedd.

On pp. 31–4 is a numerical table headed 'In this Table all the Books are Compar'd', whose intention is similar to that given for this book on pp. xiii–xv above. The triads are listed alphabetically by their key epithets, and

[32] The pagination is modern, and not quite correct. There is no leaf corresponding with pp. 35–6, though there is no corresponding lacuna in the manuscript at this point. Pages 37–8, containing *Enweu Ynys Prydein*, were intended to head the collection, but have been incorrectly bound.

[33] *Y Delyn Ledr o Gaer Gybi* (= BL Addl. 14,873; *Rep.* II, p. 1156), written by William Morris in 1738–9. On p. 53 is the following superscription: *Y Trioedd a ganlyn a gymerwyd allan o Lyfr Mr Vychan uchod yn Llyfrgell Hengwrt gan (fy) Mrawd Lewis Morris* 1738. Other copies of Lewis Morris's transcript were made by Evan Evans (= Pa. 13) and by Iolo Morganwg (Llanover MS. C36); and G. Evans implies in the *Rep.* (II, pp. 817, 1157) that both of these manuscripts are the source of the *Myvyrian* text. I think it is clear that both were used, since the notes added to the text in Pa. 13 have been incorporated in *Myvyrian*, yet an omission (of the name *Mwynfawr* after *Elidir* in triad 44) corresponds in William Morris's text and in *Myvyrian* but is not found in Pa. 13 (see MA^2 394).

[34] On Maredudd Lloyd—Vaughan's friend and relative—see *Bywgraffiadur* 552, and Nesta Lloyd's article, *Journal of the Welsh Bibliographical Society* XI, pp. 133–92, and below p. xliii, n. 38.

these are followed by the serial number of each triad in each of the manuscripts listed above in which it is included. Although this table is incomplete and occasionally faulty, it provides an invaluable clue to the identity and content of Vaughan's sources, since it makes it possible to construct a nearly complete list of the order in which the triads occur in the different manuscripts used by him. Beyond this table Vaughan gives no intimation as to his source for any individual triad. Although he follows the order of triads in several manuscripts in turn, in a manner similar to that which has been followed in this volume, yet the text he produces is sometimes an 'edited' one, in which he has selected a preferable reading from one or other of the manuscripts available to him, but without indicating its source.[35] It is clear that Pen. 16 was not available to Vaughan, although it was used by John Jones, and we must conclude that it only came into the Hengwrt library at Jones's death in 1658.[36] Thus Pen. 45 was the earliest manuscript of TYP which he had, and it is this manuscript which he entitles *llyfr Robert Vaughan* in the list of his sources, and to which he gives priority in the presentation of his text. Below is an analysis of Vaughan's collection of TYP giving the numbering of the triads in the *Myvyrian* text (second edition, pp. 388–94), intended as a guide to the origin and provenance of this text.

Myv. nos. 1–6. The collection is headed with *Enweu Ynys Prydein* from Pen. 50.
Myv. nos. 7–41 are from Pen. 45 (corresponding with nos. 1–36 in this book).

The omission of the triads *teir llynghes gynniweir* and *Tri aerfedawg* (nos. 15 and 25 in this book) correspond with the omission of these two triads from Pen. 45's text of the Early Version,[37] and leave a total of thirty-four triads—the number of triads in *llyfr Robert Vaughan.*

Myv. nos. 42–62 give the text of all additional triads from Pen. 50 which do not occur in Pen. 45, with the exception of *Enweu Ynys Prydein* which, as we have seen, was brought to the head of the series.

[35] E.g. in triad 1a below, where Vaughan's substitution of *ynghaer lleon ar uysg* for *ym Mynyw* may be presumed to derive either from *llyfr Siôn Balmer* or from *llyfr John Jones*, since according to his table of sources both of these manuscripts contained the triad.

[36] According to RBB xiii this manuscript (= Hengwrt 54) was lent to John Jones by Siaspar Griffith.

[37] The full text of *Tri overveird* (*Myv.* 18 = triad 12 below) has been supplied from another manuscript. The last name is all that is given of this triad in Pen. 45 (see above, p. xix), but this was a sufficient clue to enable Vaughan to discover which triad was missing.

Following the same plan *Myv.* nos. 63–72, 75–7, represent triads from the WR series which do not occur in Pen. 45 or Pen. 50. Vaughan's table shows that he derived these triads from *llyfr Maredudd Llwyd.*[38] A study of the text of these triads proves their ultimate source to be *Llyfr Gwyn Rhydderch*, since the readings agree with W against R in such places as the two differ (e.g. *Myv.* triad 77 (= triad 67 below) reads *riarot* with W for R's *Aranrot*; and *Caswallawn* with W where R has *-awc*). A study of Vaughan's table shows that *llyfr Maredudd Llwyd* contained a version of the WR series which was defective at the beginning, and lacked precisely those triads which are absent from W (see above, pp. xxi–xxii). Vaughan describes *llyfr Maredudd Llwyd* as being written *ar femrwm* 'on parchment', and we may therefore conclude that this version of TYP was derived from the detached fragment of the *Llyfr Gwyn* which was later known as Pen. 12 (*Rep.* I, pp. 324–5). Whether by *llyfr Maredudd Llwyd* Vaughan intended to designate the complete *Llyfr Gwyn* itself must remain doubtful: the fact that the text of TYP was mutilated as it is at the present day suggests that the fragment may have been already detached at this time.[39] The number of fifty-six triads which Vaughan states were contained in *llyfr Maredudd Llwyd* corresponds with the number in the fragment.

Vaughan cites *llyfr John Balmer*[40] as his source for *Trioedd y Meirch*, which are given as a separate group at the end of the *Myvyrian* first series (p. 394). He also appends the initials J.B. to the three triads *Tri chyndynyawc, Tri Gogyfurd llys Arthur, Tri dyn goreu wrth osp a phellenig* (*Myv.* nos. 88–90

[38] On Maredudd Llwyd see S. Jones, 'The Lives and Labours of John Jones and Rt. Vaughan' (University of Wales M.A. dissertation, 1926), and N. Lloyd, *Journal of the Welsh Bibliographical Society* XI, pp. 133–92. Maredudd Llwyd was a relative of Vaughan, and lived at Welshpool. Letters exchanged between the two survive (*Cambrian Register* III, 1818, pp. 301 ff.) from which it appears that Llwyd made an unsuccessful attempt to obtain for Vaughan the *Book of Llan Dâv*. Llwyd's books, like those of John Jones, probably came into the Hengwrt collection on his death. Vaughan's description of Pen. 12 as *llyfr Maredudd Llwyd* suggests that at the time of writing Pen. 185 it was in his friend's possession and not in his own.

[39] In *Arch. Brit.* 262, col. 1, E. Lhuyd refers to the *Llyfr Gwyn* as a book which 'ought to be' in the Hengwrt library. In his account of the contents of the manuscript there is no reference to the triads and other items contained in the detached part.

[40] It appears that John Palmer was not a contemporary of Vaughan's; but that he was a scribe who wrote a manuscript for a certain Gruffudd ap Llywelyn ap Howel; and that this manuscript later passed into the possession of John Jones. I am indebted to Mr Emrys Parry for drawing my attention to the following note in Peniarth MS. 271, p. 6: *Allan o lyfr Syon Balmer a scrifennasei ef ar femrwn i Ruff: ap llywelyn ap Howel, ac sydd eiddo fynghar Jo. Jones o Gellilyfde ym mhlwy Ysgeifiog yn sir y Fflint. Robert Vychan or Hengwrt yn sir Veirionydd a scrifennodd hyn y nawfed dydd o Vyhefin. 1654*. A further reference to this work occurs in Vaughan's hand in Pen. 194 on the back of Gruffudd Hiraethog's licence as Pencerdd, where a list of the relations of Jesus Christ is followed by the note: *felly y mae y chwe gwyr uchot yn chwe chefnderw i Grist, ac Ieuan fedyddiwr yn gyfynderyw iddaw, fal y dywed llyfr hen ar femrwn a yscrifenasei John Balmer i Ruffydd ap lywelyn ap Howel.*

= nos. 72, 73, 75 below). In addition, Vaughan's table shows that the triads *Teir gwenriein* and *Teir gohoyw riein* (*Myv.* nos. 73, 74 = triads 78, 79, below) are derived from *llyfr John Balmer*. The only manuscript in which I have found these five triads is Pen. 47 (except for no. 75, which appears also in Pen. 50), and it is apparent that both in these triads and in *Trioedd y Meirch* Vaughan's text preserves certain older and better readings than those found in Pen. 47 (see *var. lecta* to triads 45, 46B, 78C, 79C). In his table Vaughan assigns to J.B. two triads, *Tri engiryawl* and *Tri anhyfodawc* (nos. 76, 77 below), which he does not give in the body of the text; and these also appear only in Pen. 47. A reconstruction from the table of the contents and order of the triads in *llyfr John Balmer* shows that it contained all the triads in Pen. 47 (= a total of fifty-six), and in addition fourteen other triads, which came at the beginning of the series, and comprised *Enweu Ynys Prydein* and *Tri hael, glew, mat gyflavan, overveird, rudvoawc*, thus making up the specified total of seventy triads. The conclusion is therefore inescapable that *llyfr John Balmer*, the fourth of the manuscripts *ar femrwn* used by Vaughan, was the source of the triads in Pen. 47; that it contained this series in a more complete as well as a more accurate form, and that it has since been lost. It is evident from the copy in Pen. 47 that this manuscript contained a particularly interesting version of *Trioedd y Meirch*. (It should be noted that although the *Myv. Arch.* ascribes the version which it gives of *Trioedd y Meirch* to *llyfr John Balmer*, the text has been 'edited', and brings in readings from other manuscripts.)

The remaining triads in the *Myv.* text must have been derived from the manuscript of John Jones, which Vaughan cites as his final manuscript source. They are *Myv.* nos. 87, 91, 92, 78, 79, 80 (= nos. 51, 53, 87–90 in this book); and *Myv.* nos. 82–6 (= App. IV in this book). There is a difficulty about the identification of the manuscript here to referred. Vaughan states that it contained only fifty-three triads, yet in his table the serial numbers of the triads ascribed to John Jones's manuscript run up to 74. One is tempted to identify this manuscript with Pen. 267, the *Hanesyn Vlodeuog* (pp. xxxix–xl above), which contains John Jones's collection of rather less than seventy-four triads. But from his table it is evident that the manuscript to which Vaughan refers contained in addition to the contents of Pen. 267 a version of *Enweu Ynys Prydein*, and also triads 89, 90 below (=*Myv.* nos. 79, 80). Each of these items appears elsewhere in John Jones's manuscripts, though not in Pen. 267. Nor does Pen. 267 include *Trywyr Gwarth* (triad 51=*Myv.* no. 91), of which Vaughan gives the 'short' version found in manuscripts whose affinities are with the *Book of Sir Richard Wynn* (see pp. xxxvi–xxxviii above).

Vaughan made three additions to TYP from his own reading. These are *Myv.* no. 85 *Trywyr a ddianchasont o Gamlan*, from *Culhwch* (see App. IV, no. 7), *Myv.* no. 31 *Trywyr hut a Lledrith*, referred to by Dafydd ap Gwilym (see note to triad 27) and *Myv.* no. 78 (see note), which is paralleled in the *Araith Ieuan Brydydd Hir* (triad 88 below).

Vaughan's collection of TYP in Pen. 185 is described thus in Edward Lhuyd's catalogue (*Arch. Brit.* 264, col. 2):

> Y Trioedh Vaugh. in K.K. (= *Y Cwta Cyfarwydd*), Lh. Siôn Palmer etc. L(*lyfr*) K(*och*) H(*ergest*) (*col.*) 588.[41] Liber Triadum, incerto Authore, a Camdeno aliisque saepius laudatus; Tria varii generis in historia Britannorum Notabilia, complectens. Hunc exiguae Molis libellum circa finem seculi septimi scriptum asserit Vaughanus, qui rogante clarissimo Usserio (quod filius ejus, D. Gryffydius Vaughan me docuit), versione Anglicana et scholiis, si quae alia in nostra Historia, luce sane publica dignissimis, illustravit. Britannicum Codicem quod attinet, duo vidimus exemplaria hoc titulo insignata, quorum alterum tamen mancum, alienum alterum videbatur. Prius occurebat in Codice rubro Hergestiano duabus schedis constans, seculo decimo quarto in membrana exaratum. Init: Porth a aeth y gan yrp Luydaug hyd yn Lhychlyn . . . Yn y rhester a skrivennodh Mr W. Maurice o Lyvre skrivennedig Hengwrt, y mae yn henwy yn lhe ŷn lhyvyr y *Trioedh* ychod. Sev y eurie ydynt: Kant o Drioedh Ynys Bryden, wedi i kaskly, ay trevny gan dhiuyd vyvyrdod Mr Robert Vaughan, yr hwn ai trôdh yn Saesneg, ag ys(s)ydh yn i deongly yn rhyvedhol. W.M. Ond ev ai kolhwyd yr ystalm o vlynydhoedh o vysk lhyvre Hengwrt medhe G(*ruffydd*) V(*aughan*). Ann. 1698.
>
> (. . . The Book of Triads, of uncertain authorship, often praised by Camden and others, (consisting of) three different *Notabilia* in the history of the Britons. Vaughan asserts that this pamphlet of small size was written about the end of the seventh century; who when asked by the most famous Ussher (as his son D. Gruffydd Vaughan told me) illustrated it with an English version and notes, as worthy of the light of publicity as anything in our history. As regards the British (Welsh) book, we have seen two exemplars marked with this title, of which the one however is defective and the other is seen to be a variant (?). The first was found in the Red Book of Hergest, consisting of two pages written on parchment in the fourteenth century, beginning *Porth a aeth* . . . (*etc.* = triad 35 R) . . . In the list which Mr W. Maurice wrote of the books at Hengwrt, he names the above old book of the Triads. His words are 'A hundred of the Triads of the Island of Britain, collected and arranged by the assiduous study of Mr R. Vaughan, who turned them into English, and who interprets them wonderfully

[41] Vaughan did not have access to the *Red Book of Hergest*. But Lhuyd evidently concluded that the readings ascribed to *llyfr Maredudd Llwyd* were from RBH; he did not realize that they are from the *Llyfr Gwyn*.

(WM). But they have been lost for a number of years from among the books at Hengwrt, according to Gruffydd Vaughan' (1698).[42])

It is evident that the reference in the latter part of this passage is to Vaughan's notes on *Trioedd Ynys Prydein*, already lost from the Hengwrt library in Lhuyd's day. Until recently this document was only known through the intermediary of Evan Evans's transcript made in the year 1773, which is contained in Pa. 51. But in 1948 the original manuscript turned up (see *Nat. Lib. of Wales Journal* V, p. 227), and it is now classified as NLW 7857D (*Handlist* II, p. 290).[43] However, Vaughan's translation and commentary covers only the first seven triads in the order in which these are given in Pen. 185, i.e. *Enweu Ynys Prydein* (App. I) followed by *Teir Lleithiclwyth*, *Tri Hael*, and *Tri Gwyndeyrn* (triads 1–3 below). Unfortunately both the beginning and the end of Vaughan's manuscript is defective,[44] so that we still have to turn to Evan Evans's transcript for a complete version of Vaughan's work. We shall never know whether Vaughan's work ever dealt with 100 triads, as claimed by Lhuyd. If these were treated on the scale of the surviving text, the work must have been immensely long. But the transcript evidently represents all that was extant in Evan Evans's day. In so far as I have compared the transcript with Vaughan's text I have found it to be accurate; and therefore I have regarded it as a dependable reproduction of those parts of Vaughan's text which have not survived. I have cited some variants from this work (in which Vaughan's original text is distinguished from Evans's transcript by the abbreviations VN^1 and VN^2) both in the notes to the triads and in the Notes to Personal Names. Vaughan's method is to quote *Enweu Ynys Prydein* sentence by sentence, followed by a very full commentary and discussion. This commentary is of value for the light which it throws upon Vaughan's scholarship and reading, his attitude to Camden, and the respect which he shares with other seventeenth-century antiquaries for

[42] It is likely that Pen. 185 is the ultimate source for the selection of triads published by Edward Jones, Bardd y Brenin, in his *Musical and Poetical Relicks of the Welsh Bards* (London, 1794), pp. 9–12. Jones describes his source (p. 9) as 'an ancient manuscript, called *Y Trioedd Ynys Prydein*, supposed to have been begun about the third or fourth century'. Cf. Tecwyn Ellis, *Edward Jones, Bardd y Brenin 1752–1824* (Caerdydd, 1957), pp. 53, 98.

[43] The fly-leaf records earlier sales of the manuscript: by Mr Wm. Vaughan to Mr Wm. Herbert in 1767, and by the latter to Wm. Owen in 1818; finally by Wm. Owen to Evan Evans for thirty shillings on 22 January 1825.

[44] A plan for the publication of Evans's transcripts of Vaughan's notes with a translation of TYP is referred to in a letter from Daines Barrington to Bishop Percy, dated 14 June 1776; later the same year Evans writes that he is collecting subscriptions for the volume. See Aneirin Lewis (ed.), *The Correspondence of Thomas Percy and Evan Evans* (Louisiana, 1957), pp. 143 n., 176. See also letter from Evan Evans to Owen Jones (1779), Hugh Owen (ed.), *Additional Letters of the Morrises of Anglesey* (London, 1947; 1949), II, p. 780.

TYP as an important historical document. The source for some of his statements is not identifiable, for example his references to the causes of the battle of *Arfderydd* (see note to triad 84), and some of his statements about *Rhun ap Maelgwn* (see note). He has preserved some popular traditions; for example his account of *Helyg ap Gwylanog* (see n. to *G6ydno Garanhir*), and his reference to the burial of *Maelgwn* on Ynys Seiriol. But he shows no lack of imagination in the inflated and highly-coloured style which he employs on occasion in writing up his material. The notes deserve publication in full.

Llanstephan 65. This collection of triads was made by Moses Williams, and bears the date 1717. In addition to TYP the book includes the *Tri Thlws ar Ddeg* (App. III) and *Pedwar Marchog ar Hugain* (App. IV), North Welsh genealogical triads, as well as general and proverbial triads. The title-page is inscribed:

> *Liber Triadum*; Sef yw hynny, Y TRIOEDD. Wedi eu casgl allan o amrafael hen Lyfrau ar Femrwn a Phapur, a'i cymharu a'i gilydd, a'i gosod i lawr mewn Trefn egwyddorol, yn ddwy Ran. Trwy Lafur ac Asdudrwydd *Moses Wiliams*, Baglawr Celfyddydau, Ficer Dyfynog yn Sir Frycheiniog. *Si quid novisti rectius istis, candidus imperti*. Printiedig yn Llundain yn y Flwyddyn 1717 . . . . 'Gwelwch nad trosof fy hunan y cymmeraisi Boen, eithr dros bawb a geisiant Ddoethineb.' *Ecc.* 24, 34.

Although this title-page gives the impression that the work is finished and prepared for the printer (see *Rep.* II, p. 556), in reality this is far from being the case, and there exists a considerable amount of confusion among the contents of the volume. The Latin introduction (pp. 1–8) makes it plain that this book was intended merely as the first part of a much longer work, to be entitled '*Cambro-Britannica, sive Autorum Vett. Cambro-Britannicorum OPERA; quae supersunt omnia; Cum variantibus Lectionibus et Annotionibus hunc primum ex Codd. MSS. in lucem edita.*' The first volume should have contained the triads together with *Somnium Maximi Imperatoris, Praelia Ludi et Levelisis* (presumably in Latin with commentary), *et Chronicon Breve*. But the collection of triads was the only part of this ambitious work to be achieved, and even this was left in a state which is far from finished. The Latin introduction was intended to apply to the whole work. The author's words with reference to the triads deserve to be quoted, since they are characteristic of the attitude of the antiquarian scholars of his day, and explain the formation of the three great collections of TYP under discussion:

Quaerenti autem quid sibi velint istae Triades, respondeo, eas memorabilia quaedam de Britannorum rebus gestis, viris illustribus, Praeliis, *etc.*, quae a variis Authoribus variis temporum intervallis conscripta sunt, continere, in quibus etsi non nulla sint quae aniles fortasse sapiant Fabellas, multa tamen notatu dignissima quaeque verae interferenda sint Historiae, et nullibi praeterea (Quod sciam) aut saltem rarissime occurant, sagax inde decerpet Lector.

(If however it be asked what these Triads are about, I reply that they contain a number of memorable things about the deeds, heroes, and battles of the Britons, written by various authors at various distances of time; and although there is much amongst them that smacks perhaps of old wives' tales, there is also much that is worthy of attention and may be regarded as true history, and moreover occurs nowhere else (as far as I know), or only very rarely, which the intelligent reader will be able to cull from them.) See further J. Davies, *Bywyd a Gwaith Moses Williams* (Caerdydd, 1937), pp. 15, 18, 116.

There follows a list of the manuscript sources used by MW for his collection of TYP, together with abbreviations, as follows:

Ll. Du. = the *Llyfr Du o Gaerfyrddin* (used for *Trioedd y Meirch*).
R.W. = 'Richd. Wynne of Gwidr's Copy. An Syr Siôn Wynne'. (See pp. xxxvi–xxxviii above.)
L.K.H. = the *Llyfr Coch Hergest*.
C.C. = *Y Cwta Cyfarwydd o Forgannwg* (= Pen. 50).
N. = 'A Copy that follows it in M.W. A.12.' [*sic*].
F. = 'Dr Foulkes' Book.'
N.N. = 'Another Copy that follows N. out of a MS. about 700 years old.' (This is John Jones's collection of TYP in Pen. 267; see pp. xxxix–xl above.)
G.O. (= Gutun Owain) is also referred to in the body of the work for a version of *Pedwar Marchog ar Hugain* (see App. IV).

There follows a collection of 123 triads, given in alphabetical order. (This number is made up by the inclusion of App. I and IV in this volume.) To these are added the *Tri Thlws ar Ddeg* (App. III). A few brief notes are appended to the triads in Latin and Welsh. Variant readings are added beneath each triad, but only too frequently these are merely introduced by the abbreviation *m.a.* (= *medd arall*), rather than accompanied by the source of the variant. Thus it is not possible to determine the source of all MW's variant readings, or to identify with certainty the manuscripts which he refers to as F and N. It is evident that NN is Pen. 267, and MW seems to refer to this manuscript again in his introduction, when he cites John Jones's authority for dating the oldest exemplar of TYP used by him as 'about 700 years old' (i.e. Pen. 16; see John Jones's note in Pen. 267, cited above, p. xxxix–xl note). It is possible that N was another manuscript in the hand of John Jones. But I have not been able to identify 'Dr Foulkes' Book' (= F). The variants which are quoted from RW correspond with the contents of the *Book of Sir Richard Wynn*, as these can be reconstructed from the other manuscripts which contain copies of this work (see pp. xxxv–xxxviii above). Hence it is that MW includes in the body of TYP triad 92 *Tri Hynaif Byd*, and *Tri Thywysogion* and *Tri Thywysog Saint* (see above, p. xxxvii), all of which derive from the *Book of Sir Richard Wynn*. Like Robert Vaughan in Pen. 185, Moses Williams in his turn was tempted to add to his collection three triads culled from his own reading: these are nos. 93, 94, and 95 below, which are derived respectively from *Culhwch*, from a *cywydd* by Gutun Owain, and from *Branwen*.

The remaining manuscripts of TYP which I have examined are the following:

Cwrtmawr 3. This manuscript was written by William Salesbury in the years 1565–6. Pages 55–72 present the WR version of TYP from the beginning of section (3)[45] *Tri Goruchel Garcharawr* to the end. *Enweu Ynys Prydein* follows section (3) as in the text of the *Llyfr Gwyn*, and the version here given resembles that of W rather than R. It is certain that this version is derived ultimately from the *Llyfr Gwyn* and not from the *Llyfr Coch*[46] though it is evidently not a direct transcript, since the readings are mainly corrupt. The variants correspond for the most part with those in the *Book of Sir Thomas Wiliems of Trefriw*, BL Addl. 31,055.[47] On pp. 91–4 of the same manuscript are some additional triads from another source, introduced by the title: *(O'r) Trioedd y tynnwyd hynn*. There follow, according to the numbering given in this book, triads 35, 51, 52, 12, 37, 44, 82, App. I, nos. 1–4. The text breaks off abruptly at this point, in the middle of App. I, no. 4, and it is possible that additional pages may have been lost. But it is clear that the triads presented represent a selection

[45] 1564 according to *Rep.* II, p. 873. Alun Mathias gives convincing evidence for the later date ('Astudiaeth o Weithgarwch Llenyddol William Salesbury', University of Wales M.A. thesis, 1949, pp. 249–50).

[46] As stated in *Rep.* II, p. 874. The text follows W in triads 33d and 56b, where certain names have been omitted from R; cf. pp. xxix–xxx above.

[47] I am indebted to Morfydd Owen for telling me that she formed a similar conclusion to the above with respect to the manuscript affiliations of the collection of proverbial triads beginning *Teir unben cerdd etc.* (Cwrt. 3, p. 73). The text of these triads corresponds closely with that found in BL Addl. 31,055, pp. 28b–29a, except that the latter text omits the first two triads in this series and begins with the third *Tri gorefras direidi*, etc. The version of this group of triads given in both of these manuscripts clearly derives ultimately from W and not from R, though as in the case of TYP it can hardly be a direct copy. See also M. E. Owen, 'Trioedd Hefut yw yrei hynn', YB XIV (1988), pp. 87–133.

taken from a fuller text, since all but the first two and no. 82 are variants of triads given earlier from the WR series. The text of triads 35 and 51 shows affinities with the version in the *Book of Sir Richard Wynn of Gwydir* (pp. xxxiv–xxxv above), since triad 35 bears the title *Tri Arianllu* and triad 51 gives the 'short' version of *Trywyr Gwarth*. Nevertheless the differences between the two preclude the possibility that these triads can represent the source of the text of this version of TYP printed by Salesbury in *Y Diarebion Camberäec*. Triads 12, 52, and 82 do not appear either in DC or in NLW 6434, and the texts given here of triads 37, 44, do not show a close enough resemblance with that of NLW to be regarded as Salesbury's source for the triads in DC. Evidently Salesbury had access to other manuscripts of TYP than those represented by the extant versions.

PANTON 10. Written by Evan Evans *circa* 1780. The version of TYP given here is copied from the text of William Salesbury in Cwrt. 3,[48] but the two versions are presented in reverse order: pp. 1–6 bear the title *O'r Trioedd y tynnwyd hynn* and corresponds with pp. 91–4 in Cwrt. 3, while pp. 9–31 corresponds with pp. 55–72 in Cwrt. 3. Unless otherwise stated, the *var. lecta* which I have quoted from Cwrt. 3 correspond with the readings of this manuscript.

PANTON 13 (pp. 89–108). A copy by Evan Evans of Lewis Morris's copy of Pen. 185. Gwenogvryn Evans shows (*Rep.* II, p. 817) that this copy is the immediate source of the text of the *Myvyrian* first series.[49] Variants from 'the printed edition' (i.e. DC, see pp. xxxii–xxxviii above) have been inserted in this copy, and are reproduced in *Myv.*

PANTON 38. Pages 83–106 contain a copy of the *Trioedd* in the *Llyfr Coch*, which breaks off in the middle of the second version of *Tri Goruchel Garcharawr* (triad 52 below = WR no. 51). The text follows R closely, and there seems no reason to deduce an intermediary transcript, as is done in *Rep.*, especially in view of the fact that Evan Evans is known to have transcribed poetry from RBH.

PANTON 26 (pp. 7–65). A copy of TYP made in 1774 by Evan Evans from John Jones's collection in Pen. 267.

[48] See G. C. G. Thomas, 'From Manuscript to Print', in R. G. Gruffydd (ed.), *A Guide to Welsh Literature c.1530–1700* (Cardiff, 1997), pp. 250–1.

[49] I have pointed out (p. xli above) that William Morris's copy of his brother's transcript was also used by the *Myvyrian* editors. Another eighteenth-century copy of Lewis Morris's transcript, attributed to Richard Thomas, is to be found in NLW Addl. MS. 53B, pp. 71–111.

PANTON 29. This is a copy of a translation of TYP made by Lewis Morris 'out of Mr Vaughan of Hengwrt's copy in his own hand, in the year 1745' (i.e. from Pen. 185). 'This translation is not to be depended upon, Oct. 1759.'[50] 'Transcribed and corrected by me, Evan Evans, Oct. 12th. 1773.' Another copy of this translation is to be found in Cwrt. 14, pp. 131 ff. See *The Cambrian Register* III (1818), pp. 207–11, where triads 1–26 of Robert Vaughan's manuscript are reproduced from this copy.

LLANSTEPHAN 12 (sixteenth century). Page 48 gives the text of triad 37 by itself, with a variant which is of some interest, if it is not merely a slip: *esgyrn kadwaladr vendigaid* in place of *esgyrn G6erthefyr 6endigeit* (see note to triad 37).

NLW ADDL. 37B. Written by Edward Jones, *Bardd y Brenin* (1752–1824). A version of TYP is found on pp. 84–9, followed by some miscellaneous triads from another source on pp. 92–4. The readings of the first series correspond closely with those of Cwrt. 3 and the *Book of Sir Thomas Wiliems* (see above). On p. 92 is found the text of triads 82, 50, and 88 in this book. These are followed by a list of the traditional *Merched Teg* of the romances, to which is appended the note 'There ends the Triades as they are found in a MS. written in the year 1582 or 3, which I take to be a very imperfect copy.' There follows 'from another copy' an incomplete text of *Enweu Ynys Prydein* (App. I below) and of triads 37, 85.

NLW ADDL. 325E. In the hand of Dafydd Ddu o Eryri (= David Thomas, 1759–1822). On p. 92 are found two triads, versions of nos. 35 and 61 in this book.

BL ADDL. 15,034 = BL². Pages 244 ff. (= pp. 122 ff. in modern numbering). A copy of Pen. 185, in the hand of Owen Jones. The triads are preceded by a list of earlier manuscript sources, which corresponds with that appended to the *Myvyrian* first series of TYP (p. xli above). At the close (p. 132a) is the note 'Diwedd trioedd o Lyfr Mr Fychan ymgleddwr ein Hiaith a'n Breiniau ebe Mr Wm. Morris yn y Delyn Ledr'. Yet William Morris's *Telyn Ledr* (BL Addl. 14,873) does not appear to be the source of this copy, since the omission of a single word which I have noted (p. xli),

[50] BL Addl. 14,941 contains Lewis Morris's indexes to TYP. This manuscript consists of a note-book in which proper names are listed alphabetically. Names from the genealogies and other early sources are included with those from TYP. The serial numbers of the triads in Vaughan's collection are appended. It is probable that this work was a list prepared by Lewis Morris as a basis for the notes on personal names given in his *Celtic Remains.*

note 33, above), as occurring in Morris's text of triad 44 does not appear in Owen Jones's version. There seems to be no evidence that this copy was used by the printers of the *Myvyrian* first series, as is the case with the transcript of TYP in *Y Delyn Ledr.*

BL ADDL. 15,023 = BL[1]. Pages 133 ff. (= folios 71a–73a in modern numbering). A copy by Owen Jones of TYP from DC (see pp. xxxii–xxxiv above), to which the following note is prefixed 'Tri a deugain o Drioedd Ynys Prydain allan o Lyfr argraffedig a gefais fenthyg gan Richd. Morris esq. Y Llyfr hwn a argraffwyd ond odid yn amser y Frenhines Elsbeth neu gynt, fal y gellir barnu wrth y ddull yr yscrifen, canys y mae'r dechreu a'r diwedd ar goll. y mae yn cynwys heblaw y trioedd swrn o Ddiarhebion yn amherffaith am fod amryw ddail ar goll.' See p. xxxv, n. 26, above.

II. ORIGIN AND DEVELOPMENT OF *TRIOEDD YNYS PRYDEIN*

Trioedd Ynys Prydein, the 'Triads of the Island of Britain', are distinguished by this title from the mass of triadic literature which has come down in Medieval Welsh. The triad form was used as a means of cataloguing a variety of technical information: in addition to TYP triads are used extensively in the legal codes, in technical treatises on medicine, and are found in the fourteenth-century *Grammar* of Einion Offeiriad,[51] where the *Trioedd Cerdd* deal with the details of poetic craftsmanship. The text of TYP is accompanied in many of the manuscripts by short collections of triads dealing with general moral, gnomic, and proverbial statements.

I am not concerned here with the ultimate problems raised by the use of the triad as a literary device, or with a comparative investigation of the triad form as it is employed in early Irish and Welsh literature. A marked predilection for triple groupings is discernible among the Celtic peoples from the time of their earliest records, as appears in the recurrence of the triple unity in the portrayal of Celtic divinities alike in Gaul and in Ireland.[52] In Wales, a tendency towards triple groupings can be pointed out in the work of Gildas[53] and in the *Historia Brittonum*, and a few triads are found amongst the oldest Welsh verse in the *Gododdin* (CA ll. 179–93). But in the early poetry the innate bias towards the triad form is manifested most clearly in the wide range of variation in mood and manner which is expressed with a high degree of technical skill in the three-line *englyn o'r*

[51] GP 16–18. See also M. E. Owen, 'Y Trioedd Arbennig', B XXIV, pp. 434–50, and eadem and Nesta Lloyd, *Drych yr Oesoedd Canol* (Caerdydd, 1986), pp. 151–2; 211–16. Kuno Meyer dates to the period 850–900 a collection of miscellaneous Irish triads comprising geographical, moral, proverbial, and legal matter, *The Triads of Ireland* (Royal Irish Academy, Todd Lecture Series, XIII, 1906).

[52] See H. d'Arbois de Jubainville, *The Irish Mythological Cycle* (trans. R. I. Best), pp. 210–16; M. L. Sjoestedt, *Gods and Heroes of the Celts* (trans. Dillon), pp. 17, 23, 43; P. Mac Cana, *Celtic Mythology* (London, 1970), and Anne Ross, *Pagan Celtic Britain* (London, 1967), both passim. Vendryes has discussed instances in which the triple grouping of Celtic deities has survived in Old Irish saga, 'L'Unité en Trois Personnes chez les Celtes', *Comptes Rendus de l'Académie des Inscriptions*, 1935, pp. 324–42; *Choix d'Études Linguistiques et Celtiques*, pp. 233–46.

[53] Gildas names three invasions of Britain (cf. triad 36 and note). As Collingwood observes (*Roman Britain and the English Settlements* (Oxford, 1936; 1975), pp. 293–4), the three-times repeated appeal by the Britons to the Romans for help which appears in his work might be described as a popular view of previous British history expressed in triadic form.

hen ganiad.[54] My subject, however, is restricted to an examination of the *content* of *Trioedd Ynys Prydein*, and to a study of the implications of the use of triads as a means of cataloguing the early traditions of Wales. And in conclusion I shall say something about the extended life given to *Trioedd Ynys Prydein* by the use of these triads as a convenient compendium of reference on which the bards might draw for the canonical patterns of comparison demanded by their craft.

It has been long recognized that the prose narratives which have come down from medieval Ireland and Wales represent a mere fragment of an extensive oral literature which was developed, preserved and transmitted over centuries by a highly trained professional order of men of learning. The preservation of any part of this narrative material in writing was merely incidental: its life was the life of the spoken, and not of the written, word. Thus the date of the great medieval *codices*—the *Llyfr Gwyn* and the *Llyfr Coch*, the *Lebor na h-Uidre* and the *Lebor Laignech*—gives no indication as to the antiquity of their contents, since the very nature of the Celtic tradition is such that it precludes the exact dating of content by linguistic *criteria*. The advance in knowledge of the historical development of the Celtic languages which has taken place during the last century may enable us to establish the date of a text in its earliest *written* form as several centuries earlier than the oldest manuscript in which it is contained, as Sir Ifor Williams attempted to demonstrate in the case of the *Four Branches* of the *Mabinogi.* But it can offer no guidance beyond this point: we still have to reckon with the possibility—and with the *chwedlau* this is always a strong probability—that these stories are the final result of centuries of previous oral transmission: a process whose consequent possibilities in the way of fusion, alteration of purpose, and substitution, were forcibly emphasized in W. J. Gruffydd's analysis of the development of the *Four Branches.*[55]

From a variety of causes,[56] early Irish literature received a much more abundant preservation in medieval manuscripts than did the early

[54] It is worth noting that the poem LlDC no. 40 (= CLlH no. VIII), entitled *Enweu Meibon Llywarch Hen*, contains instances of *englynion* in which three personal names are grouped together, *Goreu trywir y dan new*, etc. But the names cited are those of three brothers, the sons of *Llywarch* and of *Kynvarch* (CLlH no. VIII.3, emend so, see B XVII, pp. 180–1). The *Beddau* stanzas, however, provide instances in which the *englyn* form is employed, as in TYP, as a means of grouping names from independent narratives and different traditional strata; see LlDC no. 18; ed. and trans. T. Jones, 'The Black Book of Carmarthen "Stanzas of the Graves" ', PBA LIII, pp. 97–137.

[55] *Math vab Mathonwy* (Cardiff, 1928); *Rhiannon* (Cardiff, 1953). See also W. J. Gruffydd and A. O. H. Jarman, 'Mabinogi Branwen', LlC IV, pp. 129–34.

[56] See J. F. Kenney, *Sources for the Early History of Ireland* I (New York, 1929), pp. 4–5; cf. J. E. Caerwyn Williams, *Traddodiad Llenyddol Iwerddon* (Caerdydd, 1958), p. 18; idem and P. K. Ford, *The Irish Literary Tradition* (Cardiff, 1992), pp. 3–4, P. Mac Cana, *The Mabinogi* (Cardiff, 1977, 1992), pp. 19–20.

literature of Wales. But various converging lines of evidence serve to show beyond reasonable doubt that the incomplete fragments which have come down in Welsh were once a part of a very much larger body of tradition, which must have been comparable with the narrative literature which has been preserved in Irish. The *Four Branches*, *Culhwch ac Olwen*, and the Welsh romances, represent relatively late literary adaptations of what must be regarded as a mere fragment of the cycles of narrative to which they belong. I hope to show in the following pages that the original nucleus of *Trioedd Ynys Prydein*, when separated from the late accretions which have been introduced from literary sources, consisted in an index to this body of orally preserved narrative, formed for the benefit of those whose professional duty it was to preserve and hand on the stories which embodied the oldest traditions of the Britons about themselves; stories which concerned the national past alike of the people of Wales and of the lost northern territory which was still remembered in the Middle Ages as a former home of the British race. My conclusions in this matter have been reached after a study of the content of *Trioedd Ynys Prydein* in relation to material preserved in the following sources:

(i) the corpus of early poetry preserved in the so-called *Four Ancient Books of Wales*: the *Black Book of Carmarthen*, the *Book of Taliesin*, the *Book of Aneirin*, and the poems from prose-verse narratives of the *Llywarch Hen* type mainly preserved in RBH, as well as the extremely relevant catalogue of the graves of early heroes preserved in the *Black Book*;

(ii) names and allusions found in the extant *chwedlau* (and in this *Culhwch ac Olwen* is a particularly rich source of evidence);

(iii) material preserved in the works of Gildas and the *Historia Brittonum*, and in the early genealogies;[57]

[57] These are preserved in Harl. 3859 (written *circa* 1100; ed. Phillimore, *Cy.* IX, pp. 141 ff.) and in the late fourteenth-century Jes. Coll. 20 (ed. Phillimore, *Cy.* VIII, pp. 83 ff.). Both collections derive from earlier versions written in Old Welsh orthography: the Harleian text is believed to date from the mid-tenth century (see LHEB 56). For archaic features in the Jes. Coll. text see notes to triads 2, 70; and on the date of this manuscript see B XV, p. 110, n., and D. Huws, *Nat. Lib. of Wales Journal* XXVIII, p. 21. For the thirteenth-century genealogies entitled *Bonedd Gwŷr y Gogledd* see App. II and pp. civ ff. below. Full use has also been made in the notes of the different versions of *Bonedd y Saint*, of which the printed texts are listed in EWGT 51–4. All these genealogies, with others from later MSS., have now (since 1966) been collected and authoritatively edited by P. C. Bartrum in *Early Welsh Genealogical Tracts* (EWGT). On the inaccurate use of the name 'Nennius' to denote the author of the *Historia Brittonum* see D. N. Dumville, SC X/XI, pp. 78–95, and the same writer's 'Sub-Roman Britain: History and Legend', *History* 62, pp. 173–92. Dumville regards the work of Gildas as 'the founding text' upon which early Welsh scholarship was based; a view which, if accepted, would have far-reaching consequences in relation to the narrative traditions concerning Britain's past which are reflected in TYP.

(iv) parallels with the story motives of early Irish literature, which emphasize the mutual contact and the common cultural and social background shared by the two main branches of the Celtic peoples in the early Middle Ages;

(v) references by the *Gogynfeirdd* (see CBT), which indicate that this mainly oral literature was still in some degree familiar and in current circulation down to the end of the thirteenth century; and is also recalled in references made by the *cywydd* poets of the succeeding period;[58]

(vi) the fragments of antecedent Welsh tradition preserved both by Geoffrey of Monmouth and by the Welsh adapters of his story in *Brut y Brenhinedd*, and also in the Old French poems based upon the Matter of Britain.

All these sources have yielded valuable evidence; and from them I have brought together in the notes all the information I have been able to discover about the characters and stories alluded to in TYP. A comparison of the content of the triads with the material that has come down in these other records throws into relief certain subjects and dominant themes as forming the oldest nucleus in TYP. It becomes evident that the stories referred to in the triads were focused (*a*) upon figures of the early Welsh semi-mythological tradition, who belong to the milieu of the *Mabinogi*; (*b*) upon what may be described as the medieval Welsh view of the country's history in pre-Saxon times, and in the period of the arrival of the Saxons, i.e. the traditions centred upon Caswallawn, Maxen Wledig and Gwrtheyrn (= Vortigern); and (*c*) upon characters and events of the early Welsh Heroic Age of the sixth and seventh centuries,[59] who belonged both to Wales and to North Britain. The allusions classed under both (*i*) and (*ii*) are frequently at variance with the stories preserved in the extant *Mabinogi*, in *Breudwyt Maxen*, and in *Historia Brittonum*, so

[58] The quotation of allusions by the *cywyddwyr* of the fourteenth to sixteenth centuries has necessarily been selective. I have quoted all instances that I have found in which the poets cite an actual triad, in my notes to the triad in question; and I have given in the Notes to Personal Names all references in poetry that I have discovered to the less familiar names in TYP; though I have made no attempt to give exhaustive references to all the occurrences of such names as *Arthur*, *Cai*, *Bedwyr*, *Gwalchmai*, *Rhydderch*, *Nudd*, etc. I am conscious that many allusions will have escaped my notice from the less easily accessible poetry of this later period, both in print and in manuscript.

[59] See Chadwick, *The Growth of Literature* I, p. 16 *et passim*. Apart from the remote recollections of past listed above, in which history has already been turned into legend, the earliest historical event to be commemorated in TYP appears to be the allusion to the fighting in Anglesey *circa* 500 between Cadwallawn Law Hir and the Irish: an event whose historicity seems to be corroborated by the evidence of early inscriptions in the area (see triad 62a and note).

that one is led to the conclusion that the oldest stratum in the triads refers to parallel oral versions of these tales which have not survived. In the case of (*c*) the range of reference preserved in TYP extends our knowledge of the early saga of Wales and North Britain further, perhaps, than does any other single source, so that the amount of evidence which has survived independently of the triads is in itself hardly adequate to bring to light instances of conflicting tradition.

The triads which relate to these themes undoubtedly represent the oldest stratum in TYP, and a number represent the oldest stratum in medieval Welsh tradition as a whole. It is in reference to the basic nucleus of subject matter classed under (*i*) and (*ii*) above that the title *Trioedd Ynys Prydein* is significant: the triads commemorate the traditions of the Island of Britain as a whole; they look back upon the essential and still ideal sovereign unity of the island.[60] The story of the violation of this unity is brought into full relief: Maxen Wledig led away the troops from Britain, and thus opened the way for the quisling British king Gwrtheyrn to admit the Saxons into the country to his aid. The departure of the troops from Britain finds its counterpart in the invasions which beset the country as a consequence (triads 35, 36); and the early history of Britain, in a manner comparable with that of Ireland as given in the *Lebor Gabála Érenn* ('Book of Invasions of Ireland'), is envisaged as a succession of incursions by foreign peoples from without. It is significant that in Wales as in Ireland the earliest literature reflects a genuine national and nationwide consciousness on a cultural level,[61] in spite of the fact that in neither country was this reflected in a political sphere: this outlook was undoubtedly facilitated by the freedom accorded to both Welsh and Irish poets to travel unimpeded over the whole area in which their language was spoken. It is important to recognize the full significance of the term *Ynys Prydein* if we are properly to appreciate the original character of the body of tradition to which the triads refer, as well as the milieu in which they came into being and were first transmitted. But before turning to a

[60] In the title *Trioedd Ynys Prydein* we have the earliest expression given in Welsh to the deeply rooted and fundamental concept of Britain's inviolable unity—one island, one people, one sovereign ruler (cf. E. Rowlands, LlC VI, p. 223, and B. F. Roberts, 'Geoffrey of Monmouth and Welsh Historical Tradition' (ch. 2 in his *Studies on Middle Welsh Literature* (Lampeter/Lewiston, 1992), pp. 29–34; idem, LlC XII, p. 139). Rightly or wrongly, P. Sims-Williams regards Gildas as the founding father of a 'personified' *Britannia*, from which this concept emerged (CMCS 6, p. 30). Traces of it appear also in *Branwen* and *Manawydan*; Brân is *brenin coronawc ar yr Ynys hon, ac ardyrchawc o goron Lundein* (PKM 29). For the suggestion that a continuous British king-list may have existed before Geoffrey of Monmouth's HRB and subsequently superseded by his version, see P. C. Bartrum, 'Was there a British "Book of Conquests"?', B XXIII, pp. 1–6.

[61] Cf. Kenney, op. cit., p. 6.

consideration of these problems, it will be well to note a secondary, but not insignificant, feature of the treatment of early British tradition which is found in TYP. This is the emergence of the Arthurian cycle. The triads provide ample corroborative evidence for a fact which is clearly demonstrated by certain early Welsh poems preserved in the *Black Book of Carmarthen* and the *Book of Taliesin*: it is that at a period earlier than any at which the possibility of external literary influence need be considered, the name of Arthur was already beginning to act as a luminary into whose orbit were drawn the heroes of a number of independent cycles of Welsh narrative: characters both of mythology (such as Manawydan and Mabon), and of heroic tradition who may have belonged to different periods and perhaps also to different parts of Britain from the hypothetical Arthur (see n.). Examples include traditions of Geraint, Drystan, Owain and even of Taliesin. The early poems to which I have referred enable us to trace this process as already at work at an early date. Thus the appearance of Arthur in company with Drystan already in a triad in the Early Version (no. 26) need cause no surprise. But it will be shown later that the substitution in one instance in the Early Version (no. 9), and in a number of triads in the WR version, of the purely conventional *llys Arthur* formula for the earlier *ynys Prydein* formula, bears witness to the mounting impetus with which the Arthurian material gained in popularity in Wales, once Geoffrey of Monmouth's work and the French romances based on the Matter of Britain had reached Welsh audiences through the medium of *Brut y Brenhinedd* and the three Welsh Arthurian romances.

TRIOEDD YNYS PRYDEIN AND BARDIC INSTRUCTION

The argument has been advanced elsewhere[62] that *Trioedd Ynys Prydein*, like the *Trioedd Cerdd*, were evolved as a part of the teaching given by the poets to their juniors; pupil bards being required to learn the triad sequences by heart. As such, the various groups of triads originated simply as mnemonic devices; and *Trioedd Ynys Prydein* came into being as an aid to the recollection of the repertoire of narrative material which the young bard was in process of mastering. It is easy to believe that the system of grouping the triads in sequences and contrasting pairs, and the reappearance in fifteenth-century manuscripts of 'floating sections', or short groups of triads which correspond in their order with the order of

[62] GP lxxxviii, xci; J. Lloyd-Jones, *The Court Poets of the Welsh Princes* (British Academy Rhys Memorial Lecture, 1948), p. 29, n. 31. Cf. Ifor Williams, *Hen Chwedlau,* THSC 1946, p. 33.

the triads in the Early Version are to be accounted for as survivals of this original arrangement of *Trioedd Ynys Prydein* for mnemonic purposes. The *Tri Thlws ar Ddeg* (App. III) and the *Pedwar Marchog ar Hugain* (App. IV) are lists of a similar kind formed for the use of the poets,[63] though in origin they are less ancient than *Trioedd Ynys Prydein*. We know that, down to the final years of disintegration of the bardic order,[64] bardic teaching continued to be both imparted and retained in a medium which was in the main oral—for the surviving copies of the *dwned*[65] or bardic grammar represent only a late and partial aid to instruction—and hence it is that our knowledge of the content of this instruction must remain in a great measure inferential. We have, however, the statement of the *Trioedd Cerdd* as found in the *Llyfr Coch* version of the *dwned* (attributed to Einion Offeiriad),[66] to the effect that:

> Tri pheth a beir y gerdawr uot yn amyl: kyfarwydyt ystoryaeu, a bardoniaeth, a hengerd.[67]

[63] GP xci.

[64] The invention of printing had far-reaching effects on the organization of bardic teaching. When *cywyddau* began to be obtainable in printed form (for the first time in Gruffydd Robert's *Grammar*, 1567), anyone could learn the craft of poetry without a teacher, and consequently the long-cherished and esoteric learning of the bards received a mortal wound. The old organization was approaching extinction during the sixteenth century. See D. Gwenallt Jones, 'Rhethreg yng Nghyfundrefn y Beirdd', *Y Llenor* XII, p. 172.

[65] *Dwned* < *Donatus*. Aelius Donatus was the teacher of St Jerome in the fourth century. His work was the handbook on Latin grammar in common use in medieval universities, and the recognized authority on the subject in Wales up to the time of the Renaissance. Thus *dwned* became the generic term in Welsh for a grammar, although Donatus was not the only Latin grammarian whose work was adapted by the bards to the requirements of their own language. The *dwned* brought together the native learning with that of Latin Christendom; but in addition to giving an account of the parts of speech it contained additional notes on Welsh metres, the forbidden faults, the manner in which different classes of people ought to be praised, and the *Trioedd Cerdd*. See GP xcv *et passim*; *Cy.* XXVI, p. 128, GOI, pp. 216–17 n. *Dwned* < *Donatus* implies an intermediary form, and Middle English *donet, donat* has been postulated; see NED s.v., and T. H. Parry-Williams, *The English Element in Welsh* (London, 1923), pp. 108, 241. The English word is used with a similar generalized meaning to the Welsh.

[66] In its extant form this belongs to the earlier half of the fourteenth century, but as far as the purely Welsh material in it is concerned, the rules on metre suggest that this is based on sources at least as old as the early thirteenth century; see Thomas Parry, THSC 1936, p. 158; idem, PBA XLVII, pp. 177–95; R. G. Gruffydd a Rhiannon Ifans, *Gwaith Einion Offeiriad a Dafydd Ddu o Hiraddug* (Aberystwyth, 1997).

[67] GP 18.13–15. Variants from other texts appear on pp. 37, 134, 135. These variants make it clear that *cyfarwyddyd* is used in the *Llyfr Coch* version in its primary sense of 'knowledge, familiarity', and that the word is not in this context equivalent to *chwedl*, but that *ystoryaeu* is dependent upon it. For the varied meanings of *cyfarwyddyd* see GPC 686; and for those of *ystoria* and *cyfarwydddyd* see the discussions by B. F. Roberts, B XXVI, pp. 13–20 and ch. I in his *Studies on Middle Welsh Literature*. For a different interpretation of *cyfarwyddyd* see P. K. Ford in SC X/XI, pp. 152–62.

'Three things that give amplitude to a poet: knowledge of histories, the poetic art, and old verse.'

The *ystoryaeu*[68] here referred to mean the national inheritance of ancient tradition to which *Trioedd Ynys Prydein* provided the key.[69] As employed here the words *ystorya*[70] and *cyfarwyddyd* are near equivalents to the Irish term *seanchus*, which meant the whole corpus of past records in oral form, comprising the mythology and traditional history of Ireland in the widest possible sense. In Ireland, as in Wales, the poets were required to have at their command an immense repertoire of the stories and verse in which the native record was preserved—and in so far as the narrative material is concerned, the classification of the stories according to their subject matter in saga lists bears a certain resemblance to the Welsh classification by means of triads. In both there is apparent the same basic idea of grouping according to theme, rather than according to period and cycle (as would be our modern method), and there is evidence which suggests that Irish poets were prepared to recite these catalogues spontaneously when required to enumerate their repertoire for the benefit of a patron.[71] The Irish tales are listed under such headings as Cattle-Raids, Adventures, Conception-Tales, Battles, Feasts, Elopements, Visions, Invasions, etc. The highest grades of poets, known as *filid*, were required to attain an extensive range of proficiency in the native saga, as appears from the tract in the *Book of Leinster* which sets out to list the 250 *prim-scéla* 'primary stories' and the 100 *fó-scéla* 'subordinate' stories or 'anecdotes' with which they must be conversant. Unfortunately the document has come down in an incomplete form, and we are left without illustration of the character or titles of the *fó-scéla*.[72]

[68] Cf. the title *Ystorya Peredur (ab Efrawc)*, WM 165.25–6. *Breudwyt Ronabwy* is also described as an *ystorya* (RM 161.3). The first of the three *Cof* to be preserved by the bards, according to the English version by John Jones, Gellilyfdy was 'the History of the notable Acts of the Kings and princes of this land of Bruttaen and Cambria' (LlC III, p. 235).

[69] GP xlii. Cf. Guto'r Glyn's description of the studies which he shared with his patron Rhys ap Siancyn: *Dwyn ar fyfyrdod ein dau / Drioedd ac ystoriau* (GGl 241.47–8). For *cyfarwyddyd* see B. F. Roberts, 'Oral Tradition and Welsh Literature', *Studies on Middle Welsh Literature*, ch. I.

[70] The word *ystorya* is a late borrowing from L. *historia*, which had already given *ystyr* in Welsh (see Idris Foster, PBA 1949, p. 199). Foster points out that in the *Llyfr Ancr* and elsewhere this term is applied to *Bucheddau'r Saint* as well as to more general religious treatises.

[71] Myles Dillon, *The Cycles of the Kings* (Oxford, 1946), p. 115; J. E. Caerwyn Williams, *Traddodiad Llenyddol Iwerddon*, p. 53; and J. E. Caerwyn Williams and P. K. Ford, *The Irish Literary Tradition*, pp. 36–7.

[72] These terms are discussed by P. Mac Cana, *The Learned Tales of Medieval Ireland* (DIAS, 1980), who regards the term *fó-scéla* as a scribal invention (pp. 118–22). See further his 'Conservation and Innovation in Early Celtic Literature', EC XIII, pp. 61–119. He would consider TYP as constituting a 'motif index' whereas the Irish Saga Lists are a 'type-index'. See also Seán mac Airt, *Ériu* XVIII, pp. 39f.

Although we have no such detailed information in Welsh about the range of knowledge required of the bards, it is safe to deduce from the evidence already cited that originally an extensive familiarity with the canonical corpus of national tradition was demanded as part of the bardic training. This is borne out by the allusions which the twelfth-century *Gogynfeirdd* make to the *hen chwedlau*, since the sheer volume of the traditional names with which they show familiarity indicates that their knowledge can hardly have been limited to names alone, but that they must frequently have had some knowledge of the actual stories concerning the characters concerned. Evidently it was not sufficient for Cynddelw and his contemporaries, as it was to become in an ever-increasing degree for the poets in the later centuries, to stake a claim to being the inheritors of the complete corpus of national tradition, merely by a judicious use of the powerfully evocative names preserved in *Trioedd Ynys Prydein*. The poets whose work falls within the period before 1200[73] prove by their allusions that they were familiar with the following heroes[74] and cycles of narrative: the story of the Trojan origin of the Britons (see H 14.19), and the tale of Benlli Gawr (H 127.19; 152.24; 184.5, etc.), both of which are found in the *Historia Brittonum* (and for the poets it was HB (not HRB) which stood as the authority for the major events of Britain's earlier history); the characters of the *Mabinogi*;[75] Maxen Wledig; Caswallawn and his opposition to the Romans; certain of the subsidiary tales in *Culhwch ac Olwen* (H 95.4; 110.2); the Arthurian story, with references to Arthur, Cai, Llachau, Medrawd, *Kelli Wic* (see note to triad 1), and the battles of *Baddon* (H 84.10; 96.5; 101.6 = CBT IV, no. 1.40; no. 4.238; no. 6.99; no. 13.19) and *Camlan* (see note to triad 59); Cadwallawn and his contest with the English king Edwin (see note to triad 55); much North-British material including traditions about Urien Rheged and Owain, and about the battle of *Arfderydd* (see note to triad 84); the nucleus of the Taliesin story; and a number of the names of the heroes of classical antiquity (see note to triad 47). They knew the names (and, we may assume, something of the work) of others of the *Cynfeirdd*

[73] A convenient list of these poets is given by D. S. Evans, *A Grammar of Middle Welsh* (Dublin, 1964), pp. xxv–xxix; also by J. E. Caerwyn Williams, *The Poets of the Welsh Princes* (Cardiff, 1994), pp. 74–80.

[74] For those whose names occur in TYP references will be found in the Notes to Personal Names at the end of this volume.

[75] W. J. Gruffydd implies (*Rhiannon*, pp. 4–6) that the poets at all periods made little reference to the material of the *Mabinogi*. Yet Cynddelw refers to *Lleu, Pryderi, Brân, Mallolwch* (for *Matholwch*) (CBT IV, no. 9.154n.); and Prydydd y Moch to *Mallolwch, Teyrnon* and *Brân vab Llŷr* (CBT V, no. 1.91n.) see under Notes to Personal Names. References by the *cywyddwyr* to these characters are also frequent, though by the fifteenth century the heroes of the foreign romances claimed a large share in the allusions of the poets. See below, pp. lxvi–lxvii.

from those whose poetry has come down (see notes to *Auan 6erdic*, *Arouan*, *Dygynnelw*, *Trist6ard*). Owain Cyfeiliog is distinguished from his contemporaries by his references to the matter of the *Gododdin* in his poem *Hirlas Owein* (RBP cols. 1432–5 = CBT II, no. 14.125n.; see notes to triad 31 and to *Mynyda6c Eidyn*). Llywelyn Fardd (II) refers to the *Ymarwar Lludd a Llevelys* (H 208.4 = CBT VI, no. 7.4n.); while Cynddelw's references to Urien and Owain suggest that he was acquainted with that part of the Powys *englyn* cycle which dealt with their story;[76] and it is Cynddelw too, who in his allusion to March ap Meirchion (CBT IV, no. 3.12n.) gives the earliest reference found in this poetry to a character in the *Drystan* story.

Yet in spite of the wealth of allusion preserved in the work of the *Gogynfeirdd*, there is a continual difficulty in assessing the value to be attached to this material as evidence for knowledge of the antecedent tradition. For the process by which the poets from the thirteenth century onwards progressively lost touch with the national inheritance of story was implicit from the first in the use which they made of this inheritance. The *Gogynfeirdd* wrote no narrative poems, and at no time did it form any part of their intention to give much information either about their contemporaries, or (still less) about the heroes of past ages. The way in which they utilized their acquired knowledge of *ystoryaeu a hengerdd* consisted in citing the names of the ancient heroes as standards for favourable comparison (since these names occur only in eulogy), against which to set those of their patrons.[77] It has been shown[78] that this use of the material provided by the national tradition owed something to the teaching of the medieval schools of rhetoric, in which Aristotle's book on rhetoric was expounded, with its account of the various characteristics to be expected from men in different conditions of life. Yet since this tendency is apparent already in the older poetry,[79] the influence of rhetorical teaching is not a

[76] Cf. the allusions to *aelwyd reged* (H 123.18 = CBT III, no. 5.70), *Unhwch* (112.17 = CBT IV, no. 9.155).

[77] For Cynddelw's use of complimentary epithets embodying the names of the traditional heroes, see D. Myrddin Lloyd, B VI, pp. 122, 127; idem, *Rhai Agweddau ar Ddysg y Gogynfeirdd* (Caerdydd, 1977), p. 5, etc. Seán mac Airt pointed out in an important article (*Ériu* XVIII, p. 150) that a primary use made of the traditional stories by the Irish bards was for purposes of illustration. This indicates that in both countries these stories received an extended currency for a similar reason—as an essential part of the bard's equipment for his craft. On this point in relation to the Irish bards, see also E. Knott, *Irish Classical Poetry* (Dublin, 1957), p. 57. P. Mac Cana summarizes the difference between early Irish and Welsh poets in the extent and manner in which they utilized their native traditions, *The Mabinogi*, pp. 18–20; EC XIII (1972), pp. 81–2.

[78] See D. Gwenallt Jones, *Y Llenor* XII, pp. 26–7, 158.

[79] CLlH no. XI.10a (where Cynddylan is compared with Culhwch); CA l. 1242, where the famous comparison *ceni bei ef Arthur* 'though he was not Arthur' is made of one of the warriors of the *Gododdin*. Again, in the *Marwnad Cynddylan* (B VI, p. 136, l. 24) Cynddylan is described as *clod Ceiriadawg* (= *Caradawg*), and *Cadwallon* compared

complete explanation with regard to this phenomenon in Welsh literature. Nor is it by any means clear by what channels the Latin teaching of the ecclesiastical schools was made accessible, in however rudimentary a fashion, to the bards of the twelfth and thirteenth centuries. The various versions of the *dwned* used by the bards[80] contain lists of the virtues which should properly be attributed to different classes of men and women, according to their fixed status in society. From this it was but a step for a bard to attribute to his patron the valour of Alexander or Arthur, and the generosity of Rhydderch Hael; since these ancient heroes were regarded as supreme possessors of the virtues in question.[81] And for a twelfth-century poet to name his patron in eulogistic comparison with one or all of the *Tri Hael* (triad 2) was to invoke a symbol of common knowledge shared between him and his audience,[82] which led directly back into the milieu of the North-British Heroic Age. An outstanding example of this attitude of mind is the manner in which Cynddelw implicitly conceives and recreates the figure of the twelfth-century ruler Owain Gwynedd in the form of his sixth-century predecessor, the North-British hero Owain ab Urien. This concept is already present in Gwalchmai's reference to Owain Gwynedd as *gwyndeyrn Prydein* (see note to triad 3); and it is perfected in Cynddelw's *awdlau* to Owain Gwynedd (CBT IV, nos. 1–4).[83]

But the logical outcome of this impressionistic usage of the old names as symbols of valour, generosity, and courtesy, was for these names to acquire so strong an evocative power in their own right that the poets who used them progressively lost touch with all that had given to the names their original vitality. It may be said that this process is reflected in the texts of *Trioedd Ynys Prydein* from a very early stage in the manuscript tradition, since the inept comments appended to a number of triads in the WR version (see above, p. xxiii–xxiv and n.) betray for the most part a complete ignorance on the part of the scribe who wrote them as to the real meaning of the triad in question—and yet it has been shown that these comments

with *Maelgwn* in *Marwnad Cadwallon* (B VII, p. 25, l. 23) as well as with some even remoter ancestors. See R. G. Gruffydd, 'Canu Cadwallon ap Cadfan', *Ast. H.* 28.

[80] GP 15–16, 55–6.

[81] D. Gwenallt Jones, *Y Llenor* XII, pp. 26–7.

[82] Cf. T. Parry, *Hanes Llenyddiaeth Gymraeg* (Caerdydd, 1944), p. 42. Such references were charged with the intricate appeal to sense and emotion which Saunders Lewis in discussing the bardic vocabulary describes as their *aura* (*Braslun o Hanes Llenyddiaeth Gymraeg*, p. 23).

[83] See D. Myrddin Lloyd, *Y Llenor* XIII, pp. 49–50: 'Nod yr holl awdl (= H 83–5) yw cyfleu i'r dychymyg . . . ymwybod o wir fawredd Owain Gwynedd ac ystyr ei yrfa, sef mai ef i'r ddeuddegfed ganrif oedd Hiriell, Owain ab Urien, ac Arthur; iddo ef yn Nhegeingl a gerllaw Aberteifi ail ymladd 'gwaith Faddon fawr' ac 'Argoed Llwyfain'. Cynysgaedda ei oes â holl fawredd a gwerth ei gynfyd.' Cf. to the same effect T. J. Morgan, THSC 1946, p. 283, and more generally, D. M. Lloyd, *Rhai Agweddau ar Ddysg y Gogynfeirdd* (1977).

must have been already present in an older text than that of the *Llyfr Gwyn*.[84] It is this use by the bards of the old names as a quarry for reference which is largely responsible for the continued copying of the manuscripts of TYP down to the seventeenth century, when their transmission was given fresh impetus by the awakened antiquarian interest of such humanist scholars as Robert Vaughan and John Jones Gellilyfdy. It accounts also for the fact that Gwilym Tew was prepared to copy in his own hand a corrupt and barely intelligible text of TYP (Pen. 51). But on the reverse side of the picture it must be remembered that Dafydd ap Gwilym and the *cywyddwyr* down to the sixteenth century (and later) every now and again produce a fragment of narrative which cannot be directly related to any known literary source, and which is evidently based on current popular tradition.[85]

Thus it is that as a part of the diction of bardic vocabulary the names recorded in TYP acted as symbols whose precise significance altered throughout the centuries in which they were used. To the earlier *Gogynfeirdd* they may have been highly concrete symbols pointing to a definite background in the antecedent narrative tradition. They became gradually divorced from their original context; so that in the late fourteenth century, for example, it would be interesting to know exactly what was understood by the poet or by his patron when Madog Dwygraig compared Morgan ap Dafydd to the *Tri Hael* (RBP col. 1271.25–7). And a very similar problem attaches itself to the eulogistic epithets under which these names are grouped in the triads. What is the precise shade of meaning which we should attach, in their context, to such terms as *gwyndeyrn*, *deifnyawc*, *galouyd*, *rudvoawc*, *ysgymyd aeruaeu*, etc.? These are compound words which belong to the vocabulary of bardic poetry, which was predominantly archaic, and even intentionally obscure.[86] But when they are used in the triads, do these epithets hold a particular relevance, based on stories which were known about the characters named, so that they

[84] See pp. xxvii–xxviii above.

[85] Examples: Dafydd ap Gwilym's reference to the abduction of Gwenhwyfar by Melwas (GDG no. 64.20–6), and Dafydd ab Edmwnd's reference to the same story (GDE, iv, 7. 21–8). Iolo Goch (GIG no. XXIX) recounts a miracle of St David's which is not found elsewhere, though it is obscurely alluded to in *Culhwch ac Olwen* in the episode of the *dau genau Gast Rymhi* (CO ll. 929–37). Variant forms of the *Mabinogi* of *Math* were known to the *cywyddwyr*. See also p. lxviii, n., below, and notes to *Petroc Paladrddellt, Tegeu Eururon, Merwydd.*

[86] See my chapter 'Cyfeiriadau Traddodiadol a Chwedlonol y Gogynfeirdd', in M. E. Owen and B. F. Roberts (eds), *Beirdd a Thywysogion*, pp. 208–9; T. H. Parry-Williams, PBA (1946), p. 14; J. Lloyd-Jones, PBA (1948), p. 5. D. Myrddin Lloyd has shown (B VI, pp. 120 ff.) that Cynddelw freely employed words with any one of the meanings that they had held in any previous period of their existence in Welsh, and that he not infrequently employed them differently upon different occasions, with shades of meaning which varied between the contemporary and the archaic.

possess a significance which we cannot hope to recover? Or are they merely generalized terms of encomium, a part of the linguistic repertoire to be acquired by pupil-bards? In either case, the relative scarcity with which these epithets occur, even in the bardic poetry of the twelfth and thirteenth centuries, makes it impossible for us, at this distance of time, to recover their precise *aura*. The way in which the proper names grouped under these epithets show a tendency to vary, even among the earliest texts of TYP, serves as a warning against attaching too precise a meaning to them—in contrast to other epithets in TYP which are directly linked with very definite stories (for example triads 26, 29, 30, 37). We may conclude that these are generalized terms, broadly complimentary, but intended, as part of the esoteric heritage of bardic teaching, to be ambiguous in a way which would impress the uninitiated.

A comparison of the content of TYP with the work of the *Gogynfeirdd* leads to a further conclusion. The range of reference to characters drawn from the *ystoryaeu a hengerdd* which has already been indicated as constituting the repertoire of twelfth-century poets corresponds closely with the range of reference covered by the triads in the Early Version of TYP, as presented in Pen. 16 and 45. Thus it would appear that the Early Version of TYP represents what is in substance a classified list of the content of the canonical body of national tradition with which the poets, down to the end of the twelfth century, were required to make themselves familiar.[87] It is hoped that the significance in this respect as a turning point of the years immediately preceding and following 1200 will presently appear. The allusions in the triads combined with those made by the twelfth-century *Gogynfeirdd* prove that up to almost the end of the century the canonical tradition recognized by the bards did not include any name or episode derived from Continental romance[88] or from Geoffrey of Monmouth's pseudo-history of Britain—no reference which betrays an origin in either of these sources is to be found in the Early Version of TYP, nor can any such be found in the work of the poets of the *Gogynfeirdd* before *circa* 1300.

[87] A comparison with the bardic references listed on pp. lxv–lxviii shows that there are a few omissions. Examples: there are no allusions in TYP to the story of the Trojan origin of the Britons, or to *Benlli Gawr*, or to the battle of Baddon (*Ann. Cam.* 516). Nor is there any reference to *Hiriell*, see below, p. xcviii, n. 166.

[88] Prydydd y Moch (*circa* 1173–1220) makes the earliest allusion which might possibly be interpreted as referring to romance material (to Rhodri mab Owain): *teyrnas yth lav lid gereint nyd chwith* (H 271.9 = CBT V, no. 7.9). This is the earliest allusion made by one of the *Gogynfeirdd* to Geraint, and the words suggest a reference to the romance. But Geraint was a hero well established in the Welsh tradition before his name came to be used in the romances. Some problems are also raised by the references to *Drystan mab Tallwch* in triad 26 (see n. to *Drystan m. Tallwch*).

It is a matter of controversy how far Welsh poets of the twelfth and thirteenth centuries had access to the Latin learning of the Church. G. J. Williams laid emphasis[89] on the cultural community between poets and clerics in these centuries, and drew attention to the ecclesiastical authorship of the religious poems in LlDC, while pointing out that the scribe of LlDC also had access to the poems of Cynddelw. The ninth-century Welsh glosses on Ovid's *Ars Amatoria* and *Martianus Capella* prove a degree of ecclesiastical proficiency in Latin at a date much earlier than this. From the allusions in their poetry it is clear that Gwalchmai and others of the *Gogynfeirdd* were acquainted with the pseudo-learned tradition of the settlement of Britain by Trojan fugitives descended from Aeneas, and certain verbal echoes indicate that the poets derived this knowledge, with other details, from the Latin text of the *Historia Brittonum*.[90] But it is never clear how far the knowledge of Latin penetrated beyond the confines of the monastery. Any generalization on this subject must take into account the interrelation between secular and ecclesiastical learning which is witnessed by the fact that the earliest manuscripts containing secular poetry are the work of monastic scribes. It has been shown also that twelfth-century poets were influenced by the rhetorical teaching of the ecclesiastical schools,[91] and that from an early date some familiarity with the names at least of the leading classical heroes is evinced by them (see note to triad 47). Thus it is that although twelfth-century Welsh churchmen such as Giraldus Cambrensis and Walter Map were conversant with the contents of the *Historia Regum*, yet the poets make no use of material emanating from this source before a date which can be shown to correspond approximately with the turn of the thirteenth century.[92] This is precisely the period to which the earliest versions of *Brut y Brenhinedd* have been traced back.[93] We are consequently drawn to the conclusion that the bards made no use of

[89] GP xcv–xcvi; and note the names *Turn* < *Turnus* (CBT II, no. 27.1n. = HB ch. 10, earlier than BD 18), and *Oswald*, *Osguid* (= *Oswy*) (HB ch. 64 = CBT III, no. 3.128n.).

[90] See n. to *Eneas Ysc6ydwyn*.

[91] D. Gwenallt Jones, *Y Llenor* XII, pp. 158 ff.

[92] The earliest reference found in poetry to a character from *Brut y Brenhinedd* appears to be in a poem attributed to Elidir Sais (*circa* 1195–1246) in which he addresses Llywelyn ap Iorwerth (d. 1240) as *Gwr gwraf gorsaf gwersyll Avarwy* (CBT I, no. 17.40, n.). There are a number of instances in which *avarwy* is employed as a substantive by twelfth- and thirteenth-century poets (see GPC 41). Ifor Williams has shown that *avarwy* can have the meaning 'sorrow' (CLlH 191), and this is the meaning which suits best with the word as used by Cynddelw and Prydydd y Moch; cf. CBT III, no. 16.80 (note p. 212) and CBT V, no. 22.20 (note pp. 207–8). The reference by Elidir Sais is the first in which it appears most probable that *avarwy* is used as a proper name, though even here the allusion can hardly be regarded as certain; cf. CBT I, no. 17.40n.

[93] See BD xxix, xxxv; B XXV, p. 274. For the evidence that *Enweu Meibon Llywarch Hen* (LlDC no. 40) contains a reference to *Brut y Brenhinedd* see B XVII, pp. 180–1, and a note by E. D. Jones, LlDC xv.

Geoffrey's narrative until after this had become available to them in a Welsh dress. When this happened, it is somewhat remarkable to find that the subject matter of the *Brut* became fused with the native tradition during the course of the thirteenth and fourteenth centuries, and was regarded by the poets as a part of their accepted field of reference; while it can be seen both from the later version of TYP and from *Brut y Brenhinedd* that every attempt was made to reconcile the scheme of Geoffrey's narrative with the pre-existing, but in comparison certainly much less organized, native traditions. The material of the *Historia Regum* is thus the first of the great additions made from literary and 'external'[94] sources which received the *imprimatur* of the *Ynys Prydein* formula, and became accepted as belonging to the canonical body of traditional lore.

The alteration is witnessed in the WR version of *Trioedd Ynys Prydein* (*circa* 1350–1400), which not only incorporates a complete triad (no. 51) based on the *Brut* narrative, but contains in addition a few references which are probably to be traced to the same source (see notes to triads 37d, 59). We find a marked increase in the prominence of Arthur in the WR and later versions, and an increasing tendency for the *llys Arthur* 'Arthur's Court' formula to supersede the older *Ynys Prydein* formula in the titles of the triads. This growth in popularity of the Arthurian material, although it is already beginning to be apparent in the Early Version (see p. lviii above and note to triad 9), is no doubt to be attributed to an increasing awareness of the contemporary prominence of the Arthurian cycle in the literature of medieval Europe.

Throughout the thirteenth and fourteenth centuries it becomes increasingly apparent that the poets are drawing increasingly on literary sources for their allusions; and the introduction of this material of predominantly foreign origin coincides with the evident decline in knowledge of the native Welsh tales which, as has been shown, is reflected in the successive manuscripts of TYP. From the early-fourteenth century, references in poetry include the names of such figures as *Peredur*, *Evrawc*, *Erbin*, *Eigr*, *Lunet*, *Enid*, *Drystan*, *Essyllt*—names whose comparatively late appearance in the field of bardic reference is to be attributed to the increasing popularity of the literary romance material derived from France, although this in turn was superimposed upon older British traditional narrative about these characters. In the late fourteenth century Gruffudd ap Maredudd is to be distinguished alike from his predecessors among the

[94] I.e. material which was introduced through a literary and not through an oral channel. Of course Geoffrey's source material is itself a highly complex mixture of native Welsh and Breton tradition with classical and biblical matter. Such aspects of the subject of Geoffrey's sources as bear most directly on TYP are discussed further below, pp. lxxix–lxxx.

Gogynfeirdd, and from the *cywydd* poets who were his contemporaries, by the wealth of his references to the characters of the *Brut* and of Arthurian romance, as well as to those of the older native tradition—and he even knows of the heroines of Irish saga, *Deirdre* and *Niamh* (Welsh *Nyf*).[95] In addition to the names quoted above, Gruffudd ap Maredudd refers to *Brân vab Dyfnwal* and *Dyfnwal* (*Moelmut*), *Arawn*, *Frollo* (RBP col. 1203.13; 1206.40; cf. HRB IX, 11), *Gwrleis* (1315.10), *Eudaf* (1316.30), *Yniwl, Angharat Law Eurawc* (1326.26); as well as to the classical heroes and those of the Charlemagne tales—while in one poem he draws freely on the names of the horses of early heroes which are preserved in *Trioedd y Meirch* (1328–9). Thus the accepted corpus of story material used for bardic reference was becoming progressively expanded during this period, and the additions made from foreign sources included reference to the Matter of France and Rome, as well as to the Matter of Britain. As in the case of Geoffrey's *Historia Regum*, this foreign literature had largely become known in a Welsh form already, through the translations of the Charlemagne tales, of *Amlyn and Amic*, *Dares Phrygius*, and the *Grail* romances. (It has been shown on p. xxviii that in the Pen. 50 version of TYP certain names from *Y Seint Greal* have been introduced among the older triads.) But with regard to the Arthurian cycle at least, it is apparent that fifteenth-century poets had a more extensive knowledge of the French prose romances than they can have acquired through the medium of any Welsh versions that have come down (see note to triad 86). The introduction of these names into the accepted canon of bardic reference is a reflection of the changed state of society in the fourteenth and fifteenth centuries; and it implies among the *cywyddwyr* an awareness of the thought and literature of the outside world which contrasts strongly with the mainly inward-looking national tradition of the earlier *Gogynfeirdd*. In the fifteenth century the names from foreign Arthurian material, taken back into Welsh, became in some measure also an integral part of the bardic tradition, as is shown both in the later poetry and in the group of triads known as *Pedwar Marchog ar Hugain Llys Arthur* (App. IV). But even though accepted as belonging to the field of bardic reference, these names

[95] RBP col. 1321.21, 32. Dafydd ap Gwilym is outstanding for the wide range of his *Mabinogi* references. He also refers to *Derdri* (GDG no. 139.21). For a reference to *Derdri* by Lewis Glyn Cothi see GLGC no. 51.52n.; DGG 187. The name of *Derdri* is included in a bardic vocabulary (B I, p. 330), but without explanation. For a possible reference to *Nyf* see DGG no. 25.11; IGE^2, p. 158, l.21n. P. Sims-Williams questions the suggestion made by Ifor Williams (DGG 187) that *Nyf* ('snow'<Lat. *nix*, *nivis*) is a personal name which corresponds to that of the Irish legendary heroine, *Niamh*. See Sims-Williams's discussion in B XXIX, p. 219, and in 'Irish Elements in Medieval Welsh Literature', in M. J. Ball *et alii* (eds), *Current Issues in Linguistic Theory* (Amsterdam, 1990), pp. 282–6. On French literary borrowings in medieval Welsh, see C. Lloyd-Morgan, AW ch. 9.

could hardly become endowed with the *aura* which the names of the heroes of the native Welsh *chwedlau* had possessed for the *Gogynfeirdd* and their audiences.

TRIOEDD YNYS PRYDEIN AND THE *CHWEDLAU*

Apart from a well-known passage in the *Mabinogi of Math*,[96] there is no evidence that in Wales the highest classes of bards concerned themselves with the narration of stories, as did the *filid* in Ireland. The passage referred to tells how Gwydion arrived at the court of Pryderi as the leader of a company of bards, himself bearing the appearance of a *pencerdd*, and how he entertained the court with story-telling (*cyfarwyddyd*). The narrator adds that Gwydion was the best *cyfarwydd* in the world. The Welsh *cyfarwydd* (lit. 'expert, well-informed person', hence 'story-teller') may be compared with the Irish *scélaige* ('story-teller'), for whose existence alongside the official *fili* there is some evidence in Irish sources which go back to an early date.[97] But there is no certainty that in either country these popular entertainers belonged to the bardic order; indeed, the concluding words of *Breudwyt Ronabwy*, which state that 'neither bard nor *cyfarwydd* (shall know this tale) without a book',[98] imply the existence of some kind of distinction between the two. In these instances the Welsh tales refer to the narrator of such stories as they themselves represent as a *cyfarwydd*, and there are occasional references also to the story itself as a *cyfarwyddyd*.[99] But the nature of the relation between *beirdd* and *cyfarwyddiaid* is by no means clear. There is no evidence which suggests that the twelfth-century *Gogynfeirdd* narrated stories at the courts of the princes who were their patrons, as Gwydion did at the court of Pryderi. Yet the evidence already examined proves that Cynddelw and his contemporaries were still in a great measure conversant with the corpus of traditional narrative which is indexed in *Trioedd Ynys Prydein*; and it has been shown that these and other triads were evolved for the use of the bards themselves, and not for an unofficial class of popular entertainer,

[96] PKM 69.13–16.

[97] See Chadwick, *Growth of Literature* I, 606; V. Hull, *Longes mac n-Uislenn* (Mod. Lang. Ass. America, 1949), 43, l. 2; J. E. Caerwyn Williams, 'Gildas, Maelgwn and the Bards', in R. R. Davies *et al.* (eds), *Welsh Society and Nationhood* (Cardiff, 1984), p. 30; P Mac Cana, *The Learned Tales*, p. 139 *et passim*. On the question here discussed, see further P. K. Ford, SC X/XI, pp. 152–62; B. F. Roberts, 'Oral Tradition and Welsh Literature', *Studies*, p. 3.

[98] RM 161.5. For suggestions as to the significance of this passage—perhaps a late gloss on the tale—see M. Richards, Br. Rh. xxiii–xxiv.

[99] For references see GPC 685, 686.

such as is sometimes thought to be denoted by the word *cyfarwydd* (guide, storyteller). It is possible that the passage in *Math* preserves a memory of an older state of affairs, when the *penceirddiaid* did entertain their patrons in this way, just as we are told that the *filid* did in Ireland. But the *Four Branches* as they have come down are a secondary and literary adaptation of older traditional material, and perhaps it would be unjustifiable to lay too much emphasis on the equation which is found in the passage referred to between *bardd* and *cyfarwydd.*

The prose tales themselves provide a considerable part of the evidence which goes to show that the inheritance of national traditions originally transmitted as an essential part of bardic learning was, by 1100, and probably much earlier, being retailed on a more popular level. It is no doubt the *cyfarwydd*'s work of which we have adaptations in the written *chwedlau. Culhwch ac Olwen* may be regarded as exhibiting the resources of the *cyfarwydd* in fullest measure. This story is a skilful blending of folk-tales of types which are both Celtic and international; but it has been enriched by the insertion of elements from older Welsh mythology and heroic tradition. The early Celtic mythological substratum, and the traditions of the legendary heroes of Wales and North Britain have been merged together in such a way that the protagonists from quite unrelated cycles of narrative, which differed both in their place of origin and in their essential character, could all be assembled together at Arthur's Court.[100] Within fifty years of the redaction of *Culhwch* in its present form (about 1100 or soon after),[101] Geoffrey of Monmouth's *Historia Regum Britanniæ* was given to the world (1136 or 1138).[102] This work by a Norman-Breton ecclesiastic draws to a partial extent upon the same body of tradition as did the redactors of the *chwedlau*; and Geoffrey, though his purposes were different, has manipulated his material to suit them just as, in a different way, did the narrator of *Culhwch.* The fact that the carefully-preserved and safeguarded content of the bardic tradition could have become even in a limited degree accessible to Geoffrey, and to the *cyfarwyddiaid*, from whom was ultimately drawn such knowledge as Geoffrey had of early

[100] Such unhistorical associations are characteristic of a late stage in the development of heroic stories; see H. M. and N. K. Chadwick, *The Growth of Literature* I (Cambridge, 1932), p. 238.

[101] Idris Foster, 'Astudiaeth o Chwedl Culhwch ac Olwen' (University of Wales M.A. thesis, 1935), pp. 304 ff., in part reproduced in the introduction to CO(1); and see also R. Bromwich and D. S. Evans (eds), *Culhwch and Olwen: An Edition and Study of the Oldest Arthurian Tale* (= CO(2)) (Cardiff, 1992) and *Culhwch ac Olwen* (ail argr., Caerdydd, 1997). The text, line-references and notes correspond in the English and Welsh editions. For discussion of date and provenance see CO(2), pp. lxxvii–lxxxiii.

[102] For arguments in favour of HRB's later date see Tatlock, *The Legendary History of Britain* (Los Angeles, 1950), pp. 433–7; C. Brooke, *Studies in the Early British Church* (ed. N. K. Chadwick), p. 231, n. 2.

Welsh tradition, implies that by this date a certain decline in status of the old stories had taken place—that they were being elaborated by others than the poets, and for a different audience than the courts of princes. On the *cyfarwydd* level the ancient narrative material had by this time become confused, blended with other elements, and generally transmuted into those *nugae Brittonum* to whose existence William of Malmesbury refers somewhat scathingly.[103] An examination of the relation of the *chwedlau*, and later of Geoffrey's *Historia Regum*, to *Trioedd Ynys Prydein*, may serve to provide further evidence that the triads were an essential part of the learning of the bards, and were only imperfectly known to the popular story-tellers. But the narrative material which has come down in the extant *chwedlau* stems ultimately from the same body of tradition as is referred to in the triads, and often throws valuable light upon the allusions in them.

The *Four Branches of the Mabinogi* present a marked contrast to the other *chwedlau* in that a number (ten) of triads[104] have been incorporated into all but the First Branch. It may be that these triads were introduced into the text at varying stages in the development of the stories; but I am unable to accept Sir Ifor Williams's argument[105] that they are all to be dismissed as late scribal glosses. I think that as a whole the allusions to triads have a more fundamental relation than this to the stories in which they are cited and that the triads belong essentially to the same field of tradition as the *Mabinogi*. It has been frequently pointed out that the final author of the *Four Branches* was a consummate literary artist, and I believe that one of the ways in which he displays this artistry is in the occasional use of triads (in a manner similar to the 'digressions' in *Beowulf*) to heighten the dramatic effect of his narrative by relating it to a wider field of tradition.[106] Thus the story of the death and burial of Bendigeidfran would be in no inconsiderable degree the poorer if it had not been so dramatically set in context as belonging to the group of Fortunate Concealments and Unfortunate Disclosures (PKM 47.22–4; triad 37 below). This is true also of the allusion to the perfidy of Gronwy Pefyr's *teulu*, which caused them to be placed in the triad of the Three Faithless Warbands (PKM 92.1–6; triad 30); and I believe it also to be true of the words which accompany the first introduction of Branwen into the story which bears her name, *a honno oed tryded prif rieni yn yr ynys hon*

[103] *De Rebus Gestis Regum Anglorum* (ed. Stubbs) I, ch. 8.

[104] These are conveniently listed in PKM xxv.

[105] PKM xxx.

[106] Triads are occasionally employed in the texts of Middle Irish tales in a comparable fashion, as rhetorical devices. I have pointed out some instances from the *Book of Leinster* version of the *Táin*, B XII, pp. 9–10.

(PKM 31.1) 'she was one of the Three Great Queens(?)[107] of this Island'. And in at least one instance I think it likely that an episode in the *Mabinogi* has been adapted to make it fit in with a pre-existing triad. Elsewhere[108] I have suggested that the *Four Branches* are to be distinguished from the other *chwedlau* as much by an essential difference in their basic subject matter as by the developed artistry of their narration. They are fundamentally the stories of the old Brittonic gods from whom the leading Welsh dynasties in early historical times claimed descent, and as such they are directly affiliated to the canonical tradition whose preservation was a primary concern of the bards. It may well be this special relation with the bardic inheritance which is responsible for the comparative prominence of triads in the structure of the stories, and for the significant manner in which these are employed.

Of the ten triads which are cited in the *Four Branches*, the full versions of nos. 1, 2, and 8 in Ifor Williams's list have not been preserved in any extant text of TYP. These are the triads which included Branwen as *tryded prif rieni* (PKM 31.1; 32.27); *C(a)radawc vab Bran* as *trydyd dyn a dorres y gallon o aniuyget* (PKM 46.8–9);[109] and the slaying of Dylan as *trydyd anvat ergyd* (PKM 78.2). It would appear, therefore, that there were certain triads which we should expect to find in the extant lists of TYP, but which for some reason have been omitted, and this in itself suggests the existence of a far more extended body of traditional triadic lore than has survived. The reference to the death of Dylan is one which would find a natural place in the group of triads which celebrated events which were *anfad* or 'unfortunate' (cf. triads 34, 53, 59, and p. lxxxix below). Nos. 5 and 9 in the list (*Teir Gwith Baluawt* triad 53, and *Tri Eur Gryd* triad 67) are given in TYP in a form which differs slightly from that in which they occur in the *Mabinogi*. In triad 53 (see note) it is Matholwch, and not his cook, who strikes Branwen, and the blow is presented as a single disastrous act, and not one which was repeated daily, as in the story. While in triad 67 Lleu Llaw Gyffes is named as one of the *Tri Eurgryd*, and not his companion Gwydion, whose inclusion in the triad seems to be implied in

[107] Ifor Williams advocates *rieni* 'parents', hence 'ancestresses' as the correct reading of the manuscript both here and in PKM 32.27 (see note, PKM 165). But even if this is so, *rieni* could be a scribal error for *riein*, cf. triad 56, which lists the 'three Gwenhwyfars' as Arthur's *teir prif riein*. The obscure witticism of triplicating Gwenhwyfar's name may have ousted that of Branwen in an older version of the triad, and this older version could have been the one cited by the redactor of PKM—so that originally Branwen (who did not in fact become an ancestress) was one of the 'Three Great Queens.' See note to triad 56.

[108] SEBH, ed. N. K. Chadwick, pp. 103, 131–2. In B IX, pp. 131–3, T. Jones cites instances in which *rhieni* is equivalent to L. *progenies* 'descendants, offspring'. But *riein* 'royal lady, queen' fits better here, and gains corroboration from triad 56.

[109] See note to triad 13 below and triad 95.

the text of the *Mabinogi* (PKM 81.2; see note to triad 67c). These variations indicate that the triads were based on oral versions of the underlying tales which differed slightly from the *Mabinogi* as it has come down. There remain the two allusions to Manawydan as *trydyd lledyf unben* (PKM 49.12; triad 8), and as *trydyd eurgryd* (PKM 54.18; triad 67). Ifor Williams pointed out that Pryderi's citation to Manawydan himself of the *Tri Lledyf Unben*, in which Manawydan is himself included, is in its context the height of absurdity, and he assumes that for this reason the reference is a late scribal gloss on the tale. But would not such an incongruous allusion as this be entirely consistent with the style of the narrator, who every now and again lightens his narrative by introducing similar witticisms through the mouths of his characters? I am tempted to believe that the inclusion of this triad in the text is no less deliberate than is that of the other triads referred to above. It may be observed that the redactor of the tale has interpreted *Lleddf* as having some such meaning as 'unassuming, ungrasping', and that this is also the meaning implied in the explanatory note appended to triad 8 in the WR version. The explanation appended to the triad itself and the allusion made to it in the text of *Manawydan* are thus obviously related. They may be attributed to some predecessor of the scribe who wrote the version of TYP contained in the *Llyfr Gwyn*, who had before him a copy of TYP containing the *Tri Lledyf Unben*, and who was inspired to give to *lledyf* an interpretation which fitted in with the character of *Manawydan* as it has come down in the story. The dependence upon the *Mabinogi* of the explanation given to the triad in WR is proved by the fact that in both cases this explanation is not quite adequate. The author of the tale did not fully comprehend the original meaning of *lleddf* in the older bardic vocabulary, and we ourselves must turn to the *hengerdd* in order to find it, for *lleddf* in the triad is capable of bearing the same meaning 'prostrate' as that with which the word is used in the *Gododdin* either by the original poet or by a subsequent scribe.[110] These were men who had been 'prostrated' or laid low by misfortune.

In this instance a scribe has been influenced by a triad in his redaction of *Manawydan*, and I suggest that this is what has happened also in the case of the reference to Manawydan as *trydyd eurgryd*; though in this case the allusion in the *Mabinogi* cannot be merely a gloss, but has conditioned the final shaping of the story in the form in which it has come down. *Eur* in *eurgryd* is employed in a figurative poetic manner; it is not to be taken in its

[110] See CA l. 264 and n.

literal sense of 'golden' but rather as 'noble, exalted, excellent'.[111] The portrayal of Manawydan in the story as a shoemaker is due to the supposed derivation of his name from *manawyd* 'awl';[112] and the story requires that his excellence in the craft allotted to him should have the effect of discouraging rivals. But it does not require that he should be a *golden* shoemaker,[113] and I suggest that the allusions to the gilding of the leather and the making of golden buckles by Manawydan and Lleu in the *Mabinogi* were introduced at a penultimate stage in the development of the tales to make them conform to a pre-existing triad (see note to triad 67). The original point of these episodes, and of the triad which commemorated them, was to show that Manawydan and Lleu, like Caswallawn, were obliged by circumstances to adopt the mechanical craft of shoe-making, which was entirely inconsistent with their birth and rank in life. The workmanship in gilt has come into the *Mabinogi* because the story-teller did not understand the variant meanings of *eur-* in the bardic vocabulary.

Here then, a pre-existing triad has shaped the final form of two episodes in the story. In how many other instances in the *Four Branches* may this not have been the case? There are two allusions in *Branwen* which elsewhere form the material of triads, though the triads are not cited in *Branwen* itself. One is the reference to Caradawg fab Brân as a *cynweissyat* or 'chief officer' left to guard Britain during the absence of Bendigeidfran in Ireland (PKM 39.1; see note to triad 13); the other is the apparent allusion to *Cantref y Gwaelod*, the submerged territory in Cardigan Bay, which is introduced at the point in the story at which Brân is described as crossing to Ireland, *a guedy hynny yd amlawys y weilgi, pan oreskynwys y weilgi y tyrnassoed* (PKM 39.8–14) 'and afterwards the ocean spread out, (at the time) when the ocean conquered the kingdoms'. The repetition of *gweilgi* suggests that the latter phrase has been introduced as a gloss on the text. Thomas Jones showed[114] that the allusion here is evidently to stories about the lost lands which have not come down, though in fact they were commemorated in a triad which, turned into Latin, has by chance been preserved in the thirteenth-century Exeter *Chronica de Wallia*:

[111] GPC 1256: 'coeth, gwych, rhagorol' etc. Numerous compounds in *eur-* are quoted in G 496–9. These are particularly popular with Cynddelw, so that with him *eur-* comes to have little more meaning than that of an intensive prefix, as is pointed out by Vendryes, *La Poésie Galloise des XII–XIIIe Siècles dans ses Rapports avec la Langue* (Zaharoff lecture, Oxford, 1930), p. 15. Cf. also triad 61, *Tri Eur Gelein*.

[112] See Ifor Williams, B III, p. 49.

[113] W. J. Gruffydd (*Rhiannon*, p. 85) notes the inadequacy of the incidents narrated in the *Mabinogi* as explanations for the epithet *eurgryd* in the triad.

[114] 'Triawd Lladin ar y Gorlifiadau', B XII, pp. 79–83. For the submerged kingdoms see F. J. North, *Sunken Cities* (Cardiff, 1957) and note to *G6ydno Garanhir*. For *Teithi Hen mab Gwynhan* see CO ll. 245–50, and note.

> These are the kingdoms which the sea destroyed: The kingdom of Teithi Hen, son of Gwynnan, king of Kaerrihog. That kingdom was called at the time 'Ynys Teithi Hen'; it was between St David's and Ireland. No one escaped from it, neither men nor animals, except Teithi Hen alone with his horse; afterwards for all the days of his life he was weak from fear.
>
> The second kingdom was that of Helig son of Glannog, it was between Ceredigion and Bardsey, and as far as St David's. That land was very good, fertile and level, and it was called Maes Maichgen; it lay from the mouth (of the Ystwyth?) to Llŷn, and upwards to Aberdovey.
>
> The sea destroyed a third kingdom: the kingdom of Rhedfoe son of Rheged.[115] (My translation)

These stories, if not the triad itself, must have been in the mind of the scribe who first introduced the allusion to the 'kingdoms conquered by the sea' into the text of *Branwen*. Here then is another triad which has failed to be recorded in any extant text of TYP, though the traditions about the submerged kingdoms had a sufficiently close relevance to the tale of *Branwen*—as part of the broader narrative background to which the tale is related—for a reference to them to slip easily into the text.

The frequency with which triadic groupings are employed in *Culhwch ac Olwen* does not in itself prove a close relation with TYP, and on examination it appears that this relation is much less close than is the relation between TYP and the *Four Branches*. There are instances among the list of characters at Arthur's court in which the names are given in triple groups,[116] but this grouping is based merely upon a phonetic similarity in the names, and in no instance does one of these groups include names which occur in TYP. These groups tend to be epithetical in character, and it is likely that they have been invented for the occasion, and have had no independent existence in narrative outside the list. These triadic groupings are merely one among several points of resemblance with Irish narrative technique which are prominent in the tale of *Culhwch*; though it is unlikely that they can be directly attributed to Irish influence: Cecile O'Rahilly drew attention to the frequent occurrence of similar triple groups of epithetical names in the Old Irish saga *Togail Bruidne Da*

[115] For the Latin text see Thomas Jones, loc. cit. The story behind the last item is unknown.

[116] Examples: *Bwlch a Chyuwlch a Seuwlch* (CO l. 332), *Henwas a Hen Vyneb a Hengedymdeith* 'Old Lad and Old Face and Old Companion' (CO l. 274), *Duach a Brathach a Nerthach* (CO l. 188), *Gwyn mab Esni a Gvynn mab Nwywre a Gwynn mab Nud* (CO l. 181).

Derga.[117] One triad occurs in this list, however, which cannot be so easily dismissed. This is the 'Three Men who escaped from the Battle of Camlan'.[118] There are a number of allusions to Camlan in TYP, but this triad does not appear among them; although an adaptation of it is found in *Pedwar Marchog ar Hugain* (App. IV, no. 7), where it is evidently a borrowing from *Culhwch*. It seems most likely that this triad is to be regarded as a burlesque invention by the narrator of the story, a parody of TYP whose spirit is entirely in keeping with the jocular treatment given throughout to the list of the company at Arthur's court. It should however be set against the fragments of tradition which have survived with regard to the battle of Camlan (see note to *Camlan*, triad 59); presumably the parody would not have taken this particular form if it were not for the existence of a large body of narrative concerning the battle of Camlan of which we are now ignorant, though it is referred to both in the triads and by the poets. Thus there may really have been a tradition that a saint was among the survivors, who was identified variously as *Cynwyl*, *Pedrog*, *Derfel*, etc. The allusion in the triad to St Cynwyl's escape from the battle on his horse *Hengroen* ('Old Skin') may perhaps contain a satirical allusion to triad 44b, which names certain famous horses as being present at the battle of Arfderydd.[119]

The other triad which is quoted in *Culhwch* is a version of triad 52, *Tri Goruchel Garcharawr* 'Three Exalted Prisoners' (CO ll. 913–16). I have suggested in my note to triad 52 that the narrator of the story was aware that Mabon's imprisonment formed one in a triad of famous imprisonments; but he seems not to have known of what the poem *Preiddeu Annwn* (BT 54.16–56) suggests was an equally famous story, that of the imprisonment of *Gweir*, and this indicates that he may have had, at best, only an imperfect recollection of the triad.[120] In a similar manner the allusion among the list of *anoetheu* to the *deu ychen Gwlwlyd Wineu* (CO l. 589) seems to constitute a confused reminiscence of the oxen named in triad 45 (see note). It may be concluded, therefore, that the final narrator of *Culhwch* had no very intimate knowledge of TYP, in spite of an extensive familiarity with the general narrative background which was common to

[117] *Ireland and Wales, Their Historical and Literary Relations* (London, 1924), pp. 116–17; E. Knott (ed.), *Togail Bruidne Da Derga* (DIAS, VIII), ll. 693–4, 1154–5, 1386, etc. (See CO(2) xl–xliii.)

[118] CO ll. 226–32; trans. *Mab.* 102.

[119] For another instance in the text (CO ll. 394–6) of a triadic grouping which seems more likely to be spontaneous than a genuine citation of a pre-existing triad on the part of the narrator, see note under Personal Names to *Drych eil Kibdar*.

[120] See the discussion of the two versions of Mabon's imprisonment in CO(2) lx–lxii; and for *Preiddeu Annwn* see edn. and discussion by M. Haycock, SC XVIII/XIX, pp. 52–78 (at p. 65).

the triads and the *chwedlau*. The fact that a burlesque triad is introduced into the story offers further evidence, if such were needed, for the conclusion that *Culhwch ac Olwen* originated in a milieu different (probably one more ecclesiastically orientated) from that in which the triads were evolved.

Lludd a Llefelys is itself an expanded triad. It is a version of triad 36, *Teir Gormes a doeth y'r Enys hon*; and it is thus linked with the pseudo-history of the Invasions of Britain (see p. lvii above). But as in the case of the *Culhwch* version of *Tri Goruchel Garcharawr*, the form of the triad given in the story is an imperfect rendering of the *Teir Gormes*, due either to the narrator's ignorance, or to deliberate alteration of the original triad. The first *gormes*, the *Corranyeit*, is the same in the triad and in the story. But in *Lludd a Llefelys* the folk-tale figure of the giant who consumes the king's food has been substituted for the *Gwyddyl Ffichti*, the foreign race which constitutes the second *gormes* in the triad. The third *gormes* consists of the dragons which Lludd incarcerated at *Dinas Emrys*; and these are an evident substitution for the *gormes* of the Saxons in the triad.[121] But the dragons hidden at *Dinas Emrys* are specifically named in triad 37 as constituting one of the *Tri Chud a Thri Datcud*, and it is evident that this triad also is related to the oral tradition underlying *Lludd a Llefelys*, if not to the tale in its extant form. Triad 37 presents special problems: its basic idea is the very primitive one of human talismanic burial, but as it stands it is as a whole more closely allied to material which has come down in a literary form than is the case with any other of the triads in the Early Version—though at the same time it presents certain discrepancies with these literary sources.[122] Since the Early Version merely names the *Tri Datcud*, but does not specify them further, we do not know whether the account given in R corresponds with the *tri datcud* as they were given in the oldest form of the triad, or whether they have been altered in this late version to conform with the material of the *Brut*. I have suggested (see note to triad 37) that the popularity of the tale of *Lludd a Llefelys* has led to the substitution of Lludd's dragons for an older talisman which originally constituted the third *cudd*.

[121] The explanation which links the two is given in *Lludd a Llefelys* in a somewhat perfunctory manner: *Yr eil ormes . . . dreic yv honno. a dreic estravn genedyl arall yssyd yn ymlad a hi, ac yn keissav y goresgynn. Ac vrth bynny . . . y dyt ych dreic chvi diaspat engiryavl* (RM 23–7) 'The second Oppression . . . that is a dragon, and a dragon of another foreign nation is fighting with it, and trying to conquer it. And therefore . . . your dragon raises a terrible scream'. The passage suggests that the symbolical meaning of the warring dragons, inherited from HB, was merely an embarrassment to the story-teller.

[122] The reference to the burial of the bones of Gwerthefyr shows a certain correspondence with late bardic allusions to his burial at Dover; but does not agree with HB's statement that Vortimer's instructions about his burial were disobeyed (see note to triad 37b and to *G6ertheuyr 6endigeit*).

The tale of *Lludd a Llefelys*[123] is found in certain manuscripts of the *Brut*[124] in a form which shows only very slight verbal differences from the *Mabinogion* version. It is obvious that the story as it has come down has been adapted to fit in with the structure of the *Historia Regum*, and it betrays the influence of Geoffrey's work in certain obvious but superficial ways. The question which arises in connection with triad 37 is, whether the reference which it contains to Lludd's dragons is to be attributed to the influence of the literary redaction of *Lludd a Llefelys*, influenced as it is by the *Historia Regum*, or whether it relates to an earlier oral version of the tale. In my note to the triad I have argued that the appearance in it of the word *dreigeu* (for L. *dracones*) rather than *pryfet* (the equivalent of HB's *vermes*) to denote the monsters buried by Lludd in Dinas Emrys does not necessarily prove the influence of Geoffrey's Latin, since the literal meaning of the word 'fire-breathing (reptilian) monsters' must have been implicit in HB's reference to the *duo dracones*. The reference in the triad could therefore be to an oral version of the tale anterior to Geoffrey's work. The point is one of considerable importance in relation to the provenance of the Early Version of TYP. I have already (pp. lxv–lxvi) stated my belief that the Early Version represents the range of bardic allusion to the native *ystoryaeu* before the traditions incorporated in the triads were subjected to the influence of the *Historia Regum*. This is the only instance in the text of the Early Version of TYP, which might be said to betray the influence of Geoffrey's work, since this 'literal' use of the word *dreic*, *dreigeu*, is unparalleled in the early poetry or in that of the *Gogynfeirdd*. (See G 389 for a list of the many instances in which *dreic*, *dreigeu* are used figuratively for warriors.) Yet we know from Llywelyn Fardd II's reference to *ymarwar llut a lleuelys* (H 208.3–4 = CBT VI, no. 7.4) that the story was known in some form to twelfth-century poets, and references in the earlier poetry take it back at least a century before this time (see note to *Llud mab Beli*).

In summarizing the narrative repertoire available to twelfth-century poets (pp. lv–lvi) I have included the story of Maxen Wledig.[125] Cynddelw refers once to *moes maxen* (H 135.6 = CBT III, no. 16.88); and this evidence for the antiquity of the story is supported by the occurrence of the names of both *Maxim Guletic* and *Helen Luitdauc* [*sic*] in the Harleian genealogy of the kingdom of Dyfed (see notes to *Elen Luyda6c*, *Maxen*

[123] Ed. with introduction and notes by B. F. Roberts, *Cyfranc Lludd a Llefelys* (DIAS, 1975).

[124] See J. Rhŷs and J. G. Evans, *The Text of the Bruts from the Red Book of Hergest* (Oxford, 1890), pp. xii ff.; G. J. Visser (ed.), EC I, pp. 261–74. See note to *Llud m. Beli*.

[125] On Maximus (Maxen Wledig) 'the founding figure of independent post-Roman Britain' and a figure of high significance in Gildas's account, in which his legend is already beginning to emerge, see D. N. Dumville, *History* 62, pp. 180–1.

Wledic). It is evident that this tale, like that of *Lludd a Llefelys*, is the final culmination in literary form of traditional material which is very much older than the twelfth century. *Breudwyt Maxen* in no way betrays the influence of Geoffrey's work, although in the *Historia Regum* Geoffrey has given a variant version of the tale of the emperor Maximus and his British bride, adapted from current oral tradition.[126] The allusion to the story in triad 35a is closer to *Breudwyt Maxen* than to Geoffrey's account (see note to *Maxen Wledic*), although it does not agree perfectly with either, and may be taken as evidence for the existence of parallel oral versions of the tale.

The story of the emperor Maximus[127] and his British bride as narrated by Geoffrey of Monmouth is but one of the many episodes in the *Historia Regum* which cannot be attributed entirely to Geoffrey's own fantasy, or even to the influence of his reading of classical or foreign literature. It must be derived ultimately from contact with *cyfarwydd* tradition current in Wales or Brittany—and there is evidence which suggests[128] that in the eleventh and twelfth centuries the narrative tradition was at least to some extent shared in common by both countries. Either directly or through the intermediary of his friend the archdeacon Walter, Geoffrey certainly had some access to the underlying narrative material common to the *chwedlau* and to TYP; as well as to the early genealogies and perhaps other written sources. He seems to have had a knowledge of the content of *Enweu Ynys Prydein* (App. I), either in a written or in an oral form, since his British geography presents an interesting resemblance to that which is found in this document.[129] Geoffrey was well aware of the value of the triad form as a rhetorical device, and he makes some use of it both in the *Prophecies of Merlin* (HRB book VII) and

[126] Elsewhere (SEBH, pp. 107–9), I have compared *Breudwyt Maxen* with Geoffrey's version of the story, and suggested that in certain respects Geoffrey's version represents an older tradition. See also B. F. Roberts, 'Geoffrey of Monmouth and Welsh Historical Tradition', *Studies* ch. 2.

[127] HRB V, chs. 9–16. Geoffrey follows HB ch. 27 in calling the emperor *Maximianus* and not *Maximus*, but there can be no doubt of the identity of this figure with the *Maxen Wledic* of the Welsh tale and of the *Brut* (BD 72 ff.).

[128] Some direct evidence to this effect is provided by Hermann de Tournai's account of the visit of the monks of Laon to Bodmin in 1113 (quoted by E. K. Chambers, *Arthur of Britain*, pp. 18, 249), which implies the existence of traditions about Arthur in Cornwall and Brittany at the time. Any assessment of the indirect evidence of course involves the whole question of the channels of transmission of the Matter of Britain into Continental literature. See my 'First Transmission to England and France', AW 273–98; and L. Fleuriot, J. Balcou et Yves le Gallo (eds), *Histoire Litteraire et Culturelle de la Bretagne* (HLCB), I (Paris–Geneva, 1987).

[129] See pp. c–civ below and notes to App. I.

elsewhere, for the purpose of embodying a prophecy.[130] But it seems certain that he had no direct knowledge of *Trioedd Ynys Prydein*, or he would have made a more obvious and extensive use of triads in the course of his narrative, and would have drawn upon TYP as an inventory of proper names in the same way as he did upon the early Welsh genealogies which have come down in Harl. 3859 (see, in particular, S. Piggott, *Antiquity* XV, pp. 269–76; and P. C. Bartrum, B XXIII, pp. 1–5). This apparent ignorance in itself points to the fact that in Geoffrey's day *Trioedd Ynys Prydein* was cherished as a part of the safeguarded bardic learning, which would not have been accessible to the uninitiated. But there are at least two striking instances in the course of Geoffrey's narrative in which his statements do correspond with references in certain triads; and the statements in these triads can hardly be accounted for as dependent upon Geoffrey's work. Both statements refer to what we may call the *Cadwallawn* saga: the story of the dealings between the seventh-century king Cadwallawn of Gwynedd and his English contemporary and rival, Edwin of Northumbria. Bede tells us that Edwin (see note) grew up in exile away from his own country, and this is amplified in Geoffrey's account, since he tells us that Edwin was reared in Gwynedd as a foster-brother to Cadwallawn. In triad 26 W we are told that Edwin was one of the *Teir Prif Ormes Môn a vagwyt yndi* 'one of the Three Great Oppressions of Môn, nurtured within her'. The reference is clearly to the home of the North-Welsh kings at Aberffraw in Anglesey, where Edwin may have spent some time under the protection of Cadwallawn's father king Cadfan. Again, Geoffrey is our only explicit authority for the statement that when Cadwallawn was in his turn exiled by Edwin, he crossed over the sea to Ireland. According to triad 29, one of the *Tri Diweir Deulu*, or Three Faithful War-Bands, was that of Cadwallawn son of Cadfan, 'who were with him for seven years in Ireland'. References in the early poetry corroborate the evidence for a tradition about Cadwallawn's exile in Ireland (see note to *Catwalla6n m. Catuan*).

TRIOEDD Y MEIRCH (triads 38–46c; see pp. 103–28 below)

The 'Triads of the Horses'[131] constitute a distinct group within *Trioedd Ynys Prydein*, and are presented as such in all the manuscripts. The Early

[130] The allusion to Arthur as the third British king fated to conquer Rome (HRB IX, ch. 17) is clearly Geoffrey's own invention (see note to *Custennin vab Elen*, triad 51, ll. 25–6, and B. F. Roberts, *Studies*, ch. 2, pp. 33–4). Needless to say, such a prophecy can have had no basis in the Welsh prophetic verse of which Geoffrey appears to have had some knowledge, as appears from internal evidence in his *Prophecies of Merlin*, HRB Book VII.

[131] See R. Bromwich, 'The Triads of the Horses' in Nerys Ann Jones and Sioned Davies (eds), *The Horse in Celtic Culture* (Cardiff, 1997).

Version of TYP gives these triads at the close of the series (nos. 38–46) without any separate heading; but a recognition that they represent an independent group is found in the title *Trioed y Meirch yv y rei hynn* which is given to section 5 of TYP in WR.[132]. In Pen. 47 *Trioedd y Meirch* are similarly differentiated from *Trioedd y Milwyr* and *Trioedd y Gwragedd*,[133] and this manuscript contains two additional triads (46A and B) which do not appear in the other texts. In the Early Version and certain of the later manuscripts which are based upon it, the seven *Trioedd y Meirch* are accompanied by two others, *Tri Phryf Ychen* and *Teir Pryf Uuch* (nos. 45 and 46). In Pen. 27 the seven triads are presented as a unit, unaccompanied by any others of the *Trioedd Ynys Prydein*. A fragment consisting of four *Trioedd y Meirch* is found in the *Black Book of Carmarthen* (pages 14 r.–14 v., 27–8 in the facsimile edition = LlDC no. 6). As most recently dated by E. D. Jones (LlDC xxiv) and Daniel Huws (*Nat. Lib. of Wales Journal* XXVIII, p. 19), the Black Book belongs approximately to the same period as Pen. 16—the middle or latter half of the thirteenth century.

Trioedd y Meirch lists the names of horses belonging to the traditional heroes; and the greater number of the names of the horses' owners figure elsewhere in TYP. The horses' names are all of a descriptive nature—*Myngrwn* 'Thick Mane', *Tavawt Hir* 'Long Tongue', *Arvwl Velyn* 'Huge Yellow', etc. They have fabulous characteristics: they are horned (see triad 44b and note), and cloven-hoofed (triad 40a); they swim, and carry superhuman burdens (triad 44); and while it is obvious that for the most part the names are those of battle chargers, yet names of draft-horses (triad 43) and racers (triad 46B) are also included.

A comparison of the variant manuscript readings indicates that a considerable degree of confusion has taken place in the transmission of these triads. Both the forms of the horses' names and the names of their owners are liable to differ in the various versions of each triad. This in itself may be taken as evidence for the antiquity of *Trioedd y Meirch*; since it suggests that the confusion goes far back into the oral stage of transmission, and that the extant texts may be based on variant oral versions. Further evidence supporting a belief in the antiquity of *Trioedd y Meirch* is to be had from a poem in the *Book of Taliesin* (BT 47–8), entitled by the editor *Canu y Meirch*. This opens with a reference to the 'breaking-in' of a young horse, followed by a brief description. There is an allusion to the sparks of fire cast up by the horse's hooves, which is

[132] See p. xxi above for the contents of this section. In WR certain additional triads have been brought together under this title, while no. 44, the longest and perhaps the most interesting of the *Trioedd y Meirch*, has been misplaced and is given in an earlier section of the text.

[133] See p. xxv above.

anticipatory of some of the *cywyddau i ofyn march* of the later period. The poem has unfortunately come down in a very confused and fragmentary condition.[134] Owing to the importance of its concluding section in relation to *Trioedd y Meirch*, I give below the text of BT 48.3–18 (in which I have supplied punctuation and capitals) and a tentative translation:[135]

Tri Thri nodet atcor ar henet:
A march Mayavc, a march Genethavc,
A march Karadavc, kymrvy teithiavc.
A march Gvythur, a march Gva(w)rdur,
A march Arthur, ehofyn rodi cur;
A march Taliessin, a march Lleu lletuegin,
A Phebyrllei llvynin, a Grei march Cunin;
Kornan kyneiwavc (= kynelwawc?), Awyd awydavc,
Du Moroed enwavc, march Brvyn bro(n) bradavc;
A'r tri carn aflav(*c*), nyt ant hynt hilav:
Kethin march Keidav, carn avarn arnav,
(*Y*)scvydurith yscodic, gorvyd Llemenic,
March Ryderch rydic, Llvyt lliv elleic;
A Llamrei llavn (= llamm?) elwic, a Ffroenuoll gvirenhic,
(A) march Sadyrnin, a march Custenhin,
Ac ereill yn trin rac tir allgvin(in);
Henwyn mat dyduc kychwedyl o Hiraduc . . .

'(To) the famous Threes (= triads ?), a return to ancient times(?). Mayawg's horse, Genethawg's horse, Caradawg's horse—a strong thoroughbred(?)—Gwythur's horse, Gwa(w)rddur's horse; Arthur's horse, fearless to give battle, Taliesin's horse, and the horse of Lleu Lledfegin ('half-reared Lleu' or 'the horse of Lleu, half-reared' (cf. triad 38), (and) *Pybyrllei* ('Strong Chestnut') the dejected (?), and *Grei* ('Grey') the horse of Cunin (cf. triad 42 WR). *Cornan* ('horned') the reliable(?) (triad 44b), *Awydd Awyddawg* ('Impetuous Vigour'), famous *Du Moroedd* ('Black of the Seas'), the horse of Brwyn Bro(n) Bradawg ('B. Wily Breast', cf. triads 43, 44a). And the three Cloven-Hoofed ones (cf. triad 40a)—they do not go on a journey to procreate: *Kethin* ('Roan') the horse of Ceid(y)aw (triad 44b), a hard (?)hoof on him, *Ysgwydfrith Ysgodig* ('Shying Dappled Shoulder'), the horse of Llemenig (or 'a leaping horse'), the horse of Rhydderch

[134] See PT xxiii–xxiv. The metre is similar to that of the *Trawsganu Cynan Garwyn* and of several of the oldest poems in BT. It consists of short rhyming lines or half-lines, of which each normally contains five syllables, but exceptionally four or six.

[135] My rendering owes much to suggestions originally made to me by Sir Ifor Williams and by Professor Thomas Jones, as well as to some more recent suggestions made by Marged Haycock in her study of the poem in her thesis, 'Llyfr Taliesin: Astudiaethau ar rai Agweddau' (University of Wales, Aberystwyth, 1983), which she has kindly permitted me to consult.

the Giver (? or 'very wrathful'?). *Llwyd lliw elleic*, ('Grey Tawny-Colour' triad 43c and n.), and *Llamrei llawn* (= *llam elwic* 'Swift-paced', or 'of surpassing leap' (?), and *Ffroenfoll Gwyrennig* ('Lively Full-Nostril') Sadyrnin's horse, and Custennin's horse, and others in battle before a dispirited(?) or 'a foreign'(?) land. *Henwyn* ('Old White') who well brought tidings from Hiraddug . . .'

Notes on the Horses' Names in Canu'r Meirch

l. 4. *Gvardur* should probably be emended to *Gwawrdur*, cf. CA l. 359, and ibid. *Gwaurdur* l. 1242, where the feats of this hero are compared to those of Arthur. In *Canu'r Meirch* Arthur's horse (*Llamrei* 'Swift-Paced'(?) see l. 14) is commemorated in the line following the reference to *Gwa(w)rdur*. For Llamrei see CO ll. 1016–17n., 1225n.

l. 6. With *lletuegin* applied to a young warrior cf. CA l. 329 and n., also GPC 2131. (The gift of a horse from Arianrhod may perhaps be implied in the *Mabinogi* story as having accompanied Lleu's other gifts from his mother. In triad 38 below Lleu's horse is named *Melyngan Mangre*.)

l. 7. *Pebyrllei llvynin*. On *pefyr*, *pybyr* 'strong, robust' or else 'bright, shining' see n. on *Goronwy Peuyr*, PKM 286, and on *llei* 'grey, brown, dun', (perhaps 'chestnut'?) see Ifor Williams, B XIII, pp. 196–7.

l. 8. It is not clear whether *Awyd Awydawc* 'of impetuous vigour' is a proper name, or an additional epithet referring to the horse *Cornan*. Most probably it is a variant of the horse's name in triad 38a, which names *Awydawc vreichir* 'Eager Long Foreleg(s)' as the horse of Kyhoret eil Kynan, in place of *Meinlas* or *Melynlas* in the other versions in Pen. 47's variant of triad 38a.

l. 9. *Brvyn Bro(n) Bradavc*. A mark above the *o* of *bro* indicates that this should be extended to *bron*. But if *brwyn* was originally written in the older form *Broen*, this second *bro* could have arisen as the result of careless repetition on the part of a copyist. Ifor Williams points out that *bradawg* in this instance can hardly mean 'treacherous'; cf. the personal name *Bradwen* (*Bratwen* CA l. 468, etc), in which *brad* obviously does not have a pejorative sense, but rather 'full of wiles and stratagems'. Hence 'Wily Breast'.

l. 10. With *hilav* cf. GPC 1867 on *hiliaf*, *hilio*.

l. 10. *Carn aflaw* is attested by the rhyme, as against *carn aflavc*. Cf. *Cethin Carnavlaw* in triad 42c below, and RBP col. 1329.9–10, *vn redyat karn aflaw* (GPC 429).

l. 12. The metre favours the omission of prosthetic *y*, giving the older form *scwydvrith*, and perhaps also *scodic*. With the latter cf. Davies (1632): *Ysgodigaw*; *consternari*, *De equis conterritis dicitur*; ie. 'to be frightened, to shy'. Davies gives the derivation from *ysgod* 'shadow'. For further instances see CA l. 388.

l. 13. Ifor Williams suggested that *rydic* is a mistake for *rodic*, an apt adjective for Rhydderch (Hael), rather than for his horse, whose name follows in the second half-line. Or *ry* + *dic* 'ferocious', if the epithet refers to the horse.

l. 14. *Llamrei* 'Swift Paced' (GPC 2094), or *llam* + *grei* 'Grey Leap(er)'? *Llawn elwic* (=?*llam elwic*, 'of surpassing leap' (G 471, GPC 1208). *Llamrei* is named as Arthur's mare in CO ll. 1016–17 (see n.) and l. 1225.

l. 16. With *allgvin(in)* cf. *allwyn* 'sorrow', *allwynig* 'sorrowful' (GPC 79). M. Haycock (see n. 135 above) suggests *allmyn* 'foreign' as giving better sense and rhyme with the following *henwyn* than *allwynin* (the interpretation favoured in GPC 79 for the word in this instance).

l. 17. Nothing is known of a horse named *Henwyn* or of his story. *Moel Hiraddug* is in Flintshire.

A triadic arrangement is discernible throughout the passage, though this has been obscured in some places, probably owing to the loss of certain lines from the text. This appears to contain several lacunae, and it is defective at the end. It will be seen that the first lines give the names of the horses' owners alone, and that in some instances (*Karadawg*, *Lleu*) these are names of figures to whom horses are appropriated in *Trioedd y Meirch*. Next come a group of names which present certain correspondences with *Trioedd y Meirch*, both in the names of the horses and in those of their owners. There is a complete triad of cloven-hoofed horses, and each of the three horses' names given in it occurs along with that of its respective owner in different triads in *Trioedd y Meirch*. Obviously there exists a close connection between the poem and the extant versions of *Trioedd y Meirch*; the triads in the Black Book and in Pen. 16 are in fact in manuscripts which antedate the fourteenth-century *Book of Taliesin*, so that corruptions may have occurred in either oral or written transmission: the variation between *Grei march Cunin* in the poem (l. 7) and *Grei march Edwin* in triad 42 (WR), and the equivalence between the name of Rhydderch's horse *Llvyt lliv elleic* in the poem and *Rudlwyt* in triad 43 (where the forms are partly identical, and partly parallel in meaning, see note) are less likely to be due to corruptions which took place in the process of written than of oral transmission. There is also the vexed question of the relation between the line *Du moroed enwavc, march Brvyn bro(n) bradavc* and the two horses known in the triads as *Du, march Brwyn mab Cynadaf* (triad 43a), and *Du Moro* or *Du y Moroed, march Elidir Mwynfawr* (triad 44a, see note). Both the names in these triads, as well as that of *Du, march Moro Oeruedavc* in *Culhwch ac Olwen* (l. 718), must in some way correspond with the name of the horse in the poem; but here again the variants are such that they can hardly be accounted for except on the supposition of corruption during the process of written transmission.

In addition to Arthur's mare *Llamrei*, there is another horse whose name is given in *Culhwch* (l. 689), and who recurs in *Trioedd y Meirch*. This is *Gwynn Mygdwn* ('White Dun-Mane'), horse of *Gweddw*, who is cited as *Myngrwn* ('Arched Mane') *march Gweddw* in triad 46A. Elsewhere *Arvwl Velyn* ('Huge Yellow'), the horse of Pascen fab Urien, is named in an *englyn* belonging to the group of poems concerned with the family of

Urien Rheged in CLlH no. VII.14a(n.) (cf. EWSP 503 (25)). But except for these few instances, no evidence for the role played by these horses in early Welsh narrative is to be derived from the extant *chwedlau*. This gives all the greater interest to the fact that the names of two of the horses in *Trioedd y Meirch*, in company with those of the owners to whom they are assigned in the triads, have found their way into certain Old French Arthurian poems. These are *Lluagor march Karadawc Vreichvras* (triad 38c), and *Kein Caled* ('Hard-Backed') *march Gwalchmei*, who is named in a triad in the *Black Book of Carmarthen*, which reads as follows:[136]

> Tri gohoev etystir inis pridein. Guynev godvff hir. march kei. Ruthir ehon tuth bleit. m. Gilberd mab kadgyffro. A kein caled m. gualchmei.

Lluagor reappears in the first continuation of Chrétien's *Conte del Graal* as *Lorzagor*, the horse of *Carados Briebras*; and the French poem has an elaborate but highly primitive tale to tell of the horse's being born at one birth with the hero who afterwards owned him: a tale which fits appropriately enough with the epithet *rhoddedig varch* which is bestowed on *Lluagor* in triad 38 (see note). *Kein Caled* is to be identified with the famous horse of *Gauvain* (Gwalchmai) known as (*le*) *G*(*u*)*ingalet* or (*le*) *Gringolet*,[137] who figures in Chrétien's poems, as well as in other English and Continental sources. The names of the owners of these two horses, *Gwalchmai* and *Caradawc Vreichvras* (Briebras) remain equally stable throughout all Welsh and Continental references to them.

It is unlikely, for reasons which have previously been sufficiently indicated, that the names of these horses can have made their way into the French Arthurian poems from the triads themselves. It is more probable that they were drawn into Arthurian romance from the mass of narrative material known to *cyfarwyddiaid* in Wales, and probably also in Brittany, which must be postulated as constituting the ultimate Celtic source of the Matter of Britain. The evidence already cited from *Culhwch* proves that the names of some at least of the horses listed in *Trioedd y Meirch* were known in the *cyfarwydd* milieu; though we may well be surprised that there are hardly any allusions to these horses in the extant *chwedlau*. The absence of any reference at all to *Kein Caled* in Welsh narrative outside the

[136] BBC 28.6–10 (= LlDC no. 6). The triad is a composite version of triads 39, 42; see note to triad 42c. The only other text of *Trioedd y Meirch* to name Gwalchmai's horse is Pen. 47, which includes *Meingalet* [sic] *march Gwalchmai* in triad 46a. For the connection between this version of *Trioedd y Meirch* and that found in BBC, see p. xxv above.

[137] For the use of the definite article here cf. *y Kethin Kyflym*, triad 44b. Full references to the Continental sources which mention (*le*) *Guingalet* are given by R. S. Loomis, *Arthurian Tradition and Chrétien de Troyes*, pp. 156–9. For *Gilbert m. Catgyffro*, see n. under Personal Names below.

single triad in which this horse is named has indeed been responsible for the argument put forward by the late R. S. Loomis[138] to the effect that the name of Gwalchmai's horse can only be accounted for as a borrowing from the French *Guingalet*; though the same writer does not dispute that *Guingalet* ('White Hard') is itself a Welsh name. Two main arguments have been brought forward to support this contention: (i) the fact that the name of Gwalchmai's horse is absent from the tale of *Gereint vab Erbin*, where at a corresponding point[139] in *Erec et Enide*, *Guingalet* is named; (ii) the fact that the BBC triad which names Gwalchmai's horse includes also the name of *Gilberd mab kadgyffro* [*sic*], an incontestable reference to a twelfth-century Norman Marcher lord (see note), from which it is concluded that the triad itself can be no older than this date. I have shown elsewhere (pp. xci–xcii) that the names of two well-authenticated twelfth-century figures have been introduced into TYP (*Alan Fyrgan* and *Gilbert mab Katgyffro* named in triads 24 and 29), but that their appearance cannot be taken as evidence which condemns the whole body of TYP as being no older than the twelfth century. It must be admitted that it is somewhat surprising that the Welsh redactor of *Gereint* should not have recognized in *Le Guingalet* the name of Gwalchmai's horse, if indeed this name stood in the common source of the Welsh and French versions of the tale. But against this one must consider the total absence of these horses' names in the *chwedlau*; an absence which suggests that the *cyfarwyddiaid* had little if any knowledge of the names found in *Trioedd y Meirch*. It should be noted also that all the Continental sources concur in giving the name in a slightly different form from that in which it appears in the triad, with *guin-* (the O.W. spelling of *gwyn*) or *grin-* (an obvious corruption) in the first element. The alternation between *kein-* and *guin-* is typical of the kind of variations which occur in the horses' names between the different versions of *Trioedd y Meirch*, and it is not impossible that the form *guingalet*[140] encountered in a French source would have been sufficient in itself to confuse the Welsh redactor of the tale, if he had heard this name only as *Kein Caled*. But it seems more probable that he was ignorant of the name of Gwalchmai's horse in either form. It was not the *cyfarwyddiaid* but the bards, who were the primary custodians of the traditional lore

[138] R. S. Loomis, *Arthurian Tradition*, p. 158 (see note 137 above).

[139] Cf. RM 285.1–2: *Gwalchmei . . . a esgynnavd ar y uarch*; and *Erec et Enide* (ed. Wendelus Foerster), l. 4087: *Gauvains monte an son guingalet*.

[140] *Guingalet* 'Fair' or 'White Hard' (i.e. 'bony') may even be the older form of the name, which must certainly have been borrowed into French at an earlier date than that represented by the BBC text of *Trioedd y Meirch*. R. S. Loomis cites Wolfram's portrayal of *Gringulet* as a horse with red ears, and this suggests comparison with white red-eared animals in a number of early Celtic sources; Loomis, op. cit., p. 156.

preserved in TYP; yet a certain amount of evidence is provided by the triads themselves to show that stories in which these horses played a part entered into the narrative tradition at an early date.[141] Finally, no one would argue that the name of *Lluagor*, the horse of Caradawg Freichfras (triad 38), was borrowed from that of *Lorzagor*, who belonged to *Carados Briebras*; and the analogy is important for *Kein Caled*. To claim that either of these horses' names is a borrowing from French into Welsh is to reject all the evidence for the antiquity of a body of tradition in which the names of both the horses and their owners formed an integral part. The suggestion that the *Gogynfeirdd* were more fully acquainted with the names and traditions about these horses than were the redactors of the *chwedlau* is corroborated by the number of similar epithets for horses which occur in their poetry;[142] particularly in the *Rhieingerddi*, where horses figure in occasional instances as *llateion* or love-messengers between the poet and the lady whom he is addressing. The names of a number of the horses[143] in *Trioedd y Meirch* are listed together in a *Rhieingerdd* by Gruffudd ap Maredudd.[144]

ANTIQUITY AND PROVENANCE

It has been pointed out (pp. lxxxii–lxxxiv above) that a number of correspondences exist between *Trioedd y Meirch* and the poem *Canu y Meirch* in the *Book of Taliesin* (BT 48); and that these can best be accounted for by concluding that the horses' names as they appear in the poem represent an early link in the chain of continuous transmission, whether oral or written, of the triads. There is some slight but significant additional evidence for an intimate link between individual triads and certain passages in the *hengerdd*. Thus triad 18, *Tri Chatuarcha6c*, finds a curious echo in the lines in the *Gododdin*: *tri* (*si*) *chatvarchawc . . . tri llu llurugawc* (CA ll. 182–4), since one of the Three Battle Horsemen is named *Llud Lluryga6c* in the White Book text of triad 18. The combination of these epithets cannot be fortuitous; although it is not impossible that the

[141] Cf. triads 55a, 59a, as well as triad 44.

[142] The appropriate examples are quoted in the notes to *Trioedd y Meirch*. See also T. Gwynn Jones, *Rhieingerddi'r Gogynfeirdd* (Denbigh, 1915), pp. 17–26 and Nerys Ann Jones, ch. 5 in N. A. Jones and Sioned Davies (eds), *The Horse in Celtic Culture*.

[143] For a study of the horse in pagan Celtic mythology see Anne Ross, *Pagan Celtic Britain*, pp. 321–33.

[144] RBP col. 1329. Another horse famous in tradition is mentioned on several occasions by the *cywyddwyr*. This is *y Myngwyn o Iâl* or *y Melyn o Iâl* 'the White-Maned' or the 'Yellow of Iâl' (GO no. IX.38, see note; GTA no. CVII.64; GGl no. XXI.47). But there is no mention of this horse in any extant version of *Trioedd y Meirch*.

relation between this triad and the *Gododdin* text consists in no more than in the fact that the lines quoted were responsible for instigating a poet who was familiar both with *Trioedd Ynys Prydein* and with the older poetry, to substitute *Llud Lluryga6c* for the name *Llyr Lluyda6c* which appears in this triad in the Early Version. An echo of the same kind is provided by the epithet *Tri Engiriawl* in triad 76, since in the *Gododdin* (CA ll. 1252–7) a warrior (otherwise unknown) named *Cipno mab Guengat* is described as *tridid engiriaul* 'one of the three Violent/Impetuous (?) Ones'—and once again the question arises as to whether there existed an early triad with this key epithet, or whether the reference to the *Tri Engiriawl* in the Pen. 47 version of TYP has merely been inspired by the line in the poem (see note to triad 76). There is however one instance in which an early poem in the *Book of Taliesin* preserves what is manifestly a reference to a pre-existing triad: *Pvy y tri chynweissat, a werchetwis gvlat* 'Who are the Three Chief Officers, who guarded the country?' (BT 34.24; see note to triad 13); and this allusion in *Kadeir Teyrnon* may be compared with the similar correspondences between *Trioedd y Meirch* and BT's *Canu'r Meirch*. Both suggest there is at least a possibility that the references in the *Gododdin* are to triads which were already in existence at the time when these parts of the text were first committed to writing, and that they are thus linked with the extant versions of TYP by a written or an unwritten tradition.

Certain features of *Trioedd Ynys Prydein* which indicate that the triads were originally preserved and transmitted orally have already been pointed out (see p. lviii above). These consist in the arrangement of the triads in groups and contrasting pairs, and the appearance of 'floating sections' in some of the later manuscripts which reproduce the order of certain groups of triads in the Early Version. It will be seen that the arrangement of the triads in groups and pairs is more apparent in the Early Version than in that of WR;[145] and it is inherently probable that this version preserves the triads in an older grouping, and one which in its essentials goes back to the period of oral transmission. The following triads are presented in contrasting pairs:

[145] When the triads are tabulated in the order in which they occur in WR, and compared with the arrangement in the other texts, the result is purely negative in that it does not bring to light any such 'floating sections', apart from the obvious pairs of contrasting triads which recur in all the versions. In addition triads 22 and 23 occur consecutively in a number of manuscripts, and for no very obvious reason. In chapter 11 of M. E. Owen and B. F. Roberts (eds), *Beirdd a Thywysogion* I have proposed that Pen. 16 and 45 preserve the older serial arrangement of TYP, but that WR preserves certain individual triads in a form which is at least as old. The evidence appears to show that the *Gogynfeirdd* were more familiar with the WR version than with the early version of TYP.

Tri Chud a Thri Datcud (triad 37);
Tri Diweir Deulu a Thri Anyweir Deulu (triads 29 and 30);
Teir Mat Gyflauan a Their An6at Gyflauan (triads 32 and 33);
Tri Chyuor a aeth o'r Enys hon, a Their Gormes a doeth y'r Enys hon (triads 35 and 36).

The opposition between this last pair is obscured in the WR version, which gives triad 35 in a different form, and replaces triad 36 with *Trywyr Gwarth*, the long triad based on the *Brut* (see note to triad 51). In addition to these contrasting pairs, there is apparent in the different versions of TYP a certain rudimentary grouping of the triads according to similarity of key epithet or of subject matter, though this grouping has not in every instance been preserved even in the Early Version. We can distinguish however (i) the *unben* series (triads 7–10); (ii) the *beirdd* series (triads 11, 12,[146] cf. also 87); (iii) a group of triads concerned with events which were *mat* and *anuat* (triads 32, 33, 34, 53, 59—and cf. R's version of triad 37, where the *cud a datcud* of the Early Version become *matkud ac anvat (dat)kud*); (iv) the *Tri gwrdueichyat* (triad 26) must originally have been grouped with the *Tri gwrduagla6c* (triad 16); (v) triads 27 and 28 are a pair dealing with magicians; and (vi) triads 29 and 30 dealing with *teuluoedd* are grouped in the Early Version with another triad celebrating a famous war-band, the *Teir gosgord adwy(n)*, triad 31; and in the WR version with triad 62 *Tri hualhogeon deulu*.[147] An arrangement which was originally evolved for the purpose of easily memorizing the content of TYP may have become a mere literary convention in later usage; an instance is the *Trioedd y Gwragedd* (triads 56–8, 78–80; see note to triad 56), which constitute a distinct section in Pen. 47, but one in which certain of the triads may be late additions to the group. Another feature pointing to original oral transmission of the triads is the variation which appears not infrequently in the names included under any one key epithet between the different versions of TYP. A glance at the textual variants will show that substitutions of one or more of the personal names in a given triad occur for the most part (though triad 13 is an interesting exception) in those instances where the key epithet is of the unspecific eulogistic type, and

[146] Triads 11 and 12 should probably be regarded as a contrasting pair, see note to triad 12.

[147] There is also a possibility of deliberate grouping between triad 1 *Tri Lleithiclwyth*, triad 44 *Tri Marchlwyth*, and triad 70 *Tri Gwyndorllwyth*; though it is difficult to interpret *llwyth* ('tribe, burden') as having the same meaning in the first triad as in the other two. But ambiguities in the meaning of the compound words used as key-epithets appear in some instances to be intentional in TYP.

does not imply the existence of any definite story to account for it.[148] Variations of this kind are easily accounted for by the fallibility of the human memory, though less easily by the vagaries of manuscript transmission.

At the same time it should be pointed out that the manuscript transmission of TYP can be postulated as going back to a date at least half a century earlier than that of the oldest extant text of the Early Version in Pen. 16. The textual evidence has already been discussed (pp. xvii–xix, xxvi), which indicates that the two main versions of TYP are derived from written prototypes whose orthography showed similarities to that of the *Black Book of Carmarthen*, and which may therefore be assigned to a date in the mid and later thirteenth century; while certain features of both texts suggest ultimate exemplars of an even earlier date. There is evidence also which suggests that a common *written* original may lie behind all the extant versions of certain individual triads.[149] An example is found in triad 44, where the name *Mynach* (*Naomon*) occurs in all versions: the first word in this name can best be explained as based on an original *mynach* 'monk' or was an error for *mynawc* 'courteous' (see note to *Mynach Naomon*). The standardization of the older written form *G*(*w*)*erthmul* (*Wledic*) (see note) which appears in both versions of TYP and elsewhere, may also be compared; in no instance do we find this name altered to *G*(*w*)*erthfwl*, as we should expect. The custom of leniting or failing to lenite epithets following proper names tends (with rare exceptions) to remain unaltered throughout the different manuscripts of TYP: the epithet is either lenited, according to the normal custom in Ml. Welsh, as in Cynfelyn *Drwsgyl*, Rhiwallawn *Wallt Banhadlen*, etc.; or it remains unlenited as it was in the older usage (see p. xvii–xviii above) as in Eliffer *Gosgordua6r*, G(o)ronw(y) *Peuyr*; and this suggests adherence to a spelling which became conventional in the hands of successive copyists, without reference to current spoken forms.[150]

[148] These substitutions should warn us against too unqualified an acceptance of Ifor Williams's argument (PKM xxv–xxvi) that the citation of triads in the *Four Branches* implies that the identical three names cited in such triads, as they have been transmitted to us at the present day, were in existence at the time that the citation was made. The variants which may occur between the two main versions of TYP in the proper names introduced into triads should warn us against drawing any such conclusion too hastily.

[149] In LlC VI, p. 228 Eurys Rowlands pointed out that the evidence for a common written exemplar behind the name-forms in many of the triads suggests that from the early twelfth century the primary authority for TYP lay in written texts, rather than in oral tradition, even for the purpose of bardic instruction.

[150] It is difficult to avoid the suspicion that alliteration has caused the stabilization of the radical in such names as Pabo *Post Prydein*, Mynyddawg *Mwynfawr*, Gwrtheyrn *Gwrtheneu*, Kynfawr *Catgaduc*, and in contrast has perhaps tended to stabilize the lenited form in Gwgawn *Gledyfrud*, in spite of the fact that both Pen. 45 (triad 24) and W (triad 40) read *cledyfrud*.

It remains to consider the basic internal evidence as to date and provenance which is provided by TYP. It is apparent that the first triad in the Early Version, *Teir Lleithicl6yth*, is of a character entirely different from all the others in the collection, and that it presents problems unique to itself. The place-names alluded to link it with *Enweu Ynys Prydein* (App. I), rather than with any other group of triads in TYP. But the fact that *Mynyw* is named as the seat of the third *lleithiclwyth* in place of EYP's *Aberffraw* (App. I, no. 4) at once suggests topical implications for the triad, in relation to the twelfth-century controversy as to the archi-episcopal status of St David's. We can hardly doubt that the *Teir Lleithicl6yth* is an addition made to the series by a monastic scribe, working at a date between *circa* 1120–50,[151] when this controversy was at its height. One may infer that the triad was invented at this period on the basis of such traditional material (derived from either written or oral sources) as was available to the redactor: the use of *henyf* suggests the possibility that he was acquainted with this term as it is employed in the Welsh Laws, while *Bonedd y Saint* is the most probable source for the reference to *Cyndeyrn Garthwys* (St Kentigern). It is far more natural to suppose that the original first triad in TYP was the *Tri Hael*, the most popular and widely-known of all the triads, and the one which is cited most frequently, alike by the *Gogynfeirdd* and by the *cywyddwyr*, in address to their patrons.[152] The *Teir Lleithicl6yth* leaves no doubt as to the sympathies of the scribe who committed to writing the triads of the Early Version, though not necessarily for the first time. He presented his own triad as an essential part of the canonical body of bardic tradition enshrined in *Trioedd Ynys Prydein*, and in doing so made an impassioned attempt to support his claims on behalf of St David's with the full weight of ancient authority. This topical reference to contemporary ecclesiastical politics provides evidence that the manuscript transmission of the Early Version of TYP may with some probability be taken back at least to the second quarter of the twelfth century.

This allusion to current affairs of the twelfth century leads naturally to the examination of another question, to which it bears a certain relation. This is the appearance in *Trioedd Ynys Prydein* of two recognized historical figures of the early twelfth century: Alan IV, Duke of Brittany (d. 1119), who appears as *Alan Fyrgan* or *Fergan* (explained as *ffêr* + *cant*

[151] HW 480–2, also C. Brooke, SEBC 207–8; idem, *The Church and the Welsh Border in the Central Middle Ages* (Woodbridge, 1986), pp. 20–1; R. R. Davies, *Conquest, Co-existence and Change* (Oxford, 1991), pp. 190–1. See note to triad 1 and below, p. ci.

[152] It is interesting to find that the *Tri Hael* is preserved as the first triad in DC and NLW 6434 (see table, p. xiii above), as well as in BL Addl. 15,047. See n. to triad 2.

'perfect in strength')[153] in triad 30, and Gilbert de Clare, Count of Pembroke (d. 1114)[154] who is described as *Gilbert mab Katgyffro* ('Battle-Tumult') in triads 24, 39, and LlDC no. 6. One may readily conclude that the introduction of the *teulu* of *Alan Fyrgan* into triad 30—the *Tri Anyweir Deulu* or 'Faithless War-bands'—has satirical reference to a contemporary event, and we are left to speculate as to what battle it was at which Count Alan's retainers left their lord so conspicuously in the lurch. Alan IV was the ally of William the Conqueror and later of Henry I; and he brought to the assistance of the latter a band of Breton followers at the battle of Tinchebrai, fought in 1106 against Henry's brother Robert Corthose. It is to be noted that the epithet *Fergan*(*t*) is attached to Alan IV in Breton as well as in Welsh sources, and we may probably conclude that it arose in reference to some important event in his career. He is the latest Breton ruler for whom a Breton title (or epithet) is recorded.[155] It may have been that some contemporary scandal regarding a well-known political figure has been satirically transposed into a heroic milieu; and whether or not the engagement referred to was the battle of Tinchebrai, the bitter joke consisted in conflating it with Camlan, and thus implying that the alleged defection of the Breton troops from their allies was a betrayal as great as that which had led to Arthur's downfall.

It is less easy to explain the inclusion of Gilbert de Clare in TYP along these lines, since there is nothing derogatory about the inclusion of his horse in *Trioedd y Meirch* (triad 39), even if the reference to him in triad 24 as one of the *Tri Ysgymyd Aeruaeu* 'Three Slaughter-Blocks' is more ambiguous (see note). It is as inconceivable, however, that the inclusion of a name which is said to be that of Gilbert's horse should be regarded as evidence for the original date of *Trioedd y Meirch* as it is that the presence of Alan Fyrgan's war-band among the *Tri Anyweir Deulu* should be regarded as evidence for the original date of this triad: I have already quoted evidence which indicates that a certain amount of substitution has taken place both in the names and in the narrative elements which are classified in TYP. If, as I have suggested (p. lxxi) the allusion to the *Tri Anyweir Deulu* is to be regarded as an integral part of the extant text of PKM, then the appearance in the triad, as it has come down, of the name of *Alan Fyrgan* could represent a substitution for the name of some other character—if, indeed, it is not to be taken as evidence

153 See note to *Alan Fyrgan* on this epithet.

154 There is some doubt whether the first count is intended, or his son of the same name, who died in 1147. See note to *Gilbert mab Catgyffro*.

155 See L. Fleuriot, HLCB I, 7 'Alan Fergant, le 'brave-parfait', le dernier qui porta un surnom breton, remarquable souverain qui mourut en 1119'. Fleuriot argues (HLCB I, 28) that the prowess of Alan Fergant and his Breton followers secured the victory for Henry I over his brother Robert Corthose at the battle of Tinchebrai.

for the approximate date of composition of this triad.[156] It should be pointed out, however, that both Alan Fyrgan and Gilbert fab Cadgyffro were historical figures, both of whom would have been known for the part they had played in Welsh affairs and those of Norman England,[157] and the question as to why and by whom they were introduced into the native tradition in this manner is one which has wider implications than those which concern TYP alone.

It is best to consider the allusions to both figures in the light of similar allusions to contemporary characters which are found both in the Welsh *chwedlau* and in some French Arthurian romances of the twelfth century, into which certain names of the kind appear to have made their way from Welsh sources. Thus in *Culhwch ac Olwen* the name *Gwilenhen brenhin freinc*, introduced into the list of characters at Arthur's court (CO ll. 294, 720; see notes), is an allusion to William the Conqueror. Allowing for the fantasy of the dream setting, the story of *Breudwyt Ronabwy* may also be compared: here a character in the immediate household of the twelfth-century ruler of Powys, Madog ap Maredudd, is transferred into the company of Arthur and his warriors. In Arthurian romance I have noted the following instances of a similar kind: (i) In Chrétien's *Erec* (l. 1709) the name *Yvain de Cavaliot*, given to a character at Arthur's court, apparently reproduces that of another member of the ruling family of Powys in the twelfth century, Madog's nephew the poet-prince Owain Cyfeiliog.[158] (ii) It has been suggested[159] that the character named *Brian des Illes*, who appears in Chrétien's *Erec* (*Bruianz des Illes*, l. 6730), as well as in *Perlesvaus* and elsewhere, is to be identified with *Brian filz Count*, the natural son of *Alan Fyrgan*, and perhaps also with the (*Y*)*sperin mab Fflergant brenhin Llydaw* of the Arthurian list in *Culhwch* (CO l. 216, see n.); in *Perlesvaus* he is first depicted in an unfavourable light, but eventually he also becomes a member of Arthur's household. If this identification is correct, it is particularly interesting to find that the names

[156] For references to stories concerning the battle of Camlan see note to triad 59. It is tempting, however, to speculate as to whether an allusion to the original third character who belonged to this triad may not be preserved in HB's reference to *Catgabail Catguommed* 'C. Battle-Refuser' (HB, ch. 65—see note to *Cadauel m. Kynued6*). According to HB's account, this seventh-century ruler of Gwynedd deserted his ally Penda in company with his own followers (*de nocte consurgens*, as in *hyt nos* in triad 30), *en route* for another famous battle, that of Winwæd, at which Penda was slain. But the circumstances did not perfectly fit the triad, since the betrayal was by Cadafel himself, rather than by his *teulu*.

[157] For the relevant allusions see under Notes to Personal Names.

[158] See Brugger, *Mod. Phil.* 38, p. 268.

[159] By J. L. Weston, *Mod. Phil.* 22, pp. 405–11. He is referred to as *Briano filio comitis*:, LL 93.8. On *Brian filz Count* see also Stenton, *First Century of English Feudalism*, p. 28, n.

of both father and son have been drawn into the Arthurian orbit alike in Welsh and in Old French sources. (iii) The third instance is that of *Breri*, *Bleheris*, or *Bleddri*, whom Giraldus describes as *famosus ille fabulator Bledhericus, qui tempora nostra paulo praevenit.*[160] *Breri-Bleheris* is referred to both by the Anglo-Norman poet Thomas and by the second continuator of the *Conte del Graal* as the authority for their versions of the *Tristan* and *Perceval* romances respectively. But he appears also as *Bleobleheris*, a character at Arthur's court in Chrétien's *Erec* (l. 1714), and in the *Elucidation* prefixed to the *Perceval* as a famous teller of tales at Arthur's court. Geoffrey of Monmouth's inclusion of *Bledericus dux Cornubiae* among the British rulers who opposed Ethelfrith at the battle of Chester (HRB XI, ch. 13) may likewise conceal a reference to a famous contemporary.[161]

These instances—to which it is likely that others can be added—prove that the introduction of contemporary figures into a legendary setting was a phenomenon which occurred in the twelfth century, both in early Welsh sources which are not strictly related to Arthurian material (cf. triad 24 and pp. xci–xcii above, on *Gilbert (mab) Katgyffro* and on *Alan Fyrgan*), and in an Arthurian context in Welsh and Old French narrative. As regards TYP, the introduction of such names is to be included among the secondary additions and modifications made to the original nucleus of ancient tradition. They are witticisms of a topical nature, and therefore of a kind whose finer points it is not possible for the modern reader to

[160] Gerald of Wales, *Descriptio Cambriae*, I, ch. 17. On *Bleheris* or Bleddri ap Cedifor, see HW 428, and see also the following note.

[161] K. Jackson discussed the name *Bledhericus* as a latinization of Ml.W. *Bleddri* ('king of wolves') in a brief note in *Les Romans du Graal dans les littératures des XIIe et XIIIe siècles* (Paris, 1956), p. 148. In this he showed that the Welsh name *Bleddri* became easily corrupted to *Bleri* and then by assimilation to *Breri* and *Bleheris* in the continental romances. W. J. Gruffydd had first identified the famous story-teller with *Bleddri ap Cydifor*, the custodian of a Norman castle in the vicinity of Carmarthen during the early twelfth century (RC 33, pp. 180 ff., see HW p. 535n.; EWGT 106, 18(b); AW 186–7). Evidently this *Bleddri* was fluent both in Welsh and French, and since as Bullock-Davies showed, he was officially listed in the Pipe Rolls as a *latimarius*, or high-status official interpreter, he appears to have been ideally placed to transfer traditions (in both directions) between the Welsh and the Anglo-French. Hence the fame accorded to *Breri* in the *Tristan* poem of Thomas, and in the *Conte del Graal*. See, in particular, Constance Bullock-Davies, *Professional Interpreters and the Matter of Britain* (Cardiff, 1966), and my essay in Geraint Bowen (ed.), *Y Traddodiad Rhyddiaith yn yr Oesau Canol* (Llandysul, 1974), 160–1. There must have been many other such bilingual tradition-bearers in Norman Britain, although R. S. Loomis under-rated the significance of *Bleddri–Breri* and his like, in comparison with the alleged Breton *conteurs*, in whom as tradition-bearers he unreservedly placed his faith (ALMA 57, etc.) The whole subject has been resurveyed by P. Sims-Williams, 'Did Itinerant Breton *Conteurs* transmit the *Matière de Bretagne*?' *Romania* 1998, pp. 72–111 (on pp. 99–105 the role and identity of *Bleddri* is closely examined).

evaluate. They should be classed with other jocular elements of satire and exaggeration, which appear in the presentation of a number of the triads, in the same way as these elements have been introduced into the treatment of traditional narrative in the composition of the *chwedlau*.

It would be pedantic to attempt to enumerate the triads into whose presentation these elements of humour have entered. In my note to triad 35, *Tri Chyuor a aeth o'r Enys Hon*, I have suggested the view that the detailed anecdote which is found in this triad concerning an otherwise unknown character named *Yrp Lluyddawg* 'Yrp of the Hosts' and his ingenious methods of recruitment, is a mathematical fantasy deliberately contrived to throw into relief the *size* of the armies whose departure from Britain is commemorated; and in particular the enormous size of the host whose departure depopulated the country when Maxen Wledig led away the troops—since it is Maxen's story which the triad intended to emphasize. This suggestion gains support from the fact that there are no other references, in bardic poetry or elsewhere, to the names of Yrp or his assistant, or to any similar incident to that recorded in the triad. In a number of other instances, however, we have triads which bear all the signs of originating in genuine traditional sources, but which are presented in an exaggerated or burlesque manner. This burlesque treatment is apparent in certain of the triads which have been expanded to introduce narrative elements—triad 44 *Tri Marchlwyth* is a conspicuous example—and one suspects the presence of this burlesque element also in triad 26 (although I have latterly reached the conclusion that the *Drystan* episode must inevitably derive from ultimate French influence, see n. to triad), and in triad 54 *Teir Drut Heirua*, which deals with the preliminary exchanges which took place between Arthur and Medrawd before Camlan. The appearance of these elements of humour in certain of the triads forms a link between TYP and the *chwedlau*: we are reminded of the jocular treatment of the list of Arthur's warriors in *Culhwch*, which includes the burlesque triad of the Three Escapers from Camlan (see p. lxxvi above)—and indirectly, also, of the exaggeration and buffoonery which is a characteristic frequently manifested in Old Irish tales. Although humour of this kind constitutes an essential ingredient in *Trioedd Ynys Prydein*—its presence is obvious enough among the horses' names in *Trioedd y Meirch*—I think it likely that the expanded triads in which it is most noticeable do not in their present form represent the oldest stratum in TYP. It is probable that the oldest triads are those in which the names alone are classed under an esoteric epithet of a general eulogistic type, without amplification of any kind. Such amplifications as were subsequently made are to be attributed to a period of decline in the knowledge of the traditional background of the triads, so that it was felt necessary to add notes which would serve as a guide to the content of the stories referred to, and it seems inevitable that such notes would have been on the increase during the period of manuscript transmission.

There are a few triads, in addition to those whose final form is established by topical references which link them to twelfth-century characters and interests, to which a specific date may be assigned on internal evidence. Thus in triad 68 *Tri Brenhin a vuant o Veibion Eillion*, which commemorates the three kings whose descent was from villeins, a ninth-century king of Dyfed (Asser's king *Hemeid*, or *Hyfaidd*) is set beside a treacherous seventh-century king of Gwynedd; and the circumstances suggest that this triad is a product of that nationalist opposition to the pro-English policy of the rulers of Dyfed which found voice some forty years after Hyfaidd's time in *Armes Prydein* (see note to *Hyueid m. Bleidic* and to triad 68). Here as in the case of *Alan Fyrgan*, we have a contemporary figure whose conduct is brought into comparison for the purpose of satire with that of predecessors of the Heroic Age, and the triad is instructive as showing that this process was already at work in the composition and evolution of TYP, perhaps even earlier than the twelfth century. The inclusion of the name of another ninth-century ruler, *Gwgawn Gleddyfrud*, who is recorded as the last king of Ceredigion, who died in 871—among the participants at the battle of Chester in 616—should be compared; though here in contrast to the case of *Gilbert fab Cadgyffro* the element of satire does not seem to be present (see triad 60 and note). Triad 55 refers to the raid made into Ceredigion by Hywel and Ieuaf, sons of *Idwal Foel*, in the year 954. Since the triad incorporates older material referring to the war between *Cadwallawn* and *Edwin* in the seventh century, it is difficult to know whether to regard it as having been composed in reference to the tenth-century event, or whether the latter is merely a substitution into an older triad. It should in any case be compared with triads 60, 65, 69: these triads together constitute a group dealing with the history and traditions of Powys, and they appear only in the WR version of TYP. It may be presumed that this group of triads originated in Powys: triad 65 is based entirely on the Powys *englyn* cycle, both triad 55 and triad 69 include references to battles in Powys which occurred during the campaign fought between *Cadwallawn* and *Edwin*, while triad 60 is exclusively concerned with the battle of Chester of 616—a battle whose immediate impact was on Powys rather than on any other of the Welsh kingdoms. Although these triads do not in themselves constitute evidence from which we may reasonably conclude that the WR version of TYP originated either wholly or in the main in the kingdom of Powys, yet there is a certain amount of evidence which points to an especially lively interest in the older heroic traditions at the court of Madog ap Maredudd in the mid-twelfth century. This interest may not have been entirely spontaneous, but rather implies a continuity of tradition. Since more of Cynddelw's work has survived than has that of any of his contemporaries, it would hardly be amiss to lay some stress on the fact that the *pencerdd* associated most prominently with Madog ap Maredudd evinces a wider range of reference to the characters of the *ystoryaeu a hengerdd* than does any other poet until the time of Gruffudd ap Maredudd. Cynddelw certainly had a fuller knowledge than has come down concerning the battle of *Meigen*, a major event in Cadwallawn's war with Edwin (see note to triad 55), and he knew also of *Maes Cogwy*, i.e. the battle of *Maserfeld* (Oswestry) where Oswald of Northumbria was slain by Penda in 642:[162] presumably his knowledge of both events was derived from current tradition still alive in twelfth-century Powys. The juxtaposition in *Breudwyt Ronabwy* of characters at the court of Madog ap Maredudd with those of heroic legend of an earlier epoch suggests that Madog's court was famous in some special way for its concern with the traditions of the past, and presumably also for the patronage of the bards who preserved and retailed them—whatever may be the precise significance of the specific context given to the story in the quarrel between Madog and his brother Iorwerth.[163] Some of the distinctive traditions underlying the story were known to Cynddelw, as is proved by his allusion to Owain's Flight of Ravens, *branhes Owein* (H 83.28 = CBT IV, no. 1.28n.) in a poem to Owain Gwynedd.

Cynddelw displays his familiarity with triad 29 *Tri Diweir Deulu*, which he cites in a comparison with the *teulu* of Madog himself (CBT III, no. 9.20n.). In a similar manner Madog's nephew, the poet Owain Cyfeiliog, makes use of the framework of triad 31 *Teir Gosgord Adwy(n)* in his poem *Hirlas Owein* (CBT II, no. 14), in which he exalts his own war-band by comparing it in succession to two of the renowned *gosgordd* mentioned in the triad. Here again it is evident that Owain Cyfeiliog had a fuller knowledge of the stories referred to than has come down to us. A slight indication provided by his poem, which favours a connection between the nucleus of the WR version of TYP and Powys, is the fact that he evidently knew of this triad in the form in which it is given in WR, with the name of *Belyn* instead of the Early Version's *Melyn* as the leader of one of the *teir gosgord* (see CBT II, no. 14.37n.).

[162] See B III, pp. 59 ff. On Cynddelw's familiarity with the Powys *englyn* cycle see above, p. lxii and note 76. Cynddelw knew also that Taliesin (see note) had composed poetry for Urien and Owain—he does not associate the *Cynfardd* with Elphin and Maelgwn, as do some of his contemporaries. Cf. EWSP 362–3.

[163] I have developed this theme in 'Cyfeiriadau Traddodiadol a Chwedlonol y Gogynfeirdd' in M. E. Owen and B. F. Roberts (eds), *Beirdd a Thywysogion*, pp. 211–12.

It is obvious, however, that as it stands the WR version of TYP is a composite collection of triads derived from a number of different sources of varying antiquity, which were probably assembled together at very different dates.[164] I have suggested that there is evidence that one of these constituent groups took shape in Powys, but we may safely assume that other groups originated in other areas of Wales. Thus triad 26 appears to be based entirely on the story material of the South—even if we are partially to discount, as having been accentuated during the period of transmission,[165] the strong southern and anti-North-Welsh bias which is apparent in the treatment of the episode of *Henwen*. This triad is present in both versions of TYP, and it offers an indication that the primary redaction of TYP in the form in which the text has reached us took place somewhere in South Wales.[166] It has already been seen that it is likely that the Early Version was committed to writing by a monastic scribe who supported the archiepiscopal claims of St David's; and this in itself indicates a location in South Wales as the place of redaction for these triads.

It is my belief that the triads cited in the *Four Branches* of the *Mabinogi* represent an integral part of the text, and that they have a definite function to perform in the development of the narrative, by relating it to a wider background. If this is so, then triad 30 *Tri Anyweir Deulu* and triad 37 *Tri Chud a Thri Datcud* (to cite the two most striking instances) are shown in their original form to antedate the text of the *Four Branches*, which Sir Ifor Williams dated to *circa* 1060.[167] In the light of the evidence which has been considered there need be no difficulty in accepting this conclusion. It has been shown that the manuscript transmission of *Trioedd Ynys Prydein* can be taken back to the early part of the twelfth century; that substitutions have occurred, in the course of transmission, both in the names and

[164] See pp. xx–xxi for a summary of the constituent groups of triads in the WR version. There is evidence (see p. xxix above) that triads 47–50—listing the 'Men who received Adam's qualities—were not contained in W, so this last addition to the collection was probably made by the scribe of R himself; although the antiquity of this group of triads is vouched for by Prydydd y Moch's references to them in the late twelfth century (see note to triad 47).

[165] See p. xcv above.

[166] A further suggestion which favours South Wales as the region in which the written texts of TYP originated may perhaps be obtained from the absence of all allusion in the triads to the distinctively North-Welsh hero *Hiriell*, whose name was nevertheless well known to the poets (cf. CBT I, no. 9.140n.; II, no. 27.10; IV, no. 1.33n.; IV, no. 4.152n.; VI, no. 13.17n.; BBC 57.5; and see B III, pp. 50–2; AP ix).

[167] A more recent assessment by Thomas Charles Edwards ('The Date of the Four Branches of the Mabinogi', THSC 1970, pp. 363–98) proposes that a date for the composition of PKM cannot be more closely defined than as some time between *circa* 1050–1120 (I would prefer the latter date). It is obvious that PKM and TYP are fundamentally related, and the latter date would best suit the appearance of historical Norman characters, *Alan Fergant* and *Gilbert (mab) Catgyffro* (see notes) in TYP nos. 24, 30, 39, unless these are to be explained as post-Conquest substitutions or additions.

in the incidents in the triads (so that the allusions to *Alan Fyrgan* in triad 30, and to *Ronnwen baganes* in triad 37, need not be taken as evidence for a late date of composition for the triads in which they occur); and finally that certain triads in the extant texts of TYP (including no. 13 *Tri Chynweissyat*, whose substance underlies the text of *Branwen*) are cited in the *hengerdd* in the *Book of Taliesin*. Proof of the existence of certain of TYP in either written or unwritten form might therefore be taken back to the ninth or tenth century. We may conclude that the South-Welsh redactor of the *Four Branches* quoted these triads from oral or written tradition at a date which was little, if any, earlier than that at which some of the constituent groups of triads in TYP were committed to writing for the first time. In his discussion 'Pedair Cainc y Mabinogi' in Geraint H. Jenkins (ed.), *Cof Cenedl* XI (Llandysul, 1996), Professor Gwyn Thomas has affirmed his belief that the citation of ten triads (listed PKM xxv) in the text of the *Mabinogi* is to be accepted as evidence for the prior existence and essential integration of at least a part of TYP into the written redaction of these tales. This view is contrary to that expressed by Sir Ifor Williams in 1930, when he concluded that the triadic allusions in the *Mabinogi* were to be regarded as subsequent glosses on the text. Professor Thomas's view is undoubtedly the correct one, and is a view which is increasingly recognized in the work of contemporary scholars as the result of the evidence provided by the full publication of the seven volumes of *Cyfres Beirdd y Tywysogion* (Cardiff, 1991–6).

THE APPENDICES

The content of each of the four appendices is related with a greater or lesser degree of closeness to that of *Trioedd Ynys Prydein*; and all but App. II have been introduced into earlier collections of TYP. Robert Vaughan included App. I and IV in Pen. 185 (see above, pp. xl–xli); and it is from this source that both documents were ultimately introduced into the *Myvyrian* first series of triads (MA² 388, 393). Moses Williams introduced App. I, III and IV into his collection of *Trioedd Ynys Prydein* in Ll. 65 (see above, p. xlviii). My reason for including *Bonedd Gwŷr y Gogledd* as App. II is that this important genealogical document was not easily accessible before the publication in 1966 of P. C. Bartrum's EWGT: to include it has saved the necessity for repeated quotation in the Notes to Personal Names. App. I and II are considerably older than the others. App. I is introduced into the WR version of *Trioedd Ynys Prydein*, as one of the separate sections of which this text is composed (see pp. xx–xxi above). But since *Enweu Ynys Prydein* does not appear in the Early Version, and since it is a self-contained unit which is concerned primarily with the geography, rather than with the historical and legendary traditions of Britain, it has seemed preferable to reserve this document for separate treatment in the form of an appendix. App. III and IV were in the later centuries preserved along with TYP as an integral part of the learning of the bards (see GP xci and p. lix above). Neither text has come down in any manuscript older than the fifteenth century, yet both draw upon elements derived from the older native tradition; although in the case of App. IV these have become to a considerable degree fused with material originating in the French Arthurian romances.

The personal names which occur in App. I, III, and IV have been discussed fully in the Notes to Personal Names. But since the content of App. II is essentially genealogical, the discussion has in this case been restricted to such names as occur also in *Trioedd Ynys Prydein*. (See the Bibliography below for references to some relevant works published subsequently to the first edition of this book: in particular, B. F. Roberts, 'Geoffrey of Monmouth and Welsh Historical Tradition', *Nottingham Medieval Studies* XX, reproduced as ch. 2 in his *Studies on Middle Welsh Literature* (1992), and in LlC XII, pp. 127–45.)

Appendix I (pp. 246–55). *Enweu Ynys Prydein* 'The Names of the Island of Britain' accompanies *Trioedd Ynys Prydein* in the texts of W and R,[168]

[168] The text of W was printed by Egerton Phillimore in *Cy.* VII, pp. 123–4; that of R in Evans and Rhŷs, *Red Book Mabinogion*, p. 309.

though elements in 6–10 of the document printed here appear only in Pen. 50 and in the later versions based upon this manuscript.[169] W gives nos. 1–5 of EYP; R has only nos. 1 and 2, and omits the reference to the Marvels of Britain in no. 2. In place of the latter, R gives a list of the Cities of Britain.[170] Pen. 50 also includes the Cities in its version of EYP, but gives the Marvels of Britain separately at the conclusion of the text of TYP. The earliest texts of both the *Civitates* and the *Mirabilia* are those given in HB,[171] where the names of the Cities appear in Old Welsh of the eighth or ninth century. The names of the Cities in the HB list have been discussed fully elsewhere (see B V, pp. 19 ff.; *Antiquity* XII, pp. 44 ff.; EHR LII, pp. 193 ff.). The numerous Welsh versions of the Marvels present a complicated problem, since they differ both among themselves and from the HB *Mirabilia*.[172] For brevity I have given the text of *Enweu Ynys Prydein* without either of these additions, since the origin of the Cities and Marvels is distinct from that of the rest of the document, and has no direct bearing either upon the genesis of EYP itself, or upon the content of the other triads contained in this book.

An indication as to the date of *Enweu Ynys Prydein* is given by the reference to *Mynyw* as the seat of one of the three British archbishoprics (App. I, no. 5n.). This suggests comparison with the allusion to *Mynyw* as one of the *Teir Lleithiclwyth Ynys Prydein*, in the first triad of the Early Version of TYP. It has been pointed out in the note to triad 1 below that this allusion links the triad with the controversy over the proposed archbishopric of St David's, which was at its height during the twelfth century. It is evident that the originator of *Teir Lleithiclwyth* knew of the territorial divisions of Britain as these are represented in EYP (no. 4), and had similar ideas as to desirable episcopal seats in the three *taleithiau*. This

[169] These are Robert Vaughan's collection of TYP in Pen. 185, and its copies in Pa. 13 and BL Addl. 14,873, from which the Myvyrian text was taken. See above, p. xli, n. 33.

[170] The number of the cities has been increased to thirty-three, as in certain manuscripts of HB (one name is missing from the text of R) from Gildas's original figure of twenty-eight; see AW 89, 102. Two other manuscripts, Pen. 163 and Jes. Coll. 6, combine a much inflated version of EYP with full lists of the Cities and Marvels. This version differs so much from the earlier one that I have not collated the texts. Both are closely related, though the beginning is lacking in Pen. 163. The main source of the additions in this version is Higden's *Polychronicon*; see Thomas Jones, THSC 1943–4, pp. 46–9; B. F. Roberts, 'Ystori'r Llong Foel', B XVIII, pp. 342–8. A critical edition based upon these and other manuscripts is much required.

[171] F. Lot (ed.), pp. 208–18; Morris (ed.), 80–4; Mommsen (ed.), pp. 210–19. For an outline of the textual development of the *Historia Brittonum*, see D. N. Dumville, SC X/XI, pp. 78–95.

[172] A number of manuscripts give the Marvels as a separate unit; for a list of versions see B V, p. 21. For two versions which contain only a few items in common see B V, pp. 22–4 (from RBH) and T. H. Parry-Williams (ed.), *Rhyddiaith Gymraeg* I (Caerdydd, 1954), pp. 65–7 (from Pen. 163).

proves that both EYP and the triad were in existence before the middle of the twelfth century. But EYP is composed of elements which are probably of considerably earlier date than this: the allusion to an almost obliterated tradition about the successive occupations of the country, the territorial divisions of *Ynys Prydein a'e their rac ynys*; the measurements of the Island as taken from places whose importance has long since been forgotten, and the obsolete place-names from the old British kingdoms in the north—all invite the conclusion that the text originates in a milieu more archaic than that of the twelfth century.

It is very doubtful, however, whether the concluding part of the document is as old as this twelfth-century redaction. Nos. 6–9 appear for the first time in Pen. 50, and it has already been shown (p. xxviii above) that the scribe of this manuscript was probably responsible for making certain additions and alterations to the text of TYP which lay before him, based on a wide reading in both foreign and vernacular literature. It seems likely, therefore, that the archaic elements which appear in these additional triads have been drawn from literary sources. Nos. 7 and 8 have close verbal parallels in the text of the *Brut* (see notes), and the *Teir Prif Auon* of the latter is a duplication of the reference to the *Tri Prif Aber* in the older part of the text (no. 2). The names of the *Teir Prif Porthua* (no. 9) could have been taken from the poetry of the *Gogynfeirdd* or from earlier poetry. The *Teir Ynys Prydein* 'Three Realms of Britain' of no. 6 looks like a reminiscence of the occurrence of this phrase in *Culhwch ac Olwen* (see CO, l. 282, and n.); while the occurrence in the same triad of the name *Alban* to designate Scotland, in place of the older *Prydyn*, is obviously a late feature. The division of Britain here specified—*Lloegr a Chymry a'r Alban*—can hardly be regarded as consistent with the division outlined in no. 4, in which the three parts of the kingdom are Cornwall, Wales, and *Y Gogledd*; and we have seen that this division is reproduced in triad 1, *Teir Lleithiclwyth*. This must be the older, traditional, division intended by the phrase *teir ynys Prydein*—though it is possible to wish that the redactor of *Culhwch* had been more specific in identifying the Three Realms to which he referred. Owing to the prominence of Cornwall as Arthur's home in pre-Galfredian sources it is natural to conclude that Cornwall (representing the Dumnonian peninsula as a whole) constituted one of the Three Realms; and the geography of *Culhwch* implies that *Y Gogledd* was still remembered as an extensive British territory: the third *ynys* must therefore have consisted of both Wales *and Lloegr*. It is clear, therefore, that the concept of this three-fold division of Britain is older than the time of Geoffrey of Monmouth, though traces of it survive in the *Historia Regum* itself. According to Geoffrey's account of the colonization of Britain, Cornwall was occupied by a certain *Corineus*, a companion of

Brutus; but as Geoffrey is at pains to make clear, he was one who was descended from a separate Trojan stock (HRB I, 12). Throughout the *Historia* the existence of Cornwall as an entity separate from *Logria* (England) is indicated from time to time, and in a variety of ways. The early concept of the *teir ynys Prydein* is reproduced in Lear's three-fold division of Britain among his daughters: the two elder are bestowed in the first instance upon the dukes of Cornwall and Albany, while Logria, the central realm and the richest of the three, was evidently the inheritance intended for Cordelia (HRB II, 11). In these instances, then, Geoffrey is reproducing a traditional British geography which corresponds with a concept whose existence is indicated both in *Culhwch* and in *Enweu Ynys Prydein*.[173] The *Historia Regum* offers further suggestions that Geoffrey knew and utilized the material incorporated in this document. The reference to the vertical and transverse roads made across the length and breadth of Britain by *Belinus* son of *Dunwallo Molmutius* (HRB III, 5) suggests the influence of the statement as to the vertical and transverse measurements of the Island made in EYP (see note to no. 3). It is also apparent that Geoffrey knew of the triad of the *Teir Archesgobot* (see note to no. 5), though, as we should expect, his version substitutes *Caerleon* for *Mynyw*.

The contention that these elements in *Enweu Ynys Prydein* represent a pseudo-learned Welsh tradition which is long anterior to the time of Geoffrey of Monmouth, is corroborated by a consideration of other features in the text. The allusion to the successive colonizations of the Island made in no. 1 bears no relation whatever to the fiction of the Trojan origin of the Britons, which Geoffrey adopted from HB, and considerably elaborated in his own account of the settlement of Britain. It may well represent the survival of an older tradition; and we may compare the 'takings' of Britain here outlined with the Irish pseudo-learned tradition of the successive 'takings' of Ireland which are described in the *Lebor Gabála Érenn* (see note to no. 1). It is difficult to account for the association of the name of *Myrddin* with this tradition, implied in the title *Clas Merdin*, though the form of the name in W suggests that it is derived from an older written source. The reference to the conquest of Britain by *Prydein fab Aed Mawr*, whose name is attested elsewhere in early sources (see under Notes to Personal Names), suggests an allusion to an eponymous conqueror of Britain whose name and story Geoffrey intentionally suppressed, since he would not tolerate any rival to his account of the settlement of Britain by Brutus and his Trojan companions. It has been

[173] On *teir ynys Prydein* see note to CO l. 282.

pointed out above that the obscure place-names given in nos. 3, 4, and 9[174] provide further indications for an archaic original underlying the material of EYP. The names in England and Wales either remain in current usage or else are still identifiable, though we should not now attribute the same prominence to these places as they receive in EYP. For the places situated in Scotland this is no longer the case: the exact locality of *Penryn Blathaon*, *Penryn Rionyt*, and *Porth Wytno yn y Gogledd*, may perhaps never be known. These places belong to the lost nomenclature of 'Yr Hen Ogledd' the 'Old North', long since lost to the Britons.[175]

Appendix II (pp. 256–7). The earliest text of *Bonedd Gwŷr y Gogledd* 'The Descent of the Men of the North' is found on pages 291–2 of Pen. 45 (first half of the fourteenth century). This manuscript also contains one of the two copies of the Early Version of TYP, a text of the *Brut*, *Trioedd Arbennig*, etc. (see p. xviii above, and EWGT 72–4; 146–7; *Rep.* 379–80). BGG was first printed by Skene, FAB II, p. 454, and subsequently by Wade-Evans, *Arch. Camb.* 85, pp. 339–40. BGG provides a valuable supplement to other collections of early Welsh genealogies such as those in Harl. 3859 and in Jes. Coll. 20 (EWGT 9–13; 41–50);[176] though where the genealogies are parallel the versions given in BGG differ in some respects from those found in the other collections (see notes to *Ryderch Hael*, *Pabo Post Prydein*, *Peredur m. Elifer Gosgor(d)ua6r*). BGG gives the pedigrees of a number of princes who flourished contemporaneously during the latter part of the sixth century, each of whom is represented as being descended from one or other of the founders of the two ruling dynasties in North Britain at this period—Coel Hen and Dyfnwal Hen.[177] The first group (nos. 1–6), which consists of descendants of Coel Hen, includes not only Urien Rheged, but also Llywarch Hen and Gwenddolau, of whom neither appears in the Harl. Gen.; while the second group (nos. 8–12) includes among the descendants of Dyfnwal Hen the names of Mordaf Hael and Elidyr Mwynfawr (see under Notes to Personal Names). Between the two groups (no. 7) there is interpolated a triad commemorating the valour

[174] The names in no. 9, *Teir Prif Porthva*, are obviously as archaic as those found in the earlier part of EYP, though it has been suggested that they have been derived from the references to these places found in early poetry; see note to no. 9.

[175] Cf. the lost northern place-names in the *Gododdin*, referred to in CA xci.

[176] For the background to these genealogies see EWGT 9–13; 41–50; BWP, ch. VI; K. Jackson, *Antiquity* XXIX, pp. 77–88.

[177] On these dynasties see Chadwick, 'The British Kingdoms', *Early Scotland*, ch. x, and M. Miller, 'Historicity and the Pedigrees of the Northcountrymen', B XXVI, pp. 255–80, especially 256–8.

of the tribe of Coel Hen.[178] The final item (no. 13) bears no relation to the other pedigrees, but commemorates a legendary ruler of Cornwall; it is to be associated with the narrative background of *Culhwch ac Olwen*[179] rather than with *Gwŷr y Gogledd*. Another item which is inconsistent, and even incongruous, is no. 11, which claims that *Gauran m. Aedan Uradawc* [*sic*] was a grandson of Dyfnwal Hen. Even when this pair of names is reversed (see note to *Aedan m. Gauran*) the allusion makes little sense. *Aedán mac Gabráin* was the Irish ruler of the kingdom of Dál Riada contemporary with *Rhydderch Hael* (see note), and the existence of a certain antagonism between him and the neighbouring Britons is perhaps implied by the epithet *Bradawc* 'the Wily' which is bestowed on him here and in the triads (cf. triad 54 and note). To depict him as a kinsman of Rhydderch is historically impossible in spite of the assertion in BGG 11, and the item is best explained as the kind of humour which is rarely left behind for long in the triads and *chwedlau*. The classification of the pedigrees in BGG in separate briefs which refer in turn to each of the sixth-century northern heroes concerned, or sometimes to a group of two or more brothers, is similar to the arrangement of the pedigrees in *Bonedd y Saint*. Although it necessitated a certain amount of repetition, it was a method favoured by the professional bardic genealogists, as can be seen from the arrangement given to much of the genealogical material in the later manuscripts. These late collections (Pen. 75, 127, 128, etc.; see list in EWGT 78–9) incorporate certain of the items found in BGG along with references to other characters of the early tradition, whom they relate to the same North-British milieu (see notes to *Bran Galed*, *E(n)vael Adrann*, *Gwythyr m. Greidya6l*, *Morgant Mwynua6r*). Since BGG is supplemented by these later manuscripts, it is probable that these names derived from earlier variant versions of BGG.

The genealogies in BGG are not carried down to any later date than the group of sixth-century Men of the North on whom they converge. But it can hardly be concluded from this that BGG represents a copy, even at many removes, of a document originally drawn up in the sixth or seventh century. It is more likely that it was composed at a later date[180] as a guide to the

[178] For another reference to this triad see RM 192.20–1; R. L. Thomson, *Owein* l. 820 (quoted in note to *Owein m. Uryen*). Owain's *branhes* is here associated with the *trychant cledyf kenuerchyn* in terms which indicate an allusion to the triad quoted in BGG.

[179] For *Tutuwlch Corneu* see note to *Goreu m. Kustenin*, and on *Amlawd Wledig* see note to CO l. 2.

[180] K. H. Jackson suggested (*Antiquity* XXIX, pp. 78–9) that with one or two exceptions the northern genealogies as a whole may have been put together in the ninth century out of the orally-preserved narrative material relating to the North-British Heroic Age. It is a remarkable fact that with the exceptions of Owain and Pasgent sons of Urien, later descendants of Rhydderch, Gwallawg, Morgant etc. are not named in the genealogies. See J. Rowland, EWSP 93–4, 97–8.

interrelationships of the Men of the North, since these figured so prominently in a variety of early Welsh records. It is not for this reason necessarily an unreliable guide, since at any period up to the end of the twelfth century a bardic genealogist would have had access to much traditional material which was subsequently lost. But there is at least one indication that the document is of a later date than the tenth-century Harleian Genealogies. No. II represents Dyfnwal Hen as grandson to *Maxen Wledic Amherawdyr Ruuein*, while Harl. Gen. V gives Dyfnwal a more credible descent in depicting him as grandson of *Ceredic Wledic*, who has been identified with the fifth-century North-British ruler *Coroticus*,[181] to whom St Patrick addressed his epistle. The substitution bears witness to an increase in medieval times in the popularity of claiming descent from Maxen Wledig (see note). It would perhaps be a fair estimate to attribute the composition of *Bonedd Gwŷr y Gogledd* to the twelfth century, but on the basis of earlier traditional material which was still in current circulation, either in written or in oral form. No proof is to be derived from the orthography, however, that a written exemplar prior to 1100 underlies the extant text.

Appendix III (pp. 258–65). Both *Tri Thlws ar Ddeg Ynys Prydain* 'The Thirteen Treasures of the Island of Britain' and *Pedwar Marchog ar Hugain Llys Arthur* 'The Twenty-four Knights of Arthur's Court' (App. IV, pp. 266–9 below) belong to the period of the *cywyddwyr* of the fifteenth and sixteenth centuries; and it has already been noted (pp. lix, c above) that in the later period these documents were transmitted along with TYP as an essential part of the bardic heritage. Evidence for this is to be found in the copious manuscript transmission which both documents have received. The earliest manuscripts of both date from the mid-fifteenth century, and it seems unlikely that either can be much older than this in its present form.[182] In tone and feeling both texts are of their period,[183] and their integration with the poetry and certain prose documents of the fifteenth and sixteenth centuries is fully apparent. Tudur Aled lists a selection of the Treasures in an *awdl* to Robert Salesbury (*circa* 1500; see note to nos. 10–11). The oldest version of the Thirteen Treasures is in the autograph of Gwilym Tew in Pen. 51, 169–70), a manuscript which may have been written during the

[181] See Bartrum, EWGT 10 (5) = WCD 125; HW 126–7, Chadwick, *The Growth of Literature* I, p. 274; M. Miller, B XXVI, p. 260 n.1.

[182] For subsequent editions and a full study of the *Tri Thlws ar Ddeg*, see n. 185 below, and the references given in AW 85–8.

[183] This tone has influenced the manner of presentation of material which is certainly much older in origin. No. 1 offers a cynical explanation of Rhydderch's traditional epithet *Hael* 'the Generous', which cannot be early. A similar kind of cynicism appears in the emphasis placed on the distinction between the *gwr bonheddig* and the *iangwr*, and between the brave man and the coward, which is expressed in nos. 7, 8, 9.

decade 1460–70 (see p. xxix above). This version merely lists the names of the Treasures, in the same order as in the later manuscripts, but without the explanatory comment given in the latter.[184] But the majority of manuscripts are of the sixteenth century, with some later copies of the seventeenth and eighteenth centuries. Eventually the *Tri Thlws ar Ddeg* appeared in print in E. Jones's *Bardic Museum* (London, 1808), and again from a different text in *Y Brython* for 1860. Lady Guest published a text and translation among her notes to the *Mabinogion* in 1849 (II, pp. 353–4) from 'an old MS. in the collection of Mr Justice Bosanquet'.[185] As a good representative version I have adopted the text of C 17 (late sixteenth century) with certain emendations, but I have endeavoured to note all significant variants which occur in the other versions.

The original list of the *Tri Thlws ar Ddeg* (nos. 1–13) has been altered in a few of the versions to include two items popular from the romances of the period—the Mantle of Tegau Eurfron and Eluned's Stone and Ring. I have given these items as nos. 14 and 15, though each manuscript which includes them does so by dropping one or other of the earlier items, and by counting the Crock and Dish of Rhygenydd the Scholar (nos. 10 and 11) as a single unit. Both are evidently intrusive, and can have had no place in the original list.[186]

[184] The list includes only twelve names in the original hand—*kebystr Klydno* (no.5) is omitted. No. 3 is no longer legible. *Mantell degau* and *maen a modrwy Eluned* have been added in a later hand.

[185] The manuscript of the *Tri Thlws ar Ddeg Ynys Prydain* which I selected as my basic text—Cardiff 17—is in the hand of Rowland Lewis of Mallwyd; see Rh. F. Roberts, *Nat. Lib. of Wales Journal* IX, pp. 495–6. Two subsequent editions of this tract have been published, with annotations: by P. C. Bartrum, EC X, pp. 434–77; and by Eurys Rowlands, LlC V, pp. 33–69. Both editors make use of additional manuscripts which were not known to me. A third—and a definitive—textual study of the *Tri Thlws ar Ddeg* was made by Graham Thomas in his M.A. dissertation 'Llen Arthur a Maen a Modrwy Luned' (University of Wales M.A. thesis, 1976), in which he cited thirteen additional texts unknown to previous editors. The cumulative evidence adduced by these scholars forcibly emphasizes the popularity of the *Tri Thlws ar Ddeg* among poets of the sixteenth and following centuries, and a number of unpublished references to the *tlysau* by the *cywyddwyr*, separately and collectively, have been brought to light. (In view of the subsequent appearance of these three detailed studies, I have discarded two pages of minor textual variants cited on pp. 243–4 of the earlier editions.)

[186] Moses Williams gives yet another additional item in Ll. 65: *Cwlldr Tringer fab Nuddnot: Lle rhoid ei fenthyg mywn aradr, ef a arddei yny erchid iddaw beidiaw* 'The Coulter of Tringer son of Nuddnot: where it was borrowed for use in a plough, it would plough until it was asked to stop.' The initials JJ. which are appended to this item indicate that a manuscript belonging to John Jones, Gellilyfdy, was its source, and P. C. Bartrum points out to me that this is to be found in John Jones's version of *Y Tri Thlws ar Ddeg* in Pen. 216 (pp. 96–100), where the name *Tringer vab Nuddnot* has been written in above the line as an alternative to an original *Rrun Gawr*. With *Tringer fab Nuddnot* cf. *Tringat* in CO (l. 933, see n.); *tringat yn aber cledyf* (l. 1127); also P. C. Bartrum, EC X, pp. 476–7.

It is significant that the earliest version, that of Pen. 51, introduces the list of Treasures as *Henwae y tri thlws ar ddec A oedd yny gogledd* 'The Names of the Thirteen Treasures which were in the North'. In effect, as will be seen by consulting the Notes to Personal Names, the majority of names in the list which are identifiable are attested in the genealogies as belonging to members of *Gwŷr y Gogledd.*[187] The Treasures were regarded as emanating from the old British North, and whatever may have been the precise evocative force of the term *Y Gogledd* to poets of this late period, at least it meant that the Treasures were designated by it as belonging to a most ancient substratum in the bardic tradition. By the sixteenth century there was in existence a story which told that the Thirteen Treasures had been taken by Myrddin to his *Tŷ Gwydr* or Glass House (see note to no. 3): the *Tŷ Gwydr* was already known in older bardic sources (see note to *Myrddyn Wyllt*). This story was much popularized in the later versions, and Lewis Morris refers to a tradition which localized the *Tŷ Gwydr* on *Ynys Enlli* or Bardsey (CR 170). But the evidence for this story cannot be traced back beyond the sixteenth century, and the connection of Myrddin with the Treasures suggests the influence upon it of the character of Merlin in the Arthurian romances. A text of *circa* 1500 (see EC X, p. 447) associates the Treasures with Taliesin, instead of Myrddin, and this ascription may well be the earlier of the two. The story is however of interest as showing the elaboration of earlier traditional material which took place down to quite late times (cf. App. IV). It was perhaps in connection with this story that the Treasures became fixed as thirteen in number; though there can be no doubt that many of the elements in the *Tri Thlws ar Ddeg* are of much greater antiquity than this period.

Some proof of the antiquity of a part of the material drawn upon in the document is to be had from the references to nos. 2, 7, and 13 in *Culhwch ac Olwen* (see notes), where the *mwys* of Gwyddno and the *peir Divrnach Wydel* [*sic*] are included among the *anoetheu* or 'difficult things' which the hero is required to obtain. Elsewhere in the tale (l. 159, see n.), Arthur refers to his *llen* as one of his most precious possessions. The *gwyddbwyll Gwenddoleu* is closely paralleled in *Peredur*. It is reasonable to suppose that certain other items in the list are quite as old as this. Undoubtedly those most likely to be ancient include the talismans for the satisfaction of human wishes and for supplying abundance of food and drink, and these find some less specific parallels among the *anoetheu* in *Culhwch*, in

[187] An exception is no. 13, *Llen Arthyr*, of which it is specifically said that it was *yng Nghernyw* 'in Cornwall'. *Llawfrodedd Farchog* (recte, *farfog*) and *Dyrnwch Gawr* (nos. 6 and 7) are both paralleled in CO ll. 223, 635 etc. (see notes), and *Rhygenydd Ysgolhaig* (nos. 10, 11) is unknown in any other source.

addition to those which have been referred to above. It is in these objects that R. S. Loomis noted significant analogues to the properties of the Grail as they are portrayed in medieval French sources.[188] The antiquity of the concept underlying these Welsh talismans is vouched for by the parallels which they have in early Irish sources in numerous food-producing horns, cups, and vats.[189] One may cite in particular the Cauldron of the Irish god known as the *Dagda*, of whom it is said in an eleventh-century text: *Ni tégedh dám dimdach úadh* 'No company ever went from it unsatisfied'.[190] This cauldron is described as one of the Four Treasures of the Tuatha Dé Danann; the others were the Stone of Fál at Tara, Lug's Spear, and Nuadu's Sword.[191] These were treasures which were brought into Ireland from outside, from the Otherworld inhabited by the Tuatha Dé, and this Otherworld origin of certain magic treasures has a number of parallels in Irish sources. Among these were the Cup and Branch brought back by the High-King Cormac mac Airt after an Otherworld visit.[192] But the closest Irish parallel to the *Tri Thlws ar Ddeg*, and one which brings together three objects which correspond to objects named in the Welsh text, is found in the account in the Rennes *Dindshenchus* of magic treasures brought back from an Otherworld visit by another legendary High-King, Crimthann Nía Nar:[193]

> Is é docuaid i n-echtra . . . la Nair tuaidhigh in bansidhe, coma fae caictighis ar mís (and), dia tubairt na seotu imdai, imon carpat n-oir 7 imon fi(d)chill n-óir 7 imon cétaigh Crimthainn. i. lend sainemail, 7 aroile séotu imda olchena.
>
> 'It is he that went on an adventure . . . with the witch Nár the fairy woman. With her he slept a month and a fortnight. And to him she gave many treasures including a gilt chariot, and a *fidchell* (see note to no. 12) of gold, and Crimthann's *cetach*, a beautiful mantle, and many treasures also.'

[188] See WAL 159 and references there cited.

[189] See R. S. Loomis, *Romanische Forschungen* XLV, pp. 68 ff.; idem, RC XLVII, pp. 55 ff. See also V. Hull, ZCP XVIII, pp. 73 ff.

[190] E. A. Gray (ed.), *Cath Mag Tuired*: The Battle of Moytura (Irish Texts Society LII), §6, p. 25.

[191] R. A. S. Macalister (ed.), *Lebor Gabála Érenn* (Irish Texts Society) IV, p. 107.

[192] 'The Irish Ordeals', in Windisch (ed.), *Irische Texte* III, pp. 184–221. Cf. p. 202: *is é sin in treas sed is fearr dobhi a n-Erinn. i. Cuach Cormaic agus a Craeb agus a Claideb* 'These are the three best treasures that were in Ireland: Cormac's Cup, and his Branch, and his Sword'.

[193] RC XV, p. 332. A closely similar text is given in the Book of Leinster version of *Lebor Gabála* (LL 23b; text edited by Best, Bergin, and O'Brien, I, p. 91). The *Metrical Dinnshenchas* (E. Gwynn (ed.), III, pp. 120 ff.) gives an expanded list of Crimthann's treasures, which includes a sword and a *cuach* (cup) of plenty. For other variant versions see Gwynn's note, pp. 499–500.

These parallels suggest that the original nucleus of the Welsh Treasures may also have consisted in stories concerning magic objects which had either been won from the Otherworld or bestowed on mortals by its inhabitants. In this connection R. S. Loomis has noted[194] the reference in *Preiddeu Annwfn* to the Cauldron of the Head of Annwfn, which was credited with possessing the same characteristics as are attributed to the *peir Dyrnwch Gawr* in our text (see note to no. 7). It is possible that the *Tri Thlws ar Ddeg* refer back to a group of stories in Welsh which connected not only Arthur, but a number of other early heroes with *echtrai* or Otherworld visits, from which they returned, like the Irish kings Cormac and Crimthann, in possession of magic treasures. It must remain a matter of speculation whether these stories were originally associated in some particular way with the *Gwŷr y Gogledd*, with whom they are primarily associated in the list as it has come down. But the earlier references to some of these Treasures, the *mwys Gwydneu Garanhir* and the *peir Diwrnach Wyddel* in *Culhwch* (ll. 618, 1037), do not in any way conflict with such a supposition.[195]

Appendix IV (pp. 266–9 below). The oldest text of *Pedwar Marchog ar Hugain Llys Arthur* is in the autograph of Gutun Owain on pages 4 r.–5 r. of Ll. 28. The manuscript bears the date 1455.[196] Although the corrupt forms of the proper names in this version of the *XXIV Marchog* imply that it must have been preceded by one or more older and better texts, from which the more authentic forms in certain of the later manuscripts are derived, yet it is unlikely that the text in its present shape can be much older than the mid-fifteenth century (see p. cvi above). The greater number of the many manuscripts in which the *XXIV Marchog* has been transmitted are of the sixteenth and seventeenth centuries.[197] In these manuscripts the text frequently appears in juxtaposition with genealogical material; and no doubt it is for this reason that a version came to be prefixed to Lewis Dwnn's *Heraldic Visitations of Wales*.[198] I have given the

[194] RC XLVII, p. 55.

[195] On the Otherworld voyages known as *Echtrai* and *Immrama*, see D. N. Dumville, *Ériu* XXVII, pp. 73–94. See also Seán O'Coileáin, *Celtica* XXI, and M. Haycock's study of *Preiddeu Annwfn*, SC XVIII/XIX, pp. 52–78.

[196] Gwenogvryn Evans assigns this date to the manuscript on its own authority (*Rep.* II, p. 462). See however the discussion of Gutun Owain's manuscripts by Thomas Roberts, B XV, pp. 99 ff., where it is shown that the date 1455 given in the manuscript refers more probably to the exemplar from which it was copied. A date *circa* 1475 for Ll. 28 is more consistent with the evidence provided by Gutun Owain's other writings.

[197] See AW 201–3, and cf. P. C. Bartrum, *Nat. Lib. of Wales Journal* XIV, pp. 242–5; and Ceridwen Lloyd-Morgan, *Nat. Lib. of Wales Journal* XXI, pp. 329–39.

[198] S. R. Meyrick (ed.), (Llandovery, 1846) I, p. 10. This version is not traceable to any of the extant manuscripts.

version found in Pen. 127, the *Book of Sir Thomas ap Ieuan ap Deikws* (written *circa* 1510), since this text is fuller and more accurate than that of Gutun Owain. Little variation is presented in the key epithets introducing the triads throughout the many versions, and the order of these remains constant; but there is wide variety in the wording of the explanatory comment given to each triad, so that it was only possible to record a selection of the variants.[199]

Several of the triads in the *XXIV Marchog* are fresh adaptations of older triads which appear in the body of TYP, and no. 7 is an adaptation of the 'Three Men who escaped from Camlan' in *Culhwch* (ll. 226–32; see p. lxxvi above). Even apart from these adaptations, the extent to which this group of triads draws upon older material is obvious: of the twenty-four names, two-thirds belong exclusively to the native Welsh narrative tradition, or else were known in this tradition before they were utilized by the redactor(s) of the *Brut* to render names in Geoffrey's *Historia*; while only the remaining third consist of adaptations, with varying degrees of fidelity, of names derived from the *Historia Regum*, *Y Seint Greal*, and the thirteenth-century French 'Vulgate' cycle of Arthurian prose romances. This latter group of names is interesting, since it includes at least one name which is not taken from the only 'branch' of the Vulgate cycle of which we have a complete translation into Welsh, i.e. *Y Seint Greal*.[200] The introduction in no. 6 of *Blaes mab Iarll Llychlyn* (see note) bears witness to an acquaintance with the figure of *Blaise*, who appears as Merlin's *confesseor* in the second 'branch'—the *Prose Merlin*.[201] Perhaps a full translation of the *Merlin* may once have existed in Welsh, since a fourteenth-century fragment of the *Birth of Arthur* based on this text has come down in Ll. 201.[202] Further evidence to the same

[199] For further details of the manuscripts the reader is referred to the edition of the *Pedwar Marchog ar Hugain* published by the writer in THSC 1956, pp. 120 ff. Since I published this edition I have discovered four additional texts of the *XXIV Marchog*: one in the hand of J. Jones, Gellilyfdy in Pen. 216 (p. 33), and one by the herald Hugh Thomas in Harl. 4181 (pp. 9–10). This latter text is derived from the *Book of Sir Richard Wynn of Gwydir* (see p. xxxvi above), and its readings therefore correspond with those of C 36 and of Moses Williams in Ll. 65, both of which are derived from the same source.

[200] The first part of this fourteenth-century text is a rendering of the fourth 'branch', the *Queste del Saint Graal*, the second of the *Perlesvaus* (R. Williams (ed.), *Selections from the Hengwrt MSS.*, vol. I; and Thomas Jones (ed.), *Ystoryaeu Seint Greal Rhan I: Y Keis* (Caerdydd, 1992)). See C. Lloyd-Morgan, AW 193–205.

[201] See H. O. Sommer, *The Vulgate Cycle of Arthurian Romances* II (the *Merlin*), and index volume.

[202] J. H. Davies (ed.), *Cy.* XXIV, pp. 247 ff. The text follows in an abridged form the corresponding part of the *Merlin*, though with a few interesting additions of names derived from purely Welsh sources; see note to *Gwalchmei m. Gwyar*. In the sixteenth century, the chronicler Elis Gruffudd shows his knowledge of Welsh adaptations of the material contained in the Vulgate *Merlin*; see Thomas Jones (ed.), 'The Story of Myrddin and Gwenddydd in the Chronicle of Elis Gruffudd', EC VIII, pp. 315–45.

effect is to be found in the tradition, known to fifteenth-century poets,[203] that Cai was Arthur's foster-brother. This tradition must derive ultimately from some form of the *Prose Merlin*, though Welsh poets localized the scene of Arthur's upbringing at Caer Gai in Merioneth. Yet a third 'branch' of the Vulgate cycle, the *Lancelot*, was drawn on by the fifteenth-century redactor of the Pen. 50 version of TYP (cf. triad 86 and note), and we have no evidence that this romance was ever known in a Welsh form. This range of allusion to French romance material is one of the indications of a movement in the fourteenth and fifteenth centuries towards greater awareness of the contemporary literary fashions of France and England. It is interesting to note that it was the very same collection of French texts, the Vulgate cycle of the Arthurian romances, which was rendered into English by Sir Thomas Malory in the last quarter of the fifteenth century in his *Morte D'Arthur*.

In spite of its substratum of early traditional material, the *Pedwar Marchog ar Hugain* contains allusions which link the document closely with allusions made by fifteenth-century poets, and with references in the prose literature of the same period. The few sparse references which have come down to *Drudwas fab Tryffin* (see note) suggest that in spite of a single allusion to this character in *Culhwch* (CO ll. 200–1n.), he was more prominent in the later tradition than in the early period. The story of his death at the hands of his own *adar llwch gwin* ('griffins') may be no older than the fifteenth century; though like the tale of *Petroc Paladrddellt* (see note), and the latter's escape from Camlan, it is probable that it represents a late adaptation of older traditional material, of the same kind that we have already noted (p. cviii–cix) in connection with the *Tri Thlws ar Ddeg*. Another contemporary literary source which shows obvious points of contact with the *XXIV Marchog* is the *Ystorya Trystan*;[204] in which the prose accompaniment to the older *englynion* seems to be of approximately the same date as the *XXIV Marchog*. Not only is Gwalchmai fab Gwyar given here the epithet *dafod aur* 'of the golden tongue' as in the *XXIV*

[203] B XI, p. 13; cf. EAR I, p. 145; II, p. 318. Cf. also Rhys Goch Eryri's allusion (IGE[2] no. CXI.15–20) to Myrddin's imprisonment under a stone beneath a waterfall—an episode which is unknown in Welsh sources, and must have its ultimate origin in the Vulgate *Merlin* or *Lancelot*. See also C. Lloyd-Morgan, 'Lancelot in Wales' in K. Pratt (ed.), *Shifts and Transpositions in Medieval Narrative* (Cambridge, 1994), pp. 169–79. She concludes (p. 176) that 'at least one complete manuscript of the Vulgate Cycle had reached Wales, certainly by the fifteenth century'.

[204] Ifor Williams, B V, pp. 115 ff. The description of March fab Meirchiawn as *un arall or marchogion* in the text of Pen. 96 seems to be an allusion to the *XXIV Marchog*. This manuscript is in the hand of Lewis Dwnn (*Rep.* I, p. 592), and it has already been pointed out that Dwnn prefixed a version of the *XXIV Marchog* to his *Heraldic Visitations*. (For a discussion, and other manuscript versions see now Jenny Rowland and Graham Thomas, *Nat. Lib. of Wales Journal* XXII, pp. 241–53.)

Marchog, but Trystan's *kynneddfau* ('(magical) peculiarities') are described in detail, although these do not correspond exactly with the *kynneddfau* assigned to him in the present text.

Marchog (*urddol*) is the common term for a knight in *Y Seint Greal* and in literary sources of the fifteenth and sixteenth centuries (see GPC 2357). Hence it is that in no. 3 I have rendered *Tri Chad varchoc* by 'Three Knights of Battle', although this epithet is borrowed from an older triad (no. 18 in TYP), where I have rendered it as 'Three Battle-Horsemen'. The number of twenty-four assigned to Arthur's knights may in the context of this document be purely conventional, and due to the bards' predilection for it;[205] since the only medieval Welsh source which could have offered any possible justification for it seems to be the passage in *Peredur*, in which Arthur's *marchogion* to the number of twenty-four come each in turn to oppose the hero.[206] I am indebted to R. S. Loomis, however, for pointing out to me that twenty-four is the number of the seats allotted to Arthur's Knights on the Winchester Round Table; and this number recurs also in a contemporary English Arthurian poem 'The Carl of Carlisle'.[207]

[205] See GP xxx.

[206] *Ac ol yn ol ef a doeth petwar marchaw(c) ar hugeint*, WM col. 141.6–8. The corresponding word in the text of RM is *mackwy*. Cf. also the twenty-four *marchogion* who sue for peace with Osla Gyllellfawr in *Breudwyt Ronabwy* (RM 159.11–13); and the Twenty-four Officers of the Court in the Laws.

[207] This poem dates from *circa* 1500. See Auvo Kurvinen, *Sir Gawain and the Carl of Carlisle in Two Versions*, p. 115, ll. 11–14; Hales and Furnivall, *The Percy Folio MS.*, vol. III, p. 277.

METHOD OF EDITING

In editing the texts I have supplied capitals and punctuation. The contractions *m.* for *mab*, and *e.p.*, *y.p.* for *enys* (*ynys*) *prydein* have been expanded throughout. In Pen. 16, as in the *Dingestow Brut*, the sign *6* may have the values of *u*, *w* or *v* (= *f*) and these different values have not been distinguished in the text. Kenneth Jackson drew attention to the discrepancies in WHR Special Number (1963), pp. 82–7, and these have been corrected in the main texts. Discrepancies may remain in the variant readings. *6* may have the values *w*, *u* or *v* (= *f*) also in the part of W which contains the triads, though both manuscripts employ the sign *w* for *w* as well. Nor have I distinguished between the variant forms of *r* and *s*, since the significance of the alternation between them is of palaeographical rather than of linguistic interest. Words or letters which have been added to the main text from another manuscript are shown thus: (y), and the manuscript source of such additions is given in the textual notes beneath each triad. Letters in the manuscript which are redundant are denoted thus: (*y*).

For the purposes of both the textual and the critical notes, I have headed the references to the three items in each triad as *a*, *b*, and *c* respectively, while *d* is used for any addition to the text which follows the third item.

In the translation, the spelling of proper names has been modernized where their form is recognized; but, like the old copyists, I have left the early spelling unchanged in instances where the correct form is in doubt. Though English equivalents for epithets have been offered in the translation, in the Notes to Personal Names both names and epithets are listed under the medieval forms in which they occur in the text.[208] Where the WR version of a triad differs markedly from that of the Early Version, I have printed both texts in full; alternatively, in a few instances a second form of a triad is given from some other manuscript. The order of precedence given to the three items in a triad varies considerably in the different manuscripts, and it has not seemed necessary to indicate the variations. Notes on the horses' names in *Trioedd y Meirch* are appended to the triad concerned.

The following abbreviations are employed:

The Peniarth manuscripts are cited under Pen.,

C = Cardiff;

Cwrt. = Cwrtmawr;

H = Hafod;

[208] Names which can be spelt either with initial C- or K- in medieval Welsh are indexed together under C, as is the normal practice in glossaries. Similarly names occurring in the text with medial *-t-* for *-d-* are listed with those in *-d-* (e.g. names spelt *Cat-* or *Cad-*), since in the manuscripts medial *-d-* may be represented by either letter.

Pa. = Panton;

Ll. = Llanstephan;

NLW = National Library of Wales MS. 6434;

RW = the text of the *Book of Sir Richard Wynn of Gwydir* as preserved in Harleian MS. 4181;

DC = the text of TYP contained in Salesbury's *Y Diarebion Camberäec*;

BL[1] = British Library Additional MS. 31055;

BL[2] = British Library Additional MS. 15,047;

SV = Simwnt Vychan (for triads 47–50 in his hand, which are bound up with Pen. MS. 16);

V = Robert Vaughan, i.e. Peniarth MS. 185. Since this collection contains triads 1–90 with a very few exceptions (these consist of nos. 47–50, 76, 77), I have considered it unnecessary to include V in the list of manuscripts sources appended to each triad, and I have quoted the readings of V among the variants only in cases in which it has seemed desirable to make clear which text Vaughan follows for any specific triad. Vaughan's notes in his own hand (NLW 7857D; see above, pp. xlv–xlvi) are distinguished as VN[1] from the transcript of these made by Evan Evans (Panton MS. 51), which is denoted VN[2].

MW = Moses Williams, i.e. Llanstephan MS. 65. This collection also is quoted only in a few instances where its readings provide an interesting variant of uncertain source and also as the source of triads 93–5.

The citation of NLW implies that the readings given are those of the *Book of Sir Richard Wynn*, and correspond with the copies of the same text in Harleian MS. 4181 (= RW) and C 36. The readings of these two latter manuscripts are referred to only when they differ from those of NLW.

References given to WM (*White Book Mabinogion*) and RBP (*Poetry from the Red Book of Hergest*) are to the columns, not to the pages, in the diplomatic editions of these manuscripts.

Note that the *Peniarth*, *Cwrtmawr*, *Hafod*, *Panton*, and *Llanstephan* manuscripts, and the *Llyfr Gwyn Rhydderch* are all housed in the National Library of Wales at Aberystwyth. The *Llyfr Coch Hergest* (Jes. Coll. MS. I) is in the Bodleian Library at Oxford. The contents of these manuscripts were fully described by J. Gwenogvryn Evans, *Report on Manuscripts in the Welsh Language*, published for the *Historical Manuscripts Commission* (London, 1898, 1902 = *Rep.*, RWM).

For a brief survey of some of the Renaissance copies of material collected in this book see Graham C. G. Thomas, 'From Manuscript to Print', in R. G. Gruffydd (ed.), *A Guide to Welsh Literature c.1530–1700* (Cardiff, 1997), pp. 250–1.

The commentary given in the notes which follow each triad can be further supplemented by reference to the Notes to Personal Names.

From the *varia lecta* to the Third Edition I have omitted several obviously corrupt and insignificant variants which were recorded in the earlier editions, recording only such variants as are of intrinsic interest.

TRIOEDD YNYS PRYDEIN

TEXT, TRANSLATION AND NOTES

Pen. 16, fo. 50*r*

1. (Teir Lleithicl6yth Ynys Prydein:

Arthur yn Pen Teyrned ym Mynyw, a Dewi yn Pen Esgyb, a Maelgwn Gwyned yn Pen Hyneif;
Arthur yn Pen Teyrned yg Kelli Wic yg) Kernyw, a Bytwini Esgob yn Ben Esgyb, a Charadawc Vreichuras yn Ben Henyf;
Arthur yn Ben Teyrned ym Penn Ryonyd yn y Gogled, a G(w)erthmul Wledic yn Benn Hyneif, a Chyndeyrn Garthwys yn Benn Esgyb.

1. Three Tribal Thrones (Throne-Burdens) of the Island of Britain:

Arthur as Chief of Princes in Mynyw (St David's), and Dewi as Chief of Bishops, and Maelgwn Gwynedd as Chief of Elders;
Arthur as Chief of Princes in Celliwig in Cornwall, and Bishop Bytwini as Chief of Bishops, and Caradawg Strong-Arm as Chief of Elders;
Arthur as Chief of Princes in Pen Rhionydd in the North, and G(w)erthmwl Wledig as Chief of Elders, and Cyndeyrn Garthwys as Chief of Bishops.

Manuscripts: 16, 45, 50, 51, 77, V.

1–1*b*, ( ) *supplied by* 45.

a. Arthur yn benteyrn ynghaer lleon ar wysg 77, V, (ym mynyw *deleted* 77). penescub V *throughout*. heneif V.

b. Bitwini 45, 77. a Chriada6g vrenhin 50, a Chriadawc vreichvras 77. hyneif 45, 50, hynaif 77, V *omits* yn ben henyf.

c. ym pen rionyd 45, ym Penrhyn rhionedd 50, ym Penrhyn Rhianydd 77. Gwerthm6l Wledic. 45, Gyrthmwl Wledig 50, Gythnyw *altered to* -mul 77.

For a discussion of the relation of this triad to the Pen. 16 series as a whole, see introduction p. xci and n. to triad 85. The threefold division of Britain implied here, as well as the names given to the *Teir Lleithiclwyth*, indicate that a close relation subsists between this triad and *Enweu Ynys Prydein* (App. I; cf. nos. 4, 5). But the assertion in the triad of Arthur's sovereignty (and thus of British sovereignty) in Cornwall, Wales and the North looks like an intentional contradiction of the statement made in EYP, that each of the three *taleithieu* were to be held under the crown of London. Note that *Bendigeidfran* was *ardyrchawc o goron Lundein* (PKM 29), 'exalted with the crown of London'.

a. lleithicl6yth 'Tribal Throne' or 'Throne Load/Burden' (fig. 'supporter'; GPC 2151, 2248). *Lleithic* < L. *lectica*, the seat of greatest honour in the *llys*, a couch or throne, cf. CA n. to l. 400 *tal lleithic*. 'That high degree in a king's palace, whereon is seated ye throne, and in cathedrall churches whereon ye altar standeth, we call in ye British tongue *lleithic*', VN[1]. *Pedeir gradd llys arglwydd y sydd, kyntedd ac radd a meinc a lleithig; kyntedd yr iymyn, y radd yr yscweireid, y feink yr magwyeid, lleithig yr Teyrnedd*, 'There are four degrees in a lord's court: the *kyntedd* (daïs) for the yeomen, the *gradd* (step?) for the squires, the *meinc* (bench) for the pages, the *lleithig* for the princes'; *lleithigau eureit a welei yn y neuad* (WM 180.40).

llwyth can mean both 'tribe' and 'load, burden' (GPC 2151). The meaning here is ambiguous, perhaps intentionally so: in favour of the first meaning offered are the triads *Tri Marchlwyth* (no. 44) and *Tri Gwyndorllwyth* (no. 70). This meaning was favoured by Ifor Williams in a note in *Antiquity* IX, pp. 284–5. See further E. Rowlands, LlC VI, pp. 230–1. Cynddelw uses *lleithiclwyth* and *llwyth lleithic* as epithets in address to his patrons: Iorwerth ap Maredudd is described as *Lleithicluyth hyduyth* (H 156.25 = CBT III, no. 12.21n.), and Owain Gwynedd as *Eur llyv llwyth lleithic prydytyon* (H 95.29 = CBT IV, no. 4.231), 'a golden ruler of the tribe, supporter of poets'. Cf. also Einion Wan: *Portheis alar trvm . . . am wavr llvyth a lleithic* 'I have suffered heavy grief . . . for the supporter of the tribe and of the throne' (RBP col. 1406.38 = CBT VI, no. 4.34).

Pen Teyrned 'Chief of Princes'. On first meeting Arthur, the hero Culhwch addresses him as *Pen Teyrned yr Ynys hon* 'Chief of Princes of this Island' (CO l. 142).

Pen Hyneif (*henyf, hyneif*). For *hynaf* 'chief, elder, adviser', see GPC 1974, 1976. The two words are practically synonymous, and frequently appear in the Laws. Cf. also CO ll. 221–3, *Gormant mab Ricca—brawt y Arthur o barth y uam. Pennhynef Kernyw y tat*; RBB 404.2–4, *(g)weith badvn yd ymladavd arthur ae hyneif ar saesson ac y gorvu arthur ae hyneif (pl.)*; LlDC no. 31.56–7, *Oet hyneiw guastad ar lleg ar lles gulad*, 'he (Cei) was a steadfast leader of an army for a country's good'. The examples indicate that *hynaf* and *hynefydd* are sing. (CLlH 206), while *hyneif* can be both a sing. and a pl. In construction with *pen* the following noun may be either sing. or pl.; cf. *penkygorwr, penhebogyt* (RBB 357.24) and *pengwastrawt, penkynyd* (LlB 2, 18, etc.), but *penn rianed*, 'chief of queens' (CO l. 358); *yskithyrwyn penn beid* (CO l. 639); *a theliessin penn beird* (CO l. 214); *penn gwyr* (CA l. 537) are pl. (see n., CLlH 99); *pen teyrnet* 'chief of princes' (H 315.18).

In the triad the parallelism with *pen esgyb* and *pen teyrned* indicates that *pen hyneif* is like these a pl. form. For another early instance, see Ifor Williams's discussion of *eineuyd* (BT 56.16) in PT 29, and cf. *pennhynef* in CO l. 222n.

A tenth-century gloss in Ox. 2 (Bodl. 572, fo. 46r) equates *hinham* with *patricius* (W. H. Stevenson, *Early Scholastic Colloquies* (Oxford, 1929), p. 9; LHEB 279). The reference to *Maeldaf hynaf* in the Laws seems to equate *hynaf* with *pendevic*. In later texts the meaning is 'forefather, elder, ancestor', cf. triad 92 below. But in its earlier usage the word denotes the king's close advisers who were frequently his elder relatives; perhaps originally the older members of the same kinship group from whom the *edling* or *gwrthrychiad* was selected in the younger generation, cf. CO l. 222n. For evidence that the *Maeldaf hynaf* of the Laws was Maelgwn's maternal grandfather, see n. to *Maelgwn Gwyned* under Personal Names. But it is needless to point out that the triad preserves no trace of such a relationship subsisting between Arthur and the various *pennhyneif*. Both the triad and *Culhwch* suggest, however, that the *pennhyneif* sometimes held a regional authority; cf. the usages of Anglo-Saxon *ealdormann*.

Mynyw < L. *Menevia*, St David's, or Tyddewi in Pembrokeshire, one of the four cathedral churches in early Wales, in which the office of abbot was merged with that of bishop (HW 207, 263–4; Giraldus Cambrensis (trans. L. Thorpe), *Itinerarium Cambriae*, Book 2, p. 159ff.). On the site, see D. S. Evans, *The Welsh Life of St. David*, pp. 55–6. The controversy as to the archi-episcopal status of St David's, which reached its height *circa* 1120–50, appears to be reflected in the reference here to *Mynyw*; cf. App. I, no. 5 below, *Teir Archesgobot . . . Vn yMyny6*, etc.

b. Kelli Wic 'the forest grove', according to O. J. Padel, CMCS 8, p. 19: see also triads 54, 85 below. *Kelli Wic* is the name of Arthur's Cornish capital in TYP and in *Culhwch ac Olwen* (see n. to CO l. 261), though Geoffrey of Monmouth substituted for it *Caerleon-on-Usk* (cf. triad 51) and triad 85 attempts to combine both traditions by naming *Kelli Wic* together with *Caerleon* among Arthur's *teir priflys*. There is no general agreement as to the site of *Kelli Wic* and previous suggestions range between Callington, Gweek Wood near Helston, and 'Kelly Rounds' in the parish of Egloshayle. In Welsh *celliwig* means 'woodland, forest' (GPC 459). The whole subject of the identification has been fully discussed by O. J. Padel and P. Moreton in *Cornish Archaeology* 16 (1977), pp. 118–19 and more recently by Padel in AW 234–8. The indications are that the Welsh redactor of *Culhwch ac Olwen* had no clear idea as to the details of Cornish geography, and that he envisaged *Kelli Wic* (to which he makes five allusions) as a place on the furthest western extremity of Cornwall, and that he may have mentally identified it with *Penn Pengwaed* (Penwith Point), the place from which his hero made his penetrating destructive shout which was to be heard in the furthest extremities of Britain and Ireland. Cynddelw compares the court of Owain Gwynedd to that of *Kelli Wic*: *kyrt kertynt mal kynt kelliwyc* (H 93.29 = CBT IV, no. 4.167 n.) 'companies gathered as formerly at *Kelli Wic*'. Cf. also the references by Iolo Goch, GIG no. III.44 and no. VI.68; and GLGC no. 126.47 and no. 223.74.

c. Penn Ryonyd; cf. triad 85, *Penryn Rioned*, and App. I, no. 4, *P. Rionyt*. This is one of the lost place-names of the British kingdoms in the 'Old North' (cf. introduction, p. civ) and there remains considerable doubt as to where it was situated. *Pen(ryn)* implies that its site is to be looked for on a headland, and this precludes the possibility that it is Glasgow, the episcopal seat of St Kentigern, as was suggested by Loth, RC XIII, p. 499, and Ifor Williams cited by O. G. S. Crawford, 'Arthur and his battles', *Antiquity* IX, p. 285. Watson suggests that *Penrhynn Rhionydd* is to be identified with Ptolemy's *Rerigonion* (= 'very royal place'), the capital of the *Novantae*, which stood at the head of Loch Ryan in Galloway (*The Celtic Place-names of Scotland*, p. 34); and a similar suggestion to this was made by Robert Vaughan (VN[1]), who suggested as the site the extremity of the Mull of Galloway. This is possible, and the name is no doubt to be connected with the *kaer rian* and *luch reon* referred to in two poems in BT (29.18; 34.1). *Pen(rhyn) Rhionydd* is not referred to by the *Gogynfeirdd*; nor is it known, apparently, in any early source outside the triads. VN[2] observes that some identify the place with Edinburgh, owing to the similarity between *rhionydd* and *rhianedd* 'maidens', and in the romances Edinburgh is known as *castellum puellarum* (see J. S. P. Tatlock, *The Legendary History of Britain*, p. 12, and references there cited). This identification is to be rejected on all scores, as it is by Vaughan himself; though it is possible that it may have been present in the mind of subsequent antiquarians, as for instance in that of the scribe of Pen. 77, who gives the form *Penrhyn Rhianydd*. For another sixteenth-century reference to *Penryn Rianedd* see B. F. Roberts (ed.), 'Ystori'r Llong Foel', B XVIII, p. 357.

2. Tri Hael Enys Prydein:

Nud Hael mab Senyllt,
Mordaf Hael mab Seruan,
Ryderch Hael mab Tudwal Tutclyt.
(Ac Arthur ehun oedd haelach no'r tri.)

2. Three Generous (Noble/Victorious) Men of the Island of Britain:

Nudd the Generous, son of Senyllt,
Mordaf the Generous, son of Serwan,
Rhydderch the Generous, son of Tudwal Tudglyd.
(And Arthur himself was more generous than the three.)

Manuscripts: 16, 45, 50, WR, 51, C 6, NLW, DC, Cwrt. 3, MW, BL[2].

2. Tri hael a fu yn ynys brydain nid amgen C 6, Tri dyn a gafas haelioni Adda MW, Tri hael ynys oedd y rhai hyn BL[1].

a. Senullt W, Senllt R, Seinyllt 50, Seinillt 51, Sasulld C 6, Senylt NLW, DC.

b. a mordaf ap Servan 50, mor hael 51. Serwan WR, Serfan C 6, Sernan NLW, DC.

c. Tutwal 45, Tutawal W, Tutwal R, Tudaual 50, Tudwal C 6, NLW. Tutclyd 45, Tutklyt WR, Tutglyt 50, Tutglut C 6, Tudclyd NLW, DC, Tudglud 51, Tytclyd Cwrt. *Ifor Hael medd ereill* MW.

d. *supplied from* 50, C 6; *the latter adds* eraill.

It is likely that this triad headed the series in the archetype of Pen. 16 (see p. xxxvii above), as it does in the earliest printed version of TYP in *Y Diarebion Camberäec* (p. xxxiii above). For obvious reasons it was particularly popular among the poets. Apart from separate references to the generosity of one or other of the *Tri Hael* (which will be found in the section on Personal Names under *Nud Hael m. Senyllt, Mordaf Hael m. Seruan* and *Ryderch Hael m. Tudwal Tutclyt*), allusions to the triad are made by the following poets of the twelfth and thirteenth centuries: Cynddelw (H 127.18 = CBT III, no. 21.60n.); Prydydd y Moch (H 263.5–6 = CBT V, no. 2.29–30n.); Gwilym Rhyfel (H 183.12 = CBT II, no. 28.4n.); Einion ap Gwgon (H 52.27–32 = CBT VI, no. 18.91–4); Hywel Foel (H 56.5–6 = CBT VII, no. 22.21–2n.); Bleddyn Fardd (H 58.14 = CBT VII, no. 50.24n.). Cf. also *Englynion y Clyweit: A glyweist-di a gant Ryderch / Trydyd hael serchawc serch?* (*Blodeugerdd* no. 31, *englyn* 22). In the fourteenth century, Dafydd ap Gwilym immortalized the triad by bestowing the epithet *hael* upon his patron, Ifor ap Llywelyn of Morgannwg (GDG nos. 5–10). References to the triad were also made by: Madog Dwygraig (RBP col. 1271.25–7); Dafydd y Coed (RBP col. 1375.41); and Einion Offeiriad (GEO p. 8, ll. 37–8n.). In a final *englyn* in his *marwnad* to Gruffudd ap Cynan, Prydydd y Moch associates Arthur with the *Tri Hael*: *Hael Arthur modur myd angut—am rot / hael Ryderch am eurvut, Hael*

Mordaf, hael mawrdec Nut, Haelach gretuolach Gruffut (RBP col. 1401.27–9 = CBT V, no. 11.53–7). Except for this one instance, in which Arthur's name is superimposed, the names of the 'Three Generous Men' remain identical, without any alternatives being offered, throughout all the many citations of this triad by subsequent poets.

Among the *cywyddwyr*, Gutun Owain compares a feast made by the abbot Siôn of Llanegwestl to *y trawl a wnai Tri Haelion* (GO I, no. XXI.11; cf. also XXX.25; XLIV.11); Dafydd Nanmor compliments Rhys ap Llywelyn in a similar fashion (DN no. XI.34). MW's variant of item **c** refers to Dafydd ap Gwilym's bestowal of the epithet borrowed from the triad on his own patron 'Ifor Hael': *Rhoddaf yt brifenw Rhydderch* (GDG no. 7.9; see n., p. 438). Huw Cae Llwyd includes a reference to Ifor Hael in his citation of the triad (HCLl no. XII.9, 24–6); cf. also Wiliam Llŷn no. XVI.56: *haelder Ifor*. Tudur Aled makes three allusions to the triad (GTA no. V.71–4; VI.46; CV.1); two are made by Guto'r Glyn (GGl no. XXX.56–8; LXXXII.64). Dafydd ab Edmwnd addresses Trahaearn ap Ieuan ap Meurig as *tyrhayarn gwell no'r tri hael* (GDE no. LVII.2). The names of the *Tri Hael* are cited together—evidently in direct quotation of the triad—in the passage in the Chirk codex of the Laws which describes the expedition made by the Men of the North to Arfon to avenge Elidir Mwynfawr: with Clydno Eiddyn they formed the leaders of the northern force (ZCP XX, p. 75; see nn. to *Run m. Maelgwn* under Personal Names, and to triad 44). A further reference to the triad occurs in a note appended to the fourteenth-century Jesus Genealogies (EWGT 46 (19)), in which the descent of Rhodri Mawr is traced to *Senilth Hael. Tryd hael or gogled*—perhaps the allusion here is to an earlier version in which *Senyllt* (see n. under Personal Names) took the place of his son *Nudd*. The orthographical forms of the names in the *Jes. Gens.* indicate that the source of these was written in Old Welsh orthography prior to 1200: the spelling *Senilth* indicates an exemplar in which *t* commonly stood for *th* as well as *t*, *l* for *ll*, and *i* for *y*. For a discussion of these orthographical features, and for another archaic reference to a triad preserved as a gloss on these genealogies, see n. to triad 70 below. It is significant that *Tri hael ynys Brytain* heads the series of TYP in the sixteenth-century printed text *Y Diarebion Camberäec* (see plate, p. xxxiii above).

hael 'gŵr bonheddig, urddasol: pendefig' (GPC 1804). The three personal names in the triad denote three leading princes of the 'Men of the North', and the names are distinctive in that they remain unchanged throughout all subsequent citations of this triad. The *Tri Hael* evidently became early established as the first triad in the TYP series. The evidence suggests that *Hael*, both here and elsewhere, is capable of holding some more precise meaning than 'generous' as an imprecise complimentary epithet, such as those which are frequently employed in TYP to introduce many of the triads. In the present case *Hael* seems more likely to be a term signifying a precise and recognized social status. I find it impossible to disassociate *Hael* in the triad from the epithet *Liberali*(*s*) ('generous') of the early sixth-century Yarrow Kirk inscription: HIC MEMORIA PERPETVA. IN LOCO INSIGNISIMI PRINCIPES NVDI DVMNOGENI. HIC IACENT IN TVMVLO DVO FILII LIBERALI, 'This is the eternal memorial: in this place lie the most illustrious princes *Nudus* and *Dumnogenus*. Here lie in the grave the two sons of *Liberalis*' (*Inventory of the Ancient Monuments of Selkirkshire* (Edinburgh, 1957), pp. 110–13). See further K. H. Jackson, *Angles and Britons in Northumbria and Cumbria* (O'Donnell Lectures, Cardiff, 1963), pp. 63–4. In spite of Jackson's objections, which are based on the form of the name NVDI, I do not think it possible to discount the strong probability that the inscription refers to a predecessor belonging to the family or clan of *Nudd Hael ap Senyllt*, even though the reference is more likely to be to an ancestor of *Nudd*, rather than to *Nudd Hael* himself. This view gains support from the very early allusions made in the Taliesin poetry (PT no. VIII.45n.; XII.4n.) and in the *Gododdin* (CA 1. 562n.)—the first to *Nudd Hael* and the second to his father *Senyllt* (see nn. under Personal Names below). *Hael,* as a distinctive mark of status, is already to be found in the tenth-century poem *Armes Prydein* in relation to the two foretold deliverers of the British race, *Cynan* and *Cadwaladr*, who in BT 17.26 (= AP 1.167) are designated *deu hael.* For the identity of the later 'Ifor Hael' and for a collection of poetic references to him, see Eurys Rolant, 'Ifor Hael', *Y Traethodydd* CXXXVI, pp. 115–35, and references in Meic Stephens (ed.), *Cydymaith i Lenyddiaeth Cymru* (Caerdydd, 1997).

3. Tri Gwyndeyrn Enys Prydein:

Ewein mab 6ryen,
Run mab (Ma)elgwn,
Ruua6n Beuyr mab Dewrarth Wledic.

3. Three Fortunate Princes of the Island of Britain:

Owain son of Urien,
Rhun son of Maelgwn,
Rhufawn the Radiant son of Dewrarth Wledig.

Manuscripts: 16, 45, 47, 50, R, 51, NLW, DC, Cwrt. 3 (two versions), BL[2].

3. gwynteyrn 45, gwyr deyrn Cwrt. I, guydairin Cwrt. 2.

a. Ywein 45, V, Owein 47, 50, 51, Owain NLW, Ywain DC.

b. Maelg6n *supplied from* 45 *etc.*, Malgwn NLW, Maelgwyn BL[1].

c. Rua6n 45, R, 47, Ruon 51. A pheuyr 50, Peuyr 45, pebyr R, bybyr 47, pybyr 51, bevyr NLW. deorath 45, Dorath R, Dorarth 50, 51, Deorath V, Dewrarth NLW.

---

gwyndeyrn 'fortunate lord', or 'one blessed with prosperity' (GPC 1771). The secondary meaning of *gwyn* 'blessed, holy, fortunate' appears to be intended here, rather than 'fair'. But *gwyn* 'fair' occurs in the *Mabinogion* as a courtesy title, and *Kei wyn* is the common epithet for the hero Cai, exx. LlDC no. 31.75, 81; CO l. 136 etc.

When Gwalchmai refers to Owain Gwynedd as *gwyndeyrn prydein* (H 18.8 = CBT I, no. 9.48n.) the compliment evidently has an oblique reference to the triad, and to the earlier Owain named in it. Cf. also Prydydd y Moch in an elegy to Owain Gwynedd's grandson, Gruffudd ap Hywel: *Gwae ui uod llawryt, llawen ut—gwendoryf, gwyndeyrn hep datcut* (H 304.13–14 = CBT V, no. 16.14); to Llywelyn ab Iorwerth: *gwyndeyrn Aberffraw* (V, no. 17.46n.), and to his son Dafydd: *gwyndeyrn prydein* (H 263.13 = CBT V, no. 2.37); and Gruffudd ab Yr Ynad Coch in his *marwnad* to Llywelyn ap Gruffudd (a descendant of the same dynasty): *Gwyndeyrn orthryn* (= *gortheyrn?*) *vrthaw gvendoryf gorof* (RBP col. 1418.30 = CBT VII, no. 36.101n.).

From a comparison of these poetic instances with the names in the triad (all annotated below under Personal Names) it would appear that *gwyndeyrn* may have held a certain primary significance in reference to the ruling dynasty of Gwynedd, as I have suggested elsewhere (ch. 11 of Morfydd E. Owen a Brynley F. Roberts (eds), *Beirdd a Thywysogion*, pp. 210–11 and n. 22). In contexts such as those cited above, and in the triad, it may therefore have held a more 'loaded' meaning than is apparent at first sight.

4. Tri Deifnyawc Enys Prydein:

Gwalchmei mab Gwyar,
a Llacheu mab Arthur,
a Riwallawn Wallt Banhadlen.

4. Three Well-Endowed Men of the Island of Britain:

Gwalchmai son of Gwyar,
and Llachau son of Arthur,
and Rhiwallawn Broom-Hair.

Manuscripts: 16, 45, 47, 50, WR, 51, NLW, DC, Cwrt. 3.

4. deifnia6c WR, deifna6c 45, 47, 50, deifnawc 51, deifiniawc NLW, deifiniavvc DC.
a. a gwall ap gvyar WR.
b. Llecheu 45, V, Cwrt., llocheu 47, Llachen NLW, DC.
c. Riwalla6n WR, Rialla6n 47. a pheredur mab Efravc *substituted by* 50.

---

deifnya6c 'man of substance, one who holds or inherits wealth' (cf. GPC 914, *defnydd* (4); GPC 921, *deifniog* (2); CA 345n.). From *dafn* (= *licium* D, i.e. the thread used in the shuttle for weaving, 'weft') are derived both *defnydd* 'material, substance' and *deifniog*. Vendryes (RC 41, pp. 238–40) compares with W. *defnydd* the cognate forms Ir. *damnae*, Br. *danvez*. Instances occur in which both of these latter words are employed with a personal connotation in reference to individuals who are qualified to fulfil a certain role; note in particular the Ir. term *rígdamnae*, lit. 'material of a king', i.e. a person qualified to rule by reason of his descent within four generations from a former king (see E. MacNeill, *Celtic Ireland* (Dublin, 1921), ch. viii; D. A. Binchy, 'Some Celtic Legal Terms', *Celtica* III, p. 225). With this use of *damnae* Vendryes compares the Norse use of the word *efni* 'matter, substance' in the phrases *konungs-efni* 'a crown-prince', *biskups-efni* 'a bishop-elect', *konu-efni* 'one's future-wife', *bruthar-efni* 'a bride-elect' (Cleasby-Vigfusson, *An Icelandic–English Dictionary*, second edition, p. 116). It is to be noted that W. *defnydd* is used in a similar sense in *Culhwch* in the words of the giant Ysbaddaden Pencawr: *Drycheuwch y fyrch y dan uyn deu amrant hyt pan welvyf* defnyt *uyn daw* (CO l. 518n.), 'Raise up the forks under my two eyelids so that I may see the *substance* of my son-in-law'; cf. the Breton phrase *danve me mab kaer* 'my future son-in-law' quoted by Loth (*Mab.* I, 416). Vendryes hesitates to assert that the personal usage of *efni* in Norse is borrowed from that of *damnae* and its cognates in the Celtic languages, and he suggests that both usages may have a common origin in a third language. It may be suggested, indeed, that both are *calques* upon L. *materia* in its extended meaning of 'stock, race, breed' (cf. Columella 6, 27: *generosa equorum* *materia* 'an excellent breed of horses' quoted by Lewis and Short). It is possible, as Ifor Williams suggests, that the term *deifnyawc* is employed by Cynddelw with parallel meaning to the Ir. *rígdamnae*, and he cites Cynddelw's elegy to Owain son of Madog ap Maredudd: *dyfynuet a orchut deifnyawc / detyf hael mad auael madawc* (H 155.15–16 = CBT III, no. 15.15n.) 'the deep grave covers the *offspring* of Madawg of generous manners, good his grasp'; cf. also Cynddelw's lines on Iorwerth ap Maredudd: *Haetws deifnyavc ri defnyt uy martavr* (H 156.9 = CBT III, no. 12.5) 'the *offspring* of a king has merited the substance of my verse' (i.e. to be praised). *Deifnyawc* is similarly employed by Meilyr (H 4.21 = CBT I, no. 3.105n.), Gwalchmai (CBT I, nos. 7.47n.), and Llygad Gŵr to Llywelyn ap Gruffudd: *Llew deifnyawg llidiawg* (CBT VII, no. 24.71n.). Both in these instances and in the triad, *deifnyawc* is used as a substantive, and it is probable that it is used with parallel meaning in both: etymology and cognate forms suggest that *deifnyawc* in the triad may bear a dynastic connotation similar to that of the Ir. *rígdamnae*, and may be interpreted as 'qualified by descent to rule'. This suggestion gains some support from a consideration of the identity of the characters named in the triad (see under Personal Names).

5. Tri Phost Cat Enys Prydein:

Duna6t mab Pabo Post Prydein,
a Gwalla6c mab Lleenna6c,
a Chynuelyn Drwsgyl.

5. Three Pillars of Battle of the Island of Britain:

Dunawd son of Pabo Pillar of Britain,
and Gwallawg son of Lleenawg,
and Cynfelyn the Clumsy (Leprous?).

Manuscripts: 16, 45, 47, 50, WR, C 6, NLW, DC, Cwrt. 3, BL[2].

5. tri post kat WR, tri ffost kad C 6, Tri phost YB, V.

a. Dunot W, Dunawt vwrr 47, vawr 50, dynod fawr C 6.

b. Lleena6c 45, llenna6c 50, lliennawc NLW, DC, ar ail fu wallawg ap llennawg C 6. WR *substitute* ac vryen ap kynuarch; 47 *substitutes* ac uryen reget.

c. drwsgul 50, drwscyl V, drwscwl DC, NLW, RW.

Post Cat. *Post Cad* may be compared with a number of parallel figurative expressions in both Welsh and Irish court poetry, which combine the concepts of 'ruler' and 'defender'. Exx.: CA l. 67, *colovyn glyw* reithuyw; l. 1397, catvan *colovyn greit*; CLlH no. III.11c, *Oed cledyr kat kywlat rwyt*; no. VIII.5b, *Cledir kad, kanvill o gimun*; Gwalchmai: *am bost cad ked goeth oeth ym uthrwyd* (H 22.19 = CBT I, no. 12.10). Cynddelw describes Hywel fab Owain Gwynedd as *colofyn Prydein* (H 107.1 = CBT IV, no. 6.284). Iolo Goch portrays Owain Glyndŵr as *post ardal Lloegr* 'pillar (i.e. defence) of (the border) of England' (GIG no. VIII.58). For a comparison of the use of such figurative metaphors as *colofn*, *post*, *cledr* (*cad*) in medieval Welsh praise-poetry with the parallel use in Latin of *ancora*, *columna* and *murus*, see P. Sims-Williams, 'Gildas and Vernacular Poetry' in M. Lapidge and D. N. Dumville (eds), *Gildas: New Approaches*, cited at pp. 182–3. Cf. also Saunders Lewis, 'The Tradition of Taliesin', THSC 1968, pp. 293–8 (= A. R. Jones and Gwyn Thomas (eds), *Presenting Saunders Lewis* (Cardiff, 1973), pp. 145–53). For some parallel metaphors in early Irish poetry, see the examples of the figurative use of *úaithne* 'pillar, support' cited in DIL 'U' col. 20.

6. Tri Tharw Caduc Enys Prydein:

Kyn6a6r Catgaduc mab Kynwyt Kynwydyon,
a Gwendoleu mab Keida6,
Ac 6ryen mab Kyn6arch.

6. Three Bull-Protectors (i.e. 'Armed Warriors') of the Island of Britain:

Cynfawr Host-Protector, son of Cynwyd Cynwydion,
and Gwenddolau son of Ceidiaw,
and Urien son of Cynfarch.

Manuscripts: 16, 45, 47, 50, C 6, NLW, DC, BL[2].

6. caduc 45, katgaduc 47, 50, catcaduc V, gadgaddvg C 6, tri tharw kadne DC, NLW, Radne RW.

a. Kynuarch cat caduc 45, kynwa6r katgaduc 47, Kenvawr 50, Cynfawr V. kynnvyt kynvytyon 45, kynwydd kynwydiawn 50, kynvawr Catgadne DC, NLW.

b. a Gwynddoleu 50, Gwenddolav NLW. keidya6 45.

c. ar trydydd fv riain ap kynfarch C 6. 47 *substitutes* a gwallavc mab llaenna6c.

---

tarw. A common metaphor for a warrior in early poetry, cf. the list in GP xciii; exx: *tarw trin*, BT 25.3; CA ll. 427, 433; LlDC no. 18.203; 34.1; 40.14 = CLlH no. VIII.5a, *tarv trin*, *ryuel adun* 'bull of battle, leader in war' (for *adwn* see GPC 29; EWSP 536). Cf. *post cad*, and the similar terms listed in the n. to triad 5 above. See also CBT V, no. 1.107n. on *tarw catuc*.

caduc, catgaduc. *Caddug* 'fog, gloom, darkness, covering, armour' (GPC 382), *caen, gorchudd, gwisg arfau* (G); *caligo, obscuritas, nebula* (D), cf. CA 209 n. on l. 556, *haearn gaduc*; CLlH 68, which favours *d=dd* in these words. Cf. J. E. Caerwyn Williams, B XXI, pp. 26–7n. on *caddug*, comparing PT no. II.26 *kat gwortho* < *gortho* 'battle-coverer' (used of Urien Rheged), also *kat agdo* CLlH no. I.6c, n.

Uncertainty as to the pronunciation (and hence of the spelling) of *caduc* appears in the following examples in which the word is used by the *Gogynfeirdd*: Prydydd y Moch: *dadolwch teyrn tarw catuc pryduawr* (H 260.1 = CBT V, no. 1.107n.); *Am bob treis ry duc ar bob tarw caduc* (H 279.27 = CBT V, no. 25.51); Y Prydydd Bychan: *dragon gyrchyad, gad gaduc* (H 242.19 = CBT VII, no. 6.27n.). The n. to CBT V, no. 1.107 suggests that the meaning of *tarw catuc* is 'armed warrior' or the equivalent. But I adhere to my original tentative translation of this figurative phrase, for which I was first indebted to a suggestion made to me by Professor Thomas Jones; the basic meaning of *caddug* is '(protective) covering' hence 'armour'. On *tarw* 'bull' as an epithet for a warrior, both here and in the following triad, see Anne Ross (PCB 306), who compares the mythical role of the bull in the Irish *Táin Bó Cúalnge* and elsewhere.

Loth comments on *caddug* in a note on the passage quoted above from H 260 (RC XXIX, p. 23) 'ce mot a sûrement ici et dans beaucoup de passages la valeur de *combat*. C'est un sens métaphorique comme celui d'un grand nombre de termes similaires'. A description of battle given in an Irish tale helps to reconcile the two meanings of 'combat' and 'fog' in this tale: it is said that in the press and fury of the contest no two persons could recognize each other, because of the wind-driven blood (Todd, *Cogadh Gaedhel re Gallaibh*, London, 1867, p. 182). If this is the meaning of *cad gaddug*, the *mygedorth* ('battle-fog') of Gwenddolau in triad 44 may be compared. But *cad* can mean 'host' as well as 'battle', and both the triad and the occurrences of the word as used by the *Gogynfeirdd* suggest that *cad gaddug* is an epithet parallel to *tarw caddug*, i.e. 'protector of a host' and 'bull-protector'. In a defective line in the Llywarch Hen poetry (CLlH no. I.14b), which Ifor Williams emends as [*cat g*]athuc *ny techas*, the term *cat gathuc* (= *gaddug*) could either be intended as an epithet for Gwên ap Llywarch, 'host-protector'—or else the whole line could mean figuratively 'he fled not the battle-fog'. In view of the way in which *cad caddug* is employed in the triad and in early poetry, the first alternative seems the more likely of the two. With this triad celebrating three descendants of *Coel Hen* (see n.), cf. the eulogy of the same clan in the triad *Trychan cledyf Kynuverchyn* (App. II, no. 7).

7. Tri Tharw 6nben Enys Prydein:

Elinwy mab Cadegyr,
A Chynhaual mab Argat,
Ac Auaon mab Talyessin.
Tri meib beird oedynt ell tri.

7. Three Bull-Chieftains of the Island of Britain:

Elinwy son of Cadegr,
and Cynhafal son of Argad,
and Afaon son of Taliesin.
The three of them were sons of bards (*or* 'bards').

Manuscripts: 16, 45, 47, 50, WR, 51, NLW, DC, Cwrt. 3, BL[2].
7. Tri thaer unben 47, unpen NLW, vnben DC, ynpen RW.
a. Elin6r 45, cadeir 45, kategyr 47, Elmwr mab Cadeir V, 45 Elmwy RW.
b. a chynnhaval 51, a Chynhafal Cwrt. ap Argad 51, NLW.
c. Adaon WR, aua6n 47, Addaon 51, Cwrt. Talessin 45.
d. WR, 51, NLW, DC, Cwrt., BL, *omit*.

---

tarw. For *tarw* see previous triad and no. 63 below, and for the *Unben* series of triads (nos. 7–10) cf. p. lxxxix above.

tri meib beird. 'Three bards' would be a possible alternative meaning; cf. *mab aillt*, *mab llên*, *mab claf*, etc., and n. to triad 10 below.

8. Tri Lledyf 6nben Enys Prydein:

Llywarch Hen mab Elidir Lledanwyn,
A Manaw(ydan) mab Llyr Lledyeith,
A Gwga6n Gwron mab Peredur mab Elifer Gosgor(d)ua6r.

(Ac y sef acha6s y gelwit (y) rei hynny yn (l)ledyf vnbyn: wrth na cheissint gyuoeth, ac na allei neb y ludyas vdunt.)

8. Three Prostrate ('Humble') Chieftains of the Island of Britain:

Llywarch the Old son of Elidir Llydanwyn,
and Manawydan son of Llŷr Half-Speech,
and Gwgon Gwron son of Peredur son of Eliffer of the Great Retinue.

(And this is why those were called 'Prostrate Chieftains': because they would not seek a dominion, and nobody could deny it to them.)

Manuscripts: 16, 45, 47, 50, WR, 51, 240, BL[1], C 6, NLW, DC, Cwrt. 3, NLW Addl. 37B, BL[2].

8. Tri tharw unbenn 50, tri tharw unben C 6.

a. Lowarch hen C 6, Llowarch 240. Elidyr Lydanwyn 45, Elidyr llydanwyn 47, 50.

b. manawdyan 16, manawydan WR, 51, manawydyan 45, manawedan 47, Mynwedan 50, Maddian NLW, DC. ap llyr WR, llyr lledyeith 45, lletieith 47, 50, ar ail fu fynawdan ap llvr llediaith C 6.

c. gwgon gwron WR, paredur 47, perdur ap eliffer 51, predyn C 36, RW, predur NLW, prydyr C 6. gosgoruavr 16, gosgordua6r 45, 47, 50, gosgorthvawr RW. WR *omit*.

d. *supplied by* WR. na cheissynt R. 47, 50, C 6, NLW, *omit*. am na cheissynt gyvoeth yny byd. ac na allei neb i lessteir udunt os mynnynt 51, y gelwit hwynt velly achos na cheisynt hwy gyfoeth, ac ny allai neb y lyddias yddynt BL[1], 240, Cwrt.

On this triad see introduction, pp. xxiii–xxiv, lxxiii, and cf. EWSP 61–3.

lledyf. GPC 2139: 'humble, downcast, yielding', etc. 'Unassuming' would also be appropriate here. It is clear from the reference in *Manawydan* to the hero as *trydyd lledyf unben* (PKM 49.12) that the scribe understood *lleddf* here as denoting a person who makes little or no resistance when others forcibly deprive him of his territorial rights, as Caswallawn deprived Manawydan: 'passive' is the translation suggested by W. J. Gruffydd (*Rhiannon*, p. 82). The explanation given to this epithet in WR's version of the triad coincides with the interpretation given to it in the *Pedeir Keinc* (p. 227). But *lleddf* in this sense is hardly an epithet which could properly be applied to Llywarch Hen: though he was deprived of his lands, like Manawydan, he certainly was not 'passive' in his resistance, but sent out his sons in turn to fight for their inheritance against the English invaders. I conclude therefore that the explanation which WR gives to the triad is a deduction based on Manawydan's story as given in the *Mabinogi*, and that the scribe who originally made it was ignorant of the true meaning of *lleddf*. The epithet occurs in the *Gododdin*, where it is used with a meaning which is relevant to its occurrence in the triad: *ef gwneei gwyr llydw a gwragedd gwydw kynn oe agheu* 'he laid men *low* and made women widows before his death' (CA ll. 264, 273, and n.). 'Subdued by misfortune' is another possible meaning of *lleddf* in the triad. In the cases of both Llywarch Hen and Manawydan the misfortunes which brought them low consisted in deprivation of the territorial inheritance to which they were entitled. With regard to Gwgon Gwron, the allusion can only be interpreted in the light of what the tale of *Peredur* tells us about his father 'Eliffer of the Great Retinue', one of the sixth-century princes of the North who, like Llywarch, may well have had his lands subjected to the pressure of the advancing English (see n. to *Peredur*[2] under Personal Names).

Ifor Williams interpreted *lleddf* both in the triad, and in *Manawydan*, as meaning 'Humble Lord(s)' PKM 227–8, although he recorded the older meaning of *lleddf* in its pl. form *llydw* as 'low' in CA n. to l. 264. Eurys Rowlands (LlC VI, pp. 231–2) also advocates 'humble' as the meaning in the triad, with the sense of 'not enforcing their hereditary claims to territory'. He offers an ingenious alternative suggestion to my own concerning the *genesis* of the triad, to the effect that it was evolved *circa* 850 with the purpose of strengthening Rhodri Mawr's claim to rule Powys, by asserting that his claim was even stronger on the side of his father, the descendant of Llywarch Hen, than it was on that of his mother (or his grandmother) Nest, (see EWGT p. 151 and B XIX, p. 218) who was the representative of the old Powys dynasty of Cadell. The point which was thereby emphasized was that Llywarch—like Manawydan—was 'humble' because he did not press his claim to an inheritance to which he was nevertheless entitled by right of descent. This might suggest that the relocalization in Powys of an originally North-British story concerning Llywarch and his reluctance to press his claims became transferred to Powys either at the time of Rhodri's accession, or at a slightly earlier date, in order to support this claim. I would add that this interpretation would have the further recommendation of firmly linking the triad to a small group—nos. 60, 65, and 69—which on internal evidence all clearly emanate from Powys. The question of Rhodri Mawr's descent and the legitimacy of his claim to rule Gwynedd have been frequently discussed, most recently by P. Sims-Williams, WHR 17, pp. 18–19 and J. Rowland in EWSP 61–3.

9. Tri 6nben Llys Arthur:

> (Gobrwy) mab Echel 6ordwytwll,
> a Chadr(i)eith mab Portha6r Gadw,
> a Fleudur Flam.

9. Three Chieftains of Arthur's Court:

> Gobrwy son of Echel Mighty-Thigh,
> Cadr(i)eith ('Fine-Speech') son of Porthawr Gadw,
> and Ffleudur Fflam ('Flame').

Manuscripts: 16, 45, 47, WR, 51, NLW, DC, Cwrt. 3, BL[2].

9. Tri ynben lhys brenhin Arthyr C 6, RW.

a. Govrowy 16, Goron6y 45, Gobr6y 47, Goronw W, Gron6 R, 51. Echell vordvytvll 45, mord6yt6ll 47.

b. Chadreith 16, 45, a chatdeirieith m. porthavr gado 47, porthuawr gadu 45; W *substitutes* a Chaydyrleith ap seidi, a Chaedyrieith vab Seidi R, a chadrlaith ap sseidi 51, ap Sanddi Cwrt.

c. a phleidur fflam 45, a phlewd6r fflam 47, a fleudwr flam ap godo WR.

This triad is interesting as it represents the only instance in the Early Version of TYP in which the introductory *llys Arthur* formula is employed in place of the older *ynys prydein* formula (see introduction, p. lxvii). For an instance of this formula in the WR version cf. triads 18 W, 65 below, and in later texts triads 73, 74, and Appendix IV. It is tempting to believe that the source of this triad lies in a written text of *Culhwch ac Olwen*, where each of the three names are to be found in the list of warriors present at Arthur's court (CO ll. 182–3, 195, 293—with the variant *Cas mab saidi* in WR's text of the second name). Not one of the three names recurs in the same form elsewhere in TYP, but the name *Cadyrieith uab Porthawr Gandwy* occurs in *Geraint* (R. L. Thomson (ed.), *Gereint uab Erbin* (DIAS, 1997), ll. 66, 405 etc.).

10. Tri 6nben Deiuyr a Brennych:

Gall mab Disgyfdawt,
Ac Ysgafnell mab Disgyfdawt,
A Diffydell mab Disgyfdawt.
Tri meib beird oedynt ell tri.

10. Three Chieftains of Deira and Bernicia:

Gall son of Disgyfdawd,
and Ysgafnell son of Disgyfdawd,
and Diffydell son of Disgyfdawd.
The three of them were sons of bards (*or* 'bards').

Manuscripts: 16, 45, 47, NLW, DC, BL[2].

10. Deiwyr a Brynaich NLW, deivvyr DC, Brynych 45, Bryneich 47.

a. ar gwr hwnnw R, Call NLW, Disgyuedavt 45, dyskyfda6t 47, NLW, DC, Dysgyfedawc V *throughout*.

b. ysgwnell DC, NLW.

c. Diffedell NLW, DC.

10 W. (fo. 56*r*) Tri Vnben Deiuyr a Bryneic(h), a thri beird oedynt, a thri meib Dissynynda6t, a wnaethant y Teir Mat Gyfla6an:

Diffeidell ap Dissynynda6t, a lada6t G6rgi Gar6l6yt. A'r G6r(i) h6nn6 a ladei gelein beunyd (o'r) Kymry, a d6y pob Sad6rn rac llad vn y Sul;

Sgafynell ap Dissynynda6d, a lada6d Edelflet Ffleissa6c vrenhin Lloegyr;

Gall ap Dissynynda6t, a lada6d deu ederyn G6endoleu, a oedynt yn kad6 y eur (a'e) aryant; a deudyn a yssynt (beunyt) yn eu kinia6, a'r gymint arall yn eu k6ynnos.

10 W. Three Chieftains of Deira and Bernicia, and they were three bards, and three sons of Dissynyndawd, who performed the Three Fortunate Slayings;

Diffeidell son of Dissynyndawd, who slew Gwrgi Garwlwyd ('Rough-Grey'). That man used to slay every day one of the Cymry, and two every Saturday so as not to slay one on the Sunday;

Sgafnell son of Dissynyndawd who slew Edelfled Ffleisawg ('Twister') king of Lloegr;

Gall son of Dissynyndawd who slew the two Birds of Gwenddolau, who were guarding his gold and his silver: two men they used to eat for their dinner, and as much again for their supper.

Manuscripts: WR, 51, NLW (second version), BL[2] (second version), Cwrt. 3.

10 W. *Words in brackets supplied by* R. Dei6r a brynaich 51. Tri map dysyndawd. a wnaethant y tair kyflavan NLW, Disyfyndawd MW *throughout*, dysyndawd RW.

a. Diffeidell R, 51, Diofaiddel Cwrt., Maddistell NLW, Disyfundawd Cwrt. garwlwyd 51, Garlwyd Cwrt., Gwre g. lhwyd RW. or Cembry Cwrt., a laddai Cembro NLW. bop Sadwr R, dduw ssadwrn 51, dros dri Sul NLW.

b. Sgafnell R, yssgafnell 51, Gafynnell Cwrt., Gasymelh C 36, RW, Gafynnell NLW. ap dysyndod NLW. edelfflet R, 51. ffleissiawg 51, Edelffled Laisiawc Cwrt. NLW *omits.*

c. G6all R, 51, Kulh C 36, Calh RW, Gall ap dysyndod NLW. disgyfeddawd Cwrt. y rei oedynt R, y rrai hyny a oeddynt 51. gymmeint R, gymaint 51. y rhai oeddynt yn gadw ei aur ai rai harian NLW.

Cf. triad 32: W has combined triads 10 and 32 into a single triad. See nn. to triad 32, and with *Tri meib beird* cf. triad 7 and n.

In a review of the 1961 edition of this book in *Medium Aevum* XXXI, p. 146, D. Simon Evans drew attention to a number of instances in TYP in which a pl. verb occurs in an affirmative relative clause in which the relative is subject, as here in *a oedynt, a wnaethant* (W). Cf. the similar construction in triads 29, 30, 33, 36, 44, 62, 68, 70. This, he argues, is not a native construction, but is one which characterizes translated works, and its occurrence is normally regarded as betraying Latin influence. On this point see further D. S. Evans, 'Concord in Middle Welsh', SC VI, pp. 42–56. W's *a thri beird oedynt* indicates that the Early Version's *tri meib* (= *tri mab o feirdd) oedynt i beird* should probably be interpreted as 'three bards' rather than 'three sons of bards'.

11. Tri Gwa(y)6rud Beird Enys Prydein:

Trist6ard bard 6ryen,
A Dygynnelw bard Ewein mab 6ryen,
Ac Auan 6erdic bard Catwalla6n mab Catuan.

11. Three Red-Speared Bards of the Island of Britain:

Tristfardd, bard of Urien,
and Dygynnelw, bard of Owain son of Urien,
and Afan Ferddig ('little bard'), bard of Cadwallawn son of Cadfan.

Manuscripts: 16, 45, 47, 50, WR, 51, 252, C 6, NLW, DC (two versions), Cwrt. 3, BL[2].

11. gwavrud 16, gway6rud 45, 47, g6ae6 rud WR, 51, BL[2] *all omit* beird, druy beirdd DC, gwarthrud 50, gwagfardd 252, gwrthruddfardd C 6, gwawdrvyveirth NLW, gwawdruydd beirdd BL[1]. WR, 47, 51, *omit* beird.

a. tristuard 45, 47, Tristuarth barth Yrien RW, dristfardd yr hwn oedd fardd vrien rreged ap kynfarch C 6, uryen reget 47. WR *substitute* ac arouan uard seleu ap kynan; Aro6an 51, a Rovan Cwrt., Alan 252. selen ap kynan 51, selyf ap kynon 252, Auan vardd Selau ap Kynan DC.

b. dygynel6 45, 47, 50, degynel6 WR, RW, dygynlew 51, dygyn Alw 252, a ddigefelw C 6. Ywein 45, W, Ywain DC, Owein R, Owain C 6, NLW, 51, Owen 252, barth Owen RW. WR, 45, 51, *omit* mab Vryen. ap Erion 252.

c. A mian uerdic 45, auan vedic WR, 51, a veddic Cwrt., avan vyrdic 47, avan verdic 50, Avan veredig NLW, RW, Afan wledig 252, Auan Uerdeic, A. wledic DC, Mian Ferdic V, Catwallaw 45, ac auanfardd bardd kyswallawn C 6, barth K. RW.

d. 45 *adds from end of following triad in exemplar*: a Ryhavt eil morgant.

---

gwa(y)6rud. Support for Pen. 16's reading *gwavrud* as the original form may be had from CA 1. 1220 *guaurud rac ut eidin*, in addition to LlDC no. 18.189n., *guawrut grut aten*. In a note in B XXII, p. 351 Thomas Jones cites both these occurrences of *gwawrudd* (though without comparing the triad), and while admitting the possibility of a compound *gwawr* + *udd*, or *gwawr* + *rudd* 'lordly/red-stained (ones)' or 'hero lords' suggests that both forms may be corruptions of the old pl. form *gu(aiu)awr (r)ut*—which in the case of the *englyn* in LlDC no. 18.189 would have the advantage of supplying the extra syllable required. However this may be, the occurrence of these two examples of *gwawrudd* in early sources seems sufficient to recommend the Early Version's *gwavrud* as the original form of this word, though this was early misunderstood by a succession of copyists as signifying the more familiar *gwaywrud(d)* 'red-speared'. G 604 and GPC 1607 favour this interpretation of all instances cited as *gwaywrudd*. For further instances of *(g)wae(w)rut*, see Owain Cyfeiliog, CBT II, no. 14.29n. (citing further examples of *gway(w)rut* by the *Gogynfeirdd*). With respect to the import of this triad, it is perhaps significant that both W and R and later MSS. omit from their text the word *beird*.

According to the Laws the duty of the *bardd teulu* was to sing to the *teulu* when preparing for battle, LlB 22.23–5: *ac or byd darpar ymlad arnunt, canet y canu a elwir 'Vnbeinyaeth Prydein' racdunt* 'if they are preparing for battle, let him sing before them the song which is called "The Monarchy of Britain" '. (It has been suggested that this may have been *Armes Prydein*—cf. D. Jenkins, *Hywel Dda: The Law*, pp. 227–8, though this can be no more than mere speculation.) Yet, if it were the common practice for all bards to go with the warriors to battle, it would hardly be a practice to have been singled out for comment in a triad. Among the *Gogynfeirdd*, Cynddelw and others composed as occasion required, either as *pencerdd* or as *bardd teulu*, and the same could have been true of Aneirin and Taliesin in an earlier period. The allusion in the triad could therefore be to other early bards who were regarded as having combined both functions. Or, if the reading of Pen. 16 and other manuscripts as 'hero lords' is the original one, these perhaps were bards who were of noble birth, just as the following triad (no. 12 below) in contrast to triad 11 names three princes who practised the bardic craft. (But WR's reading, by omitting *beird* would, if it be the original one, preclude the intention of such a contrasting pair of triads in nos. 12 and 13.)

Pen. 16, fo. 50*v*

12. Tri O6er6eird Enys Prydein:

Arthur,
A Chatwalla6n mab Catuan,
A Rahaut eil Morgant.

12. Three Frivolous (Amateur?) Bards of the Island of Britain:

Arthur,
and Cadwallawn son of Cadfan,
and Rahawd son of Morgant.

Manuscripts: 16, 50, R, 51, Cwrt. 3 (two versions).
12. ouer uard R, overveirdd 50, o6er6ardd 51.
c. Raawt R Ryawd V Cwrt. 1, Arawt 50, Arawdd ap Morgan Cwrt. 2.

---

o6er6eird. Perhaps 'scurrilous bards' (GPC 2630) or 'wandering poets', equating *oferfeirdd* with *clerwyr*, and with the *ofer gerddorion* referred to in the *Trioedd Cerdd*: *Tri over gerddor: klerwr, a bardd y blawd, a hudol* (GP 136, 151). The role of the *clêr* is contrasted with that of the *prydydd* in that it included satire: *kanys ar glerwr y perthyn goganu, ac agloduori, chloduori, a gwneuthur kewilid a gwaradwyd, ac ar prydyd y perthyn kanmawl, a chloduori, a gwneuthur clod, a llawenyd, a gogonyant* 'since to the *clerwr* belongs satire, and dispraise, and doing shame and dishonour; and to the *prydydd* belongs eulogy, and honour, and the making of praise, and joy, and glory' (ibid., 35). The older types of *englyn* (*ynglyn o'r hen ganiad*) were classed as *over vessurau* (ibid., 113) and were regarded as suitable for the purposes of satire and ribald songs (CD § 576). Dafydd ap Gwilym refers to himself mock-disparagingly as an *oferfardd* (GDG no. 42.11); here the meaning is merely 'poor poet'. For further instances of Arthur's traditional prowess as an *oferfardd* one may refer to the *englyn* on Dillus Varvawc's beard with which Arthur is credited in *Culhwch ac Olwen* (CO ll. 978–80), which is said to have given mortal offence to Cai. *Englynion yr Eryr* (*Blodeugerdd*, no. 31) opens with Arthur's alleged declaration *Es ryfedaf kann wyf bard* 'I marvel, since I am a bard', etc. Another satirical *englyn* is attributed to Arthur in the account of the Giants in Peniarth MS. 118, p. 140 (ed. *Cy*. XXVIII = C. Grooms, *The Welsh Giants*, p. 310): in which the following is Arthur's reply to a certain Cribwr Gawr, of Cefn Cribwr in Glamorgan, who has reproached him for killing his three sisters:

Cribwr cymer dy gribeu
A Phaid a'th gostec lidieu
O daw imi gynyg—dieu
A gawsant wy, a gey ditheu.

'Cribwr, take your combs / and cease your churlish anger. / If I can make the attempt—surely / what they have had, you shall have too.'

For a further poetic effort attributed to Arthur, cf. triad 18 (W) below. It is to be noted that the three characters named in triad 12 were all princes, or sons of princes, that is like the twelfth-century poet-princes Hywel ab Owain Gwynedd and Owain Cyfeiliog, they were not professional bards, but amateurs: hence, perhaps, the application to them of the epithet *ofer*, lit. 'vain, futile, dissolute' etc. (GPC 2630). The suggestion that *ofer* has reference to the amateur status of the persons named in the triad draws support from the fact that Guto'r Glyn quotes a variant version of it, in which Trystan and Llywarch Hen are named along with Arthur (probably because these two, like Arthur, were regarded as princes to whom extant *englynion* have been attributed, *not* professional bards). Guto adds the name of the subject of his *marwnad*, Einion ap Gruffudd, as a suitable fourth to the triad:

Trywŷr a ddug tair awen
Y tri oferfardd hardd hen;
Arthur aestew a Thrystan,
A Llywarch, pen cyfarch cân.
Pedwerydd prydydd, pe rhaid,
Fu Einion, nef i'w enaid!
(GGl no. LXIV.55–60)

'Three men who bore three poetic gifts, / the three fine old Amateur Bards: / Arthur of stout shield, and Trystan, / and Llywarch, lord of address in song. / A fourth poet, if need be, / was Einion, heaven to his soul.'

But elsewhere *oferfardd, oferwr*, etc., seems to be a general term applied to the 'unprofessional' classes of poets, and to be broadly synonymous with *clerwr*, as Morris-Jones pointed out (CD 352–6; see also GPC 2630 on *oferfardd* 'wandering poet').

Gruffudd Llwyd knew of the triad, since he describes Arthur as an *oferfardd*, in the context of his allusion to the story of Rhita Gawr in the *Brut* (BD 170):

Gwn nad haws cael, gafael Gai,
Ym marf y mab a'm eurai . . .
Un blewyn rhudd-felyn rhad,
Gynt nag y cad, tyfiad hardd,
O farf Arthur oferfardd.
(IGE[2] 128.11–16.)

'I know that it is not easier to get, with the grasp of Cai / in the beard of the lad who honoured me . . . / freely a single tawny hair; any sooner than might be obtained—a fair growth— / (one) from the beard of Arthur (Frivolous) Amateur Bard.'

Triads 11 (see n.) and 12 may perhaps be taken as forming a contrasting pair: just as the *gwaywrud beird* were bards who also took part in fighting (the proper occupation of princes)—so the *oferfeirdd* were princes who were not above occupying themselves with poetry. Cf. EWSP 356, and n. to triad 67, *Tri Eur Gryd.* For similar pairs of triads, see introduction, p. lxxxix.

On the *ofer fesurau*, which were, in some cases 'caricatures', in others personal adaptations of *englynion* and other established metres made by poets from the late fifteenth century onwards, see J. Morris-Jones, CD 352–6. Eurys Rowlands points out (LlC VI, p. 232) that in the later period *oferedd* may have denoted all bardic compositions other than the highest, which was praise-poetry—the poets' patrons were as likely as the poets themselves to compose verses which could well be described as *oferedd*, for the purposes of entertainment. Hence Dafydd Johnston's apt interpretation of *oferfardd* as 'amateur (poet)' proposed in his lecture 'Canu ar ei fwyd ei hun' (Darlith Agoriadol, Prifysgol Cymru, Abertawe, 1997), p. 2. *Oferfeirdd* and *oferwyr* were not necessarily disparaging terms, as was pointed out earlier by Eurys Rowlands, but could be used of all poetic compositions other than formal praise-poetry.

13. Tri Chynweissyat Enys Prydein:

Carada6c mab Bran,
a Chaurdaf mab Karadauc,
Ac Ewein mab Maxen Wledic.

13. Three Chief Officers / (Stewards) of the Island of Britain:

Caradawg son of Brân,
and Cawrdaf son of Caradawg,
and Owain son of Maxen Wledig.

Manuscripts: 16, 45, 47, WR, 51, Cwrt. 3.

13. Tri chynweissat 45, chynweissieit WR, kynnhwyssiad 51.

a. WR, 51 *substitute* G6ydar ap run ap Beli; Gwyddia Cwrt.

b. a Cha6rdaf 45, a cha6rdaf ap karada6c W, kradawc R, mab karada6c vreichvras 47, Caradawc frechfras V.

c. Owein 45, R, 47, 51, ywein W.

This triad is alluded to in the poem *Kadeir Teyrnon*, BT 34.24: *Pwy y tri chynweissat, a werchetwis gwlat?* 'Who are the three Chief Officers, who guarded the land?' See introduction, p. lxxxviii; PKM 39.5–6; and M. Haycock, CMCS 33, pp. 29–30.

cynweissyat (< *cynt* + *gwas* + *iad*). PKM 192; GPC 803; note the pl. form in WR. In *Branwen, cynueissat* is equated with *tywyssog* (PKM 39.6). In the Laws, it is said to be the duty of the *macuiueid et chengueiseid* 'youths and officers' to prepare the fire in the court (AL ii, 895; quoted PKM 192). Cf. also the form *kynweis* (pl. of *kynwas*) CA l. 1448, and the proper name *Conguas*, LL 173.28.

According to *Branwen,* seven was the number of the *cynweissieid* who were left in charge of Britain during the absence of Bendigeidfran and his army in Ireland. In the story, as in the triad, the leader of these was Caradawg fab Brân: *Y seith hynny a drigwys yn seith kynueissat y synyaw ar yr ynys honn, a Chradawc uab Bran yn benhaf kynweisyat arnunt* (PKM 39.5–7). Thus, in naming Caradawg, Pen. 16 provides a more satisfactory version of the triad than does W, since no story survives about Gwydar ap Rhun ab Beli. Although the reference in the triad is likely to refer to an earlier and pre-literary form of *Branwen*, it seems probable that the redactor of the tale in its present form knew of the existence of the triad but deliberately increased the number of the *cynweissieid* to seven (probably in order to link the story with the place-name Bryn Seith Marchawc, between Rhuthin and Corwen (PKM 191), but also because seven as well as three was a conventional number; see n. to *Camlan*, triad 59). On the other hand, the inclusion in the triad of the sons of

Caradawg and of Maxen Wledig may denote the existence of two other stories about *cynweissieid*, outside the framework of *Branwen*. If so, the existence of the triad is not necessarily incompatible with Caradawg being the leader of a group of seven *cynweissieid* within the tale of *Branwen* itself. It is however significant that the names of the six other *cynweissieid* are almost unknown elsewhere: *Sef seithwyr oedynt, Cradawc uab Bran, ac Euehyd Hir, ac Unic Glew Yscwyd, ac Idic uab Anarawc Walltgrwn, a Fodor uab Eruyll, ac Wlch Minasgwrn, a Llashar uab Llayssar Llaesgygwyt* (PKM 39.1–7). In favour of my suggestion that the number of the *cynweissieid* in *Branwen* has been increased to 'seven' in order to conform with the place-name Bryn Seith Marchawc, I take this opportunity of advocating a very simple emendation (based upon the most common of all scribal errors) to the text of PKM 38.25–6: I suggest that *ac eu seith marchawc* should read *ac en* (= *yn*) *seith marchawc*. The *seith marchawc* are in fact identical with the *seith cynweissyat*, whose names are then given. Apart from Caradawg fab Brân, the names of the *cynweissieid* in the tale are almost entirely unknown outside PKM: *Hyueid (Euehyd) Hir* bears a name which is recorded in CA l. 56, while the name of *Anaraw(t) Walltgrwm* is found in the Jesus Genealogies, no. 19 (EWGT 46) as *Anarawd gwalchrwn*, corresponding with *Anarant* in the corresponding Harleian Genealogy no. 4 (EWGT 10). He appears in these sources as a member of the dynasty from which Merfyn Frych descended, a dynasty which was associated with the Isle of Man. See Glyn Jones, 'Idic fab Anarawt Walltgrwn: Cynweisiad', B XXV, pp. 14–19. (Another of the group, *Unic Glew Yscwyd* is possibly a variant of *Glew fab Yscawt*, CO l. 117.)

The triad is also referred to in *Lludd a Llefelys*. After it has been said that *Dinas Ffaraon Dandde* was the earlier name for *Dinas Emrys*, the comment is added: *Trydyd cynweissat uu hwnnw a torres y gallon anniuyged* 'he (i.e. *Ffaraon Dandde*) was one of the Three Chief Officers, who broke his heart from bewilderment' (RM 98.13; on *anniuyged*, see GPC 141 'shock, bewilderment'). Little further is known of *Ffaraon Dandde* (on the name, see n. to *Llyr*[1] *Lledyeith* under Personal Names and B. F. Roberts, *Cyfranc Lludd a Llefelys*, pp. xxxvi–xxxvii), but it seems likely that the redactor of the tale has been influenced in his reference by a knowledge of *Branwen*, where Caradawg fab Brân is described first as a *cynweissiad* and then as *trydyd dyn a dorres y gallon o aniuyget* (PKM 46.8). This second triad has not been preserved in any early source, but see triad 95 below. Evidently Ffaraon Dandde was named in it as well as Caradawg fab Brân, and thus the allusion to it reminded the redactor of *Lludd a Llefelys* of the other triad in which Caradawg fab Brân figured, and he was inspired to include Ffaraon Dandde in this as well. But the allusion shows that the *cynweissieid* were known to him as three in number, not as seven. (The citation of the two triads is a gloss on the original text of *Lludd a Llefelys*, as is shown by the fact that it is absent from the story as given in the *Bruts*; see EC I, p. 270.)

TRIOEDD YNYS PRYDEIN 13

It may be significant that each of the three *cynweissieid* named in the triad could be described as the son of a father more famous in Welsh tradition than himself, and that two of these 'fathers' traditionally led away the troops from Britain. On this point, see further J. K. Bollard, 'Myth and Tradition in the Four Branches of the Mabinogi', CMCS 6, p. 81, reproduced in C. N. Sullivan (ed.), *The Mabinogi: A Book of Essays* (Garland, N.Y., 1996), ch. 13, pp. 277–302.

14. Tri Llyghessa6c Enys Prydein:

Gereint mab Erbin,
a G6enwynwyn mab Naf,
a March mab Meirchya6n.

14. Three Seafarers / Fleet Owners of the Island of Britain:

Geraint son of Erbin,
and Gwenwynwyn son of Naf,
and March son of Meirchiawn.

Manuscripts: 16, 45, 47, WR, 51, NLW, Cwrt. 3, BL².

14. llyghesswr W, llynghesswr R, 51, lhyngeswyr NLW, RW, llynghessawl Cwrt.
b. Gvenvynvyn ap nav WR, naw 51, NLW, Cwrt., Haw C 36, RW.
c. Meircha6n 45, meircha6n 47, meirthion W, meirchyon R, meirchionn 51.

---

tri llyghessa6c. Cf. GPC 2268, and Ir. *loingsech* 'sea-farer, pirate, exile', as in the proper name Labraid *Loingsech* (EIHM 106n.), borne by an early traditional ruler of Ireland whose story bears a curious resemblance to that of *March ap Meirchiawn* (see n. under Personal Names). In W. *llynghessawc* may well be capable of holding the same variety of meanings as the cognate Ir. *loingsech*. The question remains as to the particular relevance of the epithet to the characters named in the triad. Both Geraint and March were represented as early rulers in south-western Britain, and it seems possible that in naming them the triad holds a reference to the contact maintained by sea with Brittany by these princes. Traditions of Geraint were certainly known in Brittany as early as the ninth century (see G. H. Doble, *St. Gerent*, Cornish Saints Series, no. 41, pp. 7–9; cf. Jean Marx, 'Monde Brittanique et Matière de Bretagne', EC X, p. 482), and he was a ruler of the insular kingdom of Dumnonia, which may be assumed to have maintained some connection with the Breton kingdom of the same name during the early period, although these are nowhere very clearly stated. According to *Liber Landavensis*, the inhabitants of Wales and of Brittany were recognized to be *unius populi et unius linguae* 'one people and (of) one language' (LL 181.15). A kind of dual rule during the first two centuries of the Breton settlement seems to be implied by certain passages in the Breton Saints' Lives; see in particular the Life of *St Léonore*, which describes Rhiwal, the founder of the Breton kingdom of Dumnonia as *dux Britonum ultra et citra mare usque ad mortem* (*Bib. Nat. MS. Lat.* 5317, fo. 73 v; quoted LBS I, p. 46. Cf. further the Life of *St Hervé*, ed. A. de la Borderie, ch. 2; SEBH 122–3, n. 6). Geraint's capital is possibly to be associated with the site of the present-day village of Gerrans on the south-west coast of Cornwall—a village whose name must commemorate either Geraint ab Erbin or one of his successors, also named Geraint. A few miles to the east above the Fowey estuary is Castle Dore, which is presumed to have been a fortress of the Dumnonian kings between the fifth and eighth centuries (see *Journal of the Royal Institution of Cornwall*, new series, vol. I, App. 1951). But since the supposed connection between the King Mark of the romances and Castle Dore appears to be based only on Wrmonoc's statement in the Life of *St Paul Aurelian* that Marcus was another name for *Quonomorius* (Conomorus), it seems to go as far as to advocate a connection here. Traditions of both Conomorus and March have survived in Brittany (see Bartrum, WCD 141–2 and Fleuriot, HLCB I, 127–9), but the two are never identified, and have in common only the evil character imputed to each of them. I consider that March ap Meirchiawn is to be associated with Glamorgan rather than with Cornwall; but it should be remembered that this area of south Wales played a part in the Breton migration whose importance was second only to that of the western peninsula of Britain. On Castle Dore see O. J. Padel, CMCS 1, pp. 53–80, and AW 240–3 (see n. to *March m. Meirchyawn* under Personal Names).

Cf. Meilyr: *torressid gormes yn llyghessavc* 'he destroyed sea-borne invaders' (H 3.24 = CBT I, no. 3.80n.). With the construction cf. GMW 123, n. 1.

15. Teir Llyghes Kynniweir Enys Prydein:

Llyghes Llawr mab Eiryf,
a Llyghes Di6wng mab Alan,
a Llyghes Solor mab Murthach.

15. Three Roving Fleets of the Island of Britain:

The Fleet of Llawr son of Eiryf,
and the Fleet of Divwng son of Alan,
and the Fleet of Solor son of Murthach.

Manuscripts: 16, 47, R, 51, NLW, Cwrt. 3, BL[2].

15. gynniweir, *g with punctum delens and k added above line in original hand* 16, gynniweir R.

a. Lary R, laryf *altered to* lyr 51, llaryf NLW, Lleryv MW, RW, C 36, llaw Cwrt., Yryf R, 51, Eirif 47, pyr NLW, 252, MW, RW.

b. Dignif R, NLW, Dignaf Cwrt., din6gl 47, dygrif 51, dignyf 252, Difwg V, Digins C 36, MW, RW. Alban 47, V.

c. dolor 47, V, ssolor 51, Solar Cwrt., Soler NLW, RW, Cwrt. Urnach R, wrnach NLW, 51, 252, anvrchath 47, Mwrchath V, soler ap Wenach C 36, Wenach RW.

---

kynniweir 'to attack, muster, hurry to and fro' (GPC 792); D *cynniweir* = *frequentare*. Cf. PKM 82: *yd oed gyniweir ac utkyrn a lleuein yn y wlat yn gynghan* 'there was a mustering and trumpeting and clamour all together throughout the country'.

c. The occurrence of an Irish name (*Murchadh*, see HGVK 54, n. 27) as that of the father of one of the fleet-owners is suggestive. Perhaps all three fleets belonged to Irish raiders, as contrasted with the three British-owned fleets of triad 14. Some of the names may represent corruptions of other Irish names, but with *Di6wng mab Alan* cf. *Digon mab Alar*, CO l. 199, and with *Llawr mab Eiryf* cf. *Llawr eil Erw*, CO l. 217. For *llawr*[2] 'champion, hero' (*llawr* lit. 'one fighting alone'), see GPC 2118 which quotes this example.

16. Tri Gwrduagla6c Enys Prydein:

Riueri mab Tangwn,
a Dina6t Vagla6c,
a Phryder mab Dolor Deiuyr a Brennych.

16. Three Powerful Shepherds of the Island of Britain:

Riueri son of Tangwn,
and Dunawd the Shepherd,
and Pryder (= Care) son of Dolor (= Grief) of Deira and Bernicia.

Manuscripts: 16, 45, 47.
a. Rineri 45, 47, V.
b. dinwaed 45, a chinwaed 47, a Thinwaed V.
c. a phyrder 47. Brynych 45, Bryneich 47.

---

gwrduagla6c. Cf. K. Meyer, *Contributions to Irish Lexicography*, p. 161: *bachlach* Ir. = (i) a shepherd, boor, rustic, and (ii) a cleric. *Bachall* (< L. *baculum*) = 'crook, crozier'. The second meaning given for *bachlach* appears also for W. *baglawc*; the earliest attested example is in a gnomic poem which can probably be dated to the late twelfth century, EWGP VIII, st. 3: *bid gywir baglawg* 'the crozier-bearer is trusty (?)' (ibid., n., p. 46, and introduction, pp. 9–12, on the date of this poem; also *baglog* GPC 249, 1700). *Baellec, belec* 'priest' is found in Breton from the fourteenth century (*Chr. Br.* 189). The reference in the triad is most probably to 'shepherds' in the sense of ecclesiastics, if we are to place any reliance on the very slight clues provided by the names: the possible equation between *Dinawt Vagla6c* (see n.) and Bede's Abbot Dinoot (*Hist. Ecc.* II, 2), combined with the ecclesiastical context of the only other reference to *Pryder mab Dolor Deiuyr a Brennych en e Gogledd* EWGT 63 (56). In favour of the literal meaning, however, is the probability that the triad was originally intended to form a pair with *Tri Gwrdueichyat*, no. 26 below. Both *gwrdfaglawc* and *gwrdfeichiad* are compounds which are unrecorded except in the case of these two triads (GPC 1700–1).

17. Tri Huala6c Enys Prydein:

Katwaladyr 6endigeit,
a Run mab Maelg6n,
a Riwalla6n Wallt Banhadlen.

(WR: ac y sef acha6s y gelwit y g6yr hynny yn hualogyon: 6rth na cheffit meirch a berthynei vdunt, rac eu meint; namyn dodi hualeu eur am eu heg6ydled ar bedreinieu eu meirch tra'e kefneu, a d6y badell eur a dan eu glinieu; ac 6rth hynny y gelwir padellec y glin).

17. Three Fettered Men of the Island of Britain:

Cadwaladr the Blessed,
and Rhun son of Maelgwn,
and Rhiwallawn Broom-Hair.

(And this is why those men were called Fettered: because horses could not be obtained that were suited to them, owing to their size; so they put fetters of gold around the small of their legs, on the cruppers of their horses, behind their backs; and two golden plates under their knees, and because of this the knee is called 'small pan' ('knee-pan').)

Manuscripts: 16, 45, 47, 50, WR, 51, C 6, C 18, DC, Cwrt. 3, BL[2].

17. hualoc eur W, hualo eur R, eurhuala6c 47, Cwrt., eurhualog V, aurhualavvc DC.

a. a chadwaladyr R, a chydwaladr 51.

b. a run a maelgvn W, Ruon 51, maelgvn gvynedd 50, C 6.

c. rialla6n 47, Ruallon 51.

d. *supplied by* WR. y gelwid hwynt yn dri hualoc *altered to* yn hualogion 51, y gelwit hwynt velly Cwrt. meirch uddunt a wassanaetha 51, ai gwasanaethai Cwrt. digon uchel iddynt V. ar bedrein R, 51. drach e6 kefna6 51. Sef y gelwit hwy velly, am na chad meirch digon uchel uddynt, rhac ei hyd a ei maint, namyn rhoi hualau ar ei traed dros bedrenau y meirch a dwy badell aur dan ei gliniau bob un o honyn DC.

---

huala6c 'fettered, shackled' (GPC 1905). Cf. triad 62, *Tri Hualhogeon Deulu* and n. Both triads may derive from a single original. In both it is likely that the explanations of *hualawc*, *-ogyon* given by WR conceal ignorance on the part of the redactors as to the original significance of this word. T. Gwynn Jones (*Aberystwyth Studies* VIII, p. 68n.) offers the suggestion that *hual* here means 'torque'; and some such *insignia* of office as this was evidently attributed to *hual* by Iolo Morganwg; cf. MA, Third Series, 42:

> Tri Hualogion Teyrnedd ynys Prydein: Morgan Mwynfawr o Forgannwg; Elystan Glodrydd rhwng Gwy a Hafren; a Gwaithfoed brenin Ceredigion;

sef eu gelwid felly achaws y gwisgynt hualau yn holl y gwneleint brif deyrnedd ynys Prydein, ac nid *taleithiau*, sef *coronau*.

'They wore *hualau* as the chief princes of Britain used to do, and not *taleithiau*, that is diadems.' Or, according to Iolo's own translation of his Triads, 'They were so-called because each wore the Golden Torques as the *insigne* of sovereignty as did the primitive Sovereigns of the Island of Britain' (see Rachel Bromwich, THSC 1968, p. 318). Cf. the *cadwyn* worn by Cynddylan (CLIH no. XI.5b, 6b), and the *cae* worn by members of Mynyddawg's *gosgordd* (CA l. 21 *et passim*), and by Cadwallawn (B VII, p. 25 l. 42). For *taleithiawc* as an indication of rank cf. triad 21. Among the instances of *hual* cited in CA 350–1, there is one, from the *Gorhoffedd* of Gwalchmai, in which the meaning 'torque' is clearly more suitable than 'fetter': *ywein hael hual dilin* (H 17.7 = CBT I, no. 9.17n.) 'generous Owain of the shining (or 'golden') torque(?)'. In an important note on *troedog aur* (GIG no. III.57), Dafydd Johnston (op. cit., pp. 195–6) cites this triad, together with no. 62 *Tri Hualhogeon Deulu,* as evidence suggesting that the *hual* 'fetter, shackle' was synonymous with the *troedog aur*, and that both denoted *insignia* of the ruling house of Gwynedd. This would fit well with Iolo Morganwg's account, as given above, but is less clearly consistent with the (girl) *troedog* who is associated with Math fab Mathonwy at the opening of *Mabinogi Math.* Cf. Cynddelw to Hywel ab Owain Gwynedd (d. 1170, another prominent member of the Gwynedd dynasty): *Trydyd hualawc huelir yn dygyn* (H 104.5 = CBT IV, no. 6.192)—an allusion which is evidently an echo of this triad. (See n. to triad 29 for a further instance in which Cynddelw demonstrates his knowledge of a pre-existing triad, and quotes dramatically from it.) Again at a later date, Llywelyn ap Gutun may be quoting from the triad, if not from a well-known tradition which it represents: *Un o'r tri, yn wr truan, / Hualog wyf, hoywal gwan*; */ Taliesin, Awstin ystum, / Yng nghefyn Cynfelyn fum*; */ Elffin, gyda chyffin chwyrn, / Maelgwn wrth wasgu'r melgyrn.* (I am indebted to the Bedwyr Lewis Jones for referring me to this quotation in Dafydd Wyn William, 'Y Traddodiad Barddol ym Mhlwyf Bodedern' (University of Wales MA thesis, 1970).)

No other meaning of *hual* than the customary one was known to D (John Davies), who cites *hual* = *compes, pedica, periscelis.* With Dafydd ap Gwilym *hual* has attained its modern meaning of 'fetter': *Hualwyd fi, hoelied f'ais / Hual gofal a gefais* (GDG no. 102.21–2). *Hual* is used for a horse-fetter in AL I, 558: *O bop march a uo hual neu lavhethyr arnav keinnawc a tal.* In connection with W's explanation of the triad it is curious to note that Maelgwn Gwynedd, father of Rhun and ancestor of Cadwaladr, may have been remarkable for his great stature, according to Gildas. Perhaps this characteristic was transmitted to Maelgwn's descendants, and the notorious height of the Gwynedd kings subsequently gave rise to the explanation here given for an epithet whose earlier dynastic significance had become forgotten.

d. am eu hegvydled. GPC 1180 cites *egwyd*, pl. *egwydledd* (with intrusive 'l') 'fetter, shackle', and also 'fetlock, pastern' of horses, quoting this instance from RB under the last.

padellec 'knee-cap' (GPC 2666); GGl no. XLIV.13–14: *Bygythiwyd, tau annwyd teg: Byd oll am dy badelleg.*

18. Tri Chatuarcha6c Enys Prydein:

> Carada6c 6reichuras,
> a Me(n)waed o Arllechwed,
> a Llyr Lluyda6c.

18. Three Battle-Horsemen of the Island of Britain:

> Caradawg Strong-Arm,
> and Me(n)waedd of Arllechwedd,
> and Llŷr of the Hosts.

Manuscripts: 16, 45, 47, 77, C 18, DC, BL[2].

a. a Chariadawc 77, kairadawc RW.

b. Meuwaed 16, menwaed 45, RW, meiwed 47, Menwaydd 77.

c. lluryga6c 47, llwyddawc V, DC, llyrygawc 77.

18. WR. Tri Ann6yl Llys Arthur, a thri Chatwarcha6c. Ac ny mynassant benteulu arnadunt eirioet. Ac y kant Arthur eglyn:

> Sef y6 vyn tri Chat varchawc:
> Mened, a Llud Lluryga6c,
> a Cholouyn Kymry Karada6c.

18 WR. Three Favourites of Arthur's Court, and Three Battle-Horsemen: they never desired a *penteulu* over them. And Arthur sang an *englyn*:

> These are my Three Battle-Horsemen:
> Menedd, and Lludd of the Breastplate,
> and the Pillar of the Cymry, Caradawg.

Manuscripts: WR, 240, BL[1], 47, Cwrt. 3, NLW Addl. 37B.

18 W. chatuarchavc R. mynnassant pennteulu R. englyn R, ac yr tri hynny englyn 47 (*following version of 16 as above*)

a. Sef ynt y tri 47, fy nhri charfarchawc NLW Addl.

b. meiwed 47, Maydd 240, BL[2], Cwrt., Maedd NLW Addl. llyr llurygawc 47, llurugawc R.

c. a cholofyn yn kymry cradavc 47, A cholofn Cambru (Caembrû Cwrt.), Cradawc 240, BM, Cwrt.

---

catuarcha6c. Cf. GPC 378, CA ll. 182–5: *tri* (*si*)*chatvarchawc . . . tri llu llurugawc, tri eur deyrn dorchawc*. (On the link between the triads in the older poetry and those in the extant collections, see introduction, pp. lxxxvii–lxxxix.) The term *catuarchawc* is used by Cynddelw (H 157.17 = CBT III, no. 12.41n.; H 172.15 = CBT IV, no. 5.5n., 90), by Seisyll Bryffwrch (CBT

II, no. 24.32), and by Y Prydydd Bychan (H 250.25 = CBT VII no. 19.13). Possibly in some contexts it may once have held a more precise meaning than is now apparent, denoting some definite office; but the rarity with which the word occurs in the older poetry makes it difficult to feel any certainty about this and it may be merely a general term. It is interesting to find, however, that both in the *Gododdin* and in Cynddelw's *Marwnad Teulu Owein Gwynedd*, *catuarchawc* is employed as parallel to *eurdorchawc* (CBT IV, no. 5.5n.; see further on this my note in M. E. Owen and B. F. Roberts (eds), *Beirdd a Thywysogion* (Caerdydd, 1996), 214–15). Iorwerth ap Madawg, to whom Cynddelw's poem is addressed, is depicted in *Breuddwyd Rhonabwy* as having scornfully rejected the office of *penteulu* offered to him by his brother Madog (BR 1.12–15); see WR's version of the triad, and n. to *penteulu* below. The other instances in which *catuarchawc* is used by the *Gogynfeirdd* give little help in elucidating the term, but cf. the Irish saga *Togail Bruidne Da Derga*, in which the champion Mac Cecht is described as *cathmilid* or 'battle-warrior' to the king Conaire Mór (ed. E. Knott, §§ 27, 88). In later usage *cadfarchog* is merely a term for 'knight'; cf. App. IV, no. 3: *Tri Chadvarchoc Llys Arthur*. On *cadfarch* 'war-horse' see J. Rowland, CMCS 30, pp. 16–17n.

A comparison of the two versions of this triad here printed provides an instructive example of the process of Arthurianization of the triads, see introduction pp. lvii–lviii. The *englyn milwr* attributed to Arthur in WR's version is perhaps older than the prose introduction; cf. EWSP 300, and n. to triad 12 above. Other triads in the form of *englynion* are found in CLlH no. VIII.2, 3, 6, and Ifor Williams suggested (CLlH 187) that these may have belonged to a verse series of triads. With *colofn kymry* cf. *post cad*, triad 5n.

penteulu. The *penteulu* or 'Captain of the Household' was the first of the Twenty-four Court Officials, being the captain of a prince's personal warband or *teulu*. Normally he was a close relative of the prince he served, such as a son or nephew. His perquisites included receiving three pounds yearly from the king, and a horn of liquor at every feast from the queen (LlB 2, 10–11; AL I, 12–14). Owain ab Urien is made Arthur's *penteulu* in *Chwedl Iarlles y Ffynnawn* (ed. R. L. Thomson (1968), l. 818). On the duties and privileges of the *penteulu*, see D. Jenkins, *Hywel Dda: The Law*, pp. 8–11. A further collection of examples of this title will be found in GPC 2761.

19. Tri Galouyd Enys Prydein:

> Greid(y)a6l Galouyd mab E(n)6ael Adrann,
> a Gueir Gwrhyt6a6r,
> a Drystan mab Tallwch.

19. Three Enemy-Subduers of the Island of Britain:

> Greid(y)awl Enemy-Subduer son of E(n)vael Adrann,
> and Gweir of Great Valour,
> and Drystan son of Tallwch.

Manuscripts: 16, 45, 47, WR, 51, 77, 240, BL[1], C 18, NLW, DC, Cwrt. 3, NLW Addl. 37B, BL[2].

19. gallouyd 45, 47, galofydd V, Cwrt., gallovydh C 18, gallouyd W, galovyd R, ssalovydd *altered* to galovydd 51, galovydd 77, glewvryd NLW, glevvuryd DC, glew Vryd RW.

a. Greidi6l galouyd 45, Greidavl galouyd WR, greidiol 51, BL[1], 240, Greidiol Glewfryd NLW, DC. Euvael 16, enuael adran 45, Enwael Aran C 18, *all other manuscripts omit* m. Envael Adrann.

b. Gweir g6rhyt va6r 45, Gwair gyhydlawn 77, Gwawr gwrhytbhawn C 18. WR, 51, NLW, DC, NLW Addl., Cwrt., *substitute* a gwgon gwron. 47 *substitutes* a blathavn mab mvreth.

c. a thrystan 51, Trystan 77, NLW. 47 *omits* m. tallwch.

---

galouyd. This is a complimentary epithet applied by the poets to their patrons. Of the five instances recorded in GPC 1375, three are in poems by Prydydd y Moch (H 280.28; 282.18; 303.22 = CBT V, no. 13.30; 18.22; 19.30); one by Gwalchmai (H 25.22 = CBT I, no. 7.47); and one by Llygad Gŵr (H 217.5 = CBT VII, no. 24.73n.). *Gal* can mean 'enemy' as well as 'enmity' (see CLlH 76); but the second element in the compound is more difficult to ascertain. The name *Greidawl Galldouyd* found in *Culhwch ac Olwen* and *Breudwyt Ronabwy* (CO l. 176; Br Rh. 19.27) favours the belief that this element is *dofydd* 'lord, master' (verb *dofi* 'to tame, subdue'; adjective *dof* 'tame') cf. AP, l. 147: *gwyr gwychyr gwallt hiryon ergyr dofyd* 'furious long-haired men, masters of blows'. 'Lords of hostility' would therefore be a possible interpretation of *gall(d)ouyd. Dofydd* however is most frequently employed with reference to God (see G 385). Morris-Jones notes that a lenited initial *d* in the second element of a compound may be lost (WG 180), and compares the analogous compound *rec douyd* (CO l. 17n.; RM 100.19; *rec douid* LL 127.20), *rec ouyd* (H 127.1 = CBT III, no. 21.43n.; IV, no. 16.34) 'dispenser of gifts'. (As used by the *Gogynfeirdd, rec ouyt* is synonymous with *haelaf*, B XIII, p. 174.) But it should be noted that all versions of the triad, as well as the poems, concur in giving the form *gal(l)ouyd* (*-ouyt, -ouit*). The various possible meanings of *-ofydd* in compounds have been discussed by

Lloyd-Jones, B XV, p. 199. The primary meaning of *ofydd* is 'master of, skilled in' and it is therefore very close in meaning to *dofydd* 'lord, subduer etc.' (GPC 1072); it seems likely that the two words may have fallen together. Lloyd-Jones argues that a further possible meaning in compounds is *anhywaith, anfoesgar* 'harsh, unmannerly' (< *of* 'crude, raw'). Finally the second element in *gallouyd, cad ouyd, llid ouyd*, etc., may be the lenited form of *gofydd* 'afflictor, oppressor'. But it will be seen that this varied range of possible meanings makes little essential difference to the significance of *gall(d)ouyd* as an epithet in early sources.

A possible commentary on the use of the word *galofydd* in reference to Drystan is to be found in the *Ystorya Trystan*, where the hero's battle-fury is such that he passes unharmed through the ranks of his enemies (B V, p. 117 = *Nat. Lib. of Wales Journal* XXII, p. 244; see further AW 216–20; trans. R. L. Thomson in J. Hill (ed.), *The Tristan Legend* (Leeds, 1977), p. 2). In spite of references by the poets to the two other heroes named in the triad, there are no surviving allusions to any martial exploits for which these were particularly distinguished.

20. Tri Ruduoa6c Enys Prydein:

Arthur,
A Run mab Beli,
A Morgant Mwynua6r.

20. Three Red Reapers (Despoilers/Ravagers) of the Island of Britain:

Arthur,
and Rhun son of Beli,
and Morgant the Wealthy.

Manuscripts: 16, 45, WR, 50, 51, NLW, Cwrt. 3, BL[2].

a. rudvodawc 50. WR *substitute*: Llew Llaw Gyffes.

b. **WR** *add*: = ac vn a oed ruduogach no'r tri. Arthur oed y hen6; bl6ydyn ny doy na g6ellt na llysseu y ford y kerdei yr vn o'r tri. a seith mlyned ny doy y ford y kerdei Arthur.

(**WR** *adds trans.*: 'And there was one who was a Red Reaper (Despoiler) greater than all three: Arthur was his name. For a year neither grass nor plants used to come where one of the three would walk, but where Arthur went, not for seven years.')

---

ruduoa6c (< *rhudd* +**boog, boawg*; GPC 3101 *rhuddfaog, rhuddfoog* 'despoiling, plundering' later 'wealthy' cites triad 20 among its illustrative *exempla*). Ifor Williams earlier compared Ir. *boingid* 'cuts, reaps' (CA 277; cf. DIL 'B', 136, b). These three were 'red reapers' or reapers in battle. Cf. the description of Owain ab Urien as *medel galon* 'reaper of enemies' (CT/PT no. X.9), and cf. also CA ll. 161, 310 etc. With WR's addition cf. Iolo Goch's description of Owain Glyndŵr: *Ni thyfodd gwellt na thafol / hefyd na'r ŷd ar ei ôl* 'Neither grass nor dock nor corn grew in his track' (GIG no. IX.61–2), where it may be concluded that Iolo Goch is quoting this triad (cf. editor's n.).

Like *galouyd* (triad 19) *rhuddfoawg* belongs essentially to the language of praise-poetry. It is used by Cynddelw in his *marwnad* for Madog ap Maredudd (LlDC no. 38.19 = CBT III, no. 7.19): *Rutwoauc vaon ny oleith* 'who does not evade red-reaping / ravaging folk', and Cynddelw describes Hywel ab Owain Gwynedd as *rutuoawc uarchavc* (H 101.15 = CBT IV, no. 6.108). In describing Llywelyn ap Gruffudd as *ual Run ruduoavc vu y droua* (RBP col. 1382.10 = CBT VI, no. 35.54), Dafydd Benfras forcibly indicates that he is quoting from this triad, by joining the name of *R(h)un* with *ruduoawc*. (Since *Rhun* is such a common name it is uncertain, however, which *Rhun* he had in mind; for several possibilities see under Personal Names below.) Elsewhere *ruduoawc* is used once by Seisyll Bryffwrch (CBT II, no. 24.41), once by Prydydd y Moch (H 212.22 = CBT V, no. 24.6); by Llygad Gŵr (H 63.20; = CBT VII, 28.5), ibid. 24.6n.; by Phylip Brydydd (H 231.32 =

CBT VI, no. 12.22), by Y Prydydd Bychan (H 238.4 = CBT VII, no. 10.14), and by Bleddyn Fardd (H 79.12 = CBT VII, no. 53.32n.). With Dafydd ap Gwilym *rhuddfoawg* has come to be synonymous with *cyfoethawg* (GDG no. 76.8; see n.)—presumably because a plunderer might by definition be regarded as a wealthy man. 'Rich, wealthy' would also suit with Iolo Goch's employment of the word: *Helm gribawg ruddfoawg fyth* 'a helmet always crested and rich' (GIG no. IV.73n.), though it seems likely that this also preserves the older meaning of 'plundering'. In all these instances it seems more likely than not that a recollection of the triad inspired the poets.

WR's version suggests that there was a variant (perhaps an earlier form?) of the triad in which Lleu Llaw Gyffes was included in place of Arthur; but the less precise the key-epithet, the easier it was for such substitutions to take place. With the superimposition of Arthur's name as a fourth character in the WR version, cf. triads 2 and 52. W's added note shows that the scribe understood the triad to mean that no plants could even so much as germinate in the track of one of these men—let alone grow to the time of reaping. This is corroborated by the entry in Davies's dictionary (1632): *Rhuddfaog (sic) y gelwid gynt y neb a adawai ei arllwybr yn rhuddfa ar ei ôl, gan waed ei elynion, neu drwy ddiwelltu'r ddaiar gan amlder ei lu* 'Red Reaper formerly denoted a person who left his track all red behind him with the blood of his enemies, or through laying waste the ground from the number of his host'. This explanation—presumably based on that given in the WR version of the triad—maintains the association of *rhuddfoog* with the idea of reaping, and thus supports Ifor Williams's view that *boog* is cognate with Ir. *boingid*, as against that of Loth (RC XXXVIII, p. 60, repeated in n. to GDG no. 76.8) who translates *rhuddfoawg* as 'belliqueux, combatif'. As an epithet for a warrior, *rhuddfoawg/rhuddfoog* survived into the eighteenth century, retaining the implicit associations with the name of Arthur with which it is endowed in the triad.

21. Tri Thaleithya6c Cat Enys Prydein:

Drystan mab Tallwch,
a Hueil mab Caw,
a Chei mab Kenyr Keinuarua6c.
Ac 6n oed taleithya6c arnadunt wynteu ell tri:
Bedwyr mab Bedra6c oed h6nn6.

21. Three Diademed Battle-leaders of the Island of Britain:

Drystan son of Tallwch,
and Hueil son of Caw,
and Cai son of Cynyr of the Fine Beard.
And one was diademed above the three of them:
that was Bedwyr son of Bedrawc.

Manuscripts: 16, 45, 47, 50, WR, 51, 77, C 18, NLW, DC, Cwrt. 3, BL[2].

21. tri thaleithia6c ynys brydein W, Cwrt., tri thaleithavc y. b. R. NLW, RW. tri thaleithioc cad DC.

a. Trystan 45, 50, Tristan NLW. Trallvch 50.

b. huil m. ca6 45, Huail 77, Huel ap Caw NLW. WR *substitute* G6eir ap g6ystyl, Gweir ap gwesstl 51, Gwair vap Gwystl Cwrt.

c. a chai 51, a Gai 77. kynyr kynuarua6c 45, Cynyr vawrchawc NLW, Cenyr vaurchawc DC, C. farchawg RW, keinvarvawc *omitted* WR, 51, 77. 47 *substitutes* Betwyr mab bedravt.

d. *omitted by* WR, 47, 51. taleitha6c 45, taleithogawc 50, daleithiogach 77, daleithioc arnunt wy ill tri NLW, DC. pedrawt 45, Petrawc 50, a bedrawc oedd hvnv NLW, DC, bedwyr m. Bedrawc C 18, bedrawc *omitted* 77.

---

taleithya6c. *Taleith* 'coronet, chaplet'. In the earliest poetry the *talaith* appears to have been a mark of distinction worn on the head by the foremost champions in battle, perhaps as an incentive to draw the enemy's attention to them, and it may have corresponded to the *cae* worn by the young warriors in the *Gododdin*, referred to in the series of stanzas beginning *Kayawc kynhorawc* 'wearing a diadem(?), fighting in the van' (ll. 21, 30, 39, 46), as is suggested by Ifor Williams (CA 69, n. on *kayawc*). (For *cae* as later used by the *cywyddwyr* to denote 'diadem, brooch' etc., see GPC 382, *caeog* 384.) Prydydd y Moch describes Llywelyn ab Iorwerth as *kayawc kynran* 'a diademed (?) prince' (RBP col. 1420.11 = CBT V, no. 23.67). This epithet is also applied to Cynddylan (CLlH no. XI.28c), unless *Kaeawc* is in this instance to be taken as a proper name (see EWSP 586–7). But information as to the proper significance of both *talaith* and *cae* is insufficient to equate them with full assurance. Hence Eurys Rowlands suggests for *taleithyawc* the meaning 'Leaders of a Host (?)' (LlC VI, p. 232). *Cae* could also mean 'torque', and torques are mentioned as worn in battle in the *Gododdin* and in *Canu Llywarch Hen*. In earlier times these were widely worn by the Celtic peoples. Cf. triad 17 *Tri Hualawc*, and n. In the thirteenth century, Llygad Gŵr uses *taleithawc* three times in praise of Llywelyn ap Gruffudd (H 18.9, 13.17 = CBT VII, no. 24.107n., and cf. idem ll. 111, 115). In *Llywelyn ap Gruffudd Tywysog Cymru* (Caerdydd, 1986), pp. 232–3, J. Beverley Smith gives references indicating that Edward I confiscated the *talaith* belonging to Llywelyn and gave it to Westminster Abbey. In *Enweu Ynys Prydein* (App. I, no. 4, see n.), it is stated with significance that the *talaith* is worn by the subsidiary rulers of Cornwall, Aberffraw, and Penrhyn Rhionydd; and it is strangely implied that these *taleithiau* are held as tributary to the crown of London.

With the addition of *Bedwyr* (see n. under Personal Names) as a fourth to this triad, cf. the addition of the name of Arthur in the WR version of triads 20 and 52. The addition of Bedwyr's name is unique to the text of Pen. 16 and is perhaps a scribal interpolation, due to an increased interest in Arthurian stories. In CO ll. 393–4, it is stated of Bedwyr *nyt arswydwys y neges yd elhai Gei idi* 'he had no dread of any quest that Cai went upon'.

22. Tri Glew Enys Prydein, tri meib Haearn6ed 6rada6c:

> Grudnei,
> a Henben,
> ac Edena6c.

22. Three Brave Men of the Island of Britain, three sons of Haearnwedd the Treacherous:

> Gruddnei,
> and Henben ('Old Head'),
> and Edenawg ('Winged').

Manuscripts: 16, 45, 50, 77, V, C 18.
22. hayarnwed urada6c 45, Hayarnedd vaglawc 77
a. Gwydhneu C 18.
b. henpen 45, 50, V, C 18.
c. Aedenaw V.

22 W. Tri Gle6 Ynys Brydein:

> Grudnei,
> a Henben,
> ac Aedenawc;

ny doynt o gat namyn ar eu geloreu. Ac ysef oedynt y rei hynny: tri meib Gleissiar Gogled, o Haearnwed Vrada6c eu mam.

22 W. Three Brave Men of the Island of Britain:

> Gruddnei,
> and Henben,
> and Aedenawg.

They would not return from battle except on their biers. And those were three sons of Gleissiar of the North, by Haearnwedd the Treacherous their mother.

Manuscripts: WR, 51, NLW, DC, Cwrt. 3, BL[2].
22 W. tri glew unben NLW, glevv vnben DC.
henbrien R.
NLW, DC, *substitute* a Chai.
haernwed R, meibion gleissiar or gogledd 51, gleisiar or gogledd o haiarnwedd ei mam NLW, DC; eu cynneddfae oedd nad eynt o gad namyn ar eu geloreu V, ar elore DC, NLW, eu heloraw 51.

---

tri meib Gleissiar Gogled. Cynddelw makes an isolated allusion to this figure in 'Marwnad Rhirid Flaidd' (CBT III, no. 24.46), *A'r goreu a vu o ueib Gleissyar*, indicating that he either knew a lost story about Gleissiar, or else that he is quoting from this triad, as known to him from a version corresponding to that of WR. This is one of the significant indications that Cynddelw and his contemporaries were familiar with the prototype of TYP in the version of WR, rather than in that of Pen. 16. See also R. Bromwich in Morfydd E. Owen a B. F. Roberts (eds), *Beirdd a Thywysogion*, p. 202ff.

23. Tri Thrahauc Enys Prydein:

Sawyl Ben Uchel,
a Phasken mab 6ryen,
a Run mab Einya6n.

23. Three Arrogant Men of the Island of Britain:

Sawyl High-Head,
and Pasgen son of Urien,
and Rhun son of Einiawn.

Manuscripts: 16, 45, 47, 50, WR, 51, 77, 240, BL[1], C 18, Cwrt 3.

23. tri thrahaus 45, 47, 50, this was the reading of llyfr Siôn Balmer, *acc.* V, tri trahavc WR, tri thrahawc 51, 77, C 18, tri Traws 240, BM, Cwrt.

a. Sawel 47, Sawl 50, 240, BL

b. WR, 51, Cwrt., *substitute* g6ibei draha6c.

c. einavn 45, V, C 18, Eingud 77. WR *substitute* a ruua6n peuyr draha6c, a Ryvawn bevr drahaawc *altered to* Ruon 51.

---

trahauc, i.e. *traha-awc* (CA 320) 'haughty, presumptuous, arrogant'; later *trahaus*.

Ifor Williams discussed the particular meaning of *traha* 'over-weening pride or presumption' in the stories of *Cantref y Gwaelod* and in the poems of the Llywarch Hen cycle (CLlH lxvii–lxix); for subsequent discussion, see EWSP ch. 2 'The Urien Rheged Poems'. In the stories to which Williams refers, *traha* appears to have been followed invariably by a fall from prosperity. The surviving fragments of poetry indicate that the fortunes of the family of Urien Rheged (see n. to *Pasken m. 6ryen*) were in some way involved with, or parallel to, those of Llywarch Hen. The poem *Diffaith Aelwyd Rheged* (CLlH no. III) suggests that Urien's dynasty came to a disastrous end.

It is tempting to speculate as to whether the triad of the *Tri Thrahauc* / *Thrahaus* may not have been conceived at an early stage as forming a contrasting pair with triad 8, *Tri Lledyf 6nben*, the 'Three Prostrate (Humble) Chieftains'.

24. Tri Ysgymyd Aeruaeu Enys Prydein:

Gilbert mab Catgyffro,
a Moruran eil Tegit,
A G6ga6n Gledyfrud.

24. Three Slaughter-Blocks (?) of the Island of Britain:

Gilbert son of Cadgyffro,
and Morfran son of Tegid,
and Gwgawn Red-Sword.

Manuscripts: 16, 45, 47, 50, WR, 51, 77, 240, BL[1], C 18, Cwrt. 3, NLW Addl. 37B.

24. esgemyd WR, yscymyd 50, essgemydd 51, yscymydh C 18, escemydd BL, 240, yscymydd V, ysgynnyddaer 77, escemydd aerau Cwrt., NLW Addl., aereu W, 45, 47, 50, aeren R, aerau 51, BL, 240.

a. gilbert katgyffro WR, 51, ap Bradgyffro 77, Gilberw Cwrt.

c. g6gon WR, gwgon 51. Cledyfurud 45, gleifrud 47.

---

ysgymyd aeruaeu. In CBT III, no. 21.34n., the definition'Un sy'n dal ei dir yn gadarn mewn brwydr, er gwaethaf ergydion y gelyn', 'chopping-block of battles, one who holds his ground firmly in battle, in spite of the enemy's blows' was given. The meaning of *ysgymydd* had been fully discussed by Ifor Williams (B XVI, pp. 191–2): *ysgymmydd* (< **ex-com-ben-ydd*) denotes a block of wood used either for sitting upon (D. *scamnum* 'bench, stool, step'), or for chopping upon (TW *subiculum* = *cymmyn-gyff, ysgymmydd*). Both these meanings are paralleled in the variant usages of the Breton cognate word *escamet, eskemet*, on which see L. Fleuriot, DGVB 231. Old Breton *istomit* in a charter dated 833 (A. de Courson (ed.), *Cartulaire de Redon* (Paris, 1863), p. 354), appears in a context which indicates that it should probably be emended to *iscomid*, as was recommended by J. Loth (*Chr. Br.* 525; *Mab.* II, 261, n. 1) and Williams (B XVI, pp. 191–2):

> Conwoion monachus scripsit istam carticulam per commeatum et voluntatem Alvriti Mactierni, sedente super *trifocalium*, id est, *istomid*, in fronte ecclesiae, stante Rethworet in dextera eius.

With the epithet in the triad compare *post cad* (triad 5, see n.), as well as the numerous similar complimentary epithets used of their patrons by the *Gogynfeirdd*, which were conveniently collected by J. Vendryes in his lecture, *La Poésie Galloise des xii–xiii siècles dans ses rapports avec la langue*: *mur* 'wall', *argae* 'embankment', *canllaw* 'support', *colofn* 'column', *corf* 'pillar', *tŵr* 'tower', *ysgor* 'rampart', etc. In his 'Marwnad Cadwallawn mab Madawg' (H 126.24 = CBT III, no. 21.34n.), Cynddelw describes the latter as *Cadeu ysgymyt ysgymodi / Cad asgen, ysgwn ysgwyd Veli* 'one who causes injury to an army, and carries the shield of skilful Beli (?)'. *Ysgymyt* 'lleiddiad' is similarly used as a favourable epithet by Einion ap Gwgon (H 51.8 = CBT VI, no. 18.38), and by Prydydd y Moch (H 310.4 = CBT V, no. 28.20). Guto'r Glyn uses *ysgemydd* in reference, apparently, to the hilt of his dagger, in the lines: *Yn llem ar ei hysgemydd, Ys hir i gymynu hydd* (GGl no. LXXX.51–2) 'Sharp upon its hilt, long to flay a stag'; i.e. the hilt is the 'seat' of the dagger.

eil Tegit. On *eil* see n. to *Rahaut eil Morgant* under Personal Names.

Pen. 16, fo. 50*v*–51*r*

25. Tri Aer(ueda6c) Enys Prydein:

Selyf mab Kenan Garrwyn,
ac Vryen mab Kynvarch,
ac Auaon mab Talyessin.

(Sef achavs y gelwit wy yn Aeruedogeon: vrth dial eu kam oc eu bed.)

25. Three Battle-Rulers of the Island of Britain:

Selyf son of Cynan Garrwyn,
and Urien son of Cynfarch,
and Afaon son of Taliesin.

(This is why they were called *Aerfeddogion*: because they avenged their wrongs from their graves.)

Manuscripts: 16, 47, WR, 51, C 18, NLW, Cwrt. 3, BL[2].

25. aer *is the last word on p. 50 v. and there is no space for the rest of the word,* aeruedavc WR, aervodavc 47, aerveddog 51 *with e added above line*, Aerfeddawc V, arffedog kad NLW.

a. selef W. kynan garvyn WR, 47, 51.

b. WR, 51, NLW, V, RW, *substitute* a gwallavc ap llennavc, lleeiniawg NLW, Lleennawc V, Gwalhawg Lheimiawg RW.

c. Abhon C 18, Addon NLW, Adhon RW.

d *supplied by* WR, yn eruedogyon R. am ddial 51. beddeu 51.

---

aer(ueda6c) < *aer* + *meddu* 'to take possession of, to rule' (B I, p. 28), or *aer* + *gwedd* 'form, aspect', etc. (GPC 38). Cynddelw refers to Owain Cyfeiliog as *aeruetawc bennaeth* (H 135.30 = CBT III, no. 16.112), and Prydydd y Moch describes Llywelyn ab Iorwerth as *aeruetawc deyrn* (H 212.19 = CBT V, no. 24.3n.). *Aerfeddog* here may be no more than a general epithet, without any very precise significance in reference to the characters named (cf. triads 5, 19, 24), or it may indicate that these three men were traditionally renowned as generals or as strategists. Loth (*Mab.* I, 315) compares the name *Moro Oeruedawc* in *Culhwch* (CO l. 718n.), which preserves the same epithet. *Aerfeddog* is unrecorded outside the triad and the instances quoted above. Kenneth Jackson compared the Anglo-Saxon phrase *ahton waelstowe geweald* 'they possessed the place of slaughter', i.e. 'won the battle' (WHR Special Number (1963), 84; see also EWSP 77–8, n.).

The scribe of W was ignorant of the meaning of *aeruetawc*, as is apparent from his attempt to explain it as derived from *bedd* 'grave'. (Triad 17 above shows a similar attempt to explain a word not understood by the scribe; for a comment on similar attempts found in WR to explain unfamiliar epithets introducing triads, see introduction pp. xxiii–xxiv.)

26. Tri Gwrdueichyat Enys Prydein:

Drystan mab Tallwch, a gedwis moch March mab Meirchyawn hyt tra aeth y meichyat y erchi y Essyllt dyuot y'w gynnadyl; ac Arthur yn keissyaw un hwch onadunt, ae y dwyll, ae y dreis, ac nys cauas.

A Phryderi mab Pwyll Pen Annwuyn, a getwis moch Pendaran Dyuet yg Glyn C6ch yn Emlyn.

A Choll mab Collvrewy, a gedwis Henwen h6ch Dallwyr Dallben, a aeth yg gordody hyt ym Penryn Austin yg Kernyw. (Ac yna yd aeth yn y mor.) Ac yn Aber Tarogi yg Went Ys Coet y doeth y'r tir, a Choll map Coll6rewy a'e la6 yn y gwrych pa ford bynnac y kerdei, nac ar vor nac ar dir. Ac y Maes G6enith yg Went y dotwes g6enithen a g6enynen. Ac yr (hynny) y mae goreu lle y wenith ac (y) wenyn y lle hwnnw. Ac odyno yd aeth hyt yn Llonyon ym Penvro, ac yno y dotwes ar eiden a g6enynen. Ac yr hynny y mae (goreu) lle y heid Llonyon. Ac odyna y kerdws hyt yn Riw Kyuerthuch yn Eryri, ac yno y dotwes ar geneu bleid ac ar gyw eryr. A'r eryr a rodes Coll mab Collvrewy y Vre(*r*)nnach Wydel o'r Gogled, a'r bleid a rodes y 6enwaed m . . . o Arllechwed. A'r rei hynny vu (6leid) Me(n)waed ac eryr Brennach. Ac odyna yd aeth hyt y Maen Du yn Llan6eir yn Aruon, ac yno y dotwes ar geneu cath. A'r keneu hwnnv a 6wrywys Coll mab Coll6rewy y Menei. A honno wedy hynny 6u Gath Baluc.

26. Three Powerful Swineherds of the Island of Britain:

Drystan son of Tallwch, who guarded the swine of March son of Meirchiawn, while the swineherd went to ask Essyllt to come to a meeting with him. And Arthur was seeking (to obtain) one pig from among them, either by deceit or by force, but he did not get it;

And Pryderi son of Pwyll, Lord of Annwfn, who guarded the swine of Pendaran Dyfed in Glyn Cuch in Emlyn;

And Coll son of Collfrewy, who guarded Henwen, the sow of Dallwyr Dallben, who went (when) about to bring forth, to Penrhyn Awstin in Cornwall, (and there she went into the sea). And at Aber Tarogi in Gwent Is Coed she came to land. And Coll son of Collfrewy with his hand on her bristles wherever she went, whether by sea or by land. And in the Wheat Field in Gwent she brought forth a grain of wheat and a bee; and therefore that place is the best for wheat and bees. And from there she went to Llonion in Pembroke, and there she brought forth a grain of barley and a bee. And therefore Llonion is the best place for barley. From thence she made for the Hill of Cyferthwch in Eryri; and there she brought forth a wolf-cub and a young eagle. And Coll son of Collfrewy gave the eagle to Bre(*r*)nnach the Irishman of the North, and the wolf he gave to

Me(n)waedd son of . . . of Arllechwedd; and these were (the Wolf of) Me(n)waedd and the Eagle of Brennach. And from thence she went to the Black Stone in Llanfair in Arfon, and there she brought forth a kitten. And Coll son of Collfrewy threw that kitten into the Menai. And she was afterwards Palug's Cat.

Manuscripts: 16, WR, 45, 47, 77, C 18 (title only).

26. g6rdueichat 45, 47.

a. drysdan m. tall6ch 47. meircha6n 45, march ameirchion 77. y gynadyl ac ef 45, yr gynadyl 47, ymgynadl 77. ae o dvyll ae y dreis 47.

b. am6yn 45, pen an6fyn 47, a Chai hir NLW Addl, glyn cuwch 45, ynglyn kuwch 47.

c. uab Kallureuwy R. dallweir 45, datweir 47, C 18. gordodo 45, a hi a aeth i gordhodw C 18. a6stin 45. ( ) *supplied by* 45. yd aeth hi yn y mor 47. aber tarrodi 47. gwenenen 45, 47. er hynny 45. 45 *omits* ac wenyn. odyna 45. y llonwen 45. gwenenen 45, 47. er hynny 45. llonwen 45. goreu *supplied by* 45. kerd6ys 45 yd aeth 47. ac ederyn eryr 47. y Urynach vydel 45, 47. y uenwaed o arllechwed 45, y veuwaed Pen. 16, y veiwed 47, 6leid *supplied by* 45. menwaed 45. meuwaed Pen. 16, meiwed 47. brynach 45. hyt y maes du 47. a uyryvys 45. a vwyryawd 47. yn ymor C 18. cath paluc 45, A hwnnw vu gath balvc gwedy hynny 47.

26 WR. Tri G6rueichiat Ynys Brydein:

Pryderi vab P6yll Pen Annwn, 6rth voch Pendaran Dyuet y tatmeth. Ac y sef moch oedynt: y seithlydyn a duc P6yll Pen Annwn, ac a'e rodes y Pendaran Dyuet y datmaeth. Ac y sef y lle y katwei, y Glyn Kuch yn Emlyn. A sef acha6s y gelwit h6nn6 yn wrueichiat: kany allei neb na th6yll na threis arna6;

A'r eil, Drystan ap Tall6ch 6rth voch March ap Meirchion, tra aeth y meichiat yn gennat ar Essyllt. Arthur, a March, a Chei, a Bet6yr a vuant ell petwar, ac ny cha6sant kymint ac un ban6, nac o dreis, nac o d6yll, nac o ledrat y gantha6;

A('r) trydyd, Koll vab K(o)llure6y, 6rth voch Dallwyr Dallben y Glyn Dallwyr yg Kerni6. Ac vn o'r moch a oed dorroc, Henwen oed y hen6; a darogan oed yd hanuyde(i) waeth Ynys Brydein o'r torll6yth. Ac yna y kynulla6d Arthur llu Ynys Brydein, ac yd aeth y geisso y diua. Ac yna yd aeth hychen yn gordodw, ac ym Penryn Hawstin yg Kerniw yd aeth yn y mor, a'r gwr(uei)chiat yn y hol. Ac y Maes G6enith yg Went y dotwes ar wenithen a g6enynen, ac yr hynny hyt hedi6 y mae goreu lle g6enith a g6enyn Maes G6enith yg Went. Ac yn Llonyon ym Phenvro y dotwes ar heiden a g6enithen. Am hynny y diharhebir o heid Llonyon. Ac yn Riw Gyuerthwch yn Aruon y dotwes a(r) geneu *cath* (= bleid) a chy6 eryr. Ac y roet y bleid y Vergaed, ac y roet yr eryr y Vreat tywyssa6c o'r Gogled, ac 6ynt a hanuuant waeth o nadunt. Ac yn Llanueir yn Aruon adan y maen du y dotwes ar geneu kath, ac y ar y maen y b6ryoed y g6rueichat yn y mor, a meibion Paluc yMon a'e magassant, yr dr6c vdunt.

A honno vu Gath Baluc. Ac a uu vn o Deir Prif Ormes Mon a uagwyt yndi. A'r eil oed Daronwy. A'r dryded, Edwin vrenhin Lloegyr.

26 WR. Three Powerful Swineherds of the Island of Britain:

Pryderi son of Pwyll, Lord of Annwfn, with the swine of Penndaran Dyfed his foster-father. These swine were the seven animals which Pwyll Lord of Annwfn brought, and gave them to Penndaran Dyfed his foster-father. And the place where he used to keep them was in Glyn Cuch in Emlyn. And this is why he was called a Powerful Swineherd: because no one was able either to deceive or to force him;

And the second, Drystan son of Tallwch, with the swine of March son of Meirchyawn, while the swineherd went with a message to Essyllt. Arthur and March and Cai and Bedwyr were (there) all four, but they did not succeed in getting so much as one pigling—neither by force, nor by deception, nor by stealth;

And the third, Coll son of C(o)llfrewy, with the swine of Dallwyr Dallben in Glyn Dallwyr in Cornwall. And one of the swine was pregnant, Henwen was her name. And it was prophecied that the Island of Britain would be the worse for the womb-burden. Then Arthur assembled the army of the Island of Britain, and set out to seek to destroy her. And then the sow went about to farrow, and at Penrhyn Awstin in Cornwall she entered the sea, and the Powerful Swineherd after her. And in the Wheat Field in Gwent she brought forth a grain of wheat and a bee. And therefore from that day to this the Wheat Field in Gwent is the best place for wheat and for bees. And at Llonion in Pembroke she brought forth a grain of barley and a grain of wheat. Therefore, the barley of Llonion is proverbial. At the Hill of Cyferthwch in Arfon she brought forth a (wolf-cub) and a young eagle. The wolf was given to (B?)ergaed and the eagle to Breat, a prince of the North: and they were both the worse for them. And at Llanfair in Arfon under the Black Rock she brought forth a kitten, and the Powerful Swineherd threw it from the Rock into the sea. And the sons of Palug fostered it in Môn, to their own harm: and that was Palug's Cat, and it was one of the Three Great Oppressions of Môn, nurtured therein. The second was Daronwy, and the third was Edwin, king of Lloegr.

Manuscripts: WR, 51, BL[1], 240, Cwrt. 3, NLW Addl. 37B.

26 W. Tri . . . veichyad 51, Tri gwrdd veichiad BL[1], 240, Cwrt.

a. penndaran R. y datmaeth R, i datmaeth 51. glynn cuch R. ac y sef achaws R. yn wrueichat R, ni allei neb nai dwyllo nae dreissio 51, wrth na wnaed na thwyll na thrais arno BL[1], 240, Cwrt., NLW Addl.

b. a Chai hir NLW Addl. y erchi y Essyllt ddyfod y gynnal oed ac ef BL[1], 240. a vuant bedwar yn ceisio'r moch ac nys chowsant vn llwdn BL[1], 240, Cwrt. *After* ell petwar 51 *adds* yn ddisscwyl. ac ny chavssant kymmeint R. y gantav R. ac ni chowssant kymeint a banw o y arnaw nag o drais nag o ledrat 51.

c. koll ap kallurevy R, 51 goll ap kollvrewy. dorrawc R. hennwen R, 51. yd hanuyde W, yr hanuydei R. y byddai waeth 51. or torllwyth hwnnw 51, or torllwyth hynny BL[1], 240. y kynnullavd R, y cyhwnnodd Arthur BL[1], 240, cychwynnodd A, NLW Addl., hycheu W, hychen R. ym henn Brynn Awstin BL[1], Cwrt., NLW Addl. gvrdueichyat R, BL[1], 240, ar wennithen a gvenninen R. Ac hyny hyd heddiw y mae gore lle (gorau BM) gwenith a gwenyn maes y gwenith yngwent BL[1], llonyon W, llouyon R, Llovian 51, Llofion BL[1], Cwrt., NLW Addl. pennuro R. y diharebir haidd Llofion BM, 240. riw gyfuerthvch R, ym pen riw Gyfoethwch Arvon BL[1], 240, Cwrt. yn aruo R. a(r) geneu, ar geneu cath WR, ar genau Cwrt., NLW Addl., cath *sic* R, y dodwes gormes kath 51, y dydwes cath a chyw eryr a chenau blaidd BL[1], 240, Cwrt., NLW Addl., ac y rroes y gath *altered to* vread 51, Vergad . . . Vryad BL[1], 240, Cwrt. ac wyw y hun (a) vuant waeth oi caffael BL[1], 240, wy y hvn a vuant oi caffael Cwrt., ac wynt a vuant waeth o naddunt 51. y maen duy BM, 240, y man du Cwrt., dan vaen *sub punct.* y maen du 51. y byryavd R, y gvrueichyat R, y bwriodd y Gwrdd veichiad y hi yr mor BL[1], 240, ac o y ar benn y maen y vwriodd y gwrveichiad ef yn y mor 51, Palic Cwrt., NLW Addl., fu'r gath Balic Cwrt., NLW Addl.

d. Teir prif ormes Mon a fagwyd yndi. Cath Paluc. Yr eil oed Daronwy. ar trydydd Edwin frenhin lloegyr V.

---

gwrdueichyat. Cf. *gwrduagla6c*, triad 16; *gwrdd* = 'mighty, powerful', GPC 1701. W and R's *g6rueich*(*i*)*at* suggests confusion in the first element with the intensive prefix *gor-, guor-, guar*; but *gwrdueichiat* is attested as the correct form for this version also, by R's reading in 1.15. Neither epithet is recorded in GPC except in these two triads.

This triad should be considered in relation to the great importance attached to swine in the life and mythology of the Celtic nations from the earliest times. A Gaulish swine-god *Moccus* is commemorated in a dedication to *Mercurius Moccus* (J. Vendryes, *La Religion des celtes*, pp. 282, 287), and the boar is found frequently as a symbol on altars in Gaul and Britain; for references see PCB 308–21; CO (2), pp. lxiv–lxxvi. In Gaul as in Ireland swine-flesh was particularly prized; in Irish sources it is represented as constituting the food of the gods at their Other-world feasting (EIHM 122–3) and immense boars figure also at more mundane feasts in the sagas of *Mac Dathó's Pig* and *Bricriu's Feast*. In these tales the choicest parts of the pig appear as the object of contention for the *curadmír* or Champion's Portion, allotted to the warrior who was recognized by all to be pre-eminent. Boar-hunts also figure largely in the sagas. In the *Triads of Ireland* (ed. Kuno Meyer, no. 236) a wonderful boar which was hunted by Fionn mac Cumhaill is described as one of the Three Wonders of Glenn Dallán in Tyrone; while in the *Boyhood Deeds of Finn*, the hero slays a sow called Beo who has been devastating Munster (*Ériu* I, pp. 184–5; Cross and Slover, *Ancient Irish Tales*, p. 364). To hunt the boar was *geis* or taboo to Diarmaid O' Duibhne because his half-brother had been turned by magic into a wild boar (ibid., pp. 409–11). Cf. SC XIV/XV (1979/80), pp. 200–11.

This is the longest and most informative of all the triads (it is surpassed in length only by the 'literary' triad based on HRB, triad no. 51). Sir John Rhŷs has given a very full discussion to it in *Celtic Folklore*, ch. 9, which throws valuable light on the various place-names mentioned. From item **c** he deduced that the triad took shape in south Wales, 'it is remarkable as giving to S. Wales credit for certain resources, but to North Wales for pests alone and scourges' (op. cit., p. 508). Certainly all three items are to be related to the story-material of the south: the bias towards south Wales in the tale of *Henwen* is obvious, and the other items refer to the tales of the south-Welsh hero *Pryderi* and of *Drystan*. It is the only triad in the early Pen. 16 collection which shows possible overt influences from antecedent French sources with its allusion to the Drystan–Esyllt story and its further allusion to *Cath Palug* (see nn. under Personal Names).

a. On the *Drystan* episode in this triad, see my chapter 'The Tristan of the Welsh', AW 209–28, especially 214–15 and the references there cited. The incident is recorded in no other source, in spite of the fact that it accords well with the type of *fabliau* incident describing stolen meetings, dangerously contrived, between Tristan and Es(s)yllt, which appear in a number of variant forms in the Continental romances. It offers a suggestion that Drystan had become drawn into the orbit of Arthur at an early stage, though this triad is exceptional in that it is unlikely to be wholly independent of influence from the Continental Tristan romances.

Line 3, **y dwyll, y dreis** 'by deception . . . by force', where *y* represents O.W. *i* 'from' (not 'to') < *de*; DGG 183; L and P, § 226, d; cf. *y dreis y ar 6edrawt*, triad 51c; *i ddwyn gwraic Ffin vab Koed i drais, Yr Areithiau Pros* 15.9; *ae dwyn y dreis* WM 496.8; *a chanys kymereist i vy mam i y dreis* YBH, l. 294. On the phrase, see B XIII, p. 3, and cf. GMW 201 (= GPC 130–1). Also cf. PKM 39.10 *y ueis yd aeth ef*.

b. The two versions indicate a variant account from that found in *Math*, of the story of the introduction of swine into Gwynedd from Dyfed. In *Math* it is Pryderi, and not his father Pwyll, who is credited with having received the swine from *Annwfn* (PKM 68.22). Since it was the father and not the son who in the *Mabinogi* was celebrated for his intimate relations with Annwfn and its ruler, it may be that the triad alludes to a different version of the story of the introduction of the pigs into Gwynedd from the south from that which is recorded in PKM. The older text of the triad could be taken as implying that the swine were the property of Pendaran Dyfed in the first place. Perhaps, as argued by W. J. Gruffydd, there once existed a form of the story in which Pendaran Dyfed was the father of Pryderi (*Rhiannon*, pp. 19, 106 *et passim*). The triad might then preserve a memory of a time when Pendaran, as ruler of Dyfed, was the original recipient of the swine from Annwfn. In this case, the version of W would represent an attempt to bring the triad into line with the *Mabinogi* in its extant form, by the statement that the swine were given by Pwyll to Pendaran, claiming that Pendaran was Pryderi's 'foster-father'. A supernatural origin is widely attributed to domestic animals in Celtic sources (cf. n. to triad 84a); and see A. Nutt, *The Voyage of Bran* I, p. 213, and D. Jenkins, *The Law of Hywel Dda*, p. 183: 'The lineage of bees is from Paradise, and it was because of man's sin that they came from thence . . .' This triad is the only source for the information that seven was the number of the swine introduced from Annwfn. But the employment of the number seven in Ml.W. sources is often purely conventional (cf. Jarman, *Ym. M a Th.* 65), and for further instances see n. to *Camlan*, triad 59.

Line 5, **Glyn C6ch yn Emlyn.** The site of Pwyll's meeting with Arawn at the opening of PKM. The river *Cuch* forms the northern boundary of Pembrokeshire with Carmarthenshire; it runs north-west to join the Teifi between Cenarth and Llechryd. *Emlyn* is the north-easternmost *cantref* of Pembrokeshire.

Line 6, **h6ch** 'pig'. The meaning is not restricted to 'sow' as in MW; see PKM 256, *hychen* (l. 17) or *hychan* is a form of the feminine (GPC 1948).

c. The third story, particularly in the version of W, is more properly a tale of the hunt or pursuit of a magic animal than one of herding swine. In neither version is the role of Coll fab Collfrewy (see n.) as *gwrdueichiat* entirely clear, especially when he throws the offspring of his charge into the sea. Though *Henwen* ('Old White') suggests comparison with numerous magic white animals in Celtic sources, I know of no parallel elsewhere in these for a magic animal who is depicted as a kind of 'culture-hero' and credited with the introduction of grain and bees. But see n. to item **b** above. Possibly we should compare with the tale of *Henwen* those episodes which recur frequently in Celtic Saints' Lives in which the saint is directed to follow a (white) boar or sow who will lead him to a suitable building site for his church. Examples: VSB 8, 44; LL 80–1; *De Antiquitate Glastoniensis* (ed. Hearne) 16–17. (For further instances of the name *Henwen* 'Old White', see n. under Personal Names.) Henwen's career impersonates the claim of south Wales to be regarded as the home of fertile crops and honey, in contrast to the bare north which is represented as producing only wolves and eagles and other more obscure pests. Pen. 16 suggests that the tale of Coll fab Collfrewy (unknown elsewhere) was originally independent of the Arthurian cycle; but in view of the fame of the story of Arthur's hunt for the boar *Troit*, recorded first in the *Mirabilia* appended to the *Historia Brittonum*, and with great elaboration of detail in *Culhwch ac Olwen*, the story of Henwen became influenced, as we find it in W's version, by that of the more famous boar-hunt. The Irish *dinnshenchus* material provides numerous parallels to onomastic tales such as occur in the *Pursuit of Henwen* and the *Hunt of Twrch Trwyth*. For instances involving swine hunts, see the *Rennes Dinnshenchus*, RC XV, pp. 421–2, 474–5; E. Gwynn, *Metrical Dinnshenchus* III, 151, 386–95. In the last example the swine are human beings transformed by a hostile relative, cf. the *Twrch Trwyth* who was 'a king whom God transformed into a pig for his sins' (CO ll. 1075–6); and there is a suggestion that *Henwen* (see n. under Personal Names) may also have had a human origin. It is curious that the pursuit of Henwen ends at the sea (in the Menai Straits), as does that of the *Twrch Trwyth* (who embarked in the Severn estuary), but reverses the journey of the *Twrch Trwyth* by swimming from Cornwall to Wales, instead of in the opposite direction—perhaps there is here an ironical reminder of the *Twrch Trwyth*'s journey.

Line 7. **a aeth yg gordody** (WR *gordodw*). This is a compound of *gor* + *dodwi* (GPC 1471) 'to farrow, produce a litter'. *Dodwi* usually means 'to lay an egg, to hatch', but is here used of giving birth to animals, bees, etc., as well as to the eagle. *Dodwi* is however used of a sow giving birth to a piglet in AL II, 194: *pop parchell ac a dotwo yr hwch*. No instance of the compound *gorddod(w)i* other than that in the triad is cited in G 383 or GPC 1471, and earlier dictionaries translate *gorddodo* as 'burrowing'.

Line 7. **Penryn Austin yg Kernyw** (WR *P. Hawstin*). Rhŷs suggests *Aust Cliff* in Gloucestershire (CF II, 506). As he points out, this implies the use of the name *Kernyw* in its ancient sense, to denote the whole of the Dumnonian peninsula. The name is preserved in that of the former Severn ferry at *Aust* Passage.

Line 8. **Aber Tarogi.** No reference is made to the place where the sow came to land in WR; evidently a sentence has dropped out of the text at this place. The *Tarogi* is now known as the *Troggy Brook*, and it joins the sea at Caldicot Pill (CF II, 506; Owen's *Pembrokeshire* (1891), pp. 210, 237); but Sudbrook, south-east of Caldicot, was the original *Aber Tarogi* (EANC 170). The *Taroci* is mentioned several times in *Liber Landavensis*, cf. LL 236.4–5, *cum libera applicatione nauium in hostio Taroci*, which bears witness to the fact that *Aber Tarogi* was a recognized port. Close by is Portskewet, i.e. *Porth Ysgewin y Gwent* (App. I, no. 9), one of the *Teir Prif Porthua Ynys Prydein*. Henwen landed several miles downstream from her point of departure: the choice of *Aber Tarogi* was presumably made in order to explain the place-name from the fact that the sow was *torrawc* (pregnant).

Line 8. **yg Went ys Coet.** The kingdom of Gwent was divided into two *cantrefs* divided by the forest called *Coit Guent* (LL 262) or *Wentwood*. The *cantref* of *Gwent Iscoed* 'below the forest' lay along the shore of the Bristol Channel (HW I, 278–9).

Line 10. **Maes G6enith** lay at the foot of Mynydd Llwyd in Wentwood (Owen's *Pembrokeshire*, p. 237).

Line 12. **Llonyon ym Penvro.** Perhaps *Lanion* near Pembroke (CF II, 506).

LL gives as the name of a village in Pembrokeshire *Din guennhaf* (*guennhaf*) *in lonion*, LL 124.26, 255.12.

Line 12. **ar eiden a g6enynen.** The much expanded version of the triad given in *Myv.*, third series (no. 101) has removed the inconsistencies between *(h)eiden* and *gwenithen*, as well as those caused by WR's *cath* in l. 20 (see n.). For Iolo Morganwg's version in *Myv. Arch.*, see MA[2] 409–10; for his translation see THSC 1969, pp. 141–2.

Line 14. **Riw Kyuerthuch yn Eryri** (WR *Riw Gyuerthwch yn Aruon*). 'Slope of Groaning', perhaps indicating the sow's labour pains, as indicated by J. Rhŷs (CF II, 506–8, 693). W's lenition following *rhiw* characterizes Caernarfonshire dialect, according to J. Lloyd-Jones, *Enwau Lleoedd Sir Gaernarfon* (Cardiff, 1928), pp. 72–3.

Line 15. **ar gyw eryr.** No doubt there is here an onomastic reference to *Eryri*, incorrectly understood to be 'the home of eagles' (see B IV, p. 140).

Line 17. **Arllechwed.** See n. to *Me(n)waed o Arllechwed* under Personal Names.

Line 18. **y Maen Du yn Llan6eir yn Aruon.** Perhaps *Llanfair Isgaer* on the Menai Straits between Port Dinorwic and Caernarfon, though no *Maen Du* is recorded there. There is a Carreg y Gath near Tregarth, and another above Bethesda. Both seem too far inland to be likely as the place intended.

Line 20. **Cath Baluc.** See n. on *Paluc* under Personal Names.

Triad 26 WR

a. Line 1. **y tatmeth.** Cf. *y datmaeth*, l. 3 *y tatmeth* shows that the scribe of W was copying from an original in which initial lenition was not regularly shown and in which *e* represented *ae*; cf. *teirgveth* for *teirguaed* (CO l. 538).

Line 8. **nac o dreis, nac o dwyll.** The phrase here is probably a borrowing from the *Drystan* anecdote (item **a** in Pen. 16), since in Pen. 16 *twyll* and *treis* are mentioned in **a** alone. In any case the words seem hardly applicable to the story of Pryderi, since in the tale of *Math* the swine were in fact stolen from Pryderi by means of a deception successfully practised on him by Gwydion.

c. Line 12. **torllwyth**, 'womb-burden, pregnancy', normally of animals, but cf. triad 70 *Tri Gwyndorllwyth*, which lists three instances of the birth of twins.

Line 14. **yd aeth hychen** (R); (*hycheu* W). *Hychen* is the feminine form of *hwch*.

Line 19. **y dotwes a(r) genau cath.** *Cath* in WR must be emended to *bleid* with all manuscripts of the Pen. 16 version. The mistake has caused some confusion among the later texts which follow WR, and which all reproduce it in one form or another.

Lines 20–1. **y Vergaed . . . y Vreat.** The corrupt name-forms given here conceal misreadings of the *Menwaed* and *Brennach* of the earlier version, as was pointed out by Rhŷs (CF II, 507). With respect to the first name, the confusion of *n* with *r* is a common mistake made in transcription from manuscripts in Insular script (for examples see BT 134); while the retention of *g* suggests that W's exemplar preserved O.W. *gu* for *w* and thus read *Menguaed* or perhaps *Menguet*. (*B*)*reat* could represent a careless miscopying of *Brēach* in which the stroke indicating the *n* was neglected, *c* read as *t*, and the final *h* omitted. There are numerous instances of *c* for *ch* in early texts: *Aballac* in Harl Gen. I; *anoethac(h)* (CO l. 420); *Kulhwc(h) mab Kilyd* (CO l. 563). Cf. also W's *bryneic* for *Bryneich*, triad 10.

Line 25. **vn o deir prif ormes Mon.** For *gormes* cf. triad 36 and n. The scribe of W was reminded of another triad, equally uncomplimentary to Gwynedd, in which Palug's cat figured: this is not recorded separately in any early collection, though V gives it as a separate triad. The 'Three Great Oppressions of Môn' may be compared with the Three Pests (*na trí fochaide*) which afflicted Ulster in the *Death-Tale of Celtchar mac Uthechair* (ed. and trans. Kuno Meyer, *Death-Tales of the Ulster Heroes* (Dublin, 1906)). These were a mouse, a hound, and the Munster hero *Conganchness mac Dedad* (cf. *Edwin* in the triad).

Line 26. **Edwin vrenhin Lloegr.** Geoffrey of Monmouth's HRB XII, 1, is the only source apart from this triad for the tradition that Edwin was reared by King Cadfan of Gwynedd (presumably at Aberffraw) as foster-brother to his son Cadwallon, and the possibility of influence from HRB cannot be excluded here. This assertion is, however, also consistent with Bede's statement (*Hist. Ecc.* II, xii) that Edwin had spent long years wandering in exile before he came to the throne of Northumbria. See introduction, p. lxxx.

TRIOEDD YNYS PRYDEIN 27

Pen. 16, fo. 51*r*–51*v*

27. Tri Lleturitha6c Enys Prydein:

Coll mab Collvrewy,
a Menw mab Teirg6aed,
A Drych eil Kibdar.

27. Three Enchanters of the Island of Britain:

Coll son of Collfrewy,
and Menw son of Teirgwaedd,
and Drych son of Cibddar.

Manuscripts: 16, 45, 47, C 18, NLW, V, DC, BL[2].
27. tri phrif lleturitha6c 45, V, trywyr hut a lletrith V.
a. Collurewy 45, 47, kall ap kollvrwy BL.
b. meny6 45, V, C 18.
c. kiwdar 45, kebddar NLW.

This triad either follows or precedes no. 26 in all manuscripts. It contains the only example of *lledrithog* 'enchanter' recorded as a substantive in GPC 2137.

Compare the version of this triad given in App. IV, no. 4, in which the *Tri Lledrithawc Varchoc* are Menw, Drystan, and E(i)ddili(g) Corr. The version in App. IV is closer to that quoted by Dafydd ap Gwilym, though Dafydd gives *Math* in place of *Drystan* (cf. triad 28):

Tri milwr, try ym olud,
A wyddyn' cyn no hyn hud—
Cad brofiad, ceidw ei brifenw,
Cyntaf, addfwynaf oedd Fenw;
A'r ail fydd, dydd da dyall,
Eiddilig Gor, Wyddel call.
Trydydd oedd, ger moroedd Môn,
Math, rhwy eurfath, rhi Arfon.
(GDG no. 84.33–42).

'Three warriors (it brings riches to me) knew enchantment before this: first in battle experience, the gentlest was Menw—he keeps his great name—and the second (a day of good understanding) Eiddilig the Dwarf, a wily Irishman. The third was Math, a ruler of splendid kind, beside the seas of Môn, king of Arfon.'

R. Vaughan cites the names as given in Dafydd ap Gwilym's version of the triad, under the title *Trywyr hut a lletrith*. With Math's *hut* cf. the *englyn enghreifftiol* cited in each of the four early versions of the Bardic Grammar, GP 7 (RBH), 26 (Ll. 3), 46 (Pen. 20, in which the verse is attributed to *Bleddyn Ddu, circa* 1310–90), and Bangor 1 (B II, p. 191):

Un dwyll wyt o bwyll, o ball dramwy—hoed
Â hud mab Mathonwy;
Unwedd y'th wneir â Chreirwy,
Enwir fryd, rhyhir frad rhwy.

'Of like mind in deceit are you—from the failure of excessive longing—as the enchantment of the son of Mathonwy; of like nature you are formed as Creirwy, of cruel intent; too long, too great the betrayal.'

Cf. GBDd no. 8 (and n. on p. 63), and GEO Atodiad C, p. 38.

28. Teir Prif Hut Enys Prydein:

Hut Math mab Mathonwy (a dysgawd y Wydyon vab Don), a Hut 6thyr Bendragon (a dysgawd y Venw vab Teirgwaed), a Hut Gwythelin Gorr (a dysgawd y Goll vab Kollurewy y nei).

28. Three Great Enchantments of the Island of Britain:

The Enchantment of Math son of Mathonwy (which he taught to Gw(y)dion son of Dôn), and the Enchantment of Uthyr Pendragon (which he taught to Menw son of Teirgwaedd), and the Enchantment of Gwythelyn the Dwarf (WR: Rudlwm the Dwarf) (which he taught to Coll son of Collfrewy his nephew).

Manuscripts: 16, 45, WR, 47, 50, WR, 51, C 18, NLW, Cwrt. 3, DC, BL[2].

Words in brackets supplied by WR.

a. mat uab mathonvy R, Maton6y 45. y wydyon R, 51, a ddyscodd mab Don Cwrt.

b. Uthur 45, R, Uther 50, NLW, DC, Yther RW. teirgwaeth 51, i Fenyw mab Teirgwaet V.

c. WR, 51, V, Cwrt., *substitute* hut rudlwm gorr, rud llwm gorr W, Ryddlwng Gorr Cwrt., G6ydelyn Gor 45, Gwyddelyn gorr BM.

The expanded version of this triad given in WR is probably to be accounted for as an attempt to combine triads 27 and 28; since W gives no version of 27, and yet two of the *Tri Lleturithawc* there named appear as pupils of the magicians named in W's version of triad 28 (see n. to triad 27). The name of the third 'pupil' (*Gwydion*) was readily supplied from the tale of *Math.*

b. In the simple form of the triad given in Pen. 16, the *hut Uthyr Pendragon* may have reference to Uthyr's powers as a shape-shifter as these are manifested in the story of Arthur's birth, which has come down in Geoffrey of Monmouth (HRB VIII, 19–20). Here Uthyr is assisted by Merlin to take on himself the form of Gorlois, duke of Cornwall, in order to lie with his wife Igerna (Eigr). If this is so, the triad suggests that this story was known in some form in the Welsh pre-Geoffrey tradition. (The part played by Merlin in Geoffrey's version could well be Geoffrey's own addition to the tale.) With regard to W's composite version of the triad, it may be noted that in *Culhwch ac Olwen*, *Menw m. Teirgwaed* (see n. to CO l. 199) is distinguished as a shape-shifter.

29. Tri Diweir Deulu Enys Prydein:

Teulu Catwalla6n mab Catuan, a uuant seith mlyned y gyt ac (ef) yn Ywerdon; ac yn hynny o yspeit ny ouynassant dim ida6, rac goruot arnadunt y ada6;

A'r eil, Teulu Gauran mab Aedan, a aethant y'r mor dros eu harglwyd;

A thrydyd, Teulu Guendoleu mab Keida6 yn Arderyd, a gynhalyassant y 6rwydyr pythewnos a mis wedy llad eu hargl6yd. Sef oed riuedi teuluoed pob un o'r g6yr hynny, 6u can wr arugeint.

29. Three Faithful War-Bands of the Island of Britain:

The War-Band of Cadwallawn son of Cadfan, who were with him seven years in Ireland; and in all that time they did not ask him for anything, lest they should be compelled to leave him;

And the second, the War-Band of Gafran son of Aeddan, who went to the sea for their lord;

And the third, the War-Band of Gwenddolau son of Ceid(i)aw at Ar(f)derydd, who continued the battle for a fortnight and a month after their lord was slain.

The number of the War-Bands of each of those men was twenty-one hundred men.

Manuscripts: 16, 45, 47, 50, C 18, NLW, DC, BL[2], V, RW.

29. Tri diweir teulu 45, deuluy NLW, DC, deweir Deylvy RW.

a. Cydwallon NLW, Cydwallan DC, teyly kydwalhon RW. a uuant seith mlyned yn iwerdon y gyt ac ef 45. ni ofynassant ddim iawn iddaw V, heb ovyn dim o ia6n yda6 yn hynny o amser 47.

b. teuluy NLW, DC. Gawran NLW, RW. Teulu Gafran m. Aedan, a aethant yn y mor drostaw 47. V *adds* pan fu y divancoll.

c. teuluy NLW, DC, teyly RW. keidya6 45. aryteryd 47. bethewnos a mis 47. wedi lhadh i harglwydheu RW. un canhvr 45, 47, vn can ar hugain NLW, DC.

29 W. Tri Diweir Deulu Ynys Brydein:

Teulu Katwalla6n yny buant hualogeon,

a Theulu Gafran ap Aedan pan uu y diuank(o)ll,

a Theulu G6endoleu ap Keidia6 yn Arderyd, a dalyassant yr ymlad pythefnos a mis g6edy llad eu hargl6yd. Sef oed eiryf pob un o'r teuluoed, vn kan 6r ar ugeint.

29 W. Three Faithful War-Bands of the Island of Britain:

The War-Band of Cadwallawn, when they were fettered;

and the War-Band of Gafran son of Aeddan, when was his complete disappearance;

and the War-Band of Gwenddolau son of Ceidiaw at Ar(f)derydd, who continued the battle for a fortnight and a month after their lord was slain;

The number of each one of the War-Bands was twenty-one hundred men.

Manuscripts: WR, 51, C 6, Cwrt. 3.

a. kynda fu deulu kyswallan lawir pan fuont hualogion C 6, yn y lle bvant h. Cwrt., teulu kadwawn 51.

b. Gafran m. Aydan 50, ga6ran ap Aeddan 51, Gafron ap Aeddann C6. y diuankall W, pan vu y divankoll arnant 51, arnaw Cwrt., pan fuont yny difankoll C 6.

c. Gwynddole6 50, 51, arderydd 51, aerddryd C 6. un kannwr *sub punct.* pum kannwr 51.

---

diweir. Lit. 'unbending' (B XI, 82) and hence 'constant, faithful, loyal'. Cf. the meaning of *diffleis*, PKM 116.

Cynddelw refers to this triad in the final *englyn* of his poem celebrating the achievements of the *teulu* of Madog ap Maredudd:

> Godwryf a glywaf ar glawr uagu glyw
> glew Uadawc bieifu
> trinua kyua kynytu
> trydyt tri diweir deulu.
> (H 153.5–8 = CBT III, no. 9.17–20)

'I hear a clamour over the land that nurtures heroes; it (they) belonged to brave Madog; (they) won complete conquest on the battlefield; one of the Three Faithful War-Bands.'

The superscription found in the two earliest MSS of this poem claims that it is a *marwnad* for Madog ap Maredudd, ruler of Powys (d. 1160), although in celebrating Madog's war-band it makes no specific allusion to Madog's death. Whether or not the poem was in fact a *marwnad* (and this was doubted by Vendryes, EC IV, pp. 22–3), it was evidently composed either at Madog's death or at any rate before 1160. This poem therefore gives proof that in mid-twelfth-century Powys the triad of the Three Faithful War-Bands was sufficiently widely known for the significance of Cynddelw's compliment to Madog's war-band to be fully appreciated (see introduction, p. xcii), and his allusion to the *Tri Diweir Deulu* is one of the earliest, if not the very first, of all the allusions made by one of the *Gogynfeirdd* to an antecedent triad. I have discussed this in 'Cyfeiriadau Chwedlonol' in Morfydd E. Owen a Brynley F. Roberts (eds), *Beirdd a Thywysogion*, p. 206. It is likely also, by implication, that the companion triad no. 30 was also in existence at the time.

a. This triad and Geoffrey of Monmouth's HRB XII, 4, are the only early sources which state that Cadwallon spent a period of exile in Ireland, though this seems to be implied by references in Welsh poetry to Cadwallon's return across the Irish sea: on these, and on the chronology of Cadwallon's career, see *Catwalla6n*[1] under Personal Names. His exile in Ireland would be a natural consequence of Edwin's conquest of the 'Mevanian islands', i.e. Man and Anglesey, which according to Bede (*Hist. Ecc.*, II, chs. 5, 9) took place after Edwin had conquered the small kingdom of Elmet (in Yorkshire) in 616.

b. a aethant y'r mor. For a discussion of *y* = *yn* (Ir. *i – n* -) 'into', see Arwyn Watkins, B XVII, pp. 140–1. Either 'who went *to* the sea' or '*into* the sea'. Since the preposition is *y* and not *ar* or *dros*, the possibility that the journey alluded to was not by sea but merely 'as far as the sea-shore' should not be excluded. But cf. Pen. 47, *a aeth yny mor* 'who went into the sea'. I assume, in the absence of other evidence, that *Aedán mac Gabráin*, king of Scottish Dál Riada *circa* 573–608, is here intended rather than his father (see EWGT 147, n. 11). One would suppose that the inhabitants of the Scottish colony in Argyllshire would have been familiar with the sea, owing to the close political bonds which they retained in early times with the parent-kingdom in Co. Antrim; and that they would have considered a sea voyage no hardship. The *Annals of Ulster* record a victorious campaign by Aedán in the Orkneys in 580, and this might be the expedition referred to in the triad. A further victory is recorded for Aedán in the following year, at *Cath Manand*, but it remains uncertain whether the reference here is to the district of *Manau Gododdin* in the east of Scotland, or to the Isle of Man (though the allusion in *Ann. Cam.* 584 to *Bellum contra Euboniam* is in favour of the latter). T. Stephens (*The Gododdin* (1852), p. 286, n.) supposed that the allusion in the triad is to the drowning of Aedán's son Conang, recorded in the *Annals of Tigernach* under the year 622: *Conangus regis Aidani filius mari demersus.* It remains possible, however, that the reference here is to Aedán's final disastrous expedition to Degsastane, at some unidentified place in Northumbria (formerly, but with insufficient evidence, associated with Dawston in Roxburghshire) where he met with a crushing defeat at the hands of Ethelfrith in 603. The *Tri Diweir Deulu* evidently distinguished themselves for their fidelity in adversity, and there can be little doubt that Degsastane was the most outstanding disaster in Aedán's career. Moreover, the Scottish forces could well have been carried by sea on this expedition.

c. For **Ar(f)derydd** see n. to triad 84. In terms of heroic warfare, to continue a battle after the death of one's leader constituted an act of very exceptional valour. In a discussion of this point with reference to Greek and Germanic heroic society, H. M. Chadwick has said: '. . . the general object aimed at in a battle was not to gain a strategic advantage but to kill the leaders. Very often this meant the destruction of the enemy's organization. At times it appears that the death or capture of a king led forthwith to the end of hostilities. . . . And in *Beowulf* we see from more than one passage that when the king was slain the heart of the resistance was broken' (*The Heroic Age*

(Cambridge, 1912), p. 340.) The custom was the same in early Ireland: 'If the army was not led by the king in person, it was usually led by one of his sons or a near kinsman. The army fought not so much for victory as for its royal leader. Hence we find that when the prince in command is slain in battle, his followers hardly ever maintain any further resistance. As it is phrased in the story of the *Battle of Ross na Rígh*, ' "it is not usual to fight after the commander falls" ' (Eoin MacNeill, *Celtic Ireland* (Dublin, 1921), p. 7.). D. A. Binchy wrote to the same effect (*Celtic and Anglo-Saxon Kingship*, p. 17), concerning the army's unwillingness to continue fighting after the death of their leader in Celtic (specifically Irish) society. 'The king retains unimpaired his traditional function of leader in battle . . . There is even a remarkable convention, doubtless of great antiquity, that when the king has been slain the battle is lost, no matter how advantageous the position in which he has left his army—exactly as in a game of chess. Tacitus states that "as for leaving a battle alive after your chief has fallen, that means infamy and shame" (*Germania*, ch. 14).'

pythewnos a mis. 'a fortnight and a month'. On the phrase, see Br. Rh. 59; PKM 182.

d. vn can wr arugeint. The number is given for a *teulu* as three hundred men (CA, pp. liii–lviii). Cf. also the *trychan cledyf Kynuerchyn*, etc., referred to in App. II, no. 7. The fantastic figure given here and in the following triad for a *teulu* was arrived at by multiplying the usual number by seven.

Triad 29 W.

a. yny buant hualogeon. Cf. triad 62. Once more the explanation given by the redactor of W is inept, since it confuses Cadwallon ap Cadfan with his ancestor of a century earlier, Cadwallon Lawhir ab Einion Yrth. In the WR order of the triads, *Tri Hualhogeon Deulu* (62) precedes the present triad, which accounts for the confusion.

b. pan uu y diuank(o)ll. 'Total loss, disappearance for good' is the meaning offered for the rare word *difancoll* in GPC 977. Among the very infrequent parallels to be found for this word (other than with the prepositions *i* or *ar*) are Dafydd ap Gwilym (GDG no. 91.57), and Iolo Goch (GIG no. XVII.54). Both poets may well be quoting from this triad as known to them from WR's version, to which both are likely to have had access through the contact which both held with Rhydderch ap Ieuan Llwyd, the apparent owner at this time, of the White Book of Rhydderch (Rachel Bromwich, review of *Selections from the Dafydd ap Gwilym Apocrypha*, SC XXXI, p. 325).

30. Tri Anyweir Deulu Enys Prydein:

Teulu Goronwy Peuyr (o Benllyn), a omedassant eu harglwyd o erbynneit y g6enwynwayw y gan Lleu Lla6 Gyffes yn Llech Oronwy ymblaen Kynuael;

a Theulu G6rgi a Pheredur, a adawssant eu harglwyd yg Caer Greu, ac oet ymlad udunt drannoeth ac Eda Glinvawr. Ac yna y llas ell deu;

a Theulu Alan Fyrgan, a ymchuelassant y 6rtha6 hyt nos a'e ell6ng a'e weissyon Gamlan. Ac yno y llas.

(W: Riuedi pob vn o'r teuluoed vn kan6r ar ugeint.)

30. Three Faithless / Disloyal War-Bands of the Island of Britain:

The War-Band of Goronwy the Radiant of (Penllyn), who refused to receive the poisoned spear from Lleu Skilful-Hand on behalf of their lord, at the Stone of Goronwy at the head of the (river) Cynfal;

and the War-Band of Gwrgi and Peredur, who abandoned their lord at Caer Greu, when they had an appointment to fight the next day with Eda Great-Knee; and there they were both slain;

and the War-Band of Alan Fyrgan, who turned away from him by night, and let him go with his servants (subordinates) to Camlan. And there he was slain.

(W: The number of each of the War-Bands was twenty-one hundred men.)

Manuscripts: 16, 45, 47, 50, WR, 51, C 6, C 18, NLW, DC, Cwrt. 3, BL[2], RW.

30. anniweir WR, aniweir 45, 47, 50, aniwair C 6.

a. goron6 peuyr W, Gronv R, grono mab pepyr 47. o bowys *in later hand over erasure* Pen. 16, o bowys NLW, DC, Penllyn 45, 50, o benllyn 47, C 6, o bennllyn WR. ymadaussant *deleted in* Pen. 16, *and* omedassant *substituted,* ymadavssant WR, omedassant 45, 47, 50, NLW, a omeddwys C 6. o erbyn WR, 51. WR, 50, 51, C 6, *omit* yn llech oronwy, *etc.*, llech grono ymlaen kynvael yn ardudwy 47, V, yn llech ronwy ymlaen kynvaeth NLW, DC.

b. a thelu W, yr ail teuluy NLW. 47 *omits* a pheredur, a phredur DC, NLW. caer greu a chy6oeth ac ymlad udunt W, 51, a chynoeth R, a chyfnot ymladd drannoeth uddunt 50, ac a oed ynllad trannoeth udunt 45, a chyfnod i ymladd dranoeth iddunt C 6. eda glingawr WR, oda glinvawr 47, eda glingawr 51, i edwin C 6. C 6 *adds* ag a giliasont ir mor ag yno i lladdwyd ill dav.

c. ar lan fergan WR, alan fergan 47, 50, alan fergant C 6, ar lann vergan 51, alan vyrgan NLW, DC, RW. a ymchoelassant y vrth eu hargl6yd ar y ford hyt nos ae ell6ng ynteu ae weisson gamlan 45, a ymada6sant ac eu harglvyd yn lledrat y ar y fford yn mynet gamlan WR, a ymhoelassant odywrthaw hyt nos iar y ford ae ellwng ynteu ae weissyon y gamlan 47, a ymchwelant yn lledrat y ar yn mynet y gamlan hyt nos ae ellwng yntheu y gamlan ay weison ac yno y llas 50, a ymchoelasant yn lledrad y ar Arthur yn myned i Gamlan hyd nos, a'i ellwng yntau i Gamlan ae weissyon ac yno y llas RW, a ymchwelesant o wrthaw o hyd nos ai ollwng ai weison yr Gamlan ac ynos y llas NLW, DC, RW, amchwelodd yn lladrad ar faenrred y gamlan o hyd nos a chymyscu i rae oi wyr ef ag yno i llas ef C 6.

Riuedi, *etc., supplied by* WR. Rivedi y gwyr a las yno 51, *corrected above line with reading of* WR; sef oedd rifedi y tri llu hynny un kant ar higain C 6.

---

anyweir. The opposite of *diweir* (triad 29, see n.), here 'unfaithful, disloyal'. In later usage *an(n)iwair* becomes confined to 'faithless' in the sense of 'unchaste', as in triad 80 below; finally 'indecent' (GPC 143).

A reference is made to the triad at the end of the account given of the death of *G(o)ronwy Bebyr* in the *Mabinogi* of *Math*: *Ac o achaws gomed ohonunt wy diodef kymryt un ergyt dros eu harglwyd, y gelwir wynteu, yr hynny hyt hediw, trydyd Anniweir Deulu* 'because of their refusal to receive one blow on behalf of their lord, they have been called, from that day to this, one of the Three Faithless War-Bands' (PKM 92.3–6). Like the other citations of triads in PKM, the passage has been regarded as a late gloss on the story (PKM xxiv–xxx), though I have suggested (introduction, p. xcviii) that the reference to the *Tri Anyweir Deulu* has a strong claim to be regarded as bearing a more integral relation to the extant text of PKM than would be held by a gloss, and that this is a quotation from the already existing triad.

The allusion to the tale of *Goronwy Pefyr* here (like the other references in the triad) is likely to relate to an oral variant of the tale on which the *Mabinogi* is based. Evidently this would be an onomastic tale, purporting to account for the name of *Llech G(o)ronwy* in Cwm Cynfal, near Ffestiniog. This was, or is, a flat stone with a hole pierced through the centre, which according to the story was used by Goronwy as a shield to ward off Lleu's spear. The account given in *Math* indicates that this stone long remained a popular landmark: . . . *ac yno y mae y llech, ar lan Auon Gynuael yn Ardudwy, a'r twll drwydi. Ac o achaws hynny ettwa y gelwir Llech Gronwy* 'and there is the stone, beside the river Cynfal in Ardudwy, with the hole through it. And because of that it is still called the Stone of G(o)ronwy' (PKM 92.20–2). A note in B VII, pp. 352–3, reports the discovery by Frank Ward in 1934 of a stone in the bed of the river Cynfal, corresponding to that described in the story. It measured about forty by thirty inches, was seven to nine inches thick, and had a hole passing through it about one inch in diameter. The stone had by that time been washed down stream some distance from its earlier position in the Ceunant Coch, where a woman who had formerly lived in the nearby farm-house named 'Llech Ronw' remembered having seen it. She also reported that a fallen standing-stone lying about 150 yards north-west of the house was believed to mark the grave of Goronwy Pefyr. See also a later account of finding the slab with a hole through it near to the farm-house 'Llech Ronw', described (with map) by Geraint Jones of Llan Ffestiniog (LlC XVII, pp. 131–3). The traditional site of 'bedd Goronwy' was shown to him nearby.

a. Ardudwy (Pen. 47). A commote lying between the Traeth Mawr and the estuary of the Mawddach (HW 238).

b. For the death of Gwrgi and Peredur, cf. *Ann. Cam.* 580: *Guurci et Peretur moritur*. Evidently there was a tradition concerning this event, which may have been distinct from the *Arfderydd* cycle (for which see triad 84 and n.)—in which Gwrgi and Peredur also appear to have played a part.

eu harglwyd. We should expect *eu harglwydi* 'their lords', but the manuscripts all give the singular here, though both Gwrgi and Peredur are implied.

Caer Greu. From *creu* 'blood' (?). *Machreu* 'the place of blood' (or 'of the pigsty'; *creu* as in PKM 71.15) is named in LlDC no. 16.3 as a Welsh place-name but, as Ifor Williams points out in PKM, there may have been a place similarly named in the 'Old North', as is attested by several other instances. Cf. the *Mathreu* named in PT no. VII.5. It would be tempting to identify some such northern *Machreu* with the *Caer Greu* of the triad. The *Machreu* named in LlDC no. 16.3 is discussed by A. O. H. Jarman in 'Perchen Machreu', LlC III, pp. 115–18.

ac oet. *Oet* 'an appointment' has been changed by the scribe of Pen. 45 into the verbal form *ac a oed*. W: a *chyuoeth ac ymlad udunt* (R: *a chynoeth*). Pen. 50 emends the sentence to *a chyfnot ymladd udunt*, where *cyfnot* is synonymous with *oet*, cf. PKM 19.6–7: *a gwna oet a chyfnot y del Riannon i'th ol*. It is difficult to see how W's reading could have arisen as a corruption of a *chyvnot*, yet *cyfnot* or *oet* is plainly required in the context. W's exemplar probably read *a chyvoet*, a compound which could once have held the same meaning as *oet*, though *cyfoed* has survived only in the meaning of 'contemporary, companion'.

c. The problem raised by the presence in this triad of the name of *Alan Fyrgan* may be compared with that raised by *Gilbert mab Catgyffro* in triads 24, 42 (see under Personal Names and introduction, pp. xcii–xciii). Both heroes are political figures belonging to the Anglo-Norman world of the first half of the twelfth century. They may in both cases be substitutions for earlier names, but their presence in TYP undoubtedly raises fundamental questions concerning the date of redaction of the triad collections.

ae ell6ng a'e weissyon Gamlan. *Ellwng* 'release, free, let go' is included among the verbs of motion which could be directly followed by a noun denoting 'place where', without any intervening preposition. This construction is found most frequently with the verbs *myned* and *dyfod*; cf. *Gwyr a aeth Gatraeth . . . Gwyr a aeth Ododin* (CA ll. 57, 68, etc. and nn.); *a dywed an dyuod Uon . . . an dyuod Leyn*, etc. (H 314.16 = CBT II, no.15.28; TC 227–8). Thus WR gives a more usual form of this construction with *mynet* instead of *gollwng / gellwng*. In Pen. 16 a mark of omission has been inserted before *Gamlan* in a late hand, indicating that a preposition was felt to be required. The variants given in the later texts show that the scribes found difficulty in interpreting the old construction: in C 6 the scribe attempted to clarify the sentence with the variant *amchwelodd yn lladrad ar faenrred y gamlan o hyd nos a chymyscu i rae oi wyr* '(who) turned swiftly (= *buanred??*) by stealth from (*y* = o?) Camlan by night and mingled in the array of his men'. Eurys Rowlands suggests (LlC VI, p. 233) as an alternative interpretation to mine that *faenrred* is a lenited form of *maenrhed* meaning 'stone avalanche', and that it is here used figuratively for 'charge'. He suggests the translation 'who returned by stealth to Camlan in a charge (?) by night, and his men disordered his array'. Sir Idris Foster pointed out (in conversation) that *rae* here is a loan from the English aphetic form 'ray' for 'array, rank, esp. of soldiers' (NED, *Ray*, sb. 3), and William Salesbury's *Dictionary* (1547) gives 'ray = *gossodiat ar wyr ymlad, Englyshe* Array'. Cf. B XV, p. 270.19 (Elis Gruffydd).

Camlan. See n. to triad 59c and n. to *Alan Fyrgan*.

d. Riuedi pob un o'r teuluoed. Either WR has transposed this sentence from the previous triad (see n.), or else Pen. 16 has omitted it from the text of this one.

31. Teir Gosgord Adwy(n) Enys Prydein:

Gosgord Mynyda6c Eidyn,
a Gosgord Melyn mab Kynuelyn,
a Gosgord Dryon mab Nud.

31. Three Breach? / Gap? Retinues (Noble Retinues) of the Island of Britain:

The Retinue of Mynyddawg of Eidyn,
and the Retinue of Melyn son of Cynfelyn,
and the Retinue of Dryon son of Nudd.

Manuscripts: 16, 45, 47, V, C 18.
31. ad6y 16, 45, 47, V, adfwyn C 18.
a. Gosgord venyda6c eidun 47, Eiddin C 18.
b. melyn m. kynvel 47.
c. drywon 47, C 18. Nudh C 18.

31 W. Teir Gosgord Advwyn Ynys Brydein:

Gosgord Mynyda6c yg Kattraeth,
a Gosgord Dreon Le6 yn Rotwyd Arderys,
a'r dryded, Gosgord Velyn o Leyn (yn) Erethlyn yn Ros.

31 W. Three Noble Retinues of the Island of Britain:

The Retinue of Mynyddawg at Catraeth,
and the Retinue of Dreon the Brave at the Dyke of Ar(f)dery(dd),
and the third, the Retinue of Belyn of Llŷn (in?) Erethlyn in Rhos.

Manuscripts: WR, 51, 240, BL[1], C 18, Cwrt. 3.
31. gosgord adwvyn W. gosgerd adfwyn R, C 18 gosgordd add6wyn 51, BL, 240, Cwrt.
a. katraeth R, Mynydawc Eydyn yng Cattraeth V.
b. drywon V, Duwon Lew BL, 240, Cwrt. arderys WR, yn rrod wyd arderys 51, yn rodwydd Arderyt V, yr Odı wydd arvcr BL, 240, Cwrt.
c. erythlyn R, er edlyn *altered to* erythlyn 51, o lwyn northlun yn Rhos BL, 240, o lan nerthlun Ros Cwrt.

---

gosgord adwy(n). On *gosgord* see CA 380 (GPC 1510). The distinction between *gosgordd* and *teulu* is not entirely clear; perhaps *gosgordd* originally implied a larger body of troops than the *teulu* (300 men). The *Voc. Corn.* glosses *familia* by *gosgor pi* (= or) *teilu* (B XI, p. 3). In the Ox. 2 Glosses (fo. 43 v.) *casgoord* glosses *satilites*. The war-band of the Gododdin is invariably called *Gosgord* Mynydawc, never *teulu* (CA, ll. 89, 96, 355, 703, 956; so also Owain Cyfeiliog, RBP 1435.6 = CBT II, no. 14.125n.). Yet the number that went to Catraeth is said to have been 300 men (CA liii–lviii). (Cf. also the epithet of Elidir *Gosgordvawr*.) Eurys Rowlands prefers the Early Version's *adwy* to *addwyn* in this triad (LlC VI, p. 233), pointing out that the allusion seems to be to three retinues which were lost or destroyed. 'Gap' or 'Breach-Retinues' is therefore possible, or perhaps 'Retinues which left a gap or breach'. Cf. the variation between *Eidyn* and *Eiddyn*. *Eidyn* is the correct form of the name of Edinburgh, see K. Jackson in P. Clemoes (ed.), *The Anglo-Saxons* (Cambridge, 1959), pp. 39ff., OSPG 75–8. But the *varia lecta* in the manuscripts show that considerable uncertainty persisted in the later centuries between medial *-d-* and *-dd-* in this word; *Eiddyn* is the form later favoured by the poets. Since medial *d* in Pen. 16 and W normally, though not invariably, represents *dd* (see introduction, p. xvii), I have with some hesitation ventured to restore *adwyn* (= *addwyn*) in the title of the triad; cf. the *advwyn* of WR (see below). *Adwy* 'gap, breach' has however been consistently reproduced in all texts of the Pen. 16 version: Pen. 45, 47, and V. The Pen. 16 scribe must certainly have understood the word to have this meaning, since he gives it in preference to the *advwyn* of the WR version; and I feel that a certain doubt still remains as to the word intended in Pen. 16. The *Gogynfeirdd* frequently employ such phrases as *keitwat adwy* (RBP 1259.13) 'keeper of the breach', *llew yn adwy* (1291.17) 'a lion in the breach', *aer advy* 'the breach of battle' (1326.10). For further instances see G 9, GPC 29. Perhaps the 'Breach / Gap Retinues' defended some such mountain pass as Roland at Roncevaux. (Cf. Skene, FAB II, 463 'Pass Retinues'.) The two forms *addfwyn* (< *add* + *mwyn*) and *addwyn* (< *dwyn* + intensive prefix, 'fine') are synonymous in meaning and appear to be used interchangeably in early sources (GPC 35). In the present context the meaning of *addwyn* is ambiguous, since it may have reference to the valour of the three *gosgordd*, or to their splendid appearance: cf. the *Aduwyneu Taliesin* (BT 8); and the poem *Etmic Dinbych* (BT 42–4 = LlDC no. 13; BWP 162–3): *Adwin caer yssit ar lan llyant*, etc. The adjectives 'Noble' or 'Brave', which in English are capable of bearing either meaning, are for this reason preferable to 'splendid'.

The fact that in the *Hirlas Owain* (R 1432–5 = CBT II, no. 14) Owain Cyfeiliog compares his own war-band to that of Belyn, and then to that of Mynyddawg, forcibly suggests that he had this actual triad in his mind. (See introduction, pp. xcvii–xcviii.) If so, we have direct evidence that triad 31 was in existence before 1156, the date when this poem was recorded (CBT II, 221; cf. B XVI, pp. 188–9). Further, it was the version of WR rather than that of Pen. 16 which Owain knew. It is difficult to determine whether the variant forms of the names in **b** and **c**, as given in the two versions, refer to identical characters or not; see Notes to Personal Names. W and 47 show uncertainty over the lenition of proper names following the feminine noun *gosgordd* (TC § 46); the same uncertainty is found in the text of the *Gododdin*.

W: b. Rotwyd. *Rhodwydd* can mean either a ford or an earthen dyke; the latter was frequently constructed on the rising ground above a ford, and would be held instead of the ford itself. This was often the place where the fiercest battles were fought. Cf. CLlH 159–60 on *Rhodwydd Forlas.*

Arderys. *s* occurs frequently for *th* in the *Black Book of Chirk*, e.g. in the words *gueisret* (*gweithret*), *pesh* (*peth*), *kefreis(h)* (*kyfreith*), and others; see T. Lewis, *Glossary of Middle Welsh Law.* For a parallel instance in the text of the *Gododdin* see CA 212, n. to *dyfforsei.* For the battle of *Arfderydd* see n. to triad 84. With the subject-matter of item **b** of this triad, cf. *Tri Hualhogeon Deulu* triad 62 below and n.

c. (yn) Erethlyn. J. E. Lloyd points out (HW I, 184, n. 95) that *yn* must be restored before *Erethlyn,* a name which survived in the old 1-inch Ordnance map of Rhos as *Hiraethlyn* and *Pennant Ereithlyn,* now Pennant Erethlyn in Eglwys Bach (WCD 40). The omission of *yn* is, however, common to all texts of the WR version of the triad, and indicates the ultimate dependence of all upon W or R.

Pen. 16, fo. 51*v*–52*r*

32. Try Wyr a wnaeth y Teir Mat Gyflauan:

Gall mab Dysgyfda6t a lada6d deu ede(ryn) G6endoleu, ac yeu o eur a oed arnadunt: dwy gelein o'r Kymry a yssynt ar eu kinya6 a dwy ar eu kwynos;

Ac Ysgafnell mab Dysgyfda6t, a ladawt Edelflet 6renhin Lloegyr;

A Diffydell mab Dysgyfda6t (a ladawd) G6rgi Garwl6yt. A'r G6rghi h6nn6 a ladei gelein beunyd o'r Kymyry, a dwy bob Sadwrn rac (llad) y Sul vr un.

32. Three Men who performed the Three Fortunate Slaughters:

Gall son of Dysgyfdawd who slew the Two Birds of Gwenddolau. And they had a yoke of gold on them. Two corpses of the Cymry they ate for their dinner, and two for their supper;

And Ysgafnell son of Dysgyfdawd, who slew Edelfled king of Lloegr;

And Diffydell son of Dysgyfdawd who slew Gwrgi Garwlwyd ('Rough Grey'). That Gwrgi used to make a corpse of one of the Cymry every day, and two on each Saturday so as not to (slay) one on the Sunday.

Manuscripts: 16, 45, 50, C 18.

32. *For the version of WR (followed by* 51, NLW) *see no. 10 above, where this triad is combined with Tri Unben Deiuyr a Bryneic.*

a, b, c. Disgyfeda6t *throughout* 45, V, Deisysdawt 50, Disgybhdawt C 18.

a. ede(ryn) *supplied at foot of page in later hand, which adds* y rhai oeddynt yn cadw ei haur ar harian 16. a deuddyn a yssynt beunydd ar eu kinyaw a deuddyn yn y kwynos 50.

b. yscafnell 50.

c. Diffetdell 50, Diffeidell C 18. a ladavd *supplied by* 45. y Wrghi hwnnw 50, 6run Pen. 16 kymyry, y Gwr hwnnw a laddai Cembro beunydd a dair diw Sadwrn dros dri sul NLW, rrac lladd yr un dduw Sul 50.

This triad could be explained as a burlesque adaptation of triad 10W, in which the same names occur, to form a new triad, and one which would constitute a pair with triad 33. The *Teir An6at Gyflauan* (no. 33) is probably the older of the two. For W's version see triad 10 above, since W combines triads 10 and 32 into one.

mat gyflauan. In its earliest usage *mad* signifies 'fortunate' and not merely 'good' as in Ml.W. and M. Breton; see B II, pp. 121–2; PKM 223–4; and triad 37 below. In the Gaulish Coligny Calendar the days of the year are divided into those which are *matus* 'fortunate' and those which are *anm*[*atus*] 'unfortunate' (*Ériu* X, p. 1ff.). Similarly triad 37 R, *matkud* 'fortunate concealment(s)'.

a. The Two Birds of Gwenddolau are unknown elsewhere. In Irish sources birds which fly in couples, linked by a chain of gold or silver, are in reality usually human beings transformed. For example: *Serglige Con Culainn* (ed. M. Dillon, 1. 60) (trans. Cross and Slover, *Ancient Irish Tales*, p. 178); *Aislinge Oenguso* (ed. F. Shaw, p. 62) (trans. K. Jackson, *Celtic Miscellany*, no. 99); *Compert Con Culainn* (ed. Van Hamel, p. 3). See Anne Ross, 'Chain Symbolism in Pagan Celtic Religion', *Speculum* XXXIV, pp. 39 ff. Gwenddolau's ferocious birds are reminiscent of Owain ab Urien's fighting ravens in *Breudwyt Ronabwy*. For another tale of savage birds performing a murder see n. to *Drutwas m. Driffin* under Personal Names.

b. According to ASC, Ethelfrith was slain in 616 by King Raedwald of East Anglia, not by a Welsh opponent.

Pen. 16, fo. 52*r*

33. Teir An6at Gyflauan Enys Prydein:

Heidyn mab Enygan a lada6d Aneiryn Gwa6tryd Mechdeyrn Beird,
a Lla6gat Tr6m Barga6t Eidyn a lada6d Auaon mab Talyessin,
a Llouan Lla6 Diuo a lada6d 6ryen mab Kyn6arch.

33. Three Unfortunate Slaughters of the Island of Britain:

Heidyn son of Enygan, who slew Aneirin of Flowing Verse, Great Prince of Poets.

and Llawgad Trwm Bargod Eidyn ('Heavy Battle-Hand of the Border of Eidyn') who slew Afaon son of Taliesin,

and Llofan Llaw Ddifo ('Ll. Severing Hand') who slew Urien son of Cynfarch.

Manuscripts: 16, 45, 47, 50, C 18.

33. anvat gyflafyn 50.

a. Eidyn m. einygan 45, 50, Eidyn m. Eingawn 47, Heidhyn m. Heinygan C 18. gwa6drud 45, gwawtrud 50. mechderyn 45, mechteyrn 50, C 18.

b. eidyn *omitted* 45, a thrwm varga6t eidin 47, a Llawgat trwn vargawt Eiddyn 50. adaon 47, Abhaon C 18. Talessin 45.

c. Llouan Lla6 dino 45, llonan lla6 deifyo 47. 50 *substitutes a* Cynon mab Klytno Eidin a Dyfynnawl mab Mynedawc Eidin. a laddawdd Urien mab Kynvarch.

33 W. Tri G6yth6r Ynys Brydein a 6naethant y Teir Anuat Gyflauan:

Llofuan Lla6 Difuro a lada6d Vryen ap Kynuarch,
Llongad Grwm Uargot Eidin a lada6d Auaon ap Talyessin,
a Heiden ap Euengat a lada6d Aneirin G6a6tryd merchteyrn beird—y g6r a rodei gan muw pob Sadarn yg ker6yn eneint yn (=yr?) Talhaearn—a'e tre6is a b6yall gynnut yn y fen.

A honno oed y dryded v6yalla6t. A'r eil, kynuttei o Aberfra6 a dre6is Golydan a b6yall yn y ben. A'r dryded, Iago ap Beli a dre6is y 6r ehun a b6yall yn y ben.

33 W. Three Savage Men of the Island of Britain, who performed the Three Unfortunate (Ill-omened) Slaughters:

Llofan Llaw Ddifro ('Ll. Exiled Hand') who slew Urien son of Cynfarch,

Llongad Grwm Fargod Eidyn ('Ll. the Bent of the Border of Eidyn') who slew Afaon son of Taliesin, and Heiden son of Efengad who slew Aneirin of Flowing Verse, Great Prince of Poets—the man who used to give a hundred cows every Saturday in a vat of oil to (?for) Talhaearn. And he struck her (him) with a wood-hatchet on the head.

And that was one of the Three Hatchet-Blows.

The second (was) a woodcutter of Aberffraw who struck Golydan with a hatchet, on the head. And the third, one of his own men struck upon Iago, son of Beli, with a hatchet, on the head.

Manuscripts: WR, 51, NLW, Cwrt. 3, BL[2], C 36, RW.

33 W. gweithwr C 36, RW, NLW, gwythawr Cwrt. y tair anvad neu vadd gyflavan NLW, y tair anvad nevadh Gyulauan RW.

a. diffro R. llewan *altered to* llowan 51, Levan RW, C 36, Llofanaw Cwrt., lovon NLW, Llavan BL.

b. llongat R, llonn grwm *altered* to llongat grwm 51, Cwrt. bargod eithin 51, Llongat grwn argodion C 36, RW, llongam Grwm argodion NLW. avon R, Addon NLW, Adhon RW.

c. Heidia6 vab evengad 51, Haidden Cwrt. ap dyrn beirdd *altered to* verch teyrnbeirdd. gan myw R. Ar oreidiaw Evengat a ladodd Edwyn Gwawdrydd merch teirn beirdd NLW. yr talhaearn 51, Galhaiarn C 36, RW.

d. kynunttei R. Golydan varth RW. R *omits* iago. Iaco vab Beli a drewis y wr ef y hûn Cwrt.

---

teir an6at gyflauan. For *anvat* 'unfortunate', see n. to triad 32; and cf. triads 34, 59.

a. Heidyn, *(H)eidyn* in triad 34a; see n. For a discussion of this triad as a whole see EWSP 115–17, and n. to *Urien Rheged* under Personal Names below

mechdeyrn beird. On *mechteyrn*, Breton *machtiern* 'chef-garant, juge' (Cornish *mychtern, mygtern*) see L. Fleuriot, 'Un fragment en Latin de très anciennes Lois Bretonnes Armoricaines du Ve siècle', *Annales de Bretagne* 78, pp. 622–3, 650–3. Fleuriot agrees with Loth (*Chr. Br.*) in deriving *machtiern* and *mechteyrn* from *mach* 'surety' and *tiern* (= *teyrn*) 'prince', and disagrees with Ifor Williams's derivation (B X, pp. 39–40) from **mach* 'great' cognate with Ir. *mass* 'lovely' etc. which, as he points out, is not attested with this meaning in any other instance. See DGVB 253 on *meic(h)* (pl. of *mach*); see also D. Jenkins, *Hywel Dda: The Law*, p. xviii, etc. on *mach* 'surety' as a legal term. Fleuriot established this derivation beyond doubt, and showed that there was not adequate basis for Ifor Williams's suggestion that *mach* is an otherwise unknown adjective meaning 'great, magnificent'. Fleuriot's analysis subsequently formed the basis for the entry in GPC 2389, from which it appears that this triad provides the earliest written instance of *mechdeyrn* in Welsh. The cognate form in Breton *machtiern* and Cornish *myg(h)tern* establish the antiquity of the word in the Brittonic languages, but Fleuriot showed that *machtiern* developed somewhat differently in meaning in Breton from its meaning in Welsh and Cornish, in both of which it signifies 'monarch, (supreme) king, emperor' and is also used of God. These meanings are also exemplified in the examples from *Gogynfeirdd* poetry recorded in GPC. The earliest (apart from the tenth-century *Armes Prydein* (AP ll.18, n.; 100) where the *mechdeyrn* apparently denotes Athelstan, king of England) is found in Gwalchmai's *marwnad* for Madog ap Maredudd, ruler of Powys, who died in 1160, in which Gwalchmai describes the prince as *mechdeyrn Lleisiawn* ('lord of Powys' H 27.24 = CBT I, no. 7.110n.). A parallel usage is recorded for the Cornish *mychtern*, which is employed in reference to both Pharaoh and to David, as well as to Christ, who is named *mychtern Yedhewon* (R. Williams, *Lexicon Cornu-Britannicum*, p. 260). In contrast, the Breton *machtiern* had a more precise if less exalted meaning, and designated a tributary ruler under a *dux* or *comes*, and this was a local and frequently a hereditary office. To quote Fleuriot (EC VII, p. 50) 'le terme *machtiern* qualifie une categorie fort nombreuse de chefs locaux qui forment l'armature de l'administration dans l'ancien royaume de Bretagne'. GPC 2389–90 records the survival in the Welsh Law codes of the term *mechdeyrn ddylyed*, which has a meaning resembling that in Breton, signifying the tribute due to an overlord by his inferior.

To the references given above, add further L. Fleuriot, HLCB I, p. 36; E. P. Hamp, EC XXI, pp. 137–40; Wendy Davies, *Small Worlds* (London, 1988), pp. 138–42; J. G. T. Sheringham, 'Les Machtierns', *Memoires de la Société d'Histoire et d'Archeologie de Bretagne*, LVIII, pp. 61–72. (For an allusion to a presiding *machtiern* quoted from the *Cart. de Redon*, see n. to triad 24 above.)

Triad 33 W.

W's ill-conceived misinterpretations reach their height of absurdity in the rendering of this triad: *mechdeyrn* has been corrupted to *merch teyrnbeird*, and Aneirin's identity is so far forgotten that the Prince of Poets has become a girl, hit with a hatchet on *her* head—*yn y fen*. (The use of *f* for *ph* is archaic, cf. CO l. 35: *heb dant yny fenn*.) A misinterpretation seems to have arisen with respect to *Talhaearn*: it looks as though the redactor of W has mistaken for a place-name what is in fact the name of another of the renowned *Cynfeirdd* listed in HB (ch. 62)—*Talhaern Tataguen*. It is a tantalizing conclusion that the scribe of W had before him a very corrupt copy of what appears to have been a fuller version of the triad than that in Pen. 16.

c. y gwr a rodei, etc. *Y gwr* must refer to *Heidyn* (= *Heiden*).

can muw. With *can* the usual form is *mu*, GMW § 51b; but in copying *can mu* the scribe of W seems to have been influenced by the alternative singular form *buw* (GPC 342). It is difficult to visualize the payment of cows as here described, and it seems likely that one or more words have dropped from the text. In *Culhwch* (CO l. 78), *can mu* is used to denote the value of the golden balls on each of the four corners of the hero's cloak 'each worth a hundred cows'.

d. W gives here what is in effect a version of triad 34 *Teir Anvat Vwyallawt*, the 'Three Unfortunate Hatchet-Blows'. This is linked to triad 34 by the allusion to the death of Aneirin, which is given in both. Golydan's murder of Cadwaladr (see n.) is cited in triad 53 below as one of the *Teir Gwith Baluawt* 'Three Sinister (Ill-omened) Hand-Slaps', and the same story is alluded to by the poet Phylip Brydydd (H 228.19–21 = CBT VI, no. 15.11–13n.). Could the slaying of Golydan by the 'woodcutter of Aberffraw' have been an act of vengeance for the slaying of the woodcutter's overlord, the Gwynedd king whose royal estate lay at Aberffraw? As M. E. Owen points out (YB XIX, p. 18), these references point to the former existence of lost traditions, otherwise unknown, but once familiar to the poets, about the *Cynfardd* Golydan.

34. Teir Anvat 6wyalla6t Enys Prydein:

> B6yalla6t (H)eidyn ym pen Aneiryn,
> a'r 6wyalla6t ym pen Golydan Vard,
> a'r 6wyalla6t ym pen Yago mab Beli

34. Three Unfortunate Hatchet-Blows of the Island of Britain:

> The Blow of Heidyn on the Head of Aneirin,
> and the Blow on the Head of Golydan the Poet,
> and the Blow on the head of Iago son of Beli.

Manuscripts: 16, 45, 47, 51, C 18.

34. *For version of* WR, *see triad* 33. anvat u6wyella6t 45 *throughout*, anvat v6ellaut 47, Tair bwallod 51.

a. Pen. 16 Eidyn. Heidhyn C 18. talhaearn a trewis e 6eirin yni ffen 51.

b. Godlan bard 45, Ar ail kym6dei *altered to* kynuntei o aberffro A drewis golydan a bwall yni benn 51.

c. Iago 45, 47, Iago ap peli a drewis y wr ehun ym benn A bwyall 51.

For W's version see triad 33, since W has combined the two triads together.

anvat 6wyalla6t. For *anvat*, see nn. to triad 32. Cf. the reference to the death of Dylan Eil Ton as *trydyd anuat ergyt* (PKM 78.2).

a. (H)eidyn = *Heidyn m. Enygan* in triad 33a (see n.); *Heiden m. Evengat* in W. The form of this name may have been influenced by the place-name *Eid(d)yn*; see n. to *Heidyn m. Enygan* under Personal Names. Each of the murderers in triad 33 belongs to the northern British kingdoms, if not, like Aneirin himself, to the district of Manau Gododdin and Edinburgh.

There is a reference to the death of Aneirin in stanza LV(B) of the *Gododdin*:

> er pan want maws mvr trin.
> er pan aeth daear ar aneirin.
> nu neut ysgaras nat a gododin.

The first line is too short in both A and B versions, and Ifor Williams suggests it might be emended by the addition of the name of the assassin (H)eidyn as found in the triad:

> er pan want (H(e)idyn) maws mvr trin.

'Since (H(e)idyn) struck the courteous wall of battle, since earth went upon Aneirin, in truth song has departed from the *Gododdin*.' See CA n. to 1. 647, and for the references to the death of Aneirin in the *Gododdin* and in TYP, see

M. E. Owen, *Ast. H.* 134ff. For Golydan's slaughter of Cadwaladr, see reference by Phylip Brydydd (H 228.19 = CBT VI, no. 15.11–13n.):

O gwnaeth Golydan gyflauan diryeit
. . . Taraw Kadwaladr, colofyn elyflu . . .

See also nn. to *Golydan* and to *Katwaladyr* under Personal Names.

35. Tri Chyuor a aeth o'r Enys hon, ac ny doeth dracheuyn 6r un onadunt:

6n a aeth gan Elen Luyda6c a Chynan e bra6t;

Eil a aeth gan Yrp Lluyda6c yn oes Cadyal mab Eryn, a doeth eman y erchi kymorth; ac nyt archei o bob pryf gaer namyn deu kymeint ac a delei gantha6 idi. Ac ny doeth gantha6 y'r gaer gyntaf namyn ef a'e was. Ac ardustru 6u rodi hynny ida6. A h6nn6 eissyoes llwyrhaf llu a aeth o'r Enys hon. Ac ny doeth dracheuyn byth nep onadunt. Sef lle y trigws y gwyr hynny: yn dwy enys yn emyl Mor Groec. Sef yw y dwy enys hynny: Gals ac Auena.

Trydyd Kyuor a aeth gan Gaswalla6n mab Beli, a Gwenwynwyn a G6anar, meibyon Llia6s mab Nwy6re, ac Aryanrot merch 6eli eu mam. Ac o Arllechwed yd hanoed y gwyr hynny. Ac aethant y gyt a Chaswalla6n eu hewyt(h)yr drwy vor yn ol y Cesaryeit. Sef lle y mae y gwyr hynny yg Wasgwyn.

A sef eiryf a aeth ym pob 6n or lluoed hynny: 6n 6il ar ugeint. A'r rei hyny oed y *Tri Aryanllu*. Sef acha6s y gelwit y 6elly, 6rth vynet eur ac aryant yr Enys ganthunt. Ac eu dethol wynteu o oreu y oreu.

35. Three Levies that departed from this Island, and not one of them came back:

The first went with Elen of the Hosts and Cynan her brother,

The second went with Yrp of the Hosts, who came here to ask for assistance in the time of Cadial son of Eryn. And all he asked of each Chief Fortress was twice as many (men) as would come with him to it; and to the first Fortress there came only himself and his servant. (And it proved grievous to have given him that.) Nevertheless that was the most complete levy that ever went from this Island, and no (man) of them ever came back. The place where those men remained was on two islands close to the Greek sea: those islands are Gals and Avena.

The third levy went with Caswallawn son of Beli, and Gwenwynwyn and Gwanar, sons of Lliaws son of Nwyfre, and Ar(i)anrhod daughter of Beli their mother. And those men came from Arllechwedd. They went with Caswallawn their uncle across the sea in pursuit of the men of Caesar. The place where those men are is in Gascony. And the number that went in each of those Hosts was twenty-one thousand men. And those were the Three Silver Hosts: they were so called because the gold and silver of the Island went with them. And they were the best-chosen men.

Manuscripts: 16, 45, 50, C 18.

a. Helen Luyda6c 45, elen luddyawc 50. 50 *adds* a hvnnv ny ddeuth drachefyn. a ddeuth a Chonstantinus i Rufain ac ni ddoeth byth drachevyn RW.

b. a ddeuth yman yn amser cadyal m. erin y erchi kymorth yr ynys honn 50. Erynt 45, Erim C 18. namyn bob cymeint C 18. ac ny ddoeth ganthaw ef y myvn 50. Mathutafur ei was V. Ac y bu mor distru gan wyr yr ynys honn hynny. Ac y rodassant iddaw y kymorth 50. llvyraf lluyd 45. Ac ny ddeuth drachefyn na hwy nae llynys 50, neb onaddunt nae llinys V.

c. Gwenwyn 50. Nwyfre 50, C 18. Aranrot 6erch Beli 45, Arianrot C 18, aranron verch Beli 50. trwy vor a rrwysc y cesseryeit or ynys honn 50.

d. un vil a thrugeint 50. aryant llu 45. achaws mynet 50. a dethol y gwyr o oreu y oreu 50, ae hethol 45, V. Sef eiryf a aeth ym pob un or lluoedd hynny 61000 V. 50 *adds* Ac vn llu hayach vu gymeint ar tri hynny. a aeth gyda maxen wledic y lydaw. A phan ddanvonawdd kynan mairydawc at Dunavt tywyssavc kernyv y gaffel vrsula y verch y daeth or dylyedogyon un vil ar ddec o vorynyon merthyri yssyd ygholoyn. Ac hevyt deugein mil o wragedd eraill. ac ny ddeuth yr un drachefyn.

35 R. *Pann aeth Llu y Lychlyn.*

Porth a aeth y gan Yrp Luyda6c hyt yn Llychlyn; a'r g6r h6nn6 a doeth yman yn oes Gadyal y Byry y erchi dygyfuor o'r Ynys honn. Ac ny doeth ganta6 namyn ef a Mathuthauar y was. Ac ys ef a archei o dec prifgaer ar hugeint yssyd yn yr Ynys honn: deu kymmeint a elei gantha6 y bob un o nadunt y dyuot gantha6 o honunt ymeith. Ac ny doei ganta6 y'r gaer gyntaf namyn ef a'e was. (Ac y bu ardustur gan wyr yr Ynys honn hynny.) Ac y rodassant ida6. A hwnnw uu l6yraf llu o'r a aeth o'r Ynys honn. Ac ef a oresgynna6d a'r gwyr hynny y fford y kerda6d. Ac ys ef lle y trigya6d y gwyr hynny, yn y d6y ynys yn ymyl Mor Groec: nyt amgen, Clas ac Auena.

A'r eil a aeth gan Elen Luyda6c a Maxen Wledic hyt yn Llychlyn. Ac ny doethant byth y'r Ynys honn.

A'r trydyd a aeth gan Gasswalla6n uab Beli, a G6enn6ynwyn a Gwanar, veibon Llia6 uab N6yfre, ac Aryanrot verch Veli eu mam. A'r g6yr hynny o Erch a Heled pann anhoedynt. Ac a aethant gyt a Chasswalla6n eu hewythyr ar 6ysc y Kessaryeit o'r Ynys honn. Sef lle y mae y g6yr hynny: yg G6asg6yn.

Sef riuedi a aeth gan bob un o nadunt: vn vil ar hugeint. A'r rei hynny uu *Tri Aryanllu Ynys Prydein.*

35 R. *When a Host went to Llychlyn.*

An army (of assistance) went with Yrp of the Hosts to Llychlyn. And that man came here in the time of Cadyal of the Blows(?) to ask for a levy from this Island. And nobody came with him but Mathuthafar his servant. This is what he asked from the ten-and-twenty Chief Fortresses that there are in this Island: that twice as many men as went with him to each of them should come away with him (from it). And to the first Fortress there came only himself and his servant. (And that proved grievous to the men of this Island.) And they granted it to him. And that was the most complete levy that ever departed from this Island. And with those men he conquered wherever he went. Those men remained in the two islands close to the Greek sea: namely, Clas and Avena.

And the second (army) went with (H)elen of the Hosts and Maxen Wledig to Llychlyn: and they never returned to this Island.

And the third (army) went with Caswallawn son of Beli, and Gwennwynwyn and Gwanar, sons of Lliaw(s) son of Nwyfre, and Arianrhod daughter of Beli their mother. And (it was) from Erch and Heledd that those men came. And they went with Caswallawn their uncle in pursuit of the men of Caesar from this Island. The place where those men are is in Gascony.

The number that went with each of (those armies) was twenty-one thousand men. And those were the Three Silver Hosts of the Island of Britain.

Manuscripts: R, 51, 252, NLW, Cwrt. 3; NLW Addl. MS. 325E, p. 92 (titles only), BL[2], RW.

35 R. Tri arianly ynys prydein 252, Tri arianllv ynys B, NLW, Cwrt. 3, tri arianlhy C 36, RW, Tri Arianllu o'r Deyrnas hon NLW Addl. 325E.

a. luyddiawc 51, Urp Lydiddog 252, y Lhy aeth gan Yrp luydhant i Lychlyn RW, Irp vlydoc Cwrt. Cadwal map Erim Cwrt. 3, yn oed Gadal a Byry i erchy dyvyny yr ynys honn C 36, RW, ac nid oedh ond ef ai was i ddechrev erchy dybly hynny NLW. Ac ny ddoeth ohonunt 51. Mathutavir 51, Machyrhavar i was a dysgy phemp gwyr or ynys i roi hynny NLW. dec prifgaer a trigaint 51, 23 prif gaer 252. y bu ddiystyr 51, a drygstyr vu Cwrt. ac y rodassany y ddaw kymaint hynny iddaw 51. a hwnnw fu y llu mwyaf Cwrt. or ynys hon erioed 51. Ag ef a oreskynodd lawer ar lly hwn or byd 252, ag ef a orysgynoed dalym or byd ar lhy hwnnw C 36, or brys byd ar Lhy hwnnw RW. Efena Cwrt., Ynys Glas ac avena NLW, RW.

b. elen luyddioc 51, Elen Leddiawg 252, Elen luyddawg a Chonstantinus i Rufain NLW, Elen lyedhawg a Chonstantinus i Ryvain C 36, RW, Elen ferch Coel a Chonstans i Ruvain Cwrt.

c. gysswallawn 51. a Gawennyd a gwanar RW, C 36. meibion lleon NLW, lleon vab Monifre Cwrt.

d. 51 *adds* trwy warth ir ynys. achos i gelwid arianllu, o herwydd iddynt fyned a'r arian ganthynt NLW Addl. 325E.

---

tri chyuor. As verb *kyuor* (*-i*, *-yaw*) means 'to cause to flow, shed'; as noun 'an influx, flood, mustering, levy' (GPC 709); cf. its compound *dygyfuor* in R l. 2, used as a noun with precisely similar meaning. Though R's version nowhere employs the word *cyfor*, yet the use of *dygyfor* here indicates that the passage has a close underlying relationship with the *cyvor* of Pen. 16. On *cyfor, dygyfor* see Ifor Williams in B IV, p. 138. Brynley Roberts points out that the expedition of Elen Luydauc and Cynan is referred to in the Llanstephan I version of *Brut y Brenhinedd*; see his article, 'Testunau Hanes Cymraeg Canol' in Tr. Rh. 290: *Tyrdyd dekyuor a aeth or enys honn wu hwnn* (quoted from Havod 2, 82b). See also MA^2 511b: *Trydyd dekyuor or enys honn wu hwnn.* With regard to the enormous numbers of Yrp's host, K. Jackson points out (WHR 1963 (Special Number on the Welsh Laws), p. 84) that the story is an example of a 'cumulative tale', of which other examples are cited in Stith Thompson's *Motif-Index*, Z, 21.1. See also Stith Thompson's *The Folktale* (New York, 1951), pp. 230–4, which includes a similar example in a discussion of cumulative tales. R substitutes *porth* 'an army (in aid)' to designate the first host, and Pen. 16 employs *kymorth*, a compound of *porth* in l. 3 where R has *dygyfuor*. In favour of *cyvor* as the original word in the triad is the fact that triads 35 and 36 form a contrasting pair: the use of *cyvor* to designate an (outgoing) flood, a draining of the resources of the Island of Britain, is balanced by that of *gormes* in triad 36 to designate an *incoming* invasion. It is difficult to account for R's substitution of *porth* in item **a**, since this stresses the idea of *assistance* which has no counterpart in triad 36 (triad 36 is in fact omitted from all texts of the WR version). A further complication is introduced by the fact that another name for triad 35 was *Tri Aryanllu* 'Three Silver Hosts', and this title is employed in NLW and Pen. 252; cf. R: *Pan aeth llu y lychlyn.* But the idea underlying the contrasting triads 35 and 36 corresponds closely with the passage in HB about the depopulation of Britain and subsequent settlement of Armorica by Maximus' soldiers, of which the Saxon invasions were regarded as a direct result:

> Hi sunt Brittones Armorici et numquam reversi sunt huc usque in hodiernum diem. Propter hoc Brittannia occupata est ab extraneis gentibus et cives expulsi sunt, usque dum Deus auxilium dederit illis. (HB ch. 27)
>
> 'These are the Armorican Britons, and they never came back, up till the present day. That is why Britain has been occupied by foreigners, and the citizens driven out, until God shall give them help.'

Hence it seems natural to regard Pen. 16's item **a**—the removal by Maximus from Britain to the continent of all the island's protective forces—as the story which inspired the composition of the whole triad. It has its logical counterpart in items **b** and **c** of triad 36.

a. The allusion here is to the tale of the Breton settlement as it appears in *Breudwyt Maxen*, rather than to the version given in the *Bruts* and Geoffrey of Monmouth, since in these latter Cynan (*Meiriadoc*) is *cousin* and not *brother* to Elen. Yet, according to *Breudwyt Maxen*, Elen was in Rome with Maxen when Cynan and his brother Adaon joined them, and it is not implied that Elen accompanied Cynan on his subsequent career of conquest to Brittany. R names Maxen and not Cynan as Elen's companion, but both versions concur in associating Elen with the expedition, and this suggests that the triad is based on a form of the tale which differed slightly from that which has come down. In the *Brut Cleopatra* (ed. J. J. Parry, p. 101), the expedition of Maxen and Cynan to Brittany is described as *tryde(d) phla ynys brydein* 'one of the three Plagues of the Island of Britain'. One suspects here a confused reference to this triad, although *pla* corresponds more closely to the *gormes* of triad 36 than to any of the words used in this triad to denote the forces which departed from the Island of Britain. Pen. 50 brings the reference into line with Geoffrey's version of the Maximus story (HRB V, 16) in its allusion to the tale of St Ursula and the Virgins of Cologne.

b. o bob pryf gaer. The number of the *prif gaerau* (thirty) is specified only in R. This must be a mistake for thirty-three, the traditional number of the cities of Britain according to *Enweu Ynys Prydein* (see App. I; according to Gildas there were twenty-eight cities).

Line 5. **ardustru.** R: *ardustur*. The sentence is probably to be explained as the comment of a glossator, which subsequently became incorporated in the text. This is the only example of *arddustru* recorded by GPC 189: 'vexatious, grievous, sorry'; cf. the verb *arddustruaf* 'to despise, disdain, vex', and the adjective and verb *anustru, anustruaw* 'contemptible; to minimize, belittle'. In the first pair of words the preposition *ar-*, in the second the intensive particle *an-* is prefixed to *distru*; Pen. 50 retains the simple form *mor distru*. R's reading *ardustur* could alternatively be explained as composed from the root of the verb *tosturio* 'to be sorry for'; although Pen. 51's emendation of this version to *y bu ddiystyr* shows that the copyist understood the form before him as meaning 'unimportant, contemptible'.

Line 5. **llwyrhaf llu.** Cf. PKM 38.21: *llwyr wys* 'the complete levy'; CA l. 586: *llwyr genyn llu*. Cf. Cynddelw's unexplained and obscure allusion to *trydyt haearnlly* (CBT IV no. 9.80n.) and the reference to *Tri Aryanllu* in the triad under **d** above.

Line 8. **Gals ac Auena.** R: *Clas ac Auena*. These names have not been identified. It seems likely that they are corruptions of forms found in some late Latin source. *Galis* occurs for *Galicia* (French *Galice*) in DGG no. LXXIV.70 (Grufffudd Gryg); but Spain hardly fits the specification given in the triad. Perhaps Galatia(?).

c. There must have existed a much fuller tradition about Caswallawn's dealings with the Romans than that which has come down (see nn. to *Caswallawn* and *F(f)lur* under Personal Names); and there are several references to it in the triads (nos. 35, 38, 51, 67). The saga which is outlined by these certainly differed considerably from Geoffrey's account (HRB III, 20; IV, 1–11); on the other hand it is difficult to associate the references in the triads with the allusions to Caswallawn in PKM, where the latter is depicted as succeeding Bendigeidfran in the rule of Britain, but no mention is made of the Romans.

Nevertheless *Branwen* and *Manawydan* may be taken as providing corroborative evidence for the pre-Geoffrey origin of the Caswallawn saga, though these tales themselves make no more than a few casual allusions to it. As outlined in HRB IV, the Caswallawn saga found an apparent parallel in the Chartres text of HB, which reproduced a similar (unhistorical) tradition of two defeats for the Romans at the hands of 'Cassabellaunus' followed by their final victory and the death of the British leader. On the interpretation of the relevant passage from the Chartres text see D. N. Dumville, *Éigse* 16, pp. 183–6.

Line 9. **Gwenwynwyn.** If *G. mab Lliaws* is to be identified with *Gwenwynwyn mab Naf (Naw)* of triad 14 (see n. to *G6enwynwyn*[2] under Personal Names), then we have a link here with one of the stories underlying that triad. The fact that the latter *Gwenwynwyn* is one of the *Tri Llynghessawc* favours the likelihood of this identification.

Line 10. **Aryanrot.** This triad is our only source for the assertion that Ar(i)anrhod's father was Beli Mawr, and hence for the information that she was in any way connected with the Caswallawn saga. On the lenition following *merch* see n. to triad 56.

Line 11. **Arllechwed.** R 18: *Erch a Heled.* One hesitates to conclude that Pen. 16's reading is preferable here, in view of Cynddelw's allusion to *Erch a Helet* in his *marwnad* to Owain Gwynedd:

> As duch duv yny dagneuet
> A duc treis tros erch a helet.
> (H 92.16 = CBT IV, no. 4.122n.)

'May God take him into his peace, who (once) brought war across *Erch* and *Heledd.*'

Both *Erch* and *Heli* occur several times as elements in river- and place-names, see EANC 67, 163. *Heli* means 'brine', *heledd* 'salt-pit' (D: *salina*), so that the two words are perhaps close enough in meaning to be used interchangeably. *Heledd* probably refers to Cheshire with its three Heledds—Nantwich, Middlewich and Northwich, and the name *Erch* seems to be preserved in that of *Child's Ercal* in Shropshire (PT 57–8; CLlH 227). Eurys Rowlands agrees (LlC VI, p. 233) that these are the regions referred to by Cynddelw, pointing out that Owain Gwynedd pushed his borders almost as far as Chester, so that the Cheshire *Heledd* is most likely to be the place to which he alludes, while his *Erch* can be identified with *Child's Ercall* and *High Ercall.* As he also points out, it is likely that the almost forgotten names *Erch* and *Heledd* of R's version were those which were original to the triad, and that they were superseded by the more familiar name *Arllechwedd* in the Pen. 16 version. There is no reason to suppose that Cynddelw's allusion to these places is dependent on the triad itself; it is more likely that both reflect independent knowledge of the places concerned. On *Erch* and *Heledd*, see further CBT IV no. 4.122n. and GPC 1229.

Line 12. **y Cesaryeit.** This is the only reference to the Romans which is to be found in the Pen. 16 version of TYP. The form *Cesaryeit* is apparently peculiar to this triad (in both versions), but cf. *kessarogyon* BT 77.17. The story here referred to of Caswallawn's pursuit of Caesar is possibly also alluded to in Ieuan ap Sulien's poem to his father (ed. M. Lapidge, SC VIII/IX, p. 83, ll. 54–6: . . . *natus sum gente Britonum / Romane quondam classi cum uiribus obstat, / Iulus cum Caesar refugus post terga recessit*). On the reference, see Brynley Roberts, *Nottingham Mediaeval Studies* XX, pp. 33–4; idem, *Studies on Middle Welsh Literature*, p. 30. Geoffrey's account may also be compared, HRB IV, 3–9.

Line 13. **yg Wasgwyn.** *Gwasgwyn* = Gascony. In the *Bruts* the names *Gvasguyn a Pheitaw ac Angyw*, 'Gascony and Poitou and Anjou', are used to render Geoffrey's *Aquitania* (BD 15.13, 16 = HRB I, 12; BD 156.23 = HRB IX, 11; see n., BD 212). Chotzen argues (EC IV, p. 236) that these names would have become familiar in Britain after the marriage of Eleanor of Aquitaine and Henry II in 1152, when Poitou and Gascony became part of the queen's dowry. *Gwasgwyn* is used of Gascon horses by Prydydd y Moch (RBP 1420–3 = CBT V, no. 23.58), and the plural *(g)wesgwyn* is used by Cynddelw (H 118.16 = CBT III, no. 7.16n.), as well as by later poets. This suggests that the name of the country had become generally familiar through trade channels during the twelfth century. The NED does not record this word before 1375.

d. eiryf . . . 6n 6il ar ugeint, i.e. the number of each host was ten times that of each of the *Tri Diweir Deulu*, triad 29. But 21,000 is a very modest estimate of the number that must have been reached by Yrp's host, which would run into some fifteen figures. R. Vaughan evidently felt this inadequacy, and altered the figure to 61,000.

Line 15. **Tri Aryanllu.** This may have been the original title of the triad; see CBT III, p. xli and n., where Cynddelw's *trydyt haearnlly* (CBT IV, no. 9.80n.) is compared. It recalls the name *Ar(y)anrot*, and the first element is probably identical in both words: see n. to *Ar(y)anrot* and PKM 269–70 for discussion of *aran, aryan*. The emphasis throughout the triad is on the *size* of the three hosts; so that from the information we are given 'great, huge' would be an appropriate epithet for them, if this is the meaning of *aran*. Pen. 16's explanation of the epithet, 'because the gold and silver of the Island went with them', comes somewhat lamely after the allusion to the number of men which composed each of the hosts, and it could well represent a secondary attempt to explain the epithet, after the original meaning of *aran* had become forgotten. Nevertheless, all the manuscripts favour *aryanllu* as against *aranllu*. And here a curious point arises. Geoffrey (HRB V, 12) tells us with reference to Maxim(ian)us's expedition to Brittany that *superbiuit maximianus propter infinitam copiam auri et argenti que illi cotidie affluebat. parauitque nauigiam. omnemque armatum militem britannie collegit.* 'Maximus became proud because of the enormous amount of gold and silver that flowed to him daily. He prepared a fleet and conscripted every armed soldier in Britain' (cf. BD 76).

There is nothing elsewhere in Geoffrey's text which throws light on this allusion to the emperor's wealth, and it therefore seems possible that the tradition recorded in the triad of the *Tri Aryanllu* may lie behind it. And again, can the allusion to Maximus's host as one of the *Tri Aryanllu* be connected with the obscure reference in HB, ch. 25 to the wealth of Segontium, the city of *Elen Luyddog*, in gold and silver and bronze?

Line 16. **o oreu y oreu.** Lit. 'and they were chosen from best to best'. Cf. WM 432.16 (= Pen. 6, 35): *Ac o oreu y oreu y doethant attav.*

Triad 35 R.

a. Porth 'help, assistance'. *Porth* is however regularly employed in *Brut Dingestow* with a similar meaning to that found here 'an army of assistance'; cf. BD 25.10; 30.8, 13; etc.

Llychlyn Ir. *Lochlann*, earlier *Lothlind.* This name commonly denotes Scandinavia in Celtic sources. *Llychlyn* is mentioned in CO l. 120n. (pp. 59–60) and in Br. Rh. (RM 104.16; 151.13; 160.6; see n. to *March m. Meirchya6n* under Personal Names). The fact that in **b** the destination of the army of Elen Luyddog and Maxen is described as *hyt yn llychlyn* provides a strong argument in favour of the belief that Llychlyn in the triad is a corruption of *Llydaw* (Armorica), the traditional destination of the army of Maxen Wledig, and surely the nucleus around which this triad was evolved. The two strokes of the *d* in *Llydaw* could at some stage have been misread as *cl.* (The alteration of *Llychlyn* to *Llydaw* has in fact been inserted in the text of the *Red Book* by a later hand.) As for Yrp's expedition, neither the proper names nor the event itself can be associated with any other persons or events referred to in early Welsh sources; nor does it appear to be alluded to by the *Gogynfeirdd* or any of the later poets. Probably it is an invented story built up around a mathematical fantasy which appealed to the triad maker. A comparison with the vast number involved in the reckoning of Yrp's host was employed to emphasize the immense number of the other two hosts. The genesis of the triad lay in the potent tradition of Maxen's alleged withdrawal of all the Roman troops from Britain. The two other incidents, **b** and **c**, alluded to in the triad, are completely unknown. There is no need to explore the possible mythological connotations of *Llychlyn* before it came to mean Scandinavia (for these see J. Rhŷs, *Hibbert Lectures* (1898), pp. 355 ff.).

The discrepancy between the eventual destination of Yrp's forces in the islands of Clas and Avena and the destination indicated in the title given to the triad provides additional proof that its original nucleus was the host which departed to Llydaw—that of Elen Luyddog and Maxen.

Line 2. **Cadyal y Byry.** *Byry* is plural of *bwrw* 'a throw, cast, blow', GPC 357. Alternatively *y byry* might represent a verbal form *y beri* 'to cause' on which *y erchi* was a later gloss, which came to be incorporated in the text. Most likely, however, *y byry* is to be traced to a corruption of Pen. 16's *mab Eryn*. It is possible that the form has been influenced by the name of *Castell y Byri* (Bere) in Meirionnydd.

c. pann anhoedynt. On the relative use of *pan*(*n*) in clauses governed by the preposition *o*, see GMW § 87. *Anhoedynt* = *han*(*n*)*oedynt*, 3rd. pl. imp. of *hanvod*.

Pen. 16, 52*v*

36. Teir Gormes a doeth y'r Enys Hon, ac nyt aeth vrun dracheuyn:

6n o nadunt Kywda6t y Corryanyeit, a doethant eman yn oes Caswalla6n mab Beli, ac nyt aeth 6r un onadunt dracheuyn. Ac or Auia pan hanoedynt.

Eil, Gormes y Gwydyl Fychti. Ac nyt aeth 6r un onadunt dracheuyn.

Tryded, Gormes y Saesson, a Hors a Hengyst yn benaduryeit arnadunt.

36. Three Oppressions that came to this Island, and not one of them went back:

One of them (was) the people of the Cor(y)aniaid, who came here in the time of Caswallawn (= Lludd?) son of Beli: and not one of them went back. And they came from Arabia.

The second Oppression: the Gwyddyl Ffichti. And not one of them went back.

The third Oppression: the Saxons, with Horsa and Hengist as their leaders.

Manuscripts: 16, 45, 50, C 18.

a. korannyeit 45, coranyeit 50, ciwdawt o goranieat C 18. Llud mab beli 45, lludd mab beli 50, lhudh m. Beli C 18.

b. g6ydyl fichti 45, yr eil ormes nyt aeth vyth o honei. y Gwyddyl ffichti 50.

c. Trydyd gormes y saesson ac nyt aethant dracheuyn 45, V. 45, V *omit* hors a hengyst.

---

gormes. The meaning of *gormes* here, as in all the earliest occurrences of the word, is that of an oppression by an alien race or conqueror (GPC 1491). Examples: *ef diodes gormes, ef dodes fin* 'he removed an oppression, he set a boundary' (CA, l. 419); *ny nodes na maes na choedyd tut achles dy ormes pan dyuyd* 'neither field nor woods, O refuge of thy people, gave protection to thy enemy when he comes (= came)' (BT 56.20 = PT no. II.8–9; for the rendering see PT 32); *kat gormes tratrachwres bro* 'oppression of battle, while the country burns' (BT 38.15); *Gereint gelin ormes* 'G. enemy to oppression' (LlDC no. 21.7). Similarly, Hafgan king of Annwfn is a *gormes* in the eyes of his rival Arawn (PKM 3.3). But cf. the triad *Teir Prif Ormes Mon* (triad 26 W) where Palug's cat and Edwin king of England are both classed as *gormesoedd.* It is clear that here, as also in *Lludd a Llefelys, gormes* may denote an oppressive animal or monster. This meaning occurs in *Peredur*, where *gormes* is employed for the *addanc* or serpent slain by the hero (WM col. 158.28) and also for the unicorn-like creature which ravages the territory of the empress of Cristinobyl (WM col. 175.29). In *Lludd a Llefelys* the *teir gormes* are the

Coraniaid (as here), the fighting dragons, and the giant who consumes the king's food. There is plainly a close relation between triad 36 and the story, since two of the *gormesoedd* correspond: the fighting dragons in *Lludd a Llefelys* are equivalent to the *gormes* of the Saxons in the triad (see introduction, p. lxxvii). The *gormesoedd* of Britain are enumerated in the account of the settlement of the country given in BD 2–3:

> Ac o'r dywed pvmp kenedyl ysyd yn y chyuanhedu, nyd amgen, Nordmannyeyt, a Brytannyeyt, a Saesson, a Gvydyl Fychti, ac Yscoteyt. Ac o'r rei hynny nyd dyledavc neb arnei namyn y Brytannyeyt, canys vynt a'e kyuanhedassant o'r mor bwy gylyd kyn dyuod neb o'r kenedloed ereyll yn *ormes* arnadunt. A hynny y dyal eu kamwed ac eu syberwyt arnadunt y rodes Dvw y Saesson a'r Gvydyl Fychty a'r Yscoteyt yn *ormes* arnadunt.

> 'Five nations finally occupied it: the Normans, the Britons, the Saxons, and the Gwyddyl Ffichti (= the Picts), and the Scots. And of those no one has a right to it (the Island) except the Britons, since they had occupied it from the one sea to the other, before any of the other nations came as oppressors (*gormes*) on them. And then to avenge their sin and their pride God sent the Saxons and the Gwyddyl Ffichti as an oppression (*gormes*) on them.'

Only the first sentence naming the five nations is paralleled in HRB; the rest of the quotation is the contribution of the Welsh redactor, and would seem to be an echo of this triad; cf. also App. I, no. 7. (For a further reference to the triad in BD see below under *Gwydyl Fychti.*) The passage is a substitution for Geoffrey's

> Ex quibus britones olim ante ceteros a mari usque ad mare insederunt. donec ultione diuina propter ipsorum superbiam superueniente pictis et saxonibus cesserunt. (HRB I, 2)

> 'Of these the Britons formerly, before the others, occupied the land from sea to sea. Then, divine vengeance overtaking them because of their pride, they submitted to the Picts and Saxons.'

It has been suggested that another early occurrence of *gormes* with reference to the 'invasions' of Britain is to be found in the latinized form *Ormesta Britanniae*, employed by the Breton monk Wrmonoc in his *Life of St Paul Aurelian* (884) to denote Gildas's *De Excidio Britanniae* (RC V, p. 459; H. Williams, *Gildas*, p. 319 n.). If this could be taken as the title by which Gildas's work was known in Brittany in the ninth century, it would provide a welcome indication as to the origin of this triad, for if we include the Scots in place of the *Corranyeit* as the third *gormes*, as did the redactor of BD, we should have a triad which names the very same *gormesoedd* whose successive arrivals in Britain are the subject of the introductory section of Gildas's work (see introduction, p. liii, n. 53). But unfortunately the identification of *gormes* with *Ormesta* cannot be accepted. Ifor Williams has shown that the Welsh word underlying the Latin *ormesta* is not *gormes* but *ormes*, and that this occurs as a variant of *armes* (RBP col. 578.43; 580.5), which can mean not only 'prophecy' but also something like 'story of affliction'—a title well suited to the *De Excidio* (AP xlv–xlix). On *gormes*, see further P. Sims-Williams, 'Some Functions of Origin Stories in Early Medieval Wales', in Tore Nyberg *et al.* (eds), *History and Heroic Tale*, pp. 105–6, 114.

In the *Ymryson* between Dafydd Llwyd and Llywelyn ap Gutun, the latter threatens to descend upon Gwynedd in the manner of the *tair ormes gynt* (B IV, 324, l. 56.). The allusion may be to the present triad, though in its context it is more likely to have reference to *Teir Prif Ormes Mon* (see triad 26 W).

a. y Corryanyeit. *korannyeit* 45, *coranyeit* 50. RM has the forms *Coranneit, Coranyeit* (pp. 94, 18; 96, 16; 97, 24, 27); while the *Brut* version of *Lludd a Llefelys* in Llanstephan 1 has *Coraneys, Coranyeyt* (EC I, pp. 267, 269, 270). The compound *Coraniaid* (which occurs only in *Lludd a Llefelys* and in the triad) is a late formation similar to *Brytaniaid*: both names fail to show the *-i-* affection found in words whose stem is in *-a-* and to which the termination *-iaid* is added; examples: *gweiniaid, trueiniaid* (see Ifor Williams, Cyf. Ll. a Ll. xii). But in an earlier form the name may well be older, and is probably to be associated with *cor* 'a dwarf'. Ifor Williams draws attention to the similarity between the name of the *Coraniaid* and that of the Breton *Korriganed* or fairies (loc. cit., xiii, n.). If the affinity between these names is to be trusted, and the *Coraniaid* do in fact represent the fairy people, later known in Wales by the euphemism of *Tylwyth Teg*, then it is significant to find that their presence in Britain is represented both in the triad and in the story as an *invasion* into this country from abroad. We may compare the tradition of the Irish *Lebor Gabála* (Book of Invasions) which depicts the mythological Túatha Dé Danann as invading Ireland from Spain. The *Teir Gormes* reflects a tradition about the incursion into Britain of successive waves of invaders, which may be compared with the pseudo-history of Ireland which is found in the *Lebor Gabála* (see introduction, p. lvii). These traditions were beginning to be recorded in Ireland as early as the eighth century (EIHM 193), and the reference to them in HB, ch. 13 proves that they were known in Britain: thus it is not impossible that the British traditions about the successive invasions of the country (see App. I, no. 1 and n.) may have been influenced by the similar Irish material, though British sources suggest that they need not necessarily be regarded as dependent upon the Irish tradition. With regard to the *Coraniaid* as constituting one of the three *gormes*, it seems possible that their name has been confused with that of the *Cesariaid* (see triad 35); since it seems strange to find the invasion of the Romans omitted from the triad, especially since this was evidently dealt with in stories about Caswallawn (see n.) to which mere allusions have come down. The Roman invasion takes the place of that of the *Coraniaid* in triad 51a (see n.), which is a later version of the present triad; and the *Coraniaid* were conflated with the *Cesariaid* in the *Myvyrian* third series of TYP, no. 15 (MA² 402; trans., THSC 1968, p. 309), though this latter evidence is of little value. See further, B. F. Roberts, *Studies on Middle Welsh Literature*, pp. 29–30; idem, *Cyfranc Lludd a Llefelys*, pp. xix–xx; and John Carey, *The Irish National Origin Legend: Synthetic Pseudohistory* (*Quiggin Pamphlets on the sources of Medieval Gaelic History*, I) (Cambridge, 1994), pp. 7ff.

Caswalla6n mab Beli. All other manuscripts concur in restoring *Lludd mab Beli*, in conformity with the tale of *Lludd a Llefelys* as it has come down to us; cf. also triad 37c. And the occurrence of the name of *Caswallawn* in the preceding triad (no. 35) might well account for its introduction here by mistake for that of Caswallawn's brother Lludd, with whom the *gormes* of the *Coraniaid* is associated in the story. Yet I hesitate to follow the example of the later manuscripts and restore the name of Lludd. In view of the extensive traditions about Caswallawn, of which only fragments have been preserved, we can have no assurance that in an earlier version of the story the coming of this *gormes* was not associated with Caswallawn rather than with his brother.

Auia. On *Auia* = Arabia see IGE² 394. The first syllable of *Arafia* was confused with the definite article *yr*.

b. y Gwydyl Fychti. These are Geoffrey's *Picti*, but the form *Gwydyl Fychti* is used in the *Bruts* (see n. to *gormes* above) and occurs also in poetry—BT 72.16: *Pymp pennaeth dimbi o vydyl ffichti*. HB ch.12 describes the coming of the *Picti* to Britain: 'After an interval of many years, not less than 800, the Picts came and occupied the islands which are called Orkney, and afterwards from the islands they devastated many regions and occupied those in the northern part of Britain, and they still live there today. They held, and hold, a third part of Britain to this day.'

Bede (*Hist. Ecc.* I, i) describes the arrival in Britain of the Picts from Scythia, and tells how they obtained wives from the Scots, on the condition that they should institute the custom of succession through the female line. This story is greatly expanded by Geoffrey (HRB IV, 17); and after reproducing Geoffrey's account BD adds a comment which appears to contain a further reference to the triad:

> A'r bobyl honno yv Gvydyl Fichti, a llyna megys y doethant a'r achavs y kynvyssvt yn gyntaf eyroet yn yr enys hon. Ac yr hynny hyt hediw y maent yn ormes heb uynet ohonei. (BD 60.27–30.)

> 'That people are the Gwyddyl Fichti, and that is how they came and were first received in this Island. And from then till this day they have been a *gormes*, without departing from it.'

c. y Saesson. The story of Vortigern's reception of the Saxon leaders Hengest and Horsa and of their subsequent treachery is told in HB, chs. 31 ff. Cf. triad 51 below and n.

37. Tri Chud a Thri Datcud Enys Prydein:

Penn Bendigeituran mab Llyr, a gladwyt yn y G6yn6ryn yn Llundein. A hyt tra vei y Penn yn yr ansa6d yd oed yno, ny doy Ormes byth y'r Enys hon;
Eil, Esgyrn G6ertheuyr 6endigeit a gladwyt ym pryf byrth yr Enys hon;
Trydyd, y Dreigeu a gladwys Llud mab Beli yn Dinas Emreis yn Eryri.

37. Three Concealments and Three Disclosures of the Island of Britain:

The Head of Bendigeidfran, son of Llŷr, which was buried in the White Hill in London. And as long as the Head was there in that position, no Oppression would ever come to this Island;
The second: the Bones of Gwerthefyr the Blessed, which were buried in the Chief Ports of this Island;
The third: the Dragons which Lludd son of Beli buried in Dinas Emrys in Eryri.

37 R. Tri Matkud Ynys Prydein:

Penn Bendigeituran uab Llyr, a guduwyt yn y G6ynuryn yn Llundein, a'e wyneb ar Ffreinc. A hyt tra uu yn yr ansa6d y dodet yno, ny doei Ormes Saesson byth y'r Ynys honn;
Yr eil Matkud: y Dreigeu yn Ninas Emreis, a gudya6d Llud uab Beli;
A'r trydyd: Esgyrn G6ertheuyr Uendigeit, ym prif pyrth yr Ynys honn. A hyt tra vydynt yn y kud h6nn6, ny doei Ormes o Saesson byth y'r Ynys honn.
A llyna y Tri Anvat(dat)kud pan datgudwyt: A G6rtheyrn G6rtheneu a datkudyawd Esgyrn G6ertheuyr Uendigeit yr serch gwreic. Sef oed honno, Ronn6en baganes;
Ac ef a datkudya6d y Dreigeu;
Ac Arthur a datkudya6d Penn Bendigeituran o'r G6ynnvrynn. Kan nyt oed dec ganta6 kad6 yr Ynys honn o gedernit neb, namyn o'r eidaw ehun.

37 R. Three Fortunate Concealments of the Island of Britain:

The Head of Bendigeidfran, son of Llŷr, which was concealed in the White Hill in London, with its face towards France. And as long as it was in the position in which it was put there, no Saxon Oppression would ever come to this Island;
The second Fortunate Concealment: the Dragons in Dinas Emrys, which Lludd son of Beli concealed;
And the third: the Bones of Gwerthefyr the Blessed, in the Chief Ports of this Island. And as long as they remained in that concealment, no Saxon Oppression would ever come to this Island.

And they were the Three Unfortunate Disclosures when they were disclosed. And Gwrtheyrn the Thin disclosed the bones of Gwerthefyr the Blessed for the love of a woman: that was Rhonwen the pagan woman;

And he disclosed the Dragons;

And Arthur disclosed the Head of Bendigeidfran (Brân the Blessed) from the White Hill, because it did not seem right to him that this Island should be defended by the strength of anyone, but by his own.

Manuscripts: 16, R, 45, 47, 50, 51, 252, 216 (J. Jones), p. 158, Ll. 12, p. 48, Cwrt. 3 (two versions), NLW, C 18, NLW Addl. 37B, p. 94, BL[2] V.

37. Tri matkudd y. p. pan gudy6yt a thri anvatkud pan datkudy6yt 47, 50, anuat datkudd 50, tair matgydd ynys b. Ll. 12, datgladd *altered to* matgudd 51, Tri anwad matgyd ynys Brydain a oedynt anuad pan datgidwyd C 36.

a. Pen Bendigeidran Cwrt. 1, 2, vab Llud RW, a gladdwyd *altered to* a guddwyd 51, a guddiwyt NLW, 216. 216 *substitutes* yng Haerludd. yn yr ansodd honno ny ddoei ormes yr ynys vyth 50, a thra vu yno ni ddoi ssais i y. p. 51, a thra vu yno ny ddoeth y sayson yma NLW, 216, Cwrt. 2, ni ddoeth drwg yr ynys 252, a hyd y gedid yn y modd hwnnw ni ddoe ormes Sasson ir ynys hon Cwrt. 1. llu saeson BL.

b. Yr eil amatkud R, ymatgudd Cwrt. 1, eil kudd 50, ar ail ddatgladd 51, a thra vy yno ni dhoeth y Saeson yma C 36, a thra vuant yno ny ddoeth gormes NLW, Cwrt. 2. Ll. 12, NLW Addl. 37B, *substitute for esgyrn* G. Vendigeit: ag esgyrn kadwaladr vendigaid.

c. a ddaliodd llyd ap beli NLW, RW. Pa. 10, ar dreigie o ddinas emrys Ll. 12. ai rhoi yn dinas Embrys NLW, RW, 216, Cwrt. 2. yn ninas pharan 50, yn ninas Pharan yg creigiau Eryri V. 51 *adds* a thra oeddyn *altered to* wyddynt yno y mil hynny ni ddoi drais ssais ir yny(s) honn.

d *supplied by* R. Tri anvatkud R. Ar tri chudd hynny anp6yt gwaeth oe datkuddya6 50, V. Gwrtheyrn Gwrtheneu a ddatkuddyawd esgyrn Gwrthevyr Vendigeit o serch Ronwen y wreic. Ac hevyt a ddatkuddyawd y dreigeu o ddinas Pharan yr honn a elwit wedy hynny yn Ddinas Emrys 50. ag arthur ai datkuddiodd a ronwen ai perys 252, Arthur a ddadguddiodd pen Bendigeidvran am na fynnai ef gadw yr Ynys hon ond o'i rym e hun. A Rhonwen a beris ddadguddio esgyrn Gwrthefyr Fendigaid i ollwng y Seison i'r Ynys RW, NLW, C 36, 216, canys nyd oedd dec gantaw gadw o neb yr ynys hon ond evo Cwrt. 1.

Pen. 47 *and* NLW Addl. *give a shortened version of the triad*: Tri matkud y. p. pan gudy6yt a thri anvatkud pan datkudy6yt penn bendigeit ran m. llyr ac esgyrn g6rthyuyr vendigeit ac d6y dreic yn dinas emreis 47. NLW Addl. *substitutes for b* Esgyrn Cadwaladr Fendigaid.

---

tri chud a thri datcud R: *Tri matkud . . . tri anvat (dat)kud.* The citation of this triad in *Branwen* (PKM 47) gives confirmation for R's wording. On *mat, anvat*, see n. to triad 32 and cf. triads 32, 33, 34. None of the texts of the Pen. 16 version gives more than the bare title of the *tri datcud*, so that it is necessary to turn to R for a complete text of the double triad.

For the basic concept expressed by this triad, of a (human) burial which acts as a talisman for the defence of the country, there are some striking parallels to be found in early Irish sources. 'Loegaire's body was brought from the south afterwards, and he was buried with his weapons in the outer south-eastern rampart of the royal fortress of Loegaire in Tara, with his face to the south, overlooking the Leinstermen, because during his life he had been the enemy of the men of Leinster' (trans. from Bergin and Best (eds), *Lebor na h-Uidre* (Dublin, 1929) p. 295).

A later text, *Caithréim Cellaig* (ed. K. Mulchrone, DIAS, 1971) is preserved in two versions, of which the earlier, contained in the *Leabhar Breac*, is dated by its most recent editor to the twelfth century. It offers an analogy to the *datguddiau* as well as to the *cuddiau*: Eóghan Bél, king of Connacht (d. 542 Annals of Ulster), was mortally wounded in battle, and before dying he gave instructions to his people, the Uí Fiachrach, that they should bury his body on the south side of the River Sligeach (which formed the boundary of his territory) in a standing position, with his spear in his hand and with his face turned towards Ulster, as if he were fighting his traditional enemies. As long as his body was left in that position, the Connachtmen routed the Ulstermen. But when the Ulstermen learned the reason for their continued defeats, they dug up the body of Eóghan Bél and carried it northwards over the Sligeach, and buried it face downwards in the cemetery of Loch Gile on the north side of the river:

> 'Then Eógan said to bury him with his red spear in his hand, on the plain, and "turn my face towards the north, and at the side of the fort over there (i.e. the side of the Uí Fiachrach). And as long as I may be there confronting them, they shall not begin a battle against the men of Connacht, while my grave is facing them, and while I myself am in it thus arrayed". That prophecy was truly fulfilled, because every place where the Clanna Néill and the Connachtmen happened to meet, the Clanna Néill were defeated there. The Clanna Néill and (the men of) the North of Ireland made the decision to go with a great host to Ráth Ua Fiachrach, to disinter Eógan and carry off his remains northwards across the Sligeach; and he was buried over there in the cemetery of Loch Gile, face downwards, so that he would not be (the way for) a pre-ordained pathway of retreat for them in the face of the Connacht men.' (Cf. also Myles Dillon, *The Cycles of the Kings* (Dublin, 1946), p. 84.)

These parallels to the story of the burial of Brân's head, taken together with the account in HB ch. 44 of the death of Gwerthefyr / Vortimer, suggest that we have here a very primitive belief in the potency of talismanic burial. It is tempting to see an allusion to this idea in the epithet *Bendigeit* attached to both Brân (see n. to *Bendigeituran*) and to Gwerthefyr. (See further on this G. Goetinck, 'The Blessed Heroes', SC XX/XXI, pp. 87–109.) The contrast between early conditions in Ireland and Wales is highlighted by the fact that in the Irish stories the concern is with internal opponents rather than with external invaders, whereas the Welsh traditions reiterate the theme of antagonism to the foreign invaders who are regarded as having destroyed the ideal sovereign unity of the Island of Britain—the theme of triad 36. (For the pervasive cult of the human head in Celtic iconography, see PCB 61–126.)

A remarkable parallel to the instances of talismanic burial cited here is recorded by John Rhŷs (CF II, 473ff.) from folk tradition current in Gwynedd during the nineteenth century. According to this story, Arthur and his men pursued an unspecified enemy from Dinas Emrys towards the summit of Snowdon. Arthur fell dead under a shower of arrows, on the pass known as Bwlch y Saethau ('the Pass of the Arrows') between Llyn Llydaw and Snowdon. Here he was buried under a cairn known as Carnedd Arthur, 'so that no enemy might march that way so long as Arthur's dust rested there'. Nearby, above Llyn Llydaw, is a cave in which a version of the 'Arthurian Cave-legend' is located. For the story see Owen Jones, *Cymru* (1875), p. 134, where this story is attributed to oral tradition current among the shepherds of the district. Yet another parallel to the story of Laoghaire's burial is found in a report by Lewis Morris, to the effect that *Bedd Ligach*, near Bodafon, Anglesey, was the grave of an Irishman called *Lugach* who was buried there standing upright in a tumulus (*Byegones Relating to Wales*, 1886–7, p. 114). The same idea seems to underline CLlH no. I.43, *Gwercheidw llam y bwch Lloryen* 'Ll. guards the Buck's Leap' (apparently the name of a mountain pass, see Ifor Williams's note, CLlH 93–4).

It is difficult, therefore, to accept the reference to the burial of the dragons here as consistent with the other two stories referred to in the triad: if this is a talisman it is obviously one of an entirely different kind, and it is introduced in a manner which is not even consistent with the symbolical presentation of the fighting dragons as typifying the Welsh and Saxon nations, as this is given in HB ch. 42. The story of the incarceration of the dragons is told in *Lludd a Llefelys.* Here they are one of the *teir gormes* that afflicted Britain, and one would therefore conclude that the circumstance of the dragons' burial could have been 'fortunate' only in so far as it delivered the country from their oppression. It could hardly, like the other two concealments, be regarded as a burial which in itself constituted a protection. As Ifor Williams showed, the story of the burial of the dragons as given in *Lludd a Llefelys* is so closely dependent on HB's account of their disclosure as to indicate that this tale was invented subsequently to the ninth-century redaction of HB. Is it possible that in the triad the burial of the dragons has supplanted a third story of human talismanic burial? A highly suggestive parallel would be the account given in the *Brut* of the burial of Cadwallon at the west gate of London 'to cause terror and fear to the Saxons' (BD 204 = HRB XII, 13). It is significant that Cadwallon[1] (see n. to *Catwalla6n*[1] *m. Catuan*), like Brân, is given the epithet *Bendigeit* in triad 55a below.

a. The account of the burial of Brân's head in *Branwen* is followed by a citation of the triad: *Ac a gladyssant y penn yn y Gwynuryn. A hwnnw trydyd* *matcud pan gudywyt, a'r trydyd anuat datcud pann datcudywyt; cany doey ormes byth drwy uor y'r ynys honn tra uei y penn yn y cud hwnnw* (PKM 47.22–6). The phraseology here corresponds more closely with R's wording of the triad than with that of the Early Version, which does not say that the Concealments and Disclosures were *mat* and *anvat*. The addition which R makes to the triad *ae wyneb ar ffreinc* is also paralleled in the story, in Brân's instructions concerning his own burial: *a dygwch (y penn) hyt y Gwynuryn yn Llundein, a chledwch a'y wyneb ar Freinc ef* (PKM 44–5) and clearly indicates a redaction of R's text after the Norman Conquest. These words emphasize the close relation which subsists between the triad and the text of *Branwen*; see introduction, pp. xxv, lxxi.

y G6yn6ryn. Probably Tower Hill is intended, though Ifor Williams suggested as an alternative (PKM 214) the hill on which St Paul's now stands.

ny doy Ormes. On gormes see n. to triad 36 above.

b. The allusion here does not accord with HB's account of the burial of *Vortimer* (HB, ch. 44), since this account states specifically that the Britons disobeyed their leader's command that his sepulchre should be placed in the harbour whence the Saxons had fled as a result of Vortimer's victories over them. HB's *sepulchrum* becomes the 'brazen pyramid' of Geoffrey, and the *delv euydeit* of BD; and it is interesting to note the later bardic references (see n. to *G6ertheuyr 6endigeit*), which follow a tradition that a monument to Gwerthefyr was erected at Dover. But the version of the triad, with its statement that Gwerthefyr's bones were actually buried, and were dispersed throughout the *ports* of Britain, appears more primitive than that of the chronicles (HRB VI, 15 claims in contrast that Vortimer was buried at Trinovantum (London)). One can understand that at some stage a narrator may have felt that the burial story was improved by focusing it on the single port (Richborough?, see CMCS 20, p. 7, n.29), whence the routed Saxons had fled from Britain. But in view of the later tradition as known to the bards, it is more difficult to account for HB's express statement that Vortimer's instructions were disobeyed.

ym pryf byrth. See App. I, nos. 2, 9, for the *Teir Prif Porthua Ynys Prydein*.

c. All versions of *Lludd a Llefelys* conclude Llefelys's instructions as to the incarceration of the dragons with the words: *A hyt tra vont hwy yn y lle kadarn hwnnw, ny daw gormes y ynys Prydein o le arall* 'And while they may be in that strong place, no oppression will come to the Island of Britain from another place' (RM 97.13–15; Llanstephan 1, see EC 1, p. 269: *Brut Cleopatra* 68; Pen. 23: *ni daw gormes o sayson* EC 1, p. 262). This is clearly a reference to the triad itself. But since the extant text of *Lludd a Llefelys* is admittedly post-Geoffrey, it is not surprising to find that an allusion to the triad has been interpolated into it.

y Dreigeu. *dreic* < L. nom. *dracō*, while *dragon* (used as both sing. and pl.< Brit. **dracŏnem, -is*). In HB ch. 42, the Fighting Dragons are introduced as *duo vermes*, and the explanation which is later put into the mouth of Ambrosius is as follows: *duo vermes duo dracones sunt; vermis rufus tuus est . . . At ille albus draco illius gentis quae occupaverit gentes et regiones plurimas in Britannia . . . Et postea gens nostra surget et gentem Anglorum trans mare viriliter deiciet.* Ifor Williams argued that by *vermes* the author intended to render the Welsh word *pryf* 'vermin' which had a much wider meaning than *vermes*. He believed that by *vermes* the writer did not intend any kind of reptile, but rather some small wild animal such as a stoat, hare, or badger; all of which would be included under the definition of *pryfed* (Williams, Cyf. Ll. a Ll. xvii–xix; THSC 1946, pp. 56–7). It is only in Geoffrey of Monmouth's rendering of the story (HRB VI, 19; VII, 3) that the *duo dracones* clearly take the shape of fire-breathing monsters, and no trace of any earlier conception of them survives. Thus the text of *Lludd a Llefelys*, in presenting the creatures throughout as *dreigeu* (except in one single instance (RM 97.7–8) in which the intoxicated dragons are described as sinking into sleep *yn rith deu barchell* 'in the form of two piglings', a phrase which Ifor Williams believed could represent a fortuitous survival from an older form of the tale in which *vermes* = *pryfed*, i.e. *pryf llwyd, mochyn daear*), may be presumed to depend on the account that Geoffrey gives in HRB of the Fighting Dragons. Since the triad agrees with the extant text of *Lludd a Llefelys* in describing the animals hidden in Dinas Emrys as *dreigeu*, it is a matter of the first importance to determine whether *Lludd a Llefelys*, under the influence of Geoffrey's account, has given to the word *dreigeu* (= *dracones*) a meaning which the author did not intend. Ifor Williams argued that this author did not wish to imply that *dracones* was parallel to *vermes*, but that he used the former word to symbolize the military valour of the two warring nations, and in the same sense as *draco* is frequently employed in Late Latin—that is, to denote a military standard bearing a dragon device. This use of *draco* is found in Ml.Latin from the third century (Souter, *Glossary of Later Latin*, p. 113). Ifor Williams drew support for his contention from the figurative usage of *dreic*, *dragon* in the older poetry, where it denotes 'fighting-man, hero, leader' (GPC 1082). He regards this use as an extension of the employment of *draco* for a military standard: instead of the standard itself, *draco* came to be used of a leader before whom the standard was carried. But is this really how the meaning of the word developed? In Classical Latin writers such as Pliny and Cicero, *draco* is used for a serpent of unspecified kind, and this 'literal' meaning of the word remained very much alive in the Middle Ages from its use in the Bible, in particular to denote the Dragon of the Apocalypse (*Rev.* ch. xii). Thus there can be little doubt about the sense in which the word is used in a contemporary entry in the Annals of Ulster for the year 745, which reports the entry *Dracones in coelo* (T. O'Maille, *The Language of the Annals of Ulster* (Manchester, 1910), p. 18). The use of *dreic* and *dragon* for warriors in early

Welsh poetry is surely a figurative use which has developed out of the 'literal' conception of *draco* as a serpent-like monster: both *dreic* and *dragon* are already used symbolically in this way in the *Gododdin* (ll. 244, 297, 298), and in the poems of Taliesin (PT no. VII.10; XII.2), and they are used in precisely the same way as are the names of the following other creatures: *twrch* 'boar', *sarff* 'serpent', *bleid* 'wolf', *eryr* 'eagle', *tarw* 'bull', *arth* 'bear'. The figurative use of these names depends on a recognition of their literal meaning, as denoting the animals, reptiles, and birds concerned, and there seems to be no reason to suppose that *dreic, dragon* should have had a different semantic development from these words to whose use it so closely approximates. Ifor Williams further noted (CA 187) that *eryr* is used in this way as a complimentary epithet, because the eagle is the prince among birds. He does not suggest that the usage here is borrowed from the eagles borne on Roman standards, and yet the use and variant meanings of *eryr* are precisely parallel to those of *dreic*. Cf. also the figurative use of *llew* (lion) in the *Gododdin* poem CA ll. 191, 408, and possibly PT no. VI.8—a creature which, like the dragon, may have become known through literary sources, ultimately of biblical origin. *Leo nithach* 'a warlike lion' is used as an epithet for a king in an Old Irish poem which Kuno Meyer dates to the first half of the seventh century (*Alt-Irische Dichtung* I, i, v. 2 (Berlin, 1914)). In commenting on the conventional use of 'lion' and similar epithets in Irish bardic poetry, Eleanor Knott made the independent suggestion that these are derived ultimately from the Bible, perhaps through the medium of Latin hymn poetry. On the figurative use of *dreic, dragon* in early Welsh poetry, see further K. H. Jackson, CMCS 3, pp. 34–5.

When in the sixth century Gildas referred to *Maelgwn Gwynedd* (see n. under Personal Names) as *insularis draco*, he used the word *draco*, if not in its 'literal' sense ('monster of the island'), then in the same derived figurative sense ('chieftain of the island'), as that in which it is employed in the *Gododdin*. It would seem therefore that in the Latin used by HB *draco* held both the 'literal' connotation which it has in the earlier Latin writers, the early Welsh connotation of 'warrior' which was derived from this, and finally the connotation of 'military standard' which can hardly be supposed to have entirely supplanted the other two meanings. Finally, is it not more natural to suppose that the alarming and mysterious creatures incarcerated in Dinas Emrys were, from the first, monsters who resembled the Dragon of the Apocalypse more closely than they resembled badgers?

Geoffrey of Monmouth knew of *draco* only in the 'literal' sense which is given to it in the Bible, and hence he interpreted HB's *dracones* as fiery monsters. The question is, whether he gave to HB's text a different significance from that which its author intended, or whether the conception of *dracones* as denoting serpent-like creatures (*vermes* in its normal meaning 'worm') was not already present in the mind of HB and the hearers of the story. I believe that it was, and therefore that this use of *dreigeu* in the triad does not necessarily betray the influence of the literary redaction of *Lludd a Llefelys* in the form in which this story has been influenced by Geoffrey of Monmouth. The point is one of the first importance in relation to the date of the Early Version of TYP; see introduction, p. lxxviii. This conclusion as to the use of complimentary epithets in early Welsh (and Irish) poetry has subsequently been confirmed and extended by P. Sims-Williams in 'Gildas and Vernacular Poetry', especially pp. 190–2 in Lapidge and Dumville (eds), *Gildas: New Approaches*.

In addition, the 'animal symbolism' considered to be characteristic of Geoffrey's prophecies (see M. E. Griffiths, *Early Vaticination in Welsh*, p. 80), in which he veils his allusions both to his contemporaries and to historical figures, by referring to them under the form of animals, is only an extension of the common figurative use of these terms in Welsh poetry. Geoffrey must have imitated it from the Welsh predictive poems, of which he clearly had some knowledge, as is apparent from his *Prophecies of Merlin* (HRB VII). There are no instances in *Armes Prydein* or in the *Avallenau* of the use of these terms in prophetic *formulae* with reference to unspecified persons, but cf. the following from the *Oianeu: arth o deheubarth a dirchafuy* 'a bear from the south will arise' (LlDC no. 17.142). There are at least two instances in which *dreic* is employed in this manner: *dy dyrchafvy dreic o parth deheu* (BT 77.6); *dreic o wyned* (RBP col. 1049.27). But though Geoffrey seems to have developed his use of animal symbolism out of the sporadic use of this which appears in Welsh prophetic poetry, he was evidently unaware of the common conventional employment of these animal-names in bardic eulogy; hence his failure to understand correctly the title of *Uthyr Bendragon* (see n. under Personal Names), which he interpreted as *caput draconis* 'dragon's head' instead of 'foremost leader, chief hero'.

yn Dinas Emreis. The words indicate a close relation both with HB and with *Lludd a Llefelys*. HB ch. 42 records that Vortigern bestowed on Ambrosius the hill-fortress in Nant Gwynant which still bears his name, *Dinas Emrys*. As Ifor Williams pointed out (Cyf. Ll. a Ll. xix), it is an anachronism in the story to bestow on the place of the dragons' incarceration the name which it received only later as a result of their disclosure by Ambrosius (*Emreis Wledic*). Pen. 50 (followed by V) corrects the anachronism by substituting *yn ninas pharan* (cf. RM 98.11–13: *Sef ffuruf y gelwit y lle hwnnw gvedy hynny dinas emreis. A chyn no hynny dinas ffaraon dande*. For *Ffaraon Dandde* see n. to *Llyr Lledyeith* under Personal Names).

Triad 37 R.

a. *a'e wyneb ar Ffreinc*. Here, as in the quotation of this triad in *Mabinogi Branwen* (PKM 47), the threat of invasion from France which became once more imminent for Britain in the fourteenth century (see n. to triad 51) superseded the more generalized threat of invasion from overseas (and specifically by the 'Saeson') which is expressed in the earlier version in Pen. 16. The allusion to the first *datgudd* is inconsistent with the statement in HB ch. 44 (followed by HRB VI, 15) that the bones of Gwerthefyr, contrary to his instructions, were not buried in the chief ports in order that they might menace and discourage all invaders, but were instead buried inland. R's account of this *datgudd* either draws upon a different tradition from that of the chronicles, or else it is a literary elaboration without traditional basis. The allusion to *Ronnwen baganes* is clearly dependent on HRB or on the *Brut*. The portrayal in R of *Gwrtheyrn* (Vortigern) as the perpetrator of both the first and the second of the Disclosures is likewise without any known foundation, as also is the claim that Arthur disinterred Brân's Head. But the conception of Arthur as a defender of his country from dangers both internal and external is entirely consistent with the manner of his portrayal in other early sources. These include *Culhwch*, the Saints' Lives, and the early poetry.

datcud 'disclosure' (GPC 903). Two instances of this word are recorded from addresses by the *Gogynfeirdd* to their princely patrons: Prydydd y Moch (CBT V, no. 16.14n.) and Dafydd Benfras (VI, no. 35.28n.). It seems clear that both poets are recalling the triad. Otherwise *datgudd* is unrecorded before the Renaissance period.

(*Trioed y Meirch yv y rei hyn:*)

(On this section, triads 38–46, see introduction pp. lxxx–lxxxvii.)

38. (T)ri Rodedicuarch Enys Prydein:

Meinlas, march Cas6alla6n mab Beli,
Melyngan Mangre, march Lleu Lla6 Gyffes,
a Lluagor, march Carada6c 6reichuras

(*These are the Triads of the Horses:*)

38. Three Bestowed Horses of the Island of Britain:

Slender Grey, horse of Caswallawn son of Beli,
Pale Yellow of the Stud, horse of Lleu Skilful-Hand,
and Host-Splitter, horse of Caradawg Strong-Arm.

Manuscripts: 16, 47, WR, 51, C 18, BBC, 27, NLW, DC, Cwrt. 3, BL[2].

38. *Title from* R. (*space left in* 16 *for initial*) redegvarch *altered to* roddedig 51. Tri hoev etistir inis pridein BBC. Tri ymladvarch 47.

a. melynlas BBC, menilas NLW, DC. 47 *substitutes* awydawc vreichir march kyhoret eil kynan.

b. melyngan gamre R, C 36, melyngam man *altered to* gamre 51. llev ll. g. R, lle6 lla6gyffes 27, 47, 51, Cwrt.

c. llu agor m. karadauc B, BBC, karawc R, gyradoc 27, crada6c 47.

---

rodedicuarch. Ifor Williams conjectured that the phrase *ym pwyth meinlas* 'in requital for Meinlas' in triad 59 may explain the appropriateness of the key-epithet to the first of the horses named in the triad: Caswallawn's horse Meinlas was *given* (or perhaps returned) to him by the Romans in exchange for permission to set foot in Britain (PKM xxix). The two triads may therefore contain an allusion to an episode in a lost tale of Caswallawn and his dealings with the Romans. The 'Bestowed horse' belonging to Lleu Llaw Gyffes, referred to in **b**, may well have been an accompaniment in a variant version of *Math*, to the gift of weapons and armour which were extracted for him from Ar(y)anrhod—since we learn that Lleu pined *o eisseu meirch ac arueu* 'from the want of horses and arms' (PKM 81.14). *March lleu lletuegin* is referred to in *Canu'r Meirch*, p. lxxxii above.

a. Meinlas. LlDC no. 6.15: *Melynlas* 'Pale-Grey', perhaps 'Dun'. This may have been the form of the name known to Madog Benfras, who refers to a lover's plight as *melynlas o was ei wedd* 'a lad of pale-grey countenance' (DGG no. LXIX.9; note that *Fflur* (triad 67) is referred to in the previous line). *Mein* 'slender' occurs frequently in epithets for horses: CA l. 6 *mein* *vuan*; l. 620 *me(i)n llwyt*; l. 307 *meinnyell*; LlDC no. 1.9 *mein winev*. For *Meinlas* see triad 59a.

b. Melyngan Mangre. *Melyngan*, lit. 'Pale-White'. For *mangre* cf. BT 9.1: *Atwyn march mygvras man gre* 'a splendid long-maned stud-horse'. The compound consists of *man* 'spot, place' with *gre* < L. *grex*, i.e. 'stud-horse' or perhaps 'stallion'. It is used also by Prydydd y Moch in reference to a horse, *Dygychwyn, olwyn, elwaf manngre* (H 289.23 = CBT V, no. 14.3n.) 'Set forth, hoofed one, choice possession (?) of the stud' (for *olwyn* = hoof, see Ifor Williams, B VIII, p. 237; and for *elw, elwaf, see* GPC 1208). T. Gwynn Jones suggested that Prydydd y Moch's line should be emended as follows, on the analogy of names which occur in *Trioedd y Meirch*: *Dygychwyn, eil gwyn welwgan uanngre* 'Set forth, one like fair Gwelwgan Vanngre' (*Rhieingerddi'r Gogynfeirdd*, p. 21 n.). The epithet *gwelwgan* 'pale white' is found in triad 41c below.

c. Lluagor, lit. 'host-opener / splitter', an epithet descriptive of a war-horse charging in battle; unless *agor* represents *angor* used in a figurative sense (G 15), 'host-anchor'. According to the *Livre de Carados* in the First Continuation of Chrétien's *Conte del Graal*, the father of *Carados Briebras* (= *Caradoc Vreichvras*) engendered at the same time a foal called *Loriagort* (var. *Lorzagor, Levagor, Lorigal*), a boar called *Tortain* (= *Twrch Trwyth?*) and a hare called *Guinaloc* (*-ot*):

> Tout icist troi si furent frere
> Caradué Bresbras de par pere.
> (Ed. Roach, *Continuations of the Percival*, III, p. 162, ll. 2599–600.)

See Roach, *First Continuation of the Perceval* I, ll. 6202–8; II, ll. 9784–8 III, ll. 2594–8. As J. L. Weston pointed out (*Legend of Sir Perceval* I, 314), these creatures evidently belong to the class of Helpful Animal Companions engendered at the same time as a hero, and destined to assist him at some crisis in his life. The French poem may thus preserve a reminiscence of a tradition according to which *Lluagor* was 'bestowed' on Caradawg as a boy, in the same manner as were the horses of Cú Chulainn and Pryderi: for these and for another analogue, see n. to triad 70c. *Canu y Meirch* lists *a march karadavc* (see p. lxxxii, l. 3 above), but gives no name, though this reference offers evidence for the antiquity of the tradition of Caradawg's horse. For the 'congenital birth' story of the foal *Lorzagor* (with variants of the name), see R. S. Loomis, 'L'étrange Histoire de Caradoc de Vannes', *Annales de Bretagne* LXX, p. 166. Another reference to *Lluagor* (apparently used as an epithet for a warrior) is preserved in the *Beddau* stanzas in Pen. 98B, p. 50: *Bedd Ann ap lleian ymnewais fynydd / lluagor llew ymrais / prif ddewin Merddin Embrais*. See also T. Jones, 'The Stanzas of the Graves', PBA LIII, p. 136, 17b, where *lluagor* is rendered as 'causing gaps in a host'.

39. Tri Phryf Edystir Enys Prydein:

Du Hir Tynnedic march Kynan Garrwyn,
ac Awyda6c Breichir march Kyoret eil Kynan,
a Rudvreon Tuth6leid march Gilbert mab Catgyffro.

39. Three Chief Steeds of the Island of Britain:

Tall Fierce Black, horse of Cynan Garrwyn,
and Eager Long Fore-Legs, horse of Cyhored son of Cynan,
and Fearless (?) Roan (?), with Wolf's Tread, horse of Gilbert son of Cadgyffro.

Manuscripts: 16, 47, WR, 51, 27, NLW, DC, Cwrt. 3, BL[2], BBC.

39. Tri phrif varch WR, Cwrt., RW, tri ffyrf varch *altered to* phrif 51.

a. tynedic W, tyuedic R, rrynedic 27, ty6edic 51. garwyn WR, 27, 47, 51, NLW.

b. avwydavc W, Awydawc R, 47, awyddawc 27, 51, Arwyddwc NLW, DC. vreichir WR, 47, 51. kyhoret W, kyhored 27, 51, keheret 47, cyhoredd Cwrt.

c. rud dreon W, rud broen R, C 36, a rrudvron 27, ruthreon 47, A rudd a breon 51, Rhuddfron V, BL, Hyddvron Tudblaidd Cwrt., tuth bleid WR, tuthwleid DC, NLW. Gylbert tair Cad gyffro NLW, DC.

---

edystir *(eddystr)*. It is difficult at the present day to understand what difference—if any—is intended between *edystir* (Bryth. **adastrio-* 'steed, colt', GPC 1170) and *march*, since in the ten *Trioedd y Meirch* the one occurs as frequently as the other; apparently both denote war-horses. Cf. CA l. 146 *edystrawr pasc* 'well-fed horses' (see n.). Even when *eddystr* occurs in the title of a triad, the three names which follow are all separately introduced as *march*, in triads 39, 42, 43. It is tempting to suggest that in these triads the old word *edestyr* has fallen together semantically with French *destrier* (< L. *dextrarius*) which it so closely resembles, and that this has occurred in spite of the fact that *amws* (< L. *admissarius* 'stallion') is used in the law tracts as an equivalent of *dextrarius* (> *destrier*). According to Dafydd Jenkins, *Hywel Dda: The Law*, p. 312, the *dextrarius* or *destrier* 'was led by the squire's right hand until the knight mounted it to go into battle'. On *amws*, see also D. Jenkins, *Llyfr Colan*, pp. 80–1.

a. Du Hir Tynnedic. *irtinetic oceenn gulan* glosses *detincta murice lana* in *Ox. Bod. Auct. F., iv*, 32 (Lindsay, *Early Welsh Script* XI, 56). Cf. however triad 43: *Du hir terwenhit, m. selyw mab kynan garrvin* (LlDC no. 6.7). *Terwyn* 'fierce' with suffix in *-ydd* offers a less esoteric epithet for a horse, and is perhaps the correct form of the name: LlDC's reading is also in some degree favoured as the earlier by the name of the horse's owner, *Selyf m. Kynan G.*, since names are more likely to be dropped out of a text in the process of transmission than to be added to it. Possibly *Du* here represents a variant of *tu* 'side'; cf. Gwalchmai's use of the phrase *tu hir* with reference to a horse: *tu hir tref tremynyad amdyfrwys* (H 28.12 = CBT I, no. 7.128n.; cf. CLlH 141), perhaps 'Long Flank'. But triads 43 and 44 provide two analogies for horses with names in *Du* 'Black'.

b. Awyda6c Breichir. Cf. p. lxxxii, l. 8 (BT 48.10): *Kornan kyne(l)wavc, Awyd awydavc*, where *awyd a.* 'of impetuous movement', if not a name, is an epithet for the horse *Kornan* (see triad 44). *Breich* is used for a horse's fore-legs, *coes* for his hind-legs (CA 225; G 73–4). For *breichir* cf. CA ll. 619–20: *ny mat dodes y vordwyt / ar vreichir me(i)nllwyt.*

c. Rudvreon Tuth6leid. Cf. triad 42 (BBC): *Ruthir ehon tuth bleit. Ehon* = *ehofn* 'fearless' with *rhudd* 'red' or *rhuthr* 'onset'. The latter form is favoured by Iorwerth Fychan, who states that he rode *ar gefyn rutheon, ruthreis y drevyd* (H 326.6 = CBT VII, no. 30.26). R's *Rud broen* is preferable to W's *Rud Dreon*, since *broen* could be an early spelling for *brwyn* 'sad' or possibly a corruption of *ffroen* 'nostril'. But since the other manuscripts without exception favour *eo* as against *oe* in this word, I hesitate to follow R's reading as against that given by Gruffudd ap Maredudd, who also quotes this horse's name: *eil rudvreon duthvleid* (RBP col. 1329.7).

tuth, lit. 'trot', i.e. 'with stealthy tread, like a wolf'.

Pen. 16, fo. 52*v*–53*r*

40. Tri Anrei(th) varch Enys Prydein:

> Carna6la6c march Ewein mab 6ryen,
> a Thaua6thir march Catwalla6n mab Catuan,
> a Bucheslom march G6ga6n Gledyfrud.

40. Three Horses of Plunder / Plundering Horses of the Island of Britain:

> Cloven-Hoof, horse of Owain son of Urien,
> and Long Tongue, horse of Cadwallawn son of Cadfan,
> and Bucheslom, horse of Gwgawn Red Sword.

Manuscripts: 16, 47, 50, WR, 51, LlDC, 27, NLW, DC, Cwrt. 3, BL[2].

40. anreinvarch 16, awreinvarch NLW, avvreinvarch DC, arwainvarch BM, anreithuarch WR, 47, 50, anreith march LlDC, anrreith6arch 27, 51, kwreinfarch RW, C 36.

a. Karnaflavc WR, Carnawlauc LlDC, Karnavlaw 27, carnafla6c 47, 50, V, Cannalawc DC, Canalawg RW, ganalawc NLW. ywein W, 50, owein R, LlDC, owain NLW, 51, owein 47, Ywain DC, 27. ap ureen 51.

b. a thauavt hir WR, Tavautir breichir LlDC. kadwallaun fil' k. LlDC, gydwallawn 27, kydwallawn 51.

c. Bucheslum seri LlDC, bachesl6m serch 47, bvchesdom 27, Bycheslom Cwrt., Byches Lom C 36. Gugaun cletywrut LlDC, Gvgavn kledyfrud W, gwgon gleddyfrudd 27, gwgawn gleifrud 47.

---

anreith (Pen. 16: *anrein*), lit. 'booty, plunder', but also 'wealth'. If these horses were won as booty, the triad may be intended as a contrasting pair with the *Tri Rodedicuarch* 'Bestowed Horses', triad 38. The meaning is ambiguous: either 'Plundering Horses' or 'Horses won by Plunder'. But here it may mean simply 'Favourite Horses' (GPC 154; CA 359).

a. Carna6la6c. *Carn* + *gaflawc* 'forked', hence 'cloven-hoofed' (GPC 429) like a cow's hoof. Cf. *Canu y Meirch: Ar tri carn aflav(c) nyt ant hynt hilav* 'and the three cloven-hoofed (horses), they do not go on a journey to procreate' or 'on an easy journey' (*hylaw*); for the passage see introduction, p. lxxxii, l. 10. Gruffudd ap Maredudd refers to a horse *un redyat karnaflaw* (RBP col. 1329.9; note that the form *karnaflaw*, attested in the poem by the rhyme, is that given in triad 40 by Pen. 27; cf. also *Cethin Carna6law* triad 42).

b. Taua6thir. LlDC no. 6.4: *Tauautir breichir* 'Long Tongue Long Fore-Legs'. Cf. *Awyda6c Breichir* triad 39b n.

c. Bucheslom. LlDC no. 6.3: *Bucheslum seri. Sseri* is equated with *meirch* in the *Peniarth Glossaries* (B II, p. 237), and T. Gwynn Jones here compares the place-name *Serïor* in Denbigh, as representing *seriawr* 'the place of steeds'. But Ifor Williams's note on *seri* (B XI, pp. 148–9), and later in *Enwau Lleoedd*, p. 82, supersedes his earlier discussion in CA, p. 128 on the line *sarff seri alon* (CA l. 201) 'a serpent on the enemy's path'—describing the hero Cynon. He shows that *seri* corresponds to the later *sarn* and means a stone-paved causeway. Cf. also Parry's n. on *Nant-y-Seri*, GDG 520 'sarn, palmant o gerrig dros gae' and Llywarch ap Llywelyn, CBT V, no. 23.48 *meirw sengi mal seri sathar* (see n.).

Bucheslom perhaps represents *buches* + *llawn* 'full of life'. Gr. ab yr Ynad Coch refers to Llywelyn ap Gruffudd as *bucheslawn arglwyd* (RBP col. 1417.12 = CBT VII, no. 36.15); here the meaning is 'lord rich in cattle'. With *buches* in the sense of 'life', *llon* cognate with Ir. *lond* 'fierce, strong' would be a suitable second element (GPC 2206). Alternatively, a confusion with *Bucefal, Bugethal*, i.e. *Bucephalus* (G 83), is not to be ruled out, and it is perhaps significant that Casnodyn uses the epithet *aryal bugethal* (H 331.9 = GC no. 5.9n.) in his poem to Gwenlliant, only two lines after his allusion to *kein caled* (on which see n. to triad 42c below and CLlH 179). An allusion to Alexander's famous horse, and one which may be older than this triad, is found in HGVK 5.11: *Bucefal, march Alexander*. See further, M. Haycock, CMCS 13, p. 17 and p. 23, n. 85. The bestowal of 'personal' names on individual horses is extremely rare in all early literature, and in my chapter 'The Triads of the Horses' (Davies and Jones (eds), *The Horse in Celtic Culture*, p. 111), I supported the suggestion that the variant forms of *Bucheslom* / *Bucephal* have been instigated by the fame of Alexander's horse *Bucephalus*, known in Wales from at least the twelfth century, and perhaps some years earlier.

41. Tri Gorderch6arch Enys Prydein:

> Ferlas, march Dalldaf eil Cunin Cof,
> a Rudurych, march Raha6t eil Morgant,
> a Guelwgan Gohoewgein, march Moruran eil Tegit.

41. Three Lovers' Horses of the Island of Britain:

> Strong Grey, horse of Dalldaf son of Cunin Cof,
> and Dappled Roan, horse of Rahawd son of Morgant,
> and Silver-White, Proud and Fair, horse of Morfran son of Tegid.

Manuscripts: 16, 47, 50, WR, 51, 27, NLW, DC, Cwrt. 3, BL[2].

41. gorderchuarch WR, 47, gordderchvarch 27, 51, V, gordderchvaich DC, NLW.

a. fferlas 27, 50, 51, R. eil kimin W, kunin R, 51, Dalldadd ail Cynan Cwrt., dalldaf eil kwrinkof DC, Daldau dilrwircou C 36, d. dilrwirncou RW. 47 *substitutes* a ruhyr reon tuthvleid march dalldaf eil kunyn kof.

b. gvrbrith W, gwrbrith R, 51, Cwrt., Arwlvrith 27, Arv6l vrith 47, Rydhyrych RW, C 36, Ruddvrych NLW. raavt WR, Rawd Cwrt., ryhawt 47, 50. ail morgan 27. WR, 50, 51, *omit* eil morgant.

c. gwel6 gohoy6 47, gwelwgan gohoiwgam DC, NLW. *For* Morvran WR *substitute* keredic ap gvallavc, Caredig ail Gwalloc Cwrt. 47 *substitutes* drystan. 27 *substitutes* a chornach arwch march morvryn tegid.

---

gorderch6arch. Perhaps we should render 'Beloved Horses' (GPC 1469), since no tradition has survived to account for any amatory propensities attributed to their original owners. The scribe of Pen. 47 (or its source) evidently felt the lack, and substituted for **c** the name of a renowned lover: *a gvelv gohoyw march drystan* (= Tristan). This indicates that by the fifteenth century *Tri Gorderch6arch* was understood to mean 'Lovers' Horses'. And as Chotzen has pointed out (*Recherches sur la Poésie de Dafydd ab Gwilym*, p. 199), this triad may well contain an allusion to the poetic convention by which horses were employed as *llateion* or love-messengers; a convention which is found already in the twelfth-century *Gogynfeirdd* (see introduction, p. lxxxvii).

a. Ferlas. Cf. the name of *Alan Fyrgan* 'A. Perfect in Strength' (see n. under Personal Names). *Ffer* 'strong, wild' is the first element in both names. Cf. the name *Feruarch*, CA l. 1125; *Fermarch* LL 265.12. On *ffer* with this meaning see CA 172 and CLlH 88–9. Gruffudd ap Maredudd: *deissyf neityav fferlas* 'I desire (one with) the leap of Fferlas' (RBP col. 1329.12). *Fferlas* is also a river-name (G 532; Ifor Williams, *Enwau Lleoedd*, p. 57).

b. Rudurych. Perhaps used to denote a bay or chestnut horse, with a white star on the forehead (?). WR substitute *Gwrbrith*, perhaps 'Speckled Stallion';

for this use of *gwr* cf. *gwrcath* 'tom-cat'. Or *gwr-* may be simply the intensive prefix *gor-*. For Pen. 27 and 47's *Arwlvrith* cf. triad 43b, *Ar6wl 6elyn.*

c. Guelwgan Gohoewgein. This horse is variously appropriated in the MSS. to Morfran, Ceredig ap Gwallawg, and Drystan. *Gwelwgan* is a compound of synonyms 'pale white'; for its use with reference to horses cf. LlDC no. 1.8: *Rac errith a gurrith y ar welugan*; Hywel ab Owain: *ac y ar welw gann . . . gorpwyf ellygdawd* (H 316.11–12 = CBT II, no. 6.23); and PKM 9.12, where Rhiannon is seated *ar uarch canwelw*. Gwalchmai refers to *lliavs gorwyt gvelv gwalch urowys* 'many a pale steed, lively as a hawk' (H 28.9 = CBT I, no. 7.125), and Casnodyn *man ym duc gwelwlym* ('pale fast one') *ar rym redec* (H 332.4 = GC 5.32). The compound *gohoywgein* may contain *cein* 'fine', but cf. *Kein Caled* 'Hard-Backed', triad 42 (LlDC); *cein* 'back' is a possibility in this epithet also. For *cein* with this meaning, see CLlH 100. The Pen. 20 version of the Bardic Grammar (GP 47) provides an additional reference to *Gwelwgan gohoewgein* in an obscure *englyn enghreifftiol* (apparently a *cerdd llatai* addressed to a horse-messenger): *Gweilging gwas, gwanas gwaywawr / Gwelwgann gohoewgein mein mawr* (GP 47) 'A stripling lad (?), prop of spears (?), great slender Silver-White, Proud and Fair'. (Pen. 56, p. 46 ascribes the *englyn* to the twelfth-century poet Gwilym Rhyfel. Cf. CBT II, no. 30.4 n. and YB X, p. 106; Bromwich, 'The Triads of the Horses' in Davies and Jones (eds), *The Horse in Celtic Culture*, p. 116; and GEO 167.)

42. Tri Gohoew Edystyr Enys Prydein:

Llwyt, march Alser mab Maelgwn,
a G6ineu Godwfhir, march Kei,
a Chethin Carna6law, march Idon mab Enyr G6ent.

42. Three Sprightly Steeds of the Island of Britain:

Grey, horse of Alser son of Maelgwn,
and Long-Necked Chestnut, horse of Cai,
and Roan Cloven-Hoof, horse of Iddon son of Ynyr Gwent.

Manuscripts: 16, 47, WR, 51, LlDC, 27, NLW, DC (two versions), Cwrt. 3, BL[2]. V.

42. Tri thom edystyr WR, 51, Cwrt., gohoiw eddestyr NLW, gohoivv eddestyr DC.

a. lluyd W, Llwyd, Ellwyd DC. Alsych 47, alfer DC, NLW, alver C 36. maelgwnn 51. 27 *omits* mab maelgwn. LlDC no. 6.11: Ruthir ehon tuth bleit march Gilberd mab kadgyffro.

b. g6d6f hir W, gwdwc hir R, Gwiney Gwdhwhir C 36, Guyneu goduff hir BBC, gwine gyddvir 27, gwinau gwddwg hir 51, gwddw hir DC, NLW. kai hir 51, Sir Gei NLW, DC, Caithr Cwrt. 47 *substitutes* meinlas march kas6alla6n mab beli.

c. a chethin kyflym 27, a chethin carnaflawc V. Iddon 27, Iddon ap eynyr Gwent NLW, DC. WR, 47, 51, Cwrt: a Grei march edwin, Gregar march Edwin DC. LlDC 6.12: A kein caled m. gualchmei.

---

gohoew edystyr. WR: *Tri thom edystyr* 'Pack Horses', an epithet suggestive of a very different kind of horse from the *gohoyw edystyr* of the other versions, and one which has in fact probably been borrowed from the title of triad 43. But there is much confusion between the various versions of this triad, both as to the names of the horses and those of their owners; see under **c** below. On *eddystr* see n. to triad 39 above.

b. G6ineu Godwfhir. *Gwineu* ('chestnut' etc, GPC 1662) occurs frequently as a colour for horses, as in Gwalchmai's reference: *lliavs gwineu fadv fravt tywys* (H 28.11 = CBT I, no. 7.127). *Godwf* = *gwddf* 'neck' (W *gvdvf*) with *o* for later *w*. Or perhaps *godwf* < *go* + *twf* 'of good growth', so 'tall'.

c. Cethin Carna6law. There is confusion both over the name of this horse, and that of its owner. Pen. 27 reads *Cethin kyflym*, and this is the name of the horse ridden by Dinogad m. Cynan Garwyn at the battle of Arfderydd, according to triad 44 (R) (see n. to triad 44b). But the owner of the horse is here stated to be the south Wales prince Iddon m. Ynyr Gwent; yet triad 69 names Calam as the *march* (?*merch*) of *Id(d)on m. Ner* (= Ynyr) (see n.). In triad 40 *Carnavlawc* is the horse of Owein m. Urien. Instead of this doubtful name-form ('the cloven-hoofed' GPC 129), WR gives *Grei* (= 'Grey'), the horse of Edwin (cf. H 28.14 = CBT I, no. 7.130: *lliaws grei grym diffwys* 'many grey (horses) of mighty strength'). LlDC no. 6.12 gives *Kein Caled march Gualchmei*. This is the original of *le Guingalet, Gringolet*, the famous horse of *Gauvain* in the French, English and German romances. For a discussion of the implication of the unique allusion here to the famous horse belonging to *Gwalchmai* / *Gauvain* in these medieval sources see my chapter, 'The Triads of the Horses', pp. 113–15 in Davies and Jones (eds), *The Horse in Celtic Culture*. *Kein* meaning 'back' is preferable in this name to *kein* 'fair', hence 'Hard Back(ed)'. Cf. CLlH 100, n. to *Kynn bum kein vaglawc.* Cynddelw alludes to a horse-messenger whom he describes as *gorvelyn called* 'golden one, so wise' (H 122.3 = CBT III, no. 5.23n.). Casnodyn also describes his horse as *eil kein galet* (GC no. 5.7n.). Tudur Aled again alludes to this horse's traditional excellence in a *cywydd i ofyn march*:

Gorau neidiwr grwn ydyw,
Gwyliwch! ai march Gwalchmai yw?
(GTA II, no. CIX.81–2.)

'He is the best and finest leaper; look, is he not Gwalchmai's horse?'

43. Tri Thom Edystyr Enys Prydein:

> Du, march Brwyn mab Kynadaf,
> ac Ar6wl 6elyn, march Pasken mab 6ryen,
> a Rudlwyt, march Ryderch Hael.

43. Three Steeds of Burden (Draft Horses) of the Island of Britain:

> Black, horse of Brwyn son of Cunedda,
> and Huge Yellow, horse of Pasgen son of Urien,
> and Dun-Grey, horse of Rhydderch Hael.

Manuscripts: 16, 47, LlDC, 27, NLW, DC, BL².

43. etystir LlDC, eddystr 27, eddestir NLW, DC.

a. Cunedaf 27, br6ynan kynadaf 47, Dy march Bewyn ap kynadw C 36, Berwyn ap k. RW. LlDC *substitutes* A Du hir terwenhit m. selyw mab kynan garruin.

b. Arwul melin LlDC, arwl velyn 27, Achul v. 47. passcen fil' urien LlDC, pasgen 27, NLW, pascen 47, DC.

c. Drudluid LlDC, dulwyd 27, Ruddlwyd NLW, DC, Rhyd Lhwyd C 36, RW. Ryterch LlDC, rydderch hayl 27. 47 *substitutes* ac ysgwydvrith march llemenic m. mawan; a Rhuddlwyt march Rydderch Hael. medd Sion Balmwr yn lle'r olaf: ac ysgwytfrith march llemenic mab Mawan V.

Tri Thom Edystyr. In WR this is the title of triad 42, and the rest of triad 43 is not represented in that version. *Tom* means 'mound' (*tomen*), also 'heap, burden' (CLlH 142, 240). It is used with reference to horses in AL I, 706: *teithi march tom neu cassec tom yw dwyn pwn a llusgaw karr yn allt ac yg gwaeret, a hynny yn dirvygvys* 'The *teithi* "qualities" of a pack-horse or mare are, to carry a load, and draw a cart up hill and down hill, and that without swerving'. On *edystyr* see n. to triad 39 above.

a. Du. BT 48.11: *Du moroed enwavc / march brvyn bro(n) bradavc.* See n. to triad 44a and CO l. 718n.

b. Arwfl wflyn. Cf. *Arvwl vrith,* triad 41b (Pen. 47), *aruul cann* CA l. 1146, *aruul melin* CLlH no. VII.14a, n. (= LlDC no. 30.75). In each instance *arvwl* is used with reference to a horse, and in combination with an adjective denoting colour. Loth compared the Ir. adjective *adbul, adbol* 'huge, great, immense' (ACL I, p. 405), and this gives good sense here. As Ifor Williams points out, the reference in CLlH, *Kin ottei eiry hid in aruul melin* 'though snow should fall (to the cruppers (?) of) Arvwl M.' must surely be to the horse of Pasgen fab Urien named in the triad, especially since the poem consists of a dialogue in which Owain fab Urien is mentioned, and since his brother Pasgen (see n.) is named in triad 23.

c. Rudlwyt. Perhaps 'tawny'; *Drudluid*, LlDC no. 6.8 'Spirited Grey'. Pen. 47 substitutes: *ysgwydvrith march llemenic m. mawan*, and V states that this was the reading of *llyfr Siôn Balmer*. The variant is significant, since both this name and the name of Rhydderch's horse are evidently derived from two lines in *Canu y Meirch*, BT 48.13–15; for the full text see introduction, pp. lxxxii–lxxxiii. The lines imply that the two horses belong to a triad of Cloven-Hoofed Horses. It may be that *Yscvydvrith yscodic gorvyd llemenic* may in the context be taken for a series of epithets describing a horse belonging to Rhydderch, whose name follows in the next line. *Llemenic* is 'leaping' (as in CA l. 303 *y ar llemenic*), and *yscodic* 'shadowy' (CA l. 388), also 'shying' (see introduction, p. lxxxiii, n. on l. 12); one may suggest as a translation ' "Shying Dappled Shoulder", a leaping steed'. On the other hand it is perhaps more natural to take *Llemenic* here as a proper name, since there is evidence in CLlH for a character named *Llemenic mab Mawan* (see triad 65).

44. Tri Meir(ch) a dugant y Tri Marchlwyth:

[Du y Moroed] march Elidir Mwyn6a6r, a duc arna6 seith nyn a hanner o Benllech yn y Gogled hyt ym Penllech [Elidir] yMon. Sef seith nyn oedynt: Elidir Mwyn6awr, a(c) Eurgein y wreic, merch Vaelgwn Gwyned, a G6ynn Da Gy6et, a G6yn Da Reinyat, a Mynach Naomon y gyghorwr, a Phrydelaw Menestyr y wallovyat, ac Aryan6agyl y was, a Gelbeineuin y goc, a nouyes a'e dwylaw ar bedrein y march—a hwnnw 6u hanner y dyn.

Er eil Marchlwyth a duc Cornan march meibyon Elifer, a duc G6rgi a Pheredur arna6, a Duna6t 6wr, a Chyn6elyn Drwsgyl, y edrych ar 6ygedorth [llu] G6endoleu (yn) Arderyd. (Ac nys gordiwedawd neb namyn Dinogat vab Kynan Garwynn y ar y Kethin Kyflym, ac aruidiawt ac aglot a gafas yr hynny hyt hediw.)

E trydyd Marchlwyth a duc [Erch] march meibyon G6erthm6l Wledic, a duc G6eir a Gleis ac Archanat yn erbyn Allt 6aellwr yg Keredigyawn yn dial eu tat.

44. Three Horses who carried the Three Horse-Burdens:

Du y Moroedd ('the Black of the Seas'), horse of Elidir Mwynfawr, who carried on his back seven and a half people from Benllech in the North to Benllech [Elidir] in Môn. These were the seven people: Elidir Mwynfawr, and Eurgain his wife, daughter of Maelgwn Gwynedd, and Gwyn Good Companion, and Gwyn Good Distributor, and Mynach Naomon his counsellor, and Prydelaw the Cupbearer, his butler, and Silver Staff his servant, and Gelbeinefin his cook, who swam with his two hands on the horse's crupper—and he was the half-person.

Cornan ('the horned'), horse of the sons of Eliffer, bore the second Horse-Burden: he carried on his back Gwrgi and Peredur and Dunawd the Stout and Cynfelyn the Leprous/Clumsy(?), to look upon the battle-fog of (the host of) Gwenddolau (at) Ar(f)derydd. (And no one overtook him but Dinogad son of Cynan Garwyn, (riding) upon Swift Roan, and he won censure (?) and dishonour from then till today.)

The third Horse Burden was borne by [*Erch*] 'Dappled' the horse of the sons of Gwerthmwl Wledig, who carried Gweir and Gleis and Archenad up the hill of Maelawr in Ceredigion to avenge their father.

Manuscripts: 16, 47, 50, R, 51, 27, NLW, DC, Cwrt. 3 (two versions) BL[2].

44. tri meir 16, meirch 47, 50, NLW, DC, tri marchlvyth ynys prydein R, 27, 51, marchowgluyth Cwrt. 1.

a. Du Moro P 16, du y moroed R, NLW, DC, Du moroedd V, Du y moroydd 27, Dur moroed 47. o ben llech elidyr yn y gogled hyd ym penn llech elidyr ym mon R, V, o Benllech yn y Gogledd hyd ym Mhen llech elidir ym Mon R, V, o Benllech yn y

Gogledd hyd ym Mhen Llech Elidyr ym Mon Cwrt. 2. ewein gwyned *altered to* vaelgwn gwyned 16, verch Vaelgwn R, 47, 50, NLW, merch Uaelgwn DC, gwyn da gywed NLW, DC. da reimat R, rreiniad 27, reinat 50, reiniad NLW. mynach navmon R, namon C 36, NLW, manach nawmon 27. A phetrylev vynestyr R, a ffedrillaw 27, a phredesaw 47, A phedrlew 51, y walhoyad C 36, y walloyad NLW, DC. aran uagyl R. ac Albeinwyn R, gellvenieu 27, gil benevin 47. a noeues R. 50 *adds* ae draett yn y defyr. a hwnw oedd vn haner y dyn NLW, DC, hanner y dyn a duc 47.

b. *Words in brackets supplied by* R, 51. R *interpolates this passage after* gvrgi a pheredur arnav. 51 *gives in correct order. All other manuscripts omit* (*except* Cwrt. 1, *which follows* R). yr ail marchowglwyth ynys Brydain Cwrt. 1. Coruann R, karvon 51, Cornan NLW, C 36, RW, Corman DC, Gorau 27, vu Goruuan Cwrt. 2. Eliffer Gosgordvawr R, oliver gosgorddvawr 27, olver NLW, Oliuer DC, olver Gosgorddvawr Cwrt. 1. Dunawt wr vab pabo R, Dunawdwr DC, a chynvelyn drwgswl NLW. ar vygedordh llu gvendoleu yn arderyd R. Diuogat R, di6ogad 51. arfidiawt 51. Ac ef a ga6as anglod er hynny hydd heddiw 51.

c. marcha6clwyth 16, marchlwyth R. Heith P 16, Erch R, herth 51, Erth Cwrt. 2, heid 47, 50. 27 *omits name.* Grythmwl R, gwrthmwl 27, gyrthmul 50, 51, Cwrt. 1. Achleu ac Archanat R, gwair achlais ac arthenat 27, Arthynad 50, Arthanat V, Arthauad DC, arthavad C 36, archanad NLW, Cwrt. 1, riw vaelawr R, allt vaelawr 47, yn erbyn y Rhiw, Cwrt. 1. 27 *adds* kyneddf oydd ar uaylwr na chaye i borth ir vn marrchluyth ac yna i llyddasant. 51 *adds* Ar march hwnnw a elwid erchani.

WR, 51 add at end of *Trioedd y Meirch* (R col. 597): Tri penn uarch ynys brydein a dugant y tri marchlwyth y mae eu henweu dracheuyn, tri phynvarch 51, ffynvarch Cwrt. henwei R. drachefn val hyn Cwrt.

The concluding words of WR (quoted above) indicate that *Tri Pennfarch* ('Pack Horses') was the original title given to this triad. Cf. RM 307.5–7; *Cy.* vii, 131.13–14; (GPC 2963). Owing to a lost leaf this triad is only represented in W by this note.

marchlwyth. Cf. GPC 2355 and *gwyndorllwyth*, triad 70. The meaning of *llwyth* in both of these compounds is 'burden', not 'tribe' as in *lleithiclwyth*, triad 1 (see n.). The first three of the four horses named in the triad are found in *Canu y Meirch*, BT 48. See introduction, p. lxxxii.

a. The historical nucleus behind this allusion is the expedition made by Elidir Mwynfawr from the North to Wales in order to claim the rule of Gwynedd in succession to Maelgwn; from the triad we learn that he based this claim upon the fact that his wife was Maelgwn's daughter *Eurgain*. A passage in the *Black Book of Chirk* (quoted under n. to *Run m. Maelgwn*) states that Elidir met his death upon this expedition, and describes how his kinsmen from the North came to Wales to avenge him. VN[2] tells us that the reason for Elidir's pressing his claim was that Rhun was of illegitimate birth. But the authority for this assertion is of uncertain antiquity, and in any case it is not likely that illegitimacy would have been regarded as an obstacle to succession at this early date. Rhun's alleged illegitimacy is probably a deduction based upon the tradition that a disputed claim to the rule of Gwynedd arose upon the death of Maelgwn. VN[2] gives the following account of Elidir's expedition to Wales:

> After the death of Maelgwn . . . many of the nobility of Cambria disdained to yield subjection to Rhun his son, being a bastard begot upon Gwalltwen the daughter of Afallach, Maelgwn's concubine, especially the nobility of Arfon, who privately sent unto Elidir Mwynfawr aforesaid to come speedily to Cambria, to aid him in the recovery of that kingdom in the right of his children by Eurgain the daughter and heir of Maelgwn. But Rhun having had intelligence of their conspiracy came and forced them of Arfon to yield obedience and fidelity unto him against all others, so that when Elidir landed in Cambria, he found Arfon men in whom he most confided to be his utter enemies and ready to give him battle, who fought with them at Aber Mefydd in Arfon where Elidir was slain. . . . Whereof intelligence being brought to the princes of the North, *Rhydderch, Clydno Eiddin, Nudd Hael*, and *Mordaf* . . . they unanimously gathered their forces, and having a navy ready they embarked themselves and their men, and landed at Arfon in North Wales, and in revenge of Elidir's death, they burned all Arfon from *Yr Eifl* to *Hergyn*, but hearing that King Rhun was ready with a puissant army to give them battle, and had intercepted their passage to their navy, they withdrew themselves homewards, and marched by land, spoiling and killing all before them, whom Rhun pursued and overtook upon the bank of the River Ewerydd, where he gave them a great overthrow, and then passed the river and brought all the princes of the North to his subjection and succeeded his father in the rule of Cambria, as Merlin Caledonius witnesseth.

The source for much of Vaughan's story is to be found in the tract *Disgyniad Pendefigaeth Cymru* (P. C. Bartrum (ed.), *Nat. Lib. of Wales Journal* XVI, pp. 253–63) from four manuscripts of the sixteenth to the eighteenth centuries. I quote the text from Pa. 38, 137 in the hand of Evan Evans (d. 1788), where it bears the superscription *Thomas Williams allan o hen vemrwn a gowsai y cof hwnn*:

> Llyma val y descennodh pendevigaeth Gymru er yn oes Vaelgwn Gwynedd. Tri brenhin Cymru yn nessaf i Faelgwn oi flaen, ni hanoedh Maelgwn o honynt. Sef oedh y tri hynny, Urien ap Cynfarch cyn nog ef, yn nessaf attaw ef Morgan ap Saturnin, cyn no Morgan i bu Rhydderch Hael; velly i dywawd *Cyvoesi Verdhin Wyllt*. yn nessaf i Faelgwn i doeth Run ap Maelgwn. Mam Run oedh [*Walltwen*] verch *Avallach*, cariadwraig i Faelgwn, ag am hynny [ni] bu gymmeredig ef yn dywyssawc gan rai, ond val i dirprwys. Wedy hynny Elidir Mwynvawr, priodawr or Gogledd ag Eurgein verch Vaelgwn Gwynedh oedh i wreic, ai vedhwl vu orescyn Gwynedh, a dyvod a llynghes ganthaw i geisiaw yn ddisyvyt i orescyn

Gwynedh, oblegid ei vot yn dyvot o waed Rydherch, ac Urien ap Cynfarch, a bod i wraig ef Eurgain yn verch i Vaelgwn oi wraig briawt, ag nad oedh Run or gwely priawt, a thebygu or ffyrdh hynny i dylei y bendevigaeth. Ac yna i llas yn Aber Nevydh yn Arvon. ac am hynny i doeth teyrnedh y gogledh in dhial, ac i lloscassant Arvon or Eiffyl hyt yn Hergyn: pan glybu Run ap Maelgwn hynny, vo dhygyvores Wynedd yn eu hol. ac wynteu a giliassant parth a'u gwlad, ag ef a'u godhiwedhodh hwynt ar lann avon Ewerydh yn y gogledh. yno i bu gyvranc ddiwal rhyngthunt, ac or diwedh i gorvu Run, ag yna i cafas ef y bendevigaeth o hynny allan, a gwiw oedh hynny.

'This is how the sovereignty of Wales descended from the time of Maelgwn Gwynedd. There were three kings next to Maelgwn, from whom Maelgwn was not descended. These were Urien ap Cynfarch before him, next to him Morgan ap Sadernin, and before Morgan was Rhydderch Hael, as the 'Prophecy of Myrddin Wyllt' says (*see* RBP cols. 577–83). Next to Maelgwn came Rhun ap Maelgwn. The mother of Rhun was [Gwalltwen] daughter of Afallach, Maelgwn's mistress, and because of that he (Rhun) was not acceptable to some as prince, but only as a deputy. After that (came) Elidir Mwynfawr, landholder of the North. Eurgain daughter of Maelgwn Gwynedd was his wife. His idea was to conquer Gwynedd, and he came suddenly with a fleet to conquer Gwynedd, on the grounds that he came of the blood of Rhydderch (Hael) and of Urien ap Cynfarch, and that his wife was Eurgain daughter of Maelgwn by his lawful wife, while Rhun was not of lawful birth, and he thought that for those reasons he had a right to the sovereignty. And then he was slain at Aber Nefydd in Arfon. For that reason the princes of the North came to avenge him, and they burned Arfon from the Eifl as far as Hergyn. When Rhun ap Maelgwn heard this he mustered the whole of Gwynedd in pursuit of them. They returned to their (own) land, and he (Rhun) overtook them on the bank of the river Ewerydd in the North. At that place there was a savage encounter between them, and at the end Rhun was victorious, and from then on he held the sovereignty, and that was right.' (On the name *Ewerydd / Gwerydd* see Jenny Rowland, SC XVI/XVII, pp. 234–47.)

The most striking parallel to the burden carried by Elidir's horse is to be found in the fifteenth-century Irish tale *The Pursuit of the Giolla Dheacair*, in which a monstrous horse carries fifteen of Finn's companions on a journey to the Otherworld: on coming to the sea they are overtaken by yet another member of the Fian band, who catches on to the horse's tail, and being unable to relinquish his hold, is carried out to sea in this manner (Hogan, *Teacht 7 Imtheacht an Ghiolla Dheacair* (Dublin, 1905), p. 19; O. Grady, *Silva Gadelica* (1892) ii, 292 ff.). Gerard Murphy points out that this strange horse has older analogies in the horses found in other Finn tales which carry people to the realms of the dead, see idem, *Duanaire Finn* III (ITS XLVI), p. xxxii; idem, *Ossianic Lore and*

Romantic Tales of Ml. Ireland (Dublin 1955, 1971 etc.), p. 52. In the Irish tale, as in the triad, the theme is treated as comic. W gives the alternative name for this triad *Tri penuarch* (see end of textual notes), which proves that triad 44 was included in the lost pages of this version, though W like R did not include it with the other *Trioedd y Meirch*. For *pen(n)varch* 'pack-horse' cf. AL I, 78, where *penuarch brenyn* is equivalent to 'gift-horse, windfall', RBP col. 1336.18, *pyn(n)varch llu*. Cf. GPC 2964 *pynorfarch* 'packhorse'.

a. **Du y Moroed** (R); *Du Moro* Pen. 16. I have substituted in both **a** and **c** the names of the horses in the forms they bear in R, which are corroborated in the later manuscripts, as well as in the poetic allusions cited below, which appear to allude to the triad. R's forms therefore appear to be the more authentic, and probably the earlier ones. But variants exist, both in the names of this horse and of its owner: cf. BT 48.10–11 (p. lxxxii above): *Du moroed enwavc, march Brvyn bro(n) bradavc*, and *Du march Moro Oeruedawc* (CO 1. 718; see n.). It is plain that there is a connection between the names of the horse as given in *Canu'r Meirch*, in *Culhwch*, and in the triad. In each case the horse is named *Du*, though in neither of the first two instances is he appropriated to Elidir Mwynfawr. In *Canu'r Meirch* the horse's name is given simply as *Du* followed by the interjection *mor oed enwawc* 'how famous he was'; and this form of the name is supported by the occurrence of the *Du march Brwyn m. Kynadaf* in triad 43. But since *Du y Moroedd* 'the Black of the Seas' is so obviously appropriate a name for the sea-going horse referred to in the triad, it is hard to believe that this form arose simply from a textual corruption of the line in BT, and that Pen. 16's *Du Moro* has simply omitted to give the horse's full name. The reference is evidently to a mythological water-horse (cf. the Irish parallel cited above), which different stories appropriated at different times to different owners. The form of the name given in *Culhwch* is plainly connected with that given in the triad; but whereas *Moro* is part of the horse's name in Pen. 16, in *Culhwch* it is transferred to the horse's owner (for *oeruedavc* see n. to *aer(ueda6c)*, triad 25). Another reference to this horse is made in a *cywydd i ofyn ebol* by Guto'r Glyn, in which the poet compares the foal for which he is asking with the offspring of a number of legendary horses, beginning with:

> Mab i'r Du ymhob erw deg
> O Brydyn, o bai redeg.
> Merch ei fam i'r march o Fôn
> Aeth i ddwyn wyth o ddynion.
> Mae ŵyrion i Ddu'r Moroedd,
> Gwn mai un onaddun oedd.
> (GGl. no. XXII.41–6).

'Son of the Black one of Prydyn (= Scotland), if on each fair acre he were to run. His mother (was) a daughter to that horse of Môn who went to carry eight men: *Du y Moroedd* has grandsons—this one, I know, was one of them.'

Tudur Aled refers twice to *Du'r Moroedd* in two *cywyddau i ofyn march*. The second allusion makes it plain that it relates to the story given in the triad:

Mwy i arial no Du'r Moroedd
Maint i rym a'i antur oedd.
(GTA II, no. C.75–6.)

'Of greater vigour than *Du'r Moroedd*, such was his strength and daring.'

Du'r Moroedd, ar derm oerwynt,
Aeth ar i gefn wyth wyr, gynt.
(GTA II, no. CII.59–60.)

'Du y Moroedd, for a spree with the cold wind, eight men formerly went upon his back.'

Cognisance should perhaps be taken of Ml. L. *morellus* = *sub-fuscus* (i.e., 'blackish'; '*color equi*'; 'Gallice, cheval moreau' (Du Cange, s.v. *morellus*)). The corresponding Old French is *morelle* 'probably mulberry roan, that is dark chestnut, heavily overlaid with black'. Constance Bullock-Davies informed me that this term, used of a horse's colour, is to be found in Exchequer records, together with numerous other colour-names used to describe particular horses, such as *albus* 'white', *badius* 'bay', *bausandus, bauzain* 'black and white pied, skewbald', *doyn* 'dun or mouse-coloured', *flavus* 'yellow', *griesus* 'grey', *pomele* 'dappled', *Powys* 'a grey horse of a breed peculiar to Powys', *sorus* 'sorrel', etc. All of these invite comparison with the colour-names apparent in the descriptive horses' names in the *Trioedd*. She informed me further that Edward I possessed a Cornish *morelle*, as is evidenced in an (unpublished) entry in the Wardrobe Book for the year 1299–1300: *Elemosina Privata. Alemanne garcioni de stabulo Regis, qui percussus fuerat cum Morello de Cornubia dextrarie Regis, de elemosina Regis, nomine expensarum suarum prehendinande apud Eboracum*. ('Private charity. To a German lad of the King's stable who was kicked by "Morellus de Cornubia", the King's charger, from the King's alms, to cover his expenses while remaining at York.')

It is by no means clear from this passage whether 'Morellus of Cornwall' was the actual name of the King's charger or whether it merely denotes its colour. If *Moro* in the triad derives from *morellus*, *du Moro* is a precise colour-name descriptive of the shade of the horse's black. Yet since *Du (y) Moroed* appears as a variant not only in R, but also in the (perhaps earlier) *Canu y Meirch* in BT 48 (p. lxxxii. l. 9 above), it is impossible to feel complete assurance as to which is the original form of the horse's name, and which one is a corruption of the other. For a variety of descriptive terms for horses in early Welsh poetry see N. A. Jones, *The Horse in Celtic Culture*, pp. 91–7.

Line 2. **o Benllech.** R: *o ben llech Elidir*. If there was ever a place of this name in North Britain, all trace of it is now lost (cf. the lost North-British place-names mentioned in App. I). *Benllech* in Anglesey is the name of a village and headland on the east coast overlooking the *Traeth Coch*. There is no evidence other than the triad that *Benllech Elidir* was its original name; but cf. the name of the mountain *Mynydd Elidir* in Caernarfonshire. Idris Foster suggested to me that the proper name here has arisen out of a misinterpretation of the original meaning of this name, in which *(e)lidir* could represent an early borrowing from Ir. *leitir* 'side of hill, steep ascent or descent' (Hogan, *Onomasticon*, p. 482). This is the more likely since Lloyd-Jones has shown that this element is present in the name of the *Afon Lledr* (J. Lloyd-Jones, *Enwau Lleoedd Sir Gaernarfon*, p. 98), and it is inherently more probable than Lloyd-Jones's own suggestion (ibid., p. 77) that *Elidir* in the mountain-name is derived from O.Ir. *elit* 'fawn'. This mountain has in fact two summits, known as *Elidir Fawr* and *Elidir Fach*. The definite article *E* (= *y*) prefixed to *(e)lidir* became subsequently understood as the first syllable in the proper name *Elidir*. This result would have been facilitated by the influence of the personal element in the names of the adjacent mountains Carnedd Llywelyn and Carnedd Dafydd; as well as by the tradition that Elidir Mwynfawr had met his death in Arfon. A similar interpretation of the name *Benllech y lidir* as *Penllech Elidir* could have been responsible for the association of Benllech with the story of Elidir's fabulous expedition.

b. The last sentence (*ac nys gordiwedawd* etc.), which does not occur in Pen. 16, has plainly been given in the wrong order in the text of R, which interpolates it after *Gwrgi a Pheredur arnav* . . .; whereas the sense requires that it should come at the end, and not in the middle of the names listed as constituting the second *marchlwyth*. The only manuscript besides R which includes this addition is Pen. 51. In giving this sentence correctly at the end of item **b** it may be presumed that Pen. 51 is reproducing the arrangement of the *Llyfr Gwyn* (see introduction, p. xxix).

Line 8. **Cornan.** Triad 70c gives this name as *Cornan* (see n.). *Cornan* was also the reading of NLW, C 6 and RW in the present triad. It is preferable to R's *coruann*, in view of the form *kornan kyne(l)wawc* which occurs in *Canu'r Meirch* (see introduction, p. lxxxiii, n. 8). *Kornan* 'the little horned one' is the name of one of the fabulous horses of *Canu'r Meirch*, cf. *Carna6la6c* 'the Cloven-Hoofed' (triad 40), and *Cornach arwch* given by Pen. 27 as a variant in triad 41c.

Line 10. **6ygedorth.** *myged* + *orth*, i.e. the rising vapour or cloud of dust or steam which rose from a horse or an army under the stress of battle: see GPC 2530; CA 153; B VIII, pp. 232–4.

Line 10. **Arderyd.** On the battle of *Ar(f)derydd* see n. to triad 84b below.

Line 11. **y ar.** When the reference is to riding on horseback, *y ar* (< *di ar*) is equivalent to *ar*; see CA, p. 152, B XIII, p. 6, for other instances of this idiom.

Line 11. **Kethin Kyflym.** Cf. triads 42 (Pen. 27), 46B, and BT 48.12: *kethin march keidaw carnavarn arnav* ('K. the horse of Keidaw, a hard (?) hoof on him'). *Cethin Carnavlaw* of triad 42 may be influenced by this line. *Cethin* means a roan or dark colour (cf. W. Salesbury, Dictionary: *Kethin o liw val march* = *Roen*), but it can also mean 'terrible' (CA 363–4, G 138). Dinogat was riding a horse which belonged to Gwenddolau's father *Keid(i)aw*, though the allusion leaves it quite uncertain as to whether he was an opponent or an ally of Gwenddolau at Arfderydd. It is interesting to find a member of the Powys dynasty (son of Cynan Garwyn) at the battle of Arfderydd in Cumbria, since so extensive a journey recalls the warriors from Gwynedd and Devon who are named in the *Gododdin* as having been present at Catraeth. Gruffudd ap Maredudd wishes for a horse which shall be *eil kethin kyflym*, col. RBP 1329.5.

Line 12. **aruidiawt.** This word is unknown elsewhere. A. O. H. Jarman suggests (*Ym. M. a Th.* 12n.) that it is a corruption of the *awydawc* of BT 48.10: *awyd awydawc* (see introduction, p. lxxxii). But the name or epithet of a horse does not seem to be required here: the context suggests rather the absence of some word which is parallel in meaning to the following word *aglot*; hence I render it tentatively by 'censure'. The termination may be either *-awt* or *-awc*, which are readily confused in copying. Eurys Rowlands agreed with my contention that the context requires a word which is parallel in meaning with *aglot* and suggested a derivative of *gwyd* 'passion' (LlC VI, p. 334). Professor Jarman, however, adheres to his belief that *aruidiawt* is the name or epithet of a horse (*Ym. M. a Th.*, pp. vi–vi). He draws support from the *varia lecta* of another triad—no. 39—and other sources which show that *uu-*, *-vu-*, and *-vw-* were all sometimes miscopied as *-ru-* and *-rw-*, and he lays stress on the testimony of *Canu'r Meirch*, BT 48.9–10 (p. lxxxii above), where *awydawc* ('ardent, high-spirited') actually occurs in the same line as that which names *Kornan kynei(l)wawc*—probably for the same horse *Cornan* 'the horned'—as is named in the triad.

Line 12. **c.** R: **Erch** 'speckled, dappled' is likely to be the correct form, as it is used of a horse by Gwalchmai *llaws erch eruei* (H 28.1 = CBT I, no. 7.129) and by Gruffudd ap Maredudd: *cyrch erchlas dossawg* (RBP col. 1329.12). *Heith* in Pen. 16 could represent a misreading of *Herch*; for the confusion between *-t-* and *-c-* cf. the previous n. and the Ir. personal name *Erc*.

Line 13. **yn erbyn allt.** This idiom is found also in *Culhwch*: *pan elwyf yn erbyn allt* (CO l. 542); cf. *yn erbyn gvynt* (CO l. 555), and for a similar construction DN no. X.41–2: *Araf yr eir i orallt / A baich yngwrthwyneb allt*.

Line 14. **Allt 6aellwr.** R: *riw Vaelawr*. This is the British hill-top fort of *Pendinas*, which lies to the south of Aberystwyth (see HW I, 258 and n.; J. Rhŷs, *A. Leg.* 351–2n.; Owen Jones's *Cymru* I, 84–5). The following description is given in the account of the *Giants* in Pen. 118 (*circa* 1600): *Ac yghwlad Aber Teibhi ydh oedh gynt cyn no dybhod Brutus ir ynys honn, Maylor gawr, a'r lhe y preswylei yndaw a elwir etto Castelh Maylor adeiliedic ar bhrynn uchel neu dorrlann uchel a enwir y Dinas ar y nailh ystlys i'r abhon ystwyth o bhywn rhydhdir trebh Aber Ystwyth* (*Cy.* 27, 136) 'And in the land of Aber Teifi there was in former times before Brutus came to this island, the Giant *Maylor*; and the place where he lived is still called *Castell Maylor*, built upon a high hill or ridge which is called *Y Dinas*, beside the river Ystwyth, within the freehold of the town of Aberystwyth' (see Chris Grooms, *The Giants of Wales*, pp. 308–9). J. E. Lloyd (*Arch. Camb.*, 1931, 201) quotes the following lines from *Y Brython*, 1860, iii, 331—the source is a fifteenth-century poem in which the poet is faced with shipwreck between Aberystwyth and Bardsey:

Adnabod—nid anobaith
Dinas Maelor o'r mor maith.

Pen. 16, fo. 53*r–v*

45. Tri Phryf Ychen Enys Prydein:

Melyn G6aianhwyn
a G6ineu Ych Gwylwylyd,
A'r Ych Brych.

45. Three Principal Oxen of the Island of Britain:

Yellow Spring ('The one of the yellow of spring'),
and Chestnut, ox of Gwylwylyd (*or* 'a meek and gentle ox'),
and the Brindled Ox.

Manuscripts: 16, 47, 50, NLW, DC, BL[2].
45. prif uchen V.
a. gwanwyn 47, V, gwanhwyn 50, Gwaynhwyn NLW, DC.
b. Gwineu 47, 50. gwylwlydd 50, g6lwlyd 47, Gwylwlwyd NLW, DC.
c. ych brychbras y beuren 47, V, y benrhen V.

Among the *anoetheu* stipulated by the Giant Ysbaddaden in *Culhwch ac Olwen* are *Deu ychen Gwlwlyd Wineu yn deu gytbreinhawc y eredic tir dyrys draw yn wych* 'the two oxen of G.W., both yoked together, to plough well the rough ground yonder', and subsequently the Giant asks for *Y Melyn Gwanhwyn a'r ych Brych yn deu gytbrein(h)avc a uynhaf,* CO ll. 589–94 (cf. nn. to CO ll. 589, 593–4).

a. Melyn G6aianhwyn. OW *guiannuin* and Ml.W. *gwaeanhwyn* are recorded in GPC 1575–6 as archaic forms of *gwanwyn* 'spring', and see also GDG no. 14.31 and n. Hence, if *g6aianhwyn* is the correct form of this name, 'Yellow Spring' or 'Yellow of the Spring' is preferable to 'Yellow Pale-White' (given in *Mab.* 114—revised edn, Gwyn Jones and Mair Jones, 1974) as the appropriate name of this ox. (I take this opportunity to correct my translation of *gwaianhwyn* as 'Yellow Pale-White' in the two earlier editions of this book. Both were published before the relevant citation from GPC became available.)

b. G6ineu. See n. to triad 42b.

Gwylwylyd 'one meek and gentle' (*gwylwlydd,* GPC 1764). The only example of this compound cited in GPC is from a line in Gwynfardd Brycheiniog's *awdl* to Dewi Sant *ac aber gwyli bieu gwylwlyd* 'And Abergwili (which) belongs to the gentle one (i.e. St David)' occurring in a list of churches in south Wales dedicated to St David. Here *gwylwlyd* plainly designates Dewi Sant (see edn and trans. of Gwynfardd's poem by M. E. Owen, CBT II, no. 26.94n.) It is evident that Gwynfardd's poem is indebted in some way, hard to estimate, either to this triad, or to the corresponding passages quoted above from CO ll. 589–94, and it is not unlikely that in the triad 'meek and gentle' was originally intended by the epithet *gw(y)lw(y)lyd* as relating to the ox(en), though in CO it became interpreted as the name of their/its owner. (There is no evidence elsewhere for *Gwylwlydd* as a personal name, and no names are given for the owners of the other oxen in the triad. This suggests that a reference to the pre-existing triad underlies the text of CO.) Some allusion to the famous oxen of Dewi Sant is implied in all three of these references. (For the folklore relating to St David's oxen see TWS 66–8.) Elsewhere in Gwynfardd's poem (l. 54 = H 198.24), St David's oxen are described as *deu gar a gertynt yn gydpreinyawc* 'two kinsmen who walked yoked together'—echoing the phrase *yn deu gytbreinhawc*, which is twice repeated in CO ll. 590, 594. Evidently, there has been some confusion in ll. 589–98 where the oxen named in the triad are followed immediately by Ysbaddaden's demand (ll. 596–8) for the *deu ychen bannawc dan yr un aradyr*.

c. A'r Ych Brych. Cf. BT 55.21–3: *ny vdant vy yr ych brych bras y penrvy. Seith vgein kygvng yny aervy* 'They do not know the Brindled Ox, stout its collar, with seven score links to its fastening'. (See edn and study of this poem by M. Haycock, SC XVIII/XIX, pp. 52–78 and see n. to l. 39.) Pen. 47's version of this triad (see *v. lecta*) preserves the older reading of this name in a variant form, *ych brych bras y beuren*, which proves its connection with the reference in *Preiddeu Annwfn* l. 39 to *yr ych brych bras y penrwy* (see introduction, p. xxvi, and CMCS 33, p. 32, n. 77 above for Pen. 47's readings). Lewys Môn alludes to two of the *tri phryf ychen* (and evidently to this triad) in his *marwnad* to Tudur Aled:

Och finnau'r ddau Ych Fannawg:
Ych melyn cewch ym mlaen côr—
F'aeth y brych fyth heb rychor.
(LlC IV, p. 27 = GLM no. XCI.7–8)

'Woe is me for the two horned oxen:
you will find the yellow ox before the choir,
the brindled ox (will be) for ever without a mate.'

46. Teir Pryf Uuch Enys Prydein:

> Brech, buwch 6aelg6n Gwyned,
> a Thonnllwyt, buwch meibyon Eliffer Gosgord6awr,
> a Chornillo, bu6ch Llawuroded 6ar6a6c.

46. Three Principal Cows of the Island of Britain:

> Speckled, cow of Maelgwn Gwynedd,
> and Grey-Skin, cow of the sons of Eliffer of the Great War-band,
> and Cornillo, cow of Llawfrodedd the Bearded.

Manuscripts: 16, 47, 50, NLW, DC, BL[2].

46. prifvu6ch 47, 50, V, prif vwch NLW, vvvch DC, priv Vywch RW.

a. maelg6n 47.

b. meibon oliffer gosgordvawr 47, oliver NLW, DC, V. Tomlwyd NLW, DC, C 36, RW.

c. a cornillo 50, DC, tornillo NLW. llawvrodedd 50, NLW, DC, Llawrodedd varchog C 36, RW.

V *adds* Felly y terfyna Trioedd y meirch herwydd Siôn Balmwr.

---

a. Brech. Cf. the magic cows of Manannán in *Altromh Tighi Da Medar*: *da ba beann-chorra bith-blichta. i. bo breac* 7 *bo odhar* 'two cows with twisted horns always in milk, a speckled cow and a dun cow'; ZCP XVIII, p. 208. Cf. also BT 55.21–3 *yr ych brych bras y penrwy*. Note the lenition of *Maelgwn* after *buwch* (feminine), which is not shown in **b** and **c** below; but of which there are sporadic instances in Ml. prose (TC § 46, i).

b. For **Tonnllwyt** see triad 70c and n. For *meibyon Eliffer* see triad 44b.

c. Cornillo. 'Little Horn' (?). The second element is uncertain, but cf. *brithyll* 'trout' (= 'little speckled'?).

Additional Trioedd y Meirch from Pen. 47 and Pen. 252 (see introduction pp. xxv–xvi above).

46A. Tri Rodedicuarch Ynys Prydein:

Meingalet, march Gwalchmei,
a Myngr6n, march Gwed6,
. . . march Drutwas mab Driffin,
a Gwineu G6d6f Hir march Kei.

46A. Three Bestowed Horses of the Island of Britain:

Slender-Hard, horse of Gwalchmai,
and Arched Mane, horse of Gweddw,
. . . horse of Drudwas son of Tryffin,
and Chestnut Long-Neck, horse of Cai.

46B. Tri Rydecuarch Ynys Prydein:

Torllydan a Gloyn, deu uarch Colla6n mab Teichi.
a'r Kethin Kyflym, march Dinoga[t] mab Kynan [Garwyn].

46B. Three Coursing Horses of the Island of Britain:

Broad-Belly and Ember, the two horses of Collawn son of Teichi,
and Swift-Roan, horse of Dinoga(d) son of Cynan (Garwyn).

46C. Tri Eddystr Ynys Brydain:

Gwirian Groddros, varch Ga(rw)y Hir,
Gwegar, march Elinwy,
farch Ellwyd,
march ap Matheu.

46C. Three Steeds of the Island of Britain:

Gwirian Groddros, horse of Ga(rw)y the Tall,
Gwegar, horse of Elinwy,
. . . horse of Ellwyd,
. . . horse of the son of Matheu.

46A *and* B *from* Pen. 47; V *gives* B *only*; 46C *from* Pen. 252.
46A. *Cf. no.* 38 *and the* LlDC *variants of* 42.
46B. V's *variants from Book of Siôn Balmer*: Collawn mab Berchi, Cynan Garwyn. Pen. 47 *reads* Dinogan mab Kynan Kawrnwy.

46A. The title belongs to triad 38, for which Pen. 47 has substituted *Tri ymladdvarch*. V omits this triad (hence its absence from MA). *Meingalet* is clearly an error for *Kein Galet*, the name of Gwalchmei's famous horse (see LlDC no. 6.12, and R. Bromwich, 'The Triads of The Horses' in Davies and Jones (eds), *The Horse in Celtic Culture*, pp. 114–15).

Myngr6n 'Round / Arched Mane'. This name recalls *Gwynn Mygdwn* 'White Hacked-Mane *march Gwedw*' named three times in *Culhwch* (CO ll. 689, 1006, 1177), which GPC 2532 derives from *mwng* + ?*twn* 'Hacked Mane' rather than *mwng* + *ddwn* 'Russet / Dun Mane'. Since *Gwedw*, the owner's name, corresponds in the tale and in the triads, it is probable that this triad in Pen. 46 gives a variant form of the horse's name as it is found in *Culhwch*. Cf. Gwalchmai: *Lliaws du a dwn a myngdwn melyn* (H 28.17 = CBT I, no. 7.133); Cynddelw: *ni hirgeidw ar geirch meirch mygdwn* (H 137.27 = CBT III, no. 16.171).

For **Gwineu G6d6f Hir** see triad 42. The name of the horse of Drudwas is nowhere given.

46B For **Kethin Kyflym** see triad 44. Could *Gloyn* be an abbreviation for *Glöyn byw* 'butterfly' used as a horse's name? Cf. LlC VI, p. 234.

46C. This is a fragment, perhaps taken from two triads. Except for *Garwy Hir* (triad 57) none of the names appear elsewhere in TYP.

Llyfr Coch Hergest, col. 588

Tri dynyon a ga6ssant gampeu Adaf:

47. Tri Dyn a gauas Kedernit Adaf:

Ercwlf Gadarn,
Ac Ector Gadarn,
A Sompson Gadarn.
Kyn gadarnet oedynt yll tri ac Adaf e hun.

Three men who received the qualities of Adam:

47. Three Men who received the Might of Adam:

Hercules the Strong,
and Hector the Strong,
and Samson the Strong.
They were, all three, as strong as Adam himself.

Manuscripts: R, 77, Simwnt Vychan (Pen. 16, fo. 55 = SV), Hafod 3 (V *omits*).

47. Tri dyn a gafodd Gryfdwr Addaf MW. Naw nyn a wnaethbwyd yn gyflawn o Adda, Tri a gafas i gedernyd 77.

a. Ercwlph 77, Erkwlf SV, Ercwlph ymmerodr Llydaw MW.

b. Ector o droia 77, Hector o Droia MW.

c. Samson 77, Sampson gawr MW.

d. kyn gydarned oedd adda ac a hwynt ill tri H 3, kyn gadarned oedd addaf a hwynt yll tri SV, Ac nid oedd y tri hyn cyn gryfed ac Adda MW.

Triads 47–50, under their own subtitle, form an individual section, which heads the collection in R (RBH col. 588). On this group of triads, see Ceri Davies, *Welsh Literature and the Classical Tradition*, pp. 40–2. In the subtitle, Pen. 77's *Naw nyn*, etc., is preferable to R's *Tri dynyon*, etc., since evidently this title refers to the group as a whole. With the exception of triad 49, two out of the three names in each of these triads correspond with names which appear in *Dares Phrygius* (RBB, pp. 1–39). The Welsh version of *Dares* dates from the first half of the fourteenth century (RBB, p. xix; cf. M. E. Owen and N. Lloyd (eds), *Drych yr Oesoedd Canol*, pp. 33–4). But triads 47–9 were in circulation at least a century earlier than this, since they are cited fully in two poems by Prydydd y Moch (*circa* 1173–1220):

Ny bu bryd eissyeu absalon
nac alexander na iason.
bu kedeyrn or tri trinheion
treul efrei afyrdwl groecyon.

Ercwlf a samsswn seirf galon.
Ac echdor gadarn gad wyllon.
Doeth vu or trioeth treit canon.
teir colofyn y keluytodyon
Marcwlf a chadw gadyr swyson.
a selyl (= selyf) benn sywedytyon.
(H 265.11–20 = CBT V, no. 4.5–14n.)

'*Absalon* was not lacking in beauty, nor *Alexander* (= *Paris*), nor *Jason*. There were strong men (of the) Three Warriors, destruction of the Hebrews, affliction of the Greeks: *Ercwlf* and *Samson*, serpent-hearts, and *Echdor* the strong; warriors fierce in battle. It was wise, learning comes from the Three Wonders; three pillars of craftsmanship were *Marcwlf* (cf. triad 49, Pen. 77 version) and *Cadw* of powerful endowments, and *Selyf*, chief of visionaries.' (See nn. to CBT V, no. 26.108–10.)

Idem (to Rhys Gryg, clearly in reference to the triad):

yth wrhyd yth wrt gadarnhed
mal gvrhyd Ercwlf ergrynhed
A Samsvn gwytgwn gogoned achaws
ac Echdor pan broued.
ac or pryd y prouaf nad fled
nath adws Yessu eissywed.
yn hygant y Tri yn tecced Adaf.
Neud adwyf y'th ganred.
(H 288.13–19 = CBT V, no. 26.107–13)

'In your valour, in your manly strength, causing as much terror as Ercwlf's valour, and Samson (warriors fighting for fame) and Echdor when he was tested. And as regards beauty, I find it is not a deception that Jesus did not allow you to be lacking in the success of the Three, in the beauty of Adam.'

In the twelfth century we find the poets to be acquainted with the names of certain of these classical heroes: both Gwalchmai and Cynddelw refer to *Echdor* (see n. to *Ector Gadarn*), and Cynddelw to *Ercwlf* and *Alexander*; Gwalchmai and Prydydd y Moch to *Eneas* (H 14.19; 280.20); Prydydd y Moch to *Echel* (= *Achilles*) (H 304.3); see also n. to *Priaf Hen*. Gwilym Rhyfel in address to Dafydd ab Owain cites names which occur in this group of triads, as standards of comparison for the qualities of his patron:

Rotes duw dri dawn y drin wychyd naf:
nerth ercvlff yw'r trydyt,
doethinab selyf yssyt
a phryd adaf ar dauyt.
(H 183.17–20 = CBT II, no.28.11n.)

'God bestowed three gifts on the lord, hero in battle: the strength of Ercvlff is one of the three, the wisdom of Selyf, and the beauty of Adam, on Dafydd.'

Similarly Dafydd Benfras attributes to Llywelyn ap Gruffudd the wisdom of Selyf, and Adam's beauty and valour (MA 223b, 4–7 = CBT VI, no. 31.35; 34.19). We find the same virtues as typified in the names of *Samson, Selyf* (Solomon) and the Greek and Trojan heroes, appearing in the lament for the Lord Rhys (d. 1197) in Thomas Jones (ed.), *Brut y Tywysogion*: *Peniarth 20 version* (Cardiff, 1952), pp. 77, 191:

Och am ogonyant y ryueloed . . . mawrvrydrwyd herkwlff, eil achel herwyd garwder y dwy vron; hynawster nestor, glewder tydeus, kedernyt samson, dewred hector, llymder curialus, tegwch a phryt paris, huolder vlixes, doethineb selyf, mawrvryt aiax. (Pen. 20 version, 139a; RBB 340.)

'Alas for the glory of battles . . . the magnanimity of Hercules! A second Achilles in the sturdiness of his breast, the gentleness of Nestor, the doughtiness of Tydeus, the strength of Samson, the valour of Hector, the fleetness of (E)urialius, the comeliness and face of Paris, the eloquence of Ulysses, the wisdom of Solomon, the majesty of Ajax!'

We may conclude, therefore, that twelfth-century poets were familiar with the content of the Latin text of *Dares*, which was translated into Welsh not earlier than *circa* 1300 (M. E. Owen and N. Lloyd (eds), *Drych yr Oesoedd Canol*, p. 34).

As Thomas Jones emphasized in reference to the eulogy of the Lord Rhys (*Brut y Tywysogion, Darlith Agoriadol* (Aberystwyth, 1952), p. 16), the medieval convention in prose and in poetry alike was to eulogize a patron, not for his individual virtues, but for his possession of those qualities which were regarded as typifying the essential attributes of a man occupying his position in the social structure. Hence the crystallization of particular virtues in connection with the names of the accepted heroes of classical and biblical antiquity, and the consequent usefulness to the poets of the triads in which these names were conveniently tabulated. For this reason I append to triad 47 the three triads given by John Jones, Gellilyfdy, in which he cites the names of the Nine Worthies (grouped as three threes) as possessors of the typical virtues. (For an identical list of the Nine Worthies, see Caxton's preface to Malory's *Morte D'Arthur*.) His triads are not, strictly speaking, variants of triads 47–9, but their inspiration is essentially similar. For further references to the Nine Worthies see GGl no. LXIII, and *Rep*. I, p. 775.

The redactor of *Y Seint Greal*, from the seclusion of his monastery, drew attention to an additional fact about three of the men who epitomized Adam's qualities:

kanys y gwr kyntaf a vu a dwyllwyt trwy wreic. A salamon doethaf. a samson gryfaf or gwyr. ac absalon uab dd. a oed deckaf or byt a dwyllwyt oblegyt gwraged. A chanys goruuwyt ar hynn oll o wyr da oblegyt gwraged nyt oes fford yr mab racko y barhau, heb y kythreul amdanat ti. (T. Jones (ed.), *Ystoryaeu Seint Greal: Rhan 1 Y Keis* (Cardiff, 1992), ll. 2612–16)

'Since the first man that ever was, was ensnared through a woman; and Solomon the wisest, and Samson the strongest of men, and Absalom son of David who was the fairest in the world, were ensnared through women. And since all these good men were overcome because of women, it is not possible for yonder lad to endure, says the devil in regard to thee' (= SG 78).

A citation of the three triads 47–9 is made by Gruffudd Llwyd (1380–1420), who claimed that all the qualities epitomized in the three heroes of strength, beauty and wisdom were possessed by his dead patron, Rhydderch ab Ieuan Llwyd:

Trywyr gynt o'r helynt hawl
O'i bryd a fu briodawl;
Tri o'i ddoethder, brywder braw,
Tri o'i nerth, trewyn' wrthaw.
I'n oes, ni bu yn oes neb,
E' ddoeth un o'i ddoethineb,
Ac o'i nerth, ef fu'n gwiw nawdd,
Ac o'i bryd, gwae a brydawdd!
Campau Addaf gwplaf gynt,
Ar Rydderch oll yr oeddynt.
(IGE[2] no. XXXVIII.9–18.)

'Three Men formerly in the course of right possessed his (= Adam's) beauty, three his wisdom—strength of amazement—three his might; they partook from him. In our time there has not come anyone of his wisdom, or of his might—he was our fine defence—or of his beauty, woe to the singer! The qualities in which Adam excelled in former times were all to be found in Rhydderch.' (On the poem, see D. J. Bowen, LlC XII, p. 121, and my note in B XXIX, pp. 81–3 on *Marwnad Rhydderch.*)

Similarly Wiliam Llŷn draws upon these triads in a eulogy to William Games: *Boed ytt . . . doethder Salmonn gwr di donnoc / A nerth Samson bur gyssur gossoc / . . . A dewredd Ektor awdurioc* (J. C. Morrice (ed.), *Barddoniaeth William Llŷn* (1908) no. XVI.54–8).

On this late reproduction of the medieval Nine Worthies cited on p. 133, see M. Haycock's discussion of early Welsh allusions to Alexander, CMCS 13, p. 22, and her note in *Blodeugerdd Barddas o Ganu Crefyddol Cynnar*, p. 80.

The names of the classical heroes regarded as typifying human qualities made by John Jones, Gellilyfdy are given on page 133.

47b. Pen. 216 (J. Jo.), pp. 28–9:
Llyma henwae y naw milwr gwrolaf, ag urddasaf or holl vyd, or rrain y mae tri Pagan, tri Iddew, a thri Christion:
Y tri Pagan: Egtor o Droia. Alexander mawr. Julius Caesar.
Y tri Iddew: Davydd broffwyd. Judas Makabeus. duwk Josua.
Y tri Christion: Arthur. Siarlys. Godffre de bwlen.

47b. Pen. 216 (J. Jones, Gellilyfdy)
Here are the names of the nine bravest and most noble warriors of the whole world; of whom there are Three Pagans, Three Jews, and Three Christians:
The Three Pagans: Hector of Troy, Alexander the Great, Julius Caesar.
The Three Jews: David the Prophet, Judas Maccabeus, Duke Joshua.
The Three Christians: Arthur, Charles (Charlemagne), Godfrey of Boulogne.

Llyfr Coch Hergest

48. Tri dyn a gauas pryt Adaf:

Absolon ab Dauyd,
A Iason uab Eson,
A Pharis uab Priaf.
Kyn decket oedynt yll tri ac Adaf e hun.

48. Three Men who received the Beauty of Adam:

Absalom son of David,
and Jason son of Aeson,
and Paris son of Priam.
They were, all three, as comely as Adam himself.

Manuscripts: R, 77, SV, Hafod 3 (V *omits*).
48. Tri a gafas i bryd 77, Tri dyn a gafodd Tegwch Adda H 3, SV.
a. Absolon ap Dd brophwyd 77, Absalon SV.
b. Iasson ab Iasson H 3.
c. a pharis vab pryaf hen frenin Troyaf H 3, SV, Alexander paris 77.
d. kyn decked oedd adda a hwyn ill tri H 3.

See n. to triad 47. *Alexander*, in the version of this triad given by Pen. 77 and by Prydydd y Moch, is an alternative name for *Paris* (see n. and CBT V no. 4.5 and n.). It is the name given to him throughout the text of *Dares Phrygius*.

Llyfr Coch Hergest

49. Tri dyn a gauas Doethineb Adaf:

Cado Hen,
a Beda,
a Sibli Doeth.
Kyn doethet oedynt ell tri ac Adaf ehun.

49. Three People who received the Wisdom of Adam:

Cato the Old,
and Bede,
and Sibli the Wise.
They were, all three, as wise as Adam himself.

Manuscripts: R, 77, SV (title only), V *omits*.
49. Tri a gafas i ddoethineb 77.
a. Marcwlph 77, Catuan ddoeth H 3.
b. bida 77, beda yffeiriad H 3.
c. 77 *substitutes* a Selef ap Dd.
d. kyn ddoethed oedd Adda a hwynt ill tri H 3.

See n. to triad 47. Prydydd y Moch knew of this triad in a slightly variant version, and his version with both *Marcwlph* (see n.) and *Selyf* reappears in the text of Pen. 77. The name of *Selyf* (Solomon) appears to have been superseded by that of *Sibli Doeth* 'the wise Sibyl' in R's version of **c**; cf. Prydydd y Moch, Pen. 77, and the other references quoted in n. to triad 47, and n. to *Selyf (Solomon)*, as the stock figure which typifies wisdom. The substitution can probably be attributed to the fact that *Proffwydoliaeth Sibli Doeth* is found in the same manuscript as these triads (RBH cols. 571–7).

Llyfr Coch Hergest

50. Teir G6raged a gauas pryt Eua yn tri thraean:

Diadema, gorderch Eneas Ysc6ydwyn,
ac Elen Uanna6c, y wreic y bu distriwedigaeth Tro dr6y y phenn,
a Pholixena uerch Priaf hen vrenhin Tro.

50. Three Women who received the Beauty of Eve in three third-shares:

Diadema (= Dido?), mistress of Eneas White-Shield,
and Elen the Famous, the woman on whose account was the destruction of Troy,
and Polixena, daughter of Priam the Old, king of Troy.

Manuscripts: R, 47, 77, BL[1], SV, H 3, NLW Addl. 37B, p. 92 (V *omits*).

50. Tair gwragedh talediw a gowsant pryt Eva BL, NLW Addl.

a. diodema BL, Diodema (gl. Dido) NLW Addl., gorderch achilarw 47.

b. bannawc H 3, vanawc 77, vannoc SV. distryw troea 47, dystryw Tro oi hachaws 77, i distrywyd troya oi hachos H 3.

c. a pholicsena 77, a ffolixena H 3, a pholexana SV. verch hen frenin troia H 3, priaf brenhin groec 47.

H 3, SV, *add* Kyn decked oedd Efa a hwy ill tair; ag felly terfyna H 3.

This triad appears to be an addition to the original group, triads 47–9, made under the influence of *Dares Phrygius* (Welsh version *circa* 1300, see Morfydd E. Owen and Nesta Lloyd (eds), *Drych yr Oesoedd Canol*, pp. 33–4); since there is no evidence that it was known to the *Gogynfeirdd* (with the unlenited form *Priaf* cf. triad 56 and n.). There is nothing to explain **a** in either *Dares Phrygius* or in the *Brut*: if the reference is really to Aeneas it must derive from HB or some different neoclassical source, or it may be based on the brief mention of Dido in Ovid's *Metamorphoses*. The later texts, as well as the references by the poets to this triad (see below) all preserve the curious form *Diadema, Diodema*. The clue to this name may have been preserved in Pen. 47's reading: *Diadema gorderch achilarw* ('D. mistress of *Achilles*'), since as Stern pointed out (ZCP VII, p. 235) there seems to have been confusion with the name of *Diademeia*, daughter of Lykomedes, on whom Achilles begot Neoptolemos (Rose, *Handbook of Greek Mythology*, p. 239).

In *Dares Phrygius,* Achilles is rendered in Welsh as *Achelarwy*. Probably, then, we should restore *Achil*(*arwy*) in **a** in place of *Eneas Yscwydwyn*, a name popularized by the *Bruts*. The triad forms the opening lines of a *cywydd* (GDG no. 51) in which Dafydd ap Gwilym, citing the triad from R (or its prototype), makes what appears to be his personal addition to the series of triads 47–9 by including the names of three renowned women as an addition to the series of the 'Men who received Adam's qualities' (RBH 588) and by adding *Elen Uannawc* (see n.) as a fourth to this triad:

Tair gwragedd â'u gwedd fal gwawn
A gafas yn gwbl gyfiawn
Pryd cain, pan fu'r damwain da,
A roes Duw Nef ar Efa.
Cyntaf o'r tair disgleirloyw
A'i cafas, ehudras hoyw
Policsena ferch Bria,
Gwaisg o grair yn gwisgo gra.
A'r ail fu Ddiodemaf,
Gwiwbryd goleudraul haul haf.
Trydedd fun ail Rhun y rhawg
Fu Elen feinwen fannawg,
Yr hon a beris cyffro
A thrin rhwng Gröeg a Thro.
(GDG no. 51.1–14 and n.)

'Three women, their form like gossamer, received in perfect measure—the chance was fortunate—the fair form which God bestowed upon Eve. The first of the three shining ones who received it, proudly graceful, was Polixena, daughter of Priam, a noble treasure, clad in fur. The second was Diodema—a fair light form, like summer sunshine. The third maiden . . . was Helen the Famous, slender-fair, who caused tumult and battle between Greece and Troy.'

Gutun Owain makes a similar comparison:

Soniwn amdanad, Polixena, ail
Elen, Diodema,
Dy liw'n dec wrth dy lvn da
A dyvodd val pryd Eva.
(GO II.9–12).

For further instances of the ambiguous epithet *bannog* 'horned / famous' as given in *Dares Phrygius* to Helen of Troy see n. to *Elen*[2] *Uanna6c* under Personal Names below.

Llyfr Coch Hergest, col. 598

51. Trywyr G6arth a uu yn Ynys Prydein:

Vn onadunt: Auar6y uab Llud uab Beli. Ef a dyuynna6d Julius Cesar a g6yr Ruuein y'r Ynys honn yn gyntaf, ac a beris talu teir mil o bunnoed aryant bop bl6ydyn yn deyrnget o'r Ynys honn y wyr Ruuein, o gyfryssed a Chasswalla6n y ewythyr.

A'r eil y6 G6rtheyrn G6rtheneu, a rodes tir gyntaf y Saesson yn yr Ynys honn, ac a ymdywedia6d yn gyntaf ac wynt, ac a beris llad Custennin Uychan uab Custennin Uendigeit o'e vrat, a dehol y deu uroder Emrys Wledic ac Uthur Penndra(g)on o'r Ynys honn hyt yn Llyda6, a chymryt y goron a'r urenhinyaeth o'e dwyll yn y eida6 e hun. Ac yn y diwed Uthur ac Emrys a losgassant Wrtheyr(n), yg Kastell G6erthrynya6n ar lann G6y, unfflam y dial eu brawt.

Trydyd, g6aethaf, uu Vedra6t pan edewis Arthur lywodraeth Ynys Prydein gantha6, pan aeth ynteu drwy vor yn erbyn Lles amhera6dyr Ruuein, a anuonassei gennadeu att Arthur hyt yg Kaer Llion y erchi teyrnget idaw o'r Ynys honn, ac y wyr Ruuein ar y messur y talp6yt [o oes] Ga(s)wallawn uab Beli hyt yn oes Gustennin Uendigeit, teit Arthur. Sef atteb a rodes Arthur y gennadeu yr Amhera6dyr: nat oed well y dylyei wyr Ruuein deyrnget y wyr Ynys Prydein, noc y dylyei wyr Ynys Prydein udunt 6ynteu. Kanys Bran uab Dyuynwal, a Chustennin uab Elen a uuassynt amherodron yn Ruuein, a deu 6r o'r Ynys honn oedynt. Ac yna y lluyda6d Arthur gordetholwyr y gyuoeth dr6y uor yn erbyn yr Amhera6dyr. Ac y kyuaruuant y tu hwnt y uynyd Mynneu. Ac aneirif o nadunt o bop parth a las y dyd h6nn6. Ac yn y diwed y kyuaruu Arthur a'r amhera6dyr, ac Arthur a'e llada6d. Ac yno y llas goreug6yr Arthur. A phan gigleu Vedra6t g6ahanu niuer Arthur, yd ymchoelawd ynteu yn erbyn Arthur, ac y duuna6d Saesson a Ffichteit ac Yscottyeit ac ef y gad6 yr Ynys honn rac Arthur. A phan gigleu Arthur hynny, yd ymchoela6d dracheuyn ac a dihengis ganta6 o'e niuer. Ac y dreis y ar Vedra6t y kauas dyuot y dir yr Ynys honn. Ac yna y bu Weith Camlan y r6ng Arthur a Medra6t, ac y llada6d Arthur Uedra6t, ac y brath6yt Arthur yn angheua6l. Ac o hynny y bu uar6. Ac y my6n plas yn Ynys Auallach y clad6yt.

51. Three Men of Shame were in the Island of Britain:

One of them: Afarwy son of Lludd son of Beli. He first summoned Julius Caesar and the men of Rome to this Island, and he caused the payment of three thousand pounds in money as tribute from this Island every year, because of a quarrel with Caswallawn his uncle.

And the second is Gwrtheyrn the Meagre, who first gave land to the Saxons in this Island, and was the first to enter into an alliance with them. He caused the death of Custennin the Younger, son of Custennin the Blessed, by his treachery, and exiled the two brothers Emrys Wledig and Uthur Penndragon from this Island to Brittany, and deceitfully took the crown and the kingdom into his own possession. And in the end Uthur and Emrys burned Gwrtheyrn in Castell Gwerthrynion beside the Wye, in a single conflagration to avenge their brother.

The third and worst was Medrawd, when Arthur left with him the government of the Island of Britain, at the time when he himself went across the sea to oppose Lles, emperor of Rome, who had dispatched messengers to Arthur in Caerleon to demand tribute to him and to the men of Rome, from this Island, in the measure that it had been paid (from the time of) Caswallawn son of Beli until the time of Custennin the Blessed, Arthur's grandfather. This is the answer that Arthur gave to the emperor's messengers: that the men of Rome had no greater claim to tribute from the men of this Island, than the men of the Island of Britain had from them. For Brân son of Dyfnwal and Custennin son of Elen had been emperors in Rome, and they were two men of this Island. And then Arthur mustered the most select warriors of his kingdom (and led them) across the sea against the emperor. And they met beyond the mountain of Mynneu (= the Alps), and an untold number was slain on each side that day. And in the end Arthur encountered the emperor, and Arthur slew him. And Arthur's best men were slain there. When Medrawd heard that Arthur's host was dispersed, he turned against Arthur, and the Saxons and the Picts and the Scots united with him to hold this Island against Arthur. And when Arthur heard that, he turned back with all that had survived of his army, and succeeded in landing on this Island in opposition to Medrawd. And then there took place the Battle of Camlan between Arthur and Medrawd, and Arthur slew Medrawd, and was himself mortally wounded. And from that (wound) he died, and was buried in a hall on the Island of Afallach.

Manuscripts: R, 51, 252.

51. Tair gormes . . . ynys p(rydain) 51, V.

a. A6arwy 51, 252. ap Beli mawr V. a ddynnodd 51. Julius a cesar R, julwy ssussar 51, Jul cesar V, a dderbynodd ulcassar 252. kannmil *altered to* tairmil 51, teir mil o . . . kym(aint) dyrnget i ryfen 252. oe gyvryssedd 51.

b. wrtheyrn fab gwrthenau 51, gwrtheyrn frenin 252. dderbynodd y sayson (yr) ynys 252. ai vrawd *altered to* oe vrad 51, oe dwyll V. a deol y ddaw brodor or tir 51. penndradon R, Uthr benndragonn 51. losgassant wrtheyr R, ai llosges yntaw 51, ac yn y diwedd y dychwelasant ac ai llosgasant V. ynghastell gwrtheyrnion 252.

c. 6u 6edrod ap llew ap kynvarch 51, V, 252. lleon *altered to* lles 51. a anvonassei gennadeu ataw or blaen hyd ynghaer llion ar wyssc 51. ag ef a dderbynodd y sayson eylwaith . . . ar gystudd i wrthladd Arthur i Ewythyr *ends* 252. y gatwallavn R, o amsser kasswallawn ap peli hyd yn amser kusstenin vendigeit 51. y wyr ruvein *altered to* y genadeu y amherodr 51. a daw or brytaniaid oedd y gwyr hynny 51. Ac ymgarvuant y tu hwnt y vynydd mynniu ac y llas aerva o bob tu. Ac y llas yr amherawdr a goreugwyr Arthur 51. wassgaru gwyr *altered to* i gadw yr ynys honn 51. 51 *adds* Ac yna doeth idawc ap nyniaw yr hwnn a elwir idawc korn prydyn yr hwnn a wnaeth y gynnen rrwng Arthur a medrod. Ac y min y mor ydd ymgy6ar66ant. Ac yno y llas medrod, *etc.* (*This rare evocation of events in the tale of* Breudwyt Ronabwy *is not paralleled elsewhere.*)

V *substitutes* Trydyd gwaethaf oll vu Medrawd ap llew ap Cynvarch pan edewis Arthur lywodraeth Ynys Prydein ganthaw, a chwedi ei fyned ynteu trwy for yn erbyn yr emerawdr tu hwnt y fynydd Mynneu, lle i llas goreugwyr Arthur. Pan glywei Medrawd gwahanu niver Arthur . . . *ends.*

(51) C6 (c. 1550, RWM = shortened version)**.** Trywyr Gwarth Ynys Brydain:

Vn fv Afarwy ap Lludd ap Beli Mawr, a dd(yfynodd) Wlkasar ymerodr Rufain i'r Ynys hon, ag a beris (talu) tair mil o bunoedd iddo bob blwyddyn o dyhyr(nged), i gyfrwysedd a Chyswallon i ewyrth.

Yr ail, Gwrtheyrn Gwrthenau, a roddes tir i'r Saeson yn yr Ynys hon, ag amddyweddiodd a hwynt yn gynta, ag a ladodd Gonstans o dwyll. Ag Uthur ag Emrys i frodyr ai lladdodd yntau ynghastell Gwrthrynion ar lan Gwy, ag ai llosgason.

Y trydydd fv Fedrod ap Llew ap Kynfarch; a ffan edewis Arthur lywodraeth yr Ynys gantho, pan aeth yntav i ymladd a Lle(s) ymerodr Rufain am ofyn tyhyrnged or Ynys hon, ag ai lladdodd ef, ag a fynodd dyhyrngedd o Rufain. Ag yna pan clywiodd Medrod i lledid ar gwyr, i gwiscodd ef y goron, ag a ddyfynodd ato y Saeson a'r Ffichdiaid (a'r Skotiait) ar ystyried i lester Arthur i'r Ynys hon. Ag ni thyckiodd (iddo), ag yna i bu Gamlan, ag y llas Medrod, ag i brathwyd Arthur yn angiriol, ag yn Ynys Afallach i bu farw, ag y kladdwyd Arthyr.

Manuscripts: C 6, C 36, NLW, RW, Cwrt. 3, BL^{2}.

Triad 51 is the only triad in the Red Book collection whose content is drawn essentially from the narrative of Geoffrey of Monmouth. The wording of this triad closely follows that of the *Brut* (BD 166–71), though it presents certain variants which suggest that it may be based on some version of *Brut y Brenhinedd* other than those which have been published. Chief of these variants is the statement in **c** that Arthur slew the Roman emperor *Lles*, which does not agree with the account given of this incident either in HRB or by the *Brut*; see n. to *Kastell G6erthrynya6n*, line 10.

In the text of R triad 51 follows immediately after triad 35 (R) *Porth aeth . . . hyt yn Llychlyn* (RB cols. 588–90). The two triads together form a subsection to themselves, and it would thus seem that they are intended to bear a special relation to each other. In the older series, triad 35 forms a contrasting pair with triad 36 (see n. to triad 35), but triad 36 (*Teir Gormes*) is absent from all texts of the WR series. Further examination shows that triad 51 is in fact a readaptation of triad 36, and it is significant to note that Pen. 51 actually gives to this triad the heading *Tair Gormes* (see *varia lecta*). The *Trywyr Gwarth* are the men who were responsible for introducing the *teir gormes* into Britain—*Gwrtheyrn* invited in the *Saeson* and *Medrawt* brought in the *Gwydyl Fychti* (or *Ffichteit*)—but with the difference that in triad 51a the Romans have taken the place of the *gormes* of the *Corranyeit* of triad 36. It seems probable that this is merely a restoration, and that originally the *Cesaryeit* or Romans (see triad 35) formed one of the *teir gormes*—it is difficult to see how they could be excluded—and that they gave place to the *Corranyeit* under the influence of the tale of *Lludd a Llefelys* (see n. to *y Corryanyeit*, triad 36).

Since the earliest text of triad 51 is that of R, and there can be no certainty as to whether or not the triad was included in the lost pages of W, it seems possible that the triad is not very much older than *circa* 1400, the approximate date of the Red Book of Hergest. An immediate contemporary attraction in the thirteenth and fourteenth centuries of the story of Arthur's triumphant rejection of the Roman tribute, would have been the implicit parallel which existed between this tribute and the unpopular tax imposed by the Papacy, known as 'Peter's Pence' (see W. E. Lunt, *Revenues in the Middle Ages* (Columbia, 1934), I, p. 68; EHR XI, p. 746). A date shortly before 1400 would agree with the similar treatment of the theme of Arthur's continental campaign in the English alliterative poem *Mort Arthure*, composed *circa* 1360 (see n. to line 24 below). On the other hand, the presence of the triad in Pen. 51 suggests that an earlier text of it may have been contained in the lost portion of W.

R and Pen. 51 are the only manuscripts to give complete texts of this triad, and Pen. 51 is interesting as including under **c** a name known elsewhere only in the tale of *Breudwyt Ronabwy*: *Idawc ap Nynian . . . idawc korn prydyn* (see *varia lecta*). Pen. 252 and V give item **c** in an incomplete or condensed form. But six other manuscripts contain an abbreviated version of the triad, and these texts show so close an agreement between themselves as to indicate that they stem from a common archetype. I append this second version from C 6, the earliest manuscript in which it appears; but since it is clear that this version derives ultimately from that of R, I have not thought it necessary to include a translation or *varia lecta*.

Trywyr Gwarth 'Three Men of Shame'.

a. See BD 49–54; RBB 87–93 (= HRB IV, 8–10). At the feast held by Caswallawn to celebrate his second victory over Caesar, a quarrel broke out between him and his nephew Afarwy (*Androgeus* in HRB), as a result of which Afarwy dispatched a letter to Caesar in France, offering him his support. After taking hostages from Afarwy, Caesar landed at Dover, and this time achieved victory over Caswallawn. Through Afarwy's mediation, peace was made between the two, on the condition that the Britons should pay as yearly tribute to Rome *teir mil o bunhoed o aryan Lloegyr* 'three thousand pounds of English money' (BD 54.21; RBB 93.4 = HRB *tria milia librarum argenti*). *Aryan*(*t*) both here and in the triad is 'money' rather than literally 'silver'.

Line 4. **o gyfryssed.** For the preposition *o*(*c*) denoting cause, see GMW 203–4. The same phrase occurs in triad 84c below. The variant *i gyfrwysedd* 'in cunning' in C 6 is a scribal corruption due to a misunderstanding of this phrase. On the frequent confusion between *cyfrysedd* and *cywrysedd* see CLlH 239.

b. According to BD 87–90, RBB 126–30 (= HRB VI, 6–8), on the death of *Custennin Uendigeit* (= *Constantinus*, see n. under Personal Names) Gwrtheyrn fetched Custennin's eldest son *Constans* the monk from his monastery at Winchester, and caused him to be crowned king in preference to his two younger brothers. (Both the *Bruts* and Geoffrey give this name as *Constans*: I know of no occurrence of the form *Custennin Vychan* except in this triad. Brynley Roberts points out (*Modern Language Review* LVII, p. 406) that the epithet of Custennin *Vychan* here and elsewhere may stand for 'junior'; see also idem, B XXV, p. 286.) From the outset, the intention of Gwrtheyrn is represented as being to obtain the rule of Britain for himself. Thus he incited the Pictish warriors, whom he had himself placed in the king's bodyguard, to murder *Constans*. After this deed Emrys and Uthur Pendragon fled to Brittany, where they were received by the Breton ruler *Emyr Llydaw* (see n. under Personal Names) (= Geoffrey's *Boudocius*), and Gwrtheyrn was thus enabled to assume the crown unopposed. Gwrtheyrn's reception of the Saxons is described BD 91–2, RBB 131–2 (= HRB VI, 10). For the older sources on which the *Brut* account is based, see n. to *Gwrtheyrn Gwrtheneu* under Personal Names.

Line 10. **Kastell G6erthrynya6n** (= *Gwrtheyrnion*, Pen. 252). The final revenge of the brothers Emrys and Uthur, in which they burned Gwrtheyrn in his *kastell*, is described in BD 117–18, RBB 156–8 (= HRB VIII, 2). The story looks like an elaboration by Geoffrey of HB's description of the burning of Gwrtheyrn by divine fire in his fortress of *Craig Gwrtheyrn* on the Teifi (HB, ch. 47). But as J. E. Lloyd has pointed out (EHR LVII, pp. 460–1), Geoffrey's account may be based on knowledge of a local variant of the tale which identified the site of Gwrtheyrn's end as the British hill-fortress of Little Doward Hill in the parish of Gannerew (earlier Gennerew) on the Wye two miles above Monmouth. Geoffrey calls the place *opidum Genoreu* and says of it *Erat autem opidum illud natione herging. super fluuium guaie. in monte qui cloartius nuncupatur* (= BD 118: *castell Goronvy* (RBB: *c. Genorvy*) . . . *sef lle* *oed hvnnv, yn Ergyng ar glann Gwy auon, ymynyd Clorach*). As shown by Lloyd, Geoffrey's *Cloartius* seems to have arisen from a scribal corruption of *Doartius* (Doward), though it is to be noted that not one of the manuscripts of the HRB which has been published up till now actually contains this form. Gannerew lies within the borders of the old cantref of Erging (= Archenfield), over which Gwrtheyrn ruled, according to the *Brut* account (BD 87.6; see also n., ibid., 264). *Kastell Gw(e)rthrynyawn*, if it really refers to the same place, may be simply a mistake for *Kastell Gwrtheyrn*; alternatively, it may represent yet another localization of the story of Gwrtheyrn's end, at a place situated farther north, within the *cantref* of *Gwrtheyrnion*, with which HB associates Gwrtheyrn and his family. I have not seen the name *Kastell Gw(e)rthrynyawn* elsewhere; so that this name, taken in conjunction with that of *Custennin Vychan* in **a** above, suggests that triad 51 owes its origin to some text of the *Brut* other than those represented by the published versions.

c. For the Roman emperor's letter to Arthur demanding tribute from Britain see BD 162, RBB 204 (= HRB IX, 15); and for Arthur's commitment of the government of the country to Medrawd see BD 167.24–5: *gorchymyn a wnaeth ynteu llywodraeth enys Prydein y Vedrawt y nei uab y chuaer, ac y Wenhvyuar urenhines* (RBB 210 = HRB X, 2).

Line 15. **[o oes] Ga(s)wallawn uab Beli hyt yn oes Gustennin Uendigeit.** R: *y gatwallavn uab Beli.* The scribe of R has confused *Caswallawn* with *Catwallawn*. Pen. 51's reading *o amsser kasswallawn . . . hyd yn amser kusstenin* proves that *o oes* should be restored in R: the tribute was not paid *to* Caswallawn, but by him to the Romans. For the payment of the British tribute by Caswallawn see n. to **a** above. According to Geoffrey's story, when the Romans finally left Britain and abandoned the people to their fate (BD 84–6; RBB 124–5 = HRB VI, 4) the Britons appealed to *Aldwr* (= *Aldroen*), ruler of Brittany, to help them, but Aldwr refused the offer of rule over Britain because of the oppressive Roman tribute—he preferred to possess the Breton kingdom in freedom rather than to rule in Britain under the yoke of the Romans. Nevertheless he sent his brother *Custennin* (father of Uthur Pendragon) to rule in Britain in his place. (Thus Geoffrey makes it clear that his hero Arthur is of Breton descent.) The redactor of the triad evidently considered Geoffrey's account to imply that the Roman tribute ceased at the time when the Romans left Britain, and that its payment was not resumed by Custennin.

Line 18. **nat oed well y dylyei.** The words of the triad follow closely Arthur's reply to Lles as given in the *Brut*, BD 163.29 ff.: *Ac vrth hynny, can ydyv amheravdyr Ruuein trvy anylyet yn keissyav yn bot ni yn trethavl idav ef, minheu trvy dylyet yavn a holaf teyrnget idav ef o Ruuein. A'r cadarnhaf ohonam kymeret teyrnget y gan y gilid. Canys o goresgynnvs Ulkessar ac amherodron ereill oc eu kedernyt enys Prydein, ac o achavs hynny keissyav* *kymell teyrnget ohonei yr avrhon, yn gynhebic y hynny minheu a uarnaf dylyu ohonaf inheu teyrnget o Ruuein. Canys uy ryeni inheu gynt a oresgynnassant Ruuein, Beli a Bran meibyon Dyuynwal Moelmut. . . . A guedy hynny Custennyn uab Helen, a Maxen Wledic, uyg kereint inheu, a uuant amherodron yn Ruuein, ac o enys Prydein heuyt y goresgynnassant* (RBB 206 = HRB IX, 16). To give this point further emphasis, texts of the shorter version of the triad add the words *ag a fynodd (Arthur) dyhyrngedd o Rufain* 'As (A) *demanded* tribute from Rome'. For the imposition of tribute on Rome by *Beli* and *Brân*, see BD 37; RBB 75 (= HRB III, 9).

Line 20. **Custennin uab Elen,** i.e. Constantine the Great; BD 69–70; RBB 108 (= HRB V, 6). Geoffrey cites *vaticinia Sibille* 'prophecies of the Sibyl'—evidently his own invention—to the effect that Arthur was destined to be the third king of Britain to conquer Rome (HRB IX, 17; BD 165). Thus Gruffudd Llwyd names *Brân, Custennin* and *Arthur* as the three British emperors who made conquests overseas (IGE^2, no. XLII.1–6).

Line 23. **Mynneu,** *Mynyd(ed) Mynneu* (*Mynheu*) = the Alps. *Mynneu* is derived from an oblique case of L. *mons, mwnnh* + *Iou* (< L. *Iovis*), later *Mons Iovis. Myn(n)hieu* became contracted to *Myn(n)heu, Mynneu* (Ifor Williams, B XVII, pp. 96–8; *Enwau Lleoedd,* 31). HB refers to *Mons Iovis* (ch. 27), and this must have originally denoted one particular summit, such as *Mont Blanc*, though in Welsh usage the derived form came to be used for the Alps as a whole (CBT I, no. 27.39n.). According to the *Brut*, Arthur had not yet crossed the Alps when the news from Britain caused him to return home: *A phan ydoed yr haf yn dyuot, ac Arthur yn esgynnu mynyded Mynheu vrth uynet y oresgyn Ruuein, nachaf kennadeu o enys Prydein yn menegi idav bot Medravt y nei uab y chuaer wedi guisgav coron enys Prydein trvy greulonder a brat* (BD 182.18–21; *mynyd mynheeu* RBB 229.24 = HRB X, 13: *montes*). Yet it would seem that this passage was in the mind of the redactor of the triad, since elsewhere in the *Brut* the name *mynyded Mynheu* occurs only in the *Prophecies of Merlin* (BD 109.5; 110.18). This name for the Alps is used by the *cywyddwyr*: *tros warr Mynnau* (GTA I, no. VII.111); *Uwch yw ystâd y tad tau / No mann o Fynydd Mynnau* (DN no. X.47–8). See also the allusion given in the first line of the extract exemplifying the metre *cywydd llosgyrnog* in each of the four early examples in the Bardic Grammar: *Lluwch eiry manot mynyd Mynneu* 'A drift of fine snow on the mountain of the Alps' (GP 13, 31, 52), and Einion ap Gwalchmai: *Porthwyf i boen edryt Mynyt Mynnheu* (CBT I, no. 27.39n.).

Line 24. **Arthur a'e llada6d.** HRB X, 11: *Tunc tandem lucius imperator infra turmas occupatus. cuiusdam lancea confossus interiit*; BD 181.17–19: *Ac ym plith y bydinoed y guant un a gleif Lles amheravdyr Ruuein, ac o'r dyrnavt hvnnv yn diannot y bu varv. Ac ny dyweit y llyuyr pvy a'e lladavd*; RBB 228.19–20: *ac yna y dygvydvys lles amherawdyr yn vrathedic gan leif neb vn.*

ac y bu varv; *Brut. Cleo.* 189, 11–12: *y gwant vn or brutannyiet lles amheravdyr ruvein a gwayw trwydaw yny digwyd yn varw yr llawr.* Wace and Layamon are equally uncertain as to the identity of the slayer of Lucius. In the *Prose Merlin* (ed. Sommer, *Vulgate Cycle of Arthurian Romances* II, p. 440), Gawain kills the Roman emperor with Arthur's sword Escalibor. The only source other than the triad that I have discovered, in which Arthur himself is credited with having performed this deed, is the English alliterative poem *Mort Arthure* (ed. Brock, EETS, ll. 2252–5), and it is from this source that Malory derives his version of the same events (*The Works of Sir Thomas Malory*, ed. Vinaver, I, p. 223). The poem has been dated *circa* 1360 (see J. N. L. O'Loughlin, ALMA 520–4). Though it seems improbable that there could be any direct influence from the English poem on the triad, the date assigned to the poem would fit well enough with the earliest appearance of the triad in the text of R, and it is possible that both accounts may draw upon a common source for the incident. The treatment of the theme of Arthur's continental campaign both in the alliterative poem and in Malory is considered to reflect elation at contemporary English successes in the continental wars of the fourteenth and fifteenth centuries (O'Loughlin, op. cit., pp. 521, 523; E. Vinaver, *The Works of Sir Thomas Malory* (2nd edn, Oxford, 1973), I, p. 223: III, 1394 quoting source from the alliterative *Morte Arthure*). Some such elation may also be reflected in this triad in the portrayal of Arthur as the slayer of the Roman emperor, a deed which is left ambiguous in the earlier sources

Line 27. **Ffichteit.** See n. to *Gwydyl Fychti*, triad 36b.

Line 29. **y dreis** 'by violence'. On this use of the preposition *y* see n. to triad 26a.

Line 30. **Gweith Camlan.** See n. to triad 59c.

Line 32. **Ynys Auallach.** See n. to the name *Auallach* under Personal Names.

Llyfr Gwyn Rhydderch, fo. 57*r*

52. Tri Goruchel Garchara6r Ynys Brydein:

Llyr Lledyeith a uu gan Euros6yd yg karchar,
A'r eil Mabon ap Modron,
A'r trydyd Gweir ap Gweirioed.

Ac vn a oed goruchelach no'r tri, a uu deirnos yg karchar yg Kaer Oeth ac Anoeth, ac a uu deir nos yg karchar gan Wen Bendragon, ac a uu deir nos yg karchar hut a dan Lech Echemeint. Ac y sef oed y Goruchel Garchara6r h6nn6, Arthur. A'r un gwas a'e gollyga6d o'r tri charchar hynny. Ac y sef oed y g6as h6nn6, Goreu vab Kustenin y geuynder6.

52. Three Exalted (Supreme) Prisoners of the Island of Britain:

Llŷr Half-Speech, who was imprisoned by Euroswydd,
and the second, Mabon son of Modron,
and third, Gwair son of Gweirioedd.

And one (Prisoner) was more exalted than the three of them, he was three nights in prison in Caer Oeth and Anoeth, and three nights imprisoned by Gwen Pendragon, and three nights in an enchanted prison under the Rock of Echeifyeint. This Exalted Prisoner was Arthur. And the same lad released him from each of these three prisons: (that lad was) Goreu, son of Custennin, his cousin.

Manuscripts: WR, 50, 51, 252, C 6, 216 (J. Jones), p. 158, Cwrt. 3 (two versions), BL[2], V.

In R *an incomplete version of this triad heads the subsection on p.* 591 *beginning* Dechreu y trioed yv y rei hynn. *The first part of this section is lacking in* W (*see introduction, p. xxi*). *A second version corresponding to that of* W *occurs on p.* 596.

52. gorychell garcharoryon 252.

a. llyr llediaith 51, 252. vn fv amasioedd C 6. o euroswydd wledic 50, V.

b. Madoc V, mabon ap medrod C 6, m. medron 50, amhadron 51, ap Edrod 252, vap Madron Cwrt. 1.

c. Geir R (*p.* 591), geyr 50, geir 51, gayr C 6, Gveiryoed R, Geryoet 50, geirroedd 51, goreoedd C 6. Echymeint R. 252 *substitutes* Ag arthyr fy deyrnos yn y gharchor, Lecg echenaint Cwrt. 1.

d. oruchelavr R (*p.* 591), uwch *altered to* oruchelawr 51, echymeint R, dan y llech a chymeint ar un gwas ae dillygh6ys 50. y gwas gore kystenin i gefnder yw C 6.

Pen. 216, p. 158: Tri goruchel garcharor ynys Brydaen: Llyr llediaith, a Mabon ap Modron, ac Arthur a vu dair nos yngharchar ehun (= Cwrt. 2: Mabo am hedron, yngharchar hud). BL *also gives this version.*

tri goruchel garchara6r. In *Culhwch ac Olwen* (ll. 914–16), a variant of this triad is placed in the mouth of Mabon fab Modron, speaking from his prison. Cai and Gwrhyr receive the following reply to their inquiry as to who it is that is lamenting within the walls of Gloucester:

> Mabon uab Modron yssyd yma ygcarch(ar). ac ny charcharwyt neb kyn dostet yn llwrw carchar a mi. na charchar Llud Llaw Ereint. neu garchar Greit mab Eri. (WM 492–3 = RM 131.18–20, CO ll. 914–16n.)

The presence of *Mabon* in both versions shows that this is a variant version of triad 52. The other names are different, though there is a superficial resemblance between each of the two pairs. The names given in the CO version occur elsewhere in the story, though they are almost unknown outside CO. Cynddelw refers once to *Greit mab Ery* (CBT IV, no. 9.78, see n. to *Greid(y)a6l Galouyd* under Personal Names); while there is ample evidence in other sources for traditions about *Gweir* and *Llŷr Lledyeith* (see nn.). *Gwair* is known as a renowned prisoner from the poem *Preiddeu Annwfn* (he, like *Mabon*, laments bitterly from his prison, BT 54.22), while *Mabinogi Branwen* offers suggestive possibilities, at least, for a story of antagonism between *Llŷr Lledyeith* and *Euroswydd*—for we are told that the two were in turn 'husbands' of *Penardun* (PKM 29). The redactor of *Culhwch* evidently knew that *Mabon*'s story belonged to a triad of famous imprisonments, but he gave a variant form of this triad from that in triad 52, in regard to the names of the two prisoners in addition to *Mabon*. Since this triad is absent from Pen.16, and appears for the first time in WR, its authority is equivalent in the two versions , and there is no means of telling whether or not the *Culhwch* version is in origin earlier or later than the text of TYP. See CO ll. 914–16, and n. to CO[2] lx–lxi. The names *Llŷr* and *Lludd* are frequently confused (see n. to *Llŷr Lledyeith* under Personal Names). *Greit mab Eri* is included both in Arthur's court-list (CO l. 176) and among the names of those captured by Gwynn ap Nudd later in the story (CO l. 992), but it is not improbable that this inclusion represents an afterthought on the part of the narrator, and that there was not in fact any known tale of imprisonment attached to either *Llŷr Lledieth* or to *Gweir*. It remains surprising that the redactor of CO had apparently not heard of the imprisonment of Gweir.

c. See n. to *Gweir m. Gweiryoed* under Personal Names. According to EYP (App. I, no. 2), *Ynys Weir* was a name for the Isle of Wight (see n.); but Rhŷs (CF II, 679) states that *Ynys Wair* was also an old name for Lundy Island, and he records that *Ynys Wair* long survived as a name for the island in the speech of the locality. One or other of these islands may have been the traditional place of Gweir's imprisonment.

d. Cf. triad 20 W, where Arthur has similarly been added as a fourth character. Such perfunctory additions as these hardly inspire confidence in the antiquity of the narrative material thus introduced, and it must be conceded that no trace has survived elsewhere of any story of imprisonment suffered by Arthur. In CO and in *Preiddeu Annwfn* Arthur appears as a *releaser* of prisoners, and his inclusion in the triad may represent a transposition of this concept of him, cf. n. to *Mabon m. Modron* under Personal Names. But there are other points of interest in **d**. Both the place-names and the personal names indicate that the narrative background is very similar to that of *Culhwch*, though *Culhwch* gives no clue as to the incidents alluded to in **a** and **c** of the triad. The relationship of 'cousin' subsisting between Arthur, Culhwch and Goreu, the sons of three daughters of Anlawdd Wledig (see n. to CO l. 10 and n. to CO l. 811), may derive from pre-Geoffrey Arthurian tradition, and there is nothing in this triad which betrays the influence of Geoffrey's narrative; while on the other hand the triad does appear to show that, independently of HRB, Arthur had been brought into contact with members of the Dumnonian dynasty, as represented here by *Goreu fab Custennin* (see also n. to *Gereint m. Erbin* under Personal Names). It is with the name of *Custennin* (*Gorneu*) (= *Constantine*) that the *Brut* and HRB attach the Arthurian pedigree to that of the rulers of Devon (*Arthur m. Uthur m. Custennin*, etc.). Perhaps the reason for this was the existence of *Culhwch ac Olwen*, or another lost story in which Arthur and Goreu (i.e. *Custennin Gorneu*) were already brought together.

Kaer Oeth ac Anoeth. LlDC no. 18.87–92: *E beteu hir yg guanas / ny chauas ae dioes. / pvy vyntvy pvy eu neges. / Teulu oeth ac anoeth a dyuu ynoeth / y eu gur y eu guas. / ae ceisso vy clated guanas* 'The long graves in Gwanas, they who despoiled them did not discover who they were, and what their mission was. The war-band of *Oeth* and *Anoeth* came there (= *yno*) . . . whoever looks for them, let him dig in Gwanas.' (*Gwanas* is the name of a mountain tract near Cadair Idris.) Cf. also Glewlwyd's words in *Culhwch*: *Mi a uum gynt yghaer oeth ac anoeth* (CO l. 115n.). *Anoeth* as an adjective means both 'difficult' and 'wonderful'; as a noun 'a wonder' (CLlH 126, GPC 149; similarly *oeth,* GPC 2628, cf. CBT I, no. 9.112n.); either a noun or an adjective may be intended in this phrase. Since *an-* is here the intensive prefix, one cannot take *oeth* as the opposite of *anoeth*. Iolo Goch (GIG no. VI.55) describes the appearance of Môn after the death of the sons of Tudur Fychan as *eilun oeth uthr olwg*; 'strange, wonderful' would suit *oeth* here. Cf. the Gaulish *Octŏ-s* in the words *octo-gesa, octŏ-durus* (= 'château resserré', Ernault) cited by Holder, ACS II, 831, 833. The compound *cyfoeth* suggests that the basic meaning is 'something precious or difficult to acquire', *anoeth* something even more so. With reference to a fortress one might suggest 'of difficult access', though this hardly does justice to the full implications of the word. But *Caer Oeth ac Anoeth* may be an old title which, like similar phrases and titles in PKM, has become so corrupted in transmission that its original constituents are no longer recognizable.

Llech Echemeint is unknown elsewhere. *Llech* usually means a flat stone or slab. *Echemeint* is OW orthography for *Echeifyeint*, with *e* = *ei* and *m* = *f*, as shown by Glyn E. Jones, LlC X, pp. 243–4, following an earlier suggestion made by Saunders Lewis (YB V, p. 39), who drew attention to two lines in praise of Dafydd ab Owain Gwynedd by Prydydd y Moch:

O uro Echeifyeint uchelgruc
Hyd Wynnuryn Llundein, lle clodluc
(H 260.3–4 = CBT V, no. 1.109–10)

Here *Echeifyeint* is opposed to *Gwynnuryn Llundein* (where the head of Bendigeidfran was buried, according to the *Mabinogi*, PKM 47) as representing the eastern and western extremities given for the transverse measurement of Britain (though it has to be conceded that these names are not included among the names for the measurements of Britain given in *Enweu Ynys Prydein*, App. I below). Saunders Lewis's suggestion that Harlech may be the place intended by *Llech Echeifyeint* has been supported by the editors of Prydydd y Moch's poem (CBT V, no. 1.109n.) in spite of the apparent discrepancy in meaning between *llech* 'stone, rock, cliff' and *bro* 'country, homeland'. Glyn Jones rightly suggests that, in his allusion, Prydydd y Moch may well be recalling the triad itself.

y geuynder6. *Culhwch ac Olwen* explains that the mothers of both Arthur and Culhwch were daughters of the mythical Anlawdd Wledig; see CO (both English and Welsh editions) l. 2 and n.

Llyfr Gwyn Rhydderch, fo. 55*r*

53. (Teir Gwith Baluawt Ynys) Prydein:

Vn onadunt a dre6is Mathol6ch 6ydel ar Vran6en verch Lyr;
A'r eil a dre6is G6enhwy6ach ar Wenh6yuar. Ac o acha6s hynny y bu Weith Cat Gamlan g6edy hynny;
A'r dryded a drewis Golydan Vard ar Gatwaladyr Vendigeit.

53. Three Sinister (Ill-omened) Hard Slaps of the Island of Britain:

One of them Matholwch the Irishman struck upon Branwen daughter of Llŷr;
The second Gwenhwyfach struck upon Gwenhwyfar: and because of that there took place afterwards the conflict of the Battle of Camlan;
And the third Golydan the Poet struck upon Cadwaladr the Blessed.

Manuscripts: WR, 50, 51, 252, C 6, C 36, NLW, Cwrt. 3, BL[2].

( ) *supplied by* R. anvat palvawt 50, anfad balfod C 6, gwrol balvot Cwrt., gwyth balfod 51, gwyr balfod 252, gwydd balfod NLW, V.

a. palvawt Mathawch 50, balfod mythonwch C 6. ar Vrannwen 51, ar fronwen RW.

b. Gvenhvyfach R, palfawt Gwenhwyfar ar Wenhwyach 50, Gwenhwyvar ar Wenhwyfar Cwrt., yr ail rodd gwenhwyfar verch gogfran ga(wr) ag am hyn byr gadgamlan 252, yr ail a roddes wenhwyvar verch Gogvran NLW, ar drydydd balfod fu balfod wenhwyfar ar wenhwyfar arall C 6. Achos hyny y bu waith Gamblan NLW.

c. y drydedd rodd golydan fardd 252, Goludan vardd Cwrt., galydan varth RW, galudan unedd wr Cadwaladr vendigait NLW. 50, V, *substitute* palvawt Arthur ar vedrawt; C 6 ar ail balfod fu balfod arthur ar fedrod yny gadgamlan.

Teir Gwith Baluawt. *Gwith*: var. of *chwith* (GPC 858, 1673) 'sinister, harmful, unlucky'. *Palfawt*, lit. 'a hand-slap' (*palf* < L. *palma*) as opposed to *dyrnawt*, a blow with the fist. Cf. GPC 2673. This triad is recalled in PKM 48.13–14: *Paluawt Branwen yr honn a uu tryded anuat paluawt yn yr ynys honn*. For *anvat* 'unfortunate' see n. to triad 32. *Anvat balvawt* is retained in the title of the triad in Pen. 50 and C 6, but elsewhere *bonclust* is the word employed in the text. *Anvat balvawt* was evidently the original epithet, since the triad is to be associated with *anvat* in triads 33, 34; see n. to **c** below. Triads 33, 34, 53, 59 constitute a group referring to events which were *mad* or *anfad* 'fortunate' or 'unfortunate', and in an earlier version of *Trioedd Ynys Prydein* these triads may have constituted a distinct subsection (see introduction, p. lxxxix). An epithet meaning 'fateful, sinister, ill-omened' is evidently demanded by the allusions in 53a and b; since the blow given to Branwen was responsible for the destruction of Wales and Ireland, and we are told here that the blow bestowed by her sister on Gwenhwyfar led to the battle of Camlan, and thus to the destruction of Arthur's kingdom.

a. *Palfawd* 'a slap with the palm of the hand' GPC 2673. After referring to *Paluawt Branwen* the narrator of *Mabinogi Branwen* goes on to list the constituent stories from which the tale was composed (PKM 48). *Paluawt Branwen* was evidently one of these tales; as W. J. Gruffydd has shown (*Rhiannon* 58, LlC IV, p. 134), this appears to have been a version of the widespread popular tale of *The Calumniated Wife*. But the reference here shows that the details differed slightly from those in the extant *Mabinogi*. According to PKM 37.27–8, it was Matholwch's cook, and not Matholwch himself, who struck Branwen; moreover, the blow was not an isolated deed, but was repeated daily: *A pheri* (a oruc Matholwch) *y'r kygyd, gwedy bei yn dryllyaw kic, dyuot idi a tharaw bonclust arnei beunyd.*

The line *A llu Brython ag Iwerddon* from a lost poem entitled *Palvawt Branwen* is quoted by Evan Evans, *Addl. Letters of the Morrises of Anglesey* (ed. Hugh Owen, *Cy.* XLIX vol. 2, p. 641) from a notebook (otherwise unidentified) in the hand of Robert Vaughan of Hengwrt. The lost poem, which refers to the poem or story, is also listed in *Arch. Brit.* 258 and in the *Cambrian Register* III (1818), no. 98. In *Arch. Brit.* 258, 'Palvot Branwen verch Lhyr Lhediaith' is listed by Edward Lhuyd as the name of a poem in R. Vaughan's (lost) collection of early poetry entitled by him 'Y Cynfeirdd Cymreig' (later Hengwrt MS. 120). On the manuscript see Wm. Maurice Cefnybraich's catalogue of the Hengwrt Library made in 1658, *The Cambrian Register* iii (1818), 278; Wynnstay MS. 10, 258–9. Though *Palvawt Branwen* is listed in PKM 48.16 as one of the sources from which *Mabinogi Branwen* was composed, it is to be noted that *bonclust* is the word used in the body of the text, PKM 37.28.

b. Cf. triad 54a, where it is *Medrawt* and not *Gwenhwyfach* who strikes the fatal blow upon Gwenhwyfar. It is possible that the name of *Medrawt* should be restored here, in place of *Gwenhwyfach*, as Ifor Williams suggested, PKM xxvi. On the other hand, we have no evidence that Medrawd's treachery formed any part of the pre-Geoffrey tradition. References by the poets indeed suggest that the contrary was the case (see n. to *Medra6t* under Personal Names). *Culhwch ac Olwen* tells us that *Gwenhwyfach* was sister to *Gwenhwyfar* (CO ll. 358–9), but outside this story and the two triads 53 and 84 there appear to be no references to *Gwenhwyfach*. Later texts of triad 53 show a confusion between *Gwenhwyfach* and the 'Three *Gwenhwyfars*' of triad 56 (cf. the reading of C 6), and it is possible that the reason for this uncertainty is that nothing whatever was known about *Gwenhwyfach*, because her name was in fact merely a variant of that of *Gwenhwyfar* (see n. to triad 56). And if triad 53a is based on an oral version of *Branwen*, it is possible that 53b also represents an early pre-Geoffrey tradition, to the effect that the dissension which led to the battle of Camlan spread originally out of a quarrel between Arthur's women.

A blow struck upon the queen was one of the three forms of *sarhaed* or insult which demanded the payment of a heavy fine in compensation, see D. Jenkins, *Hywel Dda: The Law*, pp. 6, 379–80 and Robin Stacey, WKC 37 n.33. For *Branwen* see D. Jenkins and M. E. Owen, *The Welsh Law of Women* (Cardiff, 1980), pp. 58–60. A similar story of a blow which caused *sarhaed* to Gwenhwyfar and made by an intruder into Arthur's Court is found in *Historia Peredur* (WM 122.4–5). Here the word for the provocative blow is *bonclust mawr*, see *Drych yr Oesoedd Canol*, pp. 87–8.

b. Gweith Cat Gamlan. For the battle of Camlan see n. to triad 59c, and for a further example in R of non-lenition after *gweith* 'battle' cf. *Gweith Perllan Vangor*, triad 60. Further instances from the same manuscript are collected by Ifor Williams in B III, p. 61. Instances there quoted in which the poet Cynddelw lenites a place-name following *gweith* indicate uncertainty as to the word's gender (see GPC 1564 on the meanings of *gwaith*). An early instance in which the word is clearly regarded as feminine occurs in *Ann. Cam.* 537: *gweith cam lann in qua* (fem.) etc. On Arthur's fatal battle at *Camlan*, see nn. to triads 59c and 84c, and cf. O. J. Padel, CMCS 8.

c. Cf. triads 33W(d), 34b. It is tempting to conclude that the *Teir (Anvat) Vwyallawt* referred to in triad 34 relate to an act of vengeance taken upon Golydan for the blow with which he had struck Cadwaladr. Since both the blow given to Cadwaladr and that with which Golydan himself was slain are both described as *gwith* (*chwith*) and *anvat*, there has clearly been confusion between these two triads. Of the two it would seem the more probable that the blow with which Golydan struck the king (Cadwaladr) was the one most likely to be followed by dramatically fatal results. Apart from a very obscure allusion made by Phylip Brydydd (H 228.19–21 = CBT VI, no. 15.11–13n.), no other source throws any light on the story, and the *Cyvoesi Myrddin a Gwenddydd* (RBP cols. 577–83) gives a different account of the death of Cadwaladr (see n. on *Katwaladyr Vendigeit* under Personal Names).

Llyfr Gwyn Rhydderch

54. Teir Drut Heirua Ynys Brydein:

Vn o nadunt, pan doeth Medra6t y lys Arthur yg Kelliwig yg Kerni6; nyt edewis na b6yt na dia6t yn y llys nys (treulei), a thynu G6enh6yuar heuyt o'e chadeir vrenhiniaeth. Ac yna y trewis balua6t arnei;

Yr eil Drut Heirua, pan doeth Arthur y lys Vedra6t. Nyt ede6is yn y llys nac yn y kantref na b6yt na dia6t;

(Ar trydydd Drut (Heirua), pan ddeuth Aydan Vrada6c hyt yn Alclut y lys Rydderch Hael, ac nyt adewis na bwyt na llyn na ll6d6n yn vy6.)

54. Three Violent (reckless, costly) Ravagings of the Island of Britain:

One of them (was) when Medrawd came to Arthur's Court at Celliwig in Cornwall; he left neither food nor drink in the court that he did not consume. And he also dragged Gwenhwyfar from her royal chair, and then he struck a blow upon her;

The second Costly Ravaging (was) when Arthur came to Medrawd's court. He left neither food nor drink in the court nor in the cantref;

(And the third Costly Ravaging (was) when Aeddan the Treacherous came to the court of Rhydderch Hael at Alclud (= Dumbarton); he left neither food nor drink nor beast alive.)

Manuscripts: WR, 50, 51, 77, 240, BL[1], Cwrt. 3.

54. aerua 50, 77, dryc heirva *altered to* aerva 240, dryc heirva Cwrt.

a. kelli wic R. trewyllyei W, treulei R, 50, nys treulei *above line* 51, treuliai 77. Gvenhyuar R. oe rriein gadeir 50, rhiain gadair 77, oi chadair brenhinol 51. nid edewis na bwyd na llyn ynghwbl or llys 51, nid adewis na diod ar y ol yn y llys heb i drauliaw 240, BL, Cwrt. y trewid y baluavt arnei 240, BL, Cwrt.

b. medravt R. na b6yt na dia6t nys treulei na dyn na ll6dyn yn vy6 yn y cantref 50, nag anivail na dyn yn vyw. na dim or holl dda 77, na bwyd na llyn ynghwbl or llys 51.

c. ( ) *supplied by 50. 77 includes c, but* R, 51, *omit; W includes c in a sixteenth-century hand.* heirfa W, Aerua 50. Aeddan W. Rytherch W, Ryddyrch 77. na bwyd na diod nis trywelai 77.

---

teir drut heirua. Of the various meanings of *drud* (GPC 1086) it is difficult to decide upon the most appropriate in the present context. From its primary meaning of 'fine, brave', *drud* came to hold several extended meanings, including 'daring, bold, rash, violent', and finally 'costly, expensive' as in MW. Any of these meanings would give good sense with *heirfa* 'a squandering, prodigal consumption' (PKM xxvi; GPC 1841). *Drud* is just such an adjective as the maker of the triad would choose deliberately on account of its ambiguity, and for the overtones caused by its wide range of possible meanings. I suggest 'violent, unrestrained', but the modern meaning 'costly' should be borne in mind as well: the *Teir drut Heirua* were costly, not only in their immediate results, but also, perhaps at the same time, in their political consequences; cf. triad 53.

For *heirua* Pen. 50 and 77 read *aerua* 'slaughter(s)' throughout.

a. Kelliwig. See n. to triad 1.

nys (treulei). W: *nis trewyllyei*, which Phillimore took to be an error in copying *tryllewyei* 'he utterly consumed' (*Cy.* VII, pp. 99, 123), and suggested that R had altered the obscure *trewyllyei* into the easier *treulei* 'he consumed'. But it is likely that *treul(i)ei* and not *tryllewyei* represents the original reading, since *treul(i)ei* occurs in Pen. 50 and 77, and these manuscripts cannot have derived their text from either W or R, since both give a complete version of the triad, while item **c** was omitted from both W and R (see below). The scribe of W evidently misinterpreted the *u* in *treul(i)ei* as representing *w*, the *i* as *y*, and the *l* as *ll*, adding a second *y* between the *w* and *ll*. Ifor Williams's note, CA 224 (on l. 614), may be quoted in support of my argument here, since he cites W's reading *nis trewyllei* as an instance in which the medial *-w-* represents *-u-*. Brynley Roberts also supports this reading (*Modern Language Review* LVII, p. 406), citing the spelling of the same verb *trevlyav* as *trewllyav* (also *trewylyau, trewyllyau,* in Ll. 1); see his *Brut y Brenhinedd* (Dublin, 1971), p. 109. These all appear to be orthographical variants of the modern verb *treulio*. Eurys Rowlands however (LlC VI, p. 234) favours Phillimore's belief that the scribe of R intended to emend the archaic *trewyllyei* by changing it to a more familiar verb: he would derive *trewyllyei* from the root *taro*, giving it some such meaning as 'rend asunder'.

a thynu G6enh6yuar. Cf. RBB 229.24–9: 'Nachaf genadeu o ynys prydein yn menegi y arthur ry daruot y vedravt y nei uab y chvaer goresgyn ynys prydein a gvisgav coron y teyrnas. . . . *A thynu gwenhvyfar vrenhines oe riein gadeir* a ry gysgu genti gan lygru kyfreith dvywavl y neithoreu.' There is nothing to correspond with this phrase in BD (182.23) or in HRB X, 13: *reginamque ganhumaram uiolato iure priorum nuptiarum eidem nefando uenere copulatam fuisse*. The words in RBB are probably to be explained as an addition to the text made by a redactor who was familiar with this triad; see PKM xxvii, and GPC 3590 on *trewylliaf*.

y trewis balua6t arnei. These words may have been introduced here under the influence of triad 53, which immediately precedes this triad in the text of R. They do not necessarily imply that 54a refers to the same incident as 53b.; see n. to 53b.

c. This item was originally absent from W, as it is from R. It was subsequently written into the manuscript in a late sixteenth-century hand (*Cy.*

VII, p. 123n.). But since **c** is given in Pen. 50, a manuscript which is derived from some older sources, I give **c** from Pen. 50. (V acknowledges Pen. 50 as his source for this triad.) There is no reason to suppose **c** to be a late addition to the triad, although by some oversight it was omitted from W and from R and later texts of this series. There is indeed some independent evidence for the tradition about hostility between Aeddan and Rhydderch to which it refers. The poem *Peiryan Vaban* (B XIV, pp. 104–5) alludes obscurely to *cyfrang(c) ryderch ac aedan clotleu* (l. 52). As Professor Jarman suggested in a note accompanying his edition of the poem, the allusion here must be to a contention between the two famous contemporary rulers of Dál Riada and Strathclyde in the late sixth century (see nn. to *Aedan m. Gauran* and *Ryderch Hael*), to which the present triad also refers.

Llyfr Gwyn Rhydderch

55. Teir Neges a gaat o Bowys:

Vn o nadunt y6 kyrchu Myngan o Ueigen hyt yn Llan Silin erbyn anterth drannoeth, y gymryt y kynnedueu y gan Gatwalla6n Vendigeit, wedi llad Ieuaf a Griffri;

Yr eil y6 kyrchu Griffri hyt yMryn Griffri erbyn y bore drannoeth, 6rth ymch6elu ar Edwin;

Y trydyd y6 kyrchu Hywel ap Ieuaf hyt yg Keredigia6n o Vein G6yned, y ymlad a Ieuaf ac a Iago yn yr aerua honno.

55. Three Missions that were obtained from Powys:

One of them is the fetching of Myngan from Meigen to Llansilin, by nine the next morning, to receive privileges from Cadwallawn the Blessed, after the slaying of Ieuaf and Griffri;

The second is the fetching of Griffri to Bryn Griffri before the following morning, when attacking Edwin;

The third is the fetching of Hywel son of Ieuaf to Ceredigiawn from the Stones of Gwynedd to fight with (= on the side of?) Ieuaf and Iago in that battle.

Manuscripts: WR, 240, BL[1], Cwrt. 3, NLW Addl. 37B.

55. a gahat o bowys R, a gafad o Bowys 240, BL, Cwrt.

a. o Vangen BL, o Vangan *altered to* Veigen 240. eb anterth Cwrt.

b. ym brynn griffri R. wrth ymchoelut R, ymchoelyd Cwrt., ymwhelyd 240, ymchwelyd BL. diar Edwin V.

c. y dryded uu R. howel uab Ieuaf R. ovein g. W, owein g. R, o Owein G, Cwrt., o Owen Gwynedd 240, BL. V *omits*.

On the obscure names and events referred to in this triad, see EWSP 128–9. It should be compared with nos. 24, 30, 60, 68 since, in each of these triads, leaders who were prominent in Welsh history at various dates between the ninth and twelfth centuries have been brought together with characters belonging to the heroic legend of earlier centuries. The parallel is closest, however, with triad 60, since there, as in triad 55, a figure from a later age has been set beside characters who are associated with a prominent event in Welsh history of the early seventh century: in both cases this was an event which held a particular strategic importance for the kingdom of Powys. In triad 60 this event is the battle of Chester of 616; in triad 55 it is the battle of *Meigen* (630), which was the crowning victory of Cadwallon's career. The difficulty with regard to this battle arises from the reference in *Ann. Cam.* 630, which appears to identify *Gweith Meigen* with the battle of Heathfield, where Edwin was slain by Cadwallon and Penda in 633 (Bede, *Hist. Ecc.* II, ch. 20). On the whole it seems most probable that *Ann. Cam.* (following the account in HB ch. 61) has confused one of Cadwallon's lesser victories with Heathfield (cf. EWSP 129). It is unlikely that *Meigen* was the British name for Heathfield, or that there can have been two different places called *Meigen*. The tradition that has come down in Welsh poetry, which is not necessarily directly dependent on *Ann. Cam.*, insists that the Powys *Meigen* was the site of one of Cadwallon's main victories.

The story that lies behind the reference in the triad to the battle of *Meigen* was certainly known to Cynddelw, who refers to it in his poem *Breinyeu Gwyr Powys* 'The Privileges of the Men of Powys' (see WKC 191–223):

pedeir kynnetyf cadw cadyr urten ar dec
yr dugant o ueigen.
(H 168.27–8 = CBT no. III, 11.79–80n.; cf. ibid. 10.4n.)

'Fourteen fair privileges, honoured and upheld, they brought from Meigen'.

In other poems Cynddelw alludes more than once to *gweith ueigen*: *Gwyr yn auyrdwyth gwyth yr gweith ueigen* (H 141.6 = CBT III, no. 24.20n.; *auch breint o Veigen* H 163.18 = CBT III, no. 10.80n.); Prydydd y Moch: *gweith ueigen* (H 305.4 = CBT V, no. 10.4).

The allusions in poetry imply that *Gweith Veigen* was remembered as a supremely famous Powysian victory of the not too recent past, though the poem on Cadwallon's battles hardly gives it the prominence one would expect, if it had already been regarded as the crowning victory of Cadwallon's career (see n. to *Catwalla6n m. Catuan* under Personal Names).

teir neges. *Neges* (< L. *necesse* 'what is necessary') varies in meaning between 'mission, errand, purpose, task' and 'military expedition, raid' (GPC 2562–3).

a. kyrchu 'fetch, seek for, carry' etc. (GPC 806). The significance of both *neges* and *kyrchu* is unclear in the present context.

Myngan. It seems possible that *Myngan* ('White Mane') is the name of a horse, and not of a man (see n.), and if so his exploit may be compared with that of another horse who brought tidings from a battle; BT 48.18: *henwyn mat dyduc / kychwedyl o hiraduc* (see introduction p. lxxxii, l. 17; *Hiraddug* in Flintshire was the site of a legendary battle).

o Ueigen. *Ann. Cam.* 630: *Gueith Meicen, et ibi interfectus est Etguin cum duobus filiis suis. Catguollaun autem victor fuit* (see HB ch. 61 for the parallel reference to this battle). *Meicen / Meigen* was the old name for the district surrounding the Long Mountain or Cefn Digoll (see triad 69 n.), near

Welshpool in Montgomeryshire. The name may owe its origin to the personal name *Maig* (see n. to *Meic Mygvras* under Personal Names). It also occurs in the ninth- or tenth-century sequence of *englynion* which list fourteen victories achieved by Cadwallon over the English on Welsh soil:

Lluest gatwallawn ar hafren
ac or tu draw y dygen
abreit yn llosgi meigen
(RBP col. 1043.25–6.)

'The camp of Cadwallon on the Severn, and from the far side of Dygen, almost burning Meigen.'

Dygen Freiddyn is the old name for the Breiddin hills in Montgomeryshire, EANC 103.

For an edition and study of the poem on Cadwallon's battles see R. G. Gruffydd, 'Canu Cadwallon', *Ast. H.* 34–43, and EWSP 169–73. Cf. Gwalchmai: in the twelfth century: *Gorloes rydiau dyfr Dygen Freiddin* (H 16.26 = CBT I, no. 9.6n.), and Cynddelw in *Breinyeu Gwyr Powys*: *Pedeir kynnetyf cadw cadyr urten ar dec yr dugant o ueigen* 'Fourteen fair privileges, honoured and upheld, they brought from Meigen' (H 168.27–8 = CBT III, no. 11.79–82). Cynddelw also refers to *gweith ueigen* (H 141.6 = CBT III, no. 24.20n.); *Canaon Selyf seirff cadeu meigyen* (H 166.15 = CBT III, no. 11.9); *awch breint o ueigen* (H 163.18 = CBT III, no. 10.4n. and 10.80).

The allusions by the *Gogynfeirdd* imply that *Gweith Veigen* was remembered (and celebrated?) as one of the famous victories of Powys in the past; though the poem on Cadwallon's battles hardly gives to it the prominence we should expect, if it was really the crowning victory of Cadwallon's career. The difficulty with regard to this battle arises from the reference in *Ann. Cam.*, which apparently identifies *Gweith Meigen* with *Heathfield* (probably Hatfield Chase in Yorkshire), where Edwin was slain by Cadwallon and Penda in 633 (Bede, *Hist. Ecc.* II, 20). On the whole it seems most likely that *Ann. Cam.* (following the account in HB) has confused one of Cadwallon's lesser victories with *Heathfield* (cf. EWSP 129). It is unlikely that *Meigen* was the Welsh name for Heathfield, or that there were two places called *Meigen*. The tradition which has come down in Welsh poetry, not directly dependent on the *Annales Cambriae*, insists that the Powys *Meigen* was the site of one of Cadwallon's main victories. Yet J. E. Lloyd (HW 186) concluded that the Welsh references to *Gweith Meigen* denoted Hatfield Chase, though he neglected the evidence of the poems and the triad. *Meigen* is listed, among other events which formed historical landmarks, in a computation found in RBB 404.8–10: *O weith kaer lleon* (= B. of Chester) *hyt weith veigen. pedeir blyned ar dec. O weith veigen yny aeth kadwaladyr vendigeit y ruuein, wyth mlyned a deugeint*. The tradition handed down in Welsh poetry, which does not appear to be directly dependent on the Annals, insists that the Powys *Meigen* was the site of one of Cadwallon's victories. On the confusion between the records of the two battles, see K. H. Jackson, *Celts and Saxons*, p. 43.

Llan Silin. There is a *Llansilin* between Llanfyllin and Oswestry in the old kingdom of Powys.

anterth < L. *ante tertiam* 'the third (canonical) hour', i.e. nine a.m.

Catwallawn Vendigeit. The epithet *Bendigeit* is not given to Cadwallon in any other source, though it is bestowed frequently upon his son Cadwaladr. It is possible that there has been some confusion between the two (see n. to *Catwaladyr Vendigeit* under Personal Names) and that the epithet may have been transferred from the father to the son. The name *Bendigeitvran* may also be compared.

Griffri. This name is borne by members of the Powys dynasty in the eighth and ninth centuries, though there appears to be no other reference to a contemporary of Cadwallon who bore the name, or to the *Ieuaf* who here accompanies him. Lewis Morris (CR 253) asserts that the pair were generals who led the Powys forces against Edwin, and that after their deaths they were succeeded by 'Myngan'. But he quotes no source for this nor for his statement (CR 208) that Griffri's patronymic was *ap Heilin o'r Fron Goch yMhowys*. Nor is it clear—though it seems most probable—that the *Griffri* of **a** is the same person as the *Griffri* of **b**, whose name appears to be commemorated in *Bryn Griffri*. If the two are identical, the events referred to are in inverse order.

b. The mention of the English ruler Edwin indicates that the allusion here is also to events associated with the battle of *Meigen*; see above.

kyrchu Griffri. Lewis Morris states that *Bryn Griffri* was in Powys (CR 208), and that *Griffri ap Heilin o'r Fron Goch ym Mhowys* was present at the battle of *Meigen*.

ymch6elu ar 'to turn back on', and so 'to attack'.

c. See *Brut Tywys.* (Pen. 20 version, 9a), *Ann.* 954: *Blwyddyn wedy hynny y bu ladua vawr y rwng meibyon Idwal a meibyon Hywel yn y lle a elwir Gwrgystu: Gweith Konwy Hirmawr. Ac y llas Anarawd vab Gwry. Ac y diffeithwyd wedy hynny Keredigyawn y gan veibyon Idwal. Ac y bu varw Edwin vab Hywel.* 'A year after that, there was a great slaughter between the sons of Idwal and the sons of Hywel at the place which is called *Gwrgystu*: the Battle of Conwy Hirfawr. And Anarawd ap Gwri was slain. And after that Ceredigion was ravaged by the sons of Idwal. And Edwin ap Hywel died' (trans. T. Jones). Cf. HW 344; RBB p. 261. The reference in the triad seems to imply that Hywel's intervention led to the success of the men of Gwynedd on this raid into Ceredigion.

o Vein G6yned 'from the stones of Gwynedd'. The name of a place on the Berwyns between Llanrhaiadr ym Mochnant and Llandrillo yn Edernion, according to E. Phillimore, *Cy.* VII, p. 98. R's reading *owein g.* indicates greater familiarity on the part of the scribe with the name of the twelfth-century ruler of Gwynedd than he had with the geography of Powys; and later copyists of this version were content to follow him, and automatically to reproduce a blunder that made no sense.

y ymlad a Ieuaf ac a Iago. The scribe seems to have been dissuaded from writing *ac Ieuaf . . . ac Iago* for reasons of euphony. *Ymlad a*, though normally 'to fight against' may here mean 'to fight on the side of', unless the phrase is to be taken as implying that Hywel fought against his own father, whose imprisonment he seems later to have avenged. These events are alluded to in HW I, 344. Cf. also the *Brut* account (Pen. 20, *ann.* 978–9).

yr aerua honno apparently refers to the raid on Ceredigion.

Llyfr Gwyn Rhydderch, fo. 55*v*

56. Teir Prif Riein Arthur:

> G6enh6yuar verch G6ryt Gwent,
> A G6enh6yuar verch (Gwy)thyr ap Greidia6l,
> A G6enh6yuar verch Ocuran Ga6r.

56. Arthur's Three Great Queens:

> Gwenhwyfar daughter of (Cywryd) Gwent,
> and Gwenhwyfar daughter of (Gwythyr) son of Greidiawl,
> and Gwenhwyfar daughter of (G)ogfran the Giant.

Manuscripts: WR, 47, 50, 51, 252, 240, BL[1], NLW, RW, Cwrt. 3, NLW Addl. 37B, BL[2].

56. prif wraged 47, prif wragedd 50, V *quoting Siôn Balmer*, rriain 51, rhian NLW, ryain 252. Arthur ap Uthur BL[2].

a. gwenwyvar NLW. kywryt geint 47, gwryd keint 50, Gwryd gwent 51, 252, Gwenhwyfar Gawryd Ceint V, Gweryd Gwent RW.

b. G. uerch vthyr uab greidya6l WR, Gwythur m. greidyavl gallovyd 47, Gwythyr mab Greidyawl R 50, Gwenhwyfar verch gredawyal 252, Vthr ap Greidiol 51, Ythyr ap Gredawgol C 36, Greidawol NLW, Yther ap Gredawgol RW, Uthr ap Greidiwal NLW Addl., Cwrt.

c. ogyrvan gawr 47, 50, Ogvran gawr Cwrt., gogvran gawr 51, 240, BL[1], NLW, RW, gogfran gawr 252.

Triads 56–8, together with 78–80 (absent from R) and 50, 66 are grouped together in Pen. 47 as *Trioedd y Gwragedd* 'Triads of the Women' (see Pen. 47's addition to triad 58. Triad 88, *Tair Rhiain Ardderchog*, also seems appropriate to this group, although its antiquity is uncertain).

Teir prif riein. Rhiain <**rīganī-* (plural *rhianedd*) is cognate with L. *rēgīna*, Ir. *rígain* GPC 3068. W. Rhiannon (< *Rīgantona*) 'Great Queen'. In *Culhwch* (CO l. 358) Gwenhwyfar is described as *penn rianed yr ynys hon* 'chief of the queens of this Island'. Although in Ml.W. the meaning of *rhiain* is no longer limited to 'queen' but can mean 'maiden, (royal) lady' (cf. triad 88), there are in Ml.W. a few instances in addition to this triad, in which the word retains its original meaning: B V, p. 130, *Dyd da yt riain* (see n.) and cf. WKC 534; also in the term *rhieingylch* applied to the royal progress or circuit of the country made either by the queen or by the *rhiein freinyoc* (= privileged (royal) lady, i.e. a king's close relative); see AL ii, 604, 606; PKM xxxiv–xxxvn. Cynddelw refers to *gormesgylch riein* 'the oppressive circuit of a royal lady' (H 168.16 = CBT III, no. 11.68 n.). *Riein* in the triad, as in *Culhwch*, clearly has the same significance, and the epithet given to Gwenhwyfar in CO l. 358, *pen rianed yr ynys honn*, is paralleled by that given to Arthur as *penn teyrned yr ynys honn* (CO ll. 142–3) 'chief of princes of this Island'.

On *rhiain* see further J. E. C. Williams, LlC XIII, pp. 70–1 and n. 244. The indications are that the *Teir Prif Riein Arthur* is a semi-comic readaptation of a pre-existing triad. In view of the description of Branwen ferch Llŷr as *trydydd prif rieni* (= *riein*) *yn yr ynys hon* (PKM 31.1) it is tempting to believe that Branwen's name originally belonged in this triad, in place of one of the two 'superfluous' Gwenhwyfars, and also that *riein* 'queen, maiden, virgin', etc. (GPC 3068) rather than *rieni* 'ancestress' was the original epithet which described Branwen in PKM, in direct quotation of the pre-existing triad, in which she could have been appropriately described as one of the *Teir Prif Riein Ynys Prydein* (*pace* the somewhat contrary suggestions made by Ifor Williams in PKM 165–7, and by Thomas Jones, B IX, p. 131, who suggests that *rhieni* is equivalent in meaning to L. *progenies*). The older meaning may also have been recalled in triad 88, *Tair Rhiain Ardderchog Llys Arthur*. As K. Jackson pointed out in his review of TYP (WHR (Special number on the Welsh Laws, 1963), p. 85), the explanation given for the name *Rieingulid*: *sonat regina pudica* in the *Life of St Illtud* (VSB 194–5) gives additional support for 'queen' as the meaning of *rhiein* here. (Cf. GPC 3069 *rhieni* which cites the PKM description of Branwen.)

Some confusion has arisen in this triad, and to a lesser extent in the two following triads, in the form of the patronymics following *verch*. Such patronymics were normally lenited in Ml. W. (TC § 43, i), but this custom was already becoming obsolete in the fourteenth century; and thus since the names in these triads do not appear to have been invariably familiar, it seems that the lenited forms were sometimes mistaken for the radical, both by the bards and by later copyists of the triads. In triad 56 there is initial lenition of the first two patronymics (cf. *Branwen uerch Lyr*, triad 53, and see nn. under Personal Names concerned). But in the case of *(G)ocuran Gawr* (see n.) the evidence of the early sources as to the form of the name is not conclusive. It is not impossible that *Ogfran* represents the radical, though instances from the *cywyddwyr* cited in the Notes to Personal Names favour *Gogfran* as the original form in triad 56. Lenition after *verch* is shown where the consonants are mutable, and this appears to be the case in triad 58 (see n. to *Vsber*). But in the other *Trioedd y Gwragedd* lenited patronymics are not found, nor are they observed consistently in the list of names in *Culhwch* ll. 358–72.

The interest of triad 56 centres on the question as to whether it is to be interpreted as a witticism on the part of its originator (cf. triads 32, 44a), or whether the Three Gwenhwyfars are really derived from antecedent Welsh tradition. Welsh sources other than this triad do not consistently give the name of (*G*)*ogfran Gawr* for Gwenhwyfar's father. It is hardly possible that uncertainty as to the latter's identity can have been responsible for giving two alternative names in the triad. Nevertheless, some considerations favour the second alternative. Early Irish sources provide instances in which three brothers (sometimes born together at a single birth) receive the same name, though with a distinguishing epithet (see Vendryes, 'L'Unité en trois personnes chez les celtes', *Comptes-rendus de l'Academie des Inscriptions et Belles Lettres*, 1935, p. 325; P. MacCana, *Celtic Mythology*, pp. 48–9); and triad 70 serves as a reminder that similar triple-births were not unknown in early Welsh narrative. Irish literature also provides examples of groups of three brothers (e.g. Naoíse, Ainnle and Ardán, the three sons of Tuireann, etc.) in which the group seems to be no more than a multiplication of a single personage: one character alone acts, while the others accompany him through life, and are led by him in everything (Vendryes, op. cit., pp. 327–8). It is apparent that this literary convention has a mythological basis, since in both Irish and Gaulish mythology there are various instances in which deities are portrayed alternately either in a single or in a triple form in which the members are incompletely differentiated (Vendryes, op. cit.; Sjoestedt, *Gods and Heroes of the Celts*, trans. Dillon, pp. 17, 31, 43, *et passim*). In Wales, as in Ireland, multiple personality may be a literary convention ultimately descended from what is undoubtedly a widespread Celtic mythological concept. There are instances in *Culhwch* of groups of three or more brothers with names which are identical or which rhyme or alliterate; cf. in particular the following triad of identical names with different fathers: *Gvynn m. esni, A gvynn m. nvywre, A gvynn m. nud* (WM 460.29–30 = CO ll. 181–2). One may also compare the two Essyllts (CO l. 372) and the inseparable pair of brothers Gwrgi and Peredur (see triad 70).

A further possible indication that there may have been some early Welsh source other than the triad which gave Gwenhwyfar a multiple personality, is that a trace of such a concept may have been perpetuated into thirteenth-century continental Arthurian Romance in the characters of the true and false *Guineveres* of the Vulgate *Merlin* and *Lancelot*. According to the former text (Sommer, *Vulgate Cycle of Arthurian Romance* II, 149) the false Guinevere was conceived at the same time as her sister, and by the same father (Leodegan), but upon a different mother. In the *Lancelot* she is temporarily substituted for the true Guinevere as Arthur's wife (*Vulgate Cycle* IV, 11 ff.). With this story cf. triad 53b and n.

Llyfr Gwyn Rhydderch, fo. 55*v* b

57. A'e deir Karedicwreic oed y rei hynn:

Indec verch Ar6y Hir,
A Gar6en verch Henin Hen,
A G6yl verch Endawt.

57. And his Three Concubines were these:

Indeg daughter of Garwy the Tall,
and Garwen ('Fair Leg') daughter of Henin the Old,
and Gŵyl ('Modest') daughter of Gendawd ('Big Jaws'?).

Manuscripts: WR, 47, 50, 51, 252, 240, BL[1], NLW, Cwrt. 3, NLW Addl. 37B, BL[2]. 57. Teir prif karyatwreic arthur 47, Tair cariadwraig llys Arthur NLW, 252, RW, prif garadawc wragedd 50, Tair cariadwraig oeddyn y rhai hyn 240, BL[1], Cwrt.

a. Undeg 252, Andec NLW Addl. anarwy hir 47, Avar6y hir 50, 240, BL[1], NLW, RW, C 36, Cwrt., Avarw hir 252.

b. garwenn 51, Arwen 252, NLW, C 36, RW. henni 47, henyn 50, henyn hen 51, Heinin 240, Cwrt., NLW Addl., hini hir 252, henni hir NLW, Heni hir RW.

c. G . . . ll 47, ag wedwl 252, Gwawl endawd NLW, Gweawl Eydad RW, Gwenuwl eydad C 36, Gwawl MW, enta6t 47, 50, endawd 51, 252, BL[1], Eydawt Cwrt.

See n. to triad 56.

Llyfr Gwyn Rhydderch

58. Teir G6r Vor6yn Ynys Brydein:

Vn o nadunt, Llewei verch Seitwed,
a Rore verch Vsber,
a Mederei Badellua6r.

58. Three Amazons of the Island of Britain:

The first of them, Llewei daughter of Seithwed ('Seventh')
and Rore(i) daughter of Usber,
and Mederei Badellfawr ('Big (Mead) Dish'?).

Manuscripts: WR, 47, 51, 252, 240, BL[1], NLW, Cwrt. 3, NLW Addl. 37B, BL[2].

58. gwenuor6yn 47, V *citing Siôn Balmer*, gwiri forwyn 252, gwyry vorwyn BL[2].

a. Llewinei seithuet 47, Lleicu 240, Llai 252, Llei NLW. sseidwedd *altered to* sseithwedd 51, Setwed C 36, RW, Seithwedd NLW, Saithwedd BL[1], Cwrt.

b. Rora 240, BL[1], Ror NLW. usper 47, NLW, wssber 51, Ysper 240, NLW Addl., ysher 252, Pou verch Ysper C 36, RW.

c. medrei 47, Medrai 240, NLW, NLW Addl., Cwrt.

47 *adds* hyt hynn y dywetpwyt y trioed arbennic a thrioed y milwyr a thrioed y gvraged. traethvn bellach trioed y meirch. (See introduction, p. xxv.)

See n. to triad 56.

G6r Vor6yn. *Gwrforwyn* 'amazon, virago'. This appears to be the earliest attested example. GPC 1708 records no further example of this word until it appears in Lhuyd's *Arch. Brit.* 236a, cf. *gwrwraig* GDG no. 46.9 and n. *Gwrwrach* 'a masculine hag' also occurs in *Breudwyt Ronabwy* (RM 145.17–18).

Eurys Rowlands suggests (LlC VI, p. 234) that the three names in this triad are corrupt and that they all originally ended in *(h)ei* (= *-ai*), giving *Llafnai* (?) (or *Lleinai*) ferch *Seidfedd*, *Rhonai* (?) *ferch Ysbar*, and *Meddwai* (?) *Badellfawr*. In a context which is obviously one of broad humour, 'Big (Mead) Dish' is a more likely meaning than 'Big Knee' (as proposed in the earlier editions of this book).

Llyfr Gwyn Rhydderch, fo. 56*r* a

59. Tri Anuat Gyghor Ynys Brydein:

Rodi y Vlkessar a g6yr Ruuein lle (y) karneu blaen eu meirch ar y tir ym p6yth Meinlas;
A'r eil, gadel Hors a He(y)ngyst a Ronwen y'r Ynys hon;
A'r trydyd, rannu o Arthur y wyr teirgweith a Medra6t yg Kamlan.

59. Three Unfortunate Counsels of the Island of Britain:

To give place for their horses' fore-feet on the land to Julius Caesar and the men of Rome, in requital for Meinlas ('Slender Grey');
and the second: to allow Horsa and Hengist and Rhonwen into this Island;
and the third: the threefold division by Arthur of his men with Medrawd at Camlan.

Manuscripts: WR, 50, 51, 252, NLW, RW, Cwrt. 3, BL[2].

59. Tri chynhwysiad ynys b. NLW, RW, BL[1].

a. roi kenad i iulkaisar NLW, yn wassar 50, wJkassa 51, Vlkassar V, i Julcaissar Cwrt., Rhos kenad i Iulkaisar RW. ( ) *supplied by* R. lle karne blaen y eu meirch gwyr ruvein 51, i roi blaen karneu i meirch ar y tir manlas NLW, i ros blaen karnai i meirch RW. ymlith y meinglas 50, ar dir meunlas *altered to* ym pwyth meinlas 51, ymporth mainlas Cwrt., ar y pwyth Meinlas Panton 10.

b. gellwng 51. heigyl W, Heyngyst R, hengist 50, 51, NLW, Hengys V. ronnven R, NLW *omits.* ddyvod ir ynys hon NLW.

c. 50 *omits* deirgveith, rany o arthyr dair gwaith ei wyr rhyngthaw a Medrod NLW, RW, yn Camblan a M, Cwrt., a medrod y nai BL[1].

---

anuat gyghor. For *anuat* see nn. to triads 32, 33, 34, 53.

This triad should be compared with triad 51, which alludes to the same sequence of events: the admission into Britain, first of the Romans, then of the Saxons, and finally Arthur's disastrous dissension with Medrawd. But whereas triad 51 is based on the account of these events given in the *Brut*, it appears that triad 59 betrays the influence of HRB and the *Brut* only in item **b**, the introduction of Hors and Hengist and Hengist's daughter *Ronwen* ('Fair Lance'), which is not found in any source earlier than HRB. There is nothing in the *Brut* to correspond with the allusions in **a** and **c**, and these items would appear to derive from independent Welsh stories referring to the Roman invasion (see n. to *Caswallawn m. Beli* under Personal Names) and to the battle of Camlan. It is possible, of course, that the name of *Ronwen* was also derived from Welsh sources antecedent to the *Brut*; but, if this was not the case, the triad provides an instructive example of the manner in which the *Brut* was accepted in medieval Wales as a historical authority of equal value with native sources of tradition such as HB, though not necessarily one which was to be preferred to them. According to Giraldus Cambrensis:

> The Britons maintain that, when Gildas criticized his own people so bitterly, he wrote as he did because he was so infuriated by the fact that King Arthur had killed his own brother [i.e. Gildas's brother *Hueil mab Kaw*, see n. under Personal Names], who was a Scottish chieftain, When he heard of his brother's death, or so the Britons say, he threw into the sea a number of outstanding books which he had written in their praise and about Arthur's achievements. As a result you will find no book which gives an account of that great prince. (Trans. L. Thorpe, *Descriptio Cambriae* (1978), p. 259)

a. ym pwyth Meinlas. For *Meinlas*, the horse of Caswallawn mab Beli, see triads 38, 42 (Pen. 47). Ifor Williams has pointed out the significance of the allusion here (PKM xxix), as referring to an episode in a traditional tale which may once have been in existence concerning Caswallawn's dealings with the Romans (cf. triads 35, 71, and nn. to *Caswallawn* and *Fflur*). Perhaps Caswallawn received his horse (one of the 'Three Bestowed Horses' in triad 38) as a gift from the Romans; or else, having lost *Meinlas*, his horse was restored to him on condition that he gave permission to the Romans to land in Britain. For *pwyth* 'a requital, a return, reward, recompense', see GPC 2957; CA 158; THSC 1946, p. 42; *talu'r pwyth* is 'to pay back, to requite', cf. LlA, 9, l. 1: *ym pwyth hynny yn diannot y cadarnhawyt* 'in requital for that they were quickly strengthened'.

c. rannu o Arthur y wyr teirgweith. HRB XI, 2 states that Medrawd divided his men into six battalions, and Arthur divided his into nine. According to J. Rhŷs (*A. Leg.* 16), 'the idea (of this division) is borrowed from a tournament'.

Kamlan. The triads which allude to this battle are nos. 30, 51, 53 (= *Gweith Kat Gamlan*), 59, 84. See n. to *Medra6t* under Personal Names or the reference in *Ann. Cam.* 537 to *Gueith Camlan. Camlan* < either **Cambolanda* 'crooked enclosure', or < **Camboglanna* 'crooked bank'. On the site of the battle (perhaps the Roman fort of *Camboglanna* or Birdoswald on Hadrian's Wall), see B VII, pp. 273–4; K. H. Jackson, 'Once Again Arthur's Battles', *Modern Philology* XLIII, p. 56, and references there cited. Arthur's last battle is not mentioned in HB. HRB XI, 2 locates *Camlan* on the river Camel in Cornwall (*ad fluvium Camblam* = *ar auon Camlan* BD 184.11, *ar lan kamlan* RBB 231.15). On this localization see O. J. Padel, CMCS 8, pp. 13–14.

The triads contribute substantially to the body of evidence which proves that stories about this battle were prominent in the early Arthurian tradition. *Camlan* was well known to the *Gogynfeirdd*:

Cynddelw: *ual ymosgryn mavr gavr gamlan* (H 106.16 = CBT IV, no. 6.267).

Prydydd y Moch: *yn fravtus ual camlan* (H 274.4 = *camlann* RBP col. 1420.18 = CBT V, no. 23.80).

Llywelyn Fardd II: *Clut gamlan kynran o hil kynvrein* (1387.30–1 = CBT VI, no. 8.5).

Gr. ab yr Ynad Coch: *llawer llef druan ual ban vu gamlan* (1417.40–1 = CBT VII, no. 36.57). *atgigleu gamlan* (1053.29); and it is referred to in the *Beddau stanzas* (LlDC no. 18.36): *Bet mab ossvran yg camlan.*

The account of Arthur's excessive generosity to Medrawd before the battle, given in triad 59, recalls the same incident as is alluded to in *Breudwyt Ronabwy* by Iddawc Cord Prydein ('I. Agitator of Britain') who claims to have won his nickname by distorting the messages sent from Arthur to Medrawd before the battle: *A phan dywettei arthur yr ymadravd teckaf vrthyf or a allei, y dywedwn ynneu yr ymadravd hvnnv yn haccraf a allvn vrth vedravt. Ac o hynny y gyrrwyt arnaf ynneu idavc cord brydein. Ac o hynny yd ystovet y gatgamlan* (RM 147.24–9—a tradition not recorded elsewhere). The preliminary 'weaving' or 'plotting' of the battle is referred to in the same words in *Culhwch ac Olwen*: *Gvynn hyuar maer kernyv a dyfneint, navuet a estoues catgamlan* (WM 466.18–20 = CO l. 228n.).

Other traditions about the battle are concerned with the number and identity of the men who escaped from it. According to the burlesque (?) triad in *Culhwch* (CO ll. 225–32 see introduction, p. lxxvi) there were three survivors, Morfran eil Tegit, Sande(f) Pryt Angel and Cynwyl Sant. But a different account claims that the survivors were seven. The following lines occur in the version of the *Avallenau* printed in MA 117–18:

A mi ddysgoganaf dyddaw etwa
Medrawt ac Arthur modur tyrfa,
Camlann danner than (?) difieu yna
Namyn seith ni ddyrraith or cymmanfa.

'I prophesy that there shall come again, Medrawd and Arthur, ruler of hosts, to Camlan . . . on Thursday; only seven came from the engagement.'

In favour of taking this allusion to the seven survivors as representing a genuine tradition, and not merely an echo of *Preiddeu Annwfn*, cf. BT 54.24: *nam seith ny dyrreith o gaer sidi* (see M. Haycock, SC XVIII/XIX, p. 68 n.). According to Dafydd Nanmor's account, one of these survivors was the Cornish saint Petroc (see n. to *Petroc Baladrddellt* under Personal Names). To name a saint as one of the number who escaped recalls the Cynwyl Sant of the triad in *Culhwch*, l. 230; cf. also Iddawc's statement in *Breudwyt Ronabwy* (5.6–9 = RM 558, ll. 24–30) as to the penance done by him after the battle for having 'plotted' it. Tudur Aled gives the name of yet another saint as present at the battle: *melan yw d'arfau / Mal Derfel yng Nghamlan* (GTA I, no.

VI.30). (*Derfel* was reputed to be a son of *Emyr Llydaw*, see n. under Personal Names.) A note in one of Evan Evans's manuscripts gives the names of the seven survivors:

> Llyma henwau'r gwyr a ddiangodd or Gad Gamlan, nid amgen Sandde bryd angel rhag i decced, Morfran ap Tegid rhag i haccred, Cynfelyn Sant o bedestric ei farch. Cedwyn Sant o fendith y byd, Pedrawg Sant o nerth ei wayw, Derfel gadarn o gadernid, Geneid hir o'i bedestric. Oed Crist pan fu'r gad Gamlan 542. (Pa. 13, 117b; Mostyn 144, p. 314 (c. 1640); see *Yr Areithiau Pros*, p. 90)

> 'Here are the names of the men who escaped from the battle of Camlan: Sandde Angel's form because of his beauty, Morfran son of Tegid because of his ugliness, St. Cynfelyn from the speed of his horse. St. Cedwyn from the world's blessing, St. Pedrog from the strength of his spear, Derfel the Strong from his strength, Geneid the Tall from his speed. The year of Christ when the battle of Camlan took place was 542.'

Tudur Aled knew also of *Camlan* as one of the Three Futile Battles (see n. to triad 84), and in the following lines to Gruffudd ap Rhys his disparaging allusion to the battle reflects the view embodied in triad 84 as to the inadequacy of the motives leading to it:

> Un o'r mannau'r ymwenynt
> Yng nglan afon Gamlan gynt,
> Chwi aech i faes, o chaech fan
> Iownach ymladd na Chamlan.
> (GTA I, no. XXXVII.41; see n. to triad 84)

> 'One of the places where they contended in former times (was) on the bank of the river Camlan; *you* would go to battle, if you get a chance, to a more just fight than Camlan.'

Other allusions by the *cywyddwyr* are to the fury and intensity of *Camlan*; in *Cywydd y Sêr* the stars are compared to the sparks which sprang from the weapons at the battle, *Cad Gamlan wybr lydan lwyd* (DGG no. XL.62); in another poem a girl's hair is compared to *Lliw tân y Gadgamlan gynt* (*Barddoniaeth D. ap G.*, 1789, 14); while Gutun Owain likens the tumult in his breast caused by love to *ymladd y Gad Gamlan* (GO no. VII.14). Wm. Llŷn refers to Gwenhwyfar's alleged responsibility for the battle: *Bu gad brudd yt anllad lid / Gamlan drwy ladd ac ymlid / A Gwenhwyfar gain hoywvaeth / wallt velen gnawdwen a'i gwnaeth* (Wm. Ll., no. XCV.25–7). 'There was a sad battle, provoked by wanton passion, Camlan through slaughter and pursuit; and fair Gwenhwyfar, lively-nurtured, yellow-haired, of fair flesh, brought it about.' For further allusions to Camlan by the *cywyddwyr* see TWS 200–5.

Owing to this figurative use by the poets of the name *Camlan, cadgamlan* developed into a proverbial expression for 'a confused mob, a rabble' (*cydgymmysgfa, tryblith,* GPC 378), and this usage is recorded in the fifteenth century. Such a semantic development is in itself eloquent testimony to the widespread knowledge and popularity of traditions about Arthur's last battle.

Llyfr Gwyn Rhydderch, fo. 56*v* b

60. Tri Phortha6r G6eith Perllan Vangor:

G6gon Gledyfrud,
A Mada6c ap Run,
A G6ia6n ap Kyndr6yn.

A thri ereill o bleit Loegyr:

Ha6ystyl Draha6c,
a G6aetcym Herwuden,
a G6iner.

60. Three Gate-Keepers at the Contest of Bangor Orchard:

Gwgon Red Sword,
and Madawg son of Rhun,
and Gwiawn son of Cyndrwyn.

And three others on the side of Lloegr:

Hawystyl the Arrogant,
and Gwaetcym Herwuden,
and Gwiner.

Manuscripts: WR, 51, NLW, DC, Pen. 216 (J. Jones), 136, Cwrt. 3, BL^2.

60. Tri phorthor perllan vangor NLW, DC, Tri phorthor Perllan Vangor fawr ymaelawr 216.

a. Gwgon Gleddyfrydd 216, G. Gleddydd rudd DC, NLW.

b. madoc ap Run y kynnedvau NLW, DC, RW, 216.

c. Gviwavn R, 51, a gwgon Gyndrwyn NLW, DC, RW, 216.

d. o bleid *altered to* o bart V, o bart lloegr NLW, DC, 216, RW, o bart lloer 216. Cwrt. *adds* oeddent borthorion. hastyl drahawg NLW, DC, RW. Gwentym herwm DC, NLW, RW, Gwaedrym herwnden MW. Gwymor DC, NLW, RW, Gwynor MW, Gwinedd Cwrt., Gwenkym herdoin BL.

With this triad cf. triad 55 and n., p. xcvi.

G6eith Perllan Vangor. The only authority for identifying this battle with the battle of Chester (*Ann. Cam.* 613, *recte* 616) is that of the fifteenth-century *Brut Cleopatra* (ed. J. J. Parry), which closes its rendering of the story of the battle of Chester as given by Geoffrey of Monmouth (HRB XI, 13) with the words: *A hwnnw a elwyt gweith perllan bangor* (p. 201). This is probably an allusion to the triad itself, but it bears witness to the existence of a tradition which identified *Gweith Perllan Vangor* with the battle of Chester. Some further support for this identification may be derived from the fact that two of the three Welsh personal names given in triad 60 appear to be those of members of lesser dynasties who ruled in the kingdom of Powys in the early seventh century; for the significance of the allusion to the presence at the battle of a son of Cyndrwyn see CLlH xxxiii, EWSP pp. 126–7. *Gweith Perllan Vangor* may well represent the traditional Welsh name for the battle of Chester; cf. Cynddelw's reference to *Gweith y Berllan* (CBT IV, no. 6.271n.). *Ann. Cam.* 613 designates the battle of Chester as *Gweith Cairlegion*. With *gweith* = 'battle, combat, action' (GPC 1564) cf. *Gweith Camlann Ann. Cam.* 537. It is not unnatural that the poets should have evaded nearly all mention of a battle which was a crushing British defeat.

At or near Chester in 616 the Northumbrian king Ethelfrith defeated a coalition of British forces, whose leaders are said to have included *Selyf fab Cynan Garwyn* (see n. under Personal Names), who was slain at the battle. Both *Gwiawn ap Kyndrwyn* and *Madawc ap Run* (see nn. under Personal Names) were contemporaries of Selyf, and belonged to families who may be concluded to have held local authority under that of the main Powys dynasty to which Selyf belonged. The third name in the triad, that of *Gwgon Gledyfrud* (see n. under Personal Names), appears to belong to a different period and to a different area of Wales; if he can be identified with the *Guoc(c)aun rex Ceretician* who met his death by drowning in the year 871 (*Ann. Cam.*), then he may be classed with the small group of figures from later Welsh history whom the triads deliberately bring together with legendary heroes of the sixth and seventh centuries; see nn. to *Alan Fyrgan* and *Gilbert m. Cadgyffro* under Personal Names. Analogous instances in which such late figures have been introduced into triads (nos. 24, 30, 39, 55, 68) prove that the introduction of Gwgon's name here presents no argument against the identification of *Gweith Perllan Vangor* with the battle of Chester, or against the identification of the two other Welsh characters named in the triad with contemporary figures of the seventh century. The names of the English opponents are not identifiable.

Bede (*Hist. Ecc.* II, 2) describes the massacre of the monks of *Bancornaburg* as having immediately preceded the battle of Chester: he says that the monks had come to watch the battle and to assist the British forces with their prayers, and he implies that the monastery from whence they came was nearby. Thus *Bancornaburg* is usually taken to denote the monastery of Bangor Is-coed in Flint, about twelve miles south of Chester on the right bank of the Dee, which was situated in the commote of Maelor Saesneg (*Cy.* X, 12; cf. the v.l. of Pen. 216; *Br. Cleo.* 199: *manachloc arbennic lle gelwyt bangor vawr ym maelor*). On the battle of Chester see HW 179–81. For another reference to Bangor-is-coed, see triad 90.

It is possible that Geoffrey of Monmouth knew of the Welsh name *Gweith Perllan Vangor*, and endeavoured to bring his account of the battle of Chester

(HRB XI, ch. 12–XII, ch.1) into conformity with it, for he represents the Welsh princes as rallying at Bangor immediately after the massacre of the monks at Chester, and as turning their initial defeat into victory at this place. Bangor Is-coed rather than Chester itself may thus have been the real site of the engagement. On the other hand there is no reason to suppose (as has been suggested, HW 181) that Geoffrey had any basis for claiming that the Welsh turned their initial reversal at Chester into victory in a second engagement which followed almost immediately. All our historical evidence suggests that the battle of Chester was a strategic victory for the English of far-reaching importance: perhaps because it drove a wedge between the Welsh kingdoms and those of the Strathclyde Britons, so that henceforth the Cymry of Wales remained geographically divided from the Men of the North.

tri phortha6r. I have translated *porthawr* here as having its normal meaning of 'gate-keeper' (GPC 2857); cf. Dafydd ap Gwilym's poem *Tri Phorthor Eiddig* (GDG, no. 80). If the battle really took place in an orchard, it is possible that one side may have held the entrance against the attack of the other; but if we are to believe the triad, the gateway must have been held in this way by both sides in turn. It is interesting to find that Porth Hwgan ('the Gate of Gwgan') and Porth Clais were recorded by Leland (*Itinerary*, ed. Toulmin-Smith, 67) as the names of places where ancient trackways entered the monastic enclosure at Bangor Is-coed (*Cy.* X, p. 17). For a quotation of the passage see B VIII, p. 26. Gibson's *Camden* (1695), col. 694 names Porth Hugan, and it is tempting to connect this name with that of *Gwgon Gledyfrud* in the triad. It is possible, also, that *porthawr* in the triad is intended as the equivalent of *porthwr* 'helper' (GPC 2858), a derivative of *porth* in its alternative sense of 'help, support' (cf. triad 35 R and n.). In this case its employment here would be parallel to such bardic epithets as *post cad, colofn, cad,* etc. (cf. triad 5 and n.), and it could be translated as 'supporter, helper'. Cf. the analogous form *kynnorthwy* used of Cynddylan in reference to his presence at the battle of Maes Cogwy, CLlH no. XI.111c. It is quite likely, however, that the word *porthawr* was deliberately chosen in this triad on account of the variant possible meanings of *porth* (GPC 2854–5), which may signify either 'gate' or 'help, assistance' (*porth* bears the latter meaning in R's version of triad 35).

d. A thri ereill. The names given to the English 'gate-keepers' are obscure. But two of them may contain elements which are intended to suggest 'displaced persons', and which thus indicate a similar attitude to the English invader as appears in *Armes Prydein*, where it is stressed that the Saxons are exiles and landless men. *Gwyst(y)l* 'hostage' seems to be contained in *Hawystyl*, and *herw* 'exile, outlawry' in *Herwuden*. Thus an element of humour seems to have entered into the fabrication of these names, presumably invented as suitable for the enemy. For the epithet *Trahawc* 'Arrogant', cf. triad 23. R. G. Gruffydd suggests that the wording of Dafydd ap Gwilym's poem (GDG no. 80) is an ironic evocation of this triad (YB XIII, p. 171). For a further comment on the significance of the triad see EWSP 126–7. Cynddelw alludes once to *Gweith Berllan* (CBT IV no. 6.271n.). Otherwise this significant British defeat appears not to have been noted by the *Gogynfeirdd*. Cf. Gibson's *Camden* (1695), col. 694, and C. Grooms, *The Giants of Wales*, p. 147.

Llyfr Gwyn Rhydderch

61. Tri Eur Gelein Ynys Brydein:

Mada6c ap Br6yn,
A Chengan Peillia6c,
A Rua6n Peuyr ap G6ydno.

61. Three Noble (Golden) / Splendid Corpses of the Island of Britain:

Madawg son of Brwyn,
and Cengan Peilliawg,
and Rhu(f)awn the Radiant son of Gwyddno.

Manuscripts: WR, 51, NLW, DC, Cwrt. 3, NLW Addl. 325E, p. 92, BL[2].

61. aur gelein NLW, DC, gelain Cwrt., Ayr Gelain RW.

a. ap prwyn 51, madoc ap Brwyn NLW, DC.

b. A cheugan R, V, Kyngain ab peilliawg NLW, Cyngain DC, a Chengain NLW Addl. 325E, pelliawg BL.

c. a rruon ap gwyddno peryf 51, a Ryawn Pefer Cwrt., a Aron ap Gwyddno Befyr DC, NLW, RW *substitute* ellwyd march Alser ap Maelgwn.

---

tri eur gelein. We should expect *teir*, since *celain* is feminine. Cf. *y gelein veinwen* (CLlH no. III.20a ff.) and *gelein gymryt a hi* (CO l. 448), but presumably the sex of the persons commemorated accounts for the *tri.*

The meaning of *eur gelein* could be either (a) that the corpses wore some gold ornament, such as a torque, or (b) that these corpses were retrieved from the enemy by the payment of an immense ransom, or (c) because some such payment was exacted in compensation from the enemy who slew them. It is this latter interpretation which is given to the triad in Iolo Morganwg's adaptation of it in MA[2] p. 408 (in the *Myvyrian Archaeology Third Series* of triads no. 77. I quote the translation which Iolo himself made (reproduced in THSC 1969, p. 135) 'they were so-called because their weight in gold was given for their bodies, to purchase them out of the hands of those who had slain them'). This fanciful interpretation would be consistent with the custom of the payment of *galanas*, or commutation for homicide, as laid down in the Laws of Hywel Dda.

The allusion here may recall a memorable event at the battle of Chester, where Selyf ap Cynan Garwyn was killed (he would have been essentially a 'noble' corpse). It is therefore most probable that *eur* is employed in the triad (as frequently elsewhere) in its figurative sense 'fine, splendid, excellent, noble' (GPC 1256–8). Cf. also the numerous examples of *eur* in this figurative sense given by G 496–9. The misinterpretation of *eur* in *Math* has led to the common misinterpretation of *eurgryd* in the tale as bearing its literal rather than its figurative meaning.

Llyfr Gwyn Rhydderch

62. Tri Hualhogeon Deulu Ynys Brydein:

Teulu Katwalla6n Llawir, a dodassant hualeu eu meirch ar draet pob vn o nadunt, yn ymlad a Serygei 6ydel yg Kerric G6ydyl yMon;
Ar eil, Teulu Riwallawn ap Vryen yn ymlad a Saesson;
A Theulu Belen o Leyn, yn ymlad ac Etwin yMryn Etwin yn Ros.

62. Three Fettered ('Shackled, torqued'?) War-Bands of the Island of Britain:

The War-Band of Cadwallawn Long-Arm, who each one put the fetters of their horses on their (own) feet, when fighting with Serygei the Irishman at the Irishmens' Rocks in Môn;
And the second, the War-Band of Rhiwallawn son of Urien when fighting with the Saxons;
And the third, the War-Band of Belyn of Llŷn when fighting with Edwin at Bryn Edwin in Rhos.

Manuscripts: WR, 50, 51, 240, BL[1], C 6, DC, Cwrt. 3, NLW Addl. 37B, BL[2].

62. hualogyon 50, hualogion 240, BL[1], Cwrt., NLW Addl., halogion C 6, hualoc deulu DC, hualawg d. BL[2].

a. kasswallawn *altered to* kadwallawn 51, kyswallon lawir C 6, Caswallon DC. ar y traet pob ddeu onaddunt 50, a roesant hualeu C 6, DC, dan draed i meirch bob ddav tra fuont yn ymlad C 6. Seirigei 50, ssyrygai 51, Serigi DC, Syrigei Cwrt., Sarrigi wyddel 240, BL, NLW Addl. yghreic y g6yddyl 50, yn graig y Gwyddvl C 6, ynheric y Gwyddyl DC.

b. R6allon 51, rriallawn C 6. ar Saeson 50, 51, BL[1], NLW Addl., 240.

c. belyn 50, Belan Cwrt., NLW Addl., a theulu kyhelyn o beyn C 6. ymryn keneu 50, ymryn kenav yn ros C 6, yn ymladd Edwin C 6, BL[1], 240. ymrynn yn Rhos V, a gyru y Saeson ac Edwin ymryn Edwin yn Ros DC.

Cynddelw Brydydd Mawr appears to be quoting from this triad in his poem to Hywel ab Owain Gwynedd (d. 1170—a lineal descendant of the Gwynedd dynasty), when he addresses him as *Trydydd Hualawg* (H 104.5 = CBT IV, no. 6.192n.). Cynddelw is among the first—if not the very first—of the *Gogynfeirdd* to make such a citation from TYP. (See n. to triad 29 above, and CBT III, p.xli and n. 64.)

tri hualhogeon deulu. On the historical context of this triad see HW 120, and cf. triads 17, 29 and nn. The *hual* may have originally denoted some insignia of royal office or leadership, such as a torque, which may have been particularly associated with the Gwynedd dynasty (see n. to triad 17). The word occurs in a comparable sense in the *Gorhoffedd* of Gwalchmai (CBT I, no. 9), although in the Laws of Hywel Dda we find *hual* used of a horse-fetter (AL I, 558). Note that Pen. 16 does not include *Tri Hualhogeon Deulu*, and gives triad 17, *Tri Hualawc*, only in its simplest form without any explanation of the epithet (see CBT IV, no. 6.192 which cites this triad). The two triads evidently come from a single original, from which the variants diverged at an early date. The *Rhiwallawn* included is probably the same person in both triads; although substitution has taken place among the other names. (For confusion between the names *Cadwallawn* and *Cadwalad(y)r* see n. to triad 55a. In W's version of triad 29 there is a further confusion between *Cadwallawn Llaw(h)ir* and his descendant *Cadwallawn m. Cadfan.*) WR groups triad 62 with the triads describing *teuluoedd* or war-bands (it precedes nos. 29, 30, in this version), so that the original reference in triad 17 may have been t o the *insignia* worn by each of the men named; cf. the *cae* said to have been worn by more than one member of Mynyddawg's *gosgordd* at Catraeth. (For a further suggestion as to the significance of *hual* see D. Johnston's note, GIG 195–6.) The plural form *hualogeon* (= *-ion*) may merely have arisen as a mistake for *hualawc*, though it was taken to be a different word and subsequently glossed with an explanation inspired by the customary use of *hual* as a horse-fetter. Or it could have been inspired by the collective concept denoted by the following word *teulu*, if this stood in the original triad (cf. the masculine numeral *tri* used instead of *teir* in triad 61, because the scribe of W was thinking of the gender of the persons referred to, rather than that of *celain*, feminine).

a. Cunedda is said to have 'expelled' the Irish from Gwynedd *cum ingentissime clade* (HB ch. 62). This event is usually supposed to have occurred in the late fourth century, though recent studies suggest that it may have been somewhat later; see n. to *Cunedda Wledig*. The early inscriptions in Anglesey confirm the evidence of the triad that there were still settlements of Irish in Gwynedd at a considerably later date than can be assigned to Cunedda, i.e. as late as the first half of the sixth century (see LHEB 172 and n. 4), and thus it is perfectly credible that Cunedda's grandson should have been fighting with them. *Maelgwn Gwynedd* (see n.), the son of Cadwallawn Llawhir, is said to have died in 547 (*Ann. Cam.*); thus the contest referred to in the triad may be supposed to have occurred about the year 500. On *Serygei Wyddel*, see Bartrum, WCD 587.

yg Kerric G6ydyl. *Cerryg y Gwyddyl* is near Trefdraeth in the commote of Malldraeth in Anglesey (HW 120; CR 232). A note in Cardiff MS. 36, 19 (based on the lost book of Sir Richard Wynn of Gwydyr) gives the following note on this engagement:

> Kynyr *ne* Kevyr (o henw aralh) a Meilir ac Yneigr (meibion Gwron ap Cynhedha), a vu ill tri gida Chadwallon Lawhîr i kevnderw yn dehol y Gwydhyl Fichtied o Vôn. Ac yna i divassant hwynt yn lhwyr, pan ladhodd

> Cadwallon Lawhîr Seregi Wydhel yn Llan y Gwydhyl ynghaer Gybi ym Môn.
>
> 'Kynyr or Kevyr (by another name) and Meilir and Yneigr, sons of Gwron ap Cunedda, who were all three with Cadwallon Lawhir their cousin when he drove the Gwyddyl Ffichti from Môn. And then they destroyed them (the Gwyddyl Ffichti) completely when Cadwallon Lawhir slew Seregi Wyddel (= the Irishman) in Llan y Gwyddyl at Caer Gybi (= Holyhead) in Môn.'

This episode is referred to (with slight orthographical variants) elsewhere in genealogies, cf. *Bonedd yr Arwyr*, EWGT 92–3, and cf. WCD 338. *Caer Gybi* (Holyhead) seems a probable enough site for the engagement; there are numerous *cytiau'r Gwyddelod* ('Irishmen's huts') nearby. In LlC VI, pp. 234–5, Eurys Rowlands draws attention to ll. 35–44 in Lewys Môn's *Marwnad Siôn Gruffudd Hynaf*, a *cywydd* which corroborates the statement that the battle fought between Caswallon and the Irish of Anglesey took place near Holyhead, rather than at Trefdraeth. Since the poet was a native of Llifon, he is likely to have been drawing on a local tradition to this effect. Cf. E. Rowlands, *Gwaith Lewys Môn* (Caerdydd, 1975), pp. 24–6.

c. Belen o Leyn. With the archaic orthography of *e* for *y* in *Belen* cf. *hualhogeon* above. We may conclude that *Belyn* was an ally of Cadwallon ap Cadfan, and that the triad refers to an incident in the campaign fought on Welsh soil between Cadwallon and Edwin about the year 630 (cf. triads 55, 69, which refer to the same campaign).

yMryn Etwin. Lloyd (HW 184) connects the name *Bryn Edwin* with that of *Bryn yr Odyn*, near Llanelian in the *cantref* of Rhos. It seems more likely that *Bryn Edwin* represents a corruption of this name than that the contrary can have been the case; Thomas Jones pointed out to me the analogy of the Carmarthenshire *Rhydodyn*, which is anglicized as *Edwinsford* (*odyn* = 'lime-kiln'). Triad 31 W (see n.) states that Belyn fought at *Erethlyn* in Rhos, i.e. *Hiraethlyn* or *Ereithlyn* in the same region. Variant versions of the episode referred to in **a** are cited by Bartrum, EWGT 93 and in WCD 40. See also D. S. Evans, *Lives of the Welsh Saints*, p. 36 and n. 190.

TRIOEDD YNYS PRYDEIN 63

Llyfr Gwyn Rhydderch, fo. 57*r* a

63. Tri Thar6 Ellyll Ynys Brydein:

Ellyll G6idawl,
ac Ellyll Llyr Marini,
ac Ellyll Gyrthm6l Wledic.

63. Three Bull-Spectres of the Island of Britain:

The Spectre of Gwidawl,
and the Spectre of Llŷr Marini,
and the Spectre of Gyrthmwl Wledig.

Manuscripts: WR, 51, 252, DC, Cwrt. 3, BL[2].
63. charv ellyll R, tharw e. 51, charw ellyll Cwrt., thaer ellyll DC.
a. gwidawl 51, Gwidw DC, Gwydo BL.
b. llyr merini *altered to* marini 51, Merini DC, Cwrt., myrini 252.
c. gyrthnivl R, grythmwl *altered to* gyrthmwl 51, Grithmul DC, Gyrmwl Cwrt.

---

tri thar6 ellyll. R: *tri charv e.* 'Stag-Spectres'. (Cf. triad 64.) D renders *ellyll* by *idolum, spectrum, lemures, larvae.* The word is used to denote (a) 'spirit, phantom, ghost', and (b) 'goblin, elf'. *Ellyllon* are synonymous with *tylwyth teg* in the names *bwyd ellyllon* 'mushrooms', *menyg ellyllon* 'foxgloves', and are referred to in this sense in certain *cywyddau* (G 473). Dafydd ap Gwilym uses *ellyll* in the first sense when he contrasts it with *enaid* 'soul': *Yna y mae f' enaid glân / A'm ellyll yma allan* 'Yonder is my pure *soul*, and my *wraith* here outside' (GDG no. 89.39–40); similarly Iolo Goch depicts the soul accusing the body: *ellyll meingul wyd* 'thou art a tenuous wraith' (GIG no. XIV.28n.). These instances are relevant to triads 63, 64, in which the suggested implication of *ellyll* is that of men who became 'outside' themselves, i.e. men who had become 'gwyllt'. Cf. the Ir. epithet *geilt* in the name and story of *Suibhne Geilt*, and the related Welsh story of *Myrddin* (see n. under Personal Names) who is called *Gwyllt.* Similarly we are told in CO of *Morvran eil Tegit*, that at the battle of Camlan 'pawb a debygynt y uot yn *gythreul* canhorthwy' 'everyone thought he was an assisting *demon*' (CO ll. 226–7). There is a possible instance of *ellyll* employed with reference to behaviour in battle in CA l. 1178: *nyt oed hyll ydellyll en emwaret* 'he was not an ugly phantom in deliverance' (i.e. to whoever he assisted). Ifor Williams suggests that *ydellyll* here may represent *ellyll* + the intensive prefix *ad-* (see n., CA 333). Alternatively, could *ydellyll* in the poem be a corruption of *gwyd ellyll* as in triad 64?

For the use of *tarw* in similar metaphors cf. *tarv trin*, CLlH no. VIII.5a; *Tri Tharw 6nben*, triad 7; *Tri Tharw Caduc*, triad 6 (see n.).

64. Tri G6yd Ellyll Ynys Brydein:

Ellyll Banawc,
ac Ellyll Ednyueda6c Drythyll,
ac Ellyll Melen.

64. Three Wild Spectres of the Island of Britain:

The Spectre of Banawg,
and the Spectre of Ednyfedawg the Sprightly,
and the Spectre of Melyn.

Manuscripts: WR, 51, 252, DC, BL[2].

64. gwyddellyll 51.
a. manavc R, bannawg *altered to* manawc 51, Bannawg 252, Bamawc DC.
b. ednyveddawg ddrythyll 51, Edynyffedawc Drythyll DC.
c. Ellyll Melu DC.

---

g6yd ellyll. Cf. GPC 1753, which cites this triad as an example of *gŵydd* 'wild'. (*Gŵydd ellyll* 'goose' would, however, present an attractive pair with the *tarw ellyll* 'bull-spectre' of triad 63. Cf. Anne Ross, PCB 272–3 on geese in Celtic iconography and in folklore.) The term *ydellyll* (for *gwyd ellyll?*) occurs in the *Gododdin* in reference to furious activity in battle; see n. to triad 63 for the passage. Both terms *tarw ellyll* and *gwydd ellyll* could be related to the phenomenon described in early Irish and Welsh tales of men who became *geilt* or *gwyllt* as a result of their experiences in battle—for example, *Myrddin Wyllt* (see under Personal Names).

Llyfr Gwyn Rhydderch

65. Tri Trwydeda6c Llys Arthur, a thri Anuoda6c:

> Llywarch Hen,
> a Llemenic,
> a Heled.

65. Three Licensed Guests at Arthur's Court, and Three Homeless / Dissatisfied Ones:

> Llywarch the Old,
> and Llemenig,
> and Heledd.

Manuscripts: WR, 51, 77, 252, DC, Cwrt. 3, BL[2]. Pen. 77 *adds*: *a thri gwanwyn ai gormes y. p.*

65. Tri thrwyddedawc a thri anvoddawc a thri gwenwyn ai gormes *y. p.* 77, Tri trwyddedog llys Arthur 252, trvvyddedavvc DC, anvonawc *altered to* anvoddawc 51.

b. llemennic R, llumenic ap Mavon 77, Llwmhunic ap Mauon DC, llwmhimig ap Mawon 252.

c. Elen verch kyndrwyn 77, heledd verch gyndrwyn 252.

On this triad see CLlH lxx and EWSP 61–5, 113; and cf. triad 77.

trwydeda6c. The basic meaning of *trwydded* is 'permission' (HGC 136), but with respect to residence it has a precise meaning in the Laws 'permission to stay at a court at its lord's expense'; see CLlH 152. Hence *trwyddedog* 'a (licensed) guest'. For examples of *trwydded* see further J. E. C. Williams, B XXVII, pp. 224–34.

AL II, 548: *Tri thrwyddedawg bydavawg y sydd: oedranus, maban . . .* ac *estron anghyviaith* 'There are three freely-supported inmates: an aged person, an infant . . . and a stranger who does not know the language'. Other classes of *trwyddedog* included bards, judges, shipwrecked persons, etc. These had no offices or duties to perform in exchange for their maintenance. Elsewhere it is stated that *homo truidedauc (= permissus) in domo alterius* 'a licensed man (a guest) in the home of another) must not possess a dung-heap, nor crops, nor offspring (AL II, 892).

Prydydd y Moch (to Rhys Gryg): *Y titheu ut deheu dyred / clod wr llary om llwry yth drwyted* 'May there come to thee fame, lord of the South, generous man, from my journey for thy *trwydded* (support)' (H 288.7–8 = CBT V, no. 26.102). Another *trwyddedog* who was supported by Arthur is described in *Peredur*: *llyma y corr yn dyuot y myvn ar doethoed oed blvydyn kyn no hynny y lys arthur ef ae corres, y erchi trwydet y arthur* 'Behold the dwarf coming in, who had come a year's space before that to Arthur's court, to ask for *trwydded* from Arthur' (WM 123.1–4). For some further instances of *trvydet, trvydetavc* see BT 64.19; T. Lewis, *Glossary of Medieval Welsh Law*, pp. 282–3.

Llys Arthur. With the *llys arthur* framework cf. triads 9, 18 W, 73, 74, etc., and see introduction, p. lxvii.

anuoda6c 'wandering, unsettled, homeless, dissatisfied' (GPC 117) is negative of *bodawg* 'steadfast, staunch, reliable' (B IV, p. 60 and CLIH lxx). This triad gives the only example of *anfodog* recorded in GPC, which compares *anfod* 'vagrant, homeless'. It is therefore tempting to understand *anuodauc* here as representing *anfoddog* 'surly, discontented, dissatisfied, restless, etc.' as in the texts of the triads given in Pen. 51 and Pen. 77. For another instance cf. GIG no.XVI.21–2n., which offers the meaning *dyn anghenus* 'a needy man'.

a. A late copy of a poem belonging to the *Llywarch Hen* cycle depicts Llywarch as receiving *trwydded* from an unnamed chieftain in Powys, who thus addresses him: *Llywarch Hen, na fydd diwyl / Trwydded a geffi di anwyl* 'Ll. H., do not be dejected, you will receive kindly *trwydded*', CLlH no. V. 2. Tradition may thus have presented Llywarch as ending his days in the *llys* of a local chieftain in the country where the stories about him were famous in later generations. From this it was but a short step to transfer the tradition of his privileged *trwydded* to the more improbable surroundings of Arthur's court; and the name of Llywarch suggested the names of two other unfortunates who were famous like him in the Powys *englyn* cycle.

The following reference by Iolo Goch is evidently a citation of the triad (the poet is describing the hospitality he receives from Ieuan, bishop of Llanelwy):

Llywarch Hen llawen oll wyf,
Trwyddedog, treiddio'dd ydwyf.
(GIG no. XVI.21–2n. Cf. also EWSP 61–3)

'I am a joyful Llywarch Hen; unrestricted, I go and come.'

Llyfr Gwyn Rhydderch

66. Tri Diweir Ynys Brydein:

Ard(u)n, wreic Gatcor ap Goroluyn,
Ac Eueilian, wreic Wydyr Dr6m,
Ac Emerchret, wreic Vabon ap Dewengen.

66. Three Chaste (Wives) of the Island of Britain:

Arddun wife of Cadgor son of Gorolwyn,
and Efeilian wife of Gwydyr Drwm (the Heavy),
and Emerchred wife of Mabon son of Dewengen.

Manuscripts: WR, 51, 252, V, DC, Cwrt. 3, BL^2.

66. diwairwraig Pa. 10, divvair DC.

a. ardin W, ardun R, V, arddun 252. gatgor 51, Gatrod ap Gwrolwyn DC, Gwraig Cadwr vap Gorolvyn Cwrt., gadrod gwrelwyn 252.

b. eneilian R, eveilian 51, Efilian V, Evilia 252, Eneihan Pa. 10. wyddy drwm 51, Wydyr drwn DC.

c. Emythwydd gwraig vaban ab Dewingen 252, Emythryd DC, Dewyngen DC, Amerchred gwraic Vabon vab Deu angen Cwrt.

66. Pen. 47. Teir Diweirwreic Ynys Prydein:

Treul Diueuyl, verch Llynghessa6c La6 Hael,
a Gwenvedon merch Tudaual Tutklut,
a Thegeu Eururon.
Ac un diweirach nor teir, Hemythryd verch Vabon m. Dyfynwyn.

66. Pen. 47. Three Chaste Wives of the Island of Britain:

Treul the Blameless daughter of Llynghessawc Generous Hand,
and Gwenfedon daughter of Tud(w)al Tudglud,
and Tegau Gold-Breast.
And one more faithful than the three: Hemythryd daughter of Mabon son of Dyfynwyn.

Manuscripts: 47, 50. *Both* V (*index to* Pen. 185) *and J. Jones* (Pen. 267, p. 138) *alter title to* diweirferch.

a. Treus 47, Treul difefyl 50, V, MW.

b. Gwenfeton ferch Tudwal Tutklud 50.

d *omitted by* 50, V, MW.

In Pen. 47 this triad is followed immediately by triad 80, *Teir Anniweir Wreic.* Thus the two may have been composed as a contrasting pair, like nos. 29, 30. The pair is included in the section which Pen. 47 entitles *Trioedd y Gwragedd* (see n. to triad 56). The version of triad 66 given in Pen. 47 differs widely from that of WR, and if it were not for the addition in **d,** which supplies one of the names found in the WR version, one would conclude it to be a different triad. An early feature of the WR version is the lenition of the proper names following *(g)wreic*, though it is to be noted that the addition in **c**, which is repeated in some of the later copies, shows lenition of *Mabon* after *verch*. Another indication of lateness in this version is the inclusion of *Tegeu Eururon* (see n. under Personal names), whose description as a *diweirwreic* betrays the influence of the story told about her in continental romance. The other names in this version, however, have the appearance of having come from early tradition.

tri diweir. In the context one would expect *teir* to introduce the names of the 'Three Chaste Women', but similar slips of gender are not infrequent in TYP.

diweir 'chaste, pure; faithful, loyal' (GPC, 1054). Cf. triad 29, *Tri Diweir Deulu*, and n.

Llyfr Gwyn Rhydderch, fo. 57*v* b

67. Tri Eur Gryd Ynys Brydein:

Caswalla6n vab Beli, pan aeth y geissio Flur hyt yn Ruuein;
A Manawydan vab Llyr, pan vu hut ar Dyuet;
A Lleu Lla6gyffes, pan vu ef a G6ydyon yn keissio henw ac arueu y gan (Aran)rot y vam.

67. Three Noble (lit. Golden) Shoemakers of the Island of Britain:

Caswallawn son of Beli, when he went to Rome to seek Fflur;
and Manawydan son of Llŷr, when the Enchantment was on Dyfed;
and Lleu Skilful-Hand, when he and Gwydion were seeking a name and arms from his mother Aranrhod.

Manuscripts: WR, 240, BL[1], Cwrt. 3, NLW Addl. 37B.

67 a. Casswalla6c R. pan aeth i Ruvain i geisiaw fflir 240.

b. Manwydan BL, 240, Mannydan Cwrt., uab llud R. pan vu'n yr hyd ar Dyvet BL, 240, y Rhyd ar Ddyved Cwrt., yn yr hyd ar D. NLW Addl.

c. Llew R, lles llaw gyffes BL, Cwrt., lles *altered to* llew 240. gyda Gwdion BL, 240, Cwrt. ( ) *supplied by* R, riarot W, V, rianon BL, 240, Cwrt.

Two of the three incidents referred to here (**b** and **c**) correspond with incidents in the tales of *Manawydan* and *Math*, and in both instances the citation of triad 67 in the text proves that the triad itself was familiar to the latest redactor of the *Mabinogi.* It is likely therefore that this redactor knew also of the story referred to in **a**, which was known in the mid-twelfth century to Cynddelw (see n. to *F(f)lur* under Personal Names), and which may have formed an episode in the lost tale of Caswallon. From the scattered allusions to Caswallon in the *Mabinogi* we can tell that narratives concerning him were intergrated into the *Mabinogi* material: thus the range of reference of triad 67 presents a certain degree of unity. Nothing is known of the details of the story alluded to in **a**, but the incidents narrated in the *Mabinogi* concerning the two other 'Golden(?) Shoemakers' raise certain questions, both as to the relation subsisting between the triad and the tales in their extant form, and as to the meaning of these incidents in the tales (see introduction, pp. lxxiii–lxxiv). Neither of the two occasions on which Manawydan and Lleu figure as shoemakers require that they should be 'golden shoemakers', but merely that they should make shoes and—in the case of Manawydan—that the excellence of his workmanship should have the effect of discouraging rivals. One suspects that on both occasions the allusions to the gilding of the leather and the making of golden buckles may have been introduced to make the story conform to the already existing triad. The fact that Manawydan figures in the

Mabinogi in the role of shoemaker can probably be explained by the supposed connection between his name and *manawyd* 'awl'—a false derivation which can hardly have come into existence until after the earlier territorial associations of *Manannán-Manawydan* had become obliterated in popular tradition (see Ifor Williams, B III, p. 49). In contrast to this deduction, however, it has been suggested that the portrayal of Lleu as a shoemaker originates in the remotest antiquity, since an inscription at Uxama in Spain gives *collegium sutorum* 'the college of shoemakers' as parallel to the name *Lugoves*, thus perhaps implying that the *Lugoves* were the patrons of shoemakers. The inscription runs: *Lugovibus sacrum L. L. Urcico collegio sutorum dono dedit* (RC VI, p. 488; W. J. Gruffydd, *Math*, pp. 237–8). No doubt the *Lugoves* are to be related to the god *Lugus*, and so to *Lleu*, and though the plural form given to the name is puzzling (Holder cites two other examples in inscriptions which give nominative plural *Lugoves* and dative plural (*Do*) *mesticis* (*Lugo*)*vibus*, *Alt Celtischer Sprachschatz* II, 345), we have possible analogies for it in the presentation of deities in triple form elsewhere in Gaulish dedications. For literary analogues in Irish sources, see P. MacCana, *Celtic Mythology*, pp. 48–9. Both Rhŷs (*Hib. Lec.*, 424–5) and Gruffydd (*Math*, pp. 237–8) regarded this inscription as evidence that the association of Lleu with shoemaking could be assigned to the earliest stratum of Celtic mythology. But does it mean any more than that Lugus was the patron of *all* skilled crafts, and thus that he might be invoked on behalf of shoemakers, as of other craftsmen? If Caesar's account of the Gaulish Mercury refers to *Lugus*, as is generally supposed, then we have Caesar's evidence that *Lugus* was regarded as the patron of crafts (see n. to *Lleu* under Personal Names). Thus it seems to be no more than a coincidence that shoemaking was the particular craft selected in the tale of *Math fab Mathonwy* to supply the tool—a needle—with which Lleu displayed his excellence as a marksman. It is not Lleu's skill as a *shoemaker* which is the point of the story. The views of Rhŷs and Gruffydd on this matter were corroborated by Windisch (*Das Keltische Britannien* (Leipzig, 1912), ch. 34) and by Loth (RC XLVI, pp. 297–8) on the grounds of the improbability that a particular myth which associated Lugus with shoe-making should have survived from pagan antiquity into the Middle Ages, and in such widely separated areas. One might add that the differences between Irish and Welsh sources in the portrayal of *Lugh-Lleu* should serve as a warning against concluding that any closer connection could have existed between Gaulish and Ml. Welsh conceptions of the god.

What, then, did the maker of the triad intend by the term *eurgryd*? No doubt *eur-* should here be taken in a figurative rather than in a literal sense, 'splendid' or even 'noble shoemakers', in the same way as *eurdeyrn* is employed by poets of the twelfth and thirteenth centuries—see G 496 for *eur, euraf*, used in this sense (cf. *eurgelein*, n. to triad 61). This epithet would seem to have been originally bestowed because there were stories which told how each of the characters named, in spite of their exalted status as princes and chieftains, were obliged, at some contingency in their careers, to adopt the humble handicraft of shoe-making as a means of disguising their true identity. The attitude of the narrator of the *Mabinogi* to shoe-makers is sufficiently indicated in Cigfa's words to Manawydan (PKM 58)—shoe-making was not a craft suited to a man of his station, for it was not *glanweith* ('cleanly').

a. The references to Caswallon's quest for Fflur suggest a story of the Disguised Beggar type; cf. Gruffydd, *Rhiannon*, p. 50, and see n. to *F(f)lur* under Personal Names.

b. Cf. PKM 54.12–18: *Ac yna dechreu prynu y cordwal teccaf a gauas yn y dref . . . A dechreu a wnaeth ymgedymdeithassu a'r eurych goreu yn y dref, a pheri guaegeu y'r eskidyeu, ac euraw y guaegeu, a synnyaw e hun ar hynny yny gwybu. Ac o'r achaws hwnnw, y gelwit ef yn tryded eurgryd.* 'And then he [Manawydan] began to buy the finest cordwain he found in the town . . . And he began to associate with the best goldsmith in the town, and had buckles made for the shoes, and the buckles gilded, and he looked on at that himself until he had learned it. And for that reason he was called one of the Three Golden (Noble) Shoemakers.' Irish sources concur in presenting *Manannán* as a craftsman: *druí side dano ocus cerd ocus cennaige* 'he was a druid and a craftsman and a merchant' (*Rennes Dinnshenchus*, RC XVI, p. 276).

c. Cf. PKM 79–81: *Ac o'r guimon a'r delysc hudaw cordwal a wnaeth, a hynny llawer, ac eu brithaw a oruc hyt na welsei neb lledyr degach noc ef. . . . Ac yna dechreu llunyaw esgidyeu, ac eu gwniaw . . . . A phan doethpwyt, yd oed ef yn brithaw cordwal, a hynny yn eureit. . . . Ac o'r achaws hwnnw y gelwit ef yn drydyd eurgryd.* 'And out of the seaweed and the dulse he [Gwydion] made cordwain, and much of it, and he put colours on them so that no one had ever seen leather more lovely than that. . . . And then (they) began to fashion shoes, and to stitch them. . . . And when they came he was colouring cordwain, and that in gold. . . . And for that reason he was called one of the Three Golden Shoemakers.' The natural implication of the story is that Gwydion and not Lleu is intended as *trydyd eurgryd*; and this is how these words were interpreted by Ifor Williams in reference to triad no. 9 in his list of triads quoted in PKM (p. xxv). But this need not necessarily be the case, since the subject denoted by the pronoun may be different in successive sentences.

A further contribution to this subject, presenting a view opposite to that expressed above, was advanced in 1987 by J. T. Koch, 'Manawydan, Mandubracios' (CMCS 14, pp. 17–52). Here (pp. 32–3) Koch refers to the discovery of golden shoes in the royal Halstatt burial near Stuttgart (which was at that time recently discovered). Citing an earlier article by M. A. O'Brien (*Celtica* 2, pp. 351–3) Koch describes golden shoes as 'clearly a symbolic attribute of kingship . . . Manawydan and Lleu are both sovereigns who have been denied their birthright. The craft they practise, while thus dispossessed, serves as a badge of their thwarted kingly natures: "They make the sort of shoes proper to kings"'.

Nevertheless, I remain unconvinced that 'golden' rather than 'noble' is the correct interpretation of *eur-* in this triad, as in the comparable *eurgelein* of triad 61. The lines quoted above from PKM 51 remain ambiguous as to whether Gwydion (as Ifor Williams believed) or Lleu is intended in the triad as a 'golden/noble shoemaker'. Numerous examples from early Welsh poetry are recorded in G 496–9, which testify to the very great frequency of *eur-* 'noble, splendid' in the figurative language of the bards (cf. GPC 1256–61). See introduction p. lxxiii–lxxiv above, and n. 112.

Llyfr Gwyn Rhydderch, fo. 57*v* b–58*r* a

68. Tri Brenhin a vuant o Veibion Eillion:

Gwryat vab G6ryan yn y Gogled,
A Chadauel ap Kynued6 yGwyned,
A Hyueid ap Bleidic yn Deheubarth.

68. Three Kings who were (sprung from) Villeins:

Gwriad son of Gwrian in the North,
and Cadafel son of Cynfeddw in Gwynedd,
and Hyfaidd son of Bleiddig in Deheubarth.

Manuscripts: WR, 240, BL[1], Cwrt. 3, NLW Addl. 37B.
68 b. a Chadavael 240, BL, V, Cwrt. Cynnelw MW.
c. Hyfaidd vap Blaiddic BL, 240, Cwrt..

This triad may be compared with nos. 55, 60; in each of which the names of characters who belong to Welsh history of the ninth and tenth centuries have been set beside those of heroes of the Heroic Age (see n. to triad 55). In the present context, the naming of Hyfaidd fab Bleiddig (d. 892 *Ann. Cam.*)—who is the king *Hemeid* who submitted to Alfred's overlordship, according to Asser's *Life of Alfred* ch. 80 (trans. Keynes and Lapidge, pp. 96, 262–3) alongside a treacherous seventh-century king of Gwynedd—can only be dictated by the purpose of satire. (Whether the *Gwriad* of **a** belongs to the seventh or to the ninth century is uncertain; see n. to *Gwryat* under Personal Names.) Thus triad 68 may have originated in Dyfed during or soon after the reign of King Hyfaidd, and may be taken as a significant expression of the nationalist opposition to the pro-English policy of the rulers of Dyfed which found voice some forty years after Hyfaidd's time in *Armes Prydein* (see AP xxvi–xxx, and introduction, p. xcvi above).

o Veibion Eillion. It is difficult to assess the exact implications of the sarcasm here intended. *Aillt, mab aillt* (= *villanus*) is the term commonly used in the Gwynedd code of the Laws for an unfree landholder, while the corresponding word *taeog* is generally employed in the code of Dyfed. *Mab* in this and similar expressions merely denotes a male person (HW 298, n. 75), cf. *mabsant* 'patron saint', and the term *mab uchelwr, meibion uchelwyr* in the Laws (AL II, 100, 773). In the Laws *aillt* and *mab aillt* may be used interchangeably; see D. Jenkins, *Llyfr Colan*, p. 48, and idem, *Hywel Dda: The Law*, pp. 310–11. *Mab eyll*(*t*) is the term which is used invariably in the Gwynedd code in the *Black Book of Chirk*. *Aillt* and *taeog* participated in the ownership of land, like the free members of the *cenedl*, and thus they are to be distinguished from the *caeth* or bondsman bound to the soil, who represented the very lowest *stratum* in the population. (On the three terms see HW 292–4.) The status of the *mab aillt* in medieval society is illustrated in the tale of *Math*, when Gwydion lodges with a *mab eillt* at Pennardd in Arfon: this is a farmer living in his own house, who owns swine and employs a swineherd (presumably a *caeth*) to look after them (PKM 88.24ff.). In the *Bruts, meibyon eillyon* is employed as an equivalent term to *tirdywyllodron a llauurwyr* (BD 77.28–9 = RBB 117.9); and in RBB 235.10, *meibon eillon* corresponds with *coloni* in HRB XI, 8. But it is evident that in the Laws and in these medieval texts *aillt* has declined from its earlier status of 'subject, yeoman, vassal'; though this earlier meaning is attested in the *Gododdin* (*eillt mynydawc*; *eillt wyned* CA ll. 397, 918). The meaning is clear from the etymology of the word, which is identical with the second element in *cyfaill*(*t*), Ir. *comaltae* 'nurtured together' connected with the Ir. verb *alid* 'nurture' (Vendryes, *Lexique Etymologique* A, 57). Cf. also *macc ailte* 'a son brought up in fosterage', 'someone dependant on another', hence 'vassal' (WLW 188). Thus when Dafydd ap Gwilym addresses Ifor Hael as *Cyfaillt a mab aillt y beirdd* (GDG no. 7.12) he is playing on the difference in meaning between two words which at the time of writing were perhaps still felt to be related. The same juxtaposition is employed by Iolo Goch, in address to his patron Ithel ap Robert: *A'm caifn ydyw, a'm cyfaillt / Amau o beth, a'm mab aillt* (GIG no. XIII.90n.). But the instances cited in GPC indicate a progressive decline in status of the word *aillt* during and after the medieval period (noted in G 459); so that eventually *aillt* becomes synonymous with 'bondsman, churl'. From an original meaning of 'supporter' this word seems to have degenerated to become the equivalent of *taeog*; that is, hereditary serf or villein. *Taeog* frequently occurs in *Llyfr Colan* in contexts in which *Llyfr Iorwerth* has *mab aillt*, and this enforces the belief that any original distinction that there may have been had disappeared by the thirteenth century. In view of the uncertain significance of *mab* in phrases similar to this (GPC 2293, and D. Jenkins, *Hywel Dda: The Law*, pp. 310–11), this triad should perhaps be translated simply as 'Three Kings who were Villeins'.

It is thus uncertain what was the precise value of *aillt* in the mind of the redactor of the triad. If the triad represents contemporary or near-contemporary satire of a ninth-century king, one would expect *aillt* to have a value nearer to that which it holds in the *Gododdin* than to that attested elsewhere in medieval sources. Yet it is certain that *mab aillt* is here used as a term of opprobrium (cf. the sarcastic allusions to the English merchants as *tayogeu*, PKM 53.9; 58.20). In the poem *Etmic Dinbych* (*circa* 875–900) Ifor Williams renders *eillon* by 'yeomen' in the line *noc eillon deutraeth gwell kaeth dyfet* (BT 43.8) 'better the slave(s) of Dyfed than the yeomen of Deutraeth' (i.e. of Gwynedd) (BWP 164–5, l. 24). In view of the date and provenance of the poem, this allusion might be expected to throw important light upon the value of *aillt* in the triad, yet the most that it seems possible to say is that the *caeth* and the *aillt* are here strongly contrasted in status, and that a certain incidental opprobrium is in this context attached to the *aillt*, just as it is in the triad. *Mab aillt* is characteristic of north rather than south Wales usage, though the appearance of *eillon* in *Etmic Dinbych* and of *mab aillt* in the text of *Math* proves that these were intelligible terms in the south also—though in both instances the reference is to inhabitants of north Wales. In the triad the use of the expression implies the base descent of the persons named. The genealogies show that *Hyfaidd* derived his claim to rule Dyfed through his mother. *Cadauel* (see n. under Personal Names) in **b** appears to have ruled Gwynedd between the reigns of Cadwallon and his son Cadwaladr: since the genealogies tell us nothing of him, it may be concluded that he did not belong to the direct line of the kings descended from Maelgwn Gwynedd. One of the two possible rulers named *Gwryat* (see n. under Personal Names) who may be intended in the triad was the father of Merfyn Frych, king of Gwynedd 825–44; and Merfyn Frych, like *Hyfaidd*, derived his claim to rule the kingdom through his mother. For a further note on the historical context of this triad see D. P. Kirby, B XXVII, p. 86; and for another conjecture as to the triad's possible historical significance see R. G. Gruffydd, SC XIV, p. 97.

Llyfr Gwyn Rhydderch

69. Tri Budyr Hafren:

Katwalla6n, pan aeth y Weith Digoll, a llu Kymry gantha6; ac Etwin o'r parth arall, a llu Lloegyr gantha6. Ac yna budyra6d Hafren o'e blaen hyt y haber;

A'r eil, kyuarus Golydan y gan Eina6n ap Bed brenhin Kerni6;

A'r dryded, Calam varch Idon ap Ner y gan Vaelg6n.

69. Three Defilements of the Severn:

Cadwallawn when he went to the Contest of Digoll, and the forces of Cymry with him; and Edwin on the other side, and the forces of Lloegr with him. And then the Severn was defiled from its source to its mouth;

The second, the gift of Golydan from Einiawn son of Bedd, king of Cornwall;

And the third, Calam the horse (?) of Iddon son of Ner from Maelgwn.

Manuscripts: WR, 240, BL[1], Cwrt. 3, NLW Addl. 37B.

69. bydr 240, Cwrt.

a. y budravd R, y bydrawdd 240, BL, Cwrt. llu Lloecr ou blaen 240, llu Cembry . . . llu Lloecr gantaw BL, Cwrt. tu ai haber V.

b. kyuarvs R, cyfarvod 240, Cwrt., cyfarfws V. Einyavn R, Einion vabaidd BL, 240, Cwrt., NLW Addl.

c. uerch Idon R (varch W), varch Iddein 240, Calam Iddoin ap Ner y gan Vaelgwin BL, Calain Iddon ap Ner y gan Vaelgwin Cwrt., NLW Addl.

With this triad cf. triads 55, 60, introduction, p. xcvi, EWSP 127–8.

budyr = *Budri* GPC 345, 'a defilement, a rendering turbid' (the only recorded instance in GPC 344). The triad refers to the crossing of the Severn by unusually large companies of men or beasts.

a. The allusion appears to be to an episode in the campaign fought in Wales between Edwin and Cadwallon about the year 630. Cf. triads 55a and b, 62c, and n. to *Catwalla6n*[1] under Personal Names.

y Weith Digoll. One of Cadwallon's victories took place on the mountain of *Digoll*, according to the ninth- or tenth-century (?) poem listing his battles, RBP col. 1043.23–4 (ed. R. G. Gruffydd, *Ast. H.* 36–43): *Lluest gatwallavn glotryd / yg gvarthaf digoll uynyd / seithmis a seith gat beunyd.* 'The camp of famous Cadwallon on the summit of Digoll mountain; seven months and seven battles each day.' *Cefn Digoll* is the Long Mountain in Montgomeryshire (EANC 103); and it is mentioned also in *Breudwyt Ronabwy* (RM 151.3 = Br. Rh. 9.9). It stands on the opposite side of the

Severn from Welshpool, in the centre of the district of Powys called Meigen, where according to triad 55 and to the poem quoted above, another of Cadwallon's battles took place. There is an earthwork on the summit of the mountain called *Caer Digoll* (see M. Richards, *Breudwyt Ronabwy*, p. 47, and references there cited). According to P. C. Bartrum (WCD 82) the description suggests that *Gweith Digoll* may be the *strages Sabrinae* 'the slaughter of the Severn' listed in *Ann. Cam.* 632.

Kymry, Lloegyr. In medieval texts *Kymry* (<**Combrŏgī* 'fellow-countrymen', BWP 71n., AP 20–1) denotes both the country and the people of Wales. *Lloeg*(*y*)*r* means England (originally, perhaps, it was the name given to the midland kingdom of Mercia, see AP 50–51); *Lloegrwys* 'the English'. On the meaning of *Lloegr* see B XIX, pp. 8–23; XXII, p. 47; XXIII, pp. 26–7.

b. kyuarus. *Cyfarws* (later *cyfarwys*) meant a gift or reward given by a lord to one of his followers, generally in recognition of services rendered. The word is etymologically related to *cyfarwydd* 'a sign', etc., which clearly indicates the original meaning of *cyfarws* as denoting a gift made in recognition of the dependent status of the recipient, and one which was received in recognition of this relationship. (See B II, pp. 5–6; WKC 564; GPC 684; and the additional examples given in G 204.) Thus all three codes of the Laws speak of the *cyfarws* of three pounds given yearly by the king to the *pennteulu* (AL I, 14, 358, 636), and also of the payment of one pound yearly to members of the *teulu* as *cyfarws* (AL I, 359); cf. WKC 564. In the *chwedlau* Peredur receives *dwy iarllaeth* 'two earldoms' as a *cyfarws* from the king whose lands he has fought to regain (WM 174.15–16). The different kinds of gifts which it would be natural to give as a *cyfarws* are enumerated in BD 129.6–10, when on the occasion of the Whitsun feast held by Emrys Wledig *y gelwit ar bavb y dalu eu kyuarvs udunt herwyd eu hanryded, y rei ar dir a daear, y ereill eur ac aryant, meirch a dillat a daoed ereill herwyd y dirperynt.* A more primitive conception of *cyfarws* has survived in *Culhwch* than that which is found in the other medieval texts: here it denotes the gift made on the occasion of a youth's acceptance into the tribe, which is symbolized by Arthur's cutting of the hero's hair. (CO l. 59, see n.).

In early poetry *cyfarws* is used by Gwalchmai of the endowments given by God (H 11.4 = CBT I, no. 14.62). But in LlDC no. 3.11 we find *cyfarws* used as in the triad to denote the reward made to bards for their poetry. The reference is to false bards *a ganhont gam vardoni / A geissont gyfarvs nys deubi* 'who may sing false poetry, who seek a *cyfarws* that they will not receive'. In the triad the *cyfarws* received by the bard Golydan may have consisted of cows or horses which had to be transferred across the Severn on their way from Cornwall to Wales: this seems the only way to explain the allusion. Since our only other references to Golydan associate him with Aberffraw and with King Cadwaladr of Gwynedd, the allusion may be taken as providing an interesting sidelight on the travels made by the bards in early times between one patron and another.

c. This item is corrupt. The name *Ner* should probably be emended to *Yner*, the reference perhaps being to *Id(d)on* son of *Ynyr Gwent*, who figures in the Life of *St Beuno*. R reads *verch* instead of *varch*: if this is the correct reading it is tempting to see here a confused reminiscence of the story told in the Life of the unfortunate journey made to Aberffraw by Ynyr's daughter (see n. to *Idon m. Enyr G6ent* under Personal Names). The Life synchronizes this event with the reign of Maelgwn's descendant Cadwallon, but in such a milieu this hardly presents a serious objection. A slight indication in favour of the emendation is the fact that triad 42 names *Cethin Carna6law* as the horse of *Idon m. Enyr G6ent*: *Calam* is therefore perhaps the name of Iddon's daughter (*merch*) and not of his horse. The construction *y gan Vaelgwn* suggests that it is a word parallel in meaning to *cyfarws* in **b**. Can it be a corruption of *calan*, used in the same sense as its derivative *calennig* 'a New Year's gift'? A word equivalent to *galanas* 'payment for homicide' would however be more in accordance with the details furnished by the Life of *St Beuno*: 'the *galanas* of the daughter of (Ynyr) from Maelgwn'(?). As in **b** one must assume a payment in livestock.

If *varch* is the correct reading rather than R's *uerch*, there may be here a humorous allusion to some colossal horse (cf. triad 44, *Tri Marchlwyth*), whose passage across the Severn is compared with two other stories which concerned the passage across the river of innumerable men and beasts.

On the triad and the related poem, see EWSP 127–30.

Pen. 47, p. 17

70(i). Tri Gwyn Dorll6yth Ynys Brydein:

Vryen mab Kynuarch, ac Ara6n mab Kynuarch, a Lle6 mab Kynuarch, o Neuyn verch Brychan Brecheinya6c eu mam;
A'r eil, Owein mab Vryen a Moruud uerch Vryen ac Anarun Archesgob Llydaw, o Vodron merch Auallach eu mam;
Y trydyd oed Gwrgi a Pheredur, meibon Eliffer Gosgordua6r, ac Ardun eu chwaer, a Dyrw . . . dyl, a Chornan eu march, a Thonll6y(t) eu b6ch.

70. Three Fair (Holy, Blessed) Womb-Burdens of the Island of Britain:

Urien son of Cynfarch and Arawn son of Cynfarch and Lleu son of Cynfarch, by Nefyn daughter of Brychan Brycheiniog their mother;
The second, Owain son of Urien and Morfudd daughter of Urien and Anarun archbishop of Llydaw (Brittany), by Modron daughter of Afallach their mother;
The third was Gwrgi and Peredur sons of (E)liffer of the Great Warband, and Arddun their sister, and . . . (by Efrddyl?), and Cornan their horse and Tonllwyd (Grey-Skin) their cow.

70(ii). Pen. 50. Tri Gwyndorllwyth Ynys Prydein:

Urien ac Eurddel plant Kynvarch Hen, y vuant yn un torllwyth yghallon Nevyn verch Vrychan eu mam;
A'r eil, Owein mab Urien a Morwyd y chwaer, a vuant yn un dorllwyth yghallon Modron ferch Avallach;
Y trydyd, G6rgi a Peredur a Cheindrech Pen Askell, plant Eliffer Gosgordduawr, a vuant yghallon Eurddel verch Gynfarch y mam.

70. Pen. 50: Three Fair Womb-Burdens of the Island of Britain:

Urien and Efrddyl, children of Cynfarch the Old, who were carried together in the womb of Nefyn daughter of Brychan their mother;
The second, Owain son of Urien and Morfudd his sister who were carried together in the womb of Modron daughter of Afallach;
The third, Gwrgi and Peredur and Ceindrech Pen Asgell ('Winged Head'), children of Eliffer of the Great Warband, who were carried together in the womb of Efrddyl daughter of Cynfarch their mother.

Manuscripts: 47, 50, C 6.
70. P. 50. Tri aur dorllwyth C 6.

a. urienn ag eiddel C 6, Eurddul V. y vuant 50. torllwyth V, yn un dorllwyth a fuont yngroth nefynn ferch brychan byrcheiniog C 6.

b. yn un torllwyth V, yr ail dorllwyth a fu owain ap urien a morwydd i chwaer a fuant yn groth modron verch yfallach i mam C 6.

c. a Peredur 50, y trydydd avr dorllwyth a fu gwrgi fab prydyr a cheinddoeth ben ascell plant prydyr ap elifer gysgordd fawr a fuont yngroth aurddel merch gynvarch i mam C 6.

With **gwyndorll6yth** 'fair' or 'holy' births, womb-burdens, litter, pregnancies cf. *gwyndeyrn* 'fair 'blessed' princes', triad 3 above, and with *llwyth* cf. triads 1 and 44, nn.

The present triad is found in an abbreviated and corrupt form in a list of the daughters of Brychan Brycheiniog in Jes. Gens. 20 (= EWGT 43 (5); cf. EWSP 110–11): Drynwin verch vrachan. mam vryen. Erduduyl (= Eurdyl?) gvynndorliud. Owein m. vryen. A Morud verch vryen. Gvrgi a pheredur ac arthur penuchel. a tonlut. a hortnan. a dyrnell. trydyth gwyndorliud. The manuscript is of the turn of the 14th/15th century (D. Huws, Nat. Lib. of Wales Journal XXVIII, p. 21), but with indications of having been copied from an earlier exemplar. Note the occurrence of i for y, final -d for -th in gvynndorliud (-luid, -llwyth), and of final -t for -d in tonlut (= -llwyd). The scribe has left the final -d of his original unchanged in the case of dorliud but has altered it in trydyth (cf. WM 478.16 = CO l. 538: teirgueth for -guaed). These points suggest that the triad may be as old as any that have been preserved in the earlier collections. Further indications of an archaic original appear in the text of Pen. 50 where cal(l)on is used in its earlier meaning of 'womb' (GPC 394), and where w stands for v (f) in Morwyd, and the variant spellings torllwyt, torllwydd indicate an exemplar in which t represented th, dd. And in fact the context in which the triad is cited in Jes. Gens. 20 points to the probable source which inspired its composition. This is the allusion to the progeny of Nefyn daughter of Brychan which is contained in the tract De Situ Brecheniauc, preserved in a thirteenth-century manuscript, which has been copied from one of perhaps the eleventh century (EWGT 15 (14); Cy. VII, pp. 105–6; CLlH xxii): Nyuein filia Brachan, uxor Kenuarch Cul filii Meirchiaun, mater Vruoni, mater Euerdil, matris Estedich. (Euerdil) uxor Elidir Coscoruaur (i. magne familie. et mater Gurgi et Peredur) (EWGT 15 (14)). The text is corrupt, owing to the confusion between mater and matris, but clearly Euerdil should be supplied as the wife of Elidir Gosgorduawr (see n. under Personal Names). It seems more likely that the relationship between Nyvein and Cynfarch as here stated is more an ecclesiastical fiction than a historical fact, since it is to be noted that the various husbands allotted to Brychan's many daughters are altogether too illustrious to be credible, and that they are scattered through four generations of the Men of the North. A close family connection, whether real or imaginary, between the saints and members of the Welsh ruling dynasties is a marked feature of Bonedd y Saint.

gwyndorll6yth. For *llwyth* 'burden' cf. *Tri marchlwyth*, triad 44; and, more ambiguously, *Teir Lleithiclwyth*, triad 1 (see n.). *Gwyn* 'fair' probably has here the connotation 'blessed', as is assumed by Loth who gives 'Trois portées bénies' (*Mab.* II, 283). This is rendered the more likely since the nucleus of the triad is clearly a statement about the miraculous fertility of Nefyn daughter of Brychan Brycheiniog, one of the *Tair Gwelygordd Saint Ynys Prydain* (see triads 81, 96) herself the mother of twins, each of whom was in turn the parent of twins or triplets. This arrangement is seen clearly in the Pen. 50 version, which preserves the better text of the triad, although the variants offered by Pen. 47 are in each case of considerable interest. For *gwyn* in the title C 6 substitutes *aur* 'golden' or 'exalted' (cf. Iolo Goch's reference quoted below). With *gwyndorllwyth* cf. triad 3: *Tri gwyndeyrn e. p.*, and note that *Owein m. Uryen* is included in both triads. (The two triads in association may possibly derive from an ancient grouping.)

Torllwyth is difficult to render in English, since in Ml.W. its meaning is restricted to the litter of animals, cf. triad 26 WR, where *torll6yth* is used of the offspring of the sow Henwen. The word occurs in *Branwen*, however, with meaning similar to that which it has here: *a'r mab a aner yna o'r torllwyth hwnnw* (PKM 35.21). Cf. also GIG no. V.38n. (to sons of Tudur Vychan): *Aur dorllwyth yw'r blaendrwyth blant*. Pen. 50 shows uncertainty as to the gender of *torllwyth*, which is masculine in *Branwen*, but feminine elsewhere in Ml.W.; also the triad reads *aurdorllwyth* in C 6.

a. Pen. 47 gives the names of Urien's brothers as these appear in the *Bruts*, in place of *Efrddyl* (see n. under Personal Names) who is named as Urien's sister in CLlH no. III.30–1. It is possible that the names of the brothers with whom Urien is here credited may derive from a source antecedent to the *Brut* tradition, since these names appear first in an *englyn* in LlDC no. 40.10 (see B XVII, pp. 180–1). Nevertheless Pen. 50's version is preferable, since the inclusion of *Efrddyl* forms an essential link with item **c** of the triad. The name *Efrddyl* is probably intended also by the reading *Erduduyl* of *Jes. Gens.* 20 (see n. to *Eurddel* under Personal Names), though *Erduduyl* occurs at least once elsewhere as a woman's name, *Erduduyl merch Tryffin* (CO l. 364).

Pen. 50 **yghallon Nevyn.** The use of *calon* with the meaning of 'womb' is archaic. It occurs in the *Black Book of Chirk: y mab nas ry creus y tat y callon mam y mab hun* (facsimile edition, J. Gwenogvryn Evans (ed.), (Llanbedrog, 1909), p. 72, 6–7); and in *Culhwch: ar nyd beichavc . . . ymhoelavd eu calloneu yn vrthrwm (heint) arnadunt* (CO l. 109). *Callon* occurs in this sense also in BD and RBB, but it has been only once noted in any text of later date than the latter (G 99; GPC 394). C 6 alters it to *croth*. Similarly Queen Medb bore three sons at a single birth, to Fergus mac Roich (Windisch, *Irische Texte* II, 149, 176).

b. Modron verch Avallach. This is the only statement to be found in Welsh sources as to the name of Owain's mother, and since its occurrence here has given rise to much discussion (see nn. to *Modron* and *Auallach* under Personal Names), it should be noted that the name is absent from the *Jes. Gens.* 20 text. Whatever may be the possible age of a story about Modron and Urien, the reference which is introduced to it here is incidental to the main purpose of the triad, which is evidently to illustrate the miraculous fertility of Nefyn daughter of Brychan.

c. Ardun Pen Askell is probably the correct form of the name of the sister of Gwrgi and Peredur; cf. EWGT 59 (33), where this name occurs as that of the mother of St Tysilio. But it is likely that it is this name which has been corrupted to *arthur penuchel* in *Jes. Gens.* 20, see introductory note to this triad, above. The *dyrw . . . dyl* of Pen. 47 (the manuscript is here illegible through fading) appears to combine the name which appears as *dyrnell* in *Jes. Gens.* 20 with the latter part of the name *Eurddyl* = *Eurddel* as in Pen. 50.

a Chornan eu march a Thonllwy(t) eu b6ch. (*Jes. Gens.* 20: *tonlut a hortnan.*) See triads 44, 46, for *Cornan* 'horned' and *Tonllwyt* 'Grey skin', the horse and cow of Gwrgi and Peredur. The reference here is perhaps to a story of the widespread type in which a hero's birth is accompanied by that of congenital animal companions, born at the same time as their master and by the same magic means (Stith-Thomson, *Motif-Index of Folk Literature*, B 311), and who render him essential assistance at a critical moment of his career (cf. triad 44). These stories occur over a wide area of western Europe. The animals thus born are almost always horses or dogs or both—there appears to be no other recorded instance of a cow born in this way. Instances of this motif in Celtic sources occur in the birth-tale of Cú Chulainn, whose two famous horses were born at the same time as he, and the lives of these horses were closely bound up with his own (Thurneysen, *Heldensage* 269). Cf. also the close association of Pryderi with the foal whose birth occurred simultaneously with his own. Another early Irish tale, the *Birth of Áed Sláne*, tells how a hitherto-childless queen conceived as a result of the blessing of St Finnen, and gave birth first to a lamb, then to a trout, and finally to a boy (Bergin and Best, *Lebor na h-Uidre*, 134; Nutt, *Voyage of Bran* II, 83). But although it is supported by the reference to the triad in *Jes. Gens.* XX, it is of course possible that the allusion to the animals of Gwrgi and Peredur is a humorous addition to the original triad, which is preserved in a better form in Pen. 50. For the motif of the 'Congenital Helpful Animals', whose presence in a lost tale appears to be indicated by the reference here to the animals born concurrently with Gwrgi and Peredur, see discussion by K. H. Jackson, *The International Popular Tale and Early Welsh Tradition* (Cardiff, 1961), p. 91 (in reference to the birth-tales of Pryderi and of Cú Chulainn), and cf. Caradawg Freichfras's horse Lluagor, triad 38, n. For *Tonllwyt* see triad 46b above.

Pen. 47, p. 18

71. Tri sercha6c [Ynys Brydein:

Cynon] mab Klytno (am Foruyd uerch Uryen);
a Chaswalla6n mab Beli (am Fflur ferch Vugnach Gorr);
a Drystan (mab Tallwch am Essyllt gwreig March y ewythyr).

71. Three Lovers of the Island of Britain:

Cynon son of Clydno (for Morfudd daughter of Urien);
and Caswallawn son of Beli (for Fflur daughter of Mugnach(?) the Dwarf);
and Drystan (son of Tallwch, for Essyllt, the wife of his uncle March).

Manuscripts: 47, 50. (V *follows text of* 50.)
71. [ynys Brydein. Cynon] *written above line in later hand.*
( ) *in* a, b, *and* c *supplied from* 50.
a. Klutno 50, Clutno Eiddun V.
b. Flur verch Fugnach gorr V.
c. a Thrystan 50. Trallwch 47. Tallwch V. Marach 47. March Meirchawn V.

71. Pen. 267 (pp. 16–17 = *Book of John Jones of Gelli Lyfdy.*)

Tri rhagorawl rwym serch trigiedig a vwriodd trywyr gynt yn amser Arthur ar y tair rianedd tegcaf a serchogcaf a mwya y son amdanunt ac a oedd yn Ynys Brydain yn yr oed honno; nid amgen nog a vwriodd Trystan ap Tallwch ar Essyllt ferch Gyrmananyd Post Prydain, ag a vwriodd Cynan ap Cludnaw Eiddyn ar Forfydd ferch Urien Rheged, ag a vwriawdd Cariadawg Vreichvras ap Llyr Meirini ar Degau Eurvron ferch Nudd Llawhael vrenin y Gogledd. A llyna y tair rhianedd tegcaf a serchogcaf a mwyaf y son amdanunt ac a oedd yn Ynys Brydain yn yr oes honno.

71. Pen. 267:

Three Surpassing Bonds of Enduring Love which Three Men formerly in the time of Arthur cast upon the Three Fairest, most Lovable, and most Talked-of Maidens who were in the Island of Britain at that time; that is (the bond) which Trystan son of Tallwch cast upon Essyllt daughter of Gyrmananyd Pillar of Britain; and (the bond) which Cynon son of Clydno Eiddyn cast upon Morfudd daughter of Urien Rheged; and (the bond) which Caradawg Strong-Arm son of Llŷr M(a)rini cast upon Tegau Gold-Breast daughter of Nudd Generous-Hand, king of the North. And those were the Three Fairest, most Lovable, and most Talked-of Maidens who were in the Island of Britain at that time.

Manuscripts: 267, MW, Mostyn 110 (*printed* RC XLV, 291; Pen. 137, p. 218; *Yr Areithiau Pros*, 65), Pa. 40, NLW 5282, Wynnstay 10, pp. 6–7 (J. Jones).

71. Tri rhagorawl rwym serch a freuddwydiodd Mostyn 110, Pa. 40, NLW. serchoccaf MW, Mostyn 110, Pa. 40, NLW, Wynn. o'r a oedd MW, a oedd Mostyn 110, Pa. 40, NLW. yn yr oes MW, Wynn., yn yr amser Mostyn 110, Pa. 40, NLW.

a. Tallwch MW, Mostyn 110, Pa. 40, NLW. Gur manaw, un o bedwar post Prydein Mostyn 110, Pa. 40, NLW.

b. Clydno Eidyn MW, Clydnaw Wynn, Euddun Mostyn 110, Pa. 40, NLW.

c. Llyr Marini MW, Merini Mostyn 110. ar Degau Eurfron verch Ludd lawhawdd frenhin y Gogledd Mostyn 110. MW *adds* 'Ex Libro cui Tit. Mangofion' (*the reference is to* Wynnstay 10, *entitled* 'Mangofion' *on back*).

This triad is found in its simplest form, *Tri serchawc*, only in Pen. 47: Pen. 50 adds the names of the girls loved by the *tri serchawc*. The triad may not be old. The material for items **b** and **c** could have been supplied from other triads (nos. 26, 67) and from the foreign Tristan romances: it may be noted that with nos. 72 and 73 it forms in the MS. a consecutive group of triads referring to *Drystan*. Item **a** alludes to a story relating to Cynon's love for Morfudd daughter of Urien, which is almost unknown except for the triad and its expanded version in Pen. 267 and in other manuscripts (see D. Gwenallt Jones (ed.), *Yr Areithiau Pros*, p. 65, and the allusion in *Cerdd Freuddwyd*, Rhiannon Ifans (ed.), YB XXII (1997), p. 154, ll. 38–9 and n.). On the other hand, if the correct form of the name of *Fflur*'s father is really *Mugnach*, then the lenition of this name following *verch* might be taken as an indication that the names of all three girls are derived from an early source (see n. to triad 56). It is of course by no means improbable that early North-British narrative associated Cynon ap Clydno Eiddyn with the daughter of Urien Rheged.

The expanded version of triad 71 may date from the late sixteenth century. It appears as an isolated fragment in Pen. 267, written by John Jones, Gellilyfdy in 1635–41. Moses Williams's version agrees closely with that of John Jones. The other three manuscripts which contain this version use the expanded triad to introduce a short *araith* (i.e. a piece of rhetorical writing) entitled *Breuddwyd Llywelyn Goch ap Meurig Hen*. The oldest of these manuscripts, NLW 5282, was written by Thomas Wiliems, Trefriw, in 1609; the others are copies (see D. Gwenallt Jones, *Yr Areithiau Pros*, pp. 65, 118; introduction, pp. xv, xvi). John Jones's version must either be derived from the *araith*, or else the *araith* itself is based on a form of the triad already expanded in the manner in which it appears in his manuscript. The latter alternative seems the more probable of the two, since Jones's version preserves certain better readings than the manuscripts of the *araith*: *a vwriodd* for *a freuddwydiodd* in the first line, and the form *Gyrmananyd* given as the name of Essyllt's father, for which the *araith* texts all have *Gur manaw*. The original form of this name, as given by Cynddelw, is *Kulvanawyt* (see n. to CBT III, no. 9.8n. and cf. triad 80), and it seems easiest to explain *Gur manaw* as having been arrived at by means of the intermediary form *Gyrmananyd.*

Note the substitution in the expanded version in Pen. 267 of the reference to the romance-material about *Tegau Eururon* (see n. under Personal Names), for the older tale of *Caswallawn* and *Fflur*.

tri rhagorawl rwym serch. P. C. Bartrum has drawn my attention to an earlier version of *Tri Rhagorawl rwym serch etc.* in Pen. MS. 137, 218 (not listed in Rep. I, 865). The MS. dates from 1588, and is apparently the source used by J. Jones for the extract in Pen. 267.

72. Tri Chyndynya6c:

Edelic Corr,
a Gweir G6ryt Ua6r,
a Drystan.

72. Three Stubborn Ones:

E(i)ddilig the Dwarf,
and Gwair of Great Valour,
and Drystan.

a. Edilic corr V.

Cyndynawc 'unyielding, stubborn, obstinate, tenacious' (GPC 779). *Cindynnyauc calc dreis* (CA l. 1228); *os mab y mi uyd, kyndynnyawc uyd* (CO l. 268); *Keneu Kyndrwyn Kyndynnyawc* (CLlH no. XI.8c); *naw cad cyndyniawg* (Dafydd Benfras, CBT VI, no. 35.53).

73. Tri Gogyfurd Llys Arthur:

> Ryha6t eil Morgant,
> a Dalldaf eil Cunyn Kof,
> a Drystan eil March.

73. Three Peers of Arthur's Court:

> R(a)hawd son of Morgant,
> and Dalldaf son of Cunyn Cof,
> and Drystan son of March.

---

gogyfurd, 'of equal rank' or 'dignity' (GPC 1441 and CA l. 524n.). *Deudec Gogyfurd (o) Ffreinc* is the Welsh rendering of the 'Twelve Peers of France'; see YCM 43.9, and 215. The equivalent phrase in the *Bruts* is *deudec brenhin ar Freinc yn aruer o vn teilygdavt ac un gyureith* (BD 17.5–6, RBB 55.32 = HRB I, 13): *xii reges in gallia quorum regimine tot patria pari dignitate regebatur*; BD 158.27–8 (= HRB IX, 12): *e deudec gogyuurd o Freinc a Gereint Carnwys* ('Gerin of Chartres') *yn eu blaen*—listed among the attendants at Arthur's Whitsun festival. GPC 1441 cites further instances of *gogyfurdd* from the legal codes. But it is the parallel made with the peers of Charlemagne which is here significant. Thus the implicit parallel which was felt to exist between Arthur and Charlemagne may have led to the choice of the word *gogyfurdd* in the triad. Prydydd y Moch addresses Dafydd ab Owain as *Gogyfurt torment gogyfyaw toruoet* 'peer of a host, defence of troops' (H 264.17 = CBT V, no. 3.3).

eil March. 'Son (or "successor, heir") of March' is perhaps a mistake for *nei* 'nephew'; see n. to *March. m. Meirchya6n* under Personal Names. On the meanings of *eil*, see n. to *Rahaut eil Morgant* under Personal Names.

74. Tri An(heol) Llys Arthur:

> Vchei mab G6ryon,
> a Choleda6c mab (Gwynn),
> a Gerenhyr mab Gereinya6n Hen.

74. Three who could not be exiled from Arthur's Court:

> Uchei son of Gwryon,
> and Coledawg son of (Gwynn),
> and (C)erenhyr son of Gereinyawn the Old.

Manuscripts: 47, 50.

74. anhynoda6c *altered to* anheol 47, anheol 50 (*see 77 below*).
a. Etheu m. G6rgon 50.
b. a choleda6c 50, ( ) *supplied by 50, 47 omits.*
c. a Gereint hir m. Gemeirnon hen 50.

---

an(heol) *an* (negative) + *de(h)ol* 'to exile, expel' > *anneol, anheol* 'unexpellable'. But no other instance of this compound appears to be on record. With Pen. 47's *anhynodawc* ('not famous') cf. triad 77 below. Other sources provide little evidence on which to identify any of these three names.

75. Tri Dyn Goreu 6rth Ysp a Phellennigyon Ynys Prydein:

Gwalchmei mab G6yar,
a Gadwy mab Gereint,
a Chadeiryieith (mab) Saidi.

75. Three Men of the Island of Britain who were most courteous to Guests and Strangers:

Gwalchmai son of Gwyar,
and Cadwy son of Geraint,
and Cadrieith (Fine-Speech) (son of) Saidi.

Manuscripts: 47, 50.

75. Trywyr goreu yn llys Arthur 6rth osp a phellenic 50.
c. a chaydyryeith mab saidi 5

76. Tri Engirya6l Ynys Brydein:

Haeled,
a Llywarch,
a Llemenic.

76. Three Violent(?) Marvellous (?) Ones of the Island of Britain:

Heledd,
and Llywarch,
and Llemenig.

Triads 76 and 77 appear only in Pen. 47 and V; and the table of contents given by the latter indicates that their source is the lost *llyfr Siôn Balmer*. It is possible that the triad of the *Tri Engiryawl* has an ancient origin (see reference to CA below). These names belong to triad 77, which follows immediately in the manuscript—an instance of anticipation or *achub y blaen* on the part of the scribe of *llyfr Siôn Balmer*, which is the more unfortunate since we have no other text of the triad, and therefore the original names are lost.

engirya6l, 'wicked, angry, violent' etc. but also 'amazing, marvellous' (GPC 1215). D: *engir* 'mirabilis, intolerabilis, dirus'; *engiriawl* 'idem. vulgo *anguriol*' (i.e. 'fearful, cruel, painful'). The word however has no pejorative sense in CA l. 1252, where *Cipno mab Guengat* is described as *tridid engiriawl.* As Jackson points out (OSPG 114) the reference 'bears witness to the existence of the triad (in some form) in the ninth to tenth centuries, if not the sixth'. Clearly the existing names are irrelevant to the title of the triad, and can only be accounted for as late substitutions, taken from the succeeding triad, no. 77. See also Jarman, *Gododdin* pp. 150–1n. Alternatively, the occurrence of the reference to the *Tri engiria6l* in Pen. 47 may simply be due to the influence of this line in the *Gododdin* (see introduction, p. xxvi). For another instance of a triad cited in the *Gododdin*, cf. *Tri Chatuarcha6c* (triad 18 and n.). See also J. T. Koch, *The Gododdin of Aneirin*, p. 153, n. to l. 1252.

77. Tri Anhy(v)oda6c Llys Arthur:

Haeled,
a Llywarch,
a Llemenic.

77. Three Wanderers of Arthur's Court:

Heledd,
and Llywarch,
and Llemenig.

77. Anhynodavc 47, Anhyfodawc V (index).

This triad is a variant of triad 65; see also nn. to triads 74 and 76.

anhy(v)oda6c. V's reading *anhyfodawc* indicates that *llyfr Siôn Balmer* read *anhyvodawc*, neg. of *hyvodawc* < *bod(d)awg* 'pleasing' etc. (note that the scribe of Pen. 47 had already written this word as *anhynodawc* in triad 74, where it was subsequently altered to *anheol*). I take this to be a corruption or variant form of *anvodawc* 'wandering, homeless' (GPC 117) (triad 65), with the added prefix *hy-*, but with almost identical meaning. Cf. further EWSP 64 and n. 113.

Pen. 47, p. 23

78. Teir Gwenriein Ynys Prydein:

Kreir6y merch Keritwen,
Ac Aryanrot ver(ch) Don,
A Gwen verch Kywryt mab Krydon.

78. Three Fair (Royal) Ladies of the Island of Britain:

Creirwy, daughter of Ceridwen,
and Ar(i)anrhod daughter of Dôn,
and Gwen daughter of Cywryd son of Crydon.

b. verd don 47.
c. Gwenn ferch Cywryd ap Crydon V.

Triads 78, 79, like the two previous triads, are found only in Pen. 47 and in V. Here again V's source was *llyfr Siôn Balmer*, from which he supplies certain better readings than those preserved in Pen. 47 (cf. in particular 78c and 79c). Nos. 78–80 belong to the group which Pen. 47 entitles *Trioedd y Gwragedd* (see n. to triad 56). The absence of lenition after *verch* in triads 78 and 79 suggests that these triads are not as old as the other *Trioedd y Gwragedd* (nos. 56–8). Nevertheless, an indication of a prototype for the present triad considerably older than the date of the manuscript is preserved in the orthography of 78c (see below), and a similar indication of early date is found in 79c.

gwenriein. For *riein* see n. to triad 56. In this later text (Pen. 47), *rhiein* is no longer 'queen' as in triad 56 but has the extended meaning of 'royal lady (princess)'.

c. V gives *Cywryd,* Pen. 47 *Rywryt*; both forms evidently derive from *Kywryt* in *llyfr Siôn Balmer*. For the similarity between capital R and K in early manuscripts see CLlH lxxvii.

79. Teir Gohoy6riein Ynys Prydein:

Angharat Ton Uelen merch Ryderch Hael,
ac Auan verch Meic Mygvras,
a Pherwyr verch Run (Ryuedua6r).

79. Three Lively (Royal) Ladies of the Island of Britain:

Angharat Tawny Wave (?), daughter of Rhydderch Hael,
and Afan, daughter of Maig Myngfras (Thick Mane = Mane / Hair),
and Perwyr, daughter of Rhun of Great Wealth.

b. Mygotas 47, Anan ferch Meic Mygotwas V.
c. verch *supplied no. above line in later hand* 47. Ryneidria6r 47, Ryfeddfawr V.

See nn. to triads 56 and 78, above.

c. V's *Ryfeddfawr* ('wonderful, rich, wealthy' GPC 3132) indicates *Ryueduavr* in his original, *llyfr Siôn Balmer*, and the correctness of this form is attested by the occurrence of the name *Run ryueduawr* in CLlH no. III.33a and the female ancestry of *Rhun Rhyfeddfawr ab Einion* (see n.) (EWGT 91 (28c)); a fact which in itself points to a much older prototype for the triad. For *gohoyw*, see triad 42 (*Tri Gohoew Edystyr*) and GPC 1445.

Pen. 47

80. Teir Aniweir Wreic Ynys Prydein. Teir merchet Kuluanawyt Prydein:

Essyllt (F)yngwen, (gordderch Trystan);
a Phenarwan, (gwreic Owein mab Urien);
a Bun, gwreic Flamd6yn.

Ac un oed aniweirach nor teir hynny: Gwenh6yuar gwreic Arthur, kanys gwell g6r y gwnai hi gyweilyd ida6 no neb.

80. Three Faithless (Unchaste) Wives of the Island of Britain. Three daughters of Culfanawyd Prydein:

Essyllt Fair-Hair (Trystan's mistress),
and Penarwan (wife of Owain son of Urien),
and Bun, wife of Fflamddwyn.

And one was more faithless than those three: Gwenhwyfar, Arthur's wife, since she shamed a better man than any (of the others).

Manuscripts: 47, 50.
80. Culfynawyt V.
a. Essyllt yngwen 47, fygwen 50, Fyngwen V. ( ) *supplied from* 50.
b. ( ) *supplied from* 50.
c. Run 50.
d. 50 *omits.*

Compare Pen. 47's version of triad 66, *Teir Diweirwreic*, which immediately precedes in the manuscript, and which forms an antithetical pair with the present triad. Probably the two were composed in imitation of triads 29 and 30, *Tri Diweir I Anniweir Deulu.*

Pen. 50, p. 149

81. Tri Santeidd Linys Ynys Prydein:

Llinys Joseph o Ar(i)mathia,
a Llinys Cunedda Wledic,
a Llinys Brychan Brecheina6c.

81. Three Saintly Lineages of the Island of Britain:

The Lineage of Joseph of Ar(i)mathea,
and the Lineage of Cunedda Wledig,
and the Lineage of Brychan Brycheiniog.

Manuscripts: 50, V.
a. Arimathea V.

81. C 18(i). Tair Gwelygordh Saint (ii) Ynys Prydain o Vam Gymreig:

Plant Brychan Brycheiniawc,
a phlant Cunedha Wledic,
a phlant Caw o Bryd(yn).

81. C 18. Three Families of Saints of the Island of Britain, by Welsh mothers:

The Children of Brychan Brycheiniog,
and the Children of Cunedda Wledig,
and the Children of Caw of Pictland.

Manuscripts: C 18, C 25, Pen. 129 (p. 10), Pen. 131 (p. 112), Ll. 12 (p. 146). MW *gives both versions.*

81. C 18. C 25, Pen. 129, Pen. 131. Tair Gwehelyth saint ynys brydain o rann kymry Ll. 12.

a. brecheiniog Ll. 12.

b. kunedda Pen. 131, kynedda Ll. 12

c. o Brydain C 18, Pen. 131, Ll. 12, o Brydyn C 25, Pen. 129. MW *glosses* Soboles Brecani, soboles Cunotami regis, et soboles Covi Scoti. P. C. Bartrum informs me that the earliest version known to him is that in Llanstephan 28, ed. A. W. Wade-Evans, *Arch. Cam.* 86, p. 174. (This manuscript probably derived from the lost 'Hanesyn Hen' of the thirteenth or fourteenth centuries, Hengwrt MS 33; see EWGT 75–80.)

---

gwelygordh, 'ancestry, lineage, family' etc. (GPC 1630).

The original 'Three Kindreds of Saints' must undoubtedly have been those named in the second version of triad 81, as given in C 18, i.e. the descendants of *Brychan* in Dyfed, of *Cunedda* in Gwynedd, and of *Caw of Prydein* (Pictland) in North Britain. In this form the *Tair Gwelygordd Saint* is given as an addition to the triad of the Three Wives of Brychan Brycheiniog (triad 96 below). *Tair Gwelygordd Saint* is found in Rawlinson B 466 and in C 25, whether by itself or as an adjunct to the names of the three wives of Brychan Brycheiniog (triad 96). It seems likely that in its oldest form the triad goes back at least to the date of the fifteenth-century *Hanesyn Hen.* In the version given in Pen. 50 the lineage of Joseph of Arimathea has been substituted for that of Caw of Pictland under the influence of the Grail romances, in which the redactor of this manuscript shows a particular interest (cf. triad 86 below). Nevertheless, it was in the triad's older form, which included the name of *Caw o Brydyn*, and associated him (according to a subsequent development) with Anglesey, that the triad was known to Lewys Glyn Cothi (GLGC no. 226.49–53).

All versions of *Bonedd y Saint* begin with the genealogy of Dewi Sant, the most illustrious member of the stock of Cunedda, and follow his name with those of ten or more saints of this lineage—mainly those who, like Dewi, were descended from Ceredic ap Cunedda (VSB 320; EWGT 54–6). We do not know whether Cunedda was himself a Christian when he transferred to Gwynedd from the 'Old North' in the mid-fifth century, but it appears from the evidence of a number of dedications, combined with the hagiographical tradition, that the saints of his descent were largely responsible for building up the Celtic church in Gwynedd (E. G. Bowen, *The Settlements of the Celtic Saints in Wales*, p. 31). No reference is made in *Bonedd y Saint* to the descendants of Brychan Brycheiniog, but these are the subject of a document which was perhaps originally redacted in the eleventh century, *De Situ Brecheniauc* (see EWGT 14–16; Charles Thomas, 'The Brychan Documents', ch. 9 in *And Shall These Mute Stones Speak?*; and n. to *Brychan Brycheinya6c* under Personal Names). The prominence of the saints of both these families as pioneers of Christianity in Wales is witnessed by the number of churches dedicated to the offspring of Brychan and of Cunedda respectively, and according to E. G. Bowen 'nothing stands out more clearly than the sharp distinction made in Welsh hagiography between the *Brychan* and the *Cunedda* families, thus emphasizing the deeply-rooted cultural differences between north and south Wales even at this remote time' (op. cit., 31). *Bonedd y Saint* localizes saints of Caw's descent in north Wales, particularly at Twrcelyn in Anglesey, and thus traditions of Caw and his family, probably originally belonging to the Old North, became freshly localized in Gwynedd.

Little is known about the saints who are claimed to have belonged to the family of Caw, in contrast to the descendants of Cunedda and of Brychan, except for their most famous member, (St) Gildas. But a trace has survived of others of Caw's sons, both in the ninth-century Ruys Life of *Gildas* (H. Williams (ed.), *Gildas de Excidio Britanniae*, Cymmrodorion Record Series 3,

1901, pp. 322–88), in EWGT 85 (3) etc. (*Bonedd yr Arwyr*) and in *Culhwch ac Olwen* (see nn. to CO ll. 206–14). The significance of the episode in the Life of *St Cadog* (VSB 82–4), in which the saint brings the gigantic *Cau Pritdin* back to life and subsequently enlists him among his followers is probably to be interpreted as an attempt to reconcile the prestige of Cadog with an earlier hagiography which had given equal prestige to the saints who claimed descent from Caw. The triad puts on record the earlier prominence of *Caw of Prydein* in this role; but since the medieval sources indicate that traditions about Caw and his family were already largely obliterated at the time when these came to be committed to writing, it need cause little surprise that an attempt was made by the redactor of Pen. 50 to bring the triad up to date by substituting the family of Joseph of Arimathea (see under n. to Personal Names) for that of Caw, whose earliest traditions originated from the Old North.

But the name of Joseph of Arimathea was not the only additional name to be brought into this triad, and reference must here be made to the substitution of *Llinus Brân vab Llŷr* for *Llinus Joseph o Arimathia* in the readaptation of triad 81 printed in the *Myvyrian Archaiology*'s First Series of Triads (MA 391, no. 42). This triad constitutes a unique instance in which Iolo Morganwg has tampered with the text of the *Myvyrian* First Series. There is no manuscript authority for the substitution of the name of Brân fab Llŷr (i.e. Bendigeidfran) for that of Joseph of Arimathea, either in Vaughan's copy of the triad, which is based on Pen. 50, or in any of the intermediary copies of Vaughan's text, made by the Morris brothers and Evan Evans respectively, and on which the MA text is based (see introduction p. xli and n.). Iolo's motive in substituting the name of Brân for that of Joseph of Arimathea in his original was his predilection for the legend, largely devised by himself, concerning the introduction of Christianity into Britain by Caradog fab Brân (cf. MA 3rd Series, no. 18; *Iolo Manuscripts* 100; G. J. Williams, *Iolo Morganwg*, pp. I, 312–13). This deliberate misrepresentation of Vaughan's text of the triad by Iolo Morganwg was reproduced in turn in J. Loth's translation (*Les Mabinogion* II, 280, no. 76); and thus a wider currency has been obtained for the forged version than for the triad in its authentic form. This has led to misconceptions concerning Brân's association with the legends concerning the introduction of Christianity into Britain.

In his discussion of *Tair Gwelygordd Santaidd Ynys Prydain* (SC V, pp. 11–14), E. G. Bowen discussed Iolo Morganwg's late adaptation of this triad in MA 402, 18, in which he substituted Brân Fendigaid for Caw o Brydain as the progenitor of the Third Saintly Family. Bowen, however, did not recognize that this name does not appear in either of the two earlier versions of the triad, as given above. (For a translation of Iolo's triad and my note on it, see THSC 1968, pp. 310, 331.)

82. Tri Gwestei Gwynuededic o Ynys Prydein:

Dewi,
a Phadarn,
a Theila6.

82. Three Blessed Visitors (Guests) of the Island of Britain:

Dewi,
and Padarn,
and Teilo.

Manuscripts: 50, V, Cwrt. 3, BL Addl. 31,055 (p. 28), NLW Addl. 37B, (p. 92).
b. Patern BL, Cwrt., NLW Addl., Padern V.
c. a Theilo Cwrt., NLW Addl.

The triad names the three chief saints of south-western Wales (Bowen, *The Settlements of the Celtic Saints in Wales*, p. 50). For the introductory epithet, cf. Cynddelw to Owain Gwynedd: *ystre hynt wastad gvestei gwynuydic / Gwynn y uyd biefei* (H 95.7–8 = CBT IV, no. 4.209n. and GPC 1650) where *gwestai* is shown to mean both ‘visitor’ and ‘guest, visiting stranger’.

Pen. 50

83. Tri Chorff a wnaeth Du6 er Theila6:

Vn yssydd yn Llandaff y Morgann6c,
Yr eil yn Llan Teilo Va6r,
A'r trydydd yMhenalun yn Dyfet,
mal y dyweit yr Ystorya.

83. Three Bodies which God created for Teilo:

The first is at Llandaff in Morgannwg,
the second at Llandeilo Fawr,
and the third at Penalun in Dyfed,
as the History tells us.

Manuscripts: 50, V.
a. un sydd V. ym Morganwc V.

---

yr Ystorya, the thirteenth-century French *Queste del Saint Greal,* translated into Welsh in the following century in Pen. 11 and other MSS (Thomas Jones (ed.), *Ystoryaeu Seint Greal:* Rhan I *Y Keis* (Caerdydd, 1992)).

This triad, like the preceding two, indicates the interest taken by the redactor of Pen. 50 in ecclesiastical legend: in the present instance, in the cathedral of Llandaff, and its reputed sixth-century founder St Teilo, whose *Vita* is contained in the *Liber Landavensis* (LL). This *Vita* closes with an account of the dispute which arose after the saint's death between the three churches named in the triad, as to which should obtain possession of his body. The dispute was resolved by fasting and prayer, as a result of which there took place the miracle of the creation of three identical corpses, one of which was buried in each of the three churches. The redactor of the story leaves no doubt of the fact that he favours Llandâv as the place where the true corpse of St Teilo was buried (LL 116–17). The *ystorya* referred to in the triad is thus the *Vita* of the saint contained in LL: for a similar appeal to a written source cf. triad 86. On the legend, see further LBS IV, p. 237, and GLGC no. 149.45–6.

Vendryes suggested that the legend of Teilo's triple body represents a Christian survival of the Celtic mythological concept of triple unity, and he compared the triad of the Three Gwenhwyfars (triad 56, see n. and reference there cited; Vendryes, *Choix d'études linguistiques et celtiques* 239). A much simpler explanation of the triad seems more probable: the legend of St Teilo's three bodies was evolved in order to support the unhistorical association, dating from Norman times, between St Teilo and the cathedral of Llandaff, and at the same time to satisfy the demands of the two other churches which also claimed to possess the saint's body. See 'St Teilo' in D. S. Evans (ed.), *Lives of the Welsh Saints by G. H. Doble* and, in particular, TWS 132–3.

b. Llan Teilo Va6r in Carmarthenshire, the original centre from which the cult of St Teilo spread (Bowen, *The Settlements of the Celtic Saints in Wales*, 57).

c. Penalun. Penally near Tenby, Pembrokeshire.

Pen. 50, p. 153

84. Teir Ouergat Ynys Prydein:

Vn onaddunt a vu Gat Godeu. Sef y gwnaethp6yt, o achavs yr Ast y ar i6rch fech6ys a Chornygil;

Yr eil a vu y Gweith Arderydd, a wnaethp6yt o achavs nyth yr (E)hedydd;

A'(r) drydydd oedd waethaf. Sef oedd honno, Camlan. A honno a wnaethp6yt o gywryssedd Gwenh6yuar a Gwennh6yach. Sef acha6s y gelwit y rei hynny yn ouer: 6rth y gwneuthur o acha6s mor ddiffr6yth a h6nn6.

84. Three Futile Battles of the Island of Britain:

One of them was the Battle of Goddau: it was brought about because of the bitch, the roebuck and the plover;

The second was the Contest of Ar(f)derydd, which was brought about because of the lark's nest;

And the third was the worst: that was Camlan, which was brought about because of Gwenhwyfar's contention with Gwenhwy(f)ach.

This is why those (Battles) were called Futile: because they were brought about by such barren causes as that.

Manuscripts: 50, 77, V.

84. ouerddgat 50, overgad 77, overgat V.

a. Cad godau. sef yr achaws y gellwid yn overgadau o achos yr ast ag i wrch ffechwys a chornugyll 77, ar iwch fechwys a chornigell V.

b. yr Ychedydd, 50, yr ehedydd V, yr aderydd a wnaethbwyd o achos nyth yr ehedydd 77.

c. A drydydd 50, Drydydd Camlan a wnaethbwyd o gyfrwysudd Gwenhwyvar a Gwenhwyach 50; Gwenhwyvach 77.

77 *omits* d, yn ofer gadau V.

---

teir ouergat, *ofer* 'vain, futile, useless' (GPC 2630); cf. triad 12, *Tri O6er6eird.* The three battles had in common the fact that they were fought primarily by the Britons among themselves, rather than against a foreign enemy (though the *Bruts* credit Medrawd with foreign allies at *Camlan*, see triad 51). Thus Tudur Aled quotes this triad as an illustration of useless strife, in a *cywydd* addressed to Hwmffre ap Hywel, the purpose of which is to bring about a reconciliation between Hwmffre and his near relatives:

Duw gwyn! pam y digiai wŷr
Wrth ddireidi'r athrodwyr?
Trachas gwaed, trwy achos gwan,

A ddug ymladd i Gamlan;
Tair ofergad trwy fawrgas,
Tri amhwyll hen, trwm y llas!—
Gwaith colwyn yn dwyn y dydd,
Gweithred oer, Gwaith Arderydd,
Mwy diriaid twyll Medrod hen,
Modd y gwnâi,—am ddwy gneuen,—
Rhwng dau fugail bod ail dydd,
Er rhyw adar ehedydd.
(GTA I, no. LXVI.41–52.)

'Good God, why should men become angry at the wickedness of their slanderers? Bad blood, through feeble cause, led to the fighting at Camlan. Three futile battles, three ancient follies, were waged through great hatred, heavily were they fought! The battle at which a lap-dog carried the day (i.e. Cad Goddeu); a sad contest, the Battle of Ar(f)derydd; still more disastrous the treachery of old Medrod—the manner in which he brought about another day (of battle) between two shepherds, concerning two nuts—for the sake of a certain lark's chicks.'

Evidently the poet has misremembered the triad and has here confused the cause which was believed to have led to the battle of Arfderydd with that which led to Camlan.

a. Cat Godeu, *goddeu* 'forest' (GPC 1425). For the poem on *Kat Godeu* (BT 23–7), see edition and translation by M. Haycock in Martin J. Ball *et al.* (eds), *Celtic Linguistics*, pp. 297–331. As a place-name *Godeu* occurs twice in the early Taliesin poems, PT no. VI.4 and no. VII.44. See PT xliii–xliv for various suggestions as to the identification of the site of the battle, somewhere in lowland Scotland. Following the earlier suggestion made tentatively by Ifor Williams in PT, M. Haycock here proposes to identify the site of *Cad Goddau* with Arthur's battle of *Coed Celyddon* (HB ch. 56). The subject is a battle fought by different kinds of trees, whether in unison or against each other is not clear: in another poem (BT 33.23–4) it is stated that Lleu and Gwydion were present at *Kat Godeu* (see n. to *Gwydyon vab Don* under Personal Names). A fragment of a story about the battle, containing two early *englynion*, is preserved in a seventeenth-century manuscript, Pen. 98B, 81–2 (*Rep.* I, 613; CLlH l; MA 127b; trans. FAB I, 205–6). In this passage it is stated, in words which recall the triad, that the battle was brought about *o achos iwrch gwyn a chenau milgi a hanoeddynt o Annwn, ac Amathaon ap don a'i daliodd* 'because of a white roebuck and a greyhound pup which came from *Annwfn*, and Amathaon (= *Amaethon*) vab Don caught them'. According to this account the battle was fought between Amaethon, assisted by his brother Gwydion, and Arawn king of Annwfn. An alternative name for the battle was *Cad Achren*. It would appear, then, that there was a tradition about a mythological battle in which Lleu and the sons of Don took part, and it is tempting to connect the allusion to its cause, (i.e. to the animals which Amaethon brought from Annwfn) with the swine originating from Annwfn, which Gwydion steals in the tale of *Math*. (It should be remembered that in Celtic sources domestic animals are frequently portrayed as having an otherworld origin, see n. to triad 26b.) Perhaps originally Gwydion won the swine, as well as the dog and the white roebuck, in a raid upon Annwfn itself rather than upon Dyfed (see W. J. Gruffydd, *Math*, p. 331).

y ar (< *diar*) can mean 'besides, in addition to' (B XIII, p. 6), as well as 'upon, from upon' (see n. to triad 44b above). The former is clearly the meaning intended in the present context.

y ar i6rch fechwys. I am unable to suggest any interpretation of *fechwys*; the form is probably corrupt. Cf. GPC 2043 on *iwrch* 'roebuck'. M. Haycock, *Celtic Linguistics*, p. 133, suggests it may be connected with *ffechyn* 'ardent, fervent' (GPC 1279).

a Chornygil. *Cornygil*, i.e. *cornic(c)yll* 'lapwing, plover'. D: *Cornicyll et Cornchwigl et cornor y gweunydd* = *Vanellus avis*. The *corn* probably refers to the little tuft on the bird's head.

b. Gweith Arderydd. The triads which allude to the battle are nos. 29, 31 W, 44, 84. In the triads the form is throughout *Arderyd* (31 W, *Arderys*), and this spelling of the name is normal in poetry, except for LlDC (see below). The reference to the battle in *Ann. Cam.* 573 as *Bellum Armterid* proves that the form with the medial *-f-* is original, and this early form is preserved in the *gweith arywderit* of LlDC (see LlDC no. 11.23; 16.45; 17.214). The B text of *Ann. Cam.* gives to its notice of the battle the addition *inter filios Elifer et Gwendoleu filium Keidiau, in quo bello Guendoleu cecidit, Merlinus insanus effectus est.* Skene showed that the site of *Ar(f)derit* is to be identified with *Arthuret* near Longtown in Cumbria, a few miles north of Carlisle (FAB I, 65–6). This identification is corroborated by an apparent reference to the battle in the twelfth-century fragmentary *Life* of St Kentigern (Chadwick, *The Growth of Literature* I, p. 109). The references to the battle in the triads, as well as in the poems of the *Myrddin* cycle, indicate that it was fought between rival British factions: there is nowhere any mention of the English as participating in the conflict of Arfderydd. It is clear that this battle, and the events connected with it, were the subject of an extensive body of narrative, of which only fragments have come down to us (see nn. to *Gwendoleu, Myrddyn, Peredur*[2]). In no place do these fragments state clearly what was the cause at issue, or exactly who were the participants at the battle. The *Myrddin* poems suggest that Gwenddolau, Myrddin's patron, was the leader on one side (cf. triad 44), and the entry in *Ann. Cam.* 573 agrees with triad 29 in stating that Gwenddolau fell at the battle. It is possible that his opponents were Gwrgi and Peredur, the sons of Eliffer, as is claimed in the late text of the *Ann. Cam.*, although this addition to the early entry is rendered slightly suspect by the Latin form *Merlinus* which it contains. If Gwrgi and Peredur were Gwenddolau's opponents, the leaders on both sides were very close relatives; since the genealogies show that Gwrgi and Peredur were first cousins to Gwenddolau, as well as to Dunawt Vwr (triad 44). But HB's account of the death of Urien through the machinations of Morcant (see App. II below, no. 9) serves as a reminder that such strife between near kinsmen was not unknown among the northern Britons at this period. Triad 44 suggests that the battle was a clan skirmish among the *Coelings*, the descendants of *Coel Hen Godebog* (see App. II, nos. 1–7). There is no early evidence, apart from that of Geoffrey of Monmouth's poem the *Vita Merlini*, to show that Rhydderch Hael (see n.), who belonged to the other northern dynasty of Dyfnwal Hen, took part in the battle. Skene asserted confidently that Rhydderch was Gwenddolau's opponent at Arfderydd (FAB 1, 66), and he was followed in this statement by J. E. Lloyd (HW I, 166). It is unlikely that Skene had any evidence for this assumption other than the uncertain suggestions in the Myrddin poems. For an illuminating account of a visit made to the site of Arfderydd (Arthuret) by W. F. Skene in the 1860s, and of the traditions which he discovered were at that time still surviving locally concerning a great battle which had once been fought at this site, see Skene's fascinating 'Notice of the Battle of Ardderyd', *Proceedings of the Society of Antiquaries of Scotland* VI (1864), 91–8. On the battle of Arfderydd see further AW 121, *Ast. H.* 334–5, as well as the interesting, if controversial, speculations made by Molly Miller in 'The Commanders at Arthuret', *Transactions of the Cumberland and Westmorland Archaeological Society*, LXXV, pp. 96–118 and the n. to *Gwendoleu m. Keida6* under Personal Names below. For a seventeenth-century account—in English—which links the battle with the story of Myrddin Wyllt, see further Graham Thomas (ed.), 'Chwedl Myrddin', LlC XV, pp. 270–4.

The fame of Arfderydd might easily have drawn to it the names of the most prominent of the northern rulers whose lives were contemporary with the battle. This may account for the fact that R. Vaughan, like Skene, in his note on the battle (VN[2]), states that both Rhydderch and Aeddan of Dál Riada were present there, and he portrays them as the chief protagonists of the two opposing sides. His account is worth quoting, since it is always possible that Vaughan had a source which has not come down (note the names which he gives to Myrddin's brothers, which are found also in the poem *Peiryan Vaban*, B XIV, p. 105, ll. 50, 51). He knew of the 'lark's nest' referred to in the triad, though he gives no help in explaining the allusion, and he knew also of Tudur Aled's 'shepherds':

> It chanced that the shepherds of Rhydderch and Aeddan aforesaid, by the instigation of the Devil, fell out for no other cause than a lark's nest; who, having beaten one another to the effusion of their blood, at last acquainted

their lords of the whole strife, and they presently engaged themselves in the quarrel, entering into open hostility with such eagerness and hatred that having mustered their forces and committed some outrages, they appointed a day and place to try the matter by dint of sword; and Aeddan fearing to be too weak to encounter Rhydderch, drew to his side Gwenddoleu the son of Ceidiaw of the tribe of Coel Godeboc, a very powerful prince, and they, joining their forces, met Rhydderch at a place called Arderydd, where upon the first encounter Gwenddoleu was slain, and with him Llywelyn, Gwgawn, Einiawn, and Rhiwallawn, the sons of Morfryn, Merlin Caledonius's brethren; and in the end after a great slaughter on both sides, Rhydderch obtained the victory, and Aeddan fled the country. (VN[2]; Pa. 51, 116 r.–116 v.)

The following allusions to the battle of Arfderydd are made by the *Gogynfeirdd* and the *cywyddwyr*:

Gwalchmai: *Neu dreutysy tra lliw lleudinyawn dreuyt / neu dremyrth euravc caer arderyt* (H 21.25–6): 'I passed beyond the hue (?) of the townships of Lothian—a golden vision (?), the fortress of Arderydd'(?). This line has been differently interpreted by the editors of CBT I, no. 9.155 'I penetrated beyond the (river) *Lliw* to the townships of Lothian, on a lively (horse) (*teryt*, cf. CLlH 161n.) I visited (?) *Caer Efrawg* (=York)'. This deletes the poem's reference to *Ar(f)derydd*, previously supported by Lloyd-Jones (G 36) and Ifor Williams (LEWP 74).

Cynddelw: *Mal Gweith Arderyt gwyth ar dyruein cad / Yn argrad, yn aergrein* (H 91.23–4 = CBT IV, no. 4.97–8, n.).

Llygad Gŵr: *ny bu gad hwyllyad heuelyt – gyfred / er pan vu weithred weith arderyt* (H 217.23–4 = CBT VII, no. 24.91–2).

Tudur Aled: *Llai ydyw nifer Gwaith Arderydd* (GTA I, no. III.47).

Llywelyn ab y Moel: *Arfderydd dân* (IGE[2] 201.25).

nyth yr (E)hedydd. N. K. Chadwick suggested (*Celtic Britain* (1963), p. 64) that 'Nyth yr Ehedydd' was the original name for Caerlaverock ('Lark's Fort'), a name which has come down for a Norman castle situated near the mouth of the River Nith, on the northern shore of the Solway estuary, some twenty-five miles west of Arthuret. But K. H. Jackson showed (YB X (1977), pp. 45–50) that Caerlaverock as a parish-name is earlier than the existing medieval remains of this castle, and that it may plausibly have originally denoted the Roman *caer* whose remains are still discernible, a mile away on the nearby Wardlaw hill. This was known in Skene's day as 'the Roman camp', and here there had traditionally been fought a great battle 'between the Romans and the Picts' who occupied the *caer*, and who were all slain, to the number of three hundred. 'Caer yr Ehedydd' could have preceded the name 'Caerlaverock' in its original Cumbric form—a hybrid half-translation, made by later bilingual Northumbrian settlers in the area (who substituted 'laverock' for 'ehedydd', but preserved the Celtic *caer*). Jackson concluded that the traditions attached to the name 'Caer yr Ehedydd' might reflect confused memories of the battle, bound up with a place-name which in essentials had survived its transference from Cumbric into English, together with the remote memory of a great battle that had taken place in the dim past. Memories of controversies which had preceded and led up to this battle may be reflected both in the triad, and (perhaps independently) in the passage in R. Vaughan's *Notes*, from which I have quoted above. See further n. on *Gwendoleu mab Keid6aw* under Personal Names.

Camlan. See n. to triad 59c for references to the battle. Triad 53b states that *Camlan* was brought about because of the blow given by *Gwenhwy(f)ach* to *Gwenhwyfar*; one suspects, therefore, that triad 53 may have influenced the present triad in Pen. 50, though other indications suggest this triad may have an independent and early origin. The form *Gwenhwyach* is paralleled in CO l. 359, and Gwenhwyfar's sister is not so named elsewhere. For the phrase *o gyfrysedd* 'battle, conflict, contention, strife etc.' (GPC 722) see triad 51a, l. 5 and n.

Pen. 50, pp. 158–9

85. Teir Prif Lys Arthur:

Kaerllion ar Wysg yg Kymry,
a Chelli Wic y Ghernyw,
a Phenryn Rioned yn y Gogled.

Teir Prif 6yl yn y Teir Priflys:

Pasc a Nadolic a Sulgwyn.

85. Arthur's Three Principal Courts:

Caerleon-on-Usk in Wales,
and Celliwig in Cornwall,
and Penrhyn Rhionydd in the North.

Three Principal Festivals at the Three Principal Courts:

Easter, and Christmas, and Whitsun.

Manuscripts: 50, V, NLW Addl. 37B, p. 93. See v.l. to App. I, no. 9.
85. Tair prif Lŷs Ynys Brydain NLW Addl.
b. Llys Penwaedd ynghernyw NLW Addl.
c. Llys Penrhyn Rhianedd NLW Addl.
d. teir prif wyl yn y teir llys hyn V.

See triad 1 above and EYP, App. I, no. 4; the latter of which gives this triad in its older form, with *Aberffraw*, and not *Caerllion*, as the seat of the third of the three *taleithiau* ('coronets') of Britain. The substitution of *Caerllion* for *Mynyw* (St David's) in the older version is obviously due to the influence, directly or indirectly, of HRB. In triad 1 *Mynyw* is given as the name of Arthur's *lleithiclwyth* ('tribal throne') in Wales. But all three versions of the triad are consistent in naming *Kelli Wic* and *Pen*(*ryn*) *Rioned* as the 'principal courts' of Cornwall and the North respectively.

a. *Kaerllion* ar Wysg (Caerleon on Usk) was traditionally nominated Arthur's chief capital, and the place where he was crowned king of Britain according to HRB IX, ch. 12.

b., c. For *Kelli Wic*, *Pen*(*ryn*) *Rioned*, see nn. to triad 1 above.

d. According to the *Statute of Gruffudd ap Cynan*, prepared for the Caerwys Eisteddfod in 1523, these were the *tair gŵyl arbennig*, the principal occasions in the year for the bards, at which they resorted regularly to the homes of the *uchelwyr* with their poems of praise; and these festivals were the normal occasions for the presentation of such poems. See T. Parry, 'Statud

Gruffudd ap Cynan', B V, pp. 25–33; GTA I, xxx; D. J. Bowen, *Gruffudd Hiraethog a'i Oes* (Caerdydd, 1958), p. 11. The festivals were recorded in the Law of Hywel Dda (LlB 2.27, etc.).

Pen. 50, p. 159

86. Tri Marcha6c o Lys Arthur a enilla6d y Greal, ac eu duc y Nef:

Galaad vab La6nslot y Lac,
a Pheredur vab Efra6c Iarll,
a Bort uab Brenhin Bort.

A'(r) ddeu gyntaf oeddynt wery o gyrff. A'(r) trydydd oedd ddiweir, am na wnaeth pecha6t kna6da6l ont vnweith. A hynny drwy brouedigaeth yn yr amser y ennillawd ef . . . verch Brenyn Brangor, yr honn a vu Ymherodres yn Constinobyl, o'r honn y deuth y Genedlaeth v6yaf or byt; ag o'r genedlaeth Joseph o Arimathia y hanoedynt yll tri, ac o lin David brof6yt, mal y tystolaeth *Ystorya y Greal.*

86. Three Knights of Arthur's Court who won the Grail, and (it) brought them to Heaven:

Galaad son of Lawnslot of the Lake,
and Peredur son of Earl Efrawg,
and Bort son of King Bort.

And the two first were virgin of body. And the third was chaste, for only once had he committed bodily sin; and that, through temptation (misfortune), at the time when he won . . . daughter of King Brangor, who was Empress in Constantinople, and from whom was descended the greatest race in the world. All three were sprung of the race of Joseph of Arimathea, and of the lineage of the Prophet David, as the History of the Grail testifies.

Manuscripts: 50, C 36, NLW, V, BL².

86. a gawsant y greal V, Tri marchawg Gwyryv a gowsant, ag nid yw ond chwedl, gwaed ir Arglwydh yn Castelh Gorbyn yn y northawg C 36, NLW, RW, BL, ar Arglwydh RW.

a. Galath fab Lawnselot dy Lak V. C 36, RW, NLW, *substitute* Gwalchmai

b. Peridyr ap Evrog C 36.

c. a Bawd ap Lawnslot C 36, RW, Broed ap lawnslot NLW.

d. *The name preceding* verch brenyn Brangor *is left blank in the manuscript and also in* V. C 36, NLW, RW, BL, *omit*. Armathia V. Dafudd V.

With this triad cf. App. IV, no. 2. The names of the three Grail winners, as is noted at the conclusion of the triad, are derived from part I of *Y Seint Greal*, the fourteenth-century translation of the French Vulgate *Queste del Saint Graal.* For a triad based on part II of *Y Seint Greal* see triad 91 below. The success of the three knights in the Grail quest is prophesied by an anchoress at an early stage in the story:

> Ni a wdam yny wlat yma . . . y byd reit y orffen pererindawt y greal tri marchawc urdawl gwerthuawr, y rei a geiff y glot odieithyr pawb. Ar deu a vyd marchogyon gwyry, heb wneuthur pechawt godineb oe kyrff eiryoet nae vedylyaw. Y trydyd a vyd diweir: kystal yw hynny ac na bu idaw wreic eiryoet onyt unweith—ar weith honno y kaffat arnaw siom a phrofedigaeth—ac ny byd vyth idaw mwy. Ac am hynny y gelwir ef yn diweir. Ac un or deu wyry yw y marchawc yr wyt ti yn y geissyaw (i.e. Galaad). A thitheu (i.e. Peredur) vyd yr eil. Ar trydyd yw Bwrt: drwy y tri hynny y byd gorffennedic y keis. (SG 47–8 = T. Jones (ed.), *Ystoryaeu y Seint Greal* (Caerdydd, 1992), ll. 1580–9).

This triad is probably the contribution of the redactor of Pen. 50, whose interest in ecclesiastical legend has already been noted (triad 81, see introduction, pp. xxvii–xxix and C. Lloyd-Morgan, 'Later Arthurian Literature', AW 193–205; eadem, 'Lancelot in Wales' in Karen Pratt (ed.) *Shifts and Transpositions in Medieval Narrative*). The interest of the addition made to the triad in **d** centres on the fact that it can only be based on the full narrative of *Bo(ho)rt*'s liaison with the daughter of King Brangoire, and this is not to be found anywhere in the *Queste* or in its Welsh translation, but only in the Vulgate *Lancelot* (Sommer, *Vulgate Cycle of the Arthurian Romances* IV, pp. 269–70; EAR I, 401). It may be noted that the name of the daughter of King Brangoire is not given in the French text: hence the *lacuna* in the manuscript of the triad at this point. The child born of the union was *Helian le Blanc qui puis fu empereres de constantinople* (= *Helian wynn*, SG 97.14). We have no evidence that the *Lancelot* was ever rendered into Welsh, as was the *Queste*; and thus the allusion to the daughter of King Brangoire seems to imply a direct knowledge of the French romance. But it is also possible that there once existed other Welsh translations of the French romances, in addition to those which have come down (see introduction, pp. cxi–cxii; P. C. Bartrum, *Nat. Lib. of Wales Journal* XIV, pp. 242–5; and C. Lloyd-Morgan, *Nat. Lib. of Wales Journal* XXI, pp. 329–40). The remaining manuscripts which contain this triad introduce it differently: 'Three Virgin Knights who obtained—though it is only a story—the Blood of the Lord at the Castle of Corbyn (= *Corbenic*, EAR I, p. 394) in the North.' It may be remembered in this connection that the authenticity of the Grail romances was never accepted by the medieval Church.

ac eu duc y Nef. See SG 169 (= Thomas Jones (ed.), *Ystoryaeu Seint Greal*, ll. 5673–9) for the account of the appearance of the Grail to the three knights, and for the ensuing death of *Galaad*.

d. Ymherodres yn Constinobyl. The romance of *Peredur* attributes to its hero, one of the three Grail winners, a union with the *amherodres Cristinobyl* (WM 162.12; 165.23–5).

Joseph o Arimathia. See n. to *Joseph* under Personal Names for the information provided by the romances as to the descent claimed for the three knights descended from Joseph of Arimathea, and through him from the prophet David.

Pen. 252, p. 169

87. Tri Bardd Kaw oedd yn Llys Arthur:

Myrddyn vab Morvryn,
Myrddyn Embrys,
A Thaliessin.

87. Three Skilful Bards were at Arthur's Court:

Myrddin son of Morfryn,
Myrddin Emrys,
and Taliesin.

Manuscripts: 252, V, MW, BL[2].

87. Tri Phrif Fardd Ynys Prydein V, BL, Tri Phrif Fardd a fu gynt yn Ynys Brydain MW. MW *cites source*: *Ex Gram. Hugonis Mochno.*

a, b. Merddin V.

c. a Thaliesin Ben Beirdd V.

---

bardd kaw. *Kaw* as adjective = *cyson, cywair* 'harmonious, well-ordered, skilful'; GPC 442, G 117; *bardd caw* 'musician, minstrel' GPC 258. In the following early instances *caw* is employed with reference to music: *y cav keineid* 'harmonious singers' (LlDC no. 3.4); Cynddelw: *cathleu cleu kerteu caw* 'audible strains of skilful music' (H 100.10 = CBT IV, no. 6.71). But no doubt *Tri Phrif Fardd* represents the older form of the triad. The distinction between Merlin Ambrosius (*Myrddyn Embrys*) and Merlin Celidonius (*Myrddyn vab Morvryn*) appears first in Giraldus Cambrensis, see n. to *Myrddyn m. Morvryn* under Personal Names. In the sixteenth century, Elis Gruffydd gives a curious account in which Myrddin Emrys is portrayed as having been reincarnated, first as Taliesin, and then again as Myrddin vab Morfryn (see EC VIII, pp. 320–1).

Hafod MS. 24, p. 225, quotes this triad under the heading *Perthynasseu kerdd dafod*:

> Pwy bynnag a ddywetto ei fod yn Arwyddfardd, gwybydded achoedd brenhinedd a thowyssogion a *chyfarwyddyd* oddiwrth y tri phrifardd a fu yn ynys Brydain nid amgen Merddin ap Morfryn, Merddin Emrys, a Thaliessin Benbeirdd (quoted in *Y Llenor* XII, p. 158)
>
> 'Whoever claims that he is a Heraldic Bard, let him know the genealogies of the Kings and Princes and *cyfarwyddyd* ('tradition, history'), from the Three Principal Bards who were in the Island of Britain: that is *Myrddin ap Morfryn,* etc.

Cf. LlB 25–6: *Pan vynno y vrenhines gerd o'e gwaranndaw . . . canet y bard ydi tri chanu o gerd vangaw* (GPC 254 'free, skilful, melodious', etc.). The *kaw* of the triad evidently forms the second element in *bangaw.*

In Pen. 252 and BL[2] the triad is preceded by the following: *Tri chyfannedd fardd* ('Domestic Bards') *llys arthyr. bardd Caw, a bardd tant, a bardd phethlwm* (Pen. 252: *ffithlem* = fiddle? see GPC 1291 and cf. GDG no. 25.34, where *ffithlen* is equivalent to 'whistle'). In BL[2] there follow two more triads dealing with different types of bards; evidently, therefore, triad 87 belongs properly to such a group.

Pen. 185, fo. 56r (*R. Vaughan's manuscript*)

88. Tair Rhiain Ardderchog Llys Arthur:

Dyfyr Wallt Eureit,
Enid verch i Niwl Iarll,
a Thegeu Eurfron.

88. Three Splendid (Famous) Maidens of Arthur's Court:

Dyfyr Golden-Hair,
Enid daughter of Earl (Y)niwl,
and Tegau Gold-Breast.

Manuscripts: V, BL Addl. 31055 (p. 75), NLW Addl. 37B (p. 92).
88. oedd yn llys arthur NLW Addl.
b. verch y Niwl Iarll BL, ferch Niwl jarll NLW Addl.
The triad is incorporated in the texts of *Araith Ieuan Brydydd Hir*. The following version from Pen. 218 is quoted from D. Gwenallt Jones, *Yr Areithiau Pros*, 30:

y tair rriain ardderchawg o lys arthur nid amgen no
Dyfir wallt euraid
a Thegau eurfron
ag Enid verch yn niwl iarll
kariadau Glewlwyd gafaelfawr a Chariadog vreichfras a Geraint ab Erbin.

V gives no indication as to his source for this triad, but since *Tair Rhiain Ardderchog* does not occur in any of the extant manuscripts which Vaughan states that he used, it is probable that he derived the triad from an unacknowledged source, perhaps one of the *Araith* versions. The occurrence of the triad in the book of Sir Thomas Wiliems, Trefriw (BL Addl. 31055), written in 1594–6, provides evidence for its independent existence prior to the time of Vaughan; and other versions may well come to light to prove that the triad is older than this date. The texts of the *Araith* version date from *circa* 1600 (D. Gwenallt Jones, *Yr Areithiau Pros*, p. 99).

In his *Cywydd Gofyn Cymod* (GDG no. 52), Dafydd ap Gwilym compares Morfudd in turn to Tegau, Dyfr and Enid. This may be a coincidence; though it suggests that Dafydd may have been drawing on his knowledge of *Tair Rhiain Ardderchog*. If this is so, the triad may have belonged to the group known as *Trioedd y Gwragedd*, which is represented in several of the older manuscripts. On *Rhiain* see n. to triad 56.

Pen. 185, fo. 56*r* (*R. Vaughan's manuscript*)

89. Tri Pheth a orchfygodd Loegyr:

Cynwys Die(i)thr(i)aid,
Rhyddhau carcharorion,
ac Anrheg y Gwr Moel.

89. Three Things which conquered Lloegr:

Receiving Strangers,
Freeing Prisoners,
and the Tribute of the Bald Man.

Manuscripts: Pen. 185, Mostyn 133 (J. Jones of Gelli Lyfdy), 243:
(ii) Tri pheth a ddistrywia Lloegr: ('will destroy England')
Kynwys dieithred iddi
A rhyddhau karcharor
ac anrhegu y gwr moel

Vaughan gives no source for this triad; though since it appears in a manuscript of John Jones, Gellilyfdy, it is probable that Vaughan obtained it from the latter. I have not discovered any earlier version of the triad, or any reference which throws light upon its meaning. The implications of the wording in Jones's version are slightly different—*distrywa* 'will conquer Lloegr'.

Lloegyr. See n. to triad 69. Iolo Morganwg (MA, third series, no. 82 above and n. to AP l. 109) evidently interpreted the triad as alluding to the conquest of England from the Britons by the Saxons, since he expanded the introductory wording as follows: *Tripheth a fu achaws gorchfygu Lloegr, a'i dwyn oddiar y Cymry*, etc. This may be the correct interpretation: if so, then *Cynwys Die(i)thr(i)aid* can be explained as referring to Vortigern's reception of Hengist and Horsa. See Iolo's own translation of his version of the triad (THSC 1969, pp. 136–7). The events referred to in the triad are evidently those described in HRB VI, 10–13 (BD 91–7), which tell of the arrival of the Saxons under Hengist and Horsa. Eurys Rowlands suggests (LlC VI, p. 236) that since 'dish of food' (*saig*) is one of the meanings of *anrheg*, the reference in **c** may possibly be to Rhonwen's poisoning of Gw(e)rthefyr (Vortimer) and that in **b** to the flight of the Saxons from Thanet (BD 97). But according to Iolo, *Y Gŵr Moel* 'the Bald Man' designated Julius Caesar.

Pen. 185, fo. 56*r* (*R. Vaughan's manuscript*)

90. Tri Dyfal Gyfangan Ynys Prydein:

> un oedd yn Ynys Afallach,
> yr ail y Nghaer Garadawc,
> a'r trydydd ym Mangor.

Ymhob un o'r tri lle hynny yr oedd 2400 o Wyr Crefyddol, ac o'r rheini 100 cyfnewidiol bob awr o'r 24 yn y dydd a'r nos yn parhau mewn gweddieu a gwasanaeth i Dduw, yn ddidranc ddiorffwys byth.

90. Three Perpetual Harmonies of the Island of Britain:

> One was at the Island of Afallach,
> and the second at Caer Garadawg,
> and the third at Bangor.

In each of these three places there were 2,400 religious men; and of these 100 in turn continued each hour of the twenty-four hours of the day and night in prayer and service to God, ceaselessly and without rest for ever.

Manuscripts: V, MW, BL Addl. 14,873 (Wm. Morris).

90. oedd gynt yn ynys B. BL.

a. Ynys Wydryn MW.

b. Bangor Fawr yn Iscoed ym Maelawr BL.

c. 2400 o Fenych oedd yn canu bob awr yn y dydd ac yn y nos ym mhob un o'r tair Mynachlog. Ac yn yr amser hwnnw yn amser y Mynachlogydd yr oedd 2400 o Fynachod ym mhob un o'r tair Mynachlog a ddywetpwyd uchod yn canu ynghyfair y pedair Awr ar hugain y sydd yn y dydd a'r nos fel y bu gant am bob Awr yn canu yn y Côr fel y byddai wasanaeth Duw heb orphwys MW, BL.

Pen. 228 (*Thos. Wiliems, Trefriw*), I, xxii

90. Tri Dyfal Gyfangan oedh gynt yn amser y Brytannieit: Bangawr, a Chaer Gariadawc, ag Ynys Widrin. yn Sasonaec Continuale Songe, yn Gymraec . . . bod pedwar ar hugein o vencych yn canu bop awr yn y dydh ag yn y nos. A'r amser hwnw yr oedh pedwar cant ar hugein ymhob yn o'r tair manachloc a dhywetpwyt vchod, ynghyfeir y pedeir awr ar hugein yssydh yn y dydh a'r nos, val y bai gant bob awr yn canu'n y côr, val y bydhei wasanaeth dduw heb orphwys. Amen.

> Allan o hen lyuer Cymraec
> Er mwyn y rhai sy'n caru henafiaeth yr ynys.

Manuscripts: Pen. 228, Pen. 216 (J. Jones), p. 156.

90. Tri chyfangan ynys Brydaen Pen. 216.

a. Bangawr vawr yn fford y Maelawr.

c. Ynys Avallach.

Allan o hen lyfr Kymraec medd Sr. Tom ap Wil. Terfyn noswyl Bedr 1611.

---

cyfangan 'a harmonious song, an uninterrupted choir', etc. (GPC 677). The oldest extant text of this triad is that of Thomas Wiliems, Trefriw, *Dict. Latino-Cambricum* (Pen. 228) I, xxii. John Jones, Gellilyfdy cites Wiliems's version as his source, though he gives *Ynys Avallach* in place of *Ynys Widrin.* V does not state his source for the triad, but it seems likely that he abbreviated it from Jones's version.

a. Ynys Afallach, i.e. Glastonbury, see n. to *Auallach* under Personal Names. Thomas Wiliems and Moses Williams give the variant Welsh name for the place, which is based upon the English, *Ynys Widrin* (< *gwydr* 'glass').

b. Caer Garadawc. *Cair Caratauc* is included in the HB list of cities (ed. Morris p. 80, no. 9), but its site is uncertain. Jackson points out (*Antiquity* XII, pp. 48–9) that the name is given to hill-forts at various places in southern Britain: there is one near Church Stretton in Shropshire, and one on top of the Breiddin in Montgomery. References in early poetry indicate that there was a place called *Caer Garadawc* somewhere in North Britain, BT 65.3–4: *o gaer glut hyt gaer garadawc* 'from Caer Glud (i.e. Dumbarton) to Caer G.'; cf. also *Moliant Cadwallawn* (B VII, p. 25, ll. 36–7): *yspydawd Cadwallawn g(a)er Garadawc vre / wrth y gyfwyre gynne Efrawc* 'the company of Cadwallawn near the hill of Caradawg; at his uprising the burning of York'. On this poem, see R. G. Gruffydd, 'Canu Cadwallon ap Cadfan', *Ast. H.* 25–43, EWSP 169–73, and n. to *Catwalla6n m. Catuan* under Personal Names. If this were the place referred to in the triad, then the choice of monasteries named would repeat once more the familiar division of *Ynys Prydein* into Wales, Cornwall (in its greater sense, including the whole of the south-western peninsula) and the North; cf. triads 1, 85, and App. I, no. 4. But since Geoffrey of Monmouth expressly identifies *Caer Garadawc* with Salisbury (HRB VI, 15; VIII, 9 = BD 99.20; 125.9) it may be that Salisbury is intended in the triad.

c. ym Mangor i.e. the monastery of Bangor Is-coed in Flint, for which see n. to triad 60. The allusion here may owe something to Bede's account of this monastery (*Hist. Ecc.* II, 2), in which he says that it was divided into seven parts, each containing at least three hundred men.

Cardiff 6, fo. 4*v*

91. Tri Diofnog Ynys Brydain:

Vn fu Walchmai ap Gwyar,
a'r ail fu Llacheu ap Arthur,
a'r trydydd fu Brydyr ap Efrog Iarll.

91. Three Fearless Men of the Island of Britain:

The first was Gwalchmai son of Gwyar,
the second was Llachau son of Arthur,
and the third was Prydyr (=Peredur) son of Earl Efrog.

The combination in this triad of the name of *Llacheu* with those of *Gwalchmei* and *Peredur* indicates that its source is *Y Seint Greal*, part II (based on the French *Perlesvaus*), in which *Llacheu* (see n. under Personal Names) is used to render the name of Arthur's son *Loho*(*l*)*t* in the French text. The triad names the three heroes most prominent in *Y Seint Greal*, part II (=*Perlesvaus*). *Llacheu* plays no part in part I, nor does *Galaad*—whom we might otherwise expect to find included in the triad—appear in part II. On the provenance of the triad see introduction, p. xxvii.

For a triad based on part I of *Y Seint Greal* (= the *Queste del Saint Graal*) see triad 86 above and the references there cited.

NLW 6434, fo. 134

92. Tri Hynaif Byd:

> Tylluan Gwm Kowlwyd,
> Eryr Gwern Abwy,
> A Mwyalchen Gelli Gadarn.

92. Three Elders of the World:

> The Owl of Cwm Cowlwyd,
> the Eagle of Gwernabwy,
> and the Blackbird of Celli Gadarn.

Manuscripts: NLW, MW, BL[2].
b. o Wernabwy MW, gwern Abwydd BL.
c. y Gelli ddofn BL.

The source of this triad is the lost *Book of Sir Richard Wynn of Gwydir*; see introduction, p. xxxviii.

The most familiar Welsh version of the story of the Oldest Animals is found in *Culhwch ac Olwen* (CO ll. 847–910), where the story-teller has with considerable artistry adapted the concept of creatures who are preternaturally long-lived in such a way as to illustrate and emphasize his rendering of the myth of *Mabon fab Modron*: to show, in the words of W. J. Gruffydd (*Cy*. 42, p. 142), 'that Mabon is not only the Great Prisoner, he was also the Immemorial Prisoner—the Great Son who has been lost for aeons'. But an independent folk-tale version of the 'Oldest Animals' has come down in the hand of Thomas Wiliems of Trefriw (BL Addl. 31,055, fo. 107b, written 1594–6), in which the story is self-contained, and has an entirely different setting and motivation from the *Culhwch* version. This text has been edited by Thomas Jones, *Nat. Lib. of Wales Journal* VII, pp. 62–6, with a discussion of the various versions of the tale which have appeared in print, and which are probably all ultimately based on that of Thomas Wiliems. For further versions and discussions see CO (1997), p. lii–liv; CO[2] lx–lxiii; T. Jones, 'Y Stori Werin yng Nghymru', THSC 1970, pp. 16–32.

The names and epithets of the Oldest Animals correspond in the *Culhwch* and folk-tale versions of the tale. These are: *Eryr Gwernabwy* or *Gwern Gwy, Carw Rhedynvre, Cuan* or *Tyllvan Cwm Cowlwyd, Gleisiad Llyn Llyw* (*Ll. Lliwon* or *Llifon*), *Mwyalchen Gilgwri*; i.e. Eagle, Stag, Owl, Salmon, Blackbird. Thomas Wiliems adds to these a sixth creature *Llyffant Cors Vochno* (Toad). There are references in *cywyddau* to certain of the above creatures as types of longevity: Siôn Cent's poem *Y Ffordd i'r Nef* (IGE[2] no. XCI) names the stag and the blackbird, while Gruffudd Llwyd (IGE[2] no.

XLVII) names the stag, eagle and salmon as animals which are capable of being rejuvenated, and he cites ancient tradition as his source for this belief. In the *cywydd* beginning *Lluniais oed ddyw llun ys hir* (*Barddoniaeth Dafydd ab Gwilym*, 1789, no. LII = Helen Fulton (ed.), *Dafydd ap Gwilym Apocrypha* (Llandysul, 1996), no. 26), the poet compares himself in turn to the Eagle of Gwernabwy, the Stag of Cilgwri [*sic*] and the Owl of Cwm Cowlwyd. Wiliam Llŷn in 1561 wishes for Rhys Fychan *teiroes hydd*, and concludes *Teiroes ydiw oed derwen / Teiroes mwy ytt Rys, Amen* (Wm. Ll., no. VI.64, 83–4; cf. also idem VIII.81–4). Similarly Dafydd ab Edmwnd wishes for Rhys ap Ll. ap Tudur *teir oes yr hydd tirion* (GDE 96.24).

It can thus be demonstrated that there was in the Middle Ages a body of folklore concerning the Oldest Animals. This was drawn upon by the narrator of *Culhwch*; but it is clear that it remained in circulation until much later than the date of this tale, since the folk-tale recorded by Thomas Wiliems evidently owes nothing to the *Culhwch* version. Similarly the triad—which in fact names only the Oldest Birds—is probably derived from this folk tradition rather than from the literary tale: note the variant *Celli Gadarn*, which is given as the home of the Blackbird, and which is not found elsewhere. On *Cwm Cowlwyd* (probably the one in Arfon, but there are other possibilities) and on *Gwernabwy* (? Aberdaron), see Melville Richards, 'Arthurian Onomastics', THSC 1969, p. 256. Two more versions of the story of the Oldest Animals have been published by Dafydd Ifans, 'Chwedl yr Anifeiliaid Hynaf', B XXIV, pp. 461–4, from two seventeenth-century MSS.—Bodley E.2. pp. 59–60 and NLW 20574 A, pp. 87–9. The *Iolo Manuscripts* 188–90 print a version 'from the Book of Mr Cobb'. An analogous presentation of the Owl as a type of longevity is found in the sixteenth-century Scottish Gaelic poem *Oran na Comhachaig*, 'The Owl of Strone', ed. and discussed in *Transactions of the Gaelic Society of Glasgow*, V, pp. 122–171. D. S. Thompson *An Introduction to Gaelic Poetry* (London, 1974) points out the existence of general parallels to the poem in early Welsh and Irish.

An Irish analogy to the tale of the Oldest Animals is found in the story which narrates the transformations undergone by *Tuan mac Cairill*. This appears in the *Lebor na h-Uidre* (ed. Bergin and Best, pp. 42–5; trans. Nutt, *Voyage of Bran* II, pp. 294–301), and so it is at least as old as the eleventh century. Here the motif of the Oldest Animals (a stag, boar, hawk and salmon) has been utilized, as in *Culhwch*, for a secondary purpose—that of forming one of the group of 'bridge' tales, which purport in Irish to account for the transmission into the Christian world of the traditions of pagan Ireland. There have also come down in Irish certain 'runs' which compute the longevity of various creatures in an ascending scale which is arranged in triads. The following example is translated from such a passage preserved in the fifteenth-century *Book of Lismore*, fo. 151b: 'Three life-times of the Stag for the Blackbird; three life-times of the Blackbird for the Eagle; three life-times of the Eagle for the Salmon; three life-times of the Salmon for the Yew' (Stokes, *Lives of the Saints from the Book of Lismore*, p. xli; for some further parallels in Irish and other languages see E. Hull, 'The Hawk of Achill and the Legend of the Oldest Animals', *Folklore* XLIII, pp. 376 ff.).

The extreme antiquity of the story-motif of the Oldest Animals seems established by the Indian and Persian analogues to the tale which have been cited by E. B. Cowell (*Cy*. V, pp. 169 ff.). In one version the creatures are a vulture (or eagle) and an owl, which correspond with two of the species named in the Celtic versions, but elsewhere they are a partridge, a monkey, and an elephant. The story-setting is quite different from that given to the theme in Celtic sources.

hynaif. See n. to *Penhyneif*, triad 1.

Llanstephan 65, fo. 29*r* (*Moses Williams's manuscript*)

93. Trywyr a nodes eu gwala ar Arthur yn eu *cyfarws*:

Culhwch ab Cilydd ab Celyddon Wledig,
a Huarwar mab Aflaun,
a Gordibla Kernyw.

ex Hist. Cul. ac Olwen.

93. Three Men who specified their sufficiency from Arthur as their Gift (perquisite):

Culhwch son of Cilydd son of Celyddon Wledig,
and Huarwar son of Aflawn,
and Gordibla of Cornwall.

Triad 93 represents Moses Williams's attempt to abstract an unrecognized triad from the text of *Culhwch ac Olwen*. For *Huarwar* see CO ll. 312–15 (= WM 467.9–15). But it is unlikely that *Gordibla* (< *gor* + *di* + *pla* 'mighty plague' GPC 1470) is intended as a proper name here. The word is unrecorded except in this single instance in the text of *Culhwch* (cf. CO xviii and l. 313).

cyfarws. See n. to triad 69.

b. The heading indicates that Moses Williams obtained his text of *Culhwch* from RM or from a copy of RM. In WM 467.9–11: *Huarwar mab halvn a nodes y wala ar Arthur yny gyuarvs* = RM III.3–4: *Huarwr mab aflavn.* (= CO l. 312n.). *Aflawn* 'Not full, empty'.

c. CO ll. 313–14 (= WM 467.12): *trydyt gordibla kernyw a dyfneint* [*hyt*] *pan gahat idav y wala* 'he (Huarwar) was one of the three mighty plagues of Cornwall and Devon until his fill was found for him'.

Llanstephan 65, fo. 95*v* (*Moses Williams's manuscript*)

94. Tair Gwledd Anfeidrol[1] a fu yn Ynys Brydain:

Un o honunt fu y Wledd a wnaeth Caswallawn ab Beli yn Llundain, lle llas Ugain mil o wartheg, ac o ddefaid Can mil, a Deng mil a deugain o Wyddau a Chapylldiaid, ac adar gwylldion a dofion mwy nag a allai neb eu rhifo. (*G. Owain.*)

Ai Gwledd Arthur ynghaer Llyon ar Wysg oedd y llall, a pha wledd oedd y drydedd?

[1]Anrhydeddus medd Awdwr *Drych y Prif Oesoedd,* p. 29. (See the first edition of *Drych y Prif Oesoedd* 1716, Garfield Hughes (ed.), Cardiff, 1961.)

94. Three Immense Feasts that were in the Island of Britain:

One of them was the Feast which Caswallawn son of Beli made in London, where twenty thousand cattle were slain, and a hundred thousand sheep, and fifty thousand geese and capons, and of wild and domesticated birds more than anyone might number. (*G. Owain.*)

Was Arthur's Feast in Caerleon-on-Usk the second, and what Feast was the third? (M. Williams)

Tair gwledd anfeidrol. Caswallon's feast is referred to in the tract *Y Pedwar Brenin ar hugain a farnwyd yn gadarnaf*, ed. P. C. Bartrum, EC XII, pp. 157–94. The oldest text, in Ll. 28, is in the hand of Gutun Owain, and here (14.171) the triad is specifically referred to: *a honno vu un or tair Gwledd Anveidrol yn ynys Brydain.* Bartrum dates the composition of the tract to about the middle of the fifteenth century. He suggests (p. 190) that Moses Williams's reference to 'Gutun Owain' as his source for Caswallon's feast is merely an acknowledgement of the reference in Ll. 28, and that Moses Williams did not know of Gutun Owain's *cywydd,* since he was ignorant of the allusion to the third feast as that of Merwydd in Môn.

Moses Williams's reason for leaving this triad incomplete in Ll. 65 is difficult to understand, since he refers to Gutun Owain as his source for it, and therefore he was presumably familiar with the complete triad as given in a *cywydd* by Gutun Owain in praise of the hospitality of Dafydd, abbot of Llanegwestl:

Dy wleddav, rrif dail oeddynt
Trwy'r gost a wnai'r Trywyr gynt:
Arthur, a'r llall Kaswallon,
A'r trydydd, Merwydd y' Mon

Pab vn dwf, pawb yn d'ovyn,
Pedwerydd, Davydd, wyd ynn!
(GO no. XXIX.19–24.)

'Your feasts were numerous as the leaves, with the expenditure of the Three Men of former times: Arthur and Caswallon, and the third Merwydd of Môn. Of the stature of the Pope, with everyone soliciting you—you, Dafydd, make a fourth for us!'

The opulence of the feast of Merwydd is referred to elsewhere by the *cywyddwyr*; see GGl no. CXXIV.48, and indexes to GO, GTA, GLM no. XL.56–66, and further references idem, 443. Tudur Aled once groups the feast of Merwydd with that of *Caswallawn* (GTA no. VIII.75), and once with that of Arthur (no. CXLII.1); though in the first instance he lists also *swper Troea* (T. Gwynn Jones suggests that the reference is to an episode in *Dares Phrygius*, GTA II, 563) as another feast of proverbial lavishness. Dafydd Nanmor quotes the triad in a different form, in which Jesus feeding the multitudes takes the place of Merwydd:

Ef a borthes yr Iesu
A llai o wledd i holl lu.
Y wledd a gad yn adail
Llion ar Wysc, llyna'r ail;
A'r llall a wnaeth Caswallawn
Yn Nhre' Ludd yn reiol iawn.
Ugain mil o fwystfiledd
Yn feirw a las ban fu'r wledd.
(DN no. I.13–20.)

'Jesus fed his whole company with a lesser feast (than that of Rhys of Tywyn). The feast that was held in the hall of (Caer)leon on Usk was the second, and the other that which Caswallon made royally in London. Twenty thousand animals were slain when that feast took place.'

It seems then that this triad was known in various forms, but there is no evidence that in any of them it goes back to an earlier date than the fifteenth century. Vaughan unfortunately gives only a fragmentary version of the triad, which has not been reproduced by the *Myvyrian* editors. The evidence of the *cywyddau* shows that one well-established form persisted in including *gwledd Merwydd* along with the feasts of Arthur and Caswallawn. Merwydd can perhaps be identified from a reference in HGVK 19 (B), as an eleventh-century helper of Gruffudd ap Cynan. See further P. C. Bartrum WCD 475; EWGT 117 (9) under *Llwyth Gollwyn*. One must therefore conclude that the reference is based on some kind of oral tradition; and this is the more unexpected since the other feasts introduced into this triad are all derived from purely literary sources.

a. The immediate source for the account of the feast made by Caswallawn to celebrate his victory over Julius Caesar seems to be that described in *Drych y Prif Oesoedd*, though there are slight verbal differences between the two, and it is not clear why MW wrote *anfeidrol* while at the same time noting T. Evans's variant *anrhydeddus*: *ac fe ddywedir i ladd at y wledd fawr honno ugain mil o wartheg, deng mil a deugain o ddefaid, dau can mil o wyddau a Chapryned; ac o adar eraill gwylltion a dofion y dau cymmaint a'r a allai neb eu cyfrif neu traethu: A'r wledd hon a fu un o'r tair gwledd anrhydeddus Ynys Brydain.* (*Drych y Prif Oesoedd* by Theophilus Evans, I, ch. 2; first edition, 1716, p. 29; second edition ed. D. Thomas (1955), p. 24.)

Since Theophilus Evans follows this account by a quotation of Dafydd Nanmor's lines given above, it is clear that the *cywydd* is his source for stating that Caswallon's entertainment belonged to a triad of feasts. Thus it is not surprising to find that no version of *Brut y Brenhinedd* makes any reference to such a triad when giving the account of Caswallon's entertainment: cf. BD 49.23–8; RBB 87–8; *Br. Cleo.* 75. J. Jones, Gellilyfdy, alludes to the fame of this feast in a reference to Caswallon in his list of the twenty-four Strongest Kings: *Kyswallawn brawd Lludd a ymladdodd ag Ulkessar ymerodyr Rhufain ag a wnaeth y wledd fawr yn Llundain a ddiarhebir* (*Peniarth* 267, 208; see 'Y Pedwar Brenin ar hugain a farnwyd yn gadarnaf' ed. P. C. Bartrum, EC XII, p. 171).

b. The reference is to Arthur's coronation feast at Caerleon, which took place at Whitsun following his victories over the Picts and Scots (HRB IX, 12; BD 157; RBB 199).

In its full form this triad is quoted by Edward Jones, *Musical and Poetical Relicks of the Bards* (1794), 80: *Tair Gwledd Anrhydeddus Ynys Prydein: Gwledd Caswallon yn ôl gyrru Iwl Caesar o'r ynys hon; Gwledd Emrys Wledig ar ôl gorchvygu y Saeson; a Gwledd Arthur Vrenin yNghaer Lleon ar Wysg.* 'Three Honourable Feasts of the Island of Britain: the Feast of Caswallon after driving Julius Caesar out of this Island; the Feast of Emrys Wledig after conquering the Saxons; and the Feast of King Arthur in Caerleon on Usk.'

Llanstephan 65, fo. 89*v* (*Moses Williams's manuscript*)

95. Tri dyn y torres ei galon o Annifyged:

Branwen ferch Llyr,
a Charadog ab Bran,
a Ffaraon Dandde.

95. Three People whose heart broke from Sorrow:

Branwen daughter of Llŷr,
and Caradog son of Brân,
and Ffaraon Dandde.

95. Anniwyged, *punctum delens* beneath *w* with *u* above *w*, and *t* above *d*, MW.

---

annifyged, 'unexpectedness, bewilderment' (*an-* (neg.) + *di* + *myged*), according to GPC 141, following Ifor Williams's note on the Breton gloss *aandemecet* 'ex improviso', ZCP XXI, pp. 294–5. Cf. PKM 46.3–4: *a thorri ohonaw Gradawc y galon o aniuyget*. The other references to this triad are quoted in the n. to triad 13 *Tri Chynweissyat* above. These are the only instances of *annifyged* recorded in GPC 141. See also Brynley Roberts, *Brut y Brenhinedd*, pp. 35–6n. He cites *Enyvyget* as parallel in the text of the *Brut* to *amharch*, translating *miseriam*, and he suggests that 'sorrow, shame' would suit all the known examples in Welsh. Ifor Williams earlier proposed 'bewilderment' in view of the Breton gloss, but the word may have developed different shades of meaning in Breton from those in Welsh. The suggestion that the name of *Branwen* completed this triad in an earlier form than that given by Moses Williams, was in fact made by Ifor Williams in his edn of *Lludd and Llefelys*, p. 29.

Cardiff 36, p. 14

96. Tair Gwragedd a fu i Vrychan Vrycheiniog. Eu henwae oedd:

> Eurbrawst,
> a Rybrawst,
> a Pheresgri.

A'i blant ef sydd un or Tair Gwelygordd Saint Ynys Brydain, a'r ail yw Plant Cunedda Wledic, a'r drydedd Plant Kaw o Brydyn.

96. Three Wives whom Brychan Brycheiniog had. Their names were:

> Eurbrawst,
> and Rybrawst,
> and Peresgri.

And his Children are one of the Three Kindreds of Saints of the Island of Britain. The second is the Children of Cunedda Wledig, and the third is the Children of Caw of Pictland.

Manuscripts: C 36, MW, Pen. 131, p. 112, Pen. 127 (= RC L, p. 378), Rawl. B.466, Harl. 4181.

This triad appears in the sixteenth-century *Cognacio Brychan* (VSB 317, § 13; EWGT 17–19: see VSB introduction, xix–xx, on date): (*Brychan*) *copulavit sibi tres uxores successiue, quarum nomina sunt hec, Eurbraust, Rybraust, et Proestri, de quibus magnam sobolem procreauit*, etc. The older document concerning the progeny of Brychan, *De Situ Brecheniauc* (see n. to *Brychan* under Personal Names) gives the variant form *Praust* for the first wife, *Ribraust*, and *Proistri* (VSB 315 = EWGT 16 (14)). *Proestri* is thus to be preferred to *Peresgri* for the third name in the triad. The element *proest* (var. *prawst*?) seems to be a eulogistic epithet meaning perhaps something like 'worthy'; see PT 88. On the Brychan documents as a whole, see also Charles Thomas, *And Shall These Mute Stones Speak?*, ch. 9, 'The Brychan Documents', pp. 131–62.

d. For the *Tair Gwelygordd Saint Ynys Prydain* see triad 81, and cf. triad 70 *Tri Gwyn Dorllwyth* and n.

Cardiff 36, pp. 17–18 (Book of Sir Richard Wynn of Gwedir)

97. Llyma y tri lle y daliwyd Arglwyddiaeth Gwynedd o gogail. Nid amgen:

Un onaddunt yw Stradweul verch Gadvan ap Kynan ap Eudaf ap Caradoc ap Brân ap Llyr Llediaith. A'r Stradweul honno vy wraig i Goel (Hen) Godebog; mam Kenau ap Coel, a mam Dyfyr. Eraill a ddywaid mae Seradwen i gelwid hi verch Gynan ap Euddaf ap Caradoc.

Yr ail oedd Gwawl verch Goel (Hen) Godebog, mam Cynedda Wledig, gwraig Edyrn ap Padarn Beisrudd.

A'r drydedd vu Esyllt, verch Cynan Tindaethwy, mam Rodri Mawr, a gwraig Merfyn Vrych.

97. These are the three times when the lordship of Gwynedd was held by the Distaff (side):

One of them was Stradweul daughter of Cadfan ap Cynan ab Eudaf ap Caradog ap Brân ap Llyr Llediaith; and this Stradweul was wife of Coel Hen ('the Old') Godebog ('Protector'). She was the mother of Cenau ap Coel and the mother of Dyfyr. Others say that she was called Seradwen daughter of Cynan ab Eudaf ap Caradog.

The second was Gwawl daughter of Coel Godebog, mother of Cunedda Wledig and wife of Edyrn son of Padarn Peisrudd ('Red Tunic').

And the third was Esyllt daughter of Cynan Tindaethwy, mother of Rhodri Mawr and wife of Merfyn Vrych ('Freckled').

Manuscripts: C 36 (early eighteenth century), with variants from a number of manuscripts from the fifteenth and sixteenth centuries, listed by P. C. Bartrum, from EWGT 90–1 (17). See also B XVIII, p. 237: RWM II, 231. The triad is an interesting extension of material found in App. II (*Bonedd Gwŷr y Gogledd*) and it is worth recording for its direct assertion of the descent of the Gwynedd dynasty by the female line from Cunedda Wledig, and through him from Coel Hen, legendary progenitor of Urien Rheged and others of the 'Men of the North', on whom see WCD 136.

a. Ystradwel, Ystrawawl Pen. 131 (before 1547); Ll. 28 (Gutun Owain); Seradwen Pen. 127. verch Gadvan Pen. 127, etc. mam Ddyfr Ll. 28; Dyfferwr; Dyffrwr Pen. 131; Dyfr Pen. 75, 127, 129. See WCD 649.

b. verch Goel godebawg Pen. 182.

c. Esil C 25, Ethyll C 25, Essyll Pen. 127.

C 36 here gives a late copy of a triad which has been subsequently edited by P. C. Bartrum with genealogical notes and full *varia lecta* (B XVIII, p. 237; EWGT 90–1). As elsewhere in TYP, ancient legend in **a** and **b** is used to introduce and give emphasis to the assertion made in the third item of the triad concerning the claims of *Merfyn Vrych* to rule Gwynedd in right of his wife, or (more probably) of his mother, *Esyllt* or *Ethill*, daughter of Cynan

Dindaethwy (originally a representative of a minor ruling dynasty of Gwynedd). Two versions exist of the genealogy of Merfyn Frych, who ruled Gwynedd 825–44. If not the wife of Merfyn, Esyllt was the wife of Gwriad (see n. under Personal Names) from the Isle of Man and she was Merfyn's mother (for the two alternatives see B XIX, p. 218 = EWGT 151). The second alternative is now generally accepted as the more probable of the two. It is supported by Harleian Gen. I, and further strengthened by the discovery of the ninth-century memorial cross 'Crux Gwriad' on the Isle of Man, which allegedly commemorates Esyllt's husband Gwriad. (But Bartrum, B XVIII, regards either alternative as chronologically possible.) Merfyn Frych thus became the founder of the second Gwynedd dynasty through his mother Esyllt, a dynasty no longer represented in the direct male line of descent from Cunedda Wledig, as had traditionally been the case with all the previous rulers of Gwynedd. But whether wife or mother of Merfyn Frych, Esyllt's name became indissolubly linked to Gwynedd, for poets later commemorated Gwynedd as *tir Esyllt, brodir Esyllt. gwlad Esyllt* (B XXXIII, p. 116, cf. G 491). Merfyn's position seems to have been further strengthened by his marriage to Nest, daughter of Cadell, ruler of Powys.

a. Stradweul or *Ystradwel* is unknown elsewhere; *Gadvan* or *Gadeon* can be traced in the genealogies in EWGT. For Kynan (= *Cynan brawd Elen Luyddog*, or *Cynan Meiriadoc*), *Caradoc mab Brân Fendigaid*, and *Llŷr Llediaith* see nn. under Personal Names. For *Coel (Hen) Godebog*, progenitor of Urien Rheged and the other Coelings see n. and App. II below, WCD 136, and the genealogies which are listed in EWGT 148–51. *Divyr* may conceivably be identifiable with *Dyfyr Wallt Eureit* of triad 88 (see n.), who is celebrated by the *cywyddwyr* as a traditional paragon of beauty.

Kenau ap Coel. *Cenau* is here probably a collective 'progeny' (GPC 461) rather than a proper name; see PT no. VI.11n. and no. VIII.45n.

b. For **Gwawl** 'mother of the sons of Cunedda' see n. to *Arthur*, which lists *Gwawl* among Arthur's alleged maternal progenitors, through his mother Eigr. Other genealogical references to *Gwawl* include *Jes. Gen.* VII (EWGT 45 (7)) etc., see further references in WCD 308. *Edern* son of Padarn Peisrudd is listed in Harl. Gen. I (EWGT 9) among the ancestors of the Gwynedd dynasty. See further B. L. Jones, 'Gwriad's Heritage: Links between Wales and the Isle of Man in the Early Middle Ages', THSC 1990, pp. 29–44; D. P. Kirby, B XXVII, p. 97; P. Sims-Williams, WHR 17, pp. 20–6.

APPENDIX I

The text is based on that of *Llyfr Gwyn Rhydderch*, fo. 55*r* (RWM I, 324; *Cy.* VII, p. 124; RM col. 600) with additions supplied from Pen. 50, f. 149v (*Y Cwta Cyfarwydd*)

ENWEU YNYS BRYDEIN YW HYNN:
(see pp. c–civ above)

1. Kyntaf hen6 a uu ar yr Ynys Honn, kyn no'e chael na'e chyuanhedu: Clas Merdin. Ac 6edy y chaffel a'e chyuanhedu, Y Vel Ynys. Ac wedy y goresgyn o Brydein vab Aed Ma6r, y dodet arnei Ynys Brydein.

2. Teir Prif Rac Ynys yssyd idi, a Seith Rac Ynys ar ugeint (yssyd y danei. Sef ynt y teir rac ynys: Mon a Mana6 ac Ynys Weir). A Thri Prif Aber a Seith Ugeint adeni. A Ffedeir Prif Borth ar Dec a deugeint. A Their Prif Gaer ar Dec ar Ugeint, a Ffetwar Prif Anryued ar Dec ar Ugeint.

3. Sef y6 Hyt yr Ynys Hon: o Benryn Blat(h)aon ym Brydein hyt ym Penryn Penwaed yg Kerni6. Sef y6 hynny: na6 can milldir. Sef y6 y Llet, o Grugyll y Mon hyt yn Soram, pum can milldir y6 hynny.

4. Sef y dylyir y daly 6rthi: Coron a Their Taleith. Ac yn Llundein g6isga6 y Goron, ac ym Penryn Rionyt yn y Gogled vn o'r Taleithieu, ac yn Aberfra(6) yr eil, ac yg Kerni6 y dryded.

5. A Their Archesgobot yssyd yndi: Vn yMyny6, a'r eil yg Keint, a'r dryded yg Kaer Efra6c.

Pen. 50:

(6. Teir Ynys Prydein: Lloegyr a Chymry a'r Alban.

7. Ac nyt oes dlyet y neb ar (yr) Ynys Honn, namyn y genedyl Gymry ehun, Gweddillyon y Brutannyeit, y ddeuth gynt o Gaer Droea.

8. Teir Prif Auon Ynys Prydein: Temys, a Hafren, a H6myr.

9. Teir Prif Porthua Ynys Prydein: Porth Ys(g)ewin y Gwent, a Phorth Wygyr y Mon, a Phorth 6ytno yn y Gogledd.)

APPENDIX I

These are the Names of the Island of Britain

1. The first Name that this Island bore, before it was seized or occupied: Myrddin's Precinct. And after it was seized and occupied, the Island of Honey. And after it was conquered by Prydein son of Aedd the Great it was called the Island of Prydein (Britain).

2. Britain has Three Chief Adjacent Islands. and Twenty-seven (others) are subordinate to it. These are the Three Adjacent Islands: Anglesey, Man, and Wight. It has Three Chief Estuaries and Seven score subordinate (ones), and Forty-four Chief Ports, and Thirty-three Chief Cities, and Thirty-four Chief Marvels.

3. The Length of this Island, from the promontory of Blathaon in (Scotland) to the promontory of Penwith in Cornwall, is nine hundred miles. Its breadth from Crigyll in Anglesey to Sarre is five hundred miles.

4. There should be held therein a Crown and Three Coronets. The Crown should be worn in London, and one of the Coronets at Penrhyn Rhionydd in the North, the second at Aberffraw, and the third in Cornwall.

5. It has Three Archbishoprics: one at Mynyw, the second at Canterbury, and the third at York.

(6. Three Realms of Britain: England, Wales, and Scotland.

7. And no one has a right to this Island except only the nation of the Cymry, the remnant of the Britons, who came here formerly from Troy.

8. Three Chief Rivers of the Island of Britain: Thames, Severn, and Humber.

9. Three Chief Ports of the Island of Britain: Portskewet in Gwent, Porth Wygyr in Anglesey, and Porth Wyddno in the North.)

Manuscripts: WR, Pen. 50, 240, BL Addl. 31,055 (nos. 1–5 only), V, BL Addl. 14,873, Cwrt. 3 (two versions), Pa. 23, Ll. 12 (fragmentary) NLW Addl. 37[B], p. 93 (nos, 8, 9 only).

Title: *Enweu Ynys Prydein ae rac ynyssed ae anryuedodeu R.*

1. Tri enw yr ynys honn 50, ar ynys Brytain 240. Ynys brydain vawr y may wyth gan meilltir yn i hyd a day gant yni lled Ll. 12. Glas Merdin W, clas myrdin R, clas Merddin 240, BL kyntaf y gelwit kyn y chaffel clas mertyn 50. Ac wedy cael y chafanneddu y Vel Ynys y gelwyd BL, 50 *substitutes* o vrutus *for* o Brydein vab Aed, o vryt . . . ynys Bryt V; V *adds* mewn rhai llyfrei fal hynn, O Prydein mab Aedd Mawr . . . Ynys Prydein.

2. Sef ynt y Teir Rac Ynys: Mon, a Manaw, ac Ynys Weir *supplied from* R. Tair Rac ynys sydd iddi BL, a rugeint *altered in later hand to* a thrugeint W, a thrugeint ereill

yssydd iddi V. Ynys Weith 50, Cwrt. 2, Orc, Manaw, ac Ynys Weith V, Ynys Wair 240, BL, Ll12, Cwrt. 1. a their prif aber a deugeint a chant V, 143 o brif aberoedd BL. prif porth R, porthua 50, V, o brif borthvaoedd BL. ac wyth arugeint o brif Gaerydd . . . Rhai onaddynt sydd wedi eu diwreiddiaw yn wallus, ereill yn gyfan gyfannedd etto, V. o brif Gaeroedd BL. A phetwar prif anryvedd ar ddec 50, V.

3. hyd ynys Brydain BL. o benn blathaon ymrydein 50, o bryn Bladdon 240, BL. pymp kant milltir 50.

4. Sef y delir o honei 50. Ac hi a gynhelir tan un goron V. yn pennrhyn Rhianedd BL, 240, y dlyir un or taleithedigyon 50, o aberfraw, o gernyw 50, arall yn Aberffraw V.

5. archescoptuy BL. o Geint . . . o gaer efrawc . . . o vynyw 50. Un o lundein, yr ail o Gaer Efrawc ar drydedd o Gaer lleon ar Wysg V, *adds* llyfreu ereill fal hyn (*as* W). yn gaer Evrawc yn y gogled sef yw honno Yorc Pa. 23.

6–9 *supplied by* 50 (pp. 150–1).

6. *var.* Teir prif rann Ynys Prydein V.

7. o Caer Dro V.

8. Tri phrif Aber NLW Addl.

9. Porth Ystewin 50, Porth Yscewyn V. a phorth wegri y Mon Ll. 12, Porth Wegr NLW Addl. Ll. 12 *adds* tair pf. gaer ynys brydain. kaer lundein a chaer benwedd a chaer lliwn ar wysg. tair pf. lus ynys brydain. llys benwedd yng herniw a llys kaer lleon ar wysg a llys penryn Rianedd (*see triad* 85). NLW Addl. *adds* Tair prif Afon y Bŷd: Nŷdd, Llŷch ac Urddonen.

---

1. **kyn no'e chael.** *Cael* (W: *chaffel*) < **kab-*, Brit. variant of **ghabh-* 'gafael', Ir. *gabáil.* Cf. *Lebor Gabála Érenn*, 'The Book of the *Taking* of Ireland'. See introduction, p. ciii.

a'e chyuanhedu. Cf. WM 61.1–2 (PKM 48.6–7: *a gwledychu y wlat ay chyuanhedu*—after the destruction of the population of Ireland in the war between Brân and Matholwch).

Clas Merdin. W: *glas merdin*; but *gla(i)s* as substantive (= 'stream, valley') is feminine (see G 532), so that the proper name following it should be lenited. I therefore restore *Clas* (GPC 490), which is the reading of all the other manuscripts. *Clas* < L. *classis* means an enclosure ('precinct'?), and by extension 'people of the same country', cf. *a chlas guinet* LlDC no. 17.90; *o glas ffichti* BT 42.22; and Prydydd y Moch uses the word in this sense in addressing Llywelyn ab Iorwerth *wyt priavd tir prydein ae chlas* (H 281.9 = CBT V, no. 18.31). The most common meaning of *clas* in medieval sources is that of a monastic community or convent, and in this it has an equivalent in Ir. *class.*

Y Vel Ynys 'The Honey Island' (= Britain, GPC 2418). The construction is a close compound; all the manuscripts adhere to it, and allusions to *Y Vel Ynys* recur frequently in the poetry of the *cywyddwyr*. One would expect *Ynys Vel,* and this form actually occurs, BT 72.14–16: nur yth iolaf *veli amhanogan* . . . *Ynys vel veli,* teithiavc oed idi. This suggests that the name could have originated as a corruption of *Ynys Veli*, from the name of *Beli Mawr m. Mynogan* (see n.). *Breudwyt Maxen* alludes to the conquest of Britain by Maxen from Beli: *ac y gverescynnvys yr ynys ar Veli mab Manogan ae veibon* (WM 186.29–30). The following allusions to *Y Vel Ynys* are found in the later poetry:

> Gruffudd Gryg: *Haul y Fêl Ynys yw hon* (DGG no. LXXII.42).
> Dafydd Nanmor: *Rys o'r Vêl Ynys vlaenawr* (DN no. XI.1).
> Tudur Aled: *Yr iau flaen i'r Fêl Ynys* (GTA I, 116.68).
> To these may be added a number of allusion by Gutun Owain (GO no. XII.12; no. XLVII.51; no. LIII.46; no. LXVII.31).

2. The order of the items in no. 2 varies considerably between the version of WR and that of Pen. 50.

Teir Prif Rac Ynys. Cf. *Breudwyt Maxen*: *A hitheu a nodes ynys prydein yv that o vor rud hyt vor iwerdon. Ar teir rac ynys* (WM 187.15–18). Prydydd y Moch addresses Rhodri m. Owain Gwynedd: *O ynys brydein briawd ureint / ae their rac ynys rec hofeint* (H 271.7–8 = CBT V, no. 7.7–8). See also n. to no. 6 below. HB ch. 8 describes Britain as follows:

> It has three large islands. One of them lies towards Armorica, and is called the Isle of Wight; the second is situated in the middle of the sea between Ireland and Britain, and is named *Eubonia*, that is Man; the other is situated at the extreme edge of the world of Britain, beyond the Picts, and is called *Orc* (Orkney). So the old saying runs, when rulers and kings are mentioned 'He ruled Britain with its Three Islands'.

2. **Ynys Weir.** It is difficult to account for this name as referring to the Isle of Wight, in view of HB's *Inis Gweith* (Pen. 50: *Ynys Weith*). *Ynys Weir* was an old name for Lundy Island (see nn. to *Gweir m. Geiryoed* under Personal Names and to triad 52c), but it would be impossible to group Lundy with Anglesey and Man as a *rac ynys*. This would suggest that W and R may have some authority for giving *Ynys Weir* as a name for the Isle of Wight. According to VN[2]: 'The Britons of the last 500 years called it [Wight] *Ynys Weir*, that is the land of *Gwair*, a noble Briton sometime king thereof.' (See CF II, 679.) For references to the *teir rac ynys* see n. to no. 6 below.

A Thri Prif Aber. See no. 8 below. Gildas names only the Thames and the Severn: 'It has the benefit of the estuaries of a number of rivers , and especially two splendid rivers, the Thames and the Severn, arms of the sea along which luxuries from overseas used to be brought by ship.' (*Gildas*, ed. and trans. Winterbottom, ch. 3). It seems strange that he omits the Humber.

HB ch. 9 also names the two great rivers: 'In Britain there are many rivers, that flow in all directions—to the east, west, south and north. But two of the rivers excel beyond the rest, the Thames and the Severn, like the two arms of Britain, on which ships once travelled, carrying goods for the sake of commerce.'

Teir Prif Gaer ar Dec ar Ugeint. The 'Vatican' Recension of the *Historia Brittonum* (ed. D. N. Dumville, Woodbridge, 1985) gives the number of the Cities of Britain as thirty-three. This recension was made in England in 944, but according to Dumville (in personal correspondence) the thirty-three cities had already been reduced in number to twenty-eight in a Welsh revision made after 830. The names of the cities are listed in Pen. 50.

3. **hyt yr Ynys.** Gildas (ch. 3) gives the length of Britain as 800 miles (leaving out of account the various headlands that jut out just beyond the curving ocean bays) and the breadth as 200 miles. According to Hugh Williams (*Gildas*, 14 n.) these measurements are ultimately based on Orosius and Pliny, but with additions which may have been commonplace in Gaul and Britain (see S. Reckert, *The Matter of Britain and the Praise of Spain* (1967), p. 8). And Gildas does not name the place from which the measurements were taken. The same measurements were given in HB and by Bede (*Hist. Ecc.* 1, i), who is followed by Geoffrey of Monmouth (HRB I, 2; II, 17 = BD 2). (Bede adds that when the promontories are taken into account the distance around Britain is 3,600 miles.)

The *Kyfreith Dyfnwal Moelmut* ('Law of Dyfnwal Moelmut') ascribes the taking of the measurements of Britain as given in EYP to Geoffrey of Monmouth's legendary king and lawgiver *Dunwallo Molmutius filius clotenis regis cornubiae* (WKC 230; HRB II, 17 = BD 32.11: *Dyunywal Moel Mut mab Clydno tywyssavc Kernyw*). Cf. *Dywynwal Moel*, CO l. 254n.:

> Ew a uesurus yr ynys hon o Penryn Blathaon ym Prydein (var. Pryden = Scotland) hyt y Penryn Penwaed (var. in J: Penngwaed) y Kernyu, sew yu hynny naucan mylltyr: a hynny yu hyt yr ynys hon. ac o Grugyll y Mon hyt yn Soram yglan y Mor (Vd) pym cant mylltyr a hynny yu llet yr ynys hon. (AL I, 184. See also M. Richards, *Cyfreithiau Hywel Dda o Lawysgrif Coleg yr Iesu LVII* (1957), 119.)

For the land-measurements of Britain which are said here to have been inaugurated by the legendary *Dyfnwal Moelmut* see D. Jenkins, *Hywel Dda: The Law*, pp. 120, 268; WKC 229–32.

Kyfreith Dyfnwal Moelmut seems to draw on HRB for its description of Dyfnwal Moel Mut as *mab yarll Kernyw o uerch brenhyn Lloygyr*, but the place-names given in the passage quoted could not have been derived from HRB or the *Brut* and must come from EYP. According to HRB 17 (= BD 32–3), *Dunwallo Molmutius* gave to the roads of Britain the privilege of sanctuary; but HRB states that it was Dunwallo's son Belinus who made a stone highway from Cornwall to Caithness, linking the cities along its course, and another across Britain from Menevia (= Mynyw, St David's) to Southampton; together with two other transverse roads whose course is unspecified (HRB III, 5). It is possible from the places named that Geoffrey's account of the making of the road from the extreme south to the extreme north of Britain may be influenced by a knowledge of EYP (see introduction, p. ciii), although the names given to places at the extremities of his transverse roads do not correspond with those found in EYP; cf. however the measurements of Wales given by Giraldus Cambrensis (n. to item 9 below). The *Bruts* state that the vertical road was made *o Penryn Kernyv hyt yn traeth Cathneis* (BD 35, RBB 73; cf. *Br. Cleo.* 48: *o vor kernyv ar hyt yr ynys hyt y mor cattneis yn y gogled*).

Penryn Blat(h)aon ym Brydein. *Prydein* here, as frequently elsewhere, is a mistake for *Prydyn* 'Pictland, northern Scotland' (on the confusion between these two names see AP 21–2n. and see nn. to *Kulvanawyt Prydein* and *Caw o Brydyn* under Personal Names). It is uncertain which of the northern extremities of Scotland is here intended: probably John o' Groats or Duncansby Head in Caithness. B. F. Roberts identified *Penryn Blathaon* with Pentir Gafran in Caithness (LlC XIII, p. 280); CBT V, no. 1.112n. accepts this identification in a poem by Prydydd y Moch. John o' Groats is 860 miles from Land's End, so that in adding 100 miles to Gildas's 800 miles the compiler of EYP was not far out in his calculation. VN[2] has no specific suggestion to make as to the identification of *Penryn Blathaon*, except that it is somewhere in Caithness. Vaughan suggests that *Blathaon* is an old plural of *blaidd*, and that it means 'the promontory of wolves'. The following references to the place-name occur:

BT 70.21–2: *Gvlat uerv dyderuyd hyt valaon* (? = *vlathaon*, G 57) 'The country will be in turmoil as far as Blathaon'.

CO l. 261: *Drem mab Dremidyd a welei o gelli wic ygherniv hyt ym penn blathaon ym predein pan drychauei y gvydbedin y bore gan yr heul* 'Sight son of Seer who could see from Celliwig in Cornwall as far as Penn Blathaon in Scotland, at the time when a fly would rise in the morning with the sun'. On *Penn Blathaon* see CO l. 262 n.

Brut y Tywysogyon (Pen. 20 version, 59a) AD 1111–14: *ef a gynnullawd henri lu dros holl ynys brydein. o benryn penngwaed yng hernyw hyd ymhenryn blathaon ymhrydein a hynny yn duhun y gyd yn erbyn gwyr gwyned a phowys* 'Henry mustered a host from the whole of the Island of Britain, from Penryn Penngwaed in Cornwall to Penryn Blathaon in Scotland, and those (were) in unison together against the men of Gwynedd and Powys'. See also below under *Penryn Penwaed.*

For the western to eastern measurements of Britain see n. to *Echemeint/Echeifyeint*, triad 52 above.

Penryn Penwaed. This place can be identified with Penwith Point between Land's End and Mousehole; the name is preserved in that of the Hundred of Penwith. See B. F. Roberts, LlC XIII, pp. 278–81 for a discussion of the tract entitled *De longitudine et latitudine et prouinciis Anglie* in the thirteenth-century Exeter Cathedral Library MS.3514, ff. 58–60: *Hoc est mensura anglie.*

uel britannie in longitudine Dccc.miliaria. i. a penpenwith in cornubie qui locus distat.xv miliaris ultra montem sci.michaelis usque ketenesium litus. in pentir gauyran in scocia. in latitudine habet cc. miliaria. i de sco Dauid usquw at Doure. The interest of this is that, while enshrining learned concepts concerning the measurements of Britain which are similar to those found in EYP, it is apparent that these emanate from a south-western source; i.e. the form *penpenwith* is Cornish, in contrast to EYP's *Penryn Penwaed.* The Welsh termination *-(g)waed* in this name may be due to a misinterpretation of Old Cornish *guit* which meant both 'blood' (*gwaed*) and 'wood' (*gwŷdd*) But since it is unlikely that this bleak promontory can have been wooded at any time, the second element may be some other word, such as *gwydd* 'wild' or *gwedd* 'aspect'. The following allusion to *Penryn Penwaed* may be added to that given above:

CO ll. 105–7n.: *hyt na bo anghleuach ym penn pengvaed yg kernyw. Ac yg gwaelavt dinsol yny gogled* 'so that it (the hero's threatened shout) shall not be less audible at *Pen(ryn) Pen(g)waed* in Cornwall, and at the bottom of *Dinsol* in the North'.

Gwalchmai: *[An]gertavl uy march mavr ys proueis / (ky)frwg Pennwaed barth a Phorth Ge(meis)* (H 19.27–8 = CBT I, no. 9.97–8n.) 'Spirited my horse, and I greatly tested him, between the land of Penwaed and the port of Cemeis'.

Prydydd y Moch: *Priodavr Pennwaet pan gaffad ut ner* (H 256.29 = CBT V, no. 1.9n.); idem, *O Pennwaet Dyfneint . . . hyt pentir Gafran* (H 260.5–6 = CBT V, no.1.9n.).

In this last instance *Penwaed* in Dumnonia (i.e. the Cornish *Penwaed*) is evidently contrasted with a place in the extreme north, and thus it seems likely that *pentir gafran* is the equivalent of *Penryn Blathaon* (for *Gafran* see n. to *Aedan m. Gauran* under Personal Names). *Gafran* as a place-name occurs in Taliesin's eulogy for Gwallawg, PT no. XI.42.

Crugyll. The *Afon Crigyll* flows into the sea near Rhosneigr on the west coast of Anglesey, and gives its name to *Traeth Crigyll.* The reason for the choice of this place as that from which to take the westernmost measurement of Britain is obscure, since one would expect this to be taken from the extreme point of Caergybi (Holyhead). *Traeth Crigyll* is now a sheltered bay; can it originally have had importance as a landing place for light craft from Ireland? But no. 9 below names *Porth Wygyr* (Cemais) as the *prif porthfa* in Anglesey.

Soram. The place referred to is *Sarre*, opposite the Island of Thanet in Kent. This must have been at one time an important port of embarkation for France; cf. W. Lambard, *A Perambulation of Kent* (1596), 97: 'and there be apparent markes that Sarre (where they now go over) was a proper hauen'. VN[1] identifies *Soram* with the Kentish river *Stowre*, which divides Thanet from the mainland, but *Sarre* suits better both with the context and with the form of the name. The passage quoted above from the Laws refers to *Soram yglan y Mor Vd* 'S. upon the shore of the North Sea'. *Mor Udd* means the North Sea, but it apparently included the English Channel: it is frequently contrasted with *mor Iwerdon*, as in H 266.3: *o uor ut hyt uor iwerdon* 'from the North Sea to the Irish Sea', and in the passage from *Breudwyt Maxen* quoted in n. to item 2 above.

Soram in this passage should not be confused with the *auon Soram* referred to in BD 26.12, which denotes the River Soar in Leicestershire, beside which Llŷr built his city of Leicester. (The form here is based on the Latin accusative, cf. HRB II, 11: *super flumen Soram.*) Neither Leicester nor the River Soar could possibly be the place selected in EYP as the point from which to take the south-easternmost measurement of Britain. The distance here given of 500 miles from Anglesey to Sarre is very far from the actual measurement—Holyhead to Maidstone is only 296 miles.

4–5. Cf. triad no. 1 and n. 6 and cf. introduction, p. xci.

4–5. **Ac yn Llundein g6isga6 y Goron.** Cf. the much discussed description of *Bendigeitfran* as *ardyrchawc o goron lundein* (PKM 29)—possibly a reflection of the redactor's knowledge of EYP. Yet the remainder of the story of *Branwen* reiterates the prominence of Aberffraw as the Gwynedd capital.

Penryn Rionyt yn y Gogled. Cf. TYP no. 1 and n. on **c**; cf. also introduction, p. xci.

Aberfra(6). The chief centre of the kings of Gwynedd, in south-west Anglesey; see HW 231, 682n. Llywelyn the Great described himself as *Tywysog Aberffraw ac Arglwydd Eryri.* Cf. also the description by Gruffudd ab yr Ynad Coch of Llywelyn ab Iorwerth as *brenhin, derwin dor Aberffraw* (RBP col. 1417.2 = CBT VII, no. 36.2n.).

yg Kerni6, i.e. at *Kelli Wic*; see n. to TYP no. 1 and CO 1. 261n.

5. For **Mynyw** see introduction p. xc, and n. to triad 1 above. See further R. R. Davies, *Conquest, Co-existence and Change*, pp. 190–1. The emphasis which I laid in the earlier editions on the reference to *Mynyw* in EYP as indicative of the date of this tract should now be modified in the light of the above, and also of T. M. Charles-Edwards's discussion 'The Seven Bishop-Houses of Dyfed', B XXIV, pp. 247–62. The claim of *Mynyw* to be the leading church in Wales was already advanced in some quarters by the tenth century (as is reflected in the poem *Armes Prydein*), even though the primacy of the see lacked all basis in fact. The names in EYP appear to be older than the twelfth century, and the reference to *Mynyw* as one of the three archbishoprics in Britain reflects a controversy which was at its height during the latter half of the twelfth century.

6. **Teir Ynys Prydein.** On this phrase see Thomas Jones, B XVII, pp. 268–9. *Ynys* is here used in its derived meaning of 'realm' and is employed as parallel to L. *regnum* in the triad on the Welsh Inundations, ed. T. Jones, B XII pp. 79–83; (see introduction pp. lxxiv–lxxv above): *Istum regnum uocabatur tunc Heneys Teithy Hen.* The *Teir Ynys Prydein a'i Their Rac Ynys* are alluded to three times in *Culhwch ac Olwen* (CO ll. 282 and n.; ll. 1057–8). Thomas Jones points out that *ynys* is used to translate L. *regnum* in several instances in *Brenhinedd y Saeson* and elsewhere in sixteenth-century instances, where it translates English 'realme'. He also compares *tria regna Britanniae* in Caradog of Llancarfan's *Life of Gildas* (ed. H. Williams, 396). For further instances of *ynys* = 'region, territory' cf. LlDC no. 22.20: *Teir rac ynis. ar teir inis. ar tramordvy*. Yet since the triad does not appear in EYP in the texts of W or R, it seems most likely that the scribe of Pen. 50 based his allusion to the *Teir Ynys* on his recollection of the phrase in *Culhwch.*

6. **Lloegyr**. This may have been originally the name for Mercia, the middle (English) kingdom; see *Armes Prydein* l. 109 and n. AP 50–1 for early suggestions as to the derivation. In B XXIII, pp. 26–7, K. Jackson concluded that 'the etymology of *Lloegr* is still to seek', but in CMCS 4, pp. 83–5, E. P. Hamp advocated the meaning as 'having a nearby border, being from near the border' (as opposed to 'Welsh' which for the English denoted 'foreigners', 'people from across the border'). V quotes this triad as it is given in Pen. 50, but the *Myvyrian* editors suppressed *Teir Ynys Prydein* in favour of the variant which V himself supplied; *Teir Prif Rann Ynys Prydein* 'Three Chief parts of the Island of Britain'.

7. This passage has a close verbal counterpart in BD 2.29–30 *Ac o'r rei hynny nyd dyluedavc neb arnei namyn y Brytannyeyt* etc.; see n. to *Gormes*, triad 36.

8. Cf. HRB I, 2 (= BD 2.16–17): '(Britain) has three noble rivers, the Thames, the Severn, and the Humber and these it stretches out as though they were three arms.'

9. **Porth Ys(g)ewin y Gwent.** i.e. Portskewett, Monmouthshire; for references see CBT I, no. 3.56n.; II, no. 6.50n.; no. 25.49n.; VI, no. 25.3n. For Gwent see n. to *Aber Tarogi*, triad 26c. The following references are found in poetry:

Moliant Cadwallawn: *peuyr Porth Ysgewin kyffin aber* (B VII, p. 25, l. 43; for *Porth Ysgewin* see AW 45).

Meilyr (of Gr. ap Cynan): *can gerteu kyhoet oet arderchavc / o ysgewin barth hyd borth euravc* (H 2.27–8 = CBT I, no. 3.56n.) 'he was honoured in songs well-known from the land of Ysgewin to the gate of York'.

Hywel ab Owain Gwynedd: *o byrth kaer hyd borth ysgewin* (H 317.8 = CBT II, no. 6.50n.) 'from the gates of Chester to the harbour of Ysgewin (Ysgewydd)'.

Dafydd Benfras to Llywelyn ab Iorwerth: *Llywiadwr berth hyd borth ysgewin* (CBT VI, no. 25.31).

Porth Wygyr y Mon. The *Afon Wygyr* flows into the sea in the bay of Cemais, in north-west Anglesey. The following early references to *Porth Wygyr* occur:

BT 73.13–15: *Ys trabludyo y gath vreith ae hagyfieithon / o ryt ar taradyr hyt ym porth vygyr y mon* 'The speckled cat will make havoc with its enemies, from the ford of Taradyr to Porth Wygyr in Môn'.

Gwynfardd Brycheiniog (to Arglwydd Rhys): *Am hyfryd kymryd kymry benn baladyr / am aber tarady yn tremynu / Am byrth ysgewin yn goresgynnu / am borth wygyr y mon yn menestru* (H 207.29–32 = CBT II, no. 25.50n.) 'For the fortunate one's taking possession of the whole of Wales, roving around Aber Taradr, conquering around Porth Ysgewin, entertaining around Porth Wygyr in Môn.'

Gwalchmai: *Bid ewynavc tonn tu porth wygyr* 'Foaming is the wave beside Porth Wygyr' (H 19.21 = CBT I, no. 9.91n.).

Bleddyn Fardd (to Llywelyn fab Gruffudd): *gvr oet arbennic bennaf o uilwyr / hyd ym porth wygyr eryr araf* 'A man who was supreme chief of warriors, as far as Porth Wygyr, a courteous eagle (= lord)' (H 58.25–6 = CBT VII, no. 50.36n.).

Llywelyn Fardd addresses Owain Gwynedd as *eryr porth Wygyr* 'eagle of Porth Wygyr' (H 224.8 =CBT II, no. 2.52n.).

Giraldus Cambrensis (*Itin. Cam.* I, i, ed. Dimock, Rolls series, p. 165) gives the name *portus Yoiger* (var. *Horger*, *Gordber*) *in Monia* as the place from which he cites the longitudinal measurement of Wales; it is eight days' journey from there to *portus Eskewin in Winta* (i.e. *Porth Ysgewin yng nGwent*). *Portus Yoiger* is evidently a corrupt form of the name *Porth* (*G*)*wygyr* (trans. L. Thorpe, p. 220). In addition, Giraldus gives the transverse measurement of the country as four days' journey from *Porthmaur Meneviae* (= St David's); cf. Geoffrey's transverse road, n. to item 3 above, to *Ridhelic* (= *Rhyd Helyg*, English *Walford* (trans. Thorpe, p. 220, n. 474).

Porth 6ytno yn y Gogledd. Perhaps the Solway estuary? See n. to *G6ydno Garanhir* under Personal Names. The only reference to *Porth* (*G*)*wyddno* that I have discovered is that by Phylip Brydydd, and this is most probably to be interpreted as a reference to *Porth Wyddno yng Ngheredigion*, the old name for *Y Borth*, near Aberystwyth: *gorwerd tonn tued porth gwydno* 'very green the wave on the shore of Porth Wyddno' (H 225.15 = CBT VI, no. 11.15n.); see Chw. T. 6.

APPENDIX II

Pen. 45, 291–2
(pp. civ–cvi below)
BONHED GWYR Y GOGLED YW HYN:

('This is the Descent of the Men of the North:')

1. Vryen uab Kynuarch m. Meircha6n m. Gorust Letl6m m. Keneu m. Coel.

2. Llywarch Hen m. Elidyr Lydanwyn m. Meircha6n m. Gorust Ledl6m m. Keneu m. Coel.

3. Clydno Eidin. A Chynan Genhir. a Chynuelyn Dr6sgyl. A Chatrawt Calchuynyd. meibon Kynn6yt Kynn6ydyon m. Kynuelyn m. Arthwys m. Mar m. Keneu m. Coel.

4. Duna6t. a Cherwyd. a Sawyl Pen Uchel. meibyon Pabo Post Prydein m. Arthwys m. Mar m. Keneu m. Coel.

5. G6rgi a Pheredur meibon Eliffer Gosgordua6r. m. Arthwys (m. Mar) m. Keneu m. Coel.

6. Gwendoleu. a Nud. a Chof. meibyon Keidya6 m. Arthwys m. Mar m. Keneu m. Coel.

7. Trychan cledyf Kynuerchyn. a thrychan ysg6yt Kynn6(y)dyon. A thrycha(n) wayw Coeling: pa neges bynhac yd elynt iddi yn duun. nyt amethei hon honno.
('The three hundred swords of the (tribe of) Cynfarch, and the three hundred shields of the (tribe of) Cynwydion, and the three hundred spears of the (tribe of) Coel: on whatever expedition they might go in unison, they would never fail.')

8. Ryderch Hael m. Tutwal Tutclyt m. Kedic m. Dyuynwal Hen.

9. Mordaf m. Seruan m. Kedic m. Dyfnywal Hen.

10. Elffin m. G6ydno m. Ca6rdaf m. Garmonya6n m. Dyfynwal Hen.

11. Gauran m. Aedan Uradawc m. Dyuynwal Hen m. Idnyuet m. Maxen Wledic Amherawdyr Ruuein.

12. Elidyr M6yna6r m. Gorust Prioda6r m. Dyfynwal Hen.

13. Huallu m. Tutu6lch Cor(n)eu tywyssa6c o Kerny6. A Dywanw merch Amla6t Wledic y uam.

5. *Manuscript omits* m. Mar (*see nos.* 4, 6).
6. *Manuscript* llawfrodded.
7. Kynnwdyon. a thrycha wayv.
13. Corueu.

(A revised version of *Bonedd Bonedd Gwŷr y Gogledd* was published by P. C. Bartrum in 1966 (EWGT 72–4) and therefore after the first appearance of this book in 1961. In his edition he included a few variants of the text from later manuscripts. I have profited from his edition and from his notes to the text. See further M. Miller, 'The Lineages of the Northcountrymen', B XXVI, pp. 256–7; D. P. Kirby, B XXVII, pp. 93–4. For the general background to the pedigrees see Ifor Williams, 'Wales and the North', BWP ch. VI.)

1. **Gorust Letl6m** 'G. Half-Bare'. Cf. *Gorgwst Letlwm (*CO l. 993n.). On this and other names here cited which are of North-British origin see K. Jackson, YB XII (1982), pp. 12–22. For *Gorust / Gwrgust Ledlwm* (ancestor of Urien Rheged) see Harl. Gens nos. 8 and 12 (EWGT 10–12).

7. The possible significance of this entry is discussed by Jenny Rowland, EWSP 93–5. A late variant of BGG from Cardiff MS. 36 (see *Rep.* II, 231) supplies the following expanded version of this triad: 'from a manuscript of Sir Richard Wynne of Gwydr, with variants in the hand of Guttun Owen':

> Plant Meirchion ap Gorwst Ledlwm: Kenvarch ap Meirchiawn ap Gorwst ap Kenau ap Koel, a hwnnw a elwyd Meirchiawn Gŷl ap Gorwst Ledlwm. Ac o achos Kenvarch ap Meirchiawn i gelwid hwynt Trychan Kleddyf Kenverchyn. Ag o Gynwyd Kynwydion i doethant trychant ysgwyd Kynwydion. Ac o Koel i gelwyd wynteu Trychant Gwaew Colin. Pa negis bynnac idd elynt iddi yn ûn, ni vethai ragddynt.

13. For **Amlawdd / Anlawd Wledig** and his numerous daughters see CO l. 2 and n. *Huallu* and *Tudfwlch Cor(n)eu* are both equally unknown.

APPENDIX III

Cardiff 17, 95–6;
(in hand of Rowland Lewis o Fallwyd; see *Nat. Lib. of Wales Journal* IX, pp. 495–6.)

(see pp. cvi–cx above)

Tri Thlws ar Ddeg Ynys Brydain

(Henwae y) Tri Thlws ar Ddeg Ynis Brydain (a oedd yn y Gogledd):

1. Dyrnwyn, gleddyf Rhydderch Hael: os tynnai ddyn mwyn ef i hun, ef a ennynai yn y fflam o'i groes hyd i flaen; a ffawb o'r a'i harchai ef a'i kaei, ag o blygid y gyneddf honno, hwy a'i gwrthodynt; ag am hyn(n)u i gelwyd ef Rhydderch Hael.

2. Mwys Gwyddno Garanir: bwyd i un gwr a roid ynddo, a bwyd i ganwr a gaid ynddo pan agoryd.

3. Korn Bran Galed (o'r Gogledd): y ddiod a ddymunid i bod ynddo a gaid ynddo.

4. Kar Morgan Mwynfa(w)r: od ai ddyn ynddo, damunau fod lly mynai, ag ef a fyddai yn ebrwydd.

5. Kebystr Klydno Eiddun, a oedd mewn ystwffwl is draed i welü; a damunai y march a fynai yno, ef a'i kae(i) (yn y kebystr).

6. Kyllell Llawrfrodedd Farchog, yr honn a w(a)s(a)naethai i bedwar gwr ar higain i fwyta ar fwrdd.

7. Pair (Dyrnwch Gawr): pe rhoid ynddo gig i wr llwfwr i ferwi, ni ferwai fyth; o rhoid iddo gig i wr dewr, berwi a wnai yn ebrwydd (ag yno y caid gwahan rhwng y dewr a'r llwrf).

8. (H)ogalen Tudwal Tutklud: a hogai wr dewr i gleddyf arni, od enwaedai ar wr, marw fyddai; ag os hogai wr llwfr, ni byddai waeth.

9. Pais Badarn Beisrüdd: os gwisgai wr bonheddig, kymhessür fyddai iddo, ag os iangwr, nid ai amdano.

10, 11. Gren a desgyl Rhygenydd Ysgolhaig: dymunyd ynddynt y bwyd a fynyd, ef a'i kaid.

12. Gwyddbw(y)ll Gwenddoleu (ap Ceidio): o gosodid y werin, hwynt a chw(a)raen(t) i hunain: aur oedd y klawr, ag arian oedd y gwŷr.

13. Llen Arthür (yng Nghernyw): a fai deni, nis gwelai neb ef, ag ef a welai bawb.

(*Pen.* 77:

[14. Mantell Degau Eurvron: ni wasanaethai i'r neb a dorrai i ffriodas na'i morwyndod; ac y'r neb y byddai lân y'w gwr, y byddai hyd y llawr, ac i'r neb a dorrai i ffriodas ni ddoe hyd i harffed, ac am hyny'r oedd cenvigen wrth Degau Eurvron.]

[15. Maen a Modrwy Eluned ddedwyd, a roes i dynnu Ywain ap Urien (a) oedd rhwng yr ôg a'r porth, yn ymryson a'r Marchog Dû o'r ffynnon, yr hon oedd a maen ynddi, ac o chuddid y maen ni weled mo'r neb a'i cuddiai.])

The Thirteen Treasures of the Island of Britain

(The Names of the Thirteen Treasures of the Island of Britain, which were in the North):

1. Dyrnwyn ('White-Hilt'), the Sword of Rhydderch the Generous: if a well-born man drew it himself, it burst into flame from its hilt to its tip. And everyone who used to ask for it would receive it; but because of this peculiarity everyone used to reject it. And therefore he was called Rhydderch the Generous.

2. The Hamper of Gwyddno Long-Shank: food for one man would be put in it, and when it was opened, food for a hundred men would be found in it.

3. The Horn of Brân the Niggard from the North: whatever drink might be wished for was found in it.

4. The Chariot of Morgan the Wealthy: if a man went in it, he might wish to be wherever he would, and he would be there quickly.

5. The Halter of Clydno Eiddyn, which was fixed to a staple at the foot of his bed: whatever horse he might wish for, he would find in the halter.

6. The Knife of Llawfrodedd the Horseman, which would serve for twenty-four men to eat at table.

7. The Cauldron of Dyrnwch the Giant: if meat for a coward were put in it to boil, it would never boil; but if meat for a brave man were put in it,

it would boil quickly (and thus the brave could be distinguished from the cowardly).

8. The Whetstone of Tudwal Tudglyd: if a brave man sharpened his sword on it, if he (then) drew blood from a man, he would die. If a cowardly man (sharpened his sword on it), he (his opponent) would be no worse.

9. The Coat of Padarn Red-Coat: if a well-born man put it on, it would be the right size for him; if a churl, it would not go upon him.

10, 11. The Vat and the Dish of Rhygenydd the Cleric: whatever food might be wished for in them, it would be found.

12. The Chessboard of Gwenddolau son of Ceidio: if the pieces were set, they would play by themselves. The board was of gold, and the men of silver.

13. The Mantle of Arthur in Cornwall: whoever was under it could not be seen, and he could see everyone.

(14. The Mantle of Tegau Gold-Breast: it would not serve for any (woman) who had violated her marriage or her virginity. And for whoever was faithful to her husband it would reach to the ground, and for whoever had violated her marriage it only reached to her lap. And therefore there was jealousy towards Tegau Gold-Breast.)

(15. The Stone and Ring of Eluned the Fortunate, which she gave to save Owain son of Urien, who was between the portcullis and the gate, in the contest with the Black Knight of the Fountain: it had a stone in it, and if the stone were hidden, the person who hid it was not seen at all.)

Manuscripts which have been compared: Pen. 51, 60, 77, 138, 179, 295, C 17, C 19, C 26, C 43, Ll. 94, Ll. 145, NLW 5269B, Pa. 13, BL Addl. 14,873, Mostyn 159, E. Jones, *Bardic Museum* (London, 1808), pp. 47 ff.; *Y Brython*, 1860, p. 372; Pen. 216; Guest, *Mabinogion* (1849), II, pp. 353–4 (= G); BL Addl. 14,919, fo. 128b (= Addl. 1); BL Addl 15,020, fo. 34a–35a (= Addl. 2); BL Addl. 15,047, fo. 98a–101a (= Addl. 3); BL Addl. 15,059, fo. 228b–229b.

---

2. **Mwys Gwyddno Garanir.** On *mwys* < L. *mensa* see CLlH 129. D: *mwys bara* = *panarium, cist neu fasged fara.* This is the oldest item in *Y Tri Thlws ar Ddeg* for which there is documentary authority. For Gwyddno's *mwys* as one of the *anoethau* see CO ll. 618–20; and n. to *G6ydno Garanhir* under Personal Names, also introduction p. cviii above. This food-producing hamper should be compared with the magically productive salmon-weir which Gwyddno is

represented as owning in the *Chwedl Taliesin.* For Tudur Aled's reference to Gwyddno's *mwys*, see n. to nos. 10–11 below.

3. **Korn Bran Galed.** A story relating to *Brân Galed* (see n.) was known to Guto'r Glyn: a reference which is approximately contemporary (mid fifteenth century) with the earliest list of *Y Tri Thlws ar Ddeg* in Pen. 51. The following account of Brân's Horn appears among the contemporary *marginalia* in Pen. 147 (written *circa* 1566); see *Rep.* I, 911:

> Corn bran galed oedd vn or tri thlws ar ddeg o vrenin-dlysse ynys brydain / ag yno dayth myrddin y erchi y tlysse hyny at bawb lle ydd oyddynt. Ag y Cytynoedd pawb os efe gaffe gorn bran galed y Cae gantyn hwyntey / dan dybied nachae ef ddim or Corn / ag er hyny fo gafas myrddin y Corn ag wedy hyny vo gafas y Cwbwl ag aeth ag hwy yr ty gwydr ag yn hwy byth mwy [*sic*].
>
> Corn bran galed a gafas erculys ar ben saint tawrys gwedy y ladd / ag yno y gwlychoedd gwraic saint tawrys grys erculys yngwaed saint tawrys a ffan gwisgoedd erculys y Cris ny allwyd byth y dyny o am dano nes yr Cris y vwytta y Cic ar Croen hyd yr esgyrn a lladd erculys yn varw.
>
> 'The Horn of Brân the Niggard was one of the Thirteen Royal Treasures of the Island of Britain. And Myrddin came there to ask for those treasures of everyone who had them; and everyone agreed that if he should obtain the Horn of Brân the Niggard he should obtain theirs from them, supposing that he would never get the Horn. And nevertheless Myrddin obtained the Horn, and after that he obtained them all, and went with them to the Glass House, and they (i.e. the Treasures) remain there for ever.'
>
> 'Hercules obtained the Horn of Brân the Niggard from the head of the centaur after he was slain. And then the wife of the centaur wetted Hercules' shirt in the blood of the centaur, and when Hercules had put on the shirt it was not possible ever to take it off from him until the shirt had eaten his flesh and skin to the bone, and Hercules was slain.'

The first anecdote aptly illustrates the significance of Brân's epithet *caled* 'stingy, niggardly' (see GPC 392). On *Brân Galed* see further Glyn E. Jones, B XXV, pp. 105–12.

Gerard Murphy cites parallels in Irish folk-tales for a magical bull's horn which had the power of supplying whatever meat or drink was desired (*Duanaire Finn* III, (ITS, 1953), p. 193).

6. **Llawfrodedd Farchog.** 'Ll. the Horseman.' *Barvawc* 'the Bearded' is the epithet of *Llawfrodedd* elsewhere (see CO n. to l. 223), but since only three manuscripts of *Y Tri Thlws ar Ddeg* give *farfawc* in place of *farchog* I have not felt justified in making the emendation here. The reading of the MS. is *llawfrodded.*

7. **Pair (Dyrnwch Gawr).** R. S. Loomis first called attention (WAL 156–7) to the similar characteristics possessed by the *peir pen annwfyn . . . ny beirw bwyt llwfr* 'the Cauldron of the Head of Annwfn it does not boil the food of a coward' (BT 55.2–3; see M. Haycock, SC XVIII/XIX, p. 69). But the *pair Dyrnwch Gawr* evidently has its origin in the cauldron specified (without characteristics) among the *anoetheu* in *Culhwch: Peir divrnach Vydel maer odgar mab aed brenhin iwerdon* (CO l. 635n.) 'The Cauldron of Diwrnach the Irishman, son of Odgar mab Aedd, king of Ireland'. By the fifteenth century *Diwrnach* had become the giant *Dyrnwch*, *Dyrnog*, etc. See further P. Sims-Williams, B XXIX, pp. 663–4. The reading of the MS. is *Tyrnig*.

10–11. **Gren a desgyl.** Tudur Aled refers to these and others of the Thirteen Treasures in an *awdl* to Robert Salesbury:

A rhoi, i'w gynnal, dlysau Rhagennydd,
I Ren a'i Ddysgl, a'u rhannau i'w ddysglydd;
A rhoi Pair Tyrnog i'r côg a'r cigydd,
A Chorn Brân Galed, trai yfed trefydd,
A Mwys Gwyddno lwys, luosydd—gwindai,
A phrin yn i dai o pharhaen un dydd!
(GTA I, no. IV.95–100.)

'And give, for his support, the Treasures of Rh(y)genydd; his Vat and his Dish and their portions to his Dish-Bearer, and give the Cauldron of Tyrnog [*sic*] to the Cook and the Butcher, and the Horn of Brân the Miser (ebb of the drink of townships), and the fair Hamper of Gwyddno—hosts, wine-houses—and scarcely in his halls would they last a single day.'

12. **Gwyddbw(y)ll Gwenddoleu.** *Gwyddbwyll* = Ir. *fidchell,* lit. 'wood-sense', a game frequently mentioned in Irish and Welsh tales. The fact that the game is denoted by an identical compound in both Welsh and Irish proves that its name is of extreme antiquity. For some references to *fidchell : gwyddbwyll* in both Irish and Welsh sources see Melville Richards, *Breudwyt Ronabwy*, 50. For discussions as to the nature of this and other board-games referred to in Celtic literary sources see E. Mac White, 'Early Irish Board-Games', *Éigse*: *A Journal of Irish Studies*, V, 25 ff.; F. Lewis, 'Gwerin Ffristial a Thawlbwrdd', THSC 1941, pp. 185ff. *Gwyddbwyll* has been loosely, and it appears erroneously, identified with chess, which was not known in Europe before the twelfth century. The only resemblance seems to be that like chess it was played on a board with 'men', and the word *gwyddbwyll* is used to denote both the game itself and the board on which it was played. The *chwedlau* make several references to gold and silver chessboards like that of Gwenddolau. In *Breudwyt Ronabwy* Arthur and Owain play *gwyddbwyll* with gold pieces on a silver board (*gverin eur. a clavr aryant*, RM 153.7–8 = Br. Rh. 11.27–9). Equally lavish boards were to be seen at the court of Eudaf in *Breudwyt Maxen*, where the emperor saw *deu vaccwy wineuon ieueinc yn*

gvare gvydbvyll. clavr aryant a welei yr vydbvyll. a gverin eur arnei (WM 181.2–5, later *clavr o eur*, l. 23). It was Eudaf's own occupation to carve the men to play on his golden board (ibid., l. 25). A magic *gwyddbwyll* similar to that of Gwenddolau, on which the pieces played of their own accord, is described in *Peredur*:

> A phorth y gaer oed agoret. A phan doeth tu ar neuad, y drws oed agoret. Ac val y deuth ymywn, gvyddbvyll a welei yny neuad. A phop vn or dvy werin yn gvare yn erbyn y gilyd. Ar vn y bydei borth ef idi a gollei y gvare. Ar llall a dodei avr yn vn wed a phe bydynt gvyr. Sef a wnaeth ynteu, digyav a chymryt y werin yny arfet a thaflu y clavr y llyn. (WM 174.34–175.5)

> 'And the gate of the castle was open. And when he came to the hall, the door was open. And as he came inside, he could see *gwyddbwyll* in the hall, and each of the two sets playing against the other. And the one he would support lost the game, and the other set up a shout just as though they were men. He grew angry, and caught up the pieces in his lap, and threw the board into the lake.'

A magic chessboard similar to this appears in more than one of the Continental versions of the Grail story, but in each of these versions it is the hero himself who plays the pieces on one side, and it is only the pieces on the side opposed to him which move automatically. The French versions of the incident, as well as that in *Peredur*, have been usually regarded as having a common source in the Chessboard Castle incident in the Second Continuation of Chrétien's *Conte del Graal* (ed. Potvin, ll. 22, 395 ff.); see EAR I, 302, n. 17; Weinberg, 'The Magic Chessboard in the *Perlesvaus*', PMLA L, pp. 25–35. Yet if this is so it is remarkable that the version of *Peredur* should agree with *Y Tri Thlws ar Ddeg*, against all the French versions of the incident, in depicting the *gwerin* on both sides in the magic game of *gwyddbwyll* as being self-propelled. It is more natural to suppose that the redactor of the Welsh tale had knowledge derived from native sources of a magic chessboard similar to that of Gwenddolau.

In his article on Welsh board-games cited above, F. Lewis refers to *tawlbwrdd* and *tabler*. These names occur as variants of *gwyddbwyll* in certain manuscripts of *Y Tri Thlws ar Ddeg.* The manuscripts which substitute *tabler* provide evidence that this was a game played by casting dice, though it is only the latest texts which allude to dice in connection with *gwyddbwyll* (see v.l.).

13. **Llen Arthur.** I have supplied *yng Nghernyw*, since this is the reading of the majority of manuscripts. In *Culhwch* Arthur includes his mantle in the list of his precious possessions: *ti a geffy kyfarvs a notto dy benn ath tauavd . . . eithyr vy llong, am llenn, a Chaletvulch uyg cledyf, a Rongomyant uyg gvaev, ac Wyneb Gvrth ucher uy yscvyt. a Charnwenhan uyg kyllell. a Gvenhvyuar vyg gvreic* (WM 459.26–37 = CO ll. 156–62). 'Thou shalt obtain the boon thy head and thy tongue shall name . . . except for my ship, and my mantle, and

Caledfwlch my sword, and Rongomyant my spear, and Wynebgwrthucher my shield, and Carnwennan my dagger, and Gwenhwyfar my wife.' But the description of the magic properties of Arthur's mantle found in *Y Tri Thlws ar Ddeg* is evidently inspired by that of Arthur's mantle *Gwenn* ('Fair') in *Breudwyt Ronabwy*:

> A disgyn a oruc y gvas coch mavr rac bron arthur. a thynnu kadeir eur or swmer a llenn o pali kaeravc. A thanu y llenn a oruc rac bronn arthur. Ac (a)ual rudeur vrth bop koghyl idi. a gossot y gadeir ar y llenn. . . . Gvenn oed env y llenn. Ac vn o genedueu y llenn oed. y dyn y dottit yn y gvylch. ny welei neb euo ac euo a welei bavp. ac ny thrigyei liv arnei vyth. namyn y lliv e hun. ac eisted a oruc arthur ar y llenn. (RM 152.25; 153.4; Br. Rh. 11, 13 19.)

> 'And the big red lad dismounted before Arthur, and drew forth a golden chair from the pack, and a mantle of ribbed brocaded silk. And he spread the mantle in front of Arthur, and an apple of red gold at each of its corners, and he set the chair on the mantle . . . *Gwenn* was the name of the mantle. And one of the peculiarities of the mantle was that the man around whom it might be wrapped, no one would see him and he would see everyone. And no colour would ever stay on it, except its own colour. And Arthur sat upon the mantle.'

Gutun Owain's reference to Arthur's magic mantle is most probably derived from our text (see n. to no. 15 below): *Llwyn o wyrthie llen Arthur / Yr honn oedd rhyfedd, meddyn / A guddiai danni bob dyn* (GO no.VI.26–8). Caswallawn is endowed with a *llen hut* whose properties are described as simliar to those of Arthur's mantle (PKM 46.5–6). Further references by the *cywyddwyr* to the Thirteen Treasures are cited by Graham Thomas in 'Llen Arthur a Maen a Modrwy Luned' (University of Wales MA thesis, 1976).

14. **Mantell Degau.** For references to the story of Tegau's victory over the ladies of Arthur's court in the contest of the chastity-testing mantle, see n. to *Tegeu Eururon* under Personal Names. The tale has only come down in French sources, but references to Tegau in the triads and poetry imply a widespread knowledge of it in Wales in the fifteenth and sixteenth centuries. For a discussion of the Celtic versions of the mantle test see G. Murphy, *Duanaire Finn* III (*Irish Texts Soc* 1953), p. 153 ff., and references there cited. For the Arthurian versions see Loomis and Webster, *Ulrich von Zatzikhofen's Lanzelet* (New York, 1951), pp. 211–12. Murphy concludes that the Irish versions of this theme are more likely to have been borrowed from the Arthurian ones than *vice versa*. But these may be based ultimately on a Welsh source, cf. the passage in the Welsh Laws referred to in n. to *Tegeu*.

15. The allusion is to the episode in the romance of *Iarlles y Ffynnawn* in which Owain was caught between the outer gate and the portcullis of the

countess's castle (*Owein* (ed. Thomson), ll. 281–2). This episode was particularly popular among the *cywyddwyr*; for references see n. to *Owein m. Vryen* under Personal Names. Gutun Owain probably had *Y Tri Thlws ar Ddeg* in mind when he referred to *Luned ddedwydd* almost immediately after his reference to *llen Arthur*: *Och am y Luned ddedwyd / A'm kuddiai pan ddelai yn ddydd!* (GO no. VI.31–2.)

15. **Marchog Dû.** These words occur only in Pen. 77. Cf. WM 230–1: *ti a wely varchavc y ar varch purdu, a gwisc o bali purdu ymdanav, ac ystondard o vliant purdu ar y wayw* (*Owein* (ed. Thomson), ll. 159–61). The following note which I have found in two sixteenth-century manuscripts gives the lineage of the Knight of the Fountain: *Aegon ap koel garnach ap afri o peridon o lwyth diri yw henw marchoc y ffynnon ynghymraec, ac yn ffrangeg mwnbenyd* (Peniarth MSS. 132, p. 354; 136, p. 355). R. M. Jones has commented on the name *mwnbenyd* given in these manuscripts to the Knight of the Fountain (LlC IV, p. 220, n. 109). As he points out, it may be a compound of *mont* + *benoit*. Its application to Owain's opponent remains unexplained. It would be interesting to know if there is any extant manuscript of Chrétien's romance which contains a form of the knight's name which can account for *mwnbenyd*. The normal form of this name as given in *Yvain* is *Escaldos le Ros* (*Yvain* ed. Reid), l. 1970).

[The manuscript of the 'Tri Thlws ar Ddeg Ynys Prydain' which I selected as my basic text—Cardiff 17—is in the hand of Rowland Lewis of Mallwyd; see Rh. F. Roberts, 'Rowland Lewis o Fallwyd a'i Lawysgrifau', *Nat. Lib. of Wales Journal* IX, pp. 495–6. Two subsequent editions of this tract have been published, with annotations: by P. C. Bartrum, EC X, pp. 434–77; and by Eurys Rowlands, LlC V, pp. 33–69. Both editors make use of additional manuscripts, some of which were not known to me. A third—and probably a definitive—textual study of the 'Tri Thlws ar Ddeg' was made by Graham Thomas in his MA thesis 'Llen Arthur a Maen a Modrwy Luned' (University of Wales MA thesis, 1976), in which he cites thirteen additional texts unknown to previous editors. The cumulative evidence adduced by these scholars forcibly emphasizes the popularity of the 'Tri Thlws ar Ddeg' among poets from the second half of the fifteenth century and later, and a number of unpublished references to the *tlysau* by the *cywyddwyr*, separately and collectively, have been brought to light.]

APPENDIX IV

Pen. 127, pp. 96–7
(see pp. cx–cxiii above)

Pedwar Marchog ar Hugain Llys Arthur

Pedwar Marchoc ar hugeint o varchogion urddolion oedd yn Llys Arthur yn trigo yn wastadol, a chynneddf naturiol o orchest oedd ar bob un onaddunt, mwy noc ar ereill.

1. Tri Marchoc Aurdavodiawc oedd yn Llys Arthur: Gwalchmai ap Llew ap Kenvarch, a Drudwas ap Tryffin, ac Eliwlad ap Mad(og) ap Uthur: ac nid oedd na brenhin nac arglwydd ar y delai y rhai hynny atto, na wrandawai arnunt; a pha ryw neges bynnac a geisynt, hwynt a'i keffynt ac wynt a'i mynynt y naill ai o vodd ai o anvodd.

2. Tri Marchoc Gwyry oedd yn Llys Arthur: Bwrt ap Bwrt, brenhin Gasgwin, a Ph(e)redur ap Efroc Iarll, a Galath ap Lanslod Lak. Pa le bynnac y dalai y rhai hynny, lle bai gawr na gwiddon na dyn anysbrydal, ni allai aros yr vn o'r Tri Marchoc Gw(y)ry hynny.

3. Tri Chad varchoc oedd yn Llys Arthur: Cadwr Iarll Kernyw, a Lanslod Lak, ac Ywain ap Urien Rreget. Kynneddveu y rrai hynny: ni chilynt er ofn gwayw na chleddyf na saeth: ac ni chavas Arthur erioed gywilydd mewn brwydr y dydd i gwelai eu hwynebeu yn y maes—ac am hynny i gelwid hwynt cad varchogion.

4. Tri Lledrithawc Varchoc oedd yn Llys Arthur: Menw ap Teirgwaedd, a Thrystan ap Tallwch, ac Erddili(g) Cor; cans ymrithiaw a wneynt yn y rith y mynnynt pann vai galed arnunt, ac am hynny ni allai neb eu gorvod.

5. Tri Brenhinawl Varchoc oedd yn llys Arthur: Nasiens mab Brenhin Denmarck, a Medrod ap Llew ap Kenvarch, a Howel ap Emyr Llydaw. Kyneddveu y rrai hynny: nid oedd na brenhin nac emerodr o'r byd a allai ballu uddynt rrac eu tecked a'u doethet mewn heddwch; mewn rryvel nis arhoi na milwr na rysswr, er daed i arveu. Ac am hynny i gelwid hwynt Brenhinawl Varchogion.

6. Tri Chyvion Varchog oedd yn Llys Arthur: Blaes mab Iarll Llychlyn, a Chadawc ap Gwynlliw Varvoc, a Phetroc Baladrddellt ap Clement Tywyssawc Kernyw. Kyneddfeu y rrai hynny oedd: pwy bynnac a wnelai

gam a gwann, hwynt a ymleddynt yn erbyn a wnai gam ac ef, ynghweryl kyviawnder; a'r neb a wnelai gam hwynt a'i lleddynt er kydarnet vai. Cans ymroi ddaroedd i'r tri hynny i gadw y kyfiawnder ymhob kyfreith: Blaes o gyfraith vyd, Cadawc o gyfraith eglwys, Pedroc o gyfraith arveu, ac am hynny i gelwid hwynt kyvion varchogion.

7. Tri Gwrthniviad Varchoc oedd yn Llys Arthur: Morvran ap Tegid, a Sanddef Bryd Angel, a Glewlwyd Gavaelvawr. Kyneddveu y rhai hynny: gwrthwynebawl oedd gan neb i nackau o ddim—Sanddef rac i decked, Morvran rac i hackred, Glewlwyd rac i vaint a'i gryved a'i greuloned. Ac am hynny i gelwid hwynt yn Wrthniviawc Varchogion.

8. Tri Chynghoriad Varchoc oedd yn Llys Arthur: Kynon ap Klydno Eiddun, ac Aron ap Kenvarch, a Llywarch Hen ap Elidir Lydannwyn. A'r tri hynny a oedd gynghorwyr i Arthur, pa ryw galedi bynnac a ddelai arno, hwynt a'i kynghorynt ef val na allai neb orvod arno. Ac velly yr oedd Arthur yn gorvod ar bawb, ac ar bob gorchest, a phob kenedlaeth o'r byd—drwy gydernyd yr ysbryd kadarn, a'r ffydd a'r gobaith a oedd yn i galonn i'r gwyr hynny; a thrwy yr arveu kyssegredic a roessai Dduw iddo: Rongom(i)an(t) i waew, Caledvwlch i gleddyf, a Charnwennan i ddager.

The Twenty-four Knights of Arthur's Court

Twenty-four ordained Knights were in Arthur's Court dwelling continuously, and each one of them had an innate peculiarity of achievement beyond other people.

1. Three Golden-Tongued Knights were in Arthur's Court: Gwalchmai son of Llew son of Cynfarch, and Drudwas son of Tryffin, and Eliwlod son of Madog son of Uthur: and there was neither king nor lord to whom those came who did not listen to them; and whatever quest they sought, they wished for and obtained it, either willingly or unwillingly.

2. Three Virgin Knights were in Arthur's Court: Bwrt son of Bwrt King of Gascony, and Peredur son of Earl Efrog, and Galath son of Lanslod Lak. Wherever those might come, where there might be giant or witch or fiendish being—(such) could not withstand those Three Virgin Knights.

3. Three Knights of Battle were in Arthur's Court: Cadwr Earl of Cornwall, and Lanslod Lak, and Ywain son of Urien Rheged. The peculiarities of those were that they did not flee for fear of spear or sword or arrow; and Arthur was never shamed in battle on the day that he saw their faces in the field. And therefore they were called Knights of Battle.

4. Three Enchanter Knights were in Arthur's Court: Menw son of Teirgwaedd, and Trystan son of Tallwch, and E(i)ddilig the Dwarf; since they changed themselves into the form they wished when they were hard-pressed, and therefore no one could overcome them.

5. Three Royal Knights were in Arthur's Court: Nasiens the son of the King of Denmark, and Medrod son of Llew son of Cynfarch, and Howel son of Emyr Llydaw. The peculiarities of those were that there was neither king nor emperor in the world who could refuse them, on account of their beauty and wisdom in peace; while in war no warrior or champion could withstand them, despite the excellence of his arms. And therefore they were called Royal Knights.

6. Three Just Knights were in Arthur's Court: Blaes son of the Earl of Llychlyn, and Cadog son of Gwynlliw the Bearded, and Pedrog Splintered-Spear, son of Clement Prince of Cornwall. The peculiarities of those were that whoever might do wrong to the weak, they contended against him who did him wrong in the cause of justice; and whoever might do wrong they slew, however strong he might be. For those three had dedicated themselves to preserve justice by every Law: Blaes by earthly Law, Cadog by the Law of the Church, and Pedrog by the Law of arms. And those were called Just Knights.

7. Three Irresistible Knights were in Arthur's Court: Morfran son of Tegid, and Sanddef Angel-Face, and Glewlwyd Mighty-Grasp. The peculiarities of those were that it was repugnant to anyone to refuse them anything: Sanddef because of his beauty, Morfran because of his ugliness, and Glewlwyd because of his size and his strength and his ferocity. And therefore they were called Irresistible Knights.

8. Three Counsellor Knights were in Arthur's Court: Cynon son of Clydno Eiddyn, and Aron son of Cynfarch, and Llywarch the Old son of Elidir Lydanwyn. And those three were counsellors to Arthur: whatever hardship came upon him, they counselled him, so that nobody could overcome him. And thus Arthur triumphed over everyone, and in every feat, and over every nation in the world; through the strength of the powerful spirit and the faith and hope that were in his heart towards those men, and through the sacred weapons that God had given him: Rhongomiant his spear, Caledfwlch his sword and Carnwennan his dagger.

Manuscripts: Ll. 12, 28, 52, 65, 100, 135, Pen. 16, fo. 55 (= Simwnt Vychan, SV), Pen. 127, 77, 185 (= RV), 216, Hafod 3, 5, 8 (= H), C 36, BL Addl. 31,055 (= BL), Harl. 4181; Lewis Dwnn, *Heraldic Visitations* I, p. 10 (= LD), NLW 1599 (= NLW); BL

Addl. 14,919, fo. 126b–127a (= Addl. 1); BL Addl. 14,973, fo. 37a–b (= Addl. 2). Two additional texts found in Ll. 44 (p. 23) and Pen. 179, part 2 (p. 53) correspond with the version given in Ll. 65 unless otherwise stated. For full textual variants of all the versions of the *XXIV Marchog* that I have examined, see my earlier study and edition of *Pedwar Marchog ar Hugain Llys Arthur* THSC 1957, pp. 116–32. For a further survey of influences from French Arthurian names in Welsh sources see P. C. Bartrum, *Nat. Lib. of Wales Journal* XIV, pp. 242–5, and C. Lloyd-Morgan, *Nat. Lib. of Wales Journal* XXI, pp. 329–39. See also Notes to Personal Names below and AW 204, 210–12, etc.

Tri marchoc gwyry. Cf. no. 86 and n.

Tri chadvarchoc. Cf. no. 18 and n.

Tri lledrithawc Varchoc. Cf. nos. 27, 28 and nn.

gwrthniviad (var. *gwrthyniad, gwrthwyneb*, etc.) 'that cannot be refused or denied, irresistible, unopposable', GPC 1729. The majority of manuscripts give *gwrthwyneb* in place of the less common variants of this word. With *gwrthniviad* (>*gwrth* + *gnif* 'to fight against') and *gwrthyniad*, cf. *gwrthun*, *gwrthyn* 'offensive, repugnant' etc. Ll. 28 reads *gwrthnifiog*, which GPC presents as the original form.

kyssegredic. For Arthur's 'consecrated arms', see note to App. III, no. 13, and CO ll. 159–62; *Mab.* 100.

NOTES TO PERSONAL NAMES

(*The numbers following the names refer to triads, and are not page references. Where two or more characters with the same name are to be differentiated, superior figures immediately following the name are employed.*)

Absolon ab Dauyd (brophwyd) 48. For Absalom's great beauty see 2 Samuel xiv.25. His beauty is thus described in the fourteenth-century *Llyfr Ancr Llanddewi Brefi* (J. Rhŷs and J. Morris-Jones (eds), *The Elucidarium*, 67.6–10): 'Would it please thee if thou wert as fair as Absalon, who had no blemish on his body, any more than there is on new-fallen snow? And his hair was so fair that the women of Israel gave nine talents of gold for the excess of his hair that was cut off each year. Alas for that splendour! What was his profit from that fairness?' (trans.). The same anecdote is told of Absalom's hair in *Araith Iolo Goch* (D. Gwenallt Jones (ed.), *Yr Areithiau Pros* 14.7–10) with the substitution of *merched yr india* for *gwragedd yr israel.* For Prydydd y Moch's reference to Absalom see n. to triad 47 and CBT V, no. 4.5n. See also M. Haycock, ' "Some talk of Alexander and some of Hercules": Three early medieval poems from the Book of Taliesin', CMCS 13, p. 23, n. 82.

Adaf 47, 48, 49. This form of Adam's name appears consistently in all references to Adam in LlDC, BT and in *Llyfr Ancr*; though in texts from the latter half of the fourteenth century the form is more frequently *Adda*, since the *-f* had ceased to be pronounced (Chw. T. 18). Further references by the *Gogynfeirdd* to Adam's proverbial beauty occur as follows:

Hywel Foel ap Griffri: *Pryd Adaf prif haelon* (H 56.6 = CBT VII, no. 22.20).

Prydydd y Moch (in 'Mawl Rhys Gryg'): *Arwr Dinefwr, dinamhed—Adaf* (CBT V, no. 26.77 = H 287.15).

Dafydd Benfras: *Doethineb Selyf selwyd i'm naf / A theced eidduned Adaf / a dewred yr undyn dewraf* (CBT VI, no. 34.20 = MA 223b 115–17).

Adaon m. Talyessin, see **Auaon m. Talyessin**.

Aed Ma6r, App. I, no. 1. A legendary prehistoric ruler of Britain; see references in WCD and EWGT (index), and see n. to *Prydein m. Aed Ma6r*. The Irish name *Aed* is attested in a ninth-century poem (Stokes and Strachan, *Thesaurus Palaeohibernicus* II, 295). It is proved to have been known in Wales at an early date by the reference in *Ann. Cam.* 878: *Aed map Neill moritur. Aed* appears also in an Irish context in *Culhwch ac Olwen*: *Odgar mab Aed brenhin Iwerdon* (CO ll. 635, 644, etc.); *Gwittart mab Aed brenhin Iwerdon* (CO l. 295). Cynddelw makes a possible allusion to this legendary character: *avarwy aet vab klys* (= *Rys?*) (H 155.2 = CBT III, no. 15.2n.).

Aedan m. Gauran (= Aeddan); *Gauran m. Aedan* 29; *Aydan 6radawc* 54; *Gauran m. Aedan Uradawc* App. II, no. 11. *Bradawc* 'The Treacherous' or 'The Wily'. This is *Aedán mac Gabhráin*, ruler of Scottish Dál Riada, *circa* 574–?607/8. He is one of the very few non-Welsh historical figures who became drawn into Welsh tradition (cf. also *Edwin brenhin Lloegyr* below). His father *Gabrán* was son of Domangort, son of Fergus mac Erca, who founded the Scottish kingdom of Dál Riada as an offshoot from the Irish kingdom of the same name, *circa* 500. The form *Gauran m. Aedan*, which appears both in triad 29 and in App. II, no. 11, most probably represents an inversion between the names of father and son, which is nowhere explained (cf. EWGT p. 147, n. 11). The epithet *bradawc* is given to *Aedán*'s father in the allusion made to him in *Ann. Cam.* (B text): *Gawran Wradouc filius Dinwarch* (= *Domangort*) *obiit*. In *De Situ Brecheniauc* 15 (12) the epithet is found appropriated to *Aedan* (as in triad 54): *Luan, filia Brachan, mater Haidani (Bradouc)* (*i.insidiosi*) (EWGT 15 (12)). It is rendered in *Cognacio Brychan* (EWGT 18 (12)) as *Lluan, mater Aidan . . . et uxor Gafran (vradauc)*. No doubt the epithet *bradawc* / *insidiosi* belongs properly to *Aedán*, and not to his father *Gafran*. H. M. Chadwick suggested (*Early Scotland*, p. 152) that a historical explanation for this epithet is to be looked for in the termination of a long-standing alliance between *Aedán* and the contemporary ruler of the adjacent British kingdom of Strathclyde, *Rhydderch Hael* (see n.). This explanation is favoured also by A. O. H. Jarman, and it gains some support from the allusion to hostility between *Aedán* and Rhydderch which is found both in the poem *Peiryan Vaban* (B XIV, pp. 104 ff.) and in triad 54(n.). *Ann. Cam.* records under the year 607: *Aidan map Gabran moritur* (HB ed. Morris, p. 86). *Aedán*'s familiar contacts with the Britons are witnessed by the fact that he gave the name Arthur to one of his sons (Adamnan, *Vita Columbae* I, ch. 9), while two of his grandsons bear British names—Morgand (= *Morcant*, see EIHM 362) and Rigullon (= *Rhiwallon*). The latter is also mentioned in the poem *Peiryan Vaban* (l. 51) where he is named as one of the brothers of Myrddin (B XIV, p. 107); see n. to triad 84b.

O'Rahilly (EIHM 362n.) quotes a statement from the Life of *St Laisrén* to the effect that the saint's mother was *Edani regis Scotie filia regisque Britanniae neptis*. It is remarkable that both BGG (App. II, no. 11) and *De Situ Brecheniauc* should show a forged genealogical link between *Aedán* and two traditional British dynasties—one being the descendants of Dyfnwal Hen, the other the family of Brychan Brycheiniog. In view of the historical evidence provided by Irish sources as to *Aedán*'s true parentage, both descents may be equally spurious, though they are of interest as underlining *Aedán*'s British connections.

Aedán is said to have been inaugurated into the kingship of Dál Riada by St Columba (Anderson (ed.), *Vita Columbae* III, ch. 5). The *Vita Columbae* also refers to *Aedán's* victory at *Bellum Miathorum* (I, ch. 8) (the reference may be to *Circinn* in Pictland; see Chadwick, *Early Scotland*, p. 440). The *Annals of Ulster* record campaigns by *Aedán* in the Orkneys in 580, and the victory of Cath Manann in 581. This latter is probably to be identified as the Isle of Man: *Bellum contra Eubonium* (*Ann. Cam.* 584); on it and on the references to *Aedán* in TYP see Bedwyr L. Jones, 'Gwriad's Heritage: Links between Wales and the Isle of Man in the Early Middle Ages', THSC 1990, 29–44 (ref. to the triads at p. 39). If this is so, *Aedán*'s seaborne expedition to Man could well be that referred to in triad 29. The Dál Ríadic colony must, in any case, have been a sea-going people, maintaining, as it did, a close bond with its parent kingdom in Co. Antrim.

Bede records *Aedán*'s participation at the battle of Degsastane, at an unidentified place in Northumbria in the year 603 (*Hist. Ecc.* I, ch. xxxiv). To this place, hitherto unidentified, *Aedán* had led a large army which was defeated and put to flight by the Northumbrian king Ethelfrith. The fourteenth-century Scottish historian, John Fordun, states in his *Scottichronicon* (passage quoted by A. O. Anderson in his *Early Sources of Scottish History* I, 124) that the plan was for the Britons to attack the Northumbrians from the south, and *Aedán* from the north, but that the plan miscarried, with disastrous results for *Aedán*'s army. It is tempting to speculate as to whether the disastrous expedition to Catraeth was not undertaken by a coalition of British princes, concurrently with, and in deliberately planned support of, *Aedán*'s attack upon Ethelfrith. The failure of the two armies to co-ordinate, to which Fordun refers, might provide a sufficient reason in itself for the dubious reputation which *Aedán* bears in British tradition. There need be no special significance in the occurrence of the name of *Aedán* as that of one of Mynyddawg's warriors (CA 1. 359). The name occurs also in the Harl. Gens nos. XX and XXI (EWGT 12), and in an early twelfth-century praise-poem to Cuhelyn Fardd (CBT I, no. 2.40n.).

Iolo Morganwg was the first to suggest that the battle of Degsastane of 600 or 603 could be identified with the battle of Catraeth (*Poems Lyric and Pastoral* (1794), 5n.), and his proposal was followed by Thomas Stephens, in Thomas Powel (ed.), *The Gododdin* (1888), pp. 36–42. It is a suggestion which has attractive possibilities, though it has not subsequently won any strong support.

On *Aedán mac Gabráin* see further J. Bannerman, *Studies in the History of Dalriada* (Edinburgh, 1974), pp. 86ff.; A. M. Duncan, *Scotland: the Making of a Kingdom* (Edinburgh, 1978), pp. 43–4; K. H. Jackson, 'The Britons of Southern Scotland', pp. 77–88; H. M. Chadwick, *Early Scotland*, ch. IX;

P. Mac Cana, in Geraint Bowen (ed.), *Y Gwareiddiad Celtaidd* (Llandysul, 1987), pp. 162–3.

Auallach, *Modron verch A.* 70, *Ynys A.* 51. *Aballac / Afallach* was the son of Beli Mawr, according to Harl. Gen. I, Jesus MS. 20 (V, VI), and genealogies in the Lives of Saints *Beuno, Cadoc* etc. (full references are indexed in EWGT). Harl. Gen. X and Jesus V trace the northern dynasty of Coel Hen to *Aballach mab Amalech mab Beli et Anna* (elsewhere Anna is depicted as cousin of the Virgin Mary). For Urien Rheged and other descendants of Coel Hen see App. II above. A similar ancestry from *Beli Mawr* is given in the Life of *St Beuno* for the rulers of Powys (EWGT 30; VSB 22). As the immediate offspring of the ancestor-deity *Beli Mawr* (see n.), *Afallach* thus appears to be the mythical ancestor from whom three of the most prominent of the early dynasties of the Britons claimed descent. *Amalech* of Harl. Gen. I appears to be a doublet of *Aballac / Afallach.* Urien Rheged is portrayed both as a descendant of Coel Hen, and in triad 70 as a grandson of *Aballac / Afallach* through his mother, the mythical Modron (i.e. the goddess *Mātrona*, see n. to *Modron*).

Geoffrey of Monmouth borrowed the name *Aballac* either from Harl. Gen. I or from another genealogy, and he included him among the sons of Ebraucus (HRB II, 8 = *Auallach* BD 25.5). A similar mythical ancestry is offered for Rhun ap Maelgwn Gwynedd in *Bonedd yr Arwyr* (EWGT 91 (28d)) where Gwalltwen, daughter of *Afallach*, is named as the mother of Rhun ap Maelgwn Gwynedd (making Rhun a first cousin to Urien Rheged, and emphasizing the mythical descent which was claimed for the Gwynedd dynasty from the heroes of the 'Old North').

But since *Afallach* is also a noun meaning 'a place of apples', there is room for doubt as to whether the proper or the common noun is present in the name *Ynys Avallach*, which first appears in BD 148.27 and 185.24, rendering Geoffrey of Monmouth's *insula Avallonis* (HRB XI, 2), given as the equivalent of *insula pomorum que Fortunata vocatur* in Geoffrey's *Vita Merlini* (ed. Basil Clarke, 1. 908); and the *Brut* gives *enys Auallach* as the equivalent of HRB's *insula Avallonis*. The implication is that the meaning in both cases is 'the island of apples' in allusion to the abundant apple-trees which characterize the Celtic Otherworld scene, rather than meaning 'the Island of a (man called) *Avallo* or *Avallach*' (EC IV, p. 260; ZCP XX, p. 133; Nitze, *Perlesvaus* II, 56). As a name for the Celtic Otherworld, *Aval(l)on* may have been in existence before Geoffrey of Monmouth's time, but it is difficult to avoid the conclusion that the form has been influenced by the name *Avallon*, which existed as that of a town in Burgundy (Gaulish *Aballone*, *Avallone* 'place of apples', ACS I, 6). It is not necessary to conclude, however, that *Ynys Afallach* was a name created by the redactor of the Welsh *Brut* to render Geoffrey's *insula Avallonis*, its ending influenced by that of the proper name *Aballac / Afallach*, which was already present in Welsh. Chotzen has shown ('Emain Ablach – Ynys Avallach – Insula Avallonis – Ile d'Avalo', EC IV

(1948), pp. 255–64) that *abhlach* occurs in Irish as an adjective with reference to the Otherworld island which was the home of the god *Manannán mac Lir*, and which had come to be variously located on the Scottish island of Arran, and on the Isle of Man. It has been suggested that *Afallach* is a borrowing into Welsh from the Ir. *abhlach*; cf. the proper names Brynach, Wrnach, Diwrnach, Mwrthach, etc. On these and similar formations see P. Sims-Williams, 'The Development of the Indo-European Voiced Labiovelars in Celtic', B XXIX, pp. 615–16, and P. Russell, *Celtic Word-formation: the velar suffixes* (Dublin, 1990). For further references to *Avallo* and *insula Avallonis* see n. under *Modron verch Auallach* below. The *De Antiquitate Glastoniensis Ecclesiae* by William of Malmesbury (*circa* 1240) gives the form *insula Aballoniae*, a reformation for which either the writer or his colleagues at Glastonbury Abbey may have been responsible (E. Faral, *La Légende Arthurienne* II, p. 431). The writer states explicitly that *insula Avallonis* is equivalent to *insula pomorum*, though he appends as an afterthought the alternative explanation *vel cognominatur de quodam Avalloc, qui ibidem cum suis filiabus, propter loci secretum, fertur inhabitasse*. This double explanation of the name was reproduced from the *De Antiquitate* by Giraldus Cambrensis in his *Speculum Ecclesiae*, ch. ix (Giraldus, *Opera* IV, 49) and it would seem that it was the seemingly half-hearted support given by William of Malmesbury and Giraldus Cambrensis for the proper name *Avallo(c)* which was responsible for the subsequent misunderstanding which arose concerning the meaning of *insula Avallonis*. The *De Antiquitate*, corroborated by Giraldus Cambrensis, may have been responsible for the identification of *Avallon* with Glastonbury.

Auan, verch Meic Mygvras 79. See n. to **Meic Mygvras**.

Auan 6erdic, bard Catwalla6n m. Catuan 11. 'A. the Little Bard' or, as suggested by Bedwyr Lewis Jones, if this is a hypercoristic, 'A. the Favourite Bard' (TAAS 1973, p. 194). (The epithet *Berdic* is recorded as the personal name of the bard of Gruffudd ap Llywelyn, HW 367; GPC 273.)

Cynddelw: *Gnawd canaf y volyant ual Auan Uertic / neu uartwawd Arouan* (H 106.17 = CBT IV, no. 6.268–9).

Hywel Ystorym: *odof dauawt nyt auan vyrdic* (RBP col. 1338.25).

Gwilym Ddu o Arfon: *Meu gwawt gan auan guvydvryt—frwythlawn / o gof katwallawn brenhindawn bryd* (RBP col. 1228.12–14 = GGDT 7.45).

It is evident from these allusions that *Afan Ferddig* was known to the *Gogynfeirdd* as a renowned member of the *Cynfeirdd*; both Cynddelw and Gwilym Ddu o Arfon couple his name with the names of other famous early poets. Since tradition associates *Afan Ferddig* with Cadwallon king of Gwynedd, Ifor Williams suggested that a part of his work may have survived in the poem *Moliant Cadwallawn*, which possesses the attributes of an early bardic eulogy, although it has been transmitted only in eighteenth-century copies (B VII, pp. 23–32); R. Geraint Gruffydd (ed.), 'Canu Cadwallon ap Cadfan', *Ast. H.* 25–43.

Auaon m. Talyessin *(Adaon)* 7, 25, 33.

Br. Rh: *Y guas ieuanc kymhenaf a doethaf a wneir yn y teyrnas honn adaon uab telessin* (RM 150.16–18).

Englynion y Clyweit: *A glyweist-di a gant Auaon / Uab Talyessin, gerd gofyon . . .?* (*Blodeugerdd* no. 31, *englyn* 35).

For the variation between medial *-d-* (=*dd*) and *-f-* in this name see Ifor Williams, B II, pp. 119–20. Medial and final *f* and *dd* are frequently interchangeable: cf. such pairs as *afanc, addanc*; *Eifionydd, Eiddionydd*; *godduned, gofuned*; *Peryddon, Peryfon* (see AP xxxiv–xl). Other instances of this name occur as follows: *Auagon* LL 232.9; *adeon uab eudaf* WM 186–7 (Pen. 16) = RM 88.23. LlDC no. 27 gives the title *Cysul Adaon* ('The Advice of A.') to a series of religious *englynion*, of which a fuller version is found in the *Book of Talgarth* (*Blodeugerdd* no. 29). There is no particular reason to associate these stanzas with the son of Taliesin, or to believe that *Afaon / Addaon* was necessarily, like his father, a poet. However, J. Rowland suggests (EWSP 355–6) that triad 7 may have originally had reference to the deaths of three poets.

Auar6y m. Llud m. Beli, 51. See nn. to *Beli Mawr, Llud m. Beli.* HRB III, 20; IV, 3–11 gives *Androgeus, Andrageus* in place of *Afarwy*. Geoffrey of Monmouth's immediate source for this character was Bede (*Hist. Ecc.* I, ii) and Henry of Huntingdon (*Hist. Angl.* I, 15); both of whom give the name *Androgius* to the commander of Trinovantium (London), the first of the British cities to capitulate to the Romans. Bede's source for this incident was Orosius, who gives *Andragius* as the name of the British commander; though it seems that the episode depends ultimately on no other source than Caesar's statement (*De Bell. Gall.* V, 20) that a youth of the Trinobantes named *Mandubracios* deserted to the side of the Romans after his father had been killed by *Cassivellaunos* (= *Caswallawn m. Beli*, see n.). See also Faral, *La Légende Arthurienne* II, pp. 154 ff. The expansion of the story of *Androgeus* by Geoffrey of Monmouth is evidently motivated by the desire to account for Caesar's conquest in a way which would be the least ignominious to the Britons: under the influence of HB's account of Vortigern's invitation to Hengist and Horsa to land in Britain, he attributed the earlier conquest similarly to internal treachery.

As a common noun *afarwy* means 'sorrow', CLlH 191n.; LlDC no. 34.29; GPC 41; as a personal name the rendering of *Androgeus* by *Avarwy* in *Brut y Brenhinedd* is difficult to explain. *Afarwy* appears also as a personal name in poems by Elidir Sais (*gwersyll Avarwy*, CBT I, no. 17.40n.) and by Cynddelw (*Ar ordrech Auarwy*, III, no. 16.80n.), and it is not always easy to distinguish the sense in which the word is used in individual instances such as these. See further B. F. Roberts, B XXV, pp. 278–80; idem, *Brut y Brenhinedd*, p. 40. Cf. also the following instances:

Rhisierdyn: *iaith Afarwy* (GSRh no. 4.100n.).
Madog Dwygraig: *Cadarn Afarwy cedyrn fwriad* (MA² 322.12).
Gutun Owain: *Avarwy a glodvorrwyd* (GO no. XVII.35–6).

On the possible antecedents of the name *Afarwy* see J. T. Koch, 'A Welsh Window on the Iron Age', CMCS 14, pp. 19–52.

Angharat Ton Uelen, merch Rhydderch Hael 79. 'Yellow (or "tawny") Wave', in reference to the girl's hair, seems the likely meaning of this epithet. Such epithets as *lliw ton*, 'hue of the wave', are frequently used by the poets in their much-favoured descriptions of girls' hair.

Alan¹ Fyrgan (*Fergant*) 30. A. 'Perfect in strength' or 'Perfect Hero' (following Fleuriot's rendering 'le brave parfait', EC XI, pp. 138–42). Fleuriot has explained Alan's epithet as composed of Breton *fer* (W. *ffêr* 'brave(man), hero', GPC 1283) and *cant* 'circle', here used in its secondary abstract sense of 'perfection, completion'. Ifor Williams cites (CA 1. 391n.) the analogous Welsh personal names *Ferawc*, *Feruarch* (= *Fermarch* LL 265) as containing the same *ffêr* 'strong'. Cf. also *Bonedd y Saint* (EWGT 63 (58)) which lists *Llonyaw Llawhir m. Alan Fyrgan m. Emyr Llydaw*. For 'Awdl Llonio Sant' by Huw Arwystl (*circa* 1550–83) see LBS IV, p. 429. Cf. also *Sberin mab Flergant brenhin Llydaw* (CO 1. 216n.). Fleuriot showed that Loth's earlier interpretation (*Chr. Br.* 204) of *Fergant* as 'White Ankle' is untenable because *cant* 'white' is not attested in Breton, as it is in Welsh.

Alan IV or *Alannus Fergannus* was count of Cornouailles and then duke of Brittany 1084–1112. He died in 1119. Alan was first an opponent and then an ally of William the Conqueror, whose daughter Constance he married as his first wife (HLCB 7, 14, 28, 134, etc.; see also AW 252, 257, 279). *Alan Fergant* is said (HLCB 7) to have been the latest historical Breton ruler to be known by his Breton cognomen. His alliance with William the Conqueror was maintained during the reign of William's successor, Henry I, for whom Alan's help, as leader of a powerful Breton force, is said to have been decisive in securing victory over Robert Corthose at the battle of Tinchebrai in Normandy in 1106 (L. Fleuriot, HLCB 7, 14; E. Faral, *La Légende Arthurienne* II, p. 198). Alan's son Duke Conan III married Henry I's illegitimate daughter Maud. *Alan* remained a popular name among the dukes of Brittany, but Alan IV is not to be confused with *Alan Rufus* or *le Roux* (as by Bruce, EAR I, 70; cf. Loth in RC XIII, pp. 491–2, and AW 291, n.6). The distinction between the two branches of this Breton family is made clear in the table given by C. T. Clay, *Early Yorkshire Charters IV: The Honour of Richmond* (*Yorks. Arch. Soc. Rec. Series I* (Extra Series)), p. 84.

Alan², *Di6wng m. Alan*, 15. This name should perhaps be emended to *Alun*; cf. *mab Alun Dyuet* (CO ll. 185, 725 nn.).

Alexander Paris 48 (Pen. 77). See *Paris m. Priaf*. *Paris* is known by his alternative name of *Alexander* throughout *Dares Phrygius*, as well as in Prydydd y Moch's reference (see n. to triad 47).

Alser m. Maelgwn (Gwynedd) 42. See n. to **Maelgwn Gwyned**.

Anarun Archesgob Llydaw (m. *Urien Rheged*) 70. 'A. Archbishop of Brittany'. *Bonedd yr Arwyr* (B XVIII, pp. 234–5 = EWGT 87 (6)), in contradiction to the triad, presents *Anarun* as a son of Kynfarch and therefore as a brother to Urien 87 (97). Cf. also Rawl. B. 466 (the pages are unnumbered): *Plant Kynvarch m. meirchawn; Llew brenin llychlyn, Aron brenin ysgotland, Urien reged brenin manaw, Anarawn Archesgob llydaw.* (For a shorter version see EWGT 87 (6). Cf. LlDC 40.10: *llev. ac arav. ac vrien* and n.)

Aneiryn Gwa6tryd Mechdeyrn Beird 33, 34. 'A. of Flowing Verse, Great Prince of Poets.' (On *mechdeyrn* see n. to triad 33.) HB ch. 62 in Harleian MS. 3859 provides the earliest allusion to the *Cynfeirdd*—the first Welsh poets of whom there is record, and who together are assigned by tradition to the second half of the sixth century:

> At that time *Talhaearn Tad Awen* ('Father of Inspiration') shone in poetry, and *Neirin*, *Taliesin*, *Blwchfardd* and *Cian*, who is called *Gueinth Guaut* ('Wheat of Song') together at that time shone in British poetry. (trans.)

On the passage see CA xv; BWP 43n. Ifor Williams regarded *Neirin* as the older form of the poet's name: this view was disputed by Kenneth Jackson (B XXX, pp. 47–8) who favoured *Aneirin* as the original. Of the five named poets in the HB passage, it is poetry attributed to Aneirin and Taliesin alone that has survived which can proffer a claim to represent the genuine work of the *Cynfeirdd*. The contents of the thirteenth-century *Book of Aneirin* are introduced by the superscription *Hwn yw e gododdin. aneirin ae cant*. ('This is the Gododdin: Aneirin sang it.') The *Gododdin* consists of a series of elegies on the warriors who fell at the battle of Catraeth, which is believed to have taken place *circa* AD 600 (see n. to *Mynyda6c Eidyn*). It has long been believed that the nucleus of the poem represents a composition by the poet Aneirin, whose distinction is witnessed by the passage quoted from HB. But the inevitable corruption to which the poem became subject in the process of both oral and written transmission over many centuries, and the number of subsequent accretions to which early texts inevitably become liable, constitute problems with regard to the *Gododdin*'s original content which may prove to be ultimately insoluble.

The *Gododdin* contains two allusions to *Aneirin*. At least one of these (stanza lv) can only be accounted for as an addition to the poem, since it refers to the poet's death (see n. to triad 34). The same stanza (l. 651) alludes to the *guarchan mab dwywei* 'the poem of the son of D.', and the context confirms that this allusion can only be to Aneirin himself. The name of *Dwywi verch*

Leennawc is found in *Bonedd y Saint* (EWGT 56 (12)) as that of the wife of Dunawt Vwrr and sister to St Deinioel, and to *Gwallawc m. Lleennawc* (see n.). Ifor Williams therefore deduced that Aneirin may have been Gwallawg's nephew, and that the poet could have been the brother of Deinioel Sant. The other allusion in the poem couples Aneirin's name with that of Taliesin: *Mi na vi aneirin / ys gwyr talyessin / ovec kywrenhin / neu chein(t)e ododin* (ll. 548–51). Ifor Williams interpreted these lines (CA l. 232) as meaning that Aneirin disclaimed all credit for his work—it was the *awen* alone which inspired him: 'I—not I, Aneirin—Taliesin of powerful inspiration knows—I sang the Gododdin.' (On the allusions to Aneirin in the *Gododdin*, and on the evidence for his poetic reputation which is to be derived from later sources, see M. E. Owen's study, 'Hwn yw e Gododin: Aneirin a'e cant', *Ast. H.* 123–150.)

In the twelfth–thirteenth-century anonymous poem *Anrec Uryen*, the same epithet is bestowed upon the poet as in the triad, *Aneirin gwawtryd awenyd* 'A. of Flowing Verse, inspired' (RBP cols. 1049–50; J. Morris-Jones, *Cy*. 28, pp. 195–7; and cf. CA 206). The earliest extant allusion to Aneirin by the *Gogynfeirdd* is by Dafydd Benfras (*circa* 1220–58), who wishes for the inspiration of Myrddin or for the *awen* to inspire him to sing the praise of Llywelyn ab Iorwerth *mal aneirin gynt / Dydd y cant Ododin* 'like Aneirin, the day he sang the Gododdin' (CBT VI, no. 25.5–6n.). Later in the century Sefnyn wishes for inspiration *Med kyhoed milyoed molawt aneirin* (RBP col. 1261.8–9 = GSRh no. 2.7n.), and Rhisierdyn *Tauavt un arawt aneirin gwawtglaer* (RBP col. 1281.24–5 = GSRh no. 6.75n.).

Among the relevant works concerning Aneirin and the *Gododdin* poem are the following: CA, BWP, OSPG, *Ast. H.*; D. Simon Evans, 'Aneirin – Bardd Cristnogol?', YB X, pp. 35–44; A. O. H. Jarman, *The Cynfeirdd* (Cardiff, 1981); idem, *Aneirin: Y Gododdin*; B. F. Roberts (ed.), *Early Welsh Poetry* (Aberystwyth, 1988); A. O. H. Jarman, 'The Arthurian Allusions in the Book of Aneirin', SC XXIV/XXV; M. E. Owen, 'Hwn yw e Gododin: Aneirin a'e cant', *Ast. H.* 123–150; J. T. Koch, *The Gododdin of Aneirin*; O. J. Padel (review), 'A New Study of the *Gododdin*', CMCS 35 (1998), pp. 45–55.

Aranrot verch Don 35, 67, 78. See **Ar(y)anrot**.

Ara6n m. Kynuarch 70; *Aron ap Kenvarch*, App. IV, no. 8. See n. to *Vryen Reget*. In *Brut y Brenhinedd*, *Arawn* replaces HRB's Anguselus as the brother of Urianus and Loth (BD 152 = HRB IX, 9). The name may be derived ultimately from *Arawn brenhin Annwfn* (PKM 2ff.), yet there is no apparent connection between the two characters. It is possible that *Arawn* was known as a brother of Urien Rheged in the pre-Geoffrey tradition, since the three names *Lleu ac Araw(n) ac Vrien* appear as three brothers in LlDC no. 40.10 (where it is perhaps more likely that the names reflect the influence of the *Brut*; see LlDC xv, my note in B XVII, pp. 180–1, and the n. below on *Llew m. Kynuarch*).

Bonedd yr Arwyr (B XVIII, pp. 234–5 = EWGT 87 (6)) lists as brothers *Llew, Arawn, Urien* and *Anarun archesgob Llydaw*, in contrast to the triad, where *Anarun* is presented as a son of Urien.

Gr. ap Maredudd: *arawn ynni uryen annwyt* (RBP col. 1219.15 = GGM no. 8.9); *gedernyt aron . . . gorff uryen* (RBP col. 1323.15 = GGM no. 7.87–8). The form *Aron* with short-*o*- is used to render the biblical Aaron: *aron a moesen* LlDC no. 9.13, see also *aron mab diwinvin* LlDC no. 18.179.

Archanat 44 (var. *Arthanat*). The -*ch*- may represent -*th*- in this name. For *arth* 'bear' in personal names, cf. *Arthgen, Ann. Cam.* 807 (name of a ruler in Ceredigion, as is indicated in triad 44c).

Ardun[1] (merch Eliffer Gosgord6awr) 70 (= *Ceindrech Pen Askell* 'Wing Headed', Pen. 50).

Tyssilyaw m. Brochuael Ysgithrawc m. Kyngen m. Cadell Dyrnluc, ac Ardun Bennascell verch Pabo Post Prydein y vam (EWGT 59 (33)). It is likely that *Ardun Pen Askell* is the name to be restored in the triad, in spite of Pen. 50's *Ceindrech* (though Pen. 50 gives on the whole the better readings of this triad; see n. to triad 70, item **c**). Evidently there has been confusion between the name in the triad and the *Ardun Benn Ascell* of *Bonedd y Saint*. The problem is further complicated by the fact that Cynddelw in his *awdl* to St Tysilio describes the saint as *mab gardun ardunic vawred* (HGC no. XVI.17 = CBT III, no. 3.17n.). The note to l. 17 suggests that *Garddun* is not the correct form of the saint's mother's name since, as Ifor Williams pointed out (PKM 163–4), *Arddun* is a perfectly possible form (cf. *arddunaf* 'exalt, praise, etc.' (GPC 188)), and he referred to the place-names *Dolarddun* and *Arddunwent* (*Enwau Lleoedd*, p. 42), also perhaps found in *Arddunyon* in the 'Old North' (PT no. XI.22n.). *Penardun* (PKM 29.10) is a compound either of *Arddun* or *Garddun*. Cf. *Ardun[2]* below.

Ar(d)un[2] wreic Gatcor ap Goroluyn 66. Cf. *Ardun[1]* above.

Argat, Cynhaual m. Argat 7. *Argad* is the name of a son of Llywarch Hen, LlDC no. 40.7. Cf. also *Cynhaval Sant ap Argud* EWGT 64 (68).

Arouan uard Seleu ap Kynan (*Garwyn*) 11 (WR). Cynddelw knew of both *Arouan* and *Auan 6erdic* (see n.) as early poets, and the variation between the two names in triad 11 gains interest from the fact that Cynddelw cites the names of the two poets together in his reference (CBT IV, no. 6.268–9). This is the only surviving reference to *Arofan* other than the triad. Was the triad Cynddelw's only source for this knowledge of *Arofan*?

Aron ap Kenvarch, see **Arawn m. Kynuarch.**

Arthur 1, 2, 12, 20, 26, 37(R), *llys Arthur* 9, 18, 51, 52, 53, 54, 56, 57, 59, 65, 73, 74, 85, 86, 87, 88, App. III, no. 13; App. IV (passim); *Llacheu m. Arthur* 4.18 (WR). As 'the great hero of all the Britons' (Jackson) it is surprising to find that Arthur is given no patronymic in TYP, nor in *Culhwch ac Olwen*, nor in early poetry, nor in any Welsh or Latin sources prior to Geoffrey of Monmouth's HRB. In HRB, Arthur is presented as son to *Uthur Pendragon* (see n.), the supreme ruler of Britain, and of the latter's wife Igerna (= Eigr in *Brut y Brenhinedd*). Sixteenth-century genealogies later supply this deficiency, citing both Arthur's paternal and maternal descent (*Bonedd yr Arwyr*, B XVIII, pp. 239–40 = EWGT 93–4 (30, 33); see further P. C. Bartrum, *Nat. Library of Wales Journal* XIV, p. 243).

Arthur's name has frequently (and, I suggest, with a bare possibility) been derived from the record of a certain *Lucius Artorius Castus*, a second-century Roman prefect stationed at York, who led the VI Legion on an expedition to Armorica, and a man who may plausibly have left descendants behind him in Britain and who could thus have transmitted the name *Artorius* (K. Jackson, ALMA 2). But, as Constance Bullock-Davies pointed out to me, the name of the British hero *Arthur* is nowhere actually latinized in writing as *Artorius*, but is invariably cited either as *Art(h)ur* (Harl. 3859 and HRB), *Arcturus*, or *Arturus*—the latter in the *Vita Merlini* (see n. to *Myrddin*) and elsewhere. Geoffrey of Monmouth imaginatively recreated the story of his hero from the bare list of Arthur's eleven victorious battles won against the invading English, as these are commemorated in HB ch. 56, and from the dates given for the battles of Badon and Camlan in *Ann. Cam.* (Badon 516 and Camlan 537). He could have amplified these records from still-current popular traditions (see O. J. Padel, CMCS 27, pp. 1–31), which may have included one relating to Arthur's unknown grave, as this is remembered in the *Beddau* stanzas: *Anoeth bid bet y Arthur* 'The world's wonder is Arthur's grave' (LlDC no. 18.135). No medieval writer has anywhere used the name *Artorius* for the *Arthur* of Welsh tradition, although *Artōrius* would undoubtedly have developed regularly into *Art(h)ur* in Welsh, and it has been pointed out that the 'bear' associations of his name (*arth* cognate with L. *ursus*, GPC 212) might well account for some of the more savage characteristics that have been attributed to *Arthur* in early Welsh sources. Hence the attention which has for so long and so controversially been placed on the surviving record of the Roman legionary *Lucius Artorius Castus* (first advocated by Kemp Malone, 'Artorius', MPh XII, pp. 367–74). For this suggestion, see further A. Birley, *The People of Roman Britain* (London, 1979). Geoffrey's imaginative and popular reconstruction of his hero's life and career in HRB (*circa* 1136–8) was rendered into Welsh within a century of its composition as *Brut y Brenhinedd* (several variant versions: see H. Lewis (ed.), *Brut Dingestow*; B. F. Roberts, *Brut y Brenhinedd*; and J. J. Parry, *Brut y Brenhinedd: Cotton Cleopatra Version*).

H. M. Chadwick first pointed out (*The Growth of Literature* I, pp. 161–2) that the strongest evidence for Arthur's historical existence is to be derived from the fact that four Irish, Welsh and Scottish men are recorded as having been born during the seventh century, all of whom were given the otherwise very rarely attested name of *Arthur*. This was well within living memory of the supposed lifetime of the legendary hero (*circa* 500). The list of twelve victories won by Arthur against the Saxon invaders of Britain first appears in the Harl. 3859 text of HB (*circa* 1100), ch. 56. No mention is made in this list of Arthur's last battle of Camlan, though both Badon and Camlan are listed for the first time in the *Cambrian Annals* contained in the same manuscript as HB (Harl. 3859). On the list of Arthur's widely dispersed victories, which appears to have been derived from different and perhaps ultimately unrelated sources, see K. Jackson, 'Once Again Arthur's Battles', MPh XLIII pp. 44ff., and ALMA ch. I. It has been suggested that a very probable source for the battle-list may have been an early bardic praise-poem, comparable to the poems celebrating the victories of Cynan Garwyn or those of Urien Rheged (PT nos. 1 and 7; perhaps a poem which commemorated Arthur retrospectively as a long-dead hero of former days). Little more than a century after HRB the *Book of Aneirin* was transcribed (Cardiff MS. I, *circa* 1250), with its famous eulogy in the 'B' text (CA l. 1242) of a warrior named *Gwawrddur*, who performed great deeds of valour *ceni bei ef arthur* (CA l. 1242) 'though he was not Arthur'. (For discussion of this key reference to Arthur see A. O. H. Jarman, SC XXIV/V; idem, *The Gododdin,* pp. 149–50; OSPG 112; and T. Jones, 'Datblygiadau Cynnar Chwedl Arthur', B XVII, p. 244 (trans. Gerald Morgan, 'The Early Evolution of the Legend of Arthur', *Nottingham Mediaeval Studies* VIII, pp. 3–21). Unfortunately this allusion remains highly ambiguous, since its full significance is impossible to determine in the absence of any certainty as to when the *Gododdin* poem was first composed, or when it was first committed to writing, or as to any subsequent additions which may have been made in successive transcripts of the poem. But even if the citation of Arthur's name did not belong to the original redaction of the *Gododdin*, it is highly probable that it formed a part of the written text of the poem by at least as early as the ninth century, and it is therefore an allusion of primary importance in regard to Arthur's historicity.

Speculations have inevitably varied widely as to Arthur's ultimate identity. My own suggestion (originally published in 1961 in the first edition of this book, followed by 'Concepts of Arthur', SC X/XI) proposed that Arthur may have been the first and the most prominent of the many North-British heroes concerning whom traditions were brought south from the 'Old North' and from the ninth century onwards were freshly localized and elaborated in Wales (cf. nn. to *Llywarch Hen*, *Drystan*, *Myrddyn*, *Taliessin*, *G6ydno Garanhir*). It would seem possible that Arthur could have been in origin an early Romano-British opponent of the Anglian raiders and settlers in the Catterick area of Yorkshire, who were in process of laying the foundations of what was later to be the kingdom of Deira, since the *Gododdin* reference could imply that Arthur had been an adversary in a previous generation of the same enemies as those who are later said to have opposed *Mynyddawg*

Mwynfawr's force at Catraeth *circa* 600. This suggestion gained subsequent support from A. O. H. Jarman (SC XXIV/XXV, p. 18, and in *The Gododdin*, pp. 149–50). Contrast with this view Jackson's contention (OSPG 112) that Arthur was the 'great national hero of the entire British people' and could have had no such merely localized territorial origin in an area which belonged to the territory of the 'Old North'. (For the basic texts on Arthurian origins see further E. K. Chambers, *Arthur of Britain* (1927, 1964), and the studies contained in ALMA and AW.)

A more recent discussion which may go far to reconcile disparate theories as to the significance of the earliest allusions to Arthur, and as to the different localities in Britain with which his activities are to be associated in the earliest texts, is to be found in O. J. Padel, CMCS 27, pp. 1–31. Padel argues for the priority and widespread popular nature of the onomastic traditions which associate Arthur (in HB's 'Mirabilia', chs. 67–75, in the *Lives of the Saints*, and in *Culhwch ac Olwen*; see AW 88–93) with a variety of places within the 'Celtic fringe' in north and west Britain, in Cornwall and in Wales, as against the 'historical' tradition which is indicated in the *Cambrian Annals* and in HB's list of Arthur's victorious battles against the invaders. For this view Padel draws an important parallel with the genesis of the widespread, but essentially localized, traditions of the popular hero Fionn mac Cumhaill in Ireland, a comparison which was first promulgated by the Dutch scholar A. G. van Hamel in his British Academy lecture, 'Aspects of Celtic Mythology' PBA (1934), pp. 207–48.

The increase of interest in the figure of Arthur which is apparent between the 'Early Version' of TYP, represented by Pen. 16, and the 'later' or WR version, is paralleled by the increase in the proportion of allusions to Arthur which appear in the poetry of the *Gogynfeirdd.* These have been conveniently collected and indexed by Ann Parry Owen, LlC XX, pp. 25–45, and from them it becomes apparent that between the mid-twelfth century and *circa* 1200 there already appear more allusions to *Arthur* (ten allusions) than to any other early Brythonic hero, excluding only allusions to God, Christ, the saints, biblical characters and contemporary Welsh rulers. No doubt Arthur's early fame had developed mainly out of his battle-list as this is recorded in HB, a work with which the *Gogynfeirdd* were demonstrably familiar. (On the poets' attitude to Arthur see D. M. Lloyd, *Rhai Agweddau ar Ddysg y Gogynfeirdd*, pp. 10–11.) The allusions to Arthur by poets of the thirteenth century show a marked increase over those of the previous century, conforming in this to the general growth of interest in the Arthurian theme over Europe during the same period. Such allusions culminate in Bleddyn Fardd's twice-repeated comparison between Arthur and his own outstanding hero, Llywelyn ap Gruffudd (CBT VII, no. 51.8–9). Nor was the potent symbolism of Arthur's name neglected by Welsh poets during the subsequent centuries. (Arthur is named at least once, and with increasing frequency, in each one of the 7 vols of CBT.)

Aryan6agyl 44. 'Silver Staff'. *Bagl* '(pastoral) staff' (GPC 248, cf. CLIH 100). It is possible that the first element is not *Aryan* but *Aran* (as in RB; cf. n. to *Ar(y)anrot* below). If 'Humped/Huge Staff' is the name intended for Elidir's servant, it is possible that the epithet indicates that he was a dwarf or a hunch-back.

Ar(y)anrot 35, 67, 78. See nn. to *Don, Beli m. Mynogan, Math m. Mathonwy*. BT 36.15: *Aranrot drem clot tra gwawr hinon* 'A. famous for beauty beyond the dawn of fine weather'.

On the name see PKM 269–70. *Rot (= rhod* 'wheel') is attested as the second element by the rhyme with *clot* in the line quoted above, as against W. J. Gruffydd's suggestion (*Math vab Mathonwy*, p. 189) that this represents *-rawd* < *rāt* (= Ir. *ráth*) as in the Gaulish name for Strasbourg, *Argentoratum* 'Silver Mound'. It is more difficult to determine whether the first element is *Aryan-* or *Aran-*. *Aranrot* appears consistently throughout the Fourth Branch of the *Mabinogi* in the texts of both WB and RB. But *Aryanrot* is the spelling of the name in triad 35, in the texts of both Pen. 16 and RB (the triad is absent from W). In the mind of the triad's redactor there was clearly a connection between the name *Ar(y)anrot* and the title *Tri Aryanllu*, 'Three Silver Hosts'. If *Aryanllu* is the correct form of the compound in this title, then it may have affected the spelling of the proper name. Alternatively, there may be a genuine connection between the two names, which may have stood originally as *Aranrot, Aranllu. Aran* survives independently in the mountain names *Yr Aran Fawr, Aran Benllyn*, and in the diminutive *Aren(n)ig*, as well as in the name of the Scottish island of *Arainn* (see Watson, *The Celtic Place-Names of Scotland,* p. 97), and also as in the first element of a number of Gaulish proper names cited in Holder's *Alt-Celtischer Sprachschatz*. In all these instances the exact meaning remains uncertain, but 'huge', 'round' or 'humped' would all be possible interpretations. If some such meaning as this was originally intended by *aranllu*, one may compare the phrase *llu kyngrwn*, 'a round, compact' or 'orderly host' (see CLlH no. I.23b). The triad serves to emphasize the *size* of the *Tri Ar(y)anllu*, so that *Aranllu* may have been the original form of the epithet. And the evidence of BT 36.15 combined with that of the spelling *Aranrot*, which is uniform throughout the *Mabinogi*, strongly favours *Aranrot* as the original form, as against *Aryanrot*, and in spite of the analogy of the early Welsh and Breton names compounded in *Argant-* which appear both in *Argunhell* (LL 82.28), and in early Breton charters (*Chr. Br.* 107). (A similar doubt exists as to the first element in the name *Ar(y)an6agyl* in triad 44; see n. above.)

In *Mabinogi Math*, *Aranrot* is said to be the daughter of Don, the Welsh equivalent of the Irish goddess Danu, mother of the gods (Rhŷs, *Celtic Heathenism*, pp. 89–90; WCD 204); in the *Mabinogi* she is the mother of *Lleu Llaw Gyffes* (see n.) and of Dylan Eil Ton (WCD 218–19). Triad 35 is the only source for the alternative claim that *Aranrot*'s father was Beli, i.e. *Beli Mawr mab Mynogan* (see n.)—a statement which need not necessarily be incompatible with the *Mabinogi* tradition.

On *Caer Aranrot*, see PKM 272–3; W. J. Gruffydd, *Math vab Mathonwy*, p. 189; and F. J. North, *Sunken Cities*, pp. 226–33. Known locally as *Trega'r Anthrag*, this is the name of a rock formation visible at low tide, about a mile seaward from Dinas Dinlle on the Caernarfonshire coast. Like Dinas Dinlle, Bryn Gw(y)dion, etc, the name *Caer Aranrot* bears eloquent witness to the localization in this part of the Caernarfonshire shore of the events narrated in *Mabinogi Math.*

W. J. Gruffydd (*Math fab Mathonwy*, pp. 192–5) quotes evidence that subsequent tradition, as retailed by poets of the fifteenth and sixteenth centuries, knew of the story in a slightly different form. Lewys Môn (*circa* 1465–1527) recounts a version in which *Arianrhod* [*sic*] took the place of *Goewin* as Math's virgin foot-holder: *Mae 'ynghwyn am forwyn yn fwy / no Math Hen fab Mathonwy. / Braich un ddi-wair, brechwen, ddoeth / fu'i obennydd ef beunoeth / Arianrhod:—ni bu'r unrhyw—ni byddai Fath hebddi fyw* (GLM no. XCVII.1–7, see n.). 'My complaint concerning a maiden is greater than (that of) old Math son of Mathonwy: the arm of a chaste, white-armed wise one was his pillow each night—Arianrhod, none was like her—Math would not live without her.' Gruffydd points out that the same tradition was evidently known to Tudur Aled, Lewys Môn's close contemporary, who describes a girl *unrhyw wedd Arianrhod* 'of the same form as A.' who was closely guarded by husband, father, and mother (GTA no. CXXXIV.2).

Aydan Vrada6c 'A. the Treacherous'. See **Aedan m. Gauran**

Banawc, *Ellyll Banawc* 64, *ellyll* 'spectre, spirit, phantom' etc. (GPC 1209). *Ban(n)og* 'horned' as in *deu ychen bannawc* (CO ll. 596–7n.); but also 'famous, conspicuous', as in *Elen*[2] *Uanna6c* (triad 50). According to Ifor Williams, *Mynydd Bannawg* meant the Grampian mountains (CLlH 156–7; CA 141); similarly J. E. C. Williams on the allusion *hyd tra Bannawc* in Meilyr's poem (see below). In contrast, K. H. Jackson followed W. J. Watson (*The Celtic Place-Names of Scotland*, pp. 195–6) in identifying *Ban(n)wg* with the uplands between Stirling and Dumbarton, associating the name with that of the 'Bannock Burn' which rises from these mountains (OSPG 5–6). See n. to CO l. 597, and also n. to *Caw o Brydein* (below). In several Welsh sources, including the Life of *St Cadoc* and CLlH no. V.7a (below) *tra Bannawc* 'Beyond B.' denotes the northern borderland which divided the known world from *Prydyn*, or northern Scotland, generally regarded as the unknown and mysterious homeland of the Picts.

CA l. 255: *un maban e gian o dra bannauc.*
CLlH no. V.7a: *Ysydd Lanfawr tra bannawg.*
Meilyr (H 3.8 = CBT I, no. 3.64n.): *clywed y gyma yd tra bannawc.*
CO ll. 596–7: *Deu ychen bannawc, y lleill yssyd o'r parth hwnt y'r Mynyd*

Bannawc a'r llall o'r parth hwnn 'Two horned oxen, one of them is on the far side of *Mynydd Bannawg*, and the other on this side'.

Bed 69: *Eina6n ap Bed, brenhin Kerny6*. See under **Eina6n**[2].

Beda 49. The Venerable Bede, whose writings won for him a great reputation for wisdom in Wales; cf. BT 36.18: *Nyt vy dyweit geu llyfreu beda* 'The books of Bede tell no lies'. As Ifor Williams pointed out in reference to the poem which contains this line (LEWP 56), it could not have been composed before 768, the year in which the Welsh accepted the Roman reckoning for the date of Easter. In his writings Bede abuses the Welsh for their nonconformity with the English Church on the Easter question (see *Hist. Ecc.* II, ch. 2, etc.), so that the growth of Bede's reputation in Wales must certainly be a development which took place after the settlement of this question. *Ann. Cam.* notes the year of Bede's death, 735: *Beda presbiter dormit.*

Bede's name is coupled, as in the triad, with that of Cato the Wise (see n. to *Cado Hen*), in more than one reference in medieval poetry:

Gruffudd ap Maredudd: *Am oleuvryt kadw amyl y lyfreu da / am eirie beda mawr wybodeu* (RBP col. 1205.7–9 = GGM no. 1.36).

Meurig fab Iorwerth: *y veda a chadv gynnefodicion / am y attebion y mae tebic* (RBP col. 1374.2).

Further allusions are by Justus Llwyd: *llyna med beda byt vuedu* (RBP col. 1366.2–3).

Rhisierdyn: *Bedaf y barnaf wyf beirnyat kyfyawn* (RBP col. 1283.10 = GSRh no. 7.17n.); *kein dauawt bedaf* (RBP col. 1283.40 = GSRh no. 7.49).

The *cywyddwyr* sometimes make complimentary comparisons between their ecclesiastical patrons and Bede; see Gutun Owain: *Beda o Rys* (GO no. XII.11); ibid., *Beda Ddoeth abadoedd yw* (GO no. XXV.4).

Bedra6c 21. See **Bedwyr**.

Bedwyr m. Bedra6c 21 (Pen. 45: *m. Pedrawt*), 26. Bedwyr's patronymic is not attested in CO. It should perhaps be *Pedrawc* or *Pedrawt*, cf. *Geraint ac Enid*: *Bedwyr uab bedrawt* (WM 411.41 = RM 265.18), and cf. the epithet *pedrydant* which is attached to Bedwyr in LlDC no. 31.47: *beduir bedrydant*; and of which there are further instances such as *clod pedrydant* in LlDC no. 22.11. On this and other compounds formed with *petr(y)* 'four-square, four-angled' (L. *quadru-*), with extended meaning 'perfect, complete' see Loth, RC XLIX, p. 149; Vendryes, EC IV, pp. 284–5; and GPC 2709 'perfect, strong'. For the compound *petrylaw* see n. to *Prydelaw Menestyr* below. *Dant* as an element in a personal epithet is found in LlDC no. 1.12: *Rys undant*. *Tant* 'string' in the sense of 'sinew' is preferable here to *dant* 'tooth' as the original second element in *pedrydant*, which as a personal epithet may have originally meant 'perfect of sinew'. Hence 'complete, powerful, strong' seems to suit all GPC's examples.

Bedwyr figures in the earliest Welsh sources together with Cei as one of Arthur's two earliest companions (see n. to CO l. 175): *Galw a oruc Arthur ar Uedwyr, yr hynn nyt arswydwys y neges yd elhei Gei idi. Sef a oed ar Uedwyr, nyt oed neb kymryt* (R: *kyfret*) *ac ef yn yr Ynys honn namyn Arthur a Drych eil Kibdar. A hynn heuyt, kyt bei unllofyawc nyt anwaydwys tri aeruawc kyn noc ef yn un uaes ac ef* (CO ll. 393–6): 'Arthur called on Bedwyr, who never feared to go on the undertaking that Cei went upon. This was Bedwyr's characteristic: no one was so fair (R: 'so swift') as he in this Island, except Arthur and Drych eil Kibdar. And this, too, though he was one-handed, no three warriors in the same fight with him could draw blood sooner than he.' Similarly Cei and *Bedguir* are the two warriors who accompany Arthur in the Life of *St Cadoc*; with Arthur they witness King Gwynllyw's elopement with the saint's mother (VSB 26–7), and later they assist Arthur in the reception of the magic red-eared cows which are given him in ransom by the saint (VSB 70–1). In HRB IX, 11, etc. *Beduerus* (= *Bedwyr* BD 156.29, etc.). Though Cei is the hero of the early poem *Pa gur yw y porthaur* (LlDC no. 31.56–8; see AW 40–5), *Bedwyr* is also named: *Oet hyneiw guastad / ar lleg ar lles gulad / Beduir a Bridlaw* 'They(?) were steady leaders of an army for the benefit of their(?) country, Bedwyr and Bridlaw.' A further reference is found in the *Beddau* stanzas, LlDC no. 18.38: *guydi llauer kywlavan / Bet Bedwir in alld tryvan* 'After many a slaughter, the grave of Bedwyr is on Tryfan's height'—Tryfan is a mountain above the Ogwen valley in Gwynedd. *Ffynnawn Uetwyr* is named as the site of a camp of Cadwallon's in the poem on his battles (RBP col. 1043.29 = EWSP 446.7). Later poetic references include those by Elidir Sais: *Arfod Cai a Bedwyr* (CBT I, no. 18.18n.). Llywelyn ap y Moel laments that his heart is broken after the death of Gruffudd Llwyd, like that of Cei after *Bedwyr* (IGE[2] no. LIV.16). Bleddyn Fardd in his *marwnad* to Dafydd ap Gruffydd compares him to *Bedwyr* (CBT VII, no. 55.19n.). Cf. GDC no. 1.22n. Iolo Goch describes King Edward III as *anian Bedwyr* (GIG no. I.2). A son and daughter of Bedwyr are named in the tales: *Amren mab Bedwyr* (CO l. 285, named also in *Geraint ac Enid*, WM 465.35–6); *Eneuawc merch Uedwyr* (CO l. 362); and HRB X, 9 names *Hirelglas* nephew of *Beduerus.*

Belen *(Belyn)* **o Leyn** 31 (WR), 62 (WR) (= Pen. 16 *Melyn m. Kynvelyn*, see no. 31 and n. to Personal Names). WR's version is supported by *Ann. Cam.* 627, *Belin moritur*; and this form is further advocated as correct by Owain Cyfeiliog's poem *Hirlas Owein* in his description of his own war-band: *Ketwyr yd aethant er clod obryn / kyuoedon arvawc arvau edwyn / Talassant eu med mal gwyr Belyn gynt* (RBP col. 1433. 5–8 = CBT II, no. 14.37n.) 'warriors went out to earn fame, armed comrades with keen weapons, they earned their mead like Belyn's men of old'. It seems probable that *Belyn* of Llŷn and *Melyn fab Kynvelyn* are two distinct characters who have been conflated (with the first, cf. CA l. 1361 *y wynassed velyn*—see n., and EWGT 56 (13)).

Triad 62 suggests that *Belyn o Leyn* was an ally of *Cadwallon* (see n.) in his

Welsh campaign against Edwin of Northumbria (d. 633). This would fit well with the date of 627 given in *Ann. Cam.* for Belyn's death. J. Lloyd-Jones drew attention to the place-name *Tyddyn Belyn* near Tudweiliog in Llŷn, and to other possible occurrences of this hero's name near Llanllyfni (*Enwau Lleoedd Sir Gaernarfon*, p. 35).

Beli (Mawr m. Mynogan (*Manogan*)**)** 35: *Ar(y)anrot merch Veli* (see n. and nn. to *Caswalla6n m. Beli, Llud m. Beli, Bran Vendigeit m. Llyr*). BT 72.14–16: *nur yth iolaf budic veli amhanogan . . . ynys Vel Veli teithiawc oed idi* (see n. to *Y Vel Ynys*, App. I, no. 1), and cf. WM 186.29–32: *Ac y gwerescynnwys* (*yr amherawdr Macsen*) *yr ynys ar veli mab Manogan a'e veibon* 'And the emperor (Maxen) conquered the Island (of Britain) from Beli son of Manogan and his sons.' For the sons of *Beli* see n. to *Llud mab Beli* below.

Beli Mawr mab Manogan is the name with which the *Brut* renders Geoffrey of Monmouth's king *Heli* (HRB III, 20 = BD 44.8), though in HRB III, 1 etc. Geoffrey of Monmouth employs the name *Belinus* as that of a son of Dunwallo Molmutius. *Beli Mawr* appears in a number of early Welsh genealogies (EWGT index) as an 'ancestor deity' from whom many of the leading dynasties in early times claimed to be descended (cf. Giraldus Cambrensis, *Descr. Cam.* I, 3). Harl. Gen. no. I (EWGT 9, i) traces the ancestry of the Gwynedd line to *Aballac* [i.e. *Avallach*, see n.] *map Amalech qui fuit Beli Magni filius, et mater eius, quam dicunt esse consobrinum Mariae virginis*. Similarly Harl. Gen. no. X traces the descent of *Coel Hen* (see n.) to *Beli* and Anna; so also HGVK 1.21 and the Life of *St Cadoc* (VSB 119, EWGT 25, etc.). Thus all Coel's descendants, including Urien Rheged, Gwenddolau and Llywarch Hen (see App. II) are shown to have claimed descent from *Beli Mawr*. The Life of *St Beuno* gives a similar descent for the royal line of Powys (VSB 22). I suggested previously (SEBH 131–2) that *Beli Mawr* was the ancestor deity from whom the principal dynasties who ruled in early Wales claimed to be descended. This view gains support from Ifor Williams's suggestion (Cyf. Ll. a Ll. 12) that *Beli Mawr* is to be identified with the Gaulish god *Belenos* or *Belinos* (cf. B. F. Roberts (ed.), *Cyfranc Lludd a Llefelys*, pp. xii–xiii, and J. T. Koch, CMCS 20, pp. 4–6, who follow O'Rahilly (EIHM 67) in deriving *Beli* from the deity *Belgios*, and this gains support from the fact that the *Belgi* of Gaul and of Britain both claimed *Belgios* as their ancestor). It is a very old suggestion (see Bartrum, EWGT 126n. and idem, WCD 38–9) that the Anna who is described in the genealogies as 'cousin of the Virgin Mary' was originally identical with *Ana* or *Anu*, a variant form of the name of *Danu*, the Irish mother of the gods, who was therefore the Irish equivalent of the Welsh Dôn.

In HB ch. 19 it is said of Julius Caesar that he fought against *Dolobellus qui et ipse Bellinus vocabatur, et filius erat Minocanni. Beli fab Mynogan* thus appears under various forms and in a number of sources as the legendary

British ruler from whom the Romans conquered the country. According to Suetonius, a British prince called *Adminius Cynobellini Britannorum regis filiis* was exiled by his father and went over to the Romans in AD 40. At the hands of the fourth-century Orosius this name became *Minocynobellinus Britannorum regis filius*, which in turn resulted in the form given in HB. But *Beli Mawr* is a character too firmly rooted in early Welsh tradition for his existence to be accounted for merely as an adaptation of HB's *Bellinus* < *Belenos*. Further, Loth showed that *Manogan* itself can be explained as a Celtic name, since *Monocan* < W. *mynawg*, *mynog* 'noble, courteous' etc. (cf. CA 157; and GPC 2538 on *mynog*, *mynogan*) appears in the *Cartulaire de Redon* (RC 51, p. 10; *Chr. Br.* 152). Two further instances of this name in Celtic sources may be further noticed: *Jes. Gen.* XVIII: *Manogan m. pascen m. Cadell* (EWGT 48 (18)), and the Ogham inscription MINNACANNI (Macalister, CIIC I, no. 135). See nn. to *Llud m. Beli* and *Caswalla6n m. Beli*.

References to *Beli* and *Beli Hir* in *Gogynfeirdd* poetry suggest that Beli's name was familiar as that of a legendary ruler and proprietor of Britain (see App. I, no. 1, n.). These references have been collected by Ann Parry Owen, LlC XX, pp. 26ff., to which a number of allusions from later poetry might be added. The epithet *Mawr* is only exceptionally attached to *Beli* in poetry: as by Madog Dwygraig—*rud baladyr mal rod beli mawr* (RBP col. 1271.9), and by Einion Offeiriad, who curiously describes Sir Rhys ap Gruffudd as *Rhys rhysedd—Beli Mawr, Amherawdr Romani* (GEO no. 1.166–7nn.)—although traditionally *Beli Mawr* was the prince from whom the Romans conquered Britain, rather than himself the conqueror of the Romans.

Belyn o Leyn: = 62, see **Belen o Leyn.**

Bendigeituran; see **Bran Vendigeit m. Llŷr**. In early sources the form *Bendigeituran* appears to be confined to the text of *Mabinogi Branwen* and to TYP in the WR versions of both. *Benidigeitran* (*sic*) is employed by Bleddyn Fardd (CBT VII, no. 51.5, see n.) and subsequently by Tudur Aled (GTA no. CXXI.41), and by Lewys Môn (GLM no. VIII.19).

Blaes m. Iarll Llychlyn, App. IV, no. 6: 'B. son of the Earl of Llychlyn.' The name appears to be derived from that of the hermit *Bla(i)se* in the *Prose Merlin* (Sommer (ed.), *Vulgate Cycle of Arthurian Romances* II), to whom Merlin gave the task of writing down his prophecies and the writing of the early history of the Grail. He is described as 'li maistre de Merlin en Northumberlande', and his book 'aura a non *Li Livres du Graal*'.

Blathavn m. Mvreth 19b. (Pen. 47). *Mwreth* = *Mwrchath*, *Murchadh*, a king of Leinster; cf. HGVK 4.27n., 6.14n., lxxv, cxiv.

Bleidic 68. See n. on *Hyueid m. Bleidic*. Derivatives of *blaidd* 'wolf' are of fairly frequent occurrence in Ml.W. personal names; cf. *Bleddyn, Bleiddudd*, and the epithet of *Rhirid Flaidd*. *Bleiddig* is unknown: for possible clues as to his identity see D. P. Kirby, B XXVII, p. 86, and R. G. Gruffydd, SC XIV/XV, p. 97.

Bort m. Brenhin Bort 86, *Bwrt ap Bwrt brenhin Gasgwin*, App. IV, no. 2. 'Bwrt son of Bwrt, king of Gascony', i.e. *Bohort de Gannes* or *Bohort li Escillies*, son of king *Bohort* in the French *Vulgate Cycle*: the brother of Lionel and the cousin of Lancelot. He plays a part both in the *Lancelot* and in the *Queste del Saint Greal*; with Galahad and with Perceval he was one of the three knights who achieved the *Queste*. *Bort* / *Bwrt* became familiar in Welsh sources through the fourteenth-century *Queste del Seint Greal* (SG 96.4–5: *Ac ynteu a dywawt mae bwrt agawns* (i.e. *de Gannes*) *oed y henw. A mab brenhin bort wyf a chevynderw y lancelot*); see further P. C. Bartrum, *Nat. Lib. of Wales Journal* XIV, p. 242, and C. Lloyd-Morgan, *Nat. Lib. of Wales Journal* XXI, p. 332. For *Bort*'s alleged relationship to Joseph of Arimathea see n. to *Joseph o Arimathia*.

Bran[1] m. Dyuynwal 51. HRB III, 1ff. (= BD 33ff.) gives the story of *Brenn(i)us*, the brother of Belinus and son of Dunwallo Molmutius, who conquered the Romans and became emperor of Rome.

Bran[2] Vendigeit (Bendigeituran) m. Llyr 37, 97. See nn. to *Caradawc m. Bran*, *Llŷr Lledyeith*, *Manawydan m. Llŷr*, *Branwen ferch Lŷr*, *Beli Mawr m. Mynogan*. According to *Mabinogi Branwen*, *Brân* ('B. The Blessed') was the grandson of Beli Mawr, whose daughter Penardun was united to Llŷr Lledyeith. In reality it seems probable that *Brân* was the son of Beli's sister, from whom he succeeded to the rule of Britain, and that *Penardun verch Ueli* (PKM 46.10) should be emended to *Penardun chwaer Ueli* in accordance with the statement made elsewhere in the text (46.7; 49.10), that *Brân* and Manawydan were cousins to Caswallawn m. Beli (see J. Rhŷs and D. Brynmor-Jones, *The Welsh People* (London, 1900 etc.), pp. 39–40). *Brân* 'raven' occurs frequently in poetry as an epithet for a warrior (GPC 308; cf. CLlH 73 on *kynvrein*). In Irish sources *Bran* is the name of the hero of the eighth- (or ninth-century) tale *Immram Brain* ('The Voyage of Bran') who is perhaps ultimately to be identified with the Welsh *Brân*. The name is found also in early Breton documents (*Chr. Br.* 111). See further Glyn E. Jones, B XXV, pp. 380–6.

The portrayal of *Brân Fendigaid* in *Mabinogi Branwen* suggests that he is a euhemerized deity. His size is such that no ordinary house will hold him, he crosses the sea by wading, and carries his army on his back across the River Liffey. (The Liffey and not the Shannon is clearly the river intended in the text by the name *Llinon* (= *Lliuon*, O.Ir. *Life*); see my review of P. Mac Cana's *Branwen* in *Medium Aevum*, XXVIII, pp. 208–9.) The *clwydeu* 'hurdles' which were placed across the river are a clear onomastic reference to Dublin, the city which bestrides the Liffey and for which the Irish name is *Áth Cliath* ('the ford of the hurdles').

Brân is also the possessor of a magic cauldron of regeneration, and after his death his dismembered head serves as a marvellous talisman for the satisfaction of all human needs and, when buried, it becomes a defence to his country. Ifor Williams suggested (PKM 222) that the epithet *Bendigeid* for *Brân* and *Urddawl* for Brân's head (*Ysbydawt Urdaul Benn* 'The Hospitality of the Noble Head'), cited as one of the subtitles which relate to episodes in the *Mabinogi*, have probably replaced older epithets whose meaning had become obsolete by the time of the first written redaction of the story. Thus *Urddawl* could represent *Uthrawl* 'terrible' or *Uirdaul* < *gwyrthiol* 'miraculous'. *Bendigeit* in this phrase might be a corruption of *Penn* with a following epithet, since the marvellous qualities of *Brân*'s severed head appear to have been his most prominent characteristic in the underlying mythology associated with his name. (For some speculation as to the significance of the epithet *bendigeit* 'blessed, sacred, praiseworthy' as applied to *Brân*, Gwerthefyr and Cadwaladr, see Glenys Goetinck, 'The Blessed Heroes', SC XX/XXI, pp. 87–109.) The form *Brân Vendigeit* appears to have been restricted to PKM and to TYP, while *Brân fab Llŷr* is more commonly employed by the poets.

Whatever its original significance, the later meaning attached to *bendigeit* 'blessed' became responsible for the growth of the legend that *Brân* had first introduced Christianity into Britain (see on this G. J. Williams, *Iolo Morganwg*, pp. 312–13n.). This tradition cannot, however, be traced back to any source earlier than the eighteenth century (see n. to *Carada6c m. Bran*). It seems to have been brought about by the identification made by antiquarians of this period between *Carada6c fab Bran* and the British leader *Caratācus*. It received extended currency owing to Iolo Morganwg's substitution in the *Myvyrian Archaiology of Wales* (MA² 391, no. 42 = the *Iolo Manuscripts* (Liverpool, 1848) 100, no. 42) of the 'Lineage of Bran fab Llŷr' for that of Joseph of Arimathea in the triad *Tri Santaidd Linys Ynys Prydain* (TYP no. 81, see n.). For Iolo's adaptation of this triad see further his own English translation of his original version, and my note, THSC 1968, pp. 310, 331.

An early allusion to the tale of *Brân* is found in BT 33.25: *Bum y gan vran yn iwerdon / Gweleis pan ladwyt y mordwyt tyllon* 'I was with Brân in Ireland, I saw when the M.T. was slain' (see n. PKM 207). Cynddelw: *Rut ongir Bran vab llir lledieith / Ruit y clod in cludav anreith* (LlDC no. 38.17 = CBT III, no. 7.17n.) 'the red spear of Brân son of Llŷr; facile his fame for carrying off booty'; *Rybu Uran uab Llyr llu rwymadur mad / yg camp yg kywlad yg cad, yg cur* (CBT IV, no. 17.71–2) 'Brân son of Llŷr has lived; he was a good commander of the host; in battle, in hostile territory, in the contest, in stress'. Further allusions by Prydydd y Moch are listed in CBT V, no. 11.27n.; 20.37. In his eloquent final elegy for Llywelyn ap Gruffudd, Bleddyn Fardd (*circa* 1257–*circa* 1283) compares the overthrow of the last prince to the deaths of Llywelyn Fawr, of 'Benigeitran' and of Arthur (CBT VII, 51.5–8n.).

The memory of *Brân fab Llŷr* may have survived in the name of *Castell Dinas Brân* in Denbighshire. Alternatively, it has been suggested that this place-name may itself have given rise to the creation of the character of *Brân*, which subsequently drew to itself mythological traditions which were originally connected with other figures; see P. Mac Cana, *Branwen, Daughter of Llŷr*, pp. 137–9, who suggests further that the allusion in CA l. 1291—*ymwan bran clot lydan yg kynwyt*—may have referred to a lost tale about *Brân*, which was originally located in this area in Denbighshire.

In his article 'Bran, Brennos: Gallo-Brittonic History and Mythology' (CMCS 20, pp. 1–20), J. T. Koch proposes two intriguing parallels between the traditions recounted by Pausanius about the Celtic chieftain *Brennos* (the invader of Greece in the third century BC) and elements in the *Mabinogi* account of *Brân fab Llŷr*. He proposes that Brancaster (*Branodunum*) 'the fort of Brân' on the Norfolk coast originally preceded London as the site where *Brân*'s head was believed to have been buried, and he sees in the name of the Gaulish leader *Brennos* the prototype of *Brân Fendigaid fab Llŷr*.

Many Arthurianists have concurred in regarding *Brân Fendigaid* as the Celtic prototype of *Bron*, the 'Rich Fisher' or the 'Fisher King' of the Grail romances in European literatures. See A. Nutt, *Studies in the Legend of the Holy Grail* (London, 1888); J. Rhŷs, *The Arthurian Legend*, pp. 306 ff; WAL passim, and AW 87–8.

Bran[3] Galed o'r Gogledd, App. III, no. 3 'Brân the Niggard from the North' (*Caled* 'niggardly, stingy, illiberal', GPC 392). On *Brân Galed* see Thomas Jones, *Mod. Lang. Review* 35, pp. 403 ff. *Brân Galed*'s appearance as one of the 'Men of the North' is confirmed in a genealogy by Gruffudd Hiraethog in Pen. 176 (B XVIII, p. 237 (23), and p. 246; see also EWGT p. 150n.), as well as by Guto'r Glyn's allusion: *Bran Galed brin y gelwynt / Bonedd Gwyr y Gogledd gynt / Taliesin, ddewin ddiwael / A'i troes yn well no'r Tri Hael* 'Niggardly Brân they used to call him who was descended of old from the Nobility of the North; Taliesin, no mean magician, transformed him into one better than the *Tri Hael*' (cf. triad 2, and GGl no. LXXXII.61–4). Guto'r Glyn's mention suggests an allusion to a version of the tale in which Taliesin played a similar magician's part to that which is elsewhere attributed to Myrddin. The northern ambience of the fragment suggests that *Brân Galed* may be identical to *Bran uab Ymellyrn* (CLlH no. III.40; see EWSP 238–40), though *Brân* is too common a name to allow of any certainty in this identification. Cf. the legendary *Brân* in the *Englynion Cad Goddeu* (quoted CLlH l–li, and EWSP 238–40). See further Glyn E. Jones, B XXV, pp 105–12.

Brangor (Brenyn) 86. 'King Brangor' is derived from *Brangoire* in the *Prose Lancelot*, king of *Estregorre* or *Destregorre* (for *Destregales*?). In the *Merlin* in the French *Vulgate Cycle* it is said that his territory *marchist an roialme de Norgales*. (There is confusion as to the name of the ruler of this territory, which is alternatively given as *Carados.*) See index to Sommer's edition of the *Vulgate Cycle*, and C. Lloyd-Morgan, *Nat. Lib. of Wales Journal* XXI, p. 334.

Bran6en verch Lyr 53, 95. See *Bran Vendigeit m. Llyr, Carada6c m. Bran, Mathol6ch 6ydel. Branwen verch Lyr* is the tragic heroine of Welsh literature whose tale is given in the Second Branch of the *Mabinogi.* She was given in marriage by her brother, Brân Fendigaid, to Matholwch king of Ireland, as a pledge of alliance between Britain and Ireland. Owing to the dishonour to which she was subjected in Ireland (cf. triad 53) she became the innocent cause of strife between Brân and Matholwch, and of the disastrous war which wiped out the population of Ireland, in the course of which both her brother, the king of Britain, and her young son lost their lives. When she was brought home to Wales, Branwen broke her heart and died, and the *Mabinogi* tells that she was buried beside the River Alaw in Anglesey. In effect her name is preserved here in *Ynys Bronwen,* the site of a cromlech known traditionally as *Bedd Bronwen.* (This is referred to in a letter by R. Vaughan, see *Arch. Camb.* 1868, p. 235; and in Gough's additions to Camden (edition of 1789) II, p. 568: 'We have a tradition that the largest cromlech in this country (Anglesey) is the monument of Bronwen daughter of King Lleir who is said to have begun his reign about the year *anno mundi* 3105.') For the discovery in 1813 at this place of an urn containing calcined bones which were at that time believed to be those of a young female see PKM 217; *Arch. Cam.* 1868, p. 238. For the report of the subsequent excavation of the site of *Bedd Branwen* in the 1960s see F. Lynch and B. L. Jones, TAAS 1966, pp. 1–37. According to their concluding summary (p. 29), 'Bedd Branwen was the burial place of a group of people, probably a single large family, living at the end of the Early Bronze Age, around 1400 BC. They practised a communal burial rite in which each burial appears to have been of equal importance, whatever the personal wealth of the individual, and in which most of the urns were actually buried at the same time'. This report effectively disposes of the claim made in *Arch. Cam.* 1868 (and corresponding to that made in PKM edn. of 1930, p. 217). There is also *a Tŵr Bronwen* at Harlech which is referred to by the *Cywyddwyr*: GTP no. 16. 47–8—*Tŵr Bronwen a orffennwyd / Ferch Lyr o fewn Harddlech lwyd.* W. J. Gruffydd suggested (LlC I, pp. 132–3) that both this name and *Bedd Bronwen* appear to be older than the *Mabinogi*, so that the *Mabinogi* story may have evolved around them.

The name *Branwen* is probably to be explained as an adaptation of *Bronwen* 'White Breast' in which the vowel has been influenced by the name of her brother *Brân.* The name appears once as *Bronwen* in the White Book text of the *Mabinogi* (PKM 32.26n. = WM 42.29–30). Justus Llwyd alludes to *neithawr Vranwen* (RBP col. 1365.40 = YB XVII, 72.67), but it seems likely that Dafydd ap Gwilym is the earliest known poet to name *Branwen* when he describes Morfudd as *A'i lliw fal Branwen verch Llŷr* (GDG no. 40.14; on the absence here of lenition after *verch* see TC §43). The name *Brangien*, *Brengvein* (and variants) occurs in the *Tristan* poems by the Norman and Anglo-Norman poets Béroul and Thomas, and this name can hardly be explained as other than a written borrowing from that of the *Mabinogi* heroine (see AW 280, and n. 38, and P. Sims-Williams, *Romania* 116, p. 78).

Breat, 26 (W), see **Brennach Wydel**.

Brennach Wydel 26 (= *Breat tywyssawc o'r gogled* WR). 'B. the Irishman.' Cf. the name of St *Brynach*, the Pembrokeshire saint whose *Vita* is preserved in a twelfth-century version (VSB 2ff.). St Brynach is commemorated at *Llanfyrnach* in Pembrokeshire and at *Llanfrynach* in Brecknock; cf. LBS I, 325. It seems unlikely that there is any connection between the saint and the character named in the triad, though the correspondence in names is interesting. The termination in *-ach* suggests that this name is an Irish borrowing (see EANC I, and n. to *Auallach*). But cf. P. Sims-Williams, B XXIX, pp. 615–16 on *-ch* as a termination in medieval Welsh borrowed names as suggestive of 'uncouthness, brute vigour and primitive heroism'. The form *(B)reat* in WR has arisen as a textual corruption of *Brennach*, see n. to triad 26. Perhaps the description *tywyssawc o'r gogled* 'prince of the North' arose out of a confused recollection of the name *Bryneich*, *Brennych* (Bernicia).

Brwyn m. Kynadaf 43: *Du march B. m. K.* See n. to *Mada6c m. Brwyn*. This name appears as *brvyn bro(n) bradavc* 'B. Treacherous Breast' in *Canu y Meirch*, BT 48.10–11; see n. to triad 43. Other instances of the name are: LlDC no. 18.71: *bruin o bricheinauc*; LL 221.9: *bruin filius duta*. Cf. also *bruyno hir* in LlDC no. 18.146 (*brwyn* = 'grief').

For *Kynedaf* (= *Cunedda, Cunedag*), the progenitor of the kings of Gwynedd in the fifth century, see HB, ch. 62; Harl. Gens. nos. I, III, XXXII. *Brwyn* is, however, not listed among the sons of Cunedda in the latter genealogy.

Brychan Brecheinya6c 70, 81, 96. *Brychan* was the eponymous fifth-century ruler of the kingdom of *Brycheiniog*, which lasted until the tenth century, and comprised the modern county of Brecknock, with the exception of the district of Buellt (HW 270–1). *Brachanus* / *Brychan* figures prominently in the twelfth-century Life of *St Cadog*, as well as in the early document *De Situ Brecheniauc* and in *Cognacio Brychan* (EWGT 14–19; VSB 313–15). For a full discussion of the Brychan documents, which appear to have been copied from an original of the eleventh century or earlier, see EWGT 14; E. Phillimore, *Cy*. 7 (1886), pp. 105–6; CLlH xxii; WCD 64–7; and Charles Thomas, *And Shall These Mute Stones Speak?*, pp. 131–16. *De Situ Brecheniauc* claims that Brychan's father was an Irishman named Anlac filius Coronauc and that his mother Marchell was the daughter of a British king Teuderic. There is good evidence for the Irish origin of the dynasty, as appears from the names given to *Brychan*'s immediate ancestors in the Life of *St Cadog*: *Briscethach*, *Brusc*, *Urbf*, *Anlach* (VSB 118). Here Brychan is said to be *de optimis prosapiis regum Hibernensium*. The Irish descent of the ruling dynasty of Dyfed may be compared (*Cy*. 14, p. 112; EWGT 106 (18)).

The tract attributes to *Brychan* a family of ten sons and twenty-four daughters, most of whom became 'saints'. It is claimed that six of the daughters married 'Men of the North'; for the 'marriage' of Brychan's daughter *Nyvein* to *Kynvarch m. Meirchyawn* see n. to triad 70. Variant details concerning Brychan and his family are found in *De Situ Brecheniauc*, in *Jes. Gens*. nos. I–III (EWGT 42–4), as well as in the sixteenth-century tract *Cognacio Brychan*, EWGT 17–19. Early references to Brychan and his family are made by Gerald of Wales (*Itin. Cam*. I, 2) and by Walter Map, *De Nugis Curialium* (ed. *Cym. Record Series*), 81. Taliesin's praise-poem, *Trawsganu Cynan Garwyn*, refers to *gwlad brachan* (PT no. I.20); a later bardic reference is by Prydydd y Moch: *eil uann vrychan vrecheinyawc* (CBT V, no. 24.59n.).

Bun, gwreic Flamdwyn (merch Kulvanawyt Prydein) 80. *Bun* 'maiden'. See n. to *Fflamdwyn*.

Bwrt m. Bwrt, see **Bort m. Brenhin Bort**.

Bytwini Esgob 1. 'Bishop B.' CO l. 356: *Bitwini* (RM *Betwini*) *Escob, a uendigei uwyt a llyn (arthur)*; Br. Rh: *y gwelynt Arthur yn eisted mywn ynys wastat is y ryt. Ac o'r neill parth idaw betwin escob* (RM col. 148.23–40). *Englynion y Clyweit* (*Blodeugerdd* no. 31, *englyn* 33): *A glyweist-di a gant Bedwi, Oed escob donyawc difri*. Bishop Bytwini has been detected as the prototype of Bishop Bawdewyn in the Middle English poem *Sir Gawain and the Green Knight* (ed. Tolkien and Gordon, 1. 112). Here the name must have come through a French source, and has been assimilated to the name *Baudouin* (see editor's n.). The same character is found in two other English Arthurian poems, 'The Turk and Gowin' (Hales and Furnivall, Percy Folio MS. I, 96), and 'Sir Gawain and the Carl of Carlisle' (ed. Auvo Kurvinin, Helsinki, 1951), where the name appears under the variant forms Bishop *Bavdewyn*, *Bodwim*, *Bodwin*.

Cadauel m. Kynued6 68. On the name *Cadafel* < *Catumaglos* see K. H. Jackson, *Celt and Saxon*, pp. 38–9; idem, *Journal of Celtic Studies* I, p. 69; OSPG 72n. Jackson points out that HB's spelling *Catgabail* is a part of the sarcasm intended by the epithet *Catguommed* 'Battle-Refuser', since the Ml. W. form of the name *Cadavel* could be derived either from *Catumaglos* 'Battle Chief' or from **Catugabaglos* > O.W. *Catgabail* 'Battle-Seizer / Battle-Shirker'. According to a confused passage in HB ch. 65, King *Cadafael* of Gwynedd won this epithet because of his defection from the army of his ally Penda of Mercia, shortly before the battle of Winwaed Field (*Ann. Cam*. 657), at which Penda was killed by Oswiu of Northumbria (HW 190–1; WCD 72;

F. M. Stenton, *Anglo-Saxon England*, pp. 83–4. See further EWSP 130–1, and D. P. Kirby, B XXVII, p. 95). Jackson cited manuscript authority for his conclusion that *usque in manu Pendae* is a misplaced gloss representing *usque in Manau* 'as far as Manau, to Penda'. He identified *Iudeu* with Stirling, and suggested that Stirling was the capital of Manaw.

In seventh-century Welsh this name would be pronounced with nasalized -*v*-, and the difference in pronunciation between **Catumaglos* and **Catugabaglos* would have been sufficiently slight to invite the writer of the HB passage to achieve his pun by substituting *Catgabail* for *Catamail* (LHEB 437). Nothing is known of either *Cadafael* or his father *Cynfeddw*, and their names are absent from the Harleian genealogy of the early rulers of Gwynedd (EWGT 9(i)). It seems clear that they did not belong to Gwynedd's direct line of descent, leading through Maelgwn Gwynedd to Cunedda. The triad implies that *Cadafael* and his father were interlopers, perhaps members of that company of Britons who supported Penda of Mercia in his opposition to Oswiu of Northumbria in the events leading up to the battle of Strages Gai Campi or Winwaed, which took place near Leeds in 655–6. The battle of Strages Gai Campi is listed in *Ann. Cam.* 656. In the triad it is the war-band of the historical twelfth-century Breton ruler Alan Fergant, which is said—incongruously—to have absconded *hyd nos* 'by night' on the eve of the battle of Camlan. Several layers of innuendo may therefore underlie the use of this derogatory phrase, in reference to the opprobrious act which has been recorded of *Cadafael ap Cynfeddw* in HB ch. 65. One further allusion to Cadafael may have survived in a line of the *Cyvoesi Myrddin*: *Yngerd gadauel aui koel* 'in the song of Cadafel there will be a portent' (RBP col. 577.14–15).

Cadawc m. Gwynlliw Varvoc (*varchoc*), App. IV, no. 6 'Cadog son of G. the Bearded' or 'G. the warrior'. The reference is to the sixth-century St Cadog. For his *Vita* and that of his father *Gwynlliw* see VSB 24 ff., 172 ff. The epithets *barfawg* / *farfawg* 'bearded' and *marchawg* / *farchawg* 'horseman, warrior' are continually confused in the manuscripts; see n. to *Llawuroded 6ar6a6c* below, and cf. CO nn. to *Dillus Varchawc*, l. 700, and *Llawurodet Uaruawc*, l. 223. Cadog's inclusion in this triad is perhaps due to confusion between his name and that of *Cado Hen* (see n. below).

Catcor m. Gorolwyn 66. *Catcor* < *cad* 'battle' + *cawr* 'giant, champion, hero' (GPC 443); cf. RBP col. 1311.21: *(g)atkavr vriw*. For another suggestion see E. Rowland, LlC VI, p. 237.

Cadegyr 7: *Elinwy m. Categir*. Cf. *Cattegir* for *Cattegyrnn* > *Catteyrn ap Cadell* (*Ddyrnllug* in Harl. Gens. 22, 23, 27 (EWGT 12)). *Categyrnn* is presented as an ancestor of St Beuno, and son of Cadell Ddyrnllug (VSB 22; EWGT 30 (24)).

Catuan 12. See n. to *Catwalla6n m. Catuan. Cadfan* was great-grandson of Maelgwn Gwynedd, and ruled Gwynedd in the early seventh century. He died *circa* 625; see Harl. Gen. I (EWGT 9(i)). His name is preserved on an inscribed stone in the church at Llangadwaladr, Anglesey: *Catamanus rex sapientis(s)imus omnium regum* (ECMW no. 14; HW I, 182). Ifor Williams pointed out in *Inventory of the Ancient Mouments of Anglesey* (p. cxv) that the form CATAMANUS represents a false archaism since, by the seventh century, intervocalic lenition and the loss of the stem-vowel had already taken place, so that this name would have been pronounced approximately as at the present day. A correct restitution of the British form would have been CATUMANDUS ('wise in battle'). The relevant papers by Ifor Williams are reprinted in BWP chs. I and II, and see also LHEB 512 and CA 315.

Catgyffro 24, 39, 42 LlDC no. 6.ln.: *Gilbert m. Catgyffro* (see n.). *Catgyffro* 'Battle Inciter' or 'Army Disturber' is an epithet employed by Meilyr Brydydd for Gruffudd ap Cynan (CBT I, no. 3.123n.). In *Englynion y Clyweit* (ed. Haycock, *Blodeugerdd* no. 31, *englyn* 9), *Cadgyffro (Hen)* is a self-standing personal name rather than an epithet. *Englynion y Clyweit* evidently derives its proper names partly from TYP, and reflects the same confusion as appears in TYP as to whether *Catgyffro* is an epithet for *Gilbert* or a patronymic.

Cado Hen 49. The reputation of *Dionysius Cato* for wisdom in medieval Wales is testified by the number of Welsh versions which have come down of the *Catonis Disticha (Cynghorau Catwn)* dating from *circa* 1300 (see B II, pp. 16 ff.), and by the references made to *Cado* by the poets, e.g. in the *Cyvoesi Myrddin a Gwenddydd*: *Kyuarchaf ym diagro urawt a darllewys llyuyr cado* (RBP col. 580.24–5). In more than one instance *Cado*, *Cadw* is cited by the poets as a pattern of proverbial wisdom, as in triad 49:

> Prydydd y Moch: *Marcwlff a Chadw gadyr swyson* (CBT V, no. 4.13).
>
> Madog Dwygraig: *Na Nud o galon . . . neu gadw o synnwyr* (RBP col. 1310.36–7).
>
> Gutun Owain (*circa* 1450–98) in a *cywydd* (GO no. XLII.41–6) to Elisaf ap Gruffudd describes his patron as *fal Catw ddoeth a Selyf* (= Solomon); cf. an anonymous *marwnad* to Gutun Owain: *Gutun—ail i Gattwn oedd* (GO no. LXVII.8). It is therefore interesting to find that Ll. 28 contains a text of the *Catonis Disticha* in Gutun's hand (GO 216).
>
> Elsewhere *Kato Hen* is employed as the name of one of the 'Seven Sages of Rome' in Henry Lewis (ed.), *Seith Doethon Ruvein* (Cardiff, 1967).

Cadr(i)eith m. Portha6r Gadw 9 (W: *Caydyrleith ap Seidi*, R: *Caedyrieith ap S.*), 75 (Pen. 47: *Cadeiryeith. Cadrieith* = 'Fine Speech'). For the name cf. CA l. 1405: *Kynon a Chadreith*; and for the patronymic cf. CO l. 293n.: *Cas mab Saidi*; Br. Rh. (RM 160.12–16): *kadyrieith mab saidi . . . Ac ar hynny nachaf ueird yn dyuot y datkanu kerd y arthur, ac nyt oed dyn a adnapei y* *gerd honno. namyn kadyrieith e hun.* This description, combined with the meaning of *Cadr(i)eith*, 'Fine Speech', suggests an allusion to a poet, perhaps a recent poet or a famous contemporary. Can it be that Cynddelw Brydydd Mawr is intended by the allusion? (See my suggestion on this point in Morfydd E. Owen and Brynley F. Roberts (eds), *Beirdd a Thywysogion*, p. 215.) For *Cadrieith m. Porthawr Gadw* see *Gereint ac Enid* (RM col. 246.18–19, etc. and ed. R. L. Thomson (DIAS, 1977), 166 etc.). The meaning of this epithet is obscure, and probably corrupt. It appears also in the allusion to *Cadrieith* in *Englynion y Clyweit* (*Blodeugerdd* no. 31, *englyn* 72: *A glyweisti a gant Kad(r)eith / Uab Porthawr milwr areith?* (where the name was probably derived from TYP).

Katwaladyr 6endigeit (m. Catwalla6n m. Catuan) 17, 53. See nn. to *Catwalla6n, Golydan Vard. Catwaladr* < *Cat* + *gwaladr* 'leader, chieftain' etc. (GPC 1565). The attribution to *Cadwaladr* of the epithet *bendigeit* 'blessed', or 'worthy of praise' (GPC 271) is no doubt related to the fact that *Cadwaladr Vendigeit* is included in *Bonedd y Saint* (VSB 320.11 = EWGT 56 (11)) and is alleged to be the founder of the church of *Llangadwaladr*, near Aberffraw in Anglesey. It seems most probable that this epithet was originally bestowed on his father *Cadwallawn* (to whom it is actually appropriated in triad 55), and that from him it became transferred erroneously to his son. (On the possible significance of *bendigaid* as traditionally applied to certain legendary heroes see Glenys Goetinck, 'The Blessed Heroes', SC XX/XXI, pp. 87–109, and cf. nn. to *Bran Vendigeit, G6ertheuyr 6endigeit.*)

Cadwaladr was king of Gwynedd during the latter half of the seventh century, cf. Harl. Gen. I (EWGT 9)—*Catgualart map Catguallaun map Catman*, etc. According to *Ann. Cam.* 682 he died in the plague of that year: *Mortalitas magna fuit in Britannia, in qua catgualart filius Catgualarn obiit.* Probably this date is too late, since HB ch. 64 makes the alternative statement that *Cadwaladr* died during the reign of Oswiu of Northumbria (d. 671): *Dum ipse (Osguid) regnabat, venit mortalitas hominum, Catgualatr regnante apud Brittones, post patrem suum, et in ea periit*. The reference is probably to the great plague of 682, which the *Ann. Cam.* entry may have confused with one of the numerous lesser plagues which occurred during the course of the sixth and seventh centuries. J. E. Lloyd suggested (HW I, 230) that *Cadwaladr* died in this year (perhaps after having become a monk in the monastic settlement at *Llangadwaladr*).

References in poetry concur with TYP no. 63, however, in alluding to a tradition that *Cadwaladr* died by violence, rather than in a plague; cf. the *Cyvoesi* poem: . . . *pa leas a dvc Kadwaladyr? / As gvan gvaev o ergrywyd llog / a llav kynn diwedyd* (Pen. 3: *dyn diuedyd*) / *dybyd gymry gvarth or dyd* (RBP col. 582.7–9) 'What death will carry off *Cadwaladr*? A shaft from the splinters of a ship will pierce him by the hand of an unbaptised man(?), shame will come to the Cymry because of that day.' Phylip Brydydd: *o gwnaeth golydan gyflauan diryeit / bit ar y eneyt yr enwired / taraw kadwaladr colofyn elyflu* (H 228.19–21 = CBT VI, no. 15.11n.). 'Since Golydan performed the wicked slaughter, the iniquity will be on his soul, the striking of *Cadwaladr*, pillar of the host.'

Apart from these obscure allusions to the manner in which he met his death, no record has come down as to the career of *Cadwaladr*. This is the more tantalizing since in *Armes Prydein*, ll. 163–5, and other prophetic poems in BT and in LlDC (see G 92) his name is coupled with that of *Cynan*[1] (*Meiriadoc*) (see n.) as one of the two promised deliverers who will one day return to champion their countrymen against the English (AP l. 81n. and ll. 163–6).

Since we know nothing specific about *Cadwaladr*'s achievements, except for obscure allusions as to the manner in which he met his death (see n. to *Golydan*) his reputation as a promised deliverer in medieval poetry appears to support the view that he has been endowed not only with the epithet, but also with the fame which should properly belong to his father *Cadwallon*, the devastator of Northumbria and 'the only British king in historical times who ever overthrew an English dynasty' (Stenton, *Anglo-Saxon England*, p. 81).

Whatever the real reason for *Cadwaladr*'s subsequent reputation as a deliverer of his people, the fact that he already appears with Cynan (Meiriadoc) in this role in *Armes Prydein* (ll. 81, 163, see nn.) precludes the possibility that it can have arisen from his being the last Welsh king to be named in Geoffrey of Monmouth's HRB. Geoffrey states (XII, 17) that *Cadwaladr* was instigated by an angelic vision to end his life in Rome, and that it was foretold that the Welsh would not regain possession of Britain until such time as his relics be brought back from Rome. Geoffrey may have confused *Cadwaladr* with *Caedwalla*, king of Wessex, who died a pilgrim to Rome in 689, though this confusion seems to antedate HRB, since Bede uses the name for both the west-Saxon king of this name and for Cadwallon, *Cadwaladr*'s father (*Hist. Ecc.* II, 20; III, 1; IV, 12, 15, etc.). Geoffrey of Monmouth must have known of the British tradition about *Cadwaladr*'s promised return, since it is clear from HRB VII that he had some acquaintance with Welsh prophetic verse. On Geoffrey's treatment of this theme of the promise of eventual restoration of Welsh sovereignty over Britain see B. F. Roberts, *Studies on Middle Welsh Literature*, pp. 31–2.

Other allusions by the *Gogynfeirdd* are as follows:

Gwalchmai ap Meilyr: *Hyd pan del Kynan . . . a Chadwaladyr mawr* (H 16.19–20 = CBT I, no. 6.21–2; see n. to *Cynan*[1]).

Gr. ab yr Ynad Coch: *gwersyll katwaladr* (= *Aberffraw*, CBT no. VII, 36.11n.).

Gr. ap Maredudd: *nertheu katwaladyr rud baladyr* (RBP col. 1316.20 = GGM no. 4.69–70).

Catwalla6n[1] m. Catuan 11, 12, 29, *march C.* 40, *Katwalla6n* 69, *C.*

Vendigeit 55. See nn. to *Catuan, Catwaladr, Etwin vrenhin Lloegr*. For the epithet *Bendigeit* see nn. to *Catwaladr* and to triad 37.

Ann. Cam. 629: *Obsessio Catguallaun regis in insula Glannauc*; ibid., 630: *Gueith Meicen, etc.* (see triad 55 and n.); ibid., 631: *Bellum Cantscaul in quo Catguallaun corruit.*

HB ch. 64: *Ipse* (Oswald) *occidit Catgunblaun* (leg. *Catguollaun*) *regem Guenedotae regionis, in bello Ca(n)tscaul, cum magna clade exercitus sui.*

On *Bellum Cantscaul* (= battle of Heavenfield) see Ifor Williams, B VI, pp. 351–4; Max Foerster B VII, p. 33; and cf. also Bede, *Hist. Ecc.* III, 1.

Ifor Williams has shown (B VI, pp. 351–4) that Cantscaul 'the young warrior's enclosure' is a literal translation of Hagulstaldesham, the nearest place to the site of the battle of Heavenfield which is likely to have been known to a Welsh chronicler.

For text and discussion of the seventh-century (?) poem *Moliant Cadwallawn* see the edition by Ifor Williams (B VII, pp. 23–33) and subsequently that of R. G. Gruffydd, *Ast. H.* ch. 1. This poem was only known from eighteenth-century copies until a later and incomplete version was discovered and discussed by Graham Thomas, 'Dryll o Hen Lyfr Ysgrifen', B XXIII, pp. 309–16, and for some additional manuscript fragments of early poems relating to Cadwallon see idem, 'Llinellau o Gerddi i Gadwallon ap Cadfan', B XXXIV, pp. 67–9. In the light of these additional textual fragments, *Moliant Cadwallawn* was freshly edited and discussed, together with the other fragments, by R. G. Gruffydd in *Ast. H.* 25–43 (English summary, ibid. 3–4). Can *Moliant Cadwallon*, which is partly reminiscent in its style of the *Gododdin*, represent the surviving work of *Afan Ferddig* (see n.), who is celebrated by Cynddelw and in triad 11 as the poet of *Cadwallon*?

The contest between King *Cadwallon* of Gwynedd and Edwin of Northumbria so impressed itself on the consciousness of Welsh poets that *Edwin* (see n.) came to symbolize the typical Saxon enemy, though surprisingly, several Welsh rulers were later given his name (HW 827). After his conquest of the British kingdom of Elmet in Yorkshire in 616 (HB ch. 63) *Edwin* is said to have conquered the 'Mevanian islands' (Bede, *Hist. Ecc.* II, 5, 9), which have been taken to mean the islands of Man and Anglesey. The English conquest of Anglesey would have provided the reason for *Cadwallon*'s exile in Ireland, referred to in triad 29. Historians have regarded the *obsessio in insula Glannauc* as a prelude to *Cadwallon*'s exile, and the little island of Priestholm (*insula Glannauc*, off the shore of Anglesey) may well have given *Cadwallon* his last foothold on Welsh soil.

Moliant Cadwallawn and the other fragments, however, were evidently addressed to *Cadwallon* when he was at the height of his career: the *Moliant* is composed on a note of exultation and victory, and bears no hint of the reversal of his fortunes. It contains allusions to Edwin, to Brineich (Bernicia), to 'the burning of York' (l. 37), and to a battle in Gwynedd, which was accompanied by immense slaughter (ll. 16–17). But the context is exceedingly obscure, owing to the corrupt and fragmentary state of the texts, as much as to their archaism. There are several references to the sea and to the wind and waves, and to an encampment on a hill somewhere in Môn (l. 22). This latter allusion invites comparison with the lines in BT 73.9–10: *Pan dyfu gatwallawn dros eigyawn iwerdon / Yd atrefnwys nefwy yn ardnefon* 'When C. came (back?) across the Irish sea, he re-established his court in *Ardd Nefon*'. The ensuing lines (24–5) are: *nyt ar arch Brineich ny ry dadlas / ac Edwin arnadunt yn dad rwy twyllvras* 'He did not negotiate at the request of the men of Bernicia, since the deceitful Edwin was their leader'. It is therefore possible that the *obsessio in insula Glannauc* took place not before, but after, *Cadwallon*'s return from Ireland, and that he succeeded in driving Edwin from Anglesey (cf. l. 46: *aded gynt ethynt ynhydd irver hallt* 'the foreign tribes have gone into the salt sea'), and that he followed up his success with a victorious campaign in Wales, after which, without delay, he set upon the invasion of Northumbria. *Ann. Cam.* places its three consecutive references to *Cadwallon*'s affairs in three consecutive years (629–31). The dating of the battles of Meigen (=Heathfield?, see n. to triad 55) and Cantscaul (Heavenfield) are too early by Bede's chronology, which places these battles in the years 633 and 634 respectively.

Geoffrey of Monmouth's account of *Cadwallon* bears out that of TYP before his flight across the sea (cf. HW I, p. 184–5). Triads 26 and 29 add some important particulars such as the mutual upbringing of Edwin and *Cadwallon* at the court of Gwynedd (see introduction p. lxxx, and HRB XII, 1–2). Yet this account does not appear to be based upon TYP, so there is the more reason to believe that Geoffrey may have had some independent traditional knowledge of *Cadwallon*—which gives the more credit to his unsupported statement that *Cadwallon* married a sister of Penda (HRB XII, 14). Keating (*History of Ireland*, ITS II, p. 70) quotes the chronicle of Meredith Hanmer (Dublin 1663, 69) for the assertion that *Cadualin* 'was banished to Ireland by Edwin in 635'; and this too finds corroboration in triad 29.

Information about *Cadwallon*'s campaign in Wales is derived entirely from Welsh sources. The series of *englynion* in RBH col. 1043–4 (*Ast. H.* 36–41, see EWSP 446–7, trans. 495–6) appears to derive from a tale about this campaign: fourteen of the names of *Cadwallon*'s victories are listed, and these are mainly located beside the chief Welsh rivers—the Severn, Wye, Taf, Tywi and Teifi. The battles thus appear to have been widely distributed over the country, in Powys as well as in Gwynedd, and the English are described as the enemy, though without specifically naming Edwin. Battles at Digoll and Meigen are referred to in triads 55 and 69 (see nn.). For further discussion of sources relating to *Cadwallon* see EWSP 129, 169–73.

Welsh sources make no reference to the alliance between *Cadwallon* and Penda of Mercia which characterizes Bede's account of *Cadwallon*'s campaign. This is strange, as from the alliance between these two one might expect that Penda would have entered more prominently into Welsh tradition, as indeed did *Edwin*, or as did *Aedan uab Gauran* (see nn.). Bede's *Hist. Ecc.* is the only documentary source for the merciless ravaging of Northumbria by *Cadwallon* and Penda which followed their victory at *Gueith Meigen* (= Heathfield), and also for the account of how *Cadwallon* slew in turn the two kings Osric and Eanfrid, and ruled for a year 'not as a victorious king but as a savage tyrant, ravaging them with ghastly slaughter' (Bede, *Hist. Ecc.* III, 2), until at length he also destroyed Eanfrid, who had unwisely visited him to negotiate peace (*Hist. Ecc.* III, 1). Eanfrid was succeeded in Bernicia by his brother Oswald, who in the next year (634) with a small force achieved a remarkable victory over *Cadwallon*'s larger army at the battle of Cantscaul or Hefenfelth near Hexham (*Hist. Ecc.* III, 1; Adamnan, *Life of St Columba* I, i). Here *Cadwallon* was slain at *Cantscaul* (*Ann. Cam.* 631). Further references include:

EWGT 91 (28b): *Mam Gatwallawn ap Katfan, Tandreg ddu ferch Gynan Garwyn.*

Prydydd y Moch: *Ced wallaw, Cadwallawn amhad* (CBT V, no. 1.36n.).

An anonymous poem in praise of *Cadwallon* (CBT VI, no. 20.72n.) contains a possible reference to his victory at the battle of Meigen.

Katwalla6n² Llawir (m. Einiawn Yrth) 62 (= WR 29a). 'C. Long Arm' (father of Maelgwn Gwynedd). On *Llawhir* see TC 116–18; EWGT 9 (= Harl. Gen. I): *Mailcun map Catgolaun Lauhir map Eniaun Girt map Cuneda. Cadwallon* was the grandson of Cunedda Wledig and the father of Maelgwn Gwynedd: 'he may reasonably be regarded as the Brythonic leader who completed the North Welsh conquests of the former and prepared the way for the latter' (J. E. Lloyd, *Ancient Monuments Commission for Anglesey*, p. XXXVI; see also HW I, p. 120). HRB IX, 12: *Caduallo laurh* (= BD 158.6: *kadwallavn Llavhir*).

The genealogies claim that *Cadwallon*'s mother was Irish (or possibly Pictish); EWGT 47 (23) (= *Jes. Gen.* XXIII): *Einyav(n) a Katwallavn llavhir. Deu vroder oedynt. Ac eu dvy vam oedynt chwioryd. Merchet y didlet brenhin gvydyl fichti ym pywys.*

Gwalchmai: *Ardwyreaf hael o hil balch run / o gadwallawn llav hir llavr, uab einyavn yrth* (H 15.21–3 = CBT I, no. 8.55) 'I extol a hero of the proud line of Rhun, of Cadwallawn Long-Arm, the champion, son of Einyawn Yrth'.

Bleddyn Fardd: *Glew lew o lin Gatwallawn* (*Marwnad Owain Goch*, 'A brave lion of the race of Cadwallon', CBT VII, no. 49.19n.); idem (to the same): *Gwr beilch e ayrweilch arwymp drydar* ('a hero of strong warriors in splendid battle' CBT VII, no. 52.29).

Cadwr Iarll Kernyw, App. IV, no. 3, 'C. Earl of Cornwall'. *Cadwr* 'warrior'. *Cador dux Cornubie* (HRB IX, chs. 1, 5, 9 etc.) = *Cadwr tywyssavc*

Kernyw, *yarll Kernyw*, *brenhin Kernyw*, in the passages corresponding in *Brut y Brenhinedd* to those in HRB. In HRB *Cador* is Arthur's constant ally, and becomes the father of Arthur's successor Constantine. The name may have originated from a confusion with *Cadwy m. Gereint* (see n.).

Cadwy m. Gereint 75: *a Gadwy m. G.* See *Gereint m. Erbin*; EWGT 45 (10) = *Jes. Gen.* X: *Cado m. Gereint m. Erbin*; CO l. 182n.: *Ac adwy m. gereint*; *Br. Rh.* = RM 159.27: *Ac advy uab gereint*. In both these instances the name has been wrongly divided, and should read *a C(h)adwy* (see M. Richards, B XIII, p. 136, and *Cy.* IX, p. 90). *Cadwy* corresponds with *Cado*, *Catovius*, a figure in some Welsh and Breton Saints' Lives. In the ninth-century Life of *St Winwaloeus* his name appears in the genitive form *Catovii*, a cousin of Fracan, the saint's father (EWGT 23 (2); R. Latouche, *Mélanges d'Histoire de Cornouailles* (1911), p. 98). The Life of *St Carannog* (VSB 144 ff.) depicts Cado as a contemporary of Arthur, ruling with him in Dumnonia. It is therefore tempting to identify *Cadwy* with the *Catovius rex Britannici* of the Life of *St Winwaloeus*, and with HRB's *Cador dux Cornubie* (see n. to *Cadwr Iarll Kernyw*, and nn. to *Cadwy m. Gereint* CO l. 182 and *Berth mab Cado* CO l. 224).

Cadyal m. Eryn 35 (= *Cadyal y byry* R). R. Vaughan gives the following note to this name in his text of triad 35 in Pen. 185 (reproduced in MA^2 p. 391 n.): *Ve allai Cadell m. Gereint, y 43 brenin wedi Brutus, ogylch 300 mlwydd cyn Crist*. But the source for Vaughan's chronological reckoning is unclear: it may have come from a variant of 'The Twenty-Four Kings judged to be the Mightiest' (P. C. Bartrum, EC XII, pp. 157–94).

Carada6c[1] m. Bran 13, 95. See *Bran Vendigeit m. Llŷr*, *Branwen verch Lŷr*, *Caswalla6n m. Beli*. The name *Caradawc* occurs frequently in early sources, see: CA ll. 343, 357, 389; BT 41.23, 46.5. See also *Caradawc*[2] *Vreichfras* below.

Mabinogi Branwen tells here how Brân's son *Caradawg* was left in Britain as leader of the seven (or three, triad 13) *cynweissieit*, the 'Chief Officers' or 'Stewards' left in charge of Britain during Brân's absence in Ireland. On their return to Britain the survivors of Brân's army learn that Caswallawn has conquered the country, and they enquire as to the fate of the *cynweissieit*.

> Caswallawn attacked them, and slew the six men, and Caradawg broke his heart from shock, because he saw the sword slay his men, and he did not know who struck them. Caswallawn had put on a magic cloak, and no one could see him slay the men, but only the sword. Caswallawn did not wish to kill him [Caradawg]: he was his nephew, the son of his cousin. And he [Caradawg] was one of the Three Men who broke their hearts from shock / perplexity (cf. PKM 46.2–9; triad 95n.).

The account given in *Mabinogi Branwen* of *Caradawg* as chief *cynweissiad* left in charge of Britain during Brân's absence in Ireland has given rise to the supposition that his story may represent a survival of the story of the British hero *Caratācus* son of *Cunobelinus* (Harl. Gen. XVI = EWGT 11 (16): *Caratauc map Cinbelin*), who led the Britons unsuccessfully against Aulus Plautius in AD 43, and who was defeated by him at a battle on the River Medway (Tacitus, *Ann.* XII, 33–7, Dio Cassius LX, 20). After having been betrayed to the Romans by the Brigantian queen Cartismandua, *Caratācus* was taken as a prisoner to Rome, where he ended his life in exile. The identification between *Caradawc m. Bran* and *Caratācus* cannot, however, be traced back to any source earlier than the eighteenth century, and it appears to be without foundation, either in history or in any genuinely early tradition. In SEBH 135–6n., I suggested that this identification was one of the fabrications of Iolo Morganwg, and that the story of the first introduction of Christianity into Britain by *Caradawg ap Brân* had no genuine earlier basis (see n. to triad 81, and MA Third Series of TYP nos. 22, 34, 35, 55, 85, translated by Iolo, THSC 1968, pp. 299–338, and 1969, pp. 127–55). I am indebted to Professor G. J. Williams, however, who first drew my attention to the prior appearance of this identification in a note by the herald Hugh Thomas, *circa* 1700 in Harleian MS. 4181. As G. J. Williams showed (*Iolo Morganwg*, p. 312n.) historians had already associated *Caratācus* with the legend of the introduction of Christianity into Britain, before the identification was first made between *Caratācus* and *Caradawg fab Bran*.

Neither identification was, however, known to Theophilus Evans, who in his *Drych y Prif Oesoedd* (1716 and 1740) followed Camden in identifying *Caratācus* with *Caradawc*[2] *Vreichvras*. He should certainly have been relied on to have given the story of the introduction of Christianity into Britain by *Caratācus*, if he had known of it.

Caradawc[2] **Vreichvras (m. Llyr Marini)** 1, 18, 38, 71 (Pen. 267), 'C. Strong-Arm.' See nn. to *Llyr Marini, Tegeu Eururon, Caurdaf m. Karadawc, Drutwas m. Driffin.*

Caradawc Vreichvras is named in *Jes. Gen.* IX (EWGT 45 (9)) as an ancestor from whom the rulers of Morgannwg claimed descent. H. M. Chadwick suggested that the name may have originated as that of a historical figure of the fifth century who founded the dynasty which subsequently ruled Morgannwg (SEBH 48). But since the *Jes. Gens.* contain certain obviously fictional elements, and elsewhere betray the influence of TYP (see nn. to triads 2, 70), it remains probable that the epithet in the genealogy has been borrowed from that of the hero of romance. It is as a hero of romance that *Caradawc Vreichvras* appears in Welsh sources, as well as in French and English Arthurian romances, into which his name and epithet have been transferred. The earliest occurrence of name and epithet together is in the twelfth century *Erec et Enide* of Chrétien de Troyes, l. 1719: *Karadues Brie(f)bras. Briebras* 'short arm' is an adaptation of the Welsh epithet *Breich-bras* 'strong arm' evidently borrowed in written, rather than in oral form, owing to the unlenited initial of *bras. Bras* 'strong' was then conveniently misinterpreted for a French audience as *brie bras*, 'short arm'.

Br. Rh.: *Karadavc vreichuras uab llyr marini, penn kyghorvr (y Arthur) ae gefynderv* (RM 150.30); *a chradavc ureichuras* (159.19); *a chradavc uab llyr* (261.9). These allusions suit well with Caradawg as *penn hyneif* in Cornwall in triad 1 (see n.).

The Life of *St Collen* gives the descent of the saint from *Gwynoc ap Kydeboc ap Kowrda ap Kyriadoc Vyraichuyras* [*sic*] . . . *a vyriwodd i vyraich ynn gwneuthur adduc* (= *yngwaith Hiraddug*), *ac o'r byriw hwnnw y bu vwy i vyraich no'r llall* (Hafod 19; see EWGT 30 and T. H. Parry-Williams, *Rhyddiaith Gymraeg* I, p. 36).

The Life of *St Padarn* (VSB 260) associates *Caradawc Vreichvras* with the colonization of Brittany: *in illis diebus Caradauc, cognomento Brecbras, trans terminos etiam Brittanie regnum suum dilatauit. Et ad Letauiam veniens, illam cepit imperio*. On the questionable authenticity of this tradition see G. Paris, *Romania* XXVIII, p. 214, who believed that he was the leader of a band of British emigrants who established themselves at Vannes in the fifth century. It is, however, significant that *Carados Brie(f)bras* is depicted in the thirteenth-century *Livre de Carados* as a king ruling at Vannes (*First Continuation of the Perceval Romance*, ed. Roach, I, pp. 84 ff.). It would appear that Welsh traditions about *Caradawg* made their way into Brittany at an early date, even if the historical connection claimed in the Life of *St Padarn* (VSB 264–5) is to be rejected. The *Livre de Carados* contains some extremely primitive material, some of which came in all probability from Breton sources: a version of the Challenge or 'Beheading Game' (see EAR I, pp. 90–1), a version of the Chastity test by means of a magic drinking-horn (ATC 113–16), a tale of a serpent which attached itself to the hero's arm (evidently intended as an explanation of the epithet *breichfras* interpreted as 'Short Arm' see n. to *Tegeu Eururon* below), and—most primitive of all—a tale of the hero's congenital birth in company with his horse Lluagor (see n. to triad 38, and n. to *Tegeu Eururon*; HLCB 168–9; R. S. Loomis, 'L'étrange histoire de Caradoc de Vannes', *Annales de Bretagne* 70 (1963)).

Bonedd y Saint gives Caradawc the following saintly (but otherwise unknown) offspring: *Catuarch sant yn Abererch yn Lleyn, a Thangwn yn Llangoet yMon, a Maethlu yg Carnedawr yMon, meibyon Caradawc vreichvras m. Llyr Marini* (EWGT 59 (29); 64 (69)).

Caswalla6n m. Beli (Mawr) 35, 36 (*Lludd m. Beli*?), 38, 51, 67, 71. See nn. to *Beli Mawr m. Mynogan, Llud m. Beli, F(f)lur.*

Caswallawn < Cassivellaunos. The connection between *Caswallawn mab Beli* and the historical *Cassivellaunos*, king of the Belgic tribe of the Catuvellauni, is generally accepted. *Cassivellaunos* led a confederation of his countrymen against Caesar on his second expedition to Britain in 54 BC (*De Bell. Gall.* V, 11.18–22). The figure of *Caswallawn mab Beli* must either reflect medieval speculation about *Cassivellaunos*, or else represent a genuine traditional memory of the historical British ruler, either partly or wholly uninfluenced by the accounts found in classical writers. The identity of the two is asserted at a much earlier date than is that of *Caratacus* with *Caradawc mab Bran* (cf. n. above). *Caswallawn*'s opposition to the Romans is repeatedly expressed in TYP, and is reflected also in *Mabinogi Branwen.* But with the exception of triad 51, based directly on HRB or the *Brut*, the other triads indicate a story which differs materially from both the classical and medieval sources. According to triad 35, *Caswallawn* pursued the retreating Romans out of Britain, and his army is one of the *Tri Aryanllu* or 'Silver Hosts' which never returned. Triads 67, 71 depict *Caswallawn* as a lover, seeking Rome in the disguise of a cobbler in quest for *Fflur* (n.). With triad 38, which names *Caswallawn*'s horse Meinlas ('Slender Grey'), should be compared 59a, which, as Ifor Williams showed, may allude to an episode in *Caswallawn*'s dealings with the Romans in which his famous horse Meinlas played a part.

In the *Bruts* the name of *Cas(s)wallawn mab Beli* is used to render HRB's *Cassibellaunos filius Heli* (HRB III, 20; IV, 1–11 = BD 44–55; RBB 82–93). The romantic tale which Geoffrey tells about *Cassibellaunos* is evidently inspired by the accounts of Caesar and Dio Cassius, in addition to that of Bede (*Hist. Ecc.* I, 2), but it remains significant that the redactor of HRB identified *Caswallawn* with the son of *Beli Mawr* (n.). The allusions found in the triads to *Caswallawn* and Fflur in the Early Version of TYP, as well as those cited below by Cynddelw, provide sufficient evidence that *Caswallawn* had an independent existence in Welsh tradition, before his name was utilized in this way to render HRB's *Cassibellaunos.* (See B. F. Roberts, B XXV, p. 277.)

The portrayal of *Caswallawn vab Beli* in the tales of *Branwen* and *Manawydan* in PKM bears no very close relation to that given in TYP, nor is it related in any way to that in HRB. *Caswallawn* conquers Britain during the absence of Bendigeidfran in Ireland (PKM 45.25), slays the *cynweissieit* (cf. triad 13), and receives Pryderi's homage (PKM 50–1). There is no mention of the Romans. It is evident that these allusions, like those in TYP, relate to an extensive body of narrative concerning the dominion over Britain of *Beli Mawr* (see n.) and his sons, to which only fragmentary allusions have survived. (See J. T. Koch, 'A Welsh Window on the Iron Age', CMCS 14, pp. 17–52 at pp. 24–6.)

Cynddelw: *ked casswallavn* (H 87.24 = CBT IV, no. 3.22n.); *kedeyrned kasswallawn* (H 133.24 = CBT III, no. 24.134n.); *kaswallavn eisyor* (H 157.1 = CBT III, 12.25n.); *madauc mur tewdor cor kaswallaun* (H 144.24 = CBT III, no. 24.134n.).

Caw 21: **Caw o Bryd(yn)** 81 (C. 18), **Kaw o Brydyn** 96; *Hueil m. Caw* (see n. and n. to *Gildas*). On *Prydein* = *Prydyn*, i.e. the north of Scotland = Pictland, see AP l. 10n.; and add E. P. Hamp, B XXX, pp. 289–90. The Life of

St Cadog (*circa* 1100; VSB 23–140) has an incident in which the saint, during his visit to Scotland, resuscitates an enormous giant, who gives the following account of himself (trans.): 'Beyond the mountain *Bannog* (see n. to CO l. 597) formerly I reigned for many years. It happened that by devilish impulse I, with troops of my plunderers, arrived on these coasts with the purpose of plundering the same and wasting them. But the king who at that time reigned over this kingdom, pursuing us with his army, slew me and my host, when we had joined battle together . . . Caw of Prydyn, or *Caur* (*Cawr*), was I called formerly.' (VSB 84–5).

The gigantic dimensions assigned to *Caw* in the story are due to the hagiographer's derivation of his name from *Cawr*, 'giant' (see LHEB 306; Grooms, *The Giants of Wales*, pp. 150–1). Other hagiographical sources depict *Caw* as a ruler in north Britain and the progenitor of a numerous family of saints (cf. triads 81, 96), of whom the most illustrious was Gildas the historian. The eleventh-century Life of *Gildas* by the monk of Ruys (H. Williams (ed.), *Gildas*, p. 322 ff.) refers thus to the saint's parentage '*Nau* (emend to *Cau*), king of Scotland, was the noblest of the kings of the North. He had twenty-four sons, victorious and warlike. One of these was named Gildas . . .' So also the twelfth-century Life of *Gildas* by Caradoc of Llancarfan (op. cit., p. 394), who names Gildas as one of the twenty-four sons of '*Nau*, king of Scotia'. The Life of *St David*, ch. 5 (VSB 152), refers to *Gildas, Cau filius*; and *Bonedd y Saint* and *Achau y Saint* list as many as twenty-one of *Caw*'s other offspring (see EWGT), in later sources established at Twrcelyn in Anglesey.

A knowledge of the tradition that *Caw* was the progenitor of a large family of saints is indicated by the list of *Caw*'s nineteen sons given in CO ll. 206–19, and one daughter in CO l. 258. See also B XVIII, p. 233(3) = EWGT 84. The names which are listed in CO include Gildas, Hueil and Meilic (each of whom is also named in the Ruys, *Vita Gildae*) together with Gwyngat (= Guynnauc mab Gildas, VSB 323 (59)). Another son, *Gwarthegyt uab Kaw*, is named later in *Culhwch* (l. 1107n.) and appears also in Br. Rh. (RM 148.24; 159.18). *Kaw o Brydein* himself plays a conspicuous part in the tale (CO l. 647, see n.). Mounted on Arthur's mare Llamrei he slays the boar Ysgithrwyn Benbeidd (CO l. 1019), and at the close of the tale it is he who collects the blood of the Gwiddon Orddu ('Very Black Witch' ll. 1228–9), and scalps the giant Ysbaddaden Penkawr (ll. 1232–4). The account of the collecting of the witch's blood contains an intentional pun on the name of *Kaw*, which earlier in the story (l. 647) is given as *Kadw* / *Cado o Prydein* in W and R. The Giant makes the same pun upon the name of *Caw* / *Cadw* when he says *Nyt ymdiredaf y neb o gadw yr yskithyr namyn y Ka(d)w o Prydein* 'I will not entrust to anyone the keeping of the tusk (of the boar) but to *Ca(d)w* of Pictland'.

Lists of the sons of *Caw* are frequently found in the genealogical MSS. In these later texts *Caw* is located in Gwynedd: with *Cwm Cawlwyd* in Eryri and Twrcelyn in Anglesey. For full lists of *Caw*'s progeny see WCD 112–14; Peter

Bartrum, 'Bonedd yr Arwyr', B XVIII (1958–60), p. 233; EWGT 85 (3), and nn. to CO ll. 206–13.

It is impossible to tell whether all or any of the allusions to *Caw* in poetry are to *Caw* of *Prydyn*: e.g. LlDC no. 18.3 (*Beddau*) *kerwid a chivrid a chav*. The name is popular with Dafydd y Coed (RBP col. 1305.8; 1377.1 etc., cf. = GDC no. 1.9n.; 2.67; 3.48, 121). G cites also the place-names *Brynn Caw* (1329.6) and *Nancaw*. It is also sometimes difficult to distinguish between occurrences of the personal name and of the noun and adjective *caw* 'knot', etc. (see G 117, and n. to triad 87).

Caurdaf m. Karada6c (Vreichvras) 13. See n. to *Caradawc Vreichvras*.

Br. Rh.: *Hawrda uab karadavc vreichvras* (RM 160.4).

EWGT 62 (51) = VSB 322 (51): *Dyfnauc Sant m. Medraut m. Caurdaf m. Caradauc Ureichuras.*

EWGT 66 (88): *Iddew Korn Brydain ab Kowrda ab Kriadoc vreichvras ab llyr merini*. Although of uncertain value, the common parentage here attributed to Iddawc and to Medrawt as sons of *Cawrdaf* has a certain interest in relation to the tale of *Breudwyt Ronabwy*, which depicts Iddawc 'Kordd Prydein' or 'ap Mynyo' as doing penance for the part he took in causing the battle of Camlan (RM 146–60).

Other instances of the name *Cawrdaf* occur in Harl. Gen. XVI: *Caurtam ap Serguan*; App. II, no. 10: *Ca6rdaf m. Garmonya6n*.

Caydyrleith m. Seidi, see *Cadr(i)eith m. Portha6r Gadw*.

Cei (m. Kenyr Keinuarua6c) 21, 26 (WR), 42. On the names of both father and son see nn. to CO ll. 134, 264. *Cai* < L. *Caius*, Ml.W. *Cei* (see Vendryes, EC V, p. 34 and M. Richards, THSC 1969, p. 257). In B XIV, pp. 119–23, R. M. Jones suggested an alternative interpretation of this name, equating *Cei* with Ir. *cai*, *coi*, words which are explained in *Cormac's Glossary* (ed. O'Donovan, p. 46) as equivalent to Ir. *conair* 'path, way' (= W. *Cynyr*). Thus the combination of *Cei* and *Cynyr*, 'Path son of Way', corresponds with similar pairs in *Culhwch ac Olwen*, in which name and patronymic are synonyms, or near synonyms, see Drem vab Dremhidydd l. 261 'Sight son of Vision', Nerth mab Cadarn l. 200 'Strength son of Strong', etc. R. M. Jones compared with the Welsh *Cei* the name of the legendary Irish law-giver *Cai Cainbrethach* 'C. of Fair Judgement', and Eurys Rowlands added (LlC VI, p. 237) that if *Keinuaruawc* were a misreading for *Keinuarnawc* 'C. of Fair Judgment' the name would provide an exact equivalent of the Irish *Cai Cainbrethach*.

Cai appears together with Bedwyr (n.) as Arthur's companion in the earliest Welsh sources. The early Arthurian poem *Pa gur yw y porthaur* (LlDC no. 31; B. F. Roberts (ed.), *Ast. H.* ch. XII; trans. and discussion by P. Sims-Williams AW 40–5; and see CO(2) xxxv–xxxvii). The poem is concerned mainly with *Cai*'s exploits and gives him a clear precedence among Arthur's warriors. 'A host was futile compared with *Cai* in battle. He was a sword in battle, pledges came from his hand . . . lord of booty, the 'long man' was hostile(?) . . . When he drank from a buffalo-horn he would drink as much as four, when he came into battle, he slew for a hundred . . . On the heights of *Ystafngwn*, *Cai* slew nine witches.' The poem bestows on *Cai* the epithets of *Kei guin* and *y gur hir*, both of which are also applied to *Cai* in other Welsh sources. The poem later refers to *Cai*'s feat in slaying Palug's cat (cf. triad 26, and see n. to *Palug*).

Cai's *kynnedveu* are detailed in CO ll. 264–73:

> Kynyr Fair-Bearded. *Cei* was said to be his son. He said to his wife, 'If I have any share in your son, girl, his heart will always be cold, and there will be no heat in his hands. Another *cynneddf* ["magical peculiarity"] he will have, if he be a son of mine, he will be stubborn. Another *cynneddf* he will have: when he carries a burden, great or small, it will not be seen, neither from in front nor from behind. Another *cynneddf* he will have: no one will endure fire or water as well as he. Another *cynneddf* he will have: there will be no servant or officer like him.'

With his constant companion Bedwyr (who always plays a part secondary to *Cai*), *Cai* is the most prominent of Arthur's warriors in CO, and is the prime hero of several adventures. Culhwch slays the giants Wrnach Gawr and Dillus Farfawg, and he has a leading role in the episode of Custennin heussawr, which assists the hero Culhwch in winning his admission into the court of Ysbaddaden. An allusion to an otherwise unrecorded story concerning *Cai*'s death is included in the Arthurian court-list (CO ll. 283–4): 'Gwydawc son of Menester who slew Cai. And Arthur slew him and his brothers to avenge Cai.'

In contrast to the incidents cited, there are indications in CO of a less heroic presentation of *Cai*'s character. In the opposition which he presents to Arthur's wish to admit Culhwch into his *llys*, *Cai* appears already in what becomes his most characteristic role in the French and French-inspired Arthurian romances: the role in which he flouts and abuses young entrants to Arthur's court. This churlish characterization is already fully developed in Chrétien de Troyes' presentation of *Cai*:

> Et Kes, qui mout fu ranposneus
> Fel et poignanz et afiteus
> (*Yvain*, T. B. W. Reid (ed.), ll. 69–70)

'Cai who was very slanderous, mean, cutting, and insolent.'

This unheroic presentation is also manifested in the tale of *Peredur*, in the Welsh *Owain* or *Iarlles y Ffynnawn*, and in *Gereint ac Enid*, which all reflect the French concept of *Cai*'s character—though *Breudwyt Ronabwy* reverts to the older Welsh eulogistic portrayal: here *Cai* is *teckaf dyn a varchocka yn llys Arthur* (RM 152.6); and this heroic delineation is consistently maintained in all the allusions made to *Cai* in the work of the poets:

Cynddelw: *Gretyf greidwyr a chynyr a chei* (H 95.5 = CBT IV, no. 4.207n.) 'The might of *Greidwyr* (? unknown, cf. G 588) and *Cynyr* and *Cai*'.

Elidir Sais (in *marwnad* Ednyfed Fychan, d. 1246): *aruod Cai a Bedwyr* (CBT I, no. 18.18n.).

Trahaearn Brydydd Mawr; *pwyll kei* (RBP col. 1222.34) 'Cai's wisdom'.

(?) Einion Wan: *Mae ym gyueillt grym grymus kei* (H 193.11).

Gr. ap Maredudd: *durdwryf kei ar daerdoryf kat* (RBP col. 1210.12 = GGM no. 3.179) 'The clash of Cai in the pressing crowd of battle'; *kei deuodeu* 'Cai's customs' (RBP col. 1315.39 = GGM no. 4.42).

Meurig ab Iorwerth: *kei eil* (RBP col. 1374.17).

Dafydd y Coed: *(g)wryt kei* (RBP col. 1375.33 = GDC no. 3.47); *kei bonedigeid* (col. 1377.17 = GDC no. 3.142). Cf. GDC no. 1.9n.

Casnodyn: *Gwrhyd Cai, nid llai no Llŷr* (GC 11.44n.).

Dafydd ap Gwilym (in satire of Rhys Meigen): *nid gwrol Gai Hir* (GDG no. 21.53); to the lark: *Fry yr ai, iawn Gai angerdd* (GDG no. 114.13) 'upwards you go, with the true nature of Cai' (the allusion is to Cai's *angerdd* or *cynneddf* that he could be 'as tall as the highest tree in the forest when he wished' CO ll. 387–8, WM 171.3–4).

Further allusions to *Cai* in poetry are by Guto ap Siencyn (GGl^2 XCI.10), and by Tudur Aled (six instances, see index to GTA); *Cai ap Cynyr* GTA no. LXI.74. For further references see nn. to *Bedwyr*, *Gwenhwyuar*.

The forms in which *Cai*'s name appears in French sources are *Ke(u)s*, *Keu(x)*, *Kex*, *Keis*, *Ké*; and *Che* is the form delineated on the Modena archivolt (EAR I, 145–16). It was suggested by M. Williams (*Speculum* XIII, p. 43) that the office of steward which is consistently appropriated to *Cai* in the Continental romances owes its origin to an equation between this name and the O.F. word for 'cook'—*Keus*, *Quex*, *Queus* < *coquus*. But *Kaius* already fills the office of *dapifer* in HRB IX, 11, 13; X, 3, 9 etc, and the list quoted above from CO of *Cai*'s *cyneddfau* shows that this function, whatever its explanation, was already attributed to *Cai* in insular sources. It is probable that Geoffrey of Monmouth derived his portrayal of *Cai* from indigenous sources, and not from the Continental material, even though the French romances seem to have drawn independently on insular material.

Yet another of the facets of the story of *Cai*, which is developed fully in the Continental romances, but of which the germ is already found in the tale of *Culhwch*, is that of a latent feud between *Cai* and Arthur. This is indicated by *Cai*'s response to the satirical *englyn* which Arthur composed on the occasion of Cai's slaying Dillus Farfawg (CO ll. 981–4) when '*Cai* became angry, so that the warriors of this Island could hardly make peace between *Cai* and Arthur. And from thence forth, neither because of Arthur's weakness, nor because of the slaying of his men, *Cai* would not concern himself with him from thence forward.' In the Arthurian sources this aspect of *Cai*'s portrayal reaches its climax in the episode narrated in *Perlesvaus* (*circa* 1200) in which *Cai* is said to have treacherously slain Arthur's son Loholt (see n. to *Llacheu m. Arthur*). The bardic tradition (examples cited above) differs from that of the Welsh tales and the French romances in that it conforms to the oldest Welsh sources in presenting *Cai* invariably in a favourable light.

Cai's home was traditionally located at *Caer-gai* in the parish of Llanuwchllyn, Bala. Fifteenth-century poets knew of a story which must ultimately be based on some form of the *Prose Merlin*, to the effect that Arthur was reared at *Caer-gai* as *Cai*'s foster-brother (T. Roberts, 'Y Traddodiad am Arthur yng Nghaer gai', B XI (1941–3), pp. 12–13, and cf. references cited). *Cai*'s name is also commemorated in *Gwryt Cai* 'Cai's Span' or 'stretch' in Nant Gwynant, Gwynedd (I. Williams, 'Nodiadau Cymysg: gwryd, gwrhyd', B VIII (1935–7), pp. 235–6; idem., *Enwau Lleoedd*, pp. 32–3. See further Melville Richards, THSC 1969, pp. 257, 262 'Remembering Cai's persistent Welsh epithet of *Cai Hir* 'C. the Tall' one can envisage the gap between the mountains in Nant Gwynant as being named after him, with the tips of the fingers resting on the mountains on either side'. On the traditions of *Cai Hir* as a giant see C. Grooms, *The Giants of Wales*, pp. 148–9.

G. H. Doble refers also to *Ké* as the name of an early saint, commemorated in both Cornwall and Brittany, as at the church of *Kea* near Truro, see 'Un Saint de Cornwall dans les Côtes du Nord', *Extrait des Memoires de l'association Bretonne de Lannion* (1929).

Keid(y)a6 6, 29: *Gwendoleu m. Keida6* (n.), App. II, no. 6.

BT 48.12: *kethin march keidaw* (see n. to triad 44b).

CA l. 995: *mab keidyaw* (= a brother of Gwenddoleu?, see CA xlii).

Dafydd Benfras: *ysgvyt geidyaw* (RBP col. 1386.36 = CBT VI, no. 24.58n.).

Casnodyn: *llit erdyrn kedyrn keidyaw neu wrleis* (RBP col. 1246.15–16 = GC, no. 1.19n.).

Ceidyaw was also the name of a son of *Ynyr Gwent* (EWGT 61 (44–5)), and *Ceido* is also attested in place-names (EANC 221).

Ceindrech Pen Askell (*merch Eliffer Gosgorddfawr*) 70 (Pen. 50) 'C. Winged Head' (?). The name replaces *Ardun* in Pen. 47's text of triad 70. See n. to *Ardun merch Eliffer Gosgordva6r*.

Cengan Peillia6c 61. *Cengan* = *Cyngan* (?). *Peillio* 'to shift'. Perhaps a figurative epithet, 'sifter' of enemies', or the like (GPC 2717).

Kenyr (Kynyr) Keinuarua6c 21: *Cei m. Kenyr Keinuarua6c* (n.) 'K. Fair-Bearded'. R. M. Jones suggested (B XIV, pp. 119–21) that this name corresponds to Ir. *conair* 'path, way': cf. the name of the legendary Irish High King *Conaire Mor*. The name of Cai's father is given as *Cynyr Varvoc* in the fourteenth-century *Birth of Arthur* (*Cy*. 24, p. 7). On *Cynyr* < *Cunorix* (on an inscription at Wroxeter) see D. Ellis Evans, B XXIV, p. 420n. and CO n. to l. 264. The epithet *Keinuarua6c* 'Fair-bearded' appears to be limited to CO and to the Pen. 16 text of TYP, but *Cynyr varvoc* is attested in *Cy*. 24, p. 7.

Caer Gynyr is found as an alternative name for *Caer-gai* (B XI, p. 14). The dialogue poem between *Cai*, Melwas, and Gwenhwyfar (T. Jones, 'Melwas Gwenhwyfar a Chai', B VIII (1935–7), pp. 203–7; AW 58–61) gives the patronymic of *Cei Hir* as *ap Sefin* (a possible corruption of *Cenir*?). Cf. also LL 232.13—*Cinir*; RBP col. 1268.38—*Gwlat gynyr*; col. 1267.4—*tir kynyr*.

Cynddelw: *Gretyf Greidwyr a Chynyr a Chei* (CBT IV, no. 4.207n.).

The name *Cynyr* is found also in *Bonedd y Saint* (EWGT 54 (1)) where *Nonn verch Kenyr o Gaer Gawch yMynyw* is named as the mother of St David.

Ceredic m. Gwallawc 41 (WRc). See *Gwalla6c m. Lleenna6c*. *Ceredic m. Gwallawc* was earlier identified by Chadwick (*Early Scotland*, p. 144) with *Cer(e)dic*, the last ruler of the kingdom of Elmet in Yorks, who was expelled from his territory by King Edwin (see n.) of Deira in the early seventh century, according to HB ch. 63: 'E(d)guin, son of Aelle, reigned 17 years. He occupied Elmet and expelled Ceretic, king of that country.' This *Ceredic* seems identifiable with the *Ceretic* whose *obit* is recorded in *Ann. Cam.* 616, though it has been pointed out that the date is slightly too early, since Edwin only came to rule in Northumbria in 617.

If the identification is correct, it is not possible, as was supposed by Loth (*Mab*. II, pp. 269–70, n.6) that *Ceredig ap Gwallawg* is the *Keredic caradwy e glot* of the *Gododdin* poem (CA ll. 327, 333) who fell at the battle of Catraeth, or any other of the six or seven men named *Ceredig* (including the son of Cunedda, the alleged founder of Ceredigion) who are recorded as having lived in this same period (see WCD 123–5; EWGT 177).

J. Lloyd-Jones suggested (G 135) that the British king *Careticus* (*Ceredig*) of HRB XI, 8 and XII, 2 (= BD 188, 194) may represent a recollection of *Ceredic m. Gwallawc*.

On the subject of *Ceredig*, his kingdom and his descent, see further R. G. Gruffydd, SC XXVIII, p. 69, and references cited.

Cerenhyr m. Gereinya6n Hen 74. The scribe of Pen. 50 rendered this name as *Gereint hir*, cf. EWGT 94 (33) (in the descent of *Elen ferch Eudaf* from *Brutus*). Further instances of the proper name *Cerenhyr* are recorded: *Cerenhir* LL 239.6; *Cerennhir* 240.11, 200.12, etc; *Berwynn m. Kyrenyr* CO l. 277. CARANTORIUS is found on an inscribed stone of the sixth or seventh century at Kenfig, Glam. (ECMW no. 198; LHEB 625). Ifor Williams shows that *Carantorius* is a latinization of Brit. **Carantorix* 'king of kinsmen', *Proc. Anglesey Antiquarian Soc.* (1939), p. 32.

Keritwen 78: *Kreir6y merch K.* (n.); see also nn. to *Taliesin*, *Moruran eil Tegit*. *Ceridwen* = 'Fair and Loved'. As Ifor Williams points out (Chw. T.

3–4), the name is unsuitable for the enchantress to whom it is applied in the story, and he advocates *Cyrridfen* as the original and authentic form of the name, composed from *cyrrid* + *ben* (*cyrrid* < *cwrr* 'hooked, crooked'?), cf. Ir. *corrán* 'hook, sickle', and *ben* as in *benyw* 'woman' (GPC 271). This name would fit well enough with the traditional conception of a witch. The following references to *Ceridwen* occur in early poetry:

Neut amuc yg kadeir o peir kerritwen (BT 33.10); *autyl kyrridven* 'Ceridwen's inspiration' (LlDC no. 3.3; 4.1 = CBT I, no. 2.3n.); *Kadeir Kerritwen* BT 35.21 (title); *Kyfarchaf ym ren y ystryav awen / py dyduc aghen kyn no cherituen* 'I beseech my lord to consider the *awen*, what necessity brought it, before *Ceridwen*?' (BT 27.13–14).

Cynddelw: *mor oet gyfryw fyrt kyrt kyrridwen* (H 140.24 = CBT III, no. 24.8).

Prydydd y Moch: *Duw douyt dym ryt awen ber / ual o beir kyrriduen* 'The Lord God will give me the sweet *awen*, as from the cauldron of Ceridwen' (H 305.1–2 = CBT V, no. 10.2n.); *kyfreu kyrrituen rvyf bardoni* (RBP col. 1422.37 = CBT V, no. 25.2).

Casnodyn: *am nur pur ual peir kerituen* (RBP col. 1241.29–30 = GC no. 2.89).

The early sources all concur in presenting *Ceridwen* as the owner of a cauldron (*peir*) which was the source of poetic inspiration (*awen*). The poetic references are amplified by the folk-tale *Hanes Taliesin*, which in origin appears to go back to the ninth century, though the oldest form in which we have it is in the prose of the sixteenth-century Elis Gruffydd (*Ystorya Taliesin*, ed. P. K. Ford). Here *Ceridwen* is described as the wife of Tegid Foel of Penllyn, who lived beneath Bala lake. Their servant, Gwion Bach, drinks the magic drops from *Ceridwen*'s cauldron, which were intended for her son Afagddu. The child passes through various animal transformations, in all of which he is pursued by Ceridwen in appropriate animal form, and is eventually reborn as the infant poet Taliesin. The antiquity of this story in its essentials is borne out both by the references it contains to the Welsh poems in BT, and also by Irish parallels in the tales of *Macgnímartha Finn*, *Tochmarc Étaine*, and elsewhere. See Ifor Williams, Chw. T.; idem, LEWP; P. K. Ford, 'Gwion Bach and Taliesin' in *The Mabinogi and Other Medieval Welsh Tales* (Berkeley, 1977).

Kibdar 27: *Drych eil Kibdar*.

CO ll. 394–6n.: *nyt oed neb kymryt ac ef . . . namyn Arthur a Drych eil Kibdar*.

Prydydd y Moch (to Llywelyn ab Iorwerth): *Mal Arthur, kein modur Kybdar* (CBT V, no. 23.64n.).

Clydno Eidin App. II, no. 3. *Cynon m. Clydno Eidyn* (see n.) 33 (Pen. 50), App. IV, no. 8. *Clydno* is a derivative of *clod* 'fame' and *gno*(*u*) 'renowned'

(CA 176; CLlH 138), and may therefore be regarded as a compound of synonyms. *Eidyn* refers to the district surrounding Edinburgh, which lay adjacent to and perhaps included Manaw Gododdin (CA xxxviii). For *Eidyn* as an epithet in TYP, cf. *Mynyda6c Eidyn* and *Llawgat Trwm Bargawt Eidyn* (nn.).

In OSPG 75–6, K. H. Jackson adduced evidence that *Eidyn* is the original form of this name, although *Eiddyn* is well attested as the form later in general use by the *cywyddwyr* (cf. GIG 286n.).

Clydno Eidyn is named in the *Black Book of Chirk* among the northern rulers who came to Arfon to avenge Elidir Mwynfawr (see n. to *Run*[3] *m. Maelgwn Gwynedd*). This places *Clydno Eidyn* as a contemporary of Rhun ap Maelgwn and of Rhydderch Hael, in the latter part of the sixth century—a period which would be consistent with the presence of his son Cynon (see n. and *Ast. H.* ch. VI) at the battle of Catraeth *circa* 600. The following are among the earlier allusions made by the poets:

Llywelyn Fardd II: *o hil kywrein / mal clytno eidin prif gyfrin prein* (RBP col. 1387.31 = CBT VI, no. 8.6n.).

Gr. ap Maredudd: *klot klytno* (RBP col. 1206.4; 1327.19 = GGM no. 3.4).

Rhisierdyn: *rwyf clotnerth. ryuic clytno* (RBP col. 1287.13 = GSRh no. 6.3n.); *Clytno eidin glot ar dwydrin. glew dwr detryt* (RBP col. 1288.12–13 = GSRh, no. 6.93).

Cf. also EWGT 57 (17): *Gorwst m. Gweith Hengaer m. Elfin m. Vryen, ac Euronwy verch Klydno Eidyn y vam.*

Coel Hen 97; App. II. 'Coel the Old', or 'the Ancestor', born *circa* AD 370–400(?) is recorded in Harl. Gens. VIII–XII, XIX etc. (see EWGT 178); in BGG (= App. II) he is the progenitor of a number of dynasties in the 'Old North', including those of Urien Rheged, Llywarch Hen and Gwenddolau m. Ceidyaw, who were ruling during the sixth and seventh centuries. On the basis of the genealogies *Coel Hen* is believed to have been a dominant ruler or 'Overlord' over much of north-west England and southern Scotland in the early fifth century, and rulers in the next two centuries claimed to be descended from him. He may also have fought against the Picts in Pryden (northern Scotland). In the Genealogies *Coel Hen* bears the epithet *Guotepauc* (= *Godebog* 'Protector, Shelterer'), and a line in the *Gododdin* poem refers to *meibion Godebog, gwerin enwir* (CA l. 134n.) 'the sons of Godebog, an evil or possibly "a faithful" host'(?); see Jarman, *Y Gododdin*, p. 87, n. to l. 144. *Coel*'s name was believed by ancient tradition to be preserved in that of *Kyle* in Argyllshire, where there is a mound formerly marked as his tomb at *Coylton* (W. J. Watson, *The Celtic Place-Names of Scotland*, p. 186), but this tradition does not subsequently appear to have received general acceptance. *Coel Hen*, the historical ancestor, and presumably an overlord of Brythonic peoples, appears to have been the source of Geoffrey of Monmouth's King *Coel* (HRB V, 6, later known as 'Old King Cole').

See K. H. Jackson, 'The Britons in Southern Scotland', *Antiquity* XXIX; OSPG 121; P. C. Bartrum WCD 135–6, and EWGT *passim*; Ifor Williams, 'Wales and the North', BWP ch. VI; Chadwick, *Early Scotland*, ch. 10; A. O. H. Jarman, *Aneirin: Y Gododdin*, p. 87.

Coleda6c m. Gwynn 74. *Coleddaf* < *coleddu* ('cultivate, cherish, succour, indulge', GPC 542).

Harl. Gen. X = EWGT 10 (10): *Morcant map Coledauc map Morcant*

EWGT 62 (52): *Collen m. Petrwn m. Coleudauc m. Guynn.*

BD 158.17: *Edelyn m. Coledavc.* (The forms *Coledoc, Colezoc, Collezeuc* are attested in Breton, *Chr. Br.* 199.)

Coll m. Collvrewy 26, 27, 28 (WR). *Coll* = 'hazel', cf. *St Collen*, patron of Llangollen.

Colle tregetour ('C. the magician') is named in Chaucer's *House of Fame*, Book III, l. 1277 along with Simon Magus and other famous medieval magicians. Lady Guest noted the similarity of this name to *Coll vab Collvrewy* (*Mabinogion*, II, 176), and her identification of the two was followed by J. Loth (*Mab.* II. 271n.). F. N. Robinson in his edition of Chaucer showed that the identification is doubtful, since there are several fourteenth-century references to an English magician called *Colle tregetour*. For further speculations see J. Carey, 'Coll son of Collfrewy', SC XVI/XVII, pp. 168–74.

Collvrewy 26 (**Kallvrewy** WR), 27, 28: *Coll m. C.* (n.). With the second element in this name cf. the name *Gwenvrewy*. *Collvrewy* may similarly denote a woman's name, as is suggested by Rhŷs, CF 503n. But common elements in the names of father and son occur frequently in Welsh (CA 148), no less than in Anglo-Saxon and other languages.

Kreir6y merch Keritwen 78. See *Keritwen*; *Moruran eil Tegit*. Ifor Williams derived *Creirwy* from *crair* + *byw* 'lively treasure, darling' (Chw. T. 4). According to some versions of the story of Taliesin, *Creirfyw* was *teghaf morwyn o'r byt* 'the fairest maiden in the world'. In poetry her name is cited as a proverbial pattern of beauty:

Bleddyn Ddu: *Unwedd y'th wneir a Chreirwy* (GBDd no. 8.3n.).

Dafydd ap Gwilym: . . . *mwy Creirwy cred* (GDG no. 123.19).

Madog Benfras: *Duw a wyr pwy Creirwy cred* (DGG no. LXVII.21).

Tudur Aled: *Ceir aur rhwng Creirwy a'r hawg* (GTA no. LII.83). She is named in a further verse in the Bardic Grammar (GP 7.17).

The belief that *Garwy Hir* (see n.) was the lover of *Creirwy* appears to rest on a single allusion in an *awdl* by the fourteenth-cenury Hywel ab Einion Llygliw to Myfanwy of Dinas Brân: *Neud wyf ddihynwyf hoen Creirwy hoyged—A'm hudodd fal Garwy* (MA^2 339a, 15)—but there are further references elsewhere to *Garwy* (see n.) as a celebrated lover.

Creirwy's name is not found in the oldest version of *Ystoria Taliesin* by Elis Gruffydd, but it appears as *Creirw* in the version by Llywelyn Siôn (ed. P. K. Ford, EC XIV, pp. 454, 473–4).

Elsewhere *Chreirbia* (*Creirwy*) is the name of a sister of St Guennolé (Winwaloeus) according to the ninth-century *Vita* of the saint by Wrdisten (EWGT 23 (14)). She is described as *puella pulcherrima* (R. Latouche, *Melanges d'Histoire de Cornouailles*, p. 32n.). The name occurs also in the oldest version of *Bonedd y Saint* (Pen. 16) as an alternative to the name *Euronwy*, daughter of Clydno Eidyn (EWGT 57 (15)).

Kuluanawyt Prydein 80, *Gyrmananyd Post Prydain* 71 (Pen. 267). See nn. to *Es(s)yllt, Penarwan*. For *Prydein* = *Prydyn* 'Pictland, Scotland' see n. to *Caw o Bryd(y)n* above. The form *Kulvanawyt* is preferable to *Gyrmananyd* as the name of Esyllt's father (*pace* Chotzen, RC XLV, p. 296; on *Kulvanawyt* see AW 211). There are several instances of this name in early sources:

CO l. 253: *Kuluanawyt mab Goryon.*

Cynddelw: *Ruthyr kynon vab kulvanawyd* (H 148.10 = CBT III, no. 26.72n.

Gwgon Brydydd: *Fal rhuthyr eryr aur ysgwyd / Cynon fab Cul fanawyd* (CBT VI, no. 17.4).

Although triad 80 is the earliest source to name *Kuluanawyt* as Esyllt's father, the appearance of his name as Es(s)yllt's father in the list of the ladies at Arthur's court in *Culhwch ac Olwen* (l. 372) may support the evidence of the triad that this relationship is traditional. However, references to *Cynon fab Culfanawyd* appear to be confined to the poets quoted above.

With *Kuluanawyt* cf. the name *Manawydan* (see n.). *Manawyt* occurs as a variant of Manawydan (BT 34.9–10), and also as a form of the place-name *Manaw* (*Gododdin*), CA l. 35: *hyder gymhell ar vreithel vanawyt.* The combination with *Pryd(y)n* supports the belief that *Kuluanawyt*, like Manawydan, is derived from the place-name *Manaw*. But another interpretation is possible. The common noun *manawyd* means 'awl', and Ifor Williams has pointed out (B III, p. 49) that this word has influenced the portrayal of Manawydan in the *Mabinogi* (see introduction, pp. lxxiii–iv). *Cul* = 'narrow'. 'Slender Awl' is reminiscent of the kind of uncomplimentary nicknames applied to both English and Welsh rulers in the Saxon Genealogies appended to the HB.

Culhwch m. Cilydd m. Celyddon Wledig 93. On the name see CO n. to l. 10, and n. to triad 93; also B. F. Roberts, AW ch. 3. *Culhwch* is unknown in Welsh sources other than the story in WM and RM which bears his name.

Cunedda Wledic 81, 97, **Brwyn m. Kynadaf** 43. (On the archaic form

Kynadaf see J. E. C. Williams, *Ast. H.* 214–15 and his discussion of *Marwnad Cunedda* (BT 69–70) in *Ast. H.* ch. IX; also D. Greene, SC VI, p. 6.) For the title *Gwledig* see n. to *Maxen Wledic* below. *Cunedda* < *Cunedag* < *Couno* + *dagos* 'good lord'. With the form in triad 43 cf. *Cunedaf* BT 69.11, 18, 22, etc. J. Morris-Jones suggested (*Cy.* 1918, pp. 206–7) that in all these instances the final consonant (representing lenited *g* and rhyming with *f*) has been wrongly restored, but on this see Jackson, LHEB 458, and Ifor Williams, PT lxv. The *Kynadaf* of triad 43 is an archaic form. *Cuneda* [*sic*] is named a number of times in the Harleian Genealogies (EWGT pp. 9–13). The O.W. form *Cunedag* in HB is believed to be derived from a written source of the seventh century:

> (trans.) King Maelgwn the Great was reigning among the Britons in Gwynedd, for his ancestor *Cunedag*, with his sons to the number of eight, had come from the north, from the country called Manaw Gododdin, 146 years before Maelgwn reigned, and expelled the Irish from these countries with immense slaughter, so that they never again returned to inhabit them. (HB ch. 62; cf. LHEB 458)

The death of Maelgwn Gwynedd is recorded in *Ann. Cam.* 547, so that on the traditional reckoning of thirty years to a generation, the migration of *Cunedda* to Gwynedd may be dated approximately to the last quarter of the fourth century. If this was the case, such a spectacular migration of a whole tribe from north Britain to Wales has been regarded as explicable only as the outcome of a deliberate Roman policy, since it is unlikely to have occurred without official sanction. The intention may have been to stiffen the resistance in north Wales to incursions from Ireland, and the migration was associated by Collingwood (*Roman Britain* 289–90) with Stilicho's reconstruction, *circa* 395.

Cunedda is the traditional founder of the north Wales kingdoms: the names of three of his 'sons' according to Harl. Gen. XXXII (EWGT 13) appear as the *eponymi* of Meirionnydd, Dunoding and Ceredigion, while a fourth son named Enniaun Girt (Einyawn Yrth) appears as the progenitor of the leading Gwynedd dynasty at Aberffraw in Anglesey, and as the grandfather of Maelgwn. HB ch. 14 represents *Cunedda* and his sons as expelling the Irish from Gower and Cydweli, but this may be no more than an echo of HB ch. 62. More recent studies of the *Cunedda* story offer a revised and a more sceptical view of *Cunedda*'s migration, and regard it as an 'origin legend'. See D. N. Dumville, *History* 62; John Davies, *A History of Wales*, pp. 51–2; Wendy Davies, *Wales in the Early Middle Ages*, p. 89; P. Salway, *Roman Britain* (1984), p. 404. R. G. Gruffydd upholds the authenticity of the tradition of the migration of *Cunedda* with his sons in 'From Gododdin to Gwynedd: Reflections on the story of Cunedda', SC XXIV/XXV, pp. 1–14. Cunedda's name was unknown to the *Gogynfeirdd*, but is found in the *Beddau* stanzas: LlDC no. 18.224–5: *bet einyawn ab Cunedda / cwl ym prydein y ddiua*. Gr. ap

Dafydd ap Tudur describes his patron as *eil cuneda* (RBP col. 1254.12 = GGDT no. 2.26n.).

In *Bonedd y Saint*, a descent from Cunedda was claimed for a number of Welsh saints, including Dewi, Teilo and Seiriol (EWGT 54–67). See n. to triad 81.

The difficult and ambiguous poem *Marwnad Cunedda*, BT 69–70 (ninth or tenth century) has been edited by J. E. Caerwyn Williams, *Ast. H.* 208–33 (English summary *Ast. H.* 16–18). For discussion of the poem see R. G. Gruffydd, *loc. cit.*, 11 and nn.

Cunin Cof 41, 73, *Dalldaf eil Cunyn Kof. Cun* 'lord chief, ruler' (GPC 629), as adj. 'splendid, excellent'; *Cof* 'memory', (?) i.e. 'Lord of excellent memory'. ECMW cites two inscriptions of the fifth or sixth centuries: AVITORIA FILIA CVNIGNI (no. 142, *Eglwys Gymyn*, Carms.), and CVNEGN- (no. 172, Newchurch, Carms.; see LHEB 174). ECMW suggests that both inscriptions may commemorate the same man, and that this may be the *Cunyn Cof* who is named in *De Situ Brecheniauc* (VSB 314 §12 = EWGT 15, 12 (4)) as a grandson of Brychan Brycheiniog: *Hunyd filia Brychan . . . que fuit uxor Tudual Flaui, mater Cunin Cof* (*i. memorie*). Further instances of this name are BT 48.9: *a grei march cunin* (see introduction p. lxxxii, l. 7); Gr. ap Maredudd: *dewrdvrvf kunin dur* (RBP col. 1219.28), though this last example may be an adj. from *cun*[1] 'lord' or *cun*[3] 'dear'. App. II, no. 6 names *Cof* as a brother of Gwenddolau. There is also a *Kof* listed among the sons of Caw of Prydein (EWGT 85 (3)), and cf. *Coch mab Kaw* (CO l. 209).

Custennin Uendigeit 51. See nn. to *Goreu m. Custenin*, *Gereint m. Erbin*. (For the epithet *Bendigeit* see nn. to *Bran Vendigeit* and *G6ertheuyr 6endigeit*). *Custennin Vendigeit* (BD 85–6, 116) = *Constantinus* (HRB VI, 4, 5). In his *Constantinus* Geoffrey of Monmouth conflated the figure of Constantine the Great, the first Christian emperor, son of Constantinus Chlorus and the empress Helena (= Elen Luyddog of Welsh tradition (n.)) with that of the usurper *Constantine*, a general of Honorius, who was proclaimed emperor by the troops in Britain in the year 407. The following table illustrates the fictitious relationships which are alluded to in triad 51, and which represent the antecedents with whom Geoffrey of Monmouth endows Arthur:

Constantinus, brother of *Aldroen* (*Aldwr*), king of Armorica
(Custennin Vendigeit)

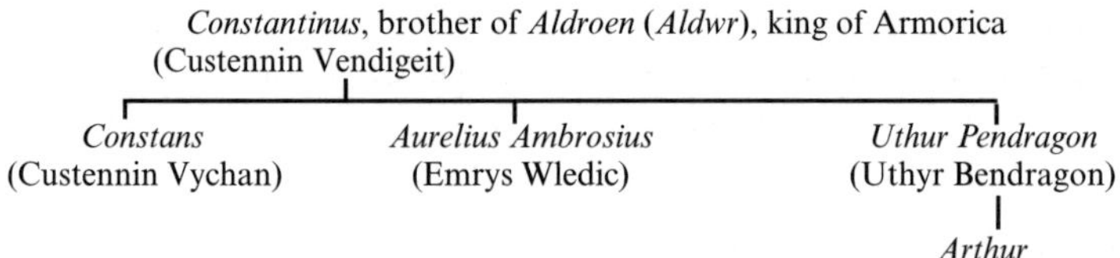

Constantine the Great was known in Welsh sources from at least the tenth century, since the ruling dynasty of Dyfed (Harl. Gen. II, EWGT 9–10) is traced back to *Constans map Constantii magni map Constantii et Helen Luitdauc*. Both the above emperors had sons named *Constans*, and Geoffrey endows his *Constantinus* with a son of this name, as well as with two additional sons, *Emrys Wledig* (Ambrosius) and *Uthyr Pendragon* (see nn.), both of whom were known independently in antecedent Welsh tradition. In HRB XI, 2 Geoffrey attributes to Cador duke of Cornwall (= *Cadwy m. Gereint*, see n.) a son *Constantine*, who eventually succeeds Arthur. By this *Constantine* Geoffrey evidently intended the *Constantinus* of Gildas's Epistle, since references follow to three other contemporary rulers who are the subjects of Gildas's diatribe (see K. H. Jackson, '*Varia*: II. Gildas and the Names of the British Princes', CMCS 3, pp. 30–40).

Geoffrey thus bestowed on Arthur as relatives three figures who each held a certain independent prominence in older Welsh sources; and, further, he attached this fictitious family to the royal Dumnonian pedigree at the point where the name of *Constantine* offered the opportunity for conflation with the characters of one or both of the earlier *Constantines*. Geoffrey evidently knew of the Dumnonian pedigree in a form resembling that in which it is given for *Gereint ab Erbin* (see n.), and cf. *Jes. Gen.* XI (EWGT 45 (11)).

Custennin[2] Uychan m. Custennin Uendigeit 51, that is 'C. the Younger' = *Constans* (HRB VI, 5 = BD 87–9; RBB 126), in contrast to his father *Constantinus Magnus*, 'C. the Great' = *C. Vendigeit* (n.). B. F. Roberts pointed out (*Modern Language Review* LVI, p. 406) that the epithet *Vychan* may here be an error for *Custennin Vynach* 'C. the Monk'. See further B. F. Roberts, B XXV, p. 286.

Geoffrey's account of the monk *Constans* being made king derives from that given by Orosius (*Histories* VII, 40) of the usurper Constantine and his son *Constans ex monacho Caesarem factum*, both of whom were slain by Constantine's general Gerontius (see n. to *Gereint m. Erbin*). Geoffrey's immediate source may, however, have been Bede, who reproduces the story (*Hist. Ecc.* I, 11).

Casnodyn: *Am gost gustennin fab elen* (RBP col. 1241.39–40 = GC 2.102n.). See also *Elen Luyada6c*.

Ky(h)oret eil Kynan 38 (Pen. 47), 39. There is no certainty as to the identity of the Cynan of the patronymic, though triad 39 suggests this may be Cynan Garwyn. For further instances of the name *Cyhoret* cf. LL XLV.5: *cohorget testis*; 199.21: *Conhorget*; LlDC no. 18.221n. (see G 227): *yn ryt gynan gyhoret.* For *eil* 'successor, descendant' see n. to *Rahaut eil Morgant*.

Kynadaf 43: *Brwyn m. Kynadaf*; see n. to *Cunedda Wledic*.

Cynan[1] (brawd Elen Luydawc) 35, 97. See nn. to *Elen Luyda6c*, *Maxen Wledic*, *Cadwaladr*. *Jes. Gen.* XI (EWGT 45 (11)) traces the descent of the Dumnonian dynasty to *Cynan m. Eudaf Hen*. This is the *Conanus Meriadocus* of HRB V, 9 (= *Kynan Meyryadavc* BD 72), where *Eudaf yarll Ergyng ac Yeuas* = *Octavius dux Gewissei*. According to HRB's account, *Maximian* (= *Maxen Wledic*) bestowed the land of Brittany upon *Cynan* as a reward for the assistance given to him in the conquest of Gaul (HRB V, 12): from him were descended the later kings of Brittany who are represented as Arthur's forebears. The Welsh account of the same events, as given in *Breudwyt Maxen*, gives to Cynan the credit both for the conquest of Brittany and also for the conquest of Rome itself on Maxen's behalf. After Elen's marriage to Maxen Wledig, her brothers *Cynan* and Adeon followed Maxen to the continent and, having re-established Maxen as emperor of Rome, *Cynan* chose to remain in the territory they had conquered, rather than to return to Britain. According to *Breudwyt Maxen* (WM 191.13–20) 'And there Cynan remained, and the other part with him to settle; and they decided to cut off the tongues of their women-folk, lest their language should be corrupted. And because the women ceased to speak their language, and the men spoke it, they were called *Llydaw*' (men < *lled-taw* 'half silent').

In B XXVI, p. 2, L. Fleuriot quoted a Latin passage from the *Cartulaire de Quimperlé* (composed between 1119 and 1128) of which the substance is: '*Beli* and *Kenan* were two brothers, sons of *Outham Senis. Kenan* held the kingdom (*Letavia*) when the Britons went to Rome . . . *Beli* son of *Anna* who is said to be the first-cousin of Mary, mother of Christ.' (*Outam Senis* is the original form of *Eudaf Hen* (EWGT 45 (11); see n. to *Gereint m. Erbin* below.) With the possible exception of a brief reference in the Life of *St Goeznovius* to Cynan's settlement (text in Chambers, *Arthur of Britain* (1927), pp. 241–3; discussion by C. Sterckz and G. Leduc, *Annales de Bretagne* LXXXVIII, pp. 277–85), this appears to be the oldest allusion to the story underlying the accounts of the Breton settlement, as found both in *Breudwyt Maxen* and in HRB.

Both versions of this story originate in the tradition that Maximus had denuded Britain of her fighting men (see n. to triad 35, and n. to *Maxen Wledic*). Although the main movement of population to Brittany from this country may be assigned to the century between AD 450–550, the earliest migrations probably began at least half a century earlier, under pressure from the raids of Picts, Scots and Saxons. The persistent tradition in early Welsh sources associates the Breton settlement with the soldiers of Maximus, and this need not be far from the truth as regards the date of the earliest settlement. A very close and continuous connection was maintained between the two countries after this, and it is natural that speculation should have been rife in Britain as to the origin of the Britons across the sea. It was an easy deduction to make that the original Breton colonizers were Maximus's lost soldiers (see I. Williams, *Breudwyt Maxen*, pp. ix–x). The result was that in

Breudwyt Maxen an onomastic fabrication has superseded the earlier traditions of the migration, as we find these outlined in Gildas and in the Lives of the Breton saints.

In Welsh prophetic verse dating from the tenth to the twelfth centuries, *Cynan* is named with Cadwaladr as one of the two promised deliverers who will one day return and lead the Britons to victory over the Saxons. It is evident from both the HRB and the *Vita Merlini* that Geoffrey of Monmouth had some knowledge of these poems, and he clearly identified the *Cynan* alluded to in them with *Cynan Meiriadoc*. I think it likely that, in this, Geoffrey was drawing on an older tradition, and that the casting of the Breton founder *Cynan* in this role is first recognized in *Armes Prydein* (*circa* 930; cf. ll. 89, 163, 182), where it is used with a particular significance. Under pressure of the Norse invasions, several members of the Breton nobility had taken refuge in England, including the duke Alan Barbetorte, Athelstan's godson. In 936 he received Athelstan's assistance in returning to his own country. This alliance must have been well known to the writer of the *Armes*, as was the allegiance of Hywel Dda to Athelstan (HW 336). Nevertheless, the poet refers more than once in the poem to the men of Llydaw, and wishes to include them in a projected pan-Celtic coalition: *A chymot Kynan gan y gilyd* ('there will be concord between Cynan and his fellow' AP l. 182). On the significance of the allegiance here claimed, see D. N. Dumville, 'Brittany and *Armes Prydein Vawr*', EC XX–XXI, pp. 153–9. Dumville points out that the allusion in this poem to the two promised deliverers, *Cynan* and *Cadwaladr*, suggests an already established tradition, and some evidence for this is to be found in early Breton sources; see L. Fleuriot, 'Old Breton Genealogies and Early British Traditions', B XXVI, pp. 1–6; ibid., HLCB 99–100; B. F. Roberts, 'Geoffrey of Monmouth and Welsh Historical Tradition', *Studies on Middle Welsh Literature*, ch. 2. Brynley Roberts has also shown that the view of *Cynan* as the returning deliverer gains corroboration from the 'Prophecy of John of Cornwall', EC XIV, pp. 31–41.

Kynan[2] Garrwyn (m. Brochfael Ysgithrog) 39 = *Selyw m. Kynan Garruin* 43 (BBC); *Selyf m. Kenan Garrwyn* 25; *Dinogat m. Kynan Garwyn* 44. See n. to *Selyf*[2] for references to *Selyf* and to his father and son in Harl. Gens. XXII, XXVII (EWGT 12; ibid. 128–9n.), and n. to *Taliesin*.

It is not certain whether *Car(r)wyn* 'of the white chariot' or *Garwyn* 'white shank' is the correct form of Cynan's epithet, and the evidence of TYP is inconclusive on the point since, in the Triads, epithets are found both in lenited and in unlenited form (see introduction p. xc; *Caruinn* / *Garwyn* are both attested in VSB, cf. B III, p. 34). See WCD 167.

Cynan's father Brochfael Ysgithrog (glossed *cum dentibus* 'of the tusks' in *De Situ Brecheniauc* (VSB 315)), was allegedly the father of St Tysilio and ruled over Powys in the mid-sixth century.

Cynan Garwyn appears in *Buchedd Beuno* (VSB 17–18) as *Kynan vrenhin vab Brochwel*, and he is said to have made a grant of land to the saint at

Gwyddelwern. The Life of *St Cadog* ch. 44 (VSB 114) refers to *rex Reinmuc* (= Dyfed? cf. CLlH 97, HW 281–2), *vocamine Cinan, cognomento Garguinn*, who was dissuaded by the saint from attacking and plundering Glamorgan.

Of primary importance as a record of the historical *Cynan Garwyn* is the early praise-poem (BT 45–6 = PT no. I) entitled *Trawsganu Cynan Garwyn mab Brochfael* (ed., trans. and discussed by Idris Foster in Foster and Daniel, *Prehistoric and Early Wales*, pp. 229ff.). This is a bardic eulogy of a familiar type, listing the famous battles won by *Cynan Garwyn* and his forebears, giving details of the rewards given by Cynan to the poet (here supposed to be the *Cynfardd* Taliesin). *Cynan* is described as *kyngen kymangan* (= *cyf-anian*) 'of the nature of Cyngen'—in an allusion to his forebear *Cyngen* (Harl. Gen. XXVII; EWGT 12 (22, 27)). The early features in the text are even more frequent than is the case in the group of poems addressed to Urien and Owain (see n. to *Taliesin*), and indicate that this is the oldest poem in the archaic group collected in PT nos. 1–12, in which the other poems relate to the northern heroes Urien Rheged, Owain and Gwallawg. It seems possible that Taliesin may have himself originated in Powys (PT lix–lx; Ifor Williams in *Bywgraffiadur*, p. 874). In a later poem Taliesin is presented as a bard attached to the court of Powys: *Keint rac ud clotleu yn doleu hafren / Rac brochuael powys a garvys vy awen* 'I sang before a lord of bright fame in the meadows of the Severn, before Brochfael of Powys who loved my *awen*' (BT 33.6–7). See further LEWP 49–70; Marged Haycock, 'Llyfr Taliesin: Astudiaeth ar rai Agweddau' (Ph.D., University of Wales, Aberystwyth 1983).

Cyndeyrn Garthwys 1. *Cyndeyrn* < **Cuno-tigernos* (LHEB 643). St Kentigern, known also as St Mungu ('my dear one'), the patron-saint of Glasgow. See nn. to *Owein m. Vryen Reget, Myrddyn Wyllt, Ryderch Hael. Ann. Cam.* 612 (= 614): *Conthigirni obitus.* O.W. *Conthigirn* > *Cyndeyrn* 'hound-like prince'. This name does not seem to be recorded in reference to any other person. I have suggested (introduction p. xci) that the reference to *Cyndeyrn* in triad 1 is derived from the following entry in *Bonedd y Saint*, EWGT 56 (14): *Kyndeyrn garthwys m. Ewein m. Vryen. a Denw verch Lewdwn luydawc o Dinas Eidyn yn y Gogled y vam.* The forms given to the saint's mother and grandfather vary throughout the different versions of *Bonedd y Saint*, but they are all approximations of the forms of these names as they appear in the *Fragmentary Life of St Kentigern* (written between 1147 and 1164 for Herbert, bishop of Glasgow), which is the oldest source for the tradition that Owain ab Urien was father to the saint. See H. M. Chadwick, *The Growth of Literature* I, pp. 118–19, 145; K. H. Jackson, 'The Sources for the Life of St Kentigern', SEBC ch. VI; Basil Clarke, *The Life of Merlin: Vita Merlini*; and P. Sims-Williams, *Romania* 116, pp. 94–5 and nn. In the twelfth-century Herbertian Life the saint's parentage is described as follows:

> King Leudonus, a semi-pagan man, from whom the province which he ruled in northern Britain got the name *Leudonia*, had a daughter with a

> step-mother, who was called *Thaney*. She had as a suitor a most distinguished young man, *Ewen* son of *Erwegende*, who was sprung from the noblest stock of the Britons . . . In historical records he is called *Ewen* son of *Ulien*. (A. P. Forbes, *Lives of St Ninian and St Kentigern*, p. 245, trans.)

For *Leudonia, Leudonesia* = Lothian, see W. J. Watson, *Celtic Place-Names of Scotland* ch. I, and CA xxxviii–xxxix. The slightly later twelfth-century Life of *St Kentigern* by Jocelyn of Furness represents the saint as having died at an advanced age in 612 (cf. *Ann. Cam.*), in the same year as did his patron *Rhydderch Hael* (see n.). But if we conclude that *Kentigern* was a comparatively young man when he died, the tradition as to his parentage is not absolutely impossible (see CLlH xxvi–vii; Chadwick, *Growth of Literature* I, pp. 145–6). However, this tradition may represent early ecclesiastical legend, rather than historical fact, as is contested by K. H. Jackson (SEBC 281–96). In this respect the story is entirely in accord with the royal parentage frequently assigned to the native saints in *Bonedd y Saint* and elsewhere. It is also the persistent tradition with regard to *Kentigern* in Welsh sources: cf. Pen. 127, 94: *Plant Ywain hael ap Vrien. Kyndeyrn Garthwys ap Ywain ap kenvarch ap Meirchiawn* (and EWGT 69 (13); 87 (7)). It is possible that Garthwys is a forgotten place-name denoting *Cyndeyrn*'s home. This was the opinion of Robert Vaughan of Hengwrt (VN[2]): '*Cyndeyrn* signifying in the British tongue the prince and the first king, and *Garthwys* the name of the place where he was born or lived in'. No such place-name has however been recorded.

Kyndr6yn 60: *G6ia6n m. Kyndr6yn* (n.). *Cyndrwyn* is associated with the district of Caereinion in Powys, over which he may have ruled during the latter part of the sixth century, together with the neighbouring border country, which is now a part of Shropshire. Thus *Cyndrwyn* was a contemporary with the Powys rulers Brochfael Ysgithrog and his son *Cynan Garwyn* (see n.). He may have been a sub-ruler under their overlordship, and his court of Pengwern may have been Shrewsbury. Fifteenth- and sixteenth-century manuscripts contain lists of the numerous sons and daughters of *Cyndrwyn* (see CLlH xxxi–xxxii; B XVIIII, p. 233 = EWGT 85 (1); and see n. below to *G6ia6n m. Kyndr6yn*). Three of *Cyndrwyn's* grandsons are said to have founded churches in Powys: *Elhayarn eg Kegitua ym Powys, a Llwchayarn eg Ketewyng, a Chynhayarn yn Eidonyd, meibyon Hygaruael m. Kyndrwyn o Lestin Wynnan eg Kereinyawn* (EWGT 60 (36); cf. VSB 322 (36)).

More famous in literary tradition than *Cyndrwyn* himself is his son Cynddylan and his daughter *Heledd* (see n.). A ninth-century Powys *cyfarwydd* composed a lengthy sequence of *englynion* concerning Cynddylan's hopeless defence of the Shropshire borderland against the English of Mercia, and these allude to Cynddylan's death in battle and the destruction of his *llys* at Pengwern. Part of the poem is portrayed as spoken by Cynddylan's daughter Heledd, the sole survivor of the family, and consists of long elegies on the deaths of her brothers in battle, of her sisters, and on the loss of their home. These and other verse passages are all that has survived of the story. The verses are preserved in RBP cols. 1044–9, and have been edited and expounded by Ifor Williams as *Canu Heledd*, in *Canu Llywarch Hen* (1935 and subsequent editions). Since the publication of *Canu Llywarch Hen*, much new light has been shed on these poems by Jenny Rowland in her extended study and edition, *Early Welsh Saga Poetry*. An allusion in these stanzas to Cynddylan's participation at the battle of Maes Cogwy (= Maserfelth, 644) where the Northumbrian king Oswald was slain by Penda (CLlH no. XI.3) is not inconsistent with the allusion in triad 60 (n.) to the presence of *Cyndrwyn*'s son Gwiawn at the battle of Chester (*Gweith Perllan Vangor*) in 616, and it corroborates a mid-seventh-century date for the events referred to. (See further EWSP ch. 3, and introduction to CLlH, especially pp. xxxi–xxxiii.)

Another poem relating to the death of the hero, 'Marwnad Cynddylan', appears to be older than the RB *englynion*, though it has been preserved only in an eighteenth-century copy (MA² 121b–122) where it is attributed to an unknown legendary poet, Meigant. (The poem is edited by Ifor Williams in B VI, pp. 134–41.) It is written in a metrical form and vocabulary similar to that of the *Gododdin*, while its orthography provides evidence of derivation from a written exemplar as old as the *Black Book of Carmarthen*. Ifor Williams believed that it may have represented a contemporary bardic elegy on Cynddylan. It contains an allusion to an attack made by the sons of *Cyndrwyn* on Caer Lwytgoed (Lichfield), which would be consistent with the border warfare described elsewhere in the *englynion* (CLlH no. XIII.45–58). *Marwnad Cynddylan* has subsequently been re-edited by R. G. Gruffydd in *Bardos* (Cardiff, 1982), pp. 10–28.

Kynuarch 5 (WR), 6, 25, 33, 70, App. II, no. 1: *Vryen m. Kynuarch*. See nn. to *Vryen*, *Arawn*, *Llew m. Kynuarch*. The O.W. form *Cinmarc* is found in Harl. Gen. no. VIII (EWGT 10 (8)), as well as in HRB IX, 12: *Kinmarc* = *Kynuarch* BD 158.5. Geoffrey of Monmouth obtained this name either from *Ann. Cam.* or from a source which was a variant of the Harleian genealogy, since it is evident that he used genealogies similar to the Harleian collection as a quarry for names, though employing them in a different context, and he does not record *Kynfarch* as the name of Urien's father (see Stuart Piggott, *Antiquity* (1941), pp. 1–18). *Kynfarch* is unknown in Welsh tradition, except as a link in the genealogies. Records of *Gwŷr y Gogledd* virtually commence with Urien's generation in the second half of the sixth century: they tell almost nothing of Urien's father's generation, with whom the struggle with the invading Angles in north Britain had first begun. It is possible that Urien inherited the kingdom of Rheged from his father, though we have no written evidence for this. *De Situ Brecheniauc* names Nyvein as wife of *Kenvarch Cul* (EWGT 15 (14)). *Kenvarch* is also named in *Englynion y Clyweit* (*Blodeugerdd* no. 31, *englyn* 12). But, according to LBS II, pp. 241–2, there was more than one saint named *Kynfarch* in early Wales, so that the records may have confused Urien's father with a saint of the same name.

Kyn6a6r Catgaduc m. Kynwyt Kynwydyon 6. 'K. Host-Protector.' On *catgaduc* see n. to triad 6. *Kynvawr* is not included among the sons of *Kynnwyt Kynnwydyon* in App. II, no. 3. Cf. however the expanded text of *Bonedd Gwŷr y Gogledd* in EWGT 74, and Pen. 127, 94 (*circa* 1510): *Clydno Eidden, kynan genhir, kynvelyn drwsgwl, kynvawr cadgaduc, cadrod calchvynydd, meibion oeddynt i kynwyd kynwydion ap kynvelyn ap Athrwys ap Mar ap Keneu ap Coel. De Situ Brecheniauc* (VSB 315) claims a union between a son of *Kynvawr* and a daughter of Brychan Brycheiniog: *Tutglid, filia Brachan, uxor Kenken filii Kenwaur Cadcathuc*; *mater Cadel et Brochuail Schitrauc, et mater Ieuab, et mater Meigh, et mater Sanand.* (For Meigh see n. to *Meic Myng(vr)as*, for *Sanand* see n. to *Maelgwn Gwynedd.*) On the unreliability of the numerous reported 'marriages' of Brychan's daughters, see n. to triad 70.

The name of *Kynvawr* was known to Casnodyn, who describes Ieuan Llwyd as *eil kynuawr catgaduc* (RBP col. 1240.6 = GC no. 2.6n).

Kynued6 68: *Cadauel m. Kynued6* (see n. to triad 68).

Cynuelyn[1] Drwsgyl 5, 44, App. II, no. 3; 'C. the Leprous' (?). *Cynvelyn* < *Cunobelinus*. On *trwsgl* 'clumsy', see B XI, pp. 140–2 where Ifor Williams cites D 'impolitus, incultus, rudis' etc. and compares Br. *trousk* 'scab' and O.Ir. *trosc* 'leper'. These cognates suggest that an earlier meaning of *trwsgl* had reference to a skin disease; cf. Eng. 'thrush'. It is this older meaning, rather than the parallel meanings of 'rough, rude' etc., which is most probably present in *Cynfelyn*'s epithet. *Trwsgl* is found in the instances of the mountain-name *Y Drosgl* in Gwynedd, describing a sharp proclivity (see Ifor Williams, *Enwau Lleoedd*, p. 18). *Cynuelyn Drwsgl* may be identifiable with the *Kinvelyn* of *Ymddiddan Myrddin a Thaliesin* (LlDC no. 1.32): *Seithued kinvelin y pop kinhuan* 'K. one of the first seven in every onset'. See also *Cynuelyn*[2].

Cynuelyn[2] 31: *Melyn m. Kynuelyn* (= *Belyn o Leyn* WR n.). See n. to *Melyn m. Kynuelyn*, and to the triad. Perhaps to be identified with the hero *Kynvelyn* who was slain at Catraeth, of whom it is said *gwyned e wlat* 'his home was Gwynedd' (CA l. 1383).

Cynhaual m. Argat 7. *Cynhafal* < *cwn* + *hafal* 'like a hound'. CUNOVALI is found on an inscription at Madron in Cornwall (CIIC I, 455). *Cynhaval* is the name of a saint: *Cynhaval sant ap Argud* (EWGT 64 (68)n.).

A variant of this name in the sixteenth-century Pen. 75 adds the following to his name, *gwayw drwsiad ynys Brydain ai thrydydd tarw unbenn* 'spear-thruster of the Island of Britain and one of her Three Bull-Chieftains', a clear reference to triad 7. *Cynhawal* (*Cin(h)aual*) occurs more than once among the names of the *Gododdin* warriors (CA ll. 507, 518, 527).

Cynon m. Clydno (Eidin) 33 (Pen. 50c), 71, App. IV, no. 8; see n. to *Clydno Eidin*. *Cynon* < **Kunonos* 'great' or 'divine hound'. *Cynon lary vronn* 'C. of the generous breast' (CA ll. 399, 409) is referred to several times in the *Gododdin* as one of the prominent heroes on the expedition to Catraeth, and in l. 416 it is stated that he was *mab klytno clot hir* 'son of Clydno of long fame'. The two opposing statements given in the poem with respect to the survivors from the expedition to Catraeth claim either that (i) there was a single survivor out of a war-band of 300, or (ii) that out of 363 warriors *Cynon* escaped with three others, of whom one was the poet Aneirin (ll. 240–1, 1405–6). On the incompatibility of the two statements, and for the argument that the allusions to the 363 and the four survivors are an accretion to the text, see CA liii–lviii. Ifor Williams suggested that the single survivor from the expedition was *Cynon ap Clydno*. A later study has interpreted the allusions in the poem differently, and has argued that *Cynon* is presented as a leading general of the *Gododdin* army: it is not implied that he survived the battle, but rather that he fell, like his companions, at Catraeth. (See R. Bromwich, 'Cynon fab Clydno', *Ast. H.* ch. VI, and introduction to *Ast. H.*, pp. 12–13. Cf. also A. O. H. Jarman, SC XXIV/XXV, p. 23.) If the *Beddau* stanzas are to be regarded as presenting evidence for Cynon's eventual fate they know nothing of his supposed death at Catraeth, but instead identify his grave in Wales: *in llan padarn bet kinon . . . Pieu y bet y dan y bryn. bet gur gurt yg kyniscin. bet Kinon mab clytno idin. . . in isel gwelitin. bet Kynon mab clytno idin. . . in oervel ig gverid. bet kinon in reon rid*. 'In Llanbadarn the grave of Cynon . . . whose is the grave under the hill, the grave of a man strong in the attack, the grave of *Cynon* son of *Clydno eidyn* . . . In a low-lying place the grave of *Cynon* etc. . . . In a cold place in the earth the grave of *Cynon* in the ford of Reon' (LlDC no. 18.26, 32). Even if the *Beddau* stanzas cannot be regarded as preserving historical evidence regarding the fate of the Men of the North, these verses nevertheless reflect the movement by which traditions of the northern heroes became freshly localized in Wales—sometimes, it is thought, by as early as the ninth or tenth centuries. (See T. Jones, PBA 53, pp. 97–116, at pp. 108–9, and cf. nn. below to *Ryderch Hael*, *Owein m. Vryen*, *Vryen Reget*.)

Cynon's fighting power is commemorated in allusions by Cynddelw (LlDC no. 37.8 = CBT III no. 9.8n.), by Llywelyn Fardd II (CBT VI, no. 7.18n.) and by Dafydd Benfras (CBT VI no. 31.64).

Neither *Cynon* nor his father are listed among the names of the warriors present at Arthur's court in *Culhwch ac Olwen*. But in *Iarlles y Ffynnawn, Cynon ap Clydno* is named as a prominent hero at Arthur's court (cf. also

App. IV, no. 8), and he is presented as the initial protagonist in the adventure of the magic fountain (corresponding to *Calogrenant* in Chrétien de Troyes' version of the tale in *Yvain*). *Bonedd y Saint* endows *Cynon* with a sister, variously named as Creirwy (Pen. 16) and as Euronwy in EWGT 57 (15): *Gorwst m. Gueith Hengaer m. Elfin m. Uryen, ac Euronwy uerch Glydno Eidin e vam*. Triad 71 claims that *Cynon* loved the daughter of Urien Rheged, though this tradition can only be traced to the fourteenth century (see n. to *Moruud verch Vryen*). The *varia lecta* show that the redactor of Pen. 50's version of triad 33 seems to have been actuated by a desire to bring together a group of warriors to whom the epithet *Eidyn* had been previously attached.

Kynwyt Kynwydyon 6, App. II, no. 3. See nn. to *Clydno Eidin, Cynuelyn Drwsgyl*. The epithet of the fourth son of *Kynwyt* named in App. II, Cadrawd Calchfynyd, has been identified with Kelso, earlier *Calchow* ('lime'); *calchfynydd* = 'lime, or chalk hill' (Watson, *The Celtic Place-Names of Scotland*, p. 343; Chadwick, *Early Scotland*, p. 144; though Jackson questions this, WHR 1963, p. 84). The place is mentioned in a poem in BT 38.11: *Kychwedyl am dodyw o galchfynyd*, etc. Thus the district of Kelso may have formed the kingdom belonging to *Kynwyd*, and later to his son Kynvawr. Like the adjoining Lothian, this kingdom must have been lost very early to Bernicia (perhaps in the early seventh century), and thus it is that no record of it but the name has survived.

Kynyr Keinuaruawc, see *Kenyr Keinvarvawc*.

K(y)6ryt[1] Gvent 56. 'K. of Gwent.' In the triad this name is lenited to *G6ryt* after *verch*, and the lenited form easily became mistaken for the radical. *Kywryt* is attested elsewhere as a personal name; *kerwid a chivrid* (LlDC no. 18.3); *kywryt vard dunawt* (RBP col. 1228.11; see n. to *Duna6t[2] m. Pabo Post Prydein*); *llywelyn vard uab kywryt* (col. 1389.32). The name in the triad should probably be emended to *Kywryt Keint* as in *Englynion y Clyweit*: *A glyweisti a gant Kywryt Keint* (*Blodeugerdd* no. 31, *englyn* 69 and n.). *Keint* is also favoured by the alliteration with *Cywryd*: here the reference is to the River *Caint* in Anglesey, rather than to the county of Kent. Cf. the variation between *Keint* and *Gwent* as epithets given to the fourteenth-century poet best known as *Siôn Cent* (IGE[2] lxx–lxxx; *Bywgraffiadur* 858). But the name of the English county is found elsewhere in Welsh sources, cf. PKM 51.2: *yg Kent y mae Caswallawn*, and *Cair Ceint* (Canterbury) is listed in the list of *Civitates* in HB ch. 66a.

Kywryt[2] mab Krydon 78: *Gwen merch K. Kerwyt m. Krydon* is listed in the paternal genealogy of Gruffudd ap Cynan among the ancestors of Beli Mawr; EWGT 36 (2) and p. 134n.; HGVK 2.5–6. P. C. Bartrum considered this name to have belonged to a pre-Geoffrey of Monmouth list of British kings; see his article in B XXIII, p. 4.

Dauyd (brophwyd) 48, *o lin David brofwyt* 86 'The prophet David'.

See Gwalchmai (H 22.11 = CBT I, no. 12.2); Dafydd Benfras (CBT VI, no. 31. 35); Madog ap Gwallter (CBT VII, no. 32. 24). To the *cywyddwyr*, *Dafydd Broffwyd* was God's poet: *A chywyddau i Dduw lwyd / Yw sallwyr Dafydd Broffwyd* (GDG no. 137.59–60); *Hoff fydd gan Ddafydd Broffwyd / Ddatganu cerdd Lleucu Llwyd / Prydydd oedd Ddafydd i Dduw* (GIG no. XXII.83–5).

Dalldaf eil Cunin Cof 41, 73. See n. to *Cunin Cof*. CO ll. 184–5: *A dalldaf eil kimin cof*. For *eil* 'son, descendant of' see T. M. Charles-Edwards, 'The Heir-apparent in Irish and Welsh Law', *Celtica* IX (1971), p. 182, and n. to *Rahaut eil Morgant* below.

Dallwyr Dallben 26. 'D. Blind-Head.' See CO l. 197n.: *a Datweir Dallpenn*. For this form of the name see the *varia lecta* to triad 26; also cf. the form *Dallmor Dallme* in Llywelyn Siôn's version of the *Ystoria Taliesin*, EC XIV, p. 452.

Daronwy 26 (WR). *Daronwy* is the title of a prophetic poem, BT 28.21, the contents of which unfortunately throw no light on the title. Sir John Rhŷs noted that *Daronwy* survives as the name of a farm in the parish of Llanfachreth, Anglesey (now named *Dronwy*, cited in the *Record of Caernarvon*: *in molendino de Darronwy et Cornewe*, CF 565–9). In G 300, Lloyd-Jones cites Ll. 6 (ed. Stanton Roberts) cxiv, 5, *o vaibion daro(nw)y*, and with the form he compares the name *Mathonwy*.

Dewengen 66: *Mabon ap Dewengen*.

Dewi 1, 82. St David lived during the latter years of the sixth century, and founded a monastery at Mynyw (St David's) in Pembrokeshire. The *Vita Beati Davidi* (*circa* 1080–90), perhaps composed by a monk of St David's named *Rhigyfarch*, was edited and translated by J. W. James (Cardiff, 1967), and it bears witness to the close contact maintained between St David's and southern Ireland. The Lives of the Irish saints corroborate the Welsh accounts of the visits of Irish monks to the Welsh monastery. Probably it was as a result of the twelfth-century controversy concerning the archi-episcopal status of St David's that its founder came to be regarded as the patron saint of all Wales (VSB xvii), though it must be noted that the protection of *Dewi* is already invoked five times in the poem *Armes Prydein* (*circa* 930), where it is claimed that *Dewi*'s banner will lead the combined Celtic armies to victory. See n. to triad 1.

All versions of *Bonedd y Saint* begin with Dewi's genealogy: *Dewi ap Sant ap Keredic ap Cuneda Wledic* (EWGT 54; VSB 320). These bear witness to the original association of the saint with the kingdom of Ceredigion. Dewi's prominence in *Bonedd y Saint* indicates that this document, like Rhigyfarch's Life, was originally drafted in support of the proposed archbishopric of St David's.

Dewrarth Wledic 3: *Ruuawn Beuyr mab D. Wledic* 'Brave Bear'. CO l. 183 *Ruawn Pebyr m. Dorath*; Br. Rh. *Deorthach Wledic* (= RM 148.17–18). For the significance of the title *Gwledic* see n. to *Maxen Wledic.*

Diadema 50 = *Dido*? (see n. to triad). The Welsh forms of this name could have arisen as corruptions based on the Latin accusative *Didonem*. But it is probable that Pen. 47's *Diadema gorderch Achilerw* may preserve the reading of the triad in its original form, and that Achilles' mistress *Diademeia* became subsequently confused with *Dido*. This result would have been facilitated by the greater prominence of Aeneas and the Trojan legend in early Wales over the story of Achilles (= *Achilarw* in the translation of *Dares Phrygius*). Cf. Ceri Davies, *Welsh Literature and the Classical Tradition*, pp. 41–2.

Diffydell m. Disgyfdawt 10 (W: *Diffeidell*), 32.

Divwng m. Alan 15 (R: *Dignif*). *Mwng* occurs as a proper name; cf. *Mwng Mawr Treuit* (CLlH no. VII.20b) and *Mwng Mawr Drefydd* in the list of *Giants* in Pen. 118 (*Cy*. 1917, p. 139 = C. Grooms, *The Giants of Wales,* pp. 203–4). *Divwng* may contain this name combined with the intensive prefix *di-*, or it may be an adj. *difwng* 'swift, destructive, invincible' (GPC 987; cf. CLlH 153; G 341). Alternatively it may represent a corruption of some other name; see n. to triad 15. Cf. *Digon mab Alar* in CO l. 199.

Dina6t Vagla6c 16. *Dinawt* = *Dunawt* (with O.W. *i* for *u* (GMW 2)) 'D. the Shepherd' or 'the Croziered' (see n. to triad 16). It is possible that *Dinawt* is to be identified with *Dinoot*, abbot of Bangor Iscoed, whom Bede names (*Hist. Ecc.* II, 2) as having presided over the company of British clerics who went to confer with St Augustine.

Dinogat m. Kynan Garwynn 44, 46B. See n. to *Kynan*[2] *Garrwyn.* The allusion in triad 44 to the presence of a son of *Cynan Garwyn* at the battle of Arfderydd in 573 is hardly consistent with the reference in *Ann. Cam.* 613 to the death of *Selyf m. Cynan Garwyn* (n.) at the battle of Chester in that year (= 616). The allusion may, however, be an addition to the triad, since it does not appear in texts based upon the Pen. 16 version. This son of *Cynan Garwyn* is not named in any other early source as far as I am aware, though there are a number of instances of the name *Din(o)gat*; *Peis dinogat e vreith* (CA l. 1101); *Dingat m. Nud Hael* EWGT 57 (18); *Dincat* LL 203.16, etc.

Disgyfdawt 10 (*disyndawd* W); *Dysgyfdawt* 32. The additional *Englynion y Beddau* in Pen. 98B give a variant of this name: *Cicleu don drom dra thywawd / am fedd Disgyrnin disgyffedawd / aches trwm anghwres pechawd* 'I have heard a heavy wave upon the sand / around the grave of Disgyrnin Disgyff(edd)awd' (T. Jones, PBA LIII, p. 136 (14)).

Dolor Deiuyr a Brennych 16: *Pryder m. D. a B.* (see n. to *Pryder*).

Don 28: *Gwydyon m. Don* (WR) (see n.); 67: *Ar(y)anrot verch Don* (n.). *Don* is to be equated with *Danu, Anu*, the mother of the gods in the Irish pantheon. Her name is preserved in that of the River Danube (*Donau*), and perhaps in that of the River Dee, for which the form *Dyfrdonwy* is attested (H 292.20 = Prydydd y Moch, CBT V, no. 22.28n.). In B VII, p. 1, W. J. Gruffydd advocated *Dono, Donwy* as the earlier form of this name. See further WCD 204.

Plant Don o Arvon are listed in *Bonedd yr Arwyr* EWGT 90 (25) = B XVIII, p. 237 (25).

Dreon Lew 31 (WR) 'D. the Brave' = Pen. 16: *Dryon m. Nud* (see n.).

Cynddelw: *Trais Dreon, trinheion nwy try* (CBT IV, no. 9.79n.).
Hywel Foel ap Griffri: *llid Dryon* (CBT VII, no. 22.16n.).

Drutwas m. Driffin 46A, App. IV, no. 1. *Drud* 'bold, reckless'; cf. *drutguas* Ll 277.26; *Drutwas m. Tryffin* CO ll. 200–1.

Mostyn MS. 146, I ff. (seventeenth century: *Rep.* I, 168; see also WCD 205–6) reports the following incident:

(trans.) Drudwas son of Treffin, son of the king of Denmark, obtained from his wife three griffins, and they would perform whatever their master demanded of them. A field (of battle) was appointed between Arthur and *Drudwas*, and nobody was to come to the field but the two of them. *Drudwas* sent his griffins before him and said 'Slay the first who may come to the field'. And as Arthur was going, there came the sister of *Drudwas* who was Arthur's mistress, and out of good will to both of them she hindered Arthur from going to the field, and in the end *Drudwas* came to the field, supposing that the griffins had slain *Arthur* according to his request. And the griffins snatched him up and slew him, and in the firmament of the sky they recognized him and descended to the earth, making the most pitful wailing, because they had slain their master *Drudwas*. And there is a song of the griffins which was made over him at that time to commemorate the event, and from it *Llywarch Hen* obtained the subject for this *englyn*:

Drudwas ap Tryffin trwm i ddiwarnawd
Rhac trallawd a gorddin
Adwyth oedd ar gyffredin
Adar ai lladdawdd llwch gwin.
Llywarch Hen ai kant.

('Drudwas son of Tryffin, sad his day / through mischance and oppression / it was a misfortune to all / the griffins slew him' – Llywarch the Old sang it. A slightly better text of the *englyn* is also found in Gutun Owain's version of the Bardic Grammar (B IV, p. 217) and since this is preferable I have substituted it here for that of Mostyn 146, for which see CLlH 185–6.)

Adar llwch gwin is the term used in heraldry for griffins, according to GPC 12. *Drudwas*'s sister, who was Arthur's mistress, is named in the court-list in CO l. 364: *Erduduyl merch Tryffin.*

Drych eil Kibdar 27. *Drych* 'aspect, mirror'. For *eil* 'son, descendant of' see n. below to *Rahaut eil Morgant.*

CO (ll. 393–6): *Galw a oruc Arthur ar Uedwyr, yr hynn . . . nyt oed neb kymryt* (R: *kyfret*) *ac ef yn yr Ynys honn namyn Arthur a Drych eil Kibdar* 'Arthur called on *Bedwyr* [see n. to *Bedwyr m. Bedra6c* above] than whom there was no one so fair (R: 'so swift') in this Island, except Arthur and Drych son of Kibdar.'

Prydydd y Moch: *Mal Arthur, kein modur Kybdar* (CBT V, no. 23.64n.).

Dryon m. Nud (WR: *Dreon Lew*) 31. Perhaps a son of *Nudd Hael* triad 2 (see n.). WR's version gives the epithet 'Dreon the Brave' but omits the patronymic. Cynddelw refers to *treis Dreon* (CBT IV, no. 9.79n.) and Hywel Foel ap Griffri to *llid Dryon* (CBT VII, no. 22.16n.).

Drystan m. Tallwch 19, 21, 26, 41 (Pen. 47), 71, 72, 73; *Trystan* 80, App. IV, no. 4. See nn. to *Tallwch, Es(s)yllt, March m. Meirchya6n. Drystan* is the usual Welsh form of this name, but the older spelling with initial *T-* appears in *Liber Landavensis* (*circa* 1120–40), where the name of a certain *Avel mab Tristan* is cited (LL 279.26). The twelfth-century French form *Tristan* may therefore have come from an early written Welsh exemplar, such as LL's *Avel mab Tristan*, but the possibility of a Breton original for this name cannot be excluded. *Drystan* is derived from prim. Celt. **Drustagnos* (see AW 210, 240–3), and is attested in variant forms in both Britain and Ireland, including the name on the early inscribed stone at Castle Dore in Cornwall, which commemorates a certain *Drusta(n)us* (AW 241–3; Macalister CIIC I, 487; see O. J. Padel, CMCS 1, pp. 78–9). The name of *Tristan* is also recorded in Brittany before the year 1050 (*Romania* LIII, pp. 96–7). I find it impossible not to associate the names of both *Drystan* and of *Tallwch* with the Pictish names *Drust, Drest, Drostan* (for an example of the latter see Padel, CMCS 9, p. 60) and *Talorc, Talorcan, Talargan*—all of which names recur in the Pictish regnal lists (Chadwick, *Early Scotland*, passim; M. O. Anderson, *Kings and Kingship in Early Scotland* (Edinburgh, 1973), pp. 271–3, 279; M. Miller, 'Pictish King-Lists', *Scottish Historical Review* LVIII (1979), pp. 1–34.) There are no other Welsh personal names which in any way resemble these names. And it remains significant that *Loenois, Loonois* (Lothian, the British territory adjacent to Pictland) adheres to Tristan's name as the name of his traditional homeland in the works of the twelfth-century French poet Béroul, in the thirteenth-century prose *Tristan*, and in other French poems and romances, including the *Brut* of Wace (*circa* 1100–75), while *Loenois* is independently recorded as the French name for Lothian in documents from the year 1158 onwards (W. J. Watson, *The Celtic Place-Names of Scotland,* pp. 101–3). No names in any way corresponding to those of *Drystan* and *Tallwch* are to be found in Welsh sources in reference to any other characters except to Drystan and to his father, and there is never any doubt that the Welsh allusions are to the character referred to as *Tristan* in the French and European romances. (This includes the strange form *Drustwrn Haearn* CO ll. 191–2, see n.) However, for the names of *Es(s)yllt* (Iseult) and *March* ('King' Mark) it is a very different matter; on these names see the notes below. (The name of Drystan's father *Tallwch* failed to be transmitted into any of the foreign texts.)

The Welsh sources are limited to the triads listed above, to two obscure fragments of verse, LlDC no. 35 (trans. and discussion SC XIV/XV, pp. 54–65; and EWSP 466, 510), and the later prose-verse tale *Ystorya Tristan.* The poems and triads are found in manuscripts of the mid-thirteenth century, and triads 19 and 21 all portray *Drystan* in complimentary but imprecise terms comparable to those used elsewhere in TYP as eulogistic epithets for other early Brythonic heroes. The significance of triad 26 is more fully open for discussion than the other two triads, and its relation to the *Drystan* story is clearly of fundamental importance for the date and content of the Peniarth 16 or 'Early Version' of TYP. The third source for the Welsh *Drystan* is the sixteenth-century *Ystorya Tristan*, composed in a mixture of prose and *englynion*, which was first edited by Ifor Williams (B V, pp. 115–21), and from a different manuscript by Jenny Rowland and Graham Thomas (*Nat. Lib. of Wales Journal* XXII, pp. 241–53). A translation of the *Ystorya Trystan* was published by R. L. Thomson, 'The Tristan Legend' in *Translation of texts from Northern and Eastern Europe* ed. Joyce Hill (University of Leeds, 1977), pp. 1–5. Some late manuscripts (incredibly) trace the descent of Cadwaladr of Gwynedd through two female lines to *Meddyf merch Tallwch ap Kwch m. Kychwein chwaer y Drystann* (B XVIII, p. 238 (28) = EWGT 91 (28f)).

But it is necessary to turn to the twelfth-century French poems attributed to Béroul, Thomas, and Marie de France (all of them earlier by a century than the manuscripts in which the Welsh triads and the *Black Book of Carmarthen* fragments are found), as well as to the slightly later *Prose Tristan* to obtain outlines of the romance of *Tristan* (*Drystan*) and *Iseult* (*Es(s)yllt*) as it has come down in the fuller continental form, which appears to underlie almost all the Welsh references to the story by poets and storytellers. The *Tristan* romance was popular throughout Europe from the twelfth century, as it was also in Wales. This is made abundantly clear from the numerous allusions to the story of *Tristan* and *Esyllt* which were made by Welsh poets from the thirteenth century onwards. In its French form the story told of *Tristan*'s love for *Es(s)yllt* (Iseult), the wife of his uncle King Mark of Cornwall (= *March ap Meirchiawn*). Significantly, Mark is presented as Tristan's mother's brother. Tristan and Iseult drank inadvertently from a charmed love-potion during the journey on which Tristan brought Iseult from her home in Ireland to be married in Cornwall to his uncle. The drink had been intended for the wedding-night of the royal pair but became responsible for the indestructible love which bound Trystan and Esyllt throughout their lives. The subsequent story in French, as in other languages, concentrates on a series of ingenious tricks and subterfuges contrived by Tristan to facilitate illicit meetings with Iseult in the face of every imaginable difficulty. Variations on the theme of the lovers' stolen meetings are explored to their ultimate limits and repeated continually throughout all the French, English and continental versions of the *Tristan* story. The flight to the forest and the lovers' idyllic woodland life are common to all the versions of the Tristan story and are among the most popular scenes in the romances. Allusions made by a number of Welsh poets prove that from the thirteenth century onwards the illegitimate love-story of *Drystan* and *Es(s)yllt* was no less familiar and popular in Wales than in England and on the continent (see references to *Drystan* in G 294, and the quotations cited below).

Contrary to my earlier views on the Welsh *Tristan* sources (THSC 1955, pp. 32–60), it is my final belief that the theme of the lovers' stolen meetings, ingeniously contrived so as to elude King Mark—and which is incessantly repeated with many variants in the continental Tristan romances—is a persistent feature of the three surviving Welsh fragments which relate to the Tristan story. One such meeting between the lovers, contrived in defiance of March ap Meirchiawn, is the manifest subject of the *Ystorya Trystan* (on the tale see EWSP 252–4, 248, 265) as it is also of the *Drystan* episode in triad 26 (see AW 214–15). I cannot now regard either of these texts as likely to be wholly independent of the twelfth-century French poems, or else of earlier lost continental versions of the *Tristan* romance. The subject-matter of the *Black Book of Carmarthen* poem is, however, more difficult to interpret, but in discussing it I have suggested that in spite of all obscurities, the two fragments reflect features of an episode frequently repeated and generally familiar to readers of the continental 'Tristan' texts as 'The Tryst beneath the Tree' (see my study 'The "Tristan" Poem in the *Black Book of Carmarthen*', SC XIV/XV, discussion and references p. 62 and n. 2). Experience has led me to conclude that the literary interrelationship between Britain and the continent of Europe in the matter of the transmission of stories, both orally and in writing, was a process which goes back many years earlier than has often been recognized and that it had been in active operation for some years before the twelfth century.

I conclude that there is a strong case for believing the earliest indigenous heroic traditions about *Drystan fab Tallwch* (as indicated in triads 19 and 21) to have originated in north Britain, in the same way as did so much else of inherited Brythonic traditions, and that this story-material moved down from the Old North to Wales during the early Middle Ages, perhaps from as early as the ninth century. As a heroic figure the early story of *Drystan*, as preserved in Old French sources, places the hero's home in the region of Lothian (*Loonois*), which lay adjacent to Pictland, so that influences permeating from the nearby Pictish kingdom could well account for Drystan's name and patronymic (preserved in the Welsh, but not in the French sources), as well as for having supplied the name of Lothian (*Loonois*) as that of Drystan's traditional home. But it must be said that a strong case has also been made by O. J. Padel (CMCS I, pp. 53–80) for the origin and development in Cornwall of the tale of *Drystan*, *March* and *Esyllt*, at least in the literary form in which the story came to be propagated in the early French poems and in the prose *Tristan*—and it is to these foreign texts alone that we have to turn in order to obtain the story in its most amplified form. Padel's view gains a certain support from the many Cornish localizations for episodes in Tristan's story, which are amplified in Béroul's twelfth-century poem. I think that the most that can be said is that Drystan was an early Brythonic hero who was famous in the 'Old North', and concerning whom stories were freshly localized at different times and in different places over western Britain. Traces of these localizations can be found to this day in the surviving topography of the country. See also O. J. Padel, CMCS 27, pp. 1–31.

References by Welsh poets from the thirteenth and subsequent centuries include the following:

Bleddyn Fardd: *deuodeu drystan* (H 68.10 = CBT VII, no. 54.26n.); idem, *kymnhebyc Drystan* (H 77.17 = CBT VII, no. 56.9).

Hywel ab Einion Llygliw: *dig drystan* (MA(2) 339b, 2).

Ll. Brydydd Hoddnant: *Cyhafal anian drystan dreistir* (GLlBH no. I.8, see n.).

Casnodyn: *I lawr Fadog fawr, fur erfid—Trystan* (GC no. 2.17). Cf. idem, no. 11.64n.: *Tyrstan.*

Dafydd ap Gwilym: *Unfryd wyf . . . a thrystan uthr ar osteg* (*marvellous* in song?) (GDG 33.8; for *gosteg*[2] see GPC 1514).

Dafydd ab Edmwnd wishes for *diod trystan im anerch / a barafi lle bo'r ferch* (GDE 3.25) 'I shall make, wherever the girl may be, Trystan's drink, that she may greet me'; idem, *Trystan wyf trosti yn wyllt / yn ymossod am Essyllt / March yw hwn a merch yw hi / am meirichion yw amherchi* 'I am (like) Trystan, madly contending for Essyllt; he is a March ap Meirchion, dishonouring her' (GDE 56.27–30).

Gr. ap Maredudd: *Trystan hir amdir yn ymdaeru* (RBP col. 1203.35 = GGM no. 2.33; cf. no. 3.19).

In *Cywydd y Sêr* (DGG no. XL) the poet describes himself as *Fal Trwstan am feingan fu* 'like Trystan (wandering) for his fair one'. (The reference to 'Drystan' here has, however, been questioned (LlC 21, p. 204. See further CMCS 1, pp. 53–81; AW chs. 10, 11, 12, 13; ALMA chs. 12, 13, 26; EAR ch. V; WCD 619–21; SC XIV/XV, pp. 54–65; and J. Bedier, *Le Roman de Tristan et Iseut* (1913).)

Dunawt[1] tywyssawc Kernyw 35 (Pen. 50). 'D. Prince of Cornwall.' *Dunawt* < *Donatus*. In BD 78–9 *Dunavt vrenhin Kernyw* is the name given to Geoffrey's *Dionotus rex Cornubie* (HRB V, 15–16), whose daughter was sought in marriage by *Conan Meiriadoc* (see n. to *Cynan brawd Elen Luydawc*). Geoffrey names the girl Ursula, thus identifying her with St Ursula, the leader of the 11,000 virgins martyred at Cologne—substituting a popular twelfth-century *Passio* for the Welsh tradition (HB ch. 27) that the Breton emigrants took as their wives native Breton women. (A full account of the Ursula legend is given in LBS IV, 312–47.) The earliest Life of *St Ursula* was written in the late tenth century, and was based on information given by the nuns of Cologne, who claimed to have had it from a Count Hrolf who had visited England about the year 928 and had learned the story from the archbishop of Canterbury. (For the text of the *Vita* see *Analecta Bollandiana* III, 7–20.) Thus the story was believed to be of insular origin, and this would have been an incentive to Geoffrey of Monmouth to find a place for it in HRB. On Geoffrey's sources for his version of the story see E. Faral, *La Légende Arthurienne* II, pp. 200–1. Geoffrey gave the name of *Dionotus* to the unnamed British ruler who, according to the *Vita*, was the father of St Ursula, and this name was rendered as *Dunawt* in the Welsh *Bruts*. Geoffrey does not, however, name Cologne as the place of the martyrdom of the virgins, but states that some of them were shipwrecked, others driven *in barbaras insulas*, where they were massacred or taken prisoner by the inhabitants. It is clear, therefore, that the redactor of Pen. 50 drew upon fuller information about this incident than is obtained either from the Welsh *Bruts* or from the available texts of HRB. Either the redactor drew upon a text of HRB so far unidentified or else he was citing an independent knowledge of the *Ursula* legend. A Welsh version of the Life of *St Ursula* was written by Syr Huw Pennant about 1514 (Pen. 182 A, 261–99; see T. H. Parry-Williams (ed.), *Rhyddiaith Gymraeg* I, pp. 18–22). There may have been earlier Welsh versions which are now lost.

Duna6t² m. Pabo Post Prydein 5; *Duna6t 6wr* 44; see n. to *Pabo Post Prydein*. For *Dunawd*'s epithet *bwr(r)* 'stout, strong, big' see GPC 354; B VII, pp. 35–6.

Ann. Cam. 595: *Dunaut* [*filius Pabo*] *rex moritur*.

It has been suggested that an allusion to the territory formerly ruled by *Dunawt fab Pabo* is to be found in the *regio Dunotinga* (modern *Dent*) in the West Riding of Yorkshire, which according to Eddius' Life of *St Wilfred* (ed. B. Colgrave) ch. 17 was presented to the church at Ripon in the year 675 (see Chadwick, *Early Scotland*, p. 143n.). If this were so, *Dunawd*'s territory would have lain close to that of Gwallawg in Elmet (cf. *bro dunawt* RBP col. 1044.1–2, and *Dunoding* (named after Cunedda's son *Dunaut*) in Meirionnydd (HW I, 238n.)). In *Canu Llywarch Hen*, *Dunawd mab Pabo* is named several times (CLlH no. III.3c, 37a, 38a; no. V.5a) in connection with fighting among the Men of the North; from the context it appears that *Dunawd* was opposed to Owain and Pasgen, sons of Urien Rheged, but was allied to Gwallawg ap Lleenawg. *Bonedd y Saint* asserts that St Deinioel, patron saint of Bangor in

Gwynedd, was Dunawd's son: *Deinnyoel m. Dunawt Vwrr m. Pabo Post Prydein a Dwywei uerch Leennauc e vam* (EWGT 56 (12)). For *Dunawd m. Pabo* see further EWSP 106–7 and *passim*; WCD 191; and G 396.

Dunawd's bard was named *Kywryt* (see n.), according to a poem by Gwilym Ddu o Arfon (*circa* 1330): *Meu ynof mawrgof . . . Mal cofein kywrein kywryt vard dunawt* 'The great memory is mine . . . like the polished memorial of Cywryd, Dunawd's bard' (RBP col. 1228.9–11 = GGDT no. 7.41–3; see 7.43n. and 6.8n.). Dunawd's bard had evidently composed a famous elegy to his patron—the lost work of one of the *Cynfeirdd*, who is otherwise unknown. Another allusion is by Bleddyn Fardd: *detyf dunawt ap Pabo* (H 78.6 = CBT VII, no. 56.26n.). With the poet's name cf. *Kywryt*[1] and *Kywryt*[2] above.

Dyfynnawl m. Mynedawc Eidin 33 (Pen. 50). *Dyfnwal* < **Dubnoualos*. Cf. *Dyuynual Hen*, App. II, nos. 7–12, and WCD 212–13. See also n. to *Mynyda6c Eidyn*. There seems to be no other reference to a son of *Mynydawc* named *Dyfnwal*.

Dyfyr Wallt Eureit 88, 97. 'Golden-Haired D.' This heroine's beauty is cited as a standard of comparison by the *cywyddwyr*, comparable with the beauty of Enid, Eigr, Luned or Creirwy. The earliest allusion to *Dyfyr*'s beauty, other than this triad, appears to be that by Gruffudd ap Maredudd: *oleune Dyfyr neu Lunet* (RBP col. 1326.20), though confusion of the name with *dyfr*, *deifr* (pl. of *dwfr* 'waters') may have obscured other allusions.

For further references to *Dyfr*, *Deifr*, see GDG no. 52.13; no. 56.33; no. 66.42; 93.32; Casnodyn: *Dyfr wledig, eilig ei wyledd—am ged* (GC no. 2.143n.); Gruffudd Llwyd: *Enw deifr, yna y dywod* (IGE[2] no. XLVIII.16); Ieuan ap Rhydderch: *Dwf eurlathrblyg Dyfr lathrbleth* (IGE[2] no. LXXV.18); Dafydd ab Edmwnd: *Dy wallt eur, Deifr Wallt Eurawg* (*Gorchestion Beirdd Cymru* 125).

Dygynnelw bard Ewein m. 6ryen 11. See n. to *Owein m. Vryen*. The name *Dygyn(n)elw* is found also as that of a son of Cynddelw Brydydd Mawr (H 179.20 = CBT III, no. 30.4, 8, 10, n.). It is tempting to conclude that Cynddelw named his son *Dygynnelw* after the earlier *Cynfardd* attached to Owain ab Urien (concerning whom nothing is known). See also GP 218.1–2: *englyn anghyfodl yr hwn a elwir 'dull Dygynelw'* (a form of the *englyn unodl union*). This appears to be the only other recorded instance of the name *Dygyn(n)elw*.

Dyrnwch Gawr App. III, no. 7. 'D. the Giant.' I restore the form from the earliest text of App. III (Pen. 51). It gains support from the inclusion of *Dyrnhwch Gawr yghwlad Euas* 'D. the Giant in the land of Ewyas' in Pen. 118, *circa* 1600 (C. Grooms, *The Giants of Wales*, p. 179; *Cy*. XXVII, p. 144). There is likely to be a connection with *Diwrnach Wydel* 'D. the Irishman' in CO l. 635n. and CO ll. 1037–52. On the name see further P. Sims-Williams, B XXIX, pp. 603–4. The variant forms of this name found in App. III and elsewhere are listed and discussed by E. Rowlands, LlC V, p. 60. See also the variants cited by P. C. Bartrum, 'Tri Thlws ar Ddeg Ynys Brydain: The Thirteen Treasures of Britain', EC X (1963), p. 468.

Dysgyfdawt 32. See *Disgyfdawt*.

Echel 6ordwytwll 9: *Gobrwy m. E.* (n.). 'E. Mighty-Thigh'. See CO ll. 195–6, 1154 (nn.), where we learn that *Echel* was killed by the boar Twrch Trwyth. *Echel*'s name may have been preserved in that of the stream *Egel* (CF 536–7; Guest, *Mabinogion* (1849) II, 364).

Br. Rh.: *a Gobrw mab Echel Uordvyt twyll* (RM 159.26).

Echel < *Achilles*. For the knowledge shown by the *Gogynfeirdd* of the names of classical heroes see n. to triad 47; D. M. Lloyd, *Rhai Agweddau ar Ddysg y Gogynfeirdd,* pp. 12–14; Ceri Davies, *Welsh Literature and the Classical Tradition,* pp. 30–43. *Echel* is alluded to a number of times by the *Gogynfeirdd*: e.g. Peryf ap Cedifor (CBT II, no. 21.10n.); Cynddelw (CBT IV, no. 6.122n.); Prydydd y Moch (CBT V, no.11.19n.). In *Brut y Brenhinedd, Echel,* (*Achel*) *urenhin Denmarch* translates HRB's *Achil, A(s)chillus rex dacorum* (BD 158.175 = HRB IX, 12; X, 6).

On the epithet *Mordwyt Twll* 'Mighty Thigh' see CLlH 70, where *twll* is equated with L. *Tullus*, *Tullius* 'thick, swollen', and cf. the name and epithet *Gwen vordwyt tylluras* (CLlH no. I.18a) where *tylluras* is evidently a compound of synonyms. The epithet of *Mordwyd Tyllyon* (PKM 44.5, see n.) need not be a plural of *twll*, but simply a variant, on the analogy of such pairs as *gwirion, gwir*. In default of further evidence, it is not possible to associate *Echel Vordwyt Twll* with the character of *Mordwyd Tyllyon*, especially since CLlH shows that *mordwyt twll* and variants could be used as honorific epithets. Proinsias Mac Cana suggested with considerable probability (*Branwen*, pp. 163–4) that *mordwyt tyllyon* in *Mabinogi Branwen* is no more than an epithet for Brân himself.

Ector Gadarn 47 = Hector of Troy. According to *Dares Phrygius*: *Ector uab Priaf gwr bloesc oed gwyn pengrych ac aelodau buan idaw ac wyneb anrydedus karedic ac adas y garyat* (RBB 13.14–17) 'Hector son of Priam was a man thick of speech, with fair curly hair and noble limbs, and a kind and noble face, deserving of love'. (For the sixth(?)-century Latin version from which the fourteenth-century Welsh *Dares Phrygius* was translated, see Owen and Lloyd, *Drych yr Oesoedd Canol*, pp. 33–4, and references cited.) But the name *Ecdor, Echtor* was employed by the poets as a standard of nobility at a much earlier date than that at which it could have become familiar to them through the Welsh version of *Dares Phrygius*: it was evidently already well known to the *Gogynfeirdd* as well as to their successors (see n. to triad 47).

> Gwalchmai: *Kyueissor echtor ach drylwyn* (H 25.8 = CBT I, no. 7.34n.).
> Cynddelw: *Echel dor Echtor gor goeluein* (H 101.29 = CBT IV, no. 6.122n.).
> Llywelyn Fardd I: *lid Echdor* (H 44.22 = CBT II, no. 1.77n.).

Dafydd Benfras: *Greddf Echdor gwawr eurdorf gwraf* (CBT VI, no. 29.102).

Einion ap Gwalchmai: *kyueissor echdor* (H 39.28 = CBT I, no. 7.34n.).

Dafydd Ddu o Hiraddug: *Milwr tŵr taerfor, fal y bu Hector* (GEO no. 2.13n.).

Gr. ap Maredudd: *aryf ector* (RBP 1316.38 = GGM no. 4.87); *eil ector* (1322.20 = GGM no. 7.31); *Deryw ector nerth diorwacter* (1209.39 = GGM no. 3.163n.).

Dafydd ap Gwilym compares Ifor Hael to *rhwyf Arthur neu Ector* (GDG no. 5.41). See G 435 for further allusions by the *cywyddwyr*.

Eda Glinvawr 30 'E . Great Knee' (= *E. glingawr* 'Giant's Knee' WR). On the name see K. H. Jackson, CS 43–4. This character is identified in the Harleian MS. 3859 of HB with the Northumbrian king *Eata* (fourth in descent from *Ida*, who was the first king of Bernicia):

> Ida genuit Eadric, genuit Ecgulf, genuit Liodguald, genuit *Aetan*—ipse est *Eata Glinmaur*—genuit Eadbyrth et Ecgbirth. (HB ch. 61. For the correct Northumbrian genealogy see D. Whitelock *et al.*, *Anglo-Saxon Chronicle*, p. 211.)

Ida was king of Bernicia (547–59), so that the association of his great-grandson *Eata* with *Gwrgi and Peredur* (see nn.) can hardly be historical, since *Ann. Cam.* notes the deaths of both in 580. The two sons of *Eata* named in HB were Edbert, king of Northumbria from 737–58, and Egbert who was consecrated bishop of York in 732. It is probable that, in the tradition on which the triad is based, the remote reputation of *Eata* as an English enemy had become confused to such an extent that his name could have represented any unspecified Northumbrian ruler who had opposed the Britons in an earlier generation. Alternatively, HB may have equated *Eata Glinmaur* with the wrong English king—perhaps it was *Ida* himself who was originally designated by this nickname (as is indicated by J. Loth, *Mab.* II, 264).

A different and apparently fanciful genealogy of *Eda Glinfawr* is found in some sixteenth-century manuscripts of *Bonedd y Saint* (it shows some echoes of *Breudwyt Ronabwy*): *Eda Glynuawr ap Gwybei drahawc ap Mwc mawr Drevydd ap Offa kyllellvawr vrenhin Lloegr, y gwr a ymladdodd yn erbyn Arthvr yNgwaith Vadon* (EWGT 64 (71n.) and see n. to *Gvibei Drahavc* below).

Edelflet Ffleissawc 6renhin Lloegyr 10 (WR), *E. vrenhin Lloegyr* 32. 'E. the Twister, king of England.' *Ipse est Aedlferd Flesaur* HB ch. 57; ch. 63.

Ethelfrith was king of Bernicia 593–617; during the latter half of his reign he was also king of Deira. The Anglo-Saxon dental spirant was rendered in Welsh by a spirant and represented by *d*; hence the Welsh rendering of his name as *Edelflet* in HB and TYP. R. G. Gruffydd suggests (SC XXVIII, p. 65) that Ethelfrith's Welsh epithet, 'The Twister' (common to both of these texts), may indicate a reputation for treaty-breaking. It is paralleled by other humorous or satirical Welsh epithets found in HB's 'Saxon Genealogies' for English kings—*Ecgfrith Ailguin* 'White Eyebrow', *Oswald Lamnguin* 'White' or perhaps 'Flashing Sword', *Eata Glinmaur* 'Great Knee' (= *E. Glinvawr*, see previous n.). On the meaning of *Flesaur*, *Ffleissawc* see PKM 116, CA xv (*ffleis* < L. *flexus* 'a bending, a turning'). Jackson points out (LHEB 49n.) 'the nickname *Flesaur* for Ethelfrith has the air of a contemporary one, but the word is in the dress of Nennius' day. About 600 it would have been **Flesor*, if not something like **Flexsor*'. D. P. Kirby *et al.* (*A Biographical Dictionary of Dark-Age Britain*, pp. 22–3) suggest that *Ethelfrith* may have been the English commander at the battle of Catraeth. For Bede's *encomium* of *Ethelfrith*, see *Hist. Ecc.* I, 34 and WCD 221.

Instances in which *Edelflet*'s name is commemorated in early Welsh historical texts are listed in G 438. The only instance in which this name is commemorated in poetry appears to be in GP 7, no. 26, which cites an *englyn enghreifftiol* in praise of Sir Rhys ap Gruffudd, in which the military strength of Sir Rhys is compared to *kedeyrned Edelf(f)let*, and the subsequent editors suggest that this was because of the strong support given by Sir Rhys to King Edward II. See GEO pp. 40–1.

Edelic Corr 72, **Erddili(g) Cor** App. IV, no. 4. 'E. the Dwarf.' Dafydd ap Gwilym gives the form *Eiddilig Gor* (see n. to triad 27). Since *eiddil* = 'weak', *Eiddilig* is perhaps a suitable name for a dwarf: alternatively, the first element may correspond with that in *(H)ediluiu* (LL 169.13). Lloyd-Jones (G 246, 455) associates *Eiddilic Cor* with the name *Kynddilic ap Cor Crud* in the *Beddau* stanzas (LlDC no. 18.126), but the confusion seems rather to be with one or other of the two dwarfs variously named as *Rudlwm Gorr* and *Gwythelyn Gorr* (see nn.) in the two main versions of triad 28. For the name *Edelic* cf. EWGT 44 (5); WCD 222.

Edena6c 22 (*adein* + *awc*) 'the Winged One'. *Anguas Edeinauc* is given as the name of one of Arthur's followers in the poem *Pa Gur* (LlDC no. 31.25); also cf. CO l. 193n.: *Ac Anwas Edeinawc*, and ll. 233–4, 237: *Henwas Edeinawc mab Erim*. The last reference seems to be a doublet of the earlier one, and is given in a triad celebrating the fleetness of foot of the three sons of Erim (with the name cf. *Eiryf* below).

Ednyueda6c Drythyll 64. *Trythyll* 'pampered, wanton, lively'.

Edwin (Etwin) vrenhin Lloegyr 26 (WR), 42 (WR), 55, 62, 69. See nn. to *Catwalla6n*[1] *m. Catuan*, *Run*[4] *m. Ryueduawr*, *Ceredic m. Gwallawc*. *Ann. Cam.* 617: *Etguin incipit regnare* 'Edwin begins to reign.'

Edwin, son of King Aelle of Deira, ruled Deira and Bernicia together, 617–33. His power extended even further than Northumbria. Bede (*Hist. Ecc.* II, 5) claims that *Edwin* 'commanded all the nations, as well of the English as of the Britons who inhabit Britain, except only the people of Kent, and he reduced also under the dominion of the English the Mevanian islands (i.e. Man and Anglesey) of the Britons, lying between Ireland and Britain'. He describes *Edwin* as the fifth of the English kings to be overlord of all the English kingdoms (except Kent) lying south of the Humber. In rendering Bede's account the ASC gives the title *Bretwalda* to these kings—a word whose significance has been much disputed, but which must bear some reference to *Edwin*'s actual or asserted power over the Britons. It is in virtue of his prolonged contest with the north Wales king Cadwallon that *Edwin*'s name has been introduced into early Welsh tradition. 'The memory of (Cadwallon's) great duel with Edwin of Northumbria, carried on with marked ill fortune for many years, but ending in the defeat and death of the English king, deeply impressed itself on the minds of his fellow-countrymen, so that Edwin became the typical English antagonist, and every bold defender of the freedom of Wales was hailed as a new Cadwallon' (HW 182). The references to *Edwin* in TYP and in early poetry (see n. to *Catwalla6n*), combined with the account of his relations with Cadwallon given by Geoffrey of Monmouth (HRB XII, 1–8), are witness to the existence of much traditional narrative concerning the antagonism between the two. Bede's account shows that, on the English side, *Edwin* had by the eighth century become established as a heroic figure, around whose name saga and folklore had grown up. Sir Frank Stenton has described *Edwin* as a 'typical king of the Heroic Age' (*Anglo-Saxon England*, 79–80).

In 'Llinellau o Gerddi i Gadwallon ap Cadfan', B XXVI, pp. 406–10, Graham Thomas quoted isolated lines from a collection of quotations made by Robert Vaughan of Hengwrt, in NLW MS. 9094, from *hengerdd* which have subsequently been lost, relating to Cadwallon. One of these quotations reads *Can dodyw pen Edwin lys Aberffraw / a dyfod Cymru yn un andaw* 'When the head of Edwin came to Aberffraw, and the Welsh (leg. *Cymry* for *Cymru*) came in a single concourse (?)' On these lines, see R. Geraint Gruffydd, 'Canu Cadwallon ap Cadfan', *Ast. H.* 42–3. Such a tradition respecting *Edwin* runs counter to Bede (*Hist. Ecc.* II, 20) who claims that *Edwin*'s dismembered head was brought to York.

The symbolical use of *Edwin*'s name to designate an English opponent is found in the poetry of the *Gogynfeirdd*, as in Gwalchmai's description of himself: *Gwalchmei y'm gelwir, gal Edwin ac Eigyl* (H 18.11 = CBT I, no. 9.51n.) 'G. I am called, enemy to Edwin and the English'. Four centuries later, William Llŷn still followed the bardic convention by calling England *gwlad Edwin* (Wm. Ll. xiii, 18). It is therefore the more surprising to find that *Edwin* was adopted as a personal name in Wales at an early date; cf. LL. 249.22: *familia etguine regis guenti filii guriat*. For the son of Hywel fab Ieuaf who bore this name in the mid-tenth century, see n. to triad 55c. Further medieval instances are cited in G and EWGT; cf. also CBT I, no. 1.23n. (= LlDC no. 22.23: *Gorwyr Edwin*).

Eua 50, Eve. For references by the *Gogynfeirdd* see Ann Parry Owen, LlC XX, p. 29, and further references in G 444. Cf. *Ag Eva addvwyna ddyn* (Wm. Ll. xcv, 29); *pryd Efa* (GO no. II.12) *Gorchestion Beirdd Cymru* (189.8).

Eueilian, wreic Wydyr Dr6m 66. More probably *Eneilian*, sister of Cadwallan ap Cadfan, see *Bonedd y Saint*; EWGT 65 (72). See n. to *Gwydyr Dr6m* below.

Euengat 33 (WR): *Heiden m. Euengat* (= *m. Enygan,* Pen. 16). See n. to *Enygan.*

Efra6c Iarll 86, **Efrog** 91, App. IV, no. 2: *Peredur (Prydyr) m. E.* See n. to *Peredur*[1] *m. Efra6c* < Romano-British *Eburācum* (= York); meaning 'the estate of *Eburos*' (LHEB 39).

Eurddel (= Efrddyl) 70 (Pen. 50). See n. to *Vryen (Reget) m. Kynuarch. Efrddyl* is named as Urien's sister, CLlH no. III.30, 31 (trans.):

> E. is sad tonight, and many (hosts) beside; in *Aber Lleu* Urien has been slain. E. is sad from the calamity tonight, and from the fate which has befallen me; in *Aber Lleu* her brother has been slain. (See also EWSP 423, 479, 561n.).

Ebrdil occurs also as the name of the mother of St Dubricius, daughter of King Pebiau of Ergyng (LL 78 ff.). This name is given in other instances in LL as *Emrdil, Eurdila, Euirdil.* Dubricius' mother was commemorated at *Lann Ebrdil* (LL 192), and perhaps this place is to be equated with Madley ('Fortunate Place') in Herefordshire (see LBS II, 414–15). The saint who bore the same name may have become partially confused in the triad with Urien's sister—so that something of the sanctity of the former became bestowed on the latter.

Eidyn 33, 34. See n. to *Heidyn m. Enygan.*

Einya6n[1] 23: *Run m. Einya6n*. See n. to *Run*[2]. The name ENNIAUN is found on an early inscription (ECMW no. 231). The reference in the triad may either be to *Einiaun Girt*, grandfather of Maelgwn Gwynedd (Harl. Gen. I = EWGT 9 (1)), or possibly to a son of Maelgwn named *Einyawn*; though G cites a large number of instances of the name *Einyawn*, so that it is impossible to feel assurance in identifying the character named, especially as *R(h)un* is also a name of frequent occurrence.

On *Einya6n*[1] see n. by E. P. Hamp ('On the Justification of Ordering in *TYP*', SC XVI/XVII, p. 109), who suggests a possible pun in the triad on *eingion* 'anvil'.

Eina6n[2] **m. Bed brenhin Kerni6** 69. This character is unidentified. *Ein(y)awn* is a name of very frequent occurrence; see above. No other instance of *Bed(d)* as a personal name has been recorded, and it seems most likely that this name arose as an orthographical corruption of *Aed*; cf. the reading of BL[1] and Pen. 240—*E. vabaidd.* The name *Aed(d)* is an Irish borrowing, but other instances of it are attested in Wales, see n. to *Aed Ma6r*.

Eiryf 15: *Llawr m. Eiryf*. If *Eiryf* is the correct form of this patronymic, we have a pair 'Solitary son of Number', which is reminiscent of similar pairs in CO. The name occurs in O.W. form as *Erim*, CO l. 235 (see P. Sims-Williams, B XXIX, p. 611). But it is possible that *Eiryf* should be emended to *Erw*, cf. CO l. 217: *Llawr eil Erw.*

Elen[1] Luyda6c 35. 'Helen of the Hosts.' See nn. to *Maxen Wledic* and to *Cynan*[1]. On *lluyddog* 'having an army, bellicose' etc. see GPC 2233.

Elen Luydawc, the heroine of *Breudwyt Maxen*, appears to have been a character of early Welsh mythology who was particularly associated with the Roman roads in Wales (hence her epithet *Lluyddog* 'of the Hosts'). The Roman roads are known to this day as *Sarn(au) Helen.* But at an early stage, as Ifor Williams showed in 1927 (in his introduction to *Breudwyt Maxen*), her identity became confused with that of the Roman St Helena, mother of Constantine the Great, who, according to a legend which goes back to the fourth century, had made a pilgrimage to Jerusalem and discovered the true Cross. Thus the Dyfed genealogy (Harl. Gen. II = EWGT p. 10) traces the descent of the royal line to Constantine the Great *map Constantii et Helen Luitdauc que de Britannia exivit ad crucem Christi querendam usque ad Ierusalem.* For a late example of this story in Welsh see also *Hystoria Adrian ac Ipotis*: *dyw gwener y kauas Elen luydyavc y groc ry daroed yr eidevonn ychudyav yny dayar achos y diodefuei crist arnei* (Morris-Jones, *The Elucidarium*, p. 137).There is, in fact, no evidence that the Roman St Helena ever came to Britain. Yet the tradition that she did so seems to have become established in this country at an early date, not only in Welsh, but also in English sources. Henry of Huntingdon, writing *circa* 1129, reports what seems to have been a local East Anglian story that Helena, the mother of Constantine, was a daughter of Coel, an eponymous ruler of Colchester (*Hist. Angl.* I, 37). This story was repeated by Geoffrey of Monmouth (HRB V, 6). It is notable that neither of these writers lays any emphasis on Helena's sanctity, nor do they refer to the legend of her discovery of the Cross. (On Geoffrey's indebtedness to Henry of Huntingdon, see Faral, *La Légende Arthurienne* II, 186–9.) Nor is there any reason to suppose that either of these writers in any way conflated St Helena with the *Elen Luyddog* of Welsh tradition, or indeed that they knew anything of the latter. With Elen's epithet *luitdauc* (*lluyddog)* cf. Cadwallawn who is entitled *lluyddog Prydain* in *Moliant Cadwallawn* (*Ast. H.* 31.29), *Yrp Luydawc* in triad 35 (R) and *Lleuddun Lluyddog* in *Bonedd y Saint*, EWGT 56 (14); 57 (18).

It remained for the redactor of *Breudwyt Maxen* to identify the *Elen Luydawc* of older Welsh tradition with the British bride with whom tradition credited the emperor Maximus (see n. to *Maxen Wledic*). The Dyfed genealogy in Harl. MS. 3859 no. 2 (= EWGT 9–10 (2)) includes the name of *Maxim Guletic* as well as that of *Helen Luitdauc*, but the name of *Maxim Guletic* is introduced seven generations higher up than that of *Helen Luitdauc*: evidently the association of the two must be subsequent to the tenth century, when the Harl. Gens. were redacted. The Welsh tale, though perhaps it is not older than the latter half of the twelfth century in its present form, is entirely uninfluenced by Geoffrey's account of Maximus' marriage. HRB gives no name to Maximus' bride, and though the account of her antecedents may in some respects preserve a trace of an older and more authentic tradition concerning her identity, it is quite clear that Geoffrey knew nothing of the Welsh figure of *Elen Luyddog*. A point which may at first seem strange in the Welsh tale is the connection of Elen and Cynan, through their father Eudaf, with the Dumnonian royal line (for the genealogy see n. to *Gereint m. Erbin*). Eudaf's court is localized at Caernarfon, and the associations of the story (apart from the anecdote about the founding of Carmarthen) are entirely with north Wales, and the manner of its narration shows local patriotism and pride in Gwynedd. But Cynan was known to tradition as the leader of the Breton colonists, and as a Dumnonian prince: hence if he were to be presented as the brother of Elen, her 'genealogy' had to be altered to conform with his, and her earlier association with the Dyfed dynasty had to be suppressed.

Elen's association with the Roman roads in Wales is evidently among the most ancient of the traditions connected with the mythical Elen Luyddog. Since the epithet *lluydawc* is first applied to her in the passage describing the making of the roads, it is clear that to the narrator of *Breudwyt Maxen* Elen's title had reference to these. The emperor Constantine the Great was responsible for a scheme of sweeping repairs to the roads in Britain (Collingwood and Myres, *Roman Britain*, p. 282). Possibly this fact may have assisted the conflation of *Elen Luydauc* with St Helena. Another explanation is however given in *Brut Cleopatra*, which explains *Lluyddog* as having reference to St Helena's pilgrimage to Jerusalem: *y kymyrth elen verch coel y phe(r)erindavt y tu gwlat gaerussalem. ac y goresgynnavd hi y wlat honno. Ac or achos hynny y gelwyd hi o hynny allan yn elen luhydawc. Ac oy rinwedawl ethrylith ay dysc y cavas hi pren y groc yr hwn y diodefawd iessu grist arney.* (J. J. Parry, *Brut Cleopatra*, 95.)

The reputed holiness that Elen derived from her conflation with St Helena was probably responsible for her appearance in *Bonedd y Saint* as the mother of St Peblig: *Peblic Sant en e Caer en Aruon m. Maxen Wledic amheradvdyr Ruuein, ac Elen uerch Eudaf e uam* (EWGT 63 (63)). See further B. F. Roberts, B XXV, pp. 286–7. The *Bruts* reserve the title *Elen Luyddog* for the earlier *Elen*, daughter of Coel (BD 69.32), and never confuse her with the second *(H)elen* (BD 75.12), Maxen's wife.

Poetic references do not distinguish between the Welsh *Elen*[1], Helen of Troy (= *Elen*[2] below), and St Helena:

Mab y Clochddyn: *eil elen y lewenyd* (RBP 1351.31).

Casnodyn: *am gost gustennin vab elen* (RBP 1241.39–40 = GC no. 2.102n.)

Another early allusion is by Gr. ap Maredudd: *pryt elen luydavc* (RBP 1327.8).

Further allusions by the *cywyddwyr* are cited in G.

Elen[2] Uanna6c 50, 'Elen the Famous' (?) i.e. Helen of Troy. *Elen uanavc chwaer (Castor a Pholux) oed gyffelyb udunt hvy; tec oed hi ac ufyd y medvl ac eskeirvreic da oed. a man oed y rvg y dvy ael. ac am hynny y gelvit hi elen uanavc* (*Dares Phrygius*, RBB 12.11–15) '*Elen Fannog*, sister of Castor and Pollux, was like unto them; she was fair and humble in mind, and a woman of good limbs. There was a mark (*man*) between her two eyebrows, and for that she was called *Elen Fannog.*' The redactor of *Dares Phrygius* thus explains Elen's epithet by reference to the 'love-spot' between her two eyebrows *notam inter duo supercilia habens* (L. C. Stern, 'Davydd ap Gwilym, ein walisischer Minnesanger', ZCP VII (1900–10), p. 235). There is no evidence that this epithet was applied to Helen in any older Welsh source than the fourteenth-century *Dares Phrygius*, so that it may merely have arisen out of the story, according to the explanation there given. But the epithet adheres persistently to *Elen*[1] in a variety of later sources (see below), so that it is possible that it may have a source antecedent to *Dares Phrygius* (see n. to triad 47 on the knowledge of the names of classical heroes in Wales at a period earlier than this text). The radical could as well be *bann-* as *man*, and for *bannawc* GPC 255 gives the meanings *aruchel, nodedig* 'noble, distinctive', as well as *bannog, corniog* 'horned'. It is likely, therefore, that *bannog* was bestowed upon Helen because of its double meaning, and contained a veiled reference to her adultery. On *Elen Fannawg* see also Lloyd and Owen, *Drych yr Oesoedd Canol*, p. 35, and n.

In 'Arthuriana from the Genealogical Manuscripts' (*Nat. Lib. of Wales Journal* XIV, p. 243), P. C. Bartrum gives citations by the *cywyddwyr*, of whom the earliest apart from Dafydd ap Gwilym (see n. to triad 50) are Guto'r Glyn and Gutun Owain, from a late triad (not included here) to *Y Tair Elen.* The three named are generally *Elen Luyddog* (ferch *Eudaf Hen*), *Elen Fannog* and *Elen ferch Coel* (i.e. St Helena), or else the *Elen* who is named as the wife of the man addressed in the poem, who may alternatively be added as a fourth. As an exceptional instance, Bartum cites from three sixteenth-century and later manuscripts an otherwise unknown *Elen chwayr Arthur* to complete the triad, in place of the *Elen* last named. See GGl. no. LXXVIII.17–24; GLM no. XXIV.71–6; GTA I, no. LXXVII.16–26; and also WCD 234–5. *Elen chwaer Arthur* (Arthur's sister) is unknown elsewhere.

Guto'r Glyn (no. LXXVIII, 17–30) compares his patron's wife to the three Elens (see editor's n.)

Gutun Owain: *Kwynfan am Elen Fannawc* (GO no. LII.23).

Tudur Aled: *Ail un, o fonedd, i Elen Fannog* (GTA I, no. II.45).

Huw Cae Llwyd: *Gwnaed rhiain lân fam Elen Fanog* (HCLI no. VII.47).

A Treatise on Heraldry (*circa* 1510) refers to: *pann ddoeth gwyr Groec i ymladd a Chaer Droea i ddyal kribddeiliad Elen Vannog* (T. H. Parry-Williams (ed.), *Rhyddiaith Gymraeg* I, p. 12).

In a *Llythyr Annerch at Ferch* (D. Gwenallt Jones, *Yr Areithiau Pros,* p. 34) a girl's embroidery is compared favourably with that of *Elen Vanog ne Degau Eurvron.*

Elidir[1] Lledanwyn 8: *Llywarch Hen m. E. Lydanwyn*, App. II, no. 2. See n. to *Llywarch Hen. Llydanwyn* 'broad and fair', i.e. 'stout and handsome'. *De Situ Brecheniauc*: *Guaur filia Brachan, uxor Lidanwen, et mater Loarch hen* (EWGT 16 (15)) and *Cognacio Brychan* = *Gwawr uxor Lledan Wyn, mater Llywarch hen* (*Cog. Brych.*, § 15, EWGT 18 (15)).

Elidir[2] Mwyn6a6r 44, App. II, no. 12. 'E. the Wealthy.' See nn. to *Run*[3] m. Maelgwn, Eurgein. On *Mwynfawr* 'rich, opulent, courteous' (GPC 2521), see B II, pp. 129–30; cf. Mynydawc *Mwynvawr* (= *Mynydawc Eidynn*).

The passage in the *Chirk Codex of the Laws* which describes *Elidir*'s expedition to Arfon to claim his right to rule Gwynedd on Maelgwn's death (because his wife Eurgein was Maelgwn's daughter) is quoted in the n. to *Run m. Maelgwn* below. *Elidir* was slain, according to this account, at Aber Meuhedus in Arfon. This has been identified with the Afon Wefus, which runs into the Desach from Bron-yr-erw, near Clynnog in Caernarfonshire (HW I, 168n.; PKM 280). Alternatively, Aneurin Owen (AL I, 105 n.) identified the Mewydus with the Cadnant, a stream which flows into the Menai straits near the town of Caernarfon, and noted that 'the place where Elidyr fell has preserved the name of "Elidyr bank"'. The grave of *Elidir* is commemorated in the additional *Beddau* stanzas in Pen. 98 B: *Bedd Elidir mwynfawr ynghlan mawr meweddus / fawd brydus briodawr / Gwen efwr (?) gwr gwrdd y gawr* (cf. MA[2], p. 65, v. 12; T. Jones, PBA LIII, pp. 136 (15)). The mountain *Mynydd Elidir* above Bangor was also popularly supposed to owe its name to the memory of *Elidir*'s expedition; but this appears to be a folk etymology, by which *y lidir* 'the (steep) hill' was misunderstood as containing the proper name (see n. to triad 44a). Nevertheless, the number of instances of the name *Elidir* in the fourteenth-century *Record of Caernarvon* (ed. H. Ellis) attest the popularity of the name in Gwynedd: *Gauell Elider*, p. 10; *Wele Elidir*, pp. 54, 58; *Elidir Loyt*, p. 62. Ieuan Deulwyn (GID, p. 75, 1. 10) in his *Moliant i Rys Awbre* makes the comparison of *(g)lewder Rhys i Elidr hen.* A variant reading *o lidir* proves that the accent in this name fell on *lídir*, and this would have facilitated the confusion with *y lidir*. Cf. also GTP no. 49.19, where *Elidir* rhymes with *hir* in a *cywydd* couplet.

Elifer (Gosgorduawr) 8, 44, *Eliffer* 46, App. II, no. 5, *Oliffer* 70 (Pen. 47): *Gwrgi a Pheredur meibion Oliffer*. See n. to *Peredur*[2]. 'E. of the Great Warband.' On *gosgordd* see n. to triad 31.

LlDC no. 1.29 alludes to *Seith meib eliffer. seith guir ban brouher / Seith guaew ny ochel in eu seithran* 'Seven sons of Eliffer, seven men when put to the test, who in their seven divisions do not avoid seven spears'. The allusion is introduced into a description of the battle of Arfderydd (see n. to triad 84). Other sources name only *two sons* of *Eliffer*—Gwrgi and Peredur—but the later vague extension of their number to the conventional figure of seven need cause no surprise in this context; cf. *Ym. M. a Th* 15.

Eliffer is the form attested both in the LlDC allusion and in the single recorded instance in which this name occurs in *cynghanedd*, Casnodyn: *gosgord loewfford eliffer* (RBP 1247.6 = GC no. 1.60n.). As Ifor Williams points out (*Arch. Camb.,* 1934, p. 349), the rhyme in LlDC proves that the final syllable of this name is *-er* and not *-ifr*. TYP illustrates some of the many variant spellings of *Eliffer* which occur; in addition to these the Harl. Gens. give the form *Eleuther* (see n. to *Peredur*[2]), and *Englynion y Clyweit* give *goliffer*: *A glyweisti a gant Goliffer / Gosgorduawr, gwymp y niuer* (*Blodeugerdd* no. 31, *englyn* 41). The name became easily confused with *Elidir*, as in *De Situ Brecheniauc* (see n. to triad 70). Further references are by Cynddelw: *Post esbyd oesbarth elifer* (H 96.32 = CBT IV, no. 4.265n.); *uaran elifer* (H 147.6 = CBT III, no. 26.36n.); and Dafydd Benfras: *trossed eliffer* (RBP 1381.5–6 = CBT VI, no. 35.3n.).

Elinwy m. Cadegyr 7, *Elinwy* 46C. LL 270.20, etc.: *Elinui* LlDC no. 18.154: *yg guernin bre bet Eilinvy.*

Eliwlad m. Mad(og) m. Uthur App. IV, no. 1. See n. to *6thyr Bendragon.* The early dialogue poem *Ymddiddan Arthur a'r Eryr* (Ifor Williams, B II, pp. 269–86; also Haycock (ed.), *Blodeugerdd* no. 30), in which *Eliwlat [sic]* figures transformed into an eagle, proves that this character belonged to the pre-Geoffrey Arthurian tradition. But it is impossible to accept T. Gwynn Jones's suggestion (*Aberystwyth Studies* VIII, p. 37) that *Eliwlat* > *Elyflath* >*Lancelot* (see n. to *La6nslot y Lac*). Bleddyn Fardd: *tyyrnwr vilwr val eliwlat* (H 69.7 = CBT VII, no. 46.7n.). For some references to *Eliwlad, Liwlad,* in *cywydd* poetry, see G 470. Add to these GTP 21.7: *Ail Liwlod o Lywelyn.* On the poem see M. Haycock, *Blodeugerdd*, pp. 297–312; P. Sims-Williams, AW 57–8; and WCD 245.

Eluned Ddedwydd, App. III, no. 15. (*Luned*). E. 'the Fortunate'. The name of the heroine of *Owein*: *Iarlles y Ffynnawn* was long supposed to have been taken from the corresponding French name *Lunette*, borne by her French counterpart in Chrétien de Troyes' poem *Yvain* (see R. L. Thomson, *Owein*, pp. lxii–lxiv). But Ifor Williams in B X, pp. 41–8, followed by J. C. Lozac'hmeur in HLCB 139, have both proposed *Iunet* ('desired one') as the original older Brythonic form of this name. Cf. also R. M. Jones, LlC IV, p. 219. *Luned* (*-t*) is the form of this name preserved in the texts of the tale *Owein* ('The Lady of the Fountain') in WM and RM. The oldest references to *Luned* are the five by Dafydd ap Gwilym (GDG no. 43.5; no. 86.9n.; no. 133.16, 44, 50)—if, as seems likely, these precede the reference by Iorwerth ab y Cyriog: *eilwed lunet* (RBP 1287.1 = GGrG no. 4.22n.) Further references are by Gr. ap Maredudd: *ail Lunet em oleuni* (RBP col. 1321.21); *oleuni Dyfr neu Lunet* (1326.20).

Emerchret, wreic Fabon m. Dewengen 66 (= *Hemythryd verch Vabon m. Dyfynwyn*, Pen. 47).

Emrys Wledic 51. See n. to *Custennin Uendigeit*. On the title *Gwledic* see n. to *Maxen Wledic*. The identification of *Emrys Wledic* with the Romano-British leader *Ambrosius Aurelianus* first appears in HB, ch. 42. It is repeated in the *Bruts* in rendering the name of Geoffrey's *Ambrosius*, whom Geoffrey presents as the brother of Uthur Bendragon and of Constans (HRB VI, 5 = BD 86). Constans is the Custennin Vychan of triad 51. Gildas describes *Aurelius Ambrosius* as 'a man of outstanding character who, alone of the Roman race, chanced to survive in the shock of such a storm (i.e. in the years following the departure of the Romans); as his parents, people undoubtedly clad in the purple, had been killed in it—whose offspring in our days have greatly degenerated from their ancestral nobleness' (*Gildas*, ed. and trans. Hugh Williams, 60). But in HB's account (chs 40–2), the Roman leader has become the miraculous infant prodigy, born without a father, who divined to Vortigern the reason for the collapse of his tower on Snowdon:

> Et rex ad adolescentem dixit: 'quo nomine vocaris?' Ille respondit 'Ambrosius vocor', id est *Embreis Guletic* ipse videbatur. Et rex dixit 'de qua progenie ortus es?' At ille 'unus est pater meus de consulibus Romanicae gentis.' (HB, ch. 42)

Rhys Goch Eryri, writing in the early fifteenth century, cites a variant tradition from that in HB and HRB about the concealed dragons under *Dinas Emrys* in Eryri (cf. triad 37), according to which it was the head of *Emrys* (Ambrosius) which was buried there. The poet invites Llywelyn ab y Moel to come *tua'r graig / Lle mae pen brawd* (= *mab,* see n.) *Cystennin / Fendigaid, lafn drafn y drin, / Yng ngwyl dderw . . . / Yng nghoed Ffaraon yng nghudd / Ar oer garreg Yryri, / . . . lle magwyd fi* 'to the crag where is the head of the son (?) of Custennin Fendigaid, a blade in the course of battle, in the darkness of the oak . . . hidden in the forest of Ffaraon on a cold rock in Eryri . . . where I was reared' (IGE^2 no. LVII.2–8). But the poet may merely have confused a memory of the other stories of talismanic burials grouped in triad 37 with the tale of the dragons buried at *Dinas Emrys*. Cf. his allusion in another poem to Gwynedd as *lle bu'r dreigiau draw* (IGE^2 no. LXI.12).

Geoffrey of Monmouth substituted *Merlinus* for *Ambrosius* when he reproduced HB's account of Vortigern's collapsing tower and the dragons (HRB VI, 19), but he reserved the name of *Ambrosius* for the brother of Uthur Pendragon. The rendering of this name as *Emrys Wledic* in the *Bruts* proves that the redactor of the *Brut* was familiar with earlier Welsh traditions about Ambrosius, whether they were traditions about the Romano-British general, or merely of the precocious boy of the folk-tale, whose identity had by the ninth century become merged with that of the 'historical' Ambrosius. Geoffrey's substitution of *Merlinus* (*Myrddin*) for *Ambrosius* caused some bewilderment to the bards, who from quite an early date were led by it to make a distinction between *Myrddin ap Morfryn* (= *Merlinus Caledonius, Merlinus Silvester*) and *Myrddin Emrys* (= *Merlinus Ambrosius*). This distinction was reproduced by Giraldus Cambrensis. (See n. to *Myrddyn Wyllt.*)

Emyr Llydaw, App. IV, no. 5: *Howel (Hywel) m. E.* (see n.). 'Emperor of Brittany.' On *emyr* as a common noun 'ymherodr, brenin, arglwydd', see J. Lloyd-Jones, B XI, pp. 34–6; B. F. Roberts, B XXV, p. 284; and EWGT 187–8.

According to *Bonedd y Saint,* Gwenn Teir Bronn (mother of the Breton saint Winwaloeus) and *Alan Fyrgan* (see n.) as well as other saints were children of *Em(h)yr Llydav* (VSB 320–3, etc., and see EWGT index). The *Beddau* stanzas give yet another character this patronymic: *beidauc rut yv hun ab emer llydau* (LlDC no. 18.117). These instances suggest that *Emyr Llydaw* was originally a generic term denoting any unspecified Breton ruler, and later came to be interpreted as a proper name denoting a particular person. It is therefore not surprising to find that the name belongs distinctively to Welsh and not to Breton tradition: the *Bruts* substitute *Emyr Llydaw* for Geoffrey's *Boudoc* (*Budicius*). (This was perhaps a historical king of Breton *Cornouaille*, named Budic in LL 110.18; 130.1: *Budic filius Cybrdan natus de Cornugallia.*) Geoffrey represents him as the father of Duke Hoel, and the fosterer of Ambrosius and Uthyr after their flight to Brittany (HRB VI, 8; IX, 2 = BD 90, 146).

Endawt 57. See **Gendawt.**

Eneas Yscwydwyn 50. 'Aeneas White-Shield.' The epithet *yscwydwyn* is consistently applied to Aeneas in the *Bruts* on the occasion of his first mention in connection with the story of the Trojan origin of the Britons (BD 3.7; RBB 41.12; *Brut Cleopatra* 6, 8). The last of the *Jes. Gens.* (LI = EWGT pp. 49–50) gives the descent of Arthur from *Eneas Ycwydwyn*—a king-list based on the *Bruts*. It is difficult, however, to account for the origin of this epithet, which does not occur in *Dares Phrygius*. Loth suggested (*Mab.* II, 230) that *yscwyddwyn* was a corruption of *ysgwydd-ddwyn* 'shoulder-bearing' and referred to Aeneas' well-known feat of filial piety. This seems unlikely, since the epithet occurs elsewhere in reference to a different character: *ysgvydwyn hovel vab kadwal* (RBP col. 578.29–30). On Aeneas' epithet see Brynley Roberts, B XXV, p. 286. He shows that 'Eneas Ysgwydwyn appears only in post-Galfridian texts, and an existing epithet may have been borrowed under the influence of *Brutus viride scutum* ('green shield') (HRB II, 9), combined with the name of the island to which Aeneas' descendants came, Albion "the White Island".'

Gwalchmai to Owain Gwynedd: *Ardwyreaf hael o hil eneas* 'I extol a generous (hero) of the race of Aeneas' (H 14.19 = CBT I, no. 8.57). This is the oldest expression in the Welsh language of the traditional belief in the Trojan origin of the Britons, which was first publicized in Latin in the ninth-century HB, from which work it probably became known to the *Gogynfeirdd.* It was, however, unexpressed in poetry before Gwalchmai. (BT 21.20 alludes to *Eneas*, but does not claim him as an ancestor as does HB, chs 10, 11, 18.)

E(n)6ael Adrann 19: *Greid(y)awl Galouyd m. E. A.* (see n.). Pen. 127, 95: *Gwydion astrus ac Envael adran a Dos, brodorion, meibion Deigr ap Dyfnwal hen ap Ednyfed) ap maxen wledic.* Cf. EWGT 89 (19).

Enid verch i Niwl Iarll 88. See n. to *Gereint m. Erbin.* The name of the heroine of the tale of *Gereint fab Erbin*, and of *Enide* in the corresponding poem *Erec et Enide* by Chrétien de Troyes, does not appear to be recorded in any antecedent source, either in Welsh or in French. The origin of *Enid(e)*'s name was long regarded as an enigma (see ATC 100–1, where Loomis rightly rejected the early suggestion that *Enid* was derived from a noun meaning 'woodlark'). In B XVII (1958), pp.181–2, I pointed out that the name *Enid(e)* arose out of a wrong division of the territorial name *Bro Wened*, the Breton name for Vannes (< *Venetis*), in the same way as the name of the Breton hero of the tale, Erec, arose out of a wrong division of the territorial name *Bro Weroc(h)*, later *Bro Werec* (as was pointed out many years ago by F. Lot, *Romania* 1896, 588–91, followed by J. Loth, RC XIII, pp. 483–4; XLIII, p. 424). Neither of these writers noted the parallelism with the name *Enid, Ened* < *Bro (Gu)ened*, and my suggestion has subsequently been widely accepted. In each case the fem. noun *bro* is responsible for the lenition of the following consonant (cf. *Chr. Br.* 101; TC 47, ii) leaving the forms *Broerec* (attested in *Cart. de Quimperlé*, *Chr. Br.* 193) and **Broened.* Though not attested in writing (as was *Bro Weroc*) earlier than in a Breton map of 1513, Professor Falc'hun has assured me that *Bro Wened* represents the most usual and widespread, as well as the most correct pronunciation of this name, in spite of an increasing tendency in the pronunciation of modern spoken Vannetais to resist lenition of the stops, so that *Bro Guened* is both heard and written in local Vannetais dialect. The explanation of *Ened* < *Bro Wened* may be the more readily accepted in view of the numerous Irish stories which depict the goddess Eriu, representing the land of Ireland, as mating with various Irish kings, for example *Lugaid Laigde*, *Niall Naoigiallacht*, and a number of their successors throughout the bardic tradition (*Ériu* XIV, pp.17–18). I have suggested (B XVII, pp. 181–2) that evidence has survived in the story of *Erec-Gereint* indicating that this was ultimately based on a narrative of a similar kind, in which the hero—the historical founder of the Breton kingdom of *Bro*

Weroc(h) or *Vannes* in the mid-sixth century—was mated to a heroine who represented the tribal goddess of the land he conquered. This pan-Celtic tale of Breton origin became transferred to insular Dumnonia, and freshly localized there around the name of the local hero Gereint fab Erbin, but the name of the heroine survived the transference unchanged. See also my discussion in 'Celtic Dynastic Themes and the Breton Lays', EC IX, pp. 439–74; J. Marx, EC X, p. 482; J. C. Lozac'hmeur, HLCB 151; and cf. also R Middleton, AW 148, 156, n.5.

Dafydd ap Gwilym alludes five times to *Enid* as a proverbial ideal of beauty: *eiliw Enid lan* (GDG no. 52.50): *tyfiad Enid* (53.1); *Enid leddf* (81.17), *eil Enid* (120.14); *Enid unrhyw* (128.6). Indeed it seems most likely that Dafydd in the fourteenth century himself inaugurated in the tradition of the *cywyddwyr* the convention of making such comparisons with traditional heroines of romance, as representatives of the ideal of female beauty.

Gr. ap Maredudd: *eil enit* (RBP col. 1326.21).

Mab y Clochyddyn: *enit vnrvyf* (1350.23); *enit vawred* (1351.37).

Enygan 33: *Heidyn m. E.* (= *Heiden m. Euengat* WR). With WR's *Euengat* cf. *Guencat* LL 145.18 and *Guengat* CA 1. 1257. The capitals *E* and *G* in Insular script were easily confused.

Erbin 14: *Gereint m. E* (see n.).

Ercwlf Gadarn 47. 'E. the Strong' (Hercules). On the poem to *Ercwlf* = Hercules (BT 65.24–66) see M. Haycock, CMCS 13, pp. 30–1, and n., pp. 38–9.

Dares Phrygius: Erkvlf Gadarn (RBB 3.4); *Erkvlff* (4.8; 16.27).

Cynddelw: *Rybu erkwlff mavr rvysc dyrawr dur* (RBP col. 1171.18 = CBT IV, no. 17.73); *grym afyrdwl erkvl ergrynitor* (H 85.30 = CBT IV, no. 2.24n.).

Prydydd y Moch: *Ercwlf a Samsswn* (H 265.15 = CBT V, no. 4.9); *Mal gwrhyd Ercwlf* (H 288.14 = CBT V, no. 26.108).

Casnodyn: *Ercwlff gryf* (RBP 1247.7 = GC no. 1.61n.).

For further instances of the employment of the name of *Erkwlff* as a model of strength and splendour, see n. to triad 47. A sixteenth-century version of the *Ystorya Erkvlff* is included in the chronicle of Elis Gruffydd, B X, p. 284–97.

Eryn 35: *Cadyal m. Eryn* (see n. to triad).

Essyllt 26: *E. verch (Kuluanawyt) Post Prydein* 71 (Pen. 267); *Essyllt (F)yngwen* 80 'Essyllt Fair-Hair.' See nn. to *Drystan m. Tallwch, March m. Meirchya6n, Kuluanawyt Prydein.*

CO l. 372 (see n.): *Essyllt Vynwen ac Essyllt Uyngul* (= *e. vinwen ac e. vin gul* RM 113.7–8). These epithets are to be interpreted as 'fair neck' and 'slender neck' (GPC 2510); *min* 'lip' (as in RM) is less likely as the first element in either compound. Cf. *mwnwgl, mynwgl* 'neck' (GPC 2510). In triad 80 the redactor of Pen. 47 misinterpreted *myn* 'neck' as *mwng* 'hair'. This last is found in a number of personal epithets which occur in the genealogies: *Mynglwyd, Myngrudd, Myngwrach* (for these see n. to *Myngan o Ueigen*) and *Myngvras* (see n. to *Meic Mygvras*). Several scholars have seen in *mynwen* the origin of the epithet applied to Tristan's wife in the French romances *Isolt aux blanches mains* (J. Loth, *Mab.* 285, RC XLIII, p. 495; F. Lot, *Romania* XXV, pp. 29–30; W. J. Gruffydd, B VIII, p. 305). This interpretation implies, however, that the original term underlying the form in CO was *meinwen* 'slender fair' (a frequent poetic epithet), and that this was half-translated, half-misinterpreted by a French redactor of the story of *Tristan,* as consisting of the French word *main* 'hand' with *(g)wen*, which he correctly translated as 'fair'. For the humorous duplication of the character of *Essyllt* in the CO allusion, cf. triad 56, which names the three Gwenhwyfars—each Arthur's queen—and note. Some have seen in this duplication the origin of the two *Isolts* of the French romances, although it seems most probable that the 'second Isolt' is an entirely French development.

The name *Essyllt* is established as indigenous and of Welsh origin by its occurrence in the earlier form *Etthil* in Harl. Gen. I: *Etthil merch Cinan* (*Tindaethwy*) as the name of the mother (or grandmother) of Rhodri Mawr (EWGT 9 (i)) = *Esyllt*[2] (triad 97). The same genealogy appears in the *Jes. Gens.* 20 (EWGT 47 (221) and HGVK 1.14), which give for this name the forms *Ethellt* and *Etill* (and see n. EWGT p. 151 on the disputed Gwynedd genealogy). That *Etthil, Ethellt* represents the earlier spelling of *Es(s)yllt* is clear from later references in poetry to this daughter of Cynan Tindaethwy as *Es(s)yllt* (see G 491 for refs., and see n. to triad 97). For this second *Es(s)yllt*, or *Etthilt*, the Gwynedd heiress, see HW 323–4 and n., and CO(2) n. to 1. 372. It is in her memory that Gwynedd is called by the poets *bro Es(s)yllt, tir Es(s)yllt*. *Esyllt*'s name is also attested independently as existing early in Cornwall by an Anglo-Saxon charter of the year 967, which lists the place-name *hryt Eselt* 'E's ford' (J. Loth, *Contributions a l'étude des Romans de la Table Ronde* (Paris, 1912), p. 29, quoting W. de Gray Birch, *Cart. Sax.* III, 473). See on this O. J. Padel, CMCS 1, pp. 66–7 and idem, AW 210–11. The earlier spellings of this name *Etthil, Etil, Ethellt* are explained by K. H. Jackson (LHEB 708–9) as due to a rare (and perhaps dialectal) survival of the dental affricate, which came to be incorporated in the O.W. genealogies, where it was variously written as *z, t*, and *tth*, but which was already normally pronounced as *-ss* by the sixth century. Jackson explains *Esyllt* as deriving from Brit. **Adsiltia* 'she who is gazed upon' (LHEB 709; EWGT 151); cf. W. *syllu* ('to gaze'). The rendering *Isolt, Iseult*, which is given for this name in the French romances, seems to represent a Germanic form—*Ishild* or *Ethylda* have been suggested. Since *Es(s)yllt* would have been accented on the first syllable by the eleventh century, it is unlikely at any stage to have been spelt with an initial *I*-or *Y*- in Welsh: *Isolt* is therefore a loose approximation of a kind not uncommon in Arthurian nomenclature, when a name comes under the influence of a similar-sounding foreign name. The *Bruts* render HRB's *Estrildis* (the name of the mistress of *Locrinus*, HRB II, 2) by *Essyllt* (BD 22.10: RBB 60.30).

The earliest citations in poetry of the heroine *Essyllt* as a figure of ideal beauty for purposes of comparison appear to be those made by Dafydd ap Gwilym. Thomas Parry lists five instances: *ail Esyllt* (GDG no. 16.14; no. 33.14; no. 120.17); *Esyllt bryd* (no. 111.29); *nith Esyllt* (no. 86.2). Other fourteenth-century references include Gr. ap Maredudd: *serchaul vryt trystan ar essyllt* (RBP 1327.7); Madog Dwygraig: *ae dewissyat dof essyllt* (1407.29). (For the use by the *cywyddwyr* of the phrase *cae Esyllt* = 'treasure' see GLGC no. 237.38 n.) In B XXV (1972), pp. 21–2, D. J. Bowen suggests that GDG no. 24.31–4 contains a reference by the poet to *Esyllt*'s *englyn* at the close of *Ystorya Trystan*.

Etwin, see n. to *Edwin urenhin Lloegyr*.

Eurbrawst 96. See n. to the triad, and to *Brychan Brecheinyauc*.

Eurgein (gwreic Elidir Mwyn6a6r) 44. See nn. to *Elidir*[2] *Mwyn6a6r*, and to *Maelgwn Gwyned. Eurgein* < *eur* + *cein* 'golden' or 'excellent', 'fair'. (For the meaning of *eur* in this and similar compounds, cf. n. on *eurgryd*, triad 67.) EWGT 63 (57) (*Bonedd y Saint*): *Eurgein uerch Vaelgwn Gwyned*, etc. Elis Gruffydd's *Chronicle* states that *Eurgain* was Maelgwn's daughter by his wife, a daughter of *Sawyl Ben Uchel* (B XVIII, p. 57; cf. also EC XII, p. 173 (22)). *St Eurgain* is commemorated at *Llaneurgain*, Flintshire. According to LBS II, 474, there was a tumulus near Rhuddlan in which she is supposed to have been buried. Lewis Morris (CR 175) records a tradition that *Eurgain* married Ethelfrith of Northumbria (= *Edelflet Ffleissawc, brenhin Lloegyr* in TYP 10 (WR)), and quotes the following saying: *Eurgain verch Maelgwn Gwynedd a roes y ganwyll wrth yr adar gwylltion i ddangos y ffordd i'w chariad* 'Eurgain, daughter of Maelgwn Gwynedd, who set the candle to the wild birds, in order to show the way to her lover'. HCLl no. XXIV.21–2: *Eurgain a gaed yn Argoed / O'r un cyff gorau'n y coed.*

Euroswyd 52. *Oswydd* = 'enemy, enemies' GPC 2660, CA 103. With *eur* in this name and in *Eurgain*, cf. n. to *eurgryd*, triad 67. *Euroswyd* = 'Splendid Enemy' (?). The meaning 'enemy' was believed to be derived from the name of the seventh-century Northumbrian king *Os(s)wy*, which is rendered as *Os(s)wyd* in *Brut Cleopatra* (ed. J. J. Parry, 211). This suggestion is however hardly consistent with the occurrence of the word *Oswyd* in the *Gododdin* (ll. 114, 414).

Our only other information about *Euroswyd* is derived from *Mabinogi Branwen*, which presents *Euroswyd* as one of the two 'husbands' of Penardun (the other being *Llŷr Lledyeith*, see n.) and father of Nyssyen and Efnyssyen

(PKM 29.10: *Eurosswyd*). A. Nutt, following a note by Lady Guest, identified *Euroswyd* with the Roman general *Ostorius Scapula* who opposed Caratācus, but his grounds for the identification are not clear (*Folklore Record* V, 8–9). A line by Gruffudd ap Maredudd contains a possible allusion to this character: *Kynnyd eur rosswyd kein y ryssed* 'the progress of E., splendid his career' (RBP col. 1315.32); though Lloyd-Jones suggests that the compound here could be *eur* + *rosswyd* (= *ros* + *Gwŷdd*) rather than the personal name (G 500). Cf. GGM no. 4.35n.

Ewein m. Maxen Wledic, see **Owein[1] m. Maxen.**

Ewein m. 6ryen, see **Owein[2] m. 6ryen.**

Ffaraon Dandde 95. 'Fiery Pharaoh' (?). See B. F. Roberts, *Cyfranc Lludd a Llefelys*, pp. xxxvi–vii; EWGT 150 (30); and n. to triad 13. See also n. to *Llyr*[1] *Lledyeith* above, and the reference by Rhys Goch Eryri quoted in the n. to *Emrys Wledic* above.

Flamdwyn 80: *Bun gwreic Flamdwyn.* 'Flamebearer.' This name appears twice in the group of early historical poems in BT: *atorelwis Flamdvyn vawr trebystawt* (PT no. VI.7, etc.) 'F. with mighty bluster shouted'; *Pan lladawd Owein Flamdwyn* (PT no. X.11) 'When Owein (ab Urien) slew Flamddwyn'. Evidently *Flamddwyn* was a nickname for an English leader or king, of the kind of which there are several other examples in HB (see n. to *Edelflet Ffleissawc*). For the suggestions that have been made as to *Flamddwyn's* identity, see Morris-Jones, *Cy.* XXVIII, p. 154. Writers of the early nineteenth century, following Lewis Morris (CR 180), identified *Fflamddwyn* with Ida, king of Bernicia 547–59, but there seems little justification for this. Skene's suggestion that *Flamddwyn* was Ida's son Theodric (FAB I, 232) has more to recommend it, since HB ch. 63 expressly states that Urien and his sons fought against Theodric. But neither suggestion can be regarded as more than a speculation. The following allusions by the *Gogynfeirdd* may refer to the English ruler so designated rather than as examples of the adjective 'fiery':

> Cynddelw: *fwyrffyscyat fal fleimyat Flamdwyn* (RBP col. 1439.3 = CBT IV, no. 9.108n.)
>
> Llygad Gwr: *hirbel ual flamddwyn y flamgyrcheu* (H 219.20 = CBT VII, no. 24.148n.).

Fleudur Flam (m. Godo) 9. CO ll. 182–3: *a fflewdwr Flam Wledic* (see n. to in CO(2); and on the significance of the title *gwledic* see n. to *Maxen Wledic*) below. *Fflam* 'flame' as a personal name is found elsewhere in the CO court-list, l. 218: *a Fflam m. Nwyfre*. *Ffleudur* also occurs later (l. 296n.), though with a different patronymic: *Atleudor mab Naf* (R: *a fflendor*). *Fleudur* may be an abbreviation for *Flewdwrn* (*dwrn* 'fist'—cf. *Cadegyr* for *Cadegyrn*, triad 7). Alternatively, cf. *Flamdur* 'with flaming sword' CA l. 934 (see n.).

Flur 67; *Fflur ferch Vugnach Gorr* 71 (= *Mugnach Gorr*, see THSC 1970, p. 147 MA 3rd Series of TYP, no. 124). The story of *Fflur* 'Flora' (cf. the name *Ystrad Fflur*, *Strata Florida*) appears to have belonged to the traditions concerning *Caswallawn fab Beli* (see n.) and his opposition to the Romans. As Ifor Williams pointed out ('Hen Chwedlau', THSC 1946, pp. 41–3) some version of the story which is referred to in triad 67 appears to have been known to Cynddelw; cf. RBP col. 1171.15–16 (= CBT IV, no. 17.69 and n.): *Rybu Ull kessar, keissyassei Fflur / y gan ut Prydein, prid y hesgur* 'There has been Julius Caesar, he had sought out Fflur, costly her care' (i.e. 'his care for her' or 'his concern for her').

The poet's subject is the transitory nature of all earthly things, and he refers in turn to the passing away of former heroes—Arthur, Brân, Hercules, Alexander, Julius Caesar. Whoever *Fflur* may have been, it would appear that she was known to tradition as an object of contention between Julius Caesar and the British prince (Caswallawn) who opposed him in his invasion of Britain. The story may even have made the quest for *Fflur* a motive in Caesar's invasion, since popular tradition frequently attributes personal motives to political events. The episode referred to in triad 67 may belong to a later (unpreserved) episode in the same story, which told how Caswallawn went to Rome in an attempt to win her back—a nobleman disguised as a beggar, like the other characters in triad 67.

Cynddelw's allusion is exceptional, since allusions to traditional heroines are notable by their absence from the poems of the *Gogynfeirdd*; see D. M. Lloyd, *Rhai Agweddau ar Ddysg y Gogynfeirdd*, p. 10; also Owen and Roberts (eds), *Beirdd a Thywysogion*, p. 212. It is the more interesting that Dafydd ap Gwilym should make three allusions to *Fflur*: *Hoen Fflur yw'r dyn a'm curia* (GDG no. 44.17n.); *Cyfliw Fflur ag eglurwawn* (GDG no. 86.5); *bryd Fflur* (GDG no. 111.8).

Madog Benfras: *Fflur dy lis, Fflur wyt o liw* (DGG no. LXIX.8).

Gruffudd ap Maredudd: *eil fflur* (RBP 1326.23).

Gauran m. Aedan 29; App. II, no. 11. The names of *Aedan* and his father *Gauran* are those of sixth-century rulers of Scottish Dál Riada. In the triad and in BGG (App. II) these names have been cited in reverse order. See n. to *Aedan m. Gauran* above.

For other instances of *Gabran* as a Welsh personal name see LL 158.18; 180.15; 204.21. *Gafran* is also the name of a Pembrokeshire river, but this may represent a diminutive of *gafr* 'goat' rather than the personal name (EANC 68).

Prydydd y Moch alludes to *O Pennwaet Dyfneint . . . hyd Pentir Gafran yd gyfyrduc* (H 260.6 = CBT V, no. 1.112n.), a comparison evidently used to contrast the two extremities of Britain. It has been suggested that *Pentir Gafran* stands for a promontory somewhere in Caithness; perhaps it represents the same place as *Penryn Blathaon* in App. I, no. 3 above (cf. B. F.

Roberts, LlC XIII, pp. 280–1). A similar juxtaposition between the northern and the southern extremities of Britain appears to be obscurely indicated in an earlier poem addressed to *Gwallawg* (PT no. XI.42–4; see n. to *Gwalla6c m. Lleenna6c*).

Galaad m. La6nslot y Lac 86; *Galath* App. IV, no. 2 = *Galahad* son of *Lancelot*. *Galaath uab Lawnslot o verch brenhin Peles* (Thomas Jones (ed.), *Ystoryeau Seint Greal*, l. 201 and n.; see AW 201–3), and n. to *La6nslot y Lac* below.

Galahad is a late introduction into the Arthurian cycle: a creation of the author of the thirteenth-century *Queste del Saint Greal* (corresponding to the first part of the Welsh translation *Y Seint Greal*), for whose religious purposes none of the older heroes of Arthurian romance would suit as hero. Pauphilet has shown in his *Études sur la Queste del Saint Greal* (Paris, 1922, pp. 135–7) that the name is derived from *Galaad* (= *Gilead*), interpreted as 'a heap of testimony' in the Vulgate Bible (Gen. xxxi.48). This made 'Mount Gilead' a symbol of Christ to medieval writers, and the instructed medieval reader would have recognized in *Gala(h)ad* (who was the perfect knight, as conceived by the Cistercian author of the *Queste*) a type of Christ. It is therefore useless to look for a Celtic prototype for this name, as was done by some early scholars. Sir John Rhŷs suggested that the name was derived from *Gwalhauet mab Gwyar* (CO l. 345), see Rhŷs's *Studies in the Arthurian Legend*, pp. 168–9, and this identification was followed in G 610, which gives references to *Galaad*, *Galath*, under *Gwalhaued*.

Some uncertainty prevailed among the bards as to the accentuation of this name: the forms *Galáth* and *Gláhath* occur with other variants. This uncertainty is reflected in the many variants of this name which appear in the manuscripts of App. IV. The trisyllabic form *Galaath* appears most frequently in the text of *Y Seint Greal*.

Llygad Gŵr: *gwalch gwrawl gwrhyd Gwalhafed* (CBT VII, no. 27.5n.).
Iolo Goch: *ail Galaath* (GIG no. XX.111 n.).
Rhys Goch Eryri: *ail Galath dda* (IGE² no. CIII.26).
Guto'r Glyn: *Pedwar-Gláth y pedeirgwlad* (GGGl no. XVII.48).
Lewys Glyn Cothi: *Galâth* (GLGC no. 169.53, 191.8).
Tudur Aled: *Brawd Galâth bro Degla wyd* (GTA I, no. LII.58).

Gall m. Disgyfdawt 10, 32. *Gall* 'foreigner'. See n. to *Disgyfdawt*.

Gar6en verch Henin Hen 57. See n. to *Henin Hen* below. *Garwen* 'Fair Leg'. This name appears in corrupt form in the additional *Beddau* stanzas from Pen. 98B written in a late hand at the end of the LlDC collection (p. 69 = LlDC nos. 43–4), and Thomas Jones (ed.), PBA LIII: *Y Beddau yn y morua ys bychan ay haelewy / y mae Sanant syberw vun / y mae Run ryuel afwy / y mae Garrwen verch Hennin / y mae Lledin a Llywy* 'The graves on the sea-strand, few are they who mourn them(?); there lies *Sanant* the proud maiden, there lies

Rhun, fervent in battle; there lies *Garwen* daughter of Henin, there lie *Lledin* and *Llywy*.' Thomas Jones suggested to me as a possibility that the *morfa* here referred to may represent Morfa Rhianedd near Llandudno, where there is a Rhiw Lledin. A further suggestion is that another allusion to *Garwen* has survived in the form *Wyrwein* which is found in a thirteenth-century English lyric, in the line *Trewe as Tegau in tour, as Wyrwein in wede* (Carlton Brown, *Thirteenth Century English Lyrics*, p. 183, l. 3). See also R. M. Wilson, *Lost Middle English Literature* (London, Methuen, 1952), p. 143, and n. to *Tegeu Eururon* below.

Garwy Hir 46C, 57: *Indec verch Ar6y Hir*. (For the lenition following *verch* see TC §43, and n. to triad 56.) With the name *Garwy* cf. LL 279.24.

LlDC no. 22 (*Mawl Hywel ap Goronwy*): *cyngor Arwy* (CBT I, no. 1.3n.).

LlDC no. 15.19 (*Y Bedwenni*): *bid y env garvy.*

Hywel ab Owain Gwynedd: *Neud athwyf o nwyf yn eil Garwy Hir* (H 319.26–7 = CBT II, no. 9.14n.).

Prydydd y Moch: *gwryd Garwy* (H 292.21–2 = CBT V, no. 22.29n.).

Dafydd y Coed: *Rhull Garwy* (GDC no. 1.6n.).

Justus Llwyd: *Hi a vu . . . am Arwy* (RBP col. 1367.14 = YB XVII, 71.34).

GDG no. 48.15: *annwyd Garwy* 'of the nature of G.' (see n. to the poem for some further references).

Gr. ap Maredudd: *Meu dogyn gur Arthur o orthir Prydein . . . Eiry hoen, am verch Arwy Hir* (RBP col. 1326.16–18). (This association of Garwy Hir's daughter (*Indec*) with Arthur suggests that the poet is citing triad no. 57.)

Further references are found in GSRh, no. 3.16n., 42; no. 6.41n. See also Pen. 67, lxix 59 (Hywel Dafi); GTA I, no. LXI.67; no. LXXVI.19–20; GTA II, no. XC.57; GO no. XIV.2; and WCD 272.

Gelbeineuin 44. Perhaps from *gylfin wyn* 'white beak', though Pen. 47's reading *gil benevin* suggests that *Gil* 'lad, servant' (Ir. *gilla*) may be present (as in the personal name *Gildas*). Cf. also the name *Gilfaethwy*, PKM 67.12, 16.

Gendawt 57: *Gŵyl verch Endawt*. *Gendawt* = 'Big chin'. For *tawd* cf. CA 259, n. on *tot*. *Tawd* (earlier *tot*) = 'whole, complete'. In *Vocabularum Cornicum (2)*, *mor tot* glosses *Oceanum*. *Blwyddyndawd* 'a complete(?) year' (Ifor Williams, B XII, p. 92). Cf. also CO l. 342: *Kynuelyn Keudawt* (for *Kendavt*? see n. to CO l. 342).

Gereint m. Erbin (< *Gerontius*) 14. See nn. to *Arthur*, *Cadwy m. Gereint*, *Custennin Uendigeit*, *Enid verch i Niwl Iarll*. *Gereint* is the hero of the tale *Gereint m. Erbin* in WM and RM (see AW, ch. 6). The story is a rendering of the popular medieval theme of the triumph of female constancy over all impediments (as in the tale of 'Faithful Grizelda'), blended with themes which are undoubtedly of Celtic origin, including a survival of the Celtic myth of the 'Sovereignty' (see my article, 'Celtic Dynastic Themes and the Breton Lays', EC IX, pp. 439–74), a theme which is also attested in early Irish. The story corresponds in outline to the French poem *Erec et Enide* by Chrétien de Troyes, and the name of the heroine *Enid* / *Enide* (see n. to *Enid verch i Niwl Iarll* above) corresponds in the two versions, while the name of *Gereint* (known more than once from the records of Dumnonia, see index to EWGT) appears to have supplanted that of the Breton hero *Weroc* (*Erec*) (Breton *Guerec*, ruler of Vannes, d. 590) in Chrétien's version of the tale (see AW 156, n.5). A number of allusions to *Gereint m. Erbin* in a variety of early sources give evidence for the prominence of this hero of the south-west in early tradition. The poem entitled *Gereint fil(ius) Erbin* (LlDC no. 21; RBP cols. 1042–3) is a eulogy of the hero, followed by references to his death in battle at Llongborth (probably Langport on the River Parret, a tidal river in Somerset—hence perhaps *Gereint*'s inclusion in triad 14 as a 'fleet-owner'). The language of the poem gives evidence for a date of composition prior to the year 1100—perhaps as much as two centuries earlier (see Thomas Jones, B XVII, pp. 246–7; and trans., NMS 8, pp. 15–16). *Gereint*'s followers are described as *guir deur o odir diwneint* 'brave men from the land of Devon' (LlDC no. 21.26), and *Arthur* is alluded to as having been present at the battle (no. 21.22). This would indicate that the Devon hero had been brought into the complex of indigenous traditions centering around the figure of Arthur at an early date in Wales. The poem appears to represent a fragment from a prose-verse tale similar in general type to the *Llywarch Hen englynion.* The poem has been edited by B. F. Roberts, *Ast. H.* 286–96; text and trans. by Jenny Rowland, EWSP 457–61, 504–6. See further P. Sims-Williams, AW 46–9; R. Middleton AW 147–57, n.5. The names of both *Constantine* and *Gerontius* (> *Gereint*) recur in the toponomy of Cornwall, and among the names of Cornwall's early rulers. (See n. to *Custennin Uendigeit.*)

The following references are also found to *Gereint ab Erbin*:

> CO l. 219: *gereint mab erbin. A dyuel mab erbin.* (On *Dyuel mab Erbin* see n. to CO l. 219.)
>
> *Englynion y Clyweit* no. 21: *A glyweist-di a gant gereint / mab erbin, kywir kywreint?* (*Blodeugerdd* no. 21, *englyn* 21).
>
> *Bonedd y Saint*: *Kebi m. Selyf m. Gereint m. Erbin m. Gustennin Gorneu; Yestin m. Gereint m. Erbin m. Gustennin Gorneu* (EWGT 58 (26, 27)); see n. to *Custennin Uendigeit* above, and n. to CO l. 435. The *Bonedd* give *Custennin Gorneu* 'C. of Cornwall' as Gereint's grandfather; cf. also *Jes. Gen.* 20 (EWGT 45 (10, 11): *Gereint m. Erbin (m. Custennin) m. Kynvawr m. Tudwawl m. Gwrwawr m. Gadeon m. Cynan m. Eudaf Hen.*

The allusion in the *Gododdin* to *Gereint rac deheu gawr a dodet* 'Geraint before the (men of the) south, a shout was raised' (CA l. 1042) has raised a problem of interpretation. The name *Gereint* suggested to Ifor Williams (CA 314) that this warrior came from Devon, though he did not go so far as positively to identify the Catraeth warrior with *Gereint m. Erbin*. Even hypothetically to suggest such an identification involves a problem which is geographical as much as it is chronological, since uncertainty as to the relative dating between events and men's careers in the latter half of the sixth century makes it impossible to know whether or not *Gereint*'s lifetime coincided with the battle of Catraeth. A. O. H. Jarman emphasized (*Aneirin: Y Gododdin*, p. 138) that the distance which exists between Devon and Catterick virtually precludes the possibility of a Devon hero having been present at the battle. With some probability, K. H. Jackson suggested that the *Geraint* of the poem came from somewhere in northern Britain to the south of the *Gododdin* territory, 'quite possibly Rheged' (OSPG 150), since we know that some members of Mynyddawg's army came from other districts, even some from as far away as Gwynedd. Allowing the normal three generations to a century, *Gereint*'s great-grandfather Kynfawr (not to be identified historically with the Cunomorus of Breton records nor with the Cunomorus of the Castle Dore stone (D. P. Kirby, B XXVII, pp. 88–9, and n. to *Drystan m. Tallwch* above)) would have been born *circa* 470–80, and the latter's great-grandfather Cynan *circa* 370–80—a date which would fit well with the alleged period of the earliest Breton settlements in the late fourth century. *Gereint*'s genealogy is presented in a slightly different form from the above in the Life of *St Cybi* (EWGT 27; VSB 234–50). Kirby asserts in B XXVII, pp. 81–114, that *Geraint fab Erbin* may have been active in resisting the Saxon advance in the south-west and that he may have lived *circa* 580–600. The earliest appearance of the name *Gereint* is in a tenth-century list of Cornish Saints; see O. J. Padel and B. Olsen, CMCS 12, p. 34.

There is no reason to believe that there is any foundation for an original relationship between Arthur and *Gereint*, such as is postulated in *Chwedl Gereint vab Erbin*. Geoffrey of Monmouth's association of Arthur with the Dumnonian dynasty was evidently quite arbitrary, and it has been shown that the earliest allusions associate Arthur with north Britain, rather than, like *Gereint*, with the south-west. In the tale of *Gereint fab Erbin*, Arthur and *Gereint* are described as cousins (WM 410.24; cf. text of Pen. 6) and *Erbin* is portrayed as Arthur's uncle (WM 409.35). But this relationship can be explained as due to the influence of HRB, which is continually apparent in the Three Romances, in a number of slight but unmistakable ways. (It is to be noted that the pedigree in Mostyn 117 (EWGT 39 (5)), which attaches Arthur to the Dumnonian ruling line, is written in the same hand as the earliest fragment of the tale of *Gereint fab Erbin* in Pen. 6; *Rep*. I, pp. 62, 316.) No suggestion of any actual kinship between Arthur and *Gereint* is to be found in the LlDC poem on *Gereint fab Erbin* (see above), although the poem is evidence that *Gereint* is to be included in the number of independent British heroes originally unconnected with the Arthurian cycle, who nevertheless became associated with Arthur in the early Middle Ages.

There is a good deal of evidence which associates *Gereint m. Erbin* with the south-west, with the territory of Dumnonia, i.e. Devon and Cornwall. His name may be preserved in that of the parish of *Ger(r)ans* on the south coast of Cornwall (see Doble, *Saint Gerent*, Cornish Saints' Series, pp. 3, 13). There is a *Killa Gerran* in the nearby parish of Roseland, and Lhuyd (*Arch. Brit.* 240) refers to a *Trev Erbin* in Cornwall, but does not say where it was. It is apparent that the name *Gerent* was borne by a number of members of the Dumnonian dynasty in later times: perhaps descendants and successors of *Gereint m. Erbin*, who bore it in memory of their ancestors. The Anglo-Saxon Chronicle alludes to a *Gerent Weala cyning*, who fought against *Ina*, king of Wessex, in the year 710 (Earle and Plummer, *Two Saxon Chronicles Parallel* I, pp. 42–3). This *Gereint* is quite probably the same as the *Geruntius* (LHEB 601n.) to whom Aldhelm wrote in 705, urging him to abolish the distinctive customs of the Celtic church. The Cornish form *Gerent* appears in yet another instance, in a list of British names (of Cornish or Breton provenance) dating from the ninth or early tenth century, preserved in *Vatican MS. Reg. Lat.* 191 (see EC III, p. 149; G. Godu and Pierre le Roux, 'Une liste des noms brittoniques', *Annales de Bretagne* 45, p. 202; CMCS 12, p. 34). A certain *Gerennius rex Cornubiensis regionis* is alluded to in the Life of *St Teilo* (LL 108.22–4, 113–14; D. S. Evans (ed.), *Lives of the Welsh Saints* by G. H. Doble, p. 185). This ruler is described as living at or near an unidentified place called *portus Din Gerein* (perhaps the Cornish *Gerrans*?), from which place news of the king's health was brought by sea to St Teilo in Brittany, and to this place a stone coffin was miraculously dispatched over the sea to him at the bidding of the saint. The story gives some evidence for the closeness of the sea-communications maintained between Cornwall and Brittany, and it is tempting to connect the miracle here narrated with the command of sea-power which is implied as belonging to *Gereint* by the term *lly(n)ghessawc* in triad 14. The name of *Gereint* is attested also in south Wales: *Din Gereint* was the name given until the end of the twelfth century to the site near the mouth of the Teifi on which the first castle of Cardigan was built (*Brut Tywys.* (Pen. 20, p. 53b, 27); HW 401, 426). Arthur is represented as holding court at Cardigan at the beginning of the poem *Erec et Enide*, and Destregales is given in the French romance as the name of *Erec*'s paternal kingdom, suggesting a genuine localization of Chrétien's poem in the south-west in post-Conquest times. See Mary Williams, EC II, pp. 220 ff.; R. M. Jones, LlC IV, p. 220; S. M. Pearce, 'The Traditions of the Royal King List of Dumnonia', THSC 1971, pp. 128–39; eadem, 'The Cornish Elements in the Arthurian Tradition', *Folklore* 85 (1974), pp. 145–63.

For the *Gereint rac deheu* alluded to in the *Gododdin* poem (CA l. 1042), see A. O. H. Jarman's *Aneirin: Y Gododdin*, p. 138n., and cf. OSPG 150. The earliest allusion to *Gereint* (see EWSP 461–2) by one of the *Gogynfeirdd* is by Prydydd y Moch in an *awdl* to Rhodri fab Owain (probably before 1190): *teyrnas yth law lid gereint nyd chwith* (H 279.9 = CBT V, no. 7.9n.) 'not unfortunate a kingdom in thy hand, (being) one with the passion of Gereint'. The combination of *Gereint*'s name with *llid* 'passion, indignation' suggests a possible allusion to the tale of *Gereint fab Erbin*, though this must remain hypothetical. Further allusions are by the following:

Bleddyn Fardd: *aruot gereint* (H 74.28 = CBT VII, no. 51.31 n.).

Justus Llwyd: *hi a vu am (er)eint ac am arwy* (RBP col. 1365.14; YB XVII, 71.34).

Dafydd y Coed: *ac aros mal gereint yng gvned* (RBP col. 1305.31 = GDC no. 1.40n.)

Ieuan Llwyd fab y Gargam: *Iawn vryt gereint gvravl ryssed* (RBP col.1415.34)

Ll. Goch ap Meurig Hen: *Hard barut hoewuard bert euell gereint* (RBP col. 1302.44 = GLlG no. 3.61n.).

Gruffudd ap Maredudd: *kymravt gereint* (RBP col. 1316.26–7 = GGM no. 4.77); *travs ereint* (RBP col. 1318.40); *llit gveir geir gereint* (RBP col. 1307.2–3 = GGM no. 3.40), *Hiraint hwyl Geraint, hael gar* (RBP col. 1325.36–7 = GGM no. 5.132).

Guto'r Glyn: *Un faint â Gereint neu gawr* (GGl 198.46).

Gereinya6n Hen 74: *Gerenhyr m. G.* 'G. the Old.' See below.

Gerenhyr m. Gereinya6n Hen. See **Cerenhyr m. Gereinya6n Hen**.

Gilbert m. Catgyffro 24 (= *G. katgyffro* WR), 39 (=*G. ap k.* WR), 42 (LlDC no. 6.11): *gilberd m. k.* 'G. son of Battle Tumult'.

Br. Rh.: *Gilbert mab katgyffro* (RM 160.3); *Englynion y Clyweit*: *A glyweist-di a gant Katgyffro Hen* (*Blodeugerdd* no. 31, *englyn* 9).

Catgyffro ('Battle Tumult / incitement / inciter') resembles an epithet rather than a personal name (cf. *Cynvawr Catgaduc* in triad 6, and CBT I no. 3.23n. where *Catgyffro* is applied to Gr. ap Cynan), but the evidence of Br. Rh. and the various texts of TYP which present it as a patronymic are supported by *Englynion y Clyweit*, which names *Catgyffro* as a separate character. The WR version of triad 24, which makes *katgyffro* an epithet, is therefore probably a slip. A possible explanation may be that this name stood originally as *Gilbert mab Gilbert Catgyffro* (*Hen*); see below.

Gilbert is a Norman name which became familiar in twelfth-century Wales because it was borne by several of the earls of Pembroke and of Gloucester, who belonged to the family of the counts of Clare (see HW, index; LL 315.24, 32: *Gilebert de Clare, Gilebert le Mareschald Conte de penbrok*). Since the Norman name was well known in Wales, it seems superfluous to look for a Welsh derivation for the form as it occurs in TYP, although a Welsh name in *Gil-* would not be impossible (cf. *Gildas* and *Gilfaethwy*, as well as *Gilla Goeshyd* (CO l. 298n.)).

On *Gilbert fitz Richard* (Gilbert de Clare, d. 1114) see J. E. Lloyd, *The Story of Ceredigion* (Cardiff, 1937), pp. 43–45; David Walker, *Medieval Wales* (Cambridge, 1990), pp. 38–40; and R. A. Griffiths, *Conquerors and Conquered* (Stroud, 1994), pp. 322–7). Gilbert was a Norman lord from Clare in Suffolk who was granted the rule of the Marcher lordship of Ceredigion by Henry I. In 1110 he started to build two castles, one on the site of the later town of Cardigan, and the other near the mouth of the Ystwyth. Gilbert's reputation for savagery is reflected in his satirical patronymic (or epithet) as one of three 'Slaughter-Blocks' of Britain (triad 24). There is, however, a possibility of confusion between Gilbert's name and that of his son, another Gilbert, who was the father of Richard 'Strongbow', and who died in 1147–8. The fact that both father and son were named *Gilbert* favours the belief that the name in TYP was originally *Gilbert mab Gilbert Katgyffro*, as suggested by Loth (*Mab.* I, p. 375, n.1), and it is possible that the identity of father and son has become confused in the reference. Both lived within fifty years of another prestigious Norman lord, *Alan Fyrgan* (see n.), who has similarly been introduced into TYP, and this offers some contributory support for the suggested identification. But too little information has come down concerning either father or son to account satisfactorily for the appearance of either in TYP in the company of earlier Welsh legendary figures, or to explain the bestowal on either of the epithet *Cadgyffro* 'Battle Tumult'. But they are not the only instances of the introduction into Welsh sources of figures belonging to the twelfth-century Norman political scene. I have cited some such instances in the introduction pp. xcii–xcv.

Gleis 44. See **Gweir a Gleis**. For *Gleis* cf. *Gleissiar* below.

Gleissiar Gogled 22 (WR). 'G. of the North.' The form of this name is attested by Cynddelw's allusions: *a goreu a vu o ueib gleissyar* (H 141.32; RBP 1429.25 = CBT III, no. 24.46n.). Except for the triad, Cynddelw's allusion in his *Marwnad Rhirid Flaidd* above is the only other known reference to this hero which has survived. It also provides an indication that Cynddelw used the version of TYP represented by WR in which alone triad 22 is found. It is possible that a further allusion to this character is concealed in a line in the *Gododdin* CA 1. 500 *ae leissyar* (see Ifor Williams's note), though the association is far from clear.

Glewlwyd Gafaelvawr 88 (Pen. 218); App. IV, no. 7. 'G. Mighty Grasp.' With *Glewlwyd* lit. 'brave grey', cf. *Gwrgi Garwlwyd* 'G. Rough Grey' (n.). LlDC no. 31.1–2: *Pa gur yw y porthaur. Gleuluid gauaeluawr*, etc. (See AW 40–5 for translation; B. F. Roberts, *Ast. H.* 296–309 for an edition and study of the poem; and CO² xxv–vi.)

CO l. 111 etc.: *Glewlwyt Gauaeluawr*

Owein: Iarlles y Ffynnawn: *Glevlvyd gyuaeluawr* (ed. Thomson, ll. 5–6 = WM 223.15–23).

Gereint vab Erbin: *Glevlvyd gyuaeluavr* (WM 385.35–6).

In the poem *Pa Gur* (LlDC no. 31) *Glewlwyd Gafaelfawr* figures as the gatekeeper of a fortress to which Arthur and his men are seeking to gain admittance. To prove their qualifications for admission Arthur gives an account of their feats and achievements, particularly emphasizing those of Cai. The names of Arthur's men include some who were originally unrelated to the Arthurian cycle, such as *Mabon* and *Manawydan* (see nn.). Evidently the narrative situation portrayed is closely related to the tale *Culhwch ac Olwen* (see Thomas Jones, B XVII, p. 248 = 'Early Evolution', pp. 16–17; AW 40–5; and CO(2) xxxv–xxxvi). In the tale Glewlwyd is presented as Arthur's own gatekeeper (CO l. 111ff.) and he demands an account of Culhwch's credentials before admitting him into the court. This incident is closely paralleled by an episode later in the same tale, in which the gatekeeper of the giant Wrnach Gawr admits Cai into his fortress after enquiring and learning from him his distinctive craft (CO ll. 765–85). It seems likely that the two gatekeepers have been interchanged, and that *Glewlwyd Gafaelfawr* originally figured as the guardian of the fortress of Wrnach Gawr. If this were so, the poem *Pa Gur* would represent an earlier version of the episode of Cai and Wrnach Gawr as told in *Culhwch* (the name of Wrnach may be concealed in the line *in neuat awarnach* (LlDC no. 31.39)). A burlesque of the poem's situation seems indeed to be intended by the complete reversal in it of the situation in the story of Culhwch's admission into Arthur's court: in this Culhwch does not state his qualifications for entrance, but instead he threatens the gatekeeper, and it is *Glewlwyd* who then enumerates Culhwch's qualifications in his discourse to Arthur. An instructive parallel to these incidents is to be found in the early Irish episode of Lug's (= Lleu's) admission to Tara in *The Battle of Moytura* (E. A. Gray (ed.), ITS vol. 52, § 53–71). Here again there is a dialogue with a gatekeeper, in which the hero is required to enumerate his distinctive qualifications and attributes before the gate of the fortress can be opened to him.

The allusions to *Glewlwyd* in the romances of *Owein* and *Gereint* appear to be based on the account given in *Culhwch*. *Glewlwyd* is the gatekeeper to Arthur's court, but according to Gereint (WM 385.5–9 = *Ystoria Gereint uab Erbin*, ed. Thomson, ll. 19–26) he performs his office only on the occasions of the three great annual festivals (for these cf. triad 85), and he is served by his deputies on other occasions. According to *Owein: Iarlles y Ffynnawn* (WM 223.15–23 = *Owein*, ed. Thomson, ll. 5–9):

> And although it was said that there was a porter to Arthur's court, there was none. *Glewlwyd Gafaelfawr* was there, however, with the rank of porter, to receive guests and far-comers, and to begin to do them honour, and to make known to them the ways and usages of the court: whoever was required to go to the hall or to the chamber, to make it known to him.

Cf. the reference in GTA I, no. XLII.75–6: *Glewlwyd, a ddug ail wely / Gafaelfawr, wyd, a'i gofl fry.* See also *Yr Areithiau Pros*, 14.13–17.

Gobrwy m. Echel 6ordwytwll 9. (Pen. 16): *Govrowy*. From the variant forms of this name in the manuscripts, I have chosen *Gobrwy* on the evidence of CO l. 195 etc. (*Gobrwy* lit. 'reward, gift', etc., GPC 1418).

CO: *A Gobrwy m. echel Uordvyt Twll* (l. 195n.).
Br. Rh.: *A gobrv mab echel uordvyt twll* (RM 159.26).

The form *Gobrwy* is attested both in CO and Pen. 47's version of triad 9. Pen. 16's *Govrowy* represents an attempt to give a contemporary spelling of a name which in O.W. orthography may have stood as *Gobroe* (with earlier *o* for *w*). Later manuscripts substitute the name *Goronwy*. See n. to *Echel 6ordwytwll*.

(G)ocuran Gawr 53 (NLW; Pen. 252), 56: *G6enh6yuar verch O*. 'G. the Giant.' See n. to *Gwenh6yuar*.

The normal lenition in Ml. Welsh of personal names following *verch* (TC §43), and the analogy of the other patronymics in triad 56 (see n.), which are lenited after *verch*, allows for doubt as to whether *Ogfran* or *Gogfran* is the correct form of the radical of this name. R. J. Thomas (EANC 80–1) regards *Ogrfran* as a compound of *ogr-* 'keen' and *-man* (as in the names *Cadfan*, *Gwrfan* etc.), and suggests that this name may be present in that of the stream *Ogran* in Monmouthshire. He regards the forms with initial *G-* as due to the secondary growth of a prosthetic *g-* in this name. And the testimony of the *Gogynfeirdd* supports the contention that *Ogrfan(n)* represents the oldest form of this name:

Cynddelw: *gwron gvrhyd ogyruan* (H 116.27 = CBT III, no. 1.3n.).
Einion Wan: *llit ogyruan* (H 187.26 = CBT VI, no. 3.5n.).
Prydydd y Moch: *gwrhydri ogyruan* (H 273.32 = CBT V, no. 23.76n.).
Hywel ab Owain Gwynedd: *yn llys ogyruann* (H 319.23, 27 = *ogyruan* RBP col. 1428.22, CBT II, no. 9.11n.).

In each of these instances, except the last (*llys* is fem.), the name occurs as a genitive following a masculine noun; a position in which lenition is not normally found. *Ogrfan* may be the original form of this name, as suggested by the Ll. 6 variant *Ogran* in GDG no.64.26. Pennant recalls that the old name for the ancient fort near Oswestry called Hen Ddinas was *Caer Ogyrfan* 'from Ogyrfan a hero co-existent with Arthur' (J. Rhŷs (ed.), *Tours in Wales*, I, p. 331; B III, p. 62). And in Owen Jones's *Cymru* (I, p. 585) it is said that 'Gogyrfan was the chief of a part of Powys in the sixth century.' Perhaps an early hero *Og(y)rfan*, known to tradition, became later confused with *Gogfran Gawr*, a giant who was the reputed father of *Gwenhwyfar* (see n.). But with the *cywyddwyr*, *Gogfran* is the usual form, and the occurrence of the name in TYP confirms the evidence that it was regarded as a compound of *brân* 'raven'; cf. *cogfran* 'jackdaw'. The following references are found in later poetry: *ail Gogran Gawr* (IGE^2 no. LXVII.4; see GSCyf p. 88, n. 81); Siôn Cent: *Mae Gwenhwyfar, gwawn hoywwedd / Merch Gogfran Gawr, fawr a fedd* (IGE², no. XC.19–20). It is found in the sixteenth-century tract on the Giants by Siôn Dafydd Rhys in Pen. MS. 118: *Gogbhran gawr a oedh yn trigo yn Aber ysgyr yn y caer uch yr abhon* (*yghwlad Brycheinawc yn agos i drebh Aber Hodni*) (*Cy.* XXVII, p. 134); *Gwenhwybhar bherch Goghbran Gawr* (ibid., p. 148). There is no connection between either of these names and the poetic term *ogyruen*, *ogrfen* = *awen*, 'inspiration, poetry' (GPC 2639), as used in early poetry (LlDC nos. 3.3, 3.35, 4.1 etc.) and by Cynddelw: *Mi gyndelw gert ogyruen* (CBT III, no. 16.92n. and n. to no. 24.6).

John Rhŷs recorded a popular rhyme: *Gwenhwyfar ferch Ogrfan gawr / Drwg yn fechan, gwaeth yn fawr* 'G. the daughter of (G)ogfran the Giant, bad when little, worse when big' (J. Rhŷs, *Studies in the Arthurian Legend*, p. 49). On the folklore of *Ogrfan/Gogrfan* see Grooms, *The Giants of Wales*, pp. 208–10, and WCD 512.

Golydan (Vard) 33 (WR), 34, 53, 69. 'G. the Poet.' See CBT VI, no. 15.11n. (Phylip Brydydd) and n. to *Katwaladyr Vendigeit* above. Ifor Williams discussed the name in B III, p. 49. *Golydan* < *Go* + *lydan* 'the broad/stout bard'. Cf. LL 199.21 where *Letan* occurs as a personal name, and also the Cornish place-name *Dind map Lethan* recorded in *Cormac's Glossary* (ed. Stokes, p. 29).

Gordibla Kernyw 93. *Gordibla* 'mighty plague' CO l. 313 (see glossary). This is not to be taken as a personal name, in spite of Moses Williams's conjecture concerning it; see n. to triad 93.

Goreu m. Kustenin 52. See nn. to *Arthur*, *Custennin Uendigeit*, *Gereint m. Erbin*.

Goreu is described in CO as *vn mab Custennhin heussawr* 'the one son of Custennin the Shepherd' (CO ll. 806–11n.). The interpretation of this name in the story as meaning 'Best' comes somewhat under suspicion owing to the early appearance of *Guoreu*, and its variants *Gurai*, *Guorai*, recorded as personal names in LL 173.28 etc. Alternatively, *Goreu* could have arisen as a corruption of *Gorneu* 'of Cornwall'; i.e. of the whole of Dumnonia (*Cornou* LL 172.26; 241–2); see K. H. Jackson LHEB 708 and CMCS 3, p. 31.

Goreu is a significant character in CO, and he acts as a kind of doublet of the hero Culhwch himself (see CO(2) xxx–xxxi, and n. to CO l. 811). In the tale, Culhwch and *Goreu* share several important features: both are cousins to King Arthur and to each other; with Gereint ab Erbin all three are descendants of Anlawd (Amlawdd) Wledig (see CO l. 2 and n.) by one or other of his numerous daughters, one of whom was Arthur's mother Eigr (= Igerna in HRB), see EWGT 94 (31). A fourth cousin was St Illtud, whose mother was Rieingulid ('gentle princess', daughter of 'Anblaud [*sic*] king of Brittannia'; VSB 196; Doble, ed. D. S. Evans, *Lives of the Welsh Saints* pp. 104 and 124, n. 83 which quotes Henry Lewis's explanation of the name Rieingulid).

Culhwch and *Goreu* are both almost unknown outside the tale of CO and triad 52, nor is there evidence that either (unlike *Geraint m. Erbin*) played any significant part in anterior Brythonic heroic traditions. In CO Goreu's claim to fame is as a giant-slayer (he assists Cai in overcoming Wrnach Gawr, and it is he (rather than Culhwch) who finally cuts off the head of the hero's arch-enemy Ysbaddaden Pencawr. *Goreu*'s name appears once in the closely related tale of *Geraint ab Erbin* (WM 411.34) and he is named also in *Breudwyt Ronabwy* (RM 159.23–4). In the triad he is presented as a releaser of Arthur from his three alleged imprisonments, a feat which seems to be an inverse reflection of the stories in which Arthur himself is distinguished as a famous releaser of prisoners (as in CO and in the poem *Preiddeu Annwfn* (BT 55–6)).

Gorolwyn 66: *Ardun, wreic Gatcor m. Goroluyn. Gorolwyn* 'Great Wheel'. Cf. the name *Eurolvyn merch Wdolwyn Gorr* (CO l. 364 n. = WM 469.39); and see nn. to *Gwythelyn Gorr* and to *Catcor m. Gorolwyn*. Lloyd-Jones suggested (by letter) that *Olwen* (fem. of *olwyn*) is cognate with Ir. *alaind* (< *al* + *find* 'beautiful') and this meaning suits well with some of the figurative occurrences of *olwyn* in early poetry (GPC 2644); cf. AW 74, and n. to *Olwen* (CO l. 364). Hence a possible meaning of *Gorolwyn* is 'Very Fair'. If, on the other hand, the normal meaning '*olwyn*' = wheel is taken, the name could mean 'Great Wheel'; cf. *Eurolwyn* 'Golden Wheel'.

Goronwy Peuyr (o Benllyn) 30. 'G. the Radiant' < *pybyr* (PKM 286n.; GPC 2958 'ardent, vigorous, shining', etc; D: *strenuus, robubstus, fortis*). Cf. nn. to *Ruua6n Beuyr* below, and cf. *Tutual Pefir* (*Tutwawl Beper*) VSB 319, EWGT 15 (11, 4) where *Tudual Flavi* translates *Tudual Pefr*; EWGT 20 (15). Either of the meanings 'handsome' or 'shining (-haired)' would appear to suit the lively adventurer featured in *Mabinogi Math*. For the tale of *G(o)ronwy Pefyr* and his intrigue with Blodeuwedd see PKM 84–92. The variant forms of the name are *Gronv pebyr* (WM 101.30–1), *Gronvy bebyr* (110.23), *Gronv bebyr* (110.10–11). Earlier forms occur in LL: *gurgoiui* (= *-nui*), p. xlvii; *guronui*, 272.5; 273.15; *guorgonui*, 222.6. Lloyd-Jones (G 571) regards the first element in this name as gw̰wr (gŵr 'man'), rather than the intensive prefix *gwor*.

The poem beginning *Tydi Dylluan tudwyll* (*Barddoniaeth Dafydd ab Gwilym* (1789) no. 121) refers to a variant version of the tale of Blodeuwedd from that which has come down in *Math* and names Blodeuwedd's abductor as *Goronwy fab Pefr Goronhir, Arglwydd Penllyn hoywyn hir* (ll. 31–2). For text and translation of the poem see H. Fulton, *Dafydd ap Gwilym: Apocrypha* (Llandysul, 1996) no. 33; also, D. H. Evans, 'Blodeuwedd', YB XX, pp. 79–89.

Greid(y)a6l Galouyd m. Envael Adrann 19, *Gwythyr m. Greidia6l* 56 (= *m. Greidyavl gallovyd*, Pen. 47). 'G. Enemy-Subduer.'

CO: *Greidawl Galldouyd* (l. 176n.).
Br. Rh.: *greidyal gall dofyd* (RM 160.3).

On *galouyd* (= *gall(d)ovyd*) see n. to triad 19. This epithet becomes corrupted to *galonn hydd* ('stag's heart') in certain late manuscript versions of BGG; see n. to *Gwythyr m. Greidya6l.*

Greidyawl = 'fierce, ardent, passionate' (G 588; GPC 1528–9). The adjective is formed from the noun *greid* 'battle, heat, passion'. Both *Greid* and *Greidyawl* occur as personal names: *Greit mab Eri* (CO ll. 176–7, 916 etc.); *Greit vab hoewgi(r)* (CA l. 266); Cynddelw: *gvr greidyavl ual greid uab ery* (H 110.2 = CBT IV, no. 9.78 n.); *Greit, confessor* (LL 3.24). *Greidyawl* occurs also as an adjective; cf. the line from Cynddelw quoted below, and also CLlH no. III.5a: *Vryen* (*Reget*) *greidyawl gauael eryr*, 'Urien Rheged the passionate, with the grasp of an eagle' (CLlH 115n.). It is not easy to distinguish in the following instances whether the reference is to the hero named in TYP or whether it is merely the adjective 'fierce', etc. that is intended:

Cynddelw: *graduuel greidyawl y vrhyt* (RBP col. 1168.35 = CBT III, no. 3.184).

Llygad Gŵr: *argae gryd greidyavl wrhydri* (H 216.10 = CBT VII, no. 24.46).

Gwilym Ddu: *parth espyt peir gryt greidyawl ffysgyat* (RBP col. 1226.38–9 = GGTD no. 6.60); LL 160.26: *nant greitiaul.* It seems likely, however, that the following allusions by Gr. ap Maredudd contain the personal name: *eil greidyawl* (RBP col. 1327.23); *(G)oronwy rwysc greidyawl* (RBP col. 1211.13 = GGM no. 5.90); *Kar dar dewrvryt gryt greidyawl dewred* (RBP col. 1315.25 = GGM 4.27n.)

Griffri 55. *Griffri* is a variant of *Gruffudd,* and is of fairly frequent occurrence in medieval sources; for examples see G 589.

Lewis Morris (CR 200) identifies this Griffri with *Griffri ap Heilin o'r Fron Goch ym Mhowys*. *Jes. Gen.* VIII: *Tevdvr m. Griffri.* In both these instances the name Griffri is associated with members of the Powys dynasty of the eighth and ninth centuries: triad 55 implies that a character of this name belonging to the same region was contemporary with Cadwallon in the seventh century, and took part in his campaign which led to the battle of Meigen (cf. EWSP 128–9, 170).

Grudnei 22. ? < *grudd* 'cheek'.

G6aetcym Herwuden 60. The names given in the triad to the English opponents at the battle of Chester are obviously invented names, rather than attempts to reproduce English forms. But they contain some recognizable elements: *gwaed* 'blood', *herw* 'exile, outlawry', basically 'the state of a man exiled from his tribe or living outside the law on the fringe of society' (on the term see GPC 1859, and cf. Br. Rh. 26). See n. to triad 60d.

Gwalchmei m. Gwyar 4, 42 (LlDC no. 6.12): *Kein caled march G.*, 46A (Pen. 47: *Meingalet march G.*), 75, 91, *G. ap Llew ap Kenvarch*, App. IV, no. 1.

Gwalch 'hawk' is employed in a number of instances by the *Gogynfeirdd* as an epithet for their patrons (for examples see G 608). It is therefore not surprising to find this word employed as an element in a personal name: the occurrence of *Brân* 'raven' as a personal name is analogous, cf. also the name *Gualchen* LL 232.10. It is unlikely, however, that *Gwalchmei* means 'Hawk of May'. Jackson (LHEB 449n.) offered the explanation that Ml. W. *Gwalchmei* < Brit. **Ṷalcos Magesos*, meaning 'The Hawk of the Plain', in which *-mei* represents an oblique case (genitive singular or plural) of *-ma* 'field, plain' < **magos*. He compares Ifor Williams's suggestion (*Enwau Lleoedd*, p. 41) that -*fai* in place-names such as *Myddfai* represents the genitive singular of *ma*. Further instances of the use of the plural of *ma* (*mei*) include *mekid meibon meigen meirch mei* 'the sons of Meigen rear horses of the plain(s)' (LlDC no. 18.145); Cynddelw: *gveiscueirch mei* 'powerful horses of the plain(s)' (H 147.4 = CBT III, no. 26.34n.); Prydydd y Moch: *a meirch meingrwn dvnn a dossavc* 'with horses of the plain(s), slender-round, brown and foaming' (H 213.26 = CBT V, no. 24.42). In LlC VI, pp. 241–3, Eurys Rowlands discussed the problems presented by this name. He regarded *mai* in place-names as more likely to be a plural 'fields, meadows' than a genitive singular (as advocated by Ifor Williams). He suggested tentatively that *Gwalchmai*'s name may after all be a close compound, and for this he drew support from the (conjectural) Breton cognate **Ualcmoe*(*i*); but proposed as an alternative derivation a compound of *gwalch* with a second element cognate with Old Irish *smech* 'chin', giving some such meaning as 'Hawk-Beak'.

Early references to *Gwalchmei* as a traditional hero are found in:

(i) the *Beddau* stanzas (LlDC no. 18.24): *bet gwalchmei ym peryton*. *Peryddon* = a tributary of the River Monnow at Monmouth is suggested by Ifor Williams (AP xl, and n. to l. 18), but it also occurs as a name for the Dee (see D. H. Evans, 'An Incident on the Dee during the Glyndŵr Rebellion?', *Denbighshire Historical Society Transactions* 38, p. 19, n. 63, and cf. Hamp in 'Peryddon', SC XVIII/XIX, pp. 132–3);

(ii) *Trioedd y Meirch* (LlDC no. 6), where *Keincaled march Gualchmei* ('Fair Hardy') reflects a name which in the form of *Guingalet* has adhered to *Gwalchmai*/*Gauvain*'s horse through an extensive range of continental romances (see n. to triad 42);

(iii) *Culhwch ac Olwen*, where *Gwalchmei* is named as Arthur's nephew, and as a leading member of Arthur's court (l. 345), one of his 'Six Helpers' (l. 404) on the quest for Olwen;

(iv) Cynddelw's *marwnad* for Owain Gwynedd (d. 1170) where the poet compares his hero to a number of legendary figures known from *Culhwch ac Olwen* and elsewhere; among them Owain Gwynedd is described as *taerualch* ('ardent and bold') *ual Gwalchmei* (CBT IV, no. 4.182n.). It is tempting to believe that Cynddelw, who was familiar with the name of *Gwalchmei* as that of a poetic predecessor, may at this date have cited *Gwalchmei fab Gwyar* from a direct knowledge of the tale of *Culhwch ac Olwen*, where he is listed as one of the members of Arthur's court (l. 345n.) and again as one of the 'Six Helpers' whom Arthur appointed to assist him in the quest for Olwen (ll. 404–7). Here it is said of *Gwalchmei* 'he was the best of walkers and the best of riders. He was Arthur's nephew, his sister's son, and his first cousin.' *Gwalchmei*'s mother was Arthur's sister Anna or *Gwyar*. It seems probable that *Gwalchmei* was an addition to the story of Culhwch (in which he plays no essential part), and that he was introduced under the influence of *Brut y Brenhinedd*. The same uncle-nephew relationship between *Gwalchmei* (= *Walwen*) and Arthur is corroborated by William of Malmesbury, in his extended and tantalizing account of Walwen in *De Rebus Gestis Anglorum* (published in 1125, ed. Stubbs III, p. 287):

> At this time was found in the province of Wales called R(h)os the tomb of Walwen, who was the not degenerate nephew of Arthur by his sister. He reigned in that part of Britain which is still called Walweitha [= Galloway < *Gall- Gaidil*]. A warrior most renowned for his valour, he was expelled from his kingdom by the brother and nephew of Hengist, of whom I spoke in the first book, but not until he had compensated for his exile by much damage wrought upon them, worthily sharing in the praise of his uncle, in that they deferred for many years the ruin of their falling country. But the tomb of Arthur is nowhere to be beheld, whence ancient ditties fable that he is yet to come. The tomb of the other, however, as I have said, was found in the time of king William upon the sea-shore, fourteen feet in length; and here some say that he was wounded by his foes and cast out in a shipwreck, but according to others he was killed by his fellow-citizens at a public banquet. Knowledge of the truth therefore remains doubtful, although neither story would be inconsistent with the defence of his fame. (Trans. by E. K. Chambers, *Arthur of Britain*, p. 17)

William of Malmesbury's sources are entirely obscure (with their strange reminder of the *Beddau* stanzas in their reference to *Gwalchmei*'s grave and to Arthur's unknown grave). Yet elsewhere William concedes the existence of *nugae Brittonum* ('the fables of the Britons') as forming a part of his source-material. Since he nowhere amplifies his allusions to these, it is impossible to tell how otherwise than by current popular tradition he may have come to hear of Arthur's unknown grave. It is worth noting too that Lewis Morris records that the site of the grave of *Gwalchmei* (the *Walwen* of the above passage) 'is shown between the Isles of Skomar and Skokham in Pembrokeshire' (CR 213). And *Kastell Gwalchmai* (Walwyn's Castle) is recorded as the name of one of the three commotes of Rhos in Pembrokeshire (*Cy.* IX, p. 330; RBB 411). This seems to provide independent evidence for the tradition recorded by William of Malmesbury (who must have had a precedent for employing *Walwen* as a Norman form corresponding to *Gwalchmai*).

Clearly the name *Walwen* corresponds to Geoffrey of Monmouth's *Gualguanus*, whom Geoffrey presents as Arthur's nephew by his sister Anna (HRB IX, 9). *Walwen/Gualguanus* also corresponds to the *Gauvains* of the French romances and to the English *Gawain*. It seems probable that Geoffrey of Monmouth knew of William of Malmesbury's account, and based on it his assertion as to the relationship claimed to subsist between his hero and Arthur. (For the importance which was implied by the uncle-nephew relationship, both in legend and in life, cf. the notes above to *Gereint m. Erbin*, *Culhwch m. Cilydd*, *Goreu m. Kustenin*, *Drystan m. Tallwch*—and the further examples in the *Mabinogi* in relation to *Math* and *Gwydion*, *Bendigeidfran* and *Gwern*.) *Gwalchmei*'s name was already familiar in Wales as that of the poet *Gwalchmai* (*circa* 1140–80), commemorated to this day in the name of the village of *Gwalchmai* in Anglesey. The cognate Breton name *Uualchmoe*(*l*) is attested in the ninth-century Breton *Cartulaire de Rédon* (J. Loth, *Chr. Br*. 152, n.5). For the variant forms of the name found on the continent in the twelfth-century (including *Galvaginus* on the Modena archivolt in Italy) see ATC 146. The continental variants of this name appear to be derived from a contamination of *Gwalchmai* in its early Breton form *Walcmoei*, as was argued earlier by Loth (RC XIII, p. 495) and Zimmer (*Zeitschrift für französische Sprache und Literatur* XIII, pp. 234–5).

Further, the significance of William's statement that Walwen 'reigned' in Galloway should not be overlooked. Any phonetic association between the two names may be set aside, yet the importance of the statement that Walwen belonged originally to north Britain still stands. One has only to compare the parallel instances of Owein ab Urien, Drystan, Llywarch Hen, and perhaps Arthur himself—characters of whom the earliest traditions come from the north, though they were subsequently relocalized in Wales—and it becomes reasonable to conclude that *Gwalchmei* also belonged originally to *Gwŷr y Gogledd*, although the tradition about him to which William refers was already partly established in Wales. Geoffrey of Monmouth tacitly recognizes this association by giving his *Gualguanus* as father of the northern ruler Lot of Lothian.

From the reference in CO l. 345 one would conclude that *Gwyar* (lit. 'blood') was the name of Arthur's brother-in-law. But the names of Math *vab Mathonwy* and Gwydion *vab Dôn* prove that matronymics were possible in Welsh, as they were in early Irish (Conchobor *mac Nessa*, Fergus *mac Roich*), and it seems evident that *Gwyar* represents a woman's name, even if this is contrary to the normal usage of the triads. In one version of *Bonedd y Saint*, *Gwyar* is listed as the name of one of the many daughters of *Amlawdd Wledig* (see EWGT p. 194 and CO n. to l. 2). Considerable confusion prevails in Welsh sources owing to the fact that Geoffrey of Monmouth gives Arthur's sister Anna as the mother of *Gualguanus*. In the fourteenth-century *Birth of Arthur* (*Cy*. XXIV, pp. 250 ff.) an attempt is made to reconcile the native tradition with that of Geoffrey by substituting the name of *Gwyar* for that of Anna as Arthur's sister:

Dwy verchet (a oeddynt i Wrleis) o Eygyr nit amgen (Gwyar a Dioneta. Gwyar) a oedd yn weddw (yn llys i that a Hywel y mab) y gyt a hi gwedy (marw Ymer llydaw i gwr) priot. Ac Uthyr (a beris i Leu vab Kynvarch) i phriodi a phlant (a gowsant nit amgen no) deu vab Gwa(lchmei a Medrawt a thair mer)chet Gracia G(raeria Dioneta).

'Gwrleis and Eigyr had two daughters, Gwyar and Dioneta. Gwyar was (living as) a widow in her father's court, and Hywel her son with her, after the death of Ymer Llydaw her husband. And Uthyr caused Lleu ap Cynfarch to marry her, and they had children: that is two sons, Gwalchmei and Medrawd, and three daughters, Gracia, Graeria, and Dioneta.' (It should be noted that the words in brackets in this passage have been supplied from the transcript made by John Jones Gellilyfdy in 1611 (Pen. 215), as the original had become too indistinct to read. These words include the name of *Gwyar*. Nevertheless, there seems no reason to reject their authenticity.)

This simple expedient did not suggest itself to the earlier redactor(s) of the *Brut*, who render Geoffrey's *Gualguanus* by *Gwalchmei*, but conform to Geoffrey's account with respect to this hero's parentage (BD 152, 154). However, the native tradition appears to have been so strong that they were obliged to divide Geoffrey's character into two: the boy *Gwalchmei* who is son of Anna and Lleu ap Kynuarch (= Lot de Lodonesia), and *Gwalchmei ap Gwyar*, whose name is used to represent that of *Gualguanus* in the later battle scenes in which he figures (BD 171, 175, 179). But in one instance the relationship is reaffirmed exactly as in CO; see BD 183: *Gualchmei uab Guyar nei y brenhin*. (On the confusion between *Gwyar* and Anna as the name of *Gwalchmei*'s mother, see B. F. Roberts, B XXV, pp. 287–8.)

Gwalchmei uab Gwyar is named in *Breudwyt Rhonabwy*, RM 159.19. Of the Three Romances, that of *Owein* differs from the others in that it depends upon the account given in the *Brut* with respect to the parentage of *Gwalchmei*, i.e. no patronymic is given, but the hero of the tale (Owein) states that he and *Gwalchmei* are first cousins (WM 248.35; Lleu (Loth) and Urien were both sons of Kynvarch). In both *Gereint* and *Peredur*, *Gwalchmei uab Gwyar* is named specifically (WM 411.28; 118.20). So also the *Ystorya Trystan* (B V, p. 123.2–3): *Gwalchmai fab Gwyar dafod aur*; but this late text still adheres to the tradition of CO, for later we have: *mi yw Gwalchmei nai Arthvr* (118.12 = 123.15). The Continental concept of *Gauvain* as a paragon of courtesy and valour is reflected in the portrayal of *Gwalchmei* in the Three Romances; cf. the description at the beginning of *Gereint* (WM 385.27–32): 'Gwalchmei above all, for he by excellence of renown, for feats of arms and dignity of noble birth was chief of the nine captains of the war-bands.' And in each of the Three Romances *Gwalchmei* figures in a scene of meeting with the hero, who has just engaged *incognito* in single combat with a series of Arthur's warriors. In each case *Gwalchmei* is the means of bringing about a reconciliation with Arthur, either as a sequel to single combat (*Owein* and *Gereint*), or as a result of his courteous intercession (*Peredur* and *Trystan*). In *Peredur*, Arthur's words on this occasion are significant: *M*(*i*) *a wydvn na bydei reit y walchmei ymlad ar marchavc. A diryfed yv idav kaffel clot. Mvy a wna ef oe eireu tec no nini o nerth an harueu* (WM 144.21–4) 'I knew it would not be necessary for Gwalchmei to fight with the knight. It is no wonder that he wins fame, for he does more with his fair words than we by force of arms'. This was the reputation of *Gauvain* in the Continental romances, and it accounts for the epithet *dafod aur* 'golden tongue' which *Gwalchmei* bears in the late Welsh texts, *Ystorya Trystan* and the *Pedwar Marchog ar Hugain* (see App. IV, no. 1).

Cynddelw (of Owain Gwynedd): *taerfalch fal Gwalchmai* (CBT IV, no. 4.182n.).

Y Prydydd Bychan (of Rhys Ieuanc): *kynnedyf Gwalchmai* (CBT VII, no. 2.15n.).

Casnodyn (of Madog Fychan): *Divei ual gwalchmei. gweilch maeth med agwin* (RBP col. 1242.39–40 = GC no. 2.145n.).

Dafydd y Coed (of Hopcyn ap Thomas): *gwiw eil gwalchmei uab gwyar* (RBP col. 1376.25 = GDC no. 3.101n.).

Einion Offeiriad (of Sir Rhys ap Gruffudd): *Gwalchmai erfai, arf ddioludd* (GEO no. 1.63; cf. *Cy*. XXVI, p. 135).

Dafydd ap Gwilym (to Rhys Meigen): *Nid un swydd â Gwalchmai* (GDG no. 21.2).

Siôn Dafydd Rhys's account of the Giants in Pen. MS. 118, fol. 831 names three wives of Welsh giants who are said to have been slain by *Gwalchmei nei Arthur* (*Cy*. XXVII, p. 130; Grooms, *The Giants of Wales*, p. 304).

Gwalla6c m. Lleenna6c 5, 6 (Pen. 47), 25 (WR). See nn. to *Lleenna6c*, *Ceredic m. Gwallawc*, *Aneiryn Gwa6tryd Mechdeyrn Beird*, *Vryen Reget*, *Kynvarch*, *Drutwas m. Driffin*.

Harl. Gen. IX: *Guallauc map Laenauc map Masguic Clop map Ceneu map Coyl Hen* (EWGT 10 (9) = *Jes. Gen.* XXXVI (EWGT 48 (36)). HB ch. 63 names *Guallauc* as one of the confederation of British kings, led by Urien Rheged, who opposed the Bernician king Hussa and other invading Saxon leaders in the mid-sixth century. Thus *Gwallawg* is well established as belonging to the early heroic tradition of north Britain: he was a descendant of Coel Hen, and a contemporary and cousin of Urien and other rulers of the late sixth century. His omission from the list of the descendants of Coel Hen in *Bonedd Gwŷr y Gogledd* (App. II) can only be accounted for as an oversight, since it is attested in the other genealogies (the *Jes. Gen.* quoted above is plainly defective; with it cf. App. II, nos. 3–6). This association is also confirmed by the allusion to *Gwallawc, marchawc trin* ('G. horseman of battle') in the *englynion* concerning the story of Urien, CLlH no. III.39a, which names

Gwallawg in connection with warfare in which the other participants were *Morgant*, *Dunawt* (*fab Pabo*) and the sons of *Urien*. Even more important evidence for *Gwallawg*'s historicity is to be found in two early poems in the Book of Taliesin (PT nos. XI and XII). These are *En env Gvledic Nef goludavc* and *En env Gvledic nef gorchordyon* (BT 29 and BT 63). The first poem consists in the main in a list of *Gwallawg*'s battles. The second, though it contains interpolated material, may represent the nucleus of a *marwnad*. In both poems it may be noted that the archaic form *Lleennavc* is found for *Gwallawg*'s father, as in triad 5. The second poem contains an apparent allusion to the small kingdom of Elmet in the Leeds area of Yorkshire, in the line *a eninat* (= *a enwat*?) *yn ygnat ac* (= *ar*) *eluet* '(?) he was named a judge (ruler) over Elmet', for it has been suggested that Elmet was *Gwallawg*'s kingdom, and that his son Ceredig (see n. to *Ceredic m. Gwallawc*) is to be identified with King Cerdic of Elmet who was expelled from his kingdom by Edwin of Bernicia (cf. *Ann. Cam.* 616).

Two poems in the *Black Book of Carmarthen* provide evidence (corroborated by the allusion quoted above from CLlH) that *Gwallawg*'s name was kept alive for a long time after his death. In a poem in which the poet claims to have visited the death-places of a number of famous early heroes appear the lines: *Ny buum lle llas gwallauc mab goholheth teithiauc / attwod lloegir mab lleyn*(*n*)*auc* (LlDC no. 34.55–7) 'I have not been where Gwallawg was slain, son of a privileged stock, the affliction of England, son of Lleynnauc.' LlDC no. 33 consists of five *englynion*, with two additional ones written across the margin of the manuscript. These may have been abstracted from a longer narrative concerning *Gwallawg ap Lleynnauc*, whose name is repeated at the end of each stanza. Such a narrative must have been of a humorous character: the hero is described as *coegauc* 'one-eyed', and a goose is said to have plucked out his other eye from his head. Then follows the *englyn*: *Nid aeth nep a uei envauc / ir gorllurv I daeth gvallauc / y valaen yr veiriauc* 'Nobody who would be famous would go in the same plight as did *Gwallawg*—ill-fated, into the brambles'. (see B XVI, p. 29, and the edition of this poem by B. F. Roberts, *Ast. H.* 309–11; trans. EWSP 509). There is only a single allusion to *Gwallawc vab Llennawc* in the Welsh *chwedlau*, where his name is included in list of *goreugwyr llys Arthur* in *Gereint fab Erbin* (WM 406.19–20 = RM 261.9).

Gwallawg appears as a personal name in LL 208.11: *gualluc*; 265.13: *guallauc*. Cf. also the place-names *Hendref Wallog* in Meirionnydd, and *Gwallog* in Ceredigion. It is therefore uncertain whether the reference to *Gwallauc Hir* ('G. the Tall') in LlDC no. 18.23—*yg karrauc bet gwallauc hir*—is to the son of *Lleennauc* or not. *Gwallawg Hir* is named in an anonymous fragment of a poem in Pen. 147 (*circa* 1566) quoted by T. Gwynn Jones (B I, p. 153): *Pan aeth Gwallawc Hir y dir mab Don*, which alludes to a crossing of the River Conwy—but this seems unlikely to be an allusion to the northern *Gwallawg ap Lleennawg*. The line appears to be a variant on a line from Iorwerth Beli's poem to the bishop of Bangor where the hero referred to is Maelgwn Hir, see GGDT no. 15.29n. and the references quoted there. A more likely allusion to *Gwallawg ap Lleennawg* is found in *Moliant Cadwallawn* (B VII, p. 25; R. G. Gruffydd (ed.), *Ast. H.* 27–34; see n. to *Catwalla6n m. Catuan*): *y digones gwychyr Gwallawc eilywed Gattraeth fawr fygedawg* 'valiant / ferocious Gwallawg caused the sorrow of great and famous Catraeth'. There is no other allusion in this poem to *Gwallawg* in connection with the battle of Catraeth. Can the allusion here be indirectly to the poet Aneirin who celebrated the battle of Catraeth, and who may in fact have been Gwallawg's nephew, according to CA l. 63 (see n.) combined with *Bonedd y Saint* (EWGT 56 (12)); cf. M. E. Owen, *Ast. H.* 134 (see n. to *Aneiryn Gwa6tryd Mechdeyrn Beirdd*). All the material relating to *Gwallawg* has subsequently been studied by Jenny Rowland, EWSP 100–6, and by R. G. Gruffydd, 'In Search of Elmet', SC XXVIII, pp. 63–79. Gruffydd suggests that *Gwallawg* (like *Cadwallawn* after him) was striving to possess the *imperium* of Britain.

G6anar 35: *Gwenwynwyn a G6anar, meibyon Llia6s m. Nwyvre. Gwanar* 'leader, warrior, prince' also 'war, battle' (GPC 1573). LL 228.3: *Guanar*. See also n. to *Gwenwynwyn*[1].

Gwed6 46A: *Myngr6n march Gwed6. Gweddw* 'widow(er)'. See n. to triad 46A.

G6eir[1] (a Gleis ac Archanat) 44 (R: *Achleu ac Archanat*). As a common noun *gwair* = 'hay' and also 'bend, circle, loop, collar' (B XI, p. 82; PKM 248–9). There are numerous instances in which *Gweir* is found as a personal name, see below, and the following instances: *Gweir hir mab feruarch* (CA l. 1124); *Tecguaret filius Gueir* (LL 277.17); and the place-name *Ynys Wair* (App. I, no. 2). See Ifor Williams's note B XI, p. 82.

Owing to the number of occurrences of the name, certain allusions by the *Gogynfeirdd* leave it uncertain which, if any, of the characters named *Gweir* in TYP is intended: Cynddelw: *angerd Weir* (CBT III, no. 20.19 n.); see *Gweir*[3] below. Cf. also Gruffudd ap Maredudd: *llit gweir* (RBP col. 1207.2 = GGM no. 3.40n.); idem, *gweir o angerd* (RBP col. 1327.40).

Gweir[2] m. Gweirioed 52. (R: *m. Gveiryoed*). The evidence of the triad confirms the identity of this *Gweir* with the *Gweir* who figures in the poem *Preiddeu Annwfn* (?pre–1100; see T. Jones, B XVII, pp. 245–6): *bu kyweir karchar gveir yg kaer sidi, trvy ebostol pvyll a phryderi* (BT 54.18) 'Prepared was the prison of *Gweir* in *Caer Sidi*, according to the story of Pwyll and Pryderi'. (For a discussion of these lines see M. Haycock, SC XVIII/XIX, pp. 64–5, and cf. CO(2) lxi.) The old title of the tale of *Manawydan fab Llŷr*, or at least that part of it which described the imprisonment of Pryderi and Rhiannon, was named *Mabinogi Mynweir a Mynord* (PKM 65) and it seems possible that this title, evidently obscure to the latest redactor of the tale, does in fact contain the proper name *Gweir* (see PKM 249).

The site of *Gweir*'s imprisonment was associated with the place-name *Ynys Wair*. But this place-name was given both to the Isle of Wight (App. I, no. 2) and to Lundy Island, off the Devon coast (see n. to triad 52c, and cf. J. Rhŷs, CF II, 679).

Gweir[3] m. Gwystyl 21 (WR).

Br. Rh.: *gveir mab gvestyl* (RM 159.26). The tale of *Peredur* names *Gveir mab gvestyl* as one of the three knights from Arthur's court whom the boy hero meets in the forest (WM 118.21).

Prydydd y Moch: *Neu'n gwneir uegys gweir uab gvestyl* (CBT V, no. 13.16n.).

Einion Wan: *gwr a wneir ual gveir uab gvestyl* (CBT VI, no. 4.27n.).

Gr. ap Maredudd: *eill rwysc gveir uab gvestyl* (RBP col. 1326.6 = GGM no. 5.149).

Gwystyl = 'hostage'. Perhaps it is this *Gweir* who is alluded to in CO ll. 256–7 (*Gwystyl mab [Nwython] a Run mab Nwython* = *Gwystyl mab Run mab nwython* RM 109.6). For a further note see P. C. Bartrum WCD 301 and *Nat. Lib. of Wales Journal* XIV, p. 242. The name *Gweir fab Gwystl* seems to have stood as a symbol of grief to the poets who cite it.

Gueir[4] Gwrhyt6a6r 19, *G. G6ryt 6awr* 72, 'G. of Great Valour'. Note that both the triads cited also include the name of Drystan (Tristan), while triad 21, which is also a Drystan triad, gives *Gweir ap Gwystyl* as a variant of the Early Version's Hueil mab Caw. This suggests the possibility that *Gueir*[4] is to be equated with *Gweir*[3], and that this character may have played some part in the Welsh Drystan stories.

CO ll. 288–92 lists four characters named *Gweir*, and *Gueir*[4] may perhaps be one of these: *a Gweir Dathar Wenidawc, a Gweir mab Kadellin Tal Aryant, a Gweir Gwrhyd Enwir, a Gweir Gwyn Paladyr* (R: *baladyr hir*)—*ywythred y arthur, brodyr y uam, meibon Llwch Llawwynnyawc o'r tu draw y Uor Terwyn* (see nn. in CO(2)). *Gereint fab Erbin* lists *Gweir gwryt uawr* (RM 265.15).

Gwen[1] Bendragon 52. For the epithet see n. to *6thyr Bendragon* below. There seems to be no reason to regard *Gwen* (= *Gwyn*) as a scribal corruption of the name of *Uthyr*, although T. Gwynn Jones drew attention to the form *Uighir* (*Ughdaire*) *Finndreaguin* in an Irish Arthurian romance (ITS vol. 10 (1907)), as a rendering of *Uthur Bendragon* (*Aberystwyth Studies* VIII, p. 48). But this could be in error for *Cinn dreaguin*, the normal Irish rendering of the epithet. *Gwen Bendragon* is unknown from any other source.

Gwen[2] verch (K)ywryt m. Krydon 78. See n. to *Kywryt m. Krydon* above. For an early instance of *Gwen* as a girl's name, cf. *Gvenn Teir Bronn* 'G. Three Breasts' (VSB 321 (19)). The name was evidently known to the Breton writer Wrdisten in the ninth century, since he gives to the mother of St Winwaloeus the name of *Alba trimammis* 'Alba Three Breasts' (Doble, *Life of St Winwaloe*, Cornish Saints Series, no. 4, p. 27).

Gwendoleu m. Keida6 6, 29, 32 (= triad 10 WR), 44, App. II, no. 6; App. III, 12. See n. to *Myrddyn (Wyllt) m. Morvryn*. With the form of this name cf. *Eudolan* LL 200.8; *Eudolen map Aballach* Harl. Gen. X (= *Eudoleu uab Auallach* in *Life of St Beuno* (*Llyfr Ancr* p. 127.10; VSB 22)); and *Guordoli* Harl. Gen. I (VSB 118.39 = EWGT 9(i)).

The allusions in TYP constitute one of the two main sources for our knowledge of *Gwenddolau*. The other source consists of the poems of the *Myrddin* cycle, which contain many allusions to him: the *Cyvoesi* (RBP col. 577.27, 32; 578.39), the *Avallenau* (LlDC no. 16.43, 63; see also the variant text from Pen. 3, which contains the additional line *neum rodes guendoleu tlysseu ym rat*, B IV, p. 122.39); the *Oianeu* (LlDC no. 17.28–31), *Peiryan Vaban* (B XIV, p. 105.32, 49). From the poems and the triads it appears that *Gwenddolau* was the patron and protector of Myrddin, and the leader of one of the factions who fought at the battle of Arfderydd (on *Gweith Arderyd* see n. to triad 84). According to the B text of *Ann. Cam.* and the *Cyvoesi* poem, *Gwenddolau* met his death at this battle. An allusion in a poem which cites the death-places of a number of sixth-century heroes gives evidence for the tradition that *Gwenddolau* was renowned in poetry (and hence, perhaps, as a patron of the poets): *Mi a wum in y lle llas guendolev / mab keidav colowin kerteu* (LlDC no. 34.43–4) 'I was present at the place where Gwenddolau was slain, the son of Keidaw, pillar of songs'.

In a brief article, 'The Site of the Battle of Arthuret', published in the *Proceedings of the Society of Antiquaries of Scotland* for 1864 (VI, pp. 91–8), W. F. Skene drew attention to the apparent preservation of *Gwenddolau*'s name in that of the *Carwinelow* burn which falls into the River Esk three miles north of Longtown in Cumbria; while Arthuret, a mile south of Longtown, can be identified with Arfderydd, the site of the famous battle with which *Gwenddolau*'s name is associated. According to Skene, *Carwinelow* (< *Caer Wenddolau*) was also the name of a mill which stood beside the burn. Chadwick suggested (*Early Scotland*, p. 143) that *Gwenddolau*'s stronghold was situated in the old Roman fortress at Netherby nearby, which was formerly known as *Castra Exploratorum*. A mile from this is the Norman fortress known as the 'Moat of Liddel', or more popularly as 'the Roman camp'. For descriptions of the site, see W. F. Skene and FAB I, pp. 65–6. According to Skene 'the old farmer of the Upper Moat, who accompanied us, informed me that the tradition of the country was that a great battle was fought here between the Romans and the Picts who held the camp, in which the Romans were victorious; that the camp was defended by 300 men, who surrendered it, and were all put to the sword, and were buried in the orchard of the Upper Moat, at a place he showed me' (loc. cit., p. 98). See also

Chadwick, *Growth of Literature* I, pp. 109–11n.; AW 118–21; and M. Miller, 'The Commanders at Arthuret', *Trans. Cumberland and Westmorland Antiq. and Arch. Soc.* LXXV, pp. 95–118.

The lines which refer to *Gwenddolau* in the *Oianeu* (LlDC no. 17.28–31) could be a surviving fragment of an elegy from a story (comparable with the early *englynion Diffaith Aelwyd Rheged* which commemorate the death of Urien Rheged (CLlH no. III; EWSP 426, 481)): *Yd weles e guendolev in perthic rieu / in cynull preitev o pop eithaw, / y dan vy guerid rut nv neud araf / pen teernet goglet llaret mvyhaw* (LlDC no. 17.28–31n.), 'I saw Gwenddolau, a marauding lord(?), collecting booty from every border; now he lies still under the brown earth; the chief of the kings of the North, of greatest generosity.'

For a suggestive analogy to this for the reworking of an ancient elegy by a subsequent court-poet cf. the discussion by R. G. Gruffydd (SC XXIV/V, p. 11) of the ninth- or tenth-century *Marwnad Cunedda*, BT 69–70 (J. E. Caerwyn Williams (ed.), *Ast. H.* ch. IX, and cf. *Ast. H.* 16–18). Further allusions to *Gwenddolau* are:

Cynddelw: *Gwrtuannyar gwrtuar Gwynndoleu* (H 113.31 = CBT IV, no. 9.202n.).

Englynion y Clyweit: *A glyweist-di a gant Gwendoleu / Wrth dramwyaw dyffrynneu* (*Blodeugerdd* no. 31, *englyn* 73).

Although there is no mention of *Gwenddolau* in the extant *chwedlau*, his development from a heroic figure into a figure of legend is evinced by the attribution to him of the possession of magic birds (triad 32), and of a magic chessboard (App. III, no. 12); cf. the allusion quoted from LlDC no. 34.43–4 to *Gwenddolau*'s fame in song, which suggests that as a legendary figure he had a prominence barely hinted at by the few surviving allusions.

Gwenvedon merch Tudaual Tutklut 66 (Pen. 47). See n. to *Tudwal Tutclyt*.

G6enhwy6ach 53, **Gwennh6yach** 84. CO ll. 358–9 and n.: *Y am Wenhwyuar . . . A Gwenhwyach y chwaer*. This reading from *Culhwch ac Olwen* and triad 84 indicate that *Gwenhwyach* is the original form of this name. (For other instances of names in *-ach*, once believed to represent Irish influence, see P. Sims-Williams B XXIX, pp. 615–16.) Evidently there is a close connection between the text of *Culhwch* and the two triads, and no other allusions to *Gwenhwy(f)ach* are extant. See n. to *Gwenh6yuar* below.

Gwenh6yuar[1] **(uerch Ocuran Gawr** see **(G)ocuran Gawr)** 53, 54, 56, 80, 84. The second element in this name is cognate with Ir. *siabair* 'phantom, spirit, fairy'; thus *Gwenhwyfar* corresponds to Ir. *Findabair*, the name of the daughter of Queen Medb in the Ulster epic *Táin Bó Cúailnge* (Thurneysen, *Heldensage* p. 95; M. Richards, 'Arthurian Onomastics', THSC 1969, p. 257).

Less likely is the suggestion that the name is to be analysed as *Gwenhwy* + *mawr* 'G. the Great' in contrast to her sister *Gwenhwy(f)ach*. *Gwenhwyfar* is named as Arthur's queen in CO l. 161 and n., and she is *Penn Rianed yr Ynys honn* 'chief of (royal) ladies of this Island', CO l. 358. She figures as *Guenièvre* in the Arthurian poems of Chrétien de Troyes, and is *Gwenhwyfar* in the corresponding three Welsh Romances: *Owein* ll. 3–4—*gwenhwyuar ae llavuoryon yn gvniaw vrth ffenestr* (WM 223.13); *Peredur*—*gvas ystauell yn gvassanaethu o orflvch ar wenhvyfar* (WM 121–2), etc.; *Gereint*—*eglvys y arthur . . . ar eil y wenhvyuar ae rianed* (WM 385.21–3 etc.). See further WCD 317–18.

The texts of HRB give the variant forms *G(u)anhumara*, *Guenhuuera*, *Gwenwara*, etc. It was pointed out by Vendryes ('La Légende del Graal', EC V, p. 34; cf. R. Thurneysen, 'Zu Nemnius', ZCP XX, p. 133n.) that the forms of this name which have an *-m-* can best be explained as derived from a *written* early Welsh *Guenhuiuar* 'white fairy' with the *-iu-* misread as *-m-*. If the forms in *-m-* represent the name as originally written by Geoffrey, they would provide good evidence for early transmission of the name in a written form. (On the variant spellings in the Berne MS. see Neil Wright, HRB I, lii, n.) But pending a full collation of the manuscripts it is impossible to establish which are the earliest forms. According to Geoffrey's account in HRB IX, 9:

> (Arthur) duxit uxorem nomine guenhuueram. ex nobile genere romanorum editam. que in thalamo cadoris ducis educta; totius insule mulieres pulchritudine superabat.
>
> '(Arthur) took a wife who was named *Gwenhuuera*, descended from a noble Roman family who had been raised in the household of duke Cador. She excelled in beauty all the women of the whole Island.'
>
> In BD 153.2–5 this passage is rendered:
>
> y kymerth y brenhin wreic a hanoed o dylyedogyon Ruuein, a Guenhvyuar oed y henv (= MA 464a: *Gwenhwyfar verch Gogvran gawr*; *Brut Cleopatra* 163: *verch Ogvran gawr*), ac yn llys Cadvr yarll Kernyw y magadoed. A phryt a thegvch y wreic honno a orchuygei holl wraged enys Prydein.
>
> 'The beauty and form of that woman surpassed all the women of the Island of Britain.'

In the absence of any references by the *Gogynfeirdd* or in earlier sources, the evidence for an authentic pre-Geoffrey tradition of *Gwenhwyfar* in Wales is highly doubtful. The triads which include her name are found only in WR and are absent from the Pen. 16 version of TYP. Early evidence therefore depends entirely on *Gwenhwyfar*'s brief appearance in *Culhwch ac Olwen*, a tale which was certainly subjected at some stage to influences from *Brut y Brenhinedd* (see CO(2) lxxxii, and notes in CO to *Gwalchmei fab Gwyar*, *Caledfwlch*, *Gwenhwyfar*).

There is also a celebrated passage in Caradog of Llancarfan's *Vita Gildae* (ed. and trans. Hugh Williams, *Gildas*, 408–11):

> He [i.e. Gildas] arrived at Glastonbury, at the time when king Melvas was reigning in the summer country . . . Glastonbury, that is, the glassy city, which took its name from glass, is a city that had its name originally in the British tongue. It was besieged by the tyrant Arthur with a countless multitude on account of his wife Gwenhwyfar, whom the aforesaid wicked king had violated and carried off, and brought there for protection, owing to the asylum afforded by the invulnerable position due to the fortifications of thickets of reed, river, and marsh. The rebellious king had searched for the queen throughout the course of one year, and at last heard that she remained there. Thereupon he roused the armies of the whole of Cornwall and Devon; war was prepared between the enemies. When he saw this, the abbot of Glastonbury, attended by the clergy and Gildas the wise, stepped in between the contending armies, and in a peaceable manner advised his king, Melvas, to restore the ravished lady. Accordingly, she who was to be restored, was restored in peace and goodwill. When these things were done, the two kings gave to the abbot a gift of many domains.

It must, however, be noted that the independence of the writings of Caradog of Llancarfan from the 'contaminations' of his contemporary Geoffrey of Monmouth have been called into question, in view of the somewhat ambiguous relationship which existed between the two writers, as attested by Geoffrey's words in the epilogue to HRB which is attributed to him in the *Berne* manuscript (HRB ed. N. Wright, p. 147; trans. Thorpe, p. 284n.). Here Geoffrey bequeaths the later history of 'the kings who have ruled in Wales' to his 'contemporary' Caradog of Llancarfan. See on this C. N. L. Brooke, SEBC 231–3, reprinted in *The Church and the Welsh Border* (1986), pp. 43–4.

There are several subsequent references to the tale of the abduction of *Gwenhwyfar* by Melwas (*Melwas* < *mael* 'prince' + *gwas* 'lad, servant'). Chrétien de Troyes names a certain *Maheloas . . . le sire de l'isle de Voirre* (*Erec*, l. 1946), and this form reproduces the Welsh name more faithfully than does the *Meleagant* of *La Charette*. (The home of Maheloas in the Isle de Voirre corresponds to Ynys Wydrin (Glastonbury), the home of Melwas.) Caradog of Llancarfan's tale of *Gwenhwyfar*'s abduction is evidently a version of that told by Chrétien in *Le Chevalier de la Charette*, in which a certain Meleagant (Malory's *Mellyagraunce*) abducts Arthur's queen *Guenièvre*. In spite of the sparse allusions to *Gwenhwyfar* in *Culhwch ac Olwen* (ll. 161, 330, 358), she must be regarded as a character who was introduced into the Arthurian story in Wales under the influence of HRB and *Brut y Brenhinedd*. Owing to the absence of verifiable pre-Geoffrey evidence concerning her, it remains highly doubtful whether *Gwenhwyfar* can properly be regarded as a Celtic 'Sovereignty' figure, as has sometimes been proposed, e.g. G. Goetinck, 'Gwenhwyfar, Guinevere, and Guenièvre', EC XI, pp. 356–7.

Dafydd ap Gwilym was familiar with *Gwenhwyfar*'s name (GDG no. 82.43) and he knew also of a story of her abduction by Melwas: in seeking access to his mistress the poet wishes for 'a window just like this (was that) through which once at Caerleon *Melwas* came, without fear and by excessive love, near the house of Giant Orgfan's daughter' (GDG no. 64.20–6; see n.). Similarly Dafydd ab Edmwnd: 'Alas that a youth's sigh avails me not to invoke the art of *Melwas*, the thief that by magic and enchantment took a girl to the end of the world, to the green wood that deceiver went, to walls (made) from a tree-top's branches—and I would wish tonight to climb as high as he' (GDE 7.21–8; cf. also GDE no. 24.15–16).

Further evidence for a tale about Melwas and *Gwenhwyfar*, dating in its earliest extant form from the sixteenth century, is to be found in the 'Dialogue of Melwas and Gwenhwyfar' (ed. and trans. by Mary Williams, 'An early ritual poem in Welsh', *Speculum* 13 (1938), pp. 38–43, and by E. D. Jones, 'Melwas, Gwenhwyfar a Chai', B VIII, pp. 203–8); see also MA² 130 *Ymddiddan Rhwng Arthur Frenhin ai ail Wraig Gwenhwyfar*: *Hon oedd y ferch a ddygodd Melwas Tywysog o'r Alban.—O'r Ll. Gwyrdd.* (See further P. Sims-Williams, AW 58–61, and K. Jackson, ALMA 18–19.) A prior redaction of this tale was probably the source of the allusions made by the two Welsh poets quoted above, and E. D. Jones believed that the version he printed of the *englynion* had a common origin with the *Llyfr Gwyrdd* text. He subjoined to his edition (B VIII, pp. 203–8) a variant version (A) which was derived from Wynnstay MS. 1 in the hand of the sixteenth-century Thomas Wiliems, Trefriw, and which bears internal evidence of having been copied from an older source, since it has a number of textual variations indicative of previous oral transmission. It therefore seems justifiable to regard this as a redaction of a much older poem, and to set it beside the older *Ymddiddanion* which it resembles in general style: those between Gwalchmai and Drystan, Taliesin and Ugnach, Gwyn ap Nudd and Gwyddno Garanhir. In origin the poem could be as old as *Ymddiddan Arthur â'r Eryr* (*Blodeugerdd* 297–312). (The Devon-Cornwall localization is another feature which the two poems share in common, suggesting that both may ultimately be of a similar provenance.) Each of the *Ymddiddanion* begins in the same way, by a meeting between the two speakers, in which the one is at first unknown to the other, followed by a mutual disclosure of identity. But apart from the fact that the poem bears this general resemblance to the other *Ymddiddanion*, textual corruption combined with our ignorance of the context makes it impossible to deduce much about *Ymddiddan Melwas a Gwenhwyfar*. It appears that a stranger has arrived at a feast at the court of Melwas, where *Gwenhwyfar* is also present; the stranger is taunted for his smallness of stature and his lack of manliness, and he is compared unfavourably with Cei. Finally he states that *Gwenhwyfar* has seen him before at the royal court in Devon. Thus the unknown stranger may represent Arthur, come to fetch back *Gwenhwyfar* from the court of Melwas (though this is not explicitly stated). The identity of Melwas appears to be established in the final *englynion* (B text) which implies recognition between the stranger and *Gwenhwyfar*—but the dialogue breaks off at this point. The claim that Melwas comes from Ynys Wydrin invites comparison with Caradog's *Vita Gildae* (see AW 58–61 and K. Jackson, ALMA 18–19).

In Geoffrey of Monmouth's account Arthur's nephew Modred (Medrawt in *Brut y Brenhinedd*) has taken the place of Melwas as *Gwenhwyfar*'s abductor, and this change appears to have brought about the degrading of *Medrawt* (see n.) in Welsh sources; he had previously been presented as a heroic figure by the *Gogynfeirdd*. In view of the general resemblances which have been noted between the Arthurian and the Fenian cycles (see A. W. van Hamel, 'Aspects of Celtic Mythology', PBA 1934; G. Murphy, *Duanaire Finn* III, 216–17; O. J. Padel, CMCS 27, pp. 1–31), it seems probable that this abduction of Arthur's wife by his own nephew may represent an early tradition: it is closely paralleled by the abduction of Finn's wife Gráinne by his nephew Diarmaid. (It has been suggested that Arthur's other nephew, Gawain (Gwalchmai), may once have played this role; see K. T. Webster, *Ulrich von Zatzikhofen's Lanzelet* 106, n. 168.) Names of yet other abductors of the queen appear in the Continental texts, of which one example is to be found on the Modena archivolt (see ALMA 60–1) and the list of abductors culminates in the portrayal of Lancelot, who in the French *Vulgate Cycle* takes over the part of Modred as the queen's abductor. The Red Knight who insults *Gwenhwyfar* by dashing wine in her face, both in *Peredur* and in the various *Perceval* romances, is presumably yet another of the queen's abductors (cf. triad 54). The story of *Guinevere*'s abduction, perhaps ultimately of early Celtic origin, remains the most prominent feature of the Continental stories about Arthur's queen. Cf. G. Goetinck, 'Gwenhwyfar, Guinevere, and Guenièvre', EC XI, pp. 351–60; the studies by K. T. Webster, *Guinevere: A Study of her Abductions* (Milton, Mass. 1951); and Cross and Nitze, *Lancelot and Guinevere* (Chicago, 1950).

Gwenhwybhar bherch Gogbhran has a small part to play in the folklore of the Welsh Giants, and their association with mountain-sites, which were preserved by tradition in mid-Wales down to the seventeenth century, and were originally collected by Siôn Dafydd Rhys (ed. Hugh Owen, *Cy.* XXVII, pp. 115–52). For texts and full discussions of the Welsh traditions of the Giants see C. Grooms, *The Giants of Wales: Cewri Cymru*. One of these tales (*Cy.* XXVII, pp. 148–9; Grooms, p. 316) describes Arthur's delivery of some brothers of queen *Gwenhwyfar verch Gogfran Gawr* who were imprisoned by giants.

G6enh6yuar[2] verch G6ryt Gwent 56. See n. to *K(y)6ryt Gwent*, and n. to the triad.

G6enh6yuar[3] verch (Gwy)thyr m. Greidia6l (*Gallovyd*) 56 (Pen. 47). See n. to the triad, and to *Gwythyr mab Greidya6l.*

Gwenwynwyn[1] (a G6anar), meibyon Llia6s mab Nwyvre 35. *Gwenwynwyn* was the name borne by a son of Owain Cyfeiliog, after whom was named *Powys Wenwynwyn*, at some date later than 1197 (*Bywgraffiadur*). This son of Owain Cyfeiliog seems to have been the only historical character recorded as having borne this somewhat exotic name (see also *G6enwynwyn mab Naf* below.) It is therefore possible that he was named after the legendary hero named in the triad of whom nothing further is known, but to whom there is the following reference by one of the *Gogynfeirdd*: Cynddelw: *gvychuar gwanar gwenwynwyn* (H 160.12 = CBT III, no. 18.24). The poem is addressed to *Gwenwynwyn* of Powys, but the conjunction of the two names can hardly be fortuitous. (Two later instances of the juxtaposition of these name-elements are however rejected by the editors of CBT VI, no. 16.9n. and no. 18.52n. as representing common nouns or adjectives (see nn.)).

G6enwynwyn[2] mab Naf 14 (WR: *Nav*; 51 *Naw*). Cf. CO ll. 194–5n., *Gwenwynwyn mab Naw mab Seithuet* in a list of the four sons of *Seithuet*, and CO ll. 250–1 (in RM only) *Gwenwynwyn mab Naf*. In RM the name *Naw* / *Naf* thus occurs twice within the same list of characters of Arthur's court; the scribe of WM expresses his uncertainty by omitting it on the second occasion. Cf. Br.Rh.: *a gvenvynnwyn uab naf* (RM 159.22). It seems likely that the *Lliaws* of triad 35 (see n.) may be derived from a corruption of the form *Naw* or *Naf*.

G6ertheuyr 6endigeit (m. Gwrtheyrn Gwrtheneu) 37. 'G. the Blessed.' *Gwerthevyr* < *Guort(h)emir* < * *Vortamorix*; where *vortamo-* is the superlative of the preposition *vor* 'above' and *rix* 'king'. The same preposition is found in *Gw(o)rtheyrn*, so that the name of father and son contain a common element, as is frequent in early genealogies. *Gurthebiriuc* (LL 201, name of a church near Monmouth) is 'the land of *Gwerthefyr* (cf. Morgan-wg); here *Gurthebir* is a variant of *Gu(o)rthemir*. *Gwerthefyr* bears the epithet *Bendigeit* 'blessed' in the *Brut* and in *Bonedd y Saint* as well as in triad 37. For a suggestion as to the significance of this, see n. to triad 37, and n. to *Bran Vendigeit* (*Bendigeituran*) *m. Llyr*. The following account of *Gwerthefyr*'s career is found in HB chs. 43–4 (trans.):

> Vortimer [= *Gwerthefyr*] fought four keen battles against them [i.e. the Saxons]. The first battle was on the River Darenth. The second was at the ford called Episford in their language, *Rhyd yr Afail* in ours, and there fell Horsa, and also Vortigern's son *Kategyrn*. The third battle was fought in the open country by the inscribed stone on the shore of the Gallic sea. The barbarians were beaten, and he was victorious. They fled to their keels and were drowned as they clambered aboard them like women. But after a short time Vortimer died, and before he died he told his war-band to set his tomb by the sea coast, in the harbour [Richborough?, cf. J. T. Koch, CMCS 20, p. 7 and n.] from which they had departed: 'Wherever else they may hold a

> British port and have settled, yet in this land they will not remain for ever.' But they neglected his command, and did not bury him in the place he had ordered. (For a note on a variant of this account see D. N. Dumville, 'Celtic-Latin Texts in Northern England, c. 1150–c. 1250', *Celtica* XII, pp. 28–9.)

The four battles here referred to correspond with the four victories which Hengist is said to have won over the Britons of the south-east in the years between 455 and 473, according to the *Anglo-Saxon Chronicle* (ed. and trans. Whitelock *et al.*, p. 10; see also H. M. Chadwick, *Origin of the English Nation*, p. 39).

In HRB VI, 12, the son of *Vortigernus* is *Vortimerus* (*Gwerthefyr*). After Vortigern's marriage with Rowen (= *Ronnwen baganes*, n.) it is said (HB ch. 48):

> He had previously three sons whose names are *Vortimer* (= *Gwerthefyr*) who fought against the barbarians, as I have said above, the second *Katigernus*, and the third *Paschent.*

Geoffrey's account of Vortimer (HRB VI, 12–15) is based on that of HB, and like HB he gives the name of three only of the four battles. He adds, however, that the Britons chose Vortimer to be king on account of his father's predilection for the Saxons; that after his four victories the Saxons sent Vortigern to his son to plead that they should have leave to return to Germany, and finally, it tells that Rowen accomplished Vortimer's death by poisoning. With respect to his burial Geoffrey tells us:

> He commanded that a brazen pyramid should be wrought for him, and that it be set in the haven wherein the Saxons were accustomed to land, and that after his death his body should be buried on the top of it, so that when the barbarians should behold his image on it they should sail back and return to Germany. He said that not one of them would dare to come near, if they were to see even his image . . . But after his death the Britons did otherwise, for they buried his body in the city of Trinovantum [= *Llundein*, BD 97–8].

The account of *Gwerthefyr*'s burial given in triad 37 differs from that of HB in affirming that his bones were actually buried according to his command in the chief ports, and there is no mention of the statue to which Geoffrey alludes. The triad gives what is evidently the more primitive version of the story. It would seem to go back to an early traditional version, also known to the redactor of HB. It is, however, to be noted that *Gwerthefyr* does not figure elsewhere in the triads or *chwedlau*, and that there are no references to him by the *Gogynfeirdd.* Later bardic tradition follows the chronicles in associating his statue with the chief *port* of entry to Britain (not the *ports*) but differs from them in implying that the statue was actually erected at Dover. Dafydd Nanmor wishes for an image of Edmund Tudur (like that of Vortimer at Dover) to be placed on the shore at Milford Haven as a terror to his enemies:

Llyna y modd i lluniwyd
Wrth Ddofyr lun Gwrthefyr lwyd.
(DN no. XV.25–6)

Lewys Morgannwg expresses a similar wish in a *marwnad* to Syr Rhys ap Tomas:

yr holl ynys fu'n lluniaw
wrth Ddofr, drych Gwrthefur draw.
(Gwyneddon 3, p. 231, ll. 5–6.)

Guto'r Glyn says of a patron *Gŵr oedd ef fal Gwrthefyr* (GGl no. LXXXIII.37); another reference is by Dafydd Llwyd: *Gwerthefyr gynt, gwarth vu'r gwaith* (Pen. 67, xxxiv, 33). Lewys Môn refers to the story that Gwerthefyr's wishes were not followed as to his burial:

Gwrthefyr, fab gwyrthfawr fu,
ar drent a roed ar untu.
(GLM no. LXXVI.35–6.)

'Gwerthefyr, he was a son of great virtue: wrongfully he was put (= buried) aside.' (See n. on *G6rtheyrn G6rtheneu.*)

G(w)erthmul Wledic 1, 44, **Gyrthm6l** 63.

Br. Rh.: *gyrthmvl wledic* (RM 160.4).

LlDC no. 18.118–20: *Bet unpen o pridein yn lleutir guynnassed / yn yd a lliw yn llychur / ig kelli uriauael bet gyrthmul* 'The grave of a chieftain of Britain' (*or* 'of the North', taking *Prydein* here for *Pryden*, as attested by the rhyme, and as advocated by T. Jones, PBA LII, p. 124, st. 39) 'in the open country of *Gwynassed*, where the *Lliw* flows into the *Llychwr*, at *Kelli Friafael* (is) the grave of *Gyrthmul*'. Robert Vaughan's note suggests he may have had a copy of the *Beddau* stanzas which read *Pryden* (Scotland) in place of LlDC's *Prydein*. VN[2]: 'Celli Friafael, unless it be somewhere in Scotland . . . the hundred of Estumanner in Merionethshire, which is called *Maes Briafael. Maes* or field doth sometimes denote the place where a battle was fought.' J. Loth suggests that the reference is to St Briavel's Castle, in the forest of Dean (*Mab.* II, p. 245n.). But the reference in the *Beddau* is specific enough: Celli Friafael is to be looked for near Pontlliw in Carmarthenshire. For the name cf. CLlH no. XI.76a: *Bei gwreic Gyrthmwl bydei gwan hediw* ('If G. were a woman, she would be weak today') and note, p. 226, where Ifor Williams points out that *Gyrthmwl* here evidently stands for the name of a place, whose form has been influenced by the fame of the character referred to in these triads. One would expect the *-m-* to be lenited in Ml.W. and then to disappear, as seems to have occurred in the place-names *Llanwrthwl*, Brecknock (LBS III, 214) and *Maes Llanwrthwl*, Carmarthenshire. Thus the termination of *G(v)erthmvl* in TYP represents an early spelling of **G(w)erthfwl.*

On the title *Gwledic*, see n. to *Maxen Wledic*.

G6ga6n[1] Gledyfrud 24, 40, 60 (= *G6gon g.* W).

Br.Rh.: *A gvgavn gledyfrud* (RM 159.5).

LlDC no. 18.134–5: *Bet y march. bet y guythur / bet y gugaun cletyfrut. Gwgawn Gleddyfrudd* was a local ruler in Ceredigion, to be identified with (*G*)*uocaun map Mouric* (EWGT 12 (26) = Harl. Gen. 26 which traces the descent of *Guocaun map Mouric* back to *Cunedda*). He was the last king of Ceredigion, whose sister Angharad married Rhodri Mawr, and who met his death by drowning (*Ann. Cam.* 871: *Guocaun mersus est, rex Ceretіciaun* (HW 257, 325)).

The following references connect *Gwgawn Gleddyfrudd* with Ceredigion: *Progenies Keredic, regis de Keredigan* (EWGT 20 (6), *circa* 1200) gives *Gugan Cledybrudh, filius Lauch, filii Lucho, filii Kedich, filii Keredic*; cf. also Jes. 20 (EWGT 49 (48) = 'Plant Ceredig': *Gwgawn m. Llawr m. Kedic m. Keredic m. Kuneda wledic*).

Dafydd ap Gwilym refers to *Gwlad Wgan, fawr union faich / Gleddyfrudd, gloyw ei ddeufraich* (GDG no. 46.67–8). Here *Gwlad Wgan* represents Ceredigion, Dafydd's home near Aberystwyth in the kingdom of Ceredigion; see further GDG no. 34.30n., where Dafydd compares Morfudd to *merch Wgon farchoges*; in *Taith i Garu* (GDG no. 83.30) he refers to *Castell Gwgawn*, a place which is mentioned in the *Calendar of Charter Rolls* as on the border of the two parishes of Llanbadarn Fawr and Llanfihangel Genau'r Glyn (GDG[2] introduction xvii). Lloyd-Jones also refers to a *Castell Gwgawn* near Aberaeron (G 676; see further GDG no. 83.31 and GLlG no. 5.46n.). Obviously, a man who died in 871 could not have been present at the battle of Chester in 616, or a contemporary with the two seventh-century men who are named in triad 60 with Gwgawn as having been present at the battle; but this does not necessarily preclude the identification (see n. to triad 60).

On the name *Gwgon, Gwgan* see B II, p. 6. It contains the same root as the noun *coned* 'pride', which is found also in *gogawn, gwogawn gogonedd*; and in the verb and adjective *digoni, dichawn, digawn*, etc. *Cadwgawn* (= *proelio potens*, D) is a compound of the same name. Other instances of this name occur CA ll. 358, 1002, and in *henn tref gucaun* LL 268.25; *Gucauno episcopo* LL 240.25; 243.14, etc.; *Gwgawn Dyuet* AL I, 342. It is found also in place-names; for references see G 675–6; J. Lloyd-Jones, *Enwau Lleoedd Sir Gaernarfon*, p. 36.

Gwga6n[2] Gwron m. Peredur m. Elifer Gosgor(d)ua6r 8, 19 (W). *Gwron* 'hero'. These triads attribute quite opposite characteristics to *Gwgawn*, but in no. 19 the name is a substitution for *Gueir Gwrhytvavr*. *Bonedd y Saint* (EWGT 65 (74)) names St Kedwyn as son of *Gwgon Gwron ap Predur ap Eliver gosgorddvawr* (*a Madrvn verch Gwrtheyrn Gwrthenev oedd i vam*). For a variant see n. to *Modron verch Auallach.*

G6ia6n ap Kyndr6yn 60. *Plant Kyndrwyn* in *Bonedd yr Arwyr* (B XVIII,

p. 233; EWGT 85(i)) includes *Gwiawn* as the third of the twenty-one sons of *Cyndrwyn* (see also CLlH xxxi). As Ifor Williams pointed out (CLlH xxxvi) these late genealogies are as likely to be based upon the poems as vice versa, and so the inclusion of *Gwion* in this list may have no authority independent of CLlH no. XI.32: *Stauell Gyndylan ys tywyll heno / o blant Kyndrwyn(yn) / Kynon a Gwiawn a Gwyn*. Other instances of the name *Gwiawn* are found in CA ll. 358, 1002; *Englynion y Clyweit* (*Blodeugerdd* 335, n. to 46a); and see EWSP 126.

G6ibei Drahavc 23 (W). 'G. the Arrogant.' *Bonedd y Saint* (EWGT 64 (71)): *Eda Glynuawr ap Gwybei Drahavc ap Mwg Mawr Drefydd ap Offa Kyllelluawr Vrenin Lloegyr, y gwr a ymladdodd yn erbyn Arthur y Ngwaith Vaddon*. The redactor of this passage appears to have listed together all the names he could find in Welsh sources for both historical and legendary Saxon opponents of the Britons; see nn. to *Eda Glinvawr, Edelflet Fleissawc*, and for *Mw(n)g Mawr Drefydd* see CLlH no. VII.20 and EWSP 235; for *Osla Gyllelluawr* see CO ll. 1193–6 and Br. Rh. 46n. (= RM 150.24). The implication is that *Gwibei Drahawc* was also a Saxon foe. With the name cf. (*G*)*wiber* (RBP col. 1165.24) and *gviber* (1339.43).

G6idawl 63. The name of the father of *Gwrtheyrn* (see n.), according to *Bonedd y Saint* (EWGT 46 (15)): *Gwrtheyrn Gwrtheneu m. Gwidawl m. Gwrdoleu m. Gloyw Gwalltir. Y gwr hwnnw a wnaeth ar ymyl Hafren tref, ac oe enw ef y gelwir yn Gaer Loew* (= Gloucester).

G6iner 60. See n. to *G6aetcym Herwuden*.

Gvrgi[1] **Garwl6yt** 32 (= 10 W) The name GURCI (lit. 'Man-Hound) is found on an inscription of the seventh to ninth century in the church at Llangors, Brycheiniog (ECMW no. 59). For the epithet *Garwlwyt* 'Rough Grey' see n. to *Bedwyr m. Bedra6c*. *Gwrgi Garwlwyt* invites comparison with Cú Chulainn's opponent *German Garbglass* ('rauh grau', Windisch, LL *Táin*, l. 4109). In both cases the allusion appears to be to a mythical antagonist: Windisch in his note (p. 584) compares the term *garb glasruad*, which occurs elsewhere in the *Táin* as an epithet for wolves. One may therefore suggest that the *garwluid* of LlDC no. 31.48 signifies a wolf, and that *Gwrgi Garwlwyt* and his Irish counterpart may have been werewolves. Sims-Williams compares the *cinbin* 'dog-heads' in l. 44 of LlDC no. 31 (AW 42). It is possible that a further reference to this figure of Welsh tradition is to be found in the giant *Urgan le Velu* of Thomas's *Tristan* poem (ed. Bédier I, pp. 219–20), cf. Harl. Gen. 18: *Guurgint barmtruch* ('thick beard'). According to the *Tristan* poem this giant lived somewhere in Dyfed and exacted a tribute of livestock from the inhabitants, but in the English poem *Sir Tristrem*, this was a human tribute (ibid., p. 227). Cf. also *Englynion y Clyweit*: *A glyweisti a gant Gwrgi* etc. (*Blodeugerdd* 335, n. to 51a).

G6rgi² a Pheredur (meibion Elif(f)er Gosgor(d)uawr) 30, 44, 46, 70. See *Peredur²* and EWSP 110–14 on *Gwrgi* and *Peredur*.

G6rtheyrn G6rthenau 37 (R), 51. *Gwrtheyrn* lit. 'overlord' came to be used as a personal name. 'G. the Thin' = *Vortigern*, the British ruler who is said to have invited the Saxons into Britain under their leaders Hengist and Horsa in the mid-fifth century (HB chs. 31–49; Bede, *Hist. Ecc.* I, 15; *Anglo-Saxon Chronicle ann.* 455). *Gwrtheyrn* < Celt. *ver-* (O.W. *gwor-*) + *tigernos* = 'Great Prince, Overlord'. For the name and its meaning see K. Jackson, CMCS 3, pp. 35–40. In the mid-eighth century the historian Bede (*Hist. Ecc.* AD 731, I, 14) gives this name in its earliest latinized form as *Uurtigernus*, and in *Hist. Ecc.* as *Vertigern*(*us*). The *Anglo-Saxon Chronicle* has *Wyrtgeorn* (Plummer, *Two Saxon Chronicles Parallel* I, pp. 12–13). Geoffrey of Monmouth gives *Uortegirnus*, *Wortegirnus* and variants (HRB VI, ch. 5 ff.), rendered in BD 87 as *Gortheyrn Gortheneu* (= RBB 127.4: *Gwrtheyrn Gwrtheneu*). (With the absence of initial lenition in the epithet cf. introduction p. xc, n. 150 above.) The name VOR(R)TIGURN is found on two Ogham inscriptions in Ireland (CIIC I, nos. 97, 297), and already in the seventh century the cognate Ir. name *Foirtgirn* appears in Adamnan's Life of *St Columba* (ed. Anderson, pp. 134, 162). In the Breton *Cartulaire de Quimperlé* there is a Life of *St Gurthiern* (text and discussion by B. Tanguy, EC XXVI, pp. 167–84). For the possible connection between these variant forms of the name and the traditions of the British king *Vortigern* see Chadwick, SEBH 27, 34–6.

The story of the invitation given by the British ruler *Gwrtheyrn* to the Saxons to enter Britain in order to enlist their help against his northern enemies, the Picts, appears first in Gildas's *De Excidio Britanniae* (ed. and trans. Winterbottom as 'The Ruin of Britain', chs. 23–6). Gildas wrote in the mid-sixth century, and therefore within a century of the date of the arrival of the Saxons in Britain. Without naming him personally, Gildas's *superbus tyrannus* has generally been recognized as constituting the Latin equivalent of *Vortigernus*. Gildas states that the Saxons arrived in three *cyulae* or longships, and that they were permitted to settle 'in the eastern parts of the island'. Here they were soon joined by further reinforcements from the continent. After the Saxons had served Vortigern for an unspecified length of time, a dispute arose between them and the Britons concerning the rations which were due to them, as the result of which the Saxons turned with the utmost ferocity upon their hosts, and ravaged the island from sea to sea. This account is amplified by Bede (*Hist. Ecc.* I, 16). Both Bede and the writer of HB made use of the text of Gildas, but both appear to have had their own additional sources of information. Both supply to Gildas's account the proper names *Uurtigernus* / *Guorthigirnus*, *Hengist*, *Hors*(*a*). HB ch. 31 gives a different reason for the arrival of Hengist and Hors(a), stating that the two were exiles and landless men (cf. AP l. 29: *nys dioes dayar*; see further AP ll. 43–4, 53, 138).

The account given in HB chs. 31–49 of the career of *Vortigern* is based in part upon popular traditions, in part (ch. 47) upon a Life of *St Germanus*, in which *Vortigern* figured in the role of the typical *rex tyrannus* of the Lives of the Saints. (Further evidence for an early traditional connection between St Germanus and *Vortigern* appears on the Valle Crucis Pillar, for which see below.) HB's chief additions to the story from secular sources are: (i) *Guorthigirn*'s infatuation for the (unnamed) daughter of Hengist, in exchange for whom he gives her father the kingdom of Kent; (ii) the story of *Guorthigirn*'s tower in Eryri (= Dinas Emrys), the fighting dragons, and the miraculous child Ambrosius (= *Emrys Wledig*, see n.); (iii) the story of *Guorthemir* (*Gwertheuyr Vendigeit*, see n.); (iv) the Treachery of the Long Knives (derived from *Widukind*, see Chadwick, *Origin of the English Nation* (1924), pp. 39–40); (v) variant traditions of the death of *Guorthigirn*, including the burning of his fortress by fire from Heaven (at *Craig Gwrtheyrn* on the Teifi). A variant tradition localized *Gwrtheyrn*'s end in *Nant Gwrtheyrn* in Llŷn (see Melville Richards, 'Nennius's Regio Guunnesi', *Trans. Caernarfonshire Historical Soc.* (1963), pp. 21–7); (vi) the genealogy of Fernmail, the ruler of Buellt and *Gwrtheyrnion* (a contemporary of 'Nennius'?), which is traced back to Pascent son of *Guorthigirn*, as Ifor Williams has shown (THSC 1946–7); the immediate source for this story must lie in indigenous tradition, and behind the Latin text can be discerned several of the characteristic devices of the native *cyfarwydd*. At the same time the story contains several elements which can only be explained as deriving from an English source, including Hengist's genealogy (ch. 31) and the incident of the 'Treachery of the Long Knives'. Geoffrey of Monmouth elaborates HB's account to a considerable extent, by introducing details which appear to be mainly fictitious, though in a few instances it seems possible that he is drawing upon local traditions which were accessible to him in Monmouthshire (see J. E. Lloyd, 'Geoffery of Monmouth', EHR 57 (1942), pp. 460–1). Geoffrey styles *Vortigern* as *consul Gewisseorum* (HRB VI, 6), and represents him as seizing the throne of Britain after murdering Constans, the legitimate heir. He gives the name of Rowen or Renwein (= *Ronnwen*, see n.) to Hengist's daughter (HRB VI, 12). He states that Ambrosius killed *Vortigern* by burning him in his castle of Genoreu (Gannerew) in Hergin (Ergyng) (HRB VIII, 2). *Gwrtheyrn*'s genealogy as given in ch. 49 appears also in *Jes. Gen.* XV (EWGT 46 (15)) as: *Gvrtheyrn Gvrtheneu m. Gwidaul m. Gvdoleu m. Glyov gvalltir y gvr a wnaeth ar ymyl hafren tref. ac oe env ef y gelwir yn gaer loev* (i.e. Gloucester). An entirely different descent of *Gorthegyrnn* (from *Beli Mawr*) is found in the Life of *St Beuno* (VSB 22; EWGT 30.)

Three disparaging allusions to *Gwrtheyrn* in early poetry reflect a portrayal of the arch-traitor who allowed the Saxons to win rule in Britain, which is similar to that expressed in HB. These are the only early allusions to *Gwrtheyrn* that are to be found in Welsh poetry (not surprisingly, no single mention of *Gwrtheyrn* is made by the *Gogynfeirdd*). The three allusions reflect a parallel attitude to *Gwrtheyrn* to that which is found in HB (and presumably they derive from the pervasive influence held in Wales by HB over the centuries, as a unique source for early events in Britain). These are:

BT 13.23 = AP l. 27: *Pell bwynt kychmyn y Wrtheyrn Gwyned* (emend to *kychmyn Gwrtheyrn*: see Ifor Williams's note on the line) 'Far be the scavengers of Gwrtheyrn Gwynedd'.

idem., l. 137: *yr amser Gwrtheyrn genhyn y sathrant* 'Since the time of Gwrtheyrn they have oppressed us'. See D. N. Dumville, 'Brittany and Armes Prydein Vawr', EC XX–I (1983), pp. 145ff.

LlDC no. 18.123: *E bet yn ystyuacheu* (?) / *y mae paup yn y amheu* / *bet gurtheyrn gurtheneu* 'The grave in Ystyvacheu which everybody doubts, i.e. "looks askance", the grave of Gwrtheyrn Gwrtheneu' (cf. HB ch. 48).

The ninth-century Pillar of Eliseg at Valle Crucis Abbey in Denbighshire (reproduced with translation in EWGT 1–3; see also CIIC vol. 2, pp. 145–9; ECMW no. 182) gives the descent of the rulers of Powys from *Cyngen ap Cadell,* grandson of Brochmail, back to *Britu* son of *Guorthigirn* 'whom Germanus blessed, and whom *Severa* bore to him the daughter of *Maximus* the king who slew the king of the Romans'. A similar genealogy is given for the Powys rulers in Harl. Gen. no. 27, but without the descent from Maximus which is asserted for Cyngen on the Pillar. The association of *Vortigern* with St Germanus, though historically unreliable, is proved to be of early date both by HB and also by the Pillar, since both testify to its existence in the ninth century. It has been suggested that St Germanus, the renowned opponent of Pelagianism, has been confused in place-names with a local saint Garmon, who is commemorated both in Llanarmon-yn-Iâl and elsewhere in the counties of Denbigh and Caernarfon. According to HB ch. 49 the rulers of *Gwrtheyrnion* (Radnorshire) claimed descent from Pascent, another son of Gwrtheyrn, and yet a third branch of *Vortigern*'s family is here said to have founded the city of Gloucester (Caer Gloiu).

In Harl. Gens. 22 and 23 the Powys dynasty is traced not to *Gwrtheyrn* but to *Cattegirn map Catel Durnluc*, a character who appears as a servant of the tyrant Benlli (Benlli Gawr?) in that part of HB (chs. 34–5) which emanates from a lost *Vita Sancti Germani.* Here Cadell Deyrnllug assists the saint who promises him that he shall himself become king, and that his heirs shall rule Powys. This is evidently a rival account of the descent of the Powys dynasty to that which is found on the Pillar, though HB's story is consistent with Harl. Gens. 22 and 23. To add to the confusion Cattegirn (Catteyrn) was also the name of one of *Vortigern*'s sons (HB chs. 44, 48), and according to Harl. Gen. 23 this Cattegirn had a son Brittu, which recalls the name which appears on the Pillar. It therefore appears that the Harl. Gens. demonstrate a deliberate attempt to suppress a tradition that the rulers of Powys were descended from *Vortigern.* This suppression is consistent with the close relation which clearly exists between the Harl. Gens. and HB, in which *Vortigern* is portrayed in so unfavourable a light. Yet the descent of the Powys ruling dynasty from

Vortigern gains strong support from the evidence of the Pillar, confirmed by the genealogies (*Jes. Gens.* XIV, XVI, and XVIII), which present *Gwrtheyrn* as the founder of the dynasties of both Powys and Morgannwg. However, both *Jes. Gen.* XVIII and the Life of *St Beuno* (EWGT 30 (24), VSB 22) name Cadell Deyrnllug as *Vortigern*'s grandson through his son Cattegyrn, so that here an attempt has evidently been made to combine both traditions. In two separate incidents in HB we are told that St Germanus blessed both Cadell Deyrnllwg (ch. 35) and also Faustus (*Vortigern*'s son by his incestuous union with his daughter, ch. 48); perhaps one or other of these sons can be identified with the Brittu whose name appears on the Pillar.

There can be little doubt that *Vortigern* was one of the most important political figures in fifth-century Britain: although the HB shows clearly that already in the ninth century he had become a legendary figure, and a focus for traditional tales. His family connections appear to have been primarily with east-central Wales, where his name was preserved in that of the cantref of *Gwrtheyrnion* (HB's *Guorthigirnion*) between the Wye and the Ieithon, near the south-west border of Powys (HW I, 254). According to HB ch. 49 it was here that *Vortigern*'s descendant Fernmail was ruling at the time of writing this work, and according to HRB and the *Bruts* it was here in his fortress of *Gwrtheyrnion* that *Vortigern* met his end (see n. to triad 51, l. 14). Nevertheless, this local connection should not allow us to lose sight of the fact that in Gildas, our earliest authority, *Vortigern* is portrayed as a ruler who also held authority in eastern Britain. In HB's account, his authority stood above that of the local ruler of Kent, whose lands he bestowed on the Saxons, but apparently it was equally valid in Wales itself. There was also a tradition that *Vortigern*'s family originated from Gloucester (cf. PKM 27 and 162n.). Even further south we find the name of *Wirtgernesburg* given by William of Malmesbury (*De Rebus Gest.* I, 19) to Bradford-on-Avon. Gildas's own words *omnes consiliarii una cum superbo tyranno caecantur* seem to suggest that *Vortigern* acted as the chairman of a Council. In any case, his action in establishing the Saxons in Kent may have been modelled on the Roman custom of enlisting *foederati* to protect their borders. From the Roman point of view his conduct would have been considered neither unusual nor dishonourable. No doubt he acted in such a way as seemed to him to be in the best interest of his country, and it was not his fault that subsequent events caused him to be regarded, above all in Wales, as an arch-traitor.

For more recent discussions and reappraisals of *Vortigern* see D. N. Dumville, *History*, 62, pp. 173–97; D. P. Kirby 'Vortigern', B XXIII; idem., B XXVII, pp. 103–5. Kirby proposes that in ninth-century Powys the traditions concerning *Vortigern* were in process of being 'collected and preserved for propaganda purposes by the family of Merfyn Frych' who were concerned to put a derogatory interpretation upon the origins of the old Powys dynasty, which had claimed descent from Vortigern. Earlier discussions are by H. M.

and N. K. Chadwick, SEBH ch. 2; Ralegh Radford, 'Vortigern', *Antiquity* XXXII, pp. 19–24; Ifor Williams, 'Hen Chwedlau', THSC 1946–7, pp. 28–58; K. H. Jackson, CMCS 3, pp. 35–40; Melville Richards, 'Nennius's Regio Guunnesi', *Trans. Caernarfonshire Historical Soc.* (1963), pp. 21–7.

Gwryat m. G6ryan 68. The name *Gwriad* (< *Viriatus*) is not uncommon, but it is not possible to identify with complete certainty the *Gwryat* of the triad with any of the early bearers of the name. The name GURIAT is found on the eighth- or ninth-century CRUX GURIAT in the Isle of Man (J. Rhŷs, ZCP I, pp. 48–53), and the name on the cross has been tentatively identified with *Guriad mab Elidyr*, listed in *Jes. Gens.* XVII and XIX (EWGT 46, see Bartrum's n. on p. 151, given also in B XIX, p. 218). Elidyr was the father of Merfyn Frych (825–44), the founder of the second Gwynedd dynasty, and grandfather of Rhodri Mawr. He was claimed as a descendant of Llywarch Hen (HW 323–4; see also CLlH xxviii, and the genealogy in HGVK 1.22 and n.). The identification of this *Gwriad* with the *Gwriad* of the cross gains some support from the reference in *Cyvoesi Myrddin a Gwenddydd* to *Meruin vrych o dir manaw* (RBP 578.40; see P. Sims-Williams, WHR 17, p. 14). But since the patronymic of the *Gwryat* referred to in the triad is not Elidyr (as in the *Jes. Gens.*) but an unknown *Gwrian*, there can be no certainty as to the identification, unless we suppose that *vab G6ryan* is a substitution. A closely similar alliterating name occurs in close juxtaposition with that of *Gwriad* in two instances in early poems, and the following lines may have influenced the form of the patronymic in the triad:

CA l. 348: *a gwryen. a gwynn. a gwryat.*
LlDC no. 18.8: *gwen a gurien a guriad.*

The above line from the *Beddau* stanzas may have been influenced by the line in the *Gododdin*, and the CA reference confirms that the name *Gwriad* was known in north Britain, and according to triad 68 it is in *Y Gogledd* that we should look for the *Gwriad* alluded to. But it remains doubtful whether the *Gwriad* of the cross and the *Gwriad* of the triad can be equated with the *Gwriad fab Elidir* of the genealogies. The whole question has been very fully discussed by Bedwyr L. Jones, 'Gwriad's Heritage: Links between Wales and the Isle of Man in the Early Middle Ages', THSC 1990, pp. 29–44, at pp. 34–7. Further instances of the name *Gwriad* are listed in G 710. There is a *Nant Guriad* in Brycheiniog (EANC 175).

Gwryon 74 = *Vchei mab G.*

G6ryt Gwent 56, see **K(y)6ryt Gvent**.

Gwyar 4, 75, 91, 97. See n. to *Gwalchmei m. Gwyar*, and n. to triad 97.

Gvydar ap Run ap Beli 13 (WR). *Ann. Cam.* 630's tantalizing reference, *Guidgar venit et non redit*, fails to throw any light upon *Gwydar*'s inclusion in the triad (though the reference is not necessarily to the same person). The name is not uncommon; cf. LL 157.19: *Guoidgar*, *Gwydyr Dr6m* below, and n. to *Run mab Beli*. A diminutive of *Gwydar* is perhaps found in the river-name *Gwydderig* (EANC 190). In WR's version of triad 13, *Gvydar ap Run* has taken the place of *Carada6c m. Bran*.

G6ydno (Garanhir) 61. 'G. Long Shank.' *Ruavn Peuyr ap Gvydno* (*ap gwyddno peryf* 51); *porth Wytno yn y gogled* App. I, no. 9; App. II, no. 10 gives the descent of *Elffin m. Gvydno* from Dyfnwal Hen (for Elffin see also BT 19.23 etc., Br. Rh. 8.18 = RM 150.19); and for Elffin's role in the *Ystorya Taliesin* see text from oldest version in the sixteenth-century *Chronicle* of Elis Gruffydd (P. K. Ford, 'A Fragment of the Hanes Taliesin by Llywelyn Siôn', EC XIV (1974–5), pp. 452–9). See further Ifor Williams, *Chwedl Taliesin* (1957); ibid. LEWP 61–3. App. III, no. 2 *mwys Gwyddno Garanhir* (see n.). Harl. Gen. V (EWGT 10 (5)) gives a confused genealogy which includes the names of Elfin and Guipno (= Guidno) and traces the family to Dyfnwal Hen (as in App. II, no. 10). In 'Pedigrees of the Welsh Tribal Patriarchs', *Nat. Lib. of Wales Journal* XIII, P. C. Bartrum on p. 95 and pp. 99–102 has listed a number of families who by the fifteenth century traced their descent to *Gwyddno Garanhir*; two of these claim descent through *Gwyddno*'s better-known son *Elfin ap Gwyddno*, and Elffin (but not his father) is alluded to several times by the *Gogynfeirdd* (CBT V, no. 25.3n.; VI, no. 15.5n., 25.10n.). Another son of *Gwyddno* is perhaps alluded to in CA l. 326; *mur greit oed moleit ef mab gwydneu* (alluding to *Isaac . . . o barth deheu*). *Gwyddneu*'s cognate Breton name *Goeznovius*, *Goueznou*, is found in the ninth-century Life of *St Paul Aurelian* (*Chr. Br.* 101).

For an edition and study of the *Ymddiddan* between *Gwyn ap Nudd* and *Gwyddno Garanhir* (LlDC no. 34), see B. F. Roberts (*Ast. H.* 311–18) and the discussion by J. Rowland (EWSP 244–5). The poem on Seithennin and the submersion of Maes Guitneu or Cantre'r Gwaelod (LlDC no. 39) is translated in EWSP 508–9 (earlier version and discussion by J. Rhŷs, CF I, 383–4). For the analogous Breton folk-tradition of the submersion of the city of Is (Ker Is) off the west coast of Brittany, associated with the legend of the Breton *St Gwennolé*, and dating perhaps from the fifteenth century, see HLCB I, 169; C. Guyot, *La Légende de la ville d'Is* (Paris, 1926), trans. and discussion by D. Kavanagh and Maria Tymoczko, *The Legend of the City of Is* (1979).

The references cited in App. I and II imply that *Gwyddno Garanhir* was one of *Gwŷr y Gogledd*, the 'Men of the North', and that the territory over which he ruled is to be looked for somewhere north of the Border. A kingdom on the northern shore of the Solway estuary was suggested by Chadwick (*Early Scotland*, p. 145) and this seems possible, though it rests on little evidence other than the questionable belief that the tale of the submersion of Cantre'r Gwaelod was already associated with *Gwyddno*'s name before the story became known in Wales. *Gwyddno*'s territory (unspecified) is alluded to in the poem *Kychwedl am dodyw* (BT 38.8–19), *Pan gyrchassam ni trwydet artir gwydno*.

The earliest recorded traditions of lands submerged by the sea in Cardigan Bay are found in *Mabinogi Branwen* (PKM 39), and in *Bonedd y Saint*, of which the earliest version is found in Pen. 16 (see pp. xvi–xviii above, a text which was first redacted in the twelfth century (VSB xvii, 320–3; EWGT 52)). Five otherwise unknown and unrecorded saints are here described (VSB 322 (40); EWGT 60 (40)) as being sons of *Seithennin vrenhin o Vaes Gwydno a oresgynnwys mor eu tir* 'sons of king *Seithennin* of *maes Gwydno* whose land the sea conquered'—repeating the identical phrase for the inundation as that employed in *Mabinogi Branwen*, and again in *Bonedd y Saint* (EWGT 60–1 (40, 42)) where three sons of Helyg ap Glannauc of Tyno Helyg (in the Conway estuary) are described as *gwyr hefyd a oresgynnwys mor eu tir* 'men also whose lands the sea conquered'. In the fifteenth century the poet Guto'r Glyn compares his grief after the death of the abbot of Ystrad Fflur to *Cwynfan Gwyddno Garanhir / Y troes Duw'r mor tros ei dir* (GGl no. XI.63–4) 'The lament of G. Garanhir / God turned the sea over his land'.

In Iolo Morganwg's Third Series of Triads (MA^2 404, no. 37) Seithennin 'king of Dyfed' is described as one of the *Tri Charnfeddwon of Britain*; in Iolo's own translation 'Detestable Drunkards of the Island of Britain' (THSC 1968, pp. 316–17; note, ibid., pp. 336–7)—because he allowed the sea to inundate his land.

A full account of the various inundation stories around the Welsh coast, and a study of their geological basis, was made by F. J. North, *Sunken Cities*, and see also the same writer's *The Legend of Llys Helig* (Llandudno 1940). Earlier discussions are by J. Rhŷs, CF ch. 12, and by R. Bromwich, 'Cantref y Gwaelod and Ker Is', in C. Fox and B. Dickins (eds), *The Early Cultures of North-West Europe: H. M. Chadwick Memorial Volume* (Cambridge, 1950), pp. 217–40. For further details, see WCD 346–8.

It was believed by F. J. North that the Cantre'r Gwaelod traditions antedate the traditions of Llys Helyg, and some traces of the former have survived in Gwynedd. There is a *cored Wyddno* 'G.'s weir' at the mouth of the River Conwy, as well as one in Ceredigion, and a stream called *Gwenwyn meirch Gwyddno* flows into the Menai near Y Felinheli (Chw. T. 5). There seems to be no certain evidence by which to know whether Cardigan Bay or the Conwy estuary was originally denoted as *maes guitneu* in the poem *Boddi Maes Gwyddneu*, LlDC no. 39.

Gwydyon vab Don 28 (W), 67. See nn. to *Math vab Mathonwy*, *Lleu Llaw Gyffes*, *Don*. There are a number of allusions to *Gwydion* in poems belonging to *Hanes Taliesin* (see n. to *Taliesin*), and, in the main, these characterize *Gwydion* in a manner similar to that in *Mabinogi Math*. Here *Gwydion* is a powerful magician, who can make horses and hounds out of toadstools, shoes out of seaweed (cf. triad 67n.), a woman out of flowers, and who can produce the illusion of a sea filled with hostile vessels. The essentials of *Gwydion*'s story are referred to in the poem *Kadeir Kerritwen* (BT 36.3–7):

> Gvydyon ap Don dygynuertheu (= oe dygyn verthur?)
> A hudvys gvreic o vlodeu
> A dyduc moch o deheu
> Kan bu idaw disgoreu (= dysc oreu?)
> Drut ymyt a gwryt pletheu
> A rithwys gorwydawt
> Y ar plagawt lys
> Ac enwerys kyfrwyeu.

'G. son of Don, out of his magic powers (?), who made by enchantment a woman from flowers, and who brought swine from the south. Since he had the best learning, he, the brave one of the world, of the interweaving of men (in battle?), who made horses in order to please the court (?), and saddles with gold fittings (?).' (For *Y ar plagawt lys* see Ifor Williams, B XVII, p. 98).

Elsewhere *Gwydion* and Lleu are referred to as magicians: *Neu leu a gwydyon a uuant geluydyon. neu a wdant lyfyryon* (RBP col. 1054.16–17). *Gwydion* is credited with the creation by magic of the poet Taliesin himself: *Am svynvys i wytyon mavnut* (= *mavr ut*?) *o brython* (BT 26.1; see Chw. T. 200) 'Gwydion created me, the great lord of the Britons'. Taken together with the various allusions to the part played by *Gwydion* at *Cad Goddeu* ('The Battles of the Trees', BT 24–7; see n. to triad 84 and references cited) these lines indicate the existence of a much fuller tradition about *Gwydion* as a magician than has survived:

> Bum yg kat godeu gan lleu a gvydyon
> Wy a rithwys gvyd eluyd ac elestron
> (BT 33.23–4)

'I was at Kat Goddeu with Lleu and Gwydion; they made by enchantment earth, trees, and irises (?).'

So also BT 24.1–3:

> Bum yg kaer nefenhir yt gryssynt wellt a gvyd
> kenynt gerdoryon kryssynt katuaon
> datvyrein y vrython [= ei vrithron? cf. Chw. T. 21–2] a oreu gvytyon.

'I was at Caer Nefenhir (when) the grasses and trees marched off. Minstrels sang, warriors marched. Gwydion lifted his magic staff.'

Gwydion is named together with his brother Amathaon (Amaethon?) son of Don in the prose fragment relating to the battle (CLlH l–li), and Amaethon is again named beside *Gwydion* in the poem *Echrys Ynys* (BT 68.15–16; Ifor Williams (ed.), *Trans. Anglesey Antiquarian Soc.*, 1941 = BWP 172–80). With

Caer Nefenhir cf. CO l. 126 and see J. Lloyd-Jones, B XIV, pp. 35–7. On *Cad Goddeu* see M. Haycock, in M. J. Ball *et al.*, *Current Issues in Linguistic Theory*, and also CBT V, no. 23.170n.

Like the references to *Gwydion*'s presence at *Cad Goddeu*, the following allusion has no explanation in the *Mabinogi*:

Gveleis ymlad taer yn nant ffrangcon
Duv sul pryt pylgeint rvg vytheint a gvydyon
Dyf ieu yn geugeint yd aethant von
y geissav yscut a hudolyon
(BT 36.11–14)

'I saw a fierce battle in Nant Ffrangcon, on Saturday at dawn between the enemies and Gwydion [or 'the vultures of Gwydion', see B IV, p. 145]; on Thursday, as appointed, they went to Môn to seek . . . with enchanters.'

Gwydion's associations are entirely with Gwynedd. Thus the poem *Echrys Ynys* designates Eryri (apparently) as *gwlat wytyon* (BT 68.11–12), and the reference in LlDC no. 36.16 to *caer lev a gwidion* may be taken as alluding to Dinas Dinlle on the coast of Caernarfonshire (see n. to *Lleu Llaw Gyffes*). Close by there is a *Bryn Gw(y)dion* near Clynnog Fawr.

Gwydion's name heads the list of twelve *Plant Don o Arfon* in *Bonedd yr Arwyr* (B XVIII, p. 237 = EWGT 90(25)), and these include Arianrhod, *Gwydion*'s sister (cf. GLGC no. 79.17). In the fifteenth century Ieuan Dyfi refers to a variant version of the *Mabinogi*, according to which the son of *Gwdion* [*sic*] was named Huan, not Lleu (HCLl no. LVII.61–2); see also W. J. Gruffydd, *Math vab Mathonwy*, pp. 198–9 (citing J. Jones, Gellilyfdy): *Mal Gwdion aml a gedwynt / ymhen gwaith am Huan gynt*. Further allusions to *Gwydion* by the poets include the following:

Justus Llwyd: hi a vu am wydyon ac eudaf (RBP col. 1365.7 = YB XVII, 71.26).

An allusion to *Gwydion*'s grave in the extra *Beddau* stanzas in Peniarth 98 B may refer to Dinas Dinlle: *Bedd Gwydion ap Don ym Morfa din(l)leu / y dan fain deveillon / Garanawg ei geiffyl meinon* (?) (ed. T. Jones, PBA LIII, p. 134).

The name *Guidian* is found in a tenth-century list of Breton-Cornish names in the Vatican manuscript *Reginensis Latinus* 191 (ed. J. Vendryes, 'Un liste de Noms Bretons', EC III, pp. 145–54; *Ann. Bret.* 45, 203, and subsequently by O. J. Padel and B. Olsen, CMCS 12, pp. 34, 49. For *Guedian* see *Chr. Br.* 208. The Breton and Cornish forms contain the medial spirant *d*; cf. the Cornish village of *Gwithian* and the later Breton *Goezian* cited by Loth in *Chr. Br.* 208. The name *Guedianus* is found in the Life of *St Samson* (ed. Fawtier, ch. 48) as that of a pagan ruler in east Cornwall.

Gwydyr Dr6m 66: *Eueilian, wreic Wydyr Drwm.* 'G. the Heavy.' On the name, cf. CA l. 387: (*g*)*wit uab peithan* and n. on p. 171, where Ifor Williams compares the Celtic name *Vitus* and cites *Gwydyr* as a compound of *Gwit* (*Gwyd*). Another instance is LL 277.21: *Guidir*. *Bonedd y Saint* (EWGT 65 (72)): *Egryn ap Gwydr drwm ap Gwedrawc ap Geraint ap Garanawc ap Glewddigar ap Kynnwac* (*Kynawc*) *ap Rychwain varvoc o Vod Rychwain yn Ros, ac Efeilian = Eneilian verch Gadvan ap Iago i vam.*

G6yl verch Endavt 57 (i.e. *Gendawt*; for the lenition after *verch* see n. to wtriad 45). *Gŵyl* 'modest'; cf. *Guilbiu* LL 148.23.

Gwylwylyd 45: ychen Gwylwylyd. See n. to triad, and GPC 1764.

Gwynlliw Varvoc App. IV, no. 6. See **Cadawc m. Gwynlliw Varvawc**.

Gwynn[1] 74: *Coleda6c mab Gwynn.*

G6ynn[2] **Da Gy6et** 44. 'G. Good Companion.' For *cy6ed* see CLlH 146, GPC 688.

G6yn[3] **Da Reinyat** 44. 'G. Good Distributor.' R's *reimat* could be a corruption of *ceim(i)ad* 'champion' (GPC 452), but *reinyat* (*rhannu*) has the support of most manuscripts.

G6ystyl 21 (W): *Gveir ap G. Gwystl* = 'hostage'. Cf. CO l. 256 *Gwystyl mab Nwython*. *Guistilianus episcopus* (= *Guisdianus*) is named in Rhigyfarch's *Life of St David* ch. 14 (ed. James), p. 34 (*Cy.* XXIV, p. 10). See n. to *Gweir*[3] *m. Gwystyl.*

Gwythelin Gorr 28 (= WR: *Rudlwm Gorr*; Pen. 45: *Gwydelyn gor*). *Gwythelyn* = *Gwyddelyn* 'little Irishman', 'G. the Dwarf'. Cf. *Guidolwyn Gorr* CO l. 657 (amongst the *Anoethau*) and n. on *Eurolvyn merch Wdolwyn Gorr* CO ll. 364–5 (in RM only); also cf. *Edelic* (*Eddili*) *Corr* in triad 72. The name *Gwidawl* (< *Vitalianus*), ancestor of *Gwrtheyrn* (HB ch. 49), should also be compared, and *Guithelinus* in HRB VI, 5. But the relationship between the various characters who bear the epithet *Corr* 'dwarf' in the different versions of triads 27 and 28 defies any satisfactory explanation. For *Gwyddelyn* as a satirical term see G 734, and GDG 555. For a suggestion that *Guidolwyn Gorr* is the original of Chrétien de Troyes' dwarf-king *Gleodalen* (*Erec* l. 2005) see ATC 141.

(Gw)ythyr m. Greidya6l 56, *Gwenhwyfar verch* (= *Vthyr m. Greidyavl* W); see *Gwenh6yuar*[3] and *Greid(y)a6l Galouyd*. *Gwythyr* rather than W's *Vthyr* is the correct form, since lenition is required after *uerch*, and is shown in the other names following *uerch* in triad 56. *Vthyr* must therefore be a substitution for *Gwythyr* < *Victor*. For an instance of the name *Victor* in Britain, cf. the bilingual Ogham-Latin inscription at Clydai, Pembrokeshire (ECMW no. 306). The following instances of *Gwythur* (without patronymic) are found in early poetry: LlDC no. 18.133: *bet y guythur*; BT 48.6: *a march gvythur*; BT 71.13–14: *Neur ordyfneis i waet am vythur*; Cynddelw: *Gwythur navs: ual traws ae treissei* (H 94.26 = CBT IV, no. 4.196n.).

Gwythyr uab Greidawl is listed in the Arthurian court-list in CO l. 176 and subsequently in the episode of the Lame Ant (l. 942), and in that of the abduction of Creidylat (l. 988), for whom *Gwythur* and Gwynn ap Nudd were to fight every May-day until the day of Judgement (ll. 370, 990 ff.), until Arthur came to the North to arbitrate between them in their quarrel (ll. 997–1004). *Gwythur* later supports Arthur in his final contest with the Gwiddon Orddu 'Very Black Witch' (ll. 1205–29).

Gwythur's genealogy is given as follows in *Bonedd yr Arwyr* (B XVIII, p. 237 (22) = EWGT 89 (22)): *Gwythyr m. Greidiawl galonyd* (= *Galouyd*? cf. triad 19) *m. Enfael addian m. Deigyr m. Dyfynwal m. Ednyfet m. Maxen m. Llywelyn.*

Gyrmananyd Post Prydein 71 (MW). See **Kulvanawyt Prydein**.

Gyrthm6l Wledic 63. See **G(w)erthmul Wledic**, n. to CLlH no. XI.76a, and EWSP 600–1.

Haearn6ed 6rada6c 22. 'Treacherous/Wily Iron Face' is the meaning, if the second element in *Haearnwedd* is to be understood as -*gwedd* and not as -*medd.* Cf. the names Blodeuwedd, Banadlfedd, Anawfedd, and Ifor Williams's notes on these names, B V, p. 136; PKM 283. *Medd* is the second element in the last two names, and perhaps also in Blodeuwedd and *Haearnwedd.* It can mean 'possession, power' and 'queen, lady' in compounds such as these: perhaps 'rich in wealth, generous'. The above examples are women's names, but it should be noted that *Haearnwedd* in the older text of the triad could be a man's name, since it is in W alone that *Haearnwedd* is definitely stated to be the name of the mother of the *Tri Glew*; cf. the reference in *Englynion y Clyweit* quoted below. Ifor Williams compares other men's names containing the element *haearn*: *Haearnin* (< *Isarninus*), and cf. also *Haerngen* (LL 207.3), *Elhaernn* 'abounding in iron' (LL 73, etc.), the three saints called *Elhaearn, Llwchaern* and *Cynhaern* (VSB 322 (36)) and the very numerous Breton names in *Hoiarn-*, *Harn-* and *Iarn-* quoted in *Chr. Br.* 141, 139, 213. In *Englynion y Clyweit*, *Haearnwedd* appears as a man: *A glyweisti a gant Haernwed Vradawc vilwr teyrned* (Haycock, *Blodeugerdd* no. 31, *englyn* 30). With *Bradawg* cf. the epithet of *Aedan Uradawc* (above).

Heidyn m. Enygan 33 (*m. Euengat* W; *m. Eingawn* 47), = *H(e)idyn*, triad 34. Since the reference in both triads is to the slayer of Aneirin, the same name is evidently intended in both. For CA l. 948 *heidyn haearnde* (? 'iron-hurling Heidyn'), see Ifor Williams's note, and cf. CLlH no. XI.88c, 89a. In *Bonedd yr Arwyr* (EWGT 85 (1) = B XVIII, p. 233), *Ehedyn* is found in a list of the sons of Cyndrwyn (also Pen. 131, p.112); cf. EWSP 166–7. It seems a likely enough explanation of the form which occurs both in the triads and in CA that the name *Heden*, *Hedyn* has been influenced by the place-name *Eid(d)yn*, though a hero's name identical with the place-name cannot be excluded; cf. the names *Mynydawc Eidyn*, *Clydno Eidyn* (nn.) and see n. to *Henben* below.

Heled (verch Kyndrwyn) 65, *Haeled* 76, 77. *Heledd* probably represents *hy-* + *ledd*; cf. *Englynion y Clyweit*: *hyled . . . merch Kyndrwyn Mawr y ryued* (Haycock, *Blodeugerdd* no. 31, *englyn* 28). Cf. the name *Llanhileth*, Monmouthshire, found in sixteenth- and seventeenth-century sources as *Llanhyledd*, *-hileth* (LBS III, 254), perhaps identical with the *llan helet* of LlDC no. 18.44. On the name *Heledd* or *Hyledd* see Ifor Williams's note, CLlH 227–8. *Heledd* was sister to the leader Cynddylan in the Powys *englyn* cycle, and she is listed among the twenty-one sons and daughters of Cyndrwyn in *Bonedd yr Arwyr* (B XVIII, p. 233 (1) = EWGT 85 (1)). For a full discussion of her part in the Cynddylan saga, see EWSP 32, 61–2 and 150–73, though Heledd's portrayal here as a 'Sovereignty' figure (see n. to *Enid verch i Niwl Iarll*) remains unconvincing. Heledd names herself as *heled hwyedic* (CLlH no. XI.78 and 79). The epithet *hwyedic* is unexplained (see GPC 1936–7 and J. Rowlands's note EWSP 601–2). Cf. also the note to *Custennin Amhynwyedic*, CO l. 435.

Henben 22 'Old Head' (*henpen* Pen. 45, 50). Cf. the name *Henin Hen* below.

> BT 71.19 (= *Marwnat Vthyr Ben* (*dragon*)): *Neu vi a rodeis i henpen* / *cledyfavr goruavr gyghallen*.
>
> LlDC no. 18.219: *Bed hennin henpen yn aelwyt dinorben*.

Hengyst 59. See **Hors a Hengyst**.

Henin Hen 57: *Garwen verch H.* See *Henben* above. R. G. Gruffydd has suggested (SC XXIV/XXV, p. 10) that we have here the name of an otherwise almost forgotten *Cynfardd* who figures as *Henin Vardd* in the story of Taliesin, as the chief poet at the court of *Maelgwn Gwynedd* (see n.), and who was routed by the genius of the young Taliesin (see P. K. Ford (ed.), *Ystorya Taliesin*, ll. 200, 374, 380; J. E. C. Williams, 'Gildas, Maelgwn and the Bards', p. 22; and cf. J. Lloyd-Jones, *Court Poets of the Welsh Princes*, PBA XXXIV, p. 4).

Henwen 26. 'Old White.' In early Celtic sources, white animals, especially those with red ears, frequently represent magic creatures of Otherworld origin, and it seems that domestic animals were generally thought of as having their origin in the Otherworld; cf. the swine which Pwyll is said to have obtained from Annwfn. A magic white boar is the object of a hunt, as in the triad, in the Breton lay of *Guingamor* (K. Warnke, *Les Lais de Marie de France*, Halle, 1925, p. 233).

Henwyn occurs elsewhere both as the name of a horse (BT 48.17, see introduction p. lxxxii) and in more than one instance as that of a man, *Bonedd y Saint* (EWGT 57 (20)): *henwyn m. gvyndaf hen o lydav. periglavr catvan* (LBS IV, p. 370). Cf. also Geoffrey of Monmouth's *Hennuinus* (*Henwinus*) *dux Cornubiae* (HRB II, 12, 15). If we compare the analogy of the Twrch Trwyth in *Culhwch ac Olwen*, this reference suggests the possibility that *Henwen* also may have been originally a prince 'enchanted for his sins'. And *Mabinogi Math* offers precedents for the idea of punishment by transformation into an animal of the opposite sex.

Hors a Hengyst 36, 59. Both names mean 'horse'. Plummer (*Two Saxon Chronicles Parallel* II, 11) suggests that *Hengest* may be an abstraction from *yþ-hengest* 'wave-horse', a figurative term for a ship. *Hengest* occurs also in *Beowulf* (ed. Klaeber ll. 1127, etc.), but possibly with reference to a different character.

For early references to the story of the arrival of the Saxons in Britain see n. to *G6rtheyrn G6rthenau*. Bede (*Hist. Ecc.* I, 15), writing in 731, is the earliest to give the names of the Saxon leaders:

> Their first chieftains are said to have been the brothers *Hengist* and *Horsa.* The latter was subsequently killed in battle against the Britons and was buried in east Kent, where a monument bearing his name still stands. (See C. Plummer, *Baedae Opera Historica* I, p. 31.)

The names *Hors et Hengist* are given in HB, ch. 31, which also traces their descent from Woden. The poet of *Armes Prydein* appears to draw upon HB in his account of the settlement of the Saxons:

> pan prynassant Danet trwy fflet called
> gan Hors a Hegys oed yng eu ryssed
> (AP ll. 31–2)

> 'When they bought Thanet through false cunning, with Hors and He(n)gys their authority was confined'.

It has been suggested that the monument bearing *Horsa*'s name to which Bede refers may be the flint-heap at Horsted, near Aylesford (Plummer, *Two Saxon Chronicles Parallel* II, 11); while Camden refers to a tradition that the nearby cromlech known as Kit's Cotty House represents the grave of Horsa's opponent Cattegirn, who fell at the same battle (Gibson's translation of *Camden*, 1695 edition, p. 194). But the name of *Hors*(*a*), which occurs for no other person elsewhere, may after all be a 'ghost' name, owing its origin to the existence of some Roman monument from which all parts of the inscription had disappeared except the letters HORS (from *cohors*). For this ingenious suggestion see Collingwood and Myres, *Roman Britain and the English Settlements*, p. 358n.

Howel m. Emyr Llydaw, App. IV, no. 5.

BD 146.18–21: *Howel uab Emyr Llydaw . . . Nei uab chuaer y Arthur oed hvnnv o Emyr Llydav y tat* (= *Hoel filius sororis arturi. ex boudocio rege armaricanorum britonum generatus*, HRB IX, 2).

RBB 220.22: *Howel uab emyr llydav. A gvalchmei uab gvyar. deu nei y arthur.*

Br. Rh.: *Howel uab emyr llydav* (RM 159.22).

Gereint: *howel uab emyr llydav* (RM 265.13 = *ymer llydavc* WM 411.32).

Peredur: *hywel vab emyr llydav* (WM 165.32 = *Howel* RM 232.10).

In HRB *Duke Hoel*(*us*) figures prominently as Arthur's close friend and ally throughout his life. His relationship to Arthur, as stated in the *Bruts*, has been rationalized in the *Birth of Arthur* fragment (*Cy.* 24, pp. 250 ff.), where Gwyar is represented as Arthur's sister, and the mother of *Howel* by Emyr Llydaw. (On these relationships see n. to *Gwalchmei m. Gwyar.*) It should be noted that Gwyar is not named in the *Brut* in connection with either *Howel* or Emyr Llydaw.

A possible explanation of the figure of Arthur's nephew *Howel*, who is unknown in pre-Geoffrey Arthurian tradition, is to be found in Geoffrey's attitude to his source-material. Sir J. E. Lloyd has shown (EHR LVII, pp. 460–8) that Geoffrey's sympathies were always with the emigrant Breton colony, as against the native Welsh themselves. Geoffrey discovered that in the insular tradition Arthur had already been equipped with that important relative, a sister's son (Gwalchmei), but since he was always anxious to enhance the prestige of Brittany in his story, he decided to provide his hero with a rival nephew, who should be of Breton birth. Therefore he invented *Hoel*(*us*) (the name was a frequent one among the dukes of Brittany) and gave him as father a traditional ruler of Breton Cornubia. (B(o)udic figures not infrequently in the ecclesiastical tradition, and may even be historical; cf. the Lives of *St Teilo*, LL 110; *St Oudoceus*, LL 130; *St Melor,* ed. Doble, p. 14; and LBS I, pp. 51, 53.) Geoffrey deliberately maintained silence as to the name of *Howel*'s mother, since this would have raised too many difficulties: he merely stated that she was Arthur's sister. Geoffrey admitted the existence of Gualguanus (Gwalchmei) as Arthur's nephew, but it will be noted that *Howel* plays a much more prominent part in his story than does Gwalchmei. The *Bruts,* ignorant of either *Howel* or his mother in any native source, countered Geoffrey's invention with the vague allusion to 'a certain ruler of Brittany' (*Emyr Llydaw,* see n.) who had married a sister of Arthur (Anna in HRB 8, 20). It was left for the *Birth of Arthur* to identify *Howel*'s mother with Gwyar.

Huarwar m. Aflaun 93; see n.

Hueil m. Caw 21. Cf. CO l. 647n. and l. 212n.

CO: *A Hueil mab Kaw—nyd asswynwys eiroet yn llaw arglwyd* (in list of the nineteen sons of Kaw, CO l. 212) 'he never submitted to a lord's hand'.

Ibid.: *A Gwydre mab Lluydeu o Wenabwy merch Kaw y uam–Hueil y ewythyr a'e gwant, ac am hynny y bu gas rwg Arthur a Hueil am yr archoll* (CO ll. 258–60) 'G. mab Ll. by Gwenabwy daughter of Kaw–Hueil his uncle stabbed him, and therefore there was hatred between Arthur and Hueil because of the wound'.

Englynion y Clyweit: *Hueil mab Kaw* (Haycock, *Blodeugerdd* no. 31, *englyn* 32).

Casnodyn: *llit durawtyr huawdyr hueil uab kaw* (RBP col. 1246.18–19 = GC no. 1.22n.).

Gruffudd ap Maredudd: *heilrwysc hueil* (RBP col. 1204.2).

Among the *cywyddwyr* there occur the following references:

Dafydd ap Gwilym: *Defodau Huail* (GDG no. 14.40).
Llywelyn ab y Moel: *Huail y glêr* (IGE[2] 178.15).
Lewys Glyn Cothi: *Dafydd fal cynnydd Huail ab Caw* (GLGC no. 38.44).

The story of *Hueil* and his relations with Arthur, which is referred to briefly in CO, is given in further detail in the early twelfth-century *Life of Gildas* by Caradog of Llancarfan:

> St. Gildas was the contemporary of Arthur, the king of the whole of Britain, whom he loved exceedingly, and whom he always desired to obey. Nevertheless his 23 brothers constantly rose up against the aforementioned rebellious king, refusing to own him as their lord, but they often routed and drove him out from forest and the battlefield. Hueil, the elder brother, an active warrior and most distinguished soldier, submitted to no king, not even to Arthur [Cf. CO ll. 212–13]. He used to harass the latter, and to provoke the greatest anger between them both. He would often sweep down from Scotland, set up conflagrations, and carry off spoils with victory and renown. In consequence, the king of all Britain, on hearing that the high-spirited youth had done such things and was doing similar things, pursued the victorious and excellent youth; who, as the inhabitants used to assert and hope, was destined to become king. In the hostile pursuit and council of war held in the island of *Minau* (the Isle of Man), he killed the young plunderer. After that murder the victorious Arthur returned, rejoicing greatly that he had overcome his bravest enemy. (H. Williams (ed.), *Gildas*, pp. 400–3)

On the date of Caradog's *Vita* see n. to *Gwenh6yuar*[1] and authorities there cited. According to the earlier *Vita* of *Gildas* by the monk of Ruys (op. cit., pp. 322 ff.), which is a century older than that by Caradog, a Scottish ruler named Caunus (= Cauu-us) had five sons, of whom the eldest was called Cuillus, and is described as *valde strenuum in armis virum, qui post mortem patris ei in regno successit.* The other sons are Gildas, Mailocus (the *Meilic mab kav* of CO l. 209), Allecus and Egreas, who with their sister Peteova all gave themselves up to religion. The name Cuillus no doubt represents the *Hueil* of the later documents. Giraldus Cambrensis makes an enigmatic allusion to Arthur's murder of *Hueil* (*Descr. Cam.* II, 2):

> The Britons maintain that, when Gildas criticized his own people so bitterly, he wrote as he did because he was so infuriated by the fact that King Arthur had killed his own (i.e. Gildas's) brother, who was a Scottish chieftain [see n. to *Caw o Brydein*]. When he heard of his brother's [i.e. *Hueil*'s death]—or so the Britons say—he threw into the sea a number of outstanding books which he had written in their praise, and about Arthur's achievements. As a result you will find no book which gives an authentic account of that great prince. (Trans. L. Thorpe, p. 259)

Another and a very different account of *Hueil*'s quarrel with Arthur appears in Elis Gruffydd's chronicle, *circa* 1530 (NLW 5276D, pp. 334 ff.). Thomas Jones has edited and discussed the story of Hueil, as summarized here from Elis Gruffydd's chronicle, together with other references to *Hueil* in Welsh and Latin sources, in 'Chwedl Huail ap Caw ac Arthur', *Astudiaethau Amrywiol a gyflwynir i Syr Thomas Parry-Williams*, pp. 48–66. He shows that Elis Gruffydd's version is a corrupt form of a much older story, and suggests that triad 21 indicates that *Hueil*, like the other characters named in the triad, was associated with Arthur from perhaps as early as the eleventh century. It is also likely that there was a cycle of stories in oral circulation about the sons of Caw of Prydyn, to which this tale belonged. *Bonedd yr Arwyr* (EWGT 85 (3) = B XVIII, p. 233 (3)) lists *Hueil*, together with Gildas and Aneirin, among the twenty-one alleged children of *Kaw o Dwrkelyn*. Several of the names correspond to names in the list of Caw's nineteen sons in CO ll. 206–13 (see n.).

It is evident that Elis Gruffydd knew of the story in a late form in which its origin in the 'Old North' was forgotten, and it had later become relocalized in Gwynedd. *Kaw o Brydein* was the name of a chieftain who ruled over Edeirnion in Gwynedd. He had two sons, Gildas and *Hueil. Hueil* was *gwr gorhewg anllad* 'cheeky and wanton'. He obtained possession of one of Arthur's mistresses. Arthur came to spy upon the pair, and a fierce combat took place between him and *Hueil*. Finally *Hueil* wounded Arthur in the knee. After this, peace was made between them, on the condition that *Hueil* should never reproach Arthur with regard to his wound. Arthur returned to his court at Caerwys, but for ever after he remained slightly lame.

On a subsequent occasion Arthur dressed himself in woman's clothes in order to visit a girl at Rhuthun. *Hueil* chanced to come there, and he recognized Arthur by his lameness, as he was dancing in a company of girls. These were his words: *Da iawn yw downshio velly oni bai'r glun* 'This dancing were all right if it were not for the knee'. Arthur heard them and knew who had spoken them. He returned to his court where he caused *Hueil* to be brought before him, and he reproached him bitterly with his faithlessness.

Hueil was taken to Rhuthun, where Arthur cut off his head on a stone in the market-place, which to this day is known as *Maen Huail.* (The stone is still to be seen, suitably inscribed, on the market-square in Rhuthun.) On Elis Gruffydd's version, see further C. Lloyd-Morgan, 'Portread Elis Gruffydd o'r Brenin Arthur', YB XXIII (1997), p. 121.

The quarrel described here no doubt represents a late variant of the tradition of hostility between *Hueil* and Arthur which is found in the older sources. Cf. the prominence of *Caw* in Gwynedd genealogies (see n. to *Caw*). It is interesting also as one of the many instances in which a story which originated in north Britain has been brought south and given a precise localization in a specific district in Wales.

Hyueid m. Bleidic (brenin Deheubarth) 68.

Ann. Cam. 892: *Himeyd moritur.*

Brut y Tywysogyon (Pen. 20, p. 6a), 891–3: *Blwydyn wedy hynny y bu varw henweith* (= *Hyfaidd* son of Bleddri); see n. to T. Jones's translation of *Brut y Tywysogion* (*Pen. 20 version*), p. 139. *Hyfaidd*'s inclusion in triad 68 is to be accounted for by the fact that he derived his claim to rule Deheubarth by the female line, in right of his descent through his mother Tancoystl (or Tangwystl); see Harl. Gen. no. II (EWGT 9 (2); 106 (18)). Cf. HW I 262, 327–8, and D. P. Kirby, B XXVII, 86: 'Hyfaidd represents a family which married into the old ruling dynasty of Dyfed, and then supplanted it, as Merfyn Frych ap *Gwriad* did in Gwynedd.' He is to be identified with the king *Hemeid* of Dyfed, who oppressed St David's, and whose submission to King Alfred's overlordship is described in Asser's *Life of King Alfred* (ed. W. H. Stevenson, chs. 79, 80; trans. Keynes and Lapidge, *Asser's Life of Alfred* (Harmondsworth, 1983), pp. 94–6). Kirby further suggested that *Bleddri* is to be identified with the *Bleiddudd* of the early poem *Etmic Dinbych* (BT 42–4; Ifor Williams (ed.), BWP 155–72; see further on this, R. Geraint Gruffydd, SC XIV/XV, p. 97, and WCD 371).

Other instances of the name *Himeid*, *Hyueid* include CA l. 56: *hyueid hir*; LL 245.15, 29: *hiueid*; *Ann. Cam.* 939: *Himeid filius Clitauc moritur*; CO l. 220: *Hyueid Unllen*. In *Mabinogi Pwyll* the name of Rhiannon's father is *Heueyd Hen* (PKM 12.23; etc.), and cf. *Eueyd, Euehyd Hir* which occurs in *Branwen* (PKM 32.20 etc.). Both forms may represent the older *Himeid*, *Hyveid* and, if so, it is interesting in view of the Dyfed associations of the name *Hyveid.* But as Ifor Williams points out (PKM 129) the identification is doubtful, since forms of this name recur frequently in the text of the *Mabinogi*, and it seems unlikely that after frequently copying it the scribe would not have eventually recognized the O.W. form before him, and transposed it as *Hyveid* in his own orthography.

In listing the lands of Llywelyn ap Gruffudd, Dafydd Benfras refers to *bro Hyueid* (CBT VI, no. 35.57n.), i.e. *Maes Hyfaidd* > *Maesyfed* (Radnorshire).

Hywel m. Ieuaf 55, king of Gwynedd 979–85 (HW I, 344). See *Iago*[2] below.

Iago[1] m. Beli 33 (W); **Yago** 34. According to Harl. Gen. I, *Iago m. Beli* was father to King Cadfan of Gwynedd, and so must have lived in the late sixth century, cf. *Ann. Cam.* 613: *Iacob filii Beli dormitatio. Dormitatio* suggests that Iago died after having retreated to end his days in a monastery (as is pointed out, HW 181): it is inconsistent alike with the account of his death given in the triads, and with the assertion in manuscript B of *Ann. Cam.* (ed. Rolls series) that *Iacob filius Beli* fell at the battle of Chester (*Ann.* 613 = 616; see n. to triad 60). Presumably the fact that the two entries came under the same year in the *Annals* has caused them to be confused together in manuscript B. J. E. Lloyd believed that the *Iago* of the triads has been confused with the eleventh-century *Iago m. Idwal*, king of Gwynedd, who according to the Irish *Annals* was killed *a suis* 'by his own people' in the year 1039 (HW 358, n.2).

Iago m. Beli is probably the *Iago o tir prydyn* of BT 70.21 (see n. to *Llud m. Beli*), as frequently *Prydyn* (Pictland) and *Prydein* are confused. Cf. also *Cyvoesi Myrddin a Gwenddydd*: *Pvy wledych wedi Beli. . . Wedy Beli y uab ef Iago* (RBP col. 578.5–7).

According to Lhuyd, *Arch. Brit.* 256, col. 3, the early fifteenth-century manuscript Hengwrt 33, known as the *Hanesyn Hen* (see introduction, p. cxl and n.) contained a poem which Lhuyd describes as *marunad Iago ab Lhodri [sic] (ne Iago ab Beli) o waith Taliesin.* This reference is the more intriguing as the date given for the death of Iago in *Ann. Cam.* 613 is not inconsistent with that of the other historical figures to whom poems have survived and which are attributed to Taliesin. But so far no trace of this poem has come to light.

Iago[2] (m. Idwal Voel) 55, king of Gwynedd, reigned with his brother 950–69; alone 969–79.

After the death of Hywel Dda in 950, the two sons of *Idwal Foel*, *Iago* and Ieuaf (= Idwal) led the men of Gwynedd against the south and won the independence of their kingdom from Dyfed. Afterwards civil war broke out between the brothers, in which *Iago* was at first successful and imprisoned Ieuaf (969), but ten years later he was in turn imprisoned by his nephew, the *Hywel m. Ieuaf* of triad 55 (HW 343–4). In this captivity *Iago* appears to have died. He was among the Welsh kings who were present at the court of the west Saxon king Edred (HW 348); and he seems to have been the only Welsh king who submitted to Edgar's overlordship at Chester in 973 (HW 349; Stenton, *Anglo-Saxon England*, p. 364; *Bywgraffiadur*).

Rawl. B 466: *Plant Idwal Voel: Ieuaf, Iago, Meurig, Kynan ag Idwal Vychan . . . Plant Iago ap Idwal Voel: Kynan, Kwstennin ddu, a las yngwaith hiraddug.* Cf. *Achau Brenhinoedd a Thywysogion* EWGT 101 (7c, 7e).

Iason m. Eson 48. *Dares Phrygius*: *Pelleas a oed urenhin yghastell a elwit pelopeus. a. bravt a o(e)d idav a elvit eson. a hvnnv a oed a mab idav a elvit Mason* (RBB 1.1–13). The story of Jason and the Golden Fleece is given in the texts of *Dares* as a prelude to that of the Trojan war. (On *Dares Phrygius* see Lloyd and Owen, *Drych yr Oesoedd Canol*, pp. 33–4.)

Idawc korn prydyn (= Kordd Prydein) 51 (Pen. 51). 'I. the Agitator of Britain.' RM 147.13: *Idavc uab mynyo*; 147.15: *Idawc Cord Prydein y'm gelwir.* Iddawg figures in Br. Rh. as Rhonabwy's guide to Arthur's court; according to his own account he wantonly provoked the battle of Camlan (see n. to triad 59). Outside Br. Rh. he appears to be almost entirely unknown. See n. to *Caurdaf m. Karadawc* (*Vreichvras*).

Idon m. Enyr G6ent 42, **Idon m. Ner** 69. *Hystoria o Uuched Beuno* (*Elucidarium* 125.18 = VSB 16–22, §20): *idon vab ynyr gvent. Ynyr < Honorius,* perhaps influenced by the name of the emperor Honorius (395–425). *Ynyr Gwent* seems to have been an early ruler of Gwent (perhaps two men, WCD 643); with the epithet, cf. such names as Maelgwn Gwynedd, Custennin Gorneu, Emyr Llydaw. According to the saint's Life, he was a disciple of *St Beuno,* and bestowed on him land in Ewyas (*Elucidarium*, pp. 119–20). *Bonedd y Saint* (EWGT 61 (44, 45): *Keidav m. Ynyr Gwent a Madrun merch Wertheuyr Uendigeit y uam.* Another possible son of *Ynyr*, Caradog, is named in the Life of *St Tatheus* (VSB 274); cf. also Br. Rh.: *Heilyn goch uab Kadwgawn uab Idon* (RM 145.8). The poet Gwalchmai refers to *gwlad ynyr* (H 19.16 = CBT I, no. 9.86n.); the reference is presumably to Gwent. Other instances of the name may be to a different character: BT 42.2: *ynyr wystlon*; CO ll. 118–20: *Mi a uum gynt yn ymlad deu Ynyr pan ducpwyt y deudec gwystyl o Lychlyn.* Owain Cyfeiliog refers also to *deu vab Ynyr* as the names of two members of his *teulu* (RBP col. 1433.34 = CBT II, no. 14.64n.).

In the records *Ynyr* is less prominent than his son *Iddon*. The Life of *St Beuno* (VSB 20–1) gives a story in which the saint raises from the dead a daughter of *Ynyr Gwent* called Digiwc, who had been slain by her husband *un o weithwyr Aberffraw,* at Pennard in Arfon, while returning to her husband's home from the south. Her brother *Idon* journeys to Aberffraw to avenge the deed. LL records several gifts of land made by *Iddon* to Llandaff (118.5; *Idon rex filius ynyr gwent* 121.7; 122.9; 166.18). Tradition thus synchronizes the lives of *Ynyr Gwent* and his son with figures of the late fifth and early sixth centuries.

Ieuaf[1] (a Griffri) 55. See n. to **Griffri**.

Ieuaf[2] (ac Iago) 55. See n. to **Iago[2]**. Rawl. B 466: *Plant Ieuaf ap Idwal Voel: Meurig, Howel, Ieuaf tad Kynan.* Cf. EWGT 101, c, d, e.

Indec verch Ar6y Hir 57. See **Garwy Hir.**

CO (l. 365): *Indec merch Arwy Hir.*

Casnodyn: *eil indec* (H 331.16 = GC no. 5.16n.).

Dafydd ap Gwilym makes five allusions to the beauty of *Indeg* (perhaps partly instigated by the convenience of her name for the rhyme with *teg* in a *cywydd* couplet: GDG no. 16.9: *cain Indeg*; 43.43: *lliw Indeg*; 54.24: *Indeg efell*; 71.41: *ail Indeg*; 79.11: *Indeg loywnwyf*; 94.6: *Indeg eirian*; 96.1: *Indeg oroen*; 103.1: *ail Indeg*.

Madog Benfras: *ail Indeg* (DGG no. LXIX.15).

Llywelyn Goch (to Lleucu Llwyd): *Iawndwf rhianedd Indeg* (DGG no. LXXXVIII.4 = GLlG no. 12.37).

Gruffudd ap Maredudd: *hoen am verch arwy hir* (RBP col. 1326.18).

Dafydd ab Edmwnd: *kyfliw Indeg* (GDE no. X.3).

Dafydd Nanmor: *undw Eigr, neu Indec* (DN no. XXXIII.26).

Lewys Glyn Cothi: *Luned ac ail Indeg yw* (GLGC no. 91.32)

But no trace has survived of the story attached to this heroine. For her name cf. LL 198.16: *hindec* (*mater*) *Cathouen*. Like the other traditional heroines, Indeg's name was unknown to the *Gogynfeirdd* (cf. D. M. Lloyd, *Rhai Agweddau ar Ddysg y Gogynfeirdd*, p. 10). The earliest recorded allusion to her may be that found among the *marginalia* in the Hendregadredd MS: *indec o uodd yn dec vun* (D. Huws, *Nat. Lib. of Wales Journal* XXII, p. 26). Owing to Dafydd ap Gwilym's close association with Ieuan Llwyd and his family, it is tempting to believe that the *englyn enghreifftiol* which contains *Indeg*'s name may itself be an early work of Dafydd ap Gwilym.

Joseph o Arimathia 81, 86. *Josep o arimathia* SG(ii) 18.640. The name, as well as the nucleus of the story of *Joseph of Arimathea*, is found in the apocryphal *Evangelium Nicodemi,* and in certain other uncanonical scriptural writings (EAR I, 238–9). But *Joseph*'s fame in European romance stems from the account given of him in the French poem which bears his name, and which was composed by Robert de Boron between the years 1180 and 1199, most probably in the earlier years of this period (EAR I, 221, 267). According to the story which is given here, *Joseph* was a soldier of Pontius Pilate, who secretly worshipped as a Christian. He collected the blood of Christ in the chalice which had been used at the Last Supper (= the *Graal*); later, he buried Christ's body. After many adventures he entrusted the *Graal* to a successor named Bron who was to carry the sacred vessel to the West, to the *vaus d'avaron* (EAR I, 266). This is all the information given in the poem. It remained for William of Malmesbury to interpret the allusions to Bron's destination as signifying Britain, and to found upon this slender basis his story of the arrival of *Joseph* of Arimathea himself in Britain, with a small body of followers, in the year AD 63; and of his foundation here of the first Christian community at *Ynys Witrin* or Glastonbury. This story first appears in the revised edition of William's *De Antiquitate Glastoniensis Ecclesiae,* which was composed in the last years of the twelfth century or in the early years of the thirteenth. See J. Armitage Robinson, *Two Glastonbury Legends*; T. D. Kendrick, *British Antiquity*, pp. 15–17.

According to this account, *Joseph* of Arimathea was descended from the prophet David, but it is only in the thirteenth-century Prose Romances, the *Estoire del Saint Graal* and the *Queste del Saint Graal* (the latter corresponds with the first part of *Y Seint Greal: Y Keis* (SGii)) that he becomes in turn the ancestor of Lancelot (Lawnslot) and of Galahad (Galaad). Since Bohort (Bort) is represented as being cousin to Lancelot, he also belonged to this illustrious kin (cf. triad 86; EAR I, 402; see also H. O. Sommer, *Vulgate Cycle of the Arthurian Romances* III, pp. 13, 88, where it appears that the fathers of Bohort and of Lancelot were brothers, and that their respective mothers were sisters).

According to *Y Seint Greal,* part 2 (based on the *Perlesvaus*), Peredur (= Perceval) was of the kindred of King Peleur (= *le Roi Pescheur*), the Graal guardian, and this was evidently taken to imply descent from Joseph (see triad 86). Once the way had been pointed out, other heroes besides Peredur-Perceval and Lancelot's kin began to have their descent traced from the stock of *Joseph* of Arimathea: Tristan (in the *Prose Tristan*, EAR I, 192), and in certain manuscripts Gawain (= Gwalchmai, see *Llew m. Kynuarch*), and even Arthur himself. In *Nat. Lib. of Wales Journal* XIV, p. 245, P. C. Bartrum quotes a version of the genealogy which gives five generations derived from John of Glastonbury's *Chronica sive Historia de Rebus Glastoniensis* (Hearne (ed.) (Oxford, 1726), pp. 56–7).

H. O. Sommer's *Vulgate Cycle* VI, p. 7 (= *Queste del Saint Greal*): *celui* [Galahad] *qui est estrais del haut lignage al roi david et del parent ioseph darrimachie* (*sic*). Cf. SG 6: *Arthur heb* [*y gwr llwyt*] *llyma vi yn dwyn attat ti y Marchawc Urdawl Damunedic* [*Galaad*] *a henyw o lin Dauyd Brofwyt ac o Iosep o Arimathia*. In the *Queste* it is implied that this relationship was derived through Galahad's mother, the daughter of King Pelles, the 'fisher king', who was also the uncle of Perceval. But it is only the relationship as explained in the *Lancelot* (Sommer, III, pp. 13, 88 and see n. to triad 86) which can account for the inclusion of Bohors (= *Bort m. Brenhin Bort*) (see n.) as belonging to the kindred of *Joseph*, as in triad 86. See also Bartrum in EWGT p. 150, n. 31.

Julius Cesar 47 (Pen. 216), 51, *6lkessar* 59, *y Gwr Moel* 89, see n. See also nn. to *F(f)lur* and *Caswallawn m. Beli.*

Cynddelw: *Rybu ull kessar. keissyassei flur / gan ut Prydein, prid y hesgur* (CBT IV, no. 17.69n.).

Casnodyn: *eil ulkessar* (RBP col. 1242.15 = GC no. 2.122n.).

Gr. ap Maredudd: *dan llachar ryssed vlkassar* (RBP col. 1316.7 = GGM no. 4.56); ibid.: *vn dremyn ulkassar* (RBP col. 1325.32 = GGM no. 5.126).

(*Ulkessar*, *-kassar* is the regular form of this name employed by the bards. So also in BD 163, *Ulkessar*; RBB 59, *ulcassar*; 83, *vlkessar.*)

La6nslot y Lac 86; **Lanslod Lak,** App. IV, no. 3. See n. to *Galaad m. La6nslot y Lac*.

SG(ii) 11.402–3: *y enw ef yw Lawnslot dy Lac, y teckaf or marchogyon urdolyon.*

Rhys Goch Eryri (IGE^2 no. CIII.25): *Gwilym Lawnslod ni 'mgilia*

GGl no. 1.48: *Lawnslod di Lag.*

DN 59.6: *Lawnslod Dvlag.*

GTA I, no. VII.91: *Lawnslot*; no. XLIII.65: *Syr Lawnslod.*

The French forms, or barely adapted French forms, in which the name of *Lancelot* appears in Welsh works of the late Middle Ages, clearly indicate that the name is a foreign importation. *Lancelot* was unknown to the *Gogynfeirdd*, and the references to him by poets of the fifteenth and following centuries owe their origin to a knowledge of the prose romances of the French *Vulgate Cycle*, whose knowledge was partly disseminated in Wales by means of the fourteenth-century version of the *Queste* (SG(ii)). Other Welsh translations of these romances may also have existed (see introduction, pp. cxi–cxii).

As an Arthurian hero, *Lancelot* is a secondary introduction of Breton-French origin into the cycle (EAR I, 192). In the thirteenth-century *Vulgate* romances he finally supersedes the earlier hero Gawain (= Gwalchmei) as the peer of Arthur's knights, just as his son Galahad (= Galaad) supersedes the earlier Perceval (= Peredur) as the Grail hero.

Lancelot first makes his appearance in medieval literature in three late twelfth-century poems: *Erec et Enide* and *Le Chevalier de la Charette* by Chrétien de Troyes, and the *Lanzelet* of Ulrich von Zatzikhofen (K. T. Webster (ed.), New York, 1951). It can hardly be denied that both these poems contain elements of mythology and folk-lore which bear every appearance, supported by a general probability, of being of ultimate Celtic origin. (See n. to *Gwenh6yuar* for the relation of Chrétien's poem to the tradition of Guinevere and her elopements, and n. to *Mabon m. Modron* for some Celtic elements in Ulrich's poem.) Yet there is no evidence that these elements were introduced into the Continental Arthurian material in conjunction with the name of any one specific Celtic antecedent of *Lancelot*. In comparison with the phenomenon of the vast corpus of narrative elements which found their way into Continental Arthurian romance, and whose probable origin is to be found in Celtic mythology, folk-lore and saga, such double transferences of a particular incident in combination with the name of a particular hero are in fact extremely rare. For this reason, and because of the absence of any convincing resemblance in the name-forms, I feel no hesitation in rejecting the derivation of *Lancelot* < *Elyflath* < *Eliwlat* proposed by T. Gwynn Jones (*Aberystwyth Studies* VIII, p. 37); and also that proposed by R. S. Loomis (ATC 187–95; *Romania* LIV, p. 517; and in notes to K. T. Webster's translation of Ulrich von Zatzikhofen's *Lanzelet*, pp. 201–2) in which he associates *Lancelot* with *Lluch Llauynnauc* of LlDC no. 31.26 (= CO l. 192n.: *Lloch Llawwynnyawc*), and ultimately with the Irish god *Lug.*

It seems most probable that *Lancelot* is a variant of the Breton *Lancelin,* a name recorded in deeds of the years 1034 and 1069 (see Zimmer in *Zeitschrift für französische Sprache und Literatur* XIII, pp. 43 ff.), with an altered suffix. Cf. also the name of the hero of Marie de France's lay *Lanval.* I know of no Ml.W. name with initial *L(l)an-*.

For critical discussion of the name and figure of *Lancelot*, see C. Lloyd-Morgan, AW 193–205, and eadem, 'Lancelot in Wales' in K. Pratt (ed.), *Shifts and Transpositions in Medieval Narrative*, pp. 169–79.

Llacheu m. Arthur 4, 91.

Br. Rh.: *a llacheu mab arthur* (RM 159.28).

LlDC no. 31.76–7: *Kei guin a llachev. digonint we kadev* 'Fair Kei and Llacheu, they performed battles'; LlDC no. 34.49: *Mi a wum lle llas llachev / mab arthur uthir ig kertev / ban ryreint brein ar crev* 'I have been where Llacheu was slain, son of Arthur marvellous in songs (or crafts), when ravens croaked over blood' (cf. AW 44).

Cynddelw: *Llacheu a llachar Gynwryc* (CBT IV, no. 11.16n. = H 99.17).

Idem: *llacheuuar* (CBT III, no. 16.38n. = H 133.20).

Idem: *Llacheu gyfred* (CBT III, no. 21.149n. = H 130.11).

Idem: *Llacheu heuelys* (CBT IV, no. 6.47n. = H 99.17).

Llygad Gŵr: *Kynnwryf tan lluch uaran Llacheu* (CBT VII, no. 24.125n. = H 218.27).

Bleddyn Fardd: *Dewr a was ban llas, yn llassar-arue6 /6al e llas Llache6 is Llech Ysgar* 'He was a brave youth when he was slain in blue-enamelled arms, as Llacheu was slain below Llech Ysgar' (CBT VII, no. 52.15–16 = H 70.18–19).

Gr. ap Maredudd: *llachau glot oleu* (RBP col. 1203.20 = GGM no. 2.19); *(l)lacheu gytwed* (RBP col. 1313.36); *rwysc llacheu vilwr* (RBP col. 1316.5 = GGM no. 4.53). Cf. GGM no. 3.50.

For *Llech Ysgar*, cf. (Llywelyn ab y Moel), IGE[2] no. LXVI.1–2: *Rho Duw, Goed, rhydeg ydwyd / Y Graig lech ysgar, grug Lwyd.* (*Llech Ysgar* was a court of Madog ap Maredudd, now identified with Crickheath Hill, Llanymynech; see CBT I, no. 7.50n.; III, no. 2.4n.)

Llywelyn Goch: *llacheu yn yn llochi* (RBP col. 1307.33 = GLlG no. 6.4; see also no. 1.34n.).

Like Cei and Bedwyr, *Llacheu* appears to have belonged to an early stratum of Arthurian tradition in Wales, although the allusions to him are limited to those quoted above. He does not appear in the long Arthurian court-list in *Culhwch ac Olwen.* (One suspects, however, that the popularity of his name among the poets was its convenience for rhyme and *cynghanedd,* since proper names alliterating in *ll-* are rare.) It is the more surprising, therefore, that like Arthur's other son Amr or Anir of the *Mirabilia* in HB ch. 73, *Llacheu is* almost unknown in the extant *chwedlau,* while the older triads afford him only a single mention.

Y Seint Greal, part 2, identifies *Llacheu* with Arthur's *son Loho(l)t* of the Continental romances. Thus SG(i) 304–5 (Pen. 111, 196r.) gives the tale of Cei's treacherous murder of *Llacheu* (a variant of the popular Dragon-Slayer folk-tale; Stith Thomson, *Types of Folk-tale* no. 300), after the latter has slain the giant *Logrin Gawr.* At the corresponding place in *Perlesvaus* (ed. Nitze, ll. 4901 ff.) *Loholt* is slain by Cei (for the conclusion of the incident see *Perlesvaus*, ll. 6292 ff.; SG(i) 339ff.). It should be noted, however, that in a back-reference to this incident later in the story, the translator of *Y Seint Greal* has forgotten that he has already rendered *Loholt* by *Llacheu*:

> Yna y brenhin a ovynnawd y walchmei a welsei *loawt* [*sic*] y vab yn lle or y buassei yndaw. A Gwalchmei a dywawt nas gwelsei ef. Ryued yw gennyf, heb y brenhin, beth a daruu idaw. kanys ny chiglef i chweith y wrthaw yr pan ladawd kei logrin gawr, yr hwnn y duc ym y penn, a minneu ae diolcheis idaw. kanys ef a dialawd ar y lleidyr mwyaf or a oed yn ryuelu arnaf ac ar vyng gallu. Eissyoes pei gwypei y brenhin ual y buassei y damchwein, ny chanmolei ef nae vilwryaeth ef nae antur. (SG(i) 278 = *Perlesvaus*, ll. 6292 ff.)

> 'Then the king asked Gwalchmei whether he had seen *Loawt* his son in any place where he had been. And Gwalchmei said he had not seen him. "I wonder", said the king, "what has happened to him. For I have not heard anything of him, since Cei slew Logrin the Giant, and brought me the head, and I thanked him—since he had brought vengeance on the greatest thief of those who waged war on me and on my might." Nevertheless, if the king had known how the affair had been, he would not have praised his (Cei's) valour nor his exploit.'

It seems unlikely that there is any genuine early association between the names and characters of *Llacheu* and Loho(l)t, even apart from the consideration that the poem LlDC no. 34.49, combined with the references by the *Gogynfeirdd,* indicate that there was in existence a well-known story about *Llacheu*'s death in battle. Loho(l)t is himself a very insubstantial figure in Arthurian romance. The earliest reference to him appears to be that in Chrétien's *Erec* l. 1732, where *Loholz, li fiz le roi Artu* is included in the muster-roll of Arthur's court. But apart from the story of his death which appears in the *Perlesvaus,* practically nothing is known of him. Ulrich von Zatzikhofen states that Ginover (Gwenhwyfar) was his mother (*Lanzelet,* translated Webster and Loomis, p. 119, and n. 205). The prose romances of the *Vulgate Cycle* make various allusions to Loho(l)t as one of the knights of the Round Table, and the *Merlin* alludes specifically to his death-tale, with the remark that this was the only deed in which Cei was guilty of treachery (H. O. Sommer, *Vulgate Cycle* II, p. 316). Elsewhere the same Branch alludes to a tradition at variance with that of Ulrich, by which a certain *Lissanor* of *Canparcorentin* (= *Quimper*) was the mother of Loholt, before Arthur married Guinevere (ibid. II, 124; III, 159). In the *Livre d'Artus* Arthur has a symbolical dream referring to the death of Loholt in terms which correspond with the tale as told in *Perlesvaus* (ibid. VII, 52). For further references see WCD 401–3, and K. Busby, 'The Enigma of Loholt' in K. Varty (ed.), *An Arthurian Tapestry* (Woodbridge, 1981).

J. Loth discovered the name *Loholt* as that of a Cornish land-holder in the twelfth century (*Contributions a l'étude des Romans de la Table Ronde*, p. 65). The name appears to be of Breton-French origin, like that of *Lancelot,* with which its termination may be compared (see n. to *La6nslot*); and it is probably one of the names which were introduced into Cornwall after the Conquest.

Llawuroded 6ar6a6c 46 'Ll. the Bearded'; App. III, no. 6: *Ll. Farchog* 'Ll. the Horseman'.

CO: *Llawurodet Uaruawc* (l. 223n.).
Br. Rh.: *llavuroded varyfavc* (RM 159.29).

Llawuroded Varvawc is named in *Bonedd y Saint* and in *Achau'r Saint* (EWGT 62 (54), 66 (85), 69 (18)), and in the genealogy of *Hedd ap Alunawg* (*Nat. Lib. of Wales Journal* XIII, p. 112(32)). See also E. Rowlands, LlC V, pp. 57–60, who in his edition of the *Tri Thlws ar Ddeg* cites a number of variant forms in which the name of *Llawuroded Varvawc* appears.

In CA 286, Ifor Williams associates this name with *llawfrydedd* 'sorrow' (GPC 2111), and suggests a derivation from *llaw* 'small' and *brodedd = brawd* 'of small or inferior judgment'. Nevertheless, *Llaw(v)rodet* is employed by the poets as a complimentary epithet, denoting 'generous' (GPC 2119):

Gruffudd ap Maredudd: *llavrodet nodet nud gystadlu* (RBP col. 1203.23; ibid., 1230.24; 1315.18)

Gwilym Ddu o Arfon: *llvybrget llawvrodet llafrud gelynyon* (RBP col. 1226.11 = GGDT no. 6.27n.)

Lla6gat Tr6m Barga6t Eidyn 33. 'Heavy Battle-Hand of the border of Eidyn'; W: *Llongad Grwm Uargot Eidin* 'Ll. the Bent of the border of Eidyn'. Cf. *Clydno Eidin*, *Mynyda6c Eidyn*, *Heidyn m. Enygan.*

Llawr m. Eiryf (R: *Lary*) 15. Cf. CO l. 217n., *Llawr eil Erw*. *Llawr* = 'alone, solitary' (B V, pp. 5–6); also 'hero, champion' (CA 107). 'Solitary son of Number' suggests such designedly comic names as *Nerth m. Cadarn, Digon m. Alar,* etc., in *Culhwch. Llawr* occurs elsewhere as a personal name in respect of one of the sons of Llywarch Hen (CLlH no. I.42c); *Lavr et filius eius* (LL 245.18); *bet llaur llu ouit* (LlDC no. 18.85); *llawr ap Llawvrodedd varvawc* (EWGT 118 (10b)). R's *Llary* 'generous' is also attested elsewhere as a proper name, CO l. 215: *Llary m. Casnar Wledic.* The general context of triad 15 suggests that an Irish name or nickname may be intended here.

Lleena6c 5: *Gwalla6c m. Ll.* (see n.); *Llaennawc* 6 (Pen. 47), *Llennawc* 25 (WR). Two daughters of *Lleenawc* are recorded as mothers of saints, EWGT 56 (12): *Deinnyoel m. Dunaut Uwrr* (see n. to *Dunawt*[2]) *m. Pabo Post Prydein o Dwywei uerch Lennauc y vam* (Pen. 16: *leenavc*). Dwywei may also have been the mother of the poet Aneirin (see n.). Pen. 45, *Bonedd: Elaeth Vrenhin m. Meuruc m. Idno ac Omen Grec* (var. *Onnen Grec*) *uerch Wallauc m. Lleennauc e vam* (EWGT 62 (48) = VSB 322 (48)). *Lleen(n)awc* represents an archaic spelling of *Lle(i)nnavc.* LlDC gives the following spellings of the name: *lleynnac* (no. 34.57); *llein(n)auc, lleynnauc* (EWGT 33 (15) etc.); *Jes. Gen.* XXXVI: *llyennavc.* These forms look as though they are derived from O.W. *Lleen(n)awc,* which evidently obtained wide currency; Harl. Gen. IX gives the variant *Laenauc.* This name is trisyllabic, as is pointed out by Eurys Rowlands (LlC VI, p. 244); the medial *-ee-* representing *-ey-* (see also Brynley Roberts, *Ast. H.* 309). Rowlands suggests the possibility of a linguistic connection with *Llŷn* < *Lleyn* (Ir. *Laighen*). For the place-name *Aberlleinawg*, see Thomas Jones, *Brenhinedd y Saeson* (Cardiff, 1971), 90 (ann. 1098).

Llemenic (m. Mawan) 43 (Pen. 47: *llemenic m. mawan*); 65, 76, 77.

BT 48.13: *Yscvydurith yscodic. gorvyd llemenic* (cf. p. lxxxii, l. 12 above).

LlDC no. 18.153: *Bet llemenic in llan elvy* (i.e. St Asaph's).

CLlH no. XI.112–13: *Llemenig mab* (*Mawan*). (Ifor Williams's conjectural emendation of the *Mahawen* of the manuscript to *Mawan*, as required by the rhyme and metre, is confirmed by Pen. 47's version of the name in *Trioedd y Meirch*, triad 43.) Cf. EWSP 168–9, 612.

Bonedd y Saint (Pen. 16): *Styphan m. mawan m. kyngen m. cadell dyrnlluc* (= VSB 322 (38): *Mawon*). Cf. Pen. 45 *Bonedd*: *Brochfael Ysgithrawc m. kyngen m. cadell dyrnllvch.* These references imply that *Mawan* was a brother of Brochfael Ysgithrawg of Powys, a relationship which fits well with the appearance of his son Llemenig as a character in the *englyn*-cycle of ninth-century Powys. *Lemenic* glosses *salax* (*Eutyches*) and is cognate with Ir. *léimnech* 'leaping'. Thus *Llemenic* 'the bounding or prancing one' (< *llam*) is a name more suited to a horse than to a man, and it is used as an epithet for a horse, CA l. 303: *y ar llemenic llwybyr dew* 'from the back of a prancing broad-tracked (?) (horse)', see n. If it were not for the occurrence of *Lemenic* as a man's name in LL 174.22, one would be tempted to take the name *Llemenig* (*m. Mawan*) in CLlH as having arisen out of a misunderstanding of the *gorvyd llemenic* of BT 48.13. It remains uncertain whether this is not itself merely an epithet 'a bounding steed', although the triad Pen. 47 (representing the readings of *Llyfr Siôn Balmer*) interpreted it as a reference to the *Llemenig* of the *englyn* cycle.

The closely related compound *lleminawc* 'the leaping one' occurs either as an adjective or a proper name BT 55.5 (see M. Haycock, SC XVIII/XIX, p. 71); as an epithet for Urien Rheged BT 42.8; and as a euphemism for a promised deliverer in a prophetic poem BT 70.25–6: *Rydybyd llyminavc auyd gvr chwannavc.* Cf. also HGVK 5.24n.: *Llyminauc lletfer a daroganer.* These last instances suggest that the *llam* which forms the first element in *llemenic, llyminawc* may perhaps be associated with *llam* in its secondary meaning of 'fate' (CLlH 124), i.e. 'the fated one', rather than with that of 'leap, bound'. But perhaps the two last allusions intend to play upon the double meaning of the word. On *llyminiog* 'keen, eager' (possibly a personal name) see GPC 2271.

Lles, amhera6dyr Ruuein 51. BD 154: *Lles amheravdyr Ruuein* = *Leo imperator* (HRB IX, 11), but elsewhere the corresponding Latin name is Lucius (BD 162 = HRB IX, 15; BD 167 = *Lucius hyberus*, HRB X, 1; BD 178 = L. *hyberius* X, 8; BD 181 = L. *imperator* X, 11). On *Lles* = *Lucius*, see B. F. Roberts, B XXV, p. 280, and on the confusion as to whether Arthur or another was credited with having slain the Roman emperor, see n. to triad 51.

Lleu[1] Lla6 Gyffes 30, 38, 67, *march Ll.* 38, *llew ll. g.* 20 (W) 'Ll. Skilful-Hand'. *Mabinogi Math* gives an account of the birth, upbringing, marriage and subsequent betrayal of *Lleu Llaw Gyffes*, including the incidents referred to in triads 30 and 67. *Lleu* 'the Bright One' (PKM 275–6) is attested against *Llew* as the correct form of this name by the rhyme in *-eu* which is found in the archaic *englynion* preserved in *Math* (*Lleu*: *geu,* PKM 89–90); Pen. 16 also preserves *Lleu* (triads 30, 38). W reads *Lleu* in the naming-incident (WM 97.15) and in triad 67, but elsewhere transliterates *u* as *w* (6); and *Llew, Lle6* appears consistently throughout the text of R.

BT 48.8: *a march lleu lletuegin* (see introduction, p. lxxxii and n. 135).

LlDC no. 18.106: *Bet llev llaugyffes y dan ach(l)es mor / yny bu y gywnes / gur oet hunnu guir y neb ny rotes* 'The grave of *Ll. Ll.* under the sea-flood, where his kinsman was: he was a man who gave right to no one'. A variant of the last two lines of the stanza is found in the *Beddau* in Pen. 98 B: *cyn dyfod ei armes / gwr oedd ef gwahoddai ormes* 'before his doom came he was a man who invited attack' (PBA LIV, p. 136).

LlDC no. 36.15: *caer lev a gwidion.* The reference here is to *Dinas Dinlle(u)* (cf. *Dinllef* PKM 81.10), the great promontory fort on the shore five miles west of Caernarfon, now partly destroyed by coast erosion.

The name of *Lleu* is cognate with that of the Irish god *Lugh,* Gaulish *Lugus* (LHEB 441). The Gaulish name is found only in the plural form *Lugoves* (see n. to triad 67), or else compounded with other elements: *Lugudiacus, Luguselva* ('devoted to Lugus'), and in the names of cities which are spread over a wide area of western Europe: *Lyons*, *Laon*, and *Leiden* all represent an earlier *Lugudunum, Lugdunum*, and the name of *Lugus* was also preserved in that of Carlisle, *Luguvalium* (see LHEB 39, 414) and perhaps in *Lothian*, Ml.W. *Lleuddiniawn* (H 21.25). *Luguvalium* is 'the place of Luguvalos' (Jackson). Caesar (*De Bell. Gall.* VI, 17) states that the Gauls worship Mercury beyond all other gods, *hunt omnium inventorem artium ferunt.* Combined with the widespread Gaulish dedications of cities to *Lugus*,

Caesar's account suggests that by Mercury he meant *Lugus*, the most widely worshipped of all Celtic deities.

The epithet *llawgyffes* 'skilful hand' (PKM 275) bestowed on *Lleu* in the naming-incident in *Math* is curiously paralleled in meaning by the Ir. *samildánach* which is given to *Lugh* in the Ir. tale *Cath Maige Tuired: the Battle of Mag Tuired* (ed. and trans. E. A. Gray, ITS LII, and Cross and Slover, *Ancient Irish Tales*, pp. 35–6). *Samildánach* means 'skilled in many arts together', and the bestowal of this epithet is accounted for by an incident in which *Lugh*, seeking admittance at the gate of Tara, gives as a reason for admission his proficiency in one craft after another, and finally, his pre-eminence in all. *Samildánach* approaches more closely in its meaning to the W. *llawgyffes* than does *lámhfhada* 'long-arm' (cf. *Kadwallawn Llaw Hir*), the epithet which is more commonly appropriated to *Lugh* in Irish sources such as the *Dinnshenchus* and *Duanaire Finn*—though *lamhfhada* approaches *llawgyffes* more closely in form. *Samildánach* appears to be the older form of *Lugh*'s epithet. The naming incidents attached to both *Lugh* and *Lleu* express to some extent the same conception of the hero's skill and dexterity, although the Welsh tale does so in a less comprehensive fashion. One can hardly doubt that the two tales are variant expressions of an identical conception of *Lugh–Lleu* as the god of craftsmanship.

BT 35.24–6, refers to *Minavc ap lleu,* who is unknown elsewhere: *Mynavc hoedyl Minavc ap lleu / A weleisi yma gynheu / Diwed yn* (*ar*)*llechued lleu / Bu gwrd y hwrd yg kateu* 'Kindly was the life of Mynawg ap Lleu, whom I saw here formerly; Lleu's end was in (Ar)llechwedd (?), mighty was his thrust in battles'. (The emendation *llechwedd* to *Arllechwedd* is suggested by W. J. Gruffydd, *Math*, p. 58, on the grounds that the line is obviously too short.) For further references to the story of *Lleu* in BT see n. to *Gwydyon.*

Cynddelw: *Gnaud om gwawd goruod yn amrysson / mal pan oruyd lleu yn llyuyr canon* (H 131.16 = CBT III, no. 21.185–6n.) 'Usual by my verse is victory in (bardic) contests, as Lleu excels in the canonical books'. (For doubt as to whether *lleu* here is the proper name, see D. Johnston, review in LlC XVIII, p. 139.) With this cf. RBP col. 1054.16–17: *neu leu a gvydyon / a uuant geluydon / neu a wdant lyfyryon* 'Do Lleu and Gwydyon who were skilled (enchanters) know, do learned men know?' etc.

Lle6[2] m. Kynuarch 70, App. IV, no. 1: *Gwalchmei m. Llew m. Kenvarch.* Cf. BD 140: *ygorchymynnvyt y Leu uab Kynuarch llu enys Brydein . . . Yarll oed hvnnv a marchavc prouedic clotuavr, a doeth a phrud y oet a'e synnvyr, ac vrth ueint y glot a'e uolyant y rodassei y brenhin* (*Uthur*) *Anna y uerch yn wreic idav, a llywodraeth y deyrnas yn y lav tra ytoed ynteu yn glaf* (= HRB VIII, 21: *Loth de lodonesia . . . miles strenuissimus. sapiencia et aetate maturus*); BD 152.20: *y Leu uab Kynuarch y rodes yarllaeth Lodoneis ac a berthynei vrthi.*

The origin of Geoffrey's *Loth* is obscure. Whatever may be the ultimate derivation of the name, Geoffrey's choice of it must have been determined by its closeness to *Lodonesia* (the regular latinized form of *Lothian*; see Watson, *The Celtic Place-Names of Scotland*, p. 101); and it looks like an attempt to reproduce the name of the legendary eponymous ruler of *Lothian*, who appears in the *Fragmentary Life of St Kentigern* as King *Leudonus* of *Leudonia* [*sic*], and elsewhere in early Welsh sources as *L(l)ewdwn lluydauc* (see n. to *Cyndeyrn Garthwys*). According to Geoffrey's account, *Loth* became king of Norway as well as Lothian, after Arthur's conquest of that country, in succession to King Sichelm, who was *Loth*'s uncle (HRB IX, 11 = BD 154). Hence the portrayal of *Lot*(*h*) as king of Orkney in the French prose romances and in Malory; and hence also the allusion to Orkney in the genealogy which appears in the fifteenth-century manuscript Harl. 200 (fo. 141) (see n. to *Joseph o Arimathia*).

Whatever the origin of Geoffrey's character *Loth*, the redactor of the Welsh *Brut* substituted for *Loth* the name of *Lleu,* which he would appear to have derived from the *Mabinogi* tradition, since the name occurs nowhere else in early Welsh sources except in reference to *Lleu Llaw Gyffes* and to the son of Kynuarch here referred to. It is possible, however, that the form of this name has also been influenced by that of the eponymous *Lleudun Lluydauc.* For the relation of *Loth*/*Lleu* to Gwalchmei (Geoffrey's Gualguanus) see n. to *Gwalchmei m. Gwyar*. The names *Llew*, *Araw*(*n*), and *Vrien* are given as those of three sons of Llywarch Hen among the *englynion* entitled *Enweu Meibon Llywarch Hen*, LlDC no. 40.10 (CLlH no. VIII.3). But these names do not occur elsewhere in the Llywarch Hen poetry, or in any list of the sons of Llywarch Hen that I have seen. I have suggested (B XVII, pp. 180–1) that the first line of the *englyn Tri meib Llywarch, tri aghimen kad* should be emended to *Tri meib Kynuarch*, etc., since *Kynuarch* gives alliteration with *kad,* and the *englyn* would then give the names of the sons of *Kynuarch* as these appear in the *Brut*. For acceptance of this, see B. F. Roberts, B XXV, pp. 283–4; E. D. Jones, LlDC xv. The latter's revised dating of the Black Book to the second half of the thirteenth century makes this emendation the more acceptable.

Llewei verch Seitwed 58. *Llewei* perhaps < *llewa* 'to devour, gobble'. The later manuscripts have nearly all emended this extraordinary name in some way; Pen. 240 changing it to the recognizable and far more attractive *Lleicu. Seitwed* = 'Seven Faces', but cf. also *seit* = *capulum* 'sword-hilt', CA 369. 'Hilt-Faced' would perhaps not be more strange as a nickname than 'Iron-Faced' (*Haearnwed*, triad 22). Perhaps, however, *Seitwed* merely represents an early spelling of *seithued* 'seventh', cf. CO ll. 193–5: *A Sinnoch mab Seithuet, a Watu mab Seithuet, a Naw mab Seithuet, a Gwenwynwyn mab Naw mab Seithuet, a Bedyw mab Seithuet*.

Llia6(s) m. Nwyvre 35 (R: *Lliaw m. N.*). 'Multitude son of Sky.' For similarly intentionally comic pairs of names, cf. *Llawr m. Eiryf.*

Prydydd y Moch: *lliavs maws mab nwyfre* (H 293.21 = CBT V, no. 9.21n. The editor takes *lliaws* as a noun, rather than a proper name, and proposes that the name in the triad is derived from this line of verse.)

Englynion y Clyweit: *A glyweist-di a gant Llyaws / Mab Nwyfre, milwr hynaws* (*Blodeugerdd* no. 31, *englyn* 61).

Prydydd y Moch's allusion to *Llia6s* gives prior authority for the form in the triad and, since the allusion belongs to the late twelfth century, it gives prior evidence for a part of the tradition on which the triad is based.

Llouan Llaw Diuo 33 (= W: *Llofuan Llav Difuro*) 'Ll. Severing Hand', see EWSP 114–17, 567. *Llouan* is itself a diminutive of *llaw.* W's *difuro* 'homeless, landless', hence 'exiled', is supported as against Pen. 16's *divo* by the rhyme in CLlH no. III.46:

Angerd Uryen ys agro gennyf
Kyrchynat ym pob bro
Yn wisc Louan Law Difro

'I grieve for the might of Urien; (he was) an attacker in every land, on the track of Llovan Exiled Hand.'

Cf. also the variant of this name, *Llovan Llaw Estrawn* 'Ll. Stranger's Hand', in Pen. 98 B 48 (CLlH no. XII.7d). Instances of the orthography: *fu-*, *fv-* for *f* occur in the *Llyfr Ancr*: *kyfuaruot* (106.7), *dwfuyr, gyfulavn* (107.7, 8) (quoted PKM 146). Nevertheless, *diuo* is the form supported by the *Beddau* stanzas in Pen. 98 B (= CLlH no. XII.9–10, T. Jones, PBA LIII, p. 134):

Bedd Llovan Llaw Ddivo yn arro Venai . . .
Odidawg a'i gwypo
Namyn Duw a mi heno

'The grave of Ll. Ll. D. on the shore of Menai; few are they who know it, except God and I tonight.'

For this form cf. also RBP col. 1055.28: *chwannavc vyd llen llwydavc llav diuo. Diuo* (= *diuoi?*) 'cut away, divide, separate' (G 339), and so this form of the name could be rendered 'Ll. of the Severing Hand' or perhaps 'Ll. One-Handed'. In B XXI, pp. 29–30, J. E. Caerwyn Williams discusses *Llouan*'s epithet and advocates W's form with medial *-r-* (*difro*) as likely to be the earlier. He compares this epithet with the early Irish phrase (evidently an idiom) *Bid lám deoraid dó* (Strachan and Bergin, *Stories from the Táin* (Dublin, 1970), p. 17) meaning 'it will be an outlaw's hand to him' implying 'it will be his death'. The Irish phrase presents a remarkable parallel to *llaw d(d)ifro*; and the variant *difo* would then have arisen as an early gloss on the latter. But the evidence is too insecure to allow of any certainty as to which is the earlier form; and for a contrary view, which favours *divo* as the original, see N. J. A. Williams, 'Canu Llywarch and the Finn Cycle', *Ast. H.* 255–8.

The tradition implied in CLlH and expressly stated in the triad that *Urien Rheged* was slain by the hand of an assassin (who was a foreigner or exile?) is not necessarily inconsistent with the narrative concerning Urien's death given in HB, ch. 63 (*Morcanto destinante pro invidia*), since *Llouan* could have been the agent employed by Morcant to perform the deed. (Cf. however the variant account of the slaying of Urien which appears in Pen. 50's version of the triad.) For the passage, see n. to *Vryen Reget.*

Llud m. Beli 37; *Auarwy m. Llud m. Beli* 51. (Perhaps *Caswallawn m. Beli* in triad 36 should be emended to *Llud*; see n. to triad.) See also *Beli Mawr m. Mynogan.* On the confusion between the names *Lludd / Nudd* see below under *Llyr Lledyiaith.*

BT 70.19–21: *Seith meib o Veli dyrchafyssyn / kaswallavn a llud a chestudyn. / diwed plo coll iago o tir prydyn.* On these lines, see B. F. Roberts, *Cyfranc Lludd a Llefelys* xiii. Since only three sons of Beli are named, it seems possible that a line or more has been dropped from the text.

The above lines inaugurate a short prophetic poem which from the historical allusions which it contains may have been composed in the last quarter of the eleventh century; for a brief discussion of these see AP xl–xliv. Two other prophetic poems in BT bear titles which associate them in some unexplained way with *Lludd:* these are *Gvavt Lud y Mawr* 'the Great Eulogy of Lludd' (BT 74) and *Ymarwar Llud Bychan* 'the Short Discussion of Lludd' (BT 78). Both poems were perhaps composed in the late eleventh century (see M. E. Griffiths, *Early Vaticination in Welsh*, pp. 125–8). A line referring to *ymarwar llud a llefelis* (BT 78.26) suggests that it is *Lludd m. Beli* who is intended in the title of these poems, but no clue has survived to account for his association in this way with political prophecy.

As regards the number of the sons of Beli, it may be noted that the *Brut*, following Geoffrey, gives the names of three only, not of seven: *Ac yn ol Manogan y doeth Beli Mavr y uab ynteu . . . . Ac y hvnnv y bu tri meib, Llud a Chaswallavn a Nynnyav* (BD 44 = HRB III, 20). We might expect, therefore, to find some form of the name *Nynnyaw / Nennius* in place of *a chestudyn* in BT 70; but there is in fact no evidence that the association of this third son with Beli Mawr goes back any earlier than Geoffrey. The number of Beli's sons is not specified in the allusion to them in *Breudwyt Maxen* (WM 186.29–31; see n. to *Beli Mawr*).

Lludd m. Beli is the hero of the tale *Cyfranc Lludd a Llefelys*, which is given in RM and in a fragmentary form in WM and also in many of the texts of *Brut y Brenhinedd.* The earlier texts of the *Brut* have in fact been classified according as to whether they do or do not include this tale (see introduction to RBB xiii–xiv). The earliest version to include it is that found in Ll. 1 (= Shirburn Castle C 18, *Rep.* II, p. 119), which was written between 1225 and 1250. The text of the story from this manuscript was printed in EC I, pp. 261–71. Here, as in all versions of the *Brut* which include the story, the reference quoted above to the three sons of *Beli Mawr* is followed by the sentence: *A megys y dyweyt rey or kyvarwydyeyt pedweryd map a wu ydaw llevelys.* The tale then follows in a form which presents only slight verbal differences from the text of the *Mabinogion* version. Although the opening words of the story in both WM and RM leave no doubt as to their dependence on the *Brut*, it is certain that the story itself is composed of elements of which some at least must belong to Welsh tradition before Geoffrey's work. Thus BT 78.26 alludes to *ymarwar llud a llefelis* (see above) 'the Discussion of Ll. and Ll.', and this may well have been the earlier title of the story which RM calls *Cyfranc Lludd a Llefelys* 'The Adventure of Ll. a Ll.'. This suggestion is borne out by Llywelyn Fardd II's allusion to the story:

handwyf huavdyl was a wys yn llys
ual ymarwar llut a lleuelys
(H 208.3–4 = CBT VI, no. 7.4n.)

'I am an eloquent lad who is known in the court, like the contention of Lludd and Llevelys.'

Other elements of undoubted antiquity in the tale are the account of the *Corranyeit* (see n. to triad 36), and that of the fighting 'dragons' buried under Dinas Emrys (see n. to triad 37). The story may thus be safely regarded as having existed in some form before Geoffrey, and as constituting the most elaborate of all the additions made to Geoffrey's text from independent material by his Welsh redactors. (For a discussion of the older elements in the tale, see introduction to Ifor Williams's edition of *Cyfranc Lludd a Llefelys*; that of B. F. Roberts; and most importantly Brinley Rees, *Ceinciau'r Mabinogi* (Bangor, 1999), 15–17.)

The *Brut* (following HRB) gives no information about *Lludd mab Beli* apart from the onomastic fiction of his alleged connection with the rebuilding of London: in *Lludd*'s honour the city was given the name of *Caer Lud* (BD 20.44 = HRB I, 17) while *Ludysgat* (*Porth Lludd*) marks the place of his burial. Henry of Huntingdon (writing in 1129) knew of a King *Liud* or *Luid* whom he represents as the father of Bellinus and Cassibelaunus (*Hist. Ang.* I, ch. 12), i.e. he had evidently some indirect knowledge of the existence of a connection between these three characters, though in respect to their relationship Geoffrey reproduces the Welsh tradition more accurately. (On Henry of Huntingdon's allusions to *Liud* see Faral, *La Légende Arthurienne* II, pp. 145–6.)

References to the story of *Lludd a Llefelys* by the *cywyddwyr* include the following:

Cywydd y Sêr (? by Gr. Gryg; see DGG cv):

Dysgais . . .
Gywydd i gyweithydd uthr
Cannawg risg mewn eurwisg-gaen
A fu yn y gerwyn faen
(DGG no. XL.33–4)

'I have learned . . . a *cywydd* about a terrible company, the scaly-skinned ones in gold-clothed covering, who were in the stone coffer.'

Lewys Môn (in praise of his patron's peaceful administration of Gwynedd):

Nad i'th garn, adwyth a gaid,
acw'r un o'r Coraniaid
lladd wenwyn fal Lludd unwaith
y dŵr-swyn wyd dros ein iaith
(LlC IV, p. 36 = GLM no. LXXI.29–32)

'Do not allow your support (?)—a misfortune would be had—yonder to one of the Coraniaid to destroy the poison as Lludd once did: you are (= you supply) the holy water on behalf of our nation.' (Cf. Eurys Rowlands, LlC VI, p. 244n.)

Rhys Goch Eryri alludes to his home *yn nhir y dreigiau* (IGE[2] 163.28): *lle bu'r dreigiau draw* (185.12).

Llynghessa6c La6 Hael 66 (Pen. 47). Cf. triad 14, *Tri Llyghessawc* 'Seafarers / Fleet-Owners'. *Llaw Hael* 'Generous Hand', cf. *Nudd Hael*, var. *Nudd Llaw Hael*, 71. Cf. Life of *St Cadog* (VSB 68§22): *Ligessauc, filius Eliman, cognomento Lau hiir, id est, longa manus* (an opponent of Arthur) described as *dux quidam Brittanorum fortissimus*.

Llyr[1] Lledyeith 'Llŷr Half-Speech' or perhaps 'Half-National' (interpreting *iaith* as 'nation, people') 8: *manawydan m. llyr llyedyeith* [*sic*]; 37: *Bendigeituran m. Llyr*; 52, 53: *Branwen verch Lyr*. See also *Llyr[3] Marini*, *Bran Vendigeit m. Llyr*.

Mostyn 117 (*circa* 1280) gives the descent of Arthur as follows: *Arthur m. Ythyr m. kustenhin m. kynuavr m. Tutwal m. Moruavr m. Eudaf m. kadvr m. kynan m. karadavc m. Bran m. Llyr lletieith* (EWGT 39 (5)). The same genealogy appears in Pen. 27, p. 167, but here both Arthur's paternal and maternal descent is traced to the same line (see n. to *Arthur*). By comparing this genealogy with the versions of *Bonedd y Saint* in Pen. 27, 127, 74 (see EWGT 65 (76) etc.; RC 50, p. 367), it becomes clear that Arthur's descent has been grafted on to that of the ruling dynasty of Dumnonia with the name of his grandfather Custennin (= Custennin Gorneu in the *Bonedd*). This dynasty claimed descent from *Llŷr Lledieith*. See nn. to *Gereint m. Erbin*, *Goreu m. Kustenin*. This genealogy is extended to include the forebears of *Llŷr Lledieith*. Peter Bartrum quotes from Mostyn 113, p. 102 as follows: *Llyr Llediaith ab Pharaon danindde ac velly mal y dycko y brif ach at Dyfnwal Moelmud* (EWGT 150 n. on *Bonedd yr Arwyr* § 30; see also B XVIII, p. 249).

Hugh Thomas (Harl. 4181, p. 37) gives a different genealogy for the forebears of *Llŷr Llediaith* as follows: *Galbean. Anny ab Albean Tirvad. Dyngad. Graydiol. Gerient. Meirion. Arthan. Keidio Bywrmwyn. Kerihir Llyngwyn. Paran. Lhyr Lhediaith or Lisping Lhyr. King of Gomery about the time of Julius Caesar's first invading and perhaps as a confederate of Caswallon ap Bely ingaged in the war against him . . . in which he had the misfortune to be taken prisoner, being called one of the Three Noble Prisoners of the Island of Britain in the Triades.*

Elsewhere (*Jes. Gen.* 51) *Llŷr Lledieith* has been interpolated into Geoffrey's pre-Roman king-list to become the son of Brutus Taryanlas (replacing *Lliwelyt m. Brutus ysgwyt ir* in the genealogy in HGVK 2.8–9). All that can fairly be deduced from these genealogical references is that *Llŷr Lledieith* was regarded as a legendary ancestor. As such he may be compared with Beli Mawr: and *Mabinogi Branwen* (PKM 29) tells us that the family of Brân Vendigeit, from whom the Dumnonian dynasty claimed descent, were in fact regarded as the progeny of both *Llŷr* and Beli.

Llŷr is used frequently by the *Cynfeirdd* and *Gogynfeirdd* as a common noun denoting the sea, and in this usage it corresponds with the cognate Ir. *ler* (CLlH 116; J. Vendryes, EC VI, pp. 247–8). But as the name of a deity, whose existence is implied in that of the sea-god *Manannán mac Lír,* the Ir. *Ler* is an even more shadowy figure than the Welsh *Llŷr.* It has even been suggested that *mac lir* means merely 'son of the sea' and that it is to this epithet of Manannán's alone that the Welsh divinity *Llŷr* owes his being (see EC VI, pp. 239 ff.). If *Manawydan fab Llŷr* is indeed to be regarded as a creation based on a semi-learned borrowing from Ireland to Wales, one is tempted to connect *Llŷr*'s epithet *lledieith* with his foreign origin. But the nature of the connection between these two characters is by no means clear; see n. to *Manawydan.*

The version of triad 52 which is given in the text of *Culhwch* (CO ll. 914–16n.) could be taken as implying the identity of *Llŷr Lledyeith* with *Lludd Llaw Ereint.* Certain considerations seem to favour their identity. Firstly, *Llŷr* and *Lludd* are interchangeable names (see note to *Llyr*[2] *Lluydawc* below). Secondly, Rhŷs showed long ago (*Celtic Heathenism,* pp. 125 ff.; CF 447–8) that the name and epithet of *Lludd Llaw Ereint* corresponds with that of the Ir. god *Nuadu Argatlám* 'N. of the Silver Hand', whose name in Welsh would become *Nudd,* but the *N.* of *Nudd* > *Ll* under the influence of the initial of *Llaw*, and *Nudd* is in turn to be identified with the Romano-British deity *Nodons*, commemorated at a fourth-century temple at Lydney Park, Gloucs. (see Wheeler, *Report on an Excavation at Lydney Park*, Soc. of Antiquaries, London, 1932; cf. Anne Ross, PCB 176–9). The attributes of this deity, inferred from the mosaic pavements at the temple, associate him with the sea and with fishing, and Vendryes associates the name *Nodons* with the Gothic root *niuta* 'to fish, fishing' (*La Religion des Celtes*, vol. III of *Les Religions de l'Europe Ancienne,* ed. A. Grenier, p. 255). If *Nodons* has descended into Ml. Welsh tradition as *Lludd Llaw Ereint,* his affinities with the sea correspond well enough with those of *Llŷr.* But in the last resort the evidence for the identification of *Llŷr* and *Lludd Llaw Ereint* rests solely on a comparison of the two versions of triad 52, as they appear in *Culhwch* and in the WR text of TYP; and to my mind this identification remains extremely doubtful. *Lludd Llaw Ereint* is unknown outside the tale of *Culhwch* (see CO l. 916n.), which depicts him as the father of Creiddylad; but no tradition has anywhere survived which associates Creiddylad with the *Llŷr* family. It is possible, then, though it is by no means certain, that the two names ultimately refer to the same mythological figure. For a more recent discussion, see J. Carey, 'Nodons in Britain and Ireland', ZCP 40, pp. 1–22.

Geoffrey of Monmouth's *Leir* appears to be derived from *Laegreceaster,* the O.E. name for Leicester, where *Leir* was said to have been buried (see BD 217 = HRB II, 14). The *Bruts* render this name by *Llŷr,* under the influence of the *Llŷr* of Welsh tradition. But beyond this there can be no connection between the two characters; and the story which Geoffrey tells of 'King Lear' is unlikely to have any basis in antecedent Welsh sources: it is a popular medieval international tale, of which a version is found in the *Gesta Romanorum.*

The allusion in BT 47.22—*Ny thric y gofel* (*hwy?*) *no neithavr llyr* 'his concealment (or "plot", G 545) does not remain (longer) than the wedding-feast of Llyr'—suggests the existence of a story to the effect that this feast was in some way interrupted or perhaps prevented. But no other source throws any light upon the allusion. BT 33.3–4: *keint rac meibon llyr yn ebyr henvelen* seems to allude to the episode of Brân's Head narrated in *Branwen.* References to *Llŷr Lledieith* by the *Gogynfeirdd* are frequent:

Cynddelw: *Rut ongyr Bran vab Llyr Dedyeith* (H 118.17 = CBT IV, no. 9.50); *baran llyr lledyeith* (H 120.16 = CBT III, no. 13.34).

Prydydd y Moch: *angert lyr a bran* (H 297.25 = CBT V, no. 20.37).

Trahaearn Brydydd Mawr: *llit llyr lletyeith* (RBP col. 1222.33)

Justus Llwyd: *Hi a vu yng gvyd llu vab 1lyr lletieith* (RBP col. 1365.5 = YB 71.23).

Other references are probably though not certainly to the same character:

Bleddyn Fardd: *aruaeth llyr* (H 79.8 = CBT VII, no. 53.28n.); *meibyon llyr* (H 68.20 = CBT VII, no. 54.36n.).

Gr. ap Maredudd: *llew oed llyr gedoed* (RBP col. 1206.31 = GGM no. 3.28); *cymrawt Llyr* (RBP col. 1318.25 = GGM no. 4.167); *Llyr bwyll* (RBP col. 1328.22); *llyr gymrodedd* (MA 294b, 28 = GGM no. 3.76).

Two references to *Tŵr Llŷr* by the *cywyddwyr* perhaps denote Harlech castle (GTA I, no. XLIV.47; DN no. XXIII.3; see n. to the latter).

Llŷr Llediaith is further referred to in: GLGC no. 171.21n. etc; GTA I, no. XLII.14; *meibion Llŷr*, ibid., l. 73; *leiddiad Lŷr*, GDG no. 44.13 (see n.). In

DGG no. XXIX.19, the Salmon is described as *ail Llŷr,* which suggests an allusion to *Llŷr* as a sea-god.

Llyr² Lluyda6c 18 (= WR: *Llud lluryga6c*) 'Ll. of the Hosts'. For *Lluydawc* cf. *Elen Luyda6c*, *Yrp Lluyda6c.* W gives a different epithet: *llurygawc* < *llurig* (< L. *lorica*) 'breastplate, corselet'. Cf. CA l. 690: *llurugogyon*; l. 897: *dyfforthes ae law luric wehyn*; ll. 182–4: *tri* (*si*) *chatvarchawc . . . tri llu llurugawc.* The resemblance between *llu llurugawc* in the last line and WR's *Llud lluryga6c* is striking, and suggests that *lluryga6c* may be the older form of the epithet: note that this is the epithet given in most versions of the triad except those of Pen. 16 and Pen. 45. On the other hand the *lluryga6c* of WR may owe its origin to a reminiscence of the lines in CA quoted above. The different versions of the triad provide a good illustration of the confusion between the names *Llŷr* and *Llud*(*d*)*;* cf. triad 67: *Manawydan uab Llyr* (R: *uab llud*); RBB col. 82.23–4: *Teneuan . . . mab Dud* (*mab Beli*); ibid. 93.19–20: *T. vab llyr.*

Llyr³ Marini 63, 71 (Pen. 267) *Llyr Merini.* On *merin* 'sea' in poetry see CA 218. According to *Bonedd y Saint* (EWGT 58 (29, 66, 88, 89)) *Llŷr Marini* was the father of *Caradawc Vreichvras.* VN² claims that his father was *Einion Yrth m. Cunedda* (see Harl. Gen. I). This connection with a north Welsh genealogy seems confirmed by RBP col. 1411.18, where Lewys Glyn Cothi describes the three sons of *Sir Rossier Vychan* as *O dir mon o rodri . . . o egin llyr merini.* See GLGC no. 131.18–19n. Huw Cae Llwyd refers to *Llŷr Merini* among the ancestors of Wiliam ap Morgan ap Syr Dafydd Gam (HCLl no. I.38). *Marini* as an epithet is found on a fifth- or early sixth-century pillar-stone at Llandysilio, Pembrokeshire: CLVTORIGI(S) FIL(I) PAULINI MARINI LATIO '(The stone) of Clutorix, son of Paulinus Marinus of Latium' (ECMW, no. 315). *Latio* here may represent no more than a claim to Roman citizenship similar to *Protector* on the sixth-century stone of *Voteporix.* As a proper name *Marin*(*us*) is found on an Ogham inscription at Colbinstown, Co. Kildare: MAQI-DDECCEDA MAQI MARIN (Macalister, *Corpus Inscriptionum Insularum Celticarum,* no. 20), on which K. H. Jackson remarks ('Notes on the Ogham Inscriptions of Southern Britain', in Cyril Fox and Bruce Dickens (eds), *H. M. Chadwick Memorial Studies: Early Cultures of North-west Europe* (Cambridge, 1950), p. 212)) that the *Marinus* here named may have been a returned emigrant of mixed Irish-British parentage. *Merin* occurs in *Bonedd y Saint*; suitably enough it is the name of one of the sons of *Seithennin Vrenhin o Vaes Gwydno* (EWGT 60 (40)). The better texts of *Bonedd y Saint* are now available in EWGT 29, 51, 52, 88, 89.

But in the case of *Llŷr Marini* the epithet may be no more than a latinization of the name *Llŷr,* and the character may be merely a doublet of *Llŷr¹ Lledyeith.* As Windisch pointed out (*Das Keltische Britannien*, p. 113) the genitive *Marini* suggests an origin in a genealogical formula, and the significant position held by *Llŷr Lledieith* in the genealogies has been noted above.

Llywarch Hen (m. Elidir Lledanwyn) 'Ll. the Old', 8, 65, 76, 77; App. II, no. 2; App. IV, no. 8. The inclusion of *Llywarch Hen* in BGG (App. II, no. 2) sets forth clearly the historical milieu to which *Llywarch* was considered to belong, according to thirteenth-century tradition: i.e. he was one of the sixth-century Men of the North—a contemporary of Rhydderch Hael and Urien Rheged, and a cousin of the latter. This date for *Llywarch*'s *floruit* is borne out by the genealogy *Jes*. XVII (= EWGT 46 (17); HGVK 1–2 and nn.), which gives the (alleged) descent of Rhodri Mawr as follows: 'Rodri mavr m. Meruyn vrych m. Gvrhyat' (see n. to *Gwryat m. G6ryan*) 'm. Elidir m. Sandef m. Alcun m. tegyth m. Ceit (m. Gweir) m. Douc m. Llewarch Hen' (etc., to *Coil Hen*; see App. II, no. 2). Since Rhodri Mawr died 877 (*Ann. Cam.*), by allowing the customary thirty years to a generation, a supposed *obit* for the 'historical' *Llywarch* is obtained *circa* 604.

Corroborative and earlier evidence for the relationship between *Llywarch* and Urien as stated in App. II, no. 2, is offered by the ninth–tenth century *englynion* of the *Llywarch Hen* cycle, which affirm this relationship (CLlH no. I.22), and give further evidence for the connection of Llywarch and his family with Urien (CLlH no. I.10; VII.16, 18; and the whole of no. III, in which Llywarch is apparently intended as the speaker throughout, cf. 21c: *Gwae vy llaw llad vyg keuynderw*). This relationship is stated once more in the tract *De Situ Brecheniauc* (EWGT 14–16 (15)) which may be as old as the eleventh century (*Cy.* XIX, p. 26). Here we have *Guaur, filia Brachan, uxor (Elidir) Lidanwen, et mater Loarch Hen.* Since Kynfarch, father of Urien, is here also said to have married a daughter of Brychan (see n. to triad 70), *Llywarch* and Urien are thus represented as first cousins on the sides of both mother and father. But the marriages attributed to the numerous daughters of Brychan in this list are altogether too consistently illustrious to be easily credible: in this instance they serve merely to confirm the existence of a tradition that *Llywarch* and Urien were believed to be close kinsmen. The relationship of 'cousin' between *Llywarch* and Urien, which is corroborated by CLlH no. III, would of course suit the link between their fathers as established in BGG (see M. Miller, B XXVI, p. 258). For the possibility that *Llywarch* was conceived as Urien's slayer in the underlying saga, of which we have merely the *disjecta membra* in CLlH, see N. J. A. Williams, *Ast. H.*, ch. X.

In his study of the poetry of the *Llywarch Hen* cycle as preserved in LlDC and RBH, Ifor Williams showed that there is no early evidence to justify a belief that *Llywarch Hen* is to be included among the *Cynfeirdd*, although the fact that he figured as a character in the *englyn*-cycle of ninth-century Powys caused him to be commonly regarded as a poet by later generations. Testimony to this belief in the fifteenth century is to be found in Guto'r Glyn's inclusion of *Llywarch* in his version of the triad *Tri Oferfardd* (see n. to triad 12). In the *englynion* poetry referred to—all that has survived of the sagas dealing with the fortunes of *Llywarch* and his family—*Llywarch Hen* figures as a character in dialogues with two of his sons, Gwen and Maenwyn, whom he incites each in turn to go out and fight in defence of their homes against the English invader. *Llywarch* is also portrayed as the speaker in laments on the deaths of Gwen and of another son, Pyll; and also of a lament on his own old age, in which he regrets the glories of the past, and compares his state with that of the withered leaf. (On the antiquity of this tradition of Llywarch as a querulous ancient, see my note in B XXII, pp. 30–7.) The scene of these poems (as distinct from that of CLlH no. III which refers to events in North Britain) is laid in Powys and on its borders, and it is here that tradition claimed that the graves of several of *Llywarch*'s sons were to be found (CLlH no. I.43). Late tradition associated *Llywarch Hen* with Llanfor in Meirionnydd (CLlH no. V), where a mound known as his *pabell* was pointed out (CLlH lxxxix). Further south again a *claud lyuarch hen* (Ll. H.'s dyke) was known near Llyn Syfaddon in the twelfth century (LL 146.24). This reappearance and fresh localization in early medieval Wales of a character who belonged to sixth-century northern heroic tradition need cause no surprise: it is in accordance with the movement southwards of many of the traditions of the old North, and has analogies in the traditions about *Taliesin*, *Myrddin*, *Drystan*, *Gwyddno Garanhir*, *Urien Rheged*, *Hueil m. Caw* (see nn.).

It is stated in the poems that the number of *Llywarch*'s sons was twenty-four, and stanzas giving the names of some of these sons are interspersed through the *englynion* sequences in LlDC and RBH. Again, lists of the names of his sons appear frequently in genealogical manuscripts, for example, Pen. 75, p. 49; Pen. 127, p. 93; Pen. 129, p. 11 (see also EWGT 86 (5) = B XVIII, p. 234; WCD 424; CLIH xxx). In the manuscripts these lists are often accompanied by the stanza *Am ei Blant* (CLlH no. X). The lists include the names of Douc, Diwc from whom Rhodri Mawr traced descent (see also CLlH no. I.46–7; HGVK 1.23n.; EWGT 46 (17) etc.), and Cenau; cf. the name *Keneu vab llywarch*, CA l. 560 and n. Another son of *Llywarch Hen*, whose name does not occur in these lists, or in the poetry, is named in *Bonedd y Saint*: *Buan m. Esgun m. Llewarch Hen* (EWGT 57 (17)).

The epithet *Hen* is bestowed in the genealogies and elsewhere on certain other characters of the early period, both in North Britain and in Wales itself; examples: *Coel Hen*, *Dyfnwal Hen*, *Rhydderch Hen* (Harl. Gens. no. 6, cf. App. II), *Bran Hen m. Dumngual Moelmut* (Harl. Gen. X = *Bran*[2] *Galed o'r Gogledd*, App. III, no. 3); *Morcant Hen* of Morgannwg (HW 338n., *Jes. Gen.* XIV, LL 240.21); *Kynvarch Hen,* triad 70 (Pen. 50). Whatever may have been the full significance of this epithet in early times (and it is possible that it may once have held some precise dynastic connotation which is not now easily discernible), it is probable that the epithet *Hen* as applied to *Llywarch* had a formative influence on the shaping of the saga of the Old Man and his sons: so that in the *englynion Llywarch* came to be portrayed as a querulous veteran and a typical figure of senility. The epithet *Hen* may well account also for *Llywarch*'s inclusion in App. IV as one of Arthur's 'counsellors'. For further instances of *hen* as title, see EWGT 226. These suggest that *Hen* once held some significance as regards status, which it is now impossible for us to recover.

Triad 65 (W) already illustrates the progressive attraction into the Arthurian orbit of unrelated characters, so that even *Llywarch*, who appears to have been at one time himself the centre of a cycle of tales, was obliged to conform in this to the later encroachment in popularity of the Arthurian material. In view of this triad it is perhaps surprising to find that *Llywarch* does not figure in the list of characters at Arthur's court in *Culhwch,* nor is he named anywhere else in the *chwedlau.* There are two recorded allusions to *Llywarch Hen* by the *Gogynfeirdd*: in a poem by Dafydd Benfras who cites *Llywarch fab Elidir* (CBT VI, no. 33.20n.) and another less certain allusion by Einion vab Gwgon in his poem to Llywelyn ab Iorwerth: *llywelyn boed hyn boed hwy dichwein / no llywarch hybarch hybar kicwein* (H 52.6 = CBT VI, no. 18.68) 'Ll., may he be older and may his course be longer than honoured Llywarch of the thrusting spear'. But the name of *Llywarch* was borne by several people in the twelfth century (it was also that of a king of Dyfed who died 903, *Ann. Cam.*; see HW 333) so that it is not possible in every instance to be certain whether or not references in poetry are to the traditional *Llywarch.* Gruffudd Gryg's allusion to *Llywarch* as one of the famous poets of the past (GDG 428) seems almost certainly to be to *Llywarch ap Llywelyn* (*Prydydd y Moch*), so also is the reference by Gwilym Ddu (RBP col. 1230.1). In B XXII, pp. 34–6, I have shown that the belief that Llywarch Hen was himself a poet rather than a warrior is first attested in two allusions to him by Guto'r Glyn in the fifteenth century. This date corresponds with the first appearance in the manuscripts of the two fragments 'March Gwên' and 'Am ei Blant' (CLlH nos. IX and X), both of which bear the subscript 'Llywarch Hen a'i cant'. Guto'r Glyn refers to *Llywarch Hen a'i awdl Wên dlos* (GGl no. XXVII.49; D. J. Bowen, *Barddoniaeth yr Uchelwyr*, 17.49).

Dafydd ab Edmwnd: *Anoeth yw a hun* (= *hŷn*) *noi thaid / hun* (*hŷn*) *no Llowarch hen llawir* (GDE 56.2–3).

Tudur Penllyn: *Oes hir i'r feinir aur fyd / I Huw oes Lywarch hefyd* (GTP no. 10.53–4).

Llywelyn ab y Moel to Rhys Goch Eryri: *ail Lywarch lân* (IGE[2] 168.7)

For *Llywarch Hen* see Ifor Williams, *Canu Llywarch Hen*; 'The Poems of Llywarch Hen', PBA 1932; *Lectures on Early Welsh Poetry* (Dublin, 1944).

Mabon[1] m. Dewengen 66: *Emerchret wreic* (*M*). For instances of *Mabon* as a proper name see LL 209.8; 75.28; 164.10. See also *Mabon*[2] below.

Mabon[2] m. Modron 52. *Mabon* 'boy' is applied to Christ, BT 47.9. But the *Mabon* of Ml.W. tradition derives his name from that of a Celtic deity, *Mapŏnos* son of *Mātrŏna* 'the youth (god) son of the mother (goddess)'. For *Mātrŏna* see n. to *Modron verch Auallach.* For further instances in which a matronymic is used in place of a patronymic as the traditional form of a name, cf. *Gwydyon m. Don* and see n. to *Gwalchmei m. Gwyar.* In this instance it is just possible that the name of a god who was associated with *Mapŏnos* as father is preserved in the name *Mabon vab Mellt* 'M. son of lightning', who is mentioned (LlDC no. 31.23; CO ll. 1007–8, 1013) in association with *Mabon vab M(o)dron*, and therefore was evidently regarded, in medieval times at least, as a distinct character from him, though in origin *Mabon m. Mellt* may well be a doublet of the same name. O'Rahilly (EIHM 52 and n.) compares the Gaulish tribe *Meldi* and infers the existence of a lightning-god **Meldos.*

Epigraphic evidence for the cult of *Mapon(us)* in Roman times is confined to north Britain. In the counties of Northumberland, Cumberland and Lancashire, five dedications dating from the second and third centuries have been discovered. Two of these are on altars which have been built into the abbey wall at Hexham, and they bear the inscription *Apollini Mapono.* They are believed to have come from Corbridge, where another altar dedicated to *Maponus* is still to be seen. It is clear from the titles of the votaries on these altars that the god's cult had won the favour of high military officials stationed in the region of Hadrian's Wall—the votary of one of the altars at Hexham is described as a *praefectus castrorum,* the other as a centurion of the Sixth Legion. Another centurion of the Sixth set up an altar to *Maponus* at Ribchester in Lancashire (*Archaeologia Aeliana,* fourth series, XXI, pp. 206–10). The fifth inscription at Brampton, Cumberland (now in the Tullie House Museum, Carlisle), is of more humble provenance: the four devotees describe themselves as Germans, and were evidently auxiliaries. The equation of *Maponus* with Apollo appears on four out of the five inscriptions. See E. P. Hamp, 'Mabinogi', THSC 1975, pp. 245–8; Ralegh Radford, 'Locus Maponi', *Trans. Dumfriesshire and Galloway Nat. Hist. and Antiquarian Soc.*, XXXI; and J. MacQueen, ibid., XXXI, pp. 53–7

In Gaul *Maponus* is attested as a proper name on a potter's stamp of the first century, and in another instance in the third century, so that it would seem that there is no reason to suppose that the cult of the god was confined to Britain. A much later document cited by Holder (ACS II, 414), of *circa* 1090, contained in a cartulary of the abbey of Savigny, Rhône, mentions *de Mabono fonte,* a reference which indicates the existence of a spring sacred to the god. In addition it may be noted that *Mātrŏna* (*Modron)* is the tutelary deity of the River Marne.

Two place-names in the Border country are thought to preserve the name of the god: these are the village of *Lochmaben* in Dumfriesshire, and the megalith known as the *Clochmabenstane* near Gretna. One or other of these may well be the site of the *locus* called *Maponi* in the seventh-century Ravenna *Cosmography,* where the reference appears to be to a north-British centre of the god's cult.

The evidence just considered for the existence of a strong cult of *Mapŏnos* among the troops garrisoning the Wall, and in north Britain as a whole, gives particular interest to the occurrence of the name *Mabon* in one of the early poems in the *Book of Taliesin*, *Kychwedyl am dodyv* (BT 38), a poem which describes the battles of Owein ab Urien and introduces the names of various places in southern Scotland:

> Gogyfarch vabon o arall vro kat
> pan amuc owein biv y vro
> (38.22–3)

'The demand of Mabon (?), battle from another land, when Owein defended the cattle of his (own) land.'

> A welei vabon ar ranwen reidavl
> rac biv reget y kymyscyn.
> Ony bei ac adaned yd ehettyn
> Rac Mabon heb galaned vy nyt eyn
> O gyfarfot discyn a chychwyn kat
> Gvlat vabon gvehenyt anoleithat
> (39.2–6)

'Whoever saw Mabon (or 'Mabon saw') on a lively, handsome (horse), they mingled before the cattle of Rheged. Unless it was with wings that they flew, they could not escape from Mabon without slaughter. In meeting of attack and battle-onset, the despoilers (?) of the land of Mabon were irresistible.'

However, Professor Thomas Jones regarded this poem as later than the lifetime of Owain (B XVII, p. 240); i.e. it is not a contemporary bardic eulogy. An earlier occurrence of the name, again in a north-British context, may be that in the poem to Gwallawg, PT no. X.26 (= BT 30.11–12). But here there is no apparent connection between the Mabon named and Urien's dynasty.

The reference in these lines may be to an otherwise unknown brother or kinsman of Owein ab Urien, who bore the name of the god who was worshipped locally (see Morris-Jones, 'Taliesin', p. 199); and in this connection it is interesting to note that triad 70 gives *Modron* as the name of Owein's mother. But apart from attesting the existence of *Mabon* as a personal name, these references are of doubtful relevance to the *Mabon* of triad 52 and of Ml.W. tradition generally. LlDC no. 31.3 includes *Mabon am Mydron* [sic] among Arthur's men, and describes him as *guas Uthir Pendragon*—a reference which seems consistent with his mythological origin (see n. to *6thyr Bendragon).* Apart from this, CO l. 685 (see n.) is the only independent source of information for the Welsh tradition of *Mabon ap Modron.* The deliverance of *Mabon* is specified among the *anoetheu* which Culhwch must obtain in order to hunt the Twrch Trwyth; *Mabon* had been taken from beside his mother when three nights old, and it was not known whether he was alive or dead. The Oldest Animal—the Salmon of Llyn Lliw—revealed that the place of *Mabon*'s imprisonment was *Caer Loyw* (Gloucester), from whence he was successfully freed by Cei and Bedwyr (CO ll. 906, 923–8). Mounted on the horse *Gwynn Mygdvn* 'Fair Dun-Mane' (see triad 46A), Mabon later in the story pursues the Twrch Trwyth into the Severn

(CO ll. 1166–1204), and takes from him the razor which lay between his ears. In view of the identification of *Maponus* with Apollo which appears on the Roman inscriptions, it is difficult to know whether to attach any importance to the portrayal here of *Mabon* as a huntsman. On the whole, the Welsh evidence does not warrant this, since for the purposes of the story a group of Arthur's chief warriors are enlisted in the hunt for the famous boar. In Welsh sources, *Mabon*'s outstanding role remains that of being the most celebrated of prisoners. There is a reference to his grave in the late *Beddau* stanzas in Pen. 98B, p. 49: *Y bedd ynghorthir nanllau / ni wyr neb ei gynneddfau / mabon vab mydron glau* (T. Jones, PBA LIII, p. 190).

The name *Mabon* reappears under several variant but easily recognizable forms in Continental Arthurian poems—*Maboun, Mabuz* and *Mabonagrain*; in each instance the reference presumably goes back ultimately to the mythological *Mabon vab Modron* of early Welsh sources. And indeed *Mabon* presents a remarkable instance of a character who retains an original characteristic independently of any transference between Welsh and Continental sources, since in these latter sources he is more than once associated with a story of imprisonment. In the *Lanzelet* of the Swiss poet Ulrich von Zatzikhofen (composed in the late twelfth century) *Mabuz* retains the role of a prisoner held captive in an enchanted castle. The Anglo-Norman form of the name *Mabuz* must have been taken over from the French poem, which Ulrich acknowledges as his source (see translation of the *Lanzelet* by Webster and Loomis (New York, 1953), pp. 73 ff., and n., p. 192). In another poem of the late twelfth century, the *Joie de la Cour* episode in Chrétien's *Erec*, *Mabonagrain* is portrayed as both prisoner and warder in an enchanted garden (ll. 5447 ff.), which is encompassed only by a wall of air (the *cae niwl* of the corresponding passage in *Gereint*: the Welsh tale preserves what is on the whole a better version of this episode, although the name of the guardian-prisoner is lacking). Chrétien claims that his source for this episode was a (Breton) *lai* (*Erec,* ll. 6187–9), and it may be that an independent reference to this source as the *lai* of *Rey Mabun* has survived in a thirteenth-century list of *lais* preserved in Shrewsbury School MS. VII (ed. Brereton, *Mod. Lang. Review*, XLV (1950), p. 41). The thirteenth-century French poem *Bel Inconnu* and its English counterpart *Ly Beaus Desconnus* give the names *Maboun* and *Eurayn* or *Irayn* as those of the guardians of a prison in an enchanted castle. It has been suggested (*Romania* 24, pp. 321–2) that Chrétien's *Mabonagrain* is a composite form made from the names of these two enchanters combined by the W. conjunction *a(c).* Chrétien's *Mabonagrain* is in fact described as the nephew of a giant called Eurain, and in *Gereint* the corresponding character to Eurain is given the name of Owein. It looks as though the form Eurain in the French sources was arrived at by corrupt transmission in a written form of an earlier Welsh Euuein, Ewe(i)n. The same pair of names in a slightly variant form are found again in the First Continuation of the *Conte del Graal*:

Saigremors, et Mabonagrain
Qui niés estoit le roi Quirain
(ed. Roach, I, ll. 9161–2; certain manuscripts give *Urien* for the last name).

For further discussion of the role of *Mabon* in Welsh and Continental sources see Phillpot, *Romania* XXV, pp. 258 ff. (1896); W. J. Gruffydd, *Cy.* XLII, pp. 129 ff.; ibid., *Rhiannon,* ch. v; J. Mac Queen in Radford *et al.*, *Trans. Dumfriesshire and Galloway Antiquarian Soc.*, XXXI, pp. 43 ff.

Mada6c[1] m. Brwyn 61. See *Brwyn m. Kynadaf.* It is possible that this name denotes a grandson of Cunedda. But alternatively it may be a corruption of the *Madawc m. Run* of the previous triad, since nos. 60 and 61 appear consecutively in the WR series.

Mada6c[2] m. Run (y Kynnedvau) 60 (see v.l.). 'M. son of Rhun of the (magical) qualities.' *Jes. Gen.* XVI (EWGT 16, p. 46) traces the descent of Morgant Hen of Morgannwg to *madavc m. run m. Kenelaph dremrud. m. Kynan m. Kasanauth wledic. Gwreic Cassanauth wledic oed Thewer merch Bredoe* (i.e. *Brittu*) *m. Kadel deernlluc m. Cedehern m. Gvrtheyrn gvrtheneu.* Although the last names in this list are legendary (for Cadell see HB, ch. 35), it may be noted that the genealogy places *Madawc m. Run* in the seventh generation after *Kadel deernlluc*; which shows that he was traditionally regarded as a contemporary of Selyf m. Kynan Garwyn, who stood in the same relation to Cadell (cf. Harl. Gen. XXII) and who is known to have been killed at the battle of Chester:

Jes. Gen. XVI is therefore that of an otherwise unknown line of Powys rulers, a member of which supported the dynasty of Cynan Garwyn at this famous battle. See P. C. Bartrum, 'Noë King of Powys', *Cy.* 43, p. 60.

Maelgwn Gwyned (m. Katwallawn[2] Llawhir) 1, 69, 42: *Alser m. M.*; 44: *Eurgein merch Vaelgwn*; 46, *Brech buwch 6aelg6n.* See also *Run[3] m. Maelgwn.* On *Maelgwn*'s name, see K. Jackson, CMCS 3, pp. 34–5.

Maelgwn < gen. **Maglocunos* of Brit. **Maglocū* (nom. > W. *Meilyg*) 'Hound Prince'; for the first element cf. Ir. *mál* 'prince'. The name is found on a fifth- or early sixth-century bilingual inscription at Nevern: MAGLOCVNI FILI CLVTORI, where the latinized gen. is given the Ogham equivalent MAGLICUNAS (ECMW no. 353; LHEB 182). On the name *Maelgwn* see BD 276, LHEB 174, *et passim.* Gildas (ch. 33) gives the vocative *Maglocune* of the latinized form of this name *Maglocunus*; Geoffrey of Monmouth renders the name as *Malgo* (HRB XI, 7 = BD 187–8: *Maelgwn Gvyned*). For some further instances of territorial names used as epithets, see CLIH 198.

Maglocun(us) is one of the five contemporary rulers of sixth-century Britain whom Gildas denounces for their crimes in his *De Excidio Britanniae* (ch. 33–6). He describes *Maglocun(us)* as *insularis draco*: the reference here is clearly to Anglesey, the traditional seat of power of the rulers of Gwynedd, who had perhaps already by the time of *Maelgwn* established their court at Aberffraw. According to HB's account (ch. 62) the north-Welsh dynasty was founded when Cunedda, *Maelgwn*'s great-grandfather (see Harl. Gen. I) came down from north Britain to Wales:

> Mailcunus magnus rex apud Brittones regnabat [*circa* 540?] id est in regione Guenedote, quia atavus illius, id est Cunedag, cum filiis suis, quorum numerus octo erat, venerat prius de parte sinistrali, id est de regione quae vocatur Manau Guotodin, centum quadraginta sex annis antequam Mailcun regnaret. Et Scottos cum ingentissima clade expulerunt ab istis regionibus, et nusquam reversi sunt iterum ad habitandum.

The *Ann. Cam.* claim that *Mailcun rex Guenedotae* died in the plague of 547 or 549 (later known as *Y Fad Felen*). But there is a difficulty in reconciling this date with HB's statement that 146 years elapsed between the arrival of Cunedda in Wales and the date at which *Maelgwn* 'reigned'. Cunedda probably arrived in Gwynedd at a date nearer 450 than 400, and since plagues were not infrequent at this period, he may have died in some later outbreak which subsequently became confused with the great plague of 547.

Gildas tells us that *Maelgwn* was exceptionally tall in stature (cf. the references to him as *Maelgwn hir* in the poems quoted below), that he was more powerful than nearly all his contemporaries and that he made many conquests. Early in his career he abandoned his kingdom to become a monk, but soon renounced this vocation: the peculiar virulence of Gildas's invective seems to be caused by the set-back to British monasticism brought about by the example of so conspicuous a defaulter. Gildas further accuses *Maelgwn*, after his return to the world, of having murdered both his wife and his nephew, and of having married the wife of the latter. He refers disparagingly to *Maelgwn*'s fondness for listening to his own praises sung by poets, but he admits his great generosity.

In the face of Gildas's express statement, therefore, we may well believe that *Maelgwn* was a great patron of bards, and that the numerous traditions which have come down concerning him and his family owe their origin to this fact. Of particular note in this connection is the (perhaps entirely unhistorical) association between *Maelgwn* and Taliesin, which had already taken shape by the ninth century (see n. to *Taliesin)*: the tradition of the contest between the youthful Taliesin and the bards of *Maelgwn* is indeed probably one of the oldest elements in this story. In the Lives of the Saints, Maelgwn is portrayed as the typical *rex tyrannus,* and acts as a foil to holy men in stories whose wide distribution over all parts of Wales is in itself highly suspect as evidence for their authenticity (VSB 72–4; 246–8; 258, etc.); cf. also the part played by *Maelgwn* in the Life of *St Kentigern* (see A. P. Forbes (ed.), *Lives of St Ninian and St Kentigern* (Edinburgh, 1874)). In this capacity, *Maelgwn*'s prominence is rivalled only by that of Arthur. The names of both were borrowed by the ecclesiastical writers of the Lives from the secular tradition; and the implication would seem to be that in the eleventh century *Maelgwn*'s fame as a heroic figure of earlier times stood out in a manner comparable with that of no other legendary character but that of Arthur himself.

Although Gildas associates *Maelgwn* primarily with Anglesey, a more persistent tradition localized his court at Degannwy on the Creuddyn peninsula (cf. the *Hanes Taliesin*), where *Bryn Maelgwn* still preserves his name. It was near here that *Maelgwn* was said to have met his death of the plague, cf. BD 187: *Ac o'r diwed yd aeth* (*Maelgwn) y myvn eglvys ger llav y castell ehun yn Dygannvy, ac yno y bu uarv.* The church referred to is that of Rhos (see n., BD 276), and a memory of the event is preserved in the proverb *Hir hun Faelgwn yn eglwys Ros* 'The long sleep of M. in the church of Rhos', which is recorded among the proverbs in Davies's dictionary in 1632. VN[2] gives an elaborate account of how Maelgwn met his death at this spot (*Ann. Cam.* records Maelgwn's death in 547):

> Maelgwn betook himself to Rhos church seated near his court, in a nook of ground, on all sides saving one environed with the sea, and therefore easy of all roads to be guarded and kept from the company of people: therefore he shut himself so that he could not see or be seen of anybody (save those which did attend upon him), causing a diligent watch to be kept, lest any should come near the place, and when he had remained there a good while, he one day looked through a chink in the church door, and was presently infected with the air, so that he soon afterwards died, and when his men thought it time to serve him with necessaries, he lay silent, that they thought he was fast asleep, but when they had staid very long, in expectation of his awaking, one of them said that his silence was too long to be one of sleep, and they went to his bed and found him dead thereon, whereupon grew the proverb which with us is yet in use, when one sleepeth beyond measure or is dead we say 'Hir hun Faelgwn yn eglwys Ros', that is to say, the long sleep of Maelgwn in the Church of Rhos, being so long that he never awakened . . . . Maelgwn's body is said to be interred in *Ynys Seiriol.* (Panton 51, ff. 110v.–111v.)

The proverb was known to Dafydd ap Gwilym, who expresses a wish for the *hirun Faelgwn* (GDG no. 135.44), and to Tudur Aled, who refers to it in a *marwnad* to Gruffudd ap Rhys who is said to have been buried in the churchyard of Rhos:

> Glasoer iawn yw Eglwys Ros,
> Gan eiry, gwae ni o'i aros!
> Aeth un o waed Mathonwy
> Mal gan hun Maelgwn neu hwy.
> (GTA II, no. LXXXV.5–8.)

So also Huw Cae Llwyd:

Eich hun sy hwy na channos
Fal hun tad Rhun yn y Rhos.
(HCLl no. XXV.13–14)

Another anecdote about *Maelgwn* has come down in the *Anomalous Laws.* This is an onomastic tale purporting to explain the name *Traeth Maelgwn* in the Dyfi estuary (AL II, 48–50; see HW 129, FAB I, 64–5 and WKC 235–6):

> Gwedy dvyn coron Lundein ae theyrnwialen y gan genedyl Gymry ac eu dehol o Loegyr y gossodassant (oet) dadleu y edrych pvy a vei vrenhin pennaf o nadunt. Sef lle y gossodassant, ar draeth Maelgvn yn A(b)er Dyui, ac yno y doethant gvyr Gvyned a gvyr Powys a gvyr Deheubarth, a Rieinvc, a Morgannvc, a Seisyllvc. Ac yna y dodes Maelda hynaf mab Unhvch Vnachen pendeuic Moel Esgityavn yn Meiryonhid kadeir winithedic (= wneuthuredic?) o adaned (cvyredic) y dan Vaelgwn; a phan doeth y llanv, ny allavd neb y arhos namyn Maelgvn ehun, o achavs y gadeir. Ac o achavs hynny y kafas ynteu bot yn vrenhin pennaf, ac Aberffraw yn ben priflys idav, a jarll Mathrafyl, a iarll Dinefvr, a iarll Kaer (Llion) y danav ynteu; ac yn eir y eir ynteu ar bavp o nadunt vy, ac yn gyfreith yr eidav, ac nyt reit idav ef kadv eu kyfreith vy. Ac o achavs Maelda hynaf y kauas Pennard y breint ae bot yn hynaf kyghelloryaeth.

At this place a contest was held to decide which of the rulers of Wales should have supreme authority. Maelgwn owed his victory to the assistance of a certain *Maeldav hynaf* (see the references in the passage on *Breiniau Arfon* quoted from the Chirk codex in the n. to *Run m. Maelgwn*) who made for him a chair of waxed wings, so that he alone could remain in his place against the incoming tide. Perhaps this curious tale may preserve the tradition of some dynastic struggle in which Maelgwn established that supremacy over the other Welsh princes to which Gildas refers. Both the site of the contest—in Cardigan Bay—and the form taken by it, are surprising.

A. O. H. Jarman suggested (*Ym. M. a Th.*, 40–4) that the first poem in LlDC (no. 1.5, 21) alludes to an otherwise unrecorded attack made by *Maelgwn* on Dyfed. In LlDC no. 34.37–8 the legendary hunter Gwyn ap Nudd praises his hound Dormach (= 'door-surety', B X, p. 41) *a fv y Maelgun* 'which belonged to Maelgwn'. It seems that the prowess of *Maelgwn*'s hunting hounds was proverbial, and this is further witnessed by later poetic references; cf. GTA II no. XCI.31 and n. and no. CXXVIII.38. For the origin of this tradition see further the Life of *St Cybi* (VSB 247–9); TWS 303–4.

BT 33.19: *Dodvyf deganhvy y amrysson / a Maelgvn uvyhaf y achvysson;* 40.7: *Medhet maelgvn mon ac an medwa*; 41.26: *Pvy atal y keinon / Ae Maelgvn o von . . .*

Cyvoesi: *pvy wledych wedy vryen . . . maelgvn hir ar dir gwyned* (RBP col. 577.35–7)

CLIH no. IV.5c: *Keissyet Uaelgwn uaer arall* (RBP col. 1042.4).

Cynddelw: *hil maelgvn milcant a dodeu* (RBP col. 1440.23, cf. CBT IV, no. 4.271n. and see also no. 2.42n., no. 9.183); *Gwenwynwyn . . . maelgwn greid* (H 161.18 = CBT III, no. 20.2n.).

Gwalchmai: *morua rianet maelgvn nebyt* (H 21.24 = CBT I, no. 9.154; cf. I, no. 8.542).

Elidir Sais: *hil mavr maelgvn* (RBP col. 1144.27 = CBT I, no. 16.28).

Phylip Brydydd: *kadeir vaelgwn hir a hu berit y veird* (H 227.3 = CBT VI, no. 14.19n.); *yr pann vu elffin yghywryssed vaelgwn* (H 228.13 = CBT VI, no. 15.5n.).

Iorwerth Beli: *Pan aeth Maelgwn Hir o dir mab Don duedd / O wledd Gwalch Gorsed(d) i Gaer Seion* (MA 318a = GGDT no. 15.29–30n.).

Gruffudd ap Maredudd: *mavl maelgvn* (RBP col. 1323.13–14).

The genealogies preserve the names of *Maelgwn*'s wife and of his mother—*De Situ Brecheniauc*: *Tutglid filia Brachan, uxor Kenken filii Kenwaur Cadcathuc, mater Cadel et Brochuail Schitrauc, et mater Ieuab, et mater Meigh* [see n. to *Meic Myg(vr)as*], *et mater Sanand, que Sanant fuit uxor Mahelgun, regis Nordwalie* (EWGT 15 (9); see also *Jes. Gen.* III).

Pen. 75, p. 30 (= Rawl. B 466): Mam Vaelgwn Gwynedd oedd Veddyf (Meddyf) vch. Vaeldaf ap Dylan draws o Nan Konwy.

On *Maelgwn*, see further Juliette Wood, 'Maelgwn Gwynedd: A Forgotten Welsh Hero', *Trivium* 19, pp. 103–17; J. E. C. Williams, 'Gildas, Maelgwn and the Bards' in R. R. Davies *et al.* (eds), *Welsh Society and Nationhood*; M. Lapidge, *Gildas: New Approaches*, ch. 3; WKC 238–45; and D. P. Kirby , B XXVII, p. 86.

With the Maeldaf here named as *Maelgwn*'s maternal grandfather, cf. the *Maeldaf hynaf* of the Laws. See n. to *Pen Hyneif*, triad 1.

Manawydan m. Llyr[1] Lledyeith 8, 67. On the name *Manawydan* see Ifor Williams, B III, p.49. See further Vendryes, EC VI, pp. 239–54.

LlDC no. 31.19–22: *Manawidan ab llyr. / oet duis y cusil. / neus tuc manauid / eis tull o trywruid.*

CO l. 215n.: *Manawedan mab Llyr.*

BT 34.9–10: *ys gayr manavyt a phryderi.*

The name of *Manawydan* is evidently related to the territorial name *Manaw,* applied in early times both to the Isle of Man and to the region of *Manaw Gododdin* which lay along the southern shore of the Firth of Forth (cf. *ar vreithel vanawyt* CA l. 35 and n., also n. above to *Kuluanawyt Prydein*). And whatever the origin of the relationship, the W. *Manawydan* undoubtedly corresponds with the Ir. sea-god *Manannán mac Lir,* who in a euhemerized form is associated with the Isle of Man in *Cormac's Glossary* (*circa* 900):

(He was) a celebrated merchant who was in the Isle of Man. He was the best pilot that was in the west of Europe. He used to know by studying the heavens (i.e. using the sky) the period which would be the fine weather and the bad weather, and when each of these two times would change. *Inde Scoti et Brittones eum deum vocaverunt maris. et filium maris esse dixerunt. i. mac lir mac mara. et de nomine Manandan Inis Manand dictus est.* (W. Stokes, *Three Irish Glossaries*, P. 31; J. O'Donovan, *Cormac's Glossary*, p. 114; cf. *Cóir Anmann* in Windisch, *Irische Texte III*, p. 356.)

In other Irish tales (*Immram Brain, Serglige Conculainn)* Manannán's mythological character is more fully apparent: he presides over the Otherworld island to which Brân and Cú Chulainn are invited. But it is only in late sources that he becomes included among the *Tuatha Dé Danann.* For a discussion of the Irish sources relating to *Manannán*, see Vendryes in EC VI, pp. 239–54.

But the exact nature of the relation between *Manannán mac Lir* and *Manawydan fab Llyr* is difficult to ascertain. The most acceptable explanation is perhaps that offered by Windisch (*Das keltische Brittanien*, pp. 112–13) who claimed that both Irish and Welsh forms were derived independently from the place-name: W. *Manaw*; Ir. *Mana, Manu*; but that whereas the W. *Manawydan* is based on the nominative case, *Manannán* is derived from the Irish stem *Manu*; cf. the surviving Scottish place-names *Clackmannan, Slamannan,* which preserve the genitive case. If this explanation is correct, *Manawydan–Manannán* can be regarded as a deity known from early times in both Ireland and Wales. And this seems on the whole more probable than the alternative explanation which is sometimes advocated, that the imperfect phonetic correspondence between the two names is to be accounted for as due to a learned borrowing from one country to the other in historical times: either from Wales to Ireland, as argued by Zimmer (*Auf welchen Wege*, p. 27, n.), or conversely from Ireland to Wales, as was advocated by W. J. Gruffydd (*Rhiannon*, p. 81). According to the former alternative, the O.W. *Manauidan* would have been misread as *Mananidán* and later syncopated to *Manandán* (> *Manannán,* with Old Irish medial *-nd-* for *-nn-*). According to Gruffydd's hypothesis the *-nd-* of Ir. *Manand(án)* was mistaken by a copyist as *-uid-* to give the O.W. form *Manauid(an).* But as A. O. H. Jarman has pointed out ('Perchen Machreu', LlC III, p. 118), an origin for the W. name in a literary borrowing of this kind is hardly likely in view of the occurrence of *Manawyd, Manawidan* in the early poems: these are forms which must antedate the earliest text of PKM by more than a century, so that this spelling is likely to represent the name as it existed in pre-literary tradition. I incline therefore to Windisch's view that both names derive independently from the identical names in Irish and Welsh of the two areas concerned.

In the story of *Manawydan* as told in the Second and Third Branches of the *Mabinogi,* all earlier territorial associations of the name have been forgotten; nor is it easy to trace any connection between the highly individualized character of *Manawydan* as it is depicted by the Welsh redactor, and the supernatural attributes of *Manannán* in the Irish sources. The episode in which Manawydan appears as a 'golden shoemaker' or more probably as 'a noble shoemaker' (see n. to triad 67) indicates that the tradition incorporated in triad 67 was older than the *Four Branches of the Mabinogi*, since the significance of *eur* here is ambiguous. The story probably owes its origin to the apparent connection between his name and the word *manawyd* 'an awl', a fiction which in itself shows how far the earlier connection of the name with *Manaw* had become obliterated by the time that the Third Branch was evolved (see Ifor Williams, B III, p. 49). This evident association of *manawyd* with *Manawydan* in the mind of the eleventh-century narrator of the tale adds additional confirmation to the evidence given by the early poems, to the effect that the medial *-d-* in *Manawydan* represents *-d-* and not *-dd-*; a matter which is left ambiguous by the orthography of WM, RM, and Pen. 16 (triad 8).

It is curious to note the aptness of the description of *Manawydan* in LlDC no. 31.20: *oet duis y cusil* 'he was profound in counsel' to the *Manawydan* of the *Mabinogi*. The traditional character assigned to *Manawydan* would thus seem to be older than the Four Branches.

Marcwlph 49 (Pen. 77); var. of *Cado Hen.* The retention of this name in one manuscript alone is interesting, because a version of the triad which contained it must have been known to Prydydd y Moch (see n. to triad 47). There is evidence that *Marcolf* was known as a disputant with Solomon early in the eleventh century, if not sooner; although the Ml. L. dialogue *Salomon et Marcolfus*, which is a collection of proverbs and anecdotes, is found only in manuscripts of the fourteenth and fifteenth centuries. *Salomon et Marcolfus* is an example of a popular medieval genre in which King Solomon was portrayed as holding conversation with demons, over whom he acquired power; (see n. to *Selyf* [1]). The Old English dialogue poems *Solomon and Saturn* (composed *circa* 900) belong to this genre; and as an interlocutor with Solomon, *Marculf* appears to be interchangeable with *Saturn,* since both represent the names of pagan deities whom the wise king confuted; see R. J. Menner, *The Poetical Dialogues of Solomon and Saturn* (New York, 1941), pp. 26–35. Menner argues that *Marcolfus* developed from *Marc(h)olus* under the influence of the common Germanic name *Marculf(us)*—and we may add, perhaps under the special influence of the reputation of a monk named *Marculfus* who composed *formulae* concerning ecclesiastical matters in Merovingian France (Zevmer, *Formulae Merowingici et Karolini Aevi, Monumenta Germaniae Historica,* 1886). *Marc(h)olus* is a latinized form of the name of the Hebrew idol *Markolis* whose identification with *Mercurius* is generally accepted by Hebrew scholars. In view of Prydydd y Moch's reference it is interesting to note that the Provençal poet Raimbaut d'Orange (*fl.* 1150–73) praises his mistress for knowing more than *Solomon* or *Marcol* (Menner, op. cit., 29). Two sixteenth-century Welsh versions of *Solomon et Marcolfus* have come down in BL Addl.

31,055, 15,047 (H. Lewis (ed.), B III, pp. 161 ff.; VI, pp. 314 ff.). Henry Lewis considered the first translation to be the work of the writer of the manuscript, Thomas Wiliems, Trefriw, and did not think it likely to be based upon an older version in Welsh. It is independent from the second, though both were written within some twenty years of each other.

March m. Meirchya6n 14, 26, *Marach* (Pen. 50) 71, 73. See nn. to *Drystan, Essyllt, Meirchya6n.*

March is the *King Mark* of the *Tristan* romances. But Welsh sources indicate that more extensive traditions about him than those which have come down were once in existence.

Br. Rh.: *Gwyr Llychlyn yw y rei hynny a March uab Meirchawn yn tywyssawc arnadunt* (RM 151.14). This statement is probably to be accounted for as a reminiscence of triad 14, since from the ninth century onwards the *Llychlynwyr* or Scandinavians would have been regarded as the *llynghessogion* 'men of fleets' *par excellence* (see n. to triad 14). *March* is further included in the list of Arthur's counsellors in Br. Rh. (RM 159.18); so also is *D(ry)stan mab talluch* (159.27), and it is curious to note that the redactor of the story appears to ignore any close connection between the two.

Cynddelw (in an *awdl to* Owain Gwynedd composed between 1155 and 1170) compares his patron to *March*: *A dyly kymrv ae kymer drwy barch / Ual y kymerth march gwedy meirchyawn* 'He who has a right to Wales will possess her in honour, as March possessed her after Meirchyawn' (H 87.13–14 = CBT IV, no. 3.12n.). This is the only allusion made by any of the *Gogynfeirdd* to March, and it is to be noted that it is a full century earlier than any mention by them of *Drystan* or *Esyllt* (see nn).

Ystorya Trystan (Pen. 96, 231; B V, p. 121): *Dyma rymddiddan fv Rrwng syr trystram vab tallwch ag esyllt Gwraig march vab meirchion vn arall or marchogion.* (See introduction, p. cxii and n. 204.)

The following references are probably if not certainly to *March m. Meirchya6n*:

LlDC no. 18.133: *Bet y march. bet y guythur. / bet y gugaun cletyfrut / anoeth bid bet y arthur* (see n. to *Arthur).*

LlDC no. 35.19: *om parth guertheisse march trod* (see n. to *Drystan*).

A ninth-century *Vita* of the sixth-century saint Paul Aurelian by the Breton Wrmonoc, monk of Landevennec (ed. Cuissard, RC V, synopsis in D. S. Evans, *Lives of the Welsh Saints* (Cardiff, 1971); see also Doble, *St Paul de Leon,* Cornish Saints series, no. 46), gives a brief account of a ruler named *Marcus* who ruled somewhere in south-west Britain, and who is usually identified with the *March* of the romances. It is here said of the saint *fama ejus regis Marci pervolat ad aures, quem alio nomine Quonomorium vocant.* Now a certain Conomorus, a ruler in Breton Dumnonia, figures in the *History* of Gregory of Tours (IV, 4), as well as in the early *Vita* of *St Samson* (ed. Fawtier), the Ruys Life of *Gildas* (ed. H. Williams), and the later *Vitae* of certain other sixth-century Breton saints: *Hervé, Leonor* and *Goeznou* (see La Borderie's edition of the Life of *St Hervé,* and his *Histoire de la Bretagne*, vol. 1 and references there cited). In these sources, as well as in recent Breton folklore, Conomorus is deeply stained in crime, and is depicted as a kind of Bluebeard. The tale 'Comorre' in E. Souvestre's *Le Foyer Breton* is based on folk-tales current about him in the early nineteenth century. From Gregory of Tours it appears that Conomorus was a contemporary of Childebert I, king of the Franks, and therefore that he may have died *circa* 560. It is this *tyrannus* of the early years of the Breton occupation, whom Wrmonoc identifies, though not necessarily correctly, with his king *Marcus.* F. Lot was the first to notice (*Romania* 25, pp. 20–1) that the name Conomorus is identical with the name which appears on a sixth-century inscribed stone at Castle Dore, near Fowey in Cornwall, which reads : HIC IACIT CUNOMORI FILIUS. But the first name has been variously interpreted as DRUSTAGNI (Rhŷs), CIRUSINIUS (Macalister), and by Ralegh Radford as DRUSTAVS (*Journal of the Royal Inst. of Cornwall,* New Series, I, Appendix, 1951). Kenneth Jackson informed me that he also read this name as DRUSTAVS. The ligatured AV represents ANV, so that we have here the early form of the name Drystan. The stone connects Drystan with Cunomorus, but Wrmonoc is the single source for identifying C(o)nomorus or Quonomorius with King *Marcus.* In the absence of further evidence, the inscription on the stone cannot be regarded as proof of the identity of *March*, and the Br. *Conomorus*, for Cynfawr (< Conomorus), is too frequent a name-form to allow of specific identification with any one bearer of it. Cf. EWGT for instances of the name *Cynfor* (= *Cynfawr*), of whom one was the great-grandfather of the Devon hero *Geraint m. Erbin* (see n.). O. J. Padel has shown good reason to doubt the identity of the historical Breton *Cunomorus* with 'King Mark' (CMCS 1, pp. 77–9). The *Vita* of *St Samson* (which may be as old as the seventh century), while it describes the opposition made by Conomorus to the Breton rulers Jonas and Judual, gives no hint of any connection between Conomorus and 'King Mark'. This is the more significant since St Samson is depicted as having crossed Cornwall by the ancient trade route from Padstow to Fowey, thus passing close by Lantyan, and the site of St Samson's church in Golant, connected by Béroul with the *Tristan* story: Béroul names Lancien as the site of King Mark's court. But in spite of the localizations of the *Tristan* story made by Béroul with places in Cornwall, I can find no indication in Wrmonoc's work that the writer intended to imply that the home of King *Marcus* was in Cornwall, or in any part of the south-western peninsula. The only place-name which Wrmonoc gives is that of King Mark's home at Villa Banhedos or Caer Banhed, but this place remains so far unidentified. It is claimed that King *Marcus* was buried there, and from there St Paulinus travelled to visit his sister 'in the furthest recesses of the land, that is, on the shores of the British sea'.

The word *march*, meaning 'horse', gave rise to the growth of a folk-tale of the Midas type around the name of *March ap Meirchyawn.* This tale is found attached to the name of *March* in north Wales folk tradition (*Cy.* VI, pp. 181–3), and also to King Mark in Béroul's poem (ed. Ewert, ll. 1306ff.); and in Brittany it is attached to a king of Porzmarc'h (or alternatively, King Guivarc'h) at several places in the neighbourhood of Quimper, as well as in other parts of the country (see J. Loth, *Contributions a l'étude des Romans de la Table Ronde*, pp. 108–10 and references there cited). (For a special study of the theme see J. Jones, 'March ap Meirchiawn', *Aberystwyth Studies* XII, 21ff.) The poet Béroul gives the story only in a corrupt form, but it may be presumed that his source was the common ancestor of the Gwynedd and Breton versions. No doubt the theme is ultimately of classical origin, derived perhaps from the version in Ovid's *Metamorphoses.* The common type of the widespread folk versions may be summarized as follows (see Stith Thomson, *The Folktale*, p. 265):

> A king has the ears of a horse, of which he is ashamed. To preserve his secret he kills successively each of those whom he has compelled to act as his barber. Finally a widow's only son is commanded to shave him. He manages to escape death by concealing his dismay at his discovery, but he falls ill under the oppression of his secret. A doctor or other helper advises him to seek relief by confiding this to some natural object or plant, usually reeds. After this has been done, a pipe or other musical instrument is constructed from the material specified, and when this is played upon, it sings the words 'The king has two horses' ears'—in Breton—
>
> ar roué Guivarc'h
> En deuz diou scouarn marc'h.

The north Wales version of this tale is preserved in Pen. 134, a collection of pedigrees dating from 1550–62 (*Rep.* I, p. 837). It is part of a family tale appended to the genealogy of *Iarddur ap Egri ap morien ap mynac ap marchap meirchion, arglwydd ar dalm o wynedd,* and may be summarized as follows:

> (March) had horses' ears, and nobody knew that except his barber, and he did not dare (confess it) for the sake of his head. And there came sickness to the barber, so that he had to seek a physician, who discovered that a secret was killing him, and he requested the barber to confess it to the earth. And so he did, and became well. And fair reeds grew in that place. And at the time of a high feast the pipers of Maelgwn Gwynedd came there and saw the fair reeds, and they cut them and made them into pipes and played them before the king, and they could play nothing but *klustiau march i varch amheirchion* 'March ap Meirchion has horse's ears.' (Jenny Rowland and Graham Thomas, 'Versions of the Trystan Englynion and Prose', *Nat. Lib.*

of Wales Journal XXII (1982), p. 373; P. C. Bartrum, 'Pedigrees of the Welsh Tribal Patriarchs', *Nat. Lib. of Wales Journal* XIII (1963), p. 119, no. 58)

John Rhŷs noted (CF I, 232–4) that this story was known in Llŷn in connection with *March ap Meirchion*, who was alleged to be the proprietor of the old mansion of *Castellmarch*, which was known to Cynddelw (see CBT I, no. 3.123n.). This may be no more than a popular folk-tradition without other authority. It is curious to find that a very similar version of the Midas-story is attached to the legendary Irish king *Labraid Loingsech,* ancestor of the kings of Leinster (RC II, p. 197; EC V, p. 32; Dillon, *Cycles of the Kings*, pp. 9–10; Keating, *The History of Ireland: Forus Feasa ar Eirinn*, (eds D. Comyn and P. S. Dinneen), ITS Vol. II, pp. 172–4). In this instance the story bears no special relevance to the name of the king concerned. See also Glasynys, *Cymru Fu* (Wrexham, 1882), pp. 465, 470. But strangely enough this king's traditional epithet *loingsech* is the exact etymological equivalent of the W. *llynghessawc* of triad 14 (see n.). It is a remarkable coincidence, if no more. An earlier version of the tale, dating from the tenth century, is attached to an Irish king who bears the name of *Eochaid* (*ech* 'horse'); see K. Meyer, *Otia Merseiana* III (1903), pp. 46–54; H. Newstead, 'King Mark of Cornwall', *Romance Philology* IX, p. 247. See also P. C. Bartrum (ed.), 'Pedwar Iarddur', *Nat. Lib. of Wales Journal* (1978), p. 373, and AW 212, for the text of this folk-tale.

The name *Marcán* is known in Ireland as that of a king of the *Uí Maine* in the west of Ireland, who figures in the two sagas *Cano Meic Gartnáin* and *Caithréim Cellaig.* The former of these presents several striking features in common with the *Tristan* saga. For a discussion of both see Dillon, *Cycles of the Kings*, pp. 79 ff.; J. Carney, *Studies in Irish Literature and History*, pp. 215ff.

Math m. Mathonwy 28. With the name cf. Gaulish *Matto(n)* (ACS II, col. 478); Ir. *Math mac Úmoir in druí,* the druid of the *Tuatha Dé Danann* according to the *Lebor Gabála* (ed. Macalister, IV, pp. 122, 132); and *Matgen,* the sorcerer (*corrguinech*) of the TDD in the (*Second*) *Battle of Moytura* (RC XII, p. 80 §78; Gray (ed.), ITS (1982), §77–8). The names *Math, Mathonwy, Matholwch* and *Mathuthavar* clearly contain an identical first element, which is also found in certain Irish names (add to the above *Matha, Met. Din.* IV, p. 172; *Mathgamhain*). But the existence of *Matto(n)* in Gaulish proves that the Welsh names are not necessarily Irish-borrowed forms, as has sometimes been claimed (cf. Zimmer, *Gottische gelehrte Anzeigen* (1890), p. 512, who derives *Mathonwy* from the genitive *Mathgamnai* of Ir. *Mathgamhain*). For the termination of *Mathonwy*, cf. the names Daronwy, Goronwy, Euronwy.

It remains uncertain whether *Mathonwy* denotes the name of *Math*'s father or mother. Perhaps it is a matronymic, cf. the girl's name Gwenonwy (although the other names in *-onwy* are male, for examples see G 663); since there are indications in *Mabinogi Math* that the dynasty to which *Math* belonged was regarded as matrilinear (cf. Chadwick, *Early Scotland*, pp. 92–3). Thus *Math* may have been supposed to have inherited the rule of Gwynedd through his mother, as he in turn is succeeded by the sister's son (Lleu) of his sister's son (Gwydion). In these circumstances a matronymic might be expected, such as in fact we find that Gwydion receives: he is known invariably as *vab Dôn.* (W's version of items (a) and (c) in triad 28 may be regarded as further evidence for the special relationship considered to subsist between a man and his sister's son, since in both instances the uncle instructs the nephew in magic. But it is possible that item (a) is no more than a deduction from the *Mabinogi* itself.) The name *Mathonwy* may after all never have denoted a specific character: it may be only a 'ghost' name like those which are found in the pairs of invented names in *Culhwch*—pairs, in which the name of the parent merely repeats that of the child with some added suffix: Drem vab Dremhidydd, Sugyn vab Sucnedyd, Brys vab Brysethach, Medyr vab Methredyd. This is in fact suggested by the allusion to *Mathonwy* BT 28.26–7: *odit ae gvypvy / hutlath vathonvy / yg koet pan tyfvy* ('Few are there who know it, the magic wand of Mathonwy, where it grows in the wood'), since here *Mathonwy* seems to be simply a doublet of the name of *Math* (for his *hutlath*, cf. PKM 75.77).

The references to *Math* in early poetry lay stress, like the triads which mention him, on his character as a magician: BT 25–6: *am swynwys i vath . . . ail math pan ymdygaed* ('Math made me by enchantment . . . a second Math'); BT 68.14–15: *Math ac euuyd hutwyt* (= *hutint?*) *geluyd* ('Math and Efydd (?) fashioned by magic a skilful poet (?)'). Both these passages allude to the creation by magic of the poet Taliesin, in which it appears that Math was regarded as having had a part. (On the first passage see Chw. T. 20; on the second see BWP 173; RBP col. 1054.35–6: *Neu bum gan wyr keluydon / gan uath hen gan gouannon gan euuyd* [= BT 3.1: *gan ievyd*] *gan elestron* 'I have been with artful men: with Math the Old, with Gofannon, with Efydd, with Elestron'.)

For Dafydd ap Gwilym's reference to *Math,* see n. to triad 27. Lewys Môn refers to *Math hen ab Mathonwy* (GLM no. XCVII.2–6, and also n. to *Aryanrot*).

The Fourth Branch of the *Mabinogi* depicts *Math* as the wizard-king of Gwynedd (cf. *Math in druí* of the Irish *Lebor Gabála*), with his court at Caer Dathyl in Arfon. The main incidents of the story take place in Gwynedd, and the names of all the chief actors—Gwydion, Lleu (also Dylan), Arianrhod—have their names preserved to this day in places situated along the Caernarfonshire coast. Dafydd ap Gwilym knew of Math as *rhi Arfon* (GDG no. 84.42; see n. to triad 27); and the references quoted above suggest that a tradition of *Math* as a supreme magician entered into the ninth-century north-Welsh Taliesin saga. The main concern of this Branch of the *Mabinogi* is to illustrate the magical powers of *Math* and his nephew Gwydion, the two great magicians of Gwynedd. Indeed, the first part of the story resolves itself into a contest in magic between the two, in which Gwydion temporarily outwits his uncle by causing the violation of *Math*'s virgin *troedawc* 'footholder'. *Math* is able to repay the injury by inflicting on his nephew a series of animal-transformations (the alternating sex of the animals into which Gwydion and his brother are transformed is obviously dictated by the intention of making the punishment fit the crime); but after this episode is concluded the two magicians are portrayed as working in collaboration rather than in rivalry. *Math*'s *cynneddf* '(magical) attribute' of being able to hear every word spoken in the open air recalls that of the *Coraniaid* (triad 36n.); and a second primitive characteristic which distinguishes him is his need to have a virgin footholder constantly with him. With his *hutlath* he is able to perform transformations, a chastity test, and the creation of Lleu's wife Blodeuwedd out of flowers. In his magic powers he is rivalled only by his nephew, but there is no indication in the story that *Math* was Gwydion's instructor, as is claimed in WR's version of triad 28.

In his study *Math vab Mathonwy*, W. J. Gruffydd argued that the Irish myth of the Fomorian giant Balor, fated to be slain by his grandson Lug, as Acrisius was by Perseus ('The King and his Prophecied Death') constitutes the main theme which underlies the Welsh tale. He equates *Math* himself with Balor, Lleu with Lug. The ultimate identity of the latter pair is undeniable (see n. to *Lleu*[1] *Llaw Gyffes*); but in the story *Math* assists rather than impedes Lleu's career, Lleu does not in fact kill *Math*, nor is there any certainty that Lleu is intended to be *Math*'s grandson. This would only be the case if Gwydion and/or Arianrhod were the offspring of an incestuous union between *Math* and his sister Don; just as Lleu (and Dylan) were the fruit of such a union between Gwydion and his sister Arianrhod. See further C. W. Sullivan, 'Inheritance and Lordship in Math', THSC 1990, pp. 45–63; idem (ed.), *The Mabinogi: A Book of Essays* (New York, 1996); and Ian Hughes, *Math uab Mathonwy*, pp. viii–xii.

Matheu 46c: *march ap Matheu.* This name may be a corruption of *Math hen* (as in RBP col. 1054.35–6, quoted above under *Math*); cf. also GO no. XVII.3: *Mathav, wyneb Mathonwy.*

Mathol6ch 6ydel 53. 'M. the Irishman.' For the name cf. note to *Math m. Mathonwy.*

Cynddelw: *Ongyr urt angert Uallowch* (CBT IV, no. 9.154n.; see *varia lecta*).

Prydydd y Moch: *Ef ua6r lly6 ma6rllit Mallol6ch* (CBT V, no. 1.91n.; and cf. PKM 165n.)

Buchedd Collen: *Mam Gollen Sant oedd Ethinen Wyddeles, verch Vathylwch, Arglwydd yn y Werddon, yr Arglwyddieth hono a elwir yr owr hon Rwngwc* (Havod 19, 141, dated 1536, printed T. H. Parry-Williams (ed.), *Rhyddiaith Gymraeg* I, 36). The version of the tale in C 36, p. 377, gives the following variant: *Ethne wyddeles ferch Matholwch Arglwydd Cŵl yn Iwerddon, yr hon a elwir yr awr hon Rwngcwl.* In a sixteenth-century tract entitled 'Ceidwedigaeth Cerdd Dant' (Pen. 147; B I, p. 143), *Matholwch*

Wydel is named as one of four *pencerdd o delyn a chrwth* who were concerned with drawing up regulations governing the twenty-four musical measures, in the time of an Irish ruler named *Mwrchan Wyddel.* This reference, like the previous one, may imply no more than that, under the influence of the *Mabinogi*, *Matholwch* had become a typical name for an Irishman.

A variant form of this name, *Mallolwch,* occurs both in the Pen. 6 fragment of *Branwen* (*circa* 1225; see PKM 305), and in Cynddelw and Prydydd y Moch as quoted above. *Mallolwch* therefore has a serious claim to consideration as the original form of this name; cf. perhaps Ir. *Maelshechlainn.* But *Matholwch* appears consistently in the WM and RM texts of *Branwen*, and the form in these texts is probably responsible both for the *Matholwch* of triad 53 (W), and for the subsequent standardization of the name in this form which is apparent from the references quoted above. Cf. also Tudur Aled's allusion to the payment of horses to Matholwch in the *Mabinogi*:

Gre wen o Fôn, gron, a fu
I Fatholwch, a'i thalu.
(GTA II, no. CV.33–4)

and Iolo Goch's reference to Ireland as *gwlad Fatholwch* (GIG no. XX.119). *Mallolwch* may have become altered to *Matholwch,* perhaps by the scribe of WM, under the influence of the names *Math*, *Mathonwy* in the Fourth Branch. In suggesting that the name of *Matholwch* corresponds with that of the Irish ruler (*Maine*) *Milscothach* in the tale *Togail Bruidne Da Derga,* Proinsias Mac Cana (*Branwen*, p. 30) overlooks the evidence of the two allusions in medieval Welsh poetry to *Mallolwch* which are cited above. These corroborate the Pen. 6 text of *Branwen* in favouring *Mallolwch* as a variant (perhaps earlier) form of this name. Mac Cana compares *Caer Vallwch* in Flintshire, see his *Branwen Daughter of Llŷr*, p. 30, n. 2.

Mathonwy. See **Math m. Mathonwy.**

Mathuthauar 35 (R). For the first element cf. *Math m. Mathonwy*; the last is perhaps *-vawr.*

Mawan. See *Llemenic m. Mawan.* EANC, p. 76, connects this name with Br. *mau* 'lively, joyful' and compares Gaulish *Mavus* (ACS II, 488); LL 155.8: *Blain Mauan*; *Rec. Caern.* 138, 140: *Nant Mawan.*

Maxen (Macsen) Wledic 35 (R); App. II, no. 11. See *Owein m. Maxen Wledic, Elen*[1] *Luyda6c, Cynan*[1] *(Meiriadawc).*

Cynddelw: *kywlad loes moes maxen* (H 135.6 = CBT III, no. 16.88 and n.)

Justus Llwyd: *Hi a doeth . . . hyt yn llys vaxen* (RBP col. 1365.40 = YB XVII, 72.67–8).

Harl. Gen. IV gives the form *Maxim Guletic* (EWGT p. 10).

The name of *Maxen Wledic* represents that of the historical emperor *Magnus Maximus,* who was proclaimed emperor in Britain by the armed forces under his command in the year 383. His nationality was Spanish. Shortly after he was proclaimed emperor he left Britain for France, taking with him the best of the Roman troops stationed in Britain, in order to have an army with which to oppose the rival western emperor, Gratian. In the same year Gratian was slain and Maximus thereupon became sole ruler of the western provinces of Gaul and Spain. Five years later he was in turn defeated and slain by the emperor Theodosius.

Both Gildas and HB in referring to Maximus's career (*De Excidio,* chs. 13–14; HB, ch. 27) place the full emphasis of their story on the assertion that in leading away the troops from Britain, Maximus left the country denuded of her protectors and at the mercy of foreign invaders—Picts, Scots, and Saxons. HB (which erroneously styles the emperor *Maximianus,* see below) states that he departed from Britain *cum omnibus militibus Brittonum* and obtained the rule of the whole of Europe (*totius Europae*) by slaying Gratian; after which victory, instead of sending his troops home to Britain, he established them in Armorica (see n. to triad 35). The historical references to the departure of the British troops with Maximus in 383 are confirmed in a striking manner by archaeological evidence: Hadrian's Wall was apparently abandoned at this time by the troops which guarded it, and no coins of a later date than 383 have been discovered there. Similar evidence is offered by the site of the Roman fort of Segontium (near Caernarfon), which is thought to have been reoccupied, for a brief period only, during the last third of the fourth century (*Cy.* 33, p. 91.)

The emperor Maximus impressed himself very strongly upon native Welsh tradition in two capacities: first, as the leader who deprived Britain of her fighting men and, secondly, as the ancestor from whom several of the early Welsh ruling dynasties claimed descent. The earliest instance of this claim appears on the ninth-century Valle Crucis pillar, the inscription on which traces the descent of the kings of Powys to *Britu, filius Guarthigirn quem benedixit Germanus quemque peperit ei Seuira filia Maximi regis qui occidit regem Romanorum* (ECMW, no. 182; *Cy.* XXI, pp. 42–3 = EWGT, pp.1–3). (See n. to *G6rtheyrn G6rtheneu.*) Other dynasties which claimed descent from Maxen included the ruling family of Dyfed and certain northern lines (see Harl. Gens. II, IV; *Jes. Gens.* IV, XIII, XIX; App. II, no. 11). In App. II, no. 11 the name of *Maxen Wledic* has replaced that of *Ceredic Wledic* in Harl. Gen. V, as that of the progenitor of the northern dynasty of Dyfnwal Hen—an indication of the increasing popularity in medieval times of the fictitious claim to descent from Maxen.

In accordance with this tradition that Maximus was the progenitor of more than one native dynasty, there evolved by the early twelfth century two distinct versions of a story describing the emperor's marriage with a British bride. One is the account given by Geoffrey of Monmouth (HRB V, 9–16) of the emperor's marriage in Britain: here his bride is unnamed except that she is the daughter of *Octavius, dux (Ge)wissei*; the other is the variant version of the same story which appears in *Breudwyt Maxen.* Here the heroine is the daughter of Eudaf (= Octavius), and her father is represented as ruling at Caer Seint (= Segontium), and she herself receives the name of Elen Luydawc 'Helen of the Hosts'. There is reason to suppose that this name belonged first to an independent figure in the native tradition (originally, perhaps, a goddess, see n.), and one who, like Maxen himself, was looked upon as a renowned ancestress. In the introduction to *Breudwyt Maxen,* Ifor Williams suggested that the union between these two independent legendary figures was the creation of the first narrator of *Breudwyt Maxen.* It is clear, indeed, that this union is an artificial one, forged by some *cyfarwydd* who wished to bring together two of the renowned royal progenitors of Welsh tradition within the framework of the *Vision* type of story.

Both *Breudwyt Maxen* and Geoffrey's version combine the account of Maximus' marriage with the story of the colonization of Brittany by Maximus' soldiers—led, not by the emperor himself, but by the heroine's brother (in HRB her cousin) Cynan Meiriadoc. There are too many discrepancies between *Breudwyt Maxen* and Geoffrey's version to enable one to believe that the Welsh tale can be derived from that of Geoffrey: it is far more likely that both represent independent versions of part of the legendary material which was current about Maximus in Wales in the early Middle Ages. (I have discussed the Welsh traditions of *Maxen Wledic* more fully in 'The Character of the Early Welsh Tradition', SEBH, pp. 107ff. The earliest allusion to *Maxen* in Welsh poetry is by Cynddelw, CBT III, no. 16.88n.)

The name *Maxen* is of learned origin: the corresponding oral form, *Massen,* is in fact preserved as the emperor's name, *Mytern* (= *W. mechteyrn*) *Massen* in the fifteenth-century Cornish miracle-play *Beunans Meriasek* (see *Breuddwyd Maxen,* p. 13). Moreover, as it stands, the form *Maxen* must derive from *Maxentius* rather than *Maximus.* But the earliest occurrence of the name in Welsh is the *Maxim Guletic* of Harl. Gens. II, IV (EWGT 10 (3 and 4)), and this form clearly indicates (*Magnus*) *Maximus* as the name of the emperor who is intended by the *Maxen Wledic* of the medieval sources. But there has been considerable confusion in Welsh-Latin sources between the names *Maximus, Maximianus, Maxentius.* Gildas correctly names the emperor who led the troops from Britain as *Maximus;* but both HB (chs. 27–31) and HRB (V, 9 ff.) give his name as *Maximianus.* The *Bruts* render both this latter name and that of the emperor *Maxentius* who appears earlier in the narrative by *Maxen* (HRB V, 7 = BD 70). But in HRB it is the later emperor of British connections who is alone distinguished in the *Brut* by the title *Gwledic.* There can be no doubt historically that *Magnus Maximus* and no other Roman emperor is intended by the Welsh *Maxen Wledic*. On *Gwledig* applied to a number of British rulers who were prominent in the defence of Britain about the time of the Roman withdrawal, see GPC 1682 and n. to CO l. 1.

It is difficult to determine the precise meaning of the title *gwledic* as employed in medieval sources with reference to rulers and chieftains of earlier times. *Gwledic* is applied freely by the *Gogynfeirdd* both to God and to temporal princes, but in earlier times it seems likely that it had a more exact significance. In the HB and in the Harl. Gens. respectively this title is given to *Emrys Wledic* (*Ambrosius Aurelianus*) and to the northern ruler *Ceredic Wledic,* who was the progenitor of the Strathclyde dynasty, and Taliesin bestows this title on Urien Rheged (BT 57.19; 56.14) and on God (PT no. II.2n., III, VII, XI, XII). The triads, *Bonedd y Saint* and *Bonedd Gwŷr y Gogledd* (App. II above), add to this list *Cunedda Wledic*, *G(w)erthmwl Wledic* and *Amlawdd Wledic.* But these additions may only reflect the more widespread and less exact use of the term in the Middle Ages; since Cunedda does not bear this title in the earliest sources. It is interesting to find, however, that *Gwledic* is nowhere applied to Gwrtheyrn (Vortigern) nor to Maelgwn Gwynedd or his successors. John Rhŷs suggested that *Gwledic* was the title borne by the successor in sub-Roman times to the offices of *Dux Brittaniarum* and *Comes Litoris Saxonici* (*Celtic Britain*, p. 104; see also HW 99–100). Yet this hardly seems likely since, as C. E. Stevens has shown (EC III, p. 89), Greek historians state categorically that Maximus 'enjoyed no honourable office'. Moreover the offices to which Rhŷs refers gave authority over areas in northern and eastern Britain alone. Stevens's own suggestion is more acceptable: that the term was originally applied to a leader of local, or native, militia. This would suit well with the 'Romans' *Magnus Maximus* and *Ambrosius Aurelianus,* and also the sub-Roman chieftains Ceredig and Cunedda; and it would also account for the loose extension of the epithet to their purely Welsh successors in medieval times. (For an instance of the Breton equivalent *gloedic* applied in a fifteenth-century document to the count of Cornouailles, see RC 33, pp. 352–3.) Stevens supports the view of E. K. Chambers (*Arthur of Britain*, p. 176) that the Roman equivalent of *gwledic* may well have been *Protector,* a title which is found both on the sixth-century tombstone of the Dyfed prince *Voteporix* (Gildas's *Uortiporius,* ECMW, no. 138) and also in the names of his ancestors, the immediate descendants of *Maxim Guletic,* according to Harl. Gen. II.

In addition to the references quoted, see C. E. Stevens, EC III, 86 ff.; M. P. Charlesworth, *The Lost Province*, pp. 28–30; D. N. Dumville, *History* 62.

Mederei Badellua6r 58. In the first edition of TYP this was translated as 'M. of the Big Knee' and *Mederei* was compared with the adjective *medrus* (< *medru*) 'skilful'. *Padell* was understood as meaning '*patella*' = knee cap. *Padell* is used for knee-cap (GPC 2665) and cf. *padellog*, triad 17. Eurys Rowlands, however, suggested (LlC VI, p. 234) that the three names in this triad are corrupt and that they all originally ended in (*h*)*ei* (= *-ai*), giving *Llafnai* (?) (or *Lleinai*) *ferch Seidfedd*, *Rhonai* (?) *ferch Ysbar*, and *Meddwai* (? 'the drunken one') *Badellfawr*. In a context which is obviously one of broad humour, 'Big

(Mead) Dish' is a more likely meaning than 'Big Knee' (as proposed in the earlier editions of this book).

Medra6t 51, 53 (Pen. 50), 54, 59; *Medrod m. Llew m. Kenvarch*, App. IV, no. 5.

> *Ann. Cam.* 537: *Gueith Camlann in qua Arthur et Medraut corruerunt* ('The Battle of Camlan in which Arthur and Medrawd fell').
>
> Meilyr (*Marwnad Gr. ap Cynan,* d. 1137): *Gwanei yg kynhor eissor medravt* (H 1.29 = CBT I, no. 3.25n.).
>
> Gwalchmai (to Madog ap Maredudd): *arthur gederned menwyd medravt* (H 16.6 = CBT I, no. 6.8n.).
>
> Gwynfardd Brycheiniog: *am gyduravd medravd* (H 207.25 = CBT II, no. 25.43).
>
> Cynddelw: *moes medravt* (H 108.11 = CBT IV, no. 9.23n.).
>
> Sefnyn: *kein ymadravd kyn no medravd* (RBP col. 1261.25: cf. GSRh no. 2.24n.).
>
> Gwilym Ddu o Arfon: *meglyt dreic llachar lluchynt medrawt* (RBP col. 1227.89 = GGDT no. 6.78n.).
>
> DGG no. XXVIII.32: *Medrud son uwch Medrod Sais*; no. XXIX.48: *Ymadrodd chwedl fal Medrod.*
>
> Tudur Aled: *twyll Medrod hen* (GTA I, no. LXVI.49; see n. to triad 84); *Medrod fawr* (I, no. LXXIII.69).

The possibility of equating *Medrawt* with the Cornish *Modred* of HRB (an equation which first appears in *Brut y Brenhinedd*) presents a difficulty. Jackson objected (WHR 1963, pp. 85–6) that **Mōdrāt-* would not give *Medrawd*, and that the *e* requires explanation, if the name is the same as that of the Cornish *Modred*, Arthur's nephew and antagonist according to HRB. (On the Cornish name *Modred* see further O. J. Padel, CMCS 8, pp. 15–16.) From the single reference to *Medrawd* in *Ann. Cam.* 537, together with the allusions made to *Medrawd* by the *Gogynfeirdd*, it remains uncertain how far *Medrawd* was a prominent figure in the pre-Geoffrey Arthurian tradition in Wales. The allusions quoted above from early medieval poems, of uncertain authorship (DGG XXVIII), support T. Gwynn Jones's assertion (*Aberystwyth Studies* VIII, pp. 43–4) that *Medrawd* was traditionally regarded as a paragon of valour and of courtesy. The four allusions quoted above from the *Gogynfeirdd* are indeterminate in their character, unless we place emphasis on Cynddelw's *moes medravt* 'M's manners, customs'. Brynley Roberts suggested (AW 112–13) that *Medrawt* took on the attributes of the personality of Melwas, the abductor of Gwenhwyfar, to become Arthur's antagonist at Camlan, from the unfavourable character of Melwas as portrayed in early poetry and in the Life of *St Gildas* (for references see AW 58–60). It is notable that prior to HRB the early sources do not claim that *Medrawd* was Arthur's nephew, or even that he was Arthur's opponent at the battle of Camlan: *Ann. Cam.* merely states that *Medrawd* and Arthur together died in 537 at this battle. There appears to be no allusion by the poets to *Medrawd*'s treachery earlier than that by Tudur Aled (see above). But the later concept of *Medrawt*'s 'courtesy' is clearly reflected by his presentation in App. IV, 5, although his patronymic there given (*ap Llew ap Cynfarch*) stems directly from HRB through *Brut y Brenhinedd.* According to HRB IX, 9 *Modredus* (= *Medrawt*, BD 152.24) was the son of *Loth of Lodonesia* (BD's *Lleu fab Cynfarch*), and he was therefore brother to *Gualguanus* = *Gwalchmai.* On these relationships see B. F. Roberts, B XXV, pp. 287–8: he concludes that Geoffrey derived the form *Modredus* from a Cornish or from a Breton source, and that he conflated it with the already existing cognate W. *Medrawt*, a name already familiar in Wales in an Arthurian context in *Ann. Cam.* (See on this O. J. Padel, CMCS 8, pp. 1–28; and cf. LHEB 300–1.) *Modrot* is in fact a name attested twice in the *Cartulaire de Redon* (A. de Courson (ed.), p. 78: *Chr. Br.* 152). Two independent instances of *Modret* as a proper name have been found in Cornish sources: the place-name *Tre-Modret* is found in *Domesday* (RC XIII, p. 481), and *Tedion Modredis sunu* is recorded in the Bodmin manumissions (AD 960–1000; RC I, p. 335; XXXIII, p. 298). C. L. Wrenn drew attention to the place-name *Carveddras* (earlier *kaervodred*) in the parish of *Kenwyn* near Truro (THSC 1959, p. 60). But the post-Geoffrey triads (nos. 51–4) here cited from the WR version, reflect a tradition of hostility between Arthur and *Medrawt* which is echoed in *Breudwyt Ronabwy*, and which may well antedate Geoffrey of Monmouth.

Meic Mygvras (= Mynguras) 79: *Auan verch M. Myngvras* = 'long- or thick-maned' as applied to horses (CA l. 3; BT 9.1), so here 'long- or thick-haired'; for the first element cf. *Essyllt Fyngwen* 'fair-haired' (triad 80 and n.); for the second cf. *Caradawc Vreichvras*[1] 'Strong-Arm'. *Myngvras* is attested as the correct form of the epithet in this name by the following:

Y Prydydd Bychan: *gwychyr lym dreic eil meic myguras* (H 236.1 = CBT VII, no. 8.7). The *Mygotas* of Pen. 47 has been obtained by misreading the *u* of *uras* as *o* and the *r* as *t*.

Jes. Gen. III: Gutuyl verch vrachan. gwreic kynger mab kynwavr (=*Kynwawr Katgaduc*) a mam brochuael yscithravc. a mam *veic mengvrac* a mam sanant gwreic vaelgwn. *Mengvrac(h)* = *'hairy* mane' (B III, p. 36), but this also is probably a corruption of *Myngvras.*

(See n. to *Maelgwn Gwyned* for the corresponding reference in *De Situ Brecheniauc,* where the name is given as *Meigh* and the epithet omitted.)

Iolo Goch describes Owain Glyndŵr as *hil Maig Mygrfras* (GIG no. VIII.37; *ail Maig* no. VIII.84). The implication is that *Meic Myngvras* (corrupted to *Mygrvras* 'fine and large', i.e. 'well set-up') was a traditional ancestor of the rulers of Glyndyfrdwy in northern Powys. These claimed descent from Madog ap Maredudd, and thus the reference by Iolo Goch gives some support to the statement of the *Jes. Gen.* that *Meic* belonged to the royal dynasty of Powys, and was a brother of Brochfael Ysgithrog. Further, Iolo calls Powys *peues Faig* (GIG no. X.21). It is possible, also, that this hero's name is preserved in that of *Meigen,* the district of Powys surrounding Cefn Digoll (the Long Mountain) where there took place the battle at which Cadwallawn slew Edwin. (For *Gueith Meigen* see n. to triad 55.) Part of *Meic's* territory may have lain across the present English border, since *Meigion* is the old name for the country adjoining Bridgnorth in Shropshire (EANC 103; GDG lxx–lxxi). This is not impossible if *Meic* was in fact the brother of the sixth-century ruler of Powys, Brochfael Ysgithrog; see n. to *Selyf m. Kenan Garrwyn.*

There are other instances of both *Meic* and *Meigen* as personal names; LL 209.9; 231.10; Harl. Gen. III: *Meic map Cinglas*; *Jes. Gen.* XXXIX: *Meic m. Ewein*; *Brut y Tywys.* (Pen. 20, 11b): *Meyc m. Yeuaf*; Prydydd y Moch (perhaps in reference to *Meic Myngvras*): *ut angut angers ueic* (H 300.10). *Meigen* may be simply a diminutive of *Meic,* but it remains possible that the following instances of the proper name arose with reference to the district of Powys named *Meigen* (GDG lxxi): *Meigen ap Rhun* (LlDC no. 18.53, 56, 59); *Rhys Meigen* GDG no. 151.70; 152.55. For *Mays Maichghen [sic]* as a name for *Cantre'r Gwaelod,* see T. Jones, 'Triawd Lladin ar y Gorlifiadau', B XII (1946–50), p. 82.

Meirchya6n, *March m. M.* 14, 26. *Meirchyawn* < *Marciānos.* Several early instances of this name occur in Britain. Brit. *Marciānos* may have become popular as a proper name in this country after the emperor *Marcianus* who reigned AD 450–7 (Chadwick, *Early Scotland,* p. 143). According to *Bonedd Gwŷr y Gogledd* (App. II, no. 2) *Meirch(y)awn* was the name of the grandfather of Llywarch Hen and of Urien Rheged, who must have been born about this period or slightly later. The Cumberland place-names *Powmaughan* and *Maughanby* preserve the name of this or some other northern *Meirchyawn* (on the names see Jackson in SEBH 74; LHEB 571).

Eight further instances of the name *Merchiaun, Merchion* are found in LL (see index). These instances indicate that the name was especially popular in south Wales. A king *Meirchiawn* of Glamorgan figures in the Life of the sixth-century *St Illtud,* whom I have suggested (AW 211, n.26) could well be the father of the *March* (see n.) of the Welsh *Tristan* romance. A further possible reference to this ruler is made by the Glamorgan poet Casnodyn, who describes his patron as *camp Meirchawn* (RBP col. 1240.2 = GC no. 2.2n.; see G. J. Williams, *Traddodiad Llenyddol Morgannwg,* p. 7). Cf. also the reference by Gwilym Ddu in his elegy on Trahaearn Brydydd Mawr, whom he describes as *da Vyrdin: ae lin o lwyth meirchyawn* (RBP col. 1229.38).

A north-Welsh *Meirchyawn* is referred to in several sources; first, there is the traditional association of *March ap Meirchyawn* with *Castellmarch* in Llŷn. An Anglesey *Meirchyawn* is named as the father of Blodeuwedd in the *cywydd* to the Owl, formerly attributed to Dafydd ap Gwilym (*Barddoniaeth Dafydd ab Gwilym*, 1789 edition, no. CLXXXIII): cf. however, D. H. Evans's view on this in YB XX, pp. 82–3. Certain late genealogies give the following: *Plant egri o dal ebolion y mon a vuant yn oes vaelgwn gwynedd. Nudd ap egri. Ronyn. iarddur. Geiriad. Trystan. Meirchion,* etc. (Pen. 75, 49). The occurrence of Trystan here beside *Meirchion* is probably an interpolation due to the popularity of the romances. But these indications suggest the existence in the past of traditions, now almost obliterated, of a celebrated north-Welsh *Meirchyawn* of early times, whose name seems to have drawn to it at some stage, under the influence of the romances, the names of both March and Tristan.

Melen 64: *Ellyll Melen.* Cf. *Melyn m. Kynuelyn* below.

Melyn m. Kynuelyn 31. (W: *gosgord Velyn o Leyn.*) See n. to *Belen o Leyn.* CA ll. 1360–4 (*Gwarchan Kynvelyn*): *a galar dwvyn dyvyd / y wynnassed velyn / e greu oe gylchyn / keledic ewyn / med mygyr melyn*; 1. 1383: *gwyned e wlat.*

It is impossible to decide whether *Belyn* or *Melyn* is the correct form of this name. *Belyn* seems to be corroborated by the references in *Ann. Cam.* and in the *Hirlas Owein,* and by W's early spelling *Belen o Leyn,* triad 62. But *Melyn* gains support from the *Gwarchan Kynvelyn,* a lament for an early Gwynedd hero whom one would like to identify with the *Kynvelyn* father of *Melyn* of triad 31. If this *Kynvelyn* was really slain at Catraeth, his son could well have been a contemporary of Edwin who died in 633. The *melyn* of l. 1364 (*med mygyr melyn* 'fine yellow (?) mead') is not necessarily an adjective referring to *med,* but it could be the proper name used as a possessive genitive. Perhaps *Melyn m. Kynvelyn* and *Belyn o Leyn* were originally two distinct characters who have become hopelessly confused in tradition.

Menw m. Teirg6aed 27, 28 (WR), App. IV, no. 4. With *Menw* cf. Ir. *menb* 'something minute or small' (for the form cf. Ir. *marb*, W. *marw*; Ir. *garb*, W. *garw*); 'Little son of Three Cries'. This rendering, as Rhŷs pointed out (CF 510n.) is consistent with the bird-form assumed by *Menw*; see below.

CO (WM 461.22, *et passim*): *Menv mab teirgvaed*; 478.16: *m. mab teirgveth*; 462.17: *anynnavc* (R: *An nyannavc*) *m. menv. m. teirgvaed*; 472.2–7: *Galv o arthur ar uenv mab teirgvaed kanys o delhynt y wlat aghred mal y gallei yrru lleturith arnadunt hyt nas gwelei neb vynt. ac vyntvy a welynt pavb*; 497–8: *ymrithav a oruc menv yn rith ederyn. A disgynnu a vnaeth uch penn y gval.*

Br. Rh. (RM 160.3–4): *A menv mab teirgvaed.*

The triads tell nothing of *Menw* which either adds to, or is inconsistent with, the portrayal of this character in CO, where *Menw* appears as an enchanter and shape-shifter. Later references to *Menw* are by Dafydd ap

Gwilym (GDG no. 84.38 ; quoted note to triad 27) and Rhys Goch Eryri: *A rhan o henw, Fenw faenol* (IGE^{2} 171.17; see n. on p. 364).

Me(n)waed o Arllechwed 18 (W: *Mened*), 26. For the name see n. to *Menw m. Teirg6aed.* W's reading *y Vergaed* (triad 26) represents a corrupt transcription of *y Venguaed* in Insular script; see n. to triad 26.

Arllechwedd was the name of the *cantref* which lay along the shore of the Menai between Arfon and Rhos, its eastern border being formed by the River Conwy. 'For the most part a rugged, stony region' (HW 235).The gift of a wolf to Menwaed is therefore intended to symbolize the produce of his territory, in contrast with the rich produce of the fertile south.

Merwydd (o Fôn). See n. to triad 94.

Modron verch Auallach 70. See n. to *Mabon m. Modron. Modron* < Celt. *Mātrŏna*, 'the 'Great Mother', the deity who gave her name to the River Marne (ACS II, 468). There was a sanctuary to the *dea Matrona* at *Bellesmes,* near the source of the river (Vendryes, *La Religion des Celtes, in* vol. III of *Les Religions de l'Europe Ancienne,* ed. A. Grenier (Paris, 1948), p. 279). It has been suggested (AT 269, WAL 127–8) that the cult of *Mātrŏna* is to be associated with that of the Three Mothers, which is found in Gaulish and British dedications; and though there can be no certainty on this point, it remains a possible hypothesis (see Vendryes, loc. cit., p. 275). The cult of the triple *matres, matrae,* or *matronae,* appears to have originated in western Europe, and it flourished in Britain among the auxiliary troops stationed along Hadrian's Wall (*Archaeologia Aeliana,* fourth series, XXI, p. 210; for a collection of the dedications see AA, second series, XV, pp. 314–39; AA, third series, VII, p. 180. On the *Matres* see also Sjoestedt, *Gods and Heroes of the Celts*, pp. 18, 20; Vendryes, op. cit., pp. 276–8 PCB 204ff). In the early Welsh occurrences of the name there is variation in the vowel in the first syllable: LlDC no. 31.13: *Mabon am mydron*; BT 26.2: *am svynvys i wytyon . . . o eurwys o euron / o euron o vodron* (the reference here is to the creation by magic of the poet Taliesin; on the passage see Chw. T. 20); VSB 322 (45): *Madrun uerch Wertheuyr urenhin Enys Brideyn*; Pen. 45 *Bonedd* (LBS IV, 372): *Keidav m. ynyr gwent a madrun merch wertheuyr uendigeit y uam* (for a variant of this genealogy see n. to *Gwga6n^{2} Gwron*). According to Wade-Evans, *St Madrun* is commemorated at Trawsfynydd (HB 66, n. 3). There is a *Garth Madrun* at Talgarth in Breconshire, and a *Carn Vadrun* in Llŷn (*Cy.* 42, p. 140). But the form *Madrun* < L. *matrōna,* with long *ō*. It remains uncertain whether it is the mythical *Mātrŏna*, *Modron,* who is commemorated in these place-names, or a person subsequently named after her, such as the saint who bore her name.

The story of the begetting of Urien's two children, Owein and Morfudd, was told in a folk-tale which has come down in summary form in Pen. 147 (pp. 10–11; see *Rep.* I, p. 911). Since the story evidently bears some relation to that which is referred to in triad 70, I quote the passage here in full:

Yn Sir ddinbych y mae plwyf a elwir llan verrys / ag yno y mae *Ryd y gyfarthfa* / ag ynyr hen amser y doe gwn y wlad y gid y lan y Ryd hono y gyfarth, ag nyd oedd y fentre vyned y sbio beth oedd yno nes dyfod Urien Reged. a ffyn doyth y lan y Ryd (n)y wele yno ddim and merch yn golchi. ag yno tewi o'r kwn a'r Cyfarth ag ymhafel o Urien Reged a'r verch ag ymweithredy a hi, ag yna y dwad hithe bendith ddyw ar y traed y'th ddygoedd yma. pam heb y(nte), achos bod ynghyngedfen i olchi yma nes enill m(ab) o griston / a merch wyfi y vrenin anyfwn a dyred di yma am ben y flwyddyn ag di y gay y mab. ag velly y dayth ynte ag y Cafas yno vab a merch nyd amgen noc owein ab eirien a morfydd verch eirien [*sic*].

'In Denbighshire there is a parish which is called Llanferres, and there is there *Rhyd y Gyfarthfa* [the Ford of Barking]. In the old days the hounds of the countryside used to come together to the side of that ford to bark, and nobody dared go to find out what was there until Urien Rheged came. And when he came to the side of the ford he saw nothing there except a woman washing. And then the hounds ceased barking, and Urien seized the woman and had his will of her; and then she said "God's blessing on the feet which brought thee here." "Why?" said he. "Because I have been fated to wash here until I should conceive a son by a Christian. And I am daughter to the King of Annwfn, and come thou here at the end of the year and then thou shalt receive the boy." And so he came and he received there a boy and a girl: that is, Owein son of Urien and Morfudd daughter of Urien.' (The passage is reprinted with a discussion by J. Rowland, EWSP 234.)

The antiquity of 'The Washer at the Ford' as a mythological tale-type in Celtic countries is witnessed by the fact that a closely similar episode is found in the eleventh-century Irish tale called *The* (*Second*) *Battle of Moytura* (RC XII, pp. 85 ff.; Gray (ed.), *Cath Maige Tuired*, ITS, §84, pp. 44–5; Cross and Slover, *Ancient Irish Tales*, p. 38), in which the god Dagda meets and has intercourse with the goddess Morrigu, who is engaged in washing at the ford of Unius in Connacht. A survival of the same myth has probably come down in the widespread Breton folk-belief in supernatural washer-women who wash in the rivers at night, which has survived to recent times (P. Yves-Sebillot, *Le Folklore de la Bretagne*, pp. 44 ff.). It is significant that in north-Welsh folk-tradition Urien should be credited with this encounter with a fairy-woman on whom he begot a son and daughter whose names are the same as those given in the triad, although the localizing of a tale about Urien in Wales rather than in north Britain must of course be regarded as a secondary development (see n. to *Vryen Reget*). The name of the ancestor-deity *Auallach* (see n.) could easily become translated into more familiar, popular terms as *brenin Annwfn,* so that it is not unnatural to conclude that *merch vrenhin ann(w)fn* is to be identified with *Modron verch Avallach* in the triad. But if this story is really so old that it was already attached to Urien before the traditions about him were transferred from the North to Wales, it becomes relevant to consider the evidence for the concentration of the cult of *Mapŏnos* son of *Mātrŏna* in the north of England, and particularly in the district north-west of Hadrian's Wall (see n. to *Mabon m. Modron*). The early historical poems in BT contain allusions in which the name Mabon appears to denote either a member of Urien's family, or else is employed as a pseudonym for Owein fab Urien himself. On the other hand there is no reference to *Modron* as the name of Urien's wife in the corpus of early poetry concerning Urien and Owein that has come down (though this poetry agrees with triad 70 in naming Urien's sister as *Efrddyl*, see n. to *Eurddel (= Efrdyyl)*). We have, however, analogies in both Ireland and Wales for the attribution of divine birth to historical figures who belong to approximately the same period as Urien, in which this attribution seems to have occurred within two or three centuries of their life-time: Taliesin, who addressed poems to Urien, was depicted as the son of the goddess Ceridwen in a north-Welsh folk-tale which Ifor Williams has shown to have existed in a literary form as early as the ninth century; and a story of divine fatherhood attributed to the seventh-century Ulster king *Mongan* was committed to writing hardly more than a century after his life-time. It is relevant also to compare the recurrent Irish conception of the rightful ruler of the land as mated to a goddess who represents Ireland herself (*Ériu* XIV, pp. 14–28; cf. AT 269–70). It is plausible, therefore, to suppose that an early offshoot from the heroic tradition of Urien Rheged and his son Owein could have been the attribution to Urien, the most renowned member of the dynasty of Coel Hen, of a myth which depicted him as mating with the locally worshipped goddess *Modron*, and which depicted his famous son Owein as a fruit of their union. Further support for this conclusion may be derived from the fact that *Auallach* (see n.) figures in the Welsh dynastic genealogies as the name of the (divine) ancestor from whom Urien's family claimed descent.

Mordaf Hael m. Seruan 2; App. II, no. 9 'M. the Generous.' *Mordaf* < **Mārotamos* (LHEB 488). For the passage in the *Black Book of Chirk* which names *Mordaf* as one of the Men of the North who went to Gwynedd to avenge Elidir Mwynfawr, see n. to *Run³ m. Maelgwn*, and cf. n. to triad 44a. Like the others of the *Tri Hael,* Mordaf's exemplary generosity constitutes a favourite standard of comparison for the bards:

Cynddelw: *Mordaf heuelyt ryt ym rotei* (H 129.23 = CBT III, no. 21.129n.).

Einion Wan: *Hawd kynnelw vy rwyf rwyd ouec mordaf* (H 192.21 = CBT VI, no. 1.32).

Llywelyn Fardd I: *anvreid gymro gymradv mordaf* (H 222.22 = CBT II, no. 36.4).

Casnodyn: *am verch ruffud ud adysc mordaf* (RBP col. 1244.19–20 = GC no. 4.13n.).

Madog Dwygraig: *Kwynvn vyt y gyt amgyved mordaf* (RBP col. 1267.6).

Gruffudd Vychan: *ehutrwyd mordaf* (1300.32–3).

Y Proll: *rysgyr mordaf mavrdec* (1311.22 = GDC no. 14.25–6n.).

Gruffudd ap Maredudd: *ner dewrder, avdurdavt mordaf* (RBP col. 1325.19–20); *mawrdal mordaf* (1317.20 = GGM no. 4.112); *medgyrn mavr deyrn mordaf* (1326.13 = GGM no. 5.159).

Dafydd ap Gwilym: *Cynnydd Mordaf a Rhydderch* (GDG no. XXV.3).

Gruffudd Llwyd: *heiliau Mordaf* (IGE^2 no.XXXIX.3).

Guto'r Glyn to Rhys Abad Ystrad Fflur: *Marw Dewi'r glod, Morda'r glêr* (GGl no. XI.26).

For further references by the bards to the *Tri Hael* together, see n. to triad 2. The *Cyvoesi Myrddin a Gwenddydd* refers to *marv mordaf* (RBP col. 583.17).

Moruran eil Tegit 24, 41; App. IV, no. 7. *Moruran* = 'Great Raven'; cf. the instances of *Brân* as a proper name, cited in n. to *Bran Vendigeit.* On *eil* see n. to *Rahaut eil Morgant.*

CO (l. 225): *Moruran eil Tegit—ny dodes dyn y araf yndav yGhamlan rac y haccred, pawb a tybygynt y uod yn gythreul canhorthwy; blew a oed arnaw mal blew hyd.* 'M. son of T.; no man set his weapon on him at Camlan because of his ugliness: everyone thought he was a supporting devil. There was hair on him like the hair of a stag.'

Br. Rh.: *Moruran eil tegit* (RM 159.30).

In the later versions of *Chwedl Taliesin*, *Morfran*'s proverbial ugliness has been transferred to a brother *Y Vagddu, Afagddu.* Ifor Williams's explanation (Chw. T. 4n.) that this name 'utter darkness' arose first as a nickname for *Morfran* himself is favoured by the description in CO l. 225n., and the evident contrast intended between *Morfran*'s ugliness and the beauty of his sister *Creirwy* (see n.). The following is the opening of the tale from the version of J. Jones, Gellilyfdy, in Pen. 111, pp. 1ff. (there is no subsequent reference in the story to Morfran):

Gwr bonheddig oedd gynt ym Penllyn a elwit Tegit Voel, ai dref tad oedd yng hanol Llyn Tegit, ai wraig priod a elwit Karidwen, ag or wraig honno i ganet map a elwit Morfran ap Tegit, a merch a elwit Greirfyw, a thegkaf merch or byt oedd honno, a brawd iddunt wy oedd y dyn hagraf or byd, a elwit y Vagddu. Ag yno Karidwen ei fam a feddyliodd nad oedd ef debyg i gael ei gynwys ym plith boneddigion rrag ei hagred oni bai arno ryw gampau neu wybodau vrddasol.

'There was a well-born man in Penllyn in former times who was called Tegid the Bald, and his home was in the middle of Llyn Tegid (Bala), and his wife was called *Ceridwen* (see n.); and from that wife there was born a son who was called Morfran son of Tegid, and a daughter who was called *Creirfyw* (*Creirwy,* see n.), and she was the fairest maiden in the world; and they had a brother who was the ugliest man in the world, who was called *Y*

Fagddu. And then Ceridwen his mother considered that he was not likely to be received among well-born people because of his ugliness, unless he had some abilities or distinguished knowledge.'

It is possible that the name of *Morfran* in the story conceals a reference to a forgotten *Cynfardd*, since Cynddelw refers to a famous early poet of this name: *Dymgwallouwy duw diheudavn awen . . . / y ganu marvnad y gadwallavn / Mal pan gant moruran marvnad einyavn* (H 125.26 = CBT III, no. 21.1–6) 'May God pour forth for me authentic inspiration, to sing a death-song for Cadwallon, as when Morfran sang the *marwnad* for Einion'. It is tempting to connect this otherwise forgotten poet with the *Morfran* of *Chwedl Taliesin*, for whom (if Ifor Williams's conjecture that *Afagddu is* a 'ghost-name' is correct) Ceridwen's magic cauldron of poetic inspiration was originally prepared, although in the event the magic drops were consumed instead by Taliesin. Cf. the Irish *Macgnímartha Finn,* in which under similar circumstances the boy Finn consumes the salmon of inspiration intended for his master *Finnéces* 'Finn the Poet' (*Ériu* I, p. 186).

Moruud verch Vryen 70, *Moruyd* 71. See nn. to *Vryen Reged, Owein m. Vryen.*

The inclusion of *Moruyd merch Uryen Reget* in the list of ladies at Arthur's court (CO l. 366) is of particular interest in view of the fact that neither Uryen nor his son Owein play any part in CO. It also provides corroborative evidence for the antiquity of the tradition referred to in the triads that Owein had a sister of this name. The story alluded to in triad 71 (or perhaps the triad itself) was known to Gr. ap Maredudd: *caryat glwysuerch uryen . . . ucheneit Cynon* (RBP col. 1326.30–2). Apart from this reference, the name of *Morfudd* appears to have been unknown to the *Gogynfeirdd*, who make no use of the name of Urien's daughter as a standard of female beauty, as they do those of Essyllt, Enid, Luned and the like. Thus in view of the scarcity of early references it seems on the whole improbable that Dafydd ap Gwilym could have derived the name of *Morfudd* from literary or traditional sources, as was suggested by Chotzen (*Recherches sur la Poésie de Dafydd ap Gwilym*, p. 227), although the reference by his contemporary Gr. ap Maredudd proves that this is not impossible. The general improbability that he had *Morvudd verch Uryen* in mind lends some slight additional weight to Thomas Parry's argument that Dafydd's *Morfudd* was a real woman who bore this name, and not a mere pseudonym (GDG xlii ff.).

Morgant Mwynua6r 20; App. III, no. 4; *Rahaut eil Morgant* 12. 'M. the Wealthy.' (For *Mwynfawr* see Ifor Williams, 'Dwy Gân o Lyfr Coch Talgarth', B II (1923–5), pp. 129–30; CA 97; and cf. *Elidir Mwynvawr, Mynydawc (Mwynvawr)*, and nn.; *Rees mvynuavr Jes. Gens.* XXIV, XXV.) *Morgant* is a man's name of fairly frequent occurrence in early Welsh sources. It was borne by two of the early kings of Morgannwg (the first in the eighth and the second in the tenth century): *Morgant m. Athrwys* and *Morgant (Hen) m. Owein* (see Harl. Gen. XXVIII; *Jes. Gens* IX, LL 248). J. E. Lloyd identified *Morgant Mwynvawr* with the first of these kings, who lived *circa* 730 (HW 274), and stated his belief that the kingdom of *Morgannwg* derived its name from him. And in fact the name *Morgan Mwynwawr* (for *Morgant m. Athrwys?*) occurs in a regnal list of the kings of Morgannwg in Pen. 134, pp. 136–7 (written 1550–62). According to G. Peredur Jones, 'A List of Epithets from Welsh Pedigrees', B III (1926–7), p. 41, the name corresponds with *Morgan Mawr* in the corresponding pedigree in Panton 28, Mostyn 134, 11. The name *Morgant Mwynvawr* also occurs several times in the Iolo MSS. to denote the founder of Morgannwg (pp. 12, 18, *et passim*), and it may be that this was Lloyd's only source for the identification.

It seems to me far more likely that the name *Morgant Mwynvawr* in the triads designates one of the Men of the North, and not an early ruler of Morgannwg. The scribe of Pen. 134 could have found the name in a northern pedigree, and transferred the epithet to a ruler of Morgannwg. In fact, certain early sixteenth-century adaptations of *Bonedd Gwŷr y Gogledd* (App. II) include *Morgant Mwynvawr* among the Men of the North, making him a brother of Rhydderch Hael; e.g. Pen. 127, p. 95 (*circa* 1510): *Rydderch hael a Chynvyn glaer ac Iarderch drut a Morgant Mwynvawr brodorion, meibion tudwal tudclut ap kedic ap dyfnwal hen Isic*, and cf. Pen. 129, 21. The relationship with Rhydderch Hael need not necessarily be genuine, but the inclusion of *Morgant*'s name in the northern genealogy shows the milieu in which he was considered by bards of the period to belong. Another indication that *Morgant Mwynvawr* belonged originally to north Britain is to be found in his inclusion in App. III; where, with the possible exception of the name of Arthur, all the names that can be identified belong to various of the Men of the North. The implications of the epithet *mwynvawr* may also be considered: two out of the three other characters to whom this epithet is attached (see above) belong to the Men of the North. It is possible, indeed, that in the triad and elsewhere the common name *Morgant* has been allowed to supersede the uncommon name *Mynydawc,* appropriating the epithet which went with it, and that the references to *Morgant Mwynvawr* originally denoted the *Mynydawc Mwynvawr* of the *Gododdin.*

But there is yet another possibility. HB, ch. 63 gives *Morcant* as the name of one of the three British kings who fought in company with *Urien Rheged* (see n.) against the Bernician kings following Ida; and, according to this account, it was *Morcant* who eventually became jealous of Urien and slew him. This is the *Morgant* of CLlH no. III.41, who is named in the same context as *Gwallawc, Dunawt mab Pabo* (see nn.), and others of the Men of the North. Cf. also, perhaps, the *Morgant Hael* of WM 464.17 (though this may be a mistake for *Mordaf,* one of the *Tri Hael* of triad 2). Lloyd suggested (HW I, 318) that this *Morcant* is the *Morgant Bulc* (*bulc*, *bwlch* 'gap', perhaps 'toothless' or 'hare-lipped', B III, p. 46) of Harl. Gen. X, which represents one of the north-British dynasties; but it could equally well be *Morcant Bulc* or his grandson *Morcant m. Coledauc* of the same genealogy. The Life of *St Kentigern* by Jocelyn of Furness (ed. A. P. Forbes, p. 69) refers to a tyrannical north-British king *Morken* who oppressed the saint: he may be identical with HB's *Morcant*, since both must have ruled in the same area during the latter half of the sixth century. As Kenneth Jackson points out (SEBH 312–13), this identification should not be too readily assumed, in view of the other instances cited above in which the name *Morcant* is attested from the same period and area. But if on the other hand the episode in the Life of *St Kentigern* is an ecclesiastical fiction, it is quite likely that the *Morken* on whom it is fathered is the same as HB's *Morcant,* who was obviously a notorious character in north-British heroic narrative.

Since *Morcant* is thus likely to have been the name of a prominent ruler among the northern Britons, contemporary with Urien and Rhydderch, it is tempting to identify *Morgant Mwynvawr* with the HB's *Morcant* in view of the later tradition which links him with *Gwŷr y Gogledd.*

(M)ugnach Gorr 'M. the Dwarf'. See n. to triad 71, *Fflur verch Vugnach Gorr*.

Murthach *Solor m. M.* 15. This is the Irish name *Murchad*; cf. HGVK 30, n.6, where *gurmlach . . . merch y vwrchath vrenhin laine* is the *Gormlaith ingen Murchada, ríg Laigen* of the *Annals of Innisfallen*, AD 840 (ed. Seán Mac Airt, p. 128). The spelling *Mwrchath* is found elsewhere in Welsh sources, cf. RBB 264.20: *Mwrchath* (son of Brian Boru), 325.16: *Diermit vab Mwrchath.* The spelling with *-th-* in place of *-ch-* in the triad and elsewhere would be a simple transposition. The name occurs also in Br. Rh.: *Blathaon uab Mwrheth* (RM 159.9–10).

Mynach Naomon 44 (R: *Navmon*). *Mynach* 'monk' can hardly be intended in this name. Probably *mynach* here is a corruption of the adjective *mynawc* 'noble, courteous' (CA 157, 171), which occurs as an epithet in CO: *Bratwen m. Moren Mynawc a Moren Mynawc e hun* (CO ll. 183–4n.). Cf. also *Chr. Br.* 153: *Morgen munuc.* Some early copyist of the triad incorrectly wrote *Mynac* as *Mynach* because he was used to altering *c* in his exemplar to *ch.* But since -*ch* appears in this name in all versions of the triad it seems probable that this mistake was already made in the common exemplar from which all written texts must be ultimately derived. In *Naomon*, Pen. 16 retains older *o* for *w*, if the word here is *naw* 'nine'. It seems likely, however, that the compound has become hopelessly corrupt in the course of transmission.

Myngan (o Ueigen) 55. *Myngan* < *mwng* + *can* 'white maned'. It is possible that *Myngan* in the triad is the name of a horse, and not of a man (see n. to triad 55; cf. also N. A. Jones, 'Horses in Medieval Welsh Court Poetry' in

Davies and Jones (eds), *The Horse in Celtic Culture*, p. 94; and CBT V, no. 1.127n.). But *myng-* occurs in a number of epithets attached to personal names in the genealogies; see nn. to *Meic Myg(vr)as* (= *Myngvras*) and *E(s)syllt* (*Fyngwen*). One may also compare with *Myngan* the name of the Irish hero *Mongan.* Nutt regarded this as a reduced hypocoristic form in which the first element *mong* 'mane' is equivalent to the Welsh *mwng;* and he compares the name *Mong-find* 'White Mane' (*Voyage of Bran* II, p. 29, n.). Perhaps the Irish *Mongan* is a borrowing from Welsh *Myngan* in which the second element has not been translated, while in the analogous *Mong-find* both elements have been rendered into Irish.

Mynyda6c Eidyn (*Mwynua6r*) 31. See n. to *Morgant Mwynua6r. Mynyddawc* < *mynydd* 'mountain' + adjectival termination. For *Eidyn* (= *Eiddyn*) see CA xxxvi–xl and cf. the names *Clydno Eidyn, Llawgat Trwm Bargawt Eidyn, Heidyn m. Einygan* and nn. For *Mwynvawr* 'wealthy' etc., see CA 97 and GPC 2521 for examples; to which may be added Y Prydydd Bychan: *mwynuavr gweilch* (H 234.9); *argae mwynuavr* (H 250.13). In *Hirlas Owein,* Owain Cyfeiliog compares the achievements of his men to those of the warriors of the *Gododdin*; with this in mind he intentionally plays upon the associations of the adjective *mwynvawr* which he applies to his brother Meurig ap Gruffudd (RBP col. 1434.341 = CBT II, no. 14.111n., see below).

Eidyn designates the old district of *Eidyn* which lay along the southern shore of the Firth of Forth, and whose name is preserved in *Edinburgh* and *Carriden.* As shown by Jackson, OSPG 75–8, *Eidyn* is the older form, but *Eiddyn* became popularized by poets in the later Middle Ages; see GIG 286n. Here *Mynyddawg* appears to have ruled during the latter part of the sixth century. The disastrous expedition of his *gosgordd* to attack the English at Catraeth (probably Catterick in Yorkshire) is the subject of Aneirin's poem the *Gododdin:* according to Ifor Williams's argument, presented in the introduction to his edition of the poem, this battle took place about the year 600. References in the poem indicate that Mynyddawg's fighting force was assembled from all parts of the British world—Elmet in Yorkshire, north Wales, and Devon, as well as Rheged and the northern British kingdoms—for as long as a year before the expedition to Catraeth took place. The assembled warriors spent the year in feasting at *Mynyddawg*'s expense (this may give significance to his epithet *mwynvawr*, see n. to *Elidir*[2] *Mwyn6a6r* above); later they paid for their mead with their lives, *talassant eu met* (CA xlix). We never hear of *Mynyddawg*'s personal presence on the expedition.

Mynyddawg's name does not occur in any of the northern genealogies. Our information about him is confined to the internal references in the *Gododdin* itself, to triad 31, and to allusions in Owain Cyfeiliog's poem *Hirlas Owein*: *Mwynuavr a garcharavr a gyrchassant / Meuric uab Gruffud* 'they sought a wealthy (or valuable) prisoner' or 'a *Mwynfawr* of a prisoner' (RBP col. 1434.34–5), and

Kigleu am dal med mynet pleid Cattraeth,
Kywir eu haruaeth, arueu lliweit,
Gosgord Vynydavc, am eu kysgeit,
Cavssant eu hadravd cas vlavd vlaenyeit,
Ny waeth wnaeth yghytwyr yghalet Vaelavr—
Dillvng carcharavr dylle(i)st woleit
(RBP col. 1435.4–10 = CBT II, no. 14.123–8)

'I have heard that for a payment of mead the foremost fighters went to Catraeth; constant their purpose, with keen weapons. The war-band of Mynyddawg—foremost fighters—because they were silenced, their praises were sung. No worse did my warriors in the battle of Maelawr—the freeing of a prisoner, in a manner worthy of fame.' (My slightly amended text and translation are indebted to the study of *Hirlas Owein* by G. A. Williams, CBT II, no. 14.)

It is likely that Owain Cyfeiliog knew more about the circumstances of the expedition to Catraeth than has come down to us. We should bear in mind the possibility that the comparison which he makes between the expedition of his own war-band and that of *Mynyddawg Mwynfawr* is intended to go further than a mere general comparison between their achievements, and has reference to a similarity in purpose between the two. No allusion to the purpose of the expedition to Catraeth is given in the mutilated text of the *Gododdin* that has survived, so that this purpose can only be deduced. But it is clear from the internal evidence of the poem that the expedition undertaken by Owain Cyfeiliog's war-band had the purpose of freeing a prisoner—Owain's brother Meurig (see Rachel Bromwich, 'Nodiadau Cymysg: the Date of Hirlas Owain', B XVI (1954–8), pp. 188–9). Is it possible that the motive of the expedition to Catraeth was not only strategic, as has been argued by Ifor Williams, but that it had also as an immediate object the freeing of a prisoner, and that this prisoner was no less than *Mynyddawg* himself? Such an explanation would account for the somewhat surprising fact that *Mynyddawg* did not accompany his warriors on the expedition, and yet he receives no opprobrium, either in the poem or in any other source, for having allowed his personal *gosgordd* to fight in his absence. T. Gwynn Jones also pointed out that the analogy of *Hirlas Owein* implies that the Catraeth expedition may also have had as an object the freeing of a prisoner (*Cy.* XXXII, pp. 9–10: cf. CBT II, no. 14). Owing to the confused state in which the text has come down, I do not consider that the references in the poem to *ancwyn Mynydawc* 'M's feast' necessarily constitute an insuperable objection to the suggestion made above. For a discussion of the questions concerning the identity and role of Mynyddawg Mwynfawr, see J. Rowland, CMCS 30, pp. 30–5. Doubts as to *Mynyddawg*'s position as lord of the Gododdin tribe, based on the ambiguity of the references in the poem, have been expressed by G. R. Isaac, B XXXVII, pp. 111–13 and by J. T. Koch, *The Gododdin of*

Aneirin, pp. xlvii, 206 and 'Re-thinking Aneirin and Mynyddawg Mwynfawr', *Language Sciences* (1993), pp. 86–7. I regret that Koch's study of the *Gododdin* poem could not be considered in detail here. See further O. J. Padel's review, 'A New Study of the *Gododdin*', CMCS 35, pp. 45–55.

Myrddyn[1] Embrys 87. See *Myrddyn (Wyllt) m. Morvryn.*

Myrddyn[2] (Wyllt) m. Morvryn 87; *Clas Merdin*, App. I, no. 1. On the meaning of *gwyllt* (Ir. *geilt*), see GPC 1766 'wild, deranged', etc.

Myrddin Wyllt 'M. the Wild' (or 'insane') figures as a political prophet in a number of medieval vaticinatory poems. In one of the earliest of these, *Armes Prydein* (*circa* 930; BT 13–18), the phrase *Dysgogan Myrdin* ('M. foretells') used to introduce one stanza, is paralleled by the opening *Dy(s)gogan awen* and *Dysgogan derwydon* at the opening of other stanzas. The allusion to *gwenwawt mirdyn* in the *Gododdin* (CA l. 466 = stanza XLIIIA) may well be as old or older than *Armes Prydein:* but since there is no corresponding reference in the B version of this stanza, no assurance can be had that the line was included in the oldest redaction of the poem, although the spelling *Mirdyn* indicates a prototype in O.W. orthography (see CA, p. 188n. and A. O. H. Jarman, *Y Gododdin*, pp. 107–8). A similar objection applies, of course, to the allusion to *Myrddin* in *Armes Prydein* (l. 17n.): we can have no certainty that this name appeared in the tenth-century composition, since it could easily have been substituted by the scribe of BT or a predecessor, for one of the parallel phrases cited above.

The group of poems concerning *Myrddin* in LlDC and RBH combine prophecy with allusions to a story about the prophet's former life. According to the story which can be reconstructed from these allusions, *Myrddin* was a north-British warrior who fought at the battle of Arfderydd in Cumbria (*Ann. Cam.,* 573), at which battle his lord *Gwenddoleu* (see n.) was slain (see triads 29, 31 (W), 44, and n. to triad 84). *Myrddin* lost his reason as a result of this battle, and for many years afterwards lived a wild life in the forest of Celyddon (situated in the western lowlands of Scotland). Here he lived in terror of *Rhydderch Hael* (see n.). One poem, the *Cyvoesi* (RBP 577–83), is in the form of a dialogue between *Myrddin* and a certain Gwenddydd, who is here represented as his sister, but elsewhere is apparently his mistress.

Of these poems, the *Cyvoesi* and the *Ymddiddan Myrddin a Thaliesin* (LlDC no. 1; ed. Jarman, *Ym. M. a Th.*) were certainly composed before 1100 (for the date of the *Cyvoesi* see K. Jackson, 'The motif of the three-fold death in the story of Suibhne Geilt' in J. Ryan (ed.) *Féilsghríbhinn Eoin Mhic Néill,* pp 535–50, n. 30). At least the nucleus of the *Avallenau* and the *Oianeu* are probably as old (cf. Jarman's note on the term *hwimleian, chwibleian,* B XVI, pp. 71–6). It is therefore impossible that the prototype of the Welsh poems could be the Latin poem called the *Vita Merlini,* which appeared in the year 1150–1, and is commonly attributed to Geoffrey of Monmouth (see Basil Clarke, *Life of Merlin*). This poem tells what is clearly a version of the same story as that which underlies the Welsh poems, and it presents certain remarkable points of correspondence with them. It has, however, been clearly demonstrated that *Vita Merlini* must be in part based upon the Welsh poems, rather than that the influence was in the opposite direction (see Chadwick, *Growth of Literature* I, pp. 123–32; J. Carney, *Studies in Irish Literature and History*, ch. IV; Jarman, 'Lailoken a Llallogan', B IX, pp. 8 ff.). Apart from the linguistic evidence afforded by the poems themselves, the argument for their prior composition and independence from the *Vita Merlini* is based on the close resemblance of the *Myrddin* story to the ninth-century Irish story of *Suibhne Geilt*, and to traditions about a certain Lailoken whose story is preserved in early hagiographical records relating to St Kentigern (= *Cyndeyrn Garthwys,* see n.), the patron saint of Glasgow. Indeed, Professor Jarman has argued (LlC IV, p. 58; *Ym. M. a Th.*, pp. 46–7) that Lailoken (W. *Llallawg*, *Llallogan*) was the prophet's name in the original north-British saga, and that it was only when the story became freshly localized in south Wales that the prophet received a new name, based on a spurious etymology given to the name of the town of *Carmarthen* (W. *Caerfyrddin* 'the city of M.'; but really *Myrddin* < *Moridunon* 'the sea fortress'). The only objection to this argument is that it hardly takes into account the possible, though uncertain, antiquity of the allusion to *Myrddin* in the *Gododdin.* The exact nature of the relation between the names and characters of *Myrddin* and Lailoken, Llallogan, remains one of the basic problems of the *Myrddin* cycle. The word *llallawg* and its diminutive *llallogan* are used by Gwenddydd as terms of address to her brother in the *Cyvoesi. Llallawg*, *llallogan*, occur also outside the *Myrddin* cycle in the poem CLlH no. V; and the two have cognates in the other Celtic languages. TYP preserves no trace of *Myrddin*'s connection with the Arfderydd campaign.

Myrddin receives the patronymic *mab Morwrynn* in the poem *Peiryan Vaban* (B XIV, p. 105, l. 28), in the *Gwasgargerd*: *myrdin yv vy env uab moruryn* (RBP col. 584.5–6), and also in the *Cyvoesi*: *myrdin vab moru(r)yn geluyd* (RBP col. 582.37), as well as in a note in a late hand in BBC 46.17: *Merddin mab Morfryn a ganodd yr hyn y sydd scrifenedic yn yr wyth ddolen sy yn canlyn*, etc. (i.e. the *Hoianeu* and the *Bedwenni*). But neither Myrddin's name nor that of his father occurs in any of the northern genealogies, and his origin therefore remains obscure. Like *Llywarch Hen* (see n.), his name has come down as that of a character in a story; but unlike Llywarch, he had also outside this story the reputation of a prophet and a poet. No fragment of his poetry appears to have been preserved, although see n. to *Gwendoleu* for a possible fragment of a *marwnad*. Lloyd-Jones regarded *Myrddin* as the domestic bard of Gwenddoleu ('The Court-Poets of the Welsh Princes', PBA, 1948, p. 4), and references by twelfth- and thirteenth-century poets prove that at that date Myrddin was looked upon as one of the *Cynfeirdd*:

Cynddelw: *uch myrtwyr uch myrtin oet kein* (H 91.25 = CBT IV, no. 4.99n.). This is Cynddelw's only allusion to Myrddin.

Prydydd y Moch: *Darogan myrdin oed dyuot / brenhin o gymry werin o gamwri . . . o hil eryron o eryri* (RBP col. 1423.29–31 = CBT V, no. 25.41–4).

Gwynfardd Brycheiniog: *myrddin darogan* (H 207.25 = CBT II, no. 25.43).

Hywel ab Owain Gwynedd: *kert uolyant ual y cant mertin* (H 317.4 = CBT II, no. 6.46n.).

Iorwerth Fychan: *no fan gant myrddin mawrddysc gwenddyd* (H 327.8).

Elidir Sais: *llathreit vy mardeir wedy myrdin* (RBP col. 1144.12–13 = CBT I, no. 16.7n.; no. 17.21n.).

Sefnyn: *paravt digrifyeith meith . . . myrdin geudavt* (RBP col. 1261.4–5 = GSRh no. 2.3–4n.).

Gwilym Ddu: *da vyrdin ae lin o lwyth meirchyawn* (RBP col. 1229.37–8 = GGDT no. 8.12n.).

Madog Dwygraig (RBP col. 1275.12–13; 1276.17); Rhisierdyn (1281.35 = GSRh no. 6.86n.); Ieuan Llwyd (RBP col. 1415.9).

Dafydd Benfras wishes for divine inspiration to make him *Cyflawn awen awydd Fyrddin* (MA 217a, 28 = Panton 53 = CBT VI, no. 24.4n.).

If the reference to *Myrddin* in *Armes Prydein* is accepted, it proves that already by the tenth or eleventh century he was regarded as a prophet. Since *Ym. M. a Th.* represents both *Myrddin* and Taliesin alike as prophets, it may be that this reputation originates in the fact that both were looked upon as famous *Cynfeirdd* and hence that it is mere chance that the verse of the one and not of the other has survived. In Wales as in Ireland the gift of poetic inspiration implied also the gift of prophecy; and Giraldus Cambrensis clearly regarded Myrddin as one of the *awenyddion* or 'inspired ones' whom he describes as being endowed with the gift of prophecy (*Descriptio Cambriae*, I, ch. xvi).

Geoffrey of Monmouth latinized *Myrddin* as *Merlinus.* (Gaston Paris explained this deliberate change in the form of the name as caused by the undesirable associations of the French word *merde*; see EAR I, 129.) Geoffrey adapts to *Merlin* the HB story of the infant prodigy Ambrosius (= *Emrys Wledig,* see n.), who revealed to Vortigern the reason for the collapse of his tower (HRB VI, chs. 17–18). Geoffrey represents his prophet as coming from Carmarthen, which shows that he was aware of the spurious etymology which connected *Myrddin* with that city—it is unlikely that Geoffrey himself could have been the first to associate *Myrddin* with Carmarthen, in view of the reference to Myrddin in AP (l. 17). Following Geoffrey's account, Giraldus Cambrensis is the first writer to attempt to make a distinction between two Merlins: i.e. *Merlinus Ambrosius* (*Myrddin Emrys*), who represents the Merlin of the HRB, and *Merlinus Celidonius* or *Merlinus Sylvester,* who is the *Myrddin Wyllt* of Welsh tradition (*Itin. Cam.* II, ch. viii). Hence the distinction made in triad 87 between *Myrddin Embrys* and the native *Myrddin fab Morvryn.* But it is the *Myrddin* of HRB and of the *Bruts* who is alluded to in one of the *Beddau* stanzas, preserved in a corrupt text in Pen. 98 B: *Bedd Ann ap lleian ymnewais fynydd / lluagor llew ymrais / prif ddewin Merddin Embrais* (T. Jones, PBA LIII, p. 136 (17); for *anap y lleian* 'nun's misfortune', see GPC 108). The poets frequently distinguish between the two Myrddins; e.g. Rhys Goch Eryri distinguishes between *Merddin fab Morfryn Frych* [*sic*] and *Merddin arall* (IGE^2 no. LXI.13–26).

The *cywyddwyr* refer to *Myrddin* as a poet, and frequently couple his name with Taliesin, both in the *cywyddau brud* (= 'prophetic poems', see B VII, p. 236) and in *marwnadau* for other poets. Thus Dafydd ap Gwilym describes Madog Benfras as *Cwplws caniatgerdd Ferddin* (GDG no. 19.27), and refers to the Echo: *Mwy y dywaid heb beidiaw / No Myrddin sonfawr mawrddig* (GDG no. 130.5–7n.). Gruffudd Gryg describes Dafydd ap Gwilym as *enw Taliesin . . . cyw Myrddin* (GDG 428.1–3); Rhys Goch compares Gruffudd Llwyd to Taliesin and *Myrddin* by turn (IGE^2 159.9, 16). Similar comparisons are made in two *marwnadau* on Tudur Penllyn (GTP, Atod. IV, 9; V, 15). For further references see n. to *Taliesin.* Dafydd ap Gwilym knew also of Myrddin as a lover: *erioed ni charawdd / Na Myrddin wenieithfin iach / Na Thaliesin ei thlysach* (GDG 118.22–4); and Guto'r Glyn plainly refers to the story behind the *Myrddin* poems in the following passage: *Merddin wyllt am ei urddas / Amhorfryn, aeth i'r glyn glas / Af yn wyllt o fewn elltydd / I eiste rhwng clustiau'r hydd* (GGl no. LIII.63–6).

Similarly Ieuan Dyfi: *Merddin Wyllt am ryw ddyn wyf . . . Awr ymhell yr amhwyllai / Awr o'i gof gan Dduw ry gai* (HCLl no. LVIII.I ff.); and he refers to the poet's madness for love: *Un naturiaeth . . . Mawrddawn wr* a *Merddin Wyllt* (HCLl no. LXV.34; cf. no. LXIII.26). Some lines from a *cywydd brud* prefixed to the text of the *Bedwenni* and the *Oianeu* (LlDC no. 17) are introduced as follows: *Merddin mab Morfryn a ganodd yr hyn y sydd scrifenedic yn yr wyth ddolen sy yn canlyn, fel y tystoliaetha llewelin ap Cynfric ddu yn y wedd hon*:

Merddin wyllt hagr orwyllt haint
am Mhorfryn amau hirfraint
Cerdd tra wamal gyfalau
gynt o goed a gant o i gau
Iw borchell ddigysbell gas
a'i fedwen fel ynfyd-was.

'Myrddin the Wild, and ugly, son of Morfryn, with a mad sickness . . . sang from his retreat from the wood a frivolous song . . . to his pigling and his birch-tree, like a fool.'

For a discussion of the significance of the references made to Myrddin by Tudur Aled, Hywel Dafi, and Lewys Môn, see Eurys Rowlands, 'Syr Rhisiart Herbert o Drefaldwyn', LlC IV, pp. 117–19. These poets make several allusions to *Myrddin* as *ar bawl* or *ar bigyn,* etc., which suggest that there may have been a story according to which *Myrddin* was transfixed by a stake, as was his counterpart Lailoken (see above) in a version of the story of the Three-Fold Death. Thomas Jones ('Myrddin ar Bawl', LlC IV, p. 180) quotes an Anglesey popular tradition about 'Merddyn ar Bawl', taken down in the eighteenth century by Lewis Morris. Elis Gruffydd's version of the tale of Myrddin and the Three-Fold Death (B XVI, pp. 184 ff.) is more likely to be based on the written French or English romances, than on Welsh material.

Gruffudd Llwyd alludes to the *Cyvoesi* (IGE[2] 114.13–18), and Gutun Owain compares his carefree existence with Dafydd, abbot of Glynegwestl, to that of *Merddin*: *Ail i Verddin wyf, ar olav vyrddydd / Aeth a'r dewrion i waith Arderydd / Vn â cherdd ynddo iawn â'i chwaer Wenddydd* (GO no. XXVI.55–60). Also, in a *marwnad* to Guto'r Glyn he compares the poet to Myrddin: *Milwr fu, mawl ar ei fin / Mwy ei urddas no Merddin* (GO no. LXIII.21–2), i.e. like Myrddin he combined the activities of warrior and poet. Wm. Llŷn speaks of his patron as asking for a poem: *Galw am gerdd o waith Merddin* (Wm. Ll., no. XXI.87). An allusion by Rhys Goch Eryri is plainly to the Merlin of the Continental romances, imprisoned beneath a rock for love of Vivien: *A'r ail* (i.e. Myrddin, see Ifor Williams's n.) *a gwsg oreulwfr / Dan ffynhonnwys o ddwys ddwfr / Yn y maen, a ni a'i mawl, / Glain o ryw glyn eiriawl. / O serch gwen, myn Dwynwen deg, / Y'i gyrrodd Duw i'r garreg* (IGE[2] no. CXI.15–20). On the Myrddin poems see further LlDC xxxiv–xl.

From the fifteenth century, references to Myrddin as a lover are combined with allusions to his *tŷ gwydr* or 'house of glass' (cf. E. I. Rowlands, LlC V, p. 52): *Gwnaf yno i hudo hen / Glos o fanadl glas feinion / Modd y gwnaeth, saerniaeth serch / Merddin dŷ gwydr am ordderch* (DGG no. XLV.17–20; perhaps by Robin Ddu o Fôn, see GDG no. clxxxix); Huw Cae Llwyd: *Merddin aeth, mawrddawn ei wedd / Mewn gwydr er mwyn ei gydwedd* (HCLl no. LVIII.69–70). A note among the *marginalia* in a sixteenth-century manuscript, Pen. 147, states that Myrddin took the Thirteen Treasures of the Island of Britain with him to his *Tŷ Gwydr*. Lewis Morris localized the *Tŷ Gwydr* on Ynys Enlli (Bardsey); he rationalizes the story with the explanation that the Tŷ Gwydr was a 'museum' and that *Myrddin* was its keeper (*Celtic Remains*, pp. 170, 326). The same tradition is repeated in E. Jones's *Bardic Museum*, and in a note in *Y Greal,* 1805, p. 188: *Merddin Emrys a aeth i'r mor mewn tŷ gwydr, am ei gariad, lle y mae etto. Medd ereill, Merddin Wyllt a aeth a'r* 13 *Thlws i'r tŷ gwydr yn Enlli.* It was known also to Iolo Morganwg; see MA[2], third series of triads, no. 10 (trans.= THSC 1968, pp. 305–6 and n.). For Myrddin's *tŷ gwydr*, see also the marginal note appended to Gwyneddon MS. III, 355 'Merddin Embrys a aeth i'r mor mewn ty gwydr am ei gariad, lle y mae eto' (LlC V, p. 52). Higden's *Polychronicon* I, ch. 38 states that 'Merlinus Silvestris' is buried on Bardsey. Eurys Rowlands quotes an earlier reference to the *Tŷ Gwydr* by Hywel Rheinallt from Ll. 125, 277 where the island is described as *Ynys lle nid erys dig / sy gaer wydr gysegredig* (LlC VI, p. 246).

Naf (WR: *Nav*; 51: *Naw*) 14: *G6enwynwyn m. Naf.* See n. to *G6enwynwyn*[2] *Naf* = 'lord, chieftain, master'. Cf. CO l. 296n., *Atleudor mab Naf.*

Nasiens m. brenhin Denmarck, App. IV, no. 5. The name *Nasiens* represents that of *Nascien li Hermites* in the *Merlin* and *Queste del Saint Graal* of the French *Vulgate Cycle* of Arthurian Romances (ed. H. O. Sommer, vols. II, VI). This figure appears as *Nasiens ueudwy* in *Y Seint Greal* (T. Jones (ed.), *Ystoryeau Seint Greal I*, l. 671). According to the French sources, *Nascien* was a descendant of the sister of Joseph of Arimathea, through his mother the 'Dame de la Blanche Nue'. But a second *Nascien* appears both in the *Estoire del Saint Graal* and in the *Queste* (Sommer, vols. I, VI). In these romances one of the ancestors of Galahad, named Seraphe, receives the baptismal name *Nascien* (= *Naciens, Y Seint Greal*, p. 21, l. 7). Thus both characters of this name were known in Welsh sources, and it is not entirely clear which is intended in the triad, nor does the patronymic *mab brenhin Denmarck* (which is not found elsewhere) throw any light on the character's identity. It is possible that this patronymic became attracted to the second *Nascien* because he was originally a pagan, since in the early poetic tradition the Danes, like all Scandinavians, would have been regarded essentially as pagans. Or there may be confusion with a certain *Melyant . . . filz au roi de Danemarche*, who is alluded to elsewhere in the *Queste* (VI, 22–37). Cf. however the variant in Pen. 216: *Nasawn a elwir yn yr estron iaith Achel brenin Denmark.* The English form *Denmar(c)k* is to be noted, since it suggests the likelihood of an English intermediary for the name.

Neuyn verch Brychan Brecheinyauc 70. See n. to the triad and nn. to *Kynvarch, Vryen* (*Reget*). This name is *Nyuein* in *De Situ Brecheniauc,* but *Nyven* in *Cognacio Brycheiniog* (a sixteenth-century adaptation of the earlier text, see VSB 317). *Jes.* III gives this name as *Drynwin ferch Brychan*, mother of *Urien Rheged* (EWGT 43 (5)). For another possible reference to Urien's mother see CLlH no. III.47c, and n.

Niwl Iarll 'Earl Niwl' 88: *Enid verch i Niwl Iarll.* This name is unknown in Welsh sources except as given to the father of *Enid* in the romance of *Gereint* (= *Liconaus* in *Erec*, l. 6896). The forms which occur are as follows: *nyvl iarll* (WM 400.9 = RM 256.15), *ynvl iarll* (WM 400.25 = RM 256.24), *ynyvl iarll* (WM 400.42; 401.13 = RM 257.4; 17, etc.).

> Rhisierdyn: ?*ynywl barabyl* (RBP col. 1290.40; cf. GSRh no. 4.96n.)
> Gr. ap Maredudd: *ynywl wryt* (RBP col. 1322.13 = GGM no. 7.20).
> Tudur Aled: *Plas Y niwl iarll* (GTA I, no. XLIV.2); *Yniwl* (no. LV.29).

It is apparent that *Nywl, Niwl* is as likely to be the basic form of this name as *Yniwl*, and in copying the triad this is what Robert Vaughan understood it to be. The prosthetic *y* which frequently developed in Ml. W. before words beginning with *n*- or *s*- (see PKM xv, 104–5; cf. *yneuad,* PKM 25.21; *yniuer*

30.26–7) could have given rise to the variant *Y niwl,* which became the more frequently used of the two, and is the form commonly employed by the poets. A similar suggestion as to the origin of the name *(Y)niwl* was made by R. S. Loomis, see also R. M. Jones (LlC IV, pp. 216–19). Jones points out that the development of the prosthetic *Y-* before the initial *N* caused the accent to shift back on to the new syllable. To the examples of *Y niwl* from GTA quoted above, he adds GID no. XIII.28. See also GLGC nos. 82.43, 91.28 and 208.20 *Enid ferch Yniwl.* The only meaning which it seems possible to attach to this name is that of the common noun *niwl* 'mist'. Can it be that in an earlier form of the story the heroine's father was identical with the *Owein iarll* (= Chrétien's *Eurain)* who presides over the adventure of the *cae nywl* ('hedge of mist', RM 292.1, *Eyvein* WM 446.42)? The importance of this episode in the structure of the story as a whole stands out more clearly in the Welsh than in the French version. *Iarll y Niwl* as a pseudonym for this character could easily have become transformed into *(Y)niwl Iarll* when the original association of Enid's father with the adventure of the *cae niwl* had become obliterated and forgotten.

In the story the home of *(Y)niwl Iarll* is located at *Kaerdyff* (Cardiff), RM 292.11.

Nud Hael m. Senyllt 2, 71 (Pen. 267). See nn. to *Senyllt*, *Run m. Maelgwn*, *Tegeu Eururon.* The *Dryon m. Nud* (W: *Dreon Lev*) who, according to the WR version of triad 31 was present at Arfderydd (in 577), could have been a son of *Nud(d) Hael.* For the name *Nudd* see n. to *Llyr*[1] *Lledyeith*.

The name *Nud(d) Hael m. Senyllt* does not appear in the Harl. Gens. or in *Bonedd Gwŷr y Gogledd* (App. II). (The *Nud Hael* of the Morgannwg line who appears in *Jes. Gen.* IX should be emended to *Iudhael*; since *Iudbail* is found in the corresponding pedigree, Harl. Gen. XXVIII. The mistake is due to the fact that the redactor of the *Jes. Gens.* was familiar with the names of the *Tri Hael*, see n. to triad 2.) The following pedigree is given in *Bonedd y Saint*: *Dingat m. Nud Hael m. Senyllt m. Kedic m. Dyuyniwal Hen m. Edneuet m. Maxen Wledic* (VSB 321 (18)). If this genealogy is to be depended on, *Nudd* was a contemporary and cousin of Rhydderch and Mordaf Hael, with whom he is grouped in triad 2 (cf. App. II, nos. 8, 9). But it is to be noted that Harl. Gen. IV and *Jes.* XIX agree in giving *Nudd*'s father *Senyllt* (*Senill, Senilth hael*) a slightly different descent, and it is likely that the name *Neidaon*, *Neithon*, which occurs in these for the son of *Senyllt*, designates the same person as *Nud Hael* in the triad and in *Bonedd y Saint* (see n. to *Senyllt*). Allowing for the uncertainty as to his pedigree, however, it is clear that *Nudd Hael* was looked upon as an historical figure who lived among the northern Britons during the latter half of the sixth century. This belief is substantiated by an allusion to him in an early bardic eulogy which purports to be addressed to Urien Rheged: *A cheneu a nud hael a hirwlat y danav* (BT 63.20–1 = CT VIII.45). There is another possible reference in the poem to Gwallawg, PT no. XII.4.

It was for long supposed that an early Christian inscribed stone at Yarrowkirk, Selkirkshire, represented a memorial to two sons of *Nudd Hael* (Macalister, *Corpus Inscriptionum Insularum Celticarum* I, no. 515). The reading of the inscription was disputed, but the following translation has been agreed upon by K. Jackson and Ralegh Radford: 'This is the everlasting memorial: in this place lie the most famous princes, Nudus and Dumnogenus; in this tomb lie the two sons of Liberalis' (*Antiquity* XXIX, p. 81; see *Inventory of the Ancient Monuments of Selkirkshire*, Royal Commission on Ancient Monuments (Scotland) (Edinburgh, 1957), pp. 110–13). Since the same authorities agree that the stone is to be dated to the early sixth century, it is clearly impossible on chronological grounds that it could commemorate two sons of *Nudd Hael*, as was supposed by Sir John Rhŷs (see *The Academy*, 29 August 1891, pp. 180–1), followed by Chadwick (*Growth of Literature* I, p. 143); or *Nudd Hael* himself, as suggested by H. Lewis, 'The Sentence in Welsh', PBA 1942, p. 9. On the other hand, the appearance of the two names (or name + epithet) *Nudus* and *Liberalis* (the Latin equivalent of *Hael)* on an inscription which can be dated to within a hundred years of the period in which the early records represent *Nudd* as having lived, and which was found within the territory of *Gwŷr y Gogledd,* is too striking to be easily accepted as a coincidence. Since the epithet *Hael* was not restricted to *Nudd* himself, but appears to have been associated with the clan to which he belonged (the genealogies show that the *Tri Hael* were all cousins) it is probable that the tombstone commemorates two relatives of Nudd who belonged to an earlier generation. See further n. to triad 2 above.

The following allusions to Nudd Hael are made by the *Gogynfeirdd* (in addition to those which commemorate the *Tri Hael* together, cited in n. to triad 2):

Cynddelw: *haelach no nut* (H 147.27 = CBT III, no. 26.57n.).

Bleddyn Fardd: *ruyt val nut* (H 76.13 = CBT VII, no. 47.8), *haelder nud* (H 79.24, 25 = CBT VII, no. 49.8–9).

Llygad Gŵr: *un eurglod wyd a nut* (H 221.6 = CBT VII, no. 25.40n.).

Hillyn: *gynedyf nud or mebyt* (H 195.20).

Gr. ap Maredudd (RBP col. 1195.8; 1203.23 = GGM no. 2.22; RBP col. 1206.16 = GGM no. 3.13); Trahaearn Brydydd Mawr (RBP col. 1225.10 = GGDT no. 11.31); Gwilym Ddu o Arfon (RBP col. 1225.34; 1227.30 = GGDT no. 6.2n., no. 7.11n.); Casnodyn (RBP col. 1247.5 = GC no. 1.58, no. 2.30 and 126nn.); Rhisierdyn (RBP col. 1290.23 = GSRh no. 4.75n. etc.); Madog Dwygraig (RBP col. 1310.36); Y Prydydd Breuan (RBP col. 1349.28); Y Proll (RBP col. 1311.29 = GDC no. 14.35n.).

References by the *cywyddwyr* to *Nudd*'s proverbial generosity are too numerous to warrant even selective quotation. These make it plain that Dafydd ap Gwilym's reason for bestowing the epithet *Hael* on his patron Ifor ap Llywelyn lay in his familiarity with TYP. Whenever triad 2 is cited, the three names are constant and remain unaltered.

For *Nudd*'s mythological background see J. Carey, 'Nodons in Britain and Ireland', ZCP (1984), pp. 1–22.

Ocuran Gawr. See **(G)ocuran Gawr.**

Owein[1] (= Ewein) m. Maxen Wledic 13. See n. to *Maxen Wledic*. On this triad see J. K. Bollard, CMCS 6, p. 81, and P. C. Bartrum, EC XII, p. 192. L. *Eugenius* > O.W. *Oug(u)ein, Eug(u)ein* (see Thurneysen, *Zeitschrift für deutsche Philologie* XXVIII, p. 91, n. 1; LHEB 324, 370, n.). This name is written variously in Ml.W. as *Ewein* (CA ll. 17, 347, 892), *Owein, Ywein*. LL gives the forms *Euguen, Iguein, Yuein, Ouein.* The corresponding form in Irish is *Eógan.*

An alternative explanation which has been advocated for the Irish and Welsh forms of this name is that both derive from Celt. *Esugenos* 'engendered of Esos', i.e. the god *Esos*, for whose cult in Gaul some evidence has survived (ACS I 1479; see for this view Vendryes, 'La Religion des Celtes', p. 263 in vol. III of A. Grenier's *Les Religions de l'Europe Ancienne,* Paris, 1948; L. and P. 24 (3); and J. Lloyd-Jones, B IV, p. 48). But it is to be noted that W. *Owein*, etc., is normally latinized as *Eugenius* (see CLIH xxvi; Chadwick, *The Growth of Literature* I, p. 145, n. 2) and it seems most natural to regard both the Welsh and Irish forms as derivatives of the Latin (see GPN 200, n. 9).

Owein appears as the name of a son of Maxen Wledic in the genealogy of St Cadog appended to the saint's Life; *Maximianus genuit Ouguein. Ouguein genuit Nor. Nor genuit Solor*, etc. (EWGT 24 (45)). This pedigree is given again, in a rather confused form, in *Jes. Gen.* IV, with the addition which purports to give Owein's maternal descent from *Caswallawn mab Beli* (see EWGT 44 (8)).

Although the Welsh pedigrees credit Maxen with various sons (*Custennin, Jes. Gen.* IV; *Ednyfed* (*Idnouet*), App. II, no. 2; and *Bonedd y Saint*: *Peblic Sant* (EWGT); *Dimet and Anthun* Harl. Gens. II, IV), historical sources mention only one son of the emperor Maximus, named Victor. According to Orosius (VII, 35), Maximus left his son Victor with the Gauls as their emperor, and Victor was slain shortly afterwards by a Gaul called Arbogastes (Prosper of Aquitaine, *Chronica Minora* III, ed. T. Mommsen, p. 169n. followed by HB, ch. 29).

A later popular tradition recorded by Edward Lhuyd associated *Owen y Mhaxen* (= ap Maxen) with Dinas Emrys in Nant Gwynant in Gwynedd. Here he is reputed to have had a battle with a giant, in which both combatants hurled steel balls at each other, and in the end Owein was slain:

> A rhwng y Dinas a'r llyn (i.e. Llyn Dinas) y mae Bedd Sr. Owen y Mhaxen, yr hwn a fy yn ymladd a'r cawr a phellenau dur. Mae pannylau yn y ddaear lle 'roedd pob un yn sefyll i'w gweled etto. Mae rhai eraill yn dywedyd mae ymladd a saethau yr oeddynt a'r pannylau a welir heddiw yno oedd lle darfu uddynt gloddio i amddiffin i hunain, ond ni escorodd yr un mo'r tro. Pan welwyd y marchog (i.e. Owein) nad oedd dim gobaith iddo fyw fawr

> hwy, fe ofynnwyd iddo ple y mynnei gael i gladdu, fy archodd saethu saeth i'r awyr, a lle y descynnai hi y gwnaent ei fedd yno. (*Cambrian Journal* III, 1859, pp. 209–10; transcription by Robert Williams of a manuscript by Edward Lhuyd dated 1693.)
>
> 'And between the Dinas (i.e. *Dinas Emrys*) and the lake, there is the grave of Sir Owen son of Maxen, who had been fighting with the giant with steel balls. There are depressions in the ground still to be seen, where each one stood. Others say that they fought with arrows, and that the depressions which are seen there today were the places where they dug to defend themselves, and neither of them survived the occasion.When the knight saw that he had no hope of living much longer, he was asked where he wished to be buried, and he asked that an arrow be shot into the air, and where it should descend, that they should make his grave there.'

For a variant version of Lhuyd's tale, see also Owen Jones's *Cymru* (London, 1875) I 133. This story should be compared with the folklore of the giants preserved in Pen. 118 (*circa* 1600), ed. *Cy.* XXVII, with which body of tradition it evidently belongs. (See also Chris Grooms's, *The Giants of Wales* and WCD 521.) A version of the story is given by Iolo Morganwg (*Iolo MSS.*, pp. 81–2), in which Owein is named *Owein Vinddu,* and the giant is named Urnach.

Rhys Goch Eryri describes Gwynedd as *tir mab Macsen* (IGE^2 172.7); the above story shows that the reference is to Owain son of Maxen, and indicates the antiquity of the tradition.

Owein[2] (= Ewein) m. Vryen (Reget) 3, 11, 40, 70; App. III, no. 15; App. IV, no. 3. See nn. to *Vryen (Reget) m. Kynuarch*, *Cyndeyrn Garthwys*, *Modron verch Auallach*, *Taliessin.* On the name see n. to *Owein*[1] above.

Owein fab Urien is prominent both in early Welsh poetry and in medieval romance. He provides one of the rare examples of the transference of a name complete with patronymic from insular Celtic sources into French Arthurian romance, virtually without change. (See Thomson (ed.), *Owein*; AW ch. V; and EWSP ch. 2.) Evidence for *Owein*'s historical existence has survived in a wide variety of early records (see SEBC VI 283–4; III 5, 67; VII 52, 32n; P. Sims-Williams, *Romania* 116, p. 94). The earliest sources in which *Owein* is named are the group of early bardic poems preserved in BT, which allude to the battles fought by Urien and *Owein* at various places in north Britain (see also the later references to the battle of Argoed Llwyfein in LlDC no. 17.148–9; CBT IV no. 4.111 and n.), and which have been regarded as representing the authentic work of the sixth-century bard Taliesin (see PT and Morris-Jones, 'Taliesin', *Cy.* 28). These poems include an elegy on the death of *Owein ab Urien*. The early bardic references to Urien and *Owein* as leading warriors among the northern Britons in the latter part of the sixth century are consistent with the statement in the *Saxon Genealogies* in HB ch. 63, which states that Urien and his sons fought bravely against the English in the time of the successors of Ida of Bernicia (547–59) during this period. It may be concluded that *Owein* was one of the sons of Urien intended by the writer. Other sources name also *Riwallawn* (see n.), *Run* (see n. to *Run*[4] *Ryueduawr*) and *Pasken* (see n.), as sons of Urien. Ifor Williams pointed out (CA xxxi–xxxii) that there is no mention of either Urien or *Owein* in the *Gododdin*: since the early sources suggest that these were leading warriors in north Britain during their lifetime, it is probable that both were dead at the time when the expedition to Catraeth took place.

Neither the Harl. Gens. nor *Bonedd Gwŷr y Gogledd* (App. II) carry the pedigree of the family of Cynfarch any further back than the name of Urien himself. Thus the only early genealogical lists to include *Owein* are those which give the descent of his alleged son Cyndeyrn (St Kentigern), which are found in all versions of *Bonedd y Saint* (for the ecclesiastical tradition to the effect that *Owein* was the father of (St.) Kentigern, see n. to *Cyndeyrn Garthwys*). To these may be added the following list of the sons of Urien which appears in a slightly variant form in a number of sixteenth-century manuscripts: *Plant Urien ap Kenvarch. Ywain ap Vrien. Rvn ap Vrien. Riwallon ap Vrien. Elffin ap Vrien. Pasgen ap Vrien. Catvael ap Vrien ap kenvarch ap meirchawn ap Gorwst ap Keneu ap Coel* (Pen. 127, p. 94; cf. the similar lists in Pen. 129 and 131 = EWGT 87 (6–7); cf. B XVIII, p. 235 (7); CLlH 137). The names of Elphin, Pasgen and Run, along with that of *Owein* himself, recur in the *englynion* concerned with the wars of Urien's family and the death of Urien, which Ifor Williams has shown to have originated in ninth-century Powys. (For references to *Owein* see CLlH no. III.37, 51, 54; no. VII.16, 18.) Belonging also to this Powys tradition of Urien and his family is the attribution to *Owein* of his personal *branhes* or 'flight of ravens' (i.e. his *gosgordd*) which figures in *Breudwyt Ronabwy* and elsewhere.

Owein appears already in *Erec et Enide,* the earliest romance of Chrétien de Troyes, as *Yvains li fiz Uriien* (1.1706). The form *Ivain(s), Yvain(s)*, in which the hero's name appears in French sources points to a *written* Welsh form *Yvein, Yuein* as its original, since the initial of this name in Ml.W. is an obscure vowel which is found written variously as *E-*, *O-*, or *Y-* (Loth, RC XIII, pp. 493–4). The name must therefore have been borrowed from a written source which can hardly have been earlier than *circa* 1100 (see n. to *Owein*[1]). The corresponding Ml. Br. form is *Ivan,* O.Br. *Ewen, Euuen* (*Chr. Br.* 129).

The Welsh tale *Owein* or *Iarlles y Ffynnawn* and the corresponding French poem *Yvain* by Chrétien de Troyes (composed *circa* 1170–5) depict *Owein ab Urien* (*Yvains . . . fiz au roi Urien*) as the hero of a series of supernatural adventures which culminate in the overthrow by *Owein* of a knight who guards a magic fountain (see App. III, no. 15, and n.). These adventures are followed by *Owein*'s marriage to the wife of the knight, whom he later deserts. It is difficult to avoid the conclusion that there is some connection between this story and the story of the events which accompanied the birth of St

Kentigern, which is given in the early twelfth-century fragmentary *Life* of the saint: both appear to draw ultimately upon some common source-material (see n. to *Cyndeyrn Garthwys*, and Chadwick, *The Growth of Literature* I, pp. 237–8, followed by John MacQueen, *Trans. of the Dumfriesshire and Galloway Natural Hist. and Antiq. Soc.*, XXXIII, pp. 107–31; and cf. Basil Clarke, *Life of Merlin*, Appendix I and nn.). On other early channels of transmission between Scotland and France see R. L. Ritchie, 'Chrétien de Troyes and Scotland', the Zaharoff Lecture (Oxford, 1952).

Geoffrey of Monmouth clearly had some knowledge, direct or indirect, of the Taliesin poetry relating to Urien and *Owein*, and he seems to have based his references to father and son upon this. He presents Urien as Arthur's contemporary, but makes it clear that '*Ywain*' belonged to a subsequent generation in the single allusion which he makes to him. This follows the reference to the death of Urien's alleged brother *Anguselus (Arawn)*, king of Scotland: *Successit autem . . . in regnum Huiuenus (Hiwenus, Iwenus) filius Uriani fratris sui. qui postea in decertacionibus istis multis probitatibus preclaruit* (HRB XI, 1). Whether Geoffrey's single allusion to Urien's son can have been solely responsible for launching *Owein* upon his career as an Arthurian hero is questionable: it may well be that he had already been drawn into Arthur's orbit in Welsh sources, like a number of other traditional Welsh heroes who originally had no connection with Arthur. Such a prior connection in a Welsh *milieu* may account for the Arthurian framework in which *Yvain* appears in Chrétien's *Erec* and in *Iarlles y Ffynnawn,* as well as in *Breudwyt Ronabwy.* But it is perhaps significant that neither *Owein* nor Urien is included in the list of heroes at Arthur's court in CO, although *Owein*'s sister *Morvudd* (see n.) is included there among Arthur's ladies (CO l. 366n.). *Breudwyt Ronabwy* gives prominence to the account of *Owein*'s *branhes,* or flight of ravens, who are depicted as being responsible for slaying Arthur's war-band. Perhaps these mysterious ravens originally denoted *Owein*'s own band of fighting men, since *brân* is used figuratively in poetry for a warrior (GPC 308). This conclusion is supported by the concluding words of *Iarlles y Ffynnawn* which state that *Owein* became Arthur's *pennteulu,* and then apparently equate the *teulu* with *Owein*'s ravens: *Sef oed hynny trychant cledyf kenuerchyn ar vranhes. Ac yr lle yd elei owein a hynny gantav. goruot a vnaei* (WM 261.30–4) 'Those were the Three Hundred Swords of the tribe of Kynfarch [cf. App. II, no. 7], and the Flight of the Ravens. And wherever *Owein* went, and they with him, he would be victorious'. Cf. *Owein* 30, but contrast the translation given by Eurys Rowlands in LlC VI, p. 246—'the 300 swords of the tribe of Cynfarch as a flight of ravens', and also *Owein*, p. 62. Three hundred was the regular number for a teulu, see n. to triad 29d and also A. J. Carr, 'Teulu a Phenteulu' in WKC 63–81. A memory of *Owein*'s ravens survived in the standard bearing three ravens which was borne by the family of Syr Rhys ap Thomas of Abermarlais, which claimed descent from *Urien*

Rheged (see n.). The *brain Urien* borne on their coat of arms, and the descent of the family from Urien, are frequently referred to by the *cywyddwyr.* On *branhes Owein* see further my chapter in Owen and Roberts (eds), *Beirdd a Thywysogion*, and references cited; also Edgar M. Stotkin, 'The Fabula, Story and Text of "Breuddwyd Rhonabwy"', CMCS 18 (1989), pp. 113–16. For further instances in the poetry of the *Gogynfeirdd* of phrases which juxtapose *brain, branhes* with *Brynaich*, see T. J. Morgan, B XIV, pp. 7–8. Bleddyn Fardd refers to *branhes Bryneich* and *kigvrein ywein* 'Owain's predatory ravens', H 71.4 = CBT VII, no. 48.16n.; no. 52.32n.

Cynddelw knew of *Owein*'s flight of ravens, and refers to them as 'riding' upon the dead warriors of Bernicia: *marchogynt ar ueirw ar uil urein / marchogyon bryneich branhes ywein* (H 83.27–8 = CBT IV, no. 1.27–8). Cynddelw was evidently in touch with the traditions about *Owein* and Urien which were transmitted in Powys, and of which fragments have survived in the Powys *englyn* cycle and in *Breudwyt Ronabwy.* His allusion to *Owein* in his *Rhieingerdd* to Eva verch Madawg is clearly an echo of the verses in the *Diffaith aelwyd Rheged* (CLlH no. III.47–59).

> Pergig kynuerchin kynn no (R: noe) vyned
> Gvedy hael ywein havl ordiued
> hwyl dihwyl diofyn am y drefret
> neud wy ae gofwy nyd gouyged
> goualon eilon aelwyd reged
> (H 123.14–18 = RBP col. 1426.27–31)

'Lord of the tribe of Cynfarch before his departure (= death?), after generous Owain—fervent his claim—there was harsh and ruthless attack (on) his dwellings; cares afflict him—it is no matter of dishonour—for the stags (= warriors?) of the hearth (= hall) of Rheged.' (Revised paraphrases (1995) following the edition CBT III, no. 5.66–70. If not fig. for 'warriors', *eilon* 'stags' may recall the abandoned *aelwyd Rheged.*)

Owein's grave is alluded to in an obscure passage in the *Beddau* stanzas: *Bet owein ab urien im pedryal bit / dan gverid llan Morvael . . . in llan helet bet Owein* (LlDC no. 18.39–44) 'The grave of *Owein* ab Urien in a four-square tomb, under the sod of Llanforfael . . . in Llan Heledd (is) the grave of Owein.' These confused lines make it difficult to tell which place is intended as the site of *Owein*'s grave; but since places in Wales and not in north Britain are evidently intended, the allusion may be taken as further evidence that traditions about *Owein*, like those about his father, became freshly localized in Wales in the medieval period. (On the places named see LBS III, pp. 254, 504. There is a Llanhiledd in Monmouthshire.)

There are a number of allusions to *Owein* by the *cywyddwyr.* Guto'r Glyn wishes for a coat of mail that shall have *Teils dur Owain ab Urien / Tebig i do cerrig hen* 'the steel plates (?) of Owain ab Urien, like to an old roof of stone'

(GGl no. LXXII.57–8). Huw Cae Llwyd compares a patron in turn to *Cai* and *Caradawg,* and says he has *bwriad Owain ab Urien* 'the purpose of O. ab U.' (HCLl no. XXIII.22). But the greater number of allusions to *Owein* by the *cywyddwyr* are to episodes in the romance of *Iarlles y Ffynnawn.* R. M. Jones has pointed out (LlC IV, pp. 214–15) that *Owein* is referred to several times by Tudur Aled as *Iarll y Cawg* 'the Earl of the Basin', and he cites the following lines from a poem addressed to Urien's alleged descendant, Sir Rhys ap Thomas:

Owain oedd, ni a wyddym,
Â chawg a llêch a gwayw llym;
Ych henw, modd yr ŷch hynaf,
Iarll y Cawg arall y caf;
Iarll yr Iâ a'r Llew a'r Ôg,
Iarll Rheged, aur llurugog.
(GTA I, no. XIII.67–72; cf. also LXI.63; II, XCVIII.66; *Owain y Cawg* I, no. VII.51.)

'Owain, we knew, had a basin and a stone and a keen spear. I find your name, in the way in which you are an elder, a second Earl of the Basin and the Ice and the Lion and the Portcullis, Earl of Rheged, gold-corsleted.'

R. M. Jones notes also that the epithet *Iarll y Cawg* occurs in the title given to the romance in Ll.58, p. 37. In LlC V, p. 69, Rowlands quotes another allusion to this incident in a poem by Bedo Aeddren; Pen. 76, p. 126, ll. 21–8. Gutun Owain compares his love to that of *Owein* for the countess of the Fountain: *Mal gvr Ywain ap Vrienn / Reged, am dy weled, Wenn* (GO no. III.3–4). Gruffudd Llwyd compares Owain Glyndŵr's prowess in the Scottish wars with the contest of Owain ab Urien with the Knight of the Fountain (IGE[2] 123.10–22). The episode in the romance in which *Owein* was caught between the outer gate and the portcullis of the countess's castle (WM 236–7) was particularly popular—cf. Gutun Owain:

Yr wyf rrwng y porth a'r ôc,
Wen verch, val Owain varchoc;
Nad ym drymder yr kerydd
Luned wen, oleuni dydd!
(GO no. VII.27–30.)

'I am between the gate and the portcullis, fair girl, like Owain the knight; do not give me sorrow by your censure, fair Luned, light of day.'

The first two lines occur in identical form in Tudur Aled's allusion to the same incident (GTA II, no. CXXIV.23–8; cf. also I, XIII.2–3), and Chotzen (*Recherches sur la Poésie de D. ap Gwilym*, p. 94) pointed out another allusion to the same incident in the lines *Caru merch nis cae'r marchog / A fu rhwng y porth a'r ôg* (*Bardd. D. ap Gwilym,* 1789, no. CLII 5–6). There is clearly a connection between all these passages. In the original incident as narrated in both the W and R texts of the romance the word for 'portcullis' is *dor dyrchauat:* the normal meaning of *ôg* is 'harrow'. (On the use of *ôg*, *og cwlis, porth ôg*, for 'portcullis', see GPC 2853.) The popularity of this incident among the bards accounts for its inclusion as an 'extra item' in App III, no. 15 (see n.)

Pabo Post Prydein 5: *Duna6t mab P.*; App. II, no. 4. 'P. Pillar of Britain.' See nn. to *Duna6t m. Pabo, Sawyl Ben Uchel.* On the epithet 'Post Prydein' see K. H. Jackson, 'Two Early Scottish Names', *Scottish Historical Review* XXXIII (1954), p. 17.

Pab(o) < L. *papa.* The epithet *Post Prydein* is applied to Urien, CLlH no. III.16c: *Penn post Prydein ryallat* 'the head of the Pillar of Britain has been carried away'. *Prydein* occurs very frequently for *Prydyn* 'Pictland, Scotland'; see n. to *Caw o Brydein* and AP 14. But in the case of both Urien and Pabo, who were rulers among the northern Britons, it is not likely that *Prydein* can have any meaning other than 'Britain'. Harl. Gens. XI, XIX (= *Jes. Gen.* XXXVIII) name *Pappo Post Priten* as a son of *Ceneu mab Coel Hen,* but it will be seen that App. II, no. 4, inserts two extra generations between *Pabo* and Ceneu, thus making *Pabo* a contemporary and first cousin of Ceidiaw and Eliffer Gosgordvawr in the mid-sixth century.

In addition to his sons Dunawt and Sawyl Benuchel, *Bonedd y Saint* credits *Pabo Post Prideyn* [*sic*] with a daughter Ardun Benn Ascell (see n. to *Ardun*[1]), mother of *St Tyssilyaw* (VSB 322 (33) = EWGT 59 (33)).

Pabo Post Prydein is reputed to have been buried at *Llanbabo* in Anglesey. Lewis Morris claimed to have seen the inscription found on his grave, and to have deciphered it as reading: *Hic iacet Pabo Post PriiD* (H. Owen, *The Life and Works of Lewis Morris,* p. 14; CR 339). Apart from the incongruity of the appearance of Pabo's epithet on his gravestone, we have no supporting evidence that the northern Pabo became an ecclesiastic, or that he died in Anglesey. Probably it is some other *Pabo* who is commemorated in the name of the church.

The following references by the *Gogynfeirdd* are possibly, though in the first two instances not certainly, to *Pabo Post Prydein*:

Prydydd y Moch: *mvyn pabo* (H 274.31 = CBT V, no. 23.107n.).

Justus Llwyd: *hi a vu yn bebyll y hen babo* (RBP col. 1365.28 = YB XVII, 71.52).

Llygad Gŵr: *gretuavl hawl hwyl gynnyt pabo* (H 221.24) and in the same poem: *Post prydein urtein wrt gyhussed* (H 220.3 = CBT VII, no. 25.5n. and 58).

Padarn[1] **Beisrudd** 97; App. III, no. 9. *Padarn* < L. *Paternus. Peisrudd* 'Red Coat' or 'Red Tunic'. Harl. Gen. I (= *Jes. Gen.* VI) names *Patern Pesrud* as the grandfather of *Cunedda* (see n.); he may therefore have lived in the mid-fourth century, and may have ruled in *Manaw Gododdin.* Rhŷs was the first to suggest that the epithet *peisrudd* may have referred to the purple worn by high-ranking Roman officials, with which *Padar*n might have been invested as part of the Roman policy of enlisting *foederati* in the government of the country (*Celtic Britain*, p. 118). The suggestion remains an attractive possibility in view of the Latin names given in Harl. Gen. I (EWGT 9) to both the father (*Tacit*) and the son (*Aetern*) of Padarn. But there may be a simpler explanation for the epithet *peisrudd* than that which connects it with Roman *insignia* of office. Nor can there be any certainty that the genealogy preserves correctly the names of fourth-century figures, or an epithet which originated at that date, and has been preserved in spite of linguistic change. See the references to *Padarn Beisrudd* cited in EWGT 208 index.

Justus Llwyd: *Hi a vu yn llymu rac llymet y charn / ar ol peis badarn rac pas bydavl* (RBP col. 1365.11–13 = YB XVII, 71.31–2). See WCD 524–5.

Padarn[2] 82. *St Padarn,* founder of *Llanbadarn Fawr,* and one of the sixth-century pioneers of the Church in Wales. For his Life, written *circa* 1120, see VSB 252 ff. See also E. G. Bowen, *The Settlements of the Celtic Saints in Wales*, pp. 50–5, and TWS 121–7. For the early *englyn* on Padarn's staff see BWP ch. X.

Paluc 26: **Cath Baluc** (WR: *meibion Paluc, cath B*) 'Palug's cat'. On *Paluc* see Lloyd-Jones, *Ériu* XVI (1952), pp. 123–31, and AW 45–6. The root of this word is 'to dig, pierce, wound, hit, scratch, claw', etc., and it appears in *palu* 'to dig', as well as *paladr* '(spear) shaft', *paladur* 'scythe', *pen palach* 'cudgel (?) head', LlDC no. 31.84 and 86. Lloyd-Jones regards *paluc* as an adjectival derivative from the root: with the termination *-uc* (*-ug*) he compares *sarruc* 'surly', *seithuc* 'futile, vain'. This meaning, 'scratching cat', would give an aptly descriptive epithet for the cat-monster of the triad, and it seems possible that in the version of the triad in Pen. 16 *paluc* may still retain its adjectival force, as in the poem quoted below, since it is only in the WR version of the triad that we have the phrase concerning *meibion Paluc.* (Lloyd-Jones pointed out (loc.cit., p. 130) that the name has survived in the herb-name *Palf y Gath Palug*, i.e. 'Palug's Paw'—in English 'Silverweed'. Cf. CR 342.) The poem *Pa gur,* etc. (LlDC no. 31), which may date from the tenth or eleventh century, contains the only other allusion in early sources to *cath paluc.*

Kei win a aeth von
y dilein lleuon
y iscuid oed mynud
erbin cath paluc.
Pan gogiueirch tud
Puy guant cath paluc
Nau ugein kinlluc
a cuytei in y buyd
Nau ugain kinran.

> 'Fair Cei went to Môn to destroy monsters (*llewon*, 'lions'?). His shield was a fragment (?) against *cath paluc.* When people ask "Who killed *cath paluc*?" Nine score fierce (men) fell for its food, nine score warriors.'

For a full translation and commentary on the poem, see B. F. Roberts, *Ast. H.* 296–309; P. Sims-Williams, AW 40–5, 214, 280; and CO(2) xxxv–vi. The poem is fragmentary, and breaks off as above. With the account it gives of *cath paluc* may be compared another allusion to a monster cat—perhaps the same one—in Anglesey; BT 73.13–15: *Ys trabludyo y gath vreith ae hagyfieithon | o ryt ar taradyr hyt ym porth Vygyr y mon* 'May the speckled cat and her strangers make an uproar, from the ford of Taradr to Porth Wygyr (= Cemais) in Môn'. See also below for a citation from the twelfth-century French poem which alludes to Arthur's fight with *le Capalu.*

Cath Baluc is probably to be associated with the *murchata* or monstrous sea-cats of Irish tradition. One of these is described in the Life of *St Brendan*:

> 'There is a great sea-cat here like a young ox or a three-year-old horse, overgrown by feeding on the fish of this sea and this island.' The monster swims in pursuit of the saint's boat: 'Bigger than a brazen cauldron was each of his eyes: a boar's tusks had he: furzy hair upon him; and he had the maw of a leopard with the strength of a lion, and the voracity of a hound.' (W. Stokes, *Lives of the Saints from the Book of Lismore,* pp. 113, 258)

It may be noted that *Cath Baluc* was enough of a sea-cat (like some which are cited in Irish traditions) to be able to swim the Menai Straits (cf. triad 26). Much material relating to monster cats has come down in Irish folk-lore: in the later sources they do not always appear to be particularly associated with the sea, though they have sinister characteristics and monstrous size. *Béaloideas: Journal of the Folklore of Ireland Society* IV, pp. 70, 79, 340, 422; VII, p. 45; XIV, pp. 254–5. See also Curtin, *Hero Tales of Ireland*, pp. 498 ff., and *Myths and Folklore of Ireland,* pp. 216 ff.; Larminie, *West Irish Folktales and Romances,* pp.72–3, 102 ff. Sometimes they are human beings who have been bewitched, or have themselves taken on a magic disguise (*Béaloideas* III, pp. 441–3; VIII, pp. 11–17; XII, pp. 106–22). They guard buried treasure, and are seen issuing from a *sidh* mound. Delargy (*The Gaelic Storyteller,* PBA XXXI (1945), p. 41) thinks that these monster-cat stories were borrowed into Icelandic tradition from Celtic sources. They appear to be of Celtic origin.

Le Capalu reappears in several French Arthurian romances of the late twelfth and thirteenth centuries, and the references to this monster in Continental sources have been the subject of a special study by E. Freymond: *Artus Kampf mit dem Katzenungetüm—Beiträge zur Romanischen Philologie, Festgabe für Gustav Gröber* (Halle, 1899). (The main points have been summarized in a review by Gaston Paris, *Romania* XXIX, pp. 121–4.)

In contrast with the LlDC poem, which is primarily concerned with the exploits of *Cei* (see n.) and which implies that Cei was the slayer of *Cath*

Baluc, the French romances allude to a fight in which Arthur slays or is slain by a cat-monster. The earliest of these to name *Capalu* is the *Romanz des Franceis* of the late twelfth century, by a certain *André,* which contains the following passage:

Rimé ont de lui li Franceis . . .
Que bote fu par Capalu
Li reis Artur en la palu,
Et que le chat l'ocist de guerre
Puis passa outre en Engleterre,
Et ne fu pas lenz de conquerre,
Ainz porta corone en la terre
Et fu sire de la contrée.
Où ont itel fable trovée?
Mençonge est, Dex le set, provée.

'The French have made a poem about him, that king Arthur was pushed by Capalu into the bog; and the cat killed him in war, then passed over to England, and was not slow to conquer it—then wore the crown in the land, and was the lord of the country. Where did they get such a tale? It is a proven lie, God knows.' (Freymond, op. cit., pp. 332–3)

In this poem the location of the fight *en la palu* shows that the French understood *cath paluc* in their own language as meaning 'the bog cat': it is the same kind of misinterpretation of a word which had a similar form but a different meaning in the two languages—the same as gave *Carados Briebras* < *Caradoc (B)reichbras*. The ensuing lines indicate that Capalu was a man transformed into animal shape: an interpretation which should be borne in mind in connection with the Welsh references. Like *Caradoc (V)reichvras*, the name must have been borrowed in written form with unlenited initial *P* (= B). Another allusion to this version of the tale is in *Galeran de Bretagne* (early thirteenth century), where it is said of Arthur *Que le chat occist par enchaus* (ed. L. Foulet, l. 5071).

Among the other romances which narrate or refer to a similar story is the *Estoire de Merlin* (Sommer, *Vulgate Version of Arthurian Romances* II, pp. 441 ff.), which depicts Arthur as fighting a victorious engagement with a monster-cat; and it appears that this fight was localized at a place near the lake of Le Bourget in France, which was known from the fourteenth century as *Mont du Chat Artus*. Similarly Finn slew *cat neimhe a nAth Cliath* 'a fierce cat in Dublin', Mac Neill, *Duanaire Finn* I (ITS VII), pp. 79, 193. For other resemblances between the portrayal of Finn and Arthur in early sources see A. G. Van Hamel, 'Aspects of Celtic Mythology', PBA XX (1934), pp. 219–22, and O. J. Padel, *Arthur in Medieval Welsh Literature*, pp. 127–8. Yet another variant of the tale claimed that Capalu abducted Arthur to Avalon—though this looks like an attempt to combine the story of the cat-monster with the more usual account of Arthur's end. As Freymond points out, *Capalu* retains the character of a water-monster in the Continental versions. It seems possible that the oldest of these tales, in which Arthur is killed by *Capalu*, reflects a genuine variant tradition of Arthur's end, which existed in antecedent Welsh and/or Breton tradition, but which by the time of the extant records has given place to other alternative traditions. Arthur's death at Camlan (*Ann. Cam.* 537) became conflated with a story of his removal to Avallon—so that the story of his terminal fight with a cat-monster is yet another variant, which survives only in certain tantalizing allusions.

Paris vab Priaf 48. Pen. 77: *Alexander paris*. An alternative name for *Paris* was *Alexandros* ('warrior, champion'—H. J. Rose, *A Handbook of Greek Mythology*, p. 234). *Paris* is known as *Alexander* throughout the Welsh version of *Dares Phrygius* (once as *Alexander Paris*, RBB 27.10), and is quoted in Prydydd y Moch's citation of the triad (see n. to triad 47). Cf. Owen and Lloyd (eds), *Drych yr Oesoedd Canol*, pp. 33–56.

Pasken m. 6ryen 23, 43. See nn. to *Vryen Reget*, *Owein m. Vryen*; also ESWP 97–8. *Pascen(n)* < O.W. *Pascent* < L. *Pascentius*. The Latin name appears on an inscribed stone of the fifth or sixth century at Towyn, Meirionnydd (ECMW, no. 286). *Pascent* is seemingly given as the name of a son of Vortigern commemorated on the ninth-century Valle Crucis pillar (ECMW, no. 182; EWGT 43g)—cf. in confirmation HB chs. 48, 49 and *Jes. Gen.* 14. (Doubts must remain on this matter, however, in view of the somewhat obscure phrasing on the pillar-stone.) Other occurrences of the name are LL *Pascen(n)*, 186.6; 209.22, etc.; *Pascent* 211.14. See EWGT 48 (34).

Pasgen(t) is named in CLlH no. III.38c, in a context which implies that the reference is to a son of Urien who participated in warfare in north Britain in company with his brothers *Owein* and *Elphin*: their opponents were *Dunawt m. Pabo* and *Gwallawc m. Lleennawc* (see nn.).

Jes. Gens. XXXIII and XXXIV (EWGT 48): *Keneu menrud m. Pascen m. urien reget,* etc. See introduction, p. cv, n. 180.

VSB 323 (55) = EWGT 62 (55): *Nidan e Mon m. Guruyw m. Pasken m. Vryen.*

Cynddelw gives to Owain Cyfeiliog the epithet *Pasgen wrys* 'of Pasgen's fury' (H 133.25 = CBT III no. 16.43n.), but the reference here is perhaps more likely to be to Owain's ancestor of the Powys dynasty, whose name appears on the Valle Crucis pillar, than to *Pascen(t) m. Uryen.* Cf. LlDC no. 6.6 'Arwul melin. march passcen fil'. Vrien'. Since there are a number of occurrences of this name, the same uncertainty is attached to Casnodyn's allusion: *am ner per paroded pasgenn* (RBP col. 1241.30 = GC no. 2.90n., 103n.).

Penarwan (gwreic Owein m. Urien) 80. VN[2]: 'His (Owein's) wife was *Penarwen* [sic] the daughter of *Culvanawyd Prydein* (see n.), with whom for her licentious and unchaste life I presume he did not long cohabit, and therefore he had no children by her.' There is no extant evidence for *Penarwan* other than the triad.

Pendaran Dyuet 26. The second element in this name could be either *taran* 'thunder' or *daran (= derwen)* 'oak tree'. Ifor Williams suggests, however, that there is another word *daran* which is equivalent to *bras*; if so, *Pendaran* might be rendered 'Huge Head' (PKM 266–7). But *Pen(n)* could also be interpreted in the sense of 'ruler, chief', as in *Penn Annwfn,* in which case the name could mean 'the Great Lord of Dyfed', as suggested by W. J. Gruffydd (*Rhiannon*, p. 34). Alternatively Lloyd-Jones suggests that *dar* may mean 'wild, fierce' (cf. *cynddaredd*, G 297), and it may be a diminutive of this *dar* which is present in the name 'Wild Head' or 'Fierce Lord'. (Cf. *dâr*, fig. 'foremost warrior', GPC 890–1.)

Gruffydd suggests (*Rhiannon*, pp. 19, 106) that in an earlier version of *Mabinogi Pwyll* the relation which subsisted between Pendaran Dyfed and Pryderi was that of father and son. This suggestion gains in interest from the indication provided by the Early Version of triad 26 that *Pendaran* was the original owner of the swine brought from Annwfn (see n. to triad 26). Both *Pendaran* and Pwyll are however shadowy figures in comparison with Pryderi (see n.), and it is worth noting that the bards refer to Pryderi, but not in any certain instance to either of his alleged progenitors.

Ifor Williams has pointed out the anachronism which exists between the allusions to *Pendaran Dyfed* in *Pwyll* and that in *Branwen.* In the First Branch of the *Mabinogi*, *Pendaran* is Pryderi's fosterer (PKM 27.5–6), but in *Branwen* he is left behind in Britain *yn was ieuanc* 'as a young boy', while Pryderi accompanies Brân to Ireland as a full-grown man (PKM 39.4; 46.9).

Peredur[1] m. Efra6c Iarll 86, 4 (var. in Pen. 50), *Prydyr* 91, *Predur* App. IV, no. 2. The name *Peredur* occurs in early sources in reference to one or more north-British heroes; see n. to *Peredur[2] m. Eliffer*, and cf. *Peredur arueu dur* 'P. of steel weapons' who is named in the *Gododdin* (CA 1. 359). The *Beddau* stanzas commemorate the grave of a certain *mab Peredur penwetic* (LlDC no. 18.68); but since the reference here must be to the *cantref* of Penweddig in Ceredigion it is clear that this character cannot be identified with either of the two men named *Peredur* in TYP—unless we are to regard this as one of the many instances of the secondary localization in Wales of a tradition concerning a northern hero. Cf. HW 257; J. E. Lloyd, *The Story of Ceredigion 400–1277* (Cardiff, 1937), pp. 13–14. See also EANC 222, quoting Lhuyd's *Parochialia*: 'Predyr Peiswyrdh Ld. of higher Cardigan had a place of Pallace, call'd Kayro, viz. Lhŷs Predyr ynghayro'. R. J. Thomas suggested (loc. cit.) that the allusion is to *Aberceiro* near Llanfihangel Genau'r Glyn, one of the commotes of Penweddig. As Thomas Jones points out (review in LlC I, p. 129), the reference shows that there was an old story connecting *Peredur* with the commote of Penweddig.

The derivation of the name *Peredur* is obscure. Line 359, 'Peredur arveu dur', in the *Gododdin* evidently contains a pun on the similarity between the name *Peredur* and *peri* (a plural form of *par* 'spear') combined with *dur* 'hard, steel'. A later fanciful explanation of the name in which it is analysed as composed from *par* + *dur* is offered in *Y Seint Greal*: *Ae henw ynteu yw peredur . . . achaws pan anet y mab y peris y dat roi arnaw yr henw hwnnw. par dur. kanys arglwyd y corsyd oed yn ryuelu ar efrawc . . . am hynny y roespwyt ar y mab peredur, yr dyuot cof idaw pan vei yn wr gymryt par o dur. neu ynteu o nerth par o dur dial ar arglwyd y corsyd a wnathoed ae dat am dwyn y dir y arnaw* (SG (i), p. 187). 'His name is Peredur . . . for the reason that when the boy was born his father caused him to be given this name "Steel Spear", because the Lord of the Fens was waging war on Efrawg. Therefore the boy was called *Peredur*, so that when he should be a grown man he should be mindful of a Steel Spear. Or else, by the might of a steel spear he should avenge on the Lord of the Fens what he had done to his father in taking his land from him.' The form *Paredur* occurs interchangeably with *Peredur* in the earliest text of the romance of *Peredur mab Efrawc* contained in Pen. 7; cf. also RM 209.13; RBB 404.7. *Paredur* is the form which occurs most frequently in *Y Seint Greal,* and it is also used frequently by the poets (see below).

The name of Peredur's father *Efrawc* is derived from *Eburācum* = *York,* named *Cair Ebrauc* in the HB List of *Civitates.* Pokorny made the ingenious suggestion (*Beiträge zur Namenforschung* I (1950), p. 38) that the pair *P(e)redur (m)ab Efrawc* is derived from the Latin title *Pr(a)etor ab Eburāco* 'a magistrate from York' (the Latin preposition *ab* becoming the Welsh word for 'son'). This explanation of the two names would solve the difficulty as to how Peredur's father came to have a name which is that of a place and not of a person: HRB employs *Ebraucus* as a proper name, denoting the eponymous founder of York, and the father of a large family of sons and daughters (HRB II, 6 = BD 24.4, *Euravc Cadarn);* but it hardly accounts for the other occurrences cited above in which *Peredur* appears as a personal name in early Welsh sources. If such a development really took place—from a Roman title of office into a character of early Welsh heroic tradition—it is evidently a unique and quite unparalleled occurrence.

Peredur mab Efrawc is the hero of the romance of *Peredur* (see Goetinck, *Historia Peredur vab Efrawc*, and the review by B. F. Roberts in SC XII/XIII (1977–81), pp. 480–4), whose main outlines correspond with the *Conte del Graal* composed by Chrétien de Troyes, with continuations by other French poets. In the Welsh romance, *Peredur* is the counterpart of the Grail hero known in the French romances as *Perceval.* But while *Peredur* is a name attested in the earliest Welsh sources, there is no occurrence of *Perceval* in any language, prior to Chrétien's poems *Erec, Cligés* and *Perceval* (*circa* 1190). *Perceval* may have been an unfamiliar name to the French redactors of the romances, judging from their clumsy attempts to analyse it (see EAR I, pp. 251–2 n.). It is likely, therefore, that *Perceval* is to be regarded as a loose approximation of the Welsh *Peredur,* and not vice-versa. (This approximation is no looser than that which is generally recognized as existing between the Welsh and French forms of other Arthurian names: Merlin = Myrddin, Gauvain = Gwalchmai, Guenièvre = Gwenhwyfar.) Further references to the story of *Peredur* by the *cywyddwyr* are cited by Gerallt Harries, 'Peredur Nai Arthur', B XXVI (1975), pp. 311–14. These indicate a belief among poets of the fifteenth and sixteenth centuries that Peredur was a nephew of Arthur. (This belief may be based merely upon an inexact memory of the romances.) Harries shows that the relationship, together with certain other details of the Welsh tale, find a parallel in some details of the fourteenth-century English poem *Sir Percyvell de Galles.*

A north-British *Peredur*—perhaps the warrior who is named in the *Gododdin*—may thus have been a local ruler of a small British kingdom in Yorkshire, before Celtic rule in these parts was annihilated by the growing power of Anglian Deira, as happened at a date not long after the battle of Catraeth (see n. to *Edwin vrenhin Lloegyr*). Some faint recollection of dynastic traditions concerning such a ruler may well lie behind the tale of *Peredur,* though the original theme of the story has been largely overlaid by the alien Grail materials which subsequently became superimposed upon it. The Welsh (and English) versions of the tale strongly suggest that the original story centered on the hero's obligation to bring about vengeance on his father's slayer. The Welsh romance emphasizes the north-British origin of its hero (*Efravc iarll bioed iarllaeth yn y gogled* WM 117.1–2; *Peredur vab efravc or gogled* 138.3–4), though Chrétien's poem insists merely on describing Perceval consistently as *li Gallois.* The tradition remained strong in Wales that the French hero *Perceval (Perlesvaus)* corresponded to the Welsh *Peredur*, so that the fourteenth-century Welsh rendering of the romance of the Grail restores to the hero his original Welsh name: *y milwr yd ydys yny ganmawl yma. y henw yn ffranghec yw peneffresvo galeif [sic] kystal yw hynny yngkymraec a pheredur . . . . A henw y dat oed efrawc iarll. o ben glyn camelot.* (SG(i), p. 172.) See further G. Goetinck, *Peredur. A Study of Welsh Tradition in the Grail Legends* (Cardiff, 1975), and earlier articles in LlC VI (1961), pp. 138–53 and LlC VIII (1964), pp. 58–64; also, C. Lloyd-Morgan, 'Peredur', ZCP 38 (1981), pp. 187–231, and 'Perceval in Wales' in *Essays in Memory of Cedric Pickford* (Woodbridge, 1986), pp. 78–96; Ian Lovecy, 'Historia Peredur ab Efrawg' in AW 171–82.

Peredur vab Efrawc is named also in the romance of *Gereint fab Erbin* (WM 411.36–7 = RM 265.16; see now R. L. Thomson's edition, DIAS 1997), and in *Breudwyt Ronabwy*, RM 159.24: *A pheredur paladyr hir.* The supposed connection of his name with *par* 'spear' may well account for the *paladyr hir* or 'long spear' which is his attribute in the romances. In addition to Br. Rh. this epithet is bestowed on him in the tale of *Peredur* (WM 160.25–6; 165.33–4), cf. also WM 140.32–3 (= RM 211.21–2): *A vdochi heb yr arthur pvy y y marchavc paladyr (hir) a seif yn y nant uchot*?

There is no mention of *Peredur* by the twelfth-century *Gogynfeirdd*, and the earliest reference to him is by Bleddyn Fardd: *Aruot peredur drymgur dromgat / aruawc ab eurawc cadyr varchawc cat* (H 69.15 = CBT VII, no. 46.15–16n.). In the following instances it is not clear whether the reference is to *Peredur*[1] or *Peredur*[2]:

Gr. ap Maredudd *kytwed paredur* (RBP col. 1207.24 = GGM no. 3.59), *ell beredur* (RBP col. 1322.14 = GGM no. 7.22), *aruot (aruoc) eir peir paredur* (RBP col. 1212.43; 1326.1). (Elsewhere Gr. ap Maredudd refers to *Angharat Law Eurawc* (RBP col. 1326.26), so that his references are most likely to be to the *Peredur* of the Romance.)

Rhisierdyn: *pridvr serch paredur svyd* (1287.35 = GSRh no. 6.32n.).

Meurig ab Iorwerth: *baredur dysc myvn brvydyr dic* (RBP col. 1373.10).

Ieuan Llwyd: *hvyl paredur* (1415.14).

Llywelyn Goch: *Peredur gystal* (1306.24 = GLlG no. 5.37n.).

Einion Offeiriad *(circa* 1320): *Peredur lafndhur mur maranedh* (*Cy.* 26, l. 35 = GEO no. 1.35n.).

With the *cywyddwyr*, however, it is evident that the *Peredur* referred to is always the hero of the romance which bears his name. Dafydd ap Gwilym makes a detailed reference to the episode in the tale in which Peredur compares his lady's colouring to a duck killed by a hawk lying on the snow (GDG no. 45.33–52, in his version the bird is a blackbird, not a duck).

Gutun Owain: *dwbled Beredur* (GO no. XVI.37).

Dafydd Nanmor: *Peredur vab hir ydwyd / Efroc Iarll y Verwic wyd* (DN no. VIII.3–4).

Iolo Goch (to Owain Glyndŵr): *Llew Prydain, llaw Peredur* (GIG no. VIII.55n.).

The episode of the *addanc* is alluded to by Tudur Aled (GTA I, no. XXXVII.53–8); *Predur anian* (GTA no. XII.49; and three other references).

Rhys Goch Eryri gives the hero's name in its French form as *Persifal*, and alludes to the episode in which the boy kept his mother's goats, and overran the wild deer in the forest, IGE[2] 184.4–12.

For a collection of essays on the tale of *Peredur*, see Sioned Davies and Peter Wynn Thomas (eds), *Canhwyll Marchogyon* (Caerdydd, 2000).

Peredur[2] m. Eliffer Gosgor(d)ua6r 8, 30, 44, 70; App. II, no. 5; *meibyon Eliffer* G. triad 46. See EWSP 110–11, 113. On the name see n. to *Peredur*[1].

Harl. Gen. XII: *Guurci ha Peretur mepion Eleuther Cascord maur* (cf. EWGT 11 (12)). (The ensuing names in this genealogy have been copied in error from those in the genealogy of Urien Rheged; see CLlH xxiii–xxiv. App. II, no. 5, gives the correct genealogy of *Elifer Gosgordvawr*.)

Ann. Cam. 580: *Guurci et Peretur moritur.*

The genealogies show that Gwrgi and *Peredur* belonged to the family of Coel Hen (App. II above), and were among the *Gwŷr y Gogledd* who lived in the last half of the sixth century. Triad 44 claims that they were present at the battle of Arfderydd in 573 (see n. to triad 84), and this is consistent with the date recorded for their death in *Ann. Cam.*, AD 580. It is consistent also with Geoffrey of Monmouth's portrayal of *Peredurus dux Venedotorum* in the *Vita Merlini* (ed. B. Clarke, l. 26n.) as an opponent of Guennolous (= Gwenddoleu) at an unnamed battle (evidently corresponding to Arfderydd) at which Merlinus became mad. A misunderstanding of the term *Y Gogledd* may have been responsible for Geoffrey's localizing the home of *Peredurus* in north Wales. Elsewhere, Gwrgi and *Peredur* are the prototypes of Geoffrey's royal brothers Peredurus and Vigenius (Iugenius) in HRB III, 18. It is not clear on what basis Stow's *Chronicle* (edition of 1615, p. 12), in retelling Geoffrey's story, claims that *Peredur* founded the Yorkshire town of Pickering. The fact that *Peredur m. Eliffer* appears in all early sources as inseparable from his brother *Gwrgi* is an argument against identifying *Peredur*[2] with *Peredur*[1], although it must be conceded that this Yorkshire connection would not be inconsistent with the patronymic *vab Efrawc Iarll* ('son of the Earl of York') given to *Peredur*[1] (see n. above). Cf. EWSP 113. References by the poets to *Peredur* are given above under *Peredur*[1].

Peresgri, gwreic Brychan Brycheiniog 96. See nn. to *Brychan* and to triad 96.

Perwyr, verch Run Ryuedua6r 79. See nn. to *Run*[3] *ap Maelg6n*, *Run*[4] *Ryuedua6r*. Cf. B XVIII, p. 248; EWGT 91 (c); B XXV, p. 280n.; also, the following references:

Hywel ab Owain: *am berweur beruet uymhechavd* (H 317.28 = CBT II, no. 6.70n.).

Perweur is one of the two names added in the Welsh version of the list of the daughters of *Euravc Gadarn* (BD 25.6), which have no corresponding name in the text of HRB. Cf. also *Peren* mother of Beuno Sant, VSB 16 = *Perferen* VSB 321 (30).

Petroc Baladrddellt ap Clement Tywyssawc Kernyw, App. IV, no. 6. 'P. of the Shattered Spear' (GPC 2671). VSB 322 (39): *Pedrauc m. Clemens tyw(y)ssauc o Gernyv.* The cult of St Petroc was widespread both in Wales and in Brittany (see G. H. Doble, *St Petroc,* Cornish Saints series, no. 11; *Analecta Bollandiana* LXXIV, pp. 131 ff.; LBS IV, 94–103; VSB 24). His name is preserved in the Cornish *Padstow.* The church and priory at Bodmin are also dedicated to him. On the traditions associated with *Petroc*, see TWS 199–205 and K. Jankulak, *The Medieval Cult of St Petroc* (Woodbridge, 2000).

Petroc < *Petrācus (cf. the name *Petr* in Harl. Gen. II) with diminutive suffix *-oc (-og).* Cf. *Bedrawc (= Pedrawc?),* the name of the father of Bedwyr. The form *Pedrogl* is found as a variant of *Petroc* in some versions of *Bonedd y Saint* and also of the triad in App. IV, no. 6. The adjective *pedrogl* < *pedwar* +

ongl 'four-cornered, square' is however used of men, as a synonym for 'strong', cf. GIG no. V.17n.: *Pedwar eglur, pedroglion* (to the four sons of Tudur Fychan); GDG 443.

The Life of *St Cadoc* (VSB 24) gives a different account of the parentage of St Petroc, according to which he was the son of Glywys, the legendary eponymous ruler of Glywysing, and brother of Gwynlliw (*G. varvoc* or *varchawc* of App. IV, no. 6), the father of St Cadoc. But it was the tradition as to Petroc's parentage which appears in the triad and in *Bonedd y Saint* which was known to Dafydd Nanmor, and which seems to have been incorporated in local Ceredigion traditions about the saint. According to these, St Petroc was one of the seven survivors from the battle of Camlan (see n. to triad 59):

Yng Nghamlan o'r Bryttaniaid
Yr oydd eb ladd o'r ddwy blaid
Seithwyr o'r maes a aethant.
Un sydd wrth i waew yn sant:
Pedroc, oedd enwoc a'i ddûr
Vawrweirthioc, wrth varw Arthvr,
Mab brenin, o vrenhinoydd
Kernyw gynt, coronawc oydd,
Gwasnaethv bv, ac y bydd,
Y Drindawd, wedy'r vndydd
Vch Dofr, a rroi diovryd
Arver byth o arfau'r byd.
Yna i troes i'r mann y tric
Duw (= dyw) i varw hyd y Verwic.
(DN no. VI.1–14)

'In Camlan there were seven men of the Britons who escaped from the field, without being slain by either side. One of them is a saint because of his spear: precious Petroc was renowned with his weapon at the death of Arthur. He was a crowned king's son, from the ancient kings of Cornwall. He served (and will serve) the Trinity after that day, above Dover, and (he) gave a vow never more to employ worldly weapons. Then he came to *y Verwig,* the place where he awaits his death-day.'

This story corresponds with nothing in the Life of *St Petroc* by John of Tynemouth in *Nova Legenda Aurea* (reprinted *Acta SS. Boll*, June I, pp. 400–2), nor in the Life translated by Doble from Bib. Nat. 9989. (St Petroc's body was believed to have been preserved at Bodmin till 1177, when it was transferred to St Meven in Brittany (LBS IV, 100).) It must therefore represent a local tradition preserved in Ceredigion (see DN 132). *Y Ferwig* (Verwick) is one of the three Welsh churches dedicated to the saint; the others are at *Llanbedrog,* Caernarfonshire, and *St Petrox*, Pembrokeshire (LBS IV, 101). St Petroc's spear, referred to in the poem, was shown at Llanbedrog in 1535 (ibid., 103). It is described as 'a Relyk callyd *Gwawe Pedrok*' in the deposition of the rector of the parish at that time. The Lives give no indication that *Petroc* was a warrior before he became a monk; and Dafydd Nanmor's account is the only one which gives any kind of explanation as to how such an epithet as *paladrddellt* 'shattered spear' (which occurs elsewhere as an epithet, IGE^2 26.9, *peleidrddellt* 20.7) could have become applied to the *St Petroc* of the *Bonedd.* The growth of the legend about *St Petroc*'s participation at the battle of Camlan and about his marvellous spear may not be early; but the Welsh Lives of the Saints suggest that there is no reason to reject the authenticity of a tradition that he, like St Gwynlliw, was a warrior before he became a monk (see now MCSP).

Tudur Aled makes two allusions to *Pedrogl* [*sic*] and his spear: *Mal Pedrogl waywddellt, mal Pedr a'i gleddau* (GTA I, no. VII.94); *Pwy a dreigl ffon Pedrogl fyrf* (GTA no. XXIX.34).

Polixena uerch Priaf 50. See n. to *Priaf Hen*. According to *Dares Phrygius*: *Polixena gvreic hirwen ffurueid vynvgylhir. a llygeit aduvyn. a gvallt melyn hir. ac aelodeu kyweir. a byssed hiryon. ac eskeired crynyon. a thraet llunyeid oed idi yr hon oe thegvch a ragorei ar bavb. anvyt mul hael oed idi diveir oed* (RBB 13–14) 'Polixena (was) a tall, fair woman, shapely and long-necked, with beautiful eyes, and long yellow hair; well-proportioned limbs, with long fingers, good legs, and comely feet; she excelled over all in beauty. In nature she was modest and generous, and she was chaste.' In post-Homeric tradition *Polixena* plays a romantic role for which there is no authority in the *Iliad.* Thus in *Dares Phrygius,* Achilles is depicted as being violently in love with her, and it is said that he was decoyed to his death by the promise of receiving her as his wife at the temple of Apollo near the gate of Troy, where he was set upon and killed by Paris (RBB 31, and see Rose, *Handbook of Greek Mythology*, p. 235).

HCLl no. LVIII.51–2: *Achos gwen Polixena / Llas o dwyll Achilles da.*

Portha6r Gadw 9: *Cadr(i)eith m. P.*; see n. W substitutes *ap Seidi* for *Porthawr* 'gatekeeper', see n. to triad 60. *Cadw* 'flock, herd' GPC 397; i.e. *Porthawr Gadw* 'Guardian of a herd'. The name is probably corrupt; cf. the variant form *Cadyrieith uab Porthawr gandvy* as in *Ystorya Gereint fab Erbin* (ed. R. L. Thomson), ll. 405, 649, etc. (WM 388.1).

Priaf Hen, vrenhin Tro 50. 'Priam the Old, king of Troy.' *Dares Phrygius*: *Priaf vrenhin troea. gvr mavr oed. ac vyneb tec idav. a llef hynavs. a chorff eryr* (RBB 13.13–14) 'Priam king of Troy was a large man, with a fair face, agreeable voice, and the body of an eagle.' BD 45.11–13 (= RBB 83.15): *gunavn yavn . . . rac codi Pryaf Hen yn hentat gan ellvng guaet an kereint* 'Let us do right . . . lest we anger Priam the Old our forefather by shedding the blood of our relatives.' (The allusion is to the alleged common ancestry of the Romans and the Britons, which was for long claimed in Welsh poetry. The common descent of the Britons and the Romans from the Trojan heroes is plainly asserted in the first lines of HB. See introduction, p. lxi.) Cf. CBT VII no. 5.85n. For parallel instances of *Hen* for ancestral figures, see n. to triad no. 1 above, n. to *Llywarch Hen*, and EWGT 226 for further examples.

Priam's name is employed, on one occasion only, as a standard of comparison by the *Gogynfeirdd*: according to Bleddyn Fardd, Ll. ap Gruffudd is *gvr brut vegys priaf* 'a man wise like Priam' (H 58.15 = CBT VII no. 50.25n.). For other references to Greek and Roman heroes in poetry which is earlier than the fourteenth-century date assigned to the Welsh version of *Dares Phrygius,* see n. to triad 47, and *Drych yr Oesoedd Canol*, pp. 33–4, which dates the Latin original to the sixth century. References to *Priam* by the *cywyddwyr* include the following:

IGE[2] 176.2 (Ll. ab y Moel): *ail Briam bryd.*
GGl no. LXVII.5–6: *Un ffunud wyd yn ffyniant . . . â Phriaf a'i blant.*
HCLl no. XV.24: *Prif gorff fal mab Priaf gynt*; no. LXIII.25: *A chwi, fal merch i Briaf* (i.e. Polixena). See above.

Tudur Aled compares five brothers to *Pum maib Priaf* (GTA I, no. XXIII.82). (See also n. to *Brutus* who was for long regarded as the legendary founder of Britain.)

Prydein m. Aed Ma6r App. I, no. 1. The names of *Prydein* and *Aed Mawr* are inserted among the predecessors of Beli Mawr (HRB's *Heli*, III, 20) in a number of Welsh versions of Geoffrey of Monmouth's pre-Roman king-list. The oldest of these is the mid-thirteenth-century Pen. 17, which contains the *Hanes Gruffudd ap Cynan* (for the genealogy see HGVK 1–2 = EWGT 36 (2); 121 (1); and nn. pp. 134, 158). Other manuscript versions of the list which include these names are Pen. 75, 28; 129, 4; 131, 77. By comparing the various versions of these king-lists it becomes apparent that *Prydein* has been inserted in the genealogy at a place corresponding to that of *Porrux* in HRB and in the *Bruts* (BD 31–2). The genealogies which substitute *Prydein* for *Porrex* insert also the name of *Aed(d) Mawr,* which has nothing to correspond to it either in HRB or in *Brut y Brenhinedd*; but in compensation these genealogies omit two names which appear in Geoffrey's account:

Pen. 131	Pen. 75, Pen. 129	Gr. ap C.	BD	HRB
Prydain	Prydein	Prydein	Porrex	Porrux
—	—	—	Goronwy-Dygu	Gorbodug
—	—	—	Kynuarch	Kinmarch
Aedd Mawr	Aedd Mawr	Aedd Mawr	—	—
Antonius	Antonius	Antonius	Yago	Iago
Seisill	Seisyll	Seiryoel	Seisill	Seisill

It seems that we may have in *Aed Mawr* (see n.) and his son (or descendant) *Prydein* a pair of names which belonged to a genuine pre-Geoffrey antiquarian tradition preserved by the poets; and that the poets did not readily relinquish these names when they considered it necessary to harmonize the antecedent native record with the scheme of British pre-history provided by HRB. Although the Welsh *Bruts* have abandoned any record of *Aedd* and his son, we find that a bardic genealogy (Pen. 17 in HGVK), which is almost as old as the earliest versions of the *Brut*, incorporates these names among the forebears of Gruffudd ap Cynan. The manner in which *Prydein m. Aed Mawr* is portrayed in TYP strongly suggests that tradition represented him at one time as an eponymous conqueror of Britain. See introduction, p. cii; P. C. Bartrum, B XXIII (1968), pp. 1–5; and B. F. Roberts, *Studies on Middle Welsh Literature*, p. 31.

Robert Vaughan felt little doubt as to the authenticity of the tradition of *Prydein ab Aedd Mawr,* as appears from his account (VN[2]):

> You must consider that after the cruel murder of Porrux king of Britain . . . this Prydain son of Aedd the Great, king or prince of Cornwall . . . subdued the whole island, the which of him took the name of *Ynys Prydain.* Although this Prydain is not mentioned in the British history of Geoffrey in Latin, nor in the ancient Catalogue of the British kings, yet this history is maintained by very good authority, as partly by the Triades, the ancient laws of the Britons, our old books of Pedigrees; he is mentioned in the Life of Gr. ap Cynan [i.e. TYP, App. I above, and cf. EWGT 95 (i)] . . . and by another parchment manuscript of my own, of the same antiquity or very near it, also by a fair British book written on vellum . . . of the handwriting of Guttyn Owen, and by other both ancient and modern writers; whereby it may appear that it is not any new invention, but a very ancient historical tradition supported with grave authority extant long before the curiosity of later ages.

From this account it appears possible that Robert Vaughan may have had other sources of information about *Prydein ab Aedd* in addition to those of which we know.

Prydelaw Menestyr 44 (R: *a phetrylev vynestyr;* Pen. 27: *a ffedrillaw v.* 'P. the Cup-bearer'). If R's reading is accepted, *pedrylaw* 'adroit, dexterous' (GPC 2710; and J. Vendryes, EC IV, p. 284) gives a good descriptive epithet for a cup-bearer. On compounds in *pedry-* see n. to *Bedwyr m. Bedrawc.* On *menestyr* < O.F. *menestr* see GPC 2430, and cf. CBT II, no.14.9n.

Pryder m. Dolor Deiuyr a Brennych 16. 'Care son of Grief of Deira and Bernicia.' *Pryder* meant formerly 'care for, concern for', later 'anxiety' (PKM 158). O.W. *preteram* glosses *perpendo* 'I give anxious thought' (Loth, *Vocabulaire Vieux Breton,* 206), and *gurprit* glosses *superstitiosa* (ibid., p. 148). VSB 323 (56) = EWGT 63 (56): *Dwyuael m. Pryder m. Dolor Deiuyr o Deivyr a Brennych ene Gogled.* The name is reminiscent of the *Nerth mab*

Cadarn, Drem vab Dremhidydd 'Strength son of Might', 'Sight son of Seer' type of name in *Culhwch ac Olwen*.

Pryderi m. Pwyll Penn Annwuyn 26. See n. to *Pendaran Dyuet. Pryderi* is the hero of the *Four Branches of the Mabinogi*; his birth being described in the First Branch, subsequent adventures in the Second and Third, and his death in the Fourth. On the names *Pryderi* and Pwyll, see PKM 157–8 and R. L. Thomson, *Pwyll Pendefic Dyved*, p. 41. Ifor Williams has drawn attention to the occurrence of a Breton gloss on *iactura* as *dampnum vel pritiri* (ed. Stokes, RC IV, 335), which proves that *pryderi* was once known as a common noun. He suggests that the words with which Rhiannon unwittingly names her son were originally *oed escor uym pryderi* (PKM 26.9–10). When the meaning of *pryderi* became forgotten, the end of the phrase became altered to *pryder + im* (suffixed pronoun) 'my care' (see n. to *Pryder* above). *Pritiri* in the gloss is parallel to *dampnum* 'loss'; hence the original meaning of Rhiannon's exclamation was 'It would be a relief from my loss', i.e. the loss of her child since the night of his birth; and it is this loss which is commemorated in the name which is thereupon given to the boy, *Pryderi.* (Cf. the similar naming incident in the Irish epic *Táin Bó Cúalnge* in which the hero is named Cú Chulainn 'Hound of Cooley' from an incident in his early career.) In the case of *Pryderi*, Thomson points out in his n. on the passage (loc. cit.) that Rhiannon's words are a pun upon the double meaning of *escor*, which is 'relief' both in the simple sense of 'a removal, a casting off', and also in the special sense of 'a bringing forth, a giving birth'. Thus the words mean both 'It would be a relief from my anxiety' and 'It would be a giving birth to my (son) Pryderi'. Cf. GPC 1244, 2917.

According to the tale of *Math*, *Pryderi* was slain by Gwydion, and his grave was to be seen at *Maen Tyuyawc* (= Maentwrog) *uch y Uelen Ryd*, PKM 73.16. Cf. the *Beddau*: *En aber gwenoli / y mae bet pryderi* (LlDC no.18.20–1). *Gwenoli* is the name of a stream which flows into the river *Y Felenrhyd,* EANC 146. Both sources refer to the same place by a different name.

References to *Pryderi* by the *Gogynfeirdd* are as follows:

Einion fab Gwalchmai: *yt wyf pryderus ual pryderi* (H 41.8 = CBT I, no. 26.38n.).

Cynddelw: *Am ywein prydein* [i.e. Owain Gwynedd], *pryderi haual* (H 127.25 = CBT III, no. 21.67n.).

Howel Foel ap Griffri: *Gwr diletyf prifddeddyf pryderi* (H 56.28 = CBT VII, no. 23.18n.).

Dafydd ap Gwilym describes his uncle Ll. ap Gwilym as *ail Bryderi* (GDG no. 12.40), and in his *Ymryson* with Gr. Gryg he refers to Dyfed as *Pryderi dir* (GDG no. 150.32).

Pwyll Penn Annwuyn 26. *Pryderi m. P.* The First Branch of the *Mabinogi* relates how *Pwyll Pendefic Dyved* won his title of *Penn Annwfn* 'Lord of

Annwfn'. With Pwyll 'wisdom, reason understanding' etc. (GPC 2948–9) as a personal name, Holder compares Gaulish *Pellus* (ACS II, 963). Cf. also the Br. verb *poellat* 'to consider'. The name appears as *Poyll* in the fourteenth-century *Cart. de Quimper* (*Chr. Br.* 227). See also *Pwyll Hanner Dyn,* CO l. 342 and n.

Rahaut eil Morgant 12, 41; *Ryha6t* 73. Cf. *Arch. Cam.* LXXX, p. 304; *Celtica* IX, p. 182.

Br. Rh.: *A ryavd eil morgant* (RM 159.30).

Gwilym Ddu o Arfon: *Mydyr eiryeu rieu raawt eil morgant* (RBP col. 1227.1–2 = GGDT no. 6.69n.).

Eil (= Ir. *aile,* L. *alter* 'other, second') can mean 'son', but also 'descendant', more correctly 'successor'; cf. Irish *tánaise rig* 'second (i.e. heir) to a king'. (On *eil* see D. A. Binchy, 'Linguistics and Legal Archaisms in the Celtic law books', *Trans. Phil. Soc.*, 1959, p. 24, reprinted in D. Jenkins (ed.), *Celtic Law Papers* (Brussels, 1973); 'Some Celtic Legal Terms', *Celtica* III (1956), p. 224.) Cf. *Dylan eil Ton* (WM 94.5); *Glinneu eil Taran* (CO l. 992); *Drych eil Kibdar* (triad 27, CO ll. 395–6n.); *Ky(h)oret eil Kynan* (triad 39). See also n. to *Llawr m. Eiryf* = Llawr eil Erw, CO l. 217n. For *Morgant* cf. *Morgant Mwynuawr* above and n.

In other instances in poetry it is not possible to be certain that the personal name is present, rather than the adjective *hawdd* + intensive prefix *ry-* 'fine, generous' (PT 40, 97): *glev ryhavt glevhaf vn yv vryen* (BT 63.1); *eurulavd y ysgwyd / mal ysgwyd rwyd rahavd* (H 107.30). Casnodyn: *Poen ryawt deuawt ot adefaf* (RBP 1244.23 = GC no. 4.17n. etc).

Riueri m. Tangwn 16 (= *Rineri,* Pen. 45, 47). If *Riueri* (Rhyferi) is the correct form of this name, it may contain *rhif* 'number'. The components of *Tangwn* are obscure, and it seems probable that both name and patronymic are corrupt.

Riwallawn Wallt Banhadlen (m. Vryen Reget) 4, 17. 'R. Broom-Hair.' *R. ab Vryen* 62 (on the identity of the characters referred to see n. to triad 62). For another reference to *Riwallawn m. Uryen* see n. to *Owein m. Vryen.*

Rhiwallon < **Rigo-vellaunos* 'most kingly' (cf. ACS I, 863; II, 1186). There are a number of instances of O.W. *Riguallaun* in LL. The name occurs also as that of a grandson of Aedán of Dalriada (Ir. *Rigullan, Rigullon,* see EIHM 362 and nn. 3, 4), and as that of the eldest of the family of physicians, according to the thirteenth-century *Meddygon Myddveu* (ed. P. Diverres, p. 6), later associated with the story of the water-nymph of Llyn y Fan Fach; also according to VN[2] as that of a brother of *Myrddin Wyllt*, mentioned in the poem *Peiryan Vaban* (see n. to *Gweith Arderydd,* triad 84). The name is found as *Rigwatlan* in ASC *ann.* 1063 (Earle and Plummer, *Two Saxon Chronicles Parallel* I, p. 191). There is particular interest in the inclusion of a possible son of Urien Rheged in triads 4, 17 (see nn.).

The colour of broom (*banadl*) appears frequently in medieval prose and poetry as a standard of comparison for beauty:

> Br. Rh. 4.13: *ac a oed velyn (o wisc y marchawc) a oed kyn uelynet a blodeu y banadyl* (RM 147.4). Consequently there is frequent reference to the broom in comparison with a girl's hair, cf. the description of Olwen: *oed melynach y fenn no blodeu y banadyl* (CO l. 490), and it may be remembered that *blodeu y banadl* were one of the components employed in the creation of *Blodeuwedd* (PKM 83.24). *Banadlwedd* ('rich in broom', 'of the appearance of broom') occurs in Pen. 127 as a girl's name (B V, pp. 135–6). Dafydd ab Edmwnd frequently employs this image: *avr fanadl ar* y *feinir* (GDE 7.10), *gwalld pen y fanadlen hir* (39.6), *banhadlen ywch yr wyneb* (46.1); *banhadlwyn* 'a grove of broom' in a similar description (D. J. Bowen, *Barddoniaeth yr Uchelwyr*, p. 88). So also Dafydd Nanmor: *Y vun hoywdlos vanhadlwallt* (DN no. XXXIII.1), *Llwyn ne ddau i'r llan a ddoeth / Llwyn banadl, Llio'n bennoeth* (no. XXIX.29–30).

Ronn6en baganes 37 (R), *Ronwen* 59. 'R. the pagan woman.' On the name, see n. to *G6rtheyrn G6rthenau.* HB (ch. 37) gives the story of Vortigern's betrothal to Hengist's daughter, but gives the girl no name. In reproducing his predecessor's account, Geoffrey (HRB VI, 12) bestows on the heroine the name *Renwein* (for which Griscom gives the variants *Renwen, Roawen, Rowen*) or *Ronwen* (*Variant Version* of HRB, ed. Hammer, pp. 113, 116). *Ronwen* is also the form given in the *Bruts* (BD 94.97; RBB 135–8). The *Romwenna* found in the chapter-summary prefaced to a single manuscript of HB (*Mon. Germ. Hist.* XIII, p. 129) is evidently a variant of *Ronwen,* and has probably been derived from HRB or the *Brut.*

It has been suggested that *Rowen* could represent the Anglo-Saxon form *Hrothwyn* (Chadwick, *The Origin of the English Nation*, p. 43, n. 2), a name which would preserve the alliteration with Hengist such as is frequently found in the names of father and child. But it is more probable that *Ronwen*, and not *Rowen*, is the authentic form of this name, and that its meaning is Welsh 'White' or 'Fair Lance', an appropriate appellation for a slender girl (Tatlock, *The Legendary History of Britain*, pp. 146–7); cf. Dafydd ap Gwilym's description of Dyddgu as *gwaywsyth*, GDG no. 37.8. Could *rhawn* 'horse-hair' be the first element (as indicated by J. Lloyd-Jones, *Enwau Lleoedd Sir Gaernarfon* p. 12)? Cf. GPC 3041 on *rhawn.* But neither *Ronwen* nor any of the variants of this name which appear in the texts of the HRB is found in any other source, or with reference to any other character than the daughter of Hengist. For further references by the poets to *Rhonwen* as the progenitress of the English, and by extension as representing the English as a nation, see J. E. Caerwyn Williams, 'Nodiadau Cymysg: Ronwen: Rhawn Gwynion', B XXI (1964–6), pp. 301–3. Leslie Richards, *Gwaith Dafydd Llwyd o Fathafarn* (Caerdydd, 1964) derives W. *Rhonwen* from Ml.E. *Ronwenne* (< *Renwein* in HRB). Her name was nevertheless understood in Wales to be a compound of *rhawn* + *gwen.* The former usually means 'horsehair' but was also used of a girl's hair: *Gwaith Dafydd Llwyd o Fathafarn* no. VI.13, *a choroni merch rawnir.*

To the poets *R(h)onwen* was regarded as essentially the progenitor of the English nation: the English are *Rhonwen wyrion* (GTA I, no. XLVII.65; GDE 95.28); *i plant Ronwen* (GGl no. XLVIII.59, GO no. XVII.44); *esilldydd Ronwen* (DN no. XXIII.57). Cf. also GDE 66.7: *dy rwn yw daear Ronwen*; 93.16: *Ronwen nod.* Thus it is probable that in the story of Vortigern's betrothal-feast as recounted in HB and in HRB, there is a mythological significance in the act by which *Ronwen* hands to Vortigern a drinking-cup. O'Rahilly has pointed out the significance in Irish sources of scenes in which the goddess who represents the land of Ireland presents to the high-king of another country a similar cup symbolizing both marriage and sovereignty (*Ériu* XIV, pp. 14–15).

Rore verch Vsber 58. Perhaps this name should be *Rorei,* to correspond with the ending in *-ei* of the other two names in the same triad; but its constituents are obscure. (On O.W. *e, ei,* see LHEB 587–8.)

Rudlwm Gorr 28 (WR) (CO l. 333): *A grudlvyn gorr.* This suggests that *Grudlwm* should be restored in the triad, 'Bare-cheeked Dwarf.' *Grudd* is feminine in Ml.W. but masculine in this same epithet as applied by Dafydd ap Gwilym to Gruffudd Gryg: *Gruffudd ruddlwm* (GDG no. 154.25). For the confusion between the names of various dwarfs in the triads and elsewhere, see nn. to *Gwythelyn Gorr* and to triad 27.

Ruua6n Beuyr m. Dewrarth Wledic 3, *Ruua6n Peuyr Draha6c* 23 (WR), *Rua6n Peuyr ap G6ydno* 61 (the other allusions indicate that *ap Gwydno* here is a mistake). 'R. the Radiant.' On *pefyr* 'shining, bright' see n. to *Goronwy Peuyr.*

CO: *A ruavn bepyr m. dorath* (CO l. 183).

Br. Rh.: *Rvavn bybyr uab deorthach wledic* (RM 148.17–18 = Br. Rh. 6.4n.).

Einion Offeiriad (to Syr Rhys ap Gruffudd): *Gair dethol reol ruawn befrwedh* (*Cy.* 26, p. 134, l. 30 = GEO no. 1.30).

In its O.W. form *Rumaun* (< *Romānus*) this name appears in Harl. Gens. III, XXXII, as the name of a son of Cunedda after whom the district of *Rhufoniog* is traditionally believed to be named. Another early instance of the name is Rumon in the list of British personal names dating from the ninth or early tenth century preserved in *Vatican MS. Reg. Lat.* 191, and thought to be of Cornish or Breton provenance (see EC III, p. 152; also Olsen and Padel, CMCS 12, p. 46). The name may occur also in the *Gododdin*: *ruuawn hir* (CA 1. 378), *ruvawn* (l. 1002). For further references see EWGT 211.

The only certain allusion to *Ruvawn Pefyr* by the *Gogynfeirdd* is in the opening lines of Hywel ab Owain's *Gorhoffedd*: *Tonn wenn orewyn a orvlych bet | gwytua ruuavn bebyr ben teyrnet* (H 315.18–19 = CBT II, no. 6.2n.) 'A foaming white wave wets the grave-mound of Rhufawn the Radiant, chief of princes.' The allusion recalls the form of the *Beddau* stanzas, in which a *Rhufawn* is mentioned, though without indication as to the site of his grave: *bet ruvaun ruyvenit ran . . . Bet ruwaun ryievanc daerin* (LlDC no. 18.129, 132) 'The grave of R, of princely portion (or "of princely mien") . . . The grave of R., too young placed in the earth.' (Cf. GGDT 78n.)

Hywel ab Owain Gwynedd's *Gorhoffedd* implies a connection between *Rhufawn Pefyr* and Gwynedd, and this association recurs in *Araith Iolo Goch*: *Cyfoeth Ruawn befr vab Drothach [sic] wledig oedd Wynedd gynt* (D. Gwenallt Jones, *Yr Areithiau Pros,* p. 12). This source may have been influenced by the *Gorhoffedd*, yet it is not unlikely that *Rhufawn Pefyr* was one of the many north-British heroes about whom traditions were subsequently relocalized in Wales. A local connection of this kind may therefore underlie Gruffudd ap Maredudd's description of Gronwy fab Tudur of Penmynydd as *rwyf ruon dewred* 'a ruler of the valour of Rhufawn' (RBP col. 1315.22). On *Rhufon Befr* see further WCD 560–1.

Run[1] m. Beli 20, *Gvydar m. Run m. Beli* 13 (WR). Hywel Foel ap Griffri: *Gwr . . . ual run uab beli* (H 56.20 = CBT VII, no. 23.10–11n.). The reference may be to a son of *Beli Mawr* (see n.). *Beli* occurs also as the name of a son of *Run[3] m. Maelgwn* (Harl. Gen. I), but the possibility that the names of father and son have been reversed in the two instances of the name which occur in TYP seems to be precluded by the independent allusion by Hywel Foel. The name *Reidwn mab Beli* in CO l. 224 may be a mistake for *Run m. Beli.* For Dafydd Benfras's allusion to *Run Ruduoawc* (CBT VI, no. 35.54) see triad 20 and n.

The name *R(h)un* is of very frequent occurrence, so that it is impossible to tell which *Run* is intended in the many instances in which the name appears without recognizable patronymic; there are six examples in the *Beddau* stanzas, LlDC no. 18. See also EWGT index, p. 211n.

Run[2] m. Einya6n 23, 79. See n. to *Einya6n[1]*. In HRB XII, 6, Geoffrey of Monmouth reproduces what is clearly a variant version of Harl. Gen. I, according to which *Run* and *Ennianus* (= *Einyawn*) are the names of two sons of Maelgwn Gwynedd (cf. EWGT 91 (28)). This statement may rest on an authentic tradition, since the sixteenth-century Elis Gruffydd also reports that Maelgwn had two sons who bore these names (Thomas Jones, 'Gwraig Maelgwn Gwynedd a'r Fodrwy', B XVIII (1958–60), p. 57). It is possible, therefore, that the *Run* of triad 23 should be identified with *Run ap Maelgwn* (see following entry), and that *Einyawn* should properly be the name of his brother, not his father. Alternatively, *Rhun* may have been a son of *Eniaun Girt*, Maelgwn's grandfather (Harl. Gen. I). Cf., however, the following allusions to *Run m. Einyawn* in certain late genealogies: Pen. 127, 94: *Run ap Enniawn ap Mar ap Keneu ap Coel*; Pen. 75, 30: *Run Ryveddvawr* [see *Run[4]*] *ap Enniawn ap Masgwic kloff ap kenau ap koel godeboc.* Cf. EWGT 48 (35); 88 (14).

Run[3] m. Maelg6n 3, 17. See n. to *Maelgwn Gwyned.* Harl. Gen. I gives *Run map Mailcun* in the genealogy of the kings of Gwynedd (cf. HGVK 40, n. 16; GIG 286n.; CMCS 23, p. 14n.; *Romania* 116, pp. 86, 89n.). Triad 44a refers to an incident in the dispute over the succession to the rule of Gwynedd which took place after Maelgwn's death between *Rhun* and Maelgwn's son-in-law *Elidir Mwynfawr* (see n., and n. to triad 44). A celebrated passage in the Gwynedd version of the Laws preserved in the Chirk codex (*circa* 1250) refers to this dispute (for further references, see M. E. Owen, WKC 235–46):

> Eman e llas elidir muhenuaur gur or kocled, ac guedi y lad e doeht guir a koclet ema oy dial. Sef guir a doedant en tehuishocyon vdhunt: Clidno Eydin a Nud Hael va(b) Senillt a Mordaf Hael vab Seruari (= Serwan), a Retherc Hael vab Tudaual Tutclit, ac e doetant Aruon. Ac vrt lat Elidir en Aber Meuhedus en Aruon e lloskasant Aruon en rachor dial. Ac odhena e lluydhaus Ru(n) uab Maelcun a guir Guinet kanthau, ac e doethant hid eglan guerit en e kocled ac ena e buant en hir, en amresson pui a heley en e blaen druy auon Guerit, ac ena ed elleghus ru(*d*)n kenat hid eGhuynet e huybod puy byeufey e blaen. Rey a deueyt panyu Maeldaf henaf, pendeuic Penart ai barnus y guir Aruon. (C)yoruert uab Madauc druy aurdurdaud e keuarhuidyt ay kadarnaha panyhu ydno hen y guir e pist pendhu ac ena ethaethant guir Aruon en e blaen ac e buant da eno. Ac e kant Delyessin: Kikleu odures eu llaueneu, Can Run en rudhur bedineu, Guir Aruon rudyon eu redyeu. (ZCP XX, p. 75; see also J. G. Evans (ed.), *Facsimile of the Chirk Codex of the Welsh Laws* (Llanbedrog, 1909), and cf. WKC 238–46)
>
> 'Elidir Mwynfawr, a man of the North, was slain here [i.e. in Gwynedd], and after his death the Men of the North came here to avenge him. The men who came as their leaders were Clydno Eidyn and Nudd Hael son of Senyllt, and Mordaf Hael son of Serwa(n), and Rhydderch Hael son of Tudawal Tudglyd. And they came to Arfon, and because Elidir was slain at Aber Meuhedus in Arfon, they burned Arfon as a further revenge. And then Rhun son of Maelgwn and the men of Gwynedd with him, rose up in arms, and came to the bank of the Gwerydd in the North, and there they were long disputing who should take the lead through the river Gwerydd [i.e. the River Lune at Lancaster. See SC XVI/XVII, pp. 234–47]. And Rhun dispatched a messenger to Gwynedd to ascertain who were entitled to lead. Some say that Maeldaf the Elder the lord of Penardd adjudged it to the men of Arfon: (I)orwerth son of Madawg by the authority of his learning affirms that it was Idno Hen to the men of the black-headed shafts. And thereupon the men of Arfon went in the van, and were good there. And Taliesin sang: "I heard the clash of their blades, With Rhun in the rush of armies, The men

of Arfon of red spears".' (Cf. EWSP 236–7; also B XX, p. 238; and B XXVII, pp. 94–5)

Another version of this episode is found in the tract *Disgyniad Pendefigaeth Cymru*, *Nat. Lib. of Wales Journal* XVI, pp. 257–8. Certain passages quoted in the n. to triad 44 above state that the dispute over the Gwynedd succession arose out of *Rhun*'s alleged illegitimacy, but this interpretation is evidently a late comment on the story, since the question of legitimate or illegitimate birth is not one which would have held much validity for descent in early times. *Rhun*'s illegitimacy is alluded to by Elis Gruffydd: *a mab arall (i Faelgwn) o ordderch, yr hwn a elwyd Hrunn* (B XVIII, p. 57). *Rhun*'s mother is named in certain texts of *Achau'r Mamau*: *Mam Run ap Maelgwn oedd Walldwen vab Avallach* (Pen. 75, 30 = *(G)wenllian vch. Afallach*, Rawl. B 466 = EWGT 91 (28d)). VN[2] gives the following information about Rhun, in addition to that quoted in n. to triad 44: 'He (Rhun) took to his wife *Perwyr* (called the Comely), daughter of Rhun Rhyfeddfawr, a northern prince of the tribe of Coel Godebog, by whom he had a son called *Beli* who succeeded him, and a daughter called *Tymyr,* the wife of Hywel the Grand, and mother of *Alan,* the first of all the kings of Little Britain in France.' With the latter part of this passage may be compared Geoffrey of Monmouth's statement about the descent of the Breton kings from *Rhun ap Maelgwn*, HRB XII, 6. On Geoffrey's adaptation or misinterpretation of this genealogy see B. F. Roberts, B XXV, p. 288. The name of *Rhun*'s wife is derived from *Achau'r Mamau*: *Mam Beli ap Run ap Maelgw(y)n Gwynedd oedd Berwefr* (var. *Perwar) vz. Run ap Ryfedfawr* (see *Run*[4] below) *ap Enigu ap Masgwic kloff ap Kenau ap Koel Godeboc.* See EWGT 91 (28c). Cynddelw refers to the Gwynedd rulers as *hil run* (H 107.16 = CBT IV, no. 6.299) and *run blant* (H 89.32 = CBT IV no. 4.42), and to Gwynedd as *(g)wlad run ap maelgvn* (H 180.17 = CBT III, no. V.12, 17). It is believed that the name of the Roman fort of *Caerhun* in Gwynedd preserves the name of *Rhun ap Maelgwn* (J. Lloyd-Jones, *Enwau Lleoedd Sir Gaernarfon*, p. 37).

Rhun ap Maelgwn appears in Br. Rh.: *Pvy y gvr gvineu . . . Run uab Maelgvn gvyned, gvr y mae o vreint idav dyuot pavp y ymgynghor ac ef* (RM 160.8–10); and is a prominent figure at the court of Maelgwn at Degannwy in *Hanes Taliesin*; see Chw. T. 10, and P. K. Ford (ed.), *Ystorya Taliesin*. A note from an unknown source in VN links *Rhun* and Maelgwn with St Kentigern: 'In Maelgwn's court at Degannwy . . . seated over against the town of Conway, there fell a debate between Rhun the king's son and Cedig Draws, who struck the king's son with an ox-horn on his head, to the effusion of his blood, and afterwards fled to Kentigern for sanctuary.' (The source seems to have been a legend preserved at St Asaph's, of which a thirteenth-century Latin version has been preserved. See SEBC 317.)

Run[4] Ryueduaór 79, *Perwyr verch Run R.* 'R. of Great Wealth' (CLlH 132; PT 44; with *ryueduawr* cf. *mwynuawr* which has similar meaning).

Perwyr was wife of *Run*[3] m. *Maelgwn Gwynedd* (see n.). A further reference to *Run*[4] occurs in CLlH no. III.33: *Neu'm rodes i Run ryued(uawr) / Cant heit a chant ysgwydawr* (where the metre attests the emendation of R's *ryuedliawr* to *ryueduawr*). From the context of this *englyn* it may be concluded that the reference is to *Run* son of Urien Rheged, who is included in the lists of 'Plant Vrien m. Kynvarch' EWGT 87 (7). This *Run mab Urien* was identified (SEBC 25) with the *Run map Urbg(h)en* who according to *Ann. Cam.* and HB, ch. 63, took part in the baptism of King Edwin and the Northumbrians in the year 626–7: *Etguin baptizatus est. Et Run filius Urbgen baptizavit eum* (*Ann. Cam.* 626). Thus in some texts of HB an attempt has been made to reconcile this statement with Bede's account by explicitly identifying *Rhun* with Paulinus: *Run mep Urbeg(h)en id est Paulinus Eboracensis archiepiscopus baptizavit eos* (HB, ed. Mommsen, p. 207). In explanation of this passage it has been suggested that *Run* was the pre-ordination name of Paulinus, who according to Bede baptized Edwin (E. W. B. Nicholson, ZCP III, pp. 107–9). For the arguments for and against identifying *Run* with the *fi(li)us Urbagen* to whom the Chartres text of the HB (pre-1100) ascribed an early draft of this work, see Nicholson's discussion, and subsequently D. N. Dumville, '"Nennius" and the *Historia Brittonum*', SC X/XI (1975–6), pp. 78–95 (p. 93, n.2). For some deductions as to the possible facts underlying the references to *Rhun* in HB see K. Jackson in CS 49–55; and for an opposite view D. Dumville, WHR 8, pp. 345–54. The evidence is hardly sufficient to make it more than a conjecture: cf. WHR 17, pp. 10–11. Another possible reference to *Run* occurs in ch. 57 of HB, where it is said that a certain *Run* was grandfather to *Riemmelth* (= *Rieinmelth*) wife of Oswiu of Northumbria: for the identification suggested between this *Run* and *Run mab Urien* see Chadwick, *The Growth of Literature* I, p. 157. As the name *R(h)un* is of such frequent occurrence, the evidence for identifying *Run Ryuedua6r* with *Run m. Urien* is not definitive, and is doubted by Jenny Rowland, EWSP 86–7.

Ryderch Hael m. Tudwal Tutclyt 2, 43, 54; *Angharat Ton Uelen verch R.* 79, App. II, no. 8; App. III, no. 1. On the origin of this name, see CA 201. *Ryderc* occurs as an adjective for which Ifor Williams suggests the meaning 'noble'. On *Rederech* as the Cumbric form of the name, preserved in Jocelyn's *Life of St Kentigern*, see Jackson SEBC 319n. and idem, 'Angles and Britons in Northumbria and Cumbria' (O'Donnell Lectures (Cardiff, 1963) pp. 60–84).

Rhydderch Hael 'the Generous' was one of the most prominent rulers of the northern Britons during the latter part of the sixth century. See EWSP 109–10. A reference to *Rodercus filius Tothail qui in petra Cloithe regnavit* in the late seventh-century *Life of St Columba* by Adamnán (ed. Anderson, I, ch. 8) attests that *Rhydderch* was reigning in Strathclyde during the life-time of the saint, who died in 597. *Petra Cloithe* 'the rock of Clyde' is Dumbarton, i.e. *Dun Breatann* 'the Fortress of the Britons'. A tradition recorded by Jocelyn of

Furness claims that *Rhydderch* died in the same year as St Kentigern, i.e. in 612 (see n. to *Cyndeyrn Garthwys).* Rhydderch's pedigree is given in App. II and in Harl. Gen. VI (EWGT 10 (6)).

HB, ch. 63 lists *Riderch hen* along with *Urbgen* (= *Urien Rheged* n.); *Guallauc* (= *Gwallawc,* see n.) and *Morcant* (see n. to *Morgant Mwynua6r*) as the four north-British rulers who opposed the Anglian successors of Ida, apparently fighting together as a confederacy. With the epithet *Hen* 'the Old', which is bestowed on *Rhydderch* both here and in the Harl. Gen., cf. the same epithet as bestowed in App. II upon *Rhydderch*'s own ancestor Dyfnwal Hen, and the additional instances cited in nos. 8–10. Perhaps this epithet originally had a dynastic connotation which is not now readily apparent: Coel Hen and Dyfnwal Hen are the names of the traditional progenitors of the two chief ruling dynasties of the northern Britons in the sixth century in App. II. In other sources *Rhydderch* normally bears the epithet *Hael* which is bestowed on him in triad 2 (see n.). *Retherc hael [sic]* is named in the Chirk codex among the north-British rulers who went to Arfon to avenge Elidir Mwynfawr (see n. to *Run*[3] *m. Maelgwn*), and this epithet is also frequently bestowed on him in medieval poetry. It is latinized *largus* in Geoffrey of Monmouth's *Vita Merlini* (ed. B Clarke, l. 730).

There are a number of allusions to *Rhydderch Hael* in the early poetry that refers to the story of Myrddin Wyllt. *Rhydderch* is mentioned in the *Cyvoesi* (RBP col. 577.18*),* the *Avallenau* and *Oianeu* (LlDC nos. 16, 17 etc.), and in *Peiryan Vaban* (B XIV, p. 105, l. 36). The allusions in the LlDC poems indicate that in this story *Rhydderch* was the ruler whom Myrddin feared beyond all others, and from whom he lurked in hiding, after the battle of Arfderydd, in Coed Celyddon. But no definite statement is to be found in any early source to the effect that *Rhydderch* was himself present at this battle (see n. to *Arfderydd,* triad 84), though this is claimed both in VN[2] and in the account found in the *Vita Merlini* of a battle which plainly corresponds to *Arfderydd,* and at which *Rodarcus rex C(u)mbrorum* is depicted as being a protagonist (*Vita Merlini* l. 33). In the *Vita* Merlin's sister, Ganieda, is depicted as being the wife of *Rodarcus.*

Chadwick suggested (*Early Scotland*, pp. 151–2) that an alliance subsisted between the Britons of Strathclyde and the contemporary ruler of Scottish Dál Riada, *Aedán mac Gabráin* (see n.), during and before the period of *Rhydderch*'s career, and that the termination of this alliance is reflected in Aedan's epithet *bradawc* 'the Treacherous', which is bestowed on him in several Ml.W. sources. A tradition of hostility between Aedan and *Rhydderch* seems to be reflected in triad 54, and is confirmed by an allusion in the poem *Peiryan Vaban* (B XIV, p. 105, l. 52).

The late twelfth-century *Life of St Kentigern* by Jocelyn of Furness (ed. A. P. Forbes, Edinburgh 1874) represents *Rhydderch* (*Rederech*) as the champion of Christianity in north Britain, and as the supporter of St Kentigern, patron of the see of Glasgow. According to this same source (ch.

29), *Rhydderch* had been baptized in Ireland by the disciples of St Patrick. An episode in ch. 37 in which *Rhydderch*, with the aid of the saint, satisfies the irrational request made by a visiting *joculator* (probably a bard is intended) for a dish of mulberries, *recte* 'blackberres' (?), in the middle of winter may owe its origin to the tradition of *Rhydderch*'s celebrated generosity. (K. Jackson points out that a corresponding tale is attached to the Irish king *Guaire Aidne* of Connacht; see M. Dillon, *The Cycles of the Kings*, p. 93.) This is the only anecdote illustrative of *Rhydderch*'s proverbial generosity that has come down: there may have once been in existence a number of similar stories which were developed to account for his epithet *hael*; examples LlDC no. 17.4, 6, 8. For an entirely fanciful explanation of this epithet see App. III, no. 1, and introduction, p. cv n. (In a late genealogy (EWGT 89 (18)), *Rhydderch* bears the epithet *claer ac ardderchddrud* 'brilliant and splendid-brave'. On this and similar epithets preserved in the genealogies, see below, n. on *Selyf*.)

The following poetic references to *Rhydderch* are found in addition to those listed in n. to triad 2:

LlDC no. 18.41 etc.: *in abererch (bet) riterch hael.* (The site is probably Afon *Erch* in Caernarfonshire.)

Prydydd y Moch: *Mordaf, Nut, Ryderch—yn detyf rot i* (CBT V, no. 2.30 = H 264.2); *Hael Ryderch am eurwut, Hael Mordaf, hael mawrdec Nut* (ibid. V, no. 11.54–5 = H. 300.26–8); *wrth Uordaf a Nut, pan roted-ruteur. A rhydderch afneued* (ibid. V, no. 26.105–6 = H 288.11–14).

Einion ap Gwgon: *Ysymy Ryterch, rotyad (*CBT VI no. 18.91n. = H 52.29)

Bleddyn Fardd: *rydderch roddyon* (H 79.7 = CBT VII, no. 53.27n.).

Gr. ap Maredudd: *arvyd orchwylyon ryderch heilyeu* (RBP col. 1204.31); *Ryderch ganmawl hawl rwylyeu ymgywrd* (RBP col. 1315.41), Ll. Goch ap Meurig Hen: RBP col. 1302.31 = GLlG no. 3.41–2, Justus Llwyd: RBP col. 1364.32 = YB XVII 70.2; cf. 72.61.

See GDG no. 7.10; no. 15.42–3; no. 25.3, as evidence that the poet was familiar with TYP. For evocations of *Rhydderch*'s proverbial generosity, see also GIG no. XIV.76–7n., 79.

According to O. E. S. Crawford (*Antiquity*, XVII, p. 22), *Rhydderch*'s name is preserved in that of Carrutherstown, near Dumfries (= Caer Ruther in 1350) where there is an earthwork believed to denote the site of his 'castle' or *llys.*

Rhygenydd Ysgolhaig, App. III, nos. 10, 11. 'R. the Cleric.' The correct form of this name remains in doubt (see *varia lecta*) but *Rhygenydd* or *R(h)egenydd* is attested by the greater number of manuscripts. D. N. Dumville points out to me the close resemblance between this name and the *Renchidus episcopus,* described in the 'Nennian' recension of HB ch. 63 as one of the two bishops responsible for the statement that Rhun ab Urien baptized the Northumbrians; see his article SC X/XI, p. 82 and nn. 1 and 5. Neither the Latin nor the Welsh names appear to be attested in any other source.

Rybrawst (wife of Brychan Brycheiniog) 96. O.W. *Ribraust* (VSB 315, §14; see n. to triad).

Sanddef Bryd Angel, App. IV, no. 7. 'S. Angel's Form.'

CO l. 228: *A Sande Pryt Angel—ny dodes neb y wayw yndaw yGhamlan rac y decket*. On the survivors from Camlan see n. to triad 59.

For further instances of the name *Sanddef* see LL 279.7; CLlH no. I.37c. In the last instance *Sandde(f)* is the name of a son of Llywarch Hen, who is named also in the lists of the sons of Llywarch; see CLlH xxx, Pen. 127, p. 93, etc. In at least one version of this list (LD I, xx; B III, p. 37, quoting the *Hanesyn Hen*), Llywarch Hen's son receives the epithet *Sandde bryd angel*: probably in recollection of the triad of the escapers from *Camlan* in the form in which this is given in *Culhwch ac Olwen*. Cf. EWGT 86 (5) for 'Plant Llywarch Hen'.

Sawyl Ben Uchel (m. Pabo Post Prydein) 23, App. II, no. 4. 'S. High-Head.' See n. to *Pabo Post Prydein. Sawyl* < **Safwyl* < *Samuelis*.

Harl. Gen. XIX: *Samuil Pennissel* ('Low-Head') *map Pappo Post Priten.* VSB 320 (13) (= EWGT 56 (13) etc.): *Assa* (i.e. St Asaph) *m. Sawyl Bennuchel m. Pabo Post Prydein, a Guenassed uerch Rein o Rieinwc e vam.* Elis Gruffydd's *Chronicle* claims that an (unnamed) daughter of *Sawl Benuchel* was married to Maelgwn Gwynedd (B XVIII, p. 57). The genealogies assert that *Sawyl* was a contemporary of Urien Rheged, and that like Urien he was fourth in descent from Coel Hen. His epithet is sufficient reason for his inclusion in triad 23 (cf. EWSP 107n.).

Geoffrey of Monmouth gives this name as *Samuil Penissel* (HRB III, 19), which indicates a source similar to the Harl. Gens. (On Geoffrey of Monmouth's indebtedness to such a genealogical source, see S. Piggott, *Antiquity* 15, pp. 269–86.) Since the genealogy is our oldest source for this name, it seems possible that *Penisel* 'Low Head' is the earlier form of the epithet, although elsewhere this is consistently *Penuchel* 'High Head'. (EWGT 32–3 quotes from a tract in the Book of Leinster (and a number of other manuscripts) on the mothers of Irish saints the following entry: *Deichter ingen Muredaig Muinderg rig Ulaid, mathair Matóc et episcopi Santain meic Samuel Chendisil (sic)* 'Deichter, d. of Muiredach Muinderg, king of Ulster, mother of Matoc and of bishop Santan, sons of Samuel Chendisil', where Cendisel is the cognate of Penisel.) In the Life of *St Cadoc* (VSB 58) *Sauuil Pennuchel* figures as a *rex tyrannus* who is swallowed by the earth in retribution for his opposition to the saint. Cf. in addition to the above references Justus Llwyd: *Hi a vu yngrassavu sawyl ben uchel* (RBP col. 1365.16 = YB XVII, 71.37).

Seidi 9 (WR). See n. to *Cadr(i)eith m. Portha6r Gadw.*

Seitwed 58: *Llewei verch Seitwed* (see n.).

Selyf[1] (Selef) m. Dafydd Broffwyd 49 (Pen. 77). 'Solomon son of David.' *Selyf* < *Solomon,* the Old Testament ruler. In medieval sources Solomon became renowned as a great magician, holding sway over all living creatures by means of his magic ring. The composition of numerous books of magic was attributed to him. His legend became immensely popular in medieval Europe, and this accounts for the popularity of *Selyf, Salomon* as a personal name in Celtic countries. Prominent in the literature concerning him are dialogues or competitions in wisdom; and the nucleus of this genre is to be found in the dialogues between Solomon and the queen of Sheba (I Kings x.1–3; 2 Chron. ix) and with Hiram of Tyre (2 Chron. ii). Two poetic dialogues of this kind exist in O.E., and there are indications that the Latin original of these poems was transmitted to England from an Irish ecclesiastical source (R. J. Menner, *The Poetical Dialogues of Solomon and Saturn*, pp. 21–6). As a disputant with Solomon, the name of Saturn is interchangeable with *Marcolfus* (see n. to *Marcwlph*).

References in early Welsh sources to the proverbial wisdom of *Selyf m. Dafydd* are cited in n. to triad 47 (cf. also GC no. 1.61n.; no. 7.192n., 213, 228n.). In the later poetry the following allusions occur:

> *O bu ddoethaf mab Dafydd / Ylisav fal Selav sydd* (GO no. XLII.45–6); IGE[2] 116.5; DGG no. XXI.25–8; HCLl no. XXI.18. Cf. also SG(i) 131.10 ff.: *Selef uab dauyd. yr hwnn a vu gyflawn o bop doethineb. ac o bop doethineb yn gymeint ac na allei dyn marwawl wybot mwy, kanys ef a wydyat gwyrtheu pob maen a phob llyssewyn, ac anyan y syr ar sygneu, hyt na wydyat neb mwy noc efo onyt duw ehun.* 'S. son of David, who was replete with all wisdom . . . so that no mortal man could know more; since he knew the virtues of every stone and herb, and the nature of the stars and the signs (of the zodiac); so that no one knew more than he except God himself.'
>
> *Amlyn ac Amic* (ed. J. G. Evans, p. 4): *ev a rodes duv (i'r mab) . . . amylder o synhwyr, a doethineb, a donyeu, val y gelwit ev ymhob gwlat yn eil Selyv o achavs y doethineb* 'God bestowed on the boy . . . abundance of intelligence and wisdom and talents, so that in all countries he was called a second Solomon because of his wisdom.'

Selyf[2] m. Kenan Garrwyn 25, 43 WR; *Arouan uard seleu ap kynan* (LlDC no. 6.7). See n. to *Kynan[2] Garrwyn.*

Harl. Gen. XXII (= EWGT 12 (22)): *Selim map Cinan map Brocmayl* (= *Jes. Gen.* XVIII: *Seliph m. Kynan garwin*).

Ann. Cam. 613 (= 616): *Gueith Cairlegion et ibi cecidit Selim fili(us) Cinan* = *Ann. Tig.: Cath Caire Legion, ubi sancti occisi sunt, et cecidit Solon mac Conain rex Bretanorum . . . Etalfraidh uictor erat, qui post statim obit* (RC

XVII, p. 171). For *Gueith Cairlegion* (the battle of Chester) see n. to *Gueith Perllan Vangor,* triad 60. At this battle it is probable that *Selyf m. Cynan* was the leader of the Welsh forces, since as J. E. Lloyd points out 'as representative of the ancient line of the kings of Powys, he was the natural defender of the valley of the Dee' (HW I, 181).

Since the genealogies represent the descendants of *Selyf* as ruling in Powys after him, little significance can be attached to the episode in *Buchedd Beuno* in which the saint lays a curse on the sons of *Selyf ap Cynan* to the effect that their posterity shall not inherit the kingdom (VSB 17–18; cf. also ibid. 288). Nevertheless, there is some doubt as to whether the descendants of *Selyf* did in fact rule in Powys after him: in a note on Harl. Gen. XXII and *Jes. Gen.* XXVII, P. C. Bartrum in EWGT 128–9 prefers the version of Gen. 22 which claims that the later rulers of Powys were descended from his brother Eiludd, thus corroborating the story of St Beuno's curse on *Selyf*'s line, but disagreeing with *Jes.* XVIII which traces the descent of Rhodri Mawr through *Selyf ap Cynan*. An echo of *Selyf*'s reputation for prowess is perhaps to be discovered in the epithet *sarffgadeu* 'serpent of battles (armies)' which he bears in *Bonedd y Saint* (EWGT 66 (79)) and in some later genealogies (EWGT 100 (k); 113 (f)). In a review of EWGT in WHR IV (1968), 179, I suggested that such eulogistic epithets as *sarffgadeu* and *ardderchddrud* (for *Rhydderch Hael*, see n. above) betray their origin as belonging to the vocabulary of bardic encomium, and therefore as being possibly derived from early praise-poetry addressed to the princes who bear them. Cynddelw refers to the men of Powys as *canaon selyf, seirff cadeu* 'Selyf's whelps, serpents of battle' (H 166.15 = CBT III, no. 11.9n.).

Br. Rh. 18.22: *Selyf uab kynan garwyn o powys* (RM 159.4).

EWGT 63 (62): *Dona yMon m. Selyf m. Kynan garwyn m. Brochuael ysgithrawc m. Kyngen m. Cadell dyrnllwch* etc.

Senyllt 2: *Nud Hael m. S.* (see n.). CA ll. 561–2: *Nid ef borthi gwarth gorsed / senyllt ae lestri llawn med* 'The court of Senyllt would not suffer shame, with its vessels full of mead'. On this passage see OSPG 135. The court of the warrior Heilyn is here compared with that of *Senyllt*, the father of *Nudd Hael* (see n.), for its liberality; the 'shame' would have been for stinting its supplies of mead.

Jes. Gen. XIX (= EWGT 46 (19)) traces the descent of Rhodri Mawr to *Run m. Neidaon m. senilth hael. Tryd hael o'r gogled. Senilth m. Dingat m. tutwavl m. Edneuet m. dunavt m. maxen wledic* (= Harl. Gen. IV: *Run map Nethon map Senill map Dinacat map Tutagual map Eidinet map Anthun map Maxim Guletic*). Evidently the names *Neidaon, Nwython* in these genealogies are to be equated with the *Nudd* of the triad. It is interesting to find, however, that the *Jes. Gen.* implies that it is not Nudd but his father *Senyllt* who is intended as one of the *Tri Hael* (see n. to triad 2); and the allusion in the *Gododdin* to the liberality of *Senyllt*'s court may be regarded as corroborative of this version of the triad, in so far as it shows that *Senyllt*'s liberality was as renowned as that of his son (see CA. 211). Although it cannot be proved that *Senyllt* the father of Nudd Hael is intended in the poem, the chronological indications favour this identification. For this family's proverbial generosity see nn. to *Nudd Hael* and to triad 2.

Seruan 2: *Mordaf Hael m. S.*; App. II, no. 9: *Seruan m. Kedic. Serwan* < *Servandus.* With reference to another character the name occurs in the O.W. form *Serguan* in Harl. Gen. XVI (= EWGT 11 (16)).

Serygei 6ydel 62, EWGT p. 93. 'S. the Irishman.' Sir John Rhŷs suggested that this name was a corrupt form of the Norse *Sitric* 'clumsily torn out of its Latin context' (*Celtic Britain* (1904), p. 246; see also to the same effect Kuno Meyer, THSC 1895–6, p. 62n.; C. O'Rahilly, *Ireland and Wales: their Historical and Literary Relations* (London, 1924), p. 70). But whatever the constituent elements of the name *Serygei,* it is more likely that it is a corruption of an Irish name than of a Norse name, and I cannot therefore regard this name as evidence *against* the antiquity of the tradition preserved in triad 62 as to fighting with the Irish in Anglesey *circa* 500. (See introduction, p. lvi, n. 59; and n. to triad 62.)

Sibli Doeth 49. 'S. the Wise' (daughter of Priam). Triad 49 existed in an older form which did not include this name (see n.); and the appearance of *Sibli (= Sibilla)* in the version of R may be accounted for as due to the influence of *Proffwydoliaeth Sibli Doeth,* which is preserved both in the *Llyfr Gwyn* and the *Llyfr Coch* (W folios 12–13, R cols. 571–7). This text begins with the words: *Sibli oed uerch y priaf urenhin, o eccuba y mam gvreic priaf,* etc. (*Rep.* II, 4). The *Oracula Sibyllina* consisted of Jewish and Christian adaptations of the Greek Sibylline verses, and were popular throughout Europe in the Middle Ages (see M. E. Griffiths, *Early Vaticination in Welsh,* pp. 14–17, 41–4). The versions which have come down in Welsh are translated from a form of the *Oracula* which was composed at least as early as the mid-eleventh century.

Geoffrey of Monmouth refers to the *uaticinia sibille* (HRB IX, 17 = *daroganneu Sibilla* BD 165.4). In later Welsh sources *Sibyl* came to be a generic term for an enchantress (D. J. Bowen, *Barddoniaeth yr Uchelwyr,* p. 109).

Solor m. Murthach 15. See n. to *Murthach.* Since *Murthach* = *Ir. Murchad,* it is natural to look for an Irish original for *Solor*. D. N. Dumville points out to me that *Solor* probably stands for *Solon,* the Irish form of *Solomon*, reflecting the common scribal error of confusion between *r* and *n,* frequent in Insular script at all periods. He draws my attention to the form given in the Irish annals *Solon mac Conain* = *Selim fili(us) Cinan* in *Ann. Cam.* 613.

Sompson Gadarn 47. 'Samson the Strong.' For references by Prydydd y

Moch, see n. to triad 47. Huw Cae Llwyd: *Samson, greulon gwroliaeth / o dwyll ei wraig dall yr aeth* (HCLl no. LVIII.17–18).

Talhaearn 33 (W), 34 (Pen. 51). Both triads refer to the slaying of Aneirin. It is possible that the allusions to *Talhaearn* in both preserve in a corrupt form a reference to one of the famous *Cynfeirdd* whom HB names in company with Aneirin, i.e. *Talhaern tataguen* 'T. Father of Inspiration' (HB, ch. 62; for the passage see n. to *Aneirin*). Two other references to the poet are found in a poem, BT 20, *Angar Kyvyndawt,* which belongs to the *Taliesin* story. There are allusions to Taliesin, Cian and Aneirin (see CA lxxxvii), and to *ieith talhayarn* 'the speech of T.' (BT 20.4), as well as to *Talhayarn yssyd mvyhaf y sywedyd* 'T. who is the greatest of the wise men' (BT 21.16). Pen. 51's version of triad 34 may have been influenced by triad 33; though it suggests the possibility of a lost story of rivalry between *Talhaearn* and Aneirin; see introduction, p. xxx. For a suggestion as to *Talhaearn*'s role, and for the survival of his name in Gwynedd place-names, and for his possible connection with Maelgwn Gwynedd, see R. G. Gruffydd, SC XXIV/XXV, p.10.

Tangwn 16: *Riueri m. Tangwn* (see n.).

Taliessin 87. See nn. to *Auaon m. T., Keritwen* and *Aneiryn Gwa6tryd Mechdeyrn Beird* (for the passages in HB and in the *Gododdin* which name both poets together).

BT 48.7: *a march taliesin* (see introduction, pp. lxxxii).
CO l. 214: *A Theliessin Penn Beird.*

HB includes *Taliessin* together with (A)neirin among the British poets who flourished in north Britain during the second half of the sixth century, and who were contemporary with *Urien Rheged* (see n.) and the other British kings who fought against Ida of Northumbria and his successors during this period. The fourteenth-century *Book of Taliesin* includes, with much later material, a small group of poems which it is possible to regard as constituting the authentic work of the poet *Taliesin*, whose name and reputation were known to the HB compiler. These are early bardic eulogies addressed to Urien and his son Owain, to *Gwallawg ap Lleennawc* (see n.), and to *Cynan Garwyn* of Powys (see n.). One of these poems offers a suggestion that *Taliesin* came only as a visitor to the court of Urien (BT 65.9–11); and triad 11 names *Tristvard*, not *Taliesin*, as the bard personally attached to Urien, and Dygynnelw as the bard of Owain. Ifor Williams has suggested (*Bywgraffiadur* 874; PT lix–lxiii) that *Taliesin* may have been a native of Powys; hence it is that the group of early poems referred to includes an address to Cynan Gar(r)wyn, the contemporary ruler of Powys in the latter part of the sixth century, as well as two poems to *Gwallawc* (see n.). The Powys origin of the poet appears to be reflected in the (much later) story about him, *Chwedl Taliesin*, which associates his origin with the district of Bala in Meirionnydd (see below). If it can be accepted that all the poems in question are the work of the same poet and that this supposition as to *Taliesin*'s origin is correct, it gives evidence for the wide area covered by a poet of the early period in his journeys between one patron and another—journeys such as we know to have been made within the limits of Wales itself by the *Gogynfeirdd*, and within the whole of the Gaelic-speaking world by the early medieval Irish poets. (For a possible reference to a poet's journey from Cornwall to Gwynedd during the early period, see n. to triad 69b.) The later traditions about the life and activities of *Taliesin*, which were elaborated in Wales from the ninth century onwards, depict him as a visitor to *Maelgwn Gwynedd* (see n.) at Degannwy. But Maelgwn was dead before the middle of the sixth century, so that it is barely possible that the poet *Taliesin* can have had direct contact with him (see Chw. T. 8).

These later traditions are alluded to in certain of the poems in BT, though the story to which they refer is preserved in complete form only in a comparatively late version, in the hand of the sixteenth-century Elis Gruffydd (see edition and discussion by P. K. Ford, *Ystorya Taliesin*). On the manuscripts and variant versions of *Hanes Taliesin* see also P. K. Ford in EC XIV (1974–5), pp. 451–60, who published from NLW 13075B a version of the tale by Llywelyn Siôn of Llangewydd, *circa* 1590—a text which is clear and readable, and is in the editor's opinion preferable to that of J. Jones in Pen. 111, and offers certain preferable variants in the personal names (see nn. above to *Keritwen* and to *Creirwy merch Keritwen*). It is evident that stories about *Taliesin* were current in north Wales in the ninth and tenth centuries (cf. LEWP 59–60) and reference should also be made to the *ymddiddan* or dialogue in *englynion* between *Taliesin* and Ugnach fab Wydno (LlDC no. 36), which appears to be connected loosely with the story of *Taliesin*'s contention with Maelgwn's poets, as this is found in *Ystorya Taliesin.* For an edition and discussion of the poem, see Brynley Roberts, *Ast. H.* 318–25. The story tells of the magic drops of poetic inspiration received by the boy *Gwion Bach* from Ceridwen's cauldron; of the successive transformations through which he passed, to be reborn later as *Taliesin*; of his fostering by Gwyddno Garanhir's son Elffin; and of his successful contest with Maelgwn's poets at the court of Degannwy. (For Ceridwen, see further, M. E. Haycock, 'Cadair Ceridwen' in R. I. Daniel *et al.*, *Cyfoeth y Testun* (Caerdydd, 2003), pp. 148–172.) The fact that the essentials of this story are of much earlier date than the sixteenth century is witnessed by the poems in BT, which evidently relate to the story in an earlier version than that which has survived, and also by allusions made by the *Gogynfeirdd* to *Taliesin*'s contest with Maelgwn's bards, through the means of which *Taliesin* succeeded in liberating his master Elffin. (The reference in the Chirk Codex of the Laws (*circa* 1200) to *Taliesin*'s presence on Rhun's punitive expedition into north Britain reflects the persistence of the tradition that associated *Taliesin* with Maelgwn's family; see n. to *Run*[3] m. Maelgwn.) Prydydd y Moch evidently knew of the story: *rwyf bardoni yn dull talyessin yn dillwng elfin* (H 278.6–7 = CBT V, no. 25.3). Phylip Brydydd referred to Taliesin's contest with the poets in a poem which is presented as a part of a contest with the *gofeirdd* or 'inferior poets' as to which of them should present a poem to Rhys Ieuanc at the Christmas festivities at Llanbadarn Fawr in 1176. For this contest see T. Gwynn Jones, THSC 1913–14, pp. 290–4, and the subsequent discussion of the poem by M. E. Owen in CBT VI, pp. 164–7, and N. A. Jones and Huw Pryce, *Yr Arglwydd Rhys* (Caerdydd, 1996): *pan vu elfin yghywryssed vaelgwn* (H 228.13 = CBT VI no. 15.33n., *hengerdd telessin*). In contrast to these allusions, Cynddelw shows his awareness that *Taliesin* had addressed poetry to members of the house of Cynfarch, i.e. *Urien Rheged* and *Owain* (see nn.), and he shows by the following allusion that the historical tradition about *Taliesin* had survived to his day alongside the fictional one (to which Cynddelw makes no reference): *Ny bu warthlef kert kynuerching werin / o benn talyessin bartrig beirtrig* (H 145.11–12 = CBT III, no. 24.154n.) 'Not a voice of shame was the song of the army of Cynfarch, from the mouth of Taliesin, versed in the lore of bardic learning'. The historical tradition was indeed known at a still later date than this since, in a poem to Ifor Hael, Dafydd ap Gwilym compares his patron's munificence with that of *neuadd Reged* for it bestows on him the blessing of *Taliesin* (GDG no. 9.34–5); Iolo Goch then compares the home of the Tuduriaid at Penmynydd to *ail drigiant aelwyd Reged* (IGE² 16.24). Similarly Guto'r Glyn: *Taliesin . . . hwyliawdd a'i gerdd . . . hyd lys Urien* (GGl no. XCI.1–6). Other references by the *cywyddwyr* are to *Chwedl Taliesin*: *I Elffin Taliesin las / A fu fardd* (GTA II, no. CX.51–2); *ni wyppai neb buw'n i ol / nef i'r awen ai'n freuach / nog awen bair gwion bach* (GDE 143.10–12); Wm. Llŷn in his elegy to Gruffudd Hiraethog: *Gwn na bu er Gwion Bach / Gau ar synnwyr gresynach* (D. J. Bowen, *Gruffudd Hiraethog a'i Oes*, 78.85–6). Thus Llywelyn ab y Moel states that the *awen* was released in the court of Maelgwn, at the time when *Taliesin* freed Elffin: *Ac yn armes Taliesin / Drud yn llys Faelgwn fu'r drin / Pan ollyngawdd, medrawdd mwy, / Elffin o eurin aerwy* (IGE² 167.25–9). *Taliesin* is celebrated as a pattern of bardic eloquence (GO no. VIII.51; no. XLII.28; GDG no. 10.34, etc.) and as a magician (*dewin ddiwael*, GGl no. LXXXII.63); and his name is frequently coupled with that of *Myrddin* (GDG no. 118.21–4; DN 110.15; IGE² 324.26–7; 159.9, 16). For further references see n. to *Myrddyn Wyllt*.

There is evidence, independent of the traditions incorporated in *Chwedl Taliesin*, that the poet figured in stories of a semi mythological character at an early date. *Mabinogi Branwen* names *Talyessin* among the seven men who escaped from Ireland after the death of Bendigeidfran (PKM 44.26). It was suggested by Thomas Jones (B XVII, p. 246 = 'Early Evolution', 14–15) that the story of Brân's expedition to Ireland is a 'rationalization' of the episode alluded to in *Preiddeu Annwfn* (BT 54): a raid made upon *Annwfn* by Arthur and his men in which the speaker (probably *Taliesin* himself) claims to have been present.

During the tenth and eleventh centuries *Taliesin* gained a popular reputation as a prophet, as is witnessed by the number of prophetic poems attributed to him which are included in the *Book of Taliesin,* and by the dialogue poem, LlDC no. 1, in which the two *Cynfeirdd* Myrddin and *Taliesin* are represented as prophesying future events. A knowledge of this poem seems to be reflected in Geoffrey of Monmouth's *Vita Merlini* (see n. to *Myrddyn Wyllt*), in which *Telgesinus [sic]* discourses with Merlinus on geography and natural phenomena—evidently Geoffrey of Monmouth had obtained some knowledge of the current medieval conception of *Taliesin*'s omniscience, as this is reflected in the poems which belong to *Chwedl Taliesin.* See further Ifor Williams, *Canu Taliesin* (trans. J. E. C. Williams, *The Poems of Taliesin*); Marged Haycock, 'Astudiaethau ar Rai Agweddau ar Lyfr Taliesin' (Ph.D. Aberystwyth); eadem, 'Preiddeu Annwn and the Figure of Taliesin', SC XVIII/XIX; P. K. Ford, *Ystorya Taliesin.*

Tallwch 19, 21, 26: *Drystan m. Tallwch* (see n.). *Tallwch* is unknown in Welsh or in Continental sources outside TYP and the derived *Ystorya Trystan* (but cf. *Drystan eil March* in triad no. 73). *Talorgan* son of *Drostan* was the name of a Pictish king *circa* 780, listed in the Pictish king-list (F. T. Wainwright, *The Problem of the Picts*, p. 22; Chadwick, *Early Scotland*, p. 16). French sources give *Loonois (= Lothian)* as the name of Tristan's patrimony: if this represents an original north-British source, it is the more understandable that the names of both *Drystan* and *Tallwch* should have been borrowed from neighbouring Pictland, in spite of the absence of exact phonetic equivalence between the two. For instances of the infiltration of Pictish names into early Welsh sources, cf. *Gwrgwst Letlwm a Dyfnarth y uab* (CO l. 993n.) and Jackson's discussion of these names in YB XII, p. 21, and also the Pictish forms which have been discerned in the Strathclyde royal genealogy, EWGT 10 (5), and Bartrum's n. on these, p. 126. J. E. Caerwyn Williams and D. P. Kirby reject the possibility of any connection subsisting between this name and the Pictish *Talorc*, SC X/XI (1975–6), p. 480: 'Any idea that the name *Tallwch* represents the Pictish *Talorc* or its diminutive *Talorcan* would seem to be unfounded, especially in view of the forms *Talorg*, *Talorgg*, *Talorggan*, etc. (see EWGT 126, n.5). Yet there are numerous parallels to the phenomenon of loose approximation, rather than of strict philological correspondence, affecting the borrowing of personal names from one language to another and such borrowing cannot be discounted' (cf. Padel in CMCS 1, p. 55).

Tegeu Eururon 66 (Pen. 47). *T. Eurvron verch Nudd Llawhael* 71 (Pen. 267), 88; *mantell T.*, App. III, no. 14; 'T. Gold-Breast.' See n. to *Caradawc*[2] *Vreichvras*. The only full version in Welsh so far discovered of the story of *Tegau* and her chastity-testing mantle (but without the complementary tale of her encounter with the serpent), which alone explains her epithet 'gold breast', is published by Graham Thomas, 'Chwedlau Tegau Eurfron a Thristfardd, bardd Urien Rheged', B XXIV (1970), pp. 1–9, from NLW 2288, a MS. of Gwallter Mechain (late eighteenth century). The story runs as follows:

> Arthur's sister was wife to Urien Rheged [= *Morgain la Fée*?] and she was killed in sorcery. She sent to Arthur's court three chastity-testing objects—a mantle, a drinking-horn, and some slices of bacon [these last would choke the husband of an unchaste wife, and are evidently the counterpart of the carving-knife referred to in the English versions]. Only Tegau was successful in the mantle-test, and only her [un-named] husband in the other two tests.

Graham Thomas points out that details of the tale find their closest parallel in the English ballad of *The Boy and the Mantle.* In spite of the late date of the manuscript, the numerous references to *Tegau*'s mantle by the *cywyddwyr* make it plain that the story was well known in Wales. Additional references were cited by Eurys Rowlands in his edition of the *Tri Thlws ar Ddeg* (LlC V, pp. 66–8). To these Graham Thomas makes further additions, including a reference in *Breuddwyd Gruffydd ab Adda* (cf. D. Gwenallt Jones, *Yr Areithiau Pros*, 18), together with some references in *cywyddau* to Caradoc (Freichfras) as *Tegau*'s husband. A note appended in a sixteenth-century MS. to a *cywydd merch* by Dafydd ab Edmwnd supplies a slight variant: *Tegau eurfron gwraig Cariadog freuchfras cystal i gair a phenelope. iddi roedd tri thlws ni wasnaethynt i neb ond iddi i hun i mantell i phiol, ai chyllell.* 'T. Gold-Breast, wife of C. Strong-Arm; her reputation was as good as that of Penelope; she had three treasures which would serve no one but her: her mantle, her cup, and her carving-knife.'

An additional instance in which the name of '*Tegau*' is used in verse as a standard of comparison, with a possible reference to her mantle, is found in an *englyn enghreifftiol*, evidently quoted from a love-poem, in the Pen. 20 version of the Bardic Grammar (GP 47): *Nyt gwiw gouyn lliw llewychweith—Tegeu, / Tegwch Mon aeth ymeith, / Yn y del, meu ryvel meith, / Bryt v'anwylyt Von eilweith* 'It avails not to ask the colour of the shining workmanship of Tegau; the beauty of Môn has gone away—until there come—long warfare is mine—my darling's form to Môn once more'.

Tegau's name is not recorded in reference to any other character. The earliest Welsh references to her (without epithet) date from the fourteenth century: there is a reference to her in a poem addressed to a girl by Goronwy Ddu ap Tudur (1320–70) . . . *neud tau gvynbryd Tegau* (MA[2] 337, 627, 2), similarly Gr. ap Maredudd: *kymavt Eigr kame(u) Degeu* (RBP col. 1326.37). Dafydd ap Gwilym employs her name six times as a standard of comparison (GDG no. 52.1: *Tegau eurfalch*, no. 53.36: *Tegau dwf*, etc.). The fact that *Tegau* is unknown in any earlier Welsh source gives particular interest to a line in the thirteenth-century English lyric *Annot and Johon*, which gives her name in a passage in which the heroine is compared in succession to a number of the heroines of romance: *Trewe as Tegeu in tour, as Wyrwein* (= *Garwen?*) *in wede* (Carlton-Brown, *English Lyrics of the Thirteenth Century*, p. 138, l. 3;

see R. M. Wilson, *The Lost Literature of Mediaeval England*, p. 143). The suggested identification with the Welsh *Tegau* is the more likely since the same stanza contains an allusion to Caradog in the line *Cud ase cradoc in court carf the brede*—an allusion which recalls the carving test in which Caradog distinguishes himself in the English ballad *The Boy and the Mantle* (see above).

Two distinct and perhaps originally unconnected stories are attached in Old French sources to the mistress of *Carados Briebras* (= *Caradawc Vreichvras,* see n.). Neither of these has been preserved in a Welsh form, yet both were evidently known in Wales, so that they must either represent Welsh traditions of Caradog and his mistress which were borrowed into French, or else they bear witness to a widespread knowledge of French romance in medieval Wales. These tales account for *Tegau*'s epithet *Eurfron* 'Gold-Breast', as well as for her constant portrayal in the triads and elsewhere as a model of chastity and fidelity. These tales are:

(i) The story of a chastity test, located at Arthur's court, in which the fidelity of each of the ladies present was put to the proof by means of a magic horn, or mantle, or both. The horn would spill wine upon any man whose wife was unchaste; the mantle was suited in size and becoming only to a wife who was chaste. The simple horn test is found attached to Carados in Biket's *Lai du Cor* (ed. F. Wulff; see ATC 17, 28, 98) written *circa* 1150, in which the scene is laid at Cirencester. The mantle test is associated with the wife of Carados Briebras in *Le Manteau Mal Taillé,* a short French romance of the late twelfth century (ed. *Romania* XIV, pp. 358 ff.). Caradog's mantle was to be seen at Dover in the fifteenth century according to Caxton's preface to his edition of Malory's *Morte D'Arthur.* Both tests are combined, and a third—that of a carving knife—is added, in the English ballad of *The Boy and the Mantle* (ed. F. J. Child, *English and Scottish Ballads,* no. 29). In none of these versions, however, is any name bestowed upon the heroine. Thus it is not possible that the allusion to *Tegau* in *Annot and Johon* could be derived from the English ballad.

(ii) A story in which the heroine sacrifices herself for her lover by relieving him of a poisonous serpent which has attached itself to his arm and is draining away his life. The serpent fastens itself instead on to the girl's breast, and in order that her life may be saved, her breast is cut off, and a gold one is substituted. This story is appropriated to Carados in the thirteenth-century *Livre de Carados*, an interpolation into the First Continuation of Chrétien's *Conte del Graal* (ed. Roach, pp. 85 ff.; see also EAR I, 90–1). In this work the heroine is named Gui(g)nier, and she is said to be sister to Cador of Cornwall (see n. to *Cadwy m. Gereint*). Independent versions of this theme (not attached to Caradog) are found in Gaelic, English and Breton. C. Harper (*Mod. Lang. Notes* XIII, pp. 418 ff.) was the first to compare with the *Caradoc* material the brief *resumé* of this tale recorded by J. F. Campbell,

Popular Tales of the West Highlands (1891) I, pp. lxxxix–xc, and that in Child's ballad (no. 301) 'The Queen of Scotland'. For a discussion of these versions see also G. Paris, *Caradoc et le Serpent*, *Romania* 28, pp. 214 ff. I would draw attention also to a Breton variant of the tale recorded in the early fifteenth-century *Chronicle of St Brieuc,* in which the episode of the serpent and the gold breast is attached to Azenor, the mother of St Budoc. This version corresponds to the others in its main particulars, except that it is Azenor's father, not her lover, whom she saves from the serpent, and she receives a gold breast by divine intervention. See G. H. Doble (ed.), *St. Budoc* in *The Saints of Cornwall* (Part Three) printed for the Dean and Chapter of Truro (Oxford, 1964), pp. 3–14.

Although it cannot be proved that these variants are uninfluenced by the literary tale, it is not unlikely that we have in them a theme which was taken into O.F. from an antecedent French source, and that the same theme continued to exist independently in Celtic tradition. The Welsh heroine *Tegau* thus corresponds with the French *Gui(g)nier*, and her epithet *eurvron* must have reference to a similar story to that outlined above. The *Livre de Carados* combines the tale of the serpent with the episode of the chastity-testing horn, in which Carados's mistress is triumphant over the ladies of Arthur's court, as in the other versions.

Morfydd Owen called my attention to the fact that *Tegau*'s mantle is referred to in one of the so-called *Trioedd Mab y Crinwas* which are found in several sixteenth-century manuscripts; examples, C 6 and 11: *Tri pheth ni wyr neb pa liw y sydd arno: rhawn paun yn kastellu, a mantell Tegau Eurfron, a cheiniog mab y krinwas* 'Three things whose colour no one knows: (that of) a peacock's tail spread out, of the cloak of Tegau Gold-Breast, and of the miser's penny'. The story of *Tegau*'s mantle is referred to by Guto'r Glyn, who compares his patron and his wife to Caradog Freichfras, *A Thegau uwch Porth Wgon / A llaes yw'r fantell i hon* (i.e. the magic mantle was for her *llaes* 'trailing', whereas for other women it was too short, GGl no. CV.11–12). Cf. also GGl no. XXVII.33–4: *Y mwyaf cuaf a'i câr / Hithau Degau a'i digar* 'Those who love her dearest, Tegau rejects'; HCLl no. LXVI.19 (where *Tegau* is a pseudonym for the girl addressed); GID 10.23: *dau gae ddof degau ddivalch*; GTA I, no. V.46 (and three other references by Tudur Aled to *Tegau Eurfron*); *dy gae aûr degav evroen [sic]* (Pen. 76, 137, 22); *mantell Degau* (GTP no. 8.28); *ail Degau* (no. 7.15; no. 20.40); *tegav oscedd* (GDE no. XXXVIII.21). Cf. also D. Gwenallt Jones, *Yr Areithiau Pros*, p. 18, l. 17: *mantel Degau newydd ddyvod or gwydd*; also references by Lewys Môn and other poets cited by Eurys Rowlands, LlC V, p. 67.

Tegit (Voel) 24, 41. 'T. the Bald.' See n. to *Moruran eil Tegit.* Other children of *Tegit* besides those named in *Ystorya Taliesin* are mentioned in the genealogies: VSB 320 (6): *Auan Buellt m. Kedic m. Keredic m. Kuneda Wledic o Decued* ('tenth') *uerch Degit Voel o Benllyn e vam;* Rawl. B 466:

Gwron ap kunedda a bleid ap kunedda broder oeddynt o dwywai vz. degid voel o benllyn oedd i mam (= EWGT 55 (6)).

Teila6 82, 83 = St Teilo. See nn. to the triads and references cited.

Teirg6aed 27, 28; App. IV, no. 4: *Menw ap Teirgwaed* = 'Three Cries'; see n. to *Menw m. Teirg6aed,* and CO l. 199.

Treul Diueuyl, verch Llynghessa6c La6 Hael 66 (Pen. 47). 'T. the Blameless.'

Triffin 46A: *Drutwas m. Driffin* (see n.); *m. Tryffin,* App. IV, no. 1. Rhisierdyn: *Drutlyryf dal traffuryf deulit Tryphin* (MA[2] 290b, the poem is defective in RBP col. 1288 = GSRh no. 6.60n.). The name *Triphun* occurs in Harl. Gen. II (= EWGT 10 (2)) as that of an early ruler of Dyfed, and it is possible that he is to be identified with the *Triphunus* named by Rhigyfarch as ruling in Dyfed at the time of the birth of St David (VSB 152, chapter 5).

Trist6ard, bard Vryen 11. See n. to *Vryen Reget m. Kynuarch.* A fragment of three *englynion milwr,* representing a dialogue between *Tristvardd*, Urien and an unnamed woman, has been preserved in Gwyneddon 4 (Ifor Williams (ed.), B VIII, pp. 331–2), and in Ll. 57 (T. Jones (ed.), B XIII, pp. 12–13). The latter text is in the hand of Moses Williams, who gives as his source J.D.R. (= Siôn Dafydd Rhys), though the poem is not found in J.D.R.'s *Grammar*, or in any of the latter's manuscripts. This text also bears the title: *Tristfardd Bardd Urien Reged* 540. *A rhai o'r Ymddiddanion rhwng Urien a'r Tristfardd yn yr amser hwn* (which establishes that the *tristfardh* of Gwyneddon 4 is a proper name and not an epithet). The fragmentary verses belong to the same general type as the other early *ymddiddanion* which have come down in *englyn* form (see n. to *Gwenh6yuar*[1] for example). These versions have been discussed briefly by Graham Thomas, B XXIV (1970), pp. 8–9 (see n. to *Tegeu Eururon* above), and by J. Rowland, EWSP 96; cf. N. Jacobs's n. in LlC XXI, p. 63. The date 540 given to *Tristvardd* in Ll. 57 is derived from Ed. Lhuyd: *Tristvardh. Bardh Yrien Reged po(eta)*; *An.* 540 (*Arch. Brit.* 264, col. 2). Cf. EWSP 252 ff.

In his *marwnad* to Ednyfed fab Madog, Cynddelw speaks of himself in the following words: *trwm ynof cof ked wallaw / tristuart uytaf am [y] daw*, 'Sad in me the memory of the bestower of gifts, I am a sad bard because (?) he is silent' (H 169.15–16 = CBT III no. 27.16n.). *Tristuard* is here presumably an epithet, but it would be fully in accord with the studied ambiguity of the *Gogynfeirdd* to use the term with an oblique reference to an early bard who bore this name. *Tristfardd* is portrayed in the tale as engaged in secretly courting Urien's wife; without recognizing her husband, he despatches Urien himself with a message to her. The *englynion* are spoken in turn by Urien, by his wife, and by *Tristfardd.* No indication is given in the story that *Tristfardd* is Urien's poet. At the conclusion, Urien slays Tristfardd at a ford, called *Rhyd Tristfardd* near Urien's supposed castle in Radnorshire. There are suggestions elsewhere that Cynddelw possessed a special knowledge of the traditions about Urien and his family; see introduction, pp. lxii, xcvii, and n. to *Taliesin.* The latter was Urien's poet in the older tradition (see PT) and none of the *Gogynfeirdd* appear to have known anything of *Tristfardd.*

Trystan m. Tallwch. See **Drystan m. Tallwch.**

Tudwal Tutclyt 2: *Ryderch Hael m. T.* (see n.); *Tutwal T.*, App. II, no. 8; App. III, no. 8; *Gwenvedon merch Tudaual Tutklyt* 66 (Pen. 47).

With *tud* cf. Ir. *túath* 'tribe, people', and the corresponding personal name *Tuathal; Tutklyd* 'defender of the people'. *Gwâl* = 'leader, ruler' (GPC 1565 *gwâl* (2)); so *Tudwal* 'leader of the people'. The name occurs at *Tothail* (genitive of *Tothal*), an archaic spelling of Ir. *Tuathal* in Adamnán's Life of *St Columba* (see n. to *Ryderch Hael*); and also K. Jackson, SEBC 319 n.

Tudwal appears in ch. IV of the twelfth-century Life of *St Ninian* by Ailred of Rievaulx—*Lives of St Ninian and St. Kentigern*, ed. A. P. Forbes, *Historians of Scotland V* (Edinburgh, 1874). A British king named *Tuduvallus* is here said to have been punished by blindness for his rejection of Christianity and later healed by the saint. The fact that both the name and the incident are derived from a much older source than the twelfth century is witnessed by the occurrence of both in a Latin poem on the Life of *St Ninian*, which has been dated to the eighth century, and shown to have been derived from a common source with Ailred's Life. The poem was edited by Karl Strecker, *Poetæ Latini Aevi Carolini* IV, pp. 943–62 (*Mon. Germ. Hist.*); see also Levison, 'An Eighth-Century Poem on St Ninian', *Antiquity* (1940), p. 280.

Vchei m. G6ryon 74 (= *Etheu m. Gwrgon,* Pen. 50).

Ul Cesar. See **Julius Cesar.**

Vryen (Reget) m. Kyn6arch 5 (WR), 6, 25, 33, 70, App. II, no. 1, 11: *Trist6ard bard Vryen.* See nn. to *Owein m. Vryen, Riwallawn Wallt Banhadlen (m. Vryen Reget), Moruud verch Vryen.*

Brit. **Ōrbogĕnos* > O.W. *Urbgen* (see below) > Ml.W. *Urien* (LHEB 439). The first element in the compound appears as Gaulish *orbius* 'heir', L. *orbus,* and survives in the Gaulish personal names *Orbaniacus,* etc. (WG 154; L. and P. 39). The meaning of *Ōrbogĕnos* is therefore perhaps 'of privileged birth'. (This interpretation is preferable to Thurneysen's suggestion that *Urien* < *Urbi-genus* 'city-born' (*Zeitschrift für deutsche Philologie* XXVIII, p. 97, n. 1), which is followed by E. W. B. Nicholson (ZCP III, p. 108). The latter suggested that the 'city' in question is York; though if this interpretation of the name is accepted, Carlisle seems a more likely birthplace for Urien Rheged.)

The name *Urien* does not appear in Welsh sources with reference to any other character but Urien Rheged, except in one doubtful instance in the *Beddau* stanzas: *madauc . . . vir vrien gorev* (LlDC no.18.64: 'Madauc, grandson of the supreme Urien'). Nicholson (ZCP III, p. 107) cites an instance of *Urbien* in a document of 869 in the Breton *Cartulaire de Redon* (ed. Courson, p. 83). HB ch. 63, names *Urbgen*[1] as the leader of the coalition of British leaders who fought against five Northumbrian rulers, including Hussa (585–92) and Theodric (572–9):

> Against them four kings fought—*Urbgen* and *Riderch hen* and *Guallauc* and *Morcant.* Deodric [i.e. the son of Ida] fought vigorously against that Urbgen with his sons. At that time sometimes the enemy, sometimes the citizens [i.e. the Cymry] were victorious and he [*Urbgen*] besieged them three days and three nights *In insula Metcaut* [i.e. Lindisfarne]. And while he was on that expedition he was murdered at the instigation of Morcant, through jealousy—because in him, beyond all (the other) kings there was the greatest skill in prosecuting warfare. (HB ch.63—discussed in CS; cf. B XXVII, pp. 110 ff.)

The form *Urbagen,* with medial vowel retained, was preserved in the note of authorship attached to the eleventh-century Chartres text of HB (destroyed by enemy action in 1940), and inscribed before the year 1100. (See ZCP III, p. 104 for the correct reading of this name in the manuscript, and n. to *Run Ryuedua6r* on the ascription of authorship in the Chartres text.) Ifor Williams has suggested that the form *Uruoen* employed interchangeably with *Uryen* in a poem by Cynddelw (H 135.15, 20 = CBT III, no. 16.97) derives from *Urbogen,* a variant form of *Urbagen* which existed simultaneously with it (B VII, p. 388). Corroboration for this is derived from the corrupt forms *uruwyn* (PT no. VIII.53) and *eurwyn* (PT no. II.32) and also *Vruoni* in *De Situ Brecheniauc* (see n. to triad 70 for the passage), all of which appear to represent incorrectly modernized forms of early W. *Uruoen*. K. H. Jackson suggested (SEBC 285) that the corrupt forms *Eufurenn* and *Erwegen* by which Urien is denoted in certain early documents relating to St Kentigern are written corruptions of **Uruegen,* a variant of the same by-form with medial vowel retained. See also PT xxxvi–xxxvii; p. 42n. on l. 32.

Harl. Gen. VIII (= EWGT 10 (8)) gives the descent of *Urbgen map Cinmarc* from Coel Hen, and the names in this genealogy correspond in all respects with that given in App. II, no. 1, except that one generation—that of Ceneu—is omitted.

A group of early bardic panegyrics addressed to *Urien Rheged* and his son Owain are preserved in the *Book of Taliesin,* and these form the greater part of the nucleus of poems in BT which have a claim to be regarded as representing the authentic work of the bard Taliesin (see PT introduction, and Morris-Jones, *Cy.* XXVIII). Three of these poems are representative bardic eulogies, comparable in general type to those of the *Gogynfeirdd* in the succeeding period, and they include a *dadolwch* or 'intercession' by the poet after estrangement from his patron; while two present graphic accounts of battles fought by Urien and his son Owain. In these poems Urien's country is designated as *Reget* (BT 60.10), and his people are the men of Rheged (BT

58.13, leg. *gan regetwys*). Urien is described as *glyv reget* (BT 57.7) 'lord of Rheged', and *Reget diffreidyat* (BT 57.24) 'defender of Rheged', and Owain as *Reget ud* (BT 67.19) 'lord of Rheged'.

The extent of *Urien*'s kingdom of *Rheged* is clearly indicated in the *Ordnance Survey Map of Britain in the Dark Ages* (1966). It stretched from Galloway (where the name of *Rheged* may have survived in *Dunragit* near Stranraer (= *Dun Recet*) *circa* 800 in the *Martyrology of Oengus*) over much of the Scottish Lowlands and Border country; and to the south it extended over Cumbria and the Lake District. But lack of precise evidence makes it impossible to define *Rheged*'s exact borders. It seems likely that its centre lay around the Solway estuary and included Carlisle, Annan and the valley of the River Eden. Carlisle may indeed have been *Urien*'s centre of rule (see BWP 82–4 and nn.; K. Jackson, *Antiquity* XXIX, p. 82). Since in the poems *Urien* is also entitled *llyw Catraeth* (BT 62.22) 'ruler of Catraeth', this may be taken as evidence that *Rheged* at some period stretched as far south as Yorkshire. Thus the extensive area covered by *Urien*'s kingdom offers some explanation for the prominence given to *Urien* and Owain in the poetry and historical documents relating to the northern Britons. Ifor Williams has argued from the reference to *Urien* as *llyw Catraeth* in the Taliesin poetry, combined with the absence of all allusion to *Urien* and his sons in the *Gododdin*, that they must all have been dead before the year 600, and that the expedition of Mynyddawg's men was undertaken after *Urien*'s death in an attempt to win back for the Britons the strategic position of Catterick, at which three Roman roads met together (CA xxxi–xxxii). In the poems *Urien* is also given the title of *gwledig,* which seems to imply that he was a commander over native, as distinct from Roman, forces (on the significance of the term *gwledig*, see n. to *Maxen Wledic*). This would suit well with HB's account of the British coalition of forces, over which it is implied that *Urien* acted as commander-in-chief. Another early poem purporting to be a eulogy of *Urien,* which may well contain some early material, is *Anrec Vryen* 'Urien's Gift' (RBP cols. 1049–50; *Cy.* VII, p. 125, from the *Llyfr Gwyn*); see Morris-Jones, *Cy.* XVIII, pp. 195–6. At the close of this poem Urien is described as one of the *tri theyrn ar dec or gogled* 'the Thirteen Princes of the North'. (Cf. the thirteen entries in *Bonedd Gwŷr y Gogledd* (Appendix II); EWSP ch. 2 'The Urien Rheged Poems'; P. Sims-Williams, CMCS 32, pp. 25–36, and references there cited.)

The opposition presented by *Urien* and his allies to the Anglian rulers of Northumbria had in Wales by the ninth century become incorporated into a traditional narrative or *cyfarwyddyd*, fragments of which have come down in the Powys *englyn* cycle (CLlH no. III). This story evidently culminated in the death of *Urien,* since the fragments include a lament for him and a poem which gives a poignant description of the desolation of his home, *aelwyd Reged*, after the deaths of *Urien* and Owain. *Llouan Llaw Diuro* (see n.) is named *Urien*'s slayer (cf. triad 33), and Aber Lleu is designated as the place of his death. Ifor Williams has identified Aber Lleu with Ross Low where the

River Low meets the sea opposite to Lindisfarne—an identification which brings the story underlying the *englynion* into line with HB's account. A reference to *Efrddyl* (see n. above) further emphasizes the common tradition about *Urien* and his family which is drawn upon by the *englynion* and by TYP. The *englynion* also amplify HB's account by implying that *Gwallawc* (see n.) and *Dunawd m. Pabo* (see n.) were *Urien*'s enemies, in addition to *Morcant* who is named in HB. *Urien*'s sons *Owein, Pascen, Rhun* (= *Run*[4], see nn.) and *Elphin* are referred to in these poems.

Geoffrey of Monmouth evidently had some extended knowledge of traditional material about *Urien*'s family in addition to that which he may have derived from HB, since he names both *Urianus* (HRB IX, 9) and *Iwenus* (= *Owain,* XI, i) as opponents of the English in the northern wars waged by the Britons, and HB makes no mention of Owain. Chrétien de Troyes knew that *Yvain* was son to *Urien* (*Erec*, l. 1706; *Yvain,* ll. 1018–19, etc.; *Graal*, ll. 149–52); but since Chrétien was evidently in possession of additional information from a British source (or Breton?) about *Owain ab Urien* (see n.) in addition to that which he could have derived from HRB, it is clear that the references in HRB were not by themselves responsible for launching Urien and his son upon their careers as Arthurian heroes. Later romance sources depict Urien *(Uryence)* as king of the unspecified territory of *Gorre* (Gore in Malory, 1, 7, etc.). The author seems to have known, either directly or at second hand, of the Taliesin poetry. He depicts *Urien* as *rex Mureifensium,* and this does at least emphasize his awareness that *Urien*'s kingdom was located somewhere in the north. D. N. Dumville proposed to me that Geoffrey of Monmouth's Mureif represents the name Monreith in Wigtonshire (rather than Moray, as has been previously understood by translators). This identification suits much better than 'Moray' with the geographical indications given in HRB IX, 6, and provides a more satisfactory interpretation of the passage in HRB IX, 9 which names the territories given to *Urien* and to his brothers. A Mureif in Galloway would of course also conform much better than Moray with the indications as to the locality of the kingdom of *Rheged* given in older sources, in particular with *Dunragit* near Stranraer. In HRB *Urianus* is brother to Anguselus (= Arawn) and Lot (= Lleu); cf. triad 70. According to the *Brut* (BD 152), these three brothers were sons of Kynuarch. The tradition that *Urien* had brothers who bore these names is cited in the *Black Book of Carmarthen* (see n. to *Llew m. Kynuarch*), and it is therefore an open question whether or not it may antedate the Welsh proto-Brut. (It is in accordance with the BD tradition that Gruffudd ap Maredudd cites the name of Arawn (Aron) together with that of his brother in both of the allusions that he makes to *Urien* (RBP col. 1219.15 = GGM no. 8.9; RBP col. 1323.15 = GGM no. 7.88). Cf. LlDC no. 40.8–10n. and ibid., p. xv.)

Further references by the *Gogynfeirdd* occur as follows:

LlDC no. 22.36 (in a poem to Hywel ap Goronwy, d. 1106): *Yrien haval* (= CBT I, no. 1.36n.).

Meilyr: *mal vryen urten ae amgyffravd* (H 1.26 = CBT I, no. 3.26).

Cynddelw: *Blaengar glew gletyfal Uryen* (H 135.20 = CBT III, no. 16.97 and 102nn.).

Casnodyn: *aryal Uryen* (RBP col. 1241.39 = GC no. 2.101n.).

Ll. Goch: *Milwryeid gorff mal vryen* (RBP col. 1308.32–3 = GLlG no. 4.5n.).

Bleddyn Ddu: *deulit uryen* (RBP col. 1253.21 = GBDd no. 6.9n.).

Gwilym Ddu o Arfon: *aryal vryen ỹggryt* (RBP col. 1228.10 = GGDT no. 7.42n.).

In the later period, Gutun Owain compares the hospitality of abbot Siôn of Llanegwestl to that of *llys Urien gynt* (GO no. XIX.25).

Certain families in Wales claimed to be descended from *Urien Rheged.* There are a number of allusions by the *cywyddwyr* to the descent of Syr Rhys ap Thomas of Abermarlais, who is described as *o ach Urien* (GID 62.18), *ffrwyth Urien* (GTA I, no. XLIX.7*)*, *Syr Rys, eryr air Urien* (HCLl no. XXXII.1), *o blaid Urien* (ibid. no. XXXII.18). This family bore three ravens on its coat of arms, which were associated with Owain's *branhes,* and are frequently referred to (GGl no. CI.34; *brân Urien* GTA I, no. XII.30; no. XIII.7–12, etc. (see n. to *Owein m. Vryen*); *brân Owain* GID no. 56.9–10). Wm. Llŷn describes Rhydderch Llwyd as *o waed Urien* (Wm. Ll. no. C.20).

A later age transposed *Urien*'s territory to mid-Wales. In 'Chwedl Tegau Eurfron, a Thristfardd Bardd Urien Rheged' referred to above (see *Tegeu Eururon*), the home of *Urien* is localized at Dinbot (now Tinbod) castle in Radnorshire. Graham Thomas shows (B XXIV, p. 8) that this association appears already in a MS. of the sixteenth century in the hand of Siôn Dafydd Rhys, Ll. 56, p. 1. See further WCD 634–5.

Gruffudd Gryg describes Einion ap Gruffudd as *Rhywiawgwalch Urien Rheged* (DGG no. 144.52).

On *Urien Rheged* see also the introduction to CLlH; BWP chs. IV, V; PT (and CT) introductions; EWSP ch. 2; K. Jackson, *The Oldest Scottish Poem: The Gododdin*; A. O. H. Jarman, *Aneirin: Y Gododdin: Britain's Oldest Heroic Poem*; P. Sims-Williams, CMCS 32 (1996), pp. 35–66; J. T. Koch's study *The Gododdin of Aneirin.*

Ursula, verch Dunawt tywyssawc Kernyw 35 (Pen. 50). See n. to *Dunawt*[1] above.

Vsber 58: *Rore verch Vsber.* On the analogy of the names in triads 56 and 57, we should expect lenition of the personal name after *verch*, giving the form *Gusber.* Can this represent a contraction of *Gwefusber* 'sweet lips'? Such a name would hardly be more incongruous than *Gendawd* (triad 57) 'Big Chin'.

6thyr Bendragon 28, U. Penndra(g)on 51. On the name see K. Jackson, CMCS 3, pp. 34–6. Cf. *(G)wen Bendragon* 52. *Pen(n)dragon* means 'Chief

Dragon' in a figurative sense; either 'foremost leader' or 'chief of warriors'. *Draig* and *dragon* are doublets with equivalent meaning, and both occur in the early poetry as euphemisms for warriors (GPC 1082, and n. to triad 37c); cf. Gwalchmai's use of both forms in his address to Rhodri m. Owain: *keinfeleic Penn dreic a phenn dragon* (H 32.4 = CBT I, no. 11.55) 'fine and valiant foremost dragon, and chief of dragons'. *Dragon* (< an oblique case of L. *draco-*) is employed both as a singular and as a plural; hence in the epithet *pen(n)dragon* it may be either singular or a dependent genitive plural. For *pen(n)* 'chief' with dependent genitive, cf. the phrases *Penn rianed, Penn beirdd, Penn Annwfn.* Geoffrey of Monmouth completely misunderstood this epithet and explained *Pendragon* as 'dragon's head' *quod britannica lingua caput draconis sonamus* (HRB VIII, 17). This explanation was in turn responsible for the fanciful origin given to Uthyr's epithet in the *Brut*: *sef yv hynny yn yavn Gymraec Vthyr Bendreic . . . canys Myrdin a'e daroganassei yn urenhin trvy y dreic a welat yn y seren* (BD 133.24–8; see n.) 'That is in correct Welsh, Uthyr Chief. Dragon . . . since Myrddin foretold he would be king through the dragon that was seen in the star'. J. J. Parry (*Speculum* XIII, pp. 276–7) suggested that Geoffrey based the name *Uthur* on a knowledge of the epithet *uthr*, 'wonderful, terrible', which he had met in Welsh verse, and that he may have misunderstood the lines which I have quoted above from LlDC 34.50, *mab Arthur uthir ig kerteu*, as containing the adjective rather than a personal name, but that the Arthurian setting in which the adjective appears 'gave him exactly the hint he needed'. This suggestion may be rejected in view of the body of evidence which points to the prior existence of *Uthyr* in Welsh tradition. Cf. n. to triad 28.

As Professor Jarman has shown (LlC II, p. 128), there is ample evidence, even apart from that afforded by triad 28, to prove that *Uthyr Pendragon* was known in Welsh tradition prior to the time of Geoffrey of Monmouth. In the tenth- or eleventh-century poem *Pa gur* in LlDC (no. 18), *Uthyr* already appears in an Arthurian context (though he is not Arthur's father in the poem): *Mabon am mydron / guas uthir pen dragon* (LlDC no. 31.13–14). It may be noted that both in this poem and in triad 28 (WR) *Uthyr's* name is found in juxtaposition with characters who occupy prominent roles in the Arthurian court-list in Culhwch ac Olwen.

In BT (p. 70) there is a poem entitled *Marvnat vthyr pen. Dragon* had been added in the margin in a later hand, and this expansion is probably justified, since among much that is obscure, the poem contains a reference to Arthur: *Neu vi arannwys vy echlessur / nawuetran yg gwrhyt arthur* (BT 71.15–16) 'I have shared my refuge, a ninth share in Arthur's valour'.

These references taken together show that *Uthyr* was known in the pre-Geoffrey Arthurian tradition. But they do not prove that, prior to HRB, he was known as Arthur's father; although the suggestion that there was a link between the two, which is provided by the poems already quoted, is further enforced by the poem *Ymddiddan Arthur a'r Eryr* 'The Colloquy of Arthur and the Eagle' (ed. by Ifor Williams from Jes. 20, B II, pp. 272–9, and by M. Haycock, *Blodeugerdd* no. 30). Though this poem cannot be dated to a period earlier than Geoffrey of Monmouth (Ifor Williams suggests that it may go back to *circa* 1150) it belongs nevertheless to a more primitive tradition, and one which is independent of Geoffrey's work: a tradition which resembles that of *Culhwch ac Olwen,* in that Arthur rules in Cornwall, and not at Caerleon. It gives the following indications as to Arthur's family connections: the transformed eagle discloses his identity as *Eliwlat vab Madawc vab Uthyr* (verses 7, 8), to which Arthur replies with the question *ae ti eliwlat vy nei?* (verse 9). These words could imply that Arthur and Madawg were both sons of *Uthyr* (to whom the epithet *Pendragon* is not here applied). Eliwlat (later *Eliwlod,* see n.) is named in App. IV, no. 1; while there is a further reference to *Madawc mab Uthyr* in BT 66.9–11: *Madawc mur menwyt. Madawc kyn bu bed . . . Mab uthyr kyn lleas oe law dywystlas* 'Madawc, a rampart of joy (?), Madawc before he was in the grave, the son of Uthyr (or "a terrible youth", see below) before he was slain gave a pledge (?) from his hand'. Neither *Madawc* nor his son *Eliwlat* are mentioned in HRB.

There is no need either to look for the origin of the name *Uthyr Pendragon* in an early gloss similar to that appended to the list of Arthur's battles in two thirteenth-century manuscripts of HB (CCCC (= Corpus Christi College, Cambridge) 139 and Cambridge Univ. Lib. Ff. I. 27)*: Mabutur britannice, id est filius horribilis latine, quoniam a pueritia sua crudelis fuit.* HB, ed. Mommsen, *Chronica Minora* iii, p. 199; Chambers, *Arthur of Britain*, p. 238n. (On the manuscripts see D. Dumville, 'The Corpus Christi "Nennius"', B XXV (1974), pp. 369–79; also, 'Celtic-Latin Texts in England', *Celtica* VII (1977), pp. 19–49.) This gloss is the work of a scribe who was familiar with the parentage attributed to Arthur in HRB; and as Jarman points out (loc. cit.), it contains a deliberate pun on the ambiguity of *uthr,* which can be interpreted either as an adjective ('terrible') or as a proper name. The fact that *uthr* occurs frequently as an adjective in early poetry (see below) has obscured the argument as to the independent Welsh origin of the character of *Uthyr Pendragon,* since in the controversy *all* the references to *Uthyr* in early poetry have at one time or another been taken to be the adjective *uthr*. It has also been suggested that Geoffrey knew of *Uthyr* as a great magician in Welsh sources (cf. triad 28), and that he saw an earlier version of the gloss on HB quoted above, which caused him to make the identification between this magician and Arthur's father, for whom he required a name (see J. Loth, RC XLII, p. 309; 49, p. 138; Vendryes, RC XLIV, p. 236; Nitze, MLN 1943, p. 3).

Jarman's argument may also be supported by two additional instances in which *Uthyr* is attested as a personal name in Welsh and Irish sources. Walter Map (*De Nugis Curialium* II, ch. 26) refers to a Welshman named *Cadolan filius Uther,* while *Uthir* (*Uithir, Uithidir*) occurs as the name of the father of the poet Adnae in the early Irish dialogue *Immacallam in dá Thuarad* 'The

Colloquy of the Two Sages' (RC XXVI, p. 8). But it must be conceded that in the occurrences of *uthyr* in the early poetry, it is by no means easy to distinguish whether the adjective or the personal name is intended, even when it appears in a context, such as the reference to Madawc quoted above, in which we should expect the personal name to be present. Cf. also the following, LlDC no. 34.48–9: *llacheu mab arthur uthir ig kerteu* (see n. to *Llacheu m. Arthur*). This objection applies also to the following allusions by the *Gogynfeirdd*:

Llygad Gŵr: *grymus uthyr yn ruthyr yn anreithyaw* (H 62.13 = CBT VII, no. 26.5n.).

The following thirteenth-century reference probably contains the proper name:

Y Prydydd Bychan: *pwyll mab uthyr* (H 237.21; see n. to CBT VII, no. 10.3n.).

From the fourteenth century onwards it is apparent that the poets knew of Uthyr's role in the *Brut* and, where any ambiguity exists, it becomes more probable that the personal name, rather than the common noun, is intended:

Gr. ap Maredudd: o *garyat eigyr dec eiryan . . . ucheneit uthur* (RBP col. 1326.30–2); *Llwydyant ruthyr llin uthur aeth lle bu ffrollo* (1203.13 = GGM no. 2.11); *uthurwed anryded yn rest* (1219.39); *eil rolant uthyr ffynnyant* (1325.18; cf. GGM no. 5.108); *nyt hael uthyr auael eithyr ef* (1330.22, 24, 27).

Dafydd y Coed: *Doeth ell uthyr gawruthyr yn gyvrein / iavn valch yn anuod eingyl llundein* (1378.17 = GDC no. 2.39–40n.).

With the *cywyddwyr* it is evident that the *Brut* account of *Uthyr Pendragon* was widely known; cf. Dafydd ap Gwilym: *Gwiw Eigr hoen a'i goroen, un gariad Uthr* (GDG no. 16.51).

Iolo Goch: *Uthr Bendragon lon lendyd* (GIG no. VII.29).

Gruffudd Llwyd: *Uthr Bendragon . . . Pan ddialawd . . . Ei frawd â'i rwysg ei frwydr ef* (IGE² 123.6–8).

See also DN no. XX.58; GO no. XXXVII.26.

Vthyr m. Greidya6l 56. See n. to *Gwythyr m. Greidya6l*. The influence of the name *6thyr Pendragon* (see above) was evidently of effect in assisting to perpetuate this incorrect form in the later texts of triad 56; the form arose originally from the lenition of *Gwythyr* after *verch* (see n. to triad 56).

Yniwl Iarll, see **Niwl Iarll.**

Ynyr Gwent see **Idon m. Enyr G6ent**.

Yrp Lluyda6c 35. 'Yrp of the Hosts.' With the epithet cf. *Elen Luyda6c* and n. Cf. WCD p. 644.

The name *Yrp* does not occur elsewhere, nor is there any other reference in Welsh sources to this character. The following forms may however be compared: *Urbf* in the saint's genealogy given in the Life of *St Cadoc* (VSB 118), listed among the Irish ancestors of the saint's mother. Similarly *Erp, Erip* and *Irb* are found among the names of kings in the *Pictish Chronicle* (Chadwick, *Early Scotland*, pp. 8, 10, 31), so that the name may be of Irish or Pictish rather than of Welsh provenance. Alternatively, the form *Yryf* (R's variant of Pen. 16*'s Eiryf*) 'Number' in triad 15 offers a parallel form with a meaning which would be appropriate to *Yrp*'s story; and suggests that *Yrp* like *Eiryf*, *Yryf*, may be a made-up name. In the n. to triad 35 I have suggested that both the character and story of *Yrp Lluydawc* arose out of a mathematical fantasy invented by the maker of this triad.

Ysgafnell m. Disgyfdawt 10 (**Sgafnell** WR), 32. The constituents of this name may be *ysgafn* 'light' + *gell* 'brown, tawny-coloured'. The form in the triads is attested by *Englynion y Clyweit*: *A glyweist di a gant yscafnell / mab dysgyfdawt kat gymmell* (B III, p. 12, verse 36). WR preserves the older form without prosthetic -*y*. Cf. Haycock, *Blodeugerdd*, p. 334.

Ywein m. Uryen. See **Owein m. Vryen.**

ABBREVIATIONS*

A. Leg.	J. Rhŷs, *Studies in the Arthurian Legend.*
AL	Aneurin Owen, *Ancient Laws and Institutes of Wales.*
Ann. Cam.	*Annales Cambriae*, ed. E. Phillimore, *Cy* 60 (1888), 141–83. See also HB.
ACL	Whitley Stokes and Kuno Meyer, *Archiv für celtische Lexicographie.*
ACS	Alfred Holder, *Alt-celtischer Sprachschatz.*
ALMA	*Arthurian Literature in the Middle Ages*, ed. R. S. Loomis.
AW	*The Arthur of the Welsh*, eds Rachel Bromwich, A. O. H. Jarman and Brynley F. Roberts.
AP	*Armes Prydein o Lyfr Taliesin,* ed. Ifor Williams; *Armes Prydein Vawr: The Prophecy of Britain*, English version by Rachel Bromwich.
Arch. Brit.	Edward Lhuyd, *Archaeologia Britannica.*
ASC	*The Anglo-Saxon Chronicle: A Revised Translation*, Dorothy Whitelock *et al.*
Ast. H.	*Astudiaethau ar yr Hengerdd: Studies in Old Welsh Poetry*, eds Rachel Bromwich and R. Brinley Jones.
ATC	R. S. Loomis, *Arthurian Tradition and Chrétien de Troyes.*
B	*The Bulletin of the Board of Celtic Studies.*
BBC	*The Black Book of Carmarthen*, J. G. Evans.
BD	*Brut Dingestow*, ed. Henry Lewis.
BDG	*Barddoniaeth Dafydd ab Gwilym*, eds Owen Jones and William Owen Pughe.
BGG	Bonedd Gwŷr y Gogledd (Appendix II above).
Br. Cleo.	*Brut y Brenhinedd. Cotton Cleopatra Version*, ed. J. J. Parry.
Blodeugerdd	*Blodeugardd Barddas o Ganu Crefyddol Cynnar*, ed. Marged Haycock.
Br. M.	*Breuddwyd Maxen*, ed. Ifor Williams.
Br. Rh.	*Breudwyt Ronabwy*, ed. Melville Richards.
BT	*Facsimile and Text of the Book of Taliesin*, ed. J. Gwenogvryn Evans.
BWP	*The Beginnings of Welsh Poetry. Studies by Sir Ifor Williams*, ed. Rachel Bromwich.
Bywgraffiadur	*Y Bywgraffiadur Cymraeg hyd 1940*, paratowyd dan nawdd Anrhydeddus Gymdeithas y Cymmrodorion (Llundain, 1953).
CA	*Canu Aneirin*, ed. Ifor Williams.

*Full details given in bibliography.

CBT	Cyfres Beirdd y Tywysogion I–VII, general editor R. Geraint Gruffydd (Caerdydd, 1991–6): I *Gwaith Meilyr Brydydd a'i Ddisgynyddion, ynghyd â Dwy Awdl Fawl Ddienw o Ddeheubarth*; II *Gwaith Llywelyn Fardd I ac Eraill o Feirdd y Ddeuddegfed Ganrif*; III *Gwaith Cynddelw Brydydd Mawr I*; IV *Gwaith Cynddelw Brydydd Mawr II*; V *Gwaith Llywarch ap Llywelyn 'Prydydd y Moch'*; VI *Gwaith Dafydd Benfras ac Eraill o Feirdd Hanner Cyntaf y Drydedd Ganrif ar Ddeg*; VII *Gwaith Bleddyn Fardd a Beirdd Eraill Ail Hanner y Drydedd Ganrif ar Ddeg*.
CD	J. Morris-Jones, *Cerdd Dafod*.
CF	John Rhŷs, *Celtic Folklore, Welsh and Manx*, 2 volumes.
Chr. Br.	Joseph Loth, *Chrestomathie Bretonne*.
Chw. T.	Ifor Williams, *Chwedl Taliesin*.
CIIC	R. A. S. Macalister, *Corpus Inscriptionum Insularum Celticarum*.
CLlH	*Canu Llywarch Hen*, ed. Ifor Williams.
CMCS	*Cambridge/Cambrian Medieval Celtic Studies*, 1981–.
CO(1)	*Culhwch ac Olwen*, eds Rachel Bromwich and D. Simon Evans (Welsh-language edition).
CO(2)	*Culhwch and Olwen; An Edition and Study of the Oldest Arthurian Tale*, eds Rachel Bromwich and D. Simon Evans.
CR	Lewis Morris, *Celtic Remains*.
CS	Kenneth Jackson *et al.*, *Celt and Saxon*: *Studies in the Early British Border*.
Cy.	*Y Cymmrodor*.
Cyf. Ll. a Ll.	*Cyfranc Lludd a Llefelys*, ed. Ifor Williams; ed. Brynley F. Roberts.
D.	John Davies, *Antiquae Linguae Britannicae Dictionarium Duplex*.
DC	*Y Diarebion Camberäec* (1567?).
DGG	*Dafydd ap Gwilym a'i Gyfoeswyr*, eds Ifor Williams and Thomas Roberts.
DGVB	Léon Fleuriot, *Dictionnaire des Gloses en Vieux Breton*.
DIAS	Dublin Institute for Advanced Studies.
DIL	*Contributions to a Dictionary of the Irish Language* (Dublin, Royal Irish Academy, 194276).
DN	*The Poetical Works of Dafydd Nanmor*, eds Thomas Roberts and Ifor Williams.
EANC	R. J. Thomas, *Enwau Afonydd a Nentydd Cymru*.
EAR	J. D. Bruce, *The Evolution of Arthurian Romance*.
EC	*Études Celtiques*.
ECMW	V. E. Nash-Williams, *The Early Christian Monuments of Wales*.
EHR	*The English Historical Review*.
EIHM	T. F. O'Rahilly, *Early Irish History and Mythology*.
EWGP	K. H. Jackson, *Early Welsh Gnomic Poems*.
EWGT	P. C. Bartrum, *Early Welsh Genealogical Tracts*.
EWSP	Jenny Rowland, *Early Welsh Saga Poetry*.
EYP	Enweu Ynys Prydein (Appendix I above).
FAB	W. F. Skene, *The Four Ancient Books of Wales*.
G	J. Lloyd-Jones, *Geirfa Barddoniaeth Gynnar Gymraeg*.

GBDd	*Gwaith Bleddyn Ddu*, ed. R. Iestyn Daniel.
GC	*Gwaith Casnodyn*, ed. R. Iestyn Daniel.
GDC	*Gwaith Dafydd y Coed a Beirdd Eraill o Lyfr Coch Hergest*, ed. R. Iestyn-Daniel.
GDE	*Gwaith Dafydd ab Edmwnd*, ed. Thomas Roberts.
GDG	*Gwaith Dafydd ap Gwilym*, ed. Thomas Parry.
GEO	*Gwaith Einion Offeiriad a Dafydd Ddu o Hiraddug*, eds R. Geraint Gruffydd and Rhiannon Ifans.
GGl	*Gwaith Guto'r Glyn*, eds Ifor Williams and Llywelyn Williams.
GGDT	*Gwaith Gruffydd ap Dafydd ap Tudur, Gwilym Ddu o Arfon,Trahaearn Brydydd Mawr ac Iorwerth Beli*, eds N. G. Costigan (Bosco), R. Iestyn Daniel and Dafydd Johnston.
GGLl	*Gwaith Gruffudd Llwyd a'r Llygliwiaid Eraill*, ed. Rhiannon Ifans
GGM	*Gwaith Gruffudd ap Maredudd: 1 – Canu i deulu Penmynydd*, ed. Barry J. Lewis.
GID	*Casgliad o Waith Ieuan Deulwyn*, ed. Ifor Williams.
GIG	*Gwaith Iolo Goch*, ed. D. R. Johnston.
GLGC	*Gwaith Lewys Glyn Cothi*, ed. Dafydd Johnston.
GLM	*Gwaith Lewys Môn*, ed. Eurys Rowlands.
GLlBH	*Gwaith Llywelyn Brydydd Hoddnant, Dafydd ap Gwilym, Hillyn ac Eraill*, eds Ann Parry Owen and Dylan Foster Evans.
GLlG	*Gwaith Llywelyn Goch ap Meurig Hen*, ed. Dafydd Johnston.
GMW	D. Simon Evans, *A Grammar of Middle Welsh.*
GO	*L'Oeuvre Poetique de Gutun Owain*, ed. E. Bachellery.
GOI	Rudolf Thurneysen, *A Grammar of Old Irish.*
GP	*Gramadegau'r Penceirddiaid*, eds G. J. Williams and E. J. Jones.
GPC	*Geiriadur Pryfysgol Cymru: A Dictionary of the Welsh Language* (Caerdydd, 1950–).
GPN	D. Ellis Evans, *Gaulish Personal Names.*
GSRh	*Gwaith Sefnyn, Rhisierdyn . . . a Llywarch Bentwrch*, eds Nerys Ann Jones and Erwain Haf Rheinallt
GTA	*Gwaith Tudur Aled*, ed. T. Gwynn Jones, 2 volumes.
GTP	*Gwaith Tudur Penllyn ac Ieuan ap Tudur Penllyn*, ed. Thomas Roberts.
H	*Llawysgrif Hendregadredd*, eds J. Morris-Jones and T. H. Parry-Williams.
Harl. Gens.	'The Welsh Dynastic Genealogies from Harleian MS. 3859', ed. Egerton Phillimore, *Cy.* IX, pp. 141ff.; see also EWGT 9–13.
HB	*Historia Brittonum.* (*Nennius: British History and the Welsh Annals*, trans. John Morris, History from the Sources 8, (Chichester 1980))
HCLl	*Gwaith Huw Cae Llwyd ac Eraill*, ed. Leslie Harries.
HGC	*Hen Gerddi Crefyddol*, ed. Henry Lewis.
HGVK	*Historia Gruffud vab Kenan*, ed. D. Simon Evans.
Hist. Ecc.	*Historia Ecclesiastica Gentis Anglorum*, transl. by Leo Shirley-Price, *Bede: A History of the English Church and People.*
HLCB	Jean Balcou et Yves le Gallo, *Histoire Littéraire et culturelle de la Bretagne.*

HRB	Geoffrey of Monmouth, *Historia Regum Britanniae*.
HW	J. E. Lloyd, *A History of Wales*.
IGE[2]	*Cywyddau Iolo Goch ac Eraill*, eds Henry Lewis, Thomas Roberts and Ifor Williams.
ITS	The Irish Texts Society.
Jes. Gens.	'The Genealogies from Jesus Coll. MS.20', ed. E. Phillimore, *Cy* viii, pp. 83ff.; see also EWGT 41–50.
JWBS	*Journal of the Welsh Bibliographical Society*.
L. and P.	Henry Lewis and Holger Pedersen, *A Concise Comparative Celtic Grammar*.
LBS	S. Baring-Gould and J. Fisher, *The Lives of the British Saints*.
LD	Lewis Dwnn, *The Heraldic Visitations of Wales*, ed. Samuel Rush Meyrick.
LEWP	Ifor Williams, *Lectures on Early Welsh Poetry* (Dublin, 1944).
LHEB	K. H. Jackson, *Language and History in Early Britain*.
LL	*The Text of the Book of Llan Dav*, eds J. Rhŷs and J. G. Evans.
LlA	*The Elucidarium and other Tracts in Welsh from Llyvyr Agkyr Llandewivrevi*, eds J. Rhŷs and J. Morris-Jones.
LlB	*Llyfr Blegywryd*, eds S . J. Williams and J. Enoch Powell.
LlC	*Llên Cymru*.
LlDC	*Llyfr Du Caerfyrddin*, ed. A. O. H. Jarman.
LU	*Lebor na h-Uidre*, eds R. I. Best and Osborn Bergin.
MA[2]	*The Myvyrian Archaiology of Wales*, eds Owen Jones, Edward Williams and William Owen Pughe.
Mab.	*The Mabinogion*.
MCSP	Karen Jankulak, *The Medieval Cult of St Petroc*.
MLN	Modern Language Notes.
Ml.W	Medieval Welsh.
MPh	*Modern Philology*.
MW	Moses Williams (in NLW Llanstephan MS 650).
MWM	Daniel Huws, *Medieval Welsh Manuscripts*.
NLW	National Library of Wales manuscript.
Nat. Lib. of Wales Journal	*Journal of the National Library of Wales/Cylchgrawn Llyfrgell Genedlaethol Cymru*.
NMS	*Nottingham Medieval Studies*.
OSPG	Kenneth H. Jackson, *The Oldest Scottish Poem: The Gododdin*.
Owein	*Owein or Chwedyl Iarlles y Ffynnawn*, ed. R. L. Thomson.
Pa.	Panton MS. in the National Library of Wales.
PBA	*Proceedings of the British Academy*.
PCB	Anne Ross, *Pagan Celtic Britain*.
Pen.	Peniarth MS. in the National Library of Wales.
PKM	*Pedeir Keinc y Mabinogi*, ed. Ifor Williams.
PT	*The Poems of Taliesin*, ed. Ifor Williams, English version by J. E. Caerwyn Williams.
RBB	*The Text of the Bruts from the Red Book of Hergest*, eds J. G. Evans and J. Rhŷs.
RBH	The Red Book of Hergest.

RBP	*The Poetry in the Red Book of Hergest*, ed. J. G. Evans.
RC	*Revue Celtique.*
Rep.	J. Gwenogvryn Evans, *Report on MSS. in the Welsh Language.*
RM	*The Text of the Mabinogion from the Red Book of Hergest*, eds J. Rhŷs and J. Gwenogvryn Evans.
SC	*Studia Celtica.*
SEBC	*Studies in the Early British Church*, ed. N. K. Chadwick.
SEBH	*Studies in Early British History*, ed. N. K. Chadwick.
SG	*Y Seint Greal,* ed. (i) R. Williams, *Selections from the Hengwrt Manuscripts, vol. I*; (ii) Thomas Jones, *Ystoryaeu Seint Greal, Rhan 1. Y Keis.*
TAAS	*Transactions of the Anglesey Antiquarian Society.*
TC	T. J. Morgan, *Y Treigladau a'u Cystrawen.*
THSC	*Transactions of the Honourable Society of Cymmrodorion.*
TW	Thomas Wiliems, 'Thesaurus Linguae Latinae et Cambro-brytannicae', abstracted in D.
TWS	Elissa R. Henken, *Traditions of the Welsh Saints.*
TYP	*Trioedd Ynys Prydein: The Welsh Triads*, ed. Rachel Bromwich.
VM	*Vita Merlini*, ed. and and transl. by (i) J. J. Parry, *The Vita Merlini*; (ii) Basil Clarke, *Life of Merlin. Vita Merlini.*
VN[1]	Robert Vaughan's Notes to Trioedd Ynys Prydein in NLW MS. 7857 D.
VN[2]	Copy of VN[1] by Evan Evans, NLW Panton MS. 51.
VSB	*Vitae Sanctorum Britanniae et Genealogiae*, ed. A. W. Wade-Evans.
WAL	R. S. Loomis, *Wales and the Arthurian Legend.*
WCD	P. C. Bartrum, *A Welsh Classical Dictionary.*
WG	J. Morris-Jones, *A Welsh Grammar.*
WHR	*Welsh History Review.*
WKC	*The Welsh King and his Court*, eds T. M. Charles-Edwards *et al.*
WM	*The White Book Mabinogion*, ed. J. G. Evans.
Wm. Ll.	*Barddoniaeth William Llŷn*, ed. J. C. Morrice.
WR	The version of TYP contained in the White Book of Rhydderch and the Red Book of Hergest.
YB	*Ysgrifau Beirniadol*, ed. J. E. Caerwyn Williams (Dinbych, 1965–99).
YBH	*Ystorya Bown de Hamtwn*, ed. Morgan Watkin.
YCM	*Ystorya de Carolo Magno*, ed. S. J. Williams.
Ym. M. a Th.	*Ymddiddan Myrddin a Thaliesin*, ed. A. O. H. Jarman.
ZCP	*Zeitschrift für celtische Philologie.*

SELECT BIBLIOGRAPHY

Anderson, A. O., *Early Sources of Scottish History, vol. 1, A.D. 500–1286* (Edinburgh, 1922).

Anderson, A. O. and M. O., *Adomnan's Life of Columba* (Edinburgh, 1961).

Bachellery, E. (ed.), *L'Oeuvre Poétique de Gutun Owain*, 2 volumes (Paris, 1950, 1951).

Balcou, Jean and Yves le Gallo, *Histoire Littéraire et culturelle de la Bretagne* (Paris/Genève, 1987).

Baring-Gould, S. and J. Fisher, *The Lives of the British Saints*, 4 volumes (London, 1907–1914).

Bartrum, P. C., 'Pedigrees of the Welsh Tribal Patriarchs', *Nat. Lib. of Wales Journal* XIII (1963), pp. 93–146.

—*Early Welsh Genealogical Tracts* (Cardiff, 1966).

—'Was there a British Book of Conquests?', B XXIII (1968–70), pp. 1–5.

—'Y Pedwar Brenin ar Hugain', EC XII (1968–9), pp. 157–94.

—*A Welsh Classical Dictionary* (Aberystwyth, 1993).

—'Arthuriana from the Genealogical Manuscripts', *Nat. Lib. of Wales Journal* XIV (1969), pp. 42–5.

Bede, *Historia Ecclesiastica Gentis Anglorum*, transl. by Leo Shirley-Price, *Bede: A History of the English Church and People* (Harmondsworth, 1955, and reprints).

Best, R. I. and Osborn Bergin (eds), *Lebor na h-Uidre* (Dublin, 1929).

Binchy, D. A., *Celtic and Anglo-Saxon Kingship*, O'Donnell Lectures (Oxford, 1970).

Bowen, D. J., *Gruffudd Hiraethog a'i Oes* (Caerdydd, 1958).

Bowen, E. G., *Saints, Seaways, and Settlements* (Cardiff, 1969; 1977).

—*The Settlements of the Celtic Saints in Wales* (Cardiff, 1954).

Bowen, Geraint (ed.), *Y Traddodiad Rhyddiaith yn yr Oesau Canol* (Llandysul, 1974).

Bromwich, Rachel, 'The Character of the Early Welsh Tradition', in SEBH 83–136.

—'The Welsh Triads', in ALMA 44–51.

—(ed.), *Trioedd Ynys Prydein: The Welsh Triads* (Cardiff, 1961, second edition 1978).

—'Celtic Dynastic Themes and the Breton Lays', EC IX (1961), pp. 440–71.

—'Y Cynfeirdd a'r Traddodiad Cymraeg', B XXII (1966–8), pp. 30–7.

—'William Camden and *Trioedd Ynys Prydein*', B XXIII (1968–70), pp. 14–17.

—'*Trioedd Ynys Prydein*: the *Myvyrian* Third series', THSC (1968), pp. 299–338; (1969), pp. 127–56.

—*Trioedd Ynys Prydain in Welsh Literature and Scholarship*, G. J. Williams Memorial Lecture (Cardiff, 1969).

—'Concepts of Arthur', SC X/XI (1975–6), pp. 163–81.

—'Cynon ap Clydno', in *Ast. H.*, pp. 151–64.

—'The "Tristan" Poem in the Black Book of Carmarthen', SC XIV/XV (1979–80), pp. 54–65.

—'The Tristan of the Welsh', in AW, pp. 209–28.

—'Cyfeiriadau Traddodiadol a Chwedlonol y Gogynfeirdd', in *Beirdd a Thywysogion: Barddoniaeth Llys yng Nghymru, Iwerddon a'r Alban cyflwynedig i R. Geraint Gruffydd*, eds Morfydd E. Owen and Brynley F. Roberts (Caerdydd, 1996), pp. 202–18.

—'The Triads of the Horses', in *The Horse in Celtic Culture*: *Medieval Welsh Perspectives*, eds Sioned Davies and Nerys Ann Jones (Cardiff, 1997), pp. 102–20.

Bromwich, Rachel and R. Brinley Jones (eds), *Astudiaethau ar yr Hengerdd: Studies in Old Welsh Poetry, cyflwynedig i Syr Idris Foster* (Cardiff, 1978).

Bromwich, Rachel, A. O. H. Jarman and Brynley F. Roberts (eds), *The Arthur of the Welsh* (Cardiff, 1991).

Bromwich, Rachel and D. Simon Evans (eds), *Culhwch ac Olwen* [Welsh-language edition] (Caerdydd, 1988; second edition with notes, 1997); line references to the notes refer both to the second edition and to the English edition.

—*Culhwch and Olwen; An Edition and Study of the Oldest Arthurian Tale*, (Cardiff, 1992).

Brooke, C. N. L., *The Church and the Welsh Border in the Central Middle Ages* (Woodbridge, 1986).

Bruce, J. D., *The Evolution of Arthurian Romance* (second edition, Göttingen, 1928).

Bullock-Davies, C., *Professional Interpreters and the Matter of Britain* (Cardiff, 1966).

Campbell, J. L., *Popular Tales of the Western Highlands* (Edinburgh, 1860–2).

Carney, James, *Studies in Irish Literature and History* (Dublin, 1955).

Chadwick, H. M., *Early Scotland: the Picts, the Scots, and the Welsh of Southern Scotland* (Cambridge, 1949).

Chadwick, H. M. and N. K., *The Growth of Literature: vol. I The Ancient Literatures of Europe* (Cambridge, 1932).

Chadwick, N. K. (ed.), *Studies in Early British History* (Cambridge, 1952, 1959).

—(ed.), *Studies in the Early British Church*, ed. (Cambridge, 1958).

—'The Colonization of Brittany from Celtic Britain', PBA LI (1965), pp. 235–99.

—*Early Brittany* (Cardiff, 1969).

Chambers, E. K., *Arthur of Britain* (London, 1927; second edition ed. B. F. Roberts, 1964).

Charles-Edwards, T. M., Morfydd E. Owen, and Paul Russell (eds), *The Welsh King and his Court* (Cardiff, 2000).

Charlesworth, M. P., *The Lost Province* (Cardiff, 1949).

Clarke, Basil, *Life of Merlin: Geoffrey of Monmouth's Vita Merlini* (Cardiff, 1973).

Coe, J. B. and Simon Young, *Celtic Sources for the Arthurian Legend* (Felinfach, 1995).

Collingwood, R. G. and J. N. L. Myres, *Roman Britain and the English Settlements* (Oxford, 1936).

Cross, T. P. and C. H. Slover, *Ancient Irish Tales* (London, 1936).

Daniel, Iestyn R. (ed.), *Gwaith Bleddyn Ddu*, Cyfres Beirdd yr Uchelwyr (Aberystwyth, 1994).

—(ed.), *Gwaith Casnodyn*, Cyfres Beirdd yr Uchelwyr (Aberystwyth, 1999).

—(ed.), *Gwaith Gwilym Ddu o Arfon* in N. G. Costigan *et al.*, *Gwaith Gruffudd ap Dafydd ap Tudur, Gwilym Ddu o Arfon, Trahaearn Brydydd Mawr ac Iorwerth Beli*, Cyfres Beirdd yr Uchelwyr (Aberystwyth, 1995).

—(ed.), *Gwaith Dafydd y Coed a Beirdd Eraill o Lyfr Coch Hergest*, Cyfres Beirdd yr Uchelwyr (Aberystwyth, 2002).

Davies, Ceri, *Welsh Literature and the Classical Tradition* (Cardiff, 1995).

Davies, John, *Antiquae Linguae Britannicae Dictionarium Duplex* (London, 1632).

Davies, John, *Hanes Cymru* (Harmondsworth, 1992).

—*A History of Wales* (Harmondsworth, 1994).

Davies, R. R., *The Age of Conquest* (Oxford, 1987).

Davies, Sioned, *Crefft y Cyfarwydd* (Caerdydd, 1995).

Davies, Sioned and Nerys Ann Jones (eds), *The Horse in Celtic Culture: Medieval Welsh Perspectives* (Cardiff, 1997).

Davies, Wendy, *Wales in the Early Middle Ages* (Leicester, 1982).

Delargy, J., 'The Gaelic Storyteller', PBA XXXI (1945), pp. 178–221.

Dillon, Myles, *The Cycles of the Kings* (Oxford, 1946).

Dumville, David N., 'Sub-Roman Britain: History and Legend', *History*, n.s. 62 (1977), pp. 173–92.

—'The Welsh Latin Annals', SC XII/XIII (1977/78), pp. 461–7.

—'On the North British Section of the *Historia Brittonum*', WHR 8 (1976–7), pp. 345–54.

—*Histories and Pseudo-Histories of the Insular Middle Ages* (Aldershot, 1990) [contains reprints of the aforementioned articles].

Dwnn, Lewis, *The Heraldic Visitations of Wales*, ed. Samuel Rush Meyrick (London, 1846).

Evans, D. Ellis, *Gaulish Personal Names* (Oxford, 1967).

Evans, D. Simon *A Grammar of Middle Welsh*, DIAS Medieval and Modern Welsh Series, supplementary vol. (Dublin, 1964).

—(ed.), *Lives of the Welsh Saints by G. H. Doble* (Cardiff, 1971).

—(ed.), *Historia Gruffud vab Kenan* (Caerdydd, 1977).

—(ed.), *The Welsh Life of St. David* (Cardiff, 1988).

Evans, Dylan Foster, *'Goganwr am Gig Ynyd': The Poet as Satirist in Medieval Wales* (Aberystwyth, 1996).

Evans, J. Gwenogvryn, *Report on MSS. in the Welsh Language*, 3 volumes (London, 1898, 1910).

—*The Black Book of Carmarthen* (Pwllheli, 1907).

—(ed.), *The White Book Mabinogion* (Pwllheli, 1907; second edition with introduction by R. M. Jones (Cardiff, 1973)).

—(ed.), *Facsimile and Text of the Book of Taliesin* (Llanbedrog, 1910).

—(ed.), *The Poetry in the Red Book of Hergest* (Llanbedrog, 1911).

Evans, J. G. and J. Rhŷs (ed.), *The Text of the Bruts from the Red Book of Hergest* (Oxford, 1890).

—*The Text of the Book of Llan Dav* (Oxford, 1893).

Fleuriot, Léon *Dictionnaire des Gloses en Vieux Breton* (Paris, 1964).

— *Les Origines de la Bretagne* (Paris, 1980).

Faral, E., *La Légende Arthurienne* (Paris, 1913).

Forbes, A. P., *The Lives of St. Ninian and St. Kentigern* (Edinburgh, 1874); translations reprinted (Lampeter, 1989).

Ford, P. K., *The Mabinogi and Other Medieval Welsh Tales* (London, 1977).

— *The Poetry of Llywarch Hen* (Los Angeles, 1974).

— *Ystorya Taliesin* (Cardiff, 1992).

Foster, I. Ll. and Glyn Daniel, *Prehistoric and Early Wales* (London, 1965).

Fulton, Helen, *Dafydd ap Gwilym: The Apocrypha*, The Welsh Classics Series (Llandysul, 1996).

Gildas: see Williams, H., and Winterbottom, M.

Glasynys (Owen Wynne Jones), *Cymru Fu, yn cynnwys Hanesion, Traddodiadau ynghyda Chwedlau a Dammegion Cymreig oddiar Lafar Gwlad a Gweithiau y Prif Awduron* (Wrexham, 1862, 1901).

Goetinck, Glenys W., *Historia Peredur vab Efrawc* (Caerdydd, 1976).

Gray, E. A., *Cath Maige Tuired: The Battle of Mag Tuired*, Irish Texts Society, vol. LII (Naas, Kildare, 1983).

Grenier, A., *Les Religions de l'Europe Ancienne* (Paris, 1948).

Griffiths, Margaret Enid, *Early Vaticination in Welsh* (Cardiff, 1937).

Grooms, Chris, *The Giants of Wales: Cewri Cymru* (Lampeter and Lewiston, 1993).

Gruffydd, R. Geraint, 'Canu Cadwallon ap Cadfan', in *Ast. H.*, pp. 25–43.

—'Cywyddau Triawdaidd Dafydd ap Gwilym', YB XIII (1985), pp. 167–77.

— 'From Gododdin to Gwynedd: Reflections on the Story of Cunedda', SC XXIV/V (1989/90), pp. 1–14.

— (gen. ed.), *Cyfres Beirdd y Tywysogion*, 7 volumes (Caerdydd, 1991–6).

—'In search of Elmet', SC XXVIII (1994), pp. 63–79.

Gruffydd, R. Geraint and Rhiannon Ifans (eds), *Gwaith Einion Offeiriad a Dafydd Ddu Hiraddug*, Cyfres Beirdd yr Uchelwyr (Aberystwyth, 1997).

Gruffydd, W. J., *Math vab Mathonwy: An Enquiry into the Fourth Branch of the Mabinogi* (Cardiff, 1928).

— *Rhiannon: An Enquiry into the First and Third Branches of the Mabinogi* (Cardiff, 1953).

Gwynn, E. J., *The Metrical Dindshenchas: Text, Translation, and Commentary*, 5 volumes (Dublin, Royal Irish Academy, 1903–35).

Hamp, E. P., 'On the Justification of Ordering in TYP', SC XVI/XVII (1981/2), pp. 104–9.

Harries, Leslie (ed.), *Gwaith Huw Cae Llwyd ac Eraill* (Caerdydd, 1957).

Haycock, Marged, 'Llyfr Taliesin: Astudiaeth ar rai Agwedddau', unpublished Ph.D. thesis, University of Wales, Aberystwyth, 1983.

— 'Llyfr Taliesin', *Nat. Lib. of Wales Journal* XXV (1988), pp. 357–86.

— '*Preiddeu Annwn* and the Figure of Taliesin', SC XVIII/XIX (1983–4), pp. 52–78.

— 'The significance of the *Cad Goddau* Tree-list in the Book of Taliesin', in *Celtic Linguistics/Ieithyddiaeth Geltaidd. Readings in the Brythonic Languages Festschrift for T. Arwyn Watkins*, eds Martin J. Ball, James Fife, Erich Poppe and Jenny Rowland (Amsterdam, 1990), pp. 297–331.

—*Blodeugerdd Barddas o Ganu Crefyddol Cynnar* (Abertawe, 1994).

—'Taliesin's Questions', CMCS 33 (1997), pp. 19–80.

Henken, Elissa R. *Traditions of the Welsh Saints* (Woodbridge, 1987).

Historia Brittonum, ed. (i) T. H. Mommsen, Monumenta Germaniae Historica, Auctores Antiquissimi, vol. xiii, *Chronica Minora*, vol. iii (Berlin, 1888); (ii) F. Lot, *Nennius et l'Historia Brittonum* (Paris, 1934); (iii) D. N. Dumville, *The Historia Brittonum,* iii, *The Vatican Recension* (Cambridge, 1985); (iv) ed. with transl., John Morris, *Nennius' British History and the Welsh Annals* (London and Chichester, 1980); translated by A. W. Wade-Evans, *Nennius's History of the Britons* (London, 1938).

***Historia Regum Britanniae*, Geoffrey of Monmouth**, ed. (i) Acton Griscom (from Camb. Univ. Lib. MS 1706, London, 1929); (ii) Neil Wright (ed.), *The Historia Regum of Geoffrey of Monmouth* (I, Bern, Burgerbibliothek, MS 568; Cambridge, 1984); (iii) E. Faral (from Trin. Coll. Camb. MS 1126), *La Legende Arthurienne*, vol. iii (Paris, 1929). Translated by Lewis Thorpe, *Geoffrey of Monmouth's History of the Kings of Britain* (Harmondsworth, 1966).

Holder, Alfred, *Alt-celtischer Sprachschatz* (Leipzig, 1896–1913).

Hughes, Ian, *Math Uab Mathonwy: Pedwaredd Gainc y Mabinogi* (Aberystwyth, 2000).

Hughes, Kathleen, 'The Welsh-Latin Chronicles: Annales Cambriae and Related Texts', Rhŷs Memorial Lecture, PBA LIX (1973), pp. 233–58, reprinted in Hughes, *Celtic Britain in the Early Middle Ages*, ed. David Dumville, Studies in Celtic History II (Woodbridge, 1980), pp. 67–85.

Huws, Daniel, 'Llyfr Gwyn Rhydderch', CMCS 21 (1991), pp. 1–37 (= MWM, chapter 13).

—'Llyfrau Cymraeg 1250–1400', *Nat. Lib, of Wales Journal* XXVIII (1993), and translated ('Welsh Vernacular Books, 1250–1400') in MWM 36–64.

—*Medieval Welsh Manuscripts* (Cardiff, 2000).

Ifans, Rhiannon (ed.), *Gwaith Gruffudd Llwyd a'r Llygliwiaid Eraill*, Cyfres Beirdd yr Uchelwyr (Aberystwyth, 2000).

Jackson, K. H., *Early Welsh Gnomic Poems* (Cardiff, 1935).

—*Language and History in Early Britain* (Edinburgh, 1953).

—'The Britons of Southern Scotland', *Antiquity* XXIX (1955), pp. 77–88.

—'The Sources for the Life of St Kentigern', in SEBC, pp. 273–357.

—*The International Popular Tale and Early Welsh Tradition* (Cardiff, 1961).

—'Once again Arthur's Battles', *Modern Philology* 43 (1945–6), pp. 44–57.

—Review of *Trioedd Ynys Prydein*, WHR Special Number (1963), pp. 82–7.

—'Angles and Britons in Northumbria and Cumbria', in J. R. R. Tolkien et al., *Angles and Britons*, O'Donnell Lectures (Cardiff, 1963), pp. 60–84.

—*The Oldest Scottish Poem: The Gododdin* (Edinburgh, 1969).

—'*Varia*: II. Gildas and the Names of the British Princes', CMCS 3 (1982), pp. 30–40.

Jackson, K. H. *et al.*, *Celt and Saxon: Studies in the Early British Border* (Cambridge, 1963, corr. repr. 1964).

Jankulak, Karen, *The Medieval Cult of St Petroc* (Woodbridge, 2000).

Jarman, A. O. H. (ed.), *Ymddiddan Myrddin a Thaliesin* (Caerdydd, 1973, 1967).

—*The Legend of Merlin* (Cardiff, 1960).

—*The Cynfeirdd: Early Welsh Poets and Poetry*, Writers of Wales Series (Cardiff, 1981).

—*Llyfr Du Caerfyrddin* (Caerdydd, 1982).

—'Y Darlun o Arthur', LlC XV (1984–6), pp. 1–17.

—'Llyfr Du Caerfyrddin: The Black Book of Carmarthen', Rhŷs Memorial Lecture, PBA LXXI (1986), pp. 333–56.

—*Aneirin: Y Gododdin, Britain's Oldest Heroic Poem*, The Welsh Classics Series, (Llandysul, 1988).

—'The Arthurian Allusions in the Book of Aneirin, SC XXIV/XXV (1989–90), pp. 15–25.

Jenkins, Dafydd, *Hywel Dda: The Law*, The Welsh Classics Series (Llandysul 1986).

—*Llyfr Colan*, History and Law Series, Board of Celtic Studies, vol. 19 (Cardiff, 1963).

Jenkins, Dafydd and Owen, Morfydd E. (eds), *The Welsh Law of Women* (Cardiff, 1980).

Johnston, D. R. (ed.), *Gwaith Iolo Goch* (Caerdydd, 1988).

Johnston, Dafydd (ed.), *Gwaith Lewys Glyn Cothi* (Caerdydd, 1995).

—'*Canu ar ei fwyd ei hun': Golwg ar y Bardd Amatur yng Nghymru'r Oesoedd Canol* (Abertawe, 1997).

—*Gwaith Llywelyn Goch ap Meurig Hen*, Cyfres Beirdd yr Uchelwyr (Aberystwyth, 1998).

Jones, D. Gwenallt, *Yr Areithiau Pros* (Caerdydd, 1934).

Jones, Glyn E., 'Bran Galed: Bran fab Ymellyrn', B XXV, pp. 105–12.

Jones, Nerys Ann and Erwain Haf Rheinallt (eds), *Gwaith Sefnyn, Rhisierdyn, Gruffudd Fychan ap Gruffudd ab Ednyfed a Llywarch Bentwrch*, Cyfres Beirdd yr Uchelwyr (Aberystwyth, 1995).

Jones, Owen and William Owen Pughe (eds), *Barddoniaeth Dafydd ab Gwilym* (London, 1789).

Jones, Owen, Edward Williams and William Owen Pughe (eds), *The Myvyrian Archaiology of Wales* (second edition, Denbigh, 1870).

Jones, R. M., 'Nodiadau Cymysg: Cai fab Cynyr', B XIV (1950–2), pp. 119–23.

—'Y Rhamantau Cymraeg a'u Cysylltiad â'r Rhamantau Ffrangeg', LlC IV (1957), pp. 208–27.

Jones, Thomas (ed.), *Brut y Tywysogyon or The Chronicle of the Princes: Peniarth Ms. 20 version*, Board of Celtic Studies History and Law Series, vol. 11 (Cardiff, 1952).

—'Chwedl yr Anifeiliaid Hynaf', *Nat. Lib. of Wales Journal* VII (1951–2), pp. 62–6.

—'Chwedl Huail ap Caw and Arthur', in *Astudiaethau Amrywiol cyflwynedig i Syr T. H. Parry-Williams* (Caerdydd, 1968), pp. 48–66.

—'Datblygiadau Cynnar Chwedl Arthur', B XVII (1958), pp. 235–52. Translated by Gerald Morgan, 'The Early Evolution of the Legend of Arthur', NMS 8 (1964), pp. 3–21.

—'The Black Book of Carmarthen "Stanzas of the Graves"', PBA LIII (1969), pp. 97–136.

— (ed.), *Ystoryaeu Seint Greal, Rhan 1. Y Keis* (Caerdydd, 1992).

Jones, T. Gwynn (ed.), *Gwaith Tudur Aled* (Caerdydd, 1926).

Kendrick, T. D., *British Antiquity* (London, 1950).

Kenney, J. F., *Sources for the Early History of Ireland* (New York, 1929).

Keynes, Simon and Michael Lapidge, *Asser's Life of King Alfred and Other Contemporary Sources* (Harmondsworth, 1993).

Kirby, D. P., 'British Dynastic History in the Pre-Viking Period', B XXVII (1976–8), pp. 81–113.

Koch, John T. (ed.), *The Gododdin of Aneirin: Text and Context from Dark-Age North Britain* (Cardiff, 1997).

Lapidge, Michael and David Dumville (eds), *Gildas: New Approaches*, Studies in Celtic History V (Woodbridge, 1984).

Lewis, Barry J. (ed.), *Gwaith Gruffudd ap Maredudd: 1 – Canu i deulu Penmynydd*, Cyfres Beirdd yr Uchelwyr (Aberystwyth, 2003).

Lewis, Henry (ed.), *Hen Gerddi Crefyddol* (Caerdydd, 1931).

—(ed.), *Brut Dingestow*, (Caerdydd, 1942).

Lewis, Henry and Holger Pedersen, *A Concise Comparative Celtic Grammar* (Göttingen, 1937, 1961).

Lewis, Henry, Thomas Roberts and Ifor Williams (eds), *Cywyddau Iolo Goch ac Eraill* (second edition, Caerdydd, 1937).

Lewis, Saunders, *Braslun o Hanes Llenyddiaeth Gymraeg* (Caerdydd, 1932).

Lewis, Timothy, *A Glossary of Mediaeval Welsh Law* (Manchester, 1913).

Lloyd, D. Myrddin, 'Barddoniaeth Cynddelw Brydydd Mawr II', *Y Llenor* XIII (1934), pp. 49–59.

—*Rhai Agweddau ar Ddysg y Gogynfeirdd*, Darlith Goffa G. J. Williams 1976 (Caerdydd, 1977).

Lloyd, J. E., *A History of Wales*, 2 volumes (London, 1911; third edition 1939).

Lloyd-Jones, J. *Geirfa Barddoniaeth Gynnar Gymraeg* (Caerdydd, 1931–63).

—*Enwau Lleoedd Sir Gaernarfon* (Caerdydd, 1928).

—*The Court Poets of the Welsh Princes* (British Academy Rhŷs Memorial Lecture, 1948).

Lloyd-Morgan, Ceridwen, '*Breuddwyd Rhonabwy* and Later Arthurian Literature', in AW, pp. 183–208.

—'Nodiadau Ychwanegol ar Achau Arthuraidd a'u Ffynonellau Ffrangeg', *Nat. Lib. of Wales Journal* XXI (1980), pp. 329–39.

—'Lancelot in Wales', in *Shifts and Transpositions in Medieval Literature*, ed. Karen Pratt (Cambridge, 1994), pp. 169–79.

Lhuyd, Edward, *Archaeologia Britannica* (Oxford, 1707). ***Arch. Brit.***

Loomis, R. S., *Arthurian Tradition and Chrétien de Troyes* (New York, 1949).

—*Wales and the Arthurian Legend* (Cardiff, 1956).

—(ed.), *Arthurian Literature in the Middle Ages* (Oxford, 1959).

Loomis, R. S. and G. T. Webster (trans.), *Ulrich von Zatzikhoven's Lanzelet* (New York, 1951).

Loth, Joseph, *Chrestomathie Bretonne* (Paris, 1890).

—*Contributions à l'étude des Romans de la Table Ronde* (Paris, 1912).

—*Les Mabinogion* (Paris, 1913).

Mabinogion, The, translations by Lady Charlotte Guest (1849, 1877); Gwyn Jones and Thomas Jones (Everyman, 1949, 1963, etc.); J. Gantz (Harmondsworth, 1976); Modern Welsh version by Dafydd and Rhiannon Ifans (Llandysul, 1980).

Macalister, R. A. S., *Corpus Inscriptionum Insularum Celticarum*, 2 volumes (Dublin, 1945 and 1949).

Mac Cana, Proinsias, 'Aspects of the Theme of King and Goddess in Irish Literature', EC VII (1957), pp. 356–433 and VIII (1958), pp. 59–65.

—'Conservation and Innovation in Early Celtic Literature', EC XIII (1972), pp. 61–119.

—*Branwen, Daughter of Llŷr* (Cardiff, 1958).

—*Celtic Mythology* (London, 1970).

—*The Learned Tales of Medieval Ireland* (Dublin, 1980).

—*The Mabinogi* , Writers of Wales Series (Cardiff, 1977, 1992).

—Notes on the English Edition of Culhwch and Olwen', CMCS 29 (1995), pp. 53–62.

Mac Culloch, J., *The Religion of the Ancient Celts* (Edinburgh, 1911).

Meyer, Kuno, *The Triads of Ireland*, Royal Irish Academy Todd Lecture Series, vol. 13 (Dublin, 1910, reprinted 1937).

Meyer, Kuno and Alfred Nutt, *The Voyage of Bran* (London, 1895).

Morgan, T. J., *Y Treigladau a'u Cystrawen* (Caerdydd, 1952).

Morrice, J. C., *Barddoniaeth William Llŷn* (Bangor, 1908).

Morris, Lewis, *Celtic Remains* (Cambrian Archaeological Assn, 1878).

Morris-Jones, John, *A Welsh Grammar* (Oxford, 1913).

—'Taliesin', Cy. XVIII (1918).

—*Cerdd Dafod* (Oxford, 1925).

Morris-Jones, J. and T. H. Parry-Williams (eds), *Llawysgrif Hendregadredd* (Caerdydd, 1957).

Murphy, Gerald, *Duanaire Finn III* , Irish Texts Society vol. XLIII (Dublin, 1953).

Nash-Williams, V. E. *The Early Christian Monuments of Wales* (Cardiff, 1950).

North, F. J., *Sunken Cities* (Cardiff, 1957).

O'Cuív, Brian (ed.), *A View of the Irish Language* (Dublin, 1969).

O'Rahilly, T. F., *Early Irish History and Mythology* (Dublin, 1946).

Owen, Aneurin, *Ancient Laws and Institutes of Wales* (London, 1841).

Owen, Ann Parry, 'Mynegai i Enwau Priod ym Marddoniaeth Beirdd y Tywysogion, LlC XX (1997), pp. 25–45.

Owen, Ann Parry and Dylan Foster Evans (eds), *Gwaith Llywelyn Brydydd Hoddnant, Dafydd ap Gwilym, Hillyn ac Eraill*, Cyfres Beirdd yr Uchelwyr (Aberystwyth, 1996).

Owen, Henry and Egerton Philimore, *The Description of Penbrokeshire by George Owen of Henllys*, Cymmrodorion Record Series, 1–4 (London, 1892, 1897; n.d.; 1936).

Owen, Hugh (ed.), *Additional Letters of the Morrises of Anglesey (1735–1786)*, Cymmrodorion Record Series, 49 (London, 1947).

Owen, Morfydd E., 'Y Trioedd Arbennig', B XXIV, pp. 434–50.

—'Trioed hefut yw y rei hyn';, YB XIV (1988), pp. 87–114.

—'Hwn yw e Gododin. Aneirin ae cant', in *Ast. H.*, pp. 123–50.

Owen, Morfydd E. and Nesta Lloyd (eds), *Drych yr Oesoedd Canol* (Caerdydd, 1986).

Owen, Morfydd E. and Brynley F. Roberts (eds), *Beirdd a Thywysogion: Barddoniaeth Llys yng Nghymru, Iwerddon a'r Alban cyflwynedig i R. Geraint Gruffydd* (Caerdydd, 1996).

Padel, Oliver, 'The Cornish Background of the Tristan Stories', CMCS 1 (1981), pp. 53–81.

—'Geoffrey of Monmouth and Cornwall', CMCS 8 (1984), pp. 1–28.

—'The Nature of Arthur', CMCS 27 (1994), pp. 1–31.

—*Arthur in Medieval Welsh Literature*, Writers of Wales Series (Cardiff, 2000).

Padel, O. J. and B. Olsen, 'A Tenth-century List of Cornish Parochial Saints', CMCS 12 (1986), pp. 33–71.

Parry, J. J. (ed.), *The Vita Merlini*, University of Illinois Studies in Language and Literature 10 (Urbana, 1925), pp. 243–80.

—(ed.), *Brut y Brenhinedd. Cotton Cleopatra Version* (Cambridge, Mass., 1937).

Parry, Thomas, *Hanes Llenyddiaeth Gymraeg hyd 1900* (Caerdydd, 1953).

—*Gwaith Dafydd ap Gwilym* (Caerdydd, 1952, 1963, etc.).

Parry, Thomas, and Merfyn Morgan, *Llyfryddiaeth Llenyddiaeth Gymraeg* (Caerdydd, 1976).

Parry-Williams, T. H. (gol.), *Rhyddiaith Gymraeg: Y Gyfrol Gyntaf 1488–1609* (Caerdydd, 1954).

Phillimore, E., *Annales Cambriae*, Cy. LX (1888), pp. 141–83.

Piggott, Stuart, 'The Sources of Geoffrey of Monmouth's Pre-Roman King List', *Antiquity* XV (1941), pp. 269–86.

Radford, Ralegh *et al*., 'Locus Maponi', *Transactions Dumfriesshire and Galloway Natural History and Antiquarian Society*, 31 (1954), pp. 35–57.

Rhŷs, John, *Celtic Heathendom*, Hibbert Lectures (London, 1892).

—*Studies in the Arthurian Legend* (Oxford, 1891).

—*Celtic Folklore, Welsh and Manx*, 2 volumes (Oxford, 1891).

—*Celtic Britain* (London, 1904).

Rhŷs, J. and J. G. Evans (eds), (ed.), *The Text of the Mabinogion from the Red Book of Hergest* (Oxford, 1887).

Rhŷs, J. and J. Morris-Jones (eds), *The Elucidarium and other Tracts in Welsh from Llyvyr Agkyr Llandewivrevi* (Oxford, 1894).

Richards, Melville (ed.), *Breudwyt Ronabwy* (Caerdydd, 1948).

Roach, W. F., *First Continuation of the Old French Perceval* (Philadelphia, 1952).

Roberts, Brynley F., Review of *Trioedd Ynys Prydein* in *Modern Language Review* 57 (1962), pp. 405–7.

—*Brut y Brenhinedd (Selections from Llanstephan MS 1)*, Medieval and Modern Welsh Series, vol. V (DIAS, 1971).

—'The Treatment of Personal Names in the Early Welsh Versions of *Historia Regum Britanniae*', B XXV (1972–4), pp. 274–90.

—*Cyfranc Lludd a Llefelys*, Medieval and Modern Welsh Series, vol. VII (DIAS, 1975).

—'Pen Penwaedd a Phentir Gafran', LlC XIII (1980–1), pp. 278–81.

—*Studies on Middle Welsh Literature* (Lampeter and Lewiston, 1992).

—'Geoffrey of Monmouth and Welsh Historical Tradition', NMS 20 (1976), pp. 29–40.

Roberts, Thomas (ed.), *Gwaith Dafydd ab Edmwnd* (Bangor, 1914).

— (ed.), *Gwaith Tudur Penllyn ac Ieuan ap Tudur Penllyn* (Caerdydd, 1958).

Roberts, Thomas and Ifor Williams (eds), *The Poetical Works of Dafydd Nanmor* (Cardiff, 1923).

Rose, H. J., *A Handbook of Greek Mythology* (London, 1928).

Ross, Anne, *Pagan Celtic Britain* (London, 1967).

Rowland, Jenny, *Early Welsh Saga Poetry* (Cambridge, 1990).

—'Warfare and Horses in the Gododdin', CMCS 30 (1995), pp. 1–40.

Rowlands, Eurys (ed.), 'Y Tri Thlws ar Ddeg', LlC V (1958), pp. 33–69.
—Review of *Trioedd Ynys Prydein* in LlC VI (1961), pp. 222–47.
—*Gwaith Lewys Môn* (Caerdydd, 1975).
Sims-Williams, Patrick, 'The Significance of the Irish Personal Names in *Culhwch ac Olwen*', B XXIX (1980–2), pp. 600–20.
—'Some Functions of Origin Stories in Early Medieval Wales', in *History and Heroic Tale: A Symposium*, eds Tore Nyberg *et al.* (Odense, 1985).
—'Historical Need and Literary Narrative', WHR 17 (1994), pp. 1–40.
—'The Death of Urien', CMCS 32 (1996), pp. 25–36.
—'Did Itinerant Breton *Conteurs* Transmit the Matière de Bretagne?', *Romania* 116 (1998), pp. 72–111.
—'Gildas and Vernacular Poetry', in Lapidge and Dumville (eds) *Gildas: New Approaches*, pp. 169–92.
—'Clas Beuno and the Four Branches of the Mabinogi', in *150 Jahre "Mabinogion" — Deutsche-walisische Kulturbeziehungen*, ed. Bernhard Maier and Stefan Zimmer (Tübingen, 2001), pp. 111–27.
Skene, W. F. (ed., with accompanying trans.), *The Four Ancient Books of Wales*, 2 volumes (Edinburgh, 1868).
Sjoestedt, M. L., *Gods and Heroes of the Celts*, transl. by Myles Dillon (London, 1949).
Smyth, Alfred P., *Warlords and Holy Men: Scotland AD 800–1000* (Edinburgh, 1984, 1989).
Stenton, Frank, *Anglo-Saxon England* (Oxford, 1946).
Stephens, Meic (ed.), *The New Companion to the Literature of Wales* (Cardiff, 1998).
—(ed.), *Cydymaith i Lenyddiaeth Cymru* (Caerdydd, 1977, 1997).
Stokes, Whitley and Kuno Meyer, *Archiv für celtische Lexicographie* (Halle, 1900–7).
Tatlock, J. S. P., *The Legendary History of Britain* (Los Angeles 1950).
Thomas, Charles, 'The Brychan Documents', ch. 9 in *And Shall These Mute Stones Speak?* (Cardiff, 1994).
Thomas, Graham C. G., 'Llen Arthur a Maen a Modrwy Luned' unpublished M.A. thesis, University of Wales, Aberystwyth, 1976.
—'From Manuscript to Print: I. Manuscript', in *A Guide to Welsh Literature c. 1530–1700*, ed. R. Geraint Gruffydd (Cardiff, 1997), pp. 241–62.
Thomas, Gwyn, 'Pedair Cainc y Mabinogi' in Geraint Jenkins (ed.), *Cof Cenedl* XI (Llandysul, 1996), pp. 1–28.
Thomas, R. J., *Enwau Afonydd a Nentydd Cymru* (Caerdydd, 1938).
Thomson, R. L. (ed.), *Ystorya Gereint uab Erbin*, DIAS Modern and Medieval Welsh Series, Vol. X (Dublin, 1996).
— (ed.), *Owein* or *Chwedl Iarlles y Ffynnawn*, DIAS Modern and Medieval Welsh Series, Vol. IV (Dublin, 1968).
Thompson, Stith, *The Folktale from Ireland to India* (revised edition, New York, 1951).
Thorpe, Lewis (trans.), *Geoffrey of Monmouth: History of the Kings of Britain* (Harmondsworth, 1966, and subsequent reprints).
— (trans.), *Gerald of Wales: The Journey through Wales and The Description of Wales* (Harmondsworth, 1978).
Thurneysen, Rudolf, *Die Irische Helden- und Königsagen bis zum 17. Jahrhundert* (Halle, 1921; reprinted Hildersheim, 1980).
—*A Grammar of Old Irish*, translated by D. A. Binchy (Dublin, 1946).

Tolkien, J. R. R., K. H. Jackson and Nora Chadwick *et al.*, *Angles and Britons*, O'Donnell Lectures (Cardiff, 1963).

Vendryes, Joseph, *La poésie galloise des XII*ᵉ–XIIIᵉ siècles dans ses rapports avec la langue, The Zaharoff Lecture (Oxford, 1930).

—*La Religion des celtes* (Paris, 1948) [= vol. 3 of *Les Religions de l'Europe Ancienne*, ed. A. Grenier].

—'Manannán mac Lir', EC VI (1953–4), pp. 238–54.

Van Hamel, A. G., 'Aspects of Celtic Mythology', PBA 20 (1934), pp. 207–48.

Wade-Evans, A. W. (trans.), *Nennius' History of the Britons* (London, 1938).

—(ed. and transl.), *Vitae Sanctorum Britanniae et Genealogiae* (Cardiff, 1944).

Wainwright, F. T., *The Problem of the Picts* (Edinburgh, 1955).

Watkin, Morgan (ed.), *Ystorya Bown de Hamtwn* (Cardiff, 1951).

Watson, W. J., *The Celtic Place-names of Scotland* (Edinburgh, 1926).

Watts, Gareth O., *Llyfryddiaeth Llenyddiaeth Gymraeg, Cyfrol 2, 1976–1986* (Caerdydd, 1993).

Whitelock, Dorothy et al., *The Anglo-Saxon Chronicle: A Revised Translation* (London, 1961).

Williams, A., A. P. Smyth and D. P. Kirby, *A Bibliographical Dictionary of Dark Age Britain: England, Scotland and Wales c. 500–c. 1050* (London, 1991).

Williams, Edward [Iolo Morganwg]: see '*Trioedd Ynys Prydein*: the *Myvyrian* 'Third series''', *THSC* (1968), 299–338; (1969), 127–54 [text by Iolo Morganwg, translated with notes by Rachel Bromwich].

Williams, G. J., *Iolo Morganwg* (Caerdydd, 1956).

—*Traddodiad Llenyddol Morgannwg* (Caerdydd, 1956).

Williams, G. J. and E. J. Jones (eds), *Gramadegau'r Penceirddiaid* (Caerdydd, 1934).

Williams, Hugh, *Gildas: De Excidio Britanniae*, 2 volumes, Cymmrodorion Record Series (London, 1899).

Williams, Ifor (ed.), *Casgliad o Waith Ieuan Deulwyn* (Bangor, 1909).

—(ed.), *Cyfranc Lludd a Llefelys* (Bangor, 1922).

—(ed.), *Breudwyt Maxen* (Bangor, 1927).

—(ed.), *Pedeir Keinc y Mabinogi* (Caerdydd, 1930, 1935; second edn 1951).

— (ed.), *Canu Aneirin* (Caerdydd, 1938).

— (ed.), *Canu Llywarch Hen* (Caerdydd 1935).

—*Lectures on Early Welsh Poetry* (Dublin, 1944).

—*Enwau Lleoedd* (Lerpwl, 1945; 1962).

—*Chwedl Taliesin* (Caerdydd, 1957).

—(ed.), *Armes Prydein o Lyfr Taliesin* (Caerdydd, 1955).

—(ed.), *Armes Prydein Vawr: The Prophecy of Britain*, English version by Rachel Bromwich, DIAS Medieval and Modern Welsh Series, vol. VI (Dublin, 1972).

—(ed.), *The Poems of Taliesin*, English version by J. E. Caerwyn Williams, DIAS Medieval and Modern Welsh Series, vol. III (Dublin, 1968, 1987).

—*The Beginnings of Welsh Poetry. Studies by Sir Ifor Williams*, ed. Rachel Bromwich (Cardiff, 1972, 1980).

Williams, Ifor and Thomas Roberts (eds), *Dafydd ap Gwilym a'i Gyfoeswyr* (second edition, Caerdydd, 1935).

Williams, Ifor and Llywelyn Williams (eds), *Gwaith Guto'r Glyn*, (Caerdydd, 1939, 1961).

Williams, J. E. Caerwyn, *Traddodiad Llenyddol Iwerddon* (Caerdydd, 1956).
—*Y Storïwr Gwyddeleg a'i Chwedlau* (Caerdydd, 1972).
—'Cerddi'r Gogynfeirdd i Wragedd a Merched, a'u Cefndir yng Nghymru a'r Cyfandir', LlC XIII (1974/9), pp. 3–112.
—'Gildas, Maelgwn and the Bards', in *Welsh Society and Nationhood: Historical Essays Presented to Glanmor Williams*, ed. by R. R. Davies *et al.* (Cardiff, 1984), pp. 19–34.
—*The Poets of the Welsh Princes*, Writers of Wales series (Cardiff, 1978; revised edn, 1994).
Williams, J. E. Caerwyn and P. K. Ford, *The Irish Literary Tradition* (Cardiff and Belmont, 1992).
Williams, R., *Selections from the Hengwrt Manuscripts, vol. I* (London, 1876).
Williams, S. J. (ed.), *Ystorya de Carolo Magno* (Caerdydd, 1930).
Williams, S. J. and J. Enoch Powell (eds), *Llyfr Blegywryd* (Caerdydd, 1941).
Winterbottom, Michael, *Gildas: The Ruin of Britain and Other Works* (Chichester, 1978).

INDEX

INDEX TO PLACES

(*The numbers are those of the triads.*)

INDEX TO *TRIOEDD Y MEIRCH*

(*Notes on these names are appended to the triads concerned.*)

GENERAL INDEX

(This index is based on the index in the second edition of Trioedd Ynys Prydein and largely follows the pattern and coverage there adopted by Dr Bromwich. Bold type indicates main references in introduction and notes.)